THE CAMBRIDGE EDITION OF THE CORRESPONDENCE OF DANIEL DEFOE

This comprehensive and authoritative edition of the correspondence of Daniel Defoe situates each letter in its biographical, literary, and historical contexts. A unique source for a turbulent period of British history, Defoe's correspondence spans topics including the first age of party marked by Tory and Whig rivalry, religious tensions between the Church and Dissenters, the uncertainty of the monarchical succession, the birth of Great Britain and its establishment as a global empire, and the use of the press to mould public opinion. As well as an introduction discussing Defoe's epistolary habits and the distinctive features of his letters, headnotes and annotations explain each document's occasion, beginning in 1703 with Defoe hunted by the government for sedition, and ending in 1730 with him again in hiding, fleeing creditors months before his death. The volume is illustrated with examples of Defoe's letters, offering a fresh window onto Defoe's manuscript habits.

Nicholas Seager is Head of the School of Humanities and Professor of English Literature at Keele University. He has published on literature of the long eighteenth century, including on Bunyan, Swift, Defoe, Haywood, Johnson, Sterne, Goldsmith, and Austen. He is co-editor of *The Oxford Handbook of Daniel Defoe* (2023).

THE CAMBRIDGE EDITION OF THE
CORRESPONDENCE OF DANIEL DEFOE

EDITOR

Nicholas Seager, *Keele University*

ASSOCIATE EDITORS

Marc Mierowsky, *University of Melbourne*
Andreas K. E. Mueller, *University of Northern Colorado*

ADVISORY EDITORS

J. A. Downie, *Goldsmiths, University of London*
James McLaverty, *Keele University*
W. R. Owens, *University of Bedfordshire*
Pat Rogers, *University of South Florida*

THE CAMBRIDGE EDITION OF THE
CORRESPONDENCE OF

DANIEL DEFOE

Edited by
NICHOLAS SEAGER
Keele University

CAMBRIDGE
UNIVERSITY PRESS

University Printing House, Cambridge CB2 8BS, United Kingdom

One Liberty Plaza, 20th Floor, New York, NY 10006, USA

477 Williamstown Road, Port Melbourne, VIC 3207, Australia

314–321, 3rd Floor, Plot 3, Splendor Forum, Jasola District Centre,
New Delhi – 110025, India

103 Penang Road, #05–06/07, Visioncrest Commercial, Singapore 238467

Cambridge University Press is part of the University of Cambridge.

It furthers the University's mission by disseminating knowledge in the pursuit of
education, learning, and research at the highest international levels of excellence.

www.cambridge.org
Information on this title: www.cambridge.org/9781107133099
DOI: 10.1017/9781316459546

© Cambridge University Press 2022

This publication is in copyright. Subject to statutory exception
and to the provisions of relevant collective licensing agreements,
no reproduction of any part may take place without the written
permission of Cambridge University Press.

First published 2022

Printed in the United Kingdom by TJ Books Limited, Padstow Cornwall

A catalogue record for this publication is available from the British Library.

ISBN 978-1-107-13309-9 Hardback

Cambridge University Press has no responsibility for the persistence or accuracy of
URLs for external or third-party internet websites referred to in this publication
and does not guarantee that any content on such websites is, or will remain,
accurate or appropriate.

CONTENTS

List of Figures viii
Acknowledgements x
Editorial Principles and Practice xii
Chronology xx
Conventions and Abbreviations xxx
Calendar of Letters xxxix
Introduction xlix

THE LETTERS 1

Select Bibliography 882
Index 897

FIGURES

Figure 1   Daniel Defoe to the Earl of Nottingham, 9 January 1703, TNA SP 34/2, fols. 48Av–Br   page 8

Figure 2   Sir Godfrey Kneller, Robert Harley, first Earl of Oxford (1714), oil on canvas, National Portrait Gallery, London   23

Figure 3   Daniel Defoe to Samuel Elisha, 31 August 1704, Harvard University, Houghton bMS Eng 870 (26)   96

Figure 4   Daniel Defoe to Edward Owen and Joseph Cater, 26–7 October 1705, Princeton University Library, Robert H. Taylor Collection, box 6, folder 3   177

Figure 5   Michael van der Gucht, Daniel Defoe, engraving, *Jure Divino: A Satyr* (London, 1706), National Portrait Gallery, London   209

Figure 6   Daniel Defoe to Robert Harley, 11 September 1707, BL Add. MS. 70291, fol. 192r–v   419

Figure 7   Daniel Defoe to Lieutenant-General James Stanhope, 8 March 1710, Kent History Centre, Maidstone, U1590/O140/17. Reproduced by kind permission of The Board of Trustees of the Chevening Estate   479

Figure 8   Daniel Defoe [Claude Guilot] to [Robert Harley], 18 November 1710, BL Add. MS. 70291, fol. 239r   545

Figure 9   Daniel Defoe to [the Earl of Oxford], 26 August 1714, BL Add. MS. 70291, fol. 2143r   819

Figure 10   Daniel Defoe to [Charles Delafaye], 7 June 1720, Historical Society of Pennsylvania, Philadelphia, Simon Gratz Autograph Collection   853

LIST OF FIGURES

Figure 11   Daniel Defoe to Henry Baker, 12 August 1730, Bodleian
Library, University of Oxford, MS. Montagu d. 12, fols.
203ᵛ–204ʳ   880

ACKNOWLEDGEMENTS

This edition began as a collaboration between Andreas Mueller and me. Circumstances intervened to limit Andreas's capacity to work on the project, but he remained as a valued associate editor. Marc Mierowsky joined as a research associate on the edition in 2017–18 and kindly remained on board as associate editor too. Their expertise has greatly enhanced the edition. The advisory editors – Alan Downie, Jim McLaverty, Bob Owens, and Pat Rogers – provided exemplary guidance for which I am deeply grateful. All errors are my own.

The research for the edition was enabled by a fellowship from the Arts and Humanities Research Council. Other funding was provided by the British Academy and Keele University. Linda Bree, Bethany Johnson, George Laver, Anna Oxbury, and Bethany Thomas at Cambridge University Press gave the project their unstinting support.

Nicole Pohl, Albert Rivero, and Marcus Walsh kindly read parts of the edition and gave generous feedback, as did an anonymous reviewer for the Press. David Hayton went far above and beyond in reading the full typescript. Aimee Merrydew and Hannah Scragg made invaluable contributions as research assistants.

A small part of the Introduction appears in a different form in *Defoe in Context*, to be published by Cambridge University Press, edited by George Justice and Albert Rivero.

The School of Humanities at Keele University provided a congenial and inspirational base for work on this edition. For guidance, advice, and friendship, I thank my current and former colleagues Rachel Adcock, David Amigoni, Ian Atherton, Ian Bell, Becky Bowler, Susan Bruce, Anthony Carrigan, Scott Dean, Oliver Harris, Ann Hughes, Beth Johnson, Tracey Lea, Tim Lustig, Scott McCracken, Scott McGowan, Ceri Morgan, Shane O'Neill, Mariangela Palladino, James Peacock, Roger Pooley, Amanda Porritt, Laura Sandy, Jonathon Shears, Joel Sodano, Siobhan Talbott, Alannah Tomkins, and Becky Yearling.

I have benefited from the generosity of a larger community of eighteenth-century scholars, and I am glad to acknowledge debts, many of long standing. Thanks, then, to Sharon Alker, Paula Backscheider, Jenny Batt, Paddy Bullard, Rebecca Bullard, Gabriel Cervantes, Robert Clark, Lucy Cooper, Katherine Ellison, Stephen Gregg, Brean Hammond, Joseph Hone, J. Paul Hunter, Thomas Keymer, Robert Mayer, Holly Faith Nelson, Maximillian Novak, Leah Orr, Benjamin Pauley, Dahlia Porter, Manushag Powell, John Richetti, Peter Sabor,

ACKNOWLEDGEMENTS

Geoffrey Sill, David Taylor, Richard Terry, Claudine van Hensbergen, David Walker, Cynthia Wall, Abigail Williams, and Joanne Wilson. I am sorry to anyone I have missed.

I thank the staff at the following libraries and archives: the British Library; the National Archives; the Bodleian Library, University of Oxford; Christ Church College Library, University of Oxford; the Houses of Parliament; the Centre for Buckinghamshire Studies; the Pierpont Morgan Library; the New York Public Library; the Huntington Library; the William Andrews Clark Memorial Library; Cornell University Library; Keele University Library; the National Art Library, Victoria and Albert Museum; Weymouth Library; John Rylands Library, University of Manchester; the National Library of Scotland; the National Records of Scotland; University of Liverpool Library; Edinburgh University Library; Glasgow University Library; Dorset History Centre; University of Birmingham Library; the Historical Society of Pennsylvania; the Library of the Society of Friends, London; the Beinecke Rare Books and Manuscripts Library and the Sterling Memorial Library, Yale University; the Houghton Library, Harvard University; Princeton University Library; the Lilly Library, Indiana University; Indiana University Archives; Folger Shakespeare Library; Kent History Centre; Senate House Library, University of London; Roderic Bowen Library and Archives, University of Wales Trinity St David; the Catholic Diocese of Birmingham Archive; Tyne and Wear Archives, Newcastle upon Tyne; the Brotherton Library, University of Leeds; Barclays Group Archives, Manchester; Staffordshire Record Office; the Samuel Johnson Birthplace Museum; University of Nottingham Library; Lincolnshire Archives, Lincoln; Cambridge University Library; Longleat House; Surrey History Centre; Essex Record Office; Liverpool Record Office; the Kenneth Spencer Research Library, University of Kansas; and Raleigh Court Branch Library, Roanoke, Virginia.

Finally, I thank my family on both sides of the Atlantic for their love, support, and interest. My parents, Peter and Susan Seager, have guided me in countless ways over many years, and their repeated queries about when it would be finished encouraged the book's completion. Ginny Weckstein, my wife, contributed to the edition by reading draft material, helping to refine the text, and giving excellent advice. The book is dedicated to our amazing children, Samuel, Edward, and Ida, who were born while I worked on the edition. The neonatal intensive care units at Leighton Hospital in Crewe, at Liverpool Women's Hospital, and at Royal Stoke University Hospital cared for Sam and Teddy following their premature birth on Christmas Eve 2016. Our gratitude to the healthcare professionals can only be imagined.

Nicholas Seager

EDITORIAL PRINCIPLES AND PRACTICE

such a case, a textual note alone explains the addition. Defoe sometimes signs his letters with monograms that cannot be replicated in print (see Figure 9): in this edition I have represented these by '[*monogram*]'. Punctuation has been supplied silently (see below).

Textual notes are denoted by superscript bold letters. As well as manuscript tears, holes, frays, and blots, textual notes record Defoe's cancellations, insertions, and amendments, and more occasionally quirks of layout, such as vertically written text. Italic text within explanatory notes explains the placement of cancellations and interlined insertions. So, 'your[a] Serviće', for which the note states 'your] *following word* 'Intrest' *cancelled*', signals that the manuscript reads: 'your ~~Intrest~~ Serviće'. Defoe typically strikes through text with a single horizontal line. The notes record the cancelled text or specify where it is illegible; they use 'probably' and 'possibly' in (respectively) cases of near-certainty and reasonable conjecture about what Defoe cancelled. Amendments within individual words are selectively recorded: where Defoe changed one word to another, or where letters are interlined within a word, that is noted; but where he merely amends the first letter, indicating a false start rather than a revision, that is not usually recorded.

Defoe's insertions in his manuscripts are usually interlined above the main line of text with a caret below the main line to pinpoint the placement. In this edition, such insertions appear as normal text and are identified by a textual note stating '*interlined*'. Occasionally in the manuscripts, words or some letters of a word appear above the main text where limitations of space necessitated it, usually when Defoe reached the edge of the page. These have neither been treated as insertions nor noted. Most of Defoe's letters use catchwords; these have been omitted and a few minor failures to catch are not recorded.

Printed copytexts have been edited conservatively, with no attempt to recapture Defoe's manuscript traits such as abbreviations that previous editors have probably expanded and standardised.

Capitalisation

This edition reproduces most of Defoe's initial capital letters, but where a lower-case letter begins a new sentence or paragraph it has been silently capitalised. Proper nouns have been given an initial capital when Defoe has not used one. Distinguishing in Defoe's handwriting between certain majuscule and miniscule graphs can be difficult, the main two problem cases being *s* and *w*. I have adopted the basic principle that an initial *s* with an ascender is miniscule if it has a significant descender coming below the baseline, designating a long *s* (i.e. double-length *s* graphs are miniscules, supralinear are majuscules). A *w* is majuscule if its left stem is an ascender (the right stem on Defoe's *w* almost always ascends above the x-height).

xiv

EDITORIAL PRINCIPLES AND PRACTICE

Orthography, Abbreviations, Diacritics, and Sigla

Defoe's original spelling is preserved, but the long *s* has been silently modernised. Dots below raised letters in Defoe's abbreviations are omitted, so that which resembles 'w:ch' is rendered 'wch' and such like. The dots have never been interpreted as a colon, as has been the case in previous printings. Contractions and abbreviations are preserved. Defoe variously signals abbreviations not involving raised letters with periods, apostrophes, and colons, which have been preserved unless specified otherwise. I retain Defoe's use of the archaic thorn, transmogrified by this period so as to be indistinguishable from *y*: 'ye' is 'the'; 'yt' is 'that', and 'ym' is 'them'.

The brevigraph resembling an enlarged miniscule *p* with a double-line, slanted spine is a version of the 'special *p*' that Defoe often uses in place of 'per' and more occasionally in place of 'par', 'pro', and 'pre', and very rarely in some other way, such as '*p*s' for 'piece'. This abbreviation has been expanded, signalled by a square-bracketed insertion, so '*p*son' becomes 'p[er]son', '*p*cell' becomes 'p[ar]cell', '*p*posed' becomes 'p[ro]posed', and such like. This symbol is amply illustrated in the figures in this edition.

Diacritics are preserved, or if they are removed that is explained in a textual note. Defoe uses macrons, usually to double a single letter, more occasionally to abbreviate: 'Com̄on', 'Im̄ediately', and 'Brō:' ('Brother'). Defoe infrequently places diereses on 'ÿ'. More commonly than macrons and diereses, he uses a tilde-like mark on 'c̃' to designate either that its pronunciation is soft ('Senc̃eible', 'Conc̃ern'd') or to stand for the 'sh' sound made by 'si', 'ti', or 'ci' (Condesenc̃on', 'Dedicac̃on', 'Spec̃all'). Defoe's practice is inconsistent, resulting in hybrids such as 'Pacenc̃e'. In this edition these stand as written. Manicules have been preserved in Letter 14 but with a limited ability to capture the appearance of the original. An array of other scribal features – including spiral swirls, elongated tails, and embellished letters – cannot be replicated in a print edition.

Symbols used in manuscripts to designate pounds, shillings, and pence have been standardised to '£', 's', and 'd' respectively, except where a printed copytext has used '*l*' for pounds. '£' is preferred to '*l*' because it more closely resembles the symbol Defoe commonly uses. These symbols tend to be superscript. Defoe occasionally places a period after numbers but this has always been silently deleted. Defoe's superscript ordinal numbers are sometimes little more than squiggles, so have been interpreted as best fits the context, but clear 'incorrect' instances such as '22th' have not been altered. Initial 'ff' is silently converted to 'F' ('ffinley' to 'Finley'). Sigla such as ampersands have been retained, as has underlining.

The practice for presenting the letters to and from Defoe outlined here has been applied to quotations from manuscript material in explanatory notes, but amendments are not recorded.

xv

EDITORIAL PRINCIPLES AND PRACTICE

Layouts

This edition neither preserves nor denotes straightforward lineation or pagination breaks in manuscripts (i.e. when the writer reaches the righthand edge or bottom of the page). It does however attempt to replicate some spatial features, such as different levels of indentation for paragraphs and lists, headings, and hanging paragraphs. Paragraph formatting has in some places been standardised. The layouts – line breaks and placements – of subscriptions ('I am | yoᵣ hearty Frᵈ & Servᵗ | DeFoe') have been replicated as far as possible, though some untypical line breaks deemed insignificant have been removed. Subscriptions are indented from the right margin. In manuscripts datings and postscripts are generally adjacent to the subscription (placed to its left, as in Figures 1, 6, 7, and 9), but in this edition they always come below it, still on the left.

Scottish Handwriting

The letters written by several of Defoe's Scottish correspondents present new challenges. Macrons over 'ū', sometimes creating *w*, are common and are preserved. Scottish secretary hand uses several abbreviations that have been silently expanded in this edition, such as a loop to signify 'es' at the end of a word. Scots use of 'quihilk' or 'qhk' for 'which' and of 'quhen' or 'qhn' for 'when' have been standardised to 'which' and 'when', respectively. Lower-case roman numeral 'i' has been converted to '1', so 'ii5' becomes '115'.

Punctuation

Adding, and more rarely removing, punctuation has been the most subjective and extensive process of preparing the text. This has been done silently to avoid an overly fussy text covered in square brackets. On occasion, Defoe's spacing has implied the punctuation mark adopted. Supplying and altering punctuation is generally less susceptible to blanket rules than are other features, though some can be stated here. Comma splices that do not risk being misread are left alone. Commas placed by Defoe between subject and verb, or between verb and object, are judged to be expressive usages that represent pauses, and so have not been adjusted to fit modern grammatical conventions. For example, 'My being Oblig'd to abandone, an Employ of Such Consequenċe, to My Own Ruine' (Letter 121). Missing possessive apostrophes have not been supplied. Apostrophes omitted from contractions that could otherwise prove confusing have been supplied (e.g., 'Il' becomes 'I'l'), but where the word seems clear it has been left (e.g., 'Youl'). Full stops at the end of paragraphs have been supplied, occasionally in place of other marks, such as colons and semi-colons; where a paragraph ends with no punctuation and leads

xvi

EDITORIAL PRINCIPLES AND PRACTICE

into an inventory, a colon has sometimes been preferred to a full stop. Omitted commas separating items in lists have been supplied (but not the serial comma before a coordinating conjunction after the penultimate item in a list). Defoe's use of quotation marks placed to the left on every line of quoted matter has been modernised: this edition gives an opening quotation mark, a running one for the start of each new paragraph, and a closing one.

In many cases Defoe's commas and full stops are indistinguishable, though he was capable of writing them in distinct ways. Instances where a mere dot could be either a full stop or a comma have been interpreted as best suits the sense. Overall, I have silently added or altered punctuation where I have judged it needful for the sense, though the approach has been minimalist. This requires some illustration.[3]

The insertion of commas has seemed needful in some cases of simple subordinate clauses and conjunctions:

About 14 days Sinċe[,] they Rabbled the wholl synod of Ross and Maltreated the Ministers[,] and this by a Made Rabble of Men Disguised in Womens Cloths ... (Letter 115)

Though without punctuation the correct reading will quickly be established, the unpunctuated sentence could easily be misread ('14 days Sinċe they Rabbled': 'they' may not have been noticed as the main subject of the sentence). The pronoun 'this' is imprecise, and its verb is elided, so to avoid its being read as conjoined to 'the Ministers' the second comma is supplied. The basis for adding commas is clarity:

This was put to yᵉ Question and past in yᵉ Negativ or Rather[,] According to yᵉ Method here[,] Delay or proceed[,] and Carryed proceed[.]

Then yᵉ Main Question was Put[,] Approv yᵉ Second Article or Not Aprove[,] and Carry'd Approv by a Majority of 58[.] (Letter 64)

Adding punctuation in this manner is fraught and I have sought to avoid it when an intention cannot be inferred:

The people who have broke this to me are few and have promised to keep it private if possible to have it Remedyed... (Letter 77)

In all likelihood 'if possible' refers to the Scottish ministers keeping private their apprehensions about the oath of allegiance: we might place commas around those words or just one after 'possible'. But a comma after 'private' alone works grammatically and transfers 'if possible' to the remedy. This and comparable instances have been left alone in this edition to avoid forcing a single sense on prose that is potentially ambiguous.

---

3 In the subsequent examples punctuation in square brackets represents an editorial addition. In the edition itself the square brackets are absent.

xvii

CHRONOLOGY

Defoe's Life and Writings

1660 Birth of Daniel Foe to Alice and James Foe of St Giles parish, Cripplegate, probably September.

1662 The Foes follow Dr Samuel Annesley out of the Church and henceforth worship as Dissenters.

c. **1668** Death of Defoe's mother, Alice.

Historical Events and Works

May: Restoration of Charles II; reestablishment of the Church of England. November: Royal Society founded. December: Royal African Company founded.

1661 January: Failed Fifth Monarchy uprising. December: Birth of Robert Harley; Corporation Act. Boyle, *The Sceptical Chymist*.

May: Marriage of Charles II and Catherine of Braganza. August: Act of Uniformity.

1663 Butler, *Hudibras* (part II 1664, part III 1678).

1664 July: Conventicle Act. Dryden, *The Indian Queen*.

1665 Second Anglo-Dutch War (until 1667). Bubonic plague in Britain. October: Five Mile Act. Head, *The English Rogue*.

1666 Great Fire of London. Bunyan, *Grace Abounding to the Chief of Sinners*. Cavendish, *The Blazing-World*.

1667 Dryden, *Annus Mirabilis*. Marvell, *Last Instructions to a Painter*. Milton, *Paradise Lost*.

Dryden, *An Essay of Dramatick Poesie*. Cavendish, *Plays*.

1671 Buckingham, *The Rehearsal*. Milton, *Paradise Regained*, *Samson Agonistes*.

CHRONOLOGY

Defoe's Life and Writings

Historical Events and Works

1672 March: Charles II's Declaration of Indulgence.

1673 February: Withdrawal of Declaration of Indulgence; Test Act. Dryden, *Marriage-a-la-Mode*.

c. **1674** Defoe attends Rev. Charles Morton's Dissenting Academy at Newington Green (until *c.* 1679).

1675 Wycherley, *The Country Wife*.

1676 Shadwell, *The Virtuoso*. Wycherley, *The Plain Dealer*.

1677 Behn, *The Rover*. Lee, *The Rival Queens*.

1678 Popish Plot. Bunyan, *The Pilgrim's Progress* (part II 1684). Dryden, *All for Love*.

1679 Exclusion Crisis (until 1681)

1680 Bunyan, *The Life and Death of Mr Badman*. Filmer, *Patriarcha* (posthumous).

1681 'Meditaçons' (manuscript verse). Defoe decides against becoming a Presbyterian minister and begins as a wholesale merchant in London.

Dryden, *Absalom and Achitophel*.

1682 Otway, *Venice Preserv'd*.

c. **1683** 'Historical Collections'.

June: Revelation of the Rye House Plot.

1684 Marries Mary Tuffley.

Behn, *Love-Letters Between a Nobleman and His Sister* (until 1687).

1685 Joins the Monmouth Rebellion.

February: Death of Charles II and accession of James II.

1687 Pardoned for his role in the Rebellion. His first child, Benjamin, is born around this time and six more children are born by 1704.

April: James issues Declaration of Indulgence. Dryden, *The Hind and the Panther*. English translation of Marana, *Letters writ by a Turkish Spy* (until 1694). Newton, *Principia Mathematica*.

xxi

CHRONOLOGY

Defoe's Life and Writings

1688 July/August: *A Letter to a Dissenter from his Friend at the Hague*, probably Defoe's first published work.

1691 January?: *A New Discovery of an Old Intreague.*

1692 Bankrupted with debts Defoe later claimed amounted to £17,000.

1694 Sets up a brick and pantile factory at Tilbury, Essex.

1695 Serves as Accomptant to the Commissioners of the Glass Duty (until *c.* 1699).

Historical Events and Works

April: James II reissues Declaration of Indulgence. November: William III lands at Torbay, beginning Revolution of 1688. Behn, *Oroonoko.*

1689 January: General election of the Convention Parliament (Whig majority). April: William III and Mary II crowned. May: Toleration Act. Formation of Grand Alliance against France and commencement of Nine Years' War (until 1697). Locke, *An Essay concerning Human Understanding, Two Treatises on Government.*

1690 February: General election (near-equality of Whigs and Tories). June: Battle of Beachy Head. July: Battle of the Boyne.

Dryden and Purcell, *King Arthur.*

Congreve, *Incognita.* L'Estrange, *Fables.*

1693 Congreve, *The Old Bachelor, The Double Dealer.* Locke, *Some Thoughts concerning Education.*

July: Establishment of Bank of England. December: Death of Mary II; Triennial Act. Astell, *A Serious Proposal to the Ladies.* Fox, *The Journal of George Fox* (posthumous).

April: Lapse of the Press Licensing Act. August–September: Siege of Namur. November: General election (Whig victory). Blackmore, *Prince Arthur.* Congreve, *Love for Love.*

1696 February: Assassination plot against William III foiled. May: Great Recoinage. Baxter, *Reliquiae Baxterianae.* Toland, *Christianity Not Mysterious.* Tyrrell, *The General History of England.* Vanbrugh, *The Relapse.*

xxii

CHRONOLOGY

Defoe's Life and Writings	Historical Events and Works

1697 January: *An Essay upon Projects*. December: Writes in support of William III's retention of a peacetime standing army (until 1698).

September–October: Treaty of Ryswick ends the Nine Years' War. Blackmore, *King Arthur*. Dampier, *New Voyage round the World*. Vanbrugh, *The Provok'd Wife*. Wotton, *Reflections upon Ancient and Modern Learning*.

1698 January: *An Enquiry into the Occasional Conformity of Dissenters*. April: *The Poor Man's Plea*.

July–August: General election (Tory gains but Whig majority). London Stock Exchange founded. Society for the Promotion of Christian Knowledge founded. Behn, *Histories and Novels* (posthumous). Sidney, *Discourses concerning Government* (posthumous). Ward, *The London Spy* (until 1700).

1699 May: *An Encomium on a Parliament*.

1700 February: *The Pacificator*. November: *The Two Great Questions Consider'd*. December or January 1701: *The True-Born Englishman*.

July: Death of Prince William, Duke of Gloucester, Princess Anne's last surviving child. Astell, *Some Reflections upon Marriage*. Congreve, *The Way of the World*. Tutchin, *The Foreigners*.

1701 January: *The Six Distinguishing Characters of a Parliament-Man*. February/March: *The Succession to the Crown of England, Consider'd*. May: *Legion's Memorial*. December: *The Original Power of the Collective Body of the People of England*.

January: General election (Tory victory). June: Act of Settlement. September: Death of James II; Louis XIV's recognition of his son as King of England. May: War of the Spanish Succession begins in Europe. November–December: General election (Whig majority). Pix, *The Double Distress*. Steele, *The Christian Hero*.

1702 May: *The Mock Mourners*. June: *A New Test of the Church of England's Loyalty*. July/August: *Reformation of Manners*. November: *An Enquiry into Occasional Conformity*. December: *The Shortest Way with the Dissenters*; *The Spanish Descent*.

March: Death of William III and accession of Queen Anne. May: England declares war on France. July: General election (Tory majority). November: Occasional Conformity Bill introduced in Commons but later defeated in Lords. Clarendon, *History of the Rebellion* (posthumous, until 1704) Tutchin, *The Observator* (until 1712).

xxiii

CHRONOLOGY

Defoe's Life and Writings

1712 January: *The Conduct of Parties in England.* May: *Wise as Serpents; The Present State of the Parties in Great Britain.*

1713 February: *Reasons against the Succession of the House of Hanover.* March: *And What if the Pretender should come?* Arrested for debt. April: *An Answer to a Question that No Body thinks of, viz. But What if the Queen Should Die?* Arrested for seditious libel. May: *Mercator* (until July 1714). June–September: *A General History of Trade.* August: *Memoirs of Count Tariff.* December: *A Letter to the Dissenters.*

1714 February: *A Letter to the Whigs.* April–August: *The Monitor.* June: *The Weakest Go to the Wall.* September: *The Secret History of the White-Staff.*

1715 January: *The Secret History of the Secret History of the White-Staff.* February: *An Appeal to Honour and Justice.* March: *The Family Instructor.* July: *A Hymn to the Mob.*

1716 Begins writing *Mercurius Politicus.*

Historical Events and Works

March: Episcopal Toleration Act. September: Death of Earl of Godolphin. Arbuthnot, *The History of John Bull.* Blackmore, *Creation.* Pope, *The Rape of the Lock.* Rogers, *A Cruising Voyage round the World.*

April: Treaty of Utrecht. June: House of Commons votes against Anglo-French Treaty of Commerce. August–November: General election (Tory victory). Barker, *Love Intrigues.* Finch, *Miscellany Poems.* Pope, *Windsor Forest.*

March: Treaty of Rastatt. June: Death of Electress Sophia of Hanover. July: Earl of Oxford dismissed as Lord Treasurer, replaced by Duke of Shrewsbury. August: Death of Queen Anne and accession of George I. Barker, *Exilius.* Centlivre, *The Wonder.* Mandeville, *The Fable of the Bees.* Rowe, *Jane Shore.* Steele, *The Crisis.*

General election (Whig victory). September: Unsuccessful Jacobite uprising begins (until the Pretender flees Scotland in February 1716); death of Louis XIV, succeeded by Louis XV. November: Battle of Preston. Pope's translation of Homer's *Iliad* (until 1720). Richardson, *An Essay on the Theory of Painting.*

April: Death of Baron Somers. Septennial Act. December: Viscount Townshend replaced as Secretary of State by Earl Stanhope. Gay, *Trivia.* Montagu, *Court Poems.*

xxvi

CHRONOLOGY

Defoe's Life and Writings

1717 April: *Memoirs of the Church of Scotland.* June: *Minutes of the Negotiations of Monsr. Mesnager.* August?: Begins writing for Mist's *Weekly Journal.*

1718 August: *A Continuation of Letters written by a Turkish Spy.* December?: *The Family Instructor, Volume II.*

1719 April: *Robinson Crusoe.* August: *Farther Adventures.* October: *The Manufacturer* (until March 1721).

1720 January–September: *The Commentator.* May: *Memoirs of a Cavalier.* June: *Captain Singleton.* August: *Serious Reflections.* October: *The Director* (until January 1721).

1722 January: *Moll Flanders.* February: *Due Preparations for the Plague; Religious Courtship.* March: *A Journal of the Plague Year.* December: *Colonel Jack.*

Historical Events and Works

January: Swedish-backed Jacobite plot uncovered; Triple Alliance between France, Britain, and Netherlands against Spain. March: Bangorian controversy begins. Handel, *Water Music.* Pope, Gay, and Arbuthnot, *Three Hours After Marriage.*

January: Repeal of Occasional Conformity Act. December: War of the Quadruple Alliance (until 1720). Addison, *Poems on Several Occasions.* Centlivre, *A Bold Stroke for a Wife.* Hearne, *The Lover's Week.* Prior, *Solomon, and Other Poems on Several Occasions.*

Haywood, *Love in Excess.* Watts, *Psalms of David.*

February: Treaty of the Hague. September: 'South Sea Bubble'. Gay, *Poems on Several Occasions.* Trenchard and Gordon, *Cato's Letters* (until 1723).

1721 April: Robert Walpole becomes Prime Minister. Montesquieu, *Persian Letters.* Wodrow, *The History of the Sufferings of the Church of Scotland.*

March–May: General election (Whig victory). June: Death of Duke of Marlborough. August: Atterbury plot uncovered. Parnell, *Poems on Several Occasions.* Steele, *The Conscious Lovers.*

1723 March: Black Act. June: Bolingbroke pardoned for Jacobitism. Aubin, *Charlotta Du Pont.* Barker, *A Patch-Work Screen for the Ladies.*

xxvii

CHRONOLOGY

Defoe's Life and Writings	Historical Events and Works

1724 February: *The Fortunate Mistress*. May: *A Tour thro' the Whole Island of Great Britain*, vol. I. November: *A New Voyage Round the World*.

May: Death of Robert Harley, Earl of Oxford. June: Death of Henry Sacheverell. Burnet, *History of His Own Time*, vol. I (vol. II 1734). Davys, *The Reform'd Coquet*. Johnson (pseud.?), *A General History of the Pyrates*, vol. I. Swift, *Drapier's Letters* (until 1725). Watts, *Logick*. Collins, *A Discourse of the Grounds and Reasons of the Christian Religion*.

1725 June: *A Tour thro' the Whole Island of Great Britain*, vol. II. September: *The Complete English Tradesman*, vol. I. October–January 1726: *A General History of Discoveries and Improvements*.

Haywood, *Secret Histories, Novels and Poems*. Pope's translation of Homer's *Odyssey* (until 1726) and edition of Shakespeare.

1726 April: *An Essay upon Literature*. May: *A Political History of the Devil*. August: *A Tour thro' the Whole Island of Great Britain*, vol. III. November: *A System of Magick*.

Swift, *Gulliver's Travels*.

1727 February: *Conjugal Lewdness*. March: *An Essay on the History and Reality of Apparitions*. May: *The Complete English Tradesman*, vol. II. September: *A New Family Instructor*.

May: Royal Bank of Scotland founded. June: Death of George I and accession of George II. August–October: General election (Whig victory). Davys, *The Accomplished Rake*. Gay, *Fables*. Swift and Pope, *Miscellanies* (until 1732).

1728 March: *A Plan of the English Commerce*.

Chambers, *Cyclopaedia*. Gay, *The Beggar's Opera*. Hutcheson, *An Essay on the Nature and Conduct of the Passions and Affections*. Johnson (pseud.?), *A General History of the Pyrates*, vol. II. Pope, *The Dunciad*. Savage, *The Bastard*. Theobald, *Double Falshood*.

1729 Composition of *The Compleat English Gentleman* (published 1890). April: Marriage of Defoe's daughter Sophia to Henry Baker.

Drury, *Madagascar*. Elizabeth Singer Rowe, *Letters on Various Occasions*. Swift, *A Modest Proposal*.

CHRONOLOGY

Defoe's Life and Writings

1730 *Christianity Not as Old as the Creation.*

1731 April: Death by a 'lethargy' (stroke) in Ropemakers' Alley, London; buried in Bunhill Fields.

Historical Events and Works

Thomson, *The Seasons* (since 1726). Tindal, *Christianity as Old as the Creation.*

Hogarth, *A Harlot's Progress. The Gentleman's Magazine* begins publication.

CONVENTIONS AND ABBREVIATIONS

Conventions

In editorial material, dates are given in old style, but the year is assumed to have started on 1 January. The place of publication in citations is London unless otherwise stated. Noblemen are named throughout the edition according to their title at that time, but the notes identify changes to titles. Robert Harley thus becomes the Earl of Oxford from May 1711 onwards, but for clarity is identified by his family name consistently in the Introduction. I do not justify Defoe attributions except where I differ from Furbank and Owens's *Critical Bibliography*. Defoe's *Review* was for a time published in both London and Edinburgh with different dates. The earliest date is always given; when that is an Edinburgh issue it is followed by '(E)'.

Abbreviations

Defoe's Writings

Appeal	*An Appeal to Honour and Justice* (1715)
Letters, ed. Healey	*The Letters of Daniel Defoe*, ed. G. H. Healey (Oxford, 1955)
Master Mercury	*The Master Mercury*, intro. Frank H. Ellis and Henry L. Snyder, Augustan Reprint Society no. 184 (Los Angeles, Cal., 1977), supplemented by Longleat House's run
Novels	*The Novels of Daniel Defoe*, 10 vols., gen. eds. P. N. Furbank and W. R. Owens (2007–8)

> Vol. I: *Robinson Crusoe*, ed. W. R. Owens
> Vol. II: *The Farther Adventures of Robinson Crusoe*, ed. W. R. Owens
> Vol. III: *Serious Reflections ... of Robinson Crusoe*, ed. G. A. Starr
> Vol. IV: *Memoirs of a Cavalier*, ed. N. H. Keeble
> Vol. V: *Captain Singleton*, ed. P. N. Furbank
> Vol. VI: *Moll Flanders*, ed. Liz Bellamy
> Vol. VII: *A Journal of the Plague Year*, ed. John Mullan
> Vol. VIII: *Colonel Jack*, ed. Maurice Hindle
> Vol. IX: *The Fortunate Mistress*, ed. P. N. Furbank

CONVENTIONS AND ABBREVIATIONS

	Vol. x: *A New Voyage Round the World*, ed. John McVeagh
PEW	*The Political and Economic Writings of Daniel Defoe*, 8 vols., gen. eds. P. N. Furbank and W. R. Owens (2000)
	Vol. I: *Constitutional Theory*, ed. P. N. Furbank
	Vol. II: *Party Politics*, ed. J. A. Downie
	Vol. III: *Dissent*, ed. W. R. Owens
	Vol. IV: *Union with Scotland*, ed. D. W. Hayton
	Vol. V: *International Relations*, ed. P. N. Furbank
	Vol. VI: *Finance*, ed. John McVeagh
	Vol. VII: *Trade*, ed. John McVeagh
	Vol. VIII: *Social Reform*, ed. W.R. Owens
RDW	*Religious and Didactic Writings of Daniel Defoe*, 10 vols., gen. eds. P. N. Furbank and W. R. Owens (2005–6)
	Vol. I: *The Family Instructor, Volume I*, ed. P. N. Furbank
	Vol. II: *The Family Instructor, Volume II*, ed. P. N. Furbank
	Vol. III: *A New Family Instructor*, ed. W. R. Owens
	Vol. IV: *Religious Courtship*, ed. G. A. Starr
	Vol. V: *Conjugal Lewdness*, ed. Liz Bellamy
	Vol. VI: *The Poor Man's Plea*, etc., ed. J. A. Downie
	Vol. VII: *The Complete English Tradesman, Volume I*, ed. John McVeagh
	Vol. VIII: *The Complete English Tradesman, Volume II*, ed. John McVeagh
	Vol. IX: *The Commentator*, ed. P. N. Furbank
	Vol. X: *The Compleat English Gentleman*, ed. W. R. Owens
Review	*Defoe's Review* (1704–13), 9 vols., ed. John McVeagh (2004–11)
SFS	*Satire, Fantasy and Writings on the Supernatural by Daniel Defoe*, 8 vols., gen. eds. P. N. Furbank and W. R. Owens (2003–4)
	Vol. I: *The True-Born Englishman and Other Poems*, ed. W. R. Owens
	Vol. II: *Jure Divino*, ed. P. N. Furbank
	Vol. III: *The Consolidator*, etc., ed. Geoffrey Sill
	Vol. IV: *Minutes of the Negotiations of Monsr. Mesnager*, etc., ed. P. N. Furbank
	Vol. V: *The Conduct of Christians made the Sport of Infidels*, etc., ed. David Blewett

CONVENTIONS AND ABBREVIATIONS

	Vol. VI: *The Political History of the Devil*, ed. John Mullan
	Vol. VII: *A System of Magick*, ed. Peter Elmer
	Vol. VIII: *An Essay on the History and Reality of Apparitions*, ed. G. A. Starr
TDH	*Writings on Travel, Discovery and History by Daniel Defoe*, 8 vols., gen. eds. P. N. Furbank and W. R. Owens (2001–2)
	Vol. I: *A Tour thro' the Whole Island of Great Britain, Volume I*, ed. John McVeagh
	Vol. II: *A Tour thro' the Whole Island of Great Britain, Volume II*, ed. John McVeagh
	Vol. III: *A Tour thro' the Whole Island of Great Britain, Volume III*, ed. John McVeagh
	Vol. IV: *A General History of Discoveries and Improvements*, etc., ed. P. N. Furbank
	Vol. V: *Due Preparations for the Plague*, ed. Andrew Wear
	Vol. VI: *Memoirs of the Church of Scotland*, ed. N. H. Keeble
	Vols. VII–VIII: *The History of the Union of Great Britain*, ed. D. W. Hayton

Other

Add. MS(S).	Additional Manuscript(s)
Addison Letters	*The Letters of Joseph Addison*, ed. Walter Graham (Oxford, 1941)
Analecta	Robert Wodrow, *Analecta: Or, Materials for a History of Remarkable Providences; Mostly Relating to Scotch Ministers and Christians*, 2 vols. (Edinburgh, 1842)
Anne Letters	*The Letters and Diplomatic Instructions of Queen Anne*, ed. Beatrice Curtis Brown (1935)
APS	*The Acts of the Parliaments of Scotland, 1124–1707*, 11 vols., ed. Thomas Thomson (Edinburgh, 1814–24)
Army Lists	*English Army Lists and Commission Registers, 1661–1714*, 6 vols., ed. Charles Dalton (1892–1904)
Backscheider, 'John Russell'	Paula R. Backscheider, 'John Russell to Daniel Defoe: Fifteen Unpublished Letters from Scotland', *PQ* 61 (1982), 161–77

xxxii

CONVENTIONS AND ABBREVIATIONS

Backscheider, *Life*	Paula R. Backscheider, *Daniel Defoe: His Life* (Baltimore, Md., 1989)
Baker	Henry Baker, 'Autobiographical Memorandum', National Art Gallery, Victoria and Albert Museum, Forster Collection MS 23
Bastian	Frank Bastian, *Defoe's Early Life* (1981)
BIHR	*Bulletin of the Institute of Historical Research*
(B)JECS	*(British) Journal for Eighteenth-Century Studies*
BL	British Library, London
BLJ	*British Library Journal*
Bodl.	Bodleian Library, University of Oxford
Bowie, *Addresses*	*Addresses against Incorporating Union, 1706–1707*, ed. Karin Bowie (Aberdeen, 2018)
Boyer	Abel Boyer, *The History of the Life and Reign of Queen Anne* (1722)
Burnet	Gilbert Burnet, *Bishop Burnet's History of his Own Time*, 6 vols. (Oxford, 1823)
C.J.	*House of Commons Journals*
Clerk	Sir John Clerk of Penicuik, *History of the Union of Scotland and England*, abr., trans., and ed. Douglas Duncan (Edinburgh, 1993)
Cobbett	William Cobbett, *Parliamentary History of England from the Earliest Time to the Year 1803*, 36 vols. (1806–20)
Coombs	Douglas Coombs, *The Conduct of the Dutch: British Opinion and the Dutch Alliance during the War of the Spanish Succession* (The Hague, 1958)
CTB	*Calendar of Treasury Books* (1897–1962)
CTP	*Calendar of Treasury Papers* (1868–1903)
Defoe–Farewell Catalogue	*The Libraries of Daniel Defoe and Phillips Farewell: Olive Payne's Sales Catalogue* (1731), ed. Helmut Heidenreich (Berlin, 1970)
Dickson	P. G. M. Dickson, *The Financial Revolution in England: A Study in the Development of Public Credit 1688–1756* (1967)
Downie, *Robert Harley*	J. A. Downie, *Robert Harley and the Press: Propaganda and Public Opinion in the Age of Swift and Defoe* (Cambridge, 1979)
Duch. Marl. Corr.	*Private Correspondence of Sarah, Duchess of Marlborough*, 2 vols. (1838)

CONVENTIONS AND ABBREVIATIONS

Dunton, *Life and Errors*	John Dunton, *The Life and Errors of John Dunton*, 2 vols. (1818)
ECL	*Eighteenth-Century Life*
ECS	*Eighteenth-Century Studies*
EHR	*English Historical Review*
EUL	Edinburgh University Library
F&O, *Bibliography*	P. N. Furbank and W. R. Owens, *A Critical Bibliography of Daniel Defoe* (1998)
F&O, *Canonisation*	P. N. Furbank and W. R. Owens, *The Canonisation of Daniel Defoe* (New Haven, Conn., 1988)
F&O, *De-attributions*	P. N. Furbank and W. R. Owens, *Defoe De-attributions: A Critique of J. R. Moore's 'Checklist'* (1994)
F&O, 'Periodicals'	P. N. Furbank and W. R. Owens, 'On the Attribution of Periodicals and Newspapers to Daniel Defoe', *Publishing History* 40 (1996), 83–98
F&O, *Political Biography*	P. N. Furbank and W. R. Owens, *A Political Biography of Daniel Defoe* (2006)
Fasti	*Fasti Ecclesiæ Scoticanæ*, 11 vols. (Edinburgh, 1866–2000)
Fraser, *Melvilles*	Sir William Fraser, *The Melvilles, Earls of Melville, and the Leslies, Earls of Leslie*, 3 vols. (Edinburgh, 1890)
Gregg, *Queen Anne*	Edward Gregg, *Queen Anne* (New Haven, Conn., 1980)
Hamilton, *Diary*	*The Diary of Sir David Hamilton*, ed. Philip Roberts (Oxford, 1975)
Hearne	*Remarks and Collections of Thomas Hearne*, 11 vols., ed. Charles Doble *et al.* (Oxford, 1885–1921)
Heinsius Corr.	*De Briefwisseling van Anthonie Heinsius*, 19 vols., ed. A. J. Veernendaal (The Hague, 1976–94)
Hill	Brian W. Hill, *Robert Harley: Speaker, Secretary of State and Premier Minister* (New Haven, Conn., 1988)
HLQ	*Huntington Library Quarterly*
H.M.C. *Bath MSS*	*Calendar of the Manuscripts of the Marquis of Bath, Preserved at Longleat, Wiltshire*, 3 vols. (1904)
H.M.C. *Dartmouth MSS*	*The Manuscripts of the Earl of Dartmouth*, 3 vols. (1887)
H.M.C. *Eighth Report MSS*	*Eighth Report of the Royal Commission on Historical Manuscripts* (1881)
H.M.C. *House of Lords MSS*	*The Manuscripts of the House of Lords*, 12 vols. (1887–1962)

xxxiv

CONVENTIONS AND ABBREVIATIONS

H.M.C. *Laing MSS*	*Report on the Laing Manuscripts Preserved in the University of Edinburgh*, 2 vols. (1914–25)
H.M.C. *Mar and Kellie MSS*	*Report on the Manuscripts of the Earl of Mar and Kellie Preserved at Alloa House* (1904)
H.M.C. *Ninth Report, Part* II	*Ninth Report of the Royal Commission on Historical Manuscripts, Part* II (1894)
H.M.C. *Ormonde MSS*	*The Manuscripts of the Marquess of Ormonde, Preserved at Kilkenny Castle*, 8 vols. (1902–20)
H.M.C. *Portland MSS*	*The Manuscripts of his Grace the Duke of Portland, Preserved at Welbeck Abbey*, 10 vols. (1891–1931)
H.M.C. *Seafield MSS*	*The Manuscripts of the Duke of Roxburghe; Sir H. H. Campbell, Bart.; the Earl of Strathmore; and the Countess Dowager of Seafield* (1894)
Holmes	Geoffrey Holmes, *British Politics in the Age of Anne* (1967)
Hooke Corr.	*Correspondence of Colonel N. Hooke, Agent from the Court of France to the Scottish Jacobites, in the Years 1703 to 1707*, 2 vols., ed. William Dunn Macray (1870–1)
HPC 1690–1715	*The History of Parliament: The House of Commons, 1690–1715*, 5 vols., ed. Eveline Cruickshanks, Stuart Handley, and D. W. Hayton (Cambridge, 2002)
HPL 1660–1715	*The History of Parliament: The House of Lords, 1660–1715*, 5 vols., ed. Ruth Paley (Cambridge, 2016)
JEH	*Journal of Ecclesiastical History*
Jerviswood Corr.	*Correspondence of George Baillie of Jerviswood, 1702–1708*, ed. G. E. M. Kynynmond, Earl of Minto (Edinburgh, 1842)
Lee	William Lee, *Daniel Defoe: His Life, and Recently Discovered Writings*, 3 vols. (1869)
Library	*The Library: Transactions of the Bibliographical Society*
Lillywhite	Bryant Lillywhite, *London Coffee Houses: A Reference Book of Coffee Houses of the Seventeenth, Eighteenth, and Nineteenth Centuries* (1963)
L.J.	*House of Lords Journals*
LMA	London Metropolitan Archives
Lockhart Letters	*Letters of George Lockhart of Carnwath, 1698–1732*, ed. Daniel Szechi (Edinburgh, 1989)
Lockhart Memoirs	George Lockhart of Carnwath, *'Scotland's Ruine': Lockhart of Carnwath's Memoirs of the Union*, ed. Daniel Szechi (Aberdeen, 1989)

xxxv

CONVENTIONS AND ABBREVIATIONS

Lockhart Papers   *Lockhart Papers: Containing Memoirs and Commentaries upon the Affairs of Scotland from 1702 to 1715, by George Lockhart, Esq. of Carnwath,* 2 vols. (1817)

Luttrell   Narcissus Luttrell, *A Brief Historical Relation of State Affairs from September 1678 to April 1714,* 6 vols. (Oxford, 1857)

Marchmont Papers   *A Selection from the Papers of the Earls of Marchmont,* 3 vols., ed. Sir George Henry Rose (1831)

Marl.–God. Corr.   *The Marlborough–Godolphin Correspondence,* 3 vols., ed. Henry L. Snyder (Oxford, 1975)

MLR   *Modern Language Review*

Moore   John Robert Moore, *Daniel Defoe: Citizen of the World* (Chicago, Ill., 1958)

MP   *Modern Philology*

Nicolson   *The London Diaries of William Nicolson, Bishop of Carlisle, 1702–1718,* ed. Clyve Jones and Geoffrey Holmes (Oxford, 1985)

NLS   National Library of Scotland

Norgate   Francis Norgate, 'Correspondence between De Foe and John Fransham, of Norwich (1704–1707)', *N&Q,* 5th ser., 66 (3 Apr. 1875), 261–3; 5th ser., 67 (10 Apr. 1875), 282–4.

Novak   Maximillian E. Novak, *Daniel Defoe, Master of Fictions: His Life and Ideas* (Oxford, 2001)

N&Q   *Notes and Queries*

NRS   National Records of Scotland

ODNB   *Oxford Dictionary of National Biography*

OED   *Oxford English Dictionary*

Oldmixon   John Oldmixon, *The History of England* (1735)

Owens and Furbank, 'Secret Agent'   W. R. Owens and P. N. Furbank, 'Defoe as Secret Agent: Three Unpublished Letters', *The Scriblerian* 25 (1993), 145–53

PBSA   *Papers of the Bibliographical Society of America*

Peterson, *Reference Guide*   Spiro Peterson, *Daniel Defoe: A Reference Guide, 1731–1924* (Boston, Mass., 1987)

PH   *Parliamentary History*

Plomer   Henry R. Plomer, *A Dictionary of the Printers and Booksellers who were at Work in England, Ireland and Scotland from 1668 to 1725* (Oxford, 1922)

PMLA   *Publications of the Modern Language Association of America*

CONVENTIONS AND ABBREVIATIONS

POAS	*Poems on Affairs of State: Augustan Satirical Verse, 1660–1714*, 7 vols., ed. George deForest Lord *et al.* (New Haven, Conn., 1963–75)
PQ	*Philological Quarterly*
RES	*Review of English Studies*
Riley, *English Ministers*	P. W. J. Riley, *The English Ministers and Scotland, 1707–1727* (1964)
Riley, *Union*	P. W. J. Riley, *The Union of England and Scotland: A Study in Anglo-Scottish Politics of the Eighteenth Century* (Manchester, 1978)
Rogers, 'Distribution Agents'	Pat Rogers, 'Defoe's Distribution Agents and Robert Harley', *EHR* 121 (2006), 146–61
Secord	A. W. Secord, 'The Correspondence of Daniel Defoe', *MP* 54 (1956), 45–52
Sharp	Thomas Sharp, *The Life of John Sharp, Archbishop of York*, ed. T. Newcombe, 2 vols. (1825)
Shipley	John B. Shipley, 'Daniel Defoe and Henry Baker: Some of their Correspondence Again and its Provenance', *Bodleian Library Record* 7 (1967), 317–29
SHR	*Scottish Historical Review*
SP	State Papers
SP	*Studies in Philology*
Speck, *Tory and Whig*	W. A. Speck, *Tory and Whig: The Struggle in the Constituencies, 1701–1715* (1970)
Steele Corr.	*The Correspondence of Richard Steele*, ed. Rae Blanchard (Oxford, 1941)
Stephen, *Scottish Presbyterians*	Jeffrey Stephen, *Scottish Presbyterians and the Act of Union, 1707* (Edinburgh, 2007)
Sutherland	James Sutherland, *Defoe* (1937)
Swift Corr.	*The Correspondence of Jonathan Swift, D. D.*, 5 vols., ed. David Woolley (Frankfurt am Main, 1999–2014)
Swift, *EPW 1711–14*	Jonathan Swift, *English Political Writings, 1711–1714*, ed. Bertrand A. Goldgar and Ian Gadd (Cambridge, 2008)
Swift Journal	Jonathan Swift, *Journal to Stella: Letters to Esther Johnson and Rebecca Dingley, 1710–1713*, ed. Abigail Williams (Cambridge, 2013)
Szechi	Daniel Szechi, *Jacobitism and Tory Politics, 1710–1714* (Edinburgh, 1984)
TNA	The National Archives

Trevelyan	George Macaulay Trevelyan, *England Under Queen Anne*, 3 vols. (1930)
Vernon Corr.	*Letters Illustrative of the Reign of William III. From 1696 to 1708. Addressed to the Duke of Shrewsbury, by James Vernon, Esq., Secretary of State*, 3 vols. (1841)
Wentworth Papers	*The Wentworth Papers 1705–1739*, ed. J. J. Cartwright (1883)
Wilson	Walter Wilson, *Memoirs of the Life and Times of Daniel De Foe*, 3 vols. (1830)
Wodrow Corr.	*The Correspondence of the Rev. Robert Wodrow*, ed. Rev. Thomas M'Crie, 3 vols. (Edinburgh, 1842)
Wright	Thomas Wright, *The Life of Daniel Defoe*, London, 1894

CALENDAR OF LETTERS

1703

1. Earl of Nottingham	9 January	3
2. William Paterson	April	10
3. [William Penn]	12 July	15
4. James Stancliffe	[*c.* 9] November	22
5. Robert Harley	9 November	26

1704

6. [Addressee unknown]	18 April	28
7. [Robert Harley]	12 May	29
8. Robert Harley	[16 May]	32
9. Robert Harley	[May–June?]	33
10. Robert Harley	[May–June?]	36
11. Robert Harley	[early July?]	40
12. Robert Harley	7 July	50
13. [Robert Harley]	[July–August?]	52
14. [Robert Harley]	[July–August?]	56
15. [Robert Harley]	[August–September?]	85
16. Samuel Elisha	31 August	94
17. [Robert Harley]	[September?]	95
18. [Robert Harley]	28 September	98
19. [Gabriel Rogers?]	[September–October?]	106
20. [Samuel Elisha]	11 October	107
21. John Fransham to Defoe	[early October]	109
22. [Robert Harley]	2 November	111
23. John Fransham to Defoe	10 November	118
24. John Fransham	[2 December]	120

1705

25. Committee of the Lords	[*c.* 30 January]	122
26. [John Relfe] to Defoe	3 March	128

xxxix

CALENDAR OF LETTERS

27. John Relfe	9 March	129
28. John Fransham to Defoe	29 March	130
29. John Fransham to Defoe	[c. 29 March]	132
30. Lord Halifax	5 April	133
31. John Fransham to Defoe	[c. 5 April]	137
32. John Fransham	[c. 1 May]	139
33. Lord Halifax	[late May?]	141
34. Robert Harley	[early July?]	144
35. Robert Harley	9 July	146
36. Robert Harley	[10 July]	150
37. Robert Harley	[16 July?]	151
38. Lord Halifax	16 July	154
39. Robert Harley	30 July	156
40. Robert Harley	14 August	160
41. Hugh Stafford	14 August	168
42. Robert Harley	10 September	170
43. Edward Owen and Joseph Cater	26–7 October	173
44. Robert Harley	[c. 15 November]	180

1706

45. John Fransham to Defoe	[c. January–April]	190
46. [Robert Harley]	[April]	193
47. [Robert Harley]	6 May	201
48. Robert Harley	21 May	206
49. John Fransham	24 May	207
50. Robert Harley	21 August	210
51. [Robert Harley]	13 September	213
52. Robert Harley	22 September	219
53. Robert Harley	30 September	221
54. Robert Harley	2 October	224
55. [Robert Harley] to [Defoe]	[October?]	225
56. Robert Harley	24 October	226
57. Robert Harley	29 October	234
58. William Melmoth to Defoe	[November?]	237
59. Robert Harley	2 November	240
60. Robert Harley	5 November	244
61. Robert Harley	9 November	247
62. Robert Harley	13 November	251
63. Robert Harley	14 November	255
64. Robert Harley	16 November	258

xl

CALENDAR OF LETTERS

65. Robert Harley	19 November	261
66. [Robert Harley] to Defoe	21 November	264
67. [Robert Harley]	[21–3] November	266
68. [Robert Harley]	[22 November]	271
69. [Robert Harley]	26 November	275
70. [Robert Harley]	28 November	278
71. Robert Harley	30 November	282
72. [Robert Harley]	5–7 December	285
73. Robert Harley	7 December	289
74. [Robert Harley]	9 December	290
75. Robert Harley	12 December	294
76. Robert Harley	14 December	296
77. [Robert Harley]	16 December	297
78. Robert Harley	17 December	301
79. [Robert Harley]	19 December	302
80. Robert Harley	21 December	306
81. Robert Harley	24 December	308
82. Robert Harley	26 December	310
83. Robert Harley	27–8 December	312
84. John Fransham	28 December	315

1707

85. Robert Harley	2 January	319
86. Robert Harley	4 January	322
87. Robert Harley	6 January	324
88. Robert Harley	9 January	325
89. Robert Harley	11 January	328
90. Robert Harley	16 January	329
91. Robert Harley	17 January	330
92. James Webster	[late January?]	334
93. James Webster	[late January?]	336
94. Robert Harley	27 January	337
95. Robert Harley	2 February	341
96. Robert Harley	[13 February]	344
97. Robert Harley	13 February	350
98. Earl of Godolphin	22 February	351
99. Robert Harley	4 March	353
100. Robert Harley	10 March	355
101. John Bell	18 March	357

xli

CALENDAR OF LETTERS

102. Robert Harley	18 March	359
103. Robert Harley	25 March	364
104. Duke of Queensberry	2 April	366
105. Robert Harley	3 April	368
106. Robert Harley	12 April	370
107. Robert Harley	22 April	371
108. Robert Harley	24 April	375
109. Robert Harley	26 April	377
110. Robert Harley	15 May	380
111. Robert Harley	21 May	384
112. Robert Harley	23 May	387
113. Robert Harley	10 [June]	390
114. Robert Harley to Defoe	12 June	391
115. Robert Harley	8 July	396
116. Robert Harley	19 July	399
117. [Robert Harley]	5 August	401
118. [Robert Harley]	7 August	404
119. [Robert Harley]	9 August	408
120. [Robert Harley]	19 August	412
121. Robert Harley	11 September	416
122. Robert Harley	18 September	421
123. Robert Harley	29 September	423
124. Robert Harley	31 October	426
125. Robert Harley	28 November	428
126. John Fransham	20 December	430

1708

127. [Robert Harley]	5 January	432
128. Robert Harley	10 February	433
129. Robert Harley	20 February	436
130. Thomas Bowrey	[9 March?]	439
131. Thomas Bowrey	14 March	442
132. [Earl of Godolphin]	20 April	443
133. Lord Belhaven to Defoe	[April–May]	445
134. [Earl of Sunderland]	20 May	449
135. [Earl of Sunderland]	25 May	455
136. [Earl of Godolphin]	26 June	458
137. [Earl of Godolphin]	29 June	463
138. [Earl of Godolphin]	3 July	465
139. [Earl of Godolphin]	3 August	470

xlii

CALENDAR OF LETTERS

1710

140. Lt.-Gen. James Stanhope	8 March	475
141. John Russell to Defoe	14 March	482
142. Earl of Wharton	7 April	484
143. John Russell to Defoe	8 June	487
144. John Dyer	17 June	489
145. [Robert Harley]	17 July	492
146. [Robert Harley]	28 July	495
147. John Russell to Defoe	8 August	497
148. [Robert Harley]	12 August	498
149. John Russell to Defoe	22 August	501
150. [Robert Harley]	2 September	502
151. [Robert Harley]	5 September	505
152. [Robert Harley]	12 September	517
153. [Robert Harley]	21 September	520
154. John Russell to Defoe	21 September	522
155. [Robert Harley]	29 September	523
156. [Robert Harley]	10 October	527
157. [Robert Harley]	10 October	528
158. [Robert Harley]	[21 October]	537
159. [Robert Harley]	16 November	539
160. [Robert Harley]	18 November	540
161. [Robert Harley]	21 November	546
162. [Robert Harley]	25 November	548
163. [Robert Harley]	3 December	551
164. [Robert Harley]	6 December	552
165. [Robert Harley]	18 December	555
166. Joseph Button to Defoe	[c. 25 December]	558
167. [Robert Harley]	26 December	560

1711

168. [Robert Harley]	1 January	563
169. [Robert Harley]	9 January	566
170. [Robert Harley]	13 February	568
171. [Robert Harley]	19 February	572
172. [Robert Harley]	26 February	577
173. [Robert Harley]	2 March	580
174. [Robert Harley]	3 March	584
175. [Author unknown] to Defoe	24 March	586

xliii

CALENDAR OF LETTERS

176. John Russell to Defoe	19 April	594
177. [Robert Harley]	25 April	596
178. [Earl of Buchan]	26–9 May	600
179. [Earl of Oxford]	7 June	603
180. [Earl of Oxford]	19 June	606
181. John Russell to Defoe	21 June	608
182. [Earl of Oxford]	26 June	609
183. John Russell to Defoe	30 June	611
184. [Earl of Oxford]	13 July	612
185. [Earl of Oxford]	17 July	618
186. [Earl of Oxford]	20 July	623
187. [Earl of Oxford]	[c. 20 July]	626
188. [Earl of Oxford]	23 July	631
189. John Russell to Defoe	26 July	638
190. John Russell to Defoe	4 August	639
191. John Russell to Defoe	10 August	641
192. T. P. to Defoe	15 August	642
193. [Earl of Oxford]	24 August	645
194. [Earl of Oxford]	27 August	646
195. [Earl of Oxford]	3 September	649
196. [Earl of Oxford]	7 September	653
197. [Earl of Oxford]	15 September	655
198. John Russell to Defoe	29 September	658
199. [Earl of Oxford]	16 October	659
200. John Russell to Defoe	13 November	662
201. [Earl of Oxford]	30 November	664
202. John Russell to Defoe	13 December	667
203. [Earl of Oxford]	20 December	667

1712

204. [Earl of Oxford]	10 January	672
205. [Earl of Oxford]	24 January	675
206. [Earl of Oxford]	14 February	678
207. [Earl of Oxford]	5 April	683
208. [Earl of Oxford]	17 April	686
209. [Earl of Oxford]	29 April	687
210. [Earl of Oxford]	27 May	689
211. [Earl of Oxford]	5 June	692
212. [Earl of Oxford]	16 June	693
213. [Earl of Oxford]	18 August	696

xliv

CALENDAR OF LETTERS

214. [Earl of Oxford]	27 August	701
215. [Earl of Oxford]	3 September	704
216. [Earl of Oxford]	20 September	706
217. [Earl of Oxford]	3 October	710
218. [Earl of Oxford]	October	714
219. John Russell to Defoe	30 October	717

1713

220. [Earl of Oxford]	7 January	719
221. [Earl of Oxford]	15 January	721
222. [Earl of Oxford]	19 January	723
223. [Earl of Oxford]	23 January	726
224. William Carstares to Defoe	10 February	727
225. [Earl of Oxford]	14 February	729
226. [Earl of Oxford]	1 April	732
227. [Earl of Oxford]	11 April	736
228. [Earl of Oxford]	12 April	739
229. [Earl of Oxford]	14 April	744
230. [Earl of Oxford]	19 April	746
231. [Earl of Oxford]	18 July	751
232. [Earl of Oxford]	1 August	756
233. [Earl of Oxford]	9 October	758
234. [Earl of Oxford]	16 October	760
235. [Earl of Oxford]	19 October	763
236. [Earl of Oxford]	[c. 22 October]	765
237. [Earl of Oxford]	26 October	770
238. [Earl of Oxford]	28 October	772
239. [Earl of Oxford]	31 October	773
240. Queen Anne	[October/November]	776
241. [Earl of Oxford]	18 November	778
242. [Earl of Oxford]	26 November	779
243. [Earl of Oxford]	7 December	780
244. [Earl of Oxford]	25 December	782
245. [Earl of Oxford]	30 December	784

1714

246. [Earl of Oxford]	19 February	786
247. [Earl of Oxford]	2 March	790
248. [Earl of Oxford]	[c. 10 March]	793

xlv

CALENDAR OF LETTERS

249. [Earl of Oxford]	11 March	805
250. [Earl of Oxford]	21 May	807
251. [Earl of Oxford]	23 June	811
252. [Earl of Oxford]	26 July	813
253. [Earl of Oxford]	3 August	815
254. [Earl of Oxford]	26 August	816
255. [Earl of Oxford]	31 August	821
256. [Earl of Oxford]	28 September	825

1717?

257. Samuel Keimer		828

1718

258. [Charles Delafaye]	12 April	831
259. [Charles Delafaye]	26 April	833
260. Charles Delafaye	10 May	839
261. [Charles Delafaye]	23 May	840
262. [Charles Delafaye]	4 June	843
263. [Charles Delafaye]	13 June	847

1719?

264. Charles Delafaye	[September]	849
265. [Charles Delafaye]	[September]	850

1720

266. [Charles Delafaye]	7 June	850

1728

267. Henry Baker	23 August	854
268. Henry Baker	27 August	858
269. Henry Baker	9 September	860

1729

270. Henry Baker to Defoe	7 January	861
271. Henry Baker	9 January	862

xlvi

CALENDAR OF LETTERS

272. Henry Baker	21 January	864
273. Henry Baker to Defoe	[21–5 January]	866
274. Henry Baker	25 January	867
275. Henry Baker	[April]	869
276. Sophia Baker	9 June	871
277. John Watts	10 September	873

1730

278. Henry Baker	12 August	875

INTRODUCTION

The Scope and Significance of Defoe's Correspondence

Daniel Defoe's (1660–1731) earliest surviving letter dates from January 1703 when he was in hiding, hunted by the government for seditious libel. His last surviving letter was written in August 1730 when, again, he was in hiding, 'about Two mile from Greenwch in Kent', this time from creditors pursuing decades-old debts. Defoe's correspondence sheds light on an elusive, fugitive personality and these letters chronicle the turbulence of Defoe's personal life and public career.[1] Those we have represent a small fraction of Defoe's total correspondence. Nothing has surfaced from his first forty-two years, considerable gaps puncture even comparatively well-covered periods, and few personal letters exist. Nothing survives to or from his wife Mary, the 'woman whose fortunes I have Ruin'd' as Defoe called her, who nonetheless remained his 'faithfull Steward' (Letters 10 and 39).[2] Defoe once wrote that to correspond with friends was 'the greatest pleasure of life' and John Fransham called their exchanges 'complemental correspondence' (Letter 45), but only a handful of letters to his own friends survive.[3] In 1706 he lamented that he had 'so little time to correspond wth my Friends that I every day loose them who cannot bear wth it' (Letter 49). The extant letters do not reflect directly on the novels written from 1719 to 1724 that have made Defoe a household name, or on other important books across a variety of genres he wrote in his later years. The majority comprises his letters in Anne's reign to the politician Robert Harley (1661–1724), Earl of Oxford from 1711, the bulk of which are addressed from Defoe to his patron, preserved because Harley was a prolific collector and state officials at this time removed their correspondence as private property when they left office. Of the 278 letters and documents collected in this edition, 245 were written by Defoe and just 33 to him. Exchanges between Defoe and Harley account for 189 of the 278, but just 3 are from Harley to Defoe.

---

1 For Defoe's biography, see Backscheider, *Life*; Novak; and Backscheider's entry in *ODNB*.
2 The closest thing to connubial correspondence that has survived is the dedicatory epistle from 'Bellmour' to 'Clarinda' with which Defoe prefaced his 'Historical Collections' (*c.* 1683), a manuscript of vignettes transcribed from his juvenile reading in classical and modern history that Defoe presented to Mary upon their marriage (William Andrews Clark Memorial Library, MS. 1951.009, fols. 4–5).
3 *The Compleat English Gentleman* (*c.* 1729), *RDW*, x, 104.

xlix

INTRODUCTION

The epistolary record is thus incomplete to a degree that to claim it as representative is questionable, at least beyond the Defoe–Harley relationship. That important association, an intense decade within Defoe's seventy-year life, gains a disproportionate emphasis in this edition. However, we also have specimens of Defoe's correspondence with other politicians, tradesmen, clergymen, publishers, fellow writers, and members of his family. The letters are vital documents for the study of Defoe and of the political, literary, religious, economic, and social history of the early eighteenth century. Defoe's correspondence illustrates the ways that eighteenth-century letter-writers performed identities in a highly codified medium. His letters are not merely functional or perspicuous documents; they are a mode through which Defoe fashioned and purveyed his selfhood in relation to cultural conditions and interpersonal contexts.[4] Letters in Defoe's time were social as much as private utterances, often written with an eye to readers besides the addressee. Defoe expected his letters to Fransham in Norwich, Samuel Elisha in Shrewsbury, and Edward Owen in Coventry to circulate in whiggish networks in those parts. He knew that Harley shared his political reports with Godolphin and others in government. He ardently hoped that Charles Delafaye showed his letters to Sunderland and Stanhope, for whose eyes Defoe truly wrote them. Defoe forwarded to Harley letters he received from his extensive network of correspondents, especially his Scottish contacts after 1710.

Defoe regarded his letters as a way of getting things done, and scholars have always emphasised their suasive aspects. He is usually trying to achieve something: a specific political objective, the more subtle swaying of his addressee's opinions, his personal advancement or (often) remuneration. He was ready with advice on every conceivable topic, drawing on extensive learning, experience, and acumen, endeavouring to demonstrate his competence, dedication, and value. His letters to Harley traverse a significant difference of status. When their connection began in 1703, Defoe was an impecunious and disgraced author with tenuous claims to gentility. He had been saved from prison and financial ruin by Harley, already one of the most powerful men in government. Harley was the Speaker of the House of Commons, working in partnership with Godolphin's ministry; he would soon be appointed Secretary of State and eventually raised to the peerage and entrusted by Queen Anne with the leadership of the nation. An

---

4 Recent scholarship argues for the 'centrality of letters to eighteenth-century social, political, and literary life', emphasising that 'letters in the eighteenth century were cultural artifacts that revealed the interplay of public and private, political and personal' and that the early modern letter is a 'technology of the self'. See Eve Tavor Bannet, 'Studies in Epistolary Culture', *ECL* 35 (2011), 89–103 (at 90); Nicole Pohl, 'The Plausible Selves of Sarah Scott', *ECL* 35 (2011), 133–48 (at 134); James Daybell, *The Material Letter in Early Modern England: Manuscript Letters and the Culture and Practices of Letter-Writing, 1512–1635* (Basingstoke, 2012).

1

THE SCOPE AND SIGNIFICANCE OF DEFOE'S CORRESPONDENCE

adept licker of spittle, Defoe was nonetheless capable of incredible presumption, abasing himself in one breath but forthrightly offering Harley recommendations on major issues in the next, everything from election management to colonial expansion, from establishing a spy network to suppressing rival journalists. This is part of the performance, which became rhythmical as the relationship developed: expressions of humility precede an over-step before an apology that ingeminates rather than withdraws the proffered counsel. In November 1704, for example, he offered Harley 'a Genuine Candid Observaċon On yᵉ Publick Affaires as Undʳ your Conduct' but quickly retreated – 'and yet who Am I that I Should Pretend to Advise you, Quallifyed to Advise a Naċon' (Letter 22). At one time he emphasised his willingness and ability to solve Harley's problems: 'I am Never Sʳ you kno' for Searching an Evill to be Amazed at it, but to Applye The Remedyes' (Letter 118). Yet elsewhere he uses identical terms but abrogates his agency: 'It is for me Onely to Represent Dangers to yoʳ Ldᵖᵖ, Not to presume to prescribe Remedies' (Letter 218). A profession that he will decline to give advice, because he is 'Affraid to be Officous' (Letter 199), usually means that counsel is coming. As well as public affairs, Defoe offered Harley guidance on preserving one's health from overwork and bearing the grief of losing a daughter. The letters move, often rapidly, between solicitude and temerity.

The period covered by the majority of Defoe's letters was a dynamic and trans-formative one in British history. Queen Anne's reign was marked by furious fighting between and within political parties divided by fundamental questions about the nature of government, the religious settlement, and foreign affairs. Hostilities were fuelled by debates about the constitution and fanned by frequent general elections. Britain was locked in an expensive war on multiple fronts, aiming to preserve the Protestant succession at home and a balance of power in Europe against the last surges of French aggrandisement under Louis XIV. The 1707 Act of Union joined England and Wales with Scotland as Great Britain, requiring delicate, ongoing negotiations regarding the economic, political, and religious composition of the new nation. Religion was at the heart of life and further div-ided the parties. With Whig support, Dissenters from the Church of England such as Defoe had enjoyed liberty of worship since 1689, but High Tories wished to consolidate the Anglican Church's statutory monopoly on political offices by strengthening legal restrictions on Dissenters. Uncertainty hung over the future direction of the nation. Due to the exhaustion of every contingency of the 1688–9 monarchical settlement, the question of the succession was open throughout Anne's reign. Parliament had decreed that a Protestant member of the House of Hanover would succeed her when she died, but Jacobites clung to the hope that the Stuart line would continue, even if that meant a return to Roman Cathol-icism at home and a reversal in foreign policy towards an alliance with France. Political, religious, economic, military, and diplomatic debates were opened up to

INTRODUCTION

much of the nation at large by an expanding press, as pamphlets, periodicals, and poems adopted partisan positions on a raft of topical matters and on the substratal ideologies that informed those viewpoints.

Defoe was one of the most prolific, percipient, and versatile commentators on public affairs in this period, aiming to shape opinion on just about every major topic from the 1690s until the 1720s, working across numerous genres. Owing to his own mobility and the regional distribution networks that he sustained through letters, his writings in Anne's reign had a considerable national reach too. His influence was widely acknowledged. Some contemporaries of course regarded Defoe as a political hireling and turncoat, 'an *Animal* who shifts his Shape oftner than *Proteus*, and goes backwards and forwards like a Hunted *Hare*; a thorough-pac'd, true-bred *Hypocrite*, an *High-Church Man* one Day, and a *Rank Whig* the next'.[5] Such invective shows that his peers struggled to pin down his politics.[6] In a combative print culture mobilised for partisan conflict, defamation of opponents was customary, but the allegations of Defoe's perfidy stand out. Few were accused, as was Defoe, both of playing 'the Old Game of *Forty One* over again' *and* of supporting the cause of '*young J—s*'.[7] In some eyes, he was 'a mean mercenary Prostitute, a State Mountebank, an Hackney Tool, a scandalous Pen, a foul Mouthed Mongrel, an Author who writes for Bread, and lives by Defamation'.[8] The letters help us to see the toll this criticism took on him: 'No Man has been Used like me by this Furious Age', he complained (Letter 221). Others admired his steadfastness in the face of opprobrium and partisanship: 'He is not daunted with Multitudes of Enemies', wrote John Dunton, 'for he faces as many (*every Tuesday, Thursday, and Saturday*) as there are foes to Moderation and Peace.'[9] John Oldmixon remarked that Harley 'paid *Foe* better than he did *Swift*, looking on him as the shrewder Head of the Two for Business', but he also put Defoe at the head of the 'lying scandalous Scriblers' who defended Harley, denouncing 'his abundance of Words, his false Thoughts, and false *English*'.[10] Defoe's letters uncover the motivations behind public writings that attracted such extreme responses. They keep alive rather than settle the debates initiated in Defoe's lifetime about his polemical skill, political convictions, and moral compass.

---

5 *Judas Discuver'd, and Catch'd at last: Or, Daniel de Foe in Lobs Pound* (1713), 3.

6 See Nicholas Seager, 'Party Politics', in *Daniel Defoe in Context*, ed. George Justice and Albert Rivero (Cambridge, forthcoming).

7 *The Review and Observator Reviewed* (1706), 6; *The Gates of Hell Opend, in a Dialogue between the Observator and the Review* (1711), 8.

8 *A Paper concerning Daniel DeFoe* (1708), 7.

9 John Dunton, *Dunton's Whipping-Post: or, A Satyr upon Every Body* (1706), 91; cf. Dunton, *The Preaching Weathercock* [1712], 79–80. He refers to the days on which the *Review* was published. Defoe and Dunton had fallen out by the end of Anne's reign (Letter 248).

10 John Oldmixon, *The Life and Posthumous Works of Arthur Maynwaring* (1715), 276; *A Detection of the Sophistry and Falsities of the Pamphlet entitul'd the Secret History of the White-Staff* (1714), 6, 7.

lii

Defoe's letters reveal aspects of his political thought, religious beliefs, and economic ideas that informed his in-the-moment contributions to debates in published writings. They also show facets of his social being and his personality. His publications famously adopt personae and were usually published without identifying his authorship; even in his long-running periodical, the *Review* (1704–13), which contemporaries knew he wrote, there is a consciously public Defoe, 'Mr Review'. The letters give a more private and often less guarded voice. It is the voice of a man enmeshed in the public events on which he commentates, trying to figure out cataclysmic developments in situ, sometimes working in the loop and at the vanguard of ministerial objectives, but often marginal, neglected, and frustrated, 'Capable of Judgeing but by Outsides of Things, and of knowing Little but without doores' (Letter 252). In the letters, we encounter Defoe on location around Britain for Harley either side of the turbid 1705 general election, on the streets of Edinburgh as protests against the Act of Union raged around him in 1706–7, reacting to attempts from his erstwhile political allies to silence him with trumped-up prosecutions in 1713–14, and undercover among Jacobite journalists when working as a double agent for the government in 1718. As with much of his writings, Defoe's letters give a flavour of the urgency with which he tried to shape circumstances in accordance with his ideals. Being an effective letter-writer was as important as being a skilled pamphleteer, poet, and periodical essayist.

Epistolary Conduct and Education

Defoe's published writings indicate his immersion in a culture that equated epistolary skill with appropriate social and ethical conduct, as well as professional effectiveness. Defoe agreed with John Locke that

the writing of Letters has so much to do in all the occurrences of Humane Life, that no Gentleman can avoid shewing himself in this kind of Writing. Occasions will daily force him to make this use of his Pen, which ... always lays him open to a severer Examination of his Breeding, Sense, and Abilities than oral Discourses.[11]

In Defoe's lifetime numerous letter-writing manuals gave directions on composing epistles to people of different ranks on various occasions, supported by samples that readers could imitate and adapt to confect their own letters. Two chapters of Defoe's *The Complete English Tradesman* (1725–7) resemble such manuals because Defoe's advice to burgeoning merchants includes guidance on writing professional correspondence as 'one of the first things a tradesman ought to be master of'.[12] To illustrate his precepts, he presents several sample letters that provide models to

---

11 John Locke, *Some Thoughts concerning Education* (1693), ed. John W. and Jean S. Yolton (Oxford, 1989), 243.
12 *RDW*, VII, 47.

liii

follow and to reject. Echoing axioms he had laid down in print thirty years earlier in *An Essay upon Projects* (1697), he urges tradesmen to adhere to an epistolary style that is 'plain, concise, and to the purpose', sufficiently detailed that meaning cannot be doubted but free of 'long harangues, compliments, and flourishes' and eschewing 'quaint expressions' and 'book-phrases'.[13] Defoe extends his recommendation of an unadorned style beyond the functional missives of tradesmen to characterise ideal communication in all walks of life:

If any man was to ask me, which would be supposed to be a perfect stile, or language, I would answer, that in which a man speaking to five hundred people, of all common and various capacities, idiots or lunaticks excepted, should be understood by them all in the same manner with one another and in the same sense which the speaker intended to be understood, this would certainly be a most perfect stile.[14]

The Complete English Tradesman equates prudence and regularity with rationality and integrity in approaches to business. Epistolary style is indicative of personal character. The tradesman who ostentatiously embellishes his prose betrays his profligacy and vacuity, showing off to his correspondent rather than cultivating a productive equality of exchange. The letter is an advertisement, a presentation of the professional self as knowledgeable, circumspect, dependable, and equally careful of his correspondent's time as of his wares. Defoe insists that this plain mode will expedite and encourage business transactions, enhance the trader's reputation and credit, and elicit the same sedulous and transparent treatment in return. Just as Defoe extends this ideal to all forms of communication, these principles undergird his self-presentation in his own letters as plain-dealing, concise, competent, attentive to detail, and considerate of his correspondent's needs.

His unfinished book *The Compleat English Gentleman* (*c.* 1729) gives a glimpse of Defoe's own education in letter-writing more than fifty years earlier. He describes the instruction offered at a 'little Academy' by 'a tutor of unquestion'd reputation for learning', appearing to refer to Charles Morton's Newington Green Dissenting Academy where Defoe studied in the 1670s.[15] Alongside a wide curriculum spanning science, rhetoric, languages, geography, and history, the students

wrote epistles twice every week upon such subjects as he prescrib'd to them or upon such as they themselves chose to write upon. Sometimes they were ambassadors and agents abroad at foreign Courts, and wrote accounts of their negotiations and reception in foreign Courts directed to the Secretary of State and some times to the Sovereign himself.

---

13 *RDW*, vii, 47–8. In similar terms in *An Essay upon Projects*, Defoe criticised 'Stiffness and Affectation' in prose, preferring a style he characterised as 'Free and Familiar' (*PEW*, viii, 110, 142).

14 *RDW*, vii, 52.

15 Lew Girdler, 'Defoe's Education at Newington Green Academy', *SP* 50 (1953), 573–91; Ilse Vickers, *Defoe and the New Sciences* (Cambridge, 1996), 32–51.

Some times they were Ministers of State, Secretaries and Commissioners at home, and wrote orders and instructions to the ministers abroad, as by order of the King in Council and the like. Thus he taught his pupils to write a masculine and manly stile, to write the most polite English, and at the same time to kno' how to suit the manner as well to the subject they were to write upon as to the persons or degrees of persons they were to write to; and all equally free and plain, without foolish flourishes and ridiculous flights of jingling bombast in stile, or dull meanesses of expression below the dignity of the subject or the character of the writer.[16]

Defoe must have reflected on how these acts of impersonation came in handy during the years when he did correspond with secretaries of state and monarchs. In his epistolary fiction, *A Continuation of Letters written by a Turkish Spy at Paris* (1718), Defoe engaged in a similar exercise. He composed a series of letters from Mahmut, a Muslim who poses as a merchant in the French capital and sends intelligence reports, in the form of general news and philosophical reflections on cultural and religious differences, back to Constantinople. Anticipating the rules on style laid out in Defoe's conduct books, the supposed translator of Mahmut's letters has endeavoured 'to make the Language plain, artless, and honest, suitable to the Story, and in a Stile easie and free, with as few exotick Phrases and obsolete Words as possible, that the meanest Reader may meet with no Difficulty in the Reading'.[17] The implication is that Mahmut's candour and directness has facilitated the translation of his letters into plain, 'masculine' English.

Defoe saw manliness, plainness, politeness, freedom and ease, and the suitability of the register to the dignity of both subject and addressee as intersecting criteria for effective letters. He animadverted on epistolary carelessness not just in the example of the pretentious tradesman but also in that of the ignorant country squire. In *The Compleat English Gentleman*, Defoe expanded on a complaint he had made in volume II of *The Family Instructor* in 1718, that 'Gentlemen of Pleasure don't care to take the Pains to write Letters'.[18] The deplorable literacy level of the aristocracy, discernible in their letters, is a particularly English defect, Defoe insists, which he sought to redress by urging gentlemen to value a practical and principally vernacular education. Defoe decries the misalignment between 'a gentleman of sense and of tolerable good discourse' and his woefully written letters. He has his laughs transcribing examples of bad orthography ('extraordinary English') and handwriting ('the most comical scrawl of a hand that can be imagin'd'), and would have had more had he published the book and inserted two sample letters he intended to include.[19] However, the point is a serious one, brought home in dialogue between two gentlemen,

16 *RDW*, x, 163–4.
17 *SFS*, v, 46.
18 *RDW*, II, 66; cf. Defoe, *An Essay upon Literature* (1726), *TDH*, IV, 299.
19 *RDW*, x, 97. Harley's scratchy handwriting may have been in Defoe's mind.

lv

INTRODUCTION

one of whom has his steward compose a letter for him to sign. Only gradually, with reluctance, does he admit delegating letter-writing to a servant not only because of a misguided sense of what constitutes drudgery beneath his dignity but also because he is illiterate.[20] The overall thrust of *The Compleat English Gentleman* is that learning, indicated among other things by epistolary competence, adorns even the grandest estate, whereas ignorance shames it and inverts social hierarchy.

Defoe's journalism shows a similar sensitivity to epistolary propriety. The first full book he wrote after his release from prison was *The Storm* in July 1704, and it shows that he regarded letters as valuable sources of 'intelligence', a capacious term in Defoe's understanding. In *The Storm* a multiplicity of reports cumulatively provides a comprehensive perspective on the event, the tempest that ravaged southern England in November 1703, anticipating in some ways the 'scheme of an Office For Secret Intelligence at home and Abroad' Defoe presented to Harley just months later (Letter 11). Even as he apologised for '*the Meanness of Stile*' exhibited by his countrified correspondents in *The Storm*, he described their contributions as 'authentick Vouchers' whose very rusticity attests to their 'Plainness and Honesty' as reliable witnesses of the tempest.[21]

In the early years of the *Review*, Defoe undertook with professed reluctance the task of '*Answering Letters of Doubts, Difficulties, Cases and Questions*' sent in by readers.[22] This is the 'Mercure Scandale' or Scandalous Club section of Defoe's periodical, later expanded first to a monthly supplement and then to *The Little Review*. John Dunton accused Defoe of stealing this 'agony uncle' idea from *The Athenian Mercury* (1691–7), though Defoe insisted that this feature was ancillary to the main design of his paper.[23] Nonetheless, it was soon an overwhelming task, as a 'Glut of Letters' came Defoe's way, some of which he answered in the *Review*, some in private.[24] By January 1705, Defoe complained that 'he has now near 300 Letters, both Publick and Private, before him'.[25] Even after he discontinued the feature, Mr Review continued to receive letters. Defoe was accused of fabricating them, which he denied.[26]

---

20 *RDW*, x, 104–5.

21 Defoe, *The Storm*, ed. Richard Hamblyn (2005), 8, 31.

22 *Review*, I, 4 (preface, Feb. 1705).

23 See Letter 248, note 40; Rachael Scarborough King, '"Interloping with my Question-Project": Debating Genre in John Dunton's and Daniel Defoe's Epistolary Periodicals', *Studies in Eighteenth-Century Culture* 44 (2015), 121–42.

24 *Review*, II, 239 (*Little Review*, no. 1, 6 June 1705).

25 *Review*, I, 719 (30 Jan. 1705).

26 Joseph Browne, *A Dialogue between Church and No-Church: Or, A Rehearsal of the Review* (1706), in *State Tracts*, 2 vols. (1715), I, 9 ff. Defoe elsewhere admitted that inventing readers' letters was common practice (*The Commentator*, no. 15 (19 Feb. 1720), *RDW*, IX, 73–4).

Irrespective of their authenticity, his commentary on the correspondence reveals what Defoe thought constituted sound letter-writing. Predictably, he censures letters that disagree with him and commends those that compliment him, but the terms in which he does so indicate Defoe's epistolary ideals. At the greatest extreme is anonymous hatemail that threatens Defoe with physical violence or assassination.[27] Other hostile letters are variously characterised as 'abusive', 'angry', 'bullying', 'gross', 'insulting', 'railing', 'scandalous', 'scurrilous', 'snarling', 'taunting', 'teizing', 'trifling', 'unmanly', and 'unmannerly'. These adjectives affirm Defoe's preference that communication, even political debate, be conducted in a respectful manner. As he wrote to the Tory author of manuscript newsletters, John Dyer, offering a truce: 'we May Differ Still, and yet preserv both the Christian and The Gentleman' (Letter 144). In the *Review*, he endeavours to treat even impolite journalistic rivals with good manners, attacking arguments, not authors; and he thought that letters readers sent in should abide by the same standards. Anonymous letters peeve Defoe even when not hostile because they frustrate exchange. Defoe spells out his distaste for letters that he feels are baiting him, trying to provoke him to speak out and entangle himself with the government; this kind of subterfuge in correspondence offends Defoe's sense of integrity. Even in his own letters that defame some third party such as Rooke (Letter 11) or Sacheverell (Letter 140), Defoe professes to adhere to a standard of fair play. Defoe describes some mail to the *Review* as 'candid', 'honest', 'ingenuous', 'judicious', 'kind', 'modest', 'plain', and 'respectful'. Notwithstanding obvious reasons for these commendations, Defoe's moralistic treatment of correspondence sent to the *Review* contributed to the cultural policing of letters and reveals the ideals for which he strove when he wrote letters himself.[28] Defoe's sense of acting with rectitude, probity, and dexterity in necessary causes – 'to Open The Eyes of The Honest and well Meaning' (Letter 216) – is reflected not just in *what* he wrote in letters to Harley, Godolphin, and Delafaye, but in *how* he wrote.

Defoe's Epistolary Styles and Personality

Notwithstanding Defoe's self-effacing apologies for his 'Tedious Epistles' (Letter 10), he had a high regard for himself as an effective letter-writer. A letter he wrote to Lord Chief Justice Thomas Parker in 1714, which he told Delafaye had averted

---

27 *Review*, II, 359 (7 July 1705); VI, 2 (preface, 25 Mar. 1710).
28 On the affective qualities of letters in the *Review*, see Jean McBain, '"Love, Marriages, Mistresses, and the Like": Daniel Defoe's Scandal Club and an Emotional Community in Print', in *Passions, Sympathy, and Print Culture: Public Opinion and Emotional Authenticity in Eighteenth-Century Britain*, ed. Heather Kerr, David Lemmings, and Robert Phiddian (Basingstoke, 2016), 68–85.

INTRODUCTION

prosecution for libel and reconciled him to the Whigs (Letter 259), is unfortunately lost. However, in an autobiographical section of Crusoe's *Serious Reflections* (1720) Defoe reflects on that letter's efficacy:

The Letter was so stren[u]ous in Argument, so pathetick in its Eloquence, and so moving and perswasive, that as soon as the Judge read it, he sent him Word he should be easie, for he would Endeavour to make that Matter light to him, and in a Word, never left, till he obtained to stop Prosecution, and restore him to his Liberty and to his Family.[29]

Among the surviving letters, that to Nottingham is the fullest exercise in the pathetic, self-exculpatory strain that Crusoe describes:

My Lord, a Body Unfitt to bear yᵉ hardships of a Prison, and a Mind Impaċent of Confinement, have been yᵉ Onely Reasons of withdrawing My Self: And My Lord The Cries of a Numerous Ruin'd Family, The Prospect of a Long Banishment from mÿ Native Country, and yᵉ hopes of her Majᵗⁱᵉˢ Merċy, Moves me to Thro' my Self at her Majᵗⁱᵉˢ Feet, and To Intreat yoʳ Lordships Intercession. (Letter 1)

Of course, this is a speech act, a dramatisation of obeisance, because, far from prostrating himself at the throne, Defoe had eluded the Queen's Messengers and fled. His request for Nottingham's mediation was not to be reciprocated by the surrender the statesman demanded, and leaving the country might be as much a threat of what Defoe would do unless negotiations start as what he feared would happen after surrender. Just as he could be laborious in trying to pin down meaning, Defoe could be cryptic and vague when it suited his purposes.[30]

In the letter to Nottingham, Defoe employs military metaphors to apologise first for 'Raiseing Warr' against the Queen by absconding and now for the audacity of requesting she 'Capitulate wᵗʰ an offending Subject'. Trusting his writerly talents, Defoe thought initiating a correspondence his best option. He asks Nottingham to send questions in writing:

I will as Soon as I Can Recieve them, give yoʳ Lordship as Plain, Full, Direct, and honest Answers, as If I were in Imediate Apprehensions of Death from yoʳ Resentments; and Perhaps my Lord my Answers may be So Satisfactory, as may Encline you to Think you have been Mis Inform'd Concerning me.

---

29 *Novels*, III, 250.

30 See for example P. N. Furbank and W. R. Owens's attention to Defoe's deliberate ambiguity about the details of his work in Letter 259 ('Defoe, the De la Faye Letters and *Mercurius Politicus*', *BJECS* 23 (2000), 13–19). Paula R. Backscheider attends to Defoe's habits in his letters of trying to preclude misunderstanding; she says that this aim accounts for the prevalence of appositive phrases, relative clauses, elucidating paraphrases, and long-winded clarifications ('Accounts of an Eyewitness: Defoe's Dispatches from the Vale of Trade and the Edinburgh Parliament House', in *Sent as a Gift: Eight Correspondences from the Eighteenth Century*, ed. Alan T. McKenzie (Athens, Ga., 1993), 21–47).

lviii

DEFOE'S EPISTOLARY STYLES AND PERSONALITY

Here is the first of many professions in the Defoe letters of straightforwardness from this self-styled 'Plain and Unpolish'd Man' (Letter 33, to Halifax), one 'Entirely Void of Ceremoney' (Letter 150, to Harley), who does 'not speak ambiguously … atall, but in words at length and Explicit, Such as were Capabl[e] of no other Meaning, So as an Honest Man Ought allways to speak' (Letter 269, to Baker). In many of his letters, Defoe uses the conceit that he writes as though in the very presence of his interlocutor, in this case proximate to the impending violence that Nottingham can inflict but which Defoe hopes his letter will forestall. He carries the conviction that his lucid letters will win over even the people he has offended. Ten years later, Defoe figuratively 'Flyes to yor Majties Clemency' (Letter 240) through another act of writing.

Although Defoe's letters give us relatively direct access to his intimate thoughts and feelings, they are contrivances that shield as much as they reveal inner personality. Modern scholars have used them to understand Defoe as a man but have recognised that the approach is fraught. Healey averred that Defoe's letters supplied 'authentic information about a fascinating and complicated personality'.[31] Secord deemed them 'often personal and always vibrant with life'.[32] It has become common to see letters in which Defoe jumps from topic to topic while living a hand-to-mouth existence as evidence of his mental characteristics including resilience, nimbleness, versatility, and indefatigability. It is equally easy to see Defoe as prone to self-pity and whining, though it is conceivable that he both exaggerates his precarity and diligence *and* that he displays remarkable perseverance. With frankness he told Harley that 'ye Anxieties and Impacence of Perplext Circumstances lessen ye Very Capascity of Service, Sink ye Spirits, and leave Neither ye hands Free, or The head Clear, for any Valluable Performance' (Letter 150). Yet Defoe persisted, as an agent and author, through adversity. He may have been trying to wheedle his son-in-law when, in his last surviving letter, he described his as 'a Mind Sinking under the Weight of an Affliccon too heavy for my strength and looking on my Self as Abandon'd of Every Comfort, Every Friend and Every Relativ, Except Such only as are Able to give me no Assistance' (Letter 278). But there is no reason not to see requests for help as both cynical coaxing *and* as sincere expressions of feelings.

The consensus has emerged that even Defoe's fullest emotional displays are rhetorical, and that his pragmatic objectives, wherever these can be ascertained, account for his self-presentation. Novak argues that Defoe's letters provide 'extensive clues to his feelings and emotions … unfortunately they are clues rather than evidence because almost all of these letters were written with particular goals'.[33]

---

31 *Letters*, ed. Healey, v.
32 Secord, 45.
33 Max Novak, 'Defoe as a Biographical Subject', *Literature Compass* 3 (2006), 1218–36 (at 1220, 1228).

lix

INTRODUCTION

It is hard to imagine Defoe writing anything in which the aim of self-revelation takes precedence over 'particular goals'. Richetti rightly says that 'the inner man, the personality, the actual Defoe, remains an elusive and even a mysterious figure'.[34] Defoe sometimes invites his correspondent to read his letters as windows onto a unique, complex, and private self, what Pope called 'the true and undisguised state of my mind', yet his recondite habits and frequent mendacity, coupled with professions of plain-dealing, discourage us from taking them at face value.[35] Defoe's casuistical definition of deceit justifies wariness: 'Dissembling does Not Consist in Puting a Different Face Upon Our Accons, but in ye further Applying That Concealment to ye Prejudice of ye Person' (Letter 14). Even when, or especially when, Defoe is conveying his emotions rather than describing events, the reader needs to have her guard up. As Starr states, Defoe's letters 'have to be read as deliberate rhetorical artefacts, not as spontaneous outpourings of his deepest feelings. This is not to say that they are *not* revealing, autobiographically, but rather that what they reveal has to come from reading between the lines.'[36]

Early in his relationship with Harley, Defoe intimated that letters allowed him to express things that he struggled to vocalise in their 'short Interviews' (Letter 9). Harley had asked Defoe for a personal account of his difficulties since *The Shortest Way with the Dissenters*. Defoe offers an apology for tediousness: 'ye Miserable are allways full of Their Own Cases and Think Nothing Impertinent. I write This for tis too Moveing for me to Speak it' (Letter 10). Defoe presents his letters as restrained but not dispassionate – the act of writing is a controlled emotional release. They brim with self-deprecatory epithets that invite sympathy; he is 'a Man Lately Made Despicable' (Letter 7, to Harley), 'a Man Crusht by Inumerable Disasters' (Letter 136, to Godolphin), and a 'Great Sufferer' (Letter 266, to Delafaye). His letters to patrons are always to be forgiven for their impertinence and importunity in describing Defoe's 'Unhappy Craveing Circumstances' (Letter 174), especially when they contain an unbecoming emotional overflow coupled with requests for money, which often fade to statements about the ineffability of feelings: 'I Cease to go On wth This Sad story, and Tho' my Case Renders me Now Next to Desperate, yet I Can not Enlarge on my Complaint' (Letter 47). For all that Defoe's letters are practical documents, they convey intense emotion.

34 John Richetti, *The Life of Daniel Defoe: A Critical Biography* (Oxford, 2005), viii; cf. Richetti, 'Writing About Defoe: What is a Critical Biography?', *Literature Compass* 3 (2006), 65–79.

35 Pope to John Caryll, 5 Dec. 1712, *The Correspondence of Alexander Pope*, ed. George Sherburn, 5 vols. (Oxford, 1956), I, 161.

36 *Novels*, III, 6. For competing approaches to inferences about Defoe's personality from the letters and wider writings, see Paula R. Backscheider, 'Defoe: The Man in the Works', in *The Cambridge Companion to Daniel Defoe*, ed. John Richetti (Cambridge, 2009), 5–24; Ashley Marshall, 'Fabricating Defoes: From Anonymous Hack to Master of Fictions', *ECL* 36 (2012), 1–35.

lx

DEFOE'S EPISTOLARY STYLES AND PERSONALITY

Backscheider argues that biblical allusion in correspondence gave Defoe a means of understanding his service as a recapitulation of scriptural paradigms and as 'a dignified means of emotional release' for someone constrained in his expression by his masculinity, social inferiority, and need to present himself as a capable worker.[37] It is telling that Defoe frequently identifies with disabled biblical figures such as the one grateful leper (Letter 5), 'ye Cripple at ye Pool' (Letter 30), or the blind man restored to sight by Christ.[38] Thriving on a religious concept of 'service', he dreaded incapacitation. Some of Defoe's most moving letters are those in which he empathises with the spiritual condition of his correspondent. He tells the afflicted Keimer that 'The Time of Sorrow is a Time to reflect, and to look and see wherefore he that is righteous is contending with you. Only remember that he is not mocked. Nothing but a deep, thorough, unfeigned, sincere Humiliation is accepted by him' (Letter 257). Defoe took it upon himself to strengthen and support the religious convictions of men he cared about, impressing upon the bereaved Harley the necessity of 'That Soveraign Specifick, That Truly Noble and Sublime Remedy I Mean <u>Resignačon</u>' (Letter 242). Defoe's style becomes rapturous and figural when he relates events to Providence. In a letter to Fransham in the wake of the defeat of the Tack in spring 1705, he expresses his confidence that 'the work I am upon is of him whose immediate hand by wonderful steps have led me through Wildernesses of Troubles and Mountains of popular Fury' (Letter 32). His letter to Harley after Guiscard's assassination attempt is a tissue of biblical allusions through which Defoe marvels at 'ye wonders of Providenče', imputing Harley's survival to God's plans for him: 'Nor can it be Doubted, But as yor preservačon beares a proporčon to The greatness of The worke you have to do, So The work beares a due proporčon to ye Greatness of The Deliveranče'. Defoe apologises for 'Goeing Thus Out of My way ... in this Manner of Discourse' and brings the letter to an unplanned conclusion not because he has exhausted his supply of biblical metaphors but because contemplating it all has overwhelmed him: 'The Subject Sr is So Moveing, My weakness Betrays it Self, and I am Forčed to break off' (Letter 177).

As in his conduct writing on epistolary style, Defoe's letters promote staid plainness as evidence of candour, which explains the embarrassment he felt about moments of emotional overflow. He thought that plainness, manifest in both the substance and style of his letters, attested to his impartiality, objectivity, and reliability, such as when he wrote to Sunderland: 'I kno' Nothing Can be More Agreeable to yor Ldpp or More Usefull to ye Publick Serviče, than plain, Naked and Unbyass't Accots both of Persons and of Things, and yor Ldpp shall allways

---

37 Paula R. Backscheider, 'Personality and Biblical Allusion in Defoe's Letters', *South Atlantic Review* 47 (1982), 1–20 (at 12).
38 *Appeal*, 12.

lxi

find me Endeavouring to act the honest Rather than ye Artfull part in My Acco^ts' (Letter 134). Defoe laid out matters to Harley with 'A plaineness wch I hope yor Ld^pp will allow to be my Duty' (Letter 194), but as well as a sign of his loyal discharging of his commissions, Defoe's letters emphasise that unvarnished style is an indication of his privileged intimate fidelity, which he continually invokes following his admittance to 'So Near and So Advantageous a Conversa\u0107on' with the Secretary (Letter 7). He recalls 'The Freedome of a plain and Direct Stateing things to you' when he needs to complain about his treatment by Harley (Letter 121). Defoe's plainness reinforces his earnestness, which extenuates the risk of social impropriety:

> The Freedome you Allwayes gave me, and which I Think it was Never More my Duty to Take, Oblidges me to Talk to you, in Terms Too Course for y^e Distan\u0107e between yor Character, yor Person, yor Merit, <u>and Me</u>. I Beseech you Pla\u0107e my want of De\u0107en\u0107y, to y^e Acco^t of my Passion if Possible to Render you Servi\u0107e. (Letter 22)

Another risk Defoe navigated with his self-styled plainness was that of constantly being a harbinger of doom, which he feared was his inevitable role as the person telling his masters things they would rather not hear. There were other risks of misconstrual, which Defoe sought to allay: 'when I give his Ld^ship [Godolphin] a Very Mellancholly Acco^t of Things, it is Neither to Enhan\u0107e his Opinion of my Servi\u0107es nor to Suggest y^t I am Either weary Or Affraid of the Undertakeing' (Letter 119). Defoe was constantly mindful of how his correspondent viewed him.

Actually, Godolphin had told Harley, 'I have often observed that [Defoe] gives you the worst side of the picture.'[39] This is largely true, especially when Defoe was writing to the politicians about the Union. The commotions he experienced in Scotland must have seemed remote and inconsequential to the politicians in London sure of a parliamentary majority in Edinburgh. The negativity of Defoe's letters is instructive for its contrast with his published writings. Regarding the apprehensions of the ministers of the Church of Scotland, Defoe wrote to Fransham, 'I endeavour in the Review … to put the best Face on the proceedings of the Kirk' (Letter 84), and this tactic of emphasising the positives in periodical and pamphlets extends to several other matters concerning the events of 1706–7. In contemporaneous letters to Harley, by contrast, he vented about these 'Unaccountable people, Humorous, Jealous, Partiall, Censorious, Haughty, Insolent and Above all Monstrously Ignorant' (Letter 105). Defoe's letters are more candid and censorious than his published writings. They show anxieties that he suppressed for the public. Cockburn astutely compares Defoe's Union letters with his *History of the Union* (1709/10):

> By comparison with these hurried epistles, with their acute perception of affairs, their frank, unrestrained expression, their bustling eagerness to prove the author's possession of the

39 H.M.C. *Bath MSS*, 178.

lxii

DEFOE'S EPISTOLARY STYLES AND PERSONALITY

key to every problem, their impatience with fearful souls whom yet he has continually to conciliate, the same writer's *History of the Union* appears tame and insipid. In the former, the individual note is everywhere, and we see men and things as the active, strenuous Defoe saw, and wished his employer to see, them; in the latter, we have the cautious historian, who has played a certain *rôle* in the events he is narrating, and dare not display his true, critical character.[40]

The stylistic vibrancy of Defoe's letters stems from the author's uncertainty about outcomes and the urgency of his need to persuade others.

A number of scholars have attended to Defoe's prose style, acknowledging that, although he champions linguistic plainness, this is inadequate by itself to account for the versatility of his writing. Starr recognises Defoe's ability to enhance 'utilitarian' prose that purports to describe things exactly with a more subjective style through which we see people perceiving things.[41] Starr shows how this works in Defoe's novels to draw attention to the narrators as shapers of their realities. Here are two paragraphs from Defoe's letter on the civil disorder in Edinburgh on 23 October 1706 which operate in a similar way:

The Mob Came up staires to his [Sir Patrick Johnston's] Door and fell to work wth sledges to break it Open, but it seems Could not, His Lady in ye Fright wth Two Candles in her hand that she might be known Opens ye Windows and Cries Out for God Sake to Call ye Guard. …

Dureing this Hurry whether they Omitted shutting ye North port as they Call it wch goes to Leith or that it was not yet Ten a Clock I kno' not But a Second Rabble of 500 Some say a Thousand stout fellows Came up from Leith and Disporting themselves in the street Continued the Hurry in a Terrible Manner. (Letter 56)

Even in the fragmentary quotations I have extracted from the letter, the account is gripping because it satisfies truths about the 'breathless' urgency of Defoe's best prose and his knack for innocuous but enlivening details such as the candles and the wife's cry for help.[42] The latent intentions Cockburn noticed are here too: Defoe is indeed demonstrating his acuity, utility, and perceptual command of even a chaotic scene. The letter gives a sense of documentary objectivity, but it is vivified by tacit evaluations that show it to be a subjective *impression* of events ('Mob', 'Rabble', 'stout fellows', 'Disporting'), and by Defoe's manner of giving the immediate, personal impression ('Terrible Manner') as well as the retrospective, collective understanding ('Some say a Thousand'). Defoe had a talent for presenting a personal outlook as purely objective reportage.

---

40 James D. Cockburn, 'Daniel Defoe in Scotland', *Scottish Review* 36 (1900), 250–69 (at 253).
41 G. A. Starr, 'Defoe's Prose Style: 1. The Language of Interpretation', *MP* 71 (1974), 277–94.
42 Bonamy Dobrée, 'Some Aspects of Defoe's Prose', in *Pope and His Contemporaries: Essays Presented to George Sherburn*, ed. James L. Clifford and Louis A. Landa (Oxford, 1949), 171–84 (at 180).

lxiii

INTRODUCTION

Furbank and Owens have challenged criticisms of Defoe's prose that hold it to inappropriate standards of 'correctness', arguing that his metier was the 'improvisatory sentence'. Of one section from *An Essay upon Projects*, they write: 'Those interpolations that keep coming thrusting in, saving the sentence ('passage'?) from expiry, are syntactically perfectly sound; the logic of the sentence's endless extension is impeccable; and in retrospect the sentence is found to be most beautifully organised and articulated.'[43] The idea applies to Defoe's letters. A small example is Defoe's account of his agent John Pierce's work among Scottish Covenanters:

He has been at Dumfreis, in yᵉ Mountaines of Galloway, in yᵉ Dales, and Allmost Every where, he has been wᵗʰ mʳ John Hepburn The Cameronian Bishop, spent Three dayes wᵗʰ him, and with his Disciples, heard him preach and pray without Intermission near 7 houres, to a Vast Congregaċon Severall of wᶜʰ Came 24 Miles on foot to hear him, he has Opened his Eyes in Severall things, and he shows us he has been Missrepresented in Severall Others, and he Authourizes me to assure you there is No Danger from him, Unless Some New Artifiċe Succeed to Inflame them. (Letter 82)

Generalisations about the non-existence of punctuation in Defoe's manuscripts persist even among critics eager to show the artfulness of his prose, but this sentence has received no editorial additions. The three independent clauses use the anaphora ('he has …') that Curtis shows was essential to Defoe's rhetorical armoury, controlling the masculine personal pronouns for Pierce and Hepburn with great skill.[44] With Defoe, we need to resist a division between 'factual' letters that report situations and 'rhetorical' letters that express selfhood: in Defoe, the presentation of detail is part of the rhetoric, such as the acceleration of 'Three dayes', '7 hours', and '24 Miles'. In sum, Defoe's letters deserve to be read for personality and style as well as for the sociohistorical significance to which I now turn.

Politics and Intelligence

When Defoe was a young man in the mid-1680s, England's political situation seemed so dire to him that he joined a ragtag rebellion led by an illegitimate son of Charles II, narrowly escaping capture as Monmouth's makeshift rebels were rounded up. Defoe was lucky to be included in a general pardon in 1687.[45] In 1720,

43 P. N. Furbank and W. R. Owens, 'Defoe and the "Improvisatory" Sentence', *English Studies* 67 (1986), 157–66 (at 159).
44 Laura A. Curtis, 'A Rhetorical Approach to the Prose of Daniel Defoe', *Rhetorica* 11 (1993), 293–319.
45 *Appeal*, 28; TNA SP 44/337, fol. 281.

lxiv

towards the end of a long career of trying to shape public opinion on current affairs, Defoe could reflect:

Whatever particular Errors or Inconveniencies People may find in our Government, or whatever Dislike they may have to the Persons of our Governors, yet I believe they have very few Objections to the general Frame of our Constitution; and would not, if it were put to their Choice, change it for any other now subsisting in the World.[46]

Defoe felt he had both chronicled and contributed to this rise of political stability. He wrote in opposition to James II's tyranny in the 1680s and defended William III and the Revolution in the following decade.[47] After one risk too many during the High Tory resurgence following Anne's accession, Defoe fell foul of the law, but thereafter he settled into supporting all her ministries, both Whig and Tory. By the time he lionised the British constitution as an ideal balance of the sovereign's authority and the subject's rights in 1720, Defoe had both served and satirised the Whig government of early Hanoverian Britain. But he was content that the fundamental question about the constitution, about whether tyranny and Popery or liberty and Protestantism would prevail, had been settled in favour of the latter.

Becoming what one detractor called the '*most chosen Privy-Counsellor*' to Robert Harley irreparably damaged Defoe's reputation.[48] ''Till he enter'd into the Service of Mr. Harley, he had been honest in his Principles, whatever his Morals were', wrote John Oldmixon.[49] His honesty in this account refers to his support for Revolution principles, and despite such slurs Defoe never relinquished those principles. As he wrote to a like-minded acquaintance, Defoe thought that 'the Collective or Representative body of This Nation May Limitt, alter or Interrupt yᵉ Succession of yᵉ Crown' (Letter 43). And the Revolution was a religious as well as a political victory: 'Persecucon was Checkt by Authourity, and Liberty of Conścience Declar'd a Native Right, yᵉ Gust of Unlimited Power was Damn'd by Parliament, and all yᵉ Depredacons on yᵉ peoples property Made Void, and Declar'd illegall' (Letter 15). Oldmixon was recalling that, towards the end of William's reign, Defoe set up his stall as a fearless Whig who defended the King against obstructive parliaments in his military and diplomatic opposition to French aggression.[50] This stage of Defoe's career climaxed with the triumphs of 1701–2: the

---

46 *The Commentator*, no. 33 (22 Apr. 1720), *RDW*, IX, 145.
47 *A Letter to a Dissenter from his Friend at the Hague* (1688), *PEW*, I, 27–36.
48 *The Welsh-Monster: or, the Rise and Downfal of That Late Upstart, the R—t H----ble Innuendo Scribble* (1708), sig. A2r.
49 Oldmixon, 301.
50 See most importantly Defoe, *An Argument Shewing, That a Standing Army, with Consent of Parliament, is not Inconsistent with a Free Government* (1698), *PEW*, I, 63–79; *An Encomium on a Parliament* (1699), *SFS*, I, 59–62; *The Six Distinguishing Characters of a Parliament-Man* (1701), *PEW*, II, 29–37.

lxv

INTRODUCTION

provocative satire *The True-Born Englishman* (1700/1), the audacious parliamentary petition dubbed *Legion's Memorial* (1701), his contribution to Whig political theory in *The Original Power of the Collective Body of the People of England* (1701), and his uncompromising charge of hypocrisy against Tory defenders of passive resistance in *A New Test of the Church of England's Loyalty* (1702). But William died in March 1702, and at the end of that year Defoe became a victim of the Tories' desire to reassert the Church's supremacy. He was prosecuted for his satire on the zeal of the Anglican clergy in *The Shortest Way with the Dissenters*, which is where the surviving letters begin. Then, less than a year after being pilloried, Defoe was writing for the ministry. He persuaded himself that he could honour Revolution principles by working with the government. In truth, he had little choice. His letters document his effort, in part successful if not wholly so, to maintain his integrity. He pointed out that it was a ministry shorn of most High Tories: it was 'the joyning of Court and Whig' under Lord Treasurer Godolphin and so represented no betrayal of principles as Defoe understood it.[51] Moreover, Defoe's fixation on gratitude as a moral virtue which forged social bonds and approximated divine worship made his service to Harley a matter of duty.[52]

Harley's was a mercurial personality: he was personable and easygoing, inspired loyalty and encouraged frankness. He enjoyed fine wine, antique books, and learned company. He was also secretive, cryptic, and dilatory. His silence, at times deafening in Defoe's correspondence, could be punishment, procrastination, or approbation. Contemporaries testified that Harley seemed intuitively to know what motivated people. He cultivated contacts across religious, political, and social divides that confused contemporaries, and he earned the nicknames Robin Trickster and Harlequin. He was regarded as the best parliamentary manager of his day. His political creed was moderation, an ingrained opposition to factionalism and corruption in public office. His Puritan heritage and upbringing made him a prospective ally to Dissenters, but he supported and conformed to the national Church. Like Defoe, he was committed to the legacy of the 1688 Revolution, but he led the Country Party in opposition to William III during the 1690s. Harley nonetheless regarded royal authority, duly limited by parliament, as a guarantor of political stability, and he transitioned to being a Court politician amidst the succession crisis of 1701, when he became Speaker of the House of Commons. He had garnered credibility from both Whigs and Tories,

---

51 *Review*, v, 482 (25 Nov. 1708).
52 'The <u>Vertue</u> which I Call Gratitude, has Allwayes So Much Pride in it, as Makes it Push at a Retribuċon, Tho' 'tis Unable to Effect it', Defoe wrote at the start of his relationship with Harley (Letter 5), and his *Appeal* emphasised the significance of gratitude to his outlook. See Maximillian E. Novak, *Defoe and the Nature of Man* (Oxford, 1963).

lxvi

but adhered thereafter to the latter party, which is why Defoe's allegiance to him seemed to contemporaries like apostasy.[53]

Following his release from prison in late 1703, Defoe's loyalty to the government was an extension of his gratitude to Harley, to whom he wrote: 'Besides my being by Inclinaćon and prinćiple heartily in yᵉ Interest of yᵉ Governmᵗ, So I am p[er]ticularly in a great Varyety of Obligaćons and More Than Commonly by my Own Affecćons link't to yoʳ p[er]sonall Intrest, and shall be Glad to Distinguish my Self in any Thing and at Any hazard for your Serviće' (Letter 9). Throughout their association Defoe was glad to have 'my Gratitude Mixt wᵗʰ the Serviće of My Country', a personal basis for his public service (Letter 145). Harley was appointed Secretary of State in May 1704 when his 'middle way' became ministerial policy, and Defoe echoed his patron's maxims back to him when he wrote that 'This Naćon is Unhappily Divided into Partyes and Facćons', and 'yᵉ Moderate Men of both Partyes are yᵉ Substantiall part of yᵉ Nacon; They are its Refuge when yᵉ Men of Heat Carry Things too farr' (Letter 15). In its first year, Defoe's *Review* 'carefully avoided medling with State Affairs, or siding with Parties', all but excluding the words 'Whig' and 'Tory' from its pages.[54] Defoe checked with Harley that his writings were agreeable to the ministry (Letter 12), but it must also be recognised that much of what he wrote in 1704 – on press regulation, Dissent, and the naval war – is by no means propaganda directed by the ministry. Harley received several adverse reports from government informants about Defoe's writings, and Defoe lied to him on occasion, such as about the grounds for his advice to remove Admiral Rooke from command (Letter 11).

Defoe insisted on his independence. Eight years into their partnership, when accusations of venality were at their height, he wrote to Harley that 'yoʳ Goodness to me was founded On No Prinćiples of Bribery, and Corrupćon, but a generous Compassion to a Man Oppressed by Power without a Crime ... Leaving me at full Liberty to Persue My Own Reason, and Prinćiple; And above all Enableing Me to Declare my Innoćenće In the Black Charge of Bribery' (Letter 213). In support of this interpretation of at least the foundation of the relationship is the fact that in 1704 Defoe sent Harley far more advice than Harley sent him directions. Yet the thrust of some of Defoe's advice does not speak to his integrity. Early in their association, Defoe guided Harley on how to 'manage' Defoe's quondam allies, the Dissenters and Whigs. The former 'are to be Pleas'd wᵗʰ words' (Letter 14),

---

53 For Harley's biography and political ideas, see *inter alia*: Angus McInnes, *Robert Harley, Puritan Politician* (1970); Sheila Biddle, *Bolingbroke and Harley* (New York, 1975); Downie, *Robert Harley*; Hill; David Hayton, 'Robert Harley's "Middle Way": The Puritan Heritage in Augustan Politics', *BLJ* 15 (1989), 158–72; W. A. Speck's entry in *ODNB*; Hayton's entry in *HPC 1690–1715*, IV, 244–80; Robin Eagles's entry in *HPL 1660–1715*, III, 230–51.

54 *Review*, I, 428 (7 Oct. 1704).

their loyalty to the government secured with vague promises rather than the easing of legal restrictions: 'They are Better kept at a Due Distance Provided Not Made Uneasÿ' (Letter 15). And, Defoe announced, 'the whigs are weak; they may be Mannag'd, and Allways have been So. What Ever you do if Possible Divide Them, and they are Easy To be Divided. Caress The Fools of Them Most, There are Enough Among Them' (Letter 22). Defoe encouraged Harley to 'Make a Vertue of Hypocrisy' in order to become prime minister: to promote his personal popularity, circumvent cabinet councils, and establish intelligence networks to accrue and consolidate power (Letter 14). One year after the ignominy of the pillory, this failed brick manufacturer brazenly told the most powerful Commoner in England that 'you Must be prime Minister with Applause, or you will be Secretary with Disgrace'. Without blinking, Defoe urged Harley to engage in gunboat diplomacy with Sweden by sending warships into the Baltic and to focus the attention of England's Austrian allies on the war with France by threatening to fund Hungarian independence fighters to the tune of £1,000,000 (Letter 14).

From these fantastical forays into international relations, Defoe's political work settled down to domestic realities. In 1705, in the *Review* and on location around England, he promoted the ministerial message of 'Moderaćon and Union', devised to oppose the election to parliament of High Tories (Letter 44). The outcome was what Defoe called the 'best Parliament this Age can remember'.[55] He regarded the Union as the capping achievement of this parliament; it was also Defoe's proudest political accomplishment, combining his desires to support the Hanoverian succession and enhance Britain's commercial progress, with the bonus of ratifying the legal establishment of the Presbyterian Church of Scotland. For all Defoe's tendencies to self-dramatise and aggrandise his role, danger, and deserving with respect to the Union, he is justified in writing that 'I Faithfully Serv'd, I baulk't No Cases, I Appear'd in print when Others Dared not to Open Their Mouths, and without boasting I Run as Much Risq of my life, as a Grenadr in storming a Counterscarp' (Letter 121). While he was there, however, fractures had formed within government over the ministry's growing dependence on the Whigs. Harley, who regarded the Junto Lords as self-interested zealots – 'reall Atheists & pretended Patriots', as he confided to Defoe (Letter 114) – lost out to Godolphin and fell from power in 1708. Defoe promptly wrote to Harley 'in Duty and Gratitude to Offer my Self to you Against all yor Enemies' (Letter 128).

He nonetheless continued to work for the now predominantly Whig ministry, apparently with Harley's blessing. What should have been a happy alliance proved otherwise. He remained diligent but Defoe never had a personal connection with Godolphin or Sunderland. As he covered the 1708 general election in Scotland,

55 *Review*, IV, 69 (13 Mar. 1707).

POLITICS AND INTELLIGENCE

Defoe saw depressing evidence of Whig in-fighting. The Junto connived with Jacobites to undermine Godolphin in what Defoe saw as an unscrupulous pursuit of control. Mismanagement resulted in a failure to secure peace with France in 1709, and then the ministry reunified the Tories with their ill-judged impeachment of the seditious clergyman Henry Sacheverell. During the ministerial revolution of 1710, when Anne ejected the Whig ministers she had grudgingly appointed, and ultimately dismissed Godolphin, Defoe rejoined the resurgent Harley's camp, where he thought he could 'Serv both wᵗʰ Principle, and Inclinaċon' (Letter 150). He wrote to Harley that 'Now is The Time to find Out and Improve Those blessed Mediums of This Naċons happyness, which lye between The wild Extremes of all Partys, and which I know you have long Wisht for' (Letter 145). Publicly he promoted 'a Third Party that must carry the Balance between the Extreams on both sides'.[56] However, Harley's aim to construct a mixed ministry was thwarted when moderate Whigs resisted his overtures – for Defoe, another mark against them – forcing Harley to collaborate with High Tories.

Regardless of Harley's expediencies, Defoe demonstrated his underlying outlook in election propaganda in 1710 when he defined a Tory as 'a Persecutor for Religion, a Bloody Destroyer without Law, a Betrayer of Liberties, and one that will give up his Nation to *Popery* and *Arbitrary Power*, under the pretence of Passive Obedience and Non Resistance'.[57] But after the Tory landslide, Defoe's tune changed – or perhaps changed back to where he stood in 1704:

I have always thought, the only true Fundamental Maxim of Politicks that will ever make this Nation happy, is this — That the Government ought to be of *no Party at all* ... Statesmen are the Nation's Guardians, their Business is not to make Sides, and divide the Nation into Parties, and draw the Factions into Battle Array, against one another, their Work ought to be to scatter and disperse Parties, as they would Tumults, and keep a Ballance among the Interfering Interests of the Nation.[58]

Trusting that, under Harley, 'Tolleraċon, Succession or Union are Not Struck at' (Letter 146), Defoe worked 'to keep up The Governmᵗˢ Intrest, and Ballanċe the Mad Men on both Sides' (Letter 194). He insisted that even a Tory government was bound by the constitution defined by the Revolution and Union, forced despite itself to act whiggishly by honouring the laws guaranteeing the Hanoverian succession, the Toleration Act, and the Church of Scotland. This stance struck the Whigs as specious: 'The profess'd Jacobites are now become his Admirers', they sneered.[59] During the next few years, though Defoe's confidence in the irrevocability of the religious legislation produced by the Revolution and the

56 *Review*, VII, 223 (8 July 1710).
57 *Review*, VII, 360 (16 Sept. 1710).
58 *Review*, VII, 1 (preface, 25 Mar. 1711).
59 *Observator*, 1–5 Dec. 1711.

lxix

INTRODUCTION

Union was proven to be misplaced, his confidence on the succession was tested but ultimately vindicated.

Defoe insisted that his alienation from the Whigs was because they, not he, had betrayed their values. Their support for the Occasional Conformity Act (1711) was a flashpoint. It was especially galling in combination with new legislation affecting the Church of Scotland, for which Defoe felt personally accountable. He had spent months in 1706–7 reassuring 'The Rigid and Refractory Clergy' of the Kirk that a British parliament would respect the terms of the Union (Letter 113). As for the Act closing the loophole of Dissenters occasionally conforming in order to qualify for public office, Defoe traced his suffering in 1703 to his un-appreciated defence of Dissenters against earlier iterations of this precise legisla-tion, even though he personally opposed the practice of occasional conformity. 'It makes me Reflect on ye wholl body of ye Dissenters wth Something of Contempt More Than Usuall', he wrote at that time, 'and gives me ye More Regrett That I Suffer for Such a People' (Letter 2). Defoe's reaction in his letters to the 1711 Act was highly commendable. He did everything in his limited power to sway the government: the public and private expressions cohere, even in hardnosed state-ments such as when he admits, 'This Makes me I Confess not atall Regrett that they Are Ruin'd in their Politick Intrest, hopeing Still that Their Religious Intrest Shall be Established by it' (Letter 209). Yet Defoe was increasingly embittered by the 'Persecuçon and Reproach' directed against him by 'whigs and Dissenters' (Letter 206). His minatory pamphlet *A Letter to the Dissenters* (1713) threatens government retribution under the veil of offering home truths. Defoe was not bluffing. As he wrote to Harley, 'Either My Lord These Men Must alter Their Conduct to ye Governm^t or ye Governm^t Must alter its Conduct to Them. There is a Time when Clemency becomes Criminall' (Letter 244). When the Schism Bill was pending a year later Defoe wrote: 'The Conduct of The Dissenters has call'd for More Than this, and This may Remind them of a hint I gave Them in <u>The Letter</u>, whether They Enjoy'd No Favours from her Maj^ties Bounty which They might not Forfeit by Their present behaviour' (Letter 250). Though he had always given Harley advice on how to manage the Dissenters, it became vindictive at the end of Anne's reign.

Rewarded with payments from secret service funds, Defoe supported the To-ries on the most contentious issue of the 1710–13 parliament: peace with France. He was assailed from both ends of the political spectrum, and the reason for this is suggested by Arthur Maynwaring, who attests to the difficulty of classifying De-foe's politics: 'He writes one Day like a violent Whig, the next Day like a rampant Tory.'[60] Two issues that illustrate the invidious position in which Defoe found himself are Marlborough's dismissal from command and the restraining orders

60 *Medley*, 14–18 July 1712.

lxx

issued to his successor at the head of the army, Ormond. Defoe wrote to Harley approving 'This Most Necessary step, of Deposeing The Idol Man, who Coveted to Set himself up as The head of a Party, and by whom They pretended to Make Themselves Formidable' (Letter 204). Marlborough's reputation had bifurcated along party lines. Tories saw him as vainglorious and covetous; Whigs thought his unsurpassed military triumphs were being betrayed by a grubby peace. Defoe's position is characteristically more ambivalent, indicated by his subtle equivocation in the *Review* following Marlborough's dismissal: 'If there is no Occasion for Displacing the Duke, I am sorry it is done, for the Nation's sake; and if there is an Occasion for it, I am doubly sorry for it, for his sake.'[61] He barely hints at the misconduct that Swift, for one, was advertising without restraint. Confounding matters, Defoe both countered the strongest Tory censure of Marlborough and turned on the Whigs who, he says, followed their campaign against Harley in 1708 by trying to remove their own confederates, Godolphin and Marlborough, too: 'These very Whig Lords, this very Juncto, that now stickle and struggle for the D— of M——, are the same who laid the Foundation of his Fall.'[62] Whig faithlessness helped Defoe to reconcile himself to supporting the ministry. To Defoe's discredit, that support was at times unconditional; time and again, he glozed his mortification by persuading himself that he approved the policies he urged. When details of the restraining orders were leaked by the Whig press, Defoe wrote to Harley that, 'If The Fact is Not True, I Need Not hint to yor Ldpp what Resentmt The publishing it calls for from ye Governmt.' The purveyors of such scandalous fake news needed to be punished. 'On The Other hand', he continues, 'if The Thing be Fact, I can Not but Think it Recieves Such a Compleat Justificaċon in practise, from ye Constant Conduct of the Dutch, of The Imperialists, and Other Confederates' (Letter 210). If the Whigs are making it up, they need to be punished. If they are telling the truth, they are wrong to be outraged. Defoe was increasingly prone to doublethink.

For all that Defoe's conscience had been stretched, he remained clear sighted and inelastic on the Hanoverian succession. He berated the Whigs for accusing the ministry of favouring the Pretender and feared that alarmist allegations could become self-fulfilling. His three ironic 'Succession' pamphlets of 1713 were maliciously misread as Jacobite propaganda – 'Wrested Against the True Design ... and Turned to a Meaning quite different From ye Intenċon of the Author' – when the Whigs orchestrated a criminal prosecution (Letter 240). The last of those works, *What If the Queen Should Die*, also cautions the ministry that, however loyal it was to the Hanoverian succession, appeasing

---

61 *Review*, VIII, 588 (22 Jan. 1712).
62 *The Conduct of Parties in England* (1712), *PEW*, II, 261.

INTRODUCTION

the Jacobite fringe of the Tory party could backfire.[63] His letters report rumours of the ministry's inclinations to St Germains in a way that suggests Defoe was trying to sound out Harley or impel him to more definitive commitments to the Hanoverian succession:

I Do Not fail to Use My Uttmost Endeavours in all places to Undeciev The people and Expose These wicked Designs. But what is The Uttmost So Mean a hand can do! Yoᵣ Ldᴘᴘ can Applye The More Iﬁediate Cure. (Letter 225)

Defoe urged every measure that could strengthen the Hanoverian succession, and he trusted Harley. After Anne's death, in *The Secret History of the White-Staff* and *An Appeal to Honour and Justice*, he maintained that the outcome justified that trust.

Defoe's political activity and objectives after 1714 confused contemporaries and remain mysterious. His version of events, in letters to Delafaye, was one of heroic undercover work, a 'Little Peiće of Secret Serviće' that saw Defoe 'Posted among Papists, Jacobites, and Enraged High Torys, a Generation who I Profess My Very Soul abhorrs' (Letter 259). As in earlier missions, Defoe was tasked with keeping 'Difficult people ... within yᵉ bounds of Duty' in his undercover work to eviscerate Tory newspapers. But he found himself apologising to his Whig paymasters: 'It is a hard Matter to please yᵉ Tory Party as their present Temper Opperates, without Abuseing not Onely The Government but yᵉ Persons of Our Governours in Every thing they Write' (Letter 261). In short, the papers Defoe influenced remained critical of the government to a degree that suggests either his ineffectuality or his complicity.[64] It is hard to believe that Defoe bit his tongue when he disagreed with the government, and his licence to contribute to Tory papers provided the perfect cover, though this was blown when he was charged with writing letters criticising the ministry's involvement of Britain in war with Spain in 1718.

Defoe's political work across the reigns of William, Anne, and George was performed in the conviction that 'Intelligenće is yᵉ Soul of all Publick bussiness' (Letter 14). The 'Scheme of Generall Intelligenće' he laid out for Harley in 1704 depended on 'Settl[ing]' a 'Correspondenće' over Britain and Europe (Letter 13). With reference to this 'Scheme', Backscheider argues that 'Defoe's letters show naivete about how sophisticated and developed English intelligence was but also an easy familiarity with and clear conception of the history and purposes of intelligence.'[65] The main purpose of intelligence, he thought, was to gain clarity on

---

63 Nicholas Seager, '"She Will Not Be That Tyrant They Desire": Daniel Defoe and Queen Anne', in *Queen Anne and the Arts*, ed. Cedric D. Reverend III (Lewisburg, Penn., 2014), 41–55 (at 49–50).
64 F&O, *Political Biography*, 159–71.
65 Paula R. Backscheider, 'Daniel Defoe and Early Modern Intelligence', *Intelligence and National Security* 11 (1996), 1–21 (at 9).

lxxii

complex, intersecting transactions occurring at a distance, which would allow the politician to make informed interventions in anticipation of events, as well as in reaction to them. Defoe later signalled his value to Harley by advertising 'yᵉ Correspondence I keep up, wᶜʰ is Now all Over Brittain' (Letter 152) and he supplemented his own observations on affairs with the 'Constant adviċes from p[er]sons of Probity and judgement' that he received in correspondence (Letter 195).

Defoe's correspondence attests to his relish for clandestine work. He prides himself as a stealthy agent, 'Perfectly Unsuspectᵈ', crafting cover stories through his ability to 'Talk to Every body in Their Own way' (Letter 69). Defoe's espionage thus connects to the writerly ideals set out in the letter-writing instructions of *The Complete English Tradesman*, as the 'True spy' must be able to adjust his register and rhetoric to suit his marks and his informants (Letter 86), and he must be able to communicate complex circumstances with lucidity and no risk of misconstrual. As Godolphin's agent in Scotland in 1708 Defoe promised 'An Open, Candid, and honest stateing the Case to your Lᵈpp', providing 'an Accoᵗ of affaires here, in Such a Manner, as I p[er]swade my Self shall be, Exact as to Truth of Fact, usefull to His Lᵈpp, and For yᵉ Good and Advantage Even of this Country too' (Letter 135). Recognising that Defoe's letters were often intelligence reports turns our attention to how they signify as material artefacts.

Defoe's Material Letters

It would be distortive to overstate the degree of Defoe's care with the verbal text of his letters, as there are understandable signs of haste to counterpose instances of meticulous attention to phrasing and structure. The same applies to his attention to detail with their physical appearances. We need not impute conscious motive to every feature, but Defoe's letters signified as material documents as well as verbal performances in a culture that cared about epistolary presentation. This section details what the letters look like, how their appearances contribute to what they communicate, and how this relates to the social and cultural practices of letter-writing and the contexts in which correspondence was composed, delivered, and read.

A typical Defoe letter is a bifolium, a sheet with a single fold producing two leaves and four sides: fols. 1ʳ, 1ᵛ, 2ʳ, and 2ᵛ. Defoe wrote on the first side, the second if needed, and the third more rarely. Ink bleeding through the third side could affect the address, written vertically on the fourth side.[66] To produce the address box, the letter was folded further, then sealed with wax. Defoe's vertical and horizontal folds creating the address box are visible on Figures 8 and 10, as are the

66 Longer documents on multiple sheets sometimes use just recto leaves (e.g. Letters 44 and 248).

lxxiii

INTRODUCTION

residues of the seals. Letter-writing manuals urged the necessity of careful folding and sealing: 'Observe to do it neat, and let your Wax or Water be fixed on gentiely, without blurring or spattering; so that your well Inditing may not be reflected on by Carelessness or Neglect in any Point, but in every thing be circumspect and cauteous to please, that you may have your Expectations answered.'[67] Defoe's addresses are always written carefully to make a good impression.

More generally, Defoe adhered to the manuals' advice of 'giving an invitation to the eye' with his letters, both as sealed objects and as texts once unfolded.[68] His handwriting is an exceptionally neat and ornate cursive.[69] It is also idiosyncratic, being replete with diacritics, abbreviations, and contractions, some of which are rather old-fashioned for the eighteenth century. Calligraphic flourishes and curlicues personalise and signalise Defoe's letters. Commentary on Defoe's manuscripts often focuses on his 'unmistakeable, highly over-capitalized hand'.[70] In a quantitative study of early modern print and manuscript capitalisation practices, Osselton remarks that Defoe's letters have 'a higher incidence of initial capitals than any printer I have come across, sometimes running at fifty per cent of all words; but even so, he does not capitalize all nouns: he is certainly never merely mechanical, and there is a selection process of some kind'.[71] In a subsequent study, Osselton doubts this selection process, concluding that 'Defoe is about as erratic in his capitals as he is in his spelling.'[72] Fitzmaurice shares Osselton's scepticism in her examination of a letter from Defoe to Halifax (Letter 30): 'Defoe uses a great deal of capitalization throughout, and it is not clear that his practice follows any system or rule ... It is possible that he assigns initial capitals to words he wishes to emphasize.'[73] My wider survey indicates that there are strong tendencies in

---

67 Thomas Goodman, *The Experienc'd Secretary: or, Citizen and Countryman's Companion* (1699), 59–60.

68 John Hill, *The Young Secretary's Guide, Or Speedy Help to Learning* (1691), 3.

69 He wrote in black ink, which has faded to brown. For Defoe's interest in palaeography, and his pride at the state of English handwriting, see *An Essay upon Literature*, *TDH*, IV, 296–301. There, Defoe champions English round hand as an expeditious, 'masculine', and business-like improvement on Italian hand. This marries with his preference for plain, clear, and unadorned communication, discussed earlier in this Introduction.

70 Frank H. Ellis, 'Defoe's "Resignaçon" and the Limitations of "Mathematical Plainness"', *RES* 36 (1985), 338–54 (at 338).

71 N. E. Osselton, 'Informal Spelling Systems in Early Modern Europe: 1500–1800', in *English Historical Linguistics: Studies in Development*, ed. N. F. Blake and Charles Jones (Sheffield, 1984), 123–37 (at 128).

72 N. E. Osselton, 'Spelling Book Rules and the Capitalization of Nouns in the Seventeenth and Eighteenth Centuries', in *Historical and Editorial Studies in Medieval and Modern English: For Johan Gerritsen*, ed. Mary-Jo Arn, Hanneke Wirtjes, and Hans Jansen Wolters-Noordhoff (Groningen, 1985), 49–61 (at 51–2).

73 Susan M. Fitzmaurice, 'Epistolary Identity: Convention and Idiosyncrasy in Late Modern English Letters', in *Studies in Late Modern English Correspondence: Methodology and Data*, ed. Marina Dossena and Ingrid Tieken-Boon van Ostade (Bern, 2008), 77–112 (at 96–7).

lxxiv

DEFOE'S MATERIAL LETTERS

Defoe's capitalisation choices but ultimately no 'system or rule', least of all emphasis.[74] His abundant initial capitalisation is related to the calligraphic flourishes and other distinctive scribal features like diacritics and brevigraphs: collectively these stamp Defoe's manuscripts with an individual identity and flair.[75]

The visual organisation of Defoe's letters shows an equivalent carefulness with 'significant space', another concern of the manuals.[76] In her survey of epistolographies during the period 1500–1900, Walker attends to the blank regions of the page that correspondents used to express deference, 'where physical space echoes social distance between writer and receiver'.[77] The area around the salutation was crucial. Defoe often applies a greater indentation to the first paragraph following his salutation (Figures 1 and 9). The elaborate formation of the enlarged salutation 'Sr' is another expression of complaisance and respect (Figures 6 and 10). The letter to Stanhope (Figure 7), in which Defoe addressed someone unknown to him, has a notable expansion of space between the salutation and the first line, as well as a spatially elongated subscription that cascades diagonally down the page to the bottom right corner of its second side. The lower right corner was the correct place for a signature to someone of superior rank. In letters to noblemen, who are addressed as 'My Lord' rather than 'Sr', space again performs courtesy and homage, such as with the embellished 'I' commencing Defoe's supplicatory letter to Nottingham (Figure 1). In the last letters he sent to Harley, by then Lord Oxford, the salutations start lower down the page than was typical of earlier letters and are followed by a space that subtly communicates his sensitivity (Figure 9). This was a time when Harley's political career was in ruins and Defoe was offering considerate expressions of continued loyalty; Defoe was thus being respectful in both language and presentation.

The *mise en page* of a Defoe letter frequently enhances its purpose. The two 1704 memoranda on the art of government (Letters 14 and 15) are lofty missives written

---

74 Defoe infringes on advice about capitalisation given in some manuals: see Goodman, *Experienc'd Secretary*, 68.

75 Examples of Defoe manuscripts intended for publication are rare, which limits meaningful comparison with the correspondence. The two pages of 'Humanum Est Errare' in Defoe's hand, evidently sent to Harley for his approbation, resemble Defoe's memoranda of 1704: the distinctive features that could not be translated into print are present, but the work was never published. See J. A. Downie, '"Mistakes on all Sides": A New Defoe Manuscript', *RES* 27 (1976), 431–7; Maximillian E. Novak, 'Humanum Est Errare', *The Clark Newsletter* 4 (1983), 1–3. *The Compleat English Gentleman* likewise retains diacritics that are redundant for print. It applies more abbreviations than the letters. All told, it is a more functional document with fewer flourishes and ostensibly less capitalisation than the correspondence (BL Add. MS. 32555). See Karl D. Bülbring's disparaging remarks in his edition of *The Compleat English Gentleman* (1890), xvii.

76 Jonathan Gibson, 'Significant Space in Manuscript Letters', *Seventeenth Century* 12 (1997), 1–10.

77 Sue Walker, 'The Manners of the Page: Prescription and Practice in the Visual Organisation of Correspondence', *HLQ* 66 (2003), 307–29 (at 313).

INTRODUCTION

when Harley was a new Secretary of State. Defoe may have been a 'broken Hosier', but he was also, purportedly, a former advisor to William III and author of ambitious works of political philosophy such as *The Original Power*.[78] The diction, syntax, rhetorical devices, 'highly patterned rhythm', and extensive aphorism of these memoranda mark them out as examples of what Curtis calls Defoe's high style.[79] Both were apparently handed to Harley rather than posted. They are also elegantly presented artefacts and demonstrate Defoe's spatial adroitness. The progression of ideas in Letter 14 is organised through various levels of indentation, and he centralises important apothegms and surrounds them with space for emphasis ('Intelligence is yͤ Soul of all Publick bussiness'). Comparable documents in later years – those we could class as 'position papers' giving advice – are more mundane in style, substance, and appearance. Position papers sent when Harley was Lord Treasurer give advice (much of it not taken) on policy matters such as Scottish appointments, the South Sea Company, and public lotteries, but are sketchier than the earliest memoranda. In the later years of Anne's reign, Defoe's memoranda give the busy Lord Treasurer executive summaries or lists of headings to allow Harley to select which topics deserved expansion: 'I beg leave to Lay Things Down in heads That yoͬ Ldͩpp May Command The Perticulars of Such first as are Most Usefull', Defoe wrote (Letter 179). If Defoe positioned himself as a visionary counsellor in 1704, he had become an efficient, practical-minded agent by 1711; and this is visible in the appearances of the longer memoranda he wrote for Harley at those different times.

What about his emotions? Without speculating about whether interior mental states are actually materialised on the page, we can say for Defoe's letters that spatial arrangement amplifies the *expression* of states of mind.[80] Physical layout served Defoe's rhetorical purposes, and this included the intensification of his presentation of emotions. Letter-writers contend with the fact of personal absence and devise compensatory strategies. Defoe's later letters during his first Scottish trip illustrate the point. The earlier letters from Edinburgh, composed in winter and spring 1706–7 when the Union was pending, were densely packed affairs, brimming with information, so are less punctilious than usual with deferential

---

78 *Have a Care What You Say* [1707], 2.

79 Curtis, 'Rhetorical Approach', 297–305.

80 Scholars of early modern letters are understandably cautious about inferring feelings from handwriting. James Daybell calls for further work that has not been forthcoming (*Material Letter*, 90). Sara Jayne Steen, though like Daybell pulling back from such emotional interpretation, offers some useful principles on when one might legitimately pursue it, especially 'that there be enough letters that we can see patterns and exercise reasonable judgment' ('Reading Beyond the Words: Material Letters and the Process of Interpretation', *Quidditas* 22 (2001), 55–69 (at 59–61)). Defoe's letters to Harley in particular qualify, but I emphasise again that I am not inferring Defoe's feelings but rather his visual presentation of his mental states, conscious or otherwise.

DEFOE'S MATERIAL LETTERS

blank space. Even so, respectful room is still created around salutations and subscriptions. However, this is noticeably reduced in later 1707, by which time Defoe
was despairing and even reproachful towards Harley, feeling abandoned and pur-
poseless, as in his letter of 11 September (Figure 6). The second paragraph of this
letter begins:

> If I were where I have had yᵉ honoʳ to be Sʳ in yoʳ Parlour, Telling you my Own Case, and
> what a Posture my Affaires are in here, it would be too Moving a Story; you Could Not,
> I am Perswaded <u>pardon my Vanity</u>, you have too much Concerne for me, and too much
> Generosity in yoʳ Nature, you Could Not bear it — (Letter 121)

Defoe intimates that his letter is a poor substitute for the emotional intensity of a
face-to-face meeting but he approximates some of the performance of an interview,
not only in phrasing, such as the restart ('you Could Not...'), but also in the shape
of the text in the letter.[81] At two moments in this paragraph he 'breaks off' with
elongated dashes that denote his inability to continue due to emotional excess.
The first dash, ending the quotation above, is about twice the length of the second
('...I allwayes struggled with yᵉ world So as Never to want till Now —'), a firmer
stroke that suggests returning composure. The underlining – 'pardon my Vanity' –
is a failure to restrain frustration in accordance with decorum. For all that Defoe's letters are never 'fair copies' free of amendments, even the interlineations
and cancellations in this letter add to its rhetorical effects: 'till Now' is inserted in
the passage I quoted above and 'Now' is inserted in 'if you were to See Me \Now/
Entertaind of Courtisy'. These deictic expressions are accusatory demands that
Harley, comfortable in London, imagine Defoe *now* in his 'Dejected' state. He
invokes the convention that a shabby servant shames his master. Towards the end,
Defoe writes, 'I~~Think~~ Tis a Very Mortifying Thought that I have Not One friend
in the World to Support me ...', pointedly lining through the qualification to his
admonition but leaving it legible.

This was September 1707: Defoe had already been palmed off to Godolphin
whose silence amplified that of Harley. Ten weeks later came a material change.
In Letter 125 (28 November 1707) Defoe acknowledged the promise of funds that
would bring him back to London. Gratitude was important to Defoe, especially in his relationship with Harley, and it is communicated through appearance
as well as expression. He wrote that 'This gives New life to my Affaires', and his
letter-writing is accordingly rejuvenated. The letter is neater than its antecedents,
with more level lines, more spaced-out characters and words, and above all more
blank space. Defoe thus reifies his obligedness and sense of relief in the letter.

---

81 The lengthier-than-normal spurs on the *d* ascenders, which encircle the preceding words,
   could be read as emphatic reproval: '*I have had* yᵉ honoʳ ... *you Could* Not ... *you Could* Not
   bear it'.

lxxvii

INTRODUCTION

A similar thing can be said about the letter dated 21 September 1710 (Letter 153), in which Defoe gratefully acknowledges the approval of his secret service stipend and is again ceremonious with the letter's layout and language. He felt that letters acknowledging a benefit required a certain convenance, which was to be rendered visually as well as verbally.[82]

The spatial evolution of Defoe's letters after he reunited with Harley in 1710 is revealing. Those of 17 and 28 July (Letters 145 and 146), reestablishing contact after a two-and-a-half-year hiatus, use ample blank space. However, greater familiarity over the coming months meant that this formality was relaxed. After Harley's elevation to the peerage in May 1711, Defoe observed spatial decorum in new ways, leaving blank the headers on the second and third pages of his letters to match the equivalent space reserved on the first for the salutation 'My Lord'. Before Harley's ennoblement, Defoe automatically wrote from the top of the second page. One senses that Harley was not precious about such observances: just as Defoe says that he was encouraged to be more frank and plain in conversations and letters than their difference of status would ordinarily allow, he sometimes dispenses with these rules of epistolary presentation.

Some of Defoe's letters achieve a highly expressive quality through their spatial composition. That of 18 July 1713 (Letter 231), in which he communicates to Harley his 'Grief and Indignacon' at the Whigs' recriminations, articulates Defoe's measured fury both in its language and appearance. It is more orderly and more spaced out than his other letters from this time. The first page contains the salutation and sixteen lines, whereas the first pages of the three extant letters preceding it comprise, in addition to the salutation, twenty-five, twenty-two, and twenty-one lines, respectively. In those three preceding letters, the average word counts for full lines of text are mean 15.4 and median 16. In the 18 July letter, the same averages are mean 14 and median 13. In the more spaced-out 18 July letter, Defoe conveyed a stoical ability to rise above his and the government's enemies, to stay his course despite discouragement. He offers up a patient prayer: 'God Allmighty for Ever Dissappoint Them and Grant Her Majtie may Out live Not So Much the Men, but The Temper.' The spatial arrangement embodies the emotional state he aimed to convey – equanimity overcoming indignation. This

---

82 Letter 90 is interesting in this vein: Defoe enlarges his writing when announcing the joyous news of the Union, so used up the whole page, signed it big, and did one of his big swirly esses for 'Sr' in the subscription. We could read this as Defoe preening himself or signalling something momentous in what he wanted to seem like a dispatch. Letter 90 is also a plea to Harley to order him back to England, and Letter 103 is similarly spaced out, as though to urge on its recipient a more attentive reading for the consideration of his recall. But the two postscripts to Letter 103, which go back to mundane business (copyright law and sniping at his rival Paterson) are more packed in.

lxxviii

is not to say that Defoe was any more mentally composed when he wrote on 18 July 1713 than at any other time: rather, it is to suggest that he encoded self-possession into the material letter as well as its language.

Our image of Defoe is that of a man writing through fatigue and of course writing prolifically into later life. Letter 50, dated 21 August 1706, starts out neat and ebullient: Defoe wrote with positive news about his bankruptcy hearing that day. But he ends with a declaration of tiredness which the handwriting corroborates. It is a short letter, but he accidentally repeats a word ('be') and his characters gradually become less well-formed and stretch out along the lines. Defoe's spurs on *d* graphs (supralineal arches that move right to left, abundantly depicted in figures in this edition) become less symmetrical and their curvature flattens as the letter proceeds.

Defoe's writing changed relatively little in his later life: his last letters (for example, Figure 11, Letter 278) and the manuscript of *The Compleat English Gentleman* remain characteristically neat and ornate. The letters onto which we may be tempted to project the cares of his years in terms of handwriting are some of those addressed to Baker at the time he was engaged to Defoe's daughter, an ordeal that strained all parties. The handwriting in Letter 269, in which Defoe is aggrieved and exasperated, is especially shaky.

In various ways Defoe's letters allude to the contexts of their composition, transportation, and reception. Some of these processes are evident in their materiality. For example, certain letters from Edinburgh are very blotchy. Defoe was writing detailed reports in small handwriting that covers the paper, so there is a greater quantity of ink, with more densely packed and more back-to-back text. These letters travelled a considerable distance, taking more than a week to reach London, and show signs of wear and tear that it is tempting to impute to the first week of their existence rather than the following centuries. From 1710 to 1714, Defoe was in more comfortable financial circumstances, usually with readier access to Harley, at least in theory, and this often shows in the material features of his letters. Not infrequently the letters of this period leave two internal blank pages, a lavish gesture when pricey paper could be cut to furnish short notes.

Internal clues suggest Defoe did much of his letter-writing in the evening after a day's work, especially when he was on location for Harley. Some letters of course are written at several reprises, covering multiple days. Defoe's letters attest to the mechanics of a letter's transportation in this period. They moved along post roads: 'I have been Out of yᵉ Reach of any post Road wᶜʰ has hindred my writeing to yoʳ Ldpp', Defoe says at one time (Letter 218). Sometimes Defoe names his location at the head of the letter, rather than at the end as was customary for him, if it is unusual: 'Glasgow' and 'Sterling' at the head of letters show he is 'off the grid' in 1707 (Letters 110 and 111). They were occasionally sent in cover via bearers and other

INTRODUCTION

intermediaries. Letters to Defoe were delivered to him (in one of his aliases) at coffee houses or post restante addresses. When Defoe was in the south east in 1705, for example, he writes: 'ye honor of a Letter from you would be a Satisfacco and Encouragemt Directed to Alexa G .. th in a Cover to ye Revrd Mr Josiah Eveleigh at mr Francis Bere, Mercha in Tiverton' (Letter 39).

When the contents are secret the means of conveyance raises questions of trust. With justification, Harley and Defoe feared interceptions and confiscations, especially for secret service work.[83] In Devon in 1705, a letter to Defoe directed to 'Captain Turner' was intercepted by a real (or another) person of that name, leading Defoe to reassure Harley that he would henceforth use trusty intermediaries such as his brother-in-law Robert Davis – 'and So No Danger of a Misscarriage' (Letter 40). In his journey in 1704, we have the earliest surviving evidence of Defoe disguising his handwriting (Letter 17), and in the 1705 trip he does this in the addresses of some letters (Letters 40 and 42). In his Scottish expedition following the ministerial revolution of 1710, he goes to greater lengths, writing in a disguised hand, using a cipher to conceal names, and employing his new alias Claude Guilot (Figure 8, Letter 160). He expressed to Harley his 'Perplexity about the Conveying my letters' when Harley's agent in Newcastle, John Bell, proved indiscreet, which caused Defoe reluctantly to use the 'Ordina Post' (Letter 161). He found new bearers: 'Mr Young ..., a faithfull and honest Man', 'Mr Bateman', and another unnamed 'Trusty Friend' (Letters 163 and 164). And he requested a new direction for any letters Harley might send, reassuring his patron that 'Any letter Directed to Mr Wm Cliff at Mr Walter Ross's to be left at Mr David Monroe in Edinb will come to my hand. The Number of Such Names is to make it Secure' (Letter 162).

Miscarriages were a reality, but Defoe exploits the prospect of his letters not reaching their destination to attempt to elicit responses from his silent masters. 'I have but One humble Peticon ... the Honor of a Line from yor Ldpp ... to Signifye in two Words the Rect of this', he wrote to Sunderland in 1708 (Letter 135). Harley got the same pleas in winter 1710–11. Harley and Defoe each made requests to one another about how correspondence and enclosures should be handled: shared, not shared, copied, returned, and so on. Harley was evidently cautious about corresponding with Defoe. He tore out signatures, sometimes taking other content too; he endorsed letters using Defoe's sobriquets, Goldsmith and Guilot; and he directed Defoe to write in cover to agents in London. The espionage letters illustrate the interest of Defoe's letters as material texts, but that interest extends to the corpus as a whole because their physical form was a potent way for Defoe to enhance their rhetorical impact.

---

83 Defoe was once interrupted by arresting officers at his home while writing to Harley, and he feared that his papers would be confiscated (Letter 227).

lxxx

Publication and Reception History

Defoe's reputation has fluctuated in response to the gradual publication of his letters. Few were published in his lifetime. Keimer printed one without naming Defoe as its author in 1717 (Letter 257). Defoe printed snippets of his correspondence with Belhaven in the *Review* (Letter 133) and two letters to Webster in a book he suppressed (Letters 92–3). In his 1785 biography of Defoe, Chalmers lamented the lack of primary documentation for his subject, adding to the epistolary record just one autograph letter, addressed to Dyer (Letter 144).[84] Chalmers's expanded 1790 biography then included an extract of Defoe's letter to Buchan, printed in full a century later (Letter 178).[85] Chalmers explains the paucity of surviving letters with a Johnsonian reflection of doubtful applicability to Defoe: 'The lives of literary men are generally passed in the obscurities of the closet, which conceal even from friendly inquiries the artifices of study.'[86] This belletristic image hardly accords with our knowledge now of how Defoe used letters to conduct his political and business affairs.

Even at the start of the twentieth century, after more than a century of heightened interest in Defoe, Wright knew of only thirty-two Defoe letters.[87] Wilson in *Memoirs of the Life and Times of Daniel De Foe* (1830) reproduced four new ones. One addressed to Harley, located in the British Museum, was the first published correspondence between the two men (Letter 11).[88] The extent of their relationship remained unknown until the end of the nineteenth century, and the lack of documentation led Wilson into misapprehensions about the letter's date and Defoe's political connections.[89] He also produced Defoe letters then in private hands, those addressed to Wharton (Letter 142), Watts (Letter 277), and Baker (Letter 278). Wilson's attention to the letters is coloured by his hagiographic evaluation of Defoe as a defender of civil and religious liberty. For example, Wilson assigns 'laudable motives' to Defoe's letter to Wharton, which might equally be seen as officious and unctuous.[90] In printing the final surviving Defoe letter, which had been kept in Baker family papers, Wilson comments that 'he who can read it with unmoistened eyes must be possessed of feelings that no man ought to

---

84 See Rodney M. Baine, 'Chalmers' First Bibliography of Daniel Defoe', *Texas Studies in Language and Literature* 10 (1969), 547–68.
85 George Chalmers, *The Life of Daniel De Foe* (1790), 33.
86 Chalmers, *Life of Daniel De Foe*, 5. Melmoth's letter to Defoe (Letter 58) was published in 1796.
87 'Literary Papers of Thomas Wright', Centre for Buckinghamshire Studies, D161/61d; Thomas Wright, 'The Letters of Daniel Defoe', *The Leisure Hour*, Nov. 1901, 29–32.
88 Wilson, ii, 358–60.
89 See William Chadwick's treatment of this letter in *The Life and Times of Daniel De Foe* (1859), 269–71.
90 Wilson, iii, 121. This is especially the case given that Defoe thought Wharton was irreligious and clerical misconduct was the subject of Defoe's letter.

envy'.[91] He was unaware of the earlier letters between Defoe and Baker in which Defoe wrangled over his daughter's dowry: these were less likely to induce tears.

Further Defoe letters came gradually to light in the nineteenth century. Button's letter to Defoe was published in 1837 (Letter 166). In 1843 were published two of the three letters Defoe sent to Halifax in 1705 (Letters 30 and 33).[92] Two to Elisha and another to Baker were printed in 1860 (Letters 16, 20, and 268).[93] Then in 1864, Defoe's 1718 correspondence with Delafaye resurfaced with major ramifications for Defoe's reputation, which had steadily risen among the Georgians and Victorians, typified in the 1850s by Chadwick's and Forster's biographies which represent the height of Defoe's reputation for probity. Five letters were published in *The London Review*, revealing Defoe's undercover work for the early Hanoverian Whig ministry to infiltrate and enervate the Tory press (Letters 259–63).[94] That did not sit well with many Victorians. 'We should have been loath to believe that the author of "Robinson Crusoe" could have descended to the baseness and dishonesty revealed in his own correspondence', states the anonymous editor. He reflects that modern commentators had resorted to ingenious explanations for Defoe's unpopularity among his contemporaries but concludes that those who in his day called him an unprincipled hireling were right: 'The man who could write these letters could have no great value for political honesty, nor be very scrupulous in the means of advancing his own interest.' Defoe's own words in *An Appeal to Honour and Justice*, about his victimisation by rival authors and quitting political work after 1714, were cited against him, exposing Defoe's capacity for 'dirty and disreputable work'. He was 'a traitor on all sides', an 'able yet corrupt writer' who had 'prostitute[d] his honour and his talents'. The journal silently applied italics to its transcriptions of the letters, emphasising the most compromising passages.[95] Defoe now seemed capable of just about anything. The *London Review* articles attributed to him the Jacobite George Lockhart's fiercely anti-Union *Memoirs* (1714), a work that even traduces Defoe.[96] The lewdness of *Moll Flanders* was recalled.[97] Eyre Crowe's painting *Defoe in the Pillory* (1862) was publicly exhibited one month after the Delafaye letters were published.[98] Its viewers might have looked askance at

91 Wilson, III, 605.
92 Wilson, III, 605.
93 John Forster, *Oliver Cromwell. Daniel De Foe. Sir Richard Steele. Charles Churchill. Samuel Foote. Biographical Essays*, 3rd ed. (1860), iv–vi, 153–4.
94 *London Review of Politics, Society, Literature, Art, and Science*, 4 and 11 June, 1864, 590–1, 617–18. Another 1718 Delafaye letter, Defoe's first to him (Letter 258), was published in Dec. 1864, when *Notes and Queries* reprinted the letters (*N&Q*, 3rd ser., 6 (31 Dec. 1864), 527–30).
95 *London Review*, 590–1, 617, 618.
96 This attribution is debated in correspondence in the paper (*London Review*, 16 July 1864, 64–5).
97 *London Review*, 2 July 1864, 11.
98 *The Art-Journal*, July 1864, 207.

Crowe's portrayal of the author as a martyred hero: the recent revelations threatened entirely to undo the image of Defoe as a sufferer in the cause of freedom enshrined a generation earlier by Wilson.

Defoe soon found a committed, if often overzealous, defender. In contributions to *Notes and Queries*, William Lee argued that *The London Review* had presented the Delafaye letters in the worst possible light. Rather than seeing Defoe as a timeserver in his Hanoverian press work, Lee stressed his service to a Whig ministry which he sincerely supported.[99] Lee examined the newspapers to which Defoe confessed he contributed, finding that 'the continual tendency of them was to promote religion and virtue. With respect to politics, he constantly aimed at impartiality; and I have not found that he actually wrote, in any Tory journal, anything contrary to the liberal principles he had all his life professed.' Focusing on what Defoe supposedly wrote, rather than what he professedly suppressed, Lee makes Defoe a self-sacrificing saint in the early Hanoverian years, reluctantly consorting with Jacobites to thwart them, the patient victim of opprobrium by Whigs unaware that he was actually their ally. 'His motives and his conduct in so trying circumstances appear to have been upright, and the consciousness of this sustained him', Lee maintains. 'Defoe unwisely consented to place himself in a very questionable position; but ... in such a position, he did nothing to disparage, positively, his moral character as a man, a patriot, and a Christian.'[100]

The next step of Lee's vindication was attribution. He argued that Defoe was responsible for material in other Tory papers not mentioned in the letters, particularly *Applebee's Original Weekly Journal*.[101] Lee's notes on Defoe had two objectives: to repair 'the injury attempted against his character and memory in the *London Review*' and to dispel 'the distorted, and discoloured caricature of Mr. Walter Wilson, who has portrayed him as a bigoted, antichurch, radical Dissenter'. Lee's Defoe was 'always a liberal Conservative in politics; and, although a Dissenter, yet a firm supporter of the Church of England'.[102]

Lee presented this image of the author in his 1869 biography. His attention to the small number of Defoe's letters then available illustrates both Lee's merits and failings as a biographer. With careful rigour, Lee corrects Wilson's errors regarding the one known Harley letter.[103] But eager to minimise Defoe's servitude to Harley, maugre the *Appeal*, Lee uses the Halifax letters to contend that Defoe

---

99 William Lee, 'Daniel Defoe and "The London Review"', *N&Q*, 3rd ser., 7 (21 Jan. 1865), 58–61.

100 Lee, 'Daniel Defoe, the News Writer', *N&Q*, 3rd ser., 7 (25 Mar. 1865), 244–6 (at 246).

101 Lee, 'Daniel Defoe the News Writer', *N&Q*, 3rd ser., 7 (29 Apr. 1865), 343–4. Cf. Letter 266, note 5.

102 Lee, 'Daniel Defoe, on the Assassination of Rulers', *N&Q*, 3rd ser., 7 (5 Aug. 1865), 101–3 (at 101).

103 Lee, 1, 111–13.

INTRODUCTION

was not a ministerial writer until 1705 when his independently conceived opposition to *The Memorial of the Church of England* caught Godolphin's or even Queen Anne's attention, prompting the approach by Halifax.[104] The gaps in Defoe's correspondence, and in our biographical knowledge as a whole, have always produced speculation. Equally, preconceptions of Defoe have led biographers to find what they are looking for. Lee reaffirms his verdict on the Delafaye letters: 'Neither in those Letters, nor in anything I have been able to discover, is there any condition or stipulation, direct or implied, that he should ever write a word contrary to his conscience, or to the principles which had directed his whole life.'[105] One instance of over-compensation through conjecture is Lee's interpretation of the final letter from Defoe to Baker. In a rare moment of concurrence with Wilson, Lee calls it 'one of the most painfully affecting in the English language'. He first argues that Defoe's implacable 'Enemy' is not his creditor Mary Brooke, as Wilson had correctly deduced, but rather a vengeful Nathaniel Mist, in league with the Jacobite Duke of Wharton (son of the Marquess to whom Defoe wrote), hellbent on assassinating Defoe!

The first of Lee's three volumes contained the biography; the second and third anthologised periodical contributions Lee newly ascribed to Defoe. Lee presented this Hanoverian journalism as barely political, actually more an extension of Defoe's wide-ranging social and moral interests, not 'dirty work', as one reviewer, who accused Lee of hero-worship, insisted on describing it.[106] Another reviewer was persuaded that Defoe's service to the Whig party was principled but finds Lee's attributions dubious, emphasising instead that Defoe identified himself as a press censor and not necessarily the author of countless anonymous articles.[107]

Despite Lee's efforts, the Delafaye letters negatively shaped Defoe's reputation. In his *History of England* (1870) Earl Stanhope published a new Defoe letter, addressed to the historian's great-great-grandfather, General Stanhope, and offering help with Sacheverell's prosecution (Letter 140). Earl Stanhope presented it as an illustration of the regrettable application of literary ability to partisan hackwork: 'Far, very far, above [rival political journalists] in genius and power stood Defoe, though not raised beyond their level in points of party rancour.' The letter, which might ten years earlier have been read as a public-spirited act, just as Wilson had viewed Defoe's fawning letter to Wharton, now registered as personal vindictiveness and gratuitous aggravation, which Earl Stanhope supposed his ancestor, its recipient, was dispassionate enough to ignore. Conveniently, Stanhope's

---

104 Lee, I, 115–18. Lee first published the third and last known Defoe letter to Halifax (Letter 38).

105 Lee, I, 257–8.

106 *The Athenæum*, 1 May 1869, 597–8. Cf. *The Saturday Review*, 15 May 1869, 651–2.

107 'The Later Life of Defoe', *British Quarterly Review*, Oct. 1869, 483–519. Cf. Peterson, *Reference Guide*, 184–90; F&O, *Canonisation*, 62–74.

lxxxiv

PUBLICATION AND RECEPTION HISTORY

History stops in 1713 so does not tackle the revelation in the Defoe–Delafaye letters that General Stanhope, by then an Earl, did not himself always operate above the grubby polemical press: he personally employed Defoe as a double agent in George's reign.[108]

Minto's *Daniel Defoe* (1879) typifies the duality in late Victorian treatments of Defoe. Modern scholars still invoke Minto's statement that Defoe 'was a great, a truly great liar, perhaps the greatest liar who ever lived', but his following words are less well known: 'If we go deeper still in his rich and strangely mixed nature, we come upon a stubborn foundation of conscience.' In this vein, Minto reappraises Defoe's final letter, dismissing Lee's speculation about Mist being Defoe's nemesis. Minto reads the letter, which previous commentators had found sincere and affecting, as 'a clever evasion of his son-in-law's attempts to make sure of his share of the inheritance'. For Minto, this subterfuge does not amount to dishonourable greed because Defoe hoped to leave the money to his unmarried daughters. Therefore, 'it might stand as a type of the most marked characteristic in Defoe's political writings. It was a masterly and unscrupulous piece of diplomacy for the attainment of a just and benevolent end.'[109] In Minto, Victorian moralism met the Delafaye letters to produce a mixed image of Defoe as unscrupulously upstanding in both personal and political transactions – happy to employ deceit to attain upright ends, whether that is duping Jacobite journalists by diluting their newspapers or lying to a covetous son-in-law to fend for his unprovided family. In the final quarter of the nineteenth century, Defoe's letters were incorporated into a view of the author as remarkably versatile and just about honest according to his own lights but with an underdeveloped moral sense.[110]

Further Defoe letters came to light in piecemeal fashion in the late nineteenth century. His correspondence with Fransham was published in 1875, albeit only a 'Part of the Letters that past between Mr. Daniel De Foe and myself from 1704 to 1707' surfaced.[111] The Historical Manuscripts Commission, appointed by royal warrant in 1869 to calendar papers in private collections, bore its first Defoe fruits in 1881 when three letters – two to Sunderland and one to Godolphin – were found at Blenheim Palace (Letters 134–5, 139). Another Defoe–Harley letter, just

---

108 Earl Stanhope, *History of England comprising the Reign of Queen Anne until the Peace of Utrecht* (1870), 549–51. Cf. Herman Merivale's review of Stanhope's *History* which uses the Defoe–Stanhope letter to confute Lee's assertion that Defoe harboured no vengeful feelings towards Sacheverell in 1709–10 (*Edinburgh Review* 132 (1870), 519–54 (at 548–53)). The 'gotcha' approach to Defoe's politics has never gone away.

109 William Minto, *Daniel Defoe* (1879), 168–9. Both parts of Minto's argument are speculative.

110 H. R. Fox Bourne, *English Newspapers: Chapters in the History of Journalism*, 2 vols. (1887), I, 108; R. Farquharson Sharp, *Architects of English Literature: Biographical Sketches of Great Writers from Shakespeare to Tennyson* (1900), 49.

111 Norgate, 261.

INTRODUCTION

the second printed to date, was published by the Commission in 1884 (Letter 59). Separately, a letter to an unknown correspondent, perhaps William Penn Jr, was published in 1890, and Defoe's letter to Penn Sr in 1902 (Letters 6 and 3).[112] In 1893 Aitken published another letter from Defoe to Delafaye, showing that their correspondence continued until 1720 at least (Letter 266).[113] The next year, Aitken published the earliest surviving Defoe letter.[114] Wright's *Life of Daniel Defoe* (1894) published Defoe and Baker's correspondence concerning the latter's marriage to Sophia Defoe, as well as one letter from Defoe to this daughter (Letters 267–76, 278). Spying for Whig paymasters seemed less flagitious than when exposed thirty years earlier, but Defoe's haggling over his daughter's dowry confirmed Victorian views of his constitutional dishonesty. As one reviewer said, 'we cannot say we find any of these letters at all endearing'.[115] Wright planned an edition of Defoe's letters and collected materials to that end. His article in *The Leisure Hour* in 1901, 'The Letters of Daniel Defoe', gives an overview of the thirty-two letters known, as well as images from some.

By the time Wright's article appeared, Defoe's epistolary corpus had dramatically swollen. The publication in 1897 and 1899 of new volumes of the Historical Manuscript Commission, focused on the Portland Papers at Welbeck Abbey, included dozens of Defoe's letters to Harley.[116] The editor J. J. Cartwright's introduction labelled the documents a 'revelation' because they record 'the very intimate relations, for public purposes, which existed for many years between Harley and De Foe'.[117] Though the Harley letters show Defoe doing yet more clandestine work, they helped recuperate his reputation because they exhibited his sustained loyalty to principles and persons, his unstinting service despite the obvious neglect of his patrons, and the considerable extent to which his abilities as an advisor and operative were trusted by powerful politicians. One reviewer of the fourth Portland volume, which covered events to 1711, wrote that Defoe 'was not only loyal to the hand which paid him, but also by conviction a patriotic politician'.[118] The fifth volume, covering years when Defoe served Anne's final Tory ministry, produced a more mixed reaction. Bateson read Defoe's letters of those years as evidence of a 'degradation of character which sprang from his relations with Harley'. Even so, he says that Scotland for Defoe was 'a sincere work, a glimpse of the real man, himself aiding the design that he approved, and here at least needing no specious

112 *A Catalogue of Autographs Formed by Ferdinand Julius Dreer*, 2 vols. (Philadelphia, Penn., 1890), I, 157; *The Friend: A Religious and Literary Journal* 76 (1902), 2.
113 G. A. Aitken, 'Defoe and Mist's "Weekly Journal"', *The Athenæum*, 26 Aug. 1893, 287–8.
114 G. A. Aitken, 'Defoe in Trouble: 1703', *The Athenæum*, 22 Dec. 1894, 862.
115 *The Speaker*, 10 Nov. 1894, 518–19.
116 H.M.C. *Portland MSS*, IV (1897) and V (1899).
117 H.M.C. *Portland MSS*, IV, iii–iv.
118 *The Athenæum*, 19 June 1897, 811.

arguments of self-consolation'.[119] By contrast, and demonstrating the turn-of-the-century bifurcation in moral assessments of Defoe's politics, Cockburn regarded Defoe's Scottish activity as grubby: 'However we may be dazzled by his courageous cleverness we must admit the reality of his moral depreciation.'[120] In a far more positive assessment of Defoe's political work, which emphasises the mutually 'creditable' and pragmatic partnership between Defoe and Harley, Roscoe described 'numerous and vivid letters, full of varied facts and fresh suggestions' that attest to 'a mind never at rest, and extraordinarily fertile and imaginative'.[121]

Important additions to the corpus of Defoe's letters followed in the early decades of the twentieth century, enhancing the image of Defoe as Harley's trusted advisor which sat alongside, but did not displace, his reputation as a hired pen. Volume VIII of the Portland Manuscripts (1907) included his strident missive calling for the removal from command of Admiral Rooke (Letter 11's enclosure).[122] In the same year was published Defoe's lengthy memorandum on government sent to Harley after his appointment as Secretary of State in 1704 (Letter 14). As Warner noted, it complemented the existing image of the 'paid secret agent of the government' with 'the more dignified part of a political Mentor' to Harley. Advising Harley to accrue to himself the power of a supreme minister, Defoe's piece is 'marked by his usual practical sagacity, showing an intimate knowledge of affairs and a keen insight into the character of the man with whom he had to deal'.[123] By the start of the twentieth century Defoe was being taken seriously as a political writer.

Yet his reputation based on the letters remained mixed. For Trent, the Defoe revealed in the Harley papers was duplicitous and callous, a man acting against his principles, especially after 1710. Trent's general theory was that Defoe's experience in the pillory was 'the regrettable prelude to the ruin of a remarkable character', initiating an ethical decline.[124] Furbank and Owens suggest that Trent's disillusioned appraisal of Defoe is the distorted product of his own idealism and sense of nobility.[125] There are, however, some fine insights in Trent's work, borne up by

---

119 Thomas Bateson, 'The Relations of Defoe and Harley', *EHR* 15 (1900), 238–50 (at 242, 241, 246).

120 Cockburn, 'Daniel Defoe in Scotland', 267. Early twentieth-century historians of the Union incorporate Defoe's letters with little negative moral judgement. See W. L. Mathieson, *Scotland and the Union: A History of Scotland from 1695 to 1747* (Glasgow, 1905); Andrew Lang, *History of Scotland: From the Roman Occupation*, 4 vols. (1900–7), IV, 109–50; P. Hume Brown, *History of Scotland*, 3 vols. (Cambridge, 1909), III, 90.

121 E. S. Roscoe, *Robert Harley, Earl of Oxford, Prime Minister: A Study of Politics and Letters in the Age of Anne* (1902), 71, 48, 54.

122 H.M.C. *Portland MSS*, VIII (1907), 135–9. Carstares's letter to Defoe (Letter 224) was published in H.M.C. *Portland MSS*, x (1931), 288–9. Wright published a new letter to Godolphin (Letter 132) in his revised biography, *The Life of Daniel Defoe* (1931), 153–4.

123 G. F. Warner, 'An Unpublished Political Paper by Daniel Defoe', *EHR* 22 (1907), 130–43 (at 132).

124 William Peterfield Trent, *Daniel Defoe: How to Know Him* (Indianapolis, Ind., 1916), 44.

125 F&O, *Canonisation*, 83–100.

INTRODUCTION

the letters. 'As [Defoe] was a proud man, who liked to emphasize his standing as a gentleman … his position must have been very trying to him', Trent surmises about Defoe accepting employment by the ministry. Looking at the 'rather scurvy services he rendered the Tory administration' after Harley's return to power in 1710, 'we must believe that Defoe's experiences as a hack writer and a spy had rendered him more or less callous, and that his ingenious, casuistical mind supplied him with excuses whenever his conscience reproached him'.[126] Trent acknowledges that Defoe adhered to certain principles and was not merely venal. He recognises that if there was disgrace in employment by Harley and Townsend, that belongs as much to the exploitative politicians as to the writer lain prone by having unjust indictments over his head.[127] Trent was guilty of projecting his own values onto Defoe, but the larger point is that Defoe was emerging as a psychological subject thanks in large part to the epistolary corpus.

Stevens reached different conclusions, finding that after 1710 Defoe was 'freed from restraining counsel', which is to say his writing was *not* dictated by Harley as Trent supposed. The Defoe–Harley correspondence, for Stevens, corroborates a great deal of what Defoe wrote in the *Appeal*, correcting the 'fixed belief in Defoe's dishonesty'.[128] Stevens places Defoe's activities in the hardboiled reality of political journalism rather than dwelling on his psychological state. He emphasises 'Defoe's importance as a secret counsellor' to Harley and finds his having written on both sides of political disputes commendable, a sign of his independence, open-mindedness, and patriotism as opposed to the blinkered partisanship or mercenary instincts imputed to him.[129] Stevens presents Defoe's Whig press work in George I's reign without censure: he observes that what seemed like a damning revelation in the 1860s had been common knowledge and commonplace activity in the 1710s. The Whig government was entering a new phase of press control, which included recruiting its quondam critics, so the arrangement with Defoe was merely business. Defoe had to make the best terms possible.[130]

Sutherland's 1937 biography first published the other important 1704 memorandum, on union at home and power abroad, with its sometimes chilling directives for managing the Dissenters (Letter 15).[131] Sutherland's treatment of Defoe, exemplified by his attention to the new item, is more nuanced than that of the

---

126 Trent, *Daniel Defoe*, 61, 108, 102.

127 Trent, 'New Light on Defoe's Life', *The Nation*, 87, no. 2255, 17 Sept. 1908, 259–61 (at 260).

128 David Stevens, *Party Politics and English Journalism, 1702–1742* (Menasha, Wisc., 1916), 59.

129 Stevens, *Party Politics*, 52, 60.

130 Stevens, *Party Politics*, 54, 110.

131 Sutherland, 277–82. Sutherland's biography can be compared to Trevelyan's *England Under Queen Anne* (1930). 'In politics, Defoe was a man of principle but not one of party … For violences of sect and faction Defoe had an instinctive dislike, partly because the extremes of denominational and party zeal seems to him to be perpetually clashing with the true interests of the country' (Trevelyan, 1, 281).

lxxxviii

PUBLICATION AND RECEPTION HISTORY

Victorian biographers. He finds pragmatic realpolitik in Defoe's 'almost immoral detachment' when advising Harley how to manipulate the Dissenters but insists that this is combined with an unflinching commitment to Nonconformity. For Sutherland, Defoe's advice admits of opposing but not irreconcilable explanations. Defoe, frustrated at his ill-treatment by his co-religionists after *The Shortest Way*, and disgusted by their indulgence in occasional conformity, seems willing to cozen the Dissenters to bring them under Harley's heel; but his advice that a persecution should be avoided because it could unite and embolden the Dissenters also suggests his concern for their interest.[132] Sutherland does justice to the trickiness of Defoe's letters, the need to read motives beneath the surface and consider particular contexts.

Time and again, Sutherland finds Defoe's letters saying things that can be read as either damning or exculpatory. A key document is the 'singularly revealing letter' of August 1712 (Letter 213), in which an emotional Defoe, wounded by Whig accusations of apostasy, explains to Harley the footing of their long association: a meeting of kindred political minds and never a mercenary arrangement. 'Can one take his claims here at face value?' asks Sutherland: 'The habit of addressing the public had become second nature to Defoe, and even in a private letter the tendency remains.' Plausibly the letter is a hint to Harley that he would not be on board with a move to more extreme Toryism, Sutherland deduces, but the simpler explanation is that 'he seems to be trying to convince *himself* that he has never sold his pen to Harley, and he is hoping that Harley will agree'.[133] Sutherland gives an unromantic yet not unsympathetic account of Defoe dealing with challenging circumstances. Admiration for Defoe's skill mingles with reprehension for how he employed it. For instance, of the 1718 letters that reveal his secret agency under the Whigs, Sutherland concludes:

> He was well accustomed by this time to bowing in the House of Rimmon; that gesture had almost become a reflex action. Indeed, one is much more inclined to say, What fun for Defoe! ... Once again he had found a unique employment for his unique talents and experience. It was a job requiring tact, firmness, secrecy, and a great deal of skill; a job unfitted for a man of scrupulous conscience, but admirably suited to one with a bold natural talent for deception, and a strong sense of political realities.[134]

This is very different to the Delafaye letters' polarised reception in the mid-Victorian period, that is, in Lee's response to *The London Review*. Given what had been learned about how he subsisted under Harley's patronage, evidence of Defoe's duplicity was evidence of his ability.

---

132 Sutherland, 140–2.
133 Sutherland, 191.
134 Sutherland, 218.

lxxxix

INTRODUCTION

In 1947, Healey completed an edition of Defoe's letters up to Harley's fall from office in 1708 as a PhD dissertation.[135] Healey planned a comprehensive published edition when convinced that Henry Hutchins's plan for an edition would not come to fruition.[136] For *The Letters of Daniel Defoe* (1955) Healey worked with original manuscripts, which had been impossible for his dissertation due to World War II. Healey's photostats of many of the letters are now deposited at Cornell University Library.[137] The rivalry with Hutchins persisted while Healey worked on the edition.[138] Healey published several items for the first time, including pieces overlooked or not transcribed in the Portland volumes.[139] The edition presented reviewers fresh opportunities to pronounce on Defoe's conduct during his political career. Thomson concluded that 'the impression left by a perusal of the letters is far from one of admiration for Defoe's character', while Carswell disapproved of 'the whining, the cant, the flattery, the skilful puffs given to his own usefulness'.[140] In *Daniel Defoe: Citizen of the Modern World* (1958), Moore gave a more charitable interpretation, writing that in his letters 'Defoe gave little space to requests for self-advantage', and his correspondence confirms that 'the vehemence of the attacks on him' by contemporaries 'was due not to his subservience but to his independence'.[141] The blend of admiration for Defoe's abilities and wariness about his veracity endures in later scholarship, biographies, and histories acknowledged elsewhere in this edition. Since Healey, several new letters have come to light, revealing new details about Defoe's secret service work and financial dealings in Scotland in 1708.[142]

Missing Letters

The number of Defoe letters lost to us is unknowable, but some inferences about the extent of the untraced corpus can be drawn from references in the surviving letters to correspondence now missing. Defoe's letter to Penn Sr mentions further

---

135 George Harris Healey, 'The Earlier Correspondence of Daniel Defoe (1703–1707)' (Cornell University PhD, 1947).

136 Healey to John Robert Moore, 12 Jan. 1941, Indiana University Archives, H140.

137 Cornell University Library Archives 4630.

138 Healey to Moore, 2 June 1949, 24 Nov. 1950, 7 Feb. 1951, 11 Jan. 1953, Indiana University Archives, H140.

139 *Letters*, ed. Healey, v.

140 Mark A. Thomson, 'Review of *The Letters of Daniel Defoe*', *EHR* 71 (1956), 296–8 (at 297); [John Carswell], 'Review of *The Letters of Daniel Defoe*', *Times Literary Supplement*, 29 Apr. 1955, 208.

141 Moore, 202, 199.

142 J. P. W. Rogers, 'Two Unrecorded Letters by Daniel Defoe', *Papers on Language and Literature* 7 (1971), 298–9; Paula R. Backscheider, 'Robert Harley to Daniel Defoe: A New Letter', *MLR* 83 (1988), 817–19; Backscheider, 'John Russell'; Owens and Furbank, 'Secret Agent'.

MISSING LETTERS

letters to Nottingham in the wake of *The Shortest Way*. In an early letter to Harley Defoe enclosed now-untraced notes of thanks to Godolphin and Queen Anne. Defoe's extant correspondence with friends in provincial towns are incomplete: letters to Elisha and Fransham refer to untraced others. Early Harley letters also indicate gaps, such as a prior letter mentioned in that of 28 September 1704 (Letter 18); and he alludes to letters addressed to other politicians, including one to Secretary of State Sir Charles Hedges sent from Bury St Edmunds in 1704. When Defoe was travelling on intelligence-gathering circuits in 1704 and 1705, he apparently sent numerous reports to Harley, but most have not been located; nor have two letters of instructions from Harley to Defoe regarding this work, one advising him to use his warrant sparingly, the other calling for his return and expressing concern that Defoe's companions might compromise the mission. Because of Harley's near-total silence when Defoe was in Scotland in following years, scholars assume that that was how their relationship always worked, but the vagaries of what has survived colour the picture before autumn 1706. On the eve of Defoe's departure for Scotland, Harley sent Defoe a note, now untraced, preventing his attendance. Even more unfortunately than the loss of Harley's brief directives, we have the fact, in a 1706 inventory (Letter 46), of Defoe's extensive correspondence with mostly Dissenting ministers and tradesmen across the breadth of England. But hardly any letters between Defoe and members of that network have survived, a great loss given Defoe's complaint, concerning the upkeep of this network, that 'the Number of Letters [are] too many for yᵉ few Undisturb'd houres wᶜʰ I have left me' (Letter 47). George Chalmers liked to imagine Defoe ensconced in his study writing books rather than letters, but for most of his life we should envisage a man cultivating extensive correspondence networks.

The greater volume and concentration of Defoe–Harley letters during the writer's first sojourn in Scotland, from autumn 1706 to early 1708, only highlights more strongly the gaps. The first letter Defoe wrote to Harley from Scotland alludes to earlier ones he had sent since his arrival in Edinburgh. Plausibly he refers to those from the journey that we do have, but references to the content of these letters suggests gaps, such as one apparently discussing Lord Chief Justice Holt. At least three letters from Defoe to Harley while the Union was pending – in November, December, and February 1706–7, respectively – are missing, as well as two the other way dating respectively from November 1706 and January 1707. There are missing letters to Harley from later in 1707 too. It is tempting to suppose that these, perhaps like the 1705 reports, were shared with Godolphin and not returned. Letters to and from others are also missing for the period of Defoe's first Scottish sojourn. On 23 October 1706, Godolphin wrote to Harley and alluded to letters from George Mason to Defoe which Godolphin forwards; we cannot be sure that they reached Defoe. Defoe's correspondence with Lord Halifax during the Union negotiations, which Defoe mentioned to Harley on 13 November 1706 (Letter 62),

xci

INTRODUCTION

is untraced. A couple of letters from this time from Defoe to Harley's Newcastle-based agent, John Bell, are also lost, as is a note to Bell's wife. A letter from Defoe to Harley alludes to one addressed to Defoe by his associate in Scotland, John Pierce, though there were surely more letters between these collaborators. And the letters that constituted an approach to Defoe from Harley's ministerial enemy, Sunderland, shortly after that man became Harley's counterpart in the secretaryship, are likewise unknown. A letter Defoe sent via Harley to Thomas Tenison, Archbishop of Canterbury, is untraced, as are letters Defoe evidently wrote to members of the Society for the Reformation of Manners in an attempt to establish a correspondence between its Scottish and English branches.

Many of the letters included in this edition were originally accompanied by handwritten or printed enclosures, most of which were Defoe's compositions, presenting Harley with a proposal or an account of some situation or topic. Some of these have been separated from the letters, and as many as fifteen to Harley alone are not accounted for. There are fewer known Defoe letters in the years in which Harley was out of government, but the letters from February 1708 to June 1710 indicate known unknowns: going only from what is mentioned in extant letters, there was another to Godolphin (there are surely more) and unanswered letters Defoe wrote to John Shute.

Surviving letters during the years of Harley's ascendancy and the resumption of Defoe's correspondence (summer 1710 to autumn 1714) alert us to further gaps, both certain losses when Defoe refers to an antecedent letter that is untraced, and probable losses when he pledges to address a topic in a subsequent communication of which we have no record. There are at least six of the first sort and at least three of the latter. Correspondences represented by sole surviving letters were clearly part of ongoing exchanges: Dyer, Button, Buchan, and the unidentified 'T.P.' are in this class. Defoe speaks in several places about his extensive correspondence with ministers of the Church of Scotland, remarking at one point that he has 'been up all Night writeing Letters', but little of that has come to light (Letter 174). Defoe alludes to other letters: a long one he sent to Thomas Bateman, one received from Scotland and sent on to Harley, and one from an unidentified Lincolnshire correspondent. The Defoe–John Russell letters we have include only those from Russell, and besides the fact that Defoe's half of the correspondence is missing, the letters mention letters from Defoe to others, such as Major James Coult.

Cotton Mather's diary alludes to correspondence with Defoe that is untraced.[143] Backscheider found a record of his correspondence with the Earl of Hyndford.[144] The letters Defoe reportedly sent to his niece Elizabeth Job in Maryland have

---

143 *The Diary of Cotton Mather*, 2 vols. (Boston, Mass., 1911), II, 74.
144 Backscheider, 'Accounts of an Eyewitness', 33.

xcii

never come to light.[145] Concerning the post-Harley years, the letter from Keimer that prompted Defoe's surviving response is untraced, as are any other letters they exchanged. Defoe evidently sent at least one letter to Sunderland via Delafaye. He exchanged letters with Sir John Dalrymple in 1718 after that man complained about being named as the source of a story in *The White-Hall Evening Post*, a newspaper Defoe was editing.[146] Finally, the letters between Defoe and Henry Baker allude to others that have not survived, including at least one more to Defoe's daughter Sophia. The missing letters of which we know indicate the vast extent of what remains undiscovered.

145 Mary E. Ireland, 'The Defoe Family in America', *Scribner's Monthly*, 12 (1876), 61–4.
146 *Annals and Correspondence of the Viscount and the First and Second Earls of Stair*, 2 vols. (Edinburgh, 1875), ii, 58–9.

THE LETTERS

I

To Daniel Finch, Second Earl of Nottingham

9 January 1703

HEADNOTE: Daniel Finch, second Earl of Nottingham (1647–1730), was Secretary of State for the Southern Department, with responsibility for prosecuting authors and publishers of seditious writings. Defoe wrote to him as a fugitive from justice following the fallout of the publication on 1 December 1702 of *The Shortest Way with the Dissenters*, an ironic pamphlet that adopted the voice of an intolerant Anglican cleric to call for stricter laws against Nonconformists, even their banishment and the execution of their pastors.

On 14 December 1702, Speaker of the House of Commons Robert Harley (1661–1724) advised Lord Treasurer Sidney Godolphin (1645–1712) that the author of *The Shortest Way* must be discovered, which Godolphin relayed to Nottingham.[1] There is no evidence that Defoe was yet suspected, but he was named as the author in the *Observator* for 30 December–2 January 1702–3, where John Tutchin (1660/4–1707) labelled *The Shortest Way* a 'pretty Sham', making clear it was a hoax.[2] Nottingham apprehended and interrogated Edward Bellamy, a Whig propaganda agent.[3] Bellamy confessed taking the manuscript to the printer, George Croome (*c.* 1643–1713), and named Defoe as the author.[4] Nottingham on 3 January issued an order to one of the Queen's Messengers, Henry Allen, 'to make strict and diligent search for Daniel Fooe and him having found you are to apprehend and seize together with his Papers for high Crimes and misdemeanours and to bring him before me to be examined concerning such matters as shall be objected against him touching the premises and be further dealt with according to Law'.[5] Unusually, Nottingham wanted to examine Defoe personally.

Having eluded the Queen's Messenger, Defoe sent his wife to parley with Nottingham and then wrote this letter to seek pardon. At about the same time he published *A Brief Explanation of a Late Pamphlet, entituled The Shortest Way with the Dissenters*, wherein '*protesting the Honesty of his intention*' Defoe says that *The Shortest Way* is 'a Banter upon the High-flying Church-Men' and 'an Irony … free from any Seditious design', an explanation 'which he hopes may allay the Anger of the Government'.[6] It did not. Advertisements offering a £50 reward for information leading to Defoe's arrest were published in *The London Gazette* on 11 and 14 January, the latter with a physical description:

> *He is a middle Sized Spare Man, about 40 years old, of a brown Complexion, and dark brown coloured Hair, but wears a Wig, a hooked Nose, a sharp Chin, grey Eyes, and a large Mould* [mole] *near his Mouth, was*

born in London, *and for many years was a Hose Factor in Freeman's-yard, in Cornhill, and now is Owner of the Brick and Pantile Works near* Tilbury-Fort *in* Essex.[7]

The government set aside £200 for the prosecution, 'The Queen ag^t De Foe & others for a libel entitled "The shortest way with the Dissenters, &c."'[8] Defoe's *A Dialogue between a Dissenter and the Observator* (probably late January) also expressed incredulity at the controversy occasioned by *The Shortest Way*. On 25 February, the House of Commons found that *The Shortest Way* was 'full of false and scandalous Reflections upon this Parliament, and tending to promote Sedition': they ordered it to be burned by the common hangman.[9] In a speech to parliament the following day, Queen Anne reaffirmed her support for the toleration of Nonconformity, advocated 'further Laws for restraining the great License which is assumed, of publishing and spreading scandalous Pamphlets and Libels', and reminded ministers of their duty 'to prevent and punish such pernicious Practices'.[10] Defoe remained at large.

My Lord

I am Exceding Senćeible That I have Given her Maj^{tie} and The Govornment Offenće, and Severall Poor and Some Innoćent People[11] being in Trouble on my Acco^t, Moves me to Address yor Lordship in This Manner, for which Rudeness I humbly Ask yor Pardon.

I had Long Sinće Surrendred to her Maj^{ties} Clemenćy, had Not ye Menaces of yor Lordships Offićers,[12] Posest me wth Such Ideas of her Maj^{ties} and yor Lordships Resentments, as were Too Terrible, and Such as Respected former Things, which I have had No Concern in, Tho' I have had ye Missfortune to pass for Guilty by Comon Fame.[13]

To Flee from her Maj^{ties} justiće, Seems my Lord to be a kind of Raiseing Warr Against her,[14] and is Very Irkesome to me. I Beseech yor Lordship to Assist me in Laying Down These Arms, Or at Least in Makeing Such a Truće, as may Thro' her Maj^{ties} Condesenćon Obtain her Pardon.

My Lord, a Body Unfitt to bear ye hardships of a Prison, and a Mind Impaćent of Confinement,[15] have been ye Onely Reasons of withdrawing My Self: And My Lord The Cries of a Numerous Ruin'd Family,[16] The Prospect of a Long Banishment from mÿ Native Country, and ye hopes of her Maj^{ties} Merćy, Moves me to

Thro' my Self at her Maj^ties Feet, and To Intreat yor Lordships Intercession.

I Beseech yor Lordship to Assure her Maj^tie, That I am Perfectly Free From any Seditious Designs,[17] and However I have Unadvisedly offended, I am, and Ever was Entirely Devoted to her Intrest, and Service.

With ye Lowest Submission I Intreat her Maj^ties Pardon For This Mistake, For which I am Ready To Make any Publick Acknowledgement, and Further humbly Beseech yor Lordships Pardon and Pacence in Makeing a Proposall on my Own Behalf, For Tho' it Must be Unusuall Condesencon, in her Maj^tie to Capitulate[18] wth an offending Subject, yet Offences Differ in Their Nature, and her Maj^ties Mercy is Unbounded.

I was Inform'd My Lord, that when my Distress'd Wife, made Application to yor Lordship, you were pleas'd to Direct, I Should Surrender, and Answer to Such questions as Should be asked me; My Lord would yor Lordship Condescend to Permitt an̈y Questions you Think Fitt, be writt Down, and Sent to, or left at my house, I will as Soon as I Can Recieve them,^**a** give yor Lordship as Plain, Full, Direct, and honest Answers, as If I were in Imediate Apprehensions of Death from yor Resentments; and Perhaps my Lord my Answers may be So Satisfactory, as may Encline you to Think you have been Mis Inform'd Concerning me.

But My Lord if after This I Should Still have ye Misfortune to Remain Und[er]^**b** her Maj^ties Displeasure, I am Then her Most Humble Peticoner, that She will please To Remitt ye Rigor of Prosecution, and That Pleading Guilty I may Reciev a Sentence from her Perticular justice, a Little More Tollerable to me as a Gentleman,[19] Than Prisons, Pillorys, and Such like, which are worse to me Than Death.

I Beg Leave To Observe to yor Lordship, that Felons, and Thieves, whose Punishm^t is Death are Frequently Spar'd upon Entring into her Maj^ties Service. If her Maj^tie will be pleased to Order me, to Serve her a year, or More at m̈y Own Charges, I will Surrend^r m̈y Self a Voluntier at ye head of her Armyes, in y^e

---

^**a** as Soon as I Can Recieve them,] *interlined*
^**b** Und[er]] *MS frayed*

Netherlands, To any Coll^{ll} of horse,[20] her Maj^{tie} Shall Direct, and without Doubt my Lord I Shall Dye There Much more To her Service than[a] in a Prison; and If by my Behaviour I Can Expiate This Offence, and Obtain her Maj^{ties} Pardon, I Shall Think it much More honourable to me Than if I had it by Peticon.

And Least I Should Seem to Prescribe to her Maj^{ties} Mercy, My Lord, If her Maj^{tie} abateing Prisons, and Corporall Punishments, shall Please To Pass any Sentence upon me, That I am Capable To Put in Excecucon, I Resolve Chearfully To Submitt To it, and Thro' my Self upon her Native Clemency.

But if her Maj^{tie} Shall Extend her Grace to a Totall Remission of This Offence, and if I may Presume to Say Shall Further be pleas'd to Accept mÿ Service, I will Raise her Maj^{tie} a Troop of horse, at mÿ Own Charges, and at ye head of Them Ile Serve her as Long as I Live.

At Least mÿ Lord This may Assure you, I am Ready wth my hand, my Pen, or mÿ head, to show her Maj^{tie} The Gratitude of a Pardoned Subject, and To Give her Maj^{tie} all The Satisfaccon I am Capable of, being Extreamly Griev'd That I have Offended her, Humbly Entreating yor Lordships Favo^r, and Intercession which Possibly yor Lordship will not Repent, when you shall find you have Gran[ted][b] it, To a Zealous, Thankfull, and Faithfull Subject, and To

> May it Please yor Lordship
> yor Most Obedient, Distressed
> Humble Peticoner and Servt
> DeFoe

Janu^a 9th 1702[21]

Text: TNA SP 34/2, fols. 48A^v–B (Figure 1). *Address* (fol. 48B^v): To The Right Honob^{le} | Heneage[22] Earle of Nottingham | Her Maj^{ties} Princ̓ipall Secretary | of State. *Endorsed by Nottingham* (fol. 48B^v): De Foe Jan 9 1702

[a] than] *interlined*
[b] Gran[ted]] *MS torn*

---

1 'I had last night some talk wth the speaker, & he had a mind to speak to you ab^t a book lately come out, called, a short way wth ye Dissenters. [H]e seem'd to think it absolutely necessary for ye service of ye Governm^t that y^r Lp. sh^d endeavour to discover who was the Author of it' (BL Add. MS. 29589, fol. 400).

DEFOE TO EARL OF NOTTINGHAM, 9 JANUARY 1703

2 Tutchin, *Observator*, 30 Dec.–2 Jan. 1702–3. In an earlier issue, Tutchin called *The Shortest Way* 'a System of the *High-Flyers* Divinity and *Politicks*', assuming its author was one of the 'Inferior Clergy' (*Observator*, 23–6 Dec. 1702).

3 His arrest was ordered on 29 Dec. 1702 (TNA SP 44/352, fol. 105). A Tory respondent to Defoe described 'Mr. *Bellamy*, the [Whig] Parties Agent, both in *England* and *Holland* (*The Shortest Way with the Dissenters … With its Author's Brief Explication Consider'd, his Name Expos'd, his Practices Detected, and his Hellish Designs set in a True Light* (1703), 22).

4 Defoe labelled Bellamy an '*Informer*' in *A Dialogue between a Dissenter and the Observator* (1703), *PEW*, III, 119. According to Dunton, 'Mr. Croom is a fair dealer; understands his business'; 'some would insinuate as though he favoured the Jacobites, but I take him for a man of more sense' (Dunton, *Life and Errors*, I, 252).

5 TNA SP 44/352, fol. 103.

6 *PEW*, III, 115, 113.

7 *The London Gazette*, 11–14 Jan. 1703.

8 *CTP 1702–1707*, LXXXIV, 106.

9 *C.J.*, XIV, 207.

10 Boyer, 48.

11 *Severall Poor and Some Innocent People*: See Defoe's reference to 'the poor People in trouble on this account' in *A Brief Explanation of a Late Pamphlet*, *PEW*, III, 115. His solicitude for the printer and publisher was dismissed as insincere in *The Shortest Way with the Dissenters … With its Author's Brief Explication Consider'd*, 2. Edward Bellamy had been arrested: he informed against Defoe. The printer, George Croome, to whom Bellamy delivered the manuscript of *The Shortest Way*, was subsequently arrested on 15 Jan. Both Bellamy and Croome were released provided they would 'personally appear … & give evidence ag: Daniel de Foe for having writt a Scandalous Pamphlet' (LMA CLA047/LJ/01/0475, fol. 14; Backscheider, *Life*, 103, 557 n. 42).

12 *Menaces of yor Lordships Officers*: Tutchin reported that Defoe 'made his Escape from the [Queen's] Messenger' (*Observator*, 30 Dec.–2 Jan. 1702–3). Another enemy alleged that he did so by jumping out of a window (*The Shortest Way with the Dissenters … With its Author's Brief Explication Consider'd*, 22).

13 *Guilty by Comon Fame*: Defoe apparently alludes to publications dating from William III's reign attributed to him most recently by Tutchin in *Observator*, 30 Dec.–2 Jan. 1702–3. They include *Memorial to the K[night]s, C[ommon]s, and B[urgesse]s in P[arliamen]t Assembled* (1701), generally known as *Legion's Memorial*, which challenged the Commons's imprisonment of five Kentish petitioners, and the notorious *Black List* (*A List of One Unanimous Club of Members of Parliament, Nov. 11. 1701*), which named 167 MPs who voted against William and were accused of being in the French interest. Defoe denied involvement with these works in his *Brief Explanation*, fearing that his reputation as a thorn in parliament's side was exacerbating his problems with the government. *Legion's Memorial* remains attributed to Defoe, but not the *Black List*.

14 *a kind of Raiseing Warr Against her*: For an exact verbal echo in a different context – Whig pamphleteers insulting Queen Anne in her final months – see Defoe, *The Monitor*, no. 7 (8 May 1714).

15 *Confinement*: Defoe had been imprisoned in the Fleet Prison for debt in 1692 and 1702 (Pat Rogers, 'Defoe in the Fleet Prison', *RES* 22 (1971), 451–5). He later wrote of 'the Dreadful Calamity of a Lingering Gaol' (*Review*, III, 159 (9 Mar. 1706)).

16 *Numerous Ruin'd Family*: Defoe's wife Mary, *née* Tuffley (1663–1732), and their six children: Benjamin (*c.* 1687–1737); Daniel (d. 1759); Hannah (d. 1759); Henrietta, *later* Boston (d. 1760); Maria, *later* Langley; and Sophia, *later* Baker (1701–62). See Defoe, *More Reformation* (1703), *SFS*, I, 209. His father James (1630–1706) and mother-in-law Elisabeth (d. 1705) probably not dependent on Defoe.

17 *Perfectly Free From any Seditious Designs*: See the near identical phrase in *A Brief Explanation of a Late Pamphlet*, *PEW*, III, 113.

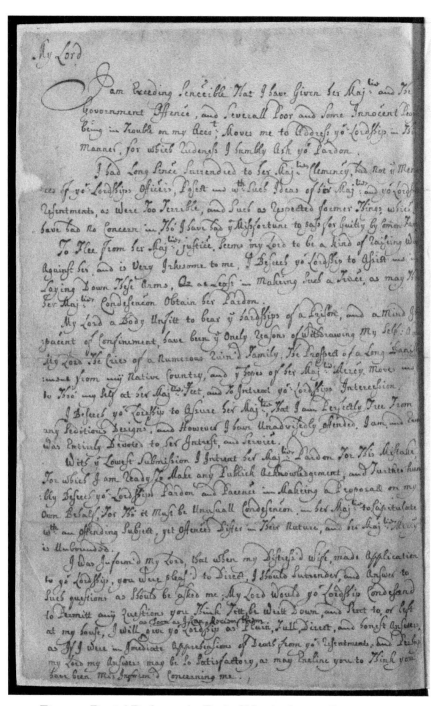

Figure 1 Daniel Defoe to the Earl of Nottingham, 9 January 1703, TNA SP 34/2, fols. 48A v–B r

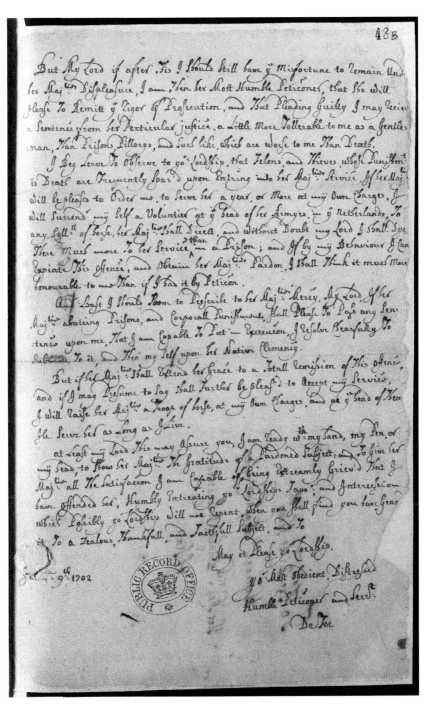

Figure 1 (continued)

18 *Capitulate*: parley.

19 *Gentleman*: One indicator of his claim to gentility is the fact that since at least 1695 Defoe had used the aristocratic sounding 'De' prefix for his surname, originally 'Foe' (Bastian, 189). It did not stick as well as he would have liked, as can be seen in the first *London Gazette* advertisement, which named 'Daniel de Fooe' and 'Daniel Fooe'. His portrait for the 1703 *True Collection of the Writings of the Author of The True Born English-man* included a coat of arms, as does the 1706 *Jure Divino* portrait (Figure 5). In his much later, unpublished, *The Compleat English Gentleman* (*c.* 1729), he wrote, 'I have the Honour to be rank'd, by the Direction of Providence, in the same Class [gentleman]' (*RDW*, x, 37). See Letter 121, note 1.

20 *Coll^ll of horse*: Commander of a cavalry division. The War of the Spanish Succession was underway in the Netherlands. Six months later, Tutchin mockingly mentions 'Colonel *Foe*', which may indicate his knowledge of this offer (*Observator*, 7–10 July 1703). Defoe had participated in Monmouth's rebellion in 1685; he joined the royal regiment of volunteer horse in July 1689 (Luttrell, I, 556). A Daniel Defoe is listed as a Captain-Lieutenant in John Desbordes's regiment of dragoons in Portugal, perhaps indicating, as Charles Dalton supposes, that Defoe acted as a recruiting agent for the regiment in Scotland (*Army Lists*, IV, vii–viii, 268). There is no evidence that he saw military action.

21 *1702*: 1703 new style.

22 *Heneage*: In error for 'Daniel'. Nottingham's father (1621–82) and younger brother (1647/8–1719) were both named Heneage. The latter was subsequently satirised as 'Banksky' in Defoe's *The Dyet of Poland* (1705), lines 997–1016, *SFS*, I, 372; and he is probably the unnamed 'Man of Arbitrary Blood' attacked in *Review*, v, 492 (30 Nov. 1708).

2

To William Paterson

April 1703

HEADNOTE: In April, when he wrote to the Presbyterian banker and political agent William Paterson (1658–1719), Defoe was still a fugitive. We lack certain knowledge of Defoe's movements while in hiding. In a late January publication Defoe relates an encounter that supposedly occurred 'in *Hackney Fields*' between himself and a bounty hunter, in which Defoe draws his sword and escapes.[1] In the letters to Nottingham and Paterson, Defoe's language suggests he was abroad: he dreads 'The Prospect of a Long Banishment from mÿ Native Country', wonders whether he will be 'Restor'd to my Native Country Or Not', and signs himself to Paterson as 'yor Exil'd Friend'. These phrases may be metaphorical or a decoy,[2] though he was rumoured to have fled to the Netherlands, for example in the dedication to John Dunton's *The Shortest-Way with Whores and Rogues* (April 1703).[3] Another enemy claimed he was being concealed by radical Whigs.[4] It is likely that his brother-in-law Robert Davis was helping him to hide. Years later, in *An Essay on the History and Reality of Apparitions* (1727), Defoe recounts a story that closely resembles his own circumstances in 1703, including the information that he was sheltered in Barnet with his brother-in-law 'Mr. *R— D—*', that he intended to go to Scotland, and that he only re-entered London (fatefully ignoring ominous dreams warning against doing so) in order 'to sign some Writings for the securing some Estate, which it was fear'd might be seiz'd by Out-law, if the Prosecution had gone on so far'.[5] We have no solid corroboration of any of these stories.

Defoe and Paterson had apparently been acquainted since the 1690s. Defoe mentions Paterson's Orphans' Fund Bank in *An Essay upon Projects* (1697), and Paterson recommends several of Defoe's books in his proposal for a library on 'Trade, Revenue, Navigation, &c.'[6] Intriguingly, a copy of two 1701 letters written by Paterson advising William III on financial and colonial subjects was kept with several personal Defoe letters and resembles plans Defoe claimed to have presented to the king.[7] Defoe was not always fulsome about Paterson, however. The two came into conflict over aspects of the economic settlement of the Anglo-Scottish Union in 1706, and Defoe was ultimately jealous at the plaudits Paterson gained in March 1707 while Defoe's service was overlooked.[8]

Paterson subsequently sent this letter on to Harley, who received it on 28 May, a week after Defoe was captured in the Spitalfields home of a French Huguenot weaver, Nathaniel Sammen (or Sammon).[9] The person who informed on him chose to remain anonymous but collected the £50 reward.[10] Defoe was committed to Newgate, a place described vividly in *Moll Flanders* (1722) as an 'Emblem of Hell itself, and a kind of an Entrance into it' – 'that horrid Place! my very Blood chills at the Mention of its Name'.[11] His interrogation by Nottingham commenced.

Sᵣ

I can Not Omitt That in yᵉ Little Informaċon I have from my Very Few Friends I Meet wᵗʰ from Every hand The Notiċes of yoᵣ Conċern for my Present Suffering, And as I am Assur'd my Gratitude for yᵉ Kindness of my friends will be yᵉ Last Vertue That will forsake me So my Senċe of yoᵣ Regard for me on whom I have Laid No Obligaċon Lays a Debt On Me I Can No Otherwise Pay Than by mÿ Thankfull Acknowledgements.

Tis Vain for me To Complain of yᵉ Misfortune of my Present Condiċon, Sinċe you Can Render me No Serviċes for wᶜʰ you Shall not Recieve Reproaches from all Partyes. Nay Even yᵉ Dissenters Like Casha To Cæsar[12] Lift up the first Dagger at me: I Confess it makes me Reflect on yᵉ wholl body of yᵉ Dissenters wᵗʰ Something of Contempt More Than Usuall, and gives me yᵉ More Regrett That I Suffer for Such a People.[13]

DEFOE TO WILLIAM PATERSON, APRIL 1703

Shall I Own to you That yᵉ Greatest Concern I have Upon me is That yᵉ Govornment whom I Profess I Did not foresee would be Displeas'd, Should Resent This Matter, I had it not in my Thoughts That yᵉ Ministers of State would Construe That as Pointing at Them, Which I Levell'd Onely at Dʳ Sachavrell,[14] Dʳ Stubbs[15] and Such People, my More Direct Antagonists; Thus Like Old Tyrrell who shot at a Stag and Killd yᵉ King[16] I Engag'd a Party, and Embroild mÿ Self with yᵉ Govornmᵗ. Sʳ, My Sencé of This has Led me to yᵉ Lowest Submissions I was Capable of in a Letter I wrott to my Lord Nottingham and Some Other Applicacóns Made Since,[17] Nor is there any Thing So Mean (which I Can Honestly Stoop to Do) That I Would not Submitt to To Obtain her Majᵗⁱᵉˢ Favour.

I Accquainted my Lᵈ Nottingham That whereas Persons Condemn'd for Capitall Offencés were Frequently Spar'd upon Their Entring Into her Majᵗⁱᵉˢ Servicé, If her Majᵗⁱᵉ would Grant me yᵉ Like Favoʳ I would Surrendʳ my Self at yᵉ head of her Armyes To any Coll. of Horse her Majᵗⁱᵉ Should Appoint and Serve her a year Two or More at my Own Charge, Not Doubting I Should Dye There more to her Majᵗⁱᵉˢ Servicé Than in a Prison, And that if by mÿ behavioʳ I Could Expiate This Folly I Should Esteem it More honour to me Than If I Obtain'd her Majᵗⁱᵉˢ Pardon by Peticón; I Omitted Nothing to Express yᵉ Unfeigned Sencé I had upon mÿ Mind of haveing offended her Majᵗⁱᵉ, and I Repeat This to you that you May kno' and be assur'd and May if you Please So farr Answer for me, that I Really am a hearty Penitent on That Accoᵗ and That I am Not asham'd, to be asham'd of it.

I Can Not but wᵗʰ Regrett Look back on yᵉ Former Discourses we have had Concérning Things Done before Now, and you Must Remember how Willingly I allwayes Offred you To make my Acknowledgements To a Certain Gentleman,[18] who I allwayes Honour For his Character Among Wise Men, More Than yᵉ Greatness of his[a] share in yᵉ Royall Favour; If I have Rendred yᵉ hopes you gave me of his Favour Desperate by This Disaster, Tis a Missfortune as Great as all yᵉ Rest. If Not, Beseech him To Suspend his Resentments Till my Future behavioʳ may Convincé

---

[a] his] *interlined*

12

DEFOE TO WILLIAM PATERSON, APRIL 1703

him That (of all yᵉ Gentlemen known to me Onely by Character) he is yᵉ Last I would Disoblige and yᵉ First I would Humble my Self To Because of The just Respect I have Entertaind of his Wisdome and Honesty.

As to mÿ Present Circumstanċes I Can Onely Say as of him yᵗ Repents without hope I Find Them Desperate and That Neither Senċe of yᵉ Offenċe Nor Future Amendment will attone, So I am Fled, and Tho' I Do allready Find Tis No Verÿ Difficult Thing for me to Get my Bread, yet as I Exprest to My Lord N: Methinks fleeing from her Majᵗⁱᵉˢ Justiċe is a Sort of Raiseing Warr against her, and I would Fain Lay Down These Arms. Nor had Death been yᵉ Punishment Should I ha[ve gone]ᵃ So Long before I had Come in and Thrown my Self upon her Majᵗⁱᵉˢ Clemenċy but Jaÿls, Pillorys and Such like w[th]ᵇ which I have been So Much Threatn'd have Convinċ't me I want Passive Courage; and I Shall Never for yᵉ Future Think my Self Injurd if I am Call'd a Coward.

I hope by my Missfortunes I Shall Not Loose yᵉ Influenċe of yoʳ Friendship, and if you Find it Necessary To Make any Postulata¹⁹ of Future Loyalty and myᶜ Obedient Submission to or Serviċe for yᵉ Govornment, If you Believ me Master of any Faith, or That I have any Prinċiples of Honour or honesty Left, you May Depend upon my Punctuall Performanċe.

If you Should Find Room for my Name in yoʳ Conversaċon wᵗʰ yᵉ Gentleman I Menċon'd, I Suppose I Need Not Name him, If you Find him Enclin'd to have Compassion for One who Offended him Onely because he Did Not kno' him, Venture in My Name in yᵉ Humblest Terms to Ask his Pardon, and whether Ever I am Restor'd to my Native Country Or Not, I Shall Never Name him but wᵗʰ Some Epethite Suited to Express his Merit; Let him kno' That I Solliċit you wᵗʰ More Earnestness To Convinċe him of my Senċe of his Resentment, and My Earnest Desire to be set Right in his Thoughts, Than I Do for the Obtaining a Recall from This Banishment Forasmuch as I Vallue yᵉ Esteem of Oneᵈ Wise man above abundanċe of Blessings.

ᵃ ha[ve gone]] *hole in MS*
ᵇ w[th]] *MS torn*
ᶜ my] *interlined*
ᵈ One] *interlined*

Accept my Repeated Thanks for ye Friendship you show in Concerning yor Self for me, my Vows for yor Welfare and Prosperity, and Continue yor Goodness and kindness To

yor Exil'd Friend
DF

Aprill. [ ]th.[a] 1703

Text: BL Add. MS. 70291, fols. 1–2. *Address* (fol. 2v): For Mr William Paterson | in | London | in Covert. *Endorsed by Harley* (fol. 2v): Received from mr Wm Paterson Fryday May 28: 1703: at one a clock

[a] [ ]th] *blank in MS*

1 *A Dialogue between a Dissenter and the Observator*, *PEW*, III, 123.

2 Looking back on *The Shortest Way* during a stay in Scotland, Defoe said 'I remain as a banish'd Man to this Day' for 'those fatal Observations I made on [Sacheverell's] Preaching and his Party's Practice', an utterance that combines literal and metaphorical exile (*Review*, VI, 576 (27 Dec. 1709)).

3 Dunton, *The Shortest-Way with Whores and Rogues* (1703), sig. A1v.

4 *The Reformer Reform'd: or, The Shortest Way with Daniel D' Fooe* (1703), 7.

5 *SFS*, VIII, 193. The property of fugitives from justice could be seized by outlaw. Outlawry proceedings against Defoe did commence (TNA T 54/18, fol. 365).

6 *PEW*, VIII, 45; Backscheider, *Life*, 105.

7 Bodl. Rawlinson MS D 132; BL Add. MS. 88618B; F&O, *Political Biography*, 31–2.

8 See Letters 68, 69, 80, and 103; *An Essay at Removing National Prejudices against a Union with Scotland ... Part II* (1706), *PEW*, IV, 79; *A Fourth Essay, at Removing National Prejudices* (1706), *PEW*, IV, 131.

9 Luttrell, V, 300–1. A year later, on 28 Sept. 1704, Secretary of State Sir Charles Hedges (*c.* 1650–1714) described to Harley 'one Sammen a weaver, a tool of De Foe's' (H.M.C. *Portland MSS*, IV, 138). See Letter 21. In 1707 and 1708, Defoe was accused of having had an affair with Sammen's wife (*The Review Review'd. In a Letter to the Prophet Daniel in Scotland* (1707), 3; *The Welsh-Monster: or, The Rise and Downfal of That Late Upstart, the R—t H—ble Innuendo Scribble* (1708?), sig. A1v).

10 *CTP 1702–1707*, LXXXV, 153; Nottingham to Godolphin, 25 May 1703, TNA SP 44/104, fol. 295; TNA T 48/17, 26 May 1703.

11 *Novels*, VI, 224. The order for Defoe's committal is TNA SP 44/352, fol. 163.

12 *Casha To Cæsar*: Servilius Casca (84–*c.* 42 BCE) was among the assassins of Julius Caesar (100–44 BCE).

13 *I Suffer for Such a People*: His unappreciated suffering for the Dissenters at this time became a regular subject for Defoe. He later wrote: 'I fell a Sacrifice for writing against the Rage and Madness of that High Party, and in the Service of the Dissenters: What Justice I met with, and above all what Mercy, is too well known to need a Repetition ... I will make no Reflections upon the Treatment I met with from the People I suffer'd for, or how I was abandon'd even in my Sufferings, at the same time that they acknowledg'd the Service it had been to their Cause' (*Appeal*, 11).

14 *Dr Sachavrell*: The High Church clergyman Henry Sacheverell (1674–1724). Defoe frequently explained his *Shortest Way* as an imitation of and satire upon the anti-Dissent rhetoric

exhibited in Sacheverell's *The Political Union* (1702). In *A Brief Explanation of a Late Pamphlet*, Defoe says that his work plainly expressed a genocidal attitude to Nonconformists that Sacheverell and others intended but tried to disguise (*PEW*, III, 114). In *More Short-Ways with the Dissenters* (1704), Defoe declares that Sacheverell was 'the Real Author of the *Shortest Way*, tho' another was Punish'd for it' (8). In *The Present State of the Parties in Great Britain* (1712), he stated that his pamphlet 'was design'd in Derision of the Standard held up by *Sacheverell* and others' (20). Before *The Shortest Way*, Defoe had attacked Sacheverell for preaching that Dissenters were a threat to political stability (*An Enquiry into Occasional Conformity* (1702), *PEW*, III, 81). After his arrest, and in the coming years, Defoe relentlessly attacked Sacheverell's politics, theology, and alleged drunkenness. See *More Reformation* (1703), lines 513–14, *SFS*, I, 228; *A Hymn to the Pillory* (1703), lines 68–74, *SFS*, I, 243; *A New Test of the Church of England's Honesty* (1704), *PEW*, III, 190–5; *Review*, I, 609 (16 Dec. 1704); *The Dyet of Poland* (1705), lines 672–7, *SFS*, I, 363; *The High-Church Legion: or, The Memorial Examin'd* (1705), *PEW*, II, 123; *Review*, II, 676 (23 Oct. 1705). For Defoe and Sacheverell in 1709 and afterwards, see Letter 140.

15 *Dr Stubbs*: The High Church clergyman Philip Stubbs (1665–1738), later Archdeacon of St Albans. Defoe attacked Stubbs in *A New Test of the Church of England's Loyalty* (1702), *PEW*, III, 60; *An Enquiry into Occasional Conformity*, *PEW*, III, 84; *The Dissenter Misrepresented and Represented* (1704?), *PEW*, III, 209; *To the Honourable the C—s of England Assembled in P—t* (1704), *PEW*, VIII, 166; and *An Elegy on the Author of the True-Born-English-Man* (1704), lines 415–23, *SFS*, I, 276.

16 *Tyrrell … King*: Walter Tirel (b. 1065) reputedly killed William II (*c.* 1056–1100) with an arrow in a hunting accident. Defoe alludes to it as an example of Providence removing a tyrant in *Jure Divino* (1706), albeit mentioning that James Tyrell had cast doubt on the incident in *The General History of England*, 3 vols. (1696–1704), II, book 11, 108–9 (*SFS*, II, 230, 307).

17 *Other Applicacons Made Since*: We do not know to whom else Defoe appealed.

18 *a Certain Gentleman*: Robert Harley, to whom Paterson sent Defoe's letter in late May. Defoe may have sought this earlier contact with Harley in 1702 when he was imprisoned for debt (Downie, *Robert Harley*, 60; Bastian, 274).

19 *Postulata*: 'demands' or 'requirements' (Latin).

3

To [William Penn]

12 July 1703

HEADNOTE: After his arrest, Defoe was examined by the imposing Nottingham, 'a huge tall Man, by his Appearance a Man of Grandeur', before being released on bail on 5 June.[1] He attempted to influence events in fresh publications. In *More Reformation* Defoe expressed his indignation at the Dissenters' misconstrual of *The Shortest Way with the Dissenters* and sought sympathy by painting himself as '*a Man of Misfortunes*'.[2] *The Shortest Way to Peace and Union* and his preface to *A True Collection of the Writings of the Author of the True Born English-man* struck a contrite and conciliatory note, again professing that his intention was not seditious.[3]

DEFOE TO [WILLIAM PENN], 12 JULY 1703

By the time these works were published in mid to late July Defoe's fate had been settled. His trial started on 7 July. With promises of clemency and on the advice of his lawyer, the Kentish petitioner William Colepeper, Defoe pleaded guilty.[4] The trial, then, was mainly a sentencing, but Defoe faced a hostile court comprising individuals he had previously satirised.[5] He was fined 200 marks (about £133), sentenced to stand in the pillory on three successive days commencing 19 July, and confined to Newgate until he could 'find good sureties to be of good behaviour for the space of seven years from thence next ensuing And that he do not depart from thence and … be of good behaviour with regard to our Lady the present Queen and her populace'.[6] An incident on 11 July further damaged Defoe's cause. Colepeper went to Windsor to petition the Queen, but while waiting was involved in a fracas with Sir Jacob Banks (1662–1724), who believed Colepeper had insulted Sir George Rooke (1650–1709), Admiral of the Fleet and MP for Portsmouth. 'After this Accident', Colepeper later wrote, 'his Lordship [Nottingham] abated of his Civility and Good-will when he was apply'd to on Mr. *De Foe's* account.'[7] Defoe's situation was bleak indeed when he wrote to William Penn (1644–1718).

Penn was a Quaker leader, founder of Pennsylvania, and promoter of religious toleration. He had himself been imprisoned three times for his faith before the 1689 Toleration Act. Defoe had referred slightingly to Penn in a 1691 poem, perhaps due to Penn's support for James II's declarations of indulgence, which Defoe had opposed.[8] Defoe's mention of Penn's colonial work in *An Essay upon Projects* (1697) is neutral, but they saw eye to eye on occasional conformity in 1703, and by the time of *A Tour thro' the Whole Island of Great Britain* (1724–6) Defoe referred to 'the great *William Penn*'.[9] Penn was friendly with the Queen, Godolphin, Nottingham, and Harley, and he decided to intercede to try to mitigate Defoe's punishment.

On 17 July, Godolphin wrote to Nottingham:

> After I had the honor to see yr Lp yesterday Mr William Penn came to mee to tell mee he had acquainted my Lord privy seal[10] that <u>de Foe</u> was ready to make oath to yr Lp of all that he knew, & to give an Account of all his Accomplices in whatsoever he has been Concerned, for the information of the Queen, & the Lords of the Councill, provided by so doing, he may be excused from the punishment of the pillory, & not produced as an Evidence against any person whatsoever, & upon my acquainting the Queen with this just now at noon, her Maty was pleased to tell mee she had received the same Account yesterday from my Lord pr— seal, & seem'd to think, this if there were no other occasion, would make it reasonable for the Cabinett Councill to meet here [Windsor] tomorrow, & has Comanded mee to tell you soe, because, she says, you seem'd to think yesterday, that it might bee an unnecessary trouble.[11]

The following day, Penn wrote to an unidentified 'Noble Friend': 'For the Queens service I beg this mans disgrace be deferr'd if not pardon'd. I inclose a lettr to Lord Treasr who desireing to be by at his examination wth Ld Nottingham, before he sufferd the Sentence, wch cannot be [if] he suffer to morrow.'[12] On the same day, Nottingham ordered the sentence to be deferred.[13]

On 21 July Defoe was examined at Windsor. The following day, Godolphin wrote to Nottingham: 'As to <u>de Foe</u>, the Queen seems to think, as she did upon your Lps first acquainting her wth what he said, that his Confession amounts to nothing, however she is willing to Leave it to ye Lords of ye Committee to lett the sentence bee executed tomorrow [Friday 23 July], or not till after Sunday [25 July], as they think proper.'[14] Nottingham's persistence in trying to extract information from Defoe continued with one final interrogation conducted, unusually, in New-gate itself, along with the Lord Privy Seal, Buckingham. Defoe was pilloried on 29 July in Cornhill at the Royal Exchange, 30 July at Cheapside Conduit, and 31 July in Temple Bar,[15] and was then returned to Newgate.

As well as wanting Defoe to give up accomplices Nottingham sought infor-mation that would discredit William III and his Whig ministers, those lords who had blocked the bill to punish occasional conformists, that is, Dissenters who circumvented the legal bars to their holding municipal or state office by taking the Anglican sacrament as a matter of form. He asked Defoe about the dissolution of parliament in November 1701[16] and about William's controversial treaties of par-tition.[17] The 'many Libells and papers found in De Foes Custody when taken' had also been seized and thoroughly examined.[18] Defoe prided himself on remaining steadfast under questioning.[19] He never forgave Nottingham for his treatment and was unremitting in his attacks in later years.[20]

July 12th, 1703

Sir

 Tho' a Long Appology Suites Neither yor Own Temper, Nor my Condicon, yet I Can Not but Let you Kno' wth all The Thankfullness I am Capable The Sence I have of your Extraordinary Kindness: — Concerning yor Self For me So Much a Stranger to you, Nor Can I Doubt whether To One who Appeares So much my Friend as to attempt being my Saviour From This Distress, I should Scruple to use the uttmost Freedome with Relacon to ye Present Case.

 Sr The Proposall you are pleas'd to hint By yor Son[21] from My Ld Nottingham, of Discovering Partyes[22] is ye same which his Lordship has often Put upon me before.

Sᵣ In Some Letters wᶜʰ I have Sent his Lordship[23] I have Answer'd him with yᵉ Same Assurance I did to yᵉ Privy Council, Vizᵗ That in yᵉ Manner which they Proposed it I really had No p[er]son to Discover: That if my Life were Concern'd in it I would Not Save it at yᵉ Price of Impeaching Innocent Men, No More would I Accuse my Friends for yᵉ Freedome of Private Conversacon.

It has been my Character Sᵣ among those who kno' me, That I Scorn to Lye, and by Gods Grace Ile preserve it while I live. I Take yᵉ Freedome to give you the Trouble of repeating it, Onely To affirm to you with yᵉ More Confidence yᵉ Protestacon I make. I Sollemnly Affirm that Other than what Passes in Conversacon, and p[er]haps There is ill blood among people of my Opinion More than Enough, but other Than that I have no Accomplices, No Sett of Men, (as my Lord Call'd Them) with whom I used to Concert Matters, of this Nature, To whom I us'd to show, or Reciev hints from them in Ordᵣ to These Matters, and Therefore to Put it upon Condicon of Such a Nature is to Offer me Nothing Attall.

But Sᵣ My Case is this, I came in upon yᵉ Honour of yᵉ Govornment, being Under Baile[24] that (at least Some of them) Consented to Let me go away, and presst me to it.[25] I agreed to give the Court No Trouble but to plead Guilty to yᵉ Indictment, Even to all yᵉ Adverbs, the Seditiously's, The Malitiously's,[26] and a Long Rapsody, of the Lawyers et Ceteras; and all this upon promises of being us'd Tenderly and Treated like a Gentleman:[27] — and with Submission to yoᵣ Judgement, I Think that yᵉ honour, of yᵉ Govornmᵗ is Concern'd in it, and No Man will Venture to Thro' himself upon their Mercy again, if I am made the Example of their Tenderness in This Manner. I am like a Prisoner of Warr yielding upon Discrecon and afterwards Cut in Peices in Cold blood wᶜʰ Tho' they may Indeed do by Law yet No Man will Trust Them after it.

As to yᵉ Church of England as I Never Meant to Insinuate That yᵐ of England as a Church did Design So to Treat yᵉ Dissenters, So Tis plain There are Members of or Rather in yᵉ Church who have Declar'd their Resolucon to do it if it was in Their Power and as these are yᵉ Men I Aim'd at So I am Ready To do yᵉ Church

DEFOE TO [WILLIAM PENN], 12 JULY 1703

of England any justice by Vindicateing her in ye Same Publick Manner They Suppose her affronted, I mean in Print.[28]

This is what I Tho^t Fitt to give you ye Trouble of, For which I ask yor Pardon, and Entreat ye Continuance of those Kind offices you have So Generously undertaken for

An Unknown Captive
yor Disstress'd Servt
Daniel De Foe

July 12

Text: Original MS untraced. The copytext is a MS copy in the Library of the Society of Friends, London, MS box 7/1/9. *Address*: For William Penn. Esqr | Humbly Pres^t

1 *Review*, VII, 78 (29 Apr. 1710).
2 *SFS*, I, 212.
3 *PEW*, III, 140; Defoe, *A True Collection of the Writings of the Author of The True Born Englishman* (1703), sig. A 4v.
4 Colepeper (d. 1726) was one of the five gentlemen from Kent incarcerated upon petitioning parliament in May 1701, urging it to vote monetary supplies to assist William III to counteract the French threat in Europe. Defoe's *Legion's Memorial* was presented to the Commons demanding the release of the petitioners, and he subsequently wrote *The History of the Kentish Petition* (1701), *PEW*, II, 39–66.
5 For details, see Backscheider, *Life*, 109–10.
6 The sessions files for 7 July in LMA, quoted in Backscheider, *Life*, 110.
7 *A True State of the Difference between Sir George Rook, Knt and William Colepeper, Esq* (1704), 6. This work has been attributed to Defoe, including at the time by Charles Leslie in *Rehearsal*, 30 Sept.–7 Oct. 1704, but the preface, here quoted, is signed William Colepeper.
8 *A New Discovery of an Old Intreague* (1691), line 544, *SFS*, I, 53. Penn was also suspected of Jacobitism during William's reign.
9 *PEW*, VIII, 43; Penn, *Considerations on the Bill depending, for Preventing Occasional Conformity* (1703?); *TDH*, II, 233.
10 John Sheffield, first Duke of Buckingham (1648–1721). Defoe admired his poetic and critical abilities (*The Pacificator* (1700), line 134, *SFS*, I, 68; *Review*, IX, 302 (28 Mar. 1713)). However, he despised his High Tory politics, his personality, and his morals. Defoe attacked Buckingham's pride, venality, sexual incontinence, and irreligion, beginning in *Reformation of Manners* (1702), line 1020, *SFS*, I, 184. Defoe satirised him as 'Bucksky', 'a Whoreing, Gaming, Swearing Chicaneer', in *The Dyet of Poland* (1705), lines 1023–49, *SFS*, I, 372–3. And he lists him among High Tory 'State Mountebanks' in *Advice to all Parties* (1705), *PEW*, II, 104. Later Defoe caricatured Buckingham as 'the Prince of *Buquinquam*' in an imagined High Church army in the *Review* for 15 Apr. 1710 (VII, 46), and as '*Buquinquhan*, a Peer of the most exquisite cunning', in *Secret Memoirs of a Treasonable Conference at S—— House* (1717), *SFS*, IV, 166.
11 BL Add. MS. 29589, fols. 28–9.
12 TNA SP 34/3, fol. 4.
13 TNA SP 44/104, fol. 316; cf. fols. 318, 320.
14 Godolphin to Nottingham, 22 July 1703, BL Add. MS. 29589 fol. 46r; Nottingham to Godolphin, 22 July 1703, BL Add. MS. 29595, fol. 239.

15 William Pittis gives a begrudging report of Defoe's triumph in the pillory – the use of the occasion to disseminate his defiant poem *A Hymn to the Pillory* and his acclamation by the crowd: 'He was deservedly plac'd where he Stood, for being a Publick Incendiary. But his Friends, the Worthy Citizens of *London*, thought him otherwise, and Hallow'd him down from his Wooden Punishment, as if he had been a *Cicero* that had made an excellent Oration in it, rather than a *Cataline* that was Expos'd and Declaim'd against There' (*Heraclitus Ridens*, no. 2 (3–7 Aug. 1703)). Pittis complains further in his poem *The True-Born Hugonot* (1703), and Leslie indignantly recalled 'the *Party* causing his Books to be *Hauk'd* and Publickly *Sold* about the *Pillory*, while he stood upon it (in *Triumph*!) for writing them ... So far is he or the *Party* from thin[k]ing the *Pillory* a *Shame*, in such a *Cause!*' (*The Wolf Stript of his Shepherd's Clothing* (1704), 59). In 1705 Defoe recalled that 'the People, that it was expected would have treated this Man very ill, on the contrary *Pitied him*' (*The Consolidator*, SFS, III, 54). And in 1712 he gave a 'triumphal' account in *The Present State of the Parties in Great Britain*, 21. But Defoe was repeatedly mocked thereafter, as he put it, for 'suffering the Indignity of the Pillory' (*Review*, IX, 366 (7 May 1713)). Contemporaneous illustrations of Defoe in the pillory emphasise shame rather than triumph (Thomas Keymer, *Poetics of the Pillory: English Literature and Seditious Libel, 1660–1820* (Oxford, 2019), 132–8).

16 Nottingham to Godolphin, 22 July 1703: 'I askt him when his advice about dissolving the Parliament was given, and he cd not at first recollect but concluded that he verily believed 'twas before the King went into Holland' (BL Add. MS. 29595, fol. 239). On this event, see Henry Horwitz, *Parliament, Policy and Politics in the Reign of William III* (Manchester, 1977), 296–7.

17 *Review*, I, 704 (23 Jan. 1705); *The Felonious Treaty* (1711), PEW, V, 167. Defoe derides Nottingham's ignorance of the partition treaties. Defoe's claims that he was personally involved in those treaties is uncorroborated.

18 *CTB 1704–5*, XIX, 408–9; TNA T 54/18, fol. 365. Defoe later mocked his interrogators' lack of penetration in examining his papers (*Advice to all Parties*, PEW, II, 89). He also burned papers, as stated in Letter 188. Enemies reported that he had been found with a bawdy poem satirising the knighting of David Hamilton (1663–1721), Queen Anne's *accoucheur* (*The Republican Bullies* (1705), 3; William Pittis, *The Whipping Post*, no. 6 (17 July 1705)). Defoe also mentioned having been 'Questioned before the Privy Counsel of *England*, in the beginning of the Queen's Reign, for a Paper of some Questions', not identified (*Review*, VII, 118 (20 May 1710)).

19 See *The Consolidator* (1705), SFS, III, 106; Letter 30; *Review*, V, 544 (25 Dec. 1708); V 683 (5 Mar. 1709); IX, 315 (4 Apr. 1713).

20 Defoe treats Nottingham's resignation as Secretary of State in 1704 as a dismissal, expressing satisfaction that Anne 'divided her self from all that sort of People, who ... shall ruine Men for speaking the Truth' (*Review*, I, 606 (16 Dec. 1704). Cf. *Review*, II, 458 (2 Aug. 1705); *The Consolidator*, SFS, III, 106; *The Conduct of Parties in England* (1712), PEW, II, 247). Defoe even depicts Nottingham reviling the Queen in *The High-Church Legion* (1705), PEW, II, 119. In *The Paralel* (1705), Defoe attacks Nottingham's role in including loyal Protestant Dissenters in an Irish Test Act (13–19). *The Dyet of Poland* (1705) satirises Nottingham as 'Finski' (lines 295–357, 1017–22, SFS, I, 353–4, 372) and dissects his political career as a whole: 'None acts so low that e'er was born so high' (line 341). In *Jure Divino* (1706), Defoe compares Nottingham to some malevolent politicians from English history: 'His *Will to Mischief's* as compleat as theirs, | His *Judgment* only in a lower Class appears' (book VII, lines 343–4, SFS, II, 227). Defoe continued to mock Nottingham as 'Dismal', the nickname occasioned by his lugubrious appearance (*Review*, IV, 865 (2 Mar. 1708)). For Defoe's later attacks on Nottingham, following his role in the 1711 Act to prevent Occasional Conformity, see Letter 203.

21 *yor Son*: William Penn, Jr (1681–1720).

DEFOE TO [WILLIAM PENN], 12 JULY 1703

22 *Discovering Partyes*: Defoe strenuously denied that he wrote *The Shortest Way* with accomplices or on behalf of a faction of radical Whigs and Dissenters. Nottingham believed otherwise: he had even received intelligence in Jan. that the 'unworthy Book was certainly contrived and hatch't by Stronger heads than the pretended author Danl. Fooe' (qtd in J. D. Alsop, 'Defoe, Toland, and *The Shortest Way with the Dissenters*', *RES* 43 (1992), 245–7). Published attacks echo the accusation that Defoe wrote the tract at the instigation of a party. See Tutchin, *Observator*, 30 Dec.–2 Jan. 1702–3 and 6–9 Jan. 1703; Leslie, *The New Association, Part II* (1703), 6; *The Fox with his Fire-brand Unkennell'd and Insnar'd: Or, A Short Answer to Mr Daniel Foe's Shortest Way with the Dissenters* (1703), 8; *The Reformer Reform'd: or, The Shortest Way with Daniel D' Fooe* (1703), 3; Ned Ward, *In Imitation of Hudibras. The Dissenting Hypocrite* (1703), 22. A decade later, Defoe spoke proudly about his steadfastness under interrogation, not implying that he had accomplices but implying that he could have given names to save himself (*Review*, IX, 315 (4 Apr. 1713)). It was common for opponents to allege that in his more effective polemics Defoe had 'Help from Men of more Brains', as one adversary, the Whig polemicist and historian, John Oldmixon (1673–1742), put it when discussing *Legion's Memorial* (Oldmixon, 235).

23 *Letters wᶜʰ I have Sent his Lordship*: Untraced.

24 *Baile*: Bail was set at £1,500 on 5 June 1703 with Defoe required to reappear on 7 July (LMA CLA047/LJ/01/047s, fol. 15). Defoe stood as surety for £500 himself; the rest was made up by Joseph Whitaker, Thomas Powell, Nicholas Morris, and Robert Davis. The last-named was Defoe's brother-in-law, married to his sister Mary (b. *c.* 1657). For information on these men, see Backscheider, *Life*, 108. Defoe later described them as '*some few friends I had then too, and who were engaged deeply enough, as Bail for me*' (*Review*, IX, 367–8 (7 May 1713)).

25 *Let me go away, and presst me to it*: Defoe repeated this claim about his good faith in appearing to answer the charge despite being advised to flee even by those who stood bail, saying he was determined to fight his cause (*Review*, IX, 369 (7 May 1713)). *A Hymn to the Pillory* (1703) has lines to the same effect: 'And yet he might ha' been secure, | Had he said less, or wou'd he ha' said more. | Tell them that this is his Reward, | And worse is yet for him prepar'd, | Because his Foolish Vertue was so nice | As not to sell his Friends, according to his Friends Advice' (lines 439–44, *SFS*, I, 252).

26 *Adverbs, the Seditiously's, The Malitiously's*: Defoe elsewhere wrote of a man who was 'found Guilty ... with all the Adverbs of the Indictment, as basely, maliciously' (*Review*, I, 143 (20 May 1704)). Looking back on events a decade later, he wrote in similar terms: 'All the Adverbs of the Indictment I deny, (*viz.*) the Maliciouslies and Seditiouslies, &c.' (*Review*, IX, 244 (24 Feb. 1713)). He uses similar phrasing a few months later, referring to 'the usual Adverbs of an Accusation, (*viz.*) The *Seditiously* and *Maliciously*' (*Review*, IX, 415 (6 June 1713)).

27 *promises ... Gentleman*: See Defoe's account in *The Consolidator*: 'They fell to *wheadling him* with good Words to throw himself into their Hands and submit, giving him that *Geu-gau* the *Publick Faith* for a Civil and Gentleman-like *Treatment*; the Man, believing *like a Coxcomb* that they spoke as they meant, *quitted his own Defence*, and threw himself on the Mercy *of the Queen as he thought*; but they abusing their Queen with false Representations, *Perjur'd all their Promises* with him, and treated him in a most barbarous manner, on pretence that there were *no such Promises made*, tho' he proved it upon them by the Oath of the Persons to whom they were made' (*SFS*, III, 106). Pittis gave little credence to Defoe's cry of foul play: 'He'll tell you likewise Promises were broke, | ... | But ne're give Credit to the Shuffling Knave, | Till he proves that was *broke* they never *gave*' (*The True-Born-Hugonot: or, Daniel de Foe* (1703), 19).

28 *Vindicateing her ... in Print*: 'I have been told he offer'd to turn the Current of his Pen another way, might he have been excus'd some little Ceremonies the Law had oblig'd him to undergo first' (Pittis, *Heraclitus Ridens*, no. 2 (3–7 Aug. 1703)).

4

To James Stancliffe

[*c.* 9] November 1703

HEADNOTE (**Letters 4 and 5**): After being pilloried at the end of July 1703, Defoe remained in Newgate. His brick and tile factory was failing,[1] and his wife was pregnant with their seventh child.[2] His isolation from the Dissenting community is indicated by the refusal of three eminent ministers to pray with him in prison.[3] In *An Appeal to Honour and Justice* (1715), Defoe wrote:

> While I lay friendless and distress'd in the Prison of *Newgate*, my Family ruin'd, and my self, without Hope of Deliverance, a Message was brought me from a Person of Honour, who, till that time, I had never had the least Acquaintance with, or Knowledge of, other than by Fame, or by Sight, as we know Men of Quality by seeing them on publick Occasions. I gave no present Answer to the Person who brought it, having not duly weighed the Import of the Message; the Message was by Word of Mouth thus: *Pray ask that Gentleman, what I can do for him?* But in return to this kind and generous Message, I immediately took my Pen and Ink, and writ the Story of the blind Man in the Gospel, who follow'd our Saviour, and to whom our Blessed Lord put the Question, *What wilt thou that I should do unto thee?* Who, as if he had made it strange that such a Question should be ask'd, or as if he had said, *Lord, doest thou see that I am blind, and yet ask me what thou shalt do for me?* My Answer is plain in my Misery, *Lord, that I may receive my Sight.*[4]

The 'Person of Honour' was Speaker of the House of Commons Robert Harley (Figure 2), to whom Defoe had already appealed via Paterson. Over the next few months Harley worked on having Defoe released.

On 13 August, Godolphin wrote to Harley, replying to a suggestion from the latter:

> I thank you for y[r] hints about Scotland, <u>De Foe</u> w[d] be the properest person in y[e] world for that transaction but I doubt the rigor of his punishm[t] to'ther day will have made it scarce practicable to engage him; if you have any means of sounding him, I wish you w[d] try it; if not, I will putt M[r] Sec[ty] Hedges upon doing it, thô he will, as well as myself, bee going to y[e] bath too soon, I doubt, to doe any in it wth Effect.
>
> Therefore it must be done by you, or not done now; Could M[r] paterson bee of no use in Scotland?[5]

Figure 2 Sir Godfrey Kneller, Robert Harley, first Earl of Oxford (1714), oil on canvas, National Portrait Gallery, London

Though in no hurry, Harley saw proper to act and engaged Defoe's friend and former business partner, James Stancliffe.[6] By 20 September, when he wrote to Godolphin, Harley had more information, as well as a developing regard for Defoe's abilities and a strategy for handling him:

> I find Foe is much oppressd in his mind with his usage, & particularly the two Lords [Nottingham and Buckingham] who examined him in Newgate: I do find he lays the harshness he hath sufferd upon

particular persons, & would be willing to serve the Qeen &c. Your L^{dp} can judg whether he be worth it; there is a private attempt amongst his friends to raise the <u>200</u> marks for his fine; he is a very capable man, and if his fine be satisfied without any other knowledg but that he alone be acquainted wth it y^t it is the Qeen's bounty to him & Grace, he may do service, & this may perhaps engage him better than any after rewards, & keep him more under the power of an obligation: This is intirely submitted to your L^{dps} judgement.[7]

On 26 September Godolphin wrote to Harley to endorse the plan: 'I have found it proper to read some paragraphs of your letter to the Queen. What you propose about Defoe may be done when you will, and how you will.'[8]

Defoe appeared before Justice Thomas Lane on 3 November with four men ready to stand as sureties for his keeping the peace: Defoe signed a bond for £200 and the others for £100 each.[9] On 4 November, Godolphin assured Harley, 'I have taken care in ye matter of de Foe',[10] and Harley wrote the same day to Stancliffe, advising him to collect the £150 that Godolphin duly assigned 'Out of Secret Service money[,] clear of all charges'.[11] Defoe's fine and prison fees were paid, he was released (probably on 8 November), and he wrote the following two letters, the first a cover, to Stancliffe, for the latter, to Harley. 'Every one is not a *Daniel de Foe* that has a Party to pay a Fine for him', sneered William Pittis, thinking that Whigs and Dissenters – not the ministry – had arranged Defoe's release: 'It's no ungainful thing to be a *Whig*, let me tell you.'[12]

Mr Stancliffe

One Trouble allwayes brings on Another, and as you have Embarkt for me in the First part of this Matter, you must not Refuse to be ye Messenger of my Acknowledgements.

I Can hardly Promise my Self that what I have wrott will Express my Sence of the Obligacon I have upon me to m^r Harley, and I wish you would make it up, by Saying Every thing you Can Immagin a Man Overcome wth Kindness Ought to Say.

I am at Some Loss about ye papers I told you I had prepar'd to publish on my Enlargement. I would do nothing of that Nature that should be offensiv to my benefactors,[13] but I am perswaded None of that party of Men which are Touch't by me have any hand in an Accon So Generous as this, and am of Opinion what was in my thoughts that way would Rather please than Dissoblidge those that Can Entertain any thoughts of kindness or Compassion for

DEFOE TO JAMES STANCLIFFE, [*C. 9*] NOVEMBER 1703

my Case, yet I shall Continue to stop yᵉ press in this Case till I hear yoʳ Opinion, tho' yᵉ substance was never So Necessary to my Own Vindication.

I am

yoʳ Oblidg'd Friend & Servᵗ

DF

No[v   ]ᵃ 1703

Text: BL Add. MS. 70291, fol. 3. *Address* (fol. 3ᵛ): To | Mʳ James Stancliffe | in Ironmonger Lane | London

---

ᵃ No[v   ]] *hole in MS*

---

1 Defoe was attending to business up until 3 July 1703, when he responded to a chancery suit brought against him by his factory clerk Paul Whitehurst for money owed (TNA C 7/377/91; G. A. Aitken, 'Defoe's Brick-Kilns', *The Athenæum*, 13 Apr. 1889, 472–3).

2 Backscheider, *Life*, 119–20; Novak, 198–9. Letter 10 specifies seven children, indicating the birth probably of Martha in spring 1704.

3 *More Reformation*, lines 892–904, *SFS*, 1, 238. The three divines were Robert Fleming (1660–*c.* 1716), John Spademan (*c.* 1648–*c.* 1708), and John Howe (1630–1705). Defoe had clashed with Howe over occasional conformity, resulting in Defoe's *A Letter to Mr. How* (1701). Defoe recalls being slighted by these three ministers in *Review*, VI, 575 (27 Dec. 1709).

4 *Appeal*, 11–12; Mark 10:51 and Luke 18:41. Paula Backscheider notes that influential biblical commentators such as Matthew Henry emphasised not only Jesus' charity but Bartimaeus' gratitude when his sight is restored because he is thereby made useful, able to work, and no longer burdensome, which suits Defoe's sentiments ('Personality and Biblical Allusion in Defoe's Letters', *South Atlantic Review* 47 (1982), 1–20 (at 3–4)).

     Defoe says he 'lay four Months in Prison after this', which if accurate places Harley's first approach in July, as Defoe was released in early Nov.

5 Godolphin to Harley, 13 Aug. [1703], Longleat House, Portland MSS Appendix II, fols. 166ʳ–167ᵛ. The consternation about Scotland was caused by acts passed there in 1703 permitting trade with France during the war and requiring the approval of the Scottish parliament for future declarations of war. A Bill of Security had been introduced which, if passed, would allow the Scottish parliament to choose Queen Anne's successor in Scotland unless trading benefits were granted Scotland; it was refused the royal assent until 1704.

6 In court in 1730, Defoe recounted some of his dealings in the 1690s with Stancliffe (d. 1727), who was his trustee for his 1706 bankruptcy (Letter 50). See TNA C 11/1473/18; James R. Sutherland, 'A Note on the Last Years of Defoe', *MLR* 29 (1934), 137–41. Defoe's biographers have treated a letter from Stancliffe to Harley concerning Defoe dated 23 Aug. 1704 as though it were from 1703, and so requesting Harley to help Defoe while imprisoned (Backscheider, *Life*, 122; Novak, 197). For details on that letter, see Letter 13.

7 BL Add. MS. 61118, fol. 60. Defoe did credit his release (and financial relief) to the Queen as well as Harley: 'Her Majesty was pleased particularly to enquire into my Circumstances and Family, and by my Lord Treasurer *Godolphin*, to send a considerable Supply to my Wife and Family, and to send me to the Prison Money to pay my Fine, and the Expences of my Discharge' (*Appeal*, 13).

8 H.M.C. *Portland MSS*, IV, 68.

9 LMA CLA047/LJ/01/0478, fol. 35. They were Robert Davis, Charles Read, John Chase, and Thomas Fry.

10 BL Add. MS. 70021, fol. 65v; H.M.C. *Portland MSS*, IV, 75.

11 The receipt survives in the receipt book of William Lowndes (1652–1724), Secretary to the Treasury and MP for Seaford. One side has Harley's instructions of 4 Nov.; the other is the receipt signed by Stancliffe, dated 8 Nov. Lowndes's note indicates the secretive proceedings: 'My Lord Trer directed this sum to be paid him [Stancliffe] for Her Maty Sec: Ser: on 5th Novr & he would give no other acqce than this' (TNA T 38/737, fol. 97; cf. TNA T 48/17, 8 Nov. 1703).

12 *Heraclitus Ridens*, no. 28, (2–6 Nov. 1703).

13 *papers … benefactors*: Defoe may refer to his *A Challenge of Peace, Address'd to the Whole Nation*, published on 22 Nov. 1703. Dedicated to the Queen, it responded to her call in her speech opening parliament on 9 Nov. for 'PERFECT PEACE AND UNION' among her subjects by suggesting the speech admonished the High Church party (Boyer, 98). Defoe was apparently not advised against publishing his views, though *A Challenge of Peace* shows some chariness about speaking freely (sig. A4v; 19).

5

To Robert Harley

9 November 1703

Sr

As there is Something Surprizeing in yor Bounty To a Mortifyed Stranger, So I am more than usually at a Loss in what Manner to Express my Sençe of it. But sr at ye Same time that you Stoop to do good you Subject yor Self to a Necessity of bearing The Impertinençe of a Thankfull Temper.

Of all ye Examples in Sacred Story None moves my Indignaçon like That of the Ten Lepers who were healed by Our Saviour.[1] I Sr Like that One Gratefull wretch am Come back to Pay the Tribute of thankfullness which this So Unexpected Goodness[2] Commands from me.

And sr Tho' I think my Self bound to Own you as the Prinçipall Agent of this Miracle, yet haveing Some Encouragement from you to Expect More Perticularly to <u>kno' my Benefactors</u>; I can Not but wish for that Discovery that my Acknowledgements may in Some Measure be Proporçon'd To ye Quallity of ye Persons, and ye Vallue of ye Favour.

DEFOE TO ROBERT HARLEY, 9 NOVEMBER 1703

It Remains for me to Conclude my Present Applicacon with This Humble Peticon[a] that if Possible I may By Some Meanes or Other know what I am capable of Doeing, that my Benefactors whoever they are May Not be Asham'd of their Bounty as Missapplyed, Not sr That I Expect to be able to Meritt So Much goodness, But as A Gratefull Temper is Allwayes Uneasy to be Loaded with Benefitts, So The <u>Vertue</u> which I Call Gratitude, has Allwayes So Much Pride in it, as Makes it Push at a Retribucon, Tho' tis Unable to Effect it.

Whoever Sr Are the Principalls in this Favour, I Can Not but Profess my Self a Debtor wholly[b] to your Self, who Till I May be Otherwise Instructed Appeares the Original <u>as to Me</u>. And in the kindness the Manner is So Oblidgeing, and all the Articles of it So Generous, that as a Man Astonish't at the Perticulars, I am Perfectly Unable to Express My Sence of it. Onely in the humblest Manner I Can, Most Earnestly Pray That I Maÿ have Some Opportunity Put into my hands by Providence to Make More Explicit Acknowledgements; And that as I have Recd Such an Obligacon as few Ever Reciev'd, I Might be Able to Make Some Such[c] Sort of Return as No Man Ever Made.

And as I am Sure I write this from an honest heart, Readyer by Farr to Perform than to Promise, So I Take The Freedome to Repeat ye Assurance of A Man Ready to Dedicate my Life and all Possible Powers to The Intrest of So Generous and So Bountifull Benefactors, Being Equally Overcome with The Nature as well as ye Vallue of The Favour I have Reciev'd, asking yor Pardon for The Freedome of This Address and For Subscribeing My Self

yor Most Obedient Infinitely Oblidged
Humble Servant
Daniel De Foe

Novembr 9° 1703

---

[a] Peticon] *interlined*
[b] wholly] *interlined*
[c] Such] *interlined*

DEFOE TO [ADDRESSEE UNKNOWN], 18 APRIL 1704

Text: BL Add. MS. 70291, fols. 4–5. *Address* (fol. 5ᵛ): To The Honoᵇˡᵉ | Robert Har-lay Esqʳ | Speaker | To yᵉ House of Commons | Humbly Present

1   *Ten Lepers who were healed by Our Saviour*: Luke 17:11–19. Defoe also alludes to it in Letter 229 and *A Journal of the Plague Year* (1722), *Novels*, VII, 210.
2   *Unexpected Goodness*: A phrase repeated in Letter 30.

6

To [Addressee Unknown]

18 April 1704

HEADNOTE: This letter to an unidentified person is addressed to someone re-cently departed from London, presumably on a voyage ('whether you Get Safe Down'), who frequently visited Defoe in Newgate. The letter has ended up in the Historical Society of Pennsylvania. Healey cautiously suggests William Penn.[1] Penn's son, William Penn Jr, is the only man apart from his lawyer William Cole-peper whom we know visited Defoe in prison,[2] and he had departed for Pennsyl-vania in autumn 1703.[3] He seems a marginally better candidate.

Sʳ

I was Very Sorry[a] To heare you were[b] So Suddainly Goeing away, and Came a great way to have Wisht you a good Journey.

This I thoᵗ my Self Oblig'd to in Return for those Many and kind Visits you bestow'd on me in a house of Bondage and affliction.[4]

As This was all my Reason for offring you yᵉ Interruption of a shake by the hand, So I Supply yoʳ absençe by putting it[c] into Writeing, Onely Assureing you I shall be Glad To hear by a Line, whether you Get Safe Down, and if it be worth your while to Correspond you may be sure Twill be welcome To

yoʳ Oblig'd Frᵈ & Servᵗ
D Foe

Aprˡˡ 18. 1704

ᵃ Sorry] *interlined*
ᵇ were] *interlined above cancelled word* 'where'
ᶜ it] *interlined*

Text: Historical Society of Pennsylvania, Philadelphia, Ferdinand J. Dreer Autograph Collection (Collection 175), English Prose Writers, box 210, folder 41.[5]
Address: none.

1 *Letters*, ed. Healey, 11 n. 1.
2 What appears to be a report for Nottingham on people who visited Defoe in Newgate lists Penn (not specifying whether father or son), Colepeper, an unnamed Presbyterian parson, and an unnamed 'Man that Squints' (TNA SP 34/24, fol. 115).
3 *Correspondence between William Penn and James Logan*, ed. Edward Armstrong (Philadelphia, Penn., 1870), 247.
4 *house of Bondage and affliction*: Exod. 20:2.
5 Dreer (1812–1902) acquired the letter from an unknown source in 1876.

7

To [Robert Harley]

12 May 1704

HEADNOTE **(Letters 7 and 8):** There is no known contact between Defoe and Harley between the letter of November 1703 and the beginning of meetings and regular letters in May 1704.[1] Defoe's published writings in this interval suggest that he was to some degree promoting policies Harley supported, but retained a great deal of autonomy. His polemics on Dissent, for instance, continued to oppose proposed legislation against occasional conformity (Godolphin, Harley, and Anne unofficially opposed a second occasional bill in the 1703–4 session, having supported the first) and to promote the ministerial message of 'moderation'.[2] However, Defoe addressed High Churchmen in ways more often antagonistic than conciliatory.[3] Unaware of the developing understanding between Defoe and Harley, Pittis labelled Defoe the Dissenters' 'Secretary', saying 'this Reprobate stands in open Defiance against Parliamentary Authority', alleging that Defoe was breaching the terms of his release in writing such works.[4]

Defoe's writings at this time on the topic of press regulation show a similar mix of what looks like government-approved restraint and a more independent streak. *An Essay on the Regulation of the Press*, published in January 1704 soberly argues against the return to press licensing being debated in the Commons.[5] But *To the Honourable, the C——s of England … Relating to the Bill for Restraining the Press*, probably written in March and intended for circulation among Defoe's Dissenting friends, savagely ironises the voice of its Tory narrator who advocates stifling Whig publications under the new legislation.[6] The secrecy of Defoe and Harley's connection is indicated by the fact that on 1 April 1704 an informer, having infiltrated

DEFOE TO [ROBERT HARLEY], 12 MAY 1704

a private meeting of Dissenters, sent Harley a copy of the printed broadside *To the Honourable, the C——s of England*, suggesting, as had Pittis on the question of Dissent, that Defoe had violated the terms of his release in writing it.[7]

The most important development for Defoe in the time since his release was the beginning of his periodical, the *Review*, on 19 February 1704. It was initially twice-weekly. For Harley, the most important development was his appointment as Secretary of State after Nottingham's resignation.[8] Harley took charge of the Northern Department, with Hedges moving by customary arrangement to the Southern office. Harley took the seals of office on 18 May but continued as Speaker of the House of Commons.

Sr

Tis a Perticular Missfortune to me That I had Not ye honour of Seeing you Last Night, and 'Tis ye More So, in that I Recd No Orders when to give My Farther Attendance.[9]

And yet Sr I had waited wth all ye Pacence became Me in This Perticular, Till yor Affaires had p[er]mitted or yor Pleasur approv'd of giveing Me Audience; had not my Uneasyness at This Time Prevail'd On Good Manners from ye Following Occasion.

I kno' ye Duty Lay on me To Conceal ye Favour I Recd in yor Admitting a Man Lately Made Despicable[10] to So Near and So Advantageous a Conversacon, and Therefore have Carefully Conceal'd from all ye world what Otherwise I should have Vallued my Self upon on all Occasions, That I had ye Honor So Much as to be known to you.

But sr It is Impossible for me to Describe ye Confusion I wa[s][a] in, when I was Publickly Told On Wednsday Last, when, where, and How often I had ye Honour of yor Conversacon, and Imagining Their Intelligence was <u>Ab Inferis</u>,[11] Expected to hear Every Mom[ent][b] ye p[er]ticulars of Our Discourse.

I am Confident you will Pardon ye Importunity of This Letter, when you Reflect how Earnest I was Not Onely to Accquat you wth This, but Also to Let you kno' ye Accident wch brought it to Pass; and ye Method by which any ill Consequence from it may be Prevented.

I am yor Most Humble Peticoner, That you will Please to abate me all Those Extasies and Extravancyes a Necessary

[a] wa[s]] *MS torn*
[b] Mom[ent]] *MS torn*

30

DEFOE TO [ROBERT HARLEY], 12 MAY 1704

Acknowlegement of yor Generous Conćern for me would
Lead me to. I Can No More Express my Self, Than I Can forgett
ye Obligaćon, And I Choose to be Perfectly Silent, from y^e
Impossibillity of Putting my Senće of it into words, and ye hopes
I have That ye Same Providenće wch I humbly Recognize[a] as y^e
first Mover of yor Thoughts in My Favour, will yet Put an Occasion
into my hands, by Faithfull, and usefull Applicaćon, to Satisfye
you, That I am ye Gratefullest wretch Allive.[12]

Fryday May. 12° 1704

S^r

If you please to Let a Note be left (or any Other way) with y^e
Maid Servt at Mr Auditors[13] Chambers I shall Call there for yor
Orders, Or Directed [to me][b] at Jones's Coffee house[14] in Finch
Lane Near ye Ex[change].[c]

Text: BL Add. MS. 70291, fols. 6–7. *Address*: torn out.

[a] Recognize] *the 'c' is interlined*
[b] [to me]] *blotted in MS by residue from the wax seal*
[c] Ex[change]] *blotted in MS*

---

1 I disagree with J. J. Cartwright, editor of H.M.C. *Portland MSS*, IV, who says 'there are references in the extant letters to previous communications and interviews between them earlier in
   that year' (iv). This letter clearly follows at least one, recent interview, but there is no evidence
   for regular contact earlier in 1704 or any correspondence between Nov. 1703 and May 1704.
2 Gregg, *Queen Anne*, 177.
3 His works on Dissent in this period are: *A Challenge of Peace, Address'd to the Whole Nation*
   (Nov. 1703); *Peace without Union* (Dec.? 1703); *The Dissenters Answer to the High-Church Challenge* (Jan. 1704); *A Serious Inquiry into this Grand Question; whether a Law to Prevent the
   Occasional Conformity of Dissenters, would not be Inconsistent with the Act of Toleration* (Jan.?
   1704); and *The Lay-Man's Sermon upon the Late Storm* (Feb. 1704).
4 *Heraclitus Ridens*, no. 45 (4–8 Jan. 1704). Pittis also suggests, perhaps scurrilously, that Defoe is
   writing from the Mint, a region of London in which criminals could not be arrested.
5 *PEW*, VIII, 143–59.
6 *PEW*, VIII, 161–6. The licensing bill was lost in committee and never became law.
7 BL Add. MS. 70267, item 41X; J. A. Downie, 'An Unknown Defoe Broadsheet on the Regulation of the Press?', *The Library* 33 (1978), 51–8.
8 Angus McInnes, 'The Appointment of Harley in 1704', *Historical Journal* 11 (1968), 255–71.
   Harley considered himself 'unfortunately pressed into the public service, in a difficult and
   dangerous post' (Harley to Richard Hill, 6 June 1704, *The Diplomatic Correspondence of the
   Right Hon. Richard Hill*, ed. Rev. W. Blackley (1845), 112; cf. Holmes, 266, 499 n. 70).
9 *Missfortune ... Attendanće*: Explained in the following letter.

DEFOE TO ROBERT HARLEY, [16 MAY 1704]

10 *a Man Lately Made Despicable*: See Defoe's reference to 'his Despicable Character' in *A Challenge of Peace* (1703), sig. A4v, and the repetition of the adjective in Letter 30.

11 *Ab Inferis*: 'From hell' (Latin).

12 *Allive*: Here half a page, the top half of the third and fourth sides (fol. 7r–v), has been torn out. That includes the signature on fol. 7r and the address on fol. 7v.

13 *Mr Auditors*: Robert Harley's younger brother, Edward (1664–1735), Auditor of the Imprest.

14 *Jones's Coffee house*: Known to be in operation from 1702 to 1714 (Lillywhite, 309). It took subscriptions for Defoe's *Jure Divino*, starting Sept. 1704 (*Review*, 1, 382 (26 Sept. 1704)).

8

To Robert Harley

[16 May 1704]

Sr

It is Very Unhappy That I, who have So Seldome ye Advantage as well as honour of yor Notice, should Meet Such United Interrupcons in ye least Occasion of its Return.

I Recd sr Last Fryday a Letter Appointing me to wait on you on Thursday Evening at 6 a Clock. I was at ye Coffee house after Four that Evening and No Letter was Come, and by ye Exactest Notice I Can have, ye Messenger did Not Leave it Till after ye Time I was to ha' been at ye Place.

As Soon as I Recd it, I Took Care by a Letter left at yor house, to Signify ye Dissapointment; and to Entreat yor farther Ordrs, but To my Surprize They Tell me ye Person who left ye Letter Call'd again, to kno' if it had been Delivred. This Causes me to Suppose Sr my Letter has Not Reach'd yor hands, Tho' left wth yor Porter Last Fryday Night.[1]

I Impacently wait to Reciev yor Ordr, and to Inform you of The Dissapointment, Wishing if Possible ye Time May Come, that you May find this Neglected fellow Servicable, or at least Make him So.

Yor Most Obedt and Humble &c [*monogram*][a]

Tuesday Noon

---

[a] [*monogram*]] *placed between and above* 'Humble' *and the ampersand because Defoe ran out of space*

Text: BL Add. MS. 70291, fol. 8. *Address* (fol. 8v): To The Right Honble | Robert Harley Esqr | One of her Majties Principll Secretarys of State | Present. *Endorsed by an unknown hand* (fol. 8v): Upon being disappointed in receiving a Letter from ye Secretary

1   *I Recd ... Fryday Night*: Defoe explains that on Friday 12 May he received Harley's letter setting an appointment at 6pm on Thursday 11 May, having last checked for mail at the coffee house at 4pm on the Thursday. The note he sent (Letter 7) seems initially to have miscarried, which is why he writes this one.

9

To Robert Harley

[May–June 1704?][1]

HEADNOTE **(Letters 9 and 10):** In early summer 1704 Defoe and Harley's relationship was evolving rather than settled. Some schemes and employments mentioned in the letters never came to pass. Defoe's finances remained straitened. He angled for some fixed position or immediate relief, but also professed his gratitude and willingness to serve the Queen and the ministry. Nonetheless, he had been involved in publications during the spring attacking the Tory-led House of Commons that he likely knew would not please Godolphin and Harley even though High Tories were gradually being removed from office. He wrote a satirical ballad, *The Address*, criticising the Commons for its partisanship, willingness to persecute Dissenters, and constitutional missteps.[2] And he very likely had a hand in *Legion's Humble Address to the Lords*, a petition asking the peers to protect constitutional rights in light of the Commons's failure to redress the disenfranchisement of an Aylesbury cobbler named Ashby.[3] A Queen's proclamation was issued for the arrest of the authors of the latter work.[4] The printer and distributors were promptly apprehended.[5] Defoe denied having written it and having absconded for so doing, but reports implicating him reached Harley.[6] In his letters to Harley, Defoe declared his eagerness to sing from the government's hymnsheet, but he also fought his own battles in the meantime.

Sr

    The Hurry of yor Affaires is my Mortification as it Deprives me of ye Opportunity of waiting On you, and I take this way to supply it, because In Our short Interviews I Omitt too Much what I would Say.

DEFOE TO ROBERT HARLEY, [MAY–JUNE 1704?]

Before I go on to what I would Now write I desire to Premise to you Sr That yor Proposall of my Goeing to H . . . .7 is Really and Sincerly Very Acceptable to me And p[er]ticularly as you were pleasd to Tell me I might do you Some Service there, the present Useless posture I am in being my p[er]ticular afflicçon.

I Entreat you to believ me wthout Complim^t That besides my being by Inclinaçon and principle heartily in ye Intrest of ye Governm^t, So I am p[er]ticularly in a great Varyety of Obligaçons and More Than Commonly by my Own Affecçons link't to yor p[er]sonall Intrest, and shall be Glad to Distinguish my Self in any Thing and at Any hazard for your^a Service.

I Confess my Own Pressures,8 wch are Sometimes Too heavy and apt to Sink ye hopes I Conciev'd from yor Goodness, Force me to Importune you, but I Can not but believ you Resolve to help me wthout my So Frequent sollicitations. I Therefore Ask pardon for my Impacence and Go On to Tell you That ye Voiage you propose is Very Acceptable to me and my Very Choice Unless I may Render you More Service Elce where, wch you will Determine for me.

But s^r This Need Not hind^r but if you please To Move my Ld Treasurer9 in mÿ behalf One Thing may be Done for me wch I humbly Represent to your Thoughts.

Either That One Branch of ye Auditors office (for I am Assur'd it is Divided)¹⁰ May be bestow'd on me, wch I Can Ord^r to be Done privately and put in a p[er]son to supply for me till my Returne, Or That his L^dship will appoint me a Convenient Private^b Allow^a for subsistence On wch I might Comfortably Depend and Continue to be servicable in a private Capascity whether abroad or at home.

I Sollicit ye first s^r On 2 accot^s: first because Matters of Accot^s are my p[er]ticular Elem^t what I have Allways been Master of¹¹ and secondly Because Twill be a Certainty in wch I may bring my Sons¹² up Under me to be in Time Servicable to Their Fathers Benefactor.

I p[er]swade my Self s^r a word from you To my Ld Treasurer would Do this for me and I Humbly tho' Earnestly press you to Consider it for me.

---

^a your] *following word* 'Intrest' *cancelled*
^b Private] *interlined*

DEFOE TO ROBERT HARLEY, [MAY–JUNE 1704?]

I beg Leav to Tell you That I will Ord^r my Affaires So in This Office that no One shall kno' me to be in it Till Something may happen to make it Reasonable to Appear in it.

If This Can Not be Then I Refer ye Case to yor Goodness that if possible I may be Delivred from ye Unsufferable Disorders of my affaires, and That my Goeing Abroad may be as speedy as you please. Pardon my Urgency in this Matter and admitt me I Entreat to as speedy an Audience as possible that I may at last Enter into yor Intrests and Service and show you whether I am quallifyed to Merit your favour or no.

I am

S^r

yor Depending but

Oblig'd Obed^t Servt

[*monogram*]

Thursday morning

Text: BL Add. MS. 70291, fols. 12–13. *Address* (fol. 13^v): To The Right Honble | Robert Harley Esqr | Principall Secretary of State | Prest

1 I follow Healey's rationale for reversing the order of this and the following letter as they appear in H.M.C. *Portland MSS*, IV, 87–9, because Letter 9 requests aid and Letter 10 acknowledges receipt of it (*Letters*, ed. Healey, 16 n. 1). Novak states that Letter 10 dates from 'sometime toward the beginning of May' (*Daniel Defoe*, 228), but both Letters 9 and 10 are addressed to Harley as Secretary of State, indicating that they were probably written after 18 May.

2 *PEW*, II, 67–76.

3 On the authorship and outcome of *Legion's Humble Address*, see W. R. Owens and P. N. Furbank, 'New Light on John Pierce, Defoe's Agent in Scotland', *Edinburgh Bibliographical Society Transactions* 6 (1998), 134–43; F&O, *Bibliography*, 271.

4 *London Gazette*, 29 May–1 June 1704.

5 Pat Rogers, 'An Eighteenth-Century Alarm: Defoe, Sir Justinian Isham and the Secretaries of State', *Northamptonshire Past and Present* 4 (1966–71), 383–7. Relevant documents are TNA SP 34/4, fols. 68–73; TNA SP 44/345, fol. 169; TNA SP 44/105, fols. 88, 90, 152.

6 'If Dan Foe be the supposed author of the libel titled "Legions Address to the Lords", you will find him at Captain Roger's at the city of Canterbury' (J.W. to Harley, 14 June 1704, H.M.C. *Portland MSS*, IV, 93).

7 *H . . . .*: Most probably Holland or Hanover. This proposal seemingly never came to pass.

8 *Pressures*: financial troubles.

9 *Ld Treasurer*: Godolphin.

10 *Branch … Divided*: There were two principal Auditors of the Imprest and two deputies; they audited the accounts of officers of the crown to whom money was issued for government expenditure. In 1703, the salary was £300, but fees were reportedly worth at least £700 more (*HPC 1690–1715*, IV, 236). Edward Harley had been appointed in 1702. The other Auditor, Brook Bridges (*c.* 1643–1717), had been appointed in 1675. He stood down in 1705. It is possible

DEFOE TO ROBERT HARLEY, [MAY–JUNE 1704?]

that Defoe knew an imminent vacancy was probable. Arthur Maynwaring (1668–1712) took over from Bridges.

11 *Matters of Accots ... Master of:* Defoe served as Accomptant to the Commissioners of the Glass Duty from 1695 to around 1699.

12 *Sons:* Benjamin and Daniel.

10

To Robert Harley

[May–June 1704?][1]

S[r]

As I Took y[e] freedome to Say to you So I Can Not but Repeat to yo[r] honor, I am at a Loss how to behave my Self und[r] y[e] Goodness and Bounty of y[e] Queen; her Maj[tie] Buyes my Small Services So Much too Dear and leaves me So Much in y[e] Dark as to my Own Merit That I am Strangely at a stand what to Say.

I have Enclos'd my humble Acknowlegem[t] to Her Maj[tie] and Perticularly to my L[d] Treasurer but when I am writing to you s[r] Pardon me to alter my Stile, I am Impacent to kno' what in my Small Service pleases and Engages. Pardon me s[r] Tis a Necessary Enquiry for a Man in y[e] Dark that I may Direct my Conduct and Push That Little Little Merit to a proper Extent.

Give me leav s[r] as at first to Say I Can Not but Think[a] Tho' her Maj[tie] is Good, and[b] My L[d] Treasurer kind, yet my wheel within all These wheels[2] must be yo[r] Self, and There I Fix my Thankfullness as I have of a Long Time my hope — as God has Thus Mov'd you to Reliev a Distrest family, Tis my Sincere Peticon to him, that he would Once Put it into my hand to Render you Some Such Signall Service, as might at least Express my Sence of it, and Encourage all Men of Power to Oblige and Espouse Gratefull and Sincere Minds.

Your farther Enquiry Into y[e] Missfortunes and afflicting Circumstances That attend and[c] Suppress me fills me wth Some

[a] Think] *following words probably* 'as at first' *cancelled*
[b] and] *interlined*
[c] and] *interlined*

36

Surprize; what Providence has Reserv'd for me he Only knows, but Sure The Gulph is too Large for me to Get ashore again.

I have Stated the black Case. Tis a Mellancholly prospect s[r] and My feares Suggest That Not less Than a Thousand Pounds will Entirely Free me.

Tis True and I am Satisfy'd 500[£] or 6 at Most Joyn'd to This I Now Reciev will Open y[e] Door to Liberty and bind all The hands of Creditors That I may have Leisure to Raise The Rest p[er]haps a year or Two but y[e] Sume is Too Large for me to Expect.

Indeed This Debt is Rais'd by Doublings of Intrest on bonds, The Length of Time haveing Encreased y[e] Burthen. I was Riseing Fairly to Clear it all when y[e] Publick Disaster you kno' of began, but s[r] That Entirely blasted all my affaires, and I Can Easily Convince you was above 2500[£] Loss to me all at Once.[3]

I forbear to Say all y[e] Moveing Things to you I Could on This head. All my prospects were built on a Manufacture I had Erected in Essex;[4] all The late kings Bounty to me[5] was Expended There. I Employ'd a hundred Poor Familys at work and it began to Pay me Very well. I Generally Made Six hundred pound proffit per Annum.

I began to live, Took a Good House,[6] bought me Coach and horses a Second Time, I paid Large Debts Gradually, small Ones wholly, and Many a Creditor after Composicon whom I found poor and Decay'd I Sent for and Paid the Remaindr to tho' Actually Discharged.[7]

But I was Ruin'd The shortest way[8] and Now s[r] had Not yo[r] Favour and her Maj[ties] Bounty Assisted it must ha' been One of y[e] worst Sorts of Ruine, I do Not mean as to Bread; I firmly and I Thank God Comfortably Depend on y[e] Divine Goodness That I Shall Never want That,[9] But a Large and Promiseing family, a Vertuous and Excellent Mother to Seaven Beautifull and hopefull Children,[10] a woman whose fortunes I have Ruin'd wth whom I have had 3700[£11] and yet who in the worst of my afflicions when my L[d] N. first Insulted her, Then Tempted her,[12] scorn'd So much as to Move me to Complye wth him, and Rather Encourag'd me to Oppose him.

Seaven Children s[r] whose Educacon Calls on me to furnish Their heads if I Can not Their Purses, and w[ch] Debt if not paid Now Can

DEFOE TO ROBERT HARLEY, [MAY–JUNE 1704?]

Never be Compounded hereafter is to me a Moveing Article and helps Very often to make me Sad.

But s^r I am I Thank God Furnisht wth Pacence, I Never Despaird and In ye Worst Condicon allways believ'd I Should be Carryed Thro' it, but wch way, has been and yet Remaines a Mystery of Providence Unexpounded.

I beg heartily yor Pardon for This Tedious Epistles; ye Miserable are allways full of Their Own Cases and Think Nothing Impertinent. I write This for tis too Moveing for me to Speak it. I Shall attend ye Ord^{rs} and houres you Appointed To morro' Even and am

S^r

yor Most Obed^t Servt

G¹³

I Presume to send ye Enclos'd¹⁴ Open for yor Approbacon; you will please to put a Seal to it —

Text: BL Add. MS. 70291, fols. 10–11. *Address* (fol. 11v): To The Right Honble | Robert Harley Esqr | Her Maj^{ties} Principall Secret^a of State | Pres^t

1 See Letter 9, note 1.

2 *wheel within all These wheels*: This image, the source of which is Ezek. 10:9–10, is used by Defoe in *Review*, I, 274 (1 Aug. 1704); III, 335 (30 May 1706); IV, 845 (21 Feb. 1708); VI, 169 (14 June 1709); *The Consolidator* (1705), *SFS*, III, 60; *The History of the Union* (1709/10), *TDH*, VII, 144; *The Secret History of the October Club* (1711), *PEW*, II, 164; *The Complete English Tradesman, Volume II* (1727), *RDW*, VIII, 46; *A Plan of the English Commerce* (1728), *PEW*, VII, 246.

3 *above 2500[£] Loss to me all at Once*: See *Review*, II, 648 (11 Oct. 1705), in which Defoe recalls being 'reduc'd by a known Disaster, and Ruin'd by a Publick Storm on his Family' at a point when 'in prosperous Circumstances, he was Gradually clearing himself of every Body'. J. A. Downie observes that the fact of Defoe's imprisonment for debt in 1702 does not tally with the account of his flourishing circumstances prior to *The Shortest Way* reported here to Harley ('Defoe in the Fleet Prison', *N&Q* 22 (1975), 343–5).

4 *Manufacture I had Erected in Essex*: Defoe's brick and pantile factory near Tilbury Fort. Enemies enjoyed belittling Defoe's business credentials, such as by calling him only 'a *Clerk* to a *wrick Kiln*' or '*Secretary* … to the *Tile-Kilns* and *Brick-Kilns* at *Tilbury*' (*Remarks on a Scandalous Libel, Entitil'd A Letter from A Member of Parliament*, 3rd ed. (1713), 5; Oldmixon, 519).

5 *late kings Bounty to me*: See *Review*, VIII, 2 (preface, July 1712) for a repeat of this claim about 'the Bounty of his late Majesty'. For sceptical takes on Defoe's self-announced ties to William III, see J. A. Downie, 'Daniel Defoe: King William's Pamphleteer?', *ECL* 12 (1988), 105–17; F&O, *Political Biography*, 26–32.

6 *Good House*: At Hackney.

38

DEFOE TO ROBERT HARLEY, [MAY–JUNE 1704?]

7 *Creditor … Discharged*: Defoe repeats in several places his claim to have continued paying his creditors beyond his legal obligation after his 1692 bankruptcy. In *A Reply to a Pamphlet entituled, The L[or]d H[aversham]'s Vindication of his Speech* (1706), 7, he writes: 'With a Numerous Family, and no helps but my own Industry, I have forc'd my way with undiscourag'd Diligence, thro' a Sea of Debt and Misfortune, and reduc'd them Exclusive of Composition from 1700*l.* to less than 5.' See also *A Dialogue between a Dissenter and the Observator* (1703), *PEW*, III, 122; Letter 49; *Review*, VIII, 7 (preface, July 1712); *Mercator*, no. 101 (12–14 Jan. 1714). In *Review*, III, 192 (26 Mar. 1706), Defoe insists that 'Paying Overplus beyond Composition' is the moral, if not the legal, obligation of the debtor.

Such fair-dealing on Defoe's part is open to dispute. Three creditors – Peter Marescoe, Robert Stamper, and John Ghiselyn – went to law in the 1690s to pursue debts, claiming that Defoe was retaining profits he should have surrendered by the terms of his composition (TNA C 5/214/5; Backscheider, *Life*, 65–6). A Tory press spy's report on Defoe, probably from 1704, says of his 1692 bankruptcy that he 'fraudulently … Concealed his effects. So that His Reputation amongst the fair Dealers of the City is very Foule' (*A Character of Daniell de Foe writer of the Pamphlett calld the Review*, BL Add. MS. 28094, fols. 165–6). Cf. *Review*, III, 119 (19 Feb. 1706), in which Defoe admits that extremity pushed him to duplicity in his early bankruptcy.

8 *Ruin'd The shortest way*: 'Nor should the Author of this Paper boast in vain, if he tells the World, that he himself, before Violence, Injury, and Barbarous Treatment Demolish'd him and his Undertaking, Employ'd 100 Poor People in making *Pan-Tiles* in *England*, a Manufacture always bought in *Holland*, and thus he pursued this Principle with his utmost Zeal for the Good of *England*; and these Gentlemen, who so eagerly persecuted him for saying what all the World since owns to be true, and which he has since a hundred times offered to prove, were particularly serviceable to the Nation, in turning that hundred of Poor People, and their Families, a begging for Work, and forcing them to turn other Poor Families out of Work, to make room for them, besides 3000 *l.* Damage to the Author of this, which he has paid for this little Experience' (*Review*, II, 55 (24 Mar. 1705)). Whereas in the present letter Defoe estimates his loss at £2,500, in 1705 he wrote to Edward Owen that he 'lost above 3000*£*' due to imprisonment for *The Shortest Way* (Letter 43). In 1712 and in 1714, he estimated his losses in the affair at '3500*l.*' (*Review*, VIII, 562 (5 Jan. 1712); *Mercator*, no. 101 (12–14 Jan. 1714)).

9 *I do Not mean as to Bread … want That*: 'He that gave me Brains, will give me Bread', Defoe wrote in *An Elegy on the Author of the True-Born-English-Man* (1704), line 577, *SFS*, I, 280.

10 *Seaven Beautifull and hopefull Children*: Since Defoe's reference to his six children in *More Reformation* (July 1703), another, perhaps Martha, had been born. *Review*, III, 513 (20 Aug. 1706) specifies seven children, though Martha died in 1707; *Review*, VIII, 7 (preface, July 1712) mentions six children.

11 *woman … 3700£*: The dowry that Mary Tuffley brought to Defoe at their marriage in 1683.

12 *L*^d *N. … Tempted her*: Some scholars have taken this as an accusation that Nottingham tried to seduce Mary Defoe, as opposed to merely offering her money. Among those who have read it this way, Trevelyan, I, 336, and Moore, 50 doubt it, whereas Novak, 228 and James Anderson Winn, *Queen Anne: Patroness of Arts* (Oxford, 2014), 377, credit it.

13 *G*: Defoe's previous letters to Harley are either unsigned or signed with his name or monogram; this signature could signify that he had started to use the pseudonym Alexander Goldsmith (see Letter 18).

14 *Enclos'd*: The notes for Queen Anne and Godolphin, now untraced.

39

To Robert Harley

[early July 1704?][1]

HEADNOTE: Defoe's smear campaign against Sir George Rooke, commander of the grand fleet, was motivated by personal and political circumstances. Later in 1704, it led him into difficulties during the tour of the eastern counties he and Harley were just now planning. Defoe's first reflections on the High Tory Rooke's incompetence came in *The Spanish Descent* (1702), a poem occasioned by Rooke's botched assault on Cadiz in 1702, a 'Baffl'd Enterprize' that degenerated into squabbling and rapine without an actual attack being mounted.[2] The mission was salvaged by a fortunate encounter with Spanish treasure ships at Vigo Bay. 'What a sorry Figure your Confederate Fleet in your World had made, after their *Andalusian Expedition*, if they had not more by Fate than Conduct, chopt upon a Booty at *Vigo* as they came back', the lunar traveller in Defoe's *Consolidator* (1705) is told.[3] Defoe kept up his criticism for years: Rooke was pusillanimous at Cadiz and lucky at Vigo Bay, the latter a French mistake rather than an English victory, for which others deserved the credit anyway.[4] Not long before the present letter, Defoe had written these lines in a poem without Harley's knowledge: 'With wonted Courage and Success | Sir *R—k* invaded *Spain*, | His wonted Conduct we confess, | And all men own the Happiness, | That he's come home again.'[5]

Defoe's personal hostility to Rooke also centred on the Admiral's refusal to fight, because Rooke had challenged Defoe's friend and lawyer William Colepeper to a duel but allegedly had then had his friends assault Colepeper. Defoe's reflections on duelling in the *Review* in May 1704 started a series of criticisms of Rooke on this matter.[6] The enclosure here is perhaps a draft of a *Review* essay or the outline of a pamphlet which never appeared. Defoe implies that he held off when he thought Harley would disapprove.[7]

Sr

I can Not but Retain a Very Deep Sen̄ce of yᵉ Candor and Goodness wᵗʰ wᶜʰ you Recᵈ me Last Night; The Perticulars Sr Admitt of No Epithets to Illustrate yᵐ; it Remaines to me Onely To Tender you all yᵉ Acknowlegemᵗ of a Gratefull Temper Highly Oblig'd.

Persuant, Sr to yᵉ Plaines I have yoʳ Leave to Use, The Enclosed Papers are written for yoʳ Perusall — They are Observac̄ons from yᵉ Discourse of yᵉ Town on yᵉ Affair of yᵉ Fleet, 'tis an Unhappy

DEFOE TO ROBERT HARLEY, [EARLY JULY 1704?]

Subject, and I assure you There is Much less than is Discours'd on that head — I have Onely One Thing to Premise, and wch I Entreat you to believ of Me, That I have No Manner of Personall Design as to Sr Geo: R ....[8] I Neither kno' him, Nor am Concern'd with him, or wth any that Does kno' him, Directly Or Indirectly; I have Not ye least Dissrespect for him, or any Personall Prejudice, on Any Acco^t whatsoever[9] — I hope you will please to give Full Credit to me in This, Otherwise It would be Very Rude and Presumeing to Offer you ye Paper.

I am Prepareing wth Joy to Execute yor Commands For Thursday Next and Furnishing my Self wth Horses &ca and Entreat ye Liberty Since ye Time is short and I Can Not Expect to See you often, of Troubling you[a] the More wth my Visits of This sort, and Fill you wth my short Requests.

First Sr That you will Please to Order ye Letter of Leave for m^r Christopher Hurt[10] to be Absent on his Private Affaires For 2 Months or More.

That you will Please to Think of Some Instruccons for my speciall Conduct and whether it may Not be Proper for me to have something About me like a Certificate, Pass, or what you Think fitt to Prevent being Question'd, Searcht or Detain'd, by an Accident, wch often happens on ye Road. ye Nature and Manner of Such a Thing I Remit to yor Judgement — It will be Very Necessary that I should be provided Against ye Impertinence of a Country Justice.

The Poem s^r of ye Diet of P .... d[11] I Omitted to Mencon to you last Night but Certainly Twill be Very Necessary to Carry in ye Country wth me, and As I am[b] Sure of its being Very Usefull I Can not but Importune you to Let me Perfect it and Turn it abroad into ye World. I Expect strange Effects from it as to ye house.

The Other Papers wch I Purpos'd to Finish I Referr, wth yor Licence, to send you Per Post — Perticularly some Notes Relateing to ye Parliam^t and a scheme of an Office For Secret Intelligence at home and Abroad.[12]

This last as I kno' you are Not Ignorant of ye Vallue, ye Magnitude and Necessity of ye Design, wth ye Want of such a Thing

---

[a] Troubling you] *following word* 'often' *cancelled*
[b] I am] *following word* 'Very' *cancelled*

DEFOE TO ROBERT HARLEY, [EARLY JULY 1704?]

in This Naćon, So I shall Take Time while I am abroad to Finish a Perfect scheme, and Such a One as I hope you will Approve, and Put in Practiće, that if Possible the Affaires of all Europe may Lye Constantly before you in a True light and you may kno'ᵃ what is a doeing all Over Europe, Even before <u>tis a doeing</u>, and In This Weighty Perticular Go beyond all that Ever were in That Plaće¹³ before you.

I Confess sʳ I had yᵉ Enclosed Papers in My Pockett when I was wᵗʰ you But was Unwilling to Rob my Self of So Much of yoʳ Obligeing Conversaćon as to Produće yᵐ. I Comitt yᵐ to your Serious Thoughts as a Subject <u>Pardon me if I Think Amiss</u> Not atall Triviall, and at Present Much Wisht for in yᵉ Naćon.

When I sʳ Take yᵉ Freedome To Lay any of these Things before you, Tis for you to Judge from as you Think Fit. I hope you will not find Me Assumeing Either a Positiv Determinaćon, or So Much as Arguing Absolutely. I may Mistake, yᵉ wholl Town may Mistake, Tho' in This Case I Doubt They do Not; however I am forward to Lay Such things before you because I Can Not but Think Tis Nećessary you should kno' in This as well as any Thing Elće what yᵉ People Say —

I am

Sʳ

yoʳ Most Obedᵗ &ca

[*monogram*]

Of The Fleet and Sʳ Geo: Rook.

It will Easily be Allow'd yᵉ Fleet May be Made more Usefull Than it is. If The Enemy did Not kno' by happy Experiençe that Our Navall Forće does Them no harm They Would Allwayes be Oblig'd to keep More Forćes on Their Coasts and Consequently Want Them Elće where.

Tis Plaine They have a Most Despicable Opinion of Our Navall Expedićons and have Too Much Reason for it.

ᵃ kno'] *interlined*

DEFOE TO ROBERT HARLEY, [EARLY JULY 1704?]

Our Fleet wth about 5000 Men on board Might keep them in Continuall Allarm. They Must have 20 Battallions at Least to Guard ye Coasts of Provençe and as Many Those of Languedoc.

We Talk of Relieving ye Camisars.[14] Nothing Can Do it So Effectually as to have Our Fleet Hovering on that Coast, Sometimes Landing a Few Men here, Sometimes There. The Mareschall De Villars[15] Must Draw Down to Monpellier and ye Sea Coast and by Consequençe give ye Camisars Room to spread Themselves and Act at Large.[16]

But Our Fleet does Nothing of all this,^{a} Tis Commanded by a Person[17] The People hate^b and all Miscarriages will lye at his Door, whether ye Fault be his or No.

No Reflecçon Can Lye Against ye Person Employ'd, but Taçitly Affects ye Govornment Employing, and Nothing Reflects on ye Govornm^t but it Touches ye Ministrÿ.

Portugall is an Instançe of This; all Our Complaints of Conduct are stopt at Onçe, by her Maj^{ties} Displaçeing ye Generall.[18] People Say her Maj^{tie} has found herself ill Serv'd,^{c} has Altred her Measures, and Chang'd ye Generall.

But when ye People Ask One Another of ye fleet, ye Common Answer is^d how should We Expect better wth Such an Admirall, A Man that Never Onçe fought Sinçe he was an Admirall, That Allwayes Embraç'd ye Party That Oppos'd ye Govornm^t, and has Constantly Favour'd, Preferrd and kept Company wth ye high furious Jacobite Party, and has Fill'd ye Fleet wth Them.[19]

How should We have Good Cap^{ts} while Such a Man Promotes Them, and This is a Reason why We have No Offiçers in ye Navy Fitt to Preferr —

The French Presume Upon This Misconduct of Ours. Tis Not to be Suppos'd ye French Admirall Durst ha' Ventur'd into ye Mediteranean wth 29 Sail when Our fleet was there before him wth a Forçe Very Superior.

It must be a Scandall on Our Admirall or On ye Naçon.

---

^{a} this] *interlined*
^{b} hate] *amended from* 'hates'
^{c} Serv'd] *following words* 'and she' *cancelled*
^{d} is] *interlined*

DEFOE TO ROBERT HARLEY, [EARLY JULY 1704?]

Either on ye Admirall that They knew he Durst not Fight Them wch Affects his Courage or That They Understood One Another wch is Worse and Affects his Fidellity.

Or it is a Scandal on ye Wholl English Naćon as if 29 French Men of war Could be a Match for 45 English.[20]

The Manner of ye Conduct afterwards is Perfectly Scandalous. Our Fleet Saw ye Enemy at ye Distanće of Three Leagues Sayes ye Relaćon.[21]

Why Did we Not fight y^m Say Our Old Tarpaulins — and all ye Exchange after them why did we not Chaće them?

<u>Why! We did Chaće y^m but found they Gain'd Upon us</u>[22]

What, do They Out Sail us Allwayes? There Never was a fleet but That Some Ships Saild better Than Others —

What! did ye worst of Their Sailers, Outgoe ye best of Ours! Then Our Navigaćon, or building, or Sailes are Defective, and should be Enquir'd into; and ye Charge of a Fleet Sav'd, Till they Are fitt to Match ye Enemye, at Sailing as Well as fighting.

But They Tow'd Away wth all Their Boates.

So Might we ha' Done too and Ought to ha' Continued ye Chaće Till We had Seen them in Port, ha' Waited On y^m to their Own doors and ha' Insulted Them there.

But at last what Can be said how They Got by us, how They Gott beyond Our Fleet, Why did Not s^r G R, when tis Plain he knew the French were in The Mediterranean, Why did he Not Post himself at ye Isle of Heires[23] and keep his Guard Upon ye Very Road of Thoulon,^a where they Must ha' Come of Course and where it had been Impossible to have Entred without Fighting him?

To Say They Might ha' fallen Upon him There and ye ships from Thoulon ha' Joyn'd in ye Fray, is Imposeing Upon us, for We all kno', They Durst Not stirr Till ye Very Aććon, Ours Lyeing before Their Port, and There Must be So Many Concurring Accidents of Wind and Tide, all wch must hitt ye Very Minute of Aććon, that ye hazard of it is Not worth Nameing.

---

^a Thoulon] *the* 'u' *is interlined*

These S^r are Some of ye Town Discourses and There are Scandalous Letters in Town from ye Fleet it Self on This head.[24]

The Accon at Barcelona[25] is Counted[a] as Monstrous as all ye Rest. To Land a Force Inferiour to ye Enemy and Indeed Disproporcon'd to ye Attempt had Some Most Scandalous Circumstances in it.

'Twas hardly Raconall To Expect ye People of Barcelona, had they Ever so much Inclinacon to ye thing, should Appear when They Saw the Force landed was Not Sufficent to Protect Them; had There been Landed 3 to 4000 Men And ye Fleet in Good Earnest Applyed themselves to Their Assistance There's No Room to Doubt ye Town had been taken.

The Country Thinking Their Friends Were Come and Not knowing Their Force was So Small began to show Themselves and as Severall Hundreds Did Come in, Many More were on ye Road and ye Wholl Province was at ye Very Point of Revolting, when ye Fleet being bound on another Expedition Resolvs to be gone, and all The Well Meaning Inhabitants are left to ye Fury of an Enrag'd Enemey to be Drag'd to Excecucon and Destruccon by the hand of ye hangman, just as ye French did at Messina.[26]

The Complaints of all Sorts of People on This head are Very Severe and The More So because not to be Answerd.

If it be Answerd ye king of Portugall Deciev'd Them,[27] Tis Reply'd Then ye attempt Should Not ha' been Made, And ye Poor People Not Expos'd.

If s^r G. R Alleages his Orders for ye Relief of Niza or Vill. Franc,[28] Then he should ha' Saild Thither First and ha' Made This Attempt at his Return when he had Leisure to ha' Carryed it[b] on. There Seems No question but if he had Stay'd, The Catalans were So Dispos'd to Joyn They would soon ha' been strong Enough to ha Force'd ye Town.

These are ye Present Grounds of Complaint as to ye Fleet wch as to ye Matter of them are Very Considerable as to Fact. As to ye Defence ye Admirall Can Make &ca:

---

[a] Counted] *interlined*
[b] it] *interlined*

DEFOE TO ROBERT HARLEY, [EARLY JULY 1704?]

This wth Submission I do not See Materiall. It Remaines
to Consider whether in Such Cases it has Not been Generally
Thought Needfull by all ye Politick Princes and states in ye World,
to Recall any Generall or Admirall who Comes Under The
Unhappyness of any of These Circumstances.

    1 Either to ha' Comitted any Capitall Mistake, Tho' Not by
    Design, want of Courage, or Negligence.

    2: That has ye Missfortune to Fall Under ye Generall Censure
    and Hatred of ye People, whether Deserv'd or No.

    3 Or That Generally Speaking is Allwayes Unfortunate.

In all these Cases The Generall may be Really Clear,[29] but yet
all Ages are Full of Instances of Such being laid by,[30] As at least
Improper Persons if Not Otherwise Culpable.

The Grecians, ye Romans and ye Carthaginians Allwayes Laid by
Unfortunate Gener^{lls} as Persons ye Gods were Angry wth and would
Not Prosper, The Turks do ye Same to This day of whom tis well
Observ'd that they Are Never Betraid.

Our Easÿ Way^a of Accquitting Men in Councils of War and by
Examinacon of Partys p[er]haps Concern'd in A Mistake gives
Room for Men to Abuse their Trust in Confidence, of Comeing
off Upon ye Artifice of Future Mannagement.

Tho' to Miscarry Ought not in justice to be Criminall, yet in
Pollicy it should Allwayes Entitle a Man to be Useless, Otherwise a
Generall shall be Indiffrent as to Success, his Own Fortunes being
Not Concern'd.

Besides who knows whether s^r G. R. has Miscarry'd for want
of Discrecon or for Want of Honesty or for want of Judgement,
Courage or any Thing Elce, and if This be Doubtfull how Can
Such a Man be Trusted with ye English Navy before ye Case is
Decided? If a Miscarriage has happend There Ought at least be a
Suspencon of Command Till ye Man Charg'd is Justifyed, For tis
an Unaccountable Risque and Such an Error in Polliticks as No
Minister of State would be Seen in to Comitt The Charge of y^e
English Fleet, ye Safety and Honour of ye Nacon to a Traytor,[31] if
Such a Thing Should Chance to^b be Made Out, what Can be Said

---

^a Way] *interlined*
^b Chance to] *following word* 'happen' *cancelled*

DEFOE TO ROBERT HARLEY, [EARLY JULY 1704?]

To Excuse So Much Credulity, For to be Suspected is Certainly Reason Enough Not to be Employ'd.

The Queen Can Not do an Accon More Agreeable or Obligeing to yᵉ Generallity of the Nacon than to Remove This Gentleman and Comitt yᵉ Navy to Another; if he be after wards Accquitted her Majtie may Restore him wth Honour to himself and Satisfaccon to yᵉ World but to Employ him while all yᵉ World Suspects him is Takeing all yᵉ blame of a Miscarriage On yᵉ Queen and Ministry if he be prov'd Guilty.

To Remove a Man from his Power Cleares yᵉ Way to Proof of Fact, wch his stacon screens him from, and wch Discourages Complaintsᵗˢ32 from Attempting.

Tis Enough to A Govornment That yᵉ People in Generall Decrye The Man, for Tho' Comon Fame is often a Lyer, yet Universall Clamour Allwayes Demands a Suitable Regard, Or is Apt to Affect yᵉ Govornmᵗ as wanting in a Due Care of Things and Careless of yᵉ Publick Dissatisfaccon.

Tis true To have Enemyes is No Crime but to have Wise Men Ones Enemy and Men of Moderacon and Temper be Uneasy is a Sufficent Ground to Suspend a Man From a Charge of Such Consequence Till it Appeares whether there is a Crime. He Ought to be Try'd Indeed before he is Condemn'd, but shall Such a Man Command Till he is Try'd?

If he Appeares Guilty then yᵉ Navy, yᵉ honour, yᵉ Safety of England is Put in yᵉ hands of a Criminall; if he be Dissmisst and yet Innocent yᵉ Injury is but to One Man,ᵃ But if he be Continued and be Guilty the Injury is to yᵉ Wholl Nacon and yᵉ hazard is too great to be Ventur'd.

The Nacons Safety, yᵉ Publick Reputacon, and yᵉ Creditt of yᵉ Ministry, Calls for a Suspencon at least of this Obnoxious Suspected Man.33

Text (letter): BL Add. MS. 4291, fols. 219–20.34 *Text (enclosure)*: BL Add. MS. 70037, fols. 286–91. [The MS is bound out of order: the correct order is fols. 286, 291, 287, 288, 289; 290 is blank.] *Address for letter* (fol. 220ᵛ): To | The Right Honble | Robert Harley Esqʳ | One of Her Majestyes Princ̄ipall Secretarys of State | Present.

ᵃ Man] *following word* 'and' *cancelled*

47

DEFOE TO ROBERT HARLEY, [EARLY JULY 1704?]

1 Healey assigns this undated letter and its enclosure to [June?], the logic being that it must precede the *Review* for 24 June 1704, and so is an approach to Harley about Rooke before the published attack on him (*Letters*, ed. Healey, 18 n. 2). H.M.C. *Portland MSS*, VIII, 135 suggests [July?]. Early July is here proposed for two reasons. First, the change of military command in Portugal, referred to by Defoe, was first reported on 27 June, so the letter probably postdates the *Review* article (Luttrell, v, 439–40). Second, Defoe in the enclosure further elaborates on the facts of Rooke's failure to intercept the French fleet as he had given in the *Review*. In the *Review* essay, he has the bare knowledge that the French Brest squadron had reached Toulon and assumes it had slipped past the confederate fleet without Rooke's being aware: 'Why did we not see them, I leave them to Answer that, when they come Home' (I, 203). Here, by contrast, Defoe is aware that Rooke saw the French but was unable to engage them – 'We did Chace yᵐ but found they Gain'd Upon us' – as was relayed in an express from Rooke that only reached London on 4 July (Luttrell, v, 442; *London Gazette*, 3–6 July 1704).

2 Line 115, *SFS*, I, 198.

3 *SFS*, III, 139.

4 Defoe's reference to 'sham Descents' in *An Elegy on the Author of the True-Born-English-Man* (1704) jibes at Rooke (line 147, *SFS*, I, 269), and *The Dyet of Poland* (1705) lampoons him as the poltroon '*Rokosky*' (lines 493–525, *SFS*, I, 358–9). See also *Master Mercury*, no. 5 (21 Aug. 1704), 19–20; *Advice to all Parties* (1705), *PEW*, II, 97; *A Reply to a Pamphlet entituled, The L[or]d H[aversham]'s Vindication of his Speech* (1706), 29; *Jure Divino* (1706), book XII, lines 526–31, *SFS*, II, 360; *Review*, IV, 472 (13 Sept. 1707); IV, 546 (16 Oct. 1707); and V, 525 (6 July 1708).

5 *The Address* (1704), lines 131–5, *PEW*, II, 73.

6 *Review*, I, 143 (20 May 1704). See also I, 597 (9 Dec. 1704); II, 224 (31 May 1705); II, 376 (12 July 1705); *The Dyet of Poland*, line 519, *SFS*, I, 359. Ultimately Rooke successfully sued Colepeper for defamation but was awarded merely a token sum in Feb. 1706 (Luttrell, VI, 17).

7 See Letter 18.

8 *Sʳ Geo: R . . . .*: Sir George Rooke (see headnote).

9 *Dissrespect ... whatsoever*. But see headnote for Defoe's earlier attacks on and personal hostility towards Rooke.

10 *mʳ Christopher Hurt*: A Dissenter and customs employee (d. 1727?), who accompanied Defoe on his tour of the eastern counties. See Letters 34 and 40.

11 *yᵉ Diet of P . . . . d*: Defoe's *The Dyet of Poland* was eventually published in mid-1705.

12 *scheme ... Abroad*: See Letter 14.

13 *Place*: Secretary of State.

14 *Camisars*: Protestant inhabitants of the Cévennes in southeastern France were rebelling against Louis XIV. They were known as Cevennois or Camisards, the latter from the white shirts they wore (*camisa*) to recognise each other during night raids. Defoe put their number at '5 or 6000' by 1704 (*Review*, I, 95 (22 Apr. 1704); cf. Trevelyan, I, 321–2). In *Lex Talionis* (1698), Defoe had argued that, though Huguenots were unjustly neglected in the previous year's Treaty of Ryswick, a fresh war on account of France's persecution of Protestants was inappropriate 'because Speaking of Right and Wrong, we are not Interested in the Quarrel' (7). He instead advocated retaliations against English Catholics. By 1704, however, supplying arms to the Camisards was seen as a good strategy for distracting France's war effort. Defoe saw this as desirable but impracticable (*Review*, I, 95–100 (22 and 25 Apr. 1704)). But he was also happy to attack Nottingham for rejecting such a scheme both at the time and later (*Master Mercury*, no. 13 (18 Sept. 1704), 52; *Advice to all Parties* (1705), *PEW*, II, 104; *Review*, III, 204 (2 Apr. 1706)). For the unjustness of this criticism, see Henry Horwitz, *Revolution Politics: The Career of Daniel Finch, Second Earl of Nottingham, 1647–1730* (Cambridge, 1968), 171.

15 *Mareschall De Villars*: Defoe reported that the French commander Villars (1653–1734) had been appointed 'with a large addition of Troops, and as some say, 30000 Men to suppress this Rebellion' (*Review*, I, 95 (22 Apr. 1704)).

16 *Camisars ... Large*: 'If ever the *Camisars* are reliev'd, it must be by strong Diversions, which must oblige the King to withdraw his Troops' (*Review*, I, 100 (25 Apr. 1704)). Defoe critiques

DEFOE TO ROBERT HARLEY, [EARLY JULY 1704?]

Rooke for providing no such diversion (*Master Mercury*, no. 7 (28 Aug. 1704), 27). Defoe reported on the death in battle of the Camisar leader, Roland (1675–1704) in *Master Mercury*, no. 9 (4 Sept. 1704), 36.

17 *Person*: Rooke.

18 *Portugall ... Generall*: In late June, Henri de Massue, Earl of Galway (1648–1720) was assigned to replace the Duke of Schomberg (1641–1719) as Commander in Chief of the British forces in Portugal.

19 *Fill'd ye Fleet wth Them*: Defoe may be alluding to Rooke's furious reaction earlier in 1704 when his flag captain James Wishart (*c*. 1659–1723) was initially overlooked for promotion to rear admiral, and Rooke secured that promotion with an appeal to the Lord High Admiral Prince George (1653–1708).

20 *29 French ... 45 English*: French Admiral Louis-Alexandre de Bourbon, Comte de Toulouse (1678–1737) had sailed the Brest squadron from northwestern France through the Strait of Gibraltar to Toulon, combining with the squadron there. Rooke sighted him off Minorca and offered to engage, but the French refused and outran the English. Defoe harps on Rooke's numerical superiority in the *Review* for 24 June 1704: 'Wiser Heads than mine, say Sir G— was strong enough to fight him, and most Men say, 45 is more than 29' (1, 202). In the *Review* essay, Defoe assumes that Rooke did not offer to fight, or never had the opportunity, but he knows better here. Defoe returned to this non-engagement in *Master Mercury*, no. 7 (28 Aug. 1704), 27 (the number of warships in the French and confederate fleets are 42 and 31). For modern accounts of the naval manoeuvres Defoe describes, see J. H. Owen, *War at Sea under Queen Anne, 1702–1708* (Cambridge, 1938), 87–9, and Julian S. Corbett, *England in the Mediterranean*, 2 vols., 2nd ed. (1917), II, 514–17. *A Narrative of Sir George Rooke's Late Voyage to the Mediterranean* (1704), a subsequent defence of Rooke, is in *Defoe-Farewell Catalogue* (item 133).

21 *Three Leagues Sayes ye Relaċon*: Defoe's source has not been identified but it is given as four leagues in *The London Gazette*, 3–6 July 1704 and *Observator*, 12–15 July 1704.

22 *We ... us*: For Defoe's hint that Rooke had no inclination to catch the French, see *Master Mercury*, no. 5 (21 Aug. 1704), 19. 'Gain'd upon' here means 'pulled away from'.

23 *Isle of Heires*: Îles d'Hyères, slightly east of Toulon.

24 *Letters ... head*: Nothing fitting this description has been traced.

25 *Aċon at Barċelona*: Before his pursuit of the Brest squadron, Rooke had landed at Barcelona with Prince George of Hesse (1669–1705), aiming to incite the Catalans to rise and declare for Archduke Charles (1685–1740), the confederates' candidate for the Spanish throne. However, the landing force of around 1,600 was too small to inspire the town to revolt. Defoe alludes to the failure at Barcelona in *Master Mercury*, no. 5 (21 Aug. 1704), 17, and *Review*, 1, 317 (22 Aug. 1704). He utterly derides Rooke's actions in *Master Mercury*, no. 7 (28 Aug. 1704), 26–8.

26 *Messina*: During the Franco-Dutch War (1672–8), Louis XIV's France supported the citizens of Messina, Sicily, in their revolt against their Spanish overlords; after the Peace of Nijmegen, however, France withdrew its support and Messina was reconquered by Spain. Defoe refers to this event in *Review*, 1, 86 (18 Apr. 1704), and he explicitly links the navy's abandonment of Catalonia to the French abandonment of Messina when attacking Rooke in *Master Mercury*, no. 7 (28 Aug. 1704), 28.

27 *king of Portugall Deciev'd Them*: Pedro II's (1648–1706) advance into Spain from Portugal, which could have helped the Catalan uprising, did not materialise. Defoe derides Portugal's military contributions in *Review*, 1, 203–4 (24 June 1704) and *Master Mercury*, no. 7 (28 Aug. 1704), 25–6.

28 *Relief of Niza or Vill. Franc.*: In Apr., Rooke received orders at Lisbon to enter the Mediterranean to assist the Savoyard ports of Nice and Villa Franca, should they require it. In the event, France did not attack them. Satirising Rooke, Defoe wrote that relieving Nice is an action befitting 'the Heroick Admiral of the *English*', his point being that Rooke did not do it (*Master Mercury*, no. 7 (28 Aug. 1704), 27). See Defoe's account of France's taking these ports in the 1690s, given in *A Continuation of Letters written by a Turkish Spy* (1718), *SFS*, V, 153–4.

49

29 *Clear*: innocent.
30 *laid by*: dismissed.
31 *Traytor*: Defoe suggests that Rooke is a traitor in *The Dyet of Poland*, lines 499–506, *SFS*, 1, 358.
32 *Complaints*: complainants.
33 *Obnoxious Suspected Man*: In the months following this letter, Defoe continued to argue that the navy was under weak management. *Master Mercury*, no. 5 (21 Aug. 1704), 17–20; *Review*, 1, 316–17 (22 Aug. 1704). Rooke was buoyed that summer by successes at Gibraltar and Vélez-Málaga.
34 The letter was published in 1830 in Wilson, 11, 358–60. It was thereafter the only letter between Defoe and Harley published for more than fifty years.

12

To Robert Harley

7 July 1704

HEADNOTE: On 29 June 1704 Godolphin wrote to Harley in the latter's capacity as Secretary of State responsible for the press to complain about the *Review*:

> The enclosed print, more scandalous in my opinion than the 'Observator' himself, is fallen into my hands. I don't know what course can be taken with effect to find out the author; but I think no pains or expense could be, or be thought, too much to bring him to the punishment he deserves … this maginifying of France is a thing so odious in England, that I can't think any jury would acquit this man if discovered.[1]

The fact that the Lord Treasurer was unaware that Defoe was the author and was working under Harley's auspices indicates the continued secrecy of this relationship. In the *Review* Defoe was not undermining the ministry's war but tracing 'the Prodigious Rise of the *French* Power' to persuade a war-weary public that France must be resisted.[2] In the 4 July number he explained his policy for those who 'mistake my Meaning, *or suspect my Principles*, thus farther to Explain my self in this particular Article of Magnifying the *French* Power'. Defoe pleads that his design is to help the English to know their enemy, which makes him more despised in France than in England. 'This is not, however, the first Time I have Wrote, what they for whose Good I Wrote it, would not understand', Defoe writes with a glance back at *The Shortest Way with the Dissenters*: 'I have here explained my self; *Wise Men* I hope will now understand me.'[3] The wise men seemed satisfied. On 31 July Godolphin advised Harley: 'I return you the blank warrant signed by the

DEFOE TO ROBERT HARLEY, 7 JULY 1704

Queen for D——'s pardon. Her Majesty commands me to tell you she approves entirely of what you have promised him, and will make it good.'[4] Defoe was now an employee of the ministry by official sanction.

S[r]

I can Easily Suppose yo[r] being Full of good News.[5] This week has Left you Little Leisure, and Und[r] That head am a Little in Pain for y[e] Dyet[6] — I Confess my Self also Something Impacent to have it from yo[r] Self, that I had Explain'd y[e] Review to yo[ra] Satisfaccon[7] and That in Reading it you have been Pleas'd to Note y[e] Caucon I Mencon'd That it was to be wrott Not as if y[e] Objectors Were of Such quallity as to whom The Stile Shou'd be Unsuitable.

But s[r] I Must Own Neither of These Mov'd me To give you This Trouble, I Can Not Put it from my Thoughts That Success of Affaires, as it is y[e] Prosperity of a Nacon, So Tis y[e] Felicity of a Ministry, Methinks This Victory Abroad Might have its Advantages at home.[8]

Tho' I Think it my Duty to give This hint I shall presume No farther without yo[r] Comand, which I shall be as Glad to Reciev as faithfull to Obey.[9]

I am
yo[r] Most Obedient faithfull Serv[t]
[*monogram*]

A New king They Say is Chosen in Poland.[10]

July. 7. 1704

Text: BL Add. MS. 70291, fols. 14–15. *Address* (fol. 15[v]): To | The Right Hon[ble] | Robert Harley Esq[r] | One of her Maj[ties] Principall Secr[a] of State. *Endorsed by Harley* (fol. 15[v]): About ye Review 7 July 1704

---

[a] yor] *interlined*

---

1   H.M.C. *Bath MSS*, I, 58–9. Despite Defoe's frequent explanations in the *Review* of why he was stressing French formidability, the memory of it as an originally Francophile paper persisted. In 1709, René Saunière de L'Hermitage's (1653–1729) despatch to the Dutch statesman Antonius Heinsius (1641–1720) stated: 'il y a beaucoup d'esprit dans son imprimé et a paru quelquefois escrire en faveur de la France et puis a changé' (*Heinsius Corr.*, IX, 535).

51

DEFOE TO [ROBERT HARLEY], [JULY–AUGUST 1704?]

2 *Review*, I, 215 (I July 1704).

3 *Review*, I, 220, 222–3 (4 July 1704).

4 H.M.C. *Bath MSS*, I, 61. This is the pardon for *The Shortest Way*.

5 *good News*: For Marlborough's victory in the Battle of Schellenberg on 21 June (see Trevelyan, I, 359–66). Defoe also celebrates it in his Blenheim poems, *A Hymn to Victory* (1704), lines 510–19, *SFS*, I, 309, and *The Double Welcome* (1705), line 86, *SFS*, I, 329. He later avers that 'the Courage and Conduct of the Duke was more Conspicuous in that Action than in the Fight at *Blenheim*' (*Remarks on the Letter to the Author of the State-Memorial* (1706), 16).

6 *ye Dyet*: *The Dyet of Poland*, for which Defoe continues to seek Harley's approval.

7 *Explain'd ye Review to yor Satisfacċon*: See headnote.

8 *Victory ... home*: To silence High Tory critics of Marlborough's march from Flanders to Bavaria, and to unite England behind the continental war; Defoe pursues this in the *Review* on the day following this letter (*Review*, I, 226–8 (8 July 1704)).

9 *yor Command ... Obey*: But see Letter 213 for Defoe's account in Aug. 1712 of how Harley never steered the content of Defoe's writing.

10 *New king ... Chosen in Poland*: During the Great Northern War (1700–21), Charles XII of Sweden (1682–1718) reacted to the Polish invasion of Swedish Livonia by invading Poland. His victories meant that in early 1704 he could pressure the Confederation of Warsaw to renounce its allegiance to the elected king, Augustus II (1670–1733), and on 2 July Stanisław Leszczyński (1677–1766) was elected to the Polish throne. Augustus was also Elector of Saxony and he allied with Russia to raise an army to try to reclaim the throne and force Sweden out of Poland. Defoe reported at length on Swedish–Polish affairs in the *Review* from 11 July to 15 Aug. 1704 (I, 234–304). He continued to praise Augustus II, notwithstanding his mistakes: 'I had always a great Regard to the Personal Valour and extraordinary Character of the King of *Poland* (*Review*, III, 741–51 (7, 10, and 12 Dec. 1706)). He calls Stanisław 'a Footboy King, a Dependent on his King-making Ally, the *Swede*' (*Review*, IV, 52 (6 Mar. 1707)). See Letter 14.

13

To [Robert Harley]

[July–August 1704?][1]

HEADNOTE: Defoe sent this letter on the eve of his departure from London on his fact-finding tour of the eastern counties, undertaken on Harley's behalf. His request for more explicit instructions was to become recurrent in the coming years. Something of the psychological effect of this neglect by Harley is indicated by a letter written from James Stancliffe to Harley on 23 August 1704: 'I saw Mr. F. yesterday, & he seemes to be much dejected by the deferring of Hope, wch the Wise man sayes makes the heart sick; but at the same tyme he & all men must know (that know any thing) that your Hurryes of late have been such as are not ordinarily met with.'[2] Defoe's financial circumstances were increasingly perilous. But his missives to Harley did not ease off. His comments at the end of the letter reflect suggestions about intervening in Sweden's war with Poland-Saxony he

DEFOE TO [ROBERT HARLEY], [JULY–AUGUST 1704?]

advanced in the *Review* in late July 1704. As Secretary of State for the Northern Department, Harley was responsible for English relations with Scandinavian and Baltic nations.

Sr

I am Convinc't you are Throng'd wth Bussiness of So Much more Weight Than ye Perticular before me, that I Ought Not to Expect you Can think this way; but Sr tis ye Debt I Owe to your Orders as well as my Willingness to Embark in yor Service which Obliges me to Accquaint you, That Persuant to yor Direccons of Getting Ready For this Very Day, I ha' been Prepareing and Fitting Out in Ordr to have been on horse-back this Morning.[3]

I Confess it Afflicts me to See ye Day Appear and My Self[a] Unfurnisht wth The Main Thing, ye Very Substance of all ye Rest, your Instruccons. Methinks I Look Like ye Muscovite Ambassador at Constantinople, who Appear'd as Envoy and had Every Thing Ready, but his Orders.[4] Indeed sr I Can not jest wth my Self heartily on this head, because I Reckon it my Great Missfortune. And tho' I shall Never Attempt to Dictate to you,[b] yet from ye Leave you have given me to Use More Freedom than Otherwise I should, I Crave a Liberty wth all Possible Respect both to your Judgement, and to yor Design, Humbly to Represent, That if This Journey be for your Service, As I hope it is or I Should be Very Sorry to be Employ'd, it Can Not be for ye Advantage of that Service to have me Straightn'd in Time, and ye Latter Part of ye Season Come on before I Shall have Room to Answer Either yor Charge or Expectacon — I Would Not be An Unprofitable Servant,[5] ye Unfortunate as I have Noted Elce where Are Criminalls in Politicks, and Ought to be Laid by;[6] if sr I have ye Season for Acting I Dare Answer for it I Won't Miscarry, but sr The Night Comes, Winter will be upon me in wch of This Affair I may Say No Man can Worke.[7]

I Acknowlege when you first did me ye honour to Converse wth me and began the Discourse of These things in Perticular, That Very Part So hit what I have had On my Thoughts Some yeares that I

---

[a] Self] *following letter 'F' cancelled*
[b] to you] *interlined*

53

DEFOE TO [ROBERT HARLEY], [JULY–AUGUST 1704?]

adjourn'd all my hopes, and all yᵉ Thoughts I had, Some of wch wereᵃ
of Much Greater Appearance; believing this a Thing So Absolutely
Usefull, So Exceedingly Profitable in its Event,[8] and So Suitable to
my Genius, that tho' I had Some Things of a More Capitall Nature
before Me,ᵇ I Clos'd wth this as <u>the Thing</u> wch I Thought yᵉ Ministry
most wanted and My Self most Capable of.

I had before Now Tendred you a Scheme of Generall
Intelligence[9] but I Thought this would Much better go before it.

I had a Designe to propose your Settling a Private Office for
yᵉ Conducting Matters of This Nature, So Directed as Neither
in Generall to be Suspected of what it should act, and yet be as
Publickly known as any Other. That in This office Openly and
without yᵉ help of Mr <u>St Johns Back staires</u>[10] a Correspondence may
be Effectually Settledᶜ wth Every Part of England, and all yᵉ World
beside, and yet yᵉ Very Clarks Employ'd Not kno' what They are a
doeing.

But all this I thought would be Better Subsequent to This
Journey and I firmly believ This Journey may be yᵉ foundacon
of Such an Intelligence as Never was in England; if I did Not
Think So I would be yor humble Peticoner Not to Let me go and
Earnestly Remonstrate Against it.

Sr I Can Not Close This Long Letter wthout Observing
Somethingᵈ from yor Last Discourse wth me.

You Were Pleas'd to Note yt yᵉ Queen held yᵉ hands of yᵉ
Dutch and yᵉ Dane from Falling on yᵉ Swede,[11] and yᵉ Reason
was just because in Case of a Rupture yᵉ Daneish, yᵉ Prussian,
and The Lunenburgh Troops must be Recall'd &ca.[12]

Sr I Entreat you to Consider whether a Squadron of English and
Dutch Men of War May Not Effectually bring yᵉ Swede to Reason
without Concerning yᵉ Dane or yᵉ Prussian in yᵉ Matter, and if
he will break wth yᵉ Rest he will be ill handled at last but I am
perswaded Our Fleet may (if well Directed) Do all yᵉ Work and yᵉ
Empire would soon have another Face.

ᵃ Some of wch were] *interlined*
ᵇ before Me] *interlined*
ᶜ Settled] *interlined*
ᵈ Something] *interlined*

DEFOE TO [ROBERT HARLEY], [JULY–AUGUST 1704?]

I Need Not Tell you ye Advantages of a Saxon Army On ye Danube and a Gratefull king in yor Intrest who will Certainly Acknowlege his being Sav'd by Our hands.[13]
I have Said too Much. I ask Pardon for ye freedome I use

and Am
&ca
[*monogram*]

Thursday Morning

Text: BL Add. MS. 70291, fols. 16–17. *Address*: none. *Endorsed by an unknown hand* (fol. 16r): A Scheme of General Intelligence &c.

1 Healey suggests [July–Aug. 1704?] (*Letters*, ed. Healey, 27 n. 1). The idea of sending a fleet to the Baltic is outlined in the *Review* on 29 July; it is likely Defoe sounded out Harley before printing it, but not impossible that the *Review* piece predates this letter.

2 BL Add. MS. 70037, fol. 298; H.M.C. *Portland MSS*, VIII, 141. Stancliffe alludes to Prov. 13:12. This letter has erroneously been treated as belonging to 1703, hence as a request for Harley's intervention while Defoe was in prison (see Letter 4, note 6).

3 *on horse-back this Morning*: In preparation for his tour of the eastern counties.

4 *Muscovite Ambassador ... Orders*: The anecdote is untraced, but it could be related to the one in the *Review* for 18 Aug. 1709: 'History relates, that when one of the Czars sent a haughty Message, threatning to declare War gainst the *Turks* – The *Turkish* Emperor bad the Messenger or Ambassador go home, and tell his Master, *he understood neither how to make War or Peace*' (VI, 302). It is retold in *Review*, VII, 243 (18 July 1710).

5 *Unprofitable Servant*: Luke 17:7–10. The phrase is used again by Defoe in Letters 102, 170, 216, and 232; Harley uses it of himself in Letter 114.

6 *Unfortunate ... Laid by*: Noted in respect to Rooke in Letter 11, and in *The Lay-Man's Sermon upon the Late Storm* (1704), 19. Compare Defoe's heavily ironic argument for dismissing unfortunate commanders in the *Review* for 11 Dec. 1707, which cuts against this advice (IV, 679).

7 *The Night Comes ... No Man can Worke*: John 9:4.

8 *Event*: outcome.

9 *Scheme of Generall Intelligence*: Letter 14.

10 *Mr St Johns Back staires*: Henry St John (1678–1751), later Viscount Bolingbroke, Secretary at War. 'Back stairs' refers to clandestine political intriguing, and Harley was often referred to as 'the backstairs dragon'.

11 *ye Swede*: Brief accounts of Defoe's view of Charles XII – freed from some problematic attributions that marred earlier accounts – are given in F&O, *Canonisation*, 20–2, and William Roosen, *Daniel Defoe and Diplomacy* (Selingsgrove, Penn., 1986), 81.

12 *Troops must be Recall'd &ca.*: Prussia (neutral in the Great Northern War) and Denmark (forced out of the anti-Swedish alliance in 1700) had Baltic interests that came under threat from Sweden's conquest of Poland; Saxony ('Lunenburgh') was allied to Poland because Augustus II ruled both. The English did not want Prussian, Danish, or Saxon troops to be withdrawn from the German front where they were fighting France and Bavaria (Denmark was not at war with France but hired troops to the confederates).

13 *king ... hands*: Augustus. In the *Review*, Defoe said that Charles XII's 'pushing this War to such violent Extremities robs the Confederacy of a powerful Member [Augustus], of a hearty and vigorous Prince, who would soon turn the Scale upon the *Danube*, and check the *French* Power, if he were disengag'd from this cruel and revengeful Enemy at his Back ... Thus it

appears to me, as Confederates, the *English*, *Dutch*, Emperor, and all the Members of the Grand Alliance, are oblig'd in Honour, and above all, by their Interest, to defend the King of *Poland*; and, if possible, to reduce the *Swede* to settle the Peace of the North' (*Review*, 1, 261–2 (25 July 1704)). He proposes dispatching a fleet to the Baltic, sending a message to Charles XII to the following effect: 'The King of *Poland* is our Ally, your pushing him to Extremities is an Injury to the Publick Good, and obliges him to withdraw those Troops which should be employ'd in the Common Cause, to defend himself against you: wherefore we desire your Majesty to hearken to good Terms, such as are both for your Honour and Advantage, which we undertake to procure for you; If your Majesty refuses this offer, you make War not with the King of *Poland*, but with us and the whole Confederacy' (*Review*, 1, 268 (29 July 1704)). Defoe's attention to Swedish naval provocations in the Baltic in *Master Mercury*, no. 1 (8 Aug. 1704) perhaps shares the aim of promoting English action against Charles. Harley's letter to Godolphin of 17 July expresses fear that the French will incite Sweden to pursue Augustus into Saxony (BL Add. MS. 28055, fol. 94).

14

To [Robert Harley]

[July–August 1704?][1]

HEADNOTE: This is Defoe's famous political memorandum addressed to Harley, which Manuel Schonhorn calls 'the bedrock of his political imagination'.[2] The document, though clearly addressed to Harley, is not collected with other Defoe–Harley correspondence and there are no physical indications that it was posted, such as folding, an address, or endorsement of receipt. Given the frank advice he offers to Harley throughout the correspondence, there is no reason to think Defoe would have shrunk from sharing it and he does mention it in prior letters. It is thus likely that Harley read it, though no firm evidence confirms he did.[3]

The memorandum seems to date from July or early August 1704. In Letter 11, probably written in very early July, Defoe says that he will complete his 'scheme of an Office For Secret Intelligence at home and Abroad' while travelling that month. It pre-dates news of the Battle of Blenheim (which reached London on 10 August) because Defoe suggests schemes that would 'Turn yᵉ Scale of yᵉ Warr On yᵉ Danube', a phrase that only makes sense coming before Marlborough's victory. In Letter 13, which seems to have been written at the end of July or start of August, Defoe refers to his 'Scheme of Generall Intelligence' as not yet having been delivered.

The *Review* since its inception four or five months earlier had set about explaining the origins of French greatness, and Defoe's counsel to Harley as Secretary of State combines what he found attractive about French absolutism and British

DEFOE TO [ROBERT HARLEY], [JULY–AUGUST 1704?]

cabinet government. The proposals about intelligence were executed to some extent by Harley in the next few years, including with the use of Defoe as a writer and agent. In his later defences of Harley after his final fall from the role of Lord Treasurer in 1714, Defoe denies that Harley acted as a prime minister, a derogatory phrase at this time, in anything like the manner he advocates here (though he also applies the title to Harley). However, the strategy Defoe advocates is to engross power without admitting to doing so; disavowals are part of the strategy.

<blockquote>

I allow That in Our Constitucon we Admit of No
Supreme Ministrÿ.
That yᵉ Nacon is Perticularly Jealous of Favourites.[4]

These Are yᵉ Two Chief Obstruccons in yᵉ Way of a Refin'd and Riseing States Man and These Are yᵉ Two Reasons why we have had No Capitall Men in yᵉ Civill Administracon, No <u>Richlieus</u>,[5] <u>Mazarines</u>[6] or <u>Colberts</u>[7] in yᵉ State.

But I must Go Back for A Reason for These Two Principles, and Must Say:

1: It wou'd be best to have a Supreme Ministry.[8]

2: The Nacon May Easily be Reconcil'd to it.

Twill be Needless to prove yᵉ Advantage of a Chief Ministry. Our Confusions in Council, Our Errors in Execcuting and Unwaryness in Directing from yᵉ Multitude and bad Conduct of Ministers make it Too plain.

To Prove yᵉ Nacon May be Easily Reconcil'd to it, Twill be Needfull to Go back for yᵉ Reasons why Former Favourites have So ill Pleas'd yᵉ Nacon, and how Others have Discharg'd Themselves wᵗʰ Honour.

The Spencers, yᵉ Gavestones[9] of Former Reigns Are too Remote; yᵉ Prime Ministers of Modern Times have been Principally yᵉ Earle of Leicester,[10] yᵉ [   ]ᵃ of Somersett,[11] Buckingham[12] &ca.

These all Incur'd yᵉ Displeasure of yᵉ people by One Crime, Persueing Their Private Intrest, Enriching and Aggrandizeing themselves and Familyes, and Raiseing Vast Estates Out of yᵉ Spoils of yᵉ Publick, and by Their Princes favour heaping up Honorˢ and Titles to Themselves from Mean Originalls.[13]

I Need Not Search hystorÿ for yᵉ Perticulars, yᵉ Fact is too plain.

</blockquote>

ᵃ yᵉ [   ] of Somersett] *blank in MS*

DEFOE TO [ROBERT HARLEY], [JULY–AUGUST 1704?]

The Consequences of this Spirit of Covetousness were[a] allwayes Extorc̄ons, Oppressions, Bribe[s],[b] Sale of Publick Employments, Intrenchments on yᵉ Publick Moneys, Exorbitant Grants of Roya[ll][c] Bounty and yᵉ like.

If any Man will sho' me yᵉ Man That Serv'd yᵉ State Abstracted from his Own Intres[t][d] Ile show Them yᵉ Man who was as Much yᵉ Peoples favourite as yᵉ kings.

Tho: Lord Cromwell was Such a One and Tho' he Fell, as who in yᵉ Reign of That Fickle Unconstant king Could stand, he Fell a Sacrifize to yᵉ Protestant Party, Universally belov'd, and Lamented of yᵉ People.[14]

Sʳ Francis[e] Wallsingham,[15] Tho' Not a Prime Minister, yet if we Read his story The ablest statesman and yᵉ Longest Employ'd, The Most Employ'd in Difficult Cases and yᵉ Greatest Master of Intelligenc̄e of yᵉ Age.

Both These Dyed Poor, They spent Their wholl Time in yᵉ Servic̄e of Their Country, and No Man would ha' Repin'd at Their Enjoying their Princ̄es favour Longer.

This Premis'd I Bring home yᵉ Matter To yᵉ Case in hand. How shall you Make your Self Prime Minister of State, Unenvy'd and Unmolested, be Neither Address'd Against by Parliament, Intreagu'd Against by Partyes, or Murmur'd at by yᵉ Mob — ?

With Submission, Tis Very feasible wᵗʰ an Accurate[16] Conduct. They Say Those Designs Require Most Polic̄y which have Least of honesty; This Design must be honest because it must be honest To Serve Our Country.

| If it be Objected, | But I wou'd Not be Prime Minister, |
| I Returne, | Then you Can Not be Secretary of State. |

The Secretaryes Offic̄e Well Discharg'd Makes a Man Prime Minister of Course; and you Must be prime Minister with Applause, or you will be Secretary with Disgrac̄e.

---

[a] were] *amended from* 'was'
[b] Bribe[s]] *MS torn*
[c] Roya[ll]] *MS torn*
[d] Intres[t]] *MS frayed*
[e] Francis] *interlined above cancelled word* 'Tho:' *(i.e.* 'Thomas')

58

DEFOE TO [ROBERT HARLEY], [JULY–AUGUST 1704?]

Popular Fame Never Thinks a Man too high, Popular Hate Never Thinks him to Lowe.

A Generous, free, Noble, Uncontracted Conduct, as Effectually Secures yᵉ affecċons of yᵉ People, as a Narrow, Covetous, Craveing Spirit Effectually Engages Their Mortall Aversion.

Tis Certainly a Noble Design to be Popular, from a Prinċiple of Reall Meritt. I Observ when all Our people Clamourd at Dutchmen, And Even yᵉ king Cou'd Not please Them, because he was a forreigner,[17] No Man Ever had a Bad word for Monsʳ Overkirk.[18]

Nothing wins This Naċon like Generous, free Open handed Courtesye.

The king of Sweden in his German Warrs, Allwayes Employ'd Trusty Persons in yᵉ Towns and Cittyes he Reduċ'd, to Inform Themselves of any known Case where one was Oppress'd, or any Family That had yᵉ Generall Pitty; and Unlook'd for, Unask'd, he would Send for,ᵃ Right, and Reliev Them.[19]

  Sʳ That Noble Soul is a Rare Pattern, he gaind his Very
  Enemyes by Surprizeing Acts of Bounty.

In your New Post[20] Joyn'd wᵗʰ yᵉ Influenċe you have on yᵉ Royall hand you will have Infinite Opportunitys, to fix an Invulnerable Reputaċon. May Not These heads be Proper.

 1: To keep a Sett of Faithfull Emissarys Selected by yoʳ Own Judgement, Let Them be yoʳ Constant Intelligenċers of Private affaires in yᵉ Court.

 2 Sett yoʳ friends by, <u>if They Are Such They'l Wait</u>, but Surprize yoʳ Enemyes if you have any wᵗʰ Voluntary kindness.

 3 Communicate yoʳ Favours wᵗʰ Unbyasst hand, That all Partyes may Court you.

 4 You have Estate Enough, and Honoʳ Enough, Let yᵉ World kno' you Covett Nothing, all Men Then will Covet you.

Let No Man Under you, Make a Profitt of yoʳ Favours. One Gehezai[21] in yoʳ Attendants, Will undo yᵉ Merit of all your Acċons, he will Gett yᵉ Money, and you yᵉ Curse of yᵉ Person yᵗ Payes it.

Tis Absolutely Neċessary to be Popular; yᵉ Peoples Darling May be a Few Mens Envy, but The peoples hate is a Statesmans Ruin.

ᵃ Send for] *following letters 'an' (for 'and') cancelled*

DEFOE TO [ROBERT HARLEY], [JULY–AUGUST 1704?]

This Opinion of yᵉ People is Easily gain'd at first, and if Lost at first Never Reestablish'd.

Tis Gaind by Little Acts of Courtisy. One Generous Man Oblig'd, One Opprest Man Reliev'd, does a Man of Trust More honour, than Twenty ill Tongues Can blott Out.

In Ordʳ To This yoʳ Trusty Servants, will Enquire you Out Occasions Enough.

A Generall forwarding, and Dispatch of Petiċons, and a Thousand Things wᶜʰ a Man in Such a Post, wᵗʰ Such a Soul, Never wants Opportunity for.

In yᵉ Old Prince of Oranges²² Army, a Captⁿ That had Long Serv'd in yᵉ Warrs Talking to a Friendᵃ was heard to Say, he would give 10000 Guilders for Such a Regiment, yᵉ Coll. being Newly Dead. Why do you Not Put in For it Sayes his Friend. Because Saies he yᵉ Prinċe has No kindness for me and I kno' he will Denye me. The Prinċe knowing him to be a Man of Meritt Sends yᵉ person who Told him yᵉ story wᵗʰ Orders to Take his bond for yᵉ 10000 Guilders Upon Condiċon that he procur'd him yᵉ Regiment, wᶜʰ he did Accordingly. The Next Day yᵉ Prinċe Sends for him, Gives him yᵉ Regimentᵇ and as he was goeing Out, here Sayes yᵉ Prinċe and here's Something for your Equipage and Threw him his bond. The Man was So Surpriz'd wᵗʰ yᵉ Generosity of it he Turn'd from a Prejudiċ'd p[er]son To yᵉ Greatest admirer yᵉ Prinċe had.

Sr

This Proposall of a Generous Bounty and Courtisye, is Not Directed because you want it, but because you have it. To Suppose you want it wou'd first be an Insolenċe Unpardonable, as it would propose yoʳ Feigningᶜ it, and So Make a Vertue of Hypocrisy; But as I have More Than Ordinary Proofs of yoʳ being Master of yᵉ Quallity, I Take yᵉ Freedome To hint yᵉ Uncommon Advantage it Gives you, to Make yoʳ Self Truly Great, and have all Men Pleas'd wᵗʰ it.

ᵃ Talking to a Friend] *interlined*
ᵇ Regiment] *illegible letter cancelled at the end of this word*
ᶜ Feigning] *amended from* 'Faning'

DEFOE TO [ROBERT HARLEY], [JULY–AUGUST 1704?]

Envy allwayes Goes with her Mouth Open,[23] and you are Not to Expect That an advanc't Post will shut it, but There is a Secret in Mannagement That Checks it Effectually, (Viz:)[a] a Generall Unaffected Goodness of Temper. Julius Cæsar was Remarkable for it, and Conquer'd More Enemyes in ye Forum Than in ye Field.

A Man Can Never be Great That is Not Popular, Especally in England. Tis Absolutely Necessary in ye Very Nature of Our Constitucon, where ye People have So Great a Share in ye Govornment.

Besides ye People here, in Recovering their Just Rights, have Usurpt Some, That are Not Their Due, Vizt Censuring Their Superiours, But ye Govornmt is bound to Submit to the Grievance because tis Incurable.

Tis True A Wise Man Will slight Popular Reproach, but No Wise Man slights ye Generall Approbacon, because Nothing but Vertue Can Obtain it.

Tis Therefore Absolutely Necessary for a States man to be Popular.

A States Man Once in ye Peoples favor has a Thousand Opportunityes to do with Freedome, what in a Contrary Circumstance he would Not Dare to Attempt; For as ye People often Condemne hastily, They Approve wth More blindness Than They Censure, and yet Generally Speaking ye Common People have been Allwayes in ye Right.

A Statesman Envy'd Dares Not Attempt a Thing, wch he knows is for ye Publick Service Least ye Miscarriage falls Upon himself.

Cardinall Richlieu Supply'd ye Want of ye Peoples favour by Meer force, and So Ruin'd those that Oppos'd him, as in ye Case of ye Duke D' Momorency,[24] and a Multitude of Others. Tho this would be Impracticable here, it showes ye Absolute Necessity of ye Thing, or of an Equivalent, And yet we find this Cardinall strove hard for ye Publick Voice, and Us'd a Thousand Artifices to Obtain it, Among wch This was One, That he Never Appear'd to his Own

---

[a] (Viz:)] *interlined*

DEFOE TO [ROBERT HARLEY], [JULY–AUGUST 1704?]

Resentments, and tho' a Multitude of Persons of all Ranks, were Sacrifiz'd to his Politick Intrest, yet he Never would be seen in a Matter of Punishment; if a Pardon was to be Granted, he Took Care yᵉ Debt should be to yᵉ Cardinall, but if Justiċe was to be Done That was In yᵉ king.[25]

A Popular States Man Shou'd have yᵉ Obtaining all yᵉ Favours, and Let Others have yᵉ Mañagement of Offenċes, and the Distribuċon of Justiċe.

In yoᵣ Perticular Case Sʳ, you have but One Publick Missfortune, Vizᵗ That yoᵣ Friends for want of Judgement are Affraid of you, Not Affraid you'l Hurt yᵐ but yoᵣ Self. Twou'd be Neċessary to Confirm yᵐ in yᵉ belief of all they hope to find.

Nᵒ 1 ☞ A Perticular Step will Absolutely Effect it — of wᶜʰ by it Self.

2 ☞ A Scheme of what I Mean by Popularity in yoᵣ Own Perticular, and how to be both Obtaind and Improv'd for yᵉ Publick Serviċe, Shall be Drawn if you Please to admitt it.

Nᵒ 3 ☞ Also A Method to Make yᵉ Offiċe of Secretary of State an Inner Cabinett, and Excecute Necessary Parts of Private affaires without yᵉ Intervenċon of yᵉ Privy Council and yet have Their Concurreñċe as farr as yᵉ Law Requires.

When a Prinċe is to Act any Thing Doubtfull or any Thing likely to be Disputed Either at Law, Or in Parliament, yᵉ Council is a Necessary Screen to yᵉ Secretaryes of State.

But in Matters of War, Treatys, Embassys, Private Instrucċons, Expediċons, how Many Such has yᵉ Delay, the Hesitaċons, yᵉ Ignoranċe, or Something worse of Privy Councelors Overthrown.

Matters Maturely Advis'd, Deliberately Concerted, and Absolutely Resolv'd, Require but Two Quallificaċons to Legitimate Their Excecuċon.

1. That They Are Legall.
2. Really for yᵉ Publick Good.

62

DEFOE TO [ROBERT HARLEY], [JULY–AUGUST 1704?]

Such Need No Council Table to Screen Them, Fear No Parliamentary Enquiry, and yet[a] the Authors are Not Answerable for yᵉ Success.

Cabinet Councils[26] in England are Modern, and Excentrick, and I Question whether an Acċon wᶜʰ is Not Justifyable Unless Transacted In[b] Council, is Justify'd by being So in yᵉ Cabinet. But Cabinets of Ten or fourteen are Monsters and Useless.

If[c] her Majᵗⁱᵉ Leaves yᵉ Course of Things to follow yᵉ Nature and Custome of English Kings, her Privy Council shou'd Take Cognizance of all Needfull Affaires, But her Treasurer and Secretary of State should be all her Cabinet Unless she had a well quallifyed Chancelour to Add to Them.

Six Sorts of Great Officers are yᵉ Moveing Springs of yᵉ State and I Can Not but Own without Flattery England was Never Capable of being better Supply'd, I Do Not Say is fully Supplyed.

a Lord Chancelor[27]   a Lord Treasurer[30]
a High Admirall[28]   a Secretary of State[31]
a Generallissimo[29]   an Arch-bishop[32] who Perhaps might
                          Expect to be Put first, but not by me

Of These   The First Should be a good Lawyer
           The Second .... a good Sailor
           The Third   a good Soldier
           The Last   a good Divine. But yᵉ Treasurer
and yᵉ Secretary Ought to be Good States Men. The Weight of all yᵉ Publick Affaires Lyes on Their shoulders.

One for Mannageing yᵉ Revenues, Provideing Needfull Funds, Maintaining Publick Credit, and Regulateing Abuses and Exacċons &ca.

The Other For Forreign Intelligences, Correspondence with yᵉ Courts Abroad, Mannageing, Settling, and Obtaining Confederates,

---

a yet] *interlined*
b In] *interlined above cancelled word* 'by'
c If] *anterior word* 'But' *cancelled*

DEFOE TO [ROBERT HARLEY], [JULY–AUGUST 1704?]

Observing and Suiting affaires wth ye Circumstances and Intrest of Princes.

Intelligence is ye Soul of all Publick bussiness.

I have heard That Our Secretaryes Office is Allow'd 12000£ p[er] Ann for This Weighty Article, And I am Credibly Inform'd ye king of France has paid 11 Millions[33] in One year for ye Same Article and Tis Allow'd he Never Spares his Money on That head, and Thereby Out does all ye World in ye knowlege of his Neighbours.

How Much of ye 12000£ Allow'd for Intelligence, is Expended in Our Secretarys Office, I Will not guess at, But This I Presume That Such a Sume being So Vastly Disproporcon'd to ye Necessary Expence, ye Work is Not Done, and Consequently ye Money yt is Given for it is Lost.

Our States Men have been So farr from Accquainting Themselves wth Other Countryes, that They are strangers to Their Own, A Certain Token That they ha' Sought Their Private Advantage Not ye Publick Service. The secretaryes Office should be an Abrigemt[34] of all Europe.

Her[a] Majties Secretary of State Ought to have Tables of all ye Following Perticulars To Referr to, Stated So Regularly, That They Might ha' Recourse to any Perticular Imediately. They Ought to have:

1st a Perfect List of all ye Gentry and Familys of Rank in England, Their Residence, Characters, and Intrest in ye Respective Countyes.

2 Of all ye Clergy of England, their Benefices, Their Character and Moralls and ye like of ye Dissenters.

3 Of all ye Leading Men in ye Cittyes and Burroughs, wth ye Partyes they Espouse.

They Ought to have a Table of Partyes, and Proper Callculacons of their Strength in Every Respective Part, wch is to be had by haveing ye Coppyes of ye Polls Sent up on all Eleccons, and All ye Circumstances of Such Eleccons Hystorically Collected by faithfull hands, and Transmitted to ye Office.

---

[a] Her] *anterior illegible word cancelled*

64

DEFOE TO [ROBERT HARLEY], [JULY–AUGUST 1704?]

They should kno' ye Names of all ye Men of Great Personall Estates, that they May kno' how and where to Direct any Occasionall Trust; they should have ye Speċall Characters of all ye Justiċes of ye Peaċe, and Men of Note in Every County, to have Recourse to on all Occasions.

Two Trusty Agents would Easily Direct all This So, if Their hands are Not too Much[a] Tyed up as to Money, and yet ye Persons Entrusted Not kno' who they Serv, Nor for what End.

The Secretary of State Should have a Table of all ye Ministers of State, Lists of ye households, The Privy Councils, and Favourites of Every Court in Europe, and Their Characters.

Wth Exact Lists of Their Forċes, Names of The Officers, State of Their Revenue, Methods of Govornment, &ca, So just and Authentick and Regularly amended as Alteraċons happen That by This he maÿ Duly Estimate Their strength, judge of Their Intrests and Proceedings, And Treat wth Them Accordingly.

He should keep a Correspondenċe of Friendship in all Courts wth Ministers of like Quallity, as far as may be honourably Obtain'd, and without Prejudiċe Carry'd on.

Mr Milton kept a Constant Epistolary Conversaċon, wth Severall forreign Ministers of State, and Men of Learning, Abstracted from Affaires of State, but So Woven wth Politicall Observaċons, that he found it as Usefull as any Part of his forreign Correspondenċe.[35]

A hundred Thousand Pounds Per Aññ: Spent Now for 3 year in forreign Intelligenċes, Might be ye[b] best Money Ever This Naċon Laid Out, and I am Persuaded I Could Name Two Articles where if Some Money had been well Apply'd, Neither ye Insurrecċon in Hungary[36] Nor ye Warr in Poland[37] should ha' been So Fatall to ye Confederaċy as Now They are.

No 4 ☞ If it may be of Serviċe I Shall give a Scheme for ye Speedy Settleing those Two Uneasy Articles, and Consequently bringing Down Such a Forċe on ye French as Should in all Probability Turn ye Scale of ye Warr On ye Danube and ye Po.[38]

---

[a] too Much] *interlined*
[b] be ye] *following illegible word beginning* 'm' *cancelled*

DEFOE TO [ROBERT HARLEY], [JULY–AUGUST 1704?]

A Settl'd Intelligence in Scotland, a Thing Strangely Neglected
There, is without Doubt yᵉ Principall Occasion of The present
Missunderstandings between yᵉ Two kingdomes; in yᵉ Last Reign it
Caus'd yᵉ king to have Many ill things Put upon him,[39] and worse
are Very likely to follow.

> I beg Leave to give a Longer Scheme of Thoughts on That
> head, than is Proper here, and a Method how yᵉ Scotts may be
> brought to Reason.[40]

There is a Large Article of Spyes abroad Among yᵉ Enemyes; this I
Suppose to be Settld, tho' by Our Defect of Intelligence, Methinks
it should Not; But It Reminds me of a Book in Eight Volumes
Published in London about 7 or 8 yeares Ago Call'd Letters writ by
a Turkish Spye[41] — The books I Take as They Are a Meer Romance,
but yᵉ Morrall is Good, A Settl'd Person of Sence and Penetracon,
of Dexterity and Courage, To Reside Constantly in Paris, Tho' As
tis a Dangerous Post he had a Larger Allowance Than Ordinary,
Might by One happy Turn Earn all yᵉ money and yᵉ Charge be well
bestow'd.

> There are 3 Towns in France where I would have yᵉ like, and
> They might all Correspond, One at <u>Thoulon</u>, One at <u>Brest</u>, One at
> <u>Dunkirk</u>. They three might Trade together as Merchants, And yᵉ
> Fourth also wᵗʰ Them.

> As Intelligence Abroad is So Considerable it follows in
> Proporcon That The Most Usefull Thing at home is Secrecy.

> For as Intelligence is yᵉ Most usefull to us, So[a] keeping Our
> Enemyes from Intelligence Among us, is As Valluable a[b] head.

> I have been in yᵉ Secretarys Office of a Post Night when Had I
> been a French Spye I Could ha' Put in My Pockett my Lord N . . . . ms
> Letters Directed to sʳ Geo: Rook and to yᵉ Duke of Marlebro'
> Laid Carelessly on a Table for yᵉ Door keepers to Carry to yᵉ Post
> Office.[42]

> How Many Miscarriages have happen'd in England for want of
> Silence and Secresy!

---

[a] So] *interlined*
[b] a] *interlined*

66

DEFOE TO [ROBERT HARLEY], [JULY–AUGUST 1704?]

Cardinall Richlieu,[43] was yᵉ Greatest Master of This Vertue That Ever I Read of, in yᵉ World, and if hystory has Not wrong'dᵃ him, has Sacrifyz'd Many a faithfull Agent, after he had Done his Duty, that he might be sure he should Not be betraid.[44]

He kept Three Offices for yᵉ Dispatch of his Affaires, and One was So Private, That None was admitted but in yᵉ Darke, and Up a pair of back Remote stairs, wᶜʰ Office being at yᵉ Apartments of his Niece Made Room for a Censure past upon her Character, wᶜʰ yᵉ Cardinall Chose to Suffer, that he might have yᵉ Liberty To Transact Affaires there of Much More Moment.[45]

This is a Principall Reason why I object Against bringing All Things before yᵉ Council, for I Will Not Affirm that yᵉ Minutes of Our Privy Council have Not been Read in yᵉ Secreatryes Office at Versailles. Tis Plain yᵉ French Out do us at These Two Things, Secrecy and Intelligence, and That we may Match yᵐ in These Points is yᵉ Design of yᵉ Proposall.

Further Schemes as to Trade, funds for Taxes, &ca Relateing to yᵉ Ldᵇ Treasurers share in yᵉ Publick Administracon I Omitt, haveing Taken up too Much Room with This —

Nᵒ 1

What I Mean by a Step to Confirm yoʳ Friends in yᵉ Belief of what They hope for From you Can Not be Explain'd without Filling yoʳ Eares wᵗʰ Some of those ill Natur'd Things They Take yᵉ Freedome to Say.

Vizᵗ

That you are a Man wholly Resolv'd to Make yoʳ fortunes and to bring it to Pass will Sacrifize your Judgement as well as yoʳ friends to yoʳ Intrest.

That you gave Proofs of this in Embraceing yᵉ Party of Those People who Pleas'd yᵐselves, and Strove to be Popular at yᵉ Expence of king William.[46]

That you forsook yᵉ king who Treated you kindly, and That his Majᵗⁱᵉ Spoke of it in Very Moveing Terms as what he was Concern'd for.

ᵃ wrong'd] *interlined above cancelled word* 'belyed'
ᵇ Ld] *interlined*

DEFOE TO [ROBERT HARLEY], [JULY–AUGUST 1704?]

That Now you have forsaken ye Dissenters, and Fallen in
with Their Enemyes and Promoted ye First Occasionall bill.[47]
Cum Multis Allijs &ca.[48]

S^r

It is Not That I Suppose ye Dissenters Ought to be Deciev'd Or
That you will Deciev Them that I Repeat it Again <u>they are to be
Pleas'd wth words</u>.

But s^r as Good words are usefull in Their Plaće So when Not
Spoken wth Design are Hono^{ble} in Themselves. There is No
Imediate Accon by wch you Can Demonstrate you will Serve
Them.

Onely Let Some Proper Persons Carefully Inform Them That
on all Occasions They may Depend On yor Good Offices wth y^e
Queen, and Give Them Some Notices by Such hands as may be
Trusted That you are Their friend.

Perticularly it May be Very Easy to Posess ye Dissenters That
They Owe ye Change of her Maj^{ties} Sentiments wth Relaćon to y^e
Occasionall bill to yor Mannagement And Councils.

And That her Maj^{ties} Changeing Sides was together wth y^e
Measures you Prescrib'd ye Onely Reason of ye Majority Obtain'd in
ye house of Lords against ye Said bill.[49]

To Effect This a short Paper Shall be handed about, Among
ye Dissenters Onely, giveing Them a Pretended View of y^e
Measures taken by Some Persons <u>Nameing None</u> to Convińce
ye Queen of ye Unreasonableness of This bill.[50]

It Can Not fail to Open their Eyes that you are their Friend and
yet if yor Affaires Should Require you to Dissown Such a Paper it
shall Easily be True that you had No knowlege of it, for you May
Really kno' Nothing of it —

If My Serviće in Another Case is Accepted I Shall Take Care to
Make Such a Paper be Read in all parts of ye kingdome.

I Allow ye Perticular Steps Menćon'd in Such a Paper May
Not be Fact, yet if it be Really Fact That you have Appear'd
Against the bill, That you have Influenc'd and Advis'd her
Maj^{tie} in Favour of The Tolleracon &ca, The Generall is Truth
and Therefore ye Design Just.

This is Part of ye Perticular Step Markt N° 1. —

No 2 Of Popularity

That wch I Call Popularity, May a Little Differ From the Thing wch Goes by That Name, in ye Generall Opinion, and Therefore Tis Needfull to Distinguish the Term.

Popularity in Generall, is ye Generall Esteem of ye People. But The Popularity I Mean Must have an Adjunct, Vizt.

A Generall Esteem Founded upon Good Accons, Truly Meriting The Love of ye People.

Tis True ye People are Not So Apt to Love, as to hate, and Therefore when ye Former is Fixt on a Person, it Ought to Implye Some Merit.

But This is Not Universally True, for ye People Sometimes Love by Antithesis, and Sho' a Generall Affeccon to One Person, to sho' Their Disesteem of his Enemy, and This May be Visible in ye Case of ye Duke of Munmouth, who Really had Not a Great Deal of Personall Merit.[51]

We Say happyness Consists in being Content; but I Must Denye it, Unless ye Contentment be fixt on a Centre of Vertue, for a Vicous Man may So, be More happy Than a Vertuous, and A Mad Man Than both; So here, A Man May be Popular without Merit, But That Popularity will Neither be usefull, nor Servicable.

For Tho' by Wicked Acts Men Gain Applause,
The Reputacon's Rotten like The Cause.[52]

A wise Man is willing to be Popular, and a wise States man will be So, but it is Such a Popular Esteem as Rises from Acts of Vertue, Bounty, and Noble Princiles.

Tis my Opinion Sr as to yor Self, and I speak it wth ye Same Plaineness as I do Things Less Smooth, That I Ought to use More Arguments wth you to Perswade you to Desire This Popular Esteem, Than to Deserv it.

And Therefore Sr I Leave ye Philosophy of ye Argument to yor Own Speculacon, and Go on to ye Present Case.

The Popularity I Mean Now, is — A Politicall Conduct of yor Self, between ye <u>Scylla</u> and ye <u>Charibdis</u>[53] of Partyes; So as to Obtain from Them all a generall Esteem.

Tho' this Part of Conduct is Call'd Dissimulacon, I am Content it shall be Call'd what They will, But as a Lye Does Not Consist in

DEFOE TO [ROBERT HARLEY], [JULY–AUGUST 1704?]

yᵉ Indirect Position of words,ᵃ but in yᵉ Design by False Speaking, to Deciev and Injure my Neighbour, So Dissembling does Not Consist in Puting a Different Faċe Upon Our Acċons, but in yᵉ further Applying That Concealment to yᵉ Prejudiċe of yᵉ Person; for Example, I Come into a persons Chamber, who on a Surprize is Apt to Fall into Dangerous Convulsions. I Come in Smileing, and Pleasant, and ask yᵉ p[er]son to Rise and Go abroad, or any Other Such question, and Press him to it Till I Prevail, whereas yᵉ Truth is I have Discovred yᵉ house to be On Fire, and I Act thus for fear ofᵇ frighting him.⁵⁴ Will any Man Tax me with Hypocrisye and Dissimulaċon?

In yoʳ Perticular Post Sʳ you may So Govorn, as That Every Party Shall believ you Their Own.

I Think I may Answer for One Side; and Shall Think Very Meanly of my Own Designs, if I Do Not bring the Dissenters to believ it firmly, if you please to give me Leave to Act as Effectuallyᶜ as I may Convinċe you will be Needfull.

The Dissenters Sʳ May be broᵗ

1. to believ better of Past Acċons, of wᶜʰ I Mean in yᵉ scheme Nᵒ. 1.
2. They Shall allwayes believ you Their Friend wᵗʰ yᵉ Queen.
3. Take you for Their Advocate and Applye to you on all Occasions.
4. Freely Accquaint you of all Circumstanċes Relateing to what They Desire, or Fear.
5. If Ever you Find Occasion, you may be yᵉ head of The wholl Party, and Consequently Influenċe them as you Please.
6. You will have yᵉ Opportunity upon all Occasions both to Represent Them Right to yᵉ Queen, and yᵉ Queen Right to Them, yᵉ Want of wᶜʰ has been Injurious to both.

ᵃ words] *following illegible word cancelled*
ᵇ of] *interlined*
ᶜ Effectually] *the 'a' is interlined*

DEFOE TO [ROBERT HARLEY], [JULY–AUGUST 1704?]

7. You Will Cauĉon Them against Indiscreĉons, and any Thing that may be to Their Dissadvantage.
8. You May at Second hand Accquaint Them of yᵉ Designs of a Party Against them**ᵃ** and have yᵉ honour of Saveing them from the Mischief Intended.

The Influenĉe yoʳ Offiĉe, as well as Personall Merit, Gives you on yᵉ Queen, will give you Opportunityes Either to bring off Many of yᵉ Hott Men on yᵉ Other Side, or So to Discourage Them that They may Cease to Disturb — and as to yᵉ Moderatest of Them you will often by Serving them Oblige Them to Acknowlege you.

Of yᵉ Moderate Men you are Secure, and They Can Not but both Aprove your Conduct as They See it Moves towards yᵉ Reall happyness of us all.

This is yᵉ Dissimulaĉon I Recomend, wᶜʰ is Not Unlike what yᵉ Apostle Sayes of himself; becoming all Things to all Men, that he might Gain Some.[55] This Hypocrise is a Vertue, and by This Conduct you Shall Make yoʳ Self Popular, you shall be Faithfull and Usefull to yᵉ Soveraign and belov'd by The People.

Nᵒ 3 Of Makeing yᵉ Secretarys**ᵇ** of State an Inner Cabinett**ᶜ** to yᵉ Queen

If The Secretarys of State have a Right Understanding and Act Entirely in Concert, it will forward it Exceedingly.

The Secretarys Should have a Sett of Able heads, Under a Secret Management, with whom to Make Generall Callculaĉons, and from whom to Recieve Such Needfull Informaĉons, as by Other Agents Under Them may be Obtain'd, in all Necessary or Difficult Cases, & yet These Secret heads Need Not Correspond.

From This fund of Adviĉe all Things Needfull to be Concerted for yᵉ Occasions of State, May be Form'd into schemes, and Come Out Perfect. The Proposalls Made by The Secretarys Shall No More be Embrios, and be brought before yᵉ Council to be Argued, and Amended, but shall be born at Onĉe, and Come before yᵐ wholl and Compleat, and

---

ᵃ them] *interlined*
ᵇ Secretarys] *amended from* 'Secreatarys'
ᶜ Cabinett] *amended from* 'Cabbinett'

71

DEFOE TO [ROBERT HARLEY], [JULY–AUGUST 1704?]

yᵉ Council have Little to do but to Approve a thingᵃ as it is Proposed.

If all yᵉ Proposalls Relateing to Publick Matters were Thus Digested, her Majᵗⁱᵉ would find There was a Secret Sufficency Some where in her Secretarys Office, that in Time would bring both her Self and Council To Depend upon yᵉ Secretarys of State, for all yᵉ Modells of Accon, as well as yᵉ Mannagement, and Thus Sʳ I have brought Out what I Affirm'd at First, That yᵉ Secretary of State Must of Course be Prime Minister.

An Essay or Two of This Nature shall be Made when you Please.

I Acknowlege yᵉ Conjunccon of yᵉ Lord Treasurer, for yᵉ Time being, would Make a Compleat Conduct, because Tis Impossible but his Lordship must be furnisht, wᵗʰ Such helps as may finish Things wᵗʰ Less Difficulty.

In This Concert All yᵉ Great Accons of State, all Orders Given to Admiralls, and Generalls, all Forreign Treatyes, and Forreign Intelligence, would Reciev Their Last Turns,ᵇ be Digested, and Finisht, and yᵉ Queen See her Self Mistress of yᵉ Most Capitall Part of her affaires, before They Come before The Council.

All Funds for Taxes, Wayes and Meanes, Projects of Trade, &ca shall be her[e]ᶜ form'd into heads, and Either be Fitted For Execucon, or Laid Aside as Impracticable, and My Lord Treasurer be Eased of yᵉ Intollerable Impertinence of Fund Maker[s]ᵈ and Projectors.

Secret Matters Relateing to Partyes, to Private Persons, home Mannagemᵗ &ca will here be Settl'd, Determin'd, and prepar'd for Execucon.

Here all yᵉ Bussiness of yᵉ Crown, yᵉ Affaires of Law Onely Excepted, will Center and yᵉ Secretarys Office be Thus yᵉ Onely Cabinett —

ᵃ a thing] *interlined. Defoe neglected to cancel* 'it' *which his insertion replaced, omitted in this edition*

ᵇ Turns] *following word* 'and' *cancelled*

ᶜ her[e]] *MS frayed*

ᵈ Maker[s]] *MS frayed*

DEFOE TO [ROBERT HARLEY], [JULY–AUGUST 1704?]

This[a] would Make Our Accŏns Uniform, Our Councils Secret, Our Orders Regular and Practicable and The Excecuc̆on Punctuall.

This would bring yᵉ Secretarys Officĕ and Above al[l][b] yᵉ Secretary into Such Reputac̆on that Orders Issued would have more Regard Sinc̆e Resentments of Miss Conduct would Lye in yᵉ Breast of yᵉ Secretary and be Very Certain and Severe —

Here would be a[c] Prime Ministry without a Grievanc̆e, The People Pleas'd, yᵉ Govornmᵗ Serv'd, Envy Asham'd, Intreagues Fruitless, Enterprizes Successfull, and all Our Measures be both better Directed and Better Excecuted.

Att home Partyes would be Suppresst, Furious Tempers on all Sides Check't and Discountenanc̆'t, Peac̆e Promoted and Union Obtain'd.

All yᵉ Leading Men of all Sides, would be Influenc̆'d here by a Rare and Secret Mannagement. They Should Never Stir or Speak as a Party but it Should be know[n].[d]

Not a Mayor or an Alderman in Any Corporac̆on, Not a shereif of a County, Not A Member of Parliamᵗ, Or Convocac̆on Could be Elected, But yᵉ Govornmᵗ Should kno' who to Oppose, and how to Do it if They Saw Fitt.

This would be The wheel of All Publick bussiness, and all yᵉ Other branches Must of Cours[e][e] Depend on yᵉ Mannagement of This Officĕ.

Nº 4 Some Considerac̆ons wᵗʰ Relation To yᵉ Affaires of Hungaria and Poland

First I Lay it Down as a Princ̆iple — That yᵉ Present[f] Insurecc̆on of yᵉ Hungarians, be Their Pretenc̆ons Never So Just, or Their Provocac̆ons Great, The Invasion of Poland by The Suede and

---

a This] *anterior letter 'T' cancelled where a normal new paragraph would have started above*
b al[l]] *MS frayed*
c a] *interlined*
d know[n]] *MS frayed*
e Cours[e]] *MS frayed*
f Present] *the first 'e' is interlined*

73

DEFOE TO [ROBERT HARLEY], [JULY–AUGUST 1704?]

Dethroneing The king, However Unjustly he may have Acted, Are Fatall Embarrasm[ts] to y[e] Present Confederacy, and in Effect Great helps to y[e] French in Their Over Runing y[e] Empire, and in Their Attempt on The Libertyes of Europe.[56]

This being Allow'd, y[e] Wholl Confederacy Are bound in y[e] Consequence to Support y[e] Emperor Against y[e] Hungarians and y[e] king of Poland Against y[e] Swedes.

If it be Objected why Not as well y[e] Swede Against y[e] Pole and y[e] Hungarians Against y[e] Emperor Since Otherwise you fight Against y[e] Protestant Religion:

I Return <u>This is Not a War of Religion</u>.[57] The Present Question is Not Protestant or Papist But Liberty Or Universall Monarchy, and if it were a War of Religion Tis Not Protestant or Papist in Hungary[58] and Poland but in England, Holand and y[e] Empire.

Now if y[e] Hungarian or Swedish Protestants will have So Little Regard to y[e] Intrest of y[e] Protestant Religion in Generall as to Make Their Private share in it Clash with y[e] Generall we Must do by Them, as We Do by Our Neighbours when y[e] Street is on fire, blow up Their houses to Save y[e] Wholl Town.[59]

Twould be preposterous Temporising if we should Suffer Our Selves to be Over Run for fear of Their being Ruin'd. These Unfortunate Christians of Hungaria have had y[e] Missfortune Once before to attempt Their Liberty in a juncture and in a Manner as Improper as This, and That was when y[ea] Turks Came Down, Or Rather when They brought The Turks Down to y[e] Siege of Vienna. Now Tho' Some People here were So Weak to wish y[e] Turks shou'd Take y[e] Citty because Thereby The Protestants would be Establish'd, yet No Man That Could See an hour before him Could Say but it were Better for all y[e] Rest of Europe That y[e] Protestants of Hungaria were Entyrely Rooted Out and Destroyd Than That y[e] Turks Should Take y[e] Citty of Vienna.[60]

And Therefore we find y[e] Protestant Princes of Germany were y[e] first and Forwardest to March to y[e] Relief of it and y[e] Hungarian Protestants Could Expect No less.

On This Accont <u>Delenda est</u>,[61] The work Must be Done; Protestant or Papist, y[e] Troubles in Hungary Must if Possible be

---

[a] when ye] *following word probably* 'Great' *cancelled*

DEFOE TO [ROBERT HARLEY], [JULY–AUGUST 1704?]

Appeas'd One way Or Other and yᵉ Onely Remaining Question is how it must or may Rather be brought to Pass.

I Grant, That as in yᵉ Simily before, Endeavours Are Allwayes Made Use of to Quench yᵉ fire before yᵉ blowing up of any houses. So here Negociacons Should first be Attempted and Accomodacons Propos'd.

The Hungarians without Doubt are an Opprest People, and On yᵉ Other hand yᵉ Emperor is in Danger and yᵉ Juncture favourable. The English and Dutch Forming a Project of Peace and Pacificacon and Entring into a Close Imediate Treaty On both hands, There is Great Reason to believ both Sides might be brought to See Their Intrest.⁶²

First the Reall Grievances of yᵉ Hungarians to be Considred, Drawn by way of Abstract from Prince Rakocsi's Declaracon,⁶³ And if any Mittigacon of Demands were Thoᵗ Reasonable, Room left to Adjust Them by a Treaty

Here it May be Considred Some are Capitall articles wᶜʰ Must be Granted on both sides.

As Restoreing The Prince, Restoreing The free Excercise of Religion, Retrenching yᵉ Usurpacons of yᵉ Romish Clergy, Calling yᵉ Assembly of yᵉ Estates & Leaving Them at Full and Entire Liberty to Act, withdrawing forreign Forces, and yᵉ like.

On yᵉ Behalf of yᵉ Emperor Some Capitall Articles Must be Insisted on, Such as Laying Down Arms, Restoreing Towns, Delivering Magazins, Renewing Alleigance and Aiding him Against yᵉ French and The like.

As toᵃ Matters of Taxes, Trade, Imposts, Freedome of Passages, Bounds of Estates and all Things Relateing to Property and Civill Justice, These may be and Must be Settled Among Themselves by Treaty or in an Assembly of Estates.

But for yᵉ Other, anᵇ Imediate Envoy to be Sent to yᵉ Emperor or Instruccons to The Resident There as Follows.

In yᵉ Name of yᵉ wholl Confederacy to Represent to yᵉ Emperor yᵉ Necessity of Complying with yᵉ Hungarians, and to Let Him kno' That On These Terms Peace is both honoᵇˡᵉ and Reasonable

---

ᵃ to] *interlined*
ᵇ an] *amended probably from* 'and'

75

DEFOE TO [ROBERT HARLEY], [JULY–AUGUST 1704?]

and That if his Imperiall Maj^{tie} will Not yield to Such a Proposall, Allowing Such Alteraçons, or Addiçons, as are Reasonable, They shall Think y^{m}selves Dissengag'd From any Extraordinary Care of y^e Empire, Any Farther Than by Treatyes They are bound, And that They will Imediately Supplye y^e Hungarians wth[a] 1000000$^£$ sterling to Enable Them to Settle Themselves Independent of y^e Empire, and Establish Prince Rakocsi king of Hungary and Transilvania, and Maintain him in The Posession of y^e Same.

At y^e Same Time a Faithfull Agent to be sent to Prince Rakocsi, to Represent to him: That as Now he has a Favourable Opportunity to Restore Religion, and Liberty, in Hungary, and Reestablish himself and his Family, So he Ought to Let his Demands be Govorn'd by The True and just Reasons of his Takeing Up Arms, and Not Build Upon ye Prosperity of his Affaires, Designes wch may Embark Other Naçons in A Necessary Quarrell Against him; That They will Concern Themselves to Mediate wth ye Emperor Such a Peace as may Secure Hungary Against Future Opressions, but That if he Pushes on his Designes beyond ye just Demands of Reason, They shall be Oblig'd to Concern Themselves against him.

That as They are Ready on ye Project of Peace Tendred y^m, to Oblige ye Emperor to Complye with it, So if Not Accepted They have Resolv'd to Assist ye Emperor wth 25000 Men to be Rais'd and Maintain'd at Their Own Charge, i.e. ye Confederates In Order to Reduce Them by Force.

These Proposalls Warmly Made, Positively Insisted on, and Resolutely Carry'd on, together wth a Dextrous Management, would in all Probabillity Soon bring ye Matter to A finall Conclusion.

It is Not Sufficent to Say This is Talking big to No Purpose, and is like Thunder at a Distance, wch Scares No body because They are Out of ye Danger, for where will ye Confederates find 25000 Men &ca for ye Service?

To This I Answer we Can find ye Money, and There's No Fear of ye Men, if ye Money be Ready; ye Emperor if he wanted Money No More Than he wants Men would Beat ye French Out of ye Empire in One Campaigne.[b]

---

[a] Hungarians wth] *following word probably* 'Mone' (*for* 'Money') *cancelled*
[b] Campaigne] *the* 'i' *is interlined*

On ye Other hand The Protestants in Hungary want No Men, They want Onely Arms, Amunic̃on, and Offic̃ers; ye last may be Supply'd Them Very well, and Money will Supply ye First wth Very Little Difficulty.

The advantage of This Peac̃e No body will Dispute.

As To Poland

The Swede is Now Agressor, and as he was Really Injur'd by The Pole in an Unjust Invasion of ye Swedish Livonia, yet he Ought to be Prevail'd wth Not to Carry his Private Resentments On, to Affect The Present Confederac̃y, of wch ye king of Poland is a Member.

When ye Swede was Embarrast wth ye Dane, ye Muscovite, and ye Pole, The English and Dutch Interpos'd, and gave ye king of Danemark ye Mortificac̃on of Seeing ye Conquest of Holstien, wch was allmost Compleat, Turn'd upon him, and a Powerfull Army allmost at ye Gates of Copenhagen.[64]

They have ye Same Right and as much Reason to Restrain ye Swede from kindling a war in ye Bowells of ye Empire, wch will Certainly be ye Effect of his Dethroneing ye King of Poland, and Marching a Swedish Army into ye Dukedome of Saxony, wch appeares Now to be ye Design.

How shall This be Done?

Embassyes and Memorialls have been Try'd Allready, and we Do Not Pretend Our Envoys In That Case have been Very well Treated, haveing been Made to follow ye Swedish Camp and been Deny'd Audienc̃e.

One Positive Memoriall Delivred him, wth Subjoyn'd Preliminarys of a Treaty between ye Poles and Their king, and Between himself and ye king of Poland, Upon Condic̃ons both honourable and Advantageous for himself — with a Resoluc̃on of ye English, The states Generall, and ye king of Danemark, to Declare Warr Against him^a In Case he Refuses to Treat,[65] would Effectually End that Warr in Two Months Time.

First, I Grant ye Condic̃ons Ought to be Very Good, and Very Mortifying to ye king of Poland, because The Swede was Injur'd in ye Invasion of his Subjects.

---

^a him] *following letters 'woul' (for 'would') cancelled*

DEFOE TO [ROBERT HARLEY], [JULY–AUGUST 1704?]

Second, But There is a Great Difference between
Demanding Satisfaccon of a Prince, and Setting his Own
Subjects To Dethrone him,[66] There is Something More
Dishonoble in That, Than in ye Injury he Recd.

But Suppose he shall Reject ye Proposall.

Act like The French, Make ye Offer wth Sword Drawn, Send a
Strong Squadron into ye Baltick, Not After ye Ambassador, but
with him.

If ye Swede Refuses Assist ye Muscovite, Let him Take Narva,[67]
wch he would Soon do if ye Swedes are kept from Relieving it. —

This fleet will Effectually Cut off his Comunicacon wth his
Own Dominions, Expose all Liefland[68] to ye Muscovites, Deliver
Dantzick[69] from ye Insults of ye Swedes, and Force him to Complye
Or be Ruin'd.

But if it be Objected he will Joyn wth France.

If he does he is Undone. France Can No way[a] Reliev him
but by Sea, and ye Confederates will Comand ye Sound & ye
Passages of ye Belt.[70]

Here a Project for Obligeing ye Swede by an Invasion of
Schonen[71] will be to ye Purpose.

Text: BL Lansdowne MS 98, fols. 223–46. *Address:* none. *Notation in an unknown
hand* (fol. 246v): Maxims & Instructions for Ministers of State. Seemingly written
about the end of ye Reign of Q. Anne, for ye use of some great man.

[a] way] 'to' *is interlined and cancelled*

---

1 For dating, see headnote.

2 Manuel Schonhorn, *Defoe's Politics: Parliament, Power, Kingship, and 'Robinson Crusoe'* (Cambridge, 1991), 101.

3 See Letter 22, note 9.

4 *ye Nacon is Perticularly Jealous of Favourites*: 'Favourites in England have always been the Subjects of the Peoples Hatred and Envy' (Defoe, *A Letter to the Whigs* (1714), 28).

5 *Richlieus*: Cardinal Richelieu (1585–1642), French chief minister under Louis XIII (1601–43). Defoe had recently read Jean Le Clerc's *Life of the Famous Cardinal-Duke de Richelieu*, 2 vols., trans. T. Browne (1695), and in the *Review* he speaks of Richelieu as 'the most exquisite Master of Politicks', a 'great Minister [who] made the Reign of a weak Prince exceedingly glorious', and 'the true Author of the present *French* Greatness' (1, 15 (26 Feb. 1704); 1, 184 (13 June 1704)). He elsewhere calls him 'the first Founder of the *Gallick* Glory' (*Eleven Opinions about Mr. H——y* (1711), *PEW*, 11, 183). And Defoe alludes to his 'exquisite Administration', in *A Brief Deduction of the Original, Progress, and Immense Greatness of the British Woollen Manufacture* (1727), 31. The hero of Defoe's *Memoirs of a Cavalier* (1720) describes Richelieu as

78

DEFOE TO [ROBERT HARLEY], [JULY–AUGUST 1704?]

'not only a supreme minister in the Church, but prime Minister in the State' (*Novels*, IV, 38). Defoe also admired his patronage of the arts (*An Essay upon Projects* (1697), *PEW*, VIII, 108). However, for Defoe, Richelieu was also an instance of an 'encroaching Instrument', adept at 'insinuating himself into the King's Favour upon his own Foot' such as in ousting his patroness Marie de Medici (*The Secret History of the White-Staff* (1714), *PEW*, II, 265; *Minutes of the Negotiations of Monsr. Mesnager* (1717), *SFS*, IV, 40). And he saw Richelieu's career as evidence of Satanic possession of powerful individuals (*The Political History of the Devil* (1726), *SFS*, VI, 178, 181). See note 43 below.

6 *Mazarines*: Cardinal Mazarin (1602–61) in 1642 succeeded his mentor, Richelieu, as chief minister under Louis XIII and then Louis XIV (1638–1714). Defoe often mentions him in the same breath as Richelieu, but indicates that even in his minority Louis XIV was less willing to be led than was Louis XIII (e.g. *Review*, VI, 42 (12 Apr. 1709)). In *A Continuation of Letters written by a Turkish Spy* (1718), Defoe illustrates Mazarin's political cunning in his suppression of a study of religious relics (*SFS*, V, 93).

7 *Colberts*: Jean-Baptiste Colbert (1619–83), chief minister following Mazarin's death. Defoe admired him for encouraging trade in France. In *A Brief Deduction*, Defoe referred to him as the 'great and successful Manager of the *French* Commerce' (33).

8 *Supreme Ministry*: I.e. a prime minister.

9 *Spencers, yᵉ Gavestones*: Piers Gaveston (*c.* 1284–1312) and father and son Hugh Despenser the elder (1261–1326) and younger (d. 1326) were the successive favourites of Edward II (1284–1327). Defoe excoriated these men in, e.g., *The High-Church Legion: or, The Memorial Examin'd* (1705), *PEW*, II, 123; *Secret Memoirs of a Treasonable Conference at S—— House* (1717), *SFS*, IV, 176; and *Of Royal Education* (*c.* 1729), *RDW*, X, 221–3.

10 *Earle of Leicester*: Robert Dudley, first Earl of Leicester (1532/3–88), favourite of Elizabeth I (1533–1603).

11 *Somersett*: Sir Edward Seymour, first Duke of Somerset (*c.* 1500–52), Lord Protector of England from 1547 to 1549, during the minority of Edward VI (1537–53). Defoe admired Somerset, unlike the others in this list. He praised Somerset's unionist attitude to Scotland (*An Essay at Removing National Prejudices against a Union with Scotland ... Part I* (1706), *PEW*, IV, 41). And he lists Somerset as an example of English monarchs' ungrateful treatment of 'Over-grown Merit' (*Review*, VII, 595 (30 Jan. 1711)).

12 *Buckingham*: George Villiers, first Duke of Buckingham (1592–1628), favourite of James I (1566–1625). Defoe calls him 'an Upstart, of mean Birth, mean Character, and worst Principles' (*A Reply to a Pamphlet entituled, The L[or]d H[aversham]'s Vindication of his Speech* (1706), 20). Defoe frequently reflects on what he deemed Buckingham's mismanagement of the relief of French Protestants at La Rochelle in 1627 (e.g. *An Argument Shewing, That a Standing Army, with Consent of Parliament, is not Inconsistent with a Free Government* (1698), *PEW*, I, 74; *The Danger of the Protestant Religion Consider'd, from the Present Prospect of a Religious War in Europe* (1701), *PEW*, V, 80; *Review*, VI, 45 (14 Apr. 1709)). He charges him with peculation and profligacy with government money (*Review*, II, 677 (23 Oct. 1705); *The Political History of the Devil*, *SFS*, VI, 181). Defoe also criticised Buckingham for his promotion of *jus divinum* theory (*Review*, II, 817 (22 Dec. 1705)), and the story in *An Essay on the History and Reality of Apparitions* (1727) of Buckingham being haunted by his father's ghost reflects on his immorality (*SFS*, VIII, 233–8).

13 *Mean Originalls*: socially inferior backgrounds.

14 *Tho: Lord Cromwell ... People*: Thomas Cromwell (1485–1540), Chief Minister under Henry VIII (1491–1547), was executed for treason. Defoe elsewhere praised Cromwell as a popular promoter of Protestantism in England (*A New Test of the Church of England's Loyalty* (1702), *PEW*, III, 73; *Review*, VIII, 590 (22 Jan. 1712)). Defoe characterised Henry VIII as 'a Prince of a haughty Spirit', 'whose Temper was (generally speaking) Bloody, Fierce, Haughty, and too apt to Insult such as fell into his Hands' (*An Enquiry into the Occasional Conformity of Dissenters, in Cases of Preferment* (1698), *PEW*, III, 41–2; *History of the Union* (1709/10), *TDH*, VII, 95). Defoe argued that 'his Lust, his Avarice, his Ambition' had 'involuntarily' initiated the Reformation

DEFOE TO [ROBERT HARLEY], [JULY–AUGUST 1704?]

despite his being 'no Protestant, *nor much of anything else*' (*Peace without Union* (1703), 14; *Royal Religion* (1704), 22; *Review*, IV, 135, 140 (12 and 15 Apr. 1707)). For Defoe, Cromwell was a victim of Henry's caprice and died for promoting true Protestantism against a king concerned only with securing the 'temporal Supremacy' of the crown in a way that had sown divisions within English Protestantism (*A Short View of the Present State of the Protestant Religion in Britain* (1707), 6–7; *Review*, IV, 146 (17 Apr. 1707)). In *Of Royal Education*, Defoe gives a more positive appraisal of Henry (*RDW*, X, 234–8).

15   *Sr Francis Wallsingham*: Walsingham (*c.* 1532–90) was Principal Secretary under Elizabeth I.

16   *Accurate*: careful.

17   *forreigner*: William III (1650–1702). Defoe defended the Dutch William from xenophobic attacks in *The True-Born Englishman* (1700/1), a response to John Tutchin's poem *The Foreigners* (1700), and elsewhere.

18   *Monsr Overkirk*: The Dutchman Henry, Count of Nassau, Lord Overkirk (1640–1708), William III's Master of Horse, and by this time 'the best of the Dutch Generals' in the allied army in Flanders (Trevelyan, I, 314).

19   *king ... Them*: Gustavus Adolphus (1594–1632), Swedish king during the Thirty Years' War (1618–48), killed in victory at the Battle of Lützen. On numerous occasions, Defoe lionised Gustavus as a 'Prodigy of War', 'the Invincible Original of Fighting', a 'Gallant King', and the 'great Champion of the Protestant Religion', responsible for 'Sealing the Liberty and Religion of the *German* Nation with his Blood' (*Review*, VI, 16 (5 Apr. 1709); *Remarks on the Letter to the Author of the State-Memorial* (1706), 16; *The Danger of the Protestant Religion Consider'd*, *PEW*, V, 63; *Review*, VI, 145 (2 June 1709); VIII, 306 (21 Aug. 1711)). The hero of *Memoirs of a Cavalier* experiences Gustavus's magnanimous attention to his soldiers when in his service (*Novels*, IV, 70–1, 81–3).

20   *New Post*: Harley became Secretary of State on 18 May 1704.

21   *Gehezai*: Elisha's dishonest servant (2 Kings 5:20–7).

22   *Old Prince of Oranges*: Maurice, Prince of Orange (1567–1625), Stadtholder of the Dutch Republic, who led the Dutch rebellion against Spain. The following anecdote is untraced. Defoe praises Maurice's military conduct in *The Danger of the Protestant Religion Consider'd*, *PEW*, V, 64, and *Review*, VII, 578–9 (20 Jan. 1711). Defoe's Cavalier observes Maurice's military feats (anachronistically in 1635, a decade after his death) but is ambivalent about his attritional tactics (*Novels*, IV, 114–15).

23   *Envy allwayes Goes with her Mouth Open*: No origin has been traced, but Defoe uses the same phrase in *Review*, I, 222 (4 July 1704); III, 861 (6 Feb. 1707); IV, 239 (31 May 1707); and *The Complete English Tradesman, Volume II* (1727), *RDW*, VIII, 119. Comparable phrases abound in Defoe's writings: 'Malice always goes with its Mouth open' (*Review*, I, 700 (20 Jan. 1705)); 'The Mouth of Slander will always be open' (*Review*, III, 751 (12 Dec. 1706)); 'Malice, that always goes with her Mouth open' (*Review*, IV, 772 (20 Jan. 1708)); '*Malice* is born with its Mouth open' (*Review*, V, 546 (25 Dec. 1708)); '*Malice goes always with its Mouth open*' (*Remarks on the Letter to the Author of the State-Memorial*, 29); 'That Maxim in Physiognomy, *that to go with the Mouth open is the certain Sign of a Fool*' (*Secret Memoirs of a Treasonable Conference at S—— House*, *SFS*, IV, 175–6); ignorant gentlemen 'go with their mouth open' (*The Compleat English Gentleman* (*c.* 1729), *RDW*, X, 82).

24   *Duke D' Momorency*: Henri, Duke of Montmorency (1595–1632), a French nobleman. Richelieu appropriated to himself Montmorency's post as Grand Admiral in 1626 and ensured his execution after the failed uprising of Gaston, Duke of Orléans (1608–60) in which Montmorency commanded the rebels at the Battle of Castelnaudary. See Le Clerc, *Richelieu*, II, 38–46. Defoe's Cavalier briefly fights under Montmorency in Savoy (*Memoirs of a Cavalier*, *Novels*, IV, 45–8). Defoe also alludes to Montmorency in *Caledonia* (1706), line 861, *PEW*, IV, 254.

25   *Cardinall ... king*: As Defoe's Cavalier says: 'This politick Minister always ordered Matters so, that if there was Success in any Thing the Glory was his; but if Things miscarried it was all laid upon the King. This Conduct was so much the more Nice, as it is the direct contrary to

DEFOE TO [ROBERT HARLEY], [JULY–AUGUST 1704?]

the Custom in like Cases, where Kings assume the Glory of all the Success in an Action; and when a Thing miscarries make themselves easie by sacrificing their Ministers and Favourites to the Complaints and Resentments of the People; but this accurate refined Statesman got over this Point' (*Novels*, IV, 41–2).

26 *Cabinet Councils*: See J. H. Plumb, 'The Organization of the Cabinet in the Reign of Queen Anne', *Transactions of the Royal Historical Society*, 5th ser., 7 (1956), 137–57.

27 *Lord Chancelor*: There had been no Lord Chancellor since 1700 when John Somers, first Baron Somers (1651–1716) was removed and the office was placed in commission.

28 *High Admirall*: Currently Rooke.

29 *Generallissimo*: Upon her accession Anne conferred the title on her husband, Prince George, but Marlborough as Captain-General was the military figurehead.

30 *Lord Treasurer*: Currently Godolphin.

31 *Secretary of State*: The office was divided into Northern and Southern departments, currently held respectively by Hedges and Harley. They acted as foreign secretaries, with the Secretary for the Southern Department also acting as Home Secretary. See Mark Thomson, *The Secretaries of State, 1681–1782* (Oxford, 1932).

32 *Arch-bishop*: I.e. Archbishop of Canterbury, a member of the cabinet at this time; currently Thomas Tenison (1636–1715).

33 *11 Millions*: 11m French livres is about £850,000, as 13 livres approximately equal £1. See *Review*, VI, 61 (21 Apr. 1709); *An Essay on the South-Sea Trade* (1711), *PEW*, VII, 39. Defoe elsewhere estimated France's expenditure on intelligence under Richelieu as two million livres per year, writing: 'The dearest Intelligence pays its own Charge; Cardinal *Richlieu* expended two Millions of *Livres* yearly, merely upon Intelligence, and by that means has his Fingers in all the Actions of *Europe*' (*Review*, IV, 610 (13 Nov. 1707)).

   In one of his apologias for Harley after his premiership had ended, Defoe laments 'that he had reduc'd that Article of *Secret Service*, from Ninety seven Thousand Pounds a Year … to under 2200*l.* a Year', an 'unseasonable Parsimony' that compromised his grip on power (*The Secret History of the White-Staff, Part III* (1715), 69–70).

34 *Abrigemt*: 'a … thing which epitomizes or embodies something, a compendium; a representation in miniature; the essence or distillation of something' (*OED*).

35 *Milton … Correspondence*: The poet John Milton (1608–74) served as Secretary of Foreign Tongues, responsible for corresponding with foreign states, answering attacks on government at home, and licensing publications. See Barbara K. Lewalski, *The Life of John Milton* (Oxford, 2000), 236–77. Defoe's knowledge of Milton's work in this office is indicated by *The Danger of the Protestant Religion Consider'd, PEW*, V, 81.

36 *Insurrecìon in Hungary*: Rákóczi's War of Independence (1703–11) saw Hungarians, led by Ferenc Rákóczi (1676–1735), resist Austrian Habsburg rule. Defoe had reported on this 'Formidable Insurrection' in Apr. and May, which he saw as pivotal because a potential distraction to Austria from the war against France (*Review*, I, 94 (22 Apr. 1704)). Subsequent to the offer in this letter to provide a scheme for solving this problem, Defoe turned the *Review* over to Hungarian affairs for over three months, from 2 Sept. to 5 Dec. 1704 (I, 335–588).

37 *Warr in Poland*: See Letter 12, note 10.

38 *Turn … Po*: This statement indicates that the memorandum was written before news of the confederate victory at Blenheim reached London on 10 Aug. 1704 (see Trevelyan, I, 378–96). As Defoe wrote in *Master Mercury*, no. 3 (14 Aug. 1704), 'the Actions of the Duke of *Marlborough* have turned the Scale of all Europe at a blow' (11). The Elector of Bavaria (1662–1726) will have to reconcile with the Empire and break with France, and the Duke of Vendôme (1654–1712) will have a much harder time battling Savoy in northern Italy, Defoe predicted. Defoe reported further on Blenheim in *Master Mercury*, nos. 4 and 6 (17 and 24 Aug. 1704), 13–15, 21–3, and *Review*, I, 307–9 (19 Aug. 1704). For Defoe's attention to the war in northern Italy, see especially *Review*, I, 43–5 (25 Mar. 1704); 262 (25 July 1704).

39 *ill things Put upon him*: William III was reproached in Scotland over the 1692 Glencoe massacre, for refusing support to the Company of Scotland in its ill-fated attempt to settle a colony

81

DEFOE TO [ROBERT HARLEY], [JULY–AUGUST 1704?]

at Darien in 1698–1700, and for settling the succession on the House of Hanover without consulting Scotland in 1701. Defoe defends William on these heads in *History of the Union, TDH*, VII, 112–22; on Glencoe, see also *Review*, IV, 197–200 (13 May 1707).

40 *Scotts may be brought to Reason*: The previous year's Bill of Security became an Act on 5 Aug. 1704 when royal assent was finally, and reluctantly, granted. Scotland had threatened to refuse raising taxes or troops to support the war unless the bill was approved. The Act gave the Scottish parliament the right to choose Anne's successor in Scotland, and mandated that this would not be the English successor unless certain economic, political, and religious conditions were met. See H.M.C. *Laing MSS*, II, 88–9.

41 *Letters writ by a Turkish Spye*: *L'Espion Turc* (1684), a fiction by Giovanni Paolo Marana (1642–93), translated into English in 1687. It depicts an Ottoman spy undercover in Paris. Seven further volumes appeared in English from 1691 to 1694. Defoe alludes to the work in *The Family Instructor, Volume II* (1718), *RDW*, II, 4; and he wrote *A Continuation of Letters written by a Turkish Spy at Paris* (1718).

42 *Secretarys Office ... Post Office*: Defoe spent time in Nottingham's office when under interrogation after *The Shortest Way*. It is reasonable to conclude that Harley failed to heed Defoe's advice, given the part played in his fall in 1708 by William Greg, a clerk in his office who was caught selling state secrets to France and executed (Trevelyan, II, 330–3).

43 *Cardinall Richlieu*: Richelieu was Defoe's exemplar in espionage and intelligence, and he referred admiringly to the 'Inscrutable Councils of Cardinal *Richlieu* and *Mazarine* ... these Eminent Ministers of State dealt too much in the Clouds, to have their Measures dissected or describ'd by the Historians, so much as copied by Posterity' (*Review*, I, 275 (1 Aug. 1704)). When he was spying in Scotland, Defoe self-identified with Richelieu (Letter 102).

44 *Cardinall ... betraid*: Defoe refers back to this in Letter 22.

45 *Niece ... Moment*: Marie de Combalet (1604–75), Duchesse d'Aiguillon from 1638. The anecdote is untraced, but for an account of her relationship to her uncle see A. Bonneau-Avenant, *La duchesse d'Aiguillon, nièce du cardinal de Richelieu* (Paris, 1879).

46 *Popular at ye Expence of king William*: Like Defoe, Harley joined in celebrations of the 1688–9 Revolution; he then entered parliament the following year as a Williamite. However, during the 1690s he led the Country party in its opposition to the Court and William III, including pressing for the reduction of the peacetime standing army in 1697–8, a topic on which Defoe supported William. Only in 1701 with the urgency of settling the succession and resisting the French threat to the European balance of power did Harley and his connection become pro-Court. See Holmes, 260; Downie, *Robert Harley*, 19–56; Hill, 34–70.

47 *First Occasionall bill*: Occasional conformity was the practice adopted by some Nonconformists of taking sacrament according to the rites of the Church of England. Some did it to circumvent the restrictions against Dissenters holding civic or military office. Defoe opposed the practice, starting with *An Enquiry into the Occasional Conformity of Dissenters, in Cases of Preferment, PEW*, III, 37–56. With the support of Anne, her ministers, and Harley (as Speaker), the first bill to prevent occasional conformity by holders of public office passed the Tory-dominated Commons in Nov. 1702. Office holders caught attending a conventicle would have faced fines and ultimately removal from office. However, the bill was frustrated by the Whig-controlled House of Lords, who diluted it with amendments unacceptable to the Commons, so that it never became law. See *HPL 1660–1715*, I, 236–7. Though he opposed occasional conformity, Defoe saw legislation against it as an infringement on the 1689 Toleration Act.

48 *Cum Multis Allijs &ca.*: 'With many others, etc.' (Latin). For the long form of the expression, see *Review*, V, 46 (15 Apr. 1708): '*Cum multis aliis quæ nunc præscribere longum est*' ('With many other matters which it would now be tedious to enumerate'). For a similar English phrase frequently used by Defoe, see Pat Rogers, '"It would be Endless": A Word Cluster in Defoe', *RES* 70 (2019), 95–110. Possibly 'Allÿs' rather than 'Allijs' in MS: the formation of the letters in this same word in the MS of *The Compleat English Gentleman* is more certainly 'Allijs' (BL Add. MS. 32555, fol. 134v).

DEFOE TO [ROBERT HARLEY], [JULY–AUGUST 1704?]

49 *Majties ... bill*: When the Commons passed a second bill to prevent occasional conformity in Nov. 1703, it was tacitly opposed by the Queen and Court and duly rejected by the Lords (Gregg, *Queen Anne*, 177).

50 *short Paper ... bill*: No such document has been traced.

51 *Munmouth ... Merit*: James Scott, first Duke of Monmouth (1649–85), the eldest illegitimate son of Charles II (1630–85), led an uprising against his uncle, James II (1633–1701), but was defeated at the Battle of Sedgemoor (1685) and executed. Defoe fought on Monmouth's side in the rebellion and was pardoned in 1687 (*Calendar of State Papers (Domestic), James II, Vol. 11: Jan. 1686–May 1687* (1964), 440, item 1833). In contrast to what he says here, in *The Succession to the Crown of England, Consider'd* (1701), 25–6, Defoe remarks that 'The Duke of *Monmouth* was a Person Valued and Beloved by the *English* Nation, at *no indifferent rate*', 'the *Darling of the People*'; 'His *Gallantry* Abroad, his *obliging Carriage* at Home, and especially his *Love to his Native Country*, Endear'd him to the Nation, and his *Memory* is Valued by them still.' In *Memoirs of the Church of Scotland* (1717), he commends Monmouth because he 'restrain'd the Rage of the Soldiery' after the government troops he commanded defeated the Scottish Covenanters at the Battle of Bothwell Bridge (1679) (*TDH*, VI, 197).

52 *For ... Cause*: From Defoe's *The Character of the Late Dr. Samuel Annesley* (1697), 7. The lines are similar to some in Defoe's 'Of Happyness Consisting in a Contented Mind', one of his youthful 'Meditaĉons' (*c.* 1681) left in MS: 'But when for Foolish Things They Get Applause, | The Satisfaĉons Rotten Like the Cause' (Huntington HM 26613, fol. 190).

53 *between ye Scylla and ye Charibdis*: Mythical sea monsters from Homer's *Odyssey* (book XI), which occupied the two sides of the narrow Straits of Messina. Odysseus had to navigate safely between them; hence, proverbially, between two evils. Defoe also makes this allusion in *Review*, V, 341 (7 Sept. 1708); VII, 492 (30 Nov. 1710); VIII, 423 (27 Oct. 1711); VIII, 808 (20 May 1712); IX, 322 (9 Apr. 1713).

54 *persons Chamber ... frighting him*: In *An Essay on the South-Sea Trade*, Defoe discusses the government's compelling its creditors to accept stocks for their debt, saying 'the Force then is no more than as you would have forc'd a Child or a Lunatick out of a House that was on Fire' (*PEW*, VII, 43).

55 *Apostle ... Some*: St Paul says, 'To the weak became I as weak, that I might gain the weak: I am made all things to all *men*, that I might by all means save some' (1 Cor. 9:22). Defoe makes the same allusion in Letter 69.

56 *Insureĉon ... Europe*: Defoe acknowledged the 'Oppressions and Tyrannies of the House of *Austria*' against the Hungarians and hence the justness of their desire to depose their king. But he insisted that their striking at the Emperor was excessive and served France's interests: 'No Man can wish the *Hungarians* Success, without wishing the Duke of *Marlborough* to be beaten' (*Review*, I, 337 (2 Sept. 1704)). Equivalently, he acknowledged that Augustus had erred in invading Livonia but again insisted that Charles XII's retaliation was excessive and harmful to the confederate war cause against France. He even calls Charles XII a French ally (*Master Mercury*, no. 15 (25 Sept. 1704), 59).

57 *Not a War of Religion*: 'The present War is not a War of Religion', Defoe emphasised in *Review*, I, 547 (28 Nov. 1704). Three years earlier, he had written: 'I see no War can be Rais'd in *Europe*, but what will of Course run into a War of Religion' (*The Danger of the Protestant Religion Consider'd, PEW*, V, 76). Hill, 87, suggests that Defoe was trying to argue Harley out of a mainly religious view of the international situation.

58 *Not Protestant or Papist in Hungary*: In the *Review*, Defoe sought to persuade his countrymen that the Hungarian rebellion was not a victory for Protestantism because it weakened the alliance against France (e.g. I, 527 (18 Nov. 1704)).

59 *Street ... Town*: Defoe uses this analogy, to explain that 'the lesser Evil must be submitted to, to avoid the greater', in *Review*, II, 350 (5 July 1705); IV, 488 (20 Sept. 1707); IV, 765 (17 Jan. 1708); V, 596 (20 Jan. 1709); VI, 425 (20 Oct. 1709); VIII, 261 (26 July 1711); IX, 391 (21 May 1713); *The Scots Nation and Union Vindicated* (1714), 7; *An Essay upon Buying and Selling of Speeches* (1716), 35; *The Question Fairly Stated* (1717), 19; and *The Director*, no. 9 (31 Oct. 1720), *PEW*, VI, 235.

DEFEO TO [ROBERT HARLEY], [JULY–AUGUST 1704?]

60 *Unfortunate Christians ... Vienna*: In the *Review* from 30 Sept. to 2 Dec. 1704, Defoe gave a lengthy account of the anti-Habsburg rebellion of the 1670s and 1680s led by Imre Thököly (1657–1705). He contended that the Hungarians merely swapped Austrian for Ottoman thraldom (*Review*, 1, 384–582). The siege of Vienna he mentions for comparison occurred in 1683, and Defoe states elsewhere that at that time he wrote a pamphlet on the topic, though this has not been identified (*Appeal*, 51).

61 *Delenda est*: As in '*Carthago delenda est*' (Latin): 'Carthage must be destroyed.' The phrase proverbially emphasises the need for action. The words were spoken by Cato the Elder (234–149 BCE), but Defoe usually assigns it to the Roman soldier Scipio (185–129 BCE), who finally razed Carthage in 146 BCE. Even if the misattribution to Scipio signals irony in *The Shortest Way with the Dissenters* (*PEW*, 111, 105), it does not do so in *Review*, IV, 326 (12 July 1707), and is simply an error.

62 *Intrest*: Defoe argued that England needed to persuade her ally, Austria, to make peace with the Hungarians in order to concentrate on the war with France, which was ultimately in the Hungarians' interest too. E.g. *Review*, 1, 343 (5 Sept. 1704).

63 *Prince Rakocsi's Declaracon*: Defoe commented on the declaration of grievances issued by the Hungarian leader Rákóczi in *Review*, 1, 355 (12 Sept. 1704).

64 *Swede ... Copenhagen*: In 1699, at the outset of the Great Northern War, Denmark besieged Tönning in Holstein-Gottorp, a Swedish ally (now in northern Germany). Seeking to preserve a balance of power between the Baltic-Scandinavian kingdoms, Britain and Holland joined with Sweden to attack Denmark, forcing her out of the alliance (formed with Poland and Russia) against Sweden by the Treaty of Travendal (1700). Defoe commended this action in *Review*, 1, 316 (22 Aug. 1704); VIII, 41 (7 Apr. 1711); VIII, 307 (21 Aug. 1711).

65 *Resolucon ... Treat*: See Letter 13.

66 *Dethrone him*: As well as what he wrote at the time, Defoe glanced back indignantly at Augustus's ouster in *Reasons against the Succession of the House of Hanover* (1713), *PEW*, 1, 169–70, and *The Compleat English Gentleman*, *RDW*, x, 42–3.

67 *Narva*: Narva, in the east of present-day Estonia, on the Russian border, was in 1700 the site of the first major Russo-Swedish battle in the Great Northern War, a Swedish victory despite being outnumbered 'One to Six' as Robinson Crusoe observes in *Farther Adventures* (1719), *Novels*, 11, 174; cf. *Review*, IX, 180 (15 Jan. 1713). At the time Defoe wrote this memorandum, in summer 1704, the town was besieged by a reorganised Russian army, and Defoe criticised Charles XII for 'pushing on his Conquests in *Poland*' rather than relieving Narva's citizens, 'who are now starving in the Service of their King' (*Review*, 1, 283 (5 Aug. 1704)). '*Narva* is at the last Extremity of Famine, and cannot hold out long', Defoe wrote in *Master Mercury*, no. 3 (14 Aug. 1704), 10; cf. *Master Mercury*, no. 7 (28 Aug. 1704), 27. In fact, it had fallen to Russia on 9 Aug. See *Master Mercury*, no. 15 (25 Sept. 1704), 60.

68 *Liefland*: Swedish territory in the eastern Baltic, comprehending parts of modern Estonia, Latvia, and Lithuania.

69 *Dantzick*: Danzig, now Gdańsk, in present-day Poland, an important independent trading city. Harley's letters in summer 1704 to the envoy at The Hague, Alexander Stanhope (1638–1707), indicate the ministry's concerns about Sweden's aggressions there (University of Nottingham Library, Pw 2Hy 666–76). Swedish forces were garrisoned on the outskirts of the city, demanding financial contributions. On 19 Sept. 1704, Harley wrote to John Robinson about the allies' 'project for Danzig, that that city shal remaine in the same relation to Poland as it hath formerly done' (Yale Beinecke, Osborne MSS Files 17650), and he wrote to the Dutch Pensionary Heinsius to the same effect the following day (*Heinsius Corr.*, 111, 365). Defoe insisted that Britain needed to intervene to protect Danzig in *Review*, 1, 267–70 (29 July 1704).

70 *Sound ... Belt*: The sea passages from the Kattegat to the Baltic.

71 *Schonen*: Modern Skåne, the southernmost region of Sweden.

84

15

To [Robert Harley]

[August–September 1704?][1]

HEADNOTE: Defoe's lengthy memorandum (Letter 14) set out some thoughts about how Harley could enhance his standing with the Dissenters at a pivotal moment in Anne's first parliament. Two Commons bills seeking to proscribe occasional conformity had been defeated in the Lords, and Anne had removed several ministers most eager for such legislation, such as Nottingham. Nonconformity remained a pressing topic for Defoe, which he addressed in numerous pamphlets during 1704, the most recent being *More Short-Ways with the Dissenters* (April 1704) and *A New Test of the Church of England's Honesty* (June 1704).[2] These attacked High Church adversaries for unchristian and disloyal tactics, expressed resentment at his own treatment over *The Shortest Way*, and set out his views of the Dissenters' current civic standing. The arguments Defoe expressed in his pamphlets overlap with those in this letter, but in the private document they are forebodingly presented as directives for the 'Mannagement of the Dissenters' by Harley as chief minister (he even notes to Harley that he would be reluctant for his ideas to be circulated).[3]

In his pamphlets, Defoe publicly styled himself as the Dissenters' defender and castigator, a writer loyal to their interests but willing to tell hard truths. He believed that the Dissenters were divided, though he hoped that a removal of the threat of renewed persecution could help them to unite. He conceded that present circumstances did not favour Dissenters' full civic participation but hoped that continued loyalty and a growth of their economic significance would achieve this in time. The Occasional Conformity Bills were less of consequence for their exclusion of Dissenters from office – that had been the situation for a long time – and more for their return to legislation that penalised Nonconformity. Defoe argued that the time since Dissenters gained toleration of their worship had weakened their unity and religiosity. He sought to incline Harley to assume a protective role towards Nonconformists.

> The First Principle of Govornment is Allow'd to be The Publick Safety.
> The Capitall Branches Whereof are
> > Union at home
> > Power Abroad

> I Humbly Conciev ye Most Difficult Point at Present is Union Among Our Selves, and as This Nacon is Unhappily Divided into

DEFOE TO [ROBERT HARLEY], [AUGUST–SEPTEMBER 1704?]

Partyes and Faccons, It Seems a Much Nicer thing to Form a Union Since Some Articles Seem Absolutely Irreconcileable.

Tis Plain Those Gentlemen who Propose This Union by Establishing One Party and Suppressing Another, Are[a] In ye Dark as to This Matter, and Offer That wch has been often Essay'd, and has as[b] Often Miscarryed.[4]

The Papist, The Church of England, and The Dissenter, have all had Their Turns in ye Publick Administracon; and when Ever Any One of Them Endeavourd their Own Settlemt by The Ruine of The Partys Dissenting, ye Consequence was Supplanting themselves.

The Papists in ye Reign of Queen Mary[5] Drove The Affair of Persecucon to that highth that They Thought to Extirpate ye Beginings of ye Reformacon, but as ye Nobillity had Entertaind a Suspicon of ye Resolucon taken to Restore ye Abbey Lands, Tis plain from ye Memoirs of those Times, the people of England had borne it but a Little while Longer, Tho' Queen Mary had liv'd.

The forwardness shown in ye Generall Establishment of ye Protestant Religion at The begining of Queen Elizabeth[6] Confirms This, For Popery Sunk So Absolutely in ye Wholl kingdome That it hardly Struggl'd at its Parting.

The Church of England had almost Enjoy'd ye Settlement of 100 yeares when in ye Civill Warrs[7] it Sunk Under ye hands of Those Dissenters it had attempted to Suppress.

These proceeding Upon ye Same Unchristian princíple, Vizt Ambicon, and Persecucon, Driving Things to Extremetyes, Overthrew Themselves and Open'd ye Door To ye Returne of The Party They Oppresst.[8]

This has allwayes been ye Fruit of Immoderate Principles.

I Might Carry On The Paralell to ye Reign of King James[9] when Popery Seem'd to Make A New Effort but Overshooting ye Mark Fell in ye Attempt.

To Bring This Home

Her Majsty Came to ye Crown on ye Foot of a Legall Settlement;[10] all ye Fatall Encroachment of Partyes wch had Embroil'd us for Some Ages, had[c] Suffred an Operacon, and Submitted to Legall Right,

---

[a] Are] *following word* 'Under' *cancelled*
[b] as] *interlined*
[c] had] *following illegible word cancelled*

DEFOE TO [ROBERT HARLEY], [AUGUST–SEPTEMBER 1704?]

Law, and Constitución; Persecución was Checkt by Authourity, and Liberty of Consćienće Declar'd a Native Right, yᵉ Gust of Unlimited Power was Damn'd by Parliament, and all yᵉ Depredaćons on yᵉ peoples property Made Void, and Declar'd illegall.

Her Majᵗⁱᵉ had yᵉ Fairest Opportunity in yᵉ World to have United us all upon her Accession to yᵉ Crown, had Not Some Unhappy Councils Directed That Early Mistake, when in her first Speech She Told yᵉ Naćon her Resolućon of Bestowing her Favours Upon yᵉ Most Zealous Church Men, in Perticular.[11]

I am Very Sure her Majᵗⁱᵉ Neither foresaw yᵉ Effect of her words, Nor Imagind that those she Designd her Favours for, would So ill Improve[12] her Goodness. But these Gentlemen[13] haveing No Power To Restrain Their Warmth, Imediately Gave a Loose to The Imoderate heat of Their Temper, and boldly Construed yᵉ Queens Perticular Favour to yᵐ as a Commission Given them to Insult yᵉ Dissenters. Tis hardly Credible wᵗʰ what Insolenće we were Treated in all soćyety, That Now we had a Church of England Queen And The Dissenters Must all Come Down, Our Ministers were Insulted in yᵉ street,[14] Down with yᵉ Whigs, was a street Phrase, and Ballads were Sung of it at Our Doors.

From Henće It proceeded to Libells, and Lampoons, and From Thenće to yᵉ Pulpitt and yᵉ Press; Till mʳ Sachavrell in a Sermon Preach't at Oxford, and Licensed by the University, Told his Hearers that whoever was a True Son of yᵉ Church or Wisht well to it, Was Oblig'd to hang Out yᵉ Bloody Flag of Deffianće Against yᵉ Dissenters.[15]

If This Treatment fill'd yᵉ Dissenters with Terrible Apprehensions of what They[a] had to Expect, Her Majᵗⁱᵉ Can Not blame Them without forgetting The use These Gentlemen Made of her first Speech, and Resenting it Accordingly.

From This Came yᵉ Book Call'd yᵉ Shortest Way, wᵗʰ all yᵉ et Ceteras of it to yᵉ Unhappy Author, Unhappy Onely in Saying too Much Truth.[16]

All her Majᵗⁱᵉ has been Able to Say Sinće, has Not been Able, Either to Check yᵉ Fury of a Party, who had posest Themselves wᵗʰ yᵉ hopes of Ruining The Dissenters, Nor Could it lessen yᵉ Feares yᵉ

ᵃ They] *following word* 'were' *cancelled*

DEFOE TO [ROBERT HARLEY], [AUGUST–SEPTEMBER 1704?]

Dissenters Too Justly Entertain'd of The Reall Design they Thot was laid for Their Destruccon.

If I am Ask'd how This wrong step is to be Retriev'd and Peace of Partyes to be Procur'd

I Must Answer in Generall

By Removeing The Dissenters Jealousyes,[17] and Checking the Destructive Fury of ye present hott party.

The Dissenters Jealousyes May Effectually be Remov'd, The wholl Party Entirely Engag'd, and Brott to an Absolute Dependence Upon her Majtie, and a Conjunccon with her Intrest, and yet No Concessions Made to Them, wch May give Reason of[a] Distast to ye Church.

Of This, if I am Ordred to give a scheme, possibly it would Appear both Reasonable and Feasible, But I wou'd be Very Loth it should be Seen but where it May be usefull.

Those Gentlemen who Are for Engrossing all ye Places of Profitt and Trust in The Kingdome in[b] The hands of Church Men, should by my Consent be Gratifyed, tho' without ye Necessity of a Law:[18] The Dissenters shou'd Content Themselves wth Their Liberty of Conscience, and I am Perswaded wou'd be So Content, and being Secur'd in Their Property and Religion, and Out of ye Feares and Taunts of Their Enemyes They wou'd of Course Correspond together, and in Time Unite.

A Bill for Occasionall Conformity would be Needless, and I am Perswaded The Gentlemen who were forwardest for it Now would ha' Thought it less Significant Than They Seem'd to do if They had Design'd to follow it with Some Other steps More Effectuall and More Perticularly Mortifying.

There Are Differences in This Unhappy Nacon which Respect ye State wholly and Not Religion; There Are High Church and Low Church as well as Conformist and Dissenter.

Tis my Opinion ye Moderate Men of both Partyes are ye Substantiall part of ye Nacon; They are its Refuge when ye Men of Heat Carry Things too farr.

---

[a] of] *amended from* 'to'
[b] in] *interlined*

88

DEFOE TO [ROBERT HARLEY], [AUGUST–SEPTEMBER 1704?]

These Are yͤ Men in whom alone yͤ Govorment Can be Safely Lodg'd and when it is So No Men That are Lovers of Their Country Can be Uneasy.

I Can Never Believ We are Safe in Any hands but These. The Lords May be Hott on One hand, and yͤ Commons On Another. So far as Either Run On to Extreams, So farr they Are to blame, Injure The Peoples Peace, Foment Partyes and Hazard Our Safety.

These Breaches May Perfectly be heal'd by The Queen. Two words at yͤ Opening the Next session shall Finish it all without a Dissolucͦn.[19]

Dissolving Parliaments Allwayes Lessens yͤ Crown, and Never lessens Grievances. Time was we Could Not have Grievances Redresst and Parliamͭˢ Could Not be Suffr'd to look into Them. Tis hard Now We have a Prince That would Make us all Easy We Can Not Correspond in Our Demands and Let her kno' wherein Our happyness Consists.

All This May be Cur'd by Wise Conduct, Wary Councils, Moderate Measures and Moderate Men.

Methods of Mannagement of yͤ Dissenters

I allow Previous to yͤ proposall That 'Tis Not Necessary in yͤ present Conjuncture to Restore The Dissenters to Offices and Preferments.

This would Make yͤ Govornͫᵗ Seem Byast in Their Favour; yͤ high Church Men would Reflect on her Majᵗⁱᵉ as Not True to her Own Princiͦples or her Promise.

I Might Possibly Grant The Temper of yͤ Dissenters Not So Well Quallify'd for yͤ Prosperity of Their Princes favour as Other Men, and Grant They are Better kept at a Due Distance Provided Not Made Uneasÿ.

But This would be Certainly the Effect of bringing yͫ into Accͦn, That it would add Nothing to Our Union; it would Onely Make One Party Easy and An Other Discontented and we should be still Divided.

I Premise Also by yͤ Way That I am Perswaded Freedom and favour to The Dissenters is The Directest Method to Lessen Their Numbers and bring Them at last into yͤ Church. I Verily Believ yͤ

DEFOE TO [ROBERT HARLEY], [AUGUST–SEPTEMBER 1704?]

18 yeares Liberty[20] They have Enjoy'd has weakn'd Their Intrest. A Tenderness and Moderaċon to Them will still Lessen Them and I Could Say Much on This head.

The Dissenters Are Divided and Impolitick. They Are Not form'd into a body. They hold No Correspondenċe among themselves. Could they ha' been brought to do So Their Numbers would ha' Made Them Formidable. But as they are Onely Numbers Irregularly Mixt They are Uncapable of Acting in Any Capasċity.

They are Consequently Passiv in all Matters of Govornment; ye Most That Ever They do is to Address by Their Ministers.

The Proceedings to Restrain Either Their Liberty as Dissenters or Their Other Privileges Must Necessarily Make Them Uneasy and Fill Them with Feares, And as Words have given Them So Much Uneasiness Words May Restore it and Cure all ye Breach without Changing ye Mannagement Other Than what is in Prospect.

The Uneasyness of ye Dissenters Consists in Their Feares That ye Queen is in ye hands of That Party of Men who would Ruin Them.

Her Majtie is Easily Able to Clear This by shifting but a Few Obnoxious hands, and Putting her Self upon ye Fidelity and Prudenċe of Such a Ministry as Neither Side Can Object Against without Manifestly Discovering that Tis ye Plaċes Not ye Men They are Concern'd About.

One Speech from Her Majtie Either in Council or at ye Next session of Parliament would Effectually Stop ye Mouth of Rallery and strife and Make us all Easy, but Such Unreasonable people on both Sides as might Easily be Silenċ't if Onċe publickly Discourag'd or if Not Silenċ't Would be Expos'd and Contemn'd.

Some Small Mannagement Among ye Dissenters by Fathfull Agents Might be Very Usefull to Settle The Generall Temper of The Party and Methods shall be propos'd at Demand.

What hands to be laid by, what p[er]ticular Expressions in Such a Speech.

DEFOE TO [ROBERT HARLEY], [AUGUST–SEPTEMBER 1704?]

What Methods to Satisfye yᵉ high Church Malecontents, I Dare Not Presume to Make an Essay at, Tho' Possibly On a Liberty Granted I Could Say what I hope would Appear Reasonable.

These Generalls Extended to Perticulars; I am Perswaded The Dissenters May be brought to be So Perfectly Easy, That if it Were in Their Power Or Choice to Alter yᵉ Face of The Govornment They would Not Attempt it. This way They Shall Convince yᵉ World that yᵉ Liberty of Their Consciences and assurance of its Continuance is a Full Satisfaccon to Them without Civill Preferments and Advantages, and That They Desire No More Than yᵉ Tolleracon They Enjoy.[21]

With This Management it shall Never Disturb Them if They Are No way Concernd in yᵉ Govornment, while They See at yᵉ Same Time, it is in yᵉ hands of Such as Sincerely Design Their Proteccon, and Not Their Destruccon.

And he That will Not be Content in Such a Case will be Dissown'd as a Hypocrite, and Pass for a Politick, Not a Religious Dissenter.[22]

Those Gentlemen of yᵉ Church who were Not Content wᵗʰ This Mannagement would Discover plainly That Twas Not yᵉ Churches Safety but yᵉ Dissenters Ruine They Aim'd at in all Their Unnecessary Clamours and Her Majᵗⁱᵉ would Easily Discern yᵉ Men.

The Gentlemen of yᵉ highest Temper in These Matters Generally Conform to yᵉ Face of yᵉ Court. Such as Continued Averse to peace Might be Either Taken off by Methods Or Discourag'd and Tho' ill Nature would Not be Suppresst at Once Twould lessen and Dye away by Time.

Should her Majᵗⁱᵉ Declare That as she had Often given her word to Maintain yᵉ Tolleracon[23] So She should Never Consent to any Act that Seem'd to Restrain The present Liberty of yᵉ Dissenters.

DEFOE TO [ROBERT HARLEY], [AUGUST–SEPTEMBER 1704?]

That she So Desired ye Generall Peaće of her People That any p[er]son That Either by Writeing, Preaching Or Printing promoted ye Fatall strife of Partyes should Meet with No Encouragement from her.

That she would Perticularly Recomend it To ye Clergy to Preach up Moderaćon, Charity and Peaće with people of Different Opinions and To strive by Their pious lives and painfull Preaching to prove whether[24] were The Best Christians. Nor Could her Maj^{tie} Need to Say Much of her Zeal or Care for ye Church. No body Doubts her Steadyness but Such a Declaraćon would Imediately Stop ye Clamours of ye Pulpitt against ye Dissenters and Care might be Taken to prevent ye Dissenters Takeing any Unjust advantages of ye Churches Silenće.

These with a Little Applicaćon and Private but Very Niće Conduct Might give ye last step to a Generall Union of Affecćon in ye Naćon and as to a Union in prinćiple As it Can Not be Expected So blessed be God it is Not So Necessary as that we Can Not be happy without it.

Text: BL Harley MS 6274, fols. 227–34. *Address*: none.

1 This letter seems to postdate slightly the longer memorandum (Letter 14) and precedes the start of the parliamentary session on 24 Oct. 1704.
2 Defoe's authorship of *A New Test of the Church of England's Honesty* was reported to Harley in a letter by an informer on 5 July 1704 (BL Add. MS. 70021, fol. 149).
3 In *The Present State of the Parties in Great Britain* (1712), Defoe looks back on this era and credits Harley as 'the Principal Agent' in defending the Dissenters to the Queen (24).
4 *Those Gentlemen ... Often Miscarryed*: This had been the theme of Defoe's *Peace without Union* (1703): he felt High Churchmen had interpreted the Queen's exhortations to peace and union as a licence to press ahead with promoting uniformity via the repression of Dissent.
5 *Queen Mary*: Mary I (1516–58). Defoe elsewhere criticised her persecution of Protestants (e.g. *Review*, VIII, 657 (28 Feb. 1712); *A Seasonable Warning and Caution against the Insinuations of Papists and Jacobites in Favour of the Pretender* (1712), 21; *Reasons against the Succession of the House of Hanover* (1713), *PEW*, I, 172).
6 *Queen Elizabeth*: Defoe greatly admired Elizabeth as a politician, 'a Princess whose Character is so established among *English* Men, for Justice, Love of her People, and especially for a most admirable Spirit of Government' (*The Monitor*, no. 9 (11 May 1714)). Defoe considered her an '*English Phoenix* ... | Who made my People rich, my Country great' (*The Mock Mourners* (1702), lines 404–5, *SFS*, I, 148). In her 'long and flourishing Reign', '*England* was entirely united, and mov'd by one regular Wheel of Government' (*Review*, III, 64 (24 Jan. 1706); III, 585 (24 Sept. 1706)). She '*Govern'd the Nation with a Matchless Prudence*' and is the monarch 'to whom this Nation as a Trading Country owes its peculiar Greatness' (*A Brief Reply to the History of Standing Armies in England* (1698), *PEW*, I, 84; *Review*, IV, 55 (6 Mar. 1707); cf.

DEFOE TO [ROBERT HARLEY], [AUGUST–SEPTEMBER 1704?]

Defoe, *A Brief Deduction of the Original, Progress, and Immense Greatness of the British Woollen Manufacture* (1727), 26; *A Plan of the English Commerce* (1728), *PEW*, VII, 195–203).

In terms of religion, Defoe commends Elizabeth as a 'Zealous Protestant Queen' who 'rescu'd the Protestant Religion' and 'gloriously finished' the English Reformation (*A New Test of the Church of England's Loyalty* (1702), *PEW*, III, 62; *An Enquiry into the Occasional Conformity of Dissenters* (1698), *PEW*, III, 43; *The Poor Man's Plea* (1698), *RDW*, VI, 26). But he laments that she 'hated, suppresss'd, and even crush'd the *Puritans*' and resisted 'a farther Reformation' of the Church (*Review*, VI, 727 (11 Mar. 1710); IV, 151 (19 Apr. 1707)). She even 'carr[ied] the Reformation back several steps towards Popery' (*The Secret History of the October-Club ... Part II* (1711), 54). In *Memoirs of the Church of Scotland* (1717), Defoe is equivocal about Elizabeth's dealings with Scotland (*TDH*, VI, 47–63).

7 *Civill Warrs ... Suppress*: The three English Civil Wars (1642–51). Following the second Civil War, England was a republican Commonwealth (1649–60). See Defoe's reference to 'the short Government of Parliament in *England*, which was erroneously called a Commonwealth' (*The Original Power of the Collective Body of the People of England* (1701), *PEW*, I, 117).

8 *Returne of The Party They Oppress*: The Restoration (1660) returned the monarchy with Charles II (1630–85) and the Anglican Church, which had been disestablished during Parliament's rule.

9 *King James*: James II.

10 *Her ... Settlement*: Queen Anne succeeded in 1702 by the terms of the Revolution settlement of 1689, which adjudged that her father James II had abdicated by desertion, both for himself and his newborn son James (1688–1766). The crown was settled jointly on William III (1650–1702) and Mary II (1662–94), thereafter their children and, in the event they both died childless, Anne. Defoe deemed '*Parliamentary Limitation*' a '*better right*' than 'Succession by Birth' (*Review*, IX, 74 (4 Oct. 1712)). As Holmes states, 'the Queen herself was always refreshingly free from any delusions about the source of her own authority', giving short shrift to divine right theory (Holmes, 187).

11 *first Speech ... Perticular*: Anne concluded her speech to both Houses, closing her first parliament on 25 May 1702 by stating: 'My own Principles must always keep me entirely firm to the Interests and Religion of the Church of England, and will incline me to countenance those who have the truest Zeal to support it' (*The History and Proceedings of the House of Commons*, 12 vols. (1742), III, 197–8). Her speech of 11 March 1702 was actually her first to parliament. Defoe wrote about this speech in similar terms in numerous places, arguing that High Church zealots mistook the Queen's meaning, wilfully ignoring her pledge to preserve the toleration of Nonconformity. See *Review*, II, 317 (26 June 1705); III, 200 (30 Mar. 1706); IV, 89–90 (22 Mar. 1707); *The Present State of the Parties in Great Britain*, 14–15.

12 *Improve*: 'Treat or portray (an action, situation, event, etc.) as something greater, better, or worse than it is, for one's profit or advantage' (*OED*).

13 *Gentlemen*: Among the High Tories he blames for providing Anne with 'Unhappy Councils', Defoe thinks especially of Laurence Hyde, first Earl of Rochester (1642–1711), removed as Lord Lieutenant of Ireland in 1703; Sir Edward Seymour (1633–1708), removed as Comptroller of the Household in 1704; and Nottingham, who resigned as Secretary of State in Apr. 1704.

14 *Our Ministers were Insulted in ye Street*: Cf. Defoe, *The Present State of the Parties in Great Britain*, 18.

15 *mr Sachavrell ... Dissenters*: Henry Sacheverell, *The Political Union* (1702), 59: 'Hang out the *Bloody Flag*, and *Banner* of Defiance'. Defoe invokes the phrase in numerous places, such as *More Short-Ways with the Dissenters* (1704), 2.

16 *ye Shortest Way ... Truth*: Defoe insisted on the 'truth' of *The Shortest Way* in several places. In the preface to *A Second Volume of the Writings of the Author of The True-Born Englishman* (1705), Defoe wrote: '*Multitudes of Occasions have since that* [his being pilloried] *serv'd to convince the World, that every Word of the Book he suffered for was both literally and interpretively the Sense of the Party pointed at, true in Fact, and true in Representation*' (sig. A5v). In *The*

Consolidator (1705), he said he had 'published some bold Truths' and 'was call'd before the Publick Authority, who could not bear the just Reflections of his *damn'd Satyrical way of Writing*' (*SFS*, III, 54). When charged with cowardice, Defoe wrote that 'if he had had the good Fortune to have been a Coward, he had never been undone for speaking the Truth' (*Review*, I, 429 (7 Oct. 1704)).

17 *Jealousyes*: suspicions.

18 *Law*: I.e. an act to prevent occasional conformity.

19 *Dissolucõn*: I.e. calling for a general election. The third session of the parliament elected in 1702 sat down on 24 Oct. 1704, was not dissolved, and rose on 14 Mar. 1705, at which time an election was required under the 1694 Triennial Act.

20 *18 yeares Liberty*: Evidently counting from James II's first declaration of indulgence in 1687, rather than the Toleration Act of 1689.

21 *Dissenters ... Enjoy*: See also *More Short-Ways with the Dissenters*, 19.

22 *Politick, Not a Religious Dissenter*: This distinction originates in Defoe's *An Enquiry into the Occasional Conformity of Dissenters*, PEW, III, 46: '*He who Dissents from an Establish'd Church on any account, but from a real Principle of Conscience, is a Politick, not a Religious Dissenter.*'

23 *Maintain ye Tolleracõn*: Defoe repeatedly invoked Anne's promise to uphold the toleration of Nonconformists, made in her speech to parliament on 25 May 1702, such as in *A New Test of the Church of England's Honesty*, PEW, III, 194–5.

24 *whether*: 'which of the two'. Defoe also uses the word in this archaic sense in *Review*, VIII, 800 (17 May 1712).

16

To Samuel Elisha

31 August 1704

HEADNOTE: Samuel Elisha (1670–1746), the son of a maltster, was an attorney and burgess in Shrewsbury and mayor in 1725.[1] Defoe wrote him a second letter on 11 October, and he is listed as Defoe's distribution agent in 1706, one of the numerous contacts in provincial towns through whom Defoe disseminated his political writings.[2]

Sr

I had yor Obligeing Letter,[3] for wch Tho' its Now Very Late I Presume to give you my Sincere Thanks.

I had Given m^r Rogers[4] Over and knew not how Matters were wth him, supposeing he was Marry'd and had forgot his friends or some thing Elce was befallen him.

This made me give you ye Trouble of a p[ar]cell yesterday by the Carryer in wch are 50 books wch you will find are a few thoughts

DEFOE TO [ROBERT HARLEY], [SEPTEMBER 1704?]

on yᵉ Late Victory⁵ — If you please to Let him have them or any Friends that Desire yᵐ. If they are to Many he may Returne what he mislikes.

I Can not Enlarge, but you'l see by yᵉ Enclosd what Wonderfull Things God is Doeing in yᵉ World of wᶜʰ I Could not forbear putting you to yᵉ Charge,ᵃ that you might let Our friends have yᵉ first of it.

Tis Midnight. I hope you will Excuse yᵉ hast.

<blockquote>
I am
Sʳ
yoʳ Sincere Friend & Hum[ble]ᵇ Servᵗ
D Foe
</blockquote>

Ultimᵒ Augᵗ. 1704

Text: Harvard University, Houghton bMS Eng 870 (26) (Figure 3). *Address*: To Mʳ Samˡˡ Elisha | in | Shrewsbury

---

ᵃ Charge] 'Charge of' *in MS*
ᵇ Hum[ble]] *MS damaged by seal*

---

1 His will was proved 24 Mar. 1746 (TNA PROB 11/745/444). See Thomas Phillips, *The History and Antiquities of Shrewsbury*, 2 vols. (1837), 1, 185; *Shrewsbury Burgess Roll*, ed. H. E. Forrest (Shrewsbury, 1924), 95.
2 See Letters 20 and 46.
3 *Letter*: Untraced.
4 *mr Rogers*: Gabriel Rogers (d. 1705), bookseller in Shrewsbury. Rogers's second wife Anne died in 1701, but no information of another marriage is known (*Chirk Castle Accounts, A.D. 1666–1753*, ed. W. M. Myddelton (Manchester, 1931), 323). See Letter 19.
5 *thoughts on yᵉ Late Victory*: Defoe's poem, *A Hymn to Victory*, which celebrated the Battle of Blenheim, was published on 29 Aug. 1704.

17

To [Robert Harley]

[September 1704?][1]

HEADNOTE: Defoe's brief for his tour of the eastern counties north of London in autumn 1704 was to discover the political feeling in these locations ahead of the general election that would take place in 1705. As well as gauging the mood,

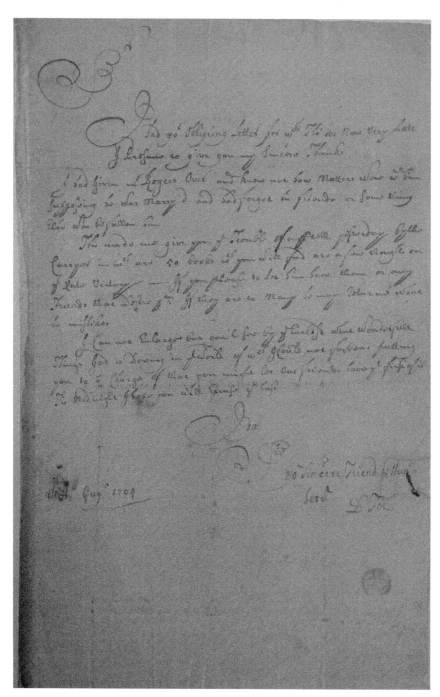

Figure 3 Daniel Defoe to Samuel Elisha, 31 August 1704,
Harvard University, Houghton bMS Eng 870 (26)

DEFOE TO [ROBERT HARLEY], [SEPTEMBER 1704?]

he was trying to influence it, 'Spreading Prinĉiples of Temper, Moderation, and Peace Thro' Countrys where I go, and Perswadeing all People That yᵉ Govornment is Resolv'd to proceed by those Rules'. He sent Harley detailed reports, only some of which have survived. Defoe evidently visited Royston, Cambridge, the vicinity of Norwich, and Bury St Edmunds. Defoe disguised his handwriting in this letter.

State of Partys in England

County of Hertford

This County is under Severall Characters.

That part of it adjoyning to Bedfordshire and Buckinghamshire is whiggish and Full of Dissenters.

That Part adjoining to Huntingdon, Cambridg and Essex Entirely Church and all of the High Sort.

The Gentlemen of the Royston Club² Settle all the affaires of the Country and carry all before them Tho' they behave wᵗʰ Something More Modesty or at least Carry it Closer than in former Dayes.

This is a Monthly Meeting of the Gentlemen of all the Neighborhood the First Thursday in Every Month. They used to Drink Excessively,³ and do a Thousand Extravagant Things, but they behave much Better now.

They have Built a large Handsome Square Room well wainscotted, and Painted, ti[s]ᵃ Hung wᵗʰ the Pictures of King Charles the 1ˢᵗ, the 2ᵈ, King James, and king William,⁴ at their Full Length, well painted in Good Frames, 10 or 12 Foot High.

They Have a Monteth⁵ of Silver of about 4 Gallons wᶜʰ cost them 50ᶜ. They raise Some Fines and Forfeitures, wᶜʰ Formerly were improved to the Encrease of Drunkeness, but now they do Some Charity's, and are much reformed.

Here Justice [   ]ᵇ and the then Club resolved the Pulling down the Quakers meeting at Hartford iñ 1683 for wᶜʰ the Proprieter afterwards Sued him and recovered Sufficient Damage to rebuild theᶜ house.⁶

Mʳ Freeman⁷ is Master of all this part of yᵉ County as to Parties.

List of the Royston Club⁸

ᵃ ti[s]] *MS torn*
ᵇ Justice [   ]] *blank in MS*
ᶜ the] *following letter probably* 'a' *cancelled*

97

DEFOE TO [ROBERT HARLEY], 28 SEPTEMBER 1704

Text: BL Add. MS. 70291, fols. 26–7. [Disguised handwriting.] *Address*: none.

1 Travelling north, Defoe was in Cambridge on 16 Sept. (Letter 18).
2 *Royston Club*: A local constituency organisation, which met in the Red Lion inn at Royston. 'The Royston Club in Hertfordshire, carefully tended by Ralph Freeman, provided the Tories in that county with a permanent committee which must have made a considerable contribution to the near monopoly of the shire seats throughout the years 1702–14' (Holmes, 315). The club selected magistrates and sheriffs, exercised the gift of church livings, and selected candidates for parliamentary elections. See *The Gentleman's Magazine* 53 (1783), 813–16.
3 *Drink Excessively*: Defoe noted the heavy drinking of the Royston Club in *Reformation of Manners* (1702), line 648, *SFS*, I, 174.
4 *king William*: Amidst the High Church resurgence in 1711, Defoe mentions the Royston Club: 'The old Drunken Laws were reviv'd already, and they resolv'd to take down King *William*'s Picture, who, they said, had been almost the Destruction of the *Club*; and set up Dr. *Sacheverell*'s there, drawn at full length, with the Church on his Back, and the Revolution at his Feet' (*The Secret History of the October-Club ... Part II* (1711), 87).
5 *Monteth*: I.e. monteith, an ornamental punchbowl with a scalloped rim.
6 *Justice [ ] ... house*: The unnamed justice was Sir Ralph Radcliffe (1633–1720). On the event Defoe describes, see Reginald L. Hine, *A Mirror for the Society of Friends: Being the Story of the Hitchin Quakers*, 2nd ed. (1930), 35.
7 *Mr Freeman*: Ralph Freman (1666–1742), Tory MP for Hertfordshire, 1697–1727. He had opposed the standing army in 1698, supported the bills against occasional conformity starting in 1702, and was one of the Tories most zealous in guarding the House of Commons's powers in determining elections in the Aylesbury case. Freman was aggrieved at being denied the Hertfordshire lieutenancy, which Harley believed spurred his activity in 1703–4 (Harley to Godolphin, 20 Sept. 1703, BL Add. MS. 61118, fol. 61; *HPC 1690–1715*, v, 67). Defoe later criticised Freman directly for his support for the tack of legislation against occasional conformity to the land tax bill (*Review*, 11, 155 (5 May 1705)). Freman and Harley evidently had an amicable relationship, judging by letters they exchanged going down to 1713 (BL Add. MS. 70197).
8 *List of the Royston Club*: Nothing is written under this heading.

18

To [Robert Harley]

28 September 1704

HEADNOTE: Defoe's tour had taken him near to Norwich and to the coastal towns of northern Norfolk. He was now lying low in Bury St Edmunds, because, as the diarist Narcissus Luttrell (1657–1732) recorded on 26 September, 'It's said, Daniel de Foe is ordered to be taken into custody for reflecting on admiral Rooke, in his Master Mercury, whereby he has forfeited his recognizance for his good behaviour.'[1] That claim had been made in a manuscript newsletter.[2] Defoe later recounted his experience in the *Review*: 'Being at *Bury* in *Suffolk*, and going into a *Coffee-house* there to read the News, I found to my Surprize an Account, that sundry Persons were taken up in *London* for scandalous Libels, that Warrants were out for *Daniel De Foe*, but he was fled from Justice – I cannot deny, but I was mov'd at this Barbarity.'[3] Defoe had been criticising Rooke since August, of course, in the *Review* and in *The Master Mercury*.[4] But more recently, the *Mercury* had on 18 and 21 September reported on the naval Battle of Vélez-Málaga, the latter issue taking a sarcastic tone and announcing it could be deemed a 'victory' only because the ill-prepared, poorly commanded English avoided a rout: 'Upon the whole the Matter is much for the Advantage of *England*, and the *French* lost the day in losing so great an Opportunity of ruining the *English* Fleet, the like of which I hope they will never have again.'[5]

It now seemed that Defoe's reflections on Rooke had caught up with him. In the *Review* on 7 October, he begrudgingly acknowledged that Vélez-Málaga was a victory for Rooke. In that and the following issue he printed this notice:

> *Whereas the Author of this Paper has been, and still is in the Country upon his Extraordinary and Lawful occasions; and some Persons Maliciously and Scandalously reported, and caus'd it to be Written in News-Letters, that he is absconded and fled from Justice.*
>
> *He gives this Notice to all Persons whom it may Concern, That as he knows no guilt, for which he has any occasion to fly; so as soon as ever he saw in the Written News, the Malice of the World, he took care to give Publick Notice to the Government where he is; and shall always be ready to shew himself to the Faces of his Enemies, let the occasion be what it will.*[6]

Defoe reported his whereabouts to the government in letters to Harley and Hedges, though he does not mention in his public notice the trip back to town he relates to Harley. Later, in November, having returned from travelling, Defoe wrote in the *Review* that the reports against him had been fabricated, amounting to '*a meer Genuine Forgery, Injuriously and Maliciously contriv'd, if possible, to bring him into Trouble*'. Only on returning to London did he find '*that no Officer, Messenger, or other Person had receiv'd any Order, Warrant, or other Direction to Search for, Enquire after, Take, Apprehend, or otherwise Disturb the said* Daniel de Foe; *or that there was any Complaint, Accusation, or Charge brought against him*'. Defoe even offered a £20 reward for anyone who could name to him the author or publisher of the news-letters that had wronged him.[7] He also recalled this experience two years later when in Scotland.[8] In the long run, it was a minor inconvenience.

Sr

I did my Self yᵉ honoʳ to write To you from Cambridge[9] on Saturday yᵉ 16th Instᵃ and was in hopes to have Recᵈ yoʳ Ordʳˢ as hinted There by Fryday — How I have Spent yᵉ Time yᵉ Last

DEFOE TO [ROBERT HARLEY], 28 SEPTEMBER 1704

week — how I Rec[d] an Odd Alarm from Lond[o] Occasion'd by m[r] Stephens y[e] Messenger of y[e] Press, who Really Treats me ill,[10] how This Occasion'd me Makeing a Trip to Town, how staying but Two dayes There I happend of a Smart Rencounter wth m[r] Toke[11] of East Greensted, These are things I Purpos'd Not to ha' Troubl'd you with, Till I had y[e] honour to finish y[e] Affair I am Upon.

As my Last[12] Signify'd my Desire to Come to This Place, and That[a] Not Recieving yo[r] Countermand I Should persue that Design, I have Accordingly Spent a few Dayes here; s[r] R Davers[13] who Rules This Town Carrys Matters Very high, s[r] ... Felton[14] y[e] Other Member we heare[b] to Day is Dead or Dying[c] and I Doubt They will make but an ill Choice. If it be possible to bring y[t] Gentleman off, it would do Great Service, his Intrest in This County being Very strong; but of This I Crave leave to be Perticular hereafter.

I Can Not but beg leave to Lay before you That I am Surpriz'd to find my Name in y[e] Written News Letters of this day[d] as Taken into Custody, and Comitted by her Maj[ties] Order for Ill Treating S[r] Geo: Rook &ca.[15] I hope if there be any Suggestion Against me, on That or any Case, you will please to Reserve me to Answer to yo[r] Self; It Can Not be, that I Can be Guilty of any Thing to Displease you, Nor of any Thing Willingly to give you Cause of Dislike; if s[r] Geo: is Scandaliz'd at me for any thing, at y[e] Same Time professing I have Not Design'd him any Affront, I beseech you S[r] to Take me into your protecc̓on, upon that head; and am Ready To Make Such Acknowledgem[t] as you shall Think Reasonable.

I have been Exceedingly Concern'd at This Case, and was Comeing Up Post to Thro' my Self at yo[r] feet and Put my Self into yo[r] hands, but being Very Unwilling to leave what I am Upon, Till it is Finisht, I have Venturd to Stay, Depending on yo[r] Goodness to me in This Case.

I Write This from Bury where I hope I have Not been Useless, Norw[ch] I have Perfectly[e] Dissected,[16] and Was Directing my Course To Lyn,[17] but This Unhappy News paper I Confess Discompos'd me, and I spend y[e] Time in Visiting The Sea Coast[f]

---

[a] That] *following word* 'my' *cancelled*
[b] heare] *the* 'a' *is interlined*
[c] or Dying] *interlined*
[d] of this day] *interlined*
[e] Perfectly] *interlined*
[f] Coast] *the* 'a' *is interlined*

DEFOE TO [ROBERT HARLEY], 28 SEPTEMBER 1704

Towns here, till I may have a line from you at This Town, where y^r farther Orders will both Comfort and Direct me.

If I do Not Reciev Some Signification from your Self by Certificate, or other wise, I shall hardly kno' how to govorn my Self, For my stirring about may be Dangerous — and I am in Danger of being Taken up as a Person fled from ye Queens justice, and in Such a Case may have my Papers Taken from me and at Least Seen, wch would be as bad. For This Reason I am Very shye of my Self, Till I have ye hono^r of yor Protection, wch I Entreat by First Post.

I am Inform'd here this News Paper is Written by one m^r Fox who they Say belongs to ye Secretarys Office.[18] If any Thing Could have been in it, I flatter my Self I Should have it from yor Self, from whom (if I were Guilty of high Treason) a Letter or a Verball Comand should Cause me To Come and Put my Self into yor Power.

I Can Not Conciev what I Can have Offended in, and shall Desire but This favour, That s^r Geo: Rook may be Referr'd to ye Law; if I have Offended him I am Willing to be left to ye Law, and Ask him no favour, but if ye Govornm^t will Espouse ye Quarrell of a Single p[er]son, against another, any Man May be Crusht.

I have Not Taken ye freedome my Inclinacon guided me to, and wch I Really Thot ye Case of s^r G R Requir'd; because I Saw you Dislik'd another man upon that head,[19] and as I hope I Act from Different Principles wth Those people, So s^r I allways Remembr'd my Obligacon to you, and believ and hope to Satisfye you, I shall Never do any Thing to Make you Think I forgett it.

Tis Something hard that while I am Spreading Principles of Temper, Moderation, and Peace Thro' Countrys where I go, and Perswadeing all People That ye Govornment is Resolv'd to proceed by those Rules, I should be Chosen Out to be made ye Object of a Private^a high flying Revenge, under Colour of ye Govornments Resentments, for be it s^r that you find s^r G. R^b faithfull, and that This fight or Victory at Sea[20] be ye first Proof of it.

I Can at This Distance Accquaint you, That ye Improvem^t[21] Made of This Victory Abroad by The Mad Men of his Party at home, is Such, that speaking of The Peace at home, wch is ye Design I am

---

^{a} Private] *following word* 'hygh' *cancelled*
^{b} s^r G. R] *following illegible word cancelled*

101

DEFOE TO [ROBERT HARLEY], 28 SEPTEMBER 1704

Upon, and wᶜʰ I Suppose her Majᵗⁱᵉ, your Self, and all Good Men Embark't in, p[er]haps we may See good Cause to wish that Victory had been a Defeat — And tho' I were to Suppose Sʳ Geo:ᵃ himself under yᵉ Mañagemᵗ of your hand, yet sʳ I am free to Tell you, that yᵉ high Church Party look on him as Their Own. The Victory at sea they look upon as Their Victory Over yᵉ Modera[te]ᵇ Party, and his health is Now Drunk by Those here, who wont Drink yᵉ Queens Nor yours,ᶜ I am Oblidg'd wᵗʰ Pacenċe to hear you Damn'd, and he Prais'd, he Exalted and her Majᵗⁱᵉ Slighted, and yᵉ Sea Victory Set up against yᵉ Land Victory, sʳ Geo: Exalted above yᵉ D of Marl .. and what Can yᵉ Reason of this be, but that they Concieve some hopes from This, that their high Church Party will Revive Under his Patronage.

Now sʳ I leave This to yoʳ judgemᵗ whether be sʳ G R Concernd or No, whether this Unreasonable Acclamaċon, be not made from Other Prinċiples than joy a Victory. If he is to be yᵉ Patron of that Party, whether he Sees it or Not, if he is to be a head for Them to Vallue yᵐselves Upon, whether Purposely or Not, he is a fatall Instrumᵗ to Ruine yᵉ Peaċe we Speak of.

Indeed sʳ Tis my Regard to your Orders, and that Onely, Restrains me On that head,²² for yᵉ Case Requires to be Spoken to, and if yᵉ Govornmᵗ Espouse yᵉ Case against me in This,ᵈ yᵉ broil will be Remov'd from high Church, and Low Church,ᵉ To Rookites and ......

The Consequenċes This has allready in yᵉ Country, and yᵉ Check it has put to yᵉ Advanċes Peaċe had Made, are Visible, and I Shall Give you Perticulars as Soonᶠ as I Come up, And Concludeᵍ wᵗʰ This presumċon — sʳ at least sʳ G. R must be won Over to Dissown yᵉ proceedings of This Party, and to Check those wᶜʰ affront yᵉ Govornment, on his behalf, or yᵉ Civill feuds of Partyes will Encrease, Rather than Diminish, my Comission will be in Vain, and you will find yᵉ Temper of yᵉ Gentlemen who are to Come up yᵉ 24ᵗʰ of Next Month,²³ less Govornable than you Expect.

ᵃ Sʳ Geo:] *following illegible word cancelled*
ᵇ Modera[te]] *MS frayed*
ᶜ Nor yours] *interlined*
ᵈ This] *following word* 'Case' *cancelled*
ᵉ Low Church] *following words* 'and Low' *cancelled*
ᶠ as Soon] *interlined*
ᵍ Conclude] *following illegible word cancelled*

DEFOE TO [ROBERT HARLEY], 28 SEPTEMBER 1704

I am Running Out s^r into ye Usuall Freedom, wth wch I hope you will not be offended. I Can not but Think it my Duty To Let you See there, what you would be Displeasd to See if you were here.

S^r I have Another Grievan̂ce to Lay before you, wth an Earnestness Perticular to my Usuall Solli̇citȧcons. Mr Chris: Hurt[24] of ye Custome house, The Same whose Name you have in yor Pocket book, has been wth me all This Journey, and a Very Usefull p[er]son I have found him in ye work I am Upon, — he is Under Concern at my staying Longer than I Expected, and haveing ask't No Leav at ye Custome house where he is Not a Little Mark't Out as a Dissenter, Expects to be ill Treated for This absen̂ce; ye Least Noti̇ce from you s^r will Remove ye Possibillity of it, and Tho' I Conceal ye bottome of ye bussiness, yet he Serves it faithfully, and I kno' Not how to want[25] him.

I Therefore Entreat you will please to get a Note of Leav^a from My Ld Treasurer Directed to ye Comiss^rs of ye Customes for <u>Christopher Hurt Key Man</u>[26] to be Absent on his Private Occasions.

I would ha' hinted that ye Magazin Runs Lowe, and is Recruited by Private Stock, wch is but Indifferent; I acknowledge myself Not a Good Husband But as my ill husbandry is Onely where I find it Absolutely Needfull, I Venture Not to be spareing and hope you will find Cause to approve it, and Trust my Choi̇ce of Instruments and Methods.

I Again Entreat yor Care of my Assistant; it would heartily Concerne me, and I believ yor Self, if he should be Divested of his Livelyhood for ye absen̂ce here while ye bottom of it is yor and ye Nȧcons Servi̇ce.

I Cease to Importune you farther and waiting to hear farther from yor Self ask yor Pardon for The length of This

> and am
> > yor Most faithfull Oblig'd
> > and Obed^t Servt
> > [*monogram*]

---

^a Leav] *following word* 'for' *cancelled*

DEFOE TO [ROBERT HARLEY], 28 SEPTEMBER 1704

yͤ Extraordinary goodness of yͤ Season (here haveing been No Rain these 3 Weeks) makes me Offer it if forᵃ yͤ Service to Stay Out as long as you please.

Bury Sept 28. 1704

If I should be straightn'd and you please to Ordͬ me To Draw for a Supply and on whom,ᵇ I hope yͤ Success of the affair will answer it beyond yoͬ Expectacon.

Please To Direct to Alexandͬ Goldsmith²⁷ at mͬ John Morleys in Bury.²⁸

Text: BL Add. MS. 70291, fols. 20–1. [A copy of the *Review* for 2 Sept. 1704 is bound in BL Add. MS. 70291, fols. 18–19, endorsed by Harley on fol. 19ᵛ: 'Sept: 5: 1704'.] *Address*: none.

ᵃ for] *interlined*
ᵇ and on whom] *interlined*

---

1 Luttrell, v, 469.
2 The newsletter Luttrell had seen is untraced; it is presumably the one Defoe attributes to Joseph Fox in the letter. On 30 Sept., another newsletter reported: 'mr. De Foe the Author of a halfe sheet of Paper Published twice a Week Entituled the Master Mercury is silenced for a Blasphemous Expression in it and Order'd to be prosecuted for that and for Reflecting on Sr George Rook and the late sea fight' (Folger Shakespeare Library, Newdigate Newsletters, L.c. 2799).
3 *Review*, III, 700 (16 Nov. 1706).
4 For Defoe's writing against Rooke, see Letter 11. Defoe attacked Rooke in *The Master Mercury*, no. 5 (21 Aug. 1704) and in the following day's *Review*, I, 316–17 (22 Aug. 1704). Subsequent issues of *The Master Mercury* grow increasingly satirical and scurrilous. Defoe ironically praises Rooke for being so careful with the Queen's ships: 'To his prudence we owe the preservation of our Navy, and the safety of all Her Majesty's Ships of War' (*Master Mercury*, no. 6 (24 Aug. 1704), 23). He highlights Rooke's miscarriages in the Mediterranean in no. 7 (28 Aug. 1704); and he prints a satirical poem on Rooke called 'The Complaisant Admirals' in no. 8 ([31] Aug. 1704).
5 *Master Mercury*, no. 14 (21 Sept. 1704), 56. In the *Review* Defoe was also hedging on the question of whether the battle represented an English victory (1, 381 (26 Sept. 1704)). See Harley's equivocal assessment of the battle in his 14 Sept. letter to John Holles, first Duke of Newcastle (1662–1711) and his 19 Sept. letter to Heinsius (H.M.C. *Portland MSS*, 11, 186; *Heinsius Corr.*, III, 366). Godolphin's to Harley on 14 Sept. calls it 'a sort of drawn battle where both sides had enough of it' (H.M.C. *Bath MSS*, 1, 62). Looking back in *The Present State of the Parties in Great Britain* (1712), Defoe alludes to it as 'a Battle at Sea, to our Advantage, in the Mediterranean' (30).
6 *Review*, I, 429–30, 436 (7 and 10 Oct. 1704).
7 *Review*, I, 507–8, 513 (4 and 7 Nov. 1704). Defoe here says that the report indicated he had 'deserted his Security' and 'forfeited *his Behaviour*'; he does not mention his pardon, which was still being kept secret.
8 *Review*, III, 700–1 (16 Nov. 1706).

DEFOE TO [ROBERT HARLEY], 28 SEPTEMBER 1704

9 *write To you from Cambridge*: Untraced.

10 *mr Stephens ... ill*: Defoe recounts his confrontation with Robert Stephens in the *Review*, which may have occurred during his two-day return in Sept. or when he was back for good in Oct.: '*The said* Daniel de Foe *... went, and in the presence of sufficient Witnesses, spoke with the said* Robert Stephens, *the Messenger, as he calls himself, of the Press; and offering himself into his Custody, Demanded of him, if he had receiv'd any Order, to Stop, Take, or Detain him; and he denyed that he had any such Order, notwithstanding he had most openly, and in Villainous Terms, Repeated before, that he would Detain him if he could find him; and he had in a Scandalous manner made Enquiries after him*' (*Review*, I, 508 (4 Nov. 1704)). Defoe recalls 'the barbarous Treatment of a certain Messenger' in this episode two years later (*Review*, III, 701 (16 Nov. 1706)). For Defoe's clashes with Stephens from the 1703 arrest onwards, see John Robert Moore, '"Robin Hog" Stephens: Messenger of the Press', *PBSA* 50 (1956), 381–7.

11 *mr Toke*: The Tory John Toke (1671–1746), MP for East Grinstead. Defoe caricatured the Tacker Toke as the wind-bag '*Tocoksi*' in *The Dyet of Poland* (1705), lines 780–811, *SFS*, I, 366–7. He also derides Toke's followers as '*Tookites*' at line 813, an insult also in *A Hymn to Victory* (1704), line 408, *SFS*, I, 306, and *The Consolidator* (1705), *SFS*, III, 158. It is sometimes assumed by 'smart Rencounter' that Defoe means that he duelled Toke, but this is doubtful. See Novak, 243.

12 *my Last*: Untraced.

13 *sr R Davers*: The Tory Sir Robert Davers (1653–1722), MP for Bury St Edmunds until 1705, then for Suffolk, 1705–22. See Letter 44, note 63.

14 *sr ... Felton*: The Whig Sir Thomas Felton (1649–1709), MP for Bury St Edmunds from 1701 until his death in 1709, indicating that Defoe's information about his health was wrong.

15 *my Name ... Rook &ca.*: See headnote.

16 *Norwch I have Perfectly Dissected*: However, Defoe's Norwich-based correspondent John Fransham implies that Defoe did not reach Norwich: 'I heard you were within a few miles of Norwich and had it not been for the impertinence of a News-Writer had made us a visit' (Letter 21).

17 *Lyn*: King's Lynn.

18 *mr Fox ... Secretarys Office*: Joseph Fox (*c.* 1663–1746), bookseller at the Seven Stars, Westminster. His obituary said he was 'eminent for sending written News Letters to most parts of the Three Kingdoms' (*General Advertiser*, 25 Nov. 1746). Defoe wrote to Hedges (letter untraced) as well as to Harley (*Review*, I, 507 (4 Nov. 1704); III, 700 (16 Nov. 1706)). However, there is no known connection of Fox to either Secretary's office. Defoe later advertised his magnanimity regarding Fox: 'I have ... been so civil, that I gave him no Trouble on that Score, which I might well have done, having, I think, very good Proof of it' (*Review*, III, 700 (16 Nov. 1706)). Fox was later one of the printers of Defoe's *A Hymn to the Mob* (1715).

19 *you Dislik'd another man upon that head*: Healey's suggestion that this refers to John Tutchin for his criticisms of the conduct of the war is plausible (*Letters*, ed. Healey, 60 n. 2), though it is plausible Defoe is himself 'another man' if Harley did not know that he wrote *The Master Mercury*. Defoe is perhaps saying he forbore publishing the enclosure to Letter 11.

20 *fight or Victory at Sea*: The Battle of Vélez-Málaga (13 Aug. 1704), the largest naval engagement of the war, in which the French failed to retake Gibraltar and retreated. Defoe's here calling it a 'fight or Victory' reflects his deliberate tergiversation on the question of Rooke's success in the *Review* (see headnote to this letter).

21 *Improvemt*: See Letter 15, note 12.

22 *Restrains me On that head*: Perhaps meaning the non-publication of the attack on Rooke Defoe sent to Harley (Letter 11).

23 *Gentlemen ... Month*: MPs to London for the new parliamentary session.

24 *Mr Chris: Hurt*: See Letter 11.

25 *want*: do without.

26 *Key Man*: I.e. 'quay man'.

27 *Alexandr Goldsmith*: Defoe's pseudonym; this is his first known use of it, though see Letter 10, note 13.

105

DEFOE TO [GABRIEL ROGERS?], [SEPTEMBER–OCTOBER 1704?]

28 *mr John Morleys in Bury*: Morley (1656–1732), a broker and later agent for the Earls of Oxford;
he was Defoe's distribution agent in 1706. See Letter 46; Rogers, 'Distribution Agents', 153–4.
In *A Brief Deduction of the Original, Progress, and Immense Greatness of the British Woollen
Manufacture* (1727), Defoe illustrates how the names of Flemish migrants to Britain were
anglicised, one example being '*Jean de Morlaix* is now *John Morley*' (17).

19

To [Gabriel Rogers?]
[September–October 1704?]¹

HEADNOTE **(Letters 19 and 20):** Defoe's letter to Samuel Elisha at the end of
August (Letter 16) mentioned 'mr Rogers'; Letter 19, whose addressee is uncertain,
seems to be written to a Shrewsbury associate, as it mentions James Owen and
Elisha. On that basis, and with the reference to books being sent, I follow Healey
in provisionally naming Gabriel Rogers as the correspondent.² As Letter 20, to
Elisha, indicates, Rogers took subscriptions in Shrewsbury for Defoe's *Jure Divino*
(1706).

Sr

I am Much Concern'd That yᵉ books are Not Come to hand. I
was Out of Town when they were Sent but They were Delivr'd at yᵉ
Falcon without Aldersgate.³ I hope you have yᵐ before this Comes
to hand, Elċe please to Give me Notiċe that I May Enquire for yᵐ.

I as Much Long To See you, where you Tell me of Friends I have
No Merit to Purchase Nor Reason to Expect, but fear yᵉ Season is
too farr spent to Expect it. Pray give my Serviċe to all that Think me
worth their Concern and Let yᵐ kno' if I Live Till spring I Purpose
to give Them Trouble Enough. My Due Respects and Serviċe to mr
Owen⁴ and Mr Elisha.⁵

I am
yoʳ hearty Frᵈ & Servᵗ
DeFoe

DEFOE TO [SAMUEL ELISHA], 11 OCTOBER 1704

Jure Divino[6] goes on. Pray forget it Not.

One of my letters about y[e] Battail[7] are here Enclosed.

Text: MS untraced. The copytext is a photostat copy at Yale University, Sterling Memorial Library, RU 387, file 7.[8] *Address*: none on the copy.

1   If Gabriel Rogers is indeed the recipient, Defoe's request that Elisha remind Rogers about *Jure Divino* on 11 Oct. (Letter 20) seems like a follow-up.
2   See Letter 16, note 4; *Letters*, ed. Healey, 62–3.
3   *y[e] Falcon without Aldersgate*: The Castle and Falcon, Aldersgate Street, from which wagons departed to the West Midlands.
4   *m[r] Owen*: James Owen (1654–1706), a Presbyterian clergyman in Shrewsbury. His *Moderation a Virtue* (1703), which argued in favour of occasional conformity by invoking Christ as the originator of the practice, was politely but firmly rebutted by Defoe in *The Sincerity of the Dissenters Vindicated, from the Scandal of Occasional Conformity* (1703). Defoe commended Owen's candour, judgement, and honest principles (sig. A2r); he invoked Owen's book in a complimentary fashion in *Review*, VIII, 544 (27 Dec. 1711).
5   *Mr Elisha*: See Letter 16.
6   *Jure Divino*: Defoe had conceived of his political poem by July 1704: an anonymous letter to Harley dated 5 July states 'De Foe's book will be called y[e] history of Superstition & is allready subscribed forr by many' (BL Add. MS. 70021, fol. 149). In the poem's preface he states that most of it was written in prison in 1703 (*SFS*, 11, 63). It was not published until July 1706.
7   *letters about the Battail*: The enclosure is untraced; it could have been *A Hymn to Victory* or a periodical essay from the *Review* or *The Master Mercury* about Blenheim. In *Master Mercury*, no. 9 (4 Sept. 1704), 34–5, Defoe printed a supposedly intercepted letter from a French officer in the wake of Blenheim, so the enclosure could conceivably have been something similar.
8   The original was auctioned by Sotheby's to Maggs Brothers for £125 from the library of an unidentified gentleman on 15 Dec. 1935 (*A Catalogue of Valuable Printed Books and Fine Bindings* (1931), 47; Secord, 47).

20

To [Samuel Elisha]

11 October 1704

S[r]

I have yo[r] kind Letter[1] and had Answerd it sooner but I have been Out of Town for above 3 Weeks.

DEFOE TO [SAMUEL ELISHA], 11 OCTOBER 1704

What Treatm^t I have had since I have been Abroad you will See in ye Review where I have been Oblig'd to Vindicate my Self by an Advertisement,[2] and had Not ye Malice of people Reported me fled from justice, wch made me think it Necessary to Come up and sho' my Self, I dont kno' but I might ha given you a short Visit.

I am Glad to hear you had ye Hymns[3] and Thank your Acceptance of the single One but I must own my self Sorry m^r Rogers is leaving you.[4]

I Thank you for yor kind proposall but tho' I have a Family Large Enough would not have my useless Accquaintance Burthensome to my Friends, Especially you of whom I have been Capable to meritt Very Little.

I Rejoyce that I shall see you in Town and wish you a good journey up — I beg ye favour of you to Remind m^r Rogers of Jure Divino wch Now Draws near putting forward.[5]

I am

S^r

yor Oblig'd Humble Servt

DF

Octobr. 11. 1704

Text: Pierpont Morgan Library, New York, MA 788.[6] *Address*: none.

1   *Letter*: Untraced.
2   *Advertisement*: See headnote to Letter 18 and *Review*, 1, 429–30, 436 (7 and 10 Oct. 1704).
3   *Hymns*: Copies of Defoe's *A Hymn to Victory*. See Letter 16.
4   *mr Rogers is leaving you*: Likely Gabriel Rogers (see Letter 19). Pat Rogers wonders if Defoe alludes to Gabriel Rogers's impending death, though the reminder that follows suggests not ('Distribution Agents', 157 n. 39).
5   *Jure Divino ... putting forward*: Rogers took subscriptions in Shrewsbury for *Jure Divino*. The poem was first announced as 'To be Printed by Subscription' in the *Review* on 26 Sept. 1704, 'The Price to be Ten Shillings, Half a Crown only to be paid Down, the Remainder on Delivery'; subscriptions were taken in across London and 'at most of the Principal Towns in England' (1, 381–2).
6   For a facsimile reproduction of the letter, see Verlyn Klinkenborg, Herbert Cahoon, and Charles Ryskamp, *British Literary Manuscripts, Series I, From 800 to 1800* (New York, 1981), item 61.

21

John Fransham to Defoe

[early October 1704][1]

HEADNOTE: John Fransham (*c.* 1670–1753) was a Dissenter and linen-draper in Norwich. We only know of his correspondence with Defoe between 1704 and 1707. One of the letters, from spring 1706, implies that they had a professional relationship from Defoe's days as a hose factor.[2] Fransham distributed Defoe's works in Norwich. His own literary efforts include contributions to *The Gentleman's Journal* in the 1690s and two whiggish polemics in 1710: *The Criterion: Or, A Touchstone, by which to Judge of the Principles of High and Low-Church* and *A Dialogue between Jack High and Will Low.* He wrote to *The Spectator* on the death of his wife in 1712, and Richard Steele (1672–1729) expanded his letter into *Spectator* no. 520.[3] Two further works have been attributed to Fransham: *An Exact Account of the Charge for Supporting the Poor in the City of Norwich* (1720) and *The World in Miniature: or, The Entertaining Traveller* (1740). He was later the rental agent to Horatio Walpole (1678–1757), the future prime minister's brother.

Sir, — I have sent you a List of the Subscribers to your Book[4] wch I have procur'd in our Town pursuant to the request you made me. I could have wish'd it longer and can assure you there was nothing wanting on my part to have made it so but when I consider First how few there are amongst Tradesmen of wch our City chiefly consists that set any great value upon Books, secondly of such as do, how many have resolv'd never to subscribe for a Book again having been bit in former Subscriptions,[5] Thirdly that the greatest part of this City would have subscribed for the contrary subject,[6] and lastly of them that like the undertaking how many of them that like their Money much better; I say when I consider these several Classes I flatter myself that you'll think I have done tollerably well.

I heard you were within a few miles of Norwich and had it not been for the impertinence of a News-Writer[7] had made us a visit. I wish you had put your designe in execution upon a double account, one the pleasure of your conversation, the other the increasing the List, for an Authors presence you know do much. If you had been here as this day you might have read in Dyers Letter[8] the following paragraph, 'The Weaver in Spittlefields that was taken up for dispersing a poem call'd the Address is admitted to Bail[9] by my

109

JOHN FRANSHAM TO DEFOE, [EARLY OCTOBER 1704]

Ld C. Just. Holt,[10] but his Tenant M^r De Foe is absconded so that a Messenger can't get to speak wth him notwithstanding he falsly asserts the contrary in his Review.'[11] T is possible (seeing it seems that you have not his Letter in London[12]) that this may prove a piece of News to you wch is all that you can be at present furnisht with by

S^r, your humble Servt
JNO. FRANSHAM.

Text: MS untraced. The copytext is Norgate, 261. *Address*: none recorded.

1 The date is inferred from Fransham's reference to reading the news of Sammen's bail, which was granted on 5 Oct.
2 Letter 49.
3 *New Letters to the Tatler and Spectator*, ed. Richmond P. Bond (Austin, Tex., 1959), 158–9.
4 *your Book*: *Jure Divino*.
5 *bit in former Subscriptions*: I.e. they had subscribed for a book that never appeared.
6 *contrary subject*: I.e. the divine right of monarchs, the doctrine that *Jure Divino* attacks.
7 *News-Writer*: Joseph Fox (see Letter 18).
8 *Dyers Letter*: The manuscript newsletter of the Tory journalist John Dyer (*c*. 1653–1713). See Henry L. Snyder, 'Newsletters in England, 1689–1715, with Special Reference to John Dyer: A Byway in the History of England', in *Newsletters to Newspapers: Eighteenth-Century Journalism*, ed. D. H. Bond and W. R. McLeod (Morgantown, W. Va., 1977), 3–19. No copy of the issue Fransham describes has been located.
9 *Weaver … Bail*: Defoe's satirical poem *The Address* (1704), *PEW*, II, 67–76. On 28 Sept. 1704, Secretary of State Sir Charles Hedges wrote to Harley: 'I have taken up ye disperser of the Address, one Sam̃en a weaver, a tool of De Foes, I can yet get nothing out of him against others, but I have sufficient evidence against him' (BL Add. MS. 70021, fol. 287). For Sammen's arrest (27 Sept. 1704), examination, and bail (5 Oct. 1704), see TNA SP 44/349, fol. 171; TNA SP 34/5, fol. 69; TNA SP 44/105, fol. 135. Defoe had been arrested at Sammen's house the previous year (see Letter 2).
10 *Ld C. Just. Holt*: Sir John Holt (1642–1710), Lord Chief Justice from 1689. When in the *Review* for 20 Apr. 1710 Defoe imagines the Whig establishment as an army with Spanish-sounding names, '*Don John de Holtio*' leads a squadron that represents the nation's lawyers (VII, 60).
11 *asserts the contrary in his Review*: This seemingly alludes to Defoe's denial earlier in the year of writing the prose pamphlet *Legion's Humble Address to the Lords*, rather than the poem now at issue, *The Address* (see Letter 9). At that time Defoe also denied having absconded, facetiously offering to show himself for public view 'Two Pence a time, *the Price of seeing a Monkey*' (*Review*, I, 168–9 (3 June 1704)). Defoe subsequently denied authorship of *The Address* in his letter to Dyer of 17 June 1710 (Letter 144), but he probably was its author (F&O, *Bibliography*, 51–2).
12 *you have not his Letter in London*: Dyer's *News-Letter* was not circulated in London. As Defoe said, 'By concealing his Letter in *London*, [Dyer] spreads continued Reproaches on the Government, round the Country' (*Review*, II, 493 (11 Aug. 1705)). Two years later, he wrote: 'As to *Dyer's* Letter, he was always Careful that it should not be seen in *London*, whether for Shame or Fear is not Material … and the Letter not being to be had in the City, he is not so easily contradicted' (*Dyers News Examined as to His Sweddish Memorial against the Review* (1707), 4).

22

To [Robert Harley]

2 November 1704

HEADNOTE: The new session of parliament commenced on 24 October 1704. Despite the fillip of Blenheim, the Godolphin ministry was insecure. The deadlocked situation with Scotland over the succession rumbled on now that the Act of Security had passed there, threatening Scotland's rejection of the Hanoverian succession.[1] In England, another divisive Tory bill against occasional conformity was anticipated.[2] Godolphin sought to hold sway with the moderate interest of his own, Harley's, and Marlborough's followers, as well as the Queen's servants (placeholders loyal to the Court).[3] However, with the dismissal of Seymour and resignation of Nottingham since parliament last sat, the ministry had ceased to represent the Tory party as a whole and had not yet forged alliances with the Whigs. It had no reliable control of either House and a Whig–Tory alliance was a real danger, with Harley the likely victim of such 'a Conjunccon of Extreams', as Defoe terms it. Defoe in his capacity of advisor had two suggestions: court Lord Somers of the Whig Junto; and divide those extremists by encouraging an occasional bill that the ministry could ultimately quash ('bring it in by Trusty hands, and blast it at last'). We have no Defoe–Harley correspondence after this letter for around seven months.

Sr

I am Very Shye of Burthening you with Triffles while ye Naçons Burthens Load you but <u>Pardon me</u> That I am Extremely Sollicitous on yor Accot; If it be So yt My Low staçon Renders my Conçern Very Useless to you, yet I Shall Not less show My Sincere Endeavour, and at worst Incur yor Censure as Impertinent Not as Unfaithfull.

The Freedome you Allwayes gave me, and which I Think it was Never More my Duty to Take, Oblidges me to Talk to you, in Terms Too Course for ye Distançe between yor Character, yor Person, yor Merit, <u>and Me</u>. I Beseech you Plaçe my want of Deçençy, to ye Accot of my Passion if Possible to Render you Serviçe.

I wish for an Occasion to Show you by any thing besides This Cheap Empty way of word Serviçe, what I would Do, Suffer, or Risque for your advantage, That ye Sincerity wth wch my Soul is Swell'd For your Serviçe Might by Some Demonstraçon Challenge

DEFOE TO [ROBERT HARLEY], 2 NOVEMBER 1704

yor belief; and I Might if Possible Discharge My Self of ye weighty Debt of Gratitude, and Please mÿ Self wth haveing Done Something worthy of you obligeing, and of me Oblig'd, beyond The Comõn Rate of Service and Obligaćon.

Among ye Croud of Things wch Press my Thoughts, and ye Various Wayes my Impotence of Thought Offers both to Discharge my Exceeding Obligaćon, and if possible be Usefull to So bountifull a benefactor, admit s^r as ye best I Can offer a Genuine Candid Observaćon On ye Publick Affaires as Und^r your Conduct — and yet who Am I that I Should Pretend to Advise you, Quallifyed to Advise a Naćon.

It Wounds me to ye Soul to hear ye Very whigs Themselves, and who for Saying So I Fancy in ye Confederacy[4] wch you hinted you had Some Notice of, Tell Me and Speak it Openly <u>you are Lost</u>, That yor Intrest in ye house wont keep you in ye Chair, That ye Party Suppressing you There, will Consequently Ruin yor Intrest in The [Queen's favour, and give a new turn to your management at Court.][a]

I Confess it Fills me with Indignaćon, to hear This Spoken wth an Air of Satisfaction, by a Party who Ought to kno', if blindness From Heaven had Not Seiz'd Their Understandings, That in yor Fall <u>Pardon my Calling it So</u> from ye Mannagem^t, The Ruin of Their Intrest is as Effectually Contain'd as tis Possible for Consequences to be in Their Originall Causes.

But ye Children of Light were allwayes Darker in Temporalls, than ye Rest of their Neighbours,[5] and we are willing to be Fools to please Our Fancys, tho' to ye Destrucćion of Our Judgements, but above all They are ye Most Implacable in Censure, — and They Can Not believ M^r H . . . honest, and True to ye Moderate Intrest, because They Once Thought him Otherwise;[6] But ye Principall Reason I Find, because They Saw[b] themselves in The Case of ye Disciples, who were Dissapointed when they Found Our Lord Did Not Restore ye Temporall Kingdome to Israell,[7] or like ye Mother of Zebedees Children who look't to have Them[c] all to be Lord

[a] [Queen's favour, and give a new turn to your management at Court.]] *illegible due to MS binding; text supplied from H.M.C. Portland MSS,* IV, *147*
[b] Saw] *interlined above cancelled word* 'find'
[c] to have Them] *interlined*

DEFOE TO [ROBERT HARLEY], 2 NOVEMBER 1704

Chancellors, and Lord Treasurers, and One to Sitt on yᵉ Right hand and yᵉ Other on yᵉ left, and were Angry Our Lord Did Not Grant it, Tho' he Declar'd <u>it was None of his to give</u>.[8]

I Rejoyċe Sʳ That I have had yᵉ honour of Doeing yoʳ Character Justiċe, and have Some Converts to boast of, but as my Little Merit Shall be yᵉ Last Thing Ile Plead, So Sʳ I Onely hint it Now to Let you kno' The blemish as they would have it be Call'd on you as a Person Not in yᵉ Right Intrest, has had a Vast Extent, and Requires Some Conduct to Rase Out; Pardon me Sʳ had your Enemys Nothing to boast of[a] but yᵉ Voiċe of Our Foolish Friends, I Grant this Not worth yoʳ Notiċe, but as it is[b] Apt to fall in wᵗʰ Other Capitall Mischiefs It Merits yoʳ Consideraċon, and Some Methods to Suppress it.

If you'l allow yᵉ Vanity of yᵉ Expression, <u>If I were a Publick Minister</u> I would if Possible kno' what Every body Said of me, and I have formerly Instanċ'd Cardˡˡ Richlieu to you on that head;[9] Please sʳ to give me leav tho'[c] yᵉ words shock my Soul as I write yᵐ and I believ yᵐ to be Impotent Forgerys, yet to Repeat Them that you may Make use of yᵐ as you See Cause.

"Mʳ Harley is <u>Out</u>, he has <u>Lost</u> his Intrest, yᵉ house will Certainly <u>lay him by</u>, and if There be Nothing Elċe in it, 'tis a Tryall of yᵉ Strength of yᵉ house, and a Proof he <u>has lost Ground</u>; besides both Sides are against him, he has Trim'd So Long On both Sides, and Caress't both Partys, Till both begin to See themselves ill Treated, and Now as he Loves Neither Side, Neither Side will Stand by him; All yᵉ Whigs of King William[s][d] Reign Expected to ha' Come In Play Again, and had Fair words Given Them, but They See it was but Wording them into a Fools Paradise, and Now The Two Ends will be Reconċil'd to Overturn his Middle Way.[10]

"If he is Out of yᵉ Chair They will Soon Work him Out of yᵉ Seales, and yᵉ Lord Godolphin Out of The Treasury." They Call The Duke of Marlebro', My Lᵈ Treasurer and your Self <u>yᵉ Triumvirate</u> who Mannage yᵉ State,[11] and That if This knot be broke in yᵉᵉ

---

[a] Nothing to boast of] *interlined*
[b] is] *interlined above cancelled illegible word*
[c] tho'] *interlined*
[d] William[s]] *MS frayed*
[e] broke in yᵉ] *following word* 'State' *cancelled*

113

DEFOE TO [ROBERT HARLEY], 2 NOVEMBER 1704

House First, They will prevail wth ye Queen to Continue ye Duke of M abroad, all This winter, Under Pretence of Goeing to Concert Measures wth ye Princes of The Empire,[12] and So they will Easyly Put by all This scheme of Mannagement.

This Ridiculous Stuff had Never Reach't yor Eares if I had Not Observ'd Some^a Coherence between it and what you were pleas'd to Mencon to me [w]as^b Design'd, and by wch it Seems Either to be publickly Concerted or at least Concluded and Talkt on as a Thing finished.

As Our Friends[13] were allwayes Fools, it Amazes me to hear Them Promise Themselves a Generall Ease^c On a Capitulacon wth ye high Church, Liberty, Occasionall Licence, and God knows what.

I Shall give you No Comments On This Ungratefull Text, I leave it To yor Sedate Thought; I Struggle wth my Uttmost to Expose ye Folly of it, and wth Encourageing Success, Nor is it ye Danger to you from These people I hear Discourse that would ha' Mov'd me thus far to assume a Post that So ill becomes me, But as These Little Capilary Veins of Mallice, Reciev ye Little Venome They Contain, from Some Fountain of Larger Dimension, so I Recomend That Fountain to yor Discovery and Prevencon.

I Remember s^r when haveing had ye honor to Serve y^e <u>Late king William</u> in a kind like this,[14] and which his Maj^tie had ye Goodness to Accept, and Over Vallue by Far, Expressing Some Concern at ye Clamour and Power of The Party, at his Express Command I had ye heart or Face or what Elce you will Please to Call it to give my [Opinion]^d in Terms like These.

> "Your Maj^tie Must Face About, Oblige yor Friends to be Content to be Laid by, and Put In your Enemyes; Put y^m into Those Posts in which They may Seem to be Employd, and Thereby Take off ye Edge and Divide The Party."[15]

---

^a Some] *following letters* 'Cho' *cancelled*
^b [w]as] *it is unclear whether* 'w' *has been deliberately cancelled or accidentally blotted; both* 'as' *and* 'was' *are plausible readings*
^c Ease] *following word* 'and' *cancelled*
^d [Opinion]] *illegible due to MS binding*

DEFOE TO [ROBERT HARLEY], 2 NOVEMBER 1704

Twould be an Unsufferable Vanity to Offer you ye Detail of That Affair, but s^r ye End of Thus Arrogantly Quoteing My Self is as Follows.

Sr The whigs are weak; they may be Mannag'd, and Allways have been So.

What Ever you do if Possible Divide Them, and they are Easy To be Divided.

Caress The Fools of Them Most, There are Enough Among Them.

Buy Them wth here and There a Pláce, it may be well bestowd.

If you have him Not allready, as all I Can Talk with That are Friends <u>Wish</u> you had, My Ld Somers[16] who all allow to be a great Man, Must if Gaind From Them, weaken and Distract ye Party.

Such a Man Can Not be bought too Dear, and if Gaind Entirely would Secure your Intrest.

'Tis Pitty Two Such Men Should Not Understand One Another[17] (if it be So). <u>United</u>, what may you Not do! <u>Divided</u>, what Mischiefs Must Ensue to both, and ye Naćon in Generall!

[S]^r[a] I Humbly Entreat your Accepting These hints. Tis my Fear of a Conjuncćon of Extreams, wch are Doubled from The Connexion of what I hear Abroad and what you Observ'd; They Talk of This Conjuncćon as of a Thing done, and you would wonder at ye Follys and hopes Some Weak People Discover at This Novelty.

I have had Some Thoughts,[b] Tho' it be but a Project,[18] That ye bringing an Occasionall Bill[19] upon The Anvill in Such a juncture would be of ye last Serviće in This Case; Twould break ye Confederaćy, Twould blacken, and Expose The Party, yours Are Sure of giveing it a Toss at last, and There are a Croud of Present Advantages[20] to be made of it.

To bring it in by Trusty hands, and blast it at last, would Confound the Thing it Self, Ruine all ye Confederaćy, Brand ye Party wth ye Scandall of Opposeing ye Queen, and breaking their Promise in The Address;[21] Twould Sink Their Character, and They would go home wth Such a Fame, as would Cause Fewer of The

---

[a] [S]^r] *MS cut*
[b] Thoughts] *following word* 'and' *cancelled*

115

Same Men to Come back Again Next session than may otherwise be Expected.[22]

These Two Things have Layn So Strongly on my Thoughts, allways Employ'd and Sollicitous to Serve yor Intrest, That I Could Not Satisfye my Self without giveing you ye Trouble of Peruseing Them, and Pardon me S^r if I Say, I Think I write of Them wth More Earnestness, and Concern, Than I Should If I were Peticoning you for a Repriev from ye Gallows.

I Beseech you Sr Place it all To ye Acco^t of my Zeal to Serve you, and to Prevent if Possible a Publick Disaster to ye Nacon, wch I Think must be ye Consequence of a blow to yor Present Greatness, and Conduct, to whom we all Owe Much of, if not all ye Present Prosperity of England.

I have Some Subsequent Thoughts On This Subject, wch if This Pleases you you May Command at a Word, as you allways May

S^r

yor Most Obedient Servt

[*monogram*]

Nov. 2. 1704

Text: BL Add. MS. 70291, fols. 22–6. *Address*: none.

1 *APS*, XI, 136.
2 Godolphin was vulnerable because he had advised giving royal assent to the Act of Security just days before news of Marlborough's victory at Blenheim reached London, making that concession to the Scottish parliament look extremely unnecessary.
3 Holmes, 373–4.
4 *Confederacy*: Between Whigs and Tories in opposition to the ministry.
5 *Children ... Neighbours*: Luke 16:8. Defoe alludes to this verse again in *Review*, v, 113 (15 May 1708).
6 *Mr H ... ... Otherwise*: See Letter 14, note 46. Defoe alludes again to Harley's time in the Country opposition to the Court during the 1690s, during which Harley criticised 'new' Whigs prepared to take office instead of remaining in permanent opposition. See Downie, *Robert Harley*, 21–3; Hill, 17–61. For a hostile contemporaneous take on Harley's moderation, see 'Moderation Display'd', lines 153–96, *POAS*, VII, 30–1.
7 *Disciples ... Israell*: Acts 1:6.
8 *Mother ... give*: Matt. 20:20–7.
9 *on that head*: See Letter 14.
10 *Mr Harley ... Way*: See the assessment of Harley's situation by James Vernon (1646–1727): 'The Tories lay the late changes at his door, and the Whigs hold themselves in suspence, not seeing any advances made towards them' (Vernon to Shrewsbury, 26 May 1704, *Vernon Corr.*, III, 260).

DEFOE TO [ROBERT HARLEY], 2 NOVEMBER 1704

11 *Triumvirate who Mannage y̆e State*: See Stanley West's letter to Harley of 29 Aug. 1704: 'The Duke, the Treasurer and yourself are called the Triumvirate, and reckoned the spring of all public affairs' (H.M.C. *Portland MSS*, IV, 119).

12 *Duke ... Empire*: After campaigning in Bavaria, Marlborough returned to Britain via a detour to Berlin and Hanover in order to persuade Britain's allies to commit more troops (*Marl.– God. Corr.*, I, 391–410). Defoe alludes to Marlborough's diplomatic journey within a lengthy panegyric on the Duke in *Jure Divino*, book XII, lines 282–92, *SFS*, II, 353. Marlborough arrived in London on 14 Dec., and Defoe's poem *The Double Welcome* appeared in Jan. 1705, celebrating Marlborough's foreign victories and the end to party strife at home that Defoe hoped his return would herald.

13 *Friends*: The Whigs in general or perhaps the Dissenters in particular.

14 *Serve ... this*: In the *Review* for 22 Feb. 1711, Defoe wrote: 'I have, within these 20 Years past, Travelled, I think I may say, to every Nook and Corner of that part of the Island, call'd *England*, either upon Publick Affairs, when I had the Honour to serve his late Majesty King *William*, of Glorious, (tho' forgotten) Memory – Or upon my private Affairs' (VII, 630–1).

15 *Your Majᵗⁱᵉ ... Party*: Compare the advice given in Letter 14.

16 *Lᵈ Somers*: Somers was Lord Chancellor under William III and a member of the Whig Junto. He and Harley were in conflict several times during the 1690s (see E. L. Ellis, 'The Whig Junto in Relation to the Development of Party Politics and Party Organization, from its Inception to 1714' (University of Oxford PhD, 1962)). Defoe admired Somers. He denounced the abortive impeachment of Somers in 1701 as a partisan Tory measure (*Legion's Memorial* (1701), *PEW*, II, 43; *The Consolidator* (1705), *SFS*, III, 146–7; *Review*, III, 209 (4 Apr. 1706); *The Felonious Treaty* (1711), *PEW*, V, 162).

   Though *persona non grata* with Queen Anne and removed from the Privy Council at her accession, Somers and the Whigs led in the House of Lords conscientiously supported the ministry in its prosecution of the war. By the start of the 1704–5 session, he and the Whigs were optimistic of gaining greater sway with the ministry (William L. Sachse, *Lord Somers: A Political Portrait* (Manchester, 1986), 226–7).

   Defoe's admiration for Somers found expression in panegyrical sections of two poems he was writing at the time of this letter: *The Dyet of Poland*, lines 246–53, *SFS*, I, 351–2; *Jure Divino*, book XII, lines 85–106, *SFS*, II, 347–8. In *Dyet* he praises Somers as '*Rigatski*', a name alluding to Somers's property in Reigate: 'High Chancellor in *Sobieski's* [William III's] Reign; | *And all true* Poles *would have him so again*' (lines 248–9).

17 *'Tis Pitty ... Another*: According to Hill, 91: 'In great secrecy [Harley] made tentative, and on the whole unproductive contact with Somers for the first time since 1701, though when the move inevitably became public it aroused Godolphin's jealousy.' Harley made firmer overtures to the more moderate Whig, the Duke of Newcastle, who was eventually approved by Godolphin, Marlborough, and Anne and eventually appointed in Mar. 1705 as Lord Privy Seal in place of Buckingham (H.M.C. *Portland MSS*, II, 186–9; Marlborough to Godolphin, 23 Oct. 1704, *Marl.–God. Corr.*, I, 392).

18 *Project*: The negative connotations of this word in Defoe's time can be gauged by two publications thirty years apart. In *An Essay upon Projects* (1697), Defoe distinguishes the various innovations his book proposes from 'Projects fram'd by subtle Heads, with a sort of *Deceptio Visus*' (*PEW*, VIII, 38). In *The Protestant Monastery* (1726), Defoe prefaces his proposal for a kind of co-operative retirement home by stating that '*a Projector*' is '*the most contemptible Character in this Part of the World*' (*PEW*, VIII, 239).

19 *Occasionall Bill*: The third Occasional Conformity Bill was introduced on 23 Nov. 1704. The Court and ministry opposed it as a divisive distraction from the prosecution of the war (Godolphin to Harley, 16 Nov. 1704, H.M.C. *Bath MSS*, I, 64–5).

20 *Present Advantages*: Defoe's suggestion that Harley encourage the bill, so as to quash it as a means of dividing his opponents, accords with evidence that Harley did advise Tory leaders to 'tack' the bill to the land tax. Tacking was controversial, as the Lords traditionally did not interfere with money bills and would not wish to jeopardise war supplies, so Harley could

117

have anticipated the backlash that did indeed ensue. The Tack was defeated in the Commons thanks to Harley's manouevres. 'Un-tacked', the occasional bill was again rejected by the Lords. Pittis alleged that Harley 'design'd to draw [the Tories] into a snare' (*The Proceedings of Both Houses of Parliament, in the Years 1702, 1703, 1704, upon the Bill to Prevent Occasional Conformity* (1710), 57). The allegation was repeated by Boyer, 161, and *An Impartial History of the Occasional Conformity and Schism Bills*, 2nd ed. (1718), 63. A letter from Sir John Pakington (1671–1727), a Tory proponent of the occasional bill, suggests Harley had confided to him his support for the bill (BL Add. MS. 29579, fol. 507; *HPC 1690–1715*, v, 67). Though it may be a *post hoc* explanation, Defoe also suggests the same in print, saying of the Tackers that Harley 'push'd them upon those Follies and Extravagances, which at the same time they ruin'd their Cause, expos'd their Politicks, turn'd 'em off the Stage, and made Fools of 'em too. ... That Great States-man handed them on to their Occasional Bills, Tackings, Dangerous Experiments, &c. and seeing beyond their Reach, drove them like *Solomon's* Fool, to the Correction of the Stocks, and made their Fury their Destruction' (*Remarks on the Letter to the Author of the State-Memorial* (1706), 30). He obliquely says the same thing in *Review*, VII, 95 (9 May 1710).
21 *Promise in The Address*: The Commons's address to the Queen of 30 Oct. pledged 'to prevent all divisions among us, and will have no contention, but who shall most promote and establish the public welfare, both in church and state' (Cobbett, VI, 357).
22 *Fewer ... Expected*: In the general election to take place in the summer of 1705.

23

John Fransham to Defoe

10 November 1704

HEADNOTE **(Letters 23 and 24)**: In November and December 1704, Defoe was engaged in opposing the Tory-dominated House of Commons's attempt to 'tack' legislation to prevent occasional conformity to a land tax bill that the Lords could not reject. It remains uncertain whether Harley encouraged the revival of the Occasional Bill as a tactic to divide the ministry's opponents, as Defoe proposed. But thanks to Harley's canvassing among moderate Tories, the Commons rejected the Tack at the end of November. When the Occasional Bill was sent up by itself it was soundly defeated in the Lords.[1] In December, Defoe started on *The Consolidator*, his satirical allegory of politics during the early years of Anne's reign, and he wrote against Sir Humphrey Mackworth's proposals for parochial factories to employ the poor. Defoe's correspondence with Fransham provides further evidence of Defoe's developing network of distribution agents for his *Review* and his occasional pamphlets in towns outside of London, which came to fuller fruition in 1705 and 1706.

> Sir, — It was with no small Sattisfaction that I read your Justification in your Review wch I doubt not on the other hand

118

JOHN FRANSHAM TO DEFOE, 10 NOVEMBER 1704

prov'd as great a Mortification to Dyer.[2] I had read it to several Gentlemen (before I receiv'd your Letter) in the chief Coffee-house[3] here where we have it as oft as it comes out and is approv'd of as the politest paper we have to entertain us with. I had some difficulty to prevail with the Master of the house to take it in but now he finds I advis'd him well, there being no paper more desir'd. If there be any that you have a mind to convey to Norwich, if it be left at my Brō: Franshams[4] and you let me know, I'll take care to have it down.

Dyer lets us know yesterday that the Observator was found Guilty and hopes that he will be exemplarily punish'd,[5] but were there such scales as could weigh Incendiaries exactly into wch put a Tutchin in one scale and a Dyer in the other and I doubt not 'twould appear that the lowest scale contain'd the lightest man.

I have nothing of news to impart but only that 2 or 3 nights since one of our worthy Justices being at the Coffee-house above nam'd was inform'd by some of the company that there was a very topping address in the Gazet from Marlborough. Ay, quoth the Justice, has the Duke sent an address? pray Mr M—— I see you have got the Gazet in your hand be so kind as to read me the Dukes address. The Gentleman pursuant to his request read (without the Title, to humour the mistake) the address from Malbrough, wch done his worship said twas a fine address truly, and so (to the great sattisfaction of the company) went away with the opinion that it was sent by the Duke notwithstanding the many high encomiums given his Grace therein. I write you this story not as a subject for your Society[6] to discant upon but only to afford you some diversion in your privet conversation, and whenever your multiplicity of business will permit you to make returns of like nature they will be gladly receiv'd by

Sr yours &c.

J. F.

Norwch Nov. 10, 1704.

Text: MS untraced. The copytext is Norgate, 261. *Address*: none recorded.

1 Henry L. Snyder, 'The Defeat of the Occasional Conformity Bill and the Tack: A Study in the Techniques of Parliamentary Management in the Reign of Queen Anne', *BIHR* 41 (1968), 172–86.

DEFOE TO JOHN FRANSHAM, [2 DECEMBER 1704]

2 *Justification ... Dyer: Review,* I, 507–8, 513 (4 and 7 Nov. 1704).

3 *chief Coffee-house:* The principal coffee houses in Norwich included Drake's, Harvey's, Frome's, and Browne's (Fiona Williamson, *Social Relations and Urban Space: Norwich, 1600–1700* (Woodbridge, 2014), 164–5).

4 *my Brō: Franshams:* Presumably Fransham's elder brother, Isaac (1660–1743), an attorney whose wall monument is in the church of St. Peter Mancroft in Norwich (his will: TNA PROB II/727/161).

5 *Dyer ... punish'd:* Tutchin's reflections on parliament's proceedings led to an arrest warrant in early 1704; he absconded until May when he gave himself up; and he was found guilty on 4 Nov. 1704 (Luttrell, v, 483–4). See Lee Sonsteng Horsley, 'The Trial of John Tutchin, Author of the *Observator*', *Yearbook of English Studies* 3 (1973), 124–40. Newdigate's copy of the 9 Nov. *Dyer's News-Letter* does not mention Tutchin; that dated 7 Nov. reports the conviction though not expectations about the punishment (Folger Shakespeare Library, Newdigate Newsletters, L.c. 2814, 7 Nov. 1704; L.c. 2815, 9 Nov. 1704).

6 *Justices ... Society: London Gazette,* 26–30 Oct. 1704, gave the address from 'the Mayor, Magistrates, and Burgesses, of the Corporation of *Marlborough*' in Wiltshire, which praised the Duke of Marlborough as a '*wise and valiant General*'. Defoe did in fact develop the story for the 'Scandalous Club' section of the *Review,* I, 583 (2 Dec. 1704).

24

To John Fransham

[2 December 1704][1]

Mr. Fransham, — I can now tell you that the dead doing Tool of Occasional Conformity having been brought into the House on Thursday was sevennight last[2] rec'd on Tuesday a fatal blow in the House of Commons by being offer'd to be consolidated or tack'd as they call it to the Land Tax Bill, wch notwithstanding a very great struggle was carried in the negative by 117 voices.[3] It has been to-day before the House as a Bill, and they have made some amendments to it, but we are in hopes that it has had a Death's wound in the last Stroke.[4] Last week I rallyed some Forces against it and brought out some thoughts on that subject in print.[5] I have sent about 25 of them to you and should be glad to hear how our Friends approve it. I have not done this that I would impose any thing of mine on you, but as my purpose of writing is to furnish our Friends with arguments to defend the cause against a clamorous noisy Enemy, so it must be necessary that they should see them as much as possible, and for this purpose we are establishing a method to send them in small parcels amongst Friends all over England.

DEFOE TO JOHN FRANSHAM, [2 DECEMBER 1704]

And yet I am so far from making a profit of it that if any are so poor as not to afford it or too narrow spirited to spare *6d.* I am very free to give them to such rather than they should not be improv'd by any thing I am able to do, and you have my free consent to give them to any body you think fit. I wish I could afford to print twenty thousand of these and give them all over the nation.

If you approve the method and think it worth while you shall have a parcel like this or a few over or under always sent you when I do any thing I think worth your while.

I have now in hand a small piece against Sʳ Humphrey Mackworth's Bill for employing the poor, which unless you contradict I'll send you some of, because it concerns you all as Manufacturers and employers and it is fit when you are to be ruin'd you should know it.[6]

In the Review of today you will find the story of the Justice of peace who thought the Malbrough address was by the Duke.[7] I wish you would send me his name and the story at large. I hope 'tis told to your Sattisfaction. Pray let me know if you receiv'd the Books.

I am, Sʳ, your sincere Friend
DE FOE.

Text: MS untraced. The copytext is Norgate, 261–2. *Address*: none recorded.

1   The date is inferred from Defoe's allusion to the *Review* of 'today', meaning that of Saturday 2 Dec. 1704, as well as references to the progress of the bill to penalise occasional conformity.
2   *Thursday was sevennight last*: Thursday 23 Nov. (*C.J.*, XIV, 433); 'was' could be Norgate's transcription error.
3   *negative by 117 voices*: On Tuesday 28 Nov., the Commons voted against tacking penalties against occasional conformity to the land tax by 251 votes to 134 (*C.J.*, XIV, 437).
4   *Bill … Stroke*: After the failed Tack, the bill to prevent occasional conformity by itself was passed in the Commons but predictably rejected by the Lords.
5   *thoughts on that subject in print*: Healey thought that Defoe referred here to *Queries upon the Bill against Occasional Conformity*, published on 5 Dec. 1704 (*Letters*, ed. Healey, 72 n. 2). But as Furbank and Owens note, that work sold for 2d., not 6d. (the price specified below), and so they propose that he means *The Dissenter Misrepresented and Represented*, a work known only from *A Second Volume of the Writings of the Author of The True-Born Englishman* (1705). See F&O, *Bibliography*, 58–9.
6   *small … know it*: Giving Alms no Charity, published on 18 Nov. 1704, was a response to the Tacker Sir Humphrey Mackworth's (1657–1727) parliamentary bill trying to reform the poor law by establishing municipal workhouses. Defoe's pamphlet objected that this scheme would undercut existing manufacturers, especially in the wool trade, because there was already an abundance of work; strengthening laws against begging would be a more effectual way of

DEFOE TO COMMITTEE OF THE LORDS, [*c.* 30 JANUARY 1705]

employing the poor. Fransham's Norwich is used among the examples Defoe offers of how Mackworth's scheme would hamper manufacture and trade. Defoe attacked Mackworth's proposal in *Review*, I, 614, 618–20 (19 and 23 Dec. 1704), and it was rejected by the Lords in Feb. 1705. Defoe had written against Mackworth before, in *The Original Power of the Collective Body of the People of England* (1701) and *Peace without Union* (1703). And he criticised Mackworth's politics in *Jure Divino* (1706), book VII, lines 388–95, *SFS*, II, 229. He again opposed Mackworth's workhouse scheme when it was reintroduced, again unsuccessfully, in the 1706–7 session (*Review*, IV, 15–65 (15 Feb.–11 Mar. 1707)); and he criticised it again in *Review*, IX, 216 (5 Feb. 1713).

Defoe also attacked Mackworth's mine adventure, a project aiming to extract silver from lead, as a cheat (*Review*, III, 270–4 (30 Apr. 1706); VII, 21–3 (4 Apr. 1710); *A New Test of the Sence of the Nation* (1710), 54; *The Secret History of the October-Club ... Part II* (1711), 5–9, 28).

7   *Review ... Duke*: *Review*, I, 583 (2 Dec. 1704). See Letter 23.

25

To [the Select Committee of the House of Lords]

[*c.* 30 January 1705]

HEADNOTE **(Letters 25–7)**: In late 1704 and early 1705 a select committee of the House of Lords examined naval underperformance. In the *Review* Defoe lamented the 'meer Misconduct, Ignorance, and want of Regulation of our Marine Affairs'.[1] Recollecting his own proposal for better manning the fleet, published in *An Essay upon Projects* (1697), Defoe asks 'what had been sav'd to this Nation, if Methods of Husbandry had been practis'd, and such Regulations had been made, as Mechanick Heads have contriv'd, but our great Managers have scorn'd to adhere to?'[2] His offer in that issue of the periodical to present his proposals was taken up by the select committee, who summoned Defoe on 25 January and requested he submit his proposal by 30 January.

Back in 1697 Defoe had argued that the state should assume a monopoly on employing sailors, who could then be hired out to merchants. He saw in this scheme a way to reduce escalating merchant marine wages, ensure a plenitude of manpower for the fleet, abolish press ganging, reduce desertion and defection, and achieve greater efficiency.[3] In its substance his plan was repeated in this proposal to the Lords. On 10 February it was read to the committee by its chair Charles Powlett, second Duke of Bolton (*c.* 1661–1722), after which Defoe was summoned and asked to write out the scheme in fuller detail for consideration by the Lord High Admiral, Prince George. On 3 March, Bolton 'acquainting the Committee that Mr De Foe desired in reguard the Session was like to be short that he might have time till the next meeting of the Parlt to prepare the schemes lately proposed by

DEFOE TO COMMITTEE OF THE LORDS, [*C.* 30 JANUARY 1705]

him, It is Ordered that Mr D'Foe doe agst the next Session prepare the Schemes he proposed for the more effectual manning the Fleet'. John Relfe (1643–1711), reading clerk at the House of Lords, relayed this to Defoe.

Nothing seems to have come of the proposal. Over twenty years later, Defoe offered his idea to the public again, and the plan proffered in *Some Considerations on the Reasonableness and Necessity of Encreasing and Encouraging the Seamen* (1728) may reflect the final proposal to the Lords in 1704. In *Some Considerations* he states: 'I remember a long and intricate Proposal, once offered to the Publick, in the Reigns of King *William*, and Queen *Anne*, which went so far as to be thought worth considering of by his Royal Highness Prince *George*, then High-Admiral, and to be laid before a Committee of Parliament.' 'It was new, and thought at first to be practicable', Defoe recalls, but 'it was at last declined only upon some Scruples about Liberty and Compulsion, which some nice People, who have got over all these Difficulties in other Cases not less dangerous, pretended to raise. Upon this Foot, I say, it was laid aside, (not rejected) and had the prince lived a little longer would, I believe, have been brought to be practicable.'[4] The related matter of the coal trade was another lifelong interest of Defoe's.[5]

Of The Seamen

Humbly Craveing yor Lordships Pardon if I mistake, I Presume yor Lordships Commands are Included in The Following Question.

Viz^t, How May the Fleet be Mann'd, without ye Delays, Expenĉe, Violenĉes, and Other Intollerable Inconvenienĉes of Impressing Seamen?[6]

It is my Humble Opinion, That Searching for ye Causes of This Evill will Imediately Direct to ye Cure.

The True, and Originall Causes of ye Scarĉity of, or Rather ye Difficulty in Procureing, Seamen, Are These Two.

1/ The Exorbitant, Unreasonable, and in All Respects Disproporĉon'd wages given to Sailors, in ye Serviĉe of The Merchant.

2/ Want of Some Due Measures to Procure Able bodyed Land Men, on any Emergenĉy of State, to Embraĉe Willingly the Serviĉe, and Thereby[a] Encrease the Number of Seamen in Time of war.

The first of these I Humbly Think to be the True, and Perhaps the Onely Reason, why Our Seamen Skulk, and hide Themselves

---

[a] Thereby] *following letters* 'Em' *cancelled*

DEFOE TO COMMITTEE OF THE LORDS, [C. 30 JANUARY 1705]

from the Publick Service; Since it can not be Expected The Sailors Should Covet to Serv the Queen at 23s Per Month, when at The Same time, they can have 55s Per Month in The Service of The Merchant.

This Premis'd I humbly Propose:

That an Act to Limit the Wages of Seamen in The Service of the Merchant May be Passt, wherein a Fixt Rate of Wages Per Month, where ye Custome of Trade is to Sail Per ye Month, and Per ye Voiage where they Sail by the Voiage, and Per Share, where the Sailors are paid by the Share, may be Appointed, Proporcon'd to, and Limited by the Rates Now paid by her Majtie in ye Navy, Or as Near Thereto as to yor Lordships Shall Seem Convenient, with Stated Penaltyes both to Masters, Owners or Seamen, who Shall give or Take beyond it.

If yor Lordships Comand me to Lay before you, any Reasonings on ye Perticulars, or Schemes for ye Performing this, your Orders Shall be Readily Obey'd; The Proposer Not Presumeing to offer Those things without yor Lordships Speciall Direccons.

For ye Supplying wth Land men on any Emergency of The State, The Proposer Humbly Represents:

That ye Act of Parliament Empowring ye Civil Magistrate to List or Enter men into ye Service, has this Defect in it.

That Many Thousands of Able body'd men, Proper Subjects for That act and Perhaps Enclin'd Enough to ye Service, are hindred from Entring or at Least are not oblig'd to Enter as ye Law Directs, The Church wardens, Overseers &c. Screening them from the Law, to prevent Their wives and Children becoming Chargeable[a] to The Parish.[7]

To Rectifye This ye Proposer humbly Offers:

That a Clause be brought in, Empowring The Proper Officers of Every Parish in Case any Man Shall Voluntarily Enter himself into The Service, who has a family in The Said Parish, to Take Such care of, and make Such allowance to Their Said Familyes, as shall be Thought fitt by yor Lordships Dureing Such time as the Said Person Continues in her

---

[a] Chargeable] *the first 'e' is interlined*

DEFOE TO COMMITTEE OF THE LORDS, [*C.* 30 JANUARY 1705]

Maj^ties Service, the Same to be Repaid Out of ye Treasury of ye Navy, or allow'd on Their Taxes, and Discounted Out of ye Pay of ye Person So Serving.

And The Said Paym^t or Such other Pension or Allow^a as Shall be Thought fitt, and for as Long Time to be Continued to ye Said Family in Case The Man should Lose his life, in The Said Service.

This tis Presum'd will not Onely Encourage Great Numbers to List, but will Remove ye Obstruccon, wch Now prevents ye Parish Officers Marking Out those That are Proper, and Some Methods for ye Makeing this yet more Effectuall shall be Laid before your Lordships if yor Commands Require Them.

By This Method the Proposer Humbly Supposes, at Least Ten Thousand able body'd Land men may be Rais'd, on Any Emergency for ye Publick Occasion without Force, Charge, or Oppression.[8]

Another Method Every way as Certain and in all its Parts
Superiour to any yet Practis'd Either here
Or Abroad
is as Follows

By an Act to Cause all ye Seamen in England at Once to be Entred into ye Publick Service, and Imediate Pay.

Under This Regulacon The proposer Offers to Satisfye yor Lordships:

1. The Navy Shall at any Time be Compleatly Mann'd at a Months Notice, all ye Seamen in ye Nation being at Command, and Easy to be Found.
2. The Merchant Never be Delay'd.
3. Trade Never Oppresst.
4. Exorbitant wages Effectually Suppresst.
5. Seamen Entring into Forreign Service Prevented.
6. The Merchants be gainers.
7. The Seamen be Pleas'd and Thankfull.
8. A Large Sume of Money Rais'd annually for The Service of the Govornment.

The Clauses of This Regulacon are too Many to Trouble yor Lordships wth here.

DEFOE TO COMMITTEE OF THE LORDS, [C. 30 JANUARY 1705]

An Abstract of Them yᵉ Proposer humbly Presents, and shall at any Time be Ready on yoʳ Lordships Commands to Enter on yᵉ Perticulars.

1 That In Proper Offiċes in Every Port, and Subjected to yᵉ Same Powers now Employ'd, all yᵉ Seamen or Seafareing Men in yᵉ Naċon, be Imediately Listed or Entred into yᵉ Queens Pay, in Classes, and Degrees, according to yᵉ usage of the Navy.

2 That They shall all Reciev half Pay when Out of Employmᵗ, 23ˢ Per Month in her Majᵗⁱᵉˢ Serviċe, 26ˢ p[er] Month in yᵉ Merchants Serviċe, 36ˢ Per Voiage to New Castle, and Proporċon'd Rates for other Voiages, and [ ]sᵃ p[er] Month half Pay, or other Rates as to your Lᵈships Shall Seem fitt.

3 That yᵉ Same Provision be made For Seamen Maim'd in yᵉ Serviċe of the Merchant as in her Majᵗⁱᵉˢ Service.

That No Man Presume to hire, Employ, or Carry to Sea, anÿ man as a Sailor, but what he shall Reciev from yᵉ Proper officers Appointed.

That yᵉ Merchᵗ Masters &ca shall Reciev any Number of Men they want at 8 Dayes Demand, wᵗʰ Liberty of Choiċe, and Refuseing, showing Reasons for it, without Delay, Fee, Payment, or any Manner of Consideraċon.

That yᵉ Merchaᵗ shall Pay The Govornmᵗ Not yᵉ Seaman, and the Seamen be paid by The Govornmᵗ.

In Time of war yᵉ Merchᵗ To Pay yᵉ Govornmᵗ 30ˢ p[er] Month for able Seamen, and No More, yᵉ Overplus of 4ˢ p[er] Month to be Reserv'd to make good yᵉ half Pay.

A Table of Regulaċons, Differenċes, Avarages, stoppage of Pay, Methods of Discharge, Rules of Subordination, allowᵃ to seamen Abroad, orders for Dissmiss of Men at Delivring Ports, Tradeing Voiages, Rules for yᵉ seamen, in Case of yᵉ Loss of ships abroad, and all yᵉ Proper Niċeties of Trade, in Such Cases, The Proposer shall be Ready to offer to yoʳ Lordships when Ever your Commands Shall Require it.

The Sum̃s yᵉ Govornment Shall Save are So Great, and will be So Easily Paid, and So willingly by The Merchᵗ, that No Proposall on Our Marine affaires can Equall: the Perticulars whereof I am Ready to offer, when Ever yoʳ Lordships Think Fitt.

ᵃ [ ]s] *blank in MS*

DEFOE TO COMMITTEE OF THE LORDS, [*c.* 30 JANUARY 1705]

By This Proposall ye Tax to be Levy'd, will be^a Easy, because all that Pay it will be gainers, and all ye advantages Proposed will be Gaind Out of ye Present Exorbitant wages of Seamen, wch is Now ye Great and most Destructive burthen of Trade, and wch Costs This Nation at This Time above a Million Per Ann.

Of The Coal Trade

The Extravagant Price of Coals[9] is Not Occasion'd as Some Imagin from Engrossments of Merchants, Pressing Their Men, or Private Combinacon among The Owners, but from ye Excessive Rate of Wages given The Seamen.[10]

This Indeed has its foundacon in ye Length of ye Voiage, and That in ye Danger of ye Passage, wch Obliges ye Colliers to wait for Convoys, Stay to go in fleets, Comp^a, and ye like.

This I Humbly Propose may be Cur'd by a Generall Assureance on ye wholl Colliery, and The scheme of which when Ever yor Lordships please to Command it, shall Make it Appear, That for The small Premio of One Per Cent, The wholl Colliery May be Assur'd, Either by The Queen or by Private hands, The assurers to find ye Necessary Convoys, and So Guard ye Passage, That ye Coliers may Run Single, as in Times of Peace, and Coles be Near^b as Cheap in The Pool as in Time of Peace,[11] and ye assured to be paid all losses, by an Imediate Method without Delays or Deduccon.

All wch is humbly Submitted to yor Lordships
May it Please yor Lordships
By yor Most Obed^t Servt
De Foe

Text: House of Lords Archive, HL/PO/JO/10/6/71, fols. 141–52. *Address*: none. *Endorsed* (fol. 148v): M^r De foe's Proposals Read 10° February 1704.[12] *Endorsed* (fol. 152v): 10° Febry 1704 M^r De Foes Proposal

---

^a will be] *following word* 'So' *cancelled*
^b Near] *interlined*

---

1   *Review*, I, 684 (13 Jan. 1705).
2   *Review*, I, 690 (16 Jan. 1705).
3   *PEW*, VIII, 135–41.

[JOHN RELFE] TO DEFOE, 3 MARCH 1705

4 *Some Considerations on the Reasonableness and Necessity of Encreasing and Encouraging the Seamen* (1728), 35, 37. Prince George died in Oct. 1708.
5 See also Letter 206.
6 *Intollerable Inconveniences of Impressing Seamen?*: Defoe deemed pressing seamen illegal and wished for parliament to prevent it (*Review*, I, 753–4 (10 Feb. 1705); II, 38–40 (17 Mar. 1705); II, 72–4 (31 Mar. 1705)).
7 *yᵉ Act of Parliament ... Parish*: Recruiting Acts were passed annually from 1703 to 1711. The acts are criticised in similar terms in *Review*, V, 594–7 (20 Jan. 1709).
8 The preceding portion of the enclosure bears its own endorsement (on fol. 148v) and is followed by three blank pages before the next section commences.
9 *Extravagant Price of Coals*: Defoe addressed coal prices in *Review*, I, 69–70 (8 Apr. 1704).
10 *Excessive Rate of Wages given The Seamen*: Compare *Review*, I, 76 (11 Apr. 1704): 'The dearness of Coals has been chiefly occasioned by the Jugling and Frauds of the *Crimps* [trepanners] *and Lighter-men* [see Letter 180, note 5], more than by Defects in Convoys, Want of Seamen, or the like'. Defoe echoed this in *Review*, VI, 420–1 (18 Oct. 1709).
11 *Coles ... Peace*: This echoes *Review*, I, 691 (16 Jan. 1705). 'The Pool' is a docking area of the Thames in London.
12 *1704*: 1705 new style.

26

[John Relfe] to Defoe

3 March 1705

Sir

His Grace the D of Bolt[1] haveing this day acquainted yᵉ Lᵈˢ Comittees appointed to consider yᵉ state of yᵉ Nation in relation to Naval Affairs that you desired, in reguard yᵉ session is like to be short, that you might[a] be allowed time till the next meeting of yᵉ Parlᵗ, to prepare yᵉ Schemes lately p[ro]posed by you, to their Ldpps, for yᵉ more effectual manning her Matyes Navy, their Ldpps ordered you should be allowed[b] the time desired, and his Grace yᵉ D of B comanded me to acquaint you therwith. I am

Sʳ

Yʳˢ

[a] might] *interlined above cancelled word* 'may'
[b] be allowed] *interlined above cancelled illegible word*

DEFOE TO JOHN RELFE, 9 MARCH 1705

3 March 1704[2]

Text: House of Lords Archive, HL/PO/JO/10/6/71, fol. 153. *Address* (fol. 153r): For Mr De foe

1   *D of Bolt*: 'Bolton preserves the Generous and Sincere' in Defoe's catalogue of praise for Whig nobles in *Jure Divino*, book XII, line 311, *SFS*, II, 353.

2   *3 March 1704*: 1705 new style; the letter is dated 3 Mar., but accompanying records indicate it was sent on 7 Mar.

27

To John Relfe

9 March 1705

Mr John Relf

According to yor Request by The Messengr who brought an Ordr of ye house of Lords for me to mr Nutts[1] I send you This to Signifye I have Recd The Said Ordr Importing That Their Ldships are pleasd to Ordr me to Prepare ye Schemes I have proposd to The Lords Comittees for ye more Effectuall Manning her Majties Navy, Against Next session of Parliament, wch I shall Carefully Obey.

Yor Humble Servt
Daniel De Foe

March. 9. 1704[2]

Text: House of Lords Archive, HL/PO/JO/10/6/71, fol. 154. *Address* (fol. 154v): To Mr John Relfe | Present | March 9. 11 a Clock | At ye House of Peers

1   *mr Nutts*: John Nutt (1667–1716) sold Defoe's works including *The Storm* (1704), for which Nutt took in the readers' accounts of the tempest that furnished Defoe's work (*Daily Courant*, 2 Dec. 1703).

2   *1704*: 1705 new style.

28

John Fransham to Defoe

29 March 1705

HEADNOTE (Letters 28 and 29): The Whig Thomas Dunch was the successful candidate for alderman of Norwich in 1704. However, the Tory Lord Mayor refused to accept his election on the grounds that he had bribed and intimidated voters and he had not taken the Anglican sacrament. Dunch went to the Queen's Bench, which ultimately gave him his mandamus.[1] This dispute came on the eve of the 1705 general election, heralding the party conflict that raged across the country and in Norwich in particular; there in 1705 the mayor again rejected the return of two candidates on a technicality before they were admitted. Defoe later criticised the mayor's misconduct in Dunch's case and in the parliamentary election in Norwich in the *Review* for 18 June 1706.[2]

Mr De Foe, — The cause of my present writing is this, a Gentleman of our Town and a great admirer of your Writings obtein'd of me sometime since a promise of sending you a Letter by him at his next going to London, for which place he sets out this day and carry's with him accordingly such a Letter which he is pleas'd to call his credentials which he'll deliver into your hands if you'll be pleas'd to direct a penny post Letter to him at the 4 Swans in Bishopgate Street[3] where he lodges or at the Garter Coffee house behind the Exchange[4] where he is 2 or 3 times a day, and in it let him know where he shall meet you any day near Change, or if it suits not your convenience there any where else you shall name.

And now to make his company the more acceptable to you (which his own merit would sufficiently do by a little acquaintance) I shall give you a brief character of him, with a short history of what has been and is still transacting in our Town relating to him.

His name is Thomas Dunch, a Wine Merchant, a person of clear Ideas, a member of the Church of England, and in fine so staunch a Whigg as to be accounted the Head of that Interest here by the Tory's who for that reason only have acted in that unaccountable manner as follow.

He was upon the 14th Instant by the Freemen of the Ward put up one of the Candidates for Alderman, the other was one of our present Sherifs.[5] The first had the Majority of 21 Votes, yet was

JOHN FRANSHAM TO DEFOE, 29 MARCH 1705

a Scrutiny demanded & granted which being gone through Mr Dunches Majority was thereby increas'd notwithstanding wch the Jack-Daw-Gentlemen[6] of the Court were so affraid of admitting him that they refus'd to swear him on his demand to be sworn, and to justify their arbitrariness pretended to bring presidents (even less to the purpose than the Commons were relating to the Ailesbury men)[7] to shew that if the Court did not approve of the Freemens choise they could order them to proceed to a new Election. When these presidents and power came to be examined into they appear'd to be founded on some obsolete charters but totally destroy'd by our last which it seems expressly says That upon the death of an Alderman the Freemen of the Ward to wch he belong'd shall by the Mayor be requir'd to proceed to a new Election and the person elected by the Majority shall be sworn Alderman for Life. Yet these Gentlemen particularly the Mayor[8] and the other Sherif[9] (who is said to have the whole management of him) have thought fit to enter Mr Dunch (thus duly elected) in their Book as a person Contentious, Seditious and pernicious and therefore not fit to be admitted amongst such Men of Peace and Moderation, so that he is now gone up an elected but unsworn Alderman. What he has farther to do he knows best.

I thought it proper to give you this brief account of this Gentlemans affair, not knowing but it might prove a subject in your conversation and for that reason you'll pardon the prolixity of

S^r yours &^c.,

J. F.

P.S. — If I have misstated the case in any particular (as I do not know I have) upon reading it to Mr. Dunch; if there be occasion he will set it right.

Norw^{ch} March 29th 1705.

Text: MS untraced. The copytext is Norgate, 262–3. *Address*: none recorded.

1 See Paul D. Halliday, *Dismembering the Body Politic: Partisan Politics in England's Towns, 1650–1730* (Cambridge, 1998), 307 n. 7 for the relevant primary sources on Dunch.
2 *Review*, III, 376.
3 *4 Swans in Bishopgate Street*: Described by John Strype as 'large, and of a considerable Trade, and resort for Waggons and Stage Coaches that go Northwards' (*A Survey of the Cities of London and Westminster*, 2 vols. (1720), I, book II, 107).

JOHN FRANSHAM TO DEFOE, [C. 29 MARCH 1705]

4   *Garter Coffee house behind the Exchange*: Lillywhite, 224–5.

5   *one of our present Sherifs*: Dunch's opponent was Benjamin Austin, elected on 24 Apr. to the office in a re-election in which Dunch's supporters protested his disqualification by refusing to vote (TNA SP 34/6, item 15).

6   *Jack-Daw-Gentlemen*: Tories. Jackdaws are considered loquacious and thievish.

7   *Ailesbury men*: Referring to the case of Matthew Ashby, a cobbler from Aylesbury, who appealed to parliament when he was prevented from voting in the 1701 general election by a constable named William White. After the Commons rejected his appeal, Ashby took it to the Lords, who in Jan. 1704 overturned the ruling, aggrieving the Commons who claimed jurisdiction in matters affecting elections. *Ashby v. White* epitomised the contest over the respective privileges of the Whig-controlled upper and Tory-controlled lower Houses during Anne's first parliament. See Eveline Cruickshanks, '*Ashby v. White*: The Case of the Men of Aylesbury', in *Party and Management in Parliament, 1660–1784*, ed. Clyve Jones (Leicester, 1984), 87–106.

8   *Mayor*: William Blythe (d. 1716). His partisan approach was punished by the Commons after the general election when on 6 Dec. 1705 he was ordered to be 'taken into the Custody of the Serjeant of Arms attending this House' (*C.J.*, xv, 56).

9   *other Sherif*: Austin was one sheriff; the other was John Riseborough.

29

John Fransham to Defoe

[*c.* 29 March 1705]

M^r De Foe, — The Gentleman who delivers you this Letter would have it of me under the notion of a credential, but you that read Mankind so much will by a little conversation quickly perceive that he's a person that wants no recommendation. His Merit is not like that of the Occasionall Conformity Bill, it wants no crutches,[1] his Character I have allready acquainted you with and therefore need nothing farther than to wish you an agreeable conversation which knowing both the Gentlemen so well is not the least doubted by

S^r yours &c.,

J. F.

Text: MS untraced. The copytext is Norgate, 262. *Address*: none recorded.

1   *Occasionall … crutches*: A reference to the Tack of the previous year.

30

To Charles Montagu, Lord Halifax

5 April 1705

HEADNOTE: Charles Montagu (1661–1715), Baron Halifax from 1700 and first Earl of Halifax from 1714, was a member of the Whig Junto who had been both Chancellor and Auditor of the Exchequer under William III. He was impeached by the Tory-led House of Commons in April 1701, but the case collapsed and the impeachment was discharged in June. He was removed from the Privy Council upon Anne's accession; Tory attempts to cashier Halifax for his former conduct proved unsuccessful at that time. Halifax remained a prominent voice in the Lords, and the Godolphin ministry was gradually establishing a more amicable relationship with the Junto, which it recognised would be necessary for prosecuting the war (the general election of May confirmed this). Harley however retained his misgivings about dealing with the Junto.

Defoe had ample praise for Montagu and in *The Poor Man's Plea* (1698) called him *'one of the Ablest and most Sensible Statesmen in the Nation'*.[1] His financial management attracted Defoe's admiration, with Defoe remarking that he was 'worthily plac'd at the Head of the Nation's Treasure' under William.[2] Defoe praised Montagu's role in upholding public credit during the Nine Years' War and his role in the 1696 recoinage.[3] Defoe wrote in opposition to the attempt to impeach Halifax for his role in the partition treaties, both at the time and subsequently.[4] He also complimented Halifax as a poet and literary patron.[5] His most fulsome and extensive panegyrics came in the wake of this contact between Halifax and Defoe in spring and summer 1705. First, in *The Dyet of Poland* (probably July 1705) Halifax is celebrated as 'Great *Taguski*', whose fidelity and abilities are acknowledged by both sides.[6] Second, in *Jure Divino* – which was in progress during 1705 and published in July 1706 – Defoe praises Halifax's poetic and political abilities at length, as well as his steadfastness and magnanimity during the attempted impeachment.[7] Defoe addressed a further two extant letters to Halifax in 1705.[8]

My Lord

I Most humbly Thank yo[r] Lordship, for Expressions of yo[r] favour and Goodness w[ch] I had as Little Reason to Expect from yo[r] L[d]ship as I have Capasċity to Merit.

My L[d] Treasur[r] has frequently Express't himself wth Concern on my behalf, and M[r] Secretary Harley The like, But I my L[d],

133

DEFOE TO LORD HALIFAX, 5 APRIL 1705

Am like yᵉ Cripple at yᵉ Pool, when yᵉ Moment happen'd No Man was at hand to put yᵉ Wretch into yᵉ water,[9] and My Talent of Sollicitaċon is absolutely a Cripple, and Unquallifyed to help it Self.

I wish yoʳ Lordship Could Understand by[a] mÿ Imperfect Expressions yᵉ Senċe I have of yoʳ Unexpected Goodness, in Menċoning me to My Lᵈ Treasurer. I Could be Very well pleas'd to wait, Till yoʳ Merit and yᵉ Naċons want of you, Shall plaċe yoʳ Lordship in yᵗ Part of yᵉ Publick affaires, where I might Owe any benefitt I shall Reciev from it, to yoʳ Goodness; and Might be able to act something for yoʳ Serviċe, as well as that of yᵉ Publick.

My Lᵈ The Proposall yoʳ Lordship was pleas'd to make by my Brother[10] yᵉ bearer, is Exceeding Pleasant to me to Perform, as well as usefull to be done, agreeable to Every Thing yᵉ Masterly Genius of yoʳ Lordship has Produċ'd in This Age; But mÿ Missfortune is, yᵉ bearer whose head is not That way, has given me So Imperfect an Accot,[11] That Makes me yoʳ Lordships most humble Petiċoner for Some hints to Ground my Observations Upon.

I was wholly Ignorant of yᵉ Design of that act, Not knowing it had Such a Noble Originall.[12]

Pardon my Importunate Applicaċon to yoʳ Lᵈship, for Some hints of the Substanċe, and Design of that act, and if yoʳ Lᵈship Please yᵉ Names Again of Some books wᶜʰ my Dull Messengʳ forgott, and wᶜʰ yoʳ Lordship was Pleas'd to Say had spoke to This head.

I The Rather Press yoʳ Ldship on This head, because The Very Next Article,[b] wᶜʰ of Course I Proposed to Enter upon in y̲ᵉ Review being that of Paper Credit, I shall at[c] Onċe do my Self yᵉ honour to Obey your Lordships Dictate, and[d] Observe yᵉ stated Order of The Discourse, I am Upon.[13]

I Shall not Presume to offer it against yoʳ Lordships Opinion, and would be farthest of all from Exposeing yoʳ Lordship to any Tongues, but if Ever yoʳ Lordship shall Think this Despicable

[a] by] *interlined*
[b] Article] *interlined above cancelled word* 'head'
[c] at] *interlined*
[d] and] *following illegible word cancelled*

DEFOE TO LORD HALIFAX, 5 APRIL 1705

Thing, who scorn'd to Come Out of Newgate at ye Price of betrayeing a Dead Master,[14] or Discovring those Things wch No body would ha' been ye worse For, fitt to be Trusted in yor Presence, Tho' Never so Much Incognito, He will Certainly, Exclusive of what he may Comunicate to yor Lordship for ye Publick Service, Recieve from you Such Instruccons as are Suitable to yor known Genius, and The Benefitt of This Nacon.

I have herew^th Sent yor Lordship Another book.[15] I kno' yor Lordship has but a Few Minutes to spare, but I am yor L^dship humble Peticoner, to bestow an hour on its Contents, because it is likely to Make Some Noise in ye World, and p[er]haps to Come before yor Lordship in Parliam^t.

I Forbear to Divert yor More Serious Thoughts wth p[er]ticulars. I humbly Thank yor L^dship for ye freedome of Access you were Pleasd to give my Messenger; and am Extreamly ambicous of Listing my Self Under yor Lordship, in That Cause, in wch yor Lordship was Allwayes Embarkt, Viz^t of Truth and Liberty.

> I am
> May it Please yor L^dship
> yor L^dships
> Most Humble and Obed^t Ser^t
> D Foe

Apr^ll 5. 1705

Text: BL Add. MS. 7121, fols. 23–4. *Address* (fol. 24^v): To The Right Honble | The Ld Hallifax. | Humbly Present. *Endorsed* (fol. 24^v): De Foe April 5 1705

1 *RDW*, VI, 23.
2 *Review*, VII, 59 (20 Apr. 1710).
3 *Review*, VII, 284 (8 Aug. 1710), where Halifax is named 'one of [credit's] especial Favourites'; *A Plan of the English Commerce* (1728), *PEW*, VII, 214.
4 See *The Original Power of the Collective Body of the People of England* (1701), *PEW*, I, 119; *Legion's Memorial* (1701), *PEW*, II, 43; *The Consolidator* (1705), *SFS*, III, 146–7; and *Review*, III, 209 (4 Apr. 1706).
5 *The Pacificator* (1700), lines 134, 293, *SFS*, I, 68, 72. But see the (disguised) jibe at Halifax as poet in *An Elegy on the Author of the True-Born-English-Man* (1704), in which Defoe discusses his forbearance as a satirist: 'I never touch'd great *M——* | Whose Follies have not been a few' (lines 357–8, *SFS*, I, 274). Swift wrote that Halifax's 'encouragements were onely good words and dinners – I never heard him say one good thing or seem to tast what was said by another' (*The Prose Writings of Jonathan Swift*, ed. Herbert Davis *et al.*, 16 vols. (Oxford, 1939–74), V, 258).

DEFOE TO LORD HALIFAX, 5 APRIL 1705

6 Lines 221–41, *SFS*, I, 351; for the publication date and circulation, see *POAS*, VII, 75.

7 Book XII, lines 107–94, *SFS*, II, 348–50.

8 For a linguistic analysis of the present letter, see Susan M. Fitzmaurice, 'Epistolary Identity: Convention and Idiosyncrasy in Late Modern English Letters', in *Studies in Late Modern English Correspondence: Methodology and Data*, ed. Marina Dossena and Ingrid Tieken-Boon van Ostade (Bern, 2008), 77–112 (at 96–100). Fitzmaurice concludes that Defoe 'demonstrates himself … distinctively adept in correspondence, particularly when trying to seek a favour from someone as socially distant as Montagu', mingling conventional self-deprecation with implications that he can be serviceable, the aim being to secure patronage (100).

9 *Cripple … water*: John 5:1–15. Defoe applies this scripture to himself again in Letter 139.

10 *Brother*: Robert Davis, Defoe's brother-in-law.

11 *bearer … Accot*: 'It was a dexterous stroke to lay the blame on his brother-in-law's memory rather than on the vagueness of Halifax's message' (Moore, 11).

12 *act … Originall*: Defoe was apparently being asked by Halifax to support the 'act for giving like remedy upon promissory notes as is now used upon bills of exchange, and for the better payment of inland bills of exchange', now often called the 1704 Promissory Notes Act. Approved in Feb. 1705 (*L.J.*, XVII, 645, 660, 664), it came into law on 1 May and effectively made promissory notes negotiable instruments of exchange by giving full legal rights to third-party recipients of endorsed notes. Before this law, a note promising to pay 'Mr A. B., or the bearer' was not assignable in law, so the bearer, if not the payee, could not sue the issuing authority in his own name.

13 *Paper … Upon*: Two weeks later, Defoe announced that the *Review* would turn to the issue of '*Publick Credit*', including 'the late Act of Parliament for the Currency and Regulation of Promisory Notes be Examin'd'; the Extensive Benefit of it Explain'd' (*Review*, II, 115 (19 Apr. 1705)). However, he did not turn to the subject until Jan. 1706, when he remarked that 'an Essay at the General Currency of Inland Bills, which came from a Noble Hand the Last Session of Parliament but one, and issued in an Act of Parliament, *tho' that Act has had little Effect*, has in it not a Test only of the true Notion that Honourable Person has of the General Interest of Trade, but is a Door Opened to all the Nation, to see their Remedy too, if they had but the Sense to close with it' (*Review*, III, 37 (12 Jan. 1706)).

14 *Dead Master*: William III. Compare *Review*, v, 683 (5 Mar. 1709): 'He that betrays his Master, tho' Dead, or exposes his Memory when he can no more reward him, tho' it be to escape a Pillory, or come out of *Newgate*, let his Reputation die the Death of a Traytor, and the World know how to shun him, as a Man of no Principle.'

15 *Another book*: *The Consolidator*, published 26 Mar. 1705. See letter 33. Defoe was clearly proud of *The Consolidator*, referring to it several times in the following years, though he modestly called it 'a little Book worth no Body's reading' in 1708 (*Review*, v, 95 (8 May 1708)).

31

John Fransham to Defoe

[*c.* 5 April 1705][1]

HEADNOTE **(Letters 31 and 32)**: Defoe's exchange with Fransham indicates that he continued to send new works to towns outside of London, and that he viewed his work as both public service and divinely approbated. Voting in the general election was imminent, and Defoe's latest publications, especially *The Consolidator*, were written to propagate the ministry's message of moderation, designed to ensure the defeats of Tackers.

Mr De Foe, — Your Consolidator (which I could have wish'd much longer) I have just now got through, which contains (according to the opinion of a high SOLUNARIAN Gentleman I had some discourse with about it) too much Wit for Mr De Foe to be the author of it; he will have it wrote by a Genius superior to any CROLIANS,[2] which shews that let a man be never so great a Bigot to his party let him but have a Tast of starling sence and ingenuity such a one must be forc'd to confess that it abounds with masterly strokes of both. I thought to have proceeded no farther in relation to this Book, but can't forbear telling you one Instance more of the approbation it met with here. Another Gentleman of my acquaintance said he was so well pleas'd wth reading it that he would have gone through had it contein'd as much as Fox's 3 Volumes.[3]

I receiv'd as mention'd in yours 6 of them,[4] 12 of Gill's case[5] and 24 of the Supplements.[6] Gill's case you perceive by my last[7] I had read before yours arriv'd and had given such a representation thereof to some topping Dissenters that they were very glad to hear I had some coming to dispose of amongst them.

The Bearer[8] of this was very desirous of having charge of it; all that I can say to recommend him to you is that I believe he is a very honest man, and one that has as great a value for the memory of King William as any man in the kingdom, and that he is one of the Subscribers for JURE DIVINO and the Review. That of this day concerning persons born deaf[9] I cannot subscribe to. I wish you had the convincing of me by word of mouth, till which time I shall not think of entring the argument.

JOHN FRANSHAM TO DEFOE, [c. 5 APRIL 1705]

You have follow'd the Heels of Truth so close in your
Consolidator that the danger of a kick[10] gave some pain to

S^r yours &c.

J. F.

Text: MS untraced. The copytext is Norgate, 262. *Address*: none recorded.

1 Fransham refers in the letter to the *Review* 'of this day', meaning 3 Apr. 1705, which Healey notes he could have been reading in Norwich by 5 Apr. (*Letters*, ed. Healey, 83 n. 1).

2 SOLUNARIAN... CROLIANS: In *The Consolidator*, Solunarians and Crolians represent, respectively, High Churchmen and Dissenters.

3 *Fox's 3 Volumes*: John Foxe's (1516/17–87) *Acts and Monuments* (1563). An expanded 1632 edition was in three volumes, but unabridged editions starting with the second (1570) were in two volumes, including that of 1702. Defoe mentions 'old *Fox's* Book of Martyrs' as a proverbially long book in *Review*, v, 390 (2 Oct. 1708).

4 *them*: Copies of *The Consolidator*.

5 *Gill's case*: Defoe's *The Experiment: or, The Shortest Way with the Dissenters Exemplified. Being the Case of Mr. Abraham Gill, a Dissenting Minister in the Isle of Ely*, published in late Mar. 1705. This is an apologia for a former Church of England minister, Gill (b. *c.* 1665), who set up a Nonconformist conventicle. He was persecuted, imprisoned, and impressed as a soldier at the instigation of High Church rivals. Defoe later explained that he wrote it at the request of a group of Gill's supporters (*Review*, IV, 802 (3 Feb. 1708)).

6 *Supplements*: *The Supplement to the Advice from the Scandal Club, for the Month of December 1704. No. 4.* The 'Scandal Club' section of the *Review* proved so popular that Defoe published monthly supplements, which were tardy; this one was published in Mar. 1705 (*Review*, II, 28 (10 Mar. 1705)).

7 *my last*: Untraced.

8 *Bearer*: Unidentified.

9 *concerning persons born deaf*: The scandal club answered in the affirmative a reader's letter asking 'Whether a Person being born Deaf and Dumb, is Capable of Learning to Write, and Understand English to Perfection' (*Review*, II, 79–80 (3 Apr. 1705)). This subject is a theme of Defoe's *Mere Nature Delineated* (1726), in which appears the poem 'On the Deaf and Dumb being taught to Speak' (*TDH*, v, 182–8).

10 *follow'd... kick*: In the *Review*, Defoe had written: 'If I can, therefore follow Truth close at the Heels, without a kick on the Face, 'twill be well; if I can't, I see no Remedy, I must venture' (I, 208 (27 June 1704)). He also uses the image in *The History of the Union* (1709/10), *TDH*, VII, 144; *The Present State of the Parties in Great Britain* (1712), 69; *The Secret History of the White-Staff* (1714), *PEW*, II, 281. Its source is Sir Walter Raleigh (1552–1618), *The History of the World* (1614), ed. C. A. Patrides (1971), 80: 'Who-so-ever in writing a moderne Historie, shall follow truth too neare the heeles, it may happily strike out his teeth.'

DEFOE TO JOHN FRANSHAM, [*c.* 1 MAY 1705]

32

To John Fransham

[*c.* 1 May 1705][1]

Sir, — I have your obligeing Letter. You can give me no greater
pleasure than to hear that any thing I can do or have done in this
world is usefull and helps to forward that good which every honest
man ought to wish and wch I believe I was brought into the world
and am suffer'd to live in it only to perform.

This is the Token for good to me that the work I am upon is
of him whose immediate hand by wonderful steps have led me
through Wildernesses of Troubles and Mountains of popular Fury[2]
to see this day in which I may in some way or other honour him
whose cause I espouse, and who is the support of that Truth and
peace of which I am the mean and unworthy advocate.

I am still farther delighted in observing by what secret steps
in his providence he has furnish'd me with or directed me to
such sincere propagators of this blessed work as you are whose
hearts he have touch'd with a sence of the obligation we have
all upon us to assist in the establishment of his Interest in
the world.

This is the glory of his infinite Wisdom that brings to pass the
great ends appointed by his foreknowledge by the agency of us his
most despicable Instruments and the interposition of the minutest
Circumstances.

To him be all the praise both of his own work and our little, little,
very little share in it, and let the success of his service encourage all
the Lovers of Truth to stand up for the Lord against the Mighty,
who knows but now is the day of our deliverance.

As to the contents of your Letter, I am glad you receiv'd the
several parcels, but I hear not whether 100 Reviews sent you every
time since according to your order came to hand.

I thank your care about the Jure Divino money, and by the
Review of to day you will see in what forwardness it is.[3]

139

DEFOE TO JOHN FRANSHAM, [C. I MAY 1705]

There is a paper come out weekly call'd Truth & Honesty, in wh if you think fit the story of your Mayor may be inserted, and I can manage it there.[4]

I am your Sincere Friend
D. F.
I hope to day's Review[5] will please you.

Text: MS untraced. The copytext is Norgate, 262. *Address*: none recorded.

1 The date is inferred from the postscript reference to the *Review*, which probably refers to the I May issue.
2 *Wildernesses of Troubles and Mountains of popular Fury*: See the temptation of Jesus in Matt. 4:I–II.
3 *Jure Divino ... is*: Under fire for the delay to *Jure Divino*, Defoe wrote, 'The said Book is now in the Press, and shall go on to be Printed with all Expedition: And for the further Satisfaction of the Subscribers, the Sheets may be seen every Day by any that please to give themselves that Trouble, at Mr. *J. Matthews*, as they come out of the Press' (*Review*, II, 148 (I May 1705)). The poem remained unpublished until July 1706. Defoe was accused of bilking his subscribers in *The Proceedings at the Tryal Examination, and Condemnation Of a Certain Scribling, Rhyming, Versifying, Poeetering Hosier, and True-born Englishman* (1705). John Matthews (d. 1716) published the *Review* at this time.
4 *Truth ... there*: 'Reflections upon the present Posture of Affairs By TRUTH and HONES-TY' was a feature in *The London Post*. On 14 May 1705, it satirised the Mayor of Norwich William Blythe for his refusal to accept Dunch's election (see Letters 28 and 29), suggesting that Fransham took up Defoe's offer. For Defoe's relationship with *The London Post*, see J. A. Downie, 'Mr. Review and his Scribbling Friends: Defoe and the Critics, 1705–1706', *HLQ* 41 (1978), 345–66 (at 349 n. 16), and F&O, 'Periodicals', 85–6. Defoe's brief reflections on the column after its demise do not suggest he was its author (*Review*, IX, 35 (30 Aug. 1712)).
5 *to day's Review*: The issue for I May 1705 attacked the recklessness of the Tackers with a view to ensuring they were not re-elected: '*Gentlemen Freeholders*, you must not Choose a *Tacker*, unless you will *Destroy* our Peace, *Divide* our Strength, *Pull Down* the Church, *let in* the *French*, and *Depose* the Queen' (II, 147).

140

33

To Charles Montagu, Lord Halifax

[late May 1705?]

HEADNOTE: On 12 May 1705, Halifax wrote with election news to Sarah Church-ill, Duchess of Marlborough (1660–1744) who, like him, was enjoying the Whigs' successes. He had sent her Defoe's *Consolidator*:

> Since I find your Grace has leasure to read the Consolidator, I have sent you some Papers that will divert you. The Review is writ by the same Author. He has a great deal of Wit, would write very well if his necessitys did not make him in too much haste, to correct. He has made two poems on Ld Marlborough; and might deserve encourage-ment. ... The verses have some turns in them that are pretty, and are very respectfull to the Queen.[1]

On 15 May, Halifax followed this letter with another, reacting to the Duchess's agreement to his plan of rewarding Defoe, acting for her in the matter:

> I find the flight your Grace has made to the moon has not at all de-prived us of your good influence here below, and you continue to shed your Bountys on poor Mortals in such a manner, that we see, the Heighth to which you are exalted, serves chiefly to make your Goodness more diffusive. I did not designe the Paper I sent, should have been so expensive to your Grace, thô I did think the Author did deserve some consideration. He has been used barbarously by Ld Nottingham, and has made sutable returns. He has complimented Ld Marlborough, and your grace has higly rewarded Him, and in my poor opinion, a little money can not be better placed by those who are in Power, than in obliging, and engaging those who have Wit, and Storys, that may be turned on Them, or the Enemy. I shall follow your Directions, till you give Me leave to let him know his Benefactresse, which I hope shall not be long concealed, since the hand that gave it, makes the greatest value of the Guift.[2]

The present letter, presumably sent by Defoe to Halifax in mid to late May, ac-knowledges the gift and fishes for the identity of his benefactor.

The Duchess later wrote on the second letter from Halifax, sometime after his death in May 1715, saying that Halifax's recommendation to remunerate Defoe was merely to gratify his own vanity. Of Defoe and her gift she says, 'the man never knew it was from me', and that 'he wrote afterwards violently against me',

DEFOE TO LORD HALIFAX, [LATE MAY 1705?]

recalling Defoe's writings for Harley's ministry from 1710, especially publications in the wake of Marlborough's dismissal at the end of 1711.[3]

Pardon Me my Lord

If to a Man that has Seen Nothing for Some yeares, but The Rough Faċe of Things, The Exceeding goodness of yor Lordsp^s discourse Softn'd me Even to a Weakness, I Could Not Conceal.

'Tis a Novelty my Lord, I have Not been Us'd to, to Reciev Obligaċons from Persons of your Lordships Character and Merit, Nor Indeed from any Part of ye world, And ye Return is a Task too hard for me to Undertake.

I am (My Lord) a Plain and Unpolish'd Man, and Perfectly Unquallify'd to Make formall Acknowlegements, and a Temper Sour'd by a Series of Affliċċons, Rendres me Still ye More Awkward in ye Rec^d Method of Common Gratitude, I Mean ye Ceremony of Thanks.

But My L^d if to be Encourag'd in gieving my Self up to That Serviċe yor Lordship is pleas'd So Much to Overvallue, if Goeing On wth ye More Cheerfullness in being usefull to and^a promoteing the Generall Peaċe and Intrest of this Naċon; If to ye Last Vigorously Opposeing a Stupid Distracted Party, that are for Ruining themselves Rather than not Destroy Their Neighbours, If This be to Merit So Much Regard, yor Lordship binds me in The Most Durable, and to me the Most pleasant Engagement in ye World, because 'tis a Serviċe that wth my Gratitude to yor Lordship, keeps an Exact Unison with my Reason, my Prinċiple,^b My Inclinaċon, and The Duty Every Man Owes to his Country, and his Posterity.

Thus My Lord Heavenly Bounty Engages Mankind, while The Commands are So far from being Grievous, that at ye Same time we Obey we promote Our Own Feliċity, and Joyn The Reward to ye Duty.

As to ye Exceeding Bounty I have now Rec^d, and wch yor Lordship Obliges me to Reserv my Acknowlegem^{ts} of For a yet Unknown Benefactor,[4] Pardon me My L^d to believ yor Lordships

---

^a and] *interlined*

^b Prinċiple] *following word* 'and' *cancelled*

DEFOE TO LORD HALIFAX, [LATE MAY 1705?]

favour to me has at Least So much share in yᵉ Conduct of it, if Not
in yᵉ Substance, that I am Perswaded I can Not be More Oblidged
to yᵉ Donor, than to your Lordships Singular goodness; which
tho' I Can not Deserve, yet I shall Allways Sencibly Reflect on, &
Improve, And Iᵃ should be Doubly blest, if Providence would put it
into my hands, to Render yoʳ Lordship Some Service, Suited to yᵉ
Sence I have of yoʳ Lordships Extraordinary Favour.

And yet I am yoʳ Lordships Most Humble Peticoner, That if
Possible I may kno' the Originalls of This Munificence; Sure That
hand That Can Suppose me to Merit So Much Regard, Must believ
me Fitt to be Trusted wᵗʰ The knowlege of my benefactor, and
Uncapable of Discovering any Part of it, That should be Conceal'd;
But I Submitt This to yoʳ Lordship and the Persons Concernd.

I Frankly Acknowlege to yoʳ Lordship, and to yᵉ Unknown
Rewarders of my Mean Performances, That I do Not See yᵉ Merit
They are Thus Pleasd to Vallue. The most I wish and wᶜʰ I hope
I Can Answer for is, That I shall Allwayes Preserv the Homely
Despicable Title of <u>an Honest Man</u>. If This will Recomend me, yoʳ
Lordship shall Never be Asham'd of giveing me that Title, Nor my
Enemys be able by Fear Or Reward to Make me Other wise.

In all Other things I justly Apprehend yoʳ Lordships
Dissappointment and That yoʳ Lᵈship will find little Elce in Me
worth yoʳ Notice.

I am
May it Please yoʳ Lordship
yoʳ Lᵈships Highly Oblig'd
Most Humble and Most Obedᵗ Servᵗ
Daniel De Foe

Text: BL Add. MS. 7121, fols. 27–8.⁵ *Address* (fol. 27ᵛ): To The Right Honᵇˡᵉ |
Charles Lᵈ Hallifax | Humbly Present. *Endorsed*: De Foes (fol. 27ᵛ) *and* From Mʳ
De Foe (fol. 28ᵛ).

ᵃ I] *interlined*

---

1   BL Add. MS. 61458, fol. 161r. The two poems are *A Hymn to Victory* and *The Double Welcome*.
2   BL Add. MS. 61458, fol. 163r.
3   BL Add. MS. 61458, fol. 162v. In *The Conduct of Parties in England* (1712) Defoe referred to 'the
   Avarice and Extortion of Queen *Zarah*' (*PEW*, II, 256); and in *The Present State of the Parties*

DEFOE TO ROBERT HARLEY, [EARLY JULY 1705?]

in Great Britain (1712) he mentioned 'the Impolitick Stiffness, not to say Rudeness, of One Old *She Favourite*' (50). In *The Secret History of the White-Staff, Part II* (1714) Defoe levelled further criticism at her, and in *The Secret History of the White-Staff, Part III* (1715) he says that 'Madam the Du---ss of ——— ... was very far mistaken in her Carriage to the Q—' (16). The Duchess is depicted as dominating the Queen in Defoe's *Minutes of the Negotiations of Monsr. Mesnager* (1717), *SFS*, IV, 40.

4   *Unknown Benefactor.* There is no evidence that Defoe ever found out that the Duchess of Marlborough was his benefactor. See headnote.

5   Unusually, the text of the letter is on the first and third page of the bifolium and the address is on the second rather than fourth page. The final part of the MS is reproduced in facsimile in R. Farquharson Sharp, *Architects of English Literature: Biographical Sketches of Great Writers from Shakespeare to Tennyson* (1900), facing 43.

34

To Robert Harley

[early July 1705?][1]

HEADNOTE **(Letters 34–7)**: Communications between Defoe and Harley from November 1704 to summer 1705 have not been traced, but the *Review* had steadily promoted the ministry's policy of 'moderation' during the 1705 general election. Defoe later boasted that 'some People' were so pleased with the issue for 17 April 1705 that they 'made me print five Thousand of that *Review* to be sent all over the Nation to move us to Peace, and paid me very frankly for them'.[2] His propaganda denounced the Tackers, whom the ministry wanted to defeat, and it encouraged support for the prosecution of the war.[3] To Defoe's mind, the election produced 'the best Parliament this Age can remember' and this was thanks to the 'Tacking Project', which backfired on the High Church party.[4] Following the election Defoe was preparing for a political fact-finding tour round England on Harley's behalf. When in retrospect he described the trip in the *Review* in October 1705, Defoe calculated that he travelled 1,100 miles on horseback, and he proclaimed his conciliatory approach:

> In all my Perambulation, my constant Endeavour, my whole Discourse has been *like my Writing*, nothing but Peace; Entreating and Perswading all Men, of what Perswasion, and of what Opinion soever, to lay aside their Party-Prejudices, to Bury former Animosities, to remember they are all *Protestants*, all *English* Men, Embark'd in the same Vessel, Environ'd and Attack'd by the same Enemies, that have no Friends, but one another to stand by them; that have the same Religious Interests, and the same Civil Interest to pursue, the

DEFOE TO ROBERT HARLEY, [EARLY JULY 1705?]

same God, and the same Government; and whose Ruine, if ever it comes, will be brought to pass by the same Methods.

He also says that he carried with him a copy of the High Church pamphlet *The Memorial of the Church of England*, published in early July, showing this as evidence of the party's beliefs.[5] The *Memorial* was a withering attack on the ministry, Dissenters, and Queen Anne, and it gave Defoe a particular object to attack in his writings, bringing together his priorities of promoting the government's agenda and opposing intolerance of Nonconformity.[6] More generally, Defoe was eager for more stable employment, particularly as political enemies were dredging up old business debts.[7]

Memorandums

To be Furnish't wth Some thing New to Informe ye people I Converse wth at Least when any Thing Extraordinary happens wch may be^a had More Authentick than Ordin^a.

To have a Certificate as from ye Office that being Travailling on my Lawfull Occasions I may not be stopt by any Malitious p[er]sons on ye Road — or wch may be worse — Search't.

To Settle a Method how To write &ca.

Charges to be Directed as Shall Reciev Ord^r —

To get Leave for ye Same Person[8] who went wth me before to be absent at ye Custome house —

To be goeing as Soon as Possible. The Assizes will Elce Not Overtake me Onely but be before me.

If May Suit wth Convenience — be gone Fryday Next.[9]

Some Specall Instruccons —

Text: BL Add. MS. 70291, fols. 28–9. *Address*: none.

---

^a be] *interlined*

145

1 Letter 44 indicates that Defoe departed London for the south-west on Monday 16 July, and in this letter he refers to his plan to 'be gone Fryday Next', suggesting this memorandum was written in the first week of July.

2 *Review*, v, 481 (25 Nov. 1708).

3 The Triumvirs' aim in the 1705 election was to capitalise on the backlash against the Tack and reduce the Tory majority in the Commons, thereby balancing the parties and ensuring that the Queen's servants (placeholders) would hold sway. As Marlborough wrote to the Duchess on 19 Apr. 1705: 'It is for the Queen's Service and the good of England, that the choyce might be such as that neither party might have a great majority, so that her Majesty might be able to influence what might be good for the common cause' (*Marl.–God. Corr.*, I, 423).

4 *Review*, IV, 69 (13 Mar. 1707). This was written with hindsight, following approval of the Act of Union.

5 *Review*, II, 649 (11 Oct. 1705). Responding to this issue, Pittis gave a malicious account of Defoe's tour, suggesting his main motivation was to sell bound copies of the first volume of the *Review* and to secure subscriptions for *Jure Divino* (*The Whipping Post*, no. 19 (2 Nov. 1705)). On the *Memorial*, see Downie, *Robert Harley*, 80–100; Joseph Hone, *The Paper Chase: The Printer, the Spymaster, and the Hunt for the Rebel Pamphleteers* (2020).

6 Two publications in which Defoe took up issues relating to Dissent are *The Experiment: or, The Shortest Way with the Dissenters Exemplified*, published in Mar. 1705, and *The Paralel: or, Persecution of Protestants the Shortest Way to Prevent the Growth of Popery in Ireland*, probably published in June 1705.

7 Unable to conceal the debts alleged against him, Defoe stated that his travels were to put himself 'out of the Reach of Implacable and Unreasonable Men', meaning creditors (*Review*, II, 649 (11 Oct. 1705)).

8 *Same Person*: Christopher Hurt (see Letter 11).

9 *Fryday Next*: Perhaps 13 July, though he seems to have gone on 16 July.

35

To Robert Harley

9 July 1705

Sʳ

When wᵗʰ yoʳ Usuall Goodness you were pleasd yᵉ Last Time I was wᵗʰ you, to Ordʳ me to Put Down in writeing any Thing I had to propose on My Private Accot, it Put me On Considering whether The Same Secret hand that first Put it into yoʳ Thoughts to do me Good, Might Not Perhaps yet Farther Move you on My behalf.

Sʳ I am Not Insensible of yᵉ Tenderness you Treat me wᵗʰ, and tho' I am Not Ever Crowding you with my Empty Acknowlegemᵗˢ as Things I kno' you are Above yᵉ Ceremoney of, yet you have bound

DEFOE TO ROBERT HARLEY, 9 JULY 1705

a Gratefull Fellow So Close to you that Nothing Can be too great for me to attempt for yor Service. I Onely want ye Occasion wch Must Come from yor Self.

When I Come to Talk of my Self s^r The story is Mellancholly Enough and yet I am Loth to give you The Trouble of it.

What I write of Peace it Seems Raises war to me and Those people who were Easy before grow Troublesome Now, tho' they Must Needs kno' me less able Than before The Last Trouble to Discharge Them, and as Those who Offer this, are Most of Them of ye Contrary Party I See The Design is if possible to put a stop to my writeing.[1]

But why do I Trouble you wth This? to Ask you Any Thing that Can Reliev This Capitall Defect, is what I have No Merit to pretend to. But I Remember when you were pleas'd, The last Bill I Rec^d from you (for wch I Ought to Repeat my Thanks), to Say Something of bringing it to a Certainty — Pardon me for Restraining My Requests tho' you Give me too Much Freedome. I kno' Not whether what I have from you be from ye Publick Or yor Own Private. Tho' ye bounty to me is Equally yo^{rs} yet This Difference it will have; That tho' I hate to be craveing, yet as I hinted Once, I was Fitter for a Pension than an Office, by wch I Meant Respecting ye Service I may do Among ye Party; So Sr Might ye Service I may do Merit a Private Allow^a by wch The Necessary Craveings of a Large Family of 7 Children[2] might be answer'd. What Elce I Can Raise in ye world would Soon Set me at Ease as to Creditors, whereas the Eager prosecucon of Enemyes will at Last Disable me Either to Support ye first or Discharge ye Last.

I kno' Not how to build this proposall but on This Foundacon, That I hope 'tis in your Power to Make me Deserve it.

I hope you have More Confidence in Me Than to Think what you Supply me wth for ye Expence of ye Service I go On, shall be in The Least Missapplyed, and Tho' I can Not Perswade mÿ Self that Good husbandry should straighten^a ye Work, and was Something too Expensive in ye Last,[3] yet Really s^r the many Perticulars Obtaind and ye short Time perform'd in Oblig'd me to Expence

---

^a straighten] *the* 'a' *is interlined*

and I Thought it well bestow'd, Nor Unless you prescribe me shall I spare where yᵉ Serviċe I am Upon Requires, Sinċe I am Satisfyed This Thing will be of Various Uses to yᵉ Publick.

All This is to Signifye to you, sʳ, that yᵉ Money you are pleas'd to Furnish, for This affair, wᶜʰ I hope is Out of yᵉ Publick stock, as yᵉ Use is for The Publick, Relates to its Proper Expenċe, Subsistenċe or allowance being hitherto Unconċern'd in it.

Nor should I Take This Freedome but wait yoʳ Leisure, to Reward meᵃ as your Own Judgement shall p[er]swade you I Merit, haveing allwayes Reason to Acknowlege you forward to Assist me, But — sʳ The Man is Demolish'd, and yᵉ Wound is too Deep [for]ᵇ Common Industry to heal; and he That made you The First Physiċan, has Entail'd The Rent Charge on you, and Makes My Lᵈ Rochesters Verses, on Women, True of me.

> That Authors Beggar like, will haunt yᵉ Door,
> Where They Recᵈ a Charity before.⁴

Make me Merit sʳ all you Do for me; if I Can do Nothing why assist me attall? if any Thing, Then yᵉ Publick Bounty will not be Lost, Tis The hopes of yᵉ Party to See me flye, and I believ They would bribe meᶜ to be gone. If my staÿ is a harm to Them, tis a use to yᵉ Contrary. My petiċon to you sʳ is, to make me Serviċable, and The Queens Bounty will follow, for No Man Servs her Majᵗⁱᵉ for Nothing.

I have Answerd This high Church Legion.⁵ I have Dedicated it to my Lᵈ Treasurer.⁶ From yoʳ hand sʳ My Lᵈ Can Not but accept it, and p[er]haps to my Advantage;⁷ if not I am Sure tis for yᵉ publick good, and if I Loose by it Ile publish it, and flatter my Self you will Not be asham'd of yᵉ performanċe.

I Forbear to Trouble you any More wᵗʰ my Cases. I Lay This at yoʳ Feet, and Throwing my Self wholly on your Goodness, humbly ask yoʳ Pardon for yᵉ Freedome and am

[monogram]

July 9. 1705

ᵃ me] *interlined*
ᵇ [for]] *MS torn*
ᶜ me] *interlined*

DEFOE TO ROBERT HARLEY, 9 JULY 1705

ye Messeng^r Stevens[8] has brought or will bring some people up for ye Dyer. I pray that a seeming Reprimand,[9] &c. may Suffize, Elċe ye Charge will lye^a — &ca.

Text: BL Add. MS. 70291, fols. 32–3. *Address*: To The Right Honble | Robert Harley Esqr

---

^a lye] *following words* 'where it' *cancelled*

---

1 *Those ... writeing*: In the *Review* for 7 July 1705, Defoe remarks that, as well as threats of physical violence and attacks in print, he had recently been harassed by old creditors. He says these 'Crowds of Sham-Actions, Arrests, Sleeping Debates in Trade of 17 Years standing' are revived 'all for the Party', even though his having been 'just strip'd Naked by the Government' in *The Shortest Way* affair makes him less able than ever to satisfy supposed debts (II, 360).

2 *Family of 7 Children*: See Letter 10.

3 *ye Last*: His trip to the eastern counties the previous year.

4 *That ... before*: 'But Women Beggarlike, still haunt the door | Where they've receiv'd a Charity before' ('A very heroical epistle in answer to Ephilia' (1679), lines 30–1, *The Works of John Wilmot, Earl of Rochester*, ed. Harold Love (Oxford, 1999), 96). Rochester (1647–80) was a poet and courtier. See John McVeagh, 'Rochester and Defoe: A Study in Influence', *Studies in English Literature 1500–1900* 14 (1974), 327–41.

5 *Answerd This high Church Legion*: Defoe's *The High-Church Legion: or, The Memorial Examin'd*, published on 17 July, responded to the High Church pamphlet *The Memorial of the Church of England*, published in early July 1705. The *Memorial* was a searing attack on the Queen and her ministry for the removal of prominent Tories, encouragement of Dissenters, and lukewarm support of the Church of England. It defended the Tack, criticised the Lords' intercession in the Aylesbury case, and threatened insurrection. As well as *The High-Church Legion*, Defoe's *Review* from 12 July to 21 Aug. 1705 attacked the *Memorial* as a 'Virulent Pamphlet' (II, 377) and derided its rallying cry of 'the Church in Danger' as 'the most Ridiculous Banter' (II, 441). Defoe frequently animadverted on the *Memorial* in later years.

6 *Dedicated it to my Ld Treasurer*: Godolphin had been criticised at length in the *Memorial* (e.g. 24–5), and he was personally upset (Sharp, 1, 365–6). Defoe's unsigned dedication defends Godolphin's 'exquisite Management of the Nations Treasure' and 'the most Punctual Untainted Fidelity to his Mistress the Queen, as well as his Mother the Church of *England*' (*The High-Church Legion, PEW*, II, 109, 120). Cf. Defoe's poetic panegyric on Godolphin in *Jure Divino*, book XII, lines 195–234, *SFS*, II, 350–1.

7 *my Advantage*: Though the dedication in question professes 'no Expectation of Reward' (*PEW*, II, 109).

8 *Messeng^r Stevens*: Robert Stephens (see Letter 18). Three days earlier, Defoe in the *Little Review* had defended Stephens's work on the behalf of the government (*Review*, II, 355–6 (6 July 1705)).

9 *seeming Reprimand*: 'Seeming' means 'suitable'. See Defoe's *Review* for 11 Aug. 1705, which angrily quotes a *Dyer's News-Letter* to the effect that the government was hunting the author of the *Memorial* but not authors of Whig attacks on the Church, and that rejoinders to the *Memorial* confirm rather than confute its assertions (II, 493–4). This could be the offensive *News-Letter*, but there may be an earlier issue. Healey (*Letters*, 90 n. 5) proposes that Defoe alludes here to a separate issue concerning the East India Company, but when Defoe takes up that matter in the *Review* on 23 Aug. he specifies that the *News-Letter* in question was dated 7 Aug., too late to be the subject of this postscript (II, 533).

149

DEFOE TO ROBERT HARLEY, [10 JULY 1705]

36

To Robert Harley

[10 July 1705]

Sᵣ

I Wrott yᵉ Enclosed¹ last Night, Tho' had I Seen you I believ mÿ heart had Faild me in Delivring it, for I Could Never yet Speak for my Self.

I Wait wᵗʰ Impaćenće yoᵣ Last Ordᵣˢ and Shall attend at 4 This afternoon According to yoᵣ Direcćon.

I Long to Accquᵗ you That I am Told Dᵣ Atterbury² is Author of The Memoriall and That Geo: Sawbridge³ and Abell Roper⁴ are yᵉ Publishers but yoᵣ Messenger Stevens (too Much a friend to That Party) Took Such Care of yᵉ Orders given him to Discover yᵉ Printers, that Some houres before his Search, a Person was Sent Privately to all yᵉ Booksellers and Gather'd Them in Again.⁵

Mᵣ Pooley⁶ in Some Compᵃ yesterday gave a great Encomium of yᵉ book very Publickly.

I have Sent you herewᵗʰ yᵉ Rough of yᵉ Answer. I hope Twill please you and any hint you please to give Shall be added. If you please to give me Leave I would address it to My Lᵈ Treasurer or to yoᵣ Self; it Should be in yᵉ press to Day if possible.

I beg yᵉ Favoᵣ of yoᵣ Perusall of it — The printing Shall Not Stop my Journey an hour — I am

Sᵣ yoᵣ Honᵣˢ Most Obedᵗ Servᵗ
[*monogram*]

Tuesday Morning

Text: BL Add. MS. 70291, fols. 34–5. *Address* (fol. 35ᵛ): To the Right Honoᵇˡᵉ | Robert Harley Esqᵣ | One of her Majᵗⁱᵉˢ Principˡˡ Secretᵃ of State | Present. *Endorsed by an unknown hand* (fol. 35ᵛ): About the Memoriall & Answer and about Subsisting yᵉ Author of the Answer 9 July 1705

1 *Enclosed*: The preceding letter.
2 *Dr Atterbury*: Francis Atterbury (1663–1732), Dean of Carlisle, later Bishop of Rochester. Defoe attacked Atterbury on later occasions: at the time of Sacheverell's trial in 1710 (*Review*,

150

DEFOE TO ROBERT HARLEY, [16 JULY 1705?]

VII, 46 (15 Apr. 1710); VII, 70 (27 Apr. 1710)). And he resumed his criticisms in the wake of the Hanoverian succession from 1715 to 1717 (*The Secret History of the Secret History of the White-Staff* (1715), *PEW*, II, 306; 'Daniel Defoe's *Some Thoughts of an Honest Tory in the Country* (1716): A Critical Edition', ed. Nicholas Seager, *Digital Defoe* 7 (2015), 1–33; *Secret Memoirs of a Treasonable Conference at S—— House* (1717), *SFS*, IV, 165).

3   *Geo: Sawbridge*: George Sawbridge the younger. He was eventually fined £200 for publishing the *Memorial* (Boyer, 286). He had published Defoe's *The Storm* in 1704.

4   *Abell Roper*: Abel Roper (1665–1726), publisher and editor of the thrice-weekly Tory periodical *The Post Boy*, with which Defoe had several run-ins. For instance, he labelled Roper's paper 'one Universal Lump of Falshood and Fiction' (*Review*, IX, 35 (3 Aug. 1712)).

5   *Messenger Stevens ... in Again*: Another messenger of the press John Gellibrand informed Harley on 13 July that 'the discovery of this book might as easily have been made as I can now go to Whitehall if you had not been trickd by mr Stephens yor messenger' (BL Add. MS. 70022, fol. 214).

6   *Mr Pooley*: Henry Poley (c. 1653–1707), lawyer and Tory MP for West Looe until the 1705 election and for Ipswich from then until his death. Defoe attacked him with fellow Tackers in *Review*, II, 155 (5 May 1705) and continued to implicate him in the production of the *Memorial* in following months (*Review*, III, 71 (26 Jan. 1706), where he is the 'Lawyer').

37

To Robert Harley

[16 July 1705?]¹

Sr

I am Sincerely Thankfull to yor Sollicitous Thots for me, tho'ᵃ I Avoid Extasies on That Subject.

I have ye Pass sr and Doubt Not its being Effectuall, and Assure you of my Makeing No use of it, but at ye Last Extremity.

I give you Joy sr of ye Good News² wch I Recd wth One hand ye Same Moment I Recd yors wth the other, and wch I Take as a good Omen, and both Contribute to Send me Outᵇ Chearfull and Easy.

I Send you herewth Six of ye High. C. Legeon. The bearer who is My Brother in Law, and who May be Depended on, and is The Same Person Carrye'd ye Coventry Affair,³ yet knows Nothing of The principall affair.

ᵃ tho'] *interlined*
ᵇ Out] *following illegible word cancelled*

DEFOE TO ROBERT HARLEY, [16 JULY 1705?]

He is Charg'd wth ye Like Number for My Ld Treasurer. But if you Demand Them will Deliver Them, Since if you would please to Concern yor Self So far as to Let my Ld Treasurer kno' They^a Come by your hand, It would be a Double Favour.

I Perswade my Self Now S^r you are Convinc't Lessly[4] has Not been ye Author of ye Memorial; I am fully posess't wth a Belief that Not him, No Nor D^r D . . . ke,[5] But ye Latter as a Tool, an Amanuensis,^b to his Grace.[6] Lætantur Lares &ca.[7] There are [h]is^c Marks, his strokes. There is his spirit, his Gall and in short his Picture.

I am Concern'd to See yor Orders betraid and Buffoon'd. That Wretch Stephens Makes ye Govornm^t perfectly Impotent in These Matters and The Booksellers and he Together make sport at yor Orders.

Indeed s^r I write This w^thout private Design or ill will to ye Man, his being a Rogue was Usefull to me, and I brib'd him[8] allways to my Advantage. But in This Case They act und^r his patronage.

An Instance of This you will have Tomorro', when^d The Memoriall is to be publish't Answer'd Paragraph by Paragraph.

As This is Done Purely to Sell ye book, wch The Town is Eager for, and wch I Think ye Govornm^t is highly Concernd to prevent, So The Answers are Allways Triffles, and ye Design wch is Dispersing the Originall is fully Answer'd.[9]

If you Send for That Fellow and Severely Reprimanding^e him Charge him in it, you May Effectually Damn This project in its Embrio, for he knows ye hand it Comes by and may Go and Seize it in ye press, and will be Frighted by your Threats, For Villains are Allways Cowards.

The License you Give me to use This Freedome, Joyn'd to My Concern For the Case, is my Excuse for This and I hope shall be Accepted So.

---

^a They] *interlined above cancelled word* 'it'
^b Amanuensis] *the* 'a' *is interlined above an illegible cancellation*
^c [h]is] 'h' *omitted*
^d when] *following word possibly* 'an' *cancelled*
^e Reprimanding] 'ing' *is interlined*

DEFOE TO ROBERT HARLEY, [16 JULY 1705?]

This Minute I go Away and shall do my Self ye honour to write at Large on all Occasions — Interim I am

&ca

[*monogram*]

Monday Morning

Text: BL Add. MS. 70291, fols. 30–1. *Address* (fol. 31v): To The Right Honble | Robert Harley Esqr | Principal Secretary of State &ca.

1 Healey's logic for dating this letter to Monday 16 July 1705 is sound (H.M.C. *Portland MSS*, IV, 200 had tentatively assigned it to 2 July). Letter 44 dates Defoe's departure on his travels to 16 July and he here says, 'This Minute I go Away.'

2 *Good News*: Marlborough's success in breaking through the lines of Brabant (a seventy-mile arc of French defences between Antwerp and Namur) at Elixheim on 7 July (Marlborough to Godolphin, 7 July 1705, *Marl.–God. Corr.*, I, 458–9). News reached London on 14 July (Luttrell, V, 573).

3 *Brother … Affair*: Robert Davis may have delivered to Harley a report from Defoe on the Coventry election riots of the previous Apr. and May. Defoe first reported on the Coventry election in *Review*, II, 169–73 (10 May 1705).

4 *Lessly*: Charles Leslie (1650–1722), a non-juror with whose periodical *The Rehearsal* (1704–9) Defoe constantly tussled, though their rivalry goes back to the start of Anne's reign. Leslie had attacked Defoe's whiggish politics as recently as *Rehearsal*, 30 June–7 July 1705, and Defoe in turn called Leslie 'an Author whose Talent is to Prevaricate, and then Equivocate' (*Review*, II, 376 (12 July 1705)).

5 *D^r D … ke*: James Drake (1667–1707), author of a High Tory periodical *Mercurius Politicus: or, An Antidote to Popular Misrepresentations* (June–Dec. 1705), was probably one of the authors of the *Memorial*. See Downie, *Robert Harley*, 83–8 for a discussion of the evidence.

6 *his Grace*: Buckingham. He had recently been removed from the post of Lord Privy Seal. Buckingham had been involved in the interrogations of Defoe in 1703 (see headnotes to Letters 3 and 4). During his campaign against the *Memorial* in the *Review*, Defoe reflected numerous times on Buckingham, including noticing the irony that the *Memorial* defends such an irreligious man (II, 402 (19 July 1705)). Defoe was not the only contemporary to suspect Buckingham's hand in the *Memorial*. The antiquarian and diarist Thomas Hearne (1678-1735) reported that 'Tis said that the Duke of Buckingham is the Author' (I, 6), and Newcastle wrote to Harley on 23 July 1705 suggesting that 'the style of this scandalous libel is as imperious as King John himself' (H.M.C. *Portland MSS*, IV, 212).

7 *Lætantur Lares &ca.*: Defoe alludes to *Sic Siti Lætantur Lares* ('the household gods delight in such a situation'), the motto on the front of Buckingham's newly built house in St James's Park (the present Buckingham Palace). Defoe satirised Buckingham House in *The Dyet of Poland*: '*Lætantur Lares* Guilds the spacious Frize, | For Houshold Gods Dwell there of every Size; | 'Twas ne're for these he Built the spacious Dome, | *For all his Graces Gods would lye in far less Room*' (lines 1046–9, *SFS*, I, 373). Defoe alludes to another of Buckingham House's mottos in *A Tour thro' the Whole Island of Great Britain*, *TDH*, III, 212.

In *Jure Divino* (1706), Defoe alludes to the 'Great Charges and Diligence' that Tory 'Party-Financiers disburse[d]' in order 'to prevent the Discovery of the Authors of the *Memorial*', putting Mackworth at the heart of this cover-up (book VII, line 390, *SFS*, II, 229).

8 *I brib'd him*: John Dunton also recalls bribing Stephens (*Life and Errors*, I, 253–4).

9 *Answers … Answer'd*: Probably *An Answer Paragraph by Paragraph, to The Memorial of the Church of England*, which reprinted and commented upon the *Memorial*. Another work, *The*

153

DEFOE TO LORD HALIFAX, 16 JULY 1705

Memorial of the Church of England … Consider'd Paragraph by Paragraph (1705) was more critical of the *Memorial*. The publication of the original had been stopped by the government. In the *Review* Defoe reflects on the production of '*pretended Answers*' to the *Memorial*, 'not Design'd to Confute' its points but to reaffirm them (*Review*, II, 493 (11 Aug. 1705)). *Dyer's News-Letter* on 21 July reported that 'the pretended Remarks that are printed with it, strengthen and not confute the Assertions of the Author' (*A Collection from Dyers Letters, Concerning the Elections of the Present Parliament* (1705), 17). Hearne likewise stated that 'ye pretended Remarks that are printed with it strengthen & not confute the Assertions of ye Author' (Hearne, I, 12). Charles Leslie called paragraph-by-paragraph answers 'a new method of dispersing *libels* more securely' (*Rehearsal*, 10 Apr. 1706).

38

To Charles Montagu, Lord Halifax

16 July 1705

HEADNOTE: Defoe's last known letter to Halifax updates him on Defoe's counter-propaganda against *The Memorial of the Church of England*. The two men evidently corresponded while Defoe was in Scotland in late 1706, but those letters have not survived, and nothing seems to have come of that resumption of contact.[1]

July. 16. 1705

My Lord

I had Gone on farther to Replye to This Most Insolent Memoriall, But yt the Subject of the[a] Review being before This book came Out, Entred Upon ye Same Article, Vizt The Danger of ye Church, I Shall handle it apart.[2]

I Think it my Duty to Lay it before yor Ldship as it is, and have Sent Six of Them,[3] Not That I Think it worth yor Ldships Recommending, but That, if yor Ldship Please to Concern yor Self for me So far, yor Own hand May Make This Empty Returne to The (to me Unknown) Benefactors of whose Goodness to me yor Lordship was Pleas'd to be a Medium, and wch I have No Other way to Acknowlege.[4]

---

[a] the] *interlined*

154

DEFOE TO LORD HALIFAX, 16 JULY 1705

If I knew how to Ask my Ld Treasurer Pardon, Either for ye Weakness of my Defence in his Case, or ye Rudeness of a Dedicaćon[5] without a Name, I Should be Glad to do it, But I am too Obscure and Remote to do it Personally, and ye Same Reason That Obliges me Not to Sign ye Dedicaćon Obliges me Not to do it Publickly.

The Writeing This book I hear is Charg'd upon Dr Drake. I Can Not forbear Assureing yor Ldship, That however he Might be The Drudge or Rather Amanuensis in ye work — his Master The Duke of Bucks is as plainly Pictur'd to me wth his Pen in his hand Correcting, Dictating and Instructing as if I had been of ye Club wth Them.[6]

I Ask your L^dships Pardon for This freedome and Am

yor L^dships Most Humble and Obed^t Servt
De Foe

Text: BL Add. MS. 7121, fols. 25–6. *Address* (fol. 26^v): To The Right Honble | Charles Ld Hallifax | Humbly Prest. *Endorsed* (fol. 26^v): 16. July 1705 From De Foe

1 See Letters 62 and 73.
2 *Subject ... apart*: Defoe's *Review* first took up the theme of 'the Danger of the Church', the High Tories' mantra during the general election, on 17 Apr. 1705: 'They certainly therefore, Delude and Impose upon the People, who offer to suggest to them, that the Church is in Danger; Choose Men of Peace, Men of Moderation, Men of Sence, Men of Morals, Men of Estates, and Men of the Church; And then Gentlemen, tell us if you can, what Danger the Church can be in' (ii, 112–13). He kept up the counter-propaganda throughout the summer: see especially *Review*, ii, 183–4 (15 May 1705); ii, 275 (14 June 1705); and ii, 351–2 (5 July 1705). In this last he says 'this Noise of the Churches Danger is a Fiction' and 'the real Danger of the Church proceeds from the very Men that thus cry out first'.
3 *Them*: Copies of *The High-Church Legion*.
4 *Empty ... Acknowlege*: The benefactor was the Duchess of Marlborough (see headnote to Letter 33). Defoe's note of thanks is untraced.
5 *Dedicaćon*: See Letter 35, note 6.
6 *Writing ... Them*: See Letter 37, note 6.

39

To Robert Harley

30 July 1705

HEADNOTE: Defoe's first letter during his travels gives Harley a prospectus of politics in the south-west – Wiltshire, Dorset, and Devon – in the wake of the contentious 1705 general election. The Godolphin ministry wanted to know what it would be dealing with when the new parliament met later in the year. Its aim had been to dislodge as many as possible of the 134 High Tories who voted for the Tack, the 'Dangerous Experiment' as Defoe called it that threatened war supplies in the previous session. The results that had come in during the summer indicated that many Tackers had indeed lost out and that the ministry could anticipate an approximately even number of Whigs and Tories in the Commons, allowing placemen to sway votes in the ministry and Court's favour.[1] The Whigs of the Junto held sway in the House of Lords, necessitating Godolphin increasingly to accommodate their objectives, a policy that generally pleased Defoe but less so Harley.

Sr

I do my Self ye honor to Accquat you That Ia Reacht This Town[2] yesterday tho' Extreamly Fatigued wth ye Violent heat, but This Country has been Cool'd wth plentifull Rains and is Nowb Very Refreshing.

I have Nothing to Complain of in ye Success of my Design Except in Dorsetshire where the Exceeding Harmony between ye Dissenters and the Low Church,[3] The Disposićon of ye former to peaće one wth Another and of ye Latter to Moderaćon, Makes my Remarks Something Useless.

The Onely 2 Warm People, Coll Strangeways and sr N Napier,[4] have acted wth More Caućon and less Success than Ever and had Lt Gen. Earle and T Freak[5] put in for ye County they had Carryed it beyond all possibillity of Miscarriage.

The Dissenters arec Indeed too Easy and Do not struggle, haveing Met wth No ill Treatment to Move ym, and Perticularly

---

a That I] *following word* 'am' *cancelled*
b Now] *interlined*
c are] *following word* 'here' *cancelled*

ye Inferr Clergy are ye Most Temperate here of any place I kno', A Certain proof that ye Difft Temper of Other Counties is Owing (at Least much of it) to Their Inflameing the Gentry.[6]

At Salisbury 'tis quite Another Thing. The Bishops Candidate for ye Town mr Harris[a] Lost it[7] and ye Bishops friends were Very ill Tr[e]ated[b] by The Clergy; at ye County Eleccon the Bishops Gentlemn,[8] ye Dukes of Somersett and Bolton[9] Recd Strange Insults and his Grace of Somersett was Insulted in ye streets of Salisbury by The[c] Mob.

Here also Things are in Terrible Disordr. The Eleccon of Honyton is an Abridgemt of Coventry,[10] and F Gwin[11] has Perticularly Distinguisht himself.

In Excester the Conquest ye Bishop made Over his Clergy and The Further Improvement his Ldship makes of his Victory Renders him Formidable and Exceedingly Chagrins the Party; But his Ldships (as they Say) still Declaring himself for ye Occa: bill Comforts Them.[12] Fisher, The former Representative of ye Clergy, was Expell'd by The Bishop last week for want of Instituçon and Induccon and had a Severe Admonicon given him to be Residt at a Small Cure he has in ye Country on pain of Suspension.[13] Severall others of ye high C Clergy feel ye Effect of his Ldships Displeasure and are Under like prosecution.

All agree here had My Ld Treasurer Given his Letter to ye Bishop[d] to ha' Set up his son, sr Ed: Seymour had lost it here;[14] if That had happen'd The Party had Recd Such a blow They would Never ha' Recovred.

I Go this day to Excester Again to finish mÿ Informations at That Place and Thence to Plymouth, shall Come Round by ye North Coast of This County and be at Tiverton in about 10 dayes where ye honor of a Letter from you would be a Satisfaccö[e] and Encouragemt Directed to Alexa G . . th[15] in a Cover to ye Revrd Mr Josiah Eveleigh[16] at mr Francis Bere, Mercha in Tiverton.[17]

---

[a] mr Harris] *interlined*
[b] Tr[e]ated] *the first 'e' is omitted*
[c] The] *following illegible word cancelled*
[d] Bishop] *following word 'here' cancelled*
[e] Satisfaccö] *Defoe ran out of space, so used the macron to abbreviate*

DEFOE TO ROBERT HARLEY, 30 JULY 1705

I Met an Express and Two Lisbone[a] Mails on y[e] Road fryday Last.[b] Some Little Perticular of That affair[18] Other than y[e] Prints Informe would furnish me wth means to Let y[m] kno' I shall be Usefull, for all Our Party here are Polititians, Espećally y[e] Parsons (God bless us) who Onće a week Settle y[e] Consćienće, Twiće a week y[e] state; and It Could not but afford me Some speculaćon, to See at This plaće, where y[e] Dissenting parson is my Friend,[19] the Post Comeing in on Sunday morning, The people Devoutly Resort to y[e] News house as they Call it first, and then to Church.

I am Allmost asham'd to Tell you how Expensive I am, and yet Not Extravagant, but I am Resolv'd not to Baulk y[e] Design, leaving all things of y[t] Sort to yo[r] kindness, and to judge by The Effect, wherefore haveing a Little Supply of my Own at Plym[o] I forbear to press you on That head; if you please to Convey to Kingslands[20] what you Think Convenient for y[e] Support of This affair against I may Reach Bristoll I shall then be Oblig'd to Draw — and My wife who is my faithfull Steward[21] will Not Diminish it One Penny.

I have Nothing More worth yo[r] Notiće Save That I am, as Allways Oblig'd

May it Please yo[r] Hon[r]
yo[r] Most Humble and Most Obedient Serv[t]
[*monogram*]

Crediton July 30. 1705

Text: BL Add. MS. 70291, fols. 36–7. *Address* (fol. 37[v]): To The Right Hon[ble] | Robert Harley Esq[r] | One of her Maj[ties] Prinćipall Secretarys of State | Present

---

[a] Lisbone] *interlined*
[b] Last] *following word* 'and' *cancelled*

---

1 On 27 July 1705, Francis Eyles (*c*. 1650–1716) advised William Bentinck, first Earl of Portland (1649–1709) that 'by the nearest computation ... the whigs and tories are equal, so that the placemen will turn the balance' (University of Nottingham Library, PwA 410).

2 *Town*: Crediton. In *A Tour thro' the Whole Island of Great Britain* (1724–6), Defoe describes the scenery of east Devon as 'the most beautiful Landskip in the World' (*TDH*, I, 252).

3 *Dorsetshire ... Church*: The narrator in Defoe's *Tour* comments: '*Dorchester* is indeed a pleasant agreeable Town to live in, and where I thought the People seem'd less Divided into Factions and Parties, than in other Places; for though here are Divisions and the People are not all of one Mind, either as to Religion, or Politicks, yet they did not seem to separate with so much Animosity as in other Places: Here I saw the Church of *England* Clergymen, and the Dissenting Minister, or Preacher drinking Tea together, and Conversing with Civility and good

DEFOE TO ROBERT HARLEY, 30 JULY 1705

Neighbourhood, like Catholick Christians, and Men of a Catholick, and extensive Charity' (*TDH*, I, 241).

4 *Coll Strangeways and s^r N Napier*: Both Tories. Thomas Strangways (1643–1713) was re-elected as MP for Dorset in 1705. Sir Nathaniel Napier (*c.* 1636–1709) was not re-elected as MP for Dorchester, though his son of the same name was returned; the Whig Awnsham Churchill (1658–1728) took the other seat.

5 *Lt Gen. Earle and T Freak*: Both Whigs. Thomas Erle (1650?–1720) and Thomas Freke (1660–1721) were re-elected as MPs for Wareham and Lyme Regis respectively in 1705. Defoe laments that neither stood for the county to defeat Strangways.

6 *Inferr Clergy … Gentry*: Defoe decried the influence of clergymen promoting Tory candidates in 1705, particularly in the *Review*, II, 210–14 (26 May 1705).

7 *m^r Harris Lost it*: At Queen Anne's instigation, the Whig Bishop of Salisbury Gilbert Burnet (1643–1715) unsuccessfully supported James Harris, a lawyer, against the Tory Charles Fox (1660–1713) in the election. Fox had in Apr. been removed as paymaster of the forces as punishment for voting for the Tack, but he was re-elected to parliament. See H. C. Foxcroft, *A Life of Gilbert Burnet, Bishop of Salisbury* (Cambridge, 1907), 417; *HPC 1690–1715*, II, 692–3.

8 *Bishops Gentlem^n*: A Mr Westfield, Burnet's steward (see Letter 44).

9 *Dukes of Somersett and Bolton*: Charles Seymour, sixth Duke of Somerset (1662–1748), Anne's Master of the Horse; for Bolton, see headnote to Letters 25–7.

10 *Eleċon of Honyton is an Abridgem^t of Coventry*: The 1705 Coventry election was marked by riots and voter intimidation. The election of two Tories – Sir Christopher Hales (1670–1717) and Thomas Gery (*c.* 1663–1727) – was eventually overturned and their two Whig opponents – Sir Orlando Bridgeman (*c.* 1679–1746) and Edward Hopkins (1675?–1736) – were returned in a 1707 re-contest (*HPC 1690–1715*, II, 628–30). Defoe reported on the riots a few weeks before the election in the *Review*, II, 169–73 (10 May 1705). His account was attacked in a Tory pamphlet, *A True State of the Case of the Election at Coventry, shewing the Misrepresentations of a Scandalous Paper, calld, The Review of the Affairs of France* (1705). Defoe looked back on the Coventry election in *Review*, III, 505–8 (17 Aug. 1706); he congratulated the city on regaining electoral freedom in *Review*, IV, 112 (1 Apr. 1707). 'Coventry Tumults' remained his shorthand for a mob election (*Review*, IV, 627 (20 Nov. 1707); IV, 727 (1 Jan. 1708); IV, 900 (18 Mar. 1708)). Defoe later described the 'Terrible Mob Election' at Honiton (Letter 44).

11 *F Gwin*: The Tory Francis Gwyn (1648?–1734), MP for Christchurch, satirised as '*Guinsky*' in Defoe's *The Dyet of Poland* (1705), lines 1050–92, *SFS*, I, 373–4.

12 *Bishop … Them*: Sir Jonathan Trelawny (1650–1721), Bishop of Exeter, had moved with the Godolphin–Marlborough ministry from the Tories to the Whigs, and induced many of the inferior clergy to join him. As a reward, he was in time promoted to the Bishopric of Winchester in 1706. In the *Review* on 14 June Defoe had suggested that Trelawny would 'Blush for his Diocese' if asked how many of his clergy voted for moderate candidates (II, 274).

13 *Fisher … Suspension*: Earlier in the year, Trelawney had contended with the High Church members of his cathedral chapter regarding elections of proctors to represent the diocese at convocation when they resisted his pressure not to elect the prebendary Peter Fisher (d. 1739), rector of Hemyock. As John Poulett, first Earl Poulett (*c.* 1668–1743) wrote to Harley on 2 May 1705, 'the Bishop himself is often named in their pulpits as an enemy to the Church' (H.M.C. *Portland MSS*, IV, 177). The clergymen published two pamphlets, *Reasons in Particular, why the Clergy of the Archdeaconry of Exon, cannot Comply with his Lordship's Present Recommendation of Proctors, to Represent them in the Ensuing Convocation* and *An Apology for the Clergy of the Diocese of Exon* (both 1705). Defoe denounced these two pamphlets and 'the Highflying Clergy of the Diocese of *Exeter*' for opposing the Bishop (*Review*, II, 351 (5 July 1705)). But at the election, Trelawney's nominees, John Hickes (1682–1762) and Robert Hoblyn (1658–1706), comfortably defeated their opponents, John Newte (1656–1716) and Fisher. See M. G. Smith, 'The Cathedral Chapter of Exeter and the Election of 1705: A Reconsideration', *Transactions of the Devonshire Association for the Advancement of Science, Literature and Art* 116 (1984), 109–26.

159

DEFOE TO ROBERT HARLEY, 14 AUGUST 1705

14 *had My Ld Treasurer ... Seymour had lost it here*: The proposal that Francis Godolphin (1678–1766) stand at Exeter in order to defeat either Tory, Sir Edward Seymour or John Snell (*c.* 1638–1717), did not come to fruition. Godolphin had first stood for the University of Cambridge, but two Tackers were re-elected. Contrary to Defoe's view that locals were confident of Godolphin's success, Lancelot Blackburne (1658–1743), Dean of Exeter, wrote to William Wake (1657–1737), Bishop of Lincoln, on 6 June 1705 that Godolphin would have lost (Wake MSS, xvii, fol. 98r, Christ Church, Oxford). Francis Godolphin was returned instead for Helston, the Godolphin family seat. For Defoe's view of Seymour, see Letter 40, note 28.

15 *Alex^a G .. th*: Defoe's pseudonym, Alexander Goldsmith.

16 *Mr Josiah Eveleigh*: Presbyterian minister at Crediton (d. 1736) and later the author of pamphlets during the trinitarian controversy of 1719. He was likely Defoe's host mentioned in the next paragraph, perhaps the Dissenter with whom Defoe travelled this circuit as mentioned in Letter 40, and certainly Defoe's distribution agent as mentioned in Letter 44.

17 *mr Francis Bere, Merch^a in Tiverton*: Bere or Bear (d. 1722) was a Presbyterian merchant and brother of Tiverton MP, Thomas Bere (1652–1725). See Backscheider, *Life*, 184; Rogers, 'Distribution Agents', 147.

18 *That affair*: Not identified.

19 *my Friend*: Probably meaning Eveleigh.

20 *Kingslands*: Defoe's residence at London, near Hackney.

21 *faithfull Steward*: The phrase is applied by Robinson Crusoe twice to the widow to whom he entrusts his money (*Novels*, 1, 264, 270) and by Captain Singleton to his Quaker companion William Walters (*Novels*, v, 220). For the biblical contexts, see 1 Cor. 4:2 and Luke 12:42–8.

40

To Robert Harley

14 August 1705

HEADNOTE (**Letters 40 and 41**): Defoe's tour of the south-west in summer 1705 was far from uneventful. The chain of events leading to the letters he sent to Harley and to Dorset JP Hugh Stafford are given in the Minute Books for Weymouth,[1] summarised by H. J. Moule:

> Jas. Turner, of the Diligence Privateer, deposes that on Monday, July 23, he received three letters in one cover, franked S. Barker, to be left at the house of Mr. Fenner, a minister in Weymouth. In one, dated Norwich, were the words, 'the Queen hath broken her Coronation oath.' The rest of the letters, 'intermixed in sundry hands,' he could make nothing of. At the Bear [inn] he delivered the letters to a stranger called, he is told, 'Mr. Daniell Dufoe,' in company with Mr. Fenner, Independent Minister. Dufoe was often named in the letters. On July 21 [sic] he received another letter, with like address, but not franked, and delivered it to

160

Mr. D. in Mr. Fenner's presence, Mr. Jonathan Edwards also coming into the room. July 26, 1705. (It would rather seem that the letters came to the wrong Capt. Turner.) Five other persons depose, saying among other things, that Mr. D. said he cared not who saw the letters, or if they were set up at the Market Cross—also that it was one of the 'Earl of Dysart's party' who spoke the above words against the Queen. A Warrant was issued, signed Ro. Price, to bring Mr. Fenner, Mr. Dufoe, Mr. Edwards, Capt. Turner, and Capt. Jas. Turner to Dorchester, as having received traitorous letters. July 27, 1705.[2]

Once he became aware of Stafford's warrant, Defoe fired off what its recipient called 'an impudent reflecting letter' (Letter 41).[3] In that letter, Defoe states that he has a pass from the Secretary of State. Stafford assumed Defoe meant Hedges rather than Harley and so wrote to the former on 27 August. He told Hedges that he had it 'from very Cridible hands, yt severall letters of dangerous Consequence to ye Queen, and Goverment were directed to Mr De' Foe att Weymouth, (wch Came to his hands)'; that after taking advice from 'Mr Baron Price[,] one of ye Judges of the Assize att Exeter', he issued a warrant for his apprehension, 'hopeing to have found some of his dangerous Letters about him'. In a postscript, Stafford proceeds to paint a colourful picture of Defoe at work on his journey, complaining about the parliamentary influence of High Tories:

> Since writing of this I have further information from very good hands that he deals very freely in his common conversation wth ye young parliamt men, in basely reflecting on them lately in my neighbourhood, by saying, as for them, they generally lay drinking att some Tavern or other near ye house [of Commons], and leave ye concerns of ye Nation to halfe a Score Old Stagers to mannage; till any business of moment, and then they are sent for, who as soon as they come into ye house imeadiatly whisper to one, and soe to another, to know how Sr Edward [Seymour], Sr Humphry [Mackworth], or Sr John [Pakington], how they voted, and haveing learnt yt, without ever hearing ye meritts of ye cause, or indeed any thing of ye matter says he, immeadiatly cry out they give their vote ye same way lett it be right or wrong soe long as Sr Edward and they vote Soe,[4] and many more Such Scandelous reflections as these are, wch makes me very much doubt [i.e. fear] he comes into our country wth noe good designe, for he keeps Company wth none but presbytarian and Independent preachers, for he has made it his business to visitt them almost in every town and p[ar]ish throughout our County, and I hear throughout all ye Countys through wch he has past.[5]

Despite acting, as he says to Hedges, 'with all possible diligence and secrecy', Stafford missed Defoe.[6] According to Defoe, this was no accident: he alleged that Stafford knew his warrant was dubious and so only issued it when Defoe was out of reach. By the time Stafford had written to Hedges, Defoe had already reflected on these events in the *Review* for 25 August 1705, writing scathingly of 'the Wisdom and Courage of a Country Justice, the Wise Esquire *S—d*', and imputing his treatment to 'Party Malice'.[7] Novak observes that Defoe projects insouciance and control over the events in his letter to Harley, but his real anger comes out in the *Review* essay.[8] He glanced back at the escapade again in the *Review* for 11 October 1705 and in the preface to volume 11, written in December. There Defoe complains of persecutory JPs, suppositious creditors, and malignant journalists, all of whom create turmoil in order to oppose the message of peace and union he conveyed in printed works and in person while travelling.[9]

Sr

I Recd but This Day ye honor of yors[10] at Tiverton; yor Concérne for me Sr fills me wth Gratefull Thoughts how to Render my Self a yet more Suitable Subject for So Much Goodness, and Encourages me to bear up undr ye Desperate Resolucóns Taken to Ruine me.[11]

Providencé and Some Dexterity of Conduct (pardon my Vanity) has hitherto Rendred all ye Measures of ye Party Impotent and Unsuccessfull and yet I have not Omitted One part of my work Nor Bauk'd One Town I purposed to Call at, Barnstaple Excepted.

I Can not however but Divert you wth ye short history of this Matter. The Misscarriage at Weymo happened by Such a Cassualty as no Man Could forsee; my Letters, Directed for ye Friend Now wth me Call'd Capt Turner,[12] to be left at Weymo, were Taken up, by One Capt Turner, Comma of a Guernsey privateer[13] Then in yt Port. The Ignorant Tarr when he found Things written Darke and Unintelligible shows ym to all ye Town; at Our Comeing however he Restores ye Letters, Drank a pint of wine wth us and Calls for One himself wch it seems afterward he went away and Never paid for; ye people of ye house Demanding Money for it next Day Put him in a frett and that Vented it[a] Self in his Railing at this Letter all about Town Till ye Mayor[14] Sent for him; ye Imperfect accot he gave fills ye Mayors as foolish head with Jealousyes, and ye

---

[a] it] *interlined above cancelled word* 'him'

DEFOE TO ROBERT HARLEY, 14 AUGUST 1705

Assises being at Dorchester away he Runs to yᵉ Judges and Getts
a summons for mʳ Fenner yᵉ Dissenting Minister[15] and Two or 3
More who I had Visited and Carryes yᵐ to Dorchester where yᵉ
Judge, Whose Name I think is Price,[16] Examin'd yᵐ and Dissmiss't
them.[17]

But This blunder has had a worse Effect Since — when I Came
to Excester and haveing[a] Appeard publickly among my Friends and
being after at Crediton[b] a Day or Two yᵉ party Thoᵗ I was Gone.
One of yᵉ Aldermen blustred that he was Sorry he Did not Take me
up and list me for a Soldier, Coll Brittons Regimᵗ[18] being There.

At my Returne I appear'd publickly, walk'd Severall Times on yᵉ[c]
Walks of yᵉ Church Call'd yᵉ Parade of yᵉ Party, went to yᵉ Church,
yᵉ Bowling Green, yᵉ Coffee house &ca with some of yᵉ Principle
of yᵉ Citizens, and mʳ Alderman & his brethren took no Notice
of it.

I went from Thence to Totness, Dartmᵒ & Plymouth and yᵉ
Day before I went yᵉ Judges Came to Town. The party then Took
heart and as I Understand applyed to mʳ Justice Price who in his
Charge to yᵉ Grand Jury Tells them There are Severall Seditious
p[er]sons Come Down into yᵉ Country spreading Libells &ca and
Embroiling yᵉ people and advises the Justices to Apprehend them.

The first Effect of This was that at Crediton a Country Justice[19]
Grants yᵉ Enclosed warrant[20] Against me and searches yᵉ Town wᵗʰ
Constables and p[er]ticularly yᵉ Dissenting Ministers house,[21] But I
was Then at Liskard in Cornwall.

The first Accoᵗ of This I mett wᵗʰ, at Bideford where Some
Gentlemen Comeing into yᵉ Town from yᵉ Assizes Told yᵉ people
yᵉ Judge had Nam'd me to yᵉ Grand Jury and Given Direccons to
Apprehend me wherever I might be found.

By This Report I had been Insulted in Bideford yᵉ Next
Morning; But yᵉ Mayor[22] being Out of Town yᵉ Next principle
Magistrate whom they[d] Call a justice, as haveing been Mayor The
year before, was my p[er]ticular Friend,[23] And here was yᵉ first and

---

[a] haveing] *interlined*
[b] after at Crediton] *interlined above cancelled word* 'Gone'
[c] Times on yᵉ] *following word* 'promenade' *cancelled*
[d] they] *interlined above cancelled word* 'yᵉ'

Onely[a] Time I show'd your Pass, Takeing ye hint from your Letter[24] of useing it wth Caucon.

This So Encourag'd ye Magistrate and all my Friends That I might have assur'd my self here of Proteccon, and ye Measures of ye Other party in ye Town Seem'd Entirely broke But I was privately Informd that[b] they had sent away a messenger Express to have me stop't at Barnstaple as I Came along.

Had not ye Danger of my Own private affaires[25] and ye warrant from London being Rouz'd by this Noise layn a Little Upon my Thoughts, I had more publickly Ventur'd the[c] Worst Effects of Their Mallice, but not knowing what of that Sort might be in it I avoided Barnstaple and haveing a p[er]ticular friend, a S. T. P. Dissenter[26] who I Carryed wth me all this Circuit from Exon, I have Visited Every Town So securely by being lodg'd among friends that I am Now under ye Nose of ye Justices Concern'd in ye Enclos'd warrant and yet Out of their Danger.

To morrow I leav this Town and County and, Presumeing your Direccons for my Returne[27] proceed from yor Apprehensions of my p[er]sonall hazards and are ye Effect of y^t Concern for me wch I Can Never Enough Acknowlege and Not from an alteracon in yor Opinion or Design of haveing this work Done, I proceed, wth Resolucon thro' More Difficultyes than these to p[er]sue all ye Ord^rs I shall at any time Reciev from you.

The success I have had in this part I p[er]swade my Self will fully Satisfye you, as it has Encouraged me to Say That Seymskyes westerne Empire[28] may wth Much Ease be Overthrown and his successor[29] Defeated, and had I Come here Sooner by half a year it had felt a great blow Ere Now.

As to Apprehensions of my Friend who is wth me betrayeing me, I assure you of the Contrary, Nor are you s^r betraid to him, Nor does he suspect I Correspond wth you or have ye honour to Converse wth you. I am not Serving a Master I have so little Vallue for; you may s^r Depend upon me That Neither by Fraud or Folly the Confidence you are pleasd to place in me shall Ever be Dissappointed.

[a] and Onely] *interlined*
[b] that] *following letter 'y' cancelled*
[c] the] *illegible letter cancelled at the end of this word*

DEFOE TO ROBERT HARLEY, 14 AUGUST 1705

I wrott you sr from Exon[30] wch I hope is Come Safe. In that I Took ye Freedome to Mençon a supplye; Indeed I have been more Expensive here than I Expected, but it has been purely to p[er]fect ye work and I Think I may Say I have a p[er]fect skeleton of this part of England and a Settled Correspondençe in Every Town and Corner of it.

I go Directly to ye Bath where my Companion leaves me and mr Davis[a] my Brother in Law,[31] who has ye honor to wait on you, Comes to me wth another Friend[32] who will Travail into ye North wth me.

By my Brother any thing you please to Convey to my Wife will Come Safe, But Rather by Bill than in speçie and Seal'd because sr I have Learnt in all these things to make Agents wthout Accquainting ym wth Perticulars.

I Humbly Entreat yor Letter wch mr Davis will bring me to ye Bath and So No Danger of a Misscarriage and Till Then forbear Troubling you any Farther

But am

yor Faithfull Obedient Servt

[*monogram*]

A Terrible storme On Fryday night Last has done Incredible Damage in ye Country besides what has been at Plymouth.[33]

Tiverton Augt. 14. 1705

Text: BL Add. MS. 70291, fols. 39–40. *Address in Defoe's disguised handwriting* (fol. 40v): To the Right Honoble | Robert Harley, Esqr | Principal Secretary of State | Present

---

[a] mr Davis] *interlined*

---

1 Weymouth Minute Book (1699–1724), Dorset History Centre DC-WYM/AD/1/5, fols. 74v–78r.

2 H. J. Moule, *Descriptive Catalogue of the Charters, Minute Books and other Documents of the Borough of Weymouth and Melcombe Regis* (Weymouth, 1883), 86–7. Thomas B. Groves, 'Daniel De Foe in Dorsetshire', *Proceedings of the Dorset Natural History and Antiquarian Field Club* 2 (1878), 67–75 contains errors.

3 Stafford to Hedges, 27 Aug. 1705, TNA SP 34/6, fol. 105. Defoe states in the *Review*, referring to himself in the third person: 'he sent him a Letter to acquaint him where he was, and which way he was going, and the Names of the Towns he would be at, if his Worship thought fit

165

DEFOE TO ROBERT HARLEY, 14 AUGUST 1705

to send for him' (II, 540 (25 Aug. 1705)). This is true, but he makes his letter to Stafford sound more civil than it in fact is.

4 This resonates with Defoe's criticisms of 'Dead Weight' MPs who mindlessly vote with some local grandee, in *The Six Distinguishing Characters of a Parliament Man* (1701), *PEW*, II, 34–5.

5 Stafford to Hedges, 27 Aug. 1705, TNA SP 34/6, fol. 105. Stafford neglected to inclose Defoe's letter, so wrote again on 17 Sept., doing so (Hedges to Stafford, 14 Sept. 1705, TNA SP 44/105, fol. 287; Stafford to Hedges, 17 Sept. 1705, TNA SP 34/6, fol. 128).

6 TNA SP 34/6, fol. 105.

7 *Review*, II, 541–2 (25 Aug. 1705).

8 Novak, 270.

9 *Review*, II, 649 (II Oct. 1705); II, 5 (preface, Dec. 1705).

10 *yors*: Untraced.

11 *Desperate Resolućons Taken to Ruine me*: See *Review*, II, 394 (17 July 1705).

12 *Capt Turner*: Unidentified. A year earlier, a Capt. Turner took subscriptions for Defoe's *Jure Divino* 'in the *Auction Room* near the House of Common's Door' (*Review*, I, 382 (26 Sept. 1704)). Defoe's account of this episode in his journey, given in the *Review*, states that he travelled 'with but one Friend, and his Friend's Servant' (II, 539 (25 Aug. 1705)). It is possible that Christopher Hurt accompanied Defoe (Defoe had requested this of Harley – see Letter 34), and Hurt may have been operating as 'Capt. Turner'. On 27 Dec. 1710, a secret service payment of £50 came to Defoe (under his sobriquet at that time, Claude Guillot) via a James Turner (TNA T 48/16, fol. 9).

13 *Capt Turner Commᵃ of a Guernsey privateer*: Capt. James Turner, commander of the privateer *Diligence* (*CTB*, XIX, 488).

14 *Mayor*: William Harding.

15 *mr Fenner yᵉ Dissenting Minister*: John Fenner (d. 1714), Independent minister in Weymouth and Melcombe Regis from 1695 to around 1712 (William Densham and Joseph Ogle, *The Story of the Congregational Churches of Dorset: From their Foundation to the Present Time* (Bournemouth, 1899), 369; Alexander Gordon, *Freedom after Ejection: A Review (1690–1692) of Presbyterian and Congregational Nonconformity in England and Wales* (Manchester, 1917), 262).

16 *Priće*: Robert Price (1653–1733), formerly MP for Weobley, and a longtime associate of Harley (*HPC 1690–1715*, v, 203–10).

17 *Dissmis't them*: Defoe's assertion that Price thought the case not worth pursuing is refuted by Price's entry in the Weymouth minute book (fol. 78r) and by Stafford's letter to Hedges. Price advised issuing the warrant.

18 *Coll Brittons Regimᵗ*: Col. William Britton. See the *Review* for 25 Aug. 1705 where Defoe warns the would-be traveller: 'Let him have a special care how he comes to *Exon*, particularly in Time of the Assizes, lest Mr. Alderman B—, Mr. —, and Mr. —, should Consult about sending an *English* Free-holder, and Livery-man of the City of *London*, for a Soldier' (II, 538).

19 *Country Justiće*: Hugh Stafford (1674–1734), Justice of the Peace in Devon. See the following letter.

20 *Enclosed warrant*: Defoe called this warrant 'a Cover to a Fiction', stating that Stafford knew its basis was dubious and so issued it only when he knew that Defoe was out of reach (*Review*, II, 541 (25 Aug. 1705)). The warrant, reproduced here, is in neither Defoe's nor Stafford's handwriting, but is signed by Stafford. Below Stafford's signature Defoe has written a note to Harley: 'Pray sʳ Do not loose this paper' (BL Add. MS. 70291, fol. 38):

> Devonsh: To all Constᵇˡᵉˢ and Tythingmen and other her majestie's officers within the County of devon and allso to Charl's Sugg.
>
> Whereas I have received Information against Daniel de Foe for spreading and publishing divers seditious and scandalous Libels and false news to the great disturbance of the Peace of this Kingdom and that He is a Person of ill Fame and Behaviour, and is now lurking within some or one of your Parishes, Tythings or Precinct's. These are in her Majᵗʸˢ name to will and require you and every of you on Sight hereof to make diligent privy Search within your said Parishes[,] Tythings

166

DEFOE TO ROBERT HARLEY, 14 AUGUST 1705

and Precincts in all suspitious Houses and Places within the same, and to be assistant to the sd Charl's Sugg in searching for and apprehending the sd. Daniel de Foe, and when found and apprehended forthwith to bring him before me to be examin'd concerning the Premises, and to be dealt with as the Law directs, Hereof you and every of you may not fail at your utmost Perils. Given under my Hand and Seal ye 9th Day of August in the 4th year of ye Reign of our soverain Lady Ann over England &c.

Anno dom: 1705.

Hugh Stafford.

21 *Dissenting Ministers house*: The minister is unidentified.

22 *Mayor*: George Strange (d. 1736?).

23 *Friend*: John Darracott (d. 1733). His spiritual diary survives but starts in 1707 (William Andrews Clark Memorial Library, MS 1950.010).

24 *Letter*: Untraced.

25 *private affaires*: The *Review* for 17 July 1705 mentions three actions, totalling £2,800, brought against Defoe for old debts, the legitimacy of which he denies (ii, 394).

26 *S. T. P. Dissenter*: *Sacrae Theologiae Professor*, i.e. professor of divinity, meaning one who studied at a university. This companion is unidentified but is possibly Eveleigh (see Letter 39).

27 *Direccons for my Returne*: Letter untraced. Presumably the direction was merely for Defoe to come out of Devon rather than return to London, as he proceeded with his national tour and only arrived back in London on 6 Nov.

28 *Seymskyes westerne Empire*: Defoe uses the same phrase in *The Dyet of Poland* (1705) for the electoral influence of Sir Edward Seymour ('Seymsky') in the south-west (line 1063, *SFS*, I, 373). See the lengthy lampoon of Seymour in that poem (lines 395–492, *SFS*, I, 355–8). Defoe attacked Seymour for his opposition to William III's standing army in *The Pacificator* (1700), line 33, *SFS*, I, 66. Defoe also accused Seymour of taking bribes, as in *Ye True-Born Englishmen Proceed* (1701), line 82, *SFS*, I, 128; *Reformation of Manners* (1702), line 563, *SFS*, I, 172. Defoe celebrated Seymour's fall from office on the basis that he was a divisive High Tory and enemy of Dissenters (e.g. *The High-Church Legion* (1705), *PEW*, II, 114; *Jure Divino* (1706), book VII, lines 380–7, *SFS*, II, 228–9).

29 *his Successor*: Francis Gwyn. See Letter 39, note II.

30 *I wrott you sr from Exon*: Presumably the preceding letter, actually from Crediton, but giving details of Defoe's time in Exeter.

31 *mr Davis my Brother in Law*: Robert Davis.

32 *another Friend*: Unidentified.

33 *Storme ... Plymouth*: Twenty years later, in the *Tour*, Defoe gives a detailed account of this storm and its aftermath, mistakenly stating that it occurred one year after the great storm of Nov. 1703 (*TDH*, I, 258–9). Cf. Defoe, *Remarks on the Bill to Prevent Frauds Committed by Bankrupts* (1706), 2.

41

To Hugh Stafford

14 August 1705

A True Coppy of Daniel De Foes Letter Sent me dated y[e] 14th of Agust 1705

S[r]

I am not att all Surprized att y[e] malice of my enemies in their vain attempts to insult me, But I am concerned to hear a man of your Character, honour, and Office, Should Soe freely grant your warrant for apprehending a man Travailing about his Lawfull Occasions, and not in the least misbehaving himselfe to any man.

I doe my Selfe y[e] Honour to acquaint you y[t], foreseeing y[e] possibillity of Such dealings, I have wth me a Certification from her mat[yes] Secretary of State of my haveing acquainted y[e] Goverment of my Occasions to travaile and of my giveing security for my Fidelity to her mat[ye], requireing you as well as all other magistrates to offer me noe disturbance or molestation in my Journey, and being att Biddeford when I had the notice of y[r] unjustice-like as well as ungentleman-like warrant,[1] I went Imeadiately to y[e] principall magistrate[2] of y[e] Town to Show my Selfe and y[e] Authority aforesd to any man y[t] had reason to question it.

By this S[r] I publickly Confute, that Scandalous Falsity affirmed in y[r] warrant of my Lurking in y[e] Countrey, and I am Sorry my Occasions will not permitt me to tell you soe to y[r] face.

As to my dispersing Libells S[r], and disturbing y[e] peace, I am extreamly desirous of knowing what Information of that Sort can be brought you Since my respect for y[r] Character forbids me to beleeve you would grant y[r] warrant for me unless it was Informed upon Oath, and if it was Sworne I shall Certainely pursue y[e] perjured Villaine as farre as y[e] law directs, assureing you it is false in fact and malicious in Suggestion.

I wish all men would pursue y[e] peace and publick Tranquillity and as earnestly perswade to it [as][a] I doe, and I Claim this Justice

---

[a] [as]] *word omitted*

DEFOE TO HUGH STAFFORD, 14 AUGUST 1705

of you y^t what is Charged on me to ye contrary may be fairly prov'd or the forgers of it detected.

I am now att Tiverton,[3] and goe from hence to Wells where I doubt not to convince y^t Honble person who tis Suggested pointed att me in publicke y^t he as well as you have been imposed upon; If you have assurance enough of y^r Information and thinke fitt to Send after me, you Shall finde I doe not Lurk about, but dare Show my face to you or any man.

If S^r you please to doe me ye honour of your reply to this and ye Justice of acquainting me who are y^r Informers, I shall receive it, if directed to me att ye Essex Coffee house att ye Temple, London.[4]

Yr humble Servt
Dan^ll De Foe.

Text: MS untraced. The copytext is the copy made by Stafford: TNA SP 34/6, fol. 128. *Address*: none. *Endorsed by an unknown hand* (fol. 128v): 1705 Augt 14

1 *unjustice-like as well as ungentleman-like warrant*: 'His Warrant was *Unjustice-like*, no Affidavit, or Information upon Oaths, being made of the Fact alledg'd' (*Review*, II, 542 (25 Aug. 1705)).
2 *principall magistrate*: John Darracott.
3 *now att Tiverton*: Defoe's itinerary in Letter 44 puts him in Tiverton on 12–13 Aug. and in Taunton on 14 Aug., the date of this letter (14 Aug.) perhaps indicating that he wrote his letters before the day's travelling.
4 *Essex Coffee house att ye Temple, London*: Lillywhite, 202. Subscriptions for *Jure Divino* were taken 'at the *Essex Coffee-house, Mitre Court Fleet-street*', starting Sept. 1704 (*Review*, I, 382 (26 Sept. 1704)).

DEFOE TO ROBERT HARLEY, 10 SEPTEMBER 1705

42

To Robert Harley

10 September 1705

HEADNOTE: Defoe's account of the 1705 elections in Wiltshire and parts of Somerset and Gloucestershire offers information and advice to Harley in equal measure. The reports he seems to have provided for the regions he subsequently visited have not been traced.

Sr

My absence from ye Bath, where I had Appointed my Brother[1] to Meet me and where having waited Two dayes I Could not Satisfy[e][a] my Self to spend my Time, Occasion'd me to Miss him Longer then I Intended and Consequently to Deferr my Giveing you an Accot That by him I Recd as well ye Supply as ye Repeated Expressions of yor Concern for my Safety, for both wch sr I Owe More Acknowlegements than I Can Express this Way.

I spent about 8 dayes, ye Intervall I Mençon above, in Goeing back into Somersetshire and yt Great Vale of Trade Extending from Warminster on ye south bordr of Wilts to Cirencester in Gloucester shire,[2] wch lyeing so Out of ye Road I Could no Otherwise take Either Goeing or Comeing without Omitting plaçes of Equall Moment.

Here I shall give you an Accot & I hope to satisfacçion of strange and Unaccountable people as well as practises in ye late Elecçons wth a survey something perticular of ye Towns of Warminster, Westbury, Bradford, Trubridge, Chipenham, Caln, Divizes, Malmsbury, Bedwin, Lutgersall, Marleboro', Cirencester &ca.[3]

Here I am to Note to you sr that <u>Watt White</u>, Member for Chipenham, is Dead,[4] and that all ye Gentry of ye high party who here act like Devills more than Men <u>pardon ye Expression</u> are Embark't to get in if possible that scandall of ye County Coll Chivers,[5] and ye Design is not So Much to have ye Man in ye house as to shelter him from ye prosecution of my Ld Bishop of Salisbury

---

[a] Satisfy[e]] *MS frayed*

170

who prosecutes him for most Impudent language,[6] of all wch I have ye p[er]ticulars.

S^r there Can not be a greater peice of Service to ye publick nor Can any Thing Tend more to Carrying future Eleccons in this County wch Now Run higher and worse than in most places in England than to prevent this project, and One step above would do it Effectually, Viz: putting Chivers Out of ye Commission of peace to wch he is Really a horrible scandall — for by being in that power he Influences ye Town, Sitts Dilligently at Every petty sessions and Aws ye people; he was at this work when I was at Chipenham — this may be done Obliquely. No Man Need kno' who hurt them, his Character will most Clearly Justifye it and No man Can Object; if he is Out of ye peace he Certainly looses the Eleccon.

My Ld Mordant stands against m^r Chivers but his Intrest is but weak yet.[7]

Bristoll, Gloucester and Bath^a are Entirely Reform'd Cittyes and the Moderate Intrest prevailes amain.[8]

Divizes and ye wholl County of Wilts are Corrupted and abused by the <u>Iron-Chest</u>, a Modern proverb now known in this Country as Universally as ye Alphabet; ye Meaning is ye Reciever Gen^ll of ye County is s^r Fra: Childs Bro:[9] whose Influence so Rules by Lending Money that who ever is Needy is sure to be bought off.

The Remove of that One Article would make 20 Members more, of wch I Reserve till I have ye honour to see you.

I am Now Moveing North, shall be at Shrewsbury to morrow and at Manchester Thursday from whence Ile do my self ye honour to write again, and where I may Reciev any Ord^rs from you if you please to Direct to Robt Davis to be left at ye post house at Manchester Till Call'd for, for I shall Go to Leverpool & Come back thither.

I am I bless God Got Clear of all ye Enemies I apprehended and am Every where Rec^d with Unusuall Respect.

It a little supriz'd me At Gloucester when m^r Forbes[10] ye Dissenting Minister bid me at parting Give his humble service to

---

^a Bath] *following words* 'and Tewxbury' *are interlined and cancelled*

DEFOE TO ROBERT HARLEY, 10 SEPTEMBER 1705

you, for he knew I had the honour [to] be known[a] to you. I Can no way Divine his Intelligen*c*e unless m*r* Auditor[11] might men*c*on it to him.

I am

S*r*

yo*r* Most Obedient Serv*t*

AG[12]

Kiderminster
Sept. 10. 1705

Text: BL Add. MS. 70291, fols. 41–2. *Address in Defoe's disguised handwriting* (fol. 42*v*): For The Right Hono*ble* | Robert Harley Esq*r* | Principall Secretary | of State

---

[a] honour [to] be known] 'honour y*e* ~~to~~ be known' *in MS; this edition restores the cancelled word and omits* 'ye'

---

1 *Brother*: Robert Davis.

2 *Great Vale … Gloucestershire*: See Defoe's discussion of the clothing trade in this region in his *Tour, TDH*, ii, 32–4. In *A Brief Deduction of the Original, Progress, and Immense Greatness of the British Woollen Manufacture* (1727), he calls it 'the richest and most fruitful Vale in all the West Part of *England*' (29).

3 *Towns … &ca*: There are some significant omissions in Defoe's tour of the south-west. In Wiltshire, he does not appear to have visited Cricklade, a fairly dependable Whig borough, or Hindon, a wonderfully corrupt one, not to mention the depopulated Old Sarum, where the outcome was contested. This is quite apart from places uncontested in 1705, like Downton, Heytesbury, and Wilton.

4 *Watt White … Dead*: Walter White (1667–1705), generally Whig, had died on 21 July.

5 *Coll Chivers*: Col. Henry Chivers (*c.* 1653–1720), Tory. In *An Encomium upon a Parliament* (1699), Defoe reflected obliquely on Chivers's actions in distributing papers listing Whigs who voted against the Disbanding Bill in 1699 (lines 56–60, *SFS*, i, 61). In *A Hymn to Peace* (1706), Defoe satirised 'Hell-born *Ch—s*' in detail (lines 557–68, *SFS*, i, 398).

6 *prosecution … language*: Bishop Burnet brought 'an action of scandalum magnatum' against Chivers in June 1705. Chivers had implied that he had seen Burnet in a brothel. The case was resolved in Nov. when Chivers apologised in a *London Gazette* notice and gave £350 for distribution among the poor (Luttrell, v, 565, 614). Defoe alludes gleefully to Chivers's humbling in *Review*, ii, 773 (4 Dec. 1705); ii, 811 (20 Dec. 1705); iii, 223 (11 Apr. 1706); and iv, 296 (28 June 1707).

7 *L*d* Mordant … yet*: John, Lord Mordaunt (*c.* 1681–1710), a Whig, who had served as MP for Chippenham before the 1705 general election, at which he unsuccessfully ran for Northamptonshire. He defeated Chivers in the Chippenham by-election.

8 *Bristoll, Gloucester and Bath … amain*: Whigs controlled the city governments. In the parliamentary election of 1705, Bristol re-elected the Whigs Sir William Daines (*c.* 1656–1724) and Robert Yate (1643–1737). Bath re-elected the Court Tory William Blathwayt (1649–1717) and the moderate Alexander Popham (*c.* 1670–1705), though the latter died shortly after the elec-

tion. Gloucester returned two Whigs: it re-elected John Hanbury (*c.* 1665–1734) and elected William Cooke (1682–1709).

Defoe crossed out Tewkesbury, denying it the positive appellation given its neighbouring towns. Its MPs were the Court-supporting Whig Edmund Bray (1678–1725) and Richard Dowdeswell (*c.* 1653–1711), who, though no Tacker, was associated with the High Tory William Bromley (1663–1732), a leading figure against occasional conformity, which may explain Defoe's cancellation. But in Letter 44 he calls it 'A Quiet Tradeing Drunken Town, a whig bayly and all well.'

9   *s^r Fra: Childs Bro:*: John Child, Receiver-General of Wiltshire since 1689, was the brother of Sir Francis Child (1642–1713), Tory MP for Devizes. Defoe may have held a grudge against Sir Francis concerning some attempted land purchases (Spiro Peterson, 'Defoe and Westminster, 1696–1706', *ECS* 12 (1979), 306–38). Looking back on the 1705 election, Defoe alludes to the 'breaking the Laws, as at *Devizes*' (*Review*, IV, 843 (21 Feb. 1708)). Sir Francis fended off a Whig challenge from Josiah Diston (*c.* 1667–1737). See Edward Bradby, 'A Deadlock in 18th-Century Devizes', *Wiltshire Archaeological and Natural History Magazine* 81 (1987), 91–110.

10   *mr Forbes*: James Forbes (*c.* 1629–1712), Independent minister at Barton Street meeting house. For his career, see *ODNB*.

11   *mr Auditor*: See Letter 7, note 13.

12   *AG*: Alexander Goldsmith, Defoe's pseudonym.

43

To Edward Owen and Joseph Cater

26–7 October 1705

HEADNOTE: Edward Owen (d. 1706), a capper and feltmaker by vocation, a Presbyterian in religion, served as Whig mayor of Coventry in 1680 and 1696. In 1702, when under-sheriff, he was tried and acquitted for illegal conduct in the previous year's election, specifically for using threatening language towards the sergeant.[1] In May 1705, he was among the aldermen who joined the mayor in writing to Robert Harley concerning Tory mobbing at the general election.[2] It is possible that he supplied Defoe with the information that furnished his *Review* article on the Coventry election. The House of Commons ultimately rejected the Coventry result.[3] Defoe lists Owen as his distribution agent in Coventry in 1706, but Owen died shortly after that.[4] Defoe was in Coventry earlier in October and in this letter recalls time spent with Owen.[5] The latter part addresses both Owen and Joseph Cater. In Furbank and Owens's words, this letter catches Defoe's 'joshing tone of voice among his cronies'.[6]

Mr Owen

I Can Not but wth Some Satisfaccon look back on ye
Conversation you had wth the Gentlemen at ye Bull.[7]

Mithinks I See all our English Gentlemen would Come to Their
Reason if They would but Allow themselves to Argue Against us
wthout Prejudice. I Can Not but Own The Sence and Parts of both
ye Gentlemen wth you and I Vallue Them as Such, and It Appear'd
Perticularly in Two Things wch as they Frankly Ownd So all ye
Gentlemen of That Party would Own[a] them also, if they were
Masters of the like Understanding.

1. The Dr[8] Allow'd That On Extraordinary Occasion The Collective
   or Representative body[b] of This Nation May Limitt, alter or
   Interupt ye Succession of ye Crown and that ye Said body of ye
   people are ye Judges of That Occasion[9] — and indeed they must
   all allow it or Denÿ ye Queens Claim to The Crown.
2. The Dr Allowed it was Scandalous to ye Church of England that
   ye Non Jurants should joyn [wth][c] and pretend to Defend the
   Church of England wch at the same Time They Denye to be a
   True Church and Declare to be scismaticall.[10]

I know but One Thing more I Could wish of those Gentlemen to
bring us all to be Of One mind, and That is That These Gentlemen
would practise what they Also Allow'd to be Reasonable, that
they might live like Christians, Neighbours and Gentlemen wth
their Brethren who Differ in some Cases and not Two Partyes
being Eternally Cutting One Anothers Throates on Chimeras of
a Presbyterian Govornmt wch I Dare Undertake to Convince Men
of their Sence and Candor No Dissenter in his witts Can Desire,[11]
and he that Does Must act against the Intrests of ye Dissenters in
Generall and be Fitter to Go to Bedlam[12] than to be a Magistrate.

I have thot Some times[d] those Gentlemen may Expect I shall
Reflect Publickly[e] on their Discourse when they may learn who I
am; Their Opinion of me I kno' Not, but pray assure them I kno

---

[a] Own] *following word* 'it' *cancelled*
[b] body] *interlined*
[c] [wth]] *hole in MS*
[d] Some times] *interlined*
[e] I shall Reflect Publickly] *interlined above cancelled words* 'me to Reflect'

DEFOE TO EDWARD OWEN AND JOSEPH CATER, 26–7 OCTOBER 1705

better Than to Invade^a Conversation or to make use of any words Gentlemen^b may Unwarily let fall when in Company they kno' not, And as I kno' Nothing said for wch they Can be justly Reproach't, ye Concessions above being I hope Their Naturall Sentiments, I wish all those we Call high Church men would act the Gentleman Equally wth these to whom^c Pray give my humble service.

Yo^r Humble Servt
D Foe

Daventry Octo. 26. Smith speaker.[13]

Pray also m^r Owen Remind those Gentlemen that, as to the Character They were pleas'd to give of me that night by Report, Viz^t that I Owe 3000[£][14] and have Taken advantage of all ye acts of parliam^t against my Creditors, it shows y^m too Credulous and too forward to Report things they can not be sure of, for that:

> 1. Tis false in Fact; I Never took advantage or indeed made Use of any act of parliam^t against any Creditor, tho' to make use of Law must be lawfull.[15]
> 2: If I do Owe 3000[£] I presume a great many men that hold up high Now if they were to fall into ye hands I have been in would hardly Come Out less in Debt, Since I Can make it appear I lost above 3000[£] in the broil they and all ye World kno' of.[16]
> 3. It is not actually a Crime to Owe 3000[£], but to Owe it and being Able to Discharge,^d Omitt or Refuse it.

So that if Debt be ye Objection and ye Occasion So plain, I think they do me Some wrong there and question not but upon Reflection they are Men of So much Sence they will own it.

Yo^r Humble serv^t
DF

---

^a Invade] *interlined above cancelled word* 'betray'
^b Gentlemen] *amended from* 'a Gentleman'
^c whom] *following illegible word beginning* 'G' *cancelled*
^d Discharge] *following word* 'or' *cancelled*

DEFOE TO EDWARD OWEN AND JOSEPH CATER, 26–7 OCTOBER 1705

What Cowards are these Coventry Whigs that now Barcelona is taken,[17] m^r Smith Chosen and all the Torys Dead hearted, yet they Dare not so Much as make a bonefire — or Ring the Bells.

Nay there's that[a] Ned Owen is such a Cowardly Ro .... that he Dares not go to Greens Coffee house[18] and Read a balad there.

Fye Ned, Coventry Men Cowards! fye! fye!

If you are So Dastardly now, what wou'd ha' become of you if B B B Bromley[19] had been Chosen?

Courage! men of blew,[20] the job[b] is Done, Rouze up Jere' Withers,[21] the Gold is all your Own.

What a Toad is this De Foe, he is old Dog[22] at a guess; he Said we should have a majority of 60 — and behold 52, wch put against 63, wch they had of us last[c] parliam^t, makes near ye 120 I Computed.[23]

And about 25 more Recovred by Controverted Elections secures ye Nation, bewildres the Jacks,[24] Disheartens ye high Church and I hope makes an End of all these brangles.

Amen

Daventry Saturday morning

m^r Cater[25] & m^r Owen

I Can not write here; you See how all things go; that affair Requires Now your Uttmost speed — Ile be in London, God willing, on Fryday.[26] Thanks and Service to all friends.

Yo^rs

DF

Text: Princeton University Library, Robert H. Taylor Collection, box 6, folder 3 (Figure 4). *Address*: To | Mr Edward Owen | in | Coventry. [*Another address in Defoe's hand, but in the corner, is cancelled*: 'm^r Steph Wright | Daventry'.[27]] *Endorsed*: Ob^r 1705 Dan: Defoe's Politicks

---

[a] there's that] *interlined*
[b] job] *following illegible word cancelled*
[c] last] *following illegible word cancelled*

---

1   *C.J.*, XIII, 763, 825–6; T. W. Whitley, *The Parliamentary Representation of the City of Coventry from the Earliest Times to the Present Date* (Coventry, 1894), 129–31; Judith J. Hurwich, "A Fanatick Town": The Political Influence of Dissenters in Coventry, 1660–1720', *Midland*

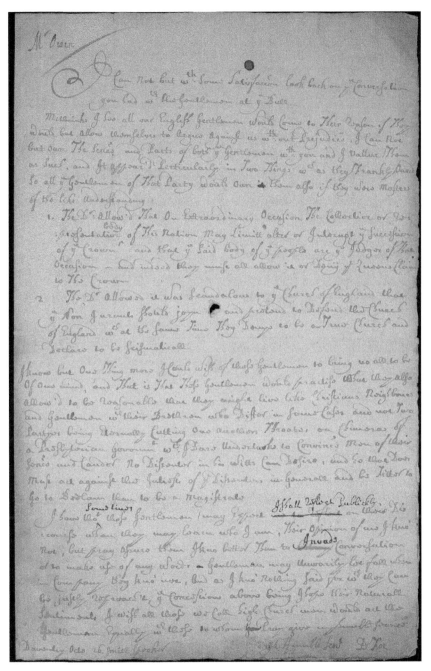

Figure 4 Daniel Defoe to Edward Owen and Joseph Cater, 26–7 October 1705, Princeton University Library, Robert H. Taylor Collection, box 6, folder 3

History 4 (1977), 15–47 (29); *The Parliamentary Diary of Sir Richard Cocks, 1698–1702*, ed. D. W. Hayton (Oxford, 1996), 257; *HPC 1690–1715*, II, 627.

2 H.M.C. *Portland MSS*, IV, 187–8; BL Add. MS. 70263, misc. 10.

3 *Review*, II, 169–73 (10 May 1705).

4 See Letter 46. Defoe apparently continued an acquaintance with Owen's son, also Edward, who in 1711 held money to pay a hostler who claimed Defoe (or at least a companion of his) had bilked him of payment for a horse three years previously (*Review*, VIII, 118 (10 May 1711)). See Letter 132.

5 Defoe's itinerary of his trip places him there from 9–14 Oct. (Letter 44), but next Apr. he stated he was there on 23 Oct., on which date his itinerary has him in Cambridge (*Review*, III, 226 (11 Apr. 1706)).

6 F&O, *Political Biography*, 52.

7 *ye Bull*: An inn in Coventry frequented by Tories (Whitley, *Parliamentary Representation*, 141–2).

8 *Dr*: Possibly Jonathan Kimberley (1651–1720), vicar of Trinity Church, Coventry, and canon of Lichfield. According to Defoe, 'the Fam'd Mr. *K—ly*' was a 'Champion against the *Dissenters*'; the Dissenters in Coventry 'liv'd in the Greatest Unity with the Reverend Ministers of the Church of *England* ... But this Gentleman, by his Violence, has Driven them all from the Church; his Fiery Spirit has made Men Abhor that place, where with Men of Temper and Moderation, they could be Content to Worship God before' (*Review*, II, 389 (14 July 1705)). Defoe accused Kimberley of contriving the bill to prevent occasional conformity in concert with Bromley, whose rector Kimberley became in 1710 (*Review*, V, 30 (8 Apr. 1708)). He is part of a High Church army Defoe imagines in *Review*, VII, 70 (27 Apr. 1710), and he is likewise targeted in *The Secret History of the October-Club ... Part II* (1711), 31–2.

9 *Collective ... Occasion*: Defoe articulated this argument most fully in *The Original Power of the Collective Body of the People of England* (1701).

10 *Scandalous ... scismaticall*: For similar sentiments, see *Review*, I, 447 (17 Oct. 1704); II, 212 (26 May 1705); *History of the Union* (1709/10), TDH, VII, 73.

11 *Chimeras ... Desire*: In *The Shortest Way to Peace and Union* (1703), Defoe observed that government by any sect of Dissenters would be untenable, and that Dissenters were rightly content with toleration under an Anglican polity: 'The Dissenters shall not only obey the present Authority, but choose it, love it, and believe it to be the best' (*PEW*, III, 152). See also Letter 15.

12 *Bedlam*: Bethlem hospital, for the insane.

13 *Smith speaker*: Reconvened after the election, the House of Commons on 25 Oct. elected the Court candidate for Speaker, the Whig John Smith (1655/6–1723), ahead of the Tory nominee William Bromley. See W. A. Speck, 'The Choice of a Speaker in 1705', *BIHR* 37 (1964), 20–46. Defoe looked back on this result at the end of the parliamentary session: 'To the Universal Joy of all good Men, whose Principles however true to the Church and its Interest, were for Moderation and Christian Temper, and to the Mortification of all those, that hop'd for Confusions and Distractions in the Councils of this Parliament, Mr. *Smith* was Chosen Speaker by a great Majority' (*Review*, III, 254 (23 Apr. 1706)). Defoe saw Bromley's defeat as the final death of the bill against occasional conformity (*Review*, IV, 70 (13 Mar. 1707); IV, 527 (7 Oct. 1707)). And, looking back, he believed the choice of Speaker paved the way for the successes of 1706–7, such as the Union with Scotland (*Review*, IV, 594 (6 Nov. 1707); *The Weakest Go to the Wall* (1714), *PEW*, III, 348).

14 *Report, Vizt that I Owe 3000ᵉ*: See *Review*, II, 394 (17 July 1705).

15 *I Never ... lawfull*: See Letter 50 for Defoe's availing himself of the parliamentary act of 1706.

16 *broil they and all ye World kno' of*: Defoe's prosecution for *The Shortest Way with the Dissenters*.

17 *Barcelona is taken*: Allied forces, commanded by Charles Mordaunt, third Earl of Peterborough (1658–1735), entered Barcelona on 9 Oct., accompanied by Charles III, the allies' candidate for the Spanish throne.

18 *Greens Coffee house*: Unidentified.

DEFOE TO EDWARD OWEN AND JOSEPH CATER, 26–7 OCTOBER 1705

19 *Bromley*: Defoe maintained a steady attack on Bromley during 1705. *The Double Welcome*, lines 479–86 (*SFS*, I, 340) lambasted his role in the bills against occasional conformity and the *Review* for 5 July 1705 identified his role in propagating the 'Church in Danger' message (II, 351). Bromley is satirised as '*Bromsky*' in *The Dyet of Poland* (1705), lines 836–77, *SFS*, i, 367–8, which mocks Bromley's *Remarkes in the Grande Tour of France and Italy* (1692). To undermine Bromley's candidacy for Speaker in 1705, Harley had had his *Remarkes* reprinted with an index drawing attention to fatuous passages, to which Defoe also alludes in the poem. Harley reputedly passed Bromley's book around the dinner table (Oldmixon, 345). Defoe further mocked Bromley's *Remarkes* in *The Consolidator* (1705), *SFS*, III, 65, 70, 157. See also the anonymous 'Declaration without Doors', *POAS*, VII, 133–41. I cannot explain why Defoe writes 'B' three times before Bromley's name.

Bromley was the Secretary of State who investigated a complaint against Defoe in 1714. See Letter 230.

20 *men of blew*: The rival factions in Coventry adopted party colours, with the Tories as 'true blue'. 'True blue', meaning steadfast and loyal, may derive from the quality of Coventry dyeing (John Ray, *Collection of English Proverbs*, 2nd ed. (1678), 230). Defoe refers to a '*true blue Specimen* of a Coventry Dye' in *Review*, III, 505 (17 Aug. 1706). But it was coming to be associated with the High Tories more generally, as with Defoe's ironic reference to 'the true Church Militants Colour, *I mean the Church Militant on Earth* whose Colour, Authors agree, must be *true Blue*' and his mention of 'stanch true blue Bigots to *Toryisme* and the *Danger of the Church*' (*Review*, VI, 385 (29 Sept. 1709); *The Secret History of the October Club* (1711), *PEW*, II, 165 – the first edition read '*Jacobitisme*' rather than '*Toryisme*').

21 *Jere' Withers*: Jeremiah Withers, an attorney in Coventry (Whitley, *Parliamentary Representation*, 125).

22 *old Dog*: Compare 'my Friend is old Dog at an Etymology' (*Review*, VIII, 739 (12 Apr. 1712)).

23 *majority … Computed*: Defoe takes the division on the Speaker as a gauge of party strength in the newly assembled Commons: High Flyers against moderate Tories, Whigs, and placemen. The vote was actually 248 to 205 (*HPC 1690–1715*, V, 503). This was not the 'great majority' Harley hoped for or which Defoe later announced in the *Review* for 23 Apr. 1706 (Harley to Marlborough, 26 July 1705, BL Add. MS. 61123, fol. 188). In that *Review*, Defoe notes that very few MPs missed this vote: '457 Voices were actually in the House' (III, 254). Eighteen months later he recalls, again incorrectly, that 'there was not above 4 Members absent' (*Review*, IV, 562–3 (23 Oct. 1707)). Defoe asserts in print that Smith enjoyed 'a Majority of above 50' (*Review*, V, 491 (30 Nov. 1708)). In *The History of the Union*, he writes, 'whereas in the other [i.e. preceding] Parliament, the High-Party had a Majority of Sixty Two or there about, … On the first Tryal of the Strength of the House, which was perhaps the Greatest that has been known of late Years, it appear'd the Whig-Party had the Majority by above Seventy Voices, and these by the turning out severals on the Trials of Elections, and other Circumstances, rose up to be above a Hundred' (*TDH*, VII, 138–9). Here, Defoe counts placemen, who usually voted with the Court, as Whigs. Godolphin's inference was: 'Of the 450 that chose the Speaker[,] Tories 190, Whigs 160, Queen's servants 100, of the last about 15 perhaps joined with the Tories in that vote of the Speaker' (Godolphin to Harley, 22 March 1706, H.M.C. *Portland MSS*, IV, 291). The best modern computation suggests that the new parliament comprised 260 Tories, 233 Whigs, and 20 unclassifiable by party, but this still amounted to a majority for the Court (*HPC 1690–1715*, I, 226–7).

24 *Jacks*: Jacobites.

25 *mr Cater*: Joseph Cater (d. 1726). He was a Dissenter and alderman in Coventry, who lost his position after the occasional conformity act (Whitley, *Parliamentary Representation*, 140). He is also used by Defoe as a post restante address in 1706 (Letter 51).

26 *Fryday*: 2 Nov., though his itinerary indicates he reached London on 6 Nov. (Letter 44).

27 Stephen Wright is unidentified.

DEFOE TO ROBERT HARLEY, [C. 15 NOVEMBER 1705]

44

To Robert Harley

[*c.* 15 November 1705][1]

HEADNOTE: In this digest of his journey, Defoe often promises Harley fuller accounts of the political situations in towns he visited, even an additional publication in the case of Coventry; these, if produced, have not survived, though earlier letters give supplementary detail, such as for Dorset. Defoe was evidently satisfied with the outcome of the election. 'Such a Harmony of Contending Partys, such a Peace, such Union, and such general Satisfaction spreads through the whole Nation', he wrote in January 1706.[2] His poem *A Hymn to Peace* (January 1706) holds out hope that national harmony will ensue from such a divisive election.

An Abstract of My Journey wth Casuall Observacons
on Publick Affaires

I Sett Out from Lond^o July 16°, haveing Concluded to Make No Observacons within 20 Miles of London. I proceed to ye Severall stages.

July

16   Brentford. Lodg'd at Justice Meriwethers[3] — he was a
        justice^a but Turn'd Out of Commission in ye Gen^{ll}
        Displaceing Moderate men.[4]
           Note.Justice Lamb of Acton who was a Goldsmith in
              Lombard street is now ye high flyeing & Ruleing
              Justice of That Side of Mids^x, ye same who swore to y^e
              flash of his pistoll in ye Case of Ni: Charleton.[5]
        Reading. They are all well there and there is No Doubt of a
           Good Member in ye Room of m^r Vachell.[6] I have ye Exact
           list of ye Magistracy of all ye Chief Towns in Berks.
17   Newbury: a large Tradeing Town but Choose no Members
        but they Influence ye Eleccons at Ludgersall[7] and^b Great
        Bedwin^c[8] and a Very Good story about ye Bruces who
        now peticon is to be told here.

---

^a he was a justice] *interlined*
^b and] *interlined*
^c Bedwin] *following illegible word cancelled*

DEFOE TO ROBERT HARLEY, [*C.* 15 NOVEMBER 1705]

18   Salisbury. Here I have yᵉ wholl accoᵗ of yᵉ County Election
        and the parsons Rustling my Lᵈ of Salisbury and mʳ
        Westfield his steward, and yᵉ Mob Insulting yᵉ Duke of
        Somersett and stopping his Coach in yᵉ street.[9]

19, 20 At Blandford — No Corporation, the County too much
        Govorn'd and this Town Entirely by Seymour Portman
        and Coll Strangeways; had Majʳ Genˡˡ Earle plyed his
        Intrest well they all Say the Other had lost it.[10]

21.   At Dorchester, a good for nothing Town. One Member
        is Churchill yᵉ bookseller, yᵉ other [   ]ᵃ Chose by
        the Intrest of Coll Strangewayes;[11] people here Very
        Moderate.[12]

22   Weymouth — here yᵉ Disorders of my letters hindred me
        stayeing to do what I purposed.[13]

23   Lyme. A Town Entirely United and all yᵉ Church men Very
        Moderate and well affected.[14]

24   Honiton: a Terrible Mob Election here but sʳ Jnᵃ Elvill of
        Excester is so Cow'd by sʳ Wᵐ Drake and Fra: Gwin that
        he Dares not peticon.[15]

25   Excester: here I have yᵉ List of all yᵉ partyes Exactly and a
        Modell how sʳ Ed Seymour may be Thrown out against
        Another Eleccon wᵗʰ out any Difficulty at all.[16]
            Here I learnt yᵉ history of yᵉ Family of Coll Rolles and
        how yᵉ young Gentleman Kᵗ of yᵉ shire for Devon will be
        brought off from high Church.[17]

Augᵗ

1   I left Excester and Went to Totness, sʳ E. S. Town as we
        Call it, tho' he has not One foot of Land nor a house in yᵉ
        Town.[18]

2   Dartmouth: a Bubbled Town Engrosst by the Herns[19] but yᵉ
        story of a ship Call'd the Constant Tacker is a Mistake.[20]

3   To Plympton, a Little Town, all Low Church and Very well
        United but a poor plačė. Lᵈ Chief <u>Baron</u>ᵇ Treebys Town.[21]

ᵃ ye other [   ]] *blank in MS*
ᵇ <u>*Baron*</u>] *'Baron' is cancelled and 'Justice' is interlined in a different hand, probably Harley's; the cancellation is apparently not Defoe's*

DEFOE TO ROBERT HARLEY, [C. 15 NOVEMBER 1705]

4   To Plymo.[22] I have ye skeleton of this Town.

5   To Saltash.[23]

6, 7   To Liskard and Bodmin.[24]

8   To Launceston:[25] there is nothing to be done in these Towns; they are wholly Guided by ye Gentlemen,[26] and ye Townsmen kno' Little but act just as they are bid, my Ld Granville Govorns severall of them, my Ld Treasurer More.[27] I Thot it was Throwing away Time to stay among them.

9, 10   Bidiford.

11.   Barstaple.[28]

12, 13.   Tiverton:[29] here ye Alarm of ye Devonshire Justice[30] Hurryed me too fast but I have Establish't Correspondence at all these Towns.

14.   Taunton:[31] have an Exact accot here.

15.   Bridgewater:[32] and here also.

16.   To Bristoll.

19.   Bath, a Contest here between ye People[a] and ye Magistracy will Come before ye house.[33]

20.   To Chippenham: here Watt White being Dead, That Scandall to all Good Manners Coll Chivers puts up; he is ye profoundest Rake and Bully in ye County and is put up here[b] by the Gentry on purpose to Skreen him from ye Bishop of Salisbury who sues[c] him for Most Impudt Scandalous lyes Raised of him.[34]

      Of This I have ye perticulars as also of his Scandalous history and Tis ye humble Request of all the County on that Side at least that he may be Out of the Commission of ye peace for he is a Scandall to ye Country.

22   To Divizes: here is ye Same petition against ye Iron Chest, ye story of wch is worth Relateing.[35]

23   To Bradford, Trubridge and Westbury;[36] ye skeletons of all these Towns are Compleat wth all ye Vale here for 50 miles.

---

[a] People] *interlined above cancelled word* 'City'
[b] here] *following illegible word cancelled*
[c] sues] 'es' *is interlined above illegible cancelled letters*

DEFOE TO ROBERT HARLEY, [*C. 15 NOVEMBER 1705*]

24 To Devizes again and from thence to Visit young Ducket, Chosen for Caln, yᵉ same sʳ Cha Hedges peticons agt;[37] of him yᵉ story how the Atheist Club at Oxford Us'd him,[38] his Character.

25 To yᵉ Bath.

26 Back to Bristoll; yᵉ history of yᵉ Revolution of this Citty[39] is large and Edifyeing and I have an Exact scale of yᵉ people, their Trade and Magistracy; stay'd here 4 dayes.

30, 31 To yᵉ Bath again, Chipenham and Caln, thence to Malmsbury, Tutbury, Nedbury[a] and Cirencester; here I had yᵉ story of yᵉ Eleccon wᶜʰ it seems mʳ Cox has Given Over or Elce the briberys on both sides would ha' Made strange work.[40]

Septembʳ

1. To Gloucester: a p[er]fect Change here, yᵉ hystory of wᶜʰ I had from mʳ Wade, Bro: to Major Wade of Bristoll,[41] and from mʳ Forbs.[42] This City and Bristoll are perfectly Reformd and New Modelled.

2. Tewxbury:[b] a Quiet Tradeing Drunken Town, a whig bayly[43] and all well.

3 Pershore and Evisham. Great Contest at yᵉ last for sʳ Richard Cox and a Great Deal of Fowl play.[44]

4 Worcester: here I forbore to Examine as to yᵉ Magistracy, you haveing full knowlege of p[er]sons and things.[45]

5 To Leominster. I went on a p[er]ticular Obligacon to Visit a Quacker, One Bowen,[46] yᵗ I had been Engag'd to by his brother here, but as being mʳ Harleys Town[47] I did nothing here.

7 Beawdly — of this Town I have a long and Usefull hystory and of the Eleccon there.[48]

8 Bridgnorth: of this Town I have a full accoᵗ and of yᵉ Throwing Out sʳ Ed Acton.[49]

10 Shrewsbury:[50] of this Town I have an Exact list.

11 Wrexam.

---

[a] Tutbury, Nedbury] *interlined*
[b] 2. Tewxbury] *In the MS, this begins a new sheet, headed* 'Septembʳ', *as Defoe restates the month, omitted in this edition*

183

DEFOE TO ROBERT HARLEY, [C. 15 NOVEMBER 1705]

12 Chester: and of this also.

13 Leverpool:[51] and here also.

16 Warrington
17 Manchester ⎫
20. Boulton   ⎬ No Magistrates in any of these Towns,
21. Rochdale   ⎬ Choose no Members nor have any officer
22. Hallifax   ⎭ but a Constable.

23, 26. Leeds, Wakefield and Sheffield — No members Chosen here neither.

Here I have made usefull Remarks on Trade and Observe that Frequent Eleccons haveing[a] no Influence here to Divide ye people They live here in Much more peace with one another than in other parts.

29. Darby:[b] the partyes were Exceeding Inveterate here but begin to Unite[c] Very much.[52]

Octob^r

2 Nottingham: this is a Violently Divided Town.[53] I have the Exact schedule of their Leaders.

6 Leicester: a monstruous story here about ye Eleccons and ye Contending partyes here Dayly together by the Eares.[54]

8 Lutterworth: here Justice Bradgate Rod a horseback into the Meeting house and Told ye parson as he was preaching he Lyed;[55] a high flyeing Town but no Corporation.

9. Coventry:[56] of this Town you will see ye history at large in print.[57]

15. Daventry. Famous for an Infamous parson who among other things swore himself a Freeholder whereas he is not the Incumbent but Curate Onely.[58]

16 Northampton.[59] Of this town I have a Draft.

18 Wellingboro'.

---

[a] haveing] *the 'e' is interlined*

[b] 29. Darby] *In the MS, this begins a new sheet, headed* 'Sept.', *as Defoe restates the month, omitted in this edition. A chain of corrections follows: Defoe had written out further late Sept. dates – '25', '26', '29' – but added '26' to the* 'Leeds, Wakefield and Sheffield' *entry and amended '25' to '29' for* 'Darby'. *Below that, he crossed through the original '26', replacing that with '2', above which he inserted* 'Octob^r', *and he wrote over '29' with '6' for* 'Leicester'. *Because he had now written it above he cancelled* 'Octob^r' *adjacent to the '8' for* 'Lutterworth'

[c] Unite] *following word* 'here' *cancelled*

184

DEFOE TO ROBERT HARLEY, [C. 15 NOVEMBER 1705]

19   Huntington.[60]

21   Cambridge: done before,[61] but yᵉ story of yᵉ Colleges Disscomoning mʳ Love, yᵉ late Mayor, and his Indiscretions are very Remarkable.[62]

25   Bury: here yᵉ Case of my Lᵈ Harvey and sʳ Dudly Cullumb and the measures taken on both sides for yᵉ Approaching Elecċon are Observable.[63]

28   Cambridge again, to Move some Friends that Came thither from London on private bussiness of my Own.

Nov.

1   To Sudbury and have yᵉ perticulars of their Mannagemᵗ of the last Elecċon.[64]

3   To Colechester.[65] 5 To Chelmsford.

6   To London.

In all Parts yᵉ Greatest hindranċe to yᵉ forming yᵉ People into Moderaċon and Union Among Themselves Next to yᵉ Clergy are yᵉ Justiċes.[66]

Wherever There happens to be Moderate Justiċes The people live Easy and The Parsons have yᵉ less Influenċe but yᵉ Conduct of yᵉ Justices in Most parts is Intollerably scandalous, Espeċally in Wilts, in Lancashire, in Nottingham, Leicester, Warrwick, Northampton, Suffolk, Essex and Middsˣ.

Text: BL Add. MS. 70291, fols. 43–9. *Address* (fol. 43ʳ): To The Right Honoᵇˡᵉ | Robert Harley Esqʳ | One of Her Majᵗⁱᵉˢ Prinċipall Secretaryes of State | Present. *Endorsed by Harley* (fol. 49ᵛ): Abstract of a jorny from July 16: to Nov: 6: 1705

---

1 Defoe alludes in this letter to Charles Coxe giving up his petition in the Cirencester election, which formally happened on 15 Nov. The letter cannot date to before 6 Nov., the date it reports Defoe arrived back in London.

2 *A Reply to a Pamphlet entituled, The L[or]d H[aversham]'s Vindication of his Speech* (1706), 21.

3 *Justiċe Meriwethers*: Richard Meriwether (d. 1714), merchant. He and Defoe were co-signatories to a petition in the early 1690s requesting greater naval protection for merchant ships in North America (Backscheider, *Life*, 48).

4 *Displaċeing Moderate men*: As Lord Keeper, Sir Nathan Wright (1654–1721) had removed around 600 Justices, replacing them mainly with Tories or '*hard Mouth'd Wretches*' as Defoe called them, alluding to this cull in *A Hymn to Peace* (1706), line 599, *SFS*, I, 399. Long earmarked by the ministry as 'a violent party man', Wright had been removed from his post in Oct. 1705 (Marlborough to the Duchess, 22 Sept. 1704, *Marl.–God. Corr.*, I, 376; Holmes, 253).

185

DEFOE TO ROBERT HARLEY, [*C.* 15 NOVEMBER 1705]

See Lionel K. J. Glassey, *Politics and the Appointment of Justices of the Peace, 1675–1720* (Oxford, 1979), 135–70.

5 *Justice Lamb ... Ni: Charleton*: Nicholas Charlton was convicted of assaulting Henry Lamb (d. 1712) in 1692, in a highway robbery that Lamb foiled by shooting one of his three assailants (Luttrell, III, 18, 25, 29, 87). Lamb left off his trade in the city in 1703 (Sir Ambrose Heal, *The London Goldsmiths 1200–1800* (Cambridge, 1935), 71). He became a JP in Acton, where he had a country house.

6 *mr Vachell*: Tanfield Vachell (1668–1705), a Whig, was re-elected for Reading in 1705 but died on 19 Oct., just before the Commons reassembled. Another Whig, Sir William Rich (*c.* 1654–1711) had already been endorsed by the corporation and was returned unopposed in Vachell's stead.

7 *Eleccions at Ludgersall*: At Ludgershall, the Tories Walter Kent (1662–1746) and Thomas Powell (1648–1709) were elected, though the latter was unseated the following year when John Richmond Webb's (1667–1724) petition was approved (*C.J.*, xv, 92–4).

8 *Great Bedwin*: At Great Bedwyn, the moderate Tory candidates (nephew and uncle) Charles, Lord Bruce (1682–1747) and James Bruce (*c.* 1670–*c.* 1732) were defeated by the Whig Sir George Byng (1664–1733) and Court Tory Nicholas Pollexfen (1678–1715). The Bruces' petition was withdrawn when a vacancy arose because Byng chose to sit for Plymouth, where he had also been elected, and Lord Bruce was elected unopposed in December 1705 (*C.J.*, xv, 8, 47).

9 *Salisbury ... Street*: See Letter 39.

10 *Blandford ... lost it*: For Strangways and Erle, see Letter 39, notes 4 and 5. The High Tory Henry Portman (*c.* 1637–1728), MP for Wells, was Sir Edward Seymour's brother (he took the name Portman in 1690 when he succeeded to the estate of his cousin Sir William Portman). Defoe refers to the 'good Families' of Dorset, including Strangways and Seymours, in *Tour, TDH*, I, 242–3.

11 *Dorchester ... Strangeways*: See Letter 39, note 4.

12 *People here Very Moderate*: See Letter 39, note 3.

13 *Weymouth ... purposed*: See Letters 40 and 41.

14 *Lyme ... affected*: At Lyme Regis, the Whigs Thomas Freke and John Burridge (*c.* 1651–1733) were returned unopposed.

15 *Honiton ... peticon*: See Letter 39 for the Honiton election and Gwyn. The Tory Sir William Drake (1658–1716) was re-elected for Honiton ahead of the Whig Sir John Elwill (*c.* 1642–1717), who had been ejected as a JP the previous year (H.M.C. *Portland MSS*, IV, 122). Defoe included Honiton in a list of boroughs that typified the heats of the 1705 general election (*Review*, III, 241 (18 Apr. 1706)).

16 *Excester ... all*: See Letter 40.

17 *Family ... Church*: Robert Rolle (*c.* 1677–1710), grandson of Col. John Rolle (1626–1706), was the Knight of the Shire; though Tory, he had voted against the Tack, but voted for Bromley for Speaker. The Rolles were 'one of the wealthiest gentry families in England' and were not turned from their Toryism: Robert voted against Sacheverell's impeachment in 1710 and his brother John (1679–1730) was in the October Club in 1711 (*HPC 1690–1715*, v, 295–6).

18 *Totness ... Town*: Seymour had sat as MP for Totnes in the 1690s, and his close associates, the High Tories Sir Humphrey Mackworth and Thomas Coulson (1645–1713) were elected on Seymour's interest in 1705. Ahead of the next general election in 1708, Defoe decried that 'the Town of *T—* has for many Years chosen whatever Sir *E— S—* bad them' (*Review*, v, 109 (15 May 1708)).

19 *Dartmouth ... Herns*: The brothers Frederick Herne (1667–1714) and Nathaniel Herne (1668–1722) held the Dartmouth seats and were Tories.

20 *Story ... Mistake*: *A Collection from Dyers Letters, Concerning the Elections of the Present Parliament* (1705), 2, gives this paragraph from *Dyer's News-Letter* for 5 May 1705: 'At *Dartmouth* they have that Veneration for the Service of their worthy Representatives, *Fred. and Nat. Hern*, Esquires, that they have *Christen'd* a Ship by the Name of *Tacker*.'

DEFOE TO ROBERT HARLEY, [C. 15 NOVEMBER 1705]

21 *Plympton ... Town*: The electoral influence of the Whig George Treby (1643–1700) passed to his son of the same name (1685–1742), but he was only twenty in 1705. Sir John Cope (1673–1749) and Richard Edgcumbe (1680–1758) were the MPs elected at Plympton Erle on the Treby interest in 1705.

22 *Plymo*: The Court Tory Major General Charles Trelawny (1653–1731) and Whig Sir George Byng were elected in Plymouth.

23 *Saltash*: Saltash returned the Tacker James Buller (1678–1710) and the Whig Joseph Moyle (1679–1742).

24 *Liskard and Bodmin*: Liskeard returned two placemen, William Bridges (d. 1714) and Thomas Dodson (*c.* 1666–1707). Bodmin returned a Tacker, John Hoblyn (*c.* 1660–1706), and a Whig, Russell Robartes (1671–1719).

25 *Launceston*: Launceston returned Rochester's son Henry, Lord Hyde (1672–1753) and William Cary (*c.* 1661–1710), both High Tories.

26 *Gentlemen*: I.e. High Tories.

27 *Ld Granville ... More*: John Granville (1665–1707) had recently broken with the administration and gone into opposition with Nottingham, and so had been removed as Lord Lieutenant of Cornwall, replaced by Godolphin.

28 *Barstaple*: Barnstaple returned the Tory Nicholas Hooper (1654–1731) and the whiggish Samuel Rolle (1669–1735).

29 *Tiverton*: Tiverton returned two Whigs unopposed, Thomas Bere and Robert Burridge (1656–1717).

30 *Alarm of ye Devonshire Justice*: See Letters 40 and 41.

31 *Taunton*: Letters 40 and 41 indicate that Defoe was at Tiverton on this date, perhaps indicating that he wrote those letters before the day's travelling. Taunton returned the Whig Edward Clarke (1650–1710) and the Tory Sir Francis Warre (1659?–1718).

32 *Bridgewater*: Bridgwater returned the Whig George Balch (d. 1738) and the Tory non-Tacker Sir Thomas Wroth (*c.* 1674–1721).

33 *Bath ... house*: See Letter 42, note 8. Members of the corporation had elected Blathwayt and Popham, but the defeated George Dashwood (1680–1758) and Richard Houblon (1672–1724) petitioned, claiming that the right of election lay with the freemen at large (*C.J.*, xv, 12). Popham's death before parliament reassembled created a vacancy. The dispute was not decided by the Commons until Jan. 1707, when it found in favour of the corporation's right to elect MPs. Samuel Trotman (1650–1720) was then elected to the vacancy.

34 *Watt White ... him*: See Letter 42.

35 *Divizes ... Relateing*: See Letter 42.

36 *Bradford, Trubridge and Westbury*: Of these towns, only Westbury returned members, these being the Tories Robert Bertie (1677–1710) and Henry Bertie (1656–1734).

37 *Ducket ... agt*: The Whig George Duckett (1684–1732) who was returned for Calne ahead of Secretary of State Sir Charles Hedges in a disputed election (*C.J.*, xv, 9). Hedges's petition was not heard because he secured election for West Looe and sat there instead. On Duckett, see *The Letters of Thomas Burnet to George Duckett*, ed. David Nichol Smith (Oxford, 1914), xiv–xxi.

38 *story ... him*: In the *Review* for 9 Oct. 1705, Defoe speaks of 'a Set or Society of Men, who openly deny their Maker, Blaspheme his Being, Insult Religion, and Abuse the Government ... known by the Name of the *Atheist Club*'. He recounts that they insulted 'an *English* Gentleman, now a Member of Parliament, and thr[e]w him out of Window, for refusing a Health that is too horrid to Name' (II, 645). See Defoe's account of a university atheist club in *Serious Reflections* (1720), *Novels*, III, 260–72, and he alludes to it briefly in *An Essay on the History and Reality of Apparitions* (1727), *SFS*, VIII, 47.

39 *Revolution of this Citty*: See Letter 42, note 8.

40 *Cirencester ... work*: At Cirencester, the High Tory ally of Bromley, Allen Bathurst (1684–1775), gained most votes; but an equality of votes cast for the Whig Henry Ireton (*c.* 1652–1711) and the Tory Charles Coxe (1661?–1728) resulted in a double return. Both Ireton and Coxe

DEFOE TO ROBERT HARLEY, [*C.* 15 NOVEMBER 1705]

complained against each other of bribery in petitions of 3 and 7 Nov., but on 15 Nov. Coxe withdrew (*C.J.*, xv, 12–13, 15, 26–7).

41 *mr Wade, Bro: to Major Wade of Bristoll*: Nathaniel Wade (*c.* 1666–1718) is 'Major Wade', a pardoned Monmouth rebel and by 1705 a city official in Bristol. Pat Rogers suggests that the brother, Defoe's informant, is more likely John Wade of Frampton (d. 1715) than Thomas Wade of Filton (d. 1716) ('Daniel Defoe on Bristol: The Description of the City in *A Tour thro' Great Britain* and its Context', *Transactions of the Bristol and Gloucestershire Archaeological Society* 136 (2018), 263–78 (at 266)). For the Gloucester result, see Letter 42, note 8.

42 *mr Forbs*: See Letter 42.

43 *whig bayly*: The two bailiffs elected for Tewkesbury in 1704–5 were the Whigs Thomas Warkman (d. before 1725?) and Abraham Farren (d. 1732), both named in the original list of burgesses when William III gave the town a new charter in 1698, which mandated two bailiffs instead of one (James Bennett, *The History of Tewkesbury* (1830), 393, 422).

44 *Evisham ... play*: At Evesham, the incumbent High Tory Hugh Parker (1673–1713) fended off the challenge of the Whig Sir Richard Cocks (*c.* 1659–1726). The other incumbent, the Whig John Rudge (1669–1740), was also re-elected.

45 *Worcester ... things*: The Whig Thomas Wylde (*c.* 1670–1740) and the (non-Tacker) Tory Samuel Swift (*c.* 1659–1718) were unopposed for parliament in Worcester.

46 *Bowen*: Probably Icabod Bowen (d. after 1726), a glover; the brother is unidentified.

47 *mr Harleys Town*: Edward Harley, brother to Robert, was MP for Leominster. The town's other MP was the Court Whig Thomas Coningsby (1656–1729), Godolphin's ally and working in cooperation with the Harleys at this time.

48 *Beawdly ... Eleccon there*: Bewdley was a single-member constituency, for which a Harley ally Salwey Winnington (1666–1736) was narrowly elected in a disputed election, though his victory was confirmed by the Commons (*HPC 1690–1715*, II, 706–7; Luttrell, VI, 18).

49 *Throwing Out s^r Ed Acton*: Sir Edward Acton (*c.* 1650–1716), longstanding Tory MP for Bridgnorth, put his son Whitmore (1678–1732) forward for the seat, but he came third behind the re-elected independent Sir Humphrey Briggs (1670?–1734) and the newly elected Whig William Whitmore (1681?–1725).

50 *Shrewsbury*: The Tories John Kynaston (1664–1733) and Richard Mytton were returned unopposed in Shrewsbury.

51 *Leverpool*: On 25 Sept. 1705, Liverpool's Whig MP and merchant Thomas Johnson (1664–1728) wrote to the unsuccessful candidate in the 1705 election, Richard Norris (1670–1730): 'We have had m^r Defoe here[.] I did not see him — mr [Samuel] Done was very bussy and invited him to his house — wch in my Opinion had been better let alone' (Liverpool Record Office, 920 NOR 1/283). Norris's brother-in-law Peter Hall wrote to him on 28 Sept.: 'Mr Dan: Defoe hath been some days in town, wch hath been the great Subject talked of and been great matter of speculation to some p[er]sons' (920 NOR 2/393). Johnson wrote to Norris again on the same day: 'I cannot be of ye opinion that mr Done did well in takeing m^r Defoe to his house — I do not like such men[,] let them be of what side they will — it's those creatures endeavours to influence us' (920 NOR 2/595). Done (d. after 1717), a ship supplier and a Dissenter, is listed as Defoe's distribution agent in the city (Letter 46). Norris had been set up in Liverpool to oppose the Tory William Clayton (after 1650–1714), but the incumbent Clayton held on.

52 *Darby ... much*: At Derby the sitting Tories John Harpur (d. 1713) and Thomas Stanhope (*c.* 1679–1730) were defeated by the Whigs Lord James Cavendish (after 1673–1751) and Sir Thomas Parker (1667–1732).

53 *Nottingham ... Town*: Nottingham returned the Tories Robert Sacheverell (1669–1714) and William Pierrepont (1669–1706) despite strong Whig opposition supported by local magnates including the Duke of Newcastle (see *HPC 1690–1715*, II, 466).

54 *Leicester ... Eares*: Two High Tories, Sir George Beaumont (1664?–1737) and James Winstanley (*c.* 1667–1719), were returned for Leicester in 1705, the latter very narrowly ahead of the Whig Lawrence Carter (1671–1741). The following year, the committee of privileges and

188

DEFOE TO ROBERT HARLEY, [C. 15 NOVEMBER 1705]

elections found in favour of Carter's petition against Winstanley, only for the Commons to overrule and confirm Winstanley's election (*C.J.*, xv, 135–7).

55 *Justice Bradgate ... Lyed*: Jarvis or Gervase Bradgate (*c.* 1659–1741) of Great Peatling, Leicestershire. Defoe alludes to this incident in *Review*, II, 716 (10 Nov. 1705), and in *A Hymn to Peace* (1706), lines 603–22, *SFS*, I, 399. The minister was probably Peter Dowley (see Letter 46).

56 *Coventry*: In *Review*, III, 226 (11 Apr. 1706), Defoe states that he was in Coventry on 23 Oct. 1705.

57 *history at large in print*: On the Coventry election, see Letter 39, note 10. Defoe had reported on it in the *Review* six months earlier (II, 169–73 (10 May 1705)). He looked back on it ten months after this letter (*Review*, III, 505–8 (17 Aug. 1706)). Otherwise, no publication concerning it is attributed to him.

58 *Infamous ... only*: Charles Allestree (1654–1707), perpetual curate at Daventry (meaning he was neither vicar nor rector). In the *Review* for 12 July 1705, Defoe refers to 'a certain Church of *England* Benefic'd Clergyman, not far from *Northampton*', having been 'Censur'd and Disown'd, for saying at a Publick Election for the County, *That the Church of* England *would never be at Ease*; or, *It would never be well with the Church, till she had an INQUISITION set up*' (II, 374). See *HPC 1690–1715*, II, 429–30. Allestree wrote a memorandum in a tithing book about the pecuniary difficulties he had had at Daventry (*A Northampton Miscellany*, ed. Edmund King (Northampton, 1983), 77–85).

59 *Northampton*: Northampton returned Halifax's nephew, the Whig George Montagu (1684–1739), and the Tory Francis Arundell (1676–1712).

60 *Huntington*: Huntingdon returned the High Tory Sir John Cotton (*c.* 1680–1731) and the Whig Edward Wortley Montagu (1678–1761), though the Whig John Pedley (*c.* 1666–1722) successfully petitioned against Cotton.

61 *Done before*: Defoe was in Cambridge the previous autumn (Letters 17–18). In the 1705 election, Cambridge returned the Tory Sir John Cotton (*c.* 1647–1713) and the Whig Anthony Thompson (*c.* 1641–1721).

62 *Colleges ... Remarkable*: Daniel Love (1655–1707) was a brewer. To 'discommon' or 'discommune' a tradesman was to prohibit members of the university from dealing with him. Defoe reports this story in his *Tour* (1724–6), *TDH*, I, 127. Both there and in this letter, Defoe is wrong to state that Love was discommuned: though guilty along with mayor James Fletcher (d. 1706) and several other aldermen of a discourtesy to Vice Chancellor John Ellys (1634?–1716), Love was omitted from the 'grace for discommuning' (Charles Henry Cooper, *Annals of Cambridge*, 5 vols. (Cambridge, 1842–1908), IV, 73–5; J. Milner Gray, *Biographical Notes on the Mayors of Cambridge* (Cambridge, 1921), 44).

63 *Bury ... Observable*: Sir Robert Davers (see Letter 18, note 13) had been elected for Bury St Edmunds, ahead of the Whig Sir Dudley Cullum (1657–1720). But Davers was also elected for Suffolk. His choice to sit for the county necessitated a by-election for the borough. On 1 Dec. 1705, John Hervey's (1665–1751) brother-in-law, the Whig Aubrey Porter (*c.* 1660–1717), was selected by the corporation in what was seen as a backlash against the Tory Davers for choosing the county seat. Despite being friendly towards Davers, in Feb. 1705 Harley wrote a memorandum regarding Davers's 1705 campaign: 'dispute – Ld Hervey to be set up' (quoted by Speck, *Tory and Whig*, 102; cf. *HPC 1690–1715*, III, 858).

64 *Sudbury ... Election*: At Sudbury, the Whigs Sir Gervase Elwes (1628–1706) and Philip Skippon (1675–1716) were elected, defeating the Tory George Dashwood (1669–1706), who petitioned on 2 Nov. but withdrew on 6 Dec. (*C.J.*, xv, 9, 53).

65 *Colchester*: At Colchester the Whigs Sir Isaac Rebow (1655–1726) and Edward Bullock (1663–1705) were elected ahead of the Tory Sir Thomas Cooke (*c.* 1648–1709). Rebow was a Williamite, praised in Defoe's *Tour* (*TDH*, I, 77–8) and *A Brief Deduction of the Original, Progress, and Immense Greatness of the British Woollen Manufacture* (1727), 28. A less favourable allusion comes in *Memoirs of Count Tariff* (1713), in which Defoe decries the opposition of provincial woollen manufacturers to the Anglo-French Commercial Treaty; he gives them a

189

JOHN FRANSHAM TO DEFOE, [*C.* JANUARY–APRIL 1706]

series of emblematic names that suggest their wares (such as '*Tom Kersie*') and among them is 'Sir *Isaac Re-Bay* of *Colchester*' (*SFS*, III, 178) – Bays (baize) was associated with Colchester.

66 *Justices*: JPs and clergymen are often blamed by Defoe for inciting the people during the 1705 election. He refers to the 'Infinite Lyes, Tricks, Shams, Illegal and Extravagant Actions of the Inferiour Clergy, Justices, Gentry and Madmen of the [High Church] Party, which … have too much been the Influencers of our Breaches, and the Preventers of the Nations Peace' (*Review*, III, 121 (19 Feb. 1706)). And he denounced 'our *High-Flyers* in *England*, our *Tackers*, our pressing Justices, and railing Clergy' (*Review*, III, 647 (24 Oct. 1706)). Long sections of *A Hymn to Peace* attacked such JPs and clergymen, with JP John Wroth (*c.* 1646–1708) of Exeter receiving particular criticism (lines 504–602, 639–61, *SFS*, I, 397–400). Defoe was accused of hypocritically magnifying the faults of the clergy in *The Review and Observator Reviewed* (1706).

45

John Fransham to Defoe

[*c.* January–April 1706][1]

HEADNOTE: The Act to Prevent Frauds frequently Committed by Bankrupts became law on 19 March 1706, with Defoe heralding it as 'one of the best Bills, that ever was produc'd in Parliament, since the *Habeas Corpus* Act, for Securing the Liberty of the Subject'.[2] By that point, Defoe had been urging bankruptcy reform in the *Review* for more than a month, arguing that the law currently 'makes no Difference between an Honest Man and a Knave, that shows no Mercy to either, but Punishes him that is Ruin'd by a Rogue, with the same Severity, as it does the Rogue that Ruin'd him'.[3] The new law, by contrast, enabled bankrupts to attain a complete discharge on condition of surrendering their effects to commissioners who arranged a composition with creditors, 'Clearing them from Vexatious Lingering of Prosecutions' and saving them from 'that Bloody Law, of Perpetual Imprisonment for Debt'.[4] Defoe had been a long-term critic of laws that disabled bankrupt merchants by incarcerating them, which disincentivised them from dealing fairly with creditors and that left them fending off lawsuits for years to come. In the *Review* campaign of 1706, he drew on his own arguments from *An Essay upon Projects* (1697), which in some ways anticipate the 1706 law.[5] Defoe wanted the Act to apply retrospectively so that those bankrupted before it passed could have their slates wiped clean; he had to counter charges of self-interest in this respect, because his own financial situation was parlous and he was being pressed by suits relating to his 1692 bankruptcy.[6] Defoe continued to extol the bill in a subsequent work, *Remarks on the Bill to Prevent Frauds Committed by Bankrupts*, published in April, roughly contemporaneous with this letter from

JOHN FRANSHAM TO DEFOE, [C. JANUARY–APRIL 1706]

Fransham reporting his defence in Norwich of Defoe's arguments and conduct regarding bankruptcy.[7] In the *Remarks*, Defoe specifies that he played a role in drafting the bill, which is acknowledged and not challenged in the anonymous attack on his ideas in *Observations on the Bankrupts Bill: Occasion'd by the … Unjust Reflections of Mr. Daniel De Foe.*

Mr De Foe, — In one of your Letters[8] you were pleas'd to promise me a correspondence tho' accounts were now ceas'd between us, but I am affraid you have forgot it or the hurry of affairs have not given you permission; however I hope now you have labour'd so heartily and gain'd your point for the publick good in the act of Bankruptcy you are a little more at leisure and will acquit yourself of the promise above, and not to make it only a complemental correspondence I will give you a subject relating to the said act. Know then that I have all along during this Bill's being the subject of all conversation been a vigorous defender of the reasonableness and justice of it, endeavouring to make the equity of it appear as clear to others as it did to me and in these little Rencounters I have sometimes occasion to defend my Friend the author of the Review and particularly last night upon my reading the Abstract of the Act and approving it I met with opponents who had receiv'd some prejudice agt you (who they suppos'd was the contriver of it[9]) by some of your creditors in these parts, vizt Mr Emperor and Mr Gibbs,[10] both whom indeed I have heard reflect upon you, but it was no great Surprise to me as well knowing that there are great numbers of persons in the World that fix the same epithet upon those that can't as on those that will not pay their Debts. However I say these Gentlemen with whom I was last night in discourse, having heard the above nam'd persons storys, were credulous enough to believe that in your case practice and principle did not exactly correspond.[11] Amongst other things in your defence I read them your Review wch contein'd advice to the Bankrupts after the Act pass'd.[12] Can it possibly be suppos'd said I that the author of this paper can have justly any thing dishonest fixt upon him — does not he here allow the Title of an Honest Man to be the most glorious that can be given and consequently the contrary to be the worst, and yet knows it belongs to himself. Can he thus in the Face of the World triumph in his Honesty which is an appeal

JOHN FRANSHAM TO DEFOE, [C. JANUARY–APRIL 1706]

to all that know him, and yet be conscious that he may easily be prov'd the contrary — have he not in his reply to Ld Haversham declar'd to all the World that he has uncompounded reduc'd his Debts from £17000 to under £5000,¹³ is not that an evident proof of his honesty? Yes reply'd the Gentleman, supposing the Fact, but where's the proof of that? His creditors in these parts are altogether unacquainted wth it. No doubt, said I, M^r De Foe has proper reasons for their coming amongst the number of the last to be paid, but I have heard tho' I can't assert it from my own knowledge that one of his creditors in Yarmouth have been fully sattisfy'd his Debt wch was considerable.¹⁴ If you could give me any proof of that, reply'd the gentleman, I shall never doubt of his being just, for I readily agree his writings are very much so.

If you think fit to enable me to give him a positive answer¹⁵ I shall receive it with a great deal of Sattisfaction because I shall be thereby likewise better able to vindicate a person whose defence is at all times undertaken with pleasure by

S^r yours &c,

J. F.

Text: MS untraced. The copytext is Norgate, 282. *Address*: none recorded.

1 Fransham refers to Defoe's *A Reply to a Pamphlet entituled, The L[or]d H[aversham]'s Vindication of his Speech*, published around 10 Jan. 1706, marking the earliest possible date for this letter; Defoe wrote extensively on bankruptcy law in the *Review* and pamphlets from Feb. to Mar. The fact that Defoe replied on 24 May suggests a date of Mar. or Apr.
2 *Review*, III, 184 (23 Mar. 1706).
3 *Review*, III, 101 (9 Feb. 1706).
4 *Review*, III, 132, 139 (26 and 28 Feb. 1706).
5 *Review*, III, 109–11 (14 Feb. 1706); *An Essay upon Projects*, *PEW*, VIII, 96–107. See W. R. Owens and P. N. Furbank, 'Defoe and Imprisonment for Debt: Some Attributions Reviewed', *RES* 37 (1986), 495–502.
6 *Review*, III, 157–64 (9 and 12 Mar. 1706).
7 *PEW*, VIII, 193–215. See also his defence of the law in *The Complete English Tradesman* (1725–7), *RDW*, VII, 80–1.
8 *one of your Letters*: Untraced.
9 *contriver of it*: Defoe claimed to have had a hand in the 1706 legislation. See headnote and *Review*, IV, 127 (8 Apr. 1707).
10 *Mr Emperor and Mr Gibbs*: Unidentified.
11 *practice and principle did not exactly correspond*: See Letter 10, note 7 for contemporaneous claims that Defoe had been less than honest in declaring his assets in his 1692 bankruptcy.
12 *Review … pass'd*: In the *Review* for 26 Mar., Defoe advises debtors to 'make an open, free, Genuine and unreserved Surrender' of their assets and suggests that if possible they 'throw

DEFOE TO [ROBERT HARLEY], [APRIL 1706]

back the Allowance of 5 *per Cent.* Granted by this Act, and give it to your Creditors' (the new act allowed 5% of his estate, up to £200, to the bankrupt as long as he could pay creditors at least 8 shillings in the pound). 'When you are deliver'd, apply Seriously and warily to Honest Endeavours to Live', Defoe's counsel continues, and 'never think yourselves discharg'd in Conscience, tho' you may be discharg'd in Law', meaning that 'Paying Overplus beyond Composition' is the duty of anyone who benefits by the new law (III, 190–2).

13 *reply ... £5000*: *A Reply to a Pamphlet entituled, The L[or]d H[aversham]'s Vindication of his Speech* (Jan. 1706), 7. See the story of a man with a £17,000 bankruptcy in *Review*, IV, 147–8 (17 Apr. 1707).
    Defoe's *Reply* was a response to *The Lord Haversham's Vindication of his Speech in Parliament* (1706), by John Thompson, first Baron Haversham (*c.* 1648–1710), itself a reply to *An Answer to the L—d H—sham's Speech. By Daniel D'Foe* (1706), a reprint of the *Review* for 24 Nov. 1705. Haversham's 15 Nov. speech in the House of Lords criticised the ministry concerning the war and trade, and he advocated bringing the heir, Sophia of Hanover (1630–1714), to reside in England, an idea Queen Anne hated. For the continuation of hostilities between Defoe and Haversham during the next four years, see Letter 125, note 4.

14 *creditors ... considerable*: The creditors are unidentified but in Mar. 1713 a Yarmouth creditor had Defoe arrested for a £1,500 debt (see Letter 226).

15 *positive answer*: Letter 49 is Defoe's response.

46

To [Robert Harley]

[April 1706][1]

HEADNOTE: During his large circuit of England in 1705, Defoe established a network of distribution agents which he used to disseminate publications across the country. The list comprises mainly Dissenting ministers, merchants, and tradesmen (many in Defoe's old line, clothing) but also two sitting MPs. Its effectiveness is indicated by the record for Harley of the wide dispersal of an April 1706 pamphlet. Defoe's *Remarks on the Letter to the Author of the State-Memorial* was a denunciation of the anonymous *A Letter to the Author of the Memorial of the State of England* (December 1705), ascribed to a radical Whig, the Rev. William Stephens (1647–1718).[2] The *Letter* itself replied to John Toland's *Memorial of the State of England* (October 1705), which had defended Marlborough and Godolphin against attacks in *The Memorial of the Church of England* (July 1705). By repeating rumours he finds himself unable to refute, the author of the *Letter* insinuates that Marlborough had deliberately mismanaged the campaign of 1705 because he was seeking to make 'an advantagious bargain for himself with *France*, by selling them a Peace to the inconceivable loss and detriment of his own Country and the Confederates'.[3] This indirection is dropped when Harley's duplicity comes under consideration: 'You

DEFOE TO [ROBERT HARLEY], [APRIL 1706]

say indeed that *he hated extremes in all Parties*, had you said he is hated extremely in all Parties you had varied less from the Mark than from the Words.'[4]

Defoe had written at length the previous year against *The Memorial of the Church of England*. He deems Toland's contribution 'honestly meant' but wrongheaded in defending the current ministers by adversely reflecting on the Whig leaders in William III's day. Defoe however denounces the response, which he assumes is by Stephens, as 'the Empty and Weak Efforts of an Expiring Party to renew their Cause'.[5] He had already denounced it as a libel in the *Review*, assuming that its author was a High Flyer.[6] When it became apparent that Stephens was a disaffected whiggish clergyman – as Leslie gleefully highlighted in *The Rehearsal* – Defoe painted him as a patsy caught in a 'Snare', who 'Copied from' the High Flyers, '*for he only was the Writer, of what his Folly had led him to hearken to, from those that took Pleasure, to give Ill turns to every thing*'.[7] In the *Remarks* Defoe even portrayed the *Letter* as a highflying *Shortest Way*, contrived to trick Dissenters into sympathy with its views: 'It was industriously spread abroad, that it was wrote by a Dissenter; the Book was secretly handed about among some of our unhappily, and too ignorantly prejudic'd Friends, and the Delusion spread a great way.'[8] For this reason, Defoe wanted to disseminate his *Remarks* as widely as possible and availed himself of his contacts across Britain.[9]

Pat Rogers remarks that Defoe's list of distribution agents purposely excludes individuals associated with Harley, guaranteeing the Secretary of State's role would remain covert. Rogers also observes that, effective as the list was in 1706, Defoe was soon after dispatched to Scotland, and Harley was out of office by February 1708. By the time Harley returned to office at the head of the Tories in 1710, Defoe's network would have been of limited use to him, because it is a decidedly Whig list, full of Dissenters and merchants.[10] The document is in two columns in manuscript, the first with a running total of 1405, the second, headed 'Ditto', with a running total of 510.

Remarks &c.[11] Sent into ye Country

100 .. to Plymo & Biddiford . . . . . mr Barron Minr[12]

100 .. to Excester . . . . mr Eveleigh Do[13]

25 . . . to Tiverton . . . . mr Bear Mercht[14]

25 . . . to Taunton . . . . mr James Mr[15]

12 . . . to Bridgewater . . . . mr Codrington[16]

100 .. Bristoll . . . . Benja Cool Quaker[17]

25 . . . Do . . . . mr Wraxall Mercha[18]

25 . . . Lime & Bridport . . . . mr Gay Mr[19]

12 . . . Weymo . . . . mr Fenner Mr[20]

12 . . . Dorchester . . . . mr Nowell Mr[21]

25 . . . Salisbury . . . . mr Sloan Mr[22]

DEFOE TO [ROBERT HARLEY], [APRIL 1706]

25 ... Divizes .... Tho: Webb Cloth[r23]
12 ... Newbury .... Ja Pearce M[r24]
25 ... Reading .... Tim[o] Westley[25]
25 ... Cirencester &c. .... m[r] Dixe[26]
12 ... Bath .... D[r] Parker[27]
12 ... Caln & Chipenham ..... by m[r] Dukett[28]
25 ... Gloucester .... by m[r] Dixe[29]
12 ... Hereford .... m[r] Bolow[30]
12 ... Worcester .... m[r] Fitzer Cloth[r31]
12 ... Leominster .... m[r] Stansbury[32]
12 ... Bewdly .... m[r] Oasland M[r33]
25 ... Evisham & Parshore ...... m[r] Gibbons[34]
50 ... Shrewsbury .... m[r] Elisha[35]
50 ... Chester .... m[r] Hinks[36]
50 ... Leverpool .... m[r] Done[37]
50[a] ... Whitehaven & preston .... m[r] Gale[38]
12 ... Warrington .... m[r] Owen M[r39]
25 ... Manchester .... m[r] Cuningham M[r40]
25 ... Bolton .... m[r] Crompton M[r41]
25 ... Hallifax .... m[r] Priestly M[r42]
25 ... Leeds & Wakefield .... m[r] Ibbetson[43]
100 .. Newcastle .... m[r] Button[44]
50 ... York and Hull .... by m[r] Ibbetson[45]
25 ... Gainsbro' .... m[r] Coates Mercha[46]
25 ... Sheffield .... m[r] Symmonds[47]
25 ... Nottingham .... D[r] Woodhouse[48]
12 ... Leicester .... m[r] Sympson[49]
12 ... Mountsorrel .... m[r] Matthews M[r50]
12 ... Wigston .... m[r] Chambers M[r51]
12 ... Lutterworth .... m[r] Dowley M[r52]
25 ... Coventry .... m[r] Owen[53]
25 ... Daventry & Northampton .. m[r] Smith[54]
50 ... Cambridge .... m[r] Jardin[55]
25 ... Wisbich .... m[r] Kinderly[56]
25 ... Bury .... m[r] Morley[57]

———

1405

[a] 50] *amended from '25'*

DEFOE TO [ROBERT HARLEY], [APRIL 1706]

Ditto

12 .... To Stamford. . . . . m[r] [   ][58]
12 .... Beccles . . . . m[r] Nokes Mr[59]
100 ...Norwich. . . . . m[r] Fransham[60]
12 .... Leostoff . . . . Cap[t] Paćy[61]
12 .... Ipswich . . . . m[r] Whitaker[62]
25 .... Sudbury . . . . Cap[t] Fenn[63]
50 ....Colechester. . . . . m[r] Wheely[64]
25 .... Canterbury. . . . . m[r] Fenner[65]
50 ....Cranbrook . . . . m[r] Jellard[66]
25 .... Maidstone . . . . m[r] Tongue[67]
50 ....Portsmo . . . . m[r] Johnson[68]
25 .... Braintry &c . . . . m[r] Ruggles[69]
25 .... Hartford &c. . . . . m[r] Smart[70]
25 .... Aylesbury. . . . . m[r] Mead[71]
50 ....to Dublin . . . . m[r] Rogers[72]
12 .... to Shirborn . . . . m[r] Dix[73]
..   Oxford . . . . m[r] Woodcock[74]

————

510
50   laid Down in Coffee houses
100[75]   Given about by hand

Text: BL Add. MS. 70291, fols. 50–1. *Address*: none.

1   The date is inferred from that of the pamphlet Defoe is sending to his distribution agents.
2   On the authorship, see J. A. Downie, 'William Stephens and the *Letter to the Author of the Memorial of the State of England* Reconsidered', *BIHR* 50 (1977), 253–9, which argues that Stephens was the printer and Thomas Rawlins the principal author.
3   [William Stephens?], *A Letter to the Author of the Memorial of the State of England* (1705), 23. See Defoe's mockery of this specific allegation against Marlborough in *Review*, v, 119 (18 May 1708).
4   [Stephens?], *Letter*, 30, quoting John Toland, *The Memorial of the State of England* (1705), 69. For an account of Stephens's arrest, prosecution, and punishment, see Douglas Coombs, 'William Stephens and the *Letter to the Author of the Memorial of the State of England* (1705)', *BIHR* 32 (1959), 24–37 (at 31–7).
5   *Remarks on the Letter to the Author of the State-Memorial*, 4, 25. Defoe attacked Stephens eight years earlier in *Some Reflections on a Pamphlet lately Publish'd, Entituled, An Argument Shewing that a Standing Army is Inconsistent with a Free Government* (1697), *PEW*, I, 41.
6   *Review*, III, 66 (24 Jan. 1706); III, 96 (7 Feb. 1706).
7   Leslie, *Rehearsal*, 10 Apr. 1706; *Review*, III, 223 (11 Apr. 1706). Cf. *Review*, III, 238–9 (16 Apr. 1706). In the preface to *Jure Divino* in summer 1706, Defoe criticises Stephens's proposal in

DEFOE TO [ROBERT HARLEY], [APRIL 1706]

the *Letter* that the Dissenters come out in support of universal religious toleration (*SFS*, II, 56–62).

8 *Remarks*, 4. Leslie's *Rehearsal* for 10 Apr. 1706 compared Stephens's *Letter* and Defoe's *Shortest Way*.

9 Harley's petty accounts indicate a payment of £20 to Alexander Goldsmith on 28 Feb. 1706 (BL Add. MS. 70269, misc. 6).

10 Rogers, 'Distribution Agents', 157–61. The annotations below draw extensively on Rogers's article.

11 *Remarks &c.*: Defoe's *Remarks on the Letter to the Author of the State-Memorial*, published in early Apr. 1706.

12 *m̃ Barron Minr̃*: Peter Baron (d. 1759), Presbyterian minister at Plymouth from 1704 and author of *A Sermon Preach'd in Exeter August the 24th 1742. Being Bartholomew-Day* (1742).

13 *m̃ Eveleigh Dᵒ*: Josiah Eveleigh (see Letter 39). 'Dᵒ' throughout the list is 'ditto', so here a minister.

14 *m̃ Bear Merchr̃*: Francis Bere (see Letter 39).

15 *m̃ James Mr̃*: Stephen James (1676–1725), Presbyterian minister at Pitminster until 1706 and thereafter at Fulwood, and divinity tutor at Taunton Dissenting Academy, an institution praised by Defoe, with respect to this period, in *Tour*, *TDH*, II, 21.

16 *m̃ Codrington*: Probably Samuel Codrington (d. 1747), a Presbyterian merchant at Bridgwater who supported the erection of a new meeting house in Dec. 1704 (Somerset Heritage Centre, D\N\bw.chch/2/1/4). He subscribed to Oldmixon's whiggish *History of England* in 1730 and 1735.

17 *Benjᵃ Cool Quaker*: Benjamin Coole (1664–1717), Quaker and merchant in Bristol, originally of Devizes. He was the author of several polemical religious tracts, an associate (like Defoe) of William Penn, and one of the founders of the Baptist Mills brass works in 1700. See Isabel Grubb, *Quakerism and Industry before 1800* (1930), 50–3. In the *Review* for 8 Mar. 1712 (VIII, 675–8), Defoe alludes to a petition presented to parliament by Coole and his associates for encouraging a brass manufacture (Defoe uses the occasion to satirise the 'brass', or brazenness, of the High Church party). Coole left a substantial manuscript autobiography, which alludes briefly to Defoe's examination for *The Shortest Way* and to *The Consolidator* (Princeton University Library, RTC01, no. 231, fols. 148, 170).

18 *m̃ Wraxall Merchᵃ*: Probably John Wraxall, linen draper in Bristol (d. 1712). In May 1705 he wrote his name on a copy of Tutchin's *The Western Martyrology*, commemorating Monmouth's rebels (John Evans, *A Chronological Outline of the History of Bristol* (1824), 240). As Rogers notes, Nathaniel Wraxall (b. 1687), a future mayor, is less likely to have been Defoe's agent ('Distribution Agents', 148).

19 *m̃ Gay Mr̃*: Matthew Gay (d. 1734), Dissenting minister at Lyme Regis.

20 *m̃ Fenner Mr̃*: John Fenner (see Letter 40).

21 *m̃ Nowell Mr̃*: Baruch Nowell (d. 1739), clerk and Dissenting minister at Dorchester from 1689 until his death. For Defoe's reflections on good relations between the Anglican and Dissenting ministers at Dorchester, see Letter 39, note 3. Cf. Jerom Merch, *A History of the Presbyterian and General Baptists Churches in the West of England* (1835), 268–70.

22 *m̃ Sloan Mr̃*: William Sloane (*c.* 1661–1717), Dissenting minister in Salisbury.

23 *Thoᵒ: Webb Clothr̃*: Not identified with certainty, but the Webbs had long been a leading family of clothiers in the south-west. Rogers, 'Distribution Agents', 149, identifies a Thomas Webb (b. 1676) active in Devizes in 1701. Defoe's contact had settled in London and was still in touch with Defoe in 1724. He left a MS dating to that year, lamenting the death of his wife: 'And poor distressed I left alone, and no one to go and speak to, save only Mr. Deffoe, who hath acted a noble and generous part towards me and my poor children. The Lord reward him and his with the blessings of upper and nether spring, with the blessings of his basket and store, &c.' (Wilson, III, 623–4). He alludes to Josh. 15:19 and Deut. 28:5.

24 *Ja Pearċe Mr̃*: James Peirce (*c.* 1674–1726), Dissenting minister in Newbury until 1713 when he moved to Exeter. He wrote *A Vindication of the Dissenters* (1717) and was a principal

197

DEFOE TO [ROBERT HARLEY], [APRIL 1706]

disputant in the Salters' Hall controversy of 1719, when he was in conflict with Defoe's contact, Josiah Eveleigh. For assessments, see Allan Brockett, *Nonconformity in Exeter, 1650–1875* (Manchester, 1962), 75–95, and Bracy V. Hill, 'The Language of Dissent: The Defense of Eighteenth-Century English Dissent in the Works and Sermons of James Peirce' (Baylor University PhD, 2010).

25 *Timo Westley*: Timothy Wesley (b. 1659), brother of Defoe's classmate at Newington Green Dissenting Academy, the Anglican clergyman and poet Samuel Wesley (1662–1735), and so the uncle of the methodists John (1703–91) and Charles Wesley (1707–88). In 1727 he or someone of the same name was a bookseller in Reading. See *CTB*, xxx, cdxii for his payment of stamp duty in 1716.

26 *mr Dixe*: Perhaps Thomas Dix (d. 1734), clothier of Cirencester, a subscriber to Oldmixon's *History* in 1735.

27 *Dr Parker*: Dr Henry Parker (1655–1736) practised medicine at Bath.

28 *mr Dukett*: George Duckett, MP for Calne (see Letters 44 and 47).

29 *mr Dixe*: Probably the same man as for Cirencester.

30 *mr Bolow*: Unidentified.

31 *mr Fitzer Clothr*: Perhaps the 'John Fitzer, late of the City of Worcester, Clothier' who was bankrupt in 1711 (*London Gazette*, 26–9 May 1711), who may as Rogers says have been a relative of Thomas Fitzer (d. 1709), a saddler ('Distribution Agents', 150).

32 *mr Stansbury*: John Stansbury (*c*. 1670–1729?), mercer and freeholder in Leominster. See Frederick Howard Wines, *The Descendants of John Stansbury of Leominster* (Springfield, Ill., 1895), 1–2.

33 *mr Oasland Mr*: Edward Oasland or Osland (d. 1752), son of the ejected minister Henry Oasland (1625–1703), graduate of Sheriffhales Dissenting Academy (also attended by Robert Harley), Independent minister in Bewdley from 1704, and subscriber to Oldmixon's *History* in 1730, though not in 1735.

34 *mr Gibbons*: Unidentified, but possibly related to William Gibbons (d. 1683) and Charles Gibbons (d. 1694), who were Worcestershire clothiers, albeit in Corsham, further south than Evesham and Pershore.

35 *mr Elisha*: Samuel Elisha (see Letters 16 and 20).

36 *mr Hinks*: Likely Edward Hincks (*c*. 1676–1734), linen draper and freeman of Chester. See Ernest Axon, 'The Hincks Family', *Transactions of the Unitarian Historical Society* 8 (1943–6), 131.

37 *mr Done*: Samuel Done (see Letter 44, note 51).

38 *mr Gale*: Likely Elisha Gale (d. 1724), a Dissenter and merchant mariner based in Whitehaven. Gale was the younger brother of John Gale (1650–1716), the steward of Lowther collieries, not his son as Rogers states ('Distribution Agents', 151). John Gale can be discounted because he was a 'bigoted Anglican, and very hostile to Whitehaven's Dissenters (who included his mother and younger brother)'. See *The Correspondence of Sir John Lowther of Whitehaven, 1693–1698: A Provincial Community in Wartime*, ed. D. R. Hainsworth (1983), 674–5. John Gale's eldest son George (1671–1712), husband of George Washington's grandmother, seems to have settled in America, where he died, by 1704. His second son John (1672–1729) is possible, but less likely than his uncle, a known Dissenter, closer to Defoe's age. See *An Exact and Industrious Tradesman: The Letter Book of Joseph Symson of Kendal, 1711–1720*, ed. S. D. Smith (2002), 713.

39 *mr Owen Mr*: Charles Owen (after 1655–1746), Presbyterian minister at Cairo Street Chapel, Warrington. He was a tutor at a Dissenting Academy in Warrington and was the younger brother of Defoe's Shrewsbury acquaintance James Owen (see Letter 19), of whom he wrote a biography, *Some Account of the Life and Writings of the Late Pious and Learned Mr. James Owen, Minister of the Gospel in Salop* (1709). Thereafter he published numerous works of divinity, religious controversy, and natural history.

40 *mr Cuningham Mr*: James Coningham (1670–1716), Presbyterian minister and tutor at a Dissenting Academy in Manchester until 1712. *A Critical Essay on Modern Medals* (1704) is

198

DEFOE TO [ROBERT HARLEY], [APRIL 1706]

attributed to him, and he published three sermons. Defoe seemingly used him as a post restante address later in 1706 (Letter 51).

41 *mr Crompton Mr*: Not identified with certainty. Joseph Crompton (1680–1729), born in Bolton and Presbyterian minister at Little Ireton in Derbyshire from around 1701, is possible if we assume that he mediated for Defoe with his Bolton connections despite residing in the Midlands. John Crompton (1673/4?–1745) was the son of a Bolton Dissenting minister, also John (1639–1703); he is possible if indeed he was a minister, or if Defoe had erroneously specified that his contact was a minister.

42 *mr Priestly Mr*: Nathaniel Priestley (*c*. 1665–1728), Presbyterian minister at Northgate End Chapel from 1696. See the panegyric in Dunton, *Life and Errors*, II, 420–1.

43 *mr Ibbetson*: James Ibbetson (1674–1739), a wealthy Dissenter and merchant in Leeds (R. G. Wilson, *Gentlemen Merchants: The Merchant Community in Leeds, 1700–1830* (Manchester, 1971), 244).

44 *mr Button*: Joseph Button, bookseller in Newcastle-upon-Tyne; Defoe's professional relationship with Button extended at least to 1715 (see Letter 166).

45 *mr Ibbetson*: Presumably the same person as for Leeds and Wakefield. One imagines that Ibbetson had a network of his own to cover these towns, given the distances.

46 *mr Coates Mercha*: John Coates, merchant in Gainsborough. He was alive as late as 1723, when he subscribed to the Nonconformist Thomas Doolittle's *A Complete Body of Practical Divinity*.

47 *mr Symmonds*: Nevill Symmons or Simmons (d. 1735), bookseller specialising in Nonconformist works, as did his father of the same name (Richard Baxter's bookseller), and as did his sons Nevill (*c*. 1692–1730) and Samuel (1703–90). See Giles Hester, *Nevill Simmons, Bookseller and Publisher: with Notices of Literature connected with Old Sheffield* (1893).

48 *Dr Woodhouse*: Dr John Woodhouse (*c*. 1677–1733), MD (Alexander Gordon, *Freedom after Ejection: A Review (1690–1692) of Presbyterian and Congregational Nonconformity in England and Wales* (Manchester, 1917), 389).

49 *mr Sympson*: Possibly Samuel Simpson (1677–1742), a grocer, Mayor of Leicester in 1735.

50 *mr Matthews Mr*: Michael Matthews (d. 1724), Presbyterian minister.

51 *mr Chambers Mr*: Abraham Chambers (d. 1735), Dissenting minister.

52 *mr Dowley Mr*: Peter Dowley (d. 1731), Dissenting minister at Lutterworth. In 1705–6 he was locked in a pamphlet controversy with the Anglican cleric Edward Wells (1667–1727) on the validity of Presbyterian ordination, a dispute that drew a series of defences of Dissent from Defoe's Newbury agent, James Peirce (Hill, 'Language of Dissent', 257–312).

53 *mr Owen*: Edward Owen (see Letter 43).

54 *mr Smith*: Obediah Smith (d. after 1723), bookseller in Daventry, active in London before 1680 (Plomer, 275). His name appears on an imprint of a 1723 book, the latest source found.

55 *mr Jardin*: Rogers proposes James Jardin (d. 1716), lace-seller, as a possibility ('Distribution Agents', 153), but the linen-draper Richard Jardine, one of two possibilities offered by Backscheider, *Life*, 184, is most probable because Defoe quotes him as a character reference for Abraham Gill in *The Experiment* (1705), 54–5.

56 *mr Kinderly*: Nathaniel Kinderley (1673–1742), a civil engineer in Wisbech. See A. W. Skempton, 'Kinderley, Nathaniel', in *A Biographical Dictionary of Civil Engineers in Great Britain and Ireland: 1500–1830*, ed. A. W. Skempton *et al.* (2002), 386–8.

57 *mr Morley*: John Morley (see Letter 18, note 28).

58 *mr [   ]*: Unidentified.

59 *mr Nokes Mr*: William Nokes (b. 1635/6), Independent minister at Beccles from about 1703 to 1710; he conformed to the Church of England in 1712. See Samuel Wilton Rix, *Brief Records of the Independent Church, at Beccles, Suffolk* (1837), 167–74. Nokes wrote several works of divinity.

60 *mr Fransham*: John Fransham (see Letter 21).

61 *Capt Pacy*: Probably John Pacy (b. 1664), merchant Nonconformist son of the wealthy fishing merchant Samuel Pacy (d. 1680). John was chosen bailiff at Dunwich in 1694 (Thomas Neale to Sir Robert Rich, 30 Nov. 1694, Folger Shakespeare Library, MS. x.d.451(142)). On the Pacy

199

DEFOE TO [ROBERT HARLEY], [APRIL 1706]

family, see David Butcher, *Lowestoft 1550–1750: Development and Change in a Suffolk Coastal Town* (Woodbridge, 2008).

62 *mr Whitaker*: Probably Charles Whitaker (*c.* 1642–1715), Whig MP for Ipswich 1695–8 and 1701–5; he did not contest the 1705 election.

63 *Capt Fenn*: As Rogers notes, likely a relative of either or both of the John Fenns, clothiers, who died in 1721 and 1724, respectively ('Distribution Agents', 155). One John Fenn left a house and land to found a charity school with the residue of the rents going to the Presbyterian chapel (William White, *History, Gazetteer, and Directory of Suffolk* (1855), 779).

64 *mr Wheely*: John Wheely, an ironmonger, who procured and began to demolish Colchester Castle; he was steward to the Colchester MP Sir Isaac Rebow (see Letter 44, note 65) to whom he sold the castle.

65 *mr Fenner*: The name Rest Fenner was passed from father to son for several generations, and the family had interests in bookselling, brewery, and clothing.

66 *mr Jellard*: Not identified. Possibly Nicholas Jellard, a Baptist preacher in Hawkhurst, near Cranbrook.

67 *mr Tongue*: Not identified, though Rogers identifies several men named John Tonge born at Tonge, near Maidstone ('Distribution Agents', 155).

68 *mr Johnson*: Not identified.

69 *mr Ruggles*: The Ruggles were a prominent family of clothiers at Bocking, near Braintree, headed by John Ruggles (d. 1709); his grandson, Thomas (1679–1743) may have been Defoe's contact. See Edith Freeman and Sir John Ruggles-Brise, 'The Ruggles of Bradford Street', *Essex Journal* 21 (1986), 13–16.

70 *mr Smart*: Likely Jonathan Smart, an ally of the new Lord Keeper, the Whig William Cowper (1665–1723). In 1705 Smart successfully led petitioners against the election of the Tory Richard Goulston (1669–1731) at Hertford, with the Whig Thomas Clarke (*c.* 1672–1754) elected in his place (*HPC 1690–1715*, III, 605). Smart gave evidence again in Clarke's successful petition after the 1722 election (*C.J.*, xx, 97). From 1703 a Dissenting congregation met at a barn he owned (William Urwick, *Nonconformity in Herts.* (1884), 541). From 1717 a congregation met at his house (W. J. Hardy, *Hertford County Records: Notes and Extracts from the Sessions Rolls*, 5 vols. (Hertford, 1905), II, 51). He (or perhaps a son of the same name) married Jane Watson in 1720 (William Brigg, *The Herts Genealogist and Antiquary*, 3 vols. (Harpenden, 1895), I, 302). He was also Receiver General of taxes in Hertfordshire.

71 *mr Mead*: William Mead (*c.* 1663–1723), Lord of the Manor of Aylesbury, High Sheriff for Buckinghamshire in 1716, and member of the Dyers' Company.

72 *mr Rogers*: Gabriel Rogers in Shrewsbury (see Letter 19) had died in early 1705; his nephew John Rogers (d. 1738?) carried on the business, so it seems likely that it was he who dispatched Defoe's pamphlet to Ireland.

73 *mr Dix*: Probably Thomas Dix of Cirencester again.

74 *mr Woodcock*: Josiah Woodcock (d. 1709), Presbyterian minister (Hearne, II, 217).

75 *100*: With the 1,405 of the first column, the list accounts for 2,065 copies of the pamphlet in total.

DEFOE TO [ROBERT HARLEY], 6 MAY 1706

47

To [Robert Harley]

6 May 1706

HEADNOTE **(Letters 47 and 48)**: Throughout 1705 Defoe complained that the renewal of claims against him for old debts were politically motivated. In the previous October Defoe wrote of himself in the *Review*: 'His Creditors [are] rouzed to a general Prosecution upon him for Debts, tho' under former Treaties and Agreements; as if he was more able to Discharge himself, now reduc'd by a known Disaster, and Ruin'd by a Publick Storm on his Family, than before; when in prosperous Circumstances, he was Gradually clearing himself of every Body, and all waited with Patience, and show'd themselves satisfied.'[1] But by spring 1706 Defoe was in hiding from bailiffs and desperate for remuneration or even an appointment that would take him out of England. In one pamphlet he reacted to allegations that he was a mercenary writer: 'Thus I am brought in for a Place; but God knows, without a Salary, I must have a Pension! I wish he was not in the wrong.'[2] He remained unsure about whether he would qualify for the new Bankruptcy Act. Though apparently without direct encouragement, he continued to promote the ministry's interests, defending the prosecution of the war and promoting the Anglo-Scottish Union.[3]

Sr

As ye last Time I had ye favor of Audience wth you, you[a] Were pleas'd to Tell me you Desir'd to Speak wth me on Accot of The Review &c. I have Often Endeavour'd to have ye like honor and began to hope Some thing might Offer in wch I might be usefull to you.

But I am Not Onely Unhappy in frequent Dissappointmts but my Unhappy Circumstances Makeing those Dissappointmts more Severe to me than I believ you Would have ym be, forces me to give you This too Tedious Narrative, Humbly to state to you My present Case and Earnest Request, and I[b] Entreat your pardon for the Importunate plainess, a Liberty you were pleas'd Frankly to give me and wch I have been too apt to Accept of.

---

[a] you] *interlined*
[b] I] *interlined*

201

DEFOE TO [ROBERT HARLEY], 6 MAY 1706

My Case Really Sr admitts no Ceremony, being Come to yt Crisis, yt without Some powerfull aid, or Some Miracle wch I Ought Not to Expect, I Shall Soon be Rendred Entirely Useless both to ye publick and My Self.

But why do I look to you, or Move you in This Matter? is a question Offers[a] Some shock in My Writeing this.

Pardon my Positive way of speaking; I don't Say I Merit, at least any Thing but Pitty — But Sr you have had ye Goodness to put me in hopes yt something was Reserv'd in My favour; If I have Mistaken you, I am Wrong Indeed, and would be Glad to be Sett Right, yt I might not Expect and make you Uneasÿ wth my Importunityes.

This Reserv sr you were pleasd to Say, wth yor Usuall Tenderness for me, you would have be Usefull to me, and therefore kept till I was free.

But sr The prospect of yt Freedome looks Every Day More Dull upon me, and I foresee I shall Never Master it, Unless I can Take off Some of the most Furious people, who Resolutely Oppose me, and which is worse I find it will be, if Contested, a Very Doubtfull point whether I am within ye Meaning of This Act or no, and am Therefore advis'd Not to attempt it.[4]

Now sr as the Risq of Disputeing is too Great, Since I must Surrender my Self first into ye hands of the Unmercifull, and that to take them off by Treaty is Absolutely Necessary, No Man yt is my Friend Advises me to attempt it by Law, Since when they in p[er]ticular are Taken off,[b] I shall be as Effectually Free as[c] by the act,[d] all ye Rest being Undr Obligation to a Composition wch they have Recd part of and Can not go from.[5]

Thus sr my Freedome Depends Upon a private Treaty, wch Treaty without assistance I Can Not Carry on, and Mean Time have been So Close persued Since I Saw you, that I am but by Miracle yet Out of their hands, and am Oblig'd to quitt all Conversation, and Make a Retreat altogether Disconsolate, and Such as Renders me useless and Uncapable.

---

[a] Offers] *following illegible word cancelled*
[b] off,] *interlined*
[c] as] *interlined above cancelled illegible word*
[d] the act] *interlined above cancelled word* 'Treaty'

DEFOE TO [ROBERT HARLEY], 6 MAY 1706

This Urges me Sr to Say, if There is Such a Thing, if her Majties Bounty has any Thing In Reserv for me, I Entreat of you One of The Two following p[er]ticulars, and tis fitt I should leave it to you to Choose.

1st   sr That I may be assisted as far as 2 or 300ℓ will do it, to Free my Self from ye Imediate fury of 5 or 6 Unreasonable Creditors, after wch I shall by my Own strength work Thro' the Rest in Time.

2dly   Or sr That According to yor kind promise wch I Can not but Claim, you will please to Send me Somewhere Abroad, Out of The Reach of Their hands, and That her Majties Bounty may be someway Applyed to ye support of my Family.

I Really kno' not Sr whether This thing I Call her Majties Bounty,[6] be what I Ought to speak of in this Manner or No; I pretend to no Merit, I have done but my Duty, — But Indeed I have been Unjustly Ruin'd and that in her Majties Name,[7] and I am Now Implacably p[er]sued purely on Accot of my Endeavours for her Majties Service: if these are Merits, I have Some Claim, And I flatter my Self yor Intercession sr will Improve it; I Cease to go On wth This Sad story, and Tho' my Case Renders me Now Next to Desperate, yet I Can not Enlarge on my Complaint.

I am not weary attending at yor Door, nor do I Repine at stayeing your Leisure — But Sr the Risque I Run So much as to pass and Repass is of ye last Consequence to me, and Tho' I Resolv if possible not to be Taken by Them, yet Theres no Defending against a Surprize.

The loss I Sustain also in ye want of Conversing wth you, appeares to me Destructive of all the Designs layd by me, for your service; The Correspondence I had Settled by your Ordr in most parts of England and from wch on all Occasions I Could have Rendred you Service, Dyes, and Declines, for want of That Assistance wch you were pleasd to Allow was necessary, to me, Vizt of a Servant to assist, and of frequent Communication of things to keep Intelligence alive.

The Very Charge is too great for my Reduc't Condition, and the Number of Letters too many for ye few Undisturb'd houres wch I have left me.

DEFOE TO [ROBERT HARLEY], 6 MAY 1706

Thus I am Rendred Useless to you, in yt wch I hoped Once to have brought to a p[er]feccon beyond Even your Own Expectation, and in wch I have been at no Inconsiderable Charge Over and Above what you have been pleasd to allot for that work.

I hope you will think all this proceeds from a mind Griev'd that I Can not be made that usefull Instrumt to ye publick I would be, and what Ever may look self Intrested, you will pardon, for tho' Tis True I Importune you in ye first, I above all Covet to show you That I would not be thought to Enjoy your favour, not to your advantage.

I have Severall things to Move you in that I Can not Comprise here; mr Ducket has been in Town; yt Affair[8] being Delay'd, not Onely sinks my Intrest and Correspondence in that Country, but puffs up the high Intrest in ye Country to a Vast Dissadvantage, and I have much to Say on that head worth Notice.

I would be yor Humble Peticoner for a private Appartmt in Whit[e]hall,[a] where I am Told It is in yor power to admitt me, and haveing an Opportunity now to Clear my Self of ye Queens bench by an Accidt wch I want to Informe you of, I might by ye shelter of Such a Retreat prevent any New attempts upon me there.

I have also Something to Informe you of, of a Design forming Agat your Self wch I should be Glad to be Instrumentall to Dissappoint, but all these things Reciev their Interruption, as I a Continued Mortification, in the Want of that Access to yor Self wch formerly I Enjoyd.

I am Impatient to Mention also ye subject of ye Three last Reviews[9] wch if you have not Seen is my Loss, Since without doubt I might be Enabld by you to have Carryed on that subject Exceedingly to ye Govornments advantage.

I humbly Referr all these things to your Consideration and wait to Dispose of[b] my Self by your Direction.

I am

Sr yor Most Obedt Servt

[*monogram*]

May. 6. 1706

---

[a] Whit[e]hall] 'e' *omitted*
[b] of] *interlined*

DEFOE TO [ROBERT HARLEY], 6 MAY 1706

Text: BL Add. MS. 70291, fols. 52–3. *Address*: none.

1 *Review*, II, 648 (II Oct. 1705). In *A Hymn to Peace* (1706), Defoe complained of the renewed financial demands on him: 'First they rifle me *the shortest Way*, | *And when they've stript me Naked, bid me Pay!*' (lines 382–3, *SFS*, I, 393).

2 *A Reply to a Pamphlet entituled, The L[or]d H[aversham]'s Vindication of his Speech* (1706), 19.

3 For details of the beginning of Union negotiations, see headnote to Letter 51.

4 *within … attempt it*: In *The British Merchant; or, Commerce Preserv'd* for 8–12 Jan. 1714, Henry Martin (d. 1721) claims he advised Defoe that he would not qualify. Defoe did, however, avail himself of the new law (see Letter 50).

5 *I Shall … from*: Defoe had negotiated compositions with most of his creditors, whereby they accepted partial payment and renounced any claim to the remainder; but creditors with whom he did not have this agreement were pursuing him. In his writing on the 1706 Bankruptcy Act, he insisted that it must obligate all creditors to come in, so that the bankrupt was not prosecuted for debts after having given up all his estate.

6 *Majties Bounty*: The only payment to Defoe of which we are certain in summer 1706 is £20 on 22 July (BL Add. MS. 70269, misc. 6).

7 *Unjustly Ruin'd and that in her Majties Name*: Referring to *The Shortest Way with the Dissenters*. See Defoe's statement that 'I was Ruin'd <u>The shortest way</u>' (Letter 10).

8 *Mr Ducket … Affair*: For Ducket, see Letter 44. This presumably refers to the fallout of the Calne election (*HPC 1690–1715*, II, 652–3).

9 *Subject of ye Three last Reviews*: With Franco-Spanish forces laying siege to Barcelona, Defoe defended the ministry's prosecution of the war in Spain in the *Review*s for 2, 4, and 7 May. Insisting that 'nothing has been wanting in the Supplies, neither as to Number or Season, for the support of the War in *Spain*', Defoe denounced attempts 'to create Jealousies among the Friends of the Government, against the Mannagement of Affairs, and against the Mannagers of them, and so if possible to remove the Men that have push'd things on with such Success both at Home and Abroad' (*Review*, III, 282, 278 (4 and 2 May 1706)). The siege was raised when the allied reinforcements that Defoe mentions in his articles arrived. Cf. *The Present State of the Parties in Great Britain* (1712), 31.

DEFOE TO ROBERT HARLEY, 21 MAY 1706

48

To Robert Harley

21 May 1706

Sr

I am Loth to break in upon yor Joy,[1] and No Man More
Sincerely Congratulates it Than I, Tho' my Clouds Darken my Own
Expression of it, and Makes me Reflect That 'tis hard all ye Queens
friends Rejoyce but I.

My Mellancholly Story however is Not ye Design of This. I Can
not Expect but you are in Hurrys too Great to Think of my Triffling
affair, but I Could not but Send you ye Enclos'd;[2] Perhaps you
may Make Use of Them to my advantage, if not Tis Fitt I should
Recomend Them to you Sr to use at yor Pleasure.

It is allways a Cordiall to me to See you but Now when So Much
more Suppress't than Ever it would be Peculiarly So.

Will a short Essay on These mighty Affaires be Accepted from
me in This juncture? is a question wch if answerd by you sr would
help Inspire ye p[er]formance.

Yor Most Obedt St

[*monogram*]

May. 21. 1706[a]

Text: BL Add. MS. 70291, fols. 54–5. *Address*: To The Right Honble | Robert Harley
Esqr | Princip^ll Secretary of State

---

[a] May. 21. 1706] *written vertically down lefthand margin*

1 *yor Joy*: For Marlborough's victory over the French in the Battle of Ramillies on 12 May 1706
(see Trevelyan, II, 102–20). Discussion of Ramillies occupies the *Review* from 21 May to 2
July (III, 315–407).

2 *Enclos'd*: Missing, but perhaps this day's *Review*, containing Defoe's admittedly hastily composed poem 'On the Fight at RAMELLIES', or the folio half-sheet reprint of that poem
under the title 'An Essay on the Great Battle at Ramellies'. The poem concludes: 'No more
insulting Tyrants shall oppress, | But *France* shall *Barter Liberty* for Peace, | By *Marlb'rough's*
Sword reduc't, he learns to fear, | And wish'd for Peace shall now conclude the War' (III, 315–18
(21 May 1706)). '*De Foe*, as ever, Execrably bad, | Throws out a Hasty *Poem*, wrote like Mad. |
'Twas the first-born, and welcome in *our Mirth*, | Tho' not *One Muse* assisted at its birth' ('An
Epistle to Sir Richard Blackmore, Kt.' (1706), lines 47–50, *POAS*, VII, 199).

206

DEFOE TO JOHN FRANSHAM, 24 MAY 1706

49

To John Fransham

24 May 1706

HEADNOTE: Defoe's reply to Fransham (Letter 45) expresses his indignation about aspersions on his reputation as a debtor. This was a constant theme of his published writings in 1706.

Sir, — I have several times been going to reply to your long Letter[1] but have been interrupted by continual hurry of business and have so little time to correspond wth my Friends that I every day loose them who cannot bear wth it.

I am sorry to see you assaulted about my Integrity, and wonder you should expect any man can be persuaded to believe a man honest whom they loose by.

I appeal to all the World, and in it to my worst Enemy's for these articles of my Honesty, and let any man in Trade shew better if they can.

1st If my Disaster was not from plain known inevitable causes wch humane wisdom could not foresee nor humane power prevent.[2]

2dly If I did not first leave off early according to my advice now to others,[3] nay while my Estate was sufficient to pay all men their full demand.

3dly If I did not immediately offer a full surrender of all I had in the World in Sattisfaction to my Creditors.

4^{thly} If after they had driven me to all extremities till all was consumed and I had not 5^s in the World but by Providence and my own Industry in the World I began to rise again, I did not pay every one according to my utmost ability.[4]

5^{thly} If notwithstanding this it has not cost me £5000 since I have been in these Troubles to maintain my Liberty to work for them and to defend myself against such as would have all their Debt before others and indeed before I could get it.

As to people paid at Yarmouth[5] I can not but admire[6] you should suffer yourself to be prevail'd upon to bring that as a proof of my honesty wch is a snare laid for me, that finding some people paid

DEFOE TO JOHN FRANSHAM, 24 MAY 1706

more than others they may have room to complain and pretend to take out a Commission of Bankrupt to recover it again.

The thing is true in Fact, and as true that these people to whom I have been so particular are now the only people who pursue me so close that I must at last I doubt quit the kingdom⁷ unless reliev'd by this late Act of Parliament, in wᶜʰ I am not yet sure that I shall find neither.

I have not time to enlarge on this melancholy story, wᶜʰ is perhaps the severest ever you heard.⁸ I desire to submit, but methinks people that call themselves protestants should be content to take all a man have and not pursue him to death.

I am now to acquaint you and all my Friends that Jure Divino at last is finished⁹ and waits only your order how many and whether bound or in sheets it shall be sent.

There is also a picture of your humble Servant prepar'd at the request of some of my Friends who are pleas'd to value it more than it deserves, but as it will cost a shilling I shall leave it free for those that please to take it or leave it.¹⁰

I am Your humble Servᵗ
D. F.

May 24, 1706.

Text: MS untraced. The copytext is Norgate, 283. *Address*: none recorded.

1 *long Letter*: Letter 45.
2 *my Disaster … prevent*: Among the causes of Defoe's 1692 bankruptcy were losses incurred in insuring merchant vessels during the Nine Years' War. In Feb. 1694 he petitioned parliament: 'the petitioner having sustained divers Losses by Insurances since the War with *France*, and having met and proposed to his Creditors a Means for their Satisfaction, some few of them will not come into these Proposals: That there being a Bill depending in the House, to enable some Merchants Insurers the better to satisfy their Creditors, the Petitioner prays his Name may be inserted in the said Bill, to have the like Benefit with them' (*C.J.*, xi, 87; see 30 for the original bill). The bill passed through the Commons but was rejected by the Lords.
3 *my advice now to others*: *Review*, iii, 123–5 (21 Feb. 1706). The advice was echoed later in *The Complete English Tradesman* (1725–7), *RDW*, vii, 83–7.
4 *pay every one according to my utmost ability*: See Letter 10, note 7.
5 *people paid at Yarmouth*: Defoe's Yarmouth debts came back to haunt him in 1713. See Letter 226.
6 *admire*: regard with wonder.
7 *quit the kingdom*: In Jan. 1706, in *A Reply to a Pamphlet entituled, The L[or]d H[aversham]'s Vindication of his Speech*, 7, Defoe says that he has contemplated moving to Spain.
8 *the severest ever you heard*: See the similar phrasing in *Review*, iii, 510 (20 Aug. 1706), which is quoted in the headnote to Letter 50.

208

Figure 5 Michael van der Gucht, Daniel Defoe, engraving, *Jure Divino: A Satyr* (London, 1706), National Portrait Gallery, London

9 *Jure Divino at last is finished*: It was published on 20 July. See Defoe's account of the reasons for its delay in the preface (*SFS*, II, 65).
10 *a picture … leave it*: The *Jure Divino* portrait of Defoe (Figure 5) was done by the Flemish engraver Michael van der Gucht (1660–1725) after a painting by Jeremiah Taverner (active 1690–1706) that is not extant. The poem's price had risen from the ten shillings projected in 1704 (of which subscribers paid down one quarter, half a crown) to fifteen shillings, so Defoe was reluctant to add further expense. A pirated edition of *Jure Divino* included a frontispiece portrait that Defoe decried amidst his fulminations against those responsible for the piracy: 'The Picture on the Book, which is but the Copy of a Copy, is about as much like the Author, as Sir *Roger L'Estrange*, was like the Dog *Towzer*' (*Review*, III, 463 (27 July 1706)). Another piracy depicted Defoe in the pillory.

50

To Robert Harley

21 August 1706

HEADNOTE: Despite his earlier doubts about whether he would qualify, Defoe applied for bankruptcy under the terms of the new law. His old business partner James Stancliffe acted as Defoe's trustee. On 22 July the following notice was printed in *The London Gazette*:

> The Commissioners in a renewed Commission of Bankrupt against Daniel Foe, late of London, Merchant, hereby give Notice, That he hath surrendred himself to the said Commissioners, and been twice examined; and that he will attend again on Tuesday the 6th of August next, at 4 in the Afternoon, at the Chamber of Mr. Robert Davis in Essex-Court in the Temple, in order to finish his Examination; when and where his Creditors may attend, to shew cause why a Certificate should not be signed pursuant to the late Act of Parliament.[1]

On 8 August, an updated notice indicated that following this third meeting his final examination would happen on 22 August.[2] 'My own Case … is now upon the Stage', wrote Defoe in the *Review* for 20 August, 'than which no Man's Case, that ever came for Relief by this new Act of Parliament, has ever been more severe; and than whom no Man is treated worse, on his flying to this Sanctuary of the law for Deliverance.'[3] In this letter of 21 August he was able to announce his 'Victory', referring to 'this afternoons Struggle', which must mean the final examination. He later looked back on his interrogations by the commission as 'four severe Trials upon Oath'.[4] Allegations of his dishonesty which he denounced as malice in the *Review* must have been disbelieved by his examiners. However, Defoe's ultimate failure to acquire the certificate that would protect him from old creditors would come back to haunt him in later years.[5] By the time Defoe returned from Scotland in 1708, a mission evidently in Harley's mind by this point, the law had been amended to require four-fifths of creditors to consent to a discharge, which was seemingly unattainable for Defoe.

Sr

Tho' I had Not ye honor to Wait on you last Night, yor Letter[6] forbiding, I Can Not but give you ye Trouble of Letting you kno', God almighty has heard ye Cries of a Disstresst Family and has

DEFOE TO ROBERT HARLEY, 21 AUGUST 1706

given me at last a Compleat Victory Over ye most Furious, Subtill and Malitious Opposicon That has been Seen in all The Instances of ye Bankrupts act.7

I Earnestly Wish and Long to give you ye perticulars, in wch Something Very Unusuall will Divert you.

S^r I Can Not but Comunicate to you One Thing, Nor Can I stay till ye Time I am to wait on you for it.

There is a Letter or Manuscript, for tis as big as a book, brought I Suppose by a Messenger Express from Scotland, to be printed here. Tis Unhappily written and full of Mischief against ye Union but p[er]ticularly address't to ye Dissenters and Insinuateing that their Destruction is Intended and will be Compass't in it. It Seems to Imply that ye presby^s in Scotland Are alarm'd at it, that ye Ministers and assistants keep Dayes of Prayer and fasting against it, that they foresee it will be fatall to their Establishm^t and would Invite the Dissenters into ye Same Notions.8

It is Something perticularly wonderfull y^t has brought this to me but I Suppose I shall be Applyed to to get it printed.9 I Encourage Them to it as far as I Can wthout appearing too forward. If I Can lay my hand Upon ye Manuscript, you will be Sure to see it, and if I Can not prevent its publication then, I shall but Ill Recomend my Capascity to you as fitt to be^a Employd abroad.

I shall more Largely Explain this when I have ye honour to See you On Saturday Night.10

I am Exceedingly Fateagu'd wth this afternoons Struggle.

> Yo^r Most Obed^t &c.
>
> [*monogram*]

Wednsday Night

Text: BL Add. MS. 70291, fols. 56–7. *Address* (fol. 57^v): To The Right Honble | Robert Harley Esqr | Princhipall Secreta of State. *Endorsed by Harley* (fol. 57^v): Mr Goldsmith R Aug: 22–23: 1706

---

^a be] 'be be' *in MS*

211

DEFOE TO ROBERT HARLEY, 21 AUGUST 1706

1 *London Gazette*, 18–22 July 1706.

2 *London Gazette*, 5–8 Aug. 1706. However, it seems to have occurred on 21 Aug.

3 *Review*, III, 510 (20 Aug. 1706). In this issue he challenges those who would accuse him of dishonesty in resigning his assets to bring their allegations to the meeting (III, 513). See Letter 49, note 8.

4 *Review*, III, 732 (3 Dec. 1706).

5 Most crucially in not gaining a discharge from his debt to James Stancliffe. After Stancliffe's death, his administrator Samuel Brooke pursued the debt; although Defoe was seemingly able to satisfy him that the debt was cleared, Brooke died, and Mary Brooke sued Defoe. See headnote to Letter 278. See also Defoe's account of his bankruptcy in *Mercator*, no. 101 (12–14 Jan. 1714).

6 *yor Letter*: Untraced.

7 *Opposicon … Bankrupts act*: Defoe reflects on the opposition presented by allegations 'that he made Concealments to defraud his Creditors' in *Review*, III, 512 (20 Aug. 1706). To illustrate the malice directed against him, Defoe later printed a letter sent to Davis on 28 Aug. 1706 alleging that Defoe had not disclosed '*an Estate of* 400*l.* per Annum' (*Review*, III, 733 (3 Dec. 1706)). Defoe rejects these imputations. His reputation on this head was poor: Defoe 'won't pay his just Debts, *and is now a Candidate for the Benefit of the late Act*', wrote one opponent in July 1706 (*Remarks on the Review, Numb. 74. Concerning the New Chappel in Russel-Court, Covent-Garden* (1706), 6).

8 *Letter … Notions*: Defoe evidently obtained the manuscript and sent it to Harley, who endorsed it ʼγολδσμιθ. Aug: 29: 1706'. The Greek signifies 'Goldsmith', Defoe's pseudonym. The manuscript survives in Harley's papers (BL Add. MS. 70039, fols. 10–27). Written as a letter from a Scottish Presbyterian to an Englishman, it says that though the 'Machiavilian Conduct of your Court' has 'made a Conquest over the Scots Com̃issioners' who negotiated the Union Treaty 'they have not conquer'd a Scots Parliament', which will preserve 'The Antient Privileges of the Scots Nation' (fols. 11r–v, 13v). It wonders at the English Dissenters' relish for the Union because 'the Ruin of Your Party and Interest lyes hid in the secret of this Design' (fol. 16r). A British parliament dominated by Anglicans would disestablish Presbyterianism and restore Episcopacy in Scotland, and the ministers who now only veil their antipathy for Dissent to quell the High Tories would 'suffer an Occasional Bill to pass, which will in its effect blow up your very Being and Constitution' (fol. 23r).

9 *printed*: No publication of this tract has been traced. In the *Review* for 26 Sept. 1706, Defoe alludes to 'the Virulence of a late Libel handed about in Manuscript, in order to perswade the *Dissenters* here against the Union, and fill them with Jealousies about it' (III, 590).

10 *Saturday Night*: 24 Aug.

51

To [Robert Harley]

13 September 1706

HEADNOTE (**Letters 51 and 52**): Harley and Godolphin had discussed using Defoe as an agent in Scotland as early as August 1703 when relations between the nations were becoming increasingly strained. As this was so soon after Defoe had stood in the pillory, and indeed while he was still in prison, the idea was passed over.[1] Defoe had since proved his loyalty and effectiveness on location in his tours of English regions in 1704 and 1705, so in autumn 1706 Harley resolved to send him to Edinburgh just as the Scottish parliament was about to debate a Treaty of Union that the English ministry and Queen Anne strongly supported.

Anglo-Scottish relations had, since 1703, further soured to the point that it seemed as though only war or union could ensue.[2] Royal assent had reluctantly been given to Scotland's Act of Security (1704) only when the Scots threatened to withhold supplies for the war. The Act allowed the Scottish parliament to nominate its own monarch after Anne's death, threatening to terminate the regnal union of 1603. The English parliament responded with the Alien Act (1705), which threatened economic sanctions – an embargo on crucial exports to England, potential confiscation of the English estates of Scots – if the Scottish parliament did not authorise either the Hanoverian succession or talks for a union treaty. Defoe denounced the Alien Act as a '*preposterous Law* ... in its Nature a Declaration of War'.[3] But out of this hostility arose the prospect of union, which Defoe first addressed in the *Review* for 11 December 1705, where he wrote: 'As a Breach between the Nations, would Compleat the Ruin of both; so an Union between them, would fix their Prosperity and Strength in so many Articles, that I am frequently sorry to see all that have hitherto wrote of it, touch so few of them, and those few so lightly.'[4]

Convinced of the public's ignorance of the benefits of a union, in early May 1706 Defoe published *An Essay at Removing National Prejudices against a Union with Scotland ... Part I.*[5] It emphasised, mainly for an English readership, that a union would aid the war against France, confirm (not alter) the religious establishment of each nation, and entail greater economic prosperity for both. By this time, negotiations for a union were being conducted by English and Scottish commissioners in Whitehall, having started on 16 April. Defoe even befriended some of the Scottish commissioners.[6] He announced on 9 May that he intended to dedicate the *Review* to the topic of the Union, 'to remove the vulgar Obstructions which are industriously thrown in the way; and if possible, Encline all Parties to a Union of Nations, that we may be henceforth one powerful Nation'.[7] However, he was immediately forced to 'adjourn' this topic in the *Review* so as to report on the continental war. Instead, Defoe produced, later in May, a second *Essay at Removing National Prejudices*.[8] On 23 July 1706 the agreed-upon articles for Union were presented to Queen Anne and their consideration by first the Scottish and then the English parliaments was to follow when they reconvened.[9]

Defoe was an ideal agent for the English government to have in Edinburgh while the Scottish parliament debated the Treaty of Union (though he was by no means the only agent). He was loyal to the government and had written in favour of the Union. His background as a tradesman gave him a plausible cause for being there, as well as the ability to relay with accuracy negotiations over commerce and taxation and to answer financial objections to the Union. And Defoe's Presbyterianism could lend him authority with the ministers of the Church of Scotland, who feared for the Kirk's security in the event of union with a larger, richer nation committed to Episcopal church government.

Defoe departed for Edinburgh on 13 September without explicit directives from Harley, leading him to lay out himself in his parting letter what he thought were his objectives.[10] Defoe's letters in September recount his trip north, noting stops in Cambridge (Stourbridge Fair), Coventry, Leicester, Nottingham, Newcastle-upon-Tyne, and Morpeth. We know he also passed through Leeds.[11] He later described his trip as 'a long Winter, a Chargeable, and as it proved, a Hazardous Journey'.[12] Travelling from London to Edinburgh, which would typically take ten to fourteen days, took Defoe around three weeks.[13] The *Review* began directly to promote the Union with the issue for 26 September.

Sr

I Was Comeing to wait Upon you and Take your Last Instruccõns, when I Met wth yor Ordr to Dispatch wthout any farther Conferenće; Tis ye More Afflicting to me because you are pleas'd to Signifye That Something Unhappy Relateing to yor Self[14] sr is ye Occasion, in wch I Condole tho' I kno' Not Directly the Occasion — But on My Own Accot sr This is a Perticular Disaster because I had a great many Enquiries to make sr in Ordr to my Conduct in The Affair I go Upon.

Not but That as Abraham went Chearfully Out Not knowing whither he went Depending on him yt Sent him,[15] So Sr I Willingly go On, Entirely Depending that I shall have Such Instruccõns as shall Not Dissable me from Effectually Answering yor Expectacõn.

I Onely Entreat yor leav to Remind you, that as you have accquainted Her Majtie & My Ld Treasr wth my goeing, The Success of my Journey is ye More my Conćerne, least want of Information

DEFOE TO [ROBERT HARLEY], 13 SEPTEMBER 1706

Rendring me Useless, The want of Capascity or Dilligence, be judg'd yᵉ Reason of my Miscarriage.

Under These Anxious Thoughts I beg you to Considʳ sʳ That I am without yᵉ heads of yᵉ Treaty, without yᵉ Characters of yᵉ Gentlemen who were here,[16] and wᵗʰout yᵉ knowlege of what has been Transacted In yᵉ Councills here, in Ordʳ to Dictate to me what I am to Obse[rve],[a] Hence I shall Seem Ignorant, of yᵉ Sence of England, and of what is Expected here, or Intended from Hence, and Thus I shall be so far from knowing yᵉ people I go to That I shall appear Not to kno' those I Come from.

However That if my Nocons are wrong, I may be Set Right by yoʳ Instruccons I beg leav, tho' it be begining at yᵉ wrong End, to Set Down how I Understand my present business — as foll.

1 To Inform My Self of yᵉ Measures Takeing Or Partys forming Against yᵉ Union and Apply my Self to prevent yᵐ.

2 In Conversation and by all Reasonable Methods to Dispose peoples minds to yᵉ Union.

3 By writeing or Discourse, to Answer any Objeccons, Libells or Refleccons on yᵉ Union, yᵉ English or yᵉ Court Relateing to the Union.

4 To Remove yᵉ Jealousies and Uneasyness of people about Secret Designs here against yᵉ Kirk &c.

Sʳ I beg yᵉ Ordʳˢ you please to give me may Mencon if I am Right in my thoughts of these Things — and that you will give me as much light as possible in yoʳ farther pleasure Concerning my Conduct.

I Can Not Quit This without Menconing yᵉ Matter of Expence. I Confess sʳ when you Told me it is Out of yoʳ private, and that the govornmᵗ should be at no Charge it straightn'd my Thoughts and I am the More Limited in My Designs — Indeed sʳ Ile put you to No[b] Expence for Extravagancies, but in yᵉ Affair if I am a good husband I shall ill Serv you.

If it be proper[c] to print any thing there — Some Charge will attend it and for Intelligence of things, I would not be spareing.

---

[a] Obse[rve]] *MS torn*
[b] No] *following letters* 'Extrem' *(for* 'Extremities'*) cancelled*
[c] proper] *rewritten due to blot*

215

DEFOE TO [ROBERT HARLEY], 13 SEPTEMBER 1706

I Entreat you to give me ye proper limits of Expence, that I may not make you Uneasy on that score; for Tho' I hope I Need Not assure you That what I shall Take shall not be Missapplyd, and That I shall bring nothing back, leaving any Consideracon for me or Mine to yor Usuall Goodness; yet I beg you will please to hint to me for my Governmt what you think fit on ye head of Charges.

I have Recd sr yor bill of £25[17] — and wth ye Uttmost Expedicon have Equipt my Self as ye Sume and ye Time will p[er]mitt.

I Mencon ye first not sr by way of Complaint, of any thing, but my Own Missfortune — who haveing as I accquainted you before Parted wth So much as horse, Saddle, bridle, pistols and Every thing[18] I am Forc't to buy all New — yet Refurnisht sr wth Two horses and all Necessarys I Assure you I have No fear of highway men.[a] Canttabit Vacuus[19] — is my Motto, and if I Reach N Castle I shall be in Condicon Very Fitt to wait upon mr Bell[20] —

As to Family, 7 Children — &c. Hei Mihi[21] —

No Man sr That Ever Serv'd you shall Trouble you less than I wth Complats of This Nature — But if I have been honest I Must be Naked & am less asham'd to Tell you So Than I should be to Tell you I am foresworn[22] and have Made Reserves.

I Need Say No More sr; you were pleasd once to Make me hope Her Majtie would have Some Concern for me when free — I have Now Naked Liberty — and Can Not but Recomend ye Circumstance to That Bounty wch I Trust you will Move on my Accot.

Thus sr you have a Widdo' and Seaven Children On yor hands, but a word I presume from you will Ease you of ye burthen.

I Ask yor Pardon for This Representacon to which My Present Circumstance Compells, I shall be No More Importunate in That affair.

I have been Considering About Treating of Union in ye Review[23] and Unless yor Judgemt and Ordrs Differ believ as I shall Mannage it it Must be Usefull, but beg hints from you if you find it Other wise.

[a] men] *following word* 'But' *cancelled*

I Entreat Letters from you Directed to Alex^a Goldsmith[24] to be left at m^r Joseph Caters[25] in Coventry where I shall be, God Willing, On Thursday or Fryday[26] at Farthest.

If any thing supplimentall offers ye Next post For Ditto to be left at^a Mr John Drury Bookseller in Nottingham[27] and ye Next at Mr John Coninghams at Manchester.[28]

yor Most Obed^t &ca [*monogram*]

Pray s^r please to give me ye positiv day ye Par^t are to Sit Down.[29]

Sept. 13. 1706, just takeing horse.

Text: BL Add. MS. 70291, fols. 58–9. *Address*: none.

---

^{a} at] *following word* 'ye' *cancelled*

---

1 Godolphin to Harley, 13 Aug. [1703], Longleat House, Portland MSS Appendix vol. II, fols. 166r–167v. See headnote to Letter 4.

2 See the narrative of Anglo-Scottish events from the 1690s to the commencement of union negotiations – including the failed Darien expeditions of 1698–1700, the breakdown of union negotiations in 1702, the Act of Security, and the Worcester affair of 1704–5 – in Defoe's *History of the Union of Great Britain* (1709/10), TDH, VII, 112–42. Defoe's reading of the hostility merely as strategic positioning for inevitable union is of course partisan.

3 *An Essay at Removing National Prejudices against a Union with Scotland ... Part I* (1706), *PEW*, IV, 43. In the *Review* for 8 Apr. 1708, he scornfully calls it 'the Act of Interruption of Trade repealed as soon as we came to our Sences' (V, 30), and he further criticises it in *History*, TDH, VII, 135–6, and *The Present State of the Parties in Great Britain* (1712), 115–16. See Nicolson, 249–52.

4 *Review*, II, 789.

5 *PEW*, IV, 37–61. Defoe was commissioned to write the first *Essay* by the Edinburgh merchant George Scott and his associates (George Scott to William Scott (1672–1735), 14 May 1706, EUL Laing II, 63; Robert Stewart to [unknown], 25 May 1706, NLS Wodrow Letters Quarto IV, fol. 74).

6 Paula R. Backscheider, 'Defoe and the Clerks of Penicuik', *MP* 84 (1987), 372–81.

7 *Review*, III, 293.

8 *PEW*, IV, 65–87. The first two *Essays at Removing National Prejudices* were reprinted together in Edinburgh as propaganda *against* the Union: the benefits envisaged for England were assumed to be at Scotland's expense. Defoe explained this in *An Essay, at Removing National Prejudices, against a Union with England. Part III* (1706), *PEW*, IV, 91–2.

9 Before he was tasked to travel to Scotland and write on the Union, Defoe supported a union in his 1705–6 writings, insisting that what looks like antagonism between the nations will eventuate in their union. See *The Consolidator* (1705), *SFS*, III, 153; *Jure Divino* (1706), book XII, lines 578–81, *SFS*, II, 361–2; *A Reply to a Pamphlet entituled, The L[or]d H[aversham]'s Vindication of his Speech* (1706), 13–17.

DEFOE TO [ROBERT HARLEY], 13 SEPTEMBER 1706

10 Defoe later dismissed 'the Suggestions of some People, of my being imployed thither, to carry on the Interest of a Party', insisting that his journey to Scotland was motivated by 'Curiosity' and the hope of being 'useful there to prompt a Work that I was fully convinced was for the general Good of the whole Island' (*History*, *TDH*, VII, 259).

11 *Review*, III, 615 (8 Oct. 1706). In a letter to an unknown recipient, George Psalmanazar (*c.* 1679–1763) wrote that 'it is say'd Daniel De Foe is gone into Scotland to apease his dearly beloved the mobb who they say is a little tumultuous upon this union' (Harvard University, Houghton bMS Eng 1473).

12 *History*, *TDH*, VII, 259. As well as the bad weather and a mishap with a horse, his route via the West Midlands was indirect.

13 For the more conventional route, via Newark and Doncaster, see NRS GD RH 9/17/266.

14 *Something Unhappy Relateing to yor Self*: Unidentified.

15 *Abraham ... him*: Gen. 12:1–9; Heb. 11:8.

16 *Gentlemen who were here*: The thirty-one commissioners from Scotland who had negotiated the Union Treaty with their English counterparts in London from April to July 1706; they are listed in Defoe's *History*, *TDH*, VII, 157–8.

17 *£25*: Harley's petty accounts show £25 was paid to Alexander Goldsmith on 10 Sept. 1706 (BL Add. MS. 70269, misc. 6).

18 *Parted ... thing*: As a consequence of his recent bankruptcy.

19 *Canttabit Vacuus*: *cantabit vacuus coram latrone viator* (Latin): 'A traveller who is empty-handed can sing in the mugger's face' (Juvenal, *Satire* x, 22, *Juvenal and Persius*, Loeb Classical Library, trans. Susanna Morton Braund (Cambridge, Mass., 2004)).

20 *mr Bell*: John Bell, Harley's agent in Newcastle, where he served as postmaster.

21 *Hei Mihi*: 'Ah me' (Latin). It is used in the Vulgate: 'Heu mihi, quia incolatus meus prolongatus est! habitavi cum habitatibus Cedar' (Psalms 119:5), translated as 'Woe is me, that I sojourn in Mesach, that I dwell in the tents of Kedar' (Psalms 120:4). This fits the context, as Defoe is going into 'exile' in Scotland.

22 *foresworn*: perjured.

23 *Treating of Union in ye Review*: The *Review* turned to the Union on 26 Sept. 1706.

24 *Alex^a Goldsmith*: See Letter 18.

25 *mr Joseph Caters in Coventry*: See Letter 43.

26 *Thursday or Fryday*: That is, 19 or 20 Sept.

27 *Mr John Drury Bookseller in Nottingham*: Probably a slip for Samuel Drewry or Drury, bookseller and printer in Nottingham (b. 1680?).

28 *Mr John Coninghams at Manchester*: Likely James Coningham, Defoe's distribution agent in Manchester (see Letter 46). The erroneous first name may arise from the fact that Coningham shared oversight of the Manchester Dissenting Academy with John Chorlton (1666–1705). In the event, Defoe did not pass through Manchester (see Letter 52).

29 *day ye Part are to Sit Down*: The Scottish parliament reconvened on 3 Oct. 1706.

DEFOE TO ROBERT HARLEY, 22 SEPTEMBER 1706

52

To Robert Harley

22 September 1706

Sr

The short Journall of my Travail hither is Not worth yor Note, Onely to Tell you I was lockt up by a Rain of 48 Houres wthout Ceasing and that we have not had One Dry Day Since I Set Out. This tho' I stayd but One Day at Sturbrige fair has made me March Very slow, The Country here being Very Deep and wett. I hope to Make More hast when I get Over ye Trent, ye Ground being hardr.

I am Dissappointed in Not Meeting yor Instruccons at Coventry as by my last. In Obedience to yor Ordr I Directed if It Meets me not at Nottingham I shall hope for it at New Castle to be left at ye post House or wth mr Bell.

I have put off my Design of Goeing to Manchester because I doubt it being late and yet kno' not ye Day ye houses will meet at Edb and ye badness of ye Ways makes it long Enough getting thither.

Sr I Entreat ye favoura that I may not fail of your letters at New Castle wthout wch I shall be Extreamly at a loss how to proceed. Till Then I go On Chearfully

as

yor Depending Obedt Servt
[*monogram*]b

Leicester Sept. 22. 1706

Sr

I think it my Duty to accquat you that there is a book published in Town whose Title I do not Remember — Norc

---

a favour] *following word* 'not' *cancelled*
b [*monogram*]] *illegible word cancelled beneath monogram, possibly a catchword at the end of the first page (fol. 60r). The following part comes on the third page (fol. 61r). Defoe wrote* 'Sr' *but nothing else at the top of the second page (fol. 60v).*
c Nor] *interlined*

219

DEFOE TO ROBERT HARLEY, 22 SEPTEMBER 1706

Unless I Could see ye Courant Can not Describe it Other than that tis S^d wrott by One that Calls himself a High Church man in wch besides a great Deal of Virulence and High Church poison I am told the wholl Memoriall is Couch't and as it were Reprinted.[1]

Tis boasted of in this Country as a Defiance to ye Court and Indeed the Impudence of the party is Intollerable in these parts[2] and such as I never met wth the like in England; they Say here that tis wrott by the Coventry parson Kinderly,[3] Others that m^r Bromley[4] & a Club are ye Authors, Others that ye Memoriall authors[5] have done it and p[er]ticularly I am told it was printed by — Taylor in Pauls C yard, I mean ye young man, Not old Taylor,[6] who I suppose has More Witt — this I thought my Duty to Accqua^t you S^r and ask yor pardon if it be Officious.

Idem &c.[7]

Text: BL Add. MS. 70291, fols. 60–1. *Address* (fol. 61v): To The Right Honble | Robert Harley Esqr | Her Maj^{ties} Principal Secret of State | Present. *Endorsed by an unknown hand* (fol. 61v): M^r De Foe

1   *book ... Reprinted*: *The History of the Church, in Respect both to its Ancient and Present Condition ... By One Call'd an High Churchman*, probably by Charles Leslie, advertised in the *Daily Courant* on 31 Aug. 1706. It defends the previous year's *Memorial of the Church of England* and airs High Church grievances against the government's failure to defend the Church against Dissent, decrying the ministry's and Court's increasingly whiggish hue. 'Couch't' means 'concealed'.

2   *Impudence ... parts*: Leicester returned two High Tories in the 1705 election (see Letter 44), and Defoe mentioned the town when describing the 'Heat and Fury of Elections', language he adopts when describing places won by Tackers (*Review*, III, 241 (18 Apr. 1706)).

3   *Coventry parson Kinderly*: Jonathan Kimberley. See Letter 43, note 8.

4   *Bromley*: See Letter 43, note 19.

5   *Memoriall authors*: See Letters 37 and 38 for Defoe's speculations on the authorship of *The Memorial of the Church of England*, now attributed principally to James Drake.

6   *Taylor ... Taylor*: 'Young' William Taylor (d. 1724) and 'old' John Taylor – either son and father or nephew and uncle – were booksellers at the Ship in St Paul's Churchyard (Plomer, 284–5). William later published several of Defoe's novels: *A Continuation of Letters written by a Turkish Spy at Paris* (1718), *Robinson Crusoe* (1719) and its sequels *The Farther Adventures* (1719) and *Serious Reflections* (1720), and *Memoirs of a Cavalier* (1720). In the *Review* for 25 Dec. 1708, Defoe offered 'Mr. *Taylor*, Bookseller in St. *Paul's Church-Yard*' as an authority for his claim that Dissenters had not 'bought up' copies of Defoe's *The Experiment* 'to prevent its being seen', as Leslie had alleged when claiming it forged documents (V, 546–7). Taylor had not published *The Experiment*, so his connection with Defoe at that time is unclear.

7   *Idem*: 'The same' (Latin), meaning the same signatory.

DEFOE TO ROBERT HARLEY, 30 SEPTEMBER 1706

53

To Robert Harley

30 September 1706

HEADNOTE (Letters 53–5): On 1 October 1706, John Bell, Harley's agent, and the postmaster at Newcastle-upon-Tyne, wrote to notify Harley:

> Yester Night Came to towne Mr Alex Goldsmith in his Jurney to Scotland & sent for me & Enquird if I had an Ordr to pay him som money[.] I told him I had a letter from a gentleman that mention'd him & would supply him with what he had Occasion for[;] he told me about 25 guineas would serve him at present & Desird a letter of Credit to my friend at Edinbrough for what he shall want there[.] I shall give him a letter to the Generall post master at Edenbᴵ to furnish him with what he has Occasion for with som Restrictions. I Dranke a botle with the gentleman & perceive he is not nice² in telling his name, & will Owne it at Edenb[;] he sa's he is so pub-licly knowne that it would not be prudence to goe under an Other name[.] I have red part of a booke under his name; it may be his Owne but be pleased to let that pass; what I write is wholly to yor selfe[.] He is to Dine with me to day and then shall be further ac-quainted with him.

Perhaps at their dinner, Defoe supplied his letter of 30 September, as Bell adds to Harley: 'Inclosed I send you a letter from Mr. Goldsmith & shall wait your Hon-ors Comands for what I have next to Doe[,] having supplyd him with money what he has occasion for at present.'³

The frustrations of Defoe's journey continued, indicated by his letter to Harley of 2 October (Letter 54) and Bell's of 4 September:

> I have had the favor of Mr A. G.'s conversation for 2 or 3 dayes & find him to be a Very Engenious man & fit for that business I guess he is goeing about. I wish him good success[.] He had occasion for more money than I mentiond to yor Honor in my Last[,] haveing Occasion to buy a horse at this place[;] he had of me forty pounds 17: 6d & I have given him a letter of Cr[edit] to the post master Generall for twenty pounds more, & if his stay be long there he is to write to me to give him fresh Cr[edit] which I shall Doe if yor Honor Approve of itt[.] Inclosed I send yor Honor his letter he left with me[;] he went for Scotland on Wedensday last.⁴

221

DEFOE TO ROBERT HARLEY, 30 SEPTEMBER 1706

By the time he arrived in Edinburgh, Defoe had a reliable supply of funds and eventually the instructions from Harley which have survived in an undated, unaddressed, and perhaps fragmentary copy in a professional hand (Letter 55).[5]

Sr

I have Every Thing here According to my Expectacon and yors Sr as to mr Bell;[6] and am Unhappy Onely in wanting yor Letter, Instruccons &c.

Yor Letter to mr Bell put me to Some Difficulty, Menconing to him That you should Draw a bill on him, whereas I had No bill, but yor Letter without yor Name and wth Some Other Circumstances in it wch were[a] Inconvenient to show him; But mr Bell was pleasd to believ me, and has Supplyd me 25$^{£7}$ [   ][b] and Given me his Letter of Credit to Edenbg for a Supply in Case of Farther Occasion in wch I shall be as Spareing as may Consist wth ye Duty I Owe to yor Service, and ye More So because you have not been pleased to limit me in Perticulars.

I have had a Severe Journey hither but it begins to Mend Now and The Two last have been ye Onely Dayes wthout Rain since I left London wch has made me longer Getting hither than I Expected.

I shall lose no Time; I came hither last night and shall go away to Morrow[c] morning for Edenbg. If you will please to favor me wth yors Directed to mr Bell Till I can write from Edenbg he will forward it to me.

Methinks I look Very Simply when to my Self I Reflect How I am yor Messengr wthout an Errand, yor Ambassador without Instructions, yor Servant wthout Ordrs. I beseech yor Honr to let me Not be to seek for any thing wch may furnish me to Answer yor Expectacons to[d] do her Majsty & ye Nacon the Service wch you Design, and for[e] Justifyeing your choice in ye honour you do me in Singling me Out for this work.

---

[a] were] *following word* 'Not' *cancelled*
[b] 25$^{£}$ [   ]] *blank in MS*
[c] Morrow] *interlined*
[d] to] *interlined above cancelled word* 'and'
[e] for] *interlined*

DEFOE TO ROBERT HARLEY, 30 SEPTEMBER 1706

I Need say no More s^r; you kno' wthout a strict Correspondence
it will be^a Impossible for me to Act by yor Measures or to kno' what
Course to steer.
I Entreat yor pardon for my Importunity on This head and Am

S^r yor Obed^t Servt [*monogram*]

New Castle Sept. 30. 1706

Text: BL Add. MS. 70291, fols. 62–3. [Defoe began on fol. 62^r, continuing perpendicularly on fol. 63^v.] *Address* (fol. 63^r): To The Right Honble | Robert Harley Esqr
| One of her Maj^{ties} Principal Secret^a of State | Present

---

^{a} be] *interlined*

---

1 George Main (d. after 1727), also a jeweller.
2 scrupulous, cautious.
3 BL Add. MS. 70023, fols. 323, 324. See H.M.C. *Portland MSS*, IV, 335.
4 BL Add. MS. 70023, fol. 327. See H.M.C. *Portland MSS*, IV, 336. Defoe departed Newcastle
   on Wednesday 2 Oct.
5 Upon Harley's fall from office eighteen months hence, a poem attacking him, *The Welsh
   Monster* [1708], mentions the arrangement between Defoe, Harley, and Bell: 'The Prophet
   Dan, | That Riming Miracle of Man, | ... Was as a chosen Friend sent forth, | So privately
   to spy the *North*, | ... And what great Sums the needy Vassal | Receiv'd at Post-house of
   New-Castle, | For Service done in Time of Need, | On th' other Side the River *Tweed*'
   (39–40).
6 *yors S^r as to m^r Bell*: Harley's letter to Bell is untraced.
7 *25$^£$*: Bell's subsequent letter to Harley (see headnote) says twenty-five guineas, which is
   £26.5s.

223

54

To Robert Harley

2 October 1706

S^r

My Last of y^e 30th past From hence Inform'd yor Hono^r of my Arrivall here;[1] I had parted from Hence This Morning but have had y^e Missfortune of One of my Horses failing, Worn Out wth the fategue of y^e Journey.

Mr Bell has however Cur'd This breach by Furnishing me wth a horse wch tho' it has Encreasd y^e Expence of The Journey, 12$^{£}$, yet The Necessity I presume will Excuse me to you and y^e Horse shall be at yor Hon^{rs} Service at Demand.

This as Now Ordred will Retard me not above half This Day and I shall God willing Reach to Morpeth to night.

I am

S^r

yor Most Obed^t Servt

[*monograms*][a]

Octo. 2. 1706

Text: BL Add. MS. 70291, fols. 66–7. *Address* (fol. 67^v): To The Right Honble | Robert Harley Esqr | One of Her Maj^{ties} Princip^{ll} Secr^s of State | Present | London[b]

[a] [*monograms*]] *two symbols: one resembles 'DF'; the other is Defoe's usual monogram*
[b] London] *this word is not in Defoe's handwriting*

1 *here*: Newcastle-upon-Tyne.

[ROBERT HARLEY] TO [DEFOE], [OCTOBER 1706?]

55

[Robert Harley] to [Defoe]

[October 1706?]¹

Instructions

1. You are to use the utmost caution that it may not be supposed you are employed by any person in England; but that you came there upon your own business, & out of love to the Country.²
2. You are to write constantly the true State how you find things, at least once a week, & you need not subscribe any name, but direct for me under Cover to Mʳˢ Collins at the Posthouse, Middle Temple Gate, London.³
   For variety you may direct under Cover to Michael Read⁴ in [   ] York Buildings.ᵃ
3. You may confidently assure those youᵇ converse with, that the Queen & all those who have Credit with her, are sincere & hearty for the Union.
4. You must shew them, this is such an opportunity that being once lost or neglected is not again to be recovered. England never was before in so good a disposition to make such large Concessions, or so heartily to unite with Scotland, & should their kindness now be slighted.⁵

Text: BL Add. MS. 70291, fols. 64–5. [This MS is written in a professional hand; it is unaddressed, undated, and perhaps incomplete.] *Address*: none.

ᵃ [   ] York Buildings] *blank in MS*
ᵇ you] *following illegible word cancelled*

1 The date is conjectural. On 30 Sept. Defoe mentions having no instructions (Letter 53); on 24 Oct. he refers to 'Commands in yᵉ Onely paper of yoʳ Ordʳˢ' (Letter 56).
2 *You ... Country*: See Defoe's account of himself in *An Essay, at Removing National Prejudices. Part III* (1706), *PEW*, IV, III: 'I Scorn the Employment of an Emissary, a Spy, or a Mercenary; my Business is known here: Which tending to Trade, Settlement, and general Improvement, I never purposed to Meddle in this Affair.'
3 *Mrs Collins ... London*: She was the receiver at the post office at Temple Bar until 1711, succeeding in that post Gabriel Collins, formerly a 'bookseller in London, at the Middle Temple Gate, 1687–90' (Plomer, 78; Hugh Feldman, *Letter Receivers of London, 1652 to 1857*, 2 vols. (1998), II, 14). She was a widow as early as 1685, described as 'an ancient tenant of a shop on the east side of the Great Gate in Fleet Street' (*Minutes of Parliament of the Middle Temple, III: 1650–1703*, ed. Charles Trice Martin (1905), 1369). Those records mention her down to 1731 ('Minutes of Parliament of the Middle Temple, IV: 1703–1747', ed. Cyril L. King (unpublished

typescript, 1975)). For a glimpse of her relationship with Harley, see the bantering anonymous letter of 23 Sept. 1700 addressed to her but concerning Harley and intended for his eyes (University of Nottingham, Pw 2Hy 312).

4 *Michael Read*: Harley's porter. Sir Michael Warton (*c.* 1648–1725) described him as a 'person of wonderful prudence and gravity' (H.M.C. *Portland MSS*, v, 17). Swift, on the other hand, implying that Read only admitted those who bribed him, called him 'an old Scotch fanatic, and the damn'dest liar in his office alive' (*Swift Journal*, 259).

5 *England ... slighted*: Defoe pursues this argument in *An Essay, at Removing National Prejudices. Part III, PEW*, IV, 104–5: 'In *England* there is a general happy disposition to this Union', but 'this happy temper in *England* has not been so easy a thing to procure'.

56

To Robert Harley

24 October 1706

HEADNOTE **(Letters 56 and 57):** Defoe's presence in Edinburgh was noticed by John Erskine, twenty-third (*de jure* sixth) Earl of Mar (1675–1732), one of the two Secretaries of State for Scotland, on 13 October, a week or so after his arrival there.[1] Defoe followed the progress of the Union Treaty through parliament, where it was being read and debated prior to the commencement of voting on each of the twenty-five articles. Parliament was divided between a pro-Union coalition of the Court party, led by James Douglas, second Duke of Queensberry (1662–1711), and the so-called Squadrone[2] on one side, and in opposition an uneasy alliance of opponents to Union nominally headed by James Douglas, fourth Duke of Hamilton (1658–1712), comprising the Country party, Episcopalians, and Jacobites. The pro-Union group enjoyed a secure parliamentary majority.[3] The opposition stoked the popular resistance to the Union that was mounting in the form of publications and protests on the streets, especially in Edinburgh. Defoe's account in his letters of the unrest he witnessed in the capital on 22 and 23 October is expanded upon in his *History of the Union*, published two years later. In the *Review* at the time, Defoe barely mentioned the violent opposition in Edinburgh.[4]

As well as hostility from the crowd on the street, Defoe witnessed dissension in the Commission of the General Assembly of the Church of Scotland. The Commission was (in Defoe's own words) 'a Deputation from the General Assembly, being a certain Number of Ministers, Impowered by an Act of the Assembly, to meet in the Intervals of their Session, to take Care of the Affairs of the Church'.[5] From its first meeting during the session, on 9 October, the Commission's members debated to what extent they should resist an incorporating union because they feared it could weaken or even imperil the Church of Scotland.[6] The Commission exasperated Defoe because he mostly did not share its members' concerns that their Church would be disadvantaged by the Union.

DEFOE TO ROBERT HARLEY, 24 OCTOBER 1706

He insinuated himself into its meetings, seeking to allay the ministers' anxieties for the Presbyterian establishment.[7] But looking back in *The History of the Union* (1709/10), Defoe commended 'the Prudence and Steadiness of the Ministers, in the Commission of the Assembly': 'The general Proceedings of that Reverend Body being always Tempered with Modesty, Calmness, and Discretion, at the same time that they were anxiously concerned for the Security of the Foundation on which they stood, and had the whole Weight of the Church of *Scotlands* Safety upon their Hands.'[8]

In October Defoe also wrote two further *Essays at Removing National Prejudices*, published in Scotland and aimed at Scottish readers, though substantially reproduced for English readers in the *Review*.[9] The third *Essay* reassures Presbyterians that the Union will not imperil but rather secure Scotland's religious settlement; the fourth impresses the need for an incorporating union, replacing the English and Scottish parliaments with a British one, as opposed to a federated union that would retain autonomous parliaments in each nation.

Sr

According to yor Commands in ye Onely paper of yor Ordrs, Vizt of writeing Constantly To you, I Continue to give you The Generll state of Things here.

I am Sorry to Tell you here is a Most Confused scene of affaires, and The Ministry have a Very Difficult Course to steer. You allow me Freedome of speaking Allegories; in such a Case it Seems to me The Presbyterians are hard at work to Restore Episcopacy and The Rabble to bring to pass ye Union.[10]

We have had Two Mobbs Since my last and Expect a Third and of these ye Following is a short accot.

The first was in ye Assembly Or Comission of Assembly where Very strange things were Talk'd of and in a strange Manner and I Confess Such as has put me Much Out of Love wth Ecclesiastic Parliamts.[11] The Power, Anglice[12] Tyranny, of ye Church was here Describd to ye life and[a] Jure Divino Insisted upon I[n][b] prejudice to Civill Authourity — but this was by some Tumultuous spirits who are Over ruld by men of More Moderation and as an Assembly they act wth more wisdom and Honesty than they do in Their private Capascities in wch I Confess they Contribute too Much

[a] and] *following letter* 'I' *or* 'J' *cancelled*
[b] I[n]] 'n' *omitted*

to yᵉ Generall Aversion wᶜʰ[a] here is to yᵉ Union; at yᵉ Same Time they Acknowlege they are Unsafe and Uneasy in Their present Establishment — I work Incessantly wᵗʰ them; they go from me seemingly Satisfyed and pretend to be Informd but are yᵉ Same Men when they Come Among Their parties — I hope what I Say to you sʳ shall Not prejudice them; in Generall They are yᵉ wisest weak men, The Falsest honest men and the steadyest Unsettled people Ever I met with. They Mean well but are blinded in their politicks and Obstinate in Opinion.

But we had yᵉ last Two Nights a worse Mob than this and that was in yᵉ street, and Certainly a Scots Rabble is yᵉ worst of its kind.

The first night[13] they Onely Threatned hard and follow'd their Patron D. Hamilton's[14] Chair wᵗʰ Huzzas from yᵉ Parliament house[15] quite Thro' yᵉ City — they Came up again Hallowing in yᵉ Dark, Threw some stones at yᵉ Guard, broke a few windows and yᵉ like and so it Ended.

I was warn'd that night that I should Take Care of my Self and not Appear in yᵉ street wᶜʰ Indeed for yᵉ last five dayes I have done Very Little, haveing been Confin'd by a Violent Cold. However I went up yᵉ street in a Friends Coach in yᵉ Evening[16] and some of yᵉ Mob Not then Gott together were heard to say when I went into a house There was One of yᵉ English Dogs &c.

I Casually stayd at yᵉ house I went then to Till Dark and Thinking to Return to my Lodging, found the wholl City in a Most Dreadfull Uproar and the high street Full of yᵉ Rabble.

Duke Hamilton Came from yᵉ House in his Chair as Usuall and Instead of Goeing Down yᵉ City to his Lodgings went up the High street <u>as was Said</u> to Visit yᵉ D of Athol.[17]

<u>This</u> whether Design'd by yᵉ D. as Most think or No,[b] but if not was Exactly Calculated to begin the Tumult[18] — For yᵉ Mob in a Vast Crow'd attending him thither waited at yᵉ Door — and as those people did not Come there to be Idle — The Duke Could have Done Nothing more Directly to point Out their bussiness, The Late Lᵈ Provost sʳ Pat. Johnston[19] liveing just upon the spot.

---

[a] wᶜʰ] *interlined*
[b] or No] *interlined*

The Mob had Threatned him before and I had been Told he[a] had
Such Notice of it That he Remov'd himself. Others Say he was in
his Lodgings with 11 or 12 Gentlemen besides Servants, Resolved to
Defend himself, but be That as it will.

The Mob Came up staires to his Door and fell to work w^th
sledges to break it Open, but it seems Could not, His Lady in y^e
Fright wth Two Candles in her hand that she might be known
Opens ye Windows and Cries Out for God Sake to Call ye Guard.

An Honest Townsman, an Apothecary that Saw ye Distress the
Family was In, went Down to ye Guard wch is kept in ye Middle
of the street, and Found ye Officers Very Indifferent in ye Matter,
whether as to ye Cause or is Rather Judg'd Thro' Reall fear of y^e
Rabble, but Applying himself to One Capt Richardson,[20] a brave
Resolute Officer, he told him he Could Not go from ye Guard
w^thout ye Ld Provosts[21] Ord^r but if he would Obtain that ord^r he
would go up — In short ye Ord^r was Obtain'd and ye Capt went
with a Party of ye Guard and made his way Thro' the Rable to s^r
Pat. Jonstons stair Case — The Generallity of them fled, some were
knock't Down and ye stair Case Clear'd and Three or four Taken in
ye Very Assaulting ye Door.[22]

Yet they fled Not far but Hallooing and Throwing stones and
sticks at ye Souldiers, Severall of Them are Very Much bruised and
the brave Capt I am Told keeps his bed.

However he brought Down his prisoners and ye Toll booth[23]
being at hand Hurryed them in and made his Retreat to ye Guard.

In This posture Things stood about 8 to 9 a Clock and the Street
seeming passable I Sallyed Out and Got to my Lodging.

I had not been Long There but I heard a Great Noise[24] and
looking Out Saw a Terrible Multitude Come up ye High street w^th
A Drum at the head of Them shouting and swearing and Cryeing
Out all Scotland would stand together, No Union, No Union,
English Dogs and the like.

I Can Not Say to you I had No Apprehensions, Nor was Monsr
De Witt[25] quite Out of my Thoughts, and perticularly when a
part of This Mob fell upon a Gentleman who had Discretion little

---

[a] he] *interlined above cancelled word* 'they'

DEFOE TO ROBERT HARLEY, 24 OCTOBER 1706

Enough to say something that Displeased them just Und[r] my Window.

He Defended himself bravely and Call'd Out lustily also for help to y[e] Guard who being within Hearing and Ready Drawn up in Close Ord[r] in the street advanc't, Rescued y[e] Gentleman and took the p[er]son he was Grappld w[th] prisoner.

The City was by this time in a Terrible fright; y[e] Guards were Insulted and stoned as they stood, y[e] Mob put out all y[e] lights, no body Could stir in y[e] streets and not a light be seen in a windo' for fear of stones.

There was a Design to have shut y[e] Gate at y[e] Nether Bow as they Call it, w[ch] is a Gate in y[e] Middle of y[e] Great street[a] as Temple barr may be, and y[e] Design was to hinder y[e] Guard in y[e] City and y[e] Guard in y[e] Cannongate[26] as they Call it from assisting one Another and Cut off their Communication.

But My L[d] Commission[r27] prevented that by sending a Detachment of his Guards up y[e] Cannon Gate street,[b] as from white hall to Temple bar,[28] who[c] seiz'd upon y[e] Nether Bow and took post there with Every Souldier a link in his hand beside his Arms.

Dureing this Hurry whether they Omitted shutting y[e] North port as they Call it w[ch] goes to Leith or that it was not yet Ten a Clock I kno' not But a Second Rabble of 500 Some say a Thousand stout fellows Came up from Leith and Disporting themselves in the street Continued the Hurry in a Terrible Manner.

About 11. a Clock My L[d] Commissioner sent for y[e] L[d] Provost and Desir'd him to let him Send a body of y[e] Guards into the City — w[ch] they Say is what Never was admitted before and some Say y[e] L[d] Provost Hesitated at it for a long time.[29]

I Can not Send you y[e] perticulars of That part — but about Midnight[30] A body of y[e] Guards[31] besides those posted at y[e] Cannon Gate Entred y[e] City Drums beating, Marcht up the High street to y[e] Parliament Close and His Grace y[e] Duke of Argyle[32] Mounted at y[e] head of y[e] Horse Guards to have Seconded them.

[a] street] *following word* 'and' *cancelled*
[b] street] *following illegible word cancelled*
[c] who] *interlined above cancelled word* 'and'

DEFOE TO ROBERT HARLEY, 24 OCTOBER 1706

After yᵉ foot Came my Lᵈ Provost, yᵉ Bayliffs and Magistrates wᵗʰ Their Officers and links and These Clearing the streets yᵉ Mob was Disspersst; they have 6 I think or there about in Prisonᵃ and The Council is Now sitting — to Take Some farther Ordʳ for preserving yᵉ Peace.[33]

Two Regiments of Foot are sent for to quarter in yᵉ City and I hope as before this Mob will like Our Tackers be aᵇ Meer plott toᶜ Hasten what They Design'd to prevent.[34]

What Further happens in This Matter I shall as it Occurs not fail to Accquaint yoʳ Honʳ wᵗʰ and am

yoʳ Most Obedᵗ Servᵗ [*monogram*] DF[35]

Edinb Octob. 24. 1706

Text: BL Add. MS. 70291, fols. 68–71. *Address* (fol. 71ᵛ): To The Right Honᵇˡᵉ | Robert Harley Esqʳ | Princ̓ipall Secretᵃ of State | Present | to be forwarded to him. *Endorsed by Harley* (fol. 71ᵛ): Edenburg oct: 24 1706 ʀ nov: 3: Riot *Endorsed by an unknown hand* (fol. 71ᵛ): Mr De Foe

---

ᵃ in Prison] *interlined*
ᵇ a] *following letters* 'pl' *(probably for* 'plot') *cancelled*
ᶜ to] *following word* 'p[er]form' *cancelled*

---

1 H.M.C. *Mar and Kellie MSS*, 292.
2 Their full name was the Squadrone Volante, which translates as 'flying squadron'; they were also called the 'New Party', a group of around twenty-four politicians who remained independent of the traditional Country/Court split, though they allied with the Court during the Union debates.
3 Riley puts 'present and active' members as 99 Court, 24 Squadrone, and 87 opposition (*Union*, 328).
4 Defoe alludes tentatively to the 23 Oct. riot in *Review*, III, 672 (5 Nov. 1706).
5 *History of the Union*, *TDH*, VII, 280. The General Assembly met for a few weeks each Apr. and at its close appointed a Commission to oversee Church affairs for the remainder of the year. The Commission for 1706–7, named on 15 Apr. 1706, comprised 143 ministers and 79 lay elders (*The Principal Acts of the General Assembly of the Church of Scotland; Convened at Edinburgh the 4th April 1706* (1706), 14–17).
6 Stephen, *Scottish Presbyterians*, 44–9.
7 Backscheider, *Life*, 219.
8 *TDH*, VII, 303, 290; cf. VII, 310–11.
9 *An Essay, at Removing National Prejudices. Part III* (1706), *PEW*, IV, 91–112 was substantially reproduced in the *Review* from 12 to 26 Nov. 1706; *A Fourth Essay, at Removing National Prejudices* (1706), *PEW*, IV, 115–44 was substantially reproduced in the *Review* from 14 Dec. 1706 to 16 Jan. 1707.
10 *Presbyterians ... Union*: With hindsight, in his *History*, Defoe intimates that the anti-Union riots in Edinburgh 'ended to the Advantage of the Government' (*TDH*, VII, 286).

DEFOE TO ROBERT HARLEY, 24 OCTOBER 1706

11 *Assembly ... Parliam^ts* : The Commission first met on 9 Oct. It addressed parliament on 17 Oct. to request greater security for the Presbyterian settlement in any union with England (NRS PA 7/20/6; NRS CH 1/3/8, 11 and 14 Oct. 1706; Bowie, *Addresses*, 37–41).

12 *Anglicè*: Usually used to introduce the English translation of a previously stated foreign phrase, but by extension 'in plain English'. It is frequently used by Defoe rhetorically to cut through jargon or euphemism. For example, 'a little out of their own Government, *Anglicè* Drunk' (*Review*, I, 147 (23 May 1704)); 'Foreign Wives, *Anglicè*, *Whores*' (*Review*, III, 492 (10 Aug. 1706)); 'Heretors *Anglicè* Lords of the Mannor' (*Review*, VIII, 140 (22 May 1711))).

13 *first night*: Tuesday 22 Oct. For Defoe's later account of the unrest in Edinburgh on 22–3 Oct., see *History*, *TDH*, VII, 283–7.

14 *D. Hamilton's*: Hamilton was Lieutenant General, Premier Peer of Scotland, and Keeper of the Palace of Holyroodhouse. He led the anti-Union Country party in Scotland. As Defoe noted elsewhere, 'God bless Duke *Ha—ton*' was a Jacobite phrase at this time (*Review*, V, 34 (10 Apr. 1708)). Hamilton's later death in a duel occasioned Defoe's condemnation of the practice (*Review*, IX, 132–4 (29 Nov. 1712)). For an appraisal of Hamilton's motivations during this session, a 'double game' to ensure his own advantage whether the Union pass or not, see Daniel Szechi, 'Playing with Fire: The 4th Duke of Hamilton's Jacobite Politics and the Union', *PH* 39 (2020), 62–84.

15 *Parliament house*: Parliament hall in Edinburgh.

16 *Evening*: The following evening, Wednesday 23 Oct.

17 *D of Athol*: John Murray (1660–1724), first Duke of Atholl, a prominent opponent of the Union and Hamilton's brother-in-law.

18 *This ... Tumult*: Defoe's account in his *History* is laced with innuendo at Hamilton's expense, implying through apophasis his deliberate agitation of the crowd: 'Far be it from me to say, the Duke of *Hamilton* desired or encouraged this Tumultuary kind of Congratulation; That sort of Popularity must be too much below a Person of his Character.' As in the letter, the rhetorical refusal to pronounce on why Hamilton altered his course guides the reader: 'Some said, he went to avoid the Mob; Others maliciously said, he went to Point them to their Work' (*TDH*, VII, 283–4). *Dyer's News-Letter* for 31 Oct. reported that Hamilton used his coach due to a sprained foot and re-directed to Atholl's house to avoid the crowd (Folger Shakespeare Library, Newdigate Newsletters, L.c. 3065).

19 *s^r Pat. Johnston*: Sir Patrick Johnston (c. 1650–1736), Lord Provost of Edinburgh (1700–2, 1704–6, 1708–10), a Union commissioner, and MP for the city. Mar informed Sir David Nairne (1655–1740) on 26 Oct. that the crowd attended Hamilton to Atholl's house and home from there, before returning to attack Johnston's house (H.M.C. *Mar and Kellie*, 298–9).

20 *Capt Richardson*: Unidentified.

21 *Ld Provosts*: Sir Samuel McClellan (c. 1650–1709), a supporter of the Union and MP for Edinburgh in the first British parliament until his death.

22 *Capt ... Door*: Richardson led thirty men and 'took six of the Rabble', according to Defoe's *History*, *TDH*, VII, 285.

23 *Toll booth*: Defined by Defoe as '*The Town House, in which is* [*the magistrates'*] *Offices, and also the Prison for the City; It is generally like the Guild Hall of a City, or the Town House in* England, *saving that the Prison is generally in the same House in* Scotland' (*History*, *TDH*, VII, 321).

24 *Great Noise*: Omitted here is this detail from *The History of the Union*: 'The Author of this had one great Stone thrown at him, for but looking out of a Window; for they suffered no Body to look out, especially with any Lights, lest they should know Faces, and Inform against them afterwards' (*TDH*, VII, 285). Defoe claims that he was personally targeted: 'The Author of this had his Share of the Danger in this Tumult, and tho unknown to him, was watch'd and set by the Mob, in order to know where to find him, had his Chamber Windows Insulted, and the Windows below him broken by Mistake. But, by the Prudence of his Friends, the Shortness of its Continuance, and GODs Providence, he escaped' (*TDH*, VII, 286).

25 *Monsr De Witt*: Johan De Witt (1625–72), Dutch politician killed by a mob, along with his brother Cornelis (1623–72). Defoe alludes to this event in several places, including *Some*

232

DEFOE TO ROBERT HARLEY, 24 OCTOBER 1706

Reflections on a Pamphlet Lately Publish'd, Entituled, An Argument Shewing that a Standing Army is Inconsistent with a Free Government (1697), *PEW*, I, 56–7; Letter 84; *The Director*, no. 26 (2 Jan. 1721), *PEW*, VI, 281; and *The Director*, no. 29 (13 Jan. 1721), *PEW*, VI, 289. See Letter 140, note 25.

26 *Gate … Cannongate*: The Nether Bow was a large gatehouse that stood across the junction between the High Street and Cannongate. It was demolished in 1764.

27 *L⁴ Commissionʳ*: The Duke of Queensberry was High Commissioner (representing the monarch) during the last session of the Scottish parliament. See headnote to Letter 104 for Defoe and Queensberry's relationship.

28 *from white hall to Temple bar*: I.e. about one mile.

29 *L⁴ Provost Hesitated at it for a long time*: According to the Squadrone MP William Bennet of Grubbet (d. 1729), 'the provost dropt tears, when he could not resist, the march of troūps into the toūn, he bewailed his misfortūne, yt it fell oūt in his administration' (NRS GD 90/2/172/2/4).

30 *about Midnight*: 'About one a Clock in the Morning', according to the *History*, *TDH*, VII, 285. Other witnesses confirm midnight, including Bennet (NRS GD 90/2/172/2/4) and Paterson (H.M.C. *Portland MSS*, VIII, 251; BL Add. MS. 70039, fol. 70v).

31 *body of yᵉ Guards*: The order specifies that fifty men guarded Cannongate and 150 marched to Parliament Close (NRS GD 26/7/124).

32 *Duke of Argyle*: John Campbell, second Duke of Argyll (1680–1743), Major-General and former Lord High Commissioner. Defoe praised him in *Caledonia* (1706), lines 905–21, *PEW*, IV, 256. For Defoe's negative views of Argyll, particularly concerning his role in the 1710 election, see Letter 160.

33 *farther Ordʳ for preserving yᵉ Peace*: On the day this letter was written, a day on which parliament was not sitting, the Privy Council convened and issued a 'Proclamation Against Tumults and Rabbles'. In his *History* Defoe speaks approvingly of the proclamation (*TDH*, VII, 287) and printed it as an appendix.

34 *Mob … prevent*: 'This Rabble was a Mine sprung before its Time, which blew backwards, and destroyed the Engineers, rather than the Enemies' (*History*, *TDH*, VII, 286). On the 1705 Tack, see Letters 23 and 24. Defoe observed with pleasure the Tack backfiring on its advocates, calling it an 'Exquisite Lampoon upon themselves' (*The Secret History of the October Club* (1711), *PEW*, II, 145).

35 *[monogram] DF*: Unusually, Defoe has signed with both his monogram and his initials.

57

To Robert Harley

29 October 1706

Sr

In my Last you had an Accot of Two Mobs, in p[er]ticular Church and street, but as you were put in Expectaċon of a Third Mob There I purposely Refer'd it to This post to let you know That this perticular Sort is Expected within ye house[1] it Self.

There is an Entire Harmony in This Country Consisting in Universall Discords, The Church men in p[er]ticular are goeing Mad, the parsons are out of their wits and those who at first were brought over and pardon me were Some of them My Converts, their Country brethren being now Come in, are all Gone back and to be brought Over by no perswasion.

The Mob you have heard of are affrighted wth ye loss of ye Scots Crown[2] — and ye parsons[a] Malitiously Humour it and a Country parson who preach't yesterday at ye high Kirk[3] before ye Comissionr took this Text <u>Behold I Come quickly: Hold fast that which thou hast; let no man take thy Crown;</u>[4] he pretended not to mean an Earthly Crown but made his wholl sermon a bald allegory against the Union.[5] I Confess I had paceṅċe to hear him but to an Ex[c]eeding[b] Mortification.

The house is Now goeing on; they have Confirmd ye act of the Council for suppressing the Rabble[6] and bringing in souldiers and thereby Suppresst a New Clamour wch was Raising Against ye bringing in souldiers into ye City at wch it was begun to Say this was not a free parliamt, but that is Over.

Now tis said this was a Mob Raisd by my Ld Comissioner and that his Graċe did it on purpose to have an Opportunity to suppress them.

The Third Mob is Expected in ye house where tis said when the party see the Articles put to ye Vote;[7] if they Can not Carry their

---

[a] parsons] 'ar' *is interlined; the 'p' is Defoe's 'special p' abbreviating 'per'/'par', so he was perhaps clarifying the word is not 'persons'*
[b] Ex[c]eeding] 'c' *omitted*

DEFOE TO ROBERT HARLEY, 29 OCTOBER 1706

part they will Protest, take Instruments as they call it here and leav the house, and then they pretend to say the Nation will take Arms and yᵉ high lands are to be brought in — and Indeed if this should Run so far I fear yᵉ Church will Joyn yᵉ Worst of their Enemies against this Union.

They are now a goeing to fast all Over yᵉ kingdome and therein to give the ministers Occasion to pray and preach against it,[8] and soon as that is done Tumultuous addresses are prepareing in severall parts of yᵉ Country.

And thus you see sʳ what a nation you have to do with here — I am as Diligent wᵗʰ Caution not to be suspected as possible. I have not yᵉ success I hop't for but I Continue to push on and think I do no harm.

I have printed One Essay[9] wᶜʰ I Transmitted yᵉ last post. I have yᵉ second in yᵉ press,[10] wᶜʰ if it does Equall Service wᵗʰ the first I shall not So much[11] Grutch yᵉ Expence.

I wrot you last post[12] how I hear I am Treated in England as to my Lᵈ C. J. Holt.[13] I beseech you sʳ to Concern yoʳ Self in the Case that I may not be Ruind while I am at this Distance, my secret Enemies being Very Vigilant and Furious. I am told they will bring the publisher[14] to a Tryall while I am absent and he Can not procure me, for which I shall be Eternally Reproacht.

Sʳ you may Depend upon it I shall be persued to the Uttmost if your power be not my screen. I Earnestly therefore Entreat you will not forget me in this Condicon.

I am
Sʳ
yoʳ Most Obed faithfull Servᵗ
D F

Edinb. Octo. 29. 1706

Text: BL Add. MS. 70291, fols. 72–3. *Address* (fol. 73ᵛ): To The Right Honᵇˡᵉ | Robert Harley Esqʳ | Prinċipall Secretᵃ of State | Present. *Endorsed by Harley* (fol. 73ᵛ): Edenburg oct: 29 1706 ℞ nov: 11

1 *house*: I.e. Parliament House.
2 *affrighted wᵗʰ yᵉ loss of yᵉ Scots Crown*: In *The History of the Union*, Defoe recalls the false rumour, believed by 'Children and most ignorant People', that 'the *Crown of Scotland*, Sword and Scepter, should be carried away to *England*' (*TDH*, VII, 274).
3 *high Kirk*: Also known as St Giles' Cathedral.

DEFOE TO ROBERT HARLEY, 29 OCTOBER 1706

4 *Behold ... Crown*: Rev. 3:11 (Defoe writes 'let' for 'that'). The verse formed the source text for the Alloa minister John Logan's (1671–1724) *A Sermon Preached before ... the Honourable Estates of Parliament in the New Church of Edinburgh upon the 27 of October 1706* (1706).

5 *allegory against the Union*: Stephen challenges Defoe's assessment of Logan's sermon, stating that it merely cautioned that the Treaty needed to guarantee the security of the Church (*Scottish Presbyterians*, 50–1). However, the sermon seems to go beyond cautioning Scots in case of Union, encouraging them to resist it.

6 *act of the Council for suppressing the Rabble*: See Letter 56, note 33.

7 *Articles put to yᵉ Vote*: Parliament had agreed to read and discuss the articles in full before commencing to vote on them one by one, which started on 4 Nov.

8 *They ... it*: On 21 Oct. 1706, the Commission of the General Assembly debated whether to ask parliament for a national fast or to recommend local days of prayer. It agreed on the latter and sent a circular letter to each presbytery, recommending they each decide on whether to appoint a 'day for Solemne national prayer and humiliation' within their own bounds (NRS Commission of the General Assembly, Scroll Minutes, CH 1/4/2, 21 Oct. 1706). Karin Bowie shows that calls for a fast were part of the parliamentary opposition's strategy of delaying the Union's progress (*Scottish Public Opinion and the Anglo-Scottish Union, 1699–1707* (Woodbridge, 2007), 119). Jeffrey Stephen qualifies the view, perpetuated by Defoe, that demands for a fast were merely tactical: fasts were as much a traditional spiritual exercise as a political expedient ('National Fasting and the Politics of Prayer: Anglo-Scottish Union, 1707', *Journal of Ecclesiastical History* 60 (2009), 294–316). Retrospectively, Defoe commended the moderation that prevented the fast from being coopted to foment opposition to the Union (*History, TDH*, VII, 280–2).

9 *Essay: An Essay, at Removing National Prejudices. Part III*. On 15 Oct., Robert Stewart of Tillicoultry (*c*. 1655–1710) reports having drunk with Defoe and remarks that 'he is printing a book here'; and on 25 Oct., he mentions 'Du foes essay which is much admired' by unionists (NLS Wodrow Letters Quarto IV, fols. 80, 81).

10 *second in yᵉ press*: *A Fourth Essay, at Removing National Prejudices*.

11 *not So much*: I.e. not so much as.

12 *I wrot you last post*: Untraced.

13 *I hear ... Holt*: Sir John Holt (see Letter 21), Lord Chief Justice. In the *Review* for 1 Oct. 1706, Defoe had discussed opposition to the Union from 'a *certain grave, great and learned Man*' (III, 599). He was accused by *Dyer's News-Letter* of reflecting on Holt and proceedings opened against him. On 24 Oct., *Dyer's News-Letter* reported that 'Daniel De Foe author of the Review being called [to the bar] appeared not. It is said he is gon to Holland' (Folger Shakespeare Library, Newdigate Newsletters, L.c. 3063). Defoe denied libelling Holt in the *Review* for 16 Nov.:

> I really took this for so empty a Slander, that I could not have the least Shaddow of Uneasiness about it, knowing my self so free, so much as in Thought, from ever having said any thing reflecting on that eminent and worthy Person, that no Man in *England* has more Honour for his Character, real Veneration for his exalted Merit, or true Respect for his Person, than my self.
>
> I was therefore the more surpriz'd, when I had Notice, that the Publisher of this Paper has been taken up, and held to Bail on this Account. I really reckon his Lordship a Glory to this Nation, an Honour to the Bench, and that great Part of the Happiness *England* enjoys by the Revolution, in being restor'd to just Judges, is exemplified in his Lordship's unbiass'd Justice, steady Courage and consummate Experience. (III, 701)

On 21 Nov., Defoe reiterated his innocence: 'The Words, I am accus'd for, had not the least Aspect towards him, they were never design'd to mean Him, or that by them others should understand his Lordship.' Defoe asks Holt to 'remit' from prosecution until he is able to return to England (*Review*, III, 709–10). On 3 Dec., Defoe again denies the charge (III, 732–3). It seems that the case was dropped. Defoe praised Holt in *The Manufacturer*, no. 30 (12 Feb. 1720), and in *A Tour thro' the Whole Island of Great Britain* (1724–6), *TDH*, I, 104; II, 161.

WILLIAM MELMOTH TO DEFOE, [NOVEMBER 1706?]

14 *publisher*: John Matthews printed and distributed the *Review*. On 21 Oct., Hearne wrote that 'ye Printer of ye *Review* was carryed by ye Messenger of ye Press before my Ld. C. Justice & bound wth two good sureties to appear ye 1st day of ye next Terme in ye Court of *Queen's Bench Westm.* to answer to wt shall be objected against him by ye Queen's Attorney General. – Mr. Foe author of yt Paper is also sought for upon ye Same Account' (1, 297). Luttrell mistakenly stated that Defoe himself had been thus summoned (1, 98). Defoe expresses concern for Matthews in *Review*, III, 701, 710 (16 and 21 Nov. 1706).

58
William Melmoth to Defoe
[November 1706?]¹

HEADNOTE: William Melmoth the elder (1665/6–1743) was a lawyer and religious polemicist, who shared Defoe's view of the immorality of the stage. The *Review* frequently animadverted on theatrical entertainments: Defoe objected to sacreligious or bawdy performances, plays that distracted and debauched youths, and vices he believed were attendant on playhouses such as prostitution and gambling.² His most recent contribution to the topic in October 1706 considered how the theatre might be reformed to promote virtue. On 26 October, Defoe published the following letter, sent to the *Review*, dated 14 August:

> *Give me leave, Sir, as a Friend to Vertue and Religion, to return you Thanks for the great Zeal you have shewn against the Enemies of both, in exposing the Wickedness of the Stage, and the Folly of those that give Encouragement to it. I assure you, Sir, your Design is highly approved of by several very worthy Gentlemen, and therefore I hope, you will still pursue it. 'Tis a copious Subject, and not easily exhausted: and as the Ladies, I doubt, are the greatest Friends to the Play-houses, it might perhaps be of some Use to spend one or two* Reviews *in an Address to them, who generally speaking are easier wrought upon than the Men. I shall not pretend to direct you in this Matter, but I believe, it would not be amiss to take Notice, how little Regard the Players have shewn to Her Majesty's Order for regulating the Stage; since (notwithstanding that) they have continued to act some of those very Plays, for which they were so justly complain'd of before, as well as others equally as scandalous — But this I must leave to your own Discretion, and shall take up no more of your Time, but to beg your Pardon for this Trouble, who am,*

WILLIAM MELMOTH TO DEFOE, [NOVEMBER 1706?]

Sir,

Yours unknown, &c.[3]

The opening of Melmoth's private letter to Defoe, preserved in his son's biography of his father published ninety years later, may point to him as the author of the letter printed in the *Review*.

Melmoth had in December 1703 brought playbills for a new version of *The Tempest* to a meeting of the Society for the Promotion of Christian Knowledge (SPCK), comdemning the performance of the play so soon after the great storm as 'done in defiance of God's heavy Judgement upon us'.[4] Around this time, he corresponded with the Archbishop of Canterbury, Thomas Tenison (1636–1715), urging that 'nothing would soe effectively contribute to check the debauchery of the present age, as the suppressing the theatre, or at least a due regulation of it'.[5] He saw Defoe as a like-minded critic.

SIR,

The regard you have shewn to the request I lately made you to persue your designe of exposeing the stage,[6] obliges me to repeat my thanks to you; which I assure you I do with great sincerity, being alwaies pleased, I must own, whenever I see the playhouses attacked; for I am persuaded they have greatly contributed to corrupting the present age. I have taken the freedome to send you Mr. Bedford's new book,[7] by which you will see my charge was not ill grounded, when I told you how little respect had been shewn to her Majesties order.[8] I am the more induced to trouble you with this book, as thinking it might be of some use to you in the designe in which you are engaged. I have likewise sent you the opinion of Archbp. Tillotson touching playes,[9] which has been lately printed, and dispersed in great numbers,[10] and which, if it were still made more public, (as it might be, if printed in one of your *Reviews*[11]) would prove, I hope, of some use. *His* opinion, perhaps, may be of weight with those who are proof against other arguments, at least one would think it should make them consider a little what they are doing, when they give countenance to a set of men who seem to bid defiance to all that is serious, &c. &c.

Text: MS untraced. The copytext is William Melmoth Jr, *Memoirs of a Late Eminent Advocate, and Member of the Honourable Society of Lincoln's Inn* (1796), 55–7. *Address*: none recorded.

WILLIAM MELMOTH TO DEFOE, [NOVEMBER 1706?]

1 The date is conjectural, supposing that the letter followed the recent correspondence in the *Review* (see headnote).

2 *Inter alia Review*, II, 150–3 (3 May 1705); III, 380–3 (20 June 1706); III, 390–3 (25 June 1706); III, 475–8 (3 Aug. 1706); III, 485–93 (8 and 10 Aug. 1706); III, 515–18 (22 Aug. 1706); III, 549–51 (7 Sept. 1706); III, 654–6 (26 Oct. 1706); III, 660–2 (29 Oct. 1706); III, 665–6 (31 Oct. 1706); IV, 515–19 (2 Oct. 1707); VI, 285–6 (9 Aug. 1709); VI, 324–7 (30 Aug. 1709); VI, 328–31 (1 Sept. 1709). See Edward G. Fletcher, 'Defoe and the Theatre', *PQ* 13 (1934), 382–9, and J. A. Downie, 'Defoe's *Review*, the Theatre, and Anti-High Church Propaganda', *Restoration and 18th-Century Theatre Research* 15 (1976), 24–32.

3 *Review*, III, 654–5 (26 Oct. 1706).

4 *A Chapter in English Church History: Being the Minutes of the Society for Promoting Christian Knowledge for the Years 1698–1704*, ed. Edmund McClure (1898), 251. See A. J. Turner, 'The Jeremy Collier Stage Controversy Again', *N&Q* 20 (1973), 409–12.

5 William Melmoth Jr, *Memoirs of a Late Eminent Advocate, and Member of the Honourable Society of Lincoln's Inn* (1796), 53.

6 *request … stage*: Perhaps the letter in the *Review* for 26 Oct., given here in the headnote.

7 *Mr. Bedford's new book*: Arthur Bedford (1668–1745), *The Evil and Danger of Stage-Plays* (Bristol, 1706). Bedford continued his antitheatricalism in *A Serious Remonstrance in Behalf of the Christian Religion* (1719) and *The Evil and Mischief of Stage-Playing* (1728).

8 *her Majesties order*: Queen Anne's proclamation against vice and impropriety in the theatre was issued on 17 Jan. 1704. It called for 'Both the Companies of Comedians, Acting in *Drury-Lane*, and *Lincolns-Inn-Fields*, to take Special Care, That Nothing be Acted in either of the Theatres contrary to Religion, or Good Manners, upon Pain of Our High Displeasure, and of being Silenc'd from further Acting: And being further desirous to Reform all other Indecencies, and Abuses of the Stage, which have Occasion'd great Disorders, and Justly give Offence' (*Daily Courant*, 24 Jan. 1704).

9 *opinion of Archbp. Tillotson touching playes*: John Tillotson (1630–94), Archbishop of Canterbury (1691–4). His sermon *The Evil of Corrupt Communication* attacks contemporary plays as 'a mighty reproach to the Age and Nation' and 'not fit to be permitted in a *civilized*, much less in a *Christian* Nation. They do most notoriously minister both to infidelity and vice. By the prophaneness of them, they are apt to instill bad Principles into the Minds of Men, and to lessen the awe and reverence which all Men ought to have for God and Religion: and by their lewdness they teach vice, and are apt to infect the minds of Men, and dispose them to lewd and dissolute Practices' (*Works*, 2 vols., 3rd ed. (1722), II, 329).

10 *dispersed in great numbers*: In Dec. 1703, the SPCK had commissioned Melmoth and Robert Nelson (1656–1715) to make a representation to leading religious figures for the suppression and regulation of playhouses; to support their campaign, they printed two paragraphs out of Tillotson's sermon to be 'Dispersed among Ladies of Quality, &c.', so it may be this that Melmoth enclosed to Defoe (*A Chapter in English Church History*, 252).

11 *if printed in one of your Reviews*: Defoe did not act upon Melmoth's suggestion. The 1721 fourth edition of Melmoth's *The Great Importance of a Religious Life Consider'd* (1711) appears in *Defoe–Farewell Catalogue* (item 664).

59

To Robert Harley

2 November 1706

HEADNOTE: Though without explicit instructions from Harley, Defoe continued his work in Edinburgh, attending parliament daily and sending reports to London. He reassured the Commission of the General Assembly of the Church of Scotland, and he worked on fresh publications responding to opponents to the Union, as well as continuing with the triweekly publication of the *Review*. As the Scottish parliament neared completion of its preliminary reading of the Treaty articles, and prepared to start voting on them, it began to receive addresses against an incorporating union from shires, burghs, towns, presbyteries, and parishes.[1] 'Most of these Addresses were worded to the same purpose', Defoe wrote, 'and in Substance contain'd a Claim of the Constituents Right, to limit and instruct their Commissioners, and a Direction to avoid an Incorporating Union.'[2] Opposition politicians promoted addressing, attempting to highlight a mismatch between public opinion and the will of parliament.

Sir

I have not faild Since I Came hither to give you a Constant and Faithfull Accot of Every thing wch Occurs on this stage of Confusion.

I am Every day a Member of ye Generall assembly[3] and I Confess I[a] make a very odd figure here, for all Day ye Commission Sitts, and all[b] night and Morning I have a Revrend Committee wth me to Answer their Cases of Conscience.

Pardon my Vanity sr, I take upon me more Mod[e]sty wh[en][c] I Argue wth the Right Revrend fathers of this Church, and if I pass for much more of an Oracle among them than I Merit, Tis Owing to that Secret Mannagement for wch I suppose my Mission hither is Designd.

And yet sr, Pardon me I do not boast my Success, they are a hardened refractory and Terrible people; They have now kept a Fast, Thursday[4] was ye Day in this City, and tho' the Ministers spoke wth

---

^a I Confess I] *interlined*
^b all] *interlined*
^c Mod[e]sty wh[en]] *MS damaged*

more Modesty than I Expected, yet in yᵉ Country they Enflame yᵉ people strangely.[5]

And yet not a man of them Can say they would Venture to stand alone, or Dare think of falling Out wᵗʰ England.

This Day Came in severall addresses from E. Louthan, Perthshire, and they say Three more, but I do not find they were sign'd by many hands.[6]

But the worst Apprehension I have is from an Association forming in yᵉ North and West[a] to wᶜʰ they say there will be 50 thousand hands; it is in yᵉ form of an Oath that they will stand by One Another in Defence of the present Establishment in Church and state — I am promised the Coppy of it wᶜʰ I shall not fail to Transmitt and as it proceeds you shall hear.

I this day fortifyed a Minister who Enclind to sign and promote it, but will now Oppose it, and I purpose to go to Sᵗ Andrews and Glasgow yᵉ next week,[7] on yᵉ same Errand, having some hopes to prevent its progress in Fife and all that side and p[er]haps as far as Perth.

The[re][b] has been no Mob here Since the proclamation[8] but at Sterlin, Glasgow and some Other places they seem forward & have been Turbulent Twice.

At Blantire, a Town in Duke Hamiltons Estate, I hear to day when[c] the minister[9] Dissmisst yᵉ people he[d] Desird the Men to stay. When the women were Gone[10] he presented an address to yᵉ parliamᵗ for them to sign, and publickly Exhorted them to it; they all signd it Except about 9 or 10 of yᵉ most Judicous who Refused. Thus you see who are the fire-brands.

One Balanton, an Incendᵃ Minister, has handed about the Enclosed paper of Queries[11] wᶜʰ I send for yoʳ p[er]usall because they are the heads of mʳ Hodges's book[12] wᶜʰ I presume you have heard of if not seen.

I think to answer these Queries to morrow — I am writeing a Poem in praise of Scotland;[13] you will say that is an odd subject, to bear a Panegyrick, but my End will be answerd. I make them believ

---

[a] and West] *interlined*
[b] The[re]] *MS damaged*
[c] when] *interlined*
[d] he] *interlined above cancelled word* 'but'

DEFOE TO ROBERT HARLEY, 2 NOVEMBER 1706

I am Come away from England, and resolv if ye Union goes on to settle in Scotland,[14] and all Conduces to p[er]swade them I am a friend to their Country.

I Confess s^r doeing all this w^thout any Instruccons or the least hint of your Approbation, I am p[er]fectly at a loss what to say — I stay[15] here for^a your Orders; I spend your Money (and that not a Little) for I have had £45 besid a horse. I beseech you s^r^b let me not Run On to any length beyond your Satisfaccon. I am Remanded wth a word, and being wholly yours, would fain act not for yor Service Onely, but by your Direccon, and to yor Content.

If you please yet to favour me wth a line Enclosed to m^r Bell he will forward it to me.

I am

yo Most Obed^t Servt

DF

Edinburgh. Novembr 2. 1706

Text: New York Public Library, Berg cased collection, A.L.S.[16] *Address*: To The Right Honble | Robert Harley Esqr | Principall Secretary of State | Pres^t. *Endorsed by Harley*: Edenburg nov: 2: 1706 R at London nov: 9: 1706 De Foe

---

^a for] *interlined*
^b s^r] *following word possibly* 'to' *cancelled*

---

1 Eighty-five addresses came to parliament from 17 Oct. 1706 to 16 Jan. 1707 (Bowie, *Addresses*, 16–17).

2 *History of the Union*, *TDH*, VII, 280.

3 *Generall assembly*: I.e. the Commission of the General Assembly of the Church of Scotland.

4 *Thursday*: 31 Oct. See Paterson to Undersecretary of State Erasmus Lewis (1671–1745), 29 Oct. 1706, H.M.C. *Portland MSS*, VIII, 254, BL Add. MS. 70039, fol. 75^v.

5 *tho' ... strangely*: See *Review*, III, 725 (30 Nov. 1706), where Defoe says the fast was peaceably observed.

6 *severall ... hands*: On 1 Nov. anti-Union addresses from Perthshire, Midlothian, and Linlithgowshire were received by parliament, and one from Forfarshire followed on 2 Nov. In his *History*, Defoe stated that 'the Address from *Mid-Lothian* was Signed by not above Twelve of the Gentlemen, or thereabout, tho' there were above Two Hundred Gentlemen in that County; And that therefore it seemed the Argument, of its being the Sense of the Nation, must be very ill Grounded' (*TDH*, VIII, 23). But see D. W. Hayton's lower calculations of the number of freeholders in the county than Defoe estimates (*TDH*, VIII, 282 n. 52).

7 *St Andrews and Glasgow ye next week*: He did not go: see Letter 65.

8 *proclamation*: See Letter 56, note 33.

9 *minister*: Perhaps Matthew Connell (*c.* 1678–1743), Presbyterian minister at Blantyre, 1704–20.

10 *women were Gone*: Women were entirely excluded from the addresses against incorporating union.

242

DEFOE TO ROBERT HARLEY, 2 NOVEMBER 1706

11 *Balanton … Queries: Some Queries, Proposed to Consideration, Relative to the Union Now Intended* (1706), by John Bannatyne (1641–1707), minister at Lanark. It argues that Union required the consent of 'every free-born Scotsman' (1). Defoe makes slighting mention of 'Queries' opposing the Union in *Review*, III, 705, 712 (19 and 23 Nov. 1706), but no full answer, as proposed here, is known. The book is in *Defoe–Farewell Catalogue* (item 1434b). The copy remained with the letter as late as 1917 (see below, note 16).

12 *mr Hodges's book*: James Hodges's *The Rights and Interests of the Two British Monarchies … Treatise III* (1706) argued for a federated union, in which Scotland would retain its independent parliament. Defoe's *Fourth Essay, at Removing National Prejudices; with some Reply to Mr. H—dges* (1706) addresses Hodges's arguments, claiming that an incorporating union would make Scotland an equal partner in constitutional terms and benefit Scotland economically. Defoe had already countered Hodges's charge that the immorality of the English should prevent Scotland uniting with them (*Review*, III, 683–96 (9, 12, and 14 Nov. 1706)). The following year, he glanced back at Hodges's arguments, rejecting Hodges's list of thirty-one competing interests that he believed made England and Scotland incompatible (*Review*, IV, 209 (17 May 1707); IV, 237 (31 May 1707); IV, 657 (2 Dec. 1707)). In his *History*, Defoe looks back on the 'Infinite Scandal and Falsity' of Hodges's book, which he says was written at the Court party's instruction (*TDH*, VII, 269–70; VIII, 49).

13 *Poem in praise of Scotland*: *Caledonia, &c. A Poem in Honour of Scotland, and the Scots Nation*, licensed by a special act of the Scottish Privy Council and published by subscription in Edinburgh in early December 1706, and then in London in January 1707.

14 *settle in Scotland*: In *An Essay, at Removing National Prejudices. Part III* (1706), Defoe alluded to 'the Treatment I have met with from Parties and Power in my Native Country' and his 'design of settling in this Kingdom' (*PEW*, IV, 111). In the *Review*, Defoe referred to his 'private, lawful and known Design of settling my Family abroad, and letting the World know, I do not live by Scribbling, as is suggested' (III, 701 (16 Nov. 1706)).

15 *stay*: wait.

16 In 1885, this letter was in the possession of Alfred Morrison (1821–97) (*Catalogue of the Collection of Autograph Letters and Historical Documents formed between 1865 and 1882 by Alfred Morrison*, 6 vols. (1885), II, 13; cf. H.M.C. *Ninth Report, Part II*, 469; H.M.C. *Portland MSS*, IV, vii). Images of the letter are produced in the Morrison catalogue. The letter was then auctioned in 1917 (*Catalogue of the Renowned Collection of Autograph Letters and Historical Manuscripts, formed by the Late Alfred Morrison, Esq. of Fonthill … The First Portion* (1917), 36). It went to the New York Public Library as part of the collection of W. T. H. Howe (1874–1939) purchased by Dr Albert Berg (1872–1950) in 1940.

60

To Robert Harley

5 November 1706

HEADNOTE: From 1 to 4 November 1706, the Scottish parliament debated and then voted on the first article of the Union Treaty. That article confirmed that the English and Scottish kingdoms would from 1 May 1707 be joined as Great Britain in an incorporating rather than federated union. Anti-Union members tried to derail or delay the vote. On 1 November, they objected that the Union should first be approved by the English parliament and only then by Scotland. When that failed, they argued that the first article, being the fundamental one, should be approved last, again without success. On 2 November, opposition leaders delivered speeches decrying an incorporating union, notably John Hamilton, second Lord Belhaven and Stenton (1656–1708). Belhaven's oration projected an image of ruined Caledonia, prompting Defoe's response in a lampooning ballad, *The Vision* (1706).[1] Parliament approved article one by 116 votes to 83 on 4 November.

Sr

Since my Last ye Face of affaires I hope are a little Mended and after a Very Long and Warm Debate On Fryday whether they should proceed on ye Union or Go first on ye security of ye Church it was past proceed.[2] On Saturday they sat till near 8 at night and the speeches on both Sides were long and warm.[3]

D Hamilton Rav'd,[4] Fletcher[a] of Saltoun,[5] and the Earle of Belhaven, Made long speeches, the Latter of wch will be printed[6] — the Clamour without was so great That a Rabble was feared tho' ye Guards are Numerous and were Drawn Out in Readyness.

Addresses are Delivred in from Severall places and More prepareing but tis observ'd the addresses Discover a Fraud wch shows ye party here at their shifts.

The addresses are found in ye Cant of ye Old Times, Deploreing ye Misery of Scotland for want of a Further Reformation and ye security of the Church and the Lords Covenanted people,[7] but when ye Names Come to be Examin'd they Are all sign'd by known Jacobites and Episcopall men.[8]

---

[a] Fletcher] *the 'c' is interlined above illegible cancelled letter*

DEFOE TO ROBERT HARLEY, 5 NOVEMBER 1706

There has been a farther Expectation of a Mob and some practises have been used to Infect ye souldiers but ye E of Leven[9] Call'd ye Guards together to day and made a speech to them; they had been posesst wth a Notion that they should be sent to the west Indees as soon as ye Union was Over.

My Ld Leven I hope has Reestablisht them, and the^a proceeding since is more favourable.

Last night ye Grand question was put whether the first Article — Or in short ye Union it self should be approved or Not — and Carryed in ye Affirmativ wch being On King Williams Birthday[10] is to me Very Remarkable and Encourageing.

I had to day the Honour to be sent for by the L^ds Comittee for Examining the Equivalents[11] and to assist them in the Calculateing the Draw back[12] on ye Salt, ye proporcon of ye Excise and some addenda About Trade.

They profess themselves Oblig'd to me more than I Merit[13] and at their next Committee I am Desir'd to Dine wth them. I am lookt on as an English man that Designs to settle here and I think am p[er]fectly Un[su]spected^b and hope on that foot I do some Service — Onely I spend you a great Deal of Money at wch I am Concern'd but see no Remedy if I will go thro' wth the work.

I have Now Great hopes of it, tho' to day the assembly men make a great stir; in short ye Kirk are <u>Au Wood</u>,[14] pardon ye Scotticisme.

Yo^r Most Obed^t Servt

D F

Edinb. Nov. 5. 1706

Text: BL Add. MS. 70291, fols. 74–5. *Address* (fol. 75^v): To The Right Honble | Robert Harley Esqr | Principall Secret^a of State | Present. *Endorsed by Harley* (fol. 75^v): Edenburg nov: 5 1706 R nov: 11:

---

^a the] *following word* 'Vote' *cancelled*
^b Un[su]spected] 'su' *omitted*

---

1 For discussion, see Leith Davis, *Acts of Union: Scotland and the Literary Negotiation of the British Nation, 1707–1830* (Stanford, Cal., 1998), 30–8.
2 *whether ... proceed*: See *History of the Union*, *TDH*, VIII, 22–4. There, Defoe erroneously indicates that the issue of the Church of Scotland's security came up on Saturday 2 Nov. rather than Friday 1 Nov., as he says here.

3 *speeches ... warm*: See *History, TDH*, VIII, 24–7. Defoe mentions only the anti-Union speeches here, but William Seton of Pitmedden (1673–1744) spoke in favour of approving the first article, and Defoe reprinted that speech in *History, TDH*, VIII, 27–32. Writing to Erasmus Lewis, also on 5 Nov., Paterson complimented in particular the pro-Union speech of the Squadrone leader John Ker (*c.* 1680–1741), fifth Earl of Roxburghe (H.M.C. *Portland MSS*, VIII, 262; BL Add. MS. 70039, fols. 86–7).

4 *D Hamilton Rav'd*: Mar said 'Hamilton spoke too with a great deal of force (I mean loud speaking)' (H.M.C. *Mar and Kellie MSS*, 309). In annotations to Lockhart's *Memoirs*, Clerk of Penicuik alleged that it was all show, as Hamilton was collaborating with Queensberry (NRS GD 18/6080, 252).

5 *Fletcher of Saltoun*: Andrew Fletcher of Saltoun (1653?–1716), writer and politician, a long-standing supporter of Scottish independence. See Paul H. Scott, *Andrew Fletcher and the Treaty of Union* (Edinburgh, 1992). Paterson summarises Fletcher's speech, which Mar disparagingly called 'study'd' (H.M.C. *Portland MSS*, VIII, 261; BL Add. MS. 70039, fols. 86–7; H.M.C. *Mar and Kellie MSS*, 309).

Fletcher had earlier accused the Scottish Union commissioners of treachery (*Dyer's News-Letter*, 5 Nov. 1706, Folger Shakespeare Library, Newdigate Newsletters, L.c. 3067). In the coming months, Defoe's pro-Union writings frequently reacted to Fletcher's 'patriotic' arguments opposing an incorporating union. Defoe responded to Fletcher's *State of the Controversy betwixt United and Separate Parliaments* (1706), denying Fletcher's claim that the Churches of England and Scotland could not coexist under one polity (*Review*, III, 673 (5 Nov. 1706)). Defoe opposed Fletcher's claim that England would renege on its financial obligations to Scotland and that Scottish interests would be subordinated to English ones (*An Essay, at Removing National Prejudices. Part III* (1706), *PEW*, IV, 108). And, apropos the anti-Union addresses presented to Scotland's parliament, Defoe rejected Fletcher's arguments that legislators were constrained by the popular will (*Review*, III, 848 (30 Jan. 1707)). A decade earlier, Defoe had written against Fletcher's anonymous *Discourse Concerning Militia's and Standing Armies* (1697) in *An Argument, Shewing, That a Standing Army, with Consent of Parliament, is not Inconsistent with a Free Government* (1698), *PEW*, I, 64. Fletcher is omitted almost entirely from Defoe's *History of the Union*.

6 *Earle ... printed*: It was published as *The Lord Beilhaven's Speech* (1706). The Lord Chancellor in Scotland, James Ogilvy, first Earl of Seafield (1664–1730), advised Godolphin that Belhaven's speech was 'contrived to incense the common people' but 'had no great influence in the House' (*Letters relating to Scotland in the reign of Queen Anne by James Ogilvy, First Earl of Seafield and Others*, ed. P. Hume Brown (Edinburgh, 1915), 100). In his *History*, where he reprinted Belhaven's speech, Defoe called it 'a long premeditate Speech' (*TDH*, VIII, 32). He elsewhere mocked the sentimental, lachrymose, and ponderous delivery (*Review*, IV, 79 (18 Mar. 1707); IV, 664–9 (6 Dec. 1707); V, 29 (8 Apr. 1708)). See Letters 67 and 70 for the subsequent poetic exchange between Defoe and Belhaven. Defoe and Belhaven were reconciled in 1708 (see Letter 133).

7 *addresses ... people*: In the *Review*, Defoe made the same argument that 'Addresses to the Parliament against the Union [are] full of apparent Zeal for Religion, for the Kirk, and for the Reformation, reciting in general the Covenant, and a great many Kirk-Phrases, or as call'd here *Presbyterian* Cant; and when the Names come to be canvass'd and examin'd, it appears to be sign'd by *Non-jurors* and *Episcopal* People, or in general Malecontents at the Government' (*Review*, III, 715 (23 Nov. 1706); cf. III, 709 (21 Nov. 1706)).

8 *sign'd by known Jacobites and Episcopall men*: The anti-Union Jacobite George Lockhart of Carnwath (1673–1731) countered Defoe's attack on the validity of the addresses:

> I know very well that ... that vile monster and wretch Daniel Defoe, and other mercenary tools and trumpeters of rebellion, have often asserted that these addresses and other instances of the nation's aversion to the Union, proceeded from the false glosses and underhand dealings of those that opposed it in Parliament, whereby the meaner sort were impos'd upon and deluded into those jealousies and measures.
>
> I shall not deny but perhaps this measure of addressing had its first original, as they report. But it is absolutely false to say that any sinister means were used to bring in subscribers.

DEFOE TO ROBERT HARLEY, 9 NOVEMBER 1706

The contrary is notoriously known, for the people flocked together to sign them and expressed their resentments with the greatest indignation. (*Lockhart Memoirs*, 147)
Lockhart's *Memoirs* appears in *Defoe–Farewell Catalogue* (item 908).

9 *E of Leven*: David Leslie (1660–1728), third Earl of Leven, Commander-in-Chief in Scotland. Defoe praises him in *Caledonia* (1706), lines 965–71, *PEW*, IV, 257–8. He had met him in London in summer 1706 (Backscheider, *Life*, 240).

10 *King Williams Birthday*: See *History*, *TDH*, VIII, 45–50. William III was born on 4 Nov. 1650, and Defoe elaborated on this auspicious coincidence of dates in *Review*, III, 706 (19 Nov. 1706), an issue probably written at a similar time to this letter. Defoe again recalls the coincidence of dates in *Review*, IV, 588–9 (4 Nov. 1708), and *History*, *TDH*, VII, 300–1, where he notes that it was also the date in 1688 that William landed in England.

11 *L^{ds} Committee for Examining the Equivalents*: On 23 Oct. 1706, the Scottish parliament established a nine-man committee to examine the treaters' calculation of the Equivalent, a one-off, upfront payment of £398,085.10s from England to recompense Scotland for its future contributions to the repayment of the English national debt, to mitigate the effects of tax increases in the short term, and to stimulate Scottish industry. For the committee's membership, see *History*, *TDH*, VIII, 14. On its members' pro-Union attitudes, see Letter 74. Defoe's naming it a 'L^{ds} Comittee' is misleading, as there were three representatives each from the nobility, shires, and burghs. The plural 'Equivalents' was common because the fund would be paid to various beneficiaries.

12 *Draw back*: A reimbursement of import duty paid upon re-exportation.

13 *They … Merit*: ''Tis for those Gentlemen [of the committee] to say, whether I was useful or not', says Defoe in his *History*, *TDH*, VII, 259.

14 *Au Wood*: 'wuid' adj. 'Mad, insane, out of one's mind, demented' (*Dictionary of the Scots Language*, sv. 'Wuid' 1). With the determiner 'a', the phrase translates as 'all mad'. Defoe uses it ('*Wod*') in *The Vision* (1706), line 112, *PEW*, IV, 204.

61

To Robert Harley

9 November 1706

HEADNOTE **(Letters 61 and 62)**: The passage of article one on 4 November intensified two of the most pressing concerns concerning the Union: the security and independence of the Church of Scotland, and the recompense to Scotland for short-term financial losses in bringing together two systems of excise and customs.

The Union commissioners were not authorised to discuss church affairs, and Scottish Presbyterians feared that the Treaty devised in London made insufficient guarantees for the Kirk. On 17 October 1706, the Commission of the General Assembly issued an address asking parliament to guarantee the establishment of the Presbyterian Church after the Union. To allay such concerns, an overture for an Act for Securing of the Protestant Religion and Presbyterian Church Government (the Act of Security) was introduced in parliament after the passage of article one. In the meantime, the Commission had begun to prepare a second address, giving more particular concerns with the Treaty, which it presented to parliament on 8 November.[1] In works such as *An Essay, at Removing National*

DEFOE TO ROBERT HARLEY, 9 NOVEMBER 1706

Prejudices, against a Union with England. Part III, Defoe maintained that the Union secured rather than endangered the Church of Scotland by establishing it within a British constitution.[2]

Questions of finance were as pressing as those of religion. Defoe commenced writing on the calculation of the Equivalent in his *Fourth Essay, at Removing National Prejudices*, as well as in the *Review*.[3] Defoe was first summoned by the committee established by the Scottish Parliament to calculate the Equivalent on 5 November. Parliament subsequently remitted other matters of taxation and customs to this committee. Defoe managed to install himself as an unofficial advisor to the committee and in this role reported crucial aspects of the economic negotiations back to Harley.[4] He continued to speak about this aspect of his work in Scotland with great pride.[5]

Sr

In my last[6] I hinted to you what ye Church was doeing as to Their Address or protest against ye Church of England Constitution.

I here wth Send you the thing it Self[7] — and as to the Generall Opinion it gains here I must Own it does some harm — but Not what it[a] Was Expected,[8] for while it was in Debate like ye English Fleet while it lay at Torbay it kept all France in suspence[9] so ye Country Expected the Kirk would have protested as ye Burghs have done[10] Against the Union in Generall as Destructiv to ye Civill Intrest and the Intrest of ye Church in Generall but Instead of That It Containes Six heads[11] as you will see, all which suppose the Union as Reall and Certain.

I had this Day the Honor to be in ye Committee of parliamt[b] Appointed to Examine the Drawbacks and Equivalents and they have Desird me to assist them; their Debates will End in makeing Explications on ye heads of Excise and Drawbacks and I believ I shall have the honour to form them. I shall in my next I hope be Able to give you a scheme of their Demands and as I believ I shall have the Honour to Draw them out for them I Would be Glad that after I send you a Draft of the subject I might be Instructed what will Or will Not be Conceded in England since it is so Ordred that

---

[a] it] *following word* 'might' *cancelled*
[b] parliamt] *following letters possibly* 'abo' *(for* 'about'*) cancelled*

I am in their Cabinet by some Mannagem^t and Can Influen&e them more than I Expected.

Now to Lead them to anything wch England will Not Complye wth or to put them off of anything wch Makes a Difficulty here and may be Complyed wth is Equally acting against ye Union.

Their L^dships have Resolved to Committ ye Drawing up the Explanations[12] to me and if Directed I might do more servi&e to both Kingdomes than I Could have Expected; if therefore my servi&e here be of any Moment I shall beg to be Instructed or If I take wrong Aim to be Excused.

Next post I shall Transmitt a Draft of ye things in Debate.

I am

yor Most Obed^t Servt

D F

Nov. 9. 1706

All ye Gentlemen Lay Elders protested in ye assembly against the address.[13]

Text: BL Add. MS. 70291, fols. 76–7. *Address* (fol. 77^v): To The Right Honble | Robert Harley Esqr | Her Maj^ties Prinċipall Secret^a of State | Present. *Endorsed by Harley* (fol. 77^v): Edenburg nov: 9 1706 ℞ nov: 18

1   NRS PA 7/20/19; Bowie, *Addresses*, 42–50.
2   *PEW*, IV, 96–108.
3   *PEW*, IV, 139–40; *Review*, III, 681 (9 Nov. 1706).
4   Backscheider, *Life*, 219.
5   *Review*, IX, 409 (2 June 1713).
6   *my last*: Untraced.
7   *the thing it Self*: Though now missing from the correspondence, the Kirk's second address to the Scottish parliament and Defoe's comments upon it are included in the *Review* for 30 Nov. 1706. There, Defoe argued that the Revolution settlement protected the current constitutional make up of Scotland as much as it did England, and he insisted that the Union would confirm this:

> *Scotland* being thus legally establish'd, as we do not in *England* pretend to object against her Settlement, so neither does *England* desire to invade it; the QUEEN has been pleas'd to add to them frequent gracious and repeated Assurances of maintaining and supporting their Church-Government, as by Law establish'd, and at last on the Supposition of this Establishment to be continued and confirm'd, the Treaty of Union is begun.
>
> In the Treaty there is not one Word of the Church concern'd, it being an express Preliminary, that the Treaters should not meddle with that Affair, but either Parliament are left to settle their respective Churches by Acts of Parliament, which afterward being incorporated into the Treaty, become part of the same, and are the Foundation of the Union. Thus both Churches are effectually and equally established. (III, 725–9)

249

DEFOE TO ROBERT HARLEY, 9 NOVEMBER 1706

Whereas the Commission's second address expressed its fear that the Church of Scotland would become a Dissenting church in an Anglican Britain, Defoe countered that it would be recognised as an equivalent establishment in a bi-confessional state.

8 *it ... Expected*: Nairne reported to Mar on the 'uneasyness' felt by the ministry in London upon this address (H.M.C. *Mar and Kellie MSS*, 320).

9 *like ... suspence*: Earlier in 1706, the position of the English fleet off Bourdeaux was so well kept a secret that in France 'the alarm was general. It put all the maritime counties of France to a vast charge, and under dismal apprehensions' (Burnet, v, 266).

10 *protested as ye Burghs have done*: The address against the Union from the Convention of Royal Burghs was presented to parliament on 6 Nov. 1706. It is printed in *Review*, III, 717–20 (26 Nov. 1706), along with Defoe's commentary stating that although a majority of burghs present at the Convention endorsed the address (24 to 20) this was a minority of the total number (64), and those burghs that supported it accounted for just 14% of the total tax paid by the burgh estate.

11 *Six heads*: The six concerns listed in the second address are: (1) the requirement that public office holders take the Anglican sacramental test; (2) the potential imposition by a British parliament of new oaths contradictory to the Church of Scotland's principles; (3) the absence from the monarch's coronation oath of a guarantee of protection for the Scottish Church; (4) the need, in case the Union passèd, for a commission for plantation of kirks, which would fill vacant livings, and a judicatory to decide matters currently dealt with by the Scottish Privy Council; (5) references to obscure acts of the English parliament in the current oath of abjuration; (6) the fact that twenty-six bishops sat in the House of Lords.

12 *Explanations*: Clarifications of or adjustments to articles of the Union Treaty that concerned commerce. Subsequent letters detail such finer points relating to salt, oats, and beer. The pro-Union groups feared that changes requested prior to ratification of the Treaty in Scotland would be rejected in England, especially if changes necessitated a recalculation of the Equivalent.

13 *all ... address*: Echoed in *Review*, III, 724 (28 Nov. 1706). The lay elders characterised the second address as 'but the deed of a pack't club and not the general sense of the church of Scotland' (NLS Wodrow Quarto LXXIII, fol. 271). They argued that 'since the ministers had already won parliament's assurance that any union treaty would confirm the Church's established status and legislate for its future security, they had little to gain by bringing these specific concerns to parliament's attention, and could be suspected of disaffection and mistrust' (Clerk, 119).

250

62

To Robert Harley

13 November 1706[1]

Sr

In my Last I Accquainted you with ye present posture of ye Affair before ye Comittee of Parliamt. The Difficulties before Them are The Draw backs and The Equivalents, The Taxes and The Trade.

The First head is — Viz, speaking as themselvs:

We have Some Difficulties, how Can we Remedy Them, We Can Not add any Article or Take off any, That will Require a New Treaty, and Consequently a New delay and ye Lord ha' Mercy On us if we have another Session here.

Will England admitt of Explanacons?

My Answer (Pardon me, Uninstructed in ye Case) without Doubt England will admitt ye Parliamt of Scotland to Declare Their Construccon of any Article of ye Treaty, provided it be agreeable to ye True Intent and Meaning of The Treaty and to Reason and justice.

Upon This foot sr you will have an Explanacon Offred on ye following heads and were I better Informd from England I Could p[er]haps lessen, Encourage or Disscourage Those Explanacons.

1. That Their Twopenny Ale wch is sold but for 2.4d p[er] Gallon[a] More Than our small beer should pay as small beer Onely, Or (as I offer) be advanced to a Middle Rate of Excise between strong and small in Proporcon to its advance of Price wch Seems just.[2]

2. That Their Own acts of Parliamt Obligeing Them to Cure fish wth forreign Salt, and those Acts[b] being by the Union to be Continued, They are to Understand English Salt as forreign Salt in ye Sence of those Acts, It being So Now, Or Elce After ye Union they shall be prohibited useing The Rock Salt of England wch will be to ye Loss of England as well as a hardship on Scotland.[3]

---

[a] Gallon] *following letters* 'Shoul' *cancelled*
[b] those Acts] *interlined*

DEFOE TO ROBERT HARLEY, 13 NOVEMBER 1706

3 That Whereas They are Obliged to Salt all flesh for
Exportaċon or for Victualling their ships,[a] with forreign Salt,
They may Use Their Own or English Salt, Paying yᵉ Duty for
it. Elċe They are Not on Equallity in Trade wᵗʰ England who
Salt Most of The[i]r[b] ships beef with English Salt.[4]
4 That yᵉ Tax Upon Coals payable by The Chalder[5] in England
be Explain'd On yᵉ Weight of Scots Coal in proporċon,[c] They
Not Selling by Measure, (5)[d] and the Bountyes on Corn[6] be[e]
Explain'd to Include a Grain Call'd Bear[7] wᶜʰ is much yᵉ Same
as Barly but Differs a little.

These are what are at present before Them and as yᵉ Rest
offer (for There will be More) I shall Accquaᵗ yoʳ Honoʳ. Mean
Time It would be Very Serviċable if I might kno'[f] whether These
Explanaċons are Agreeable to England or No, Sinċe it will be in
My power to shorten yᵐ Very much, tho' if allow'd it will give some
Ease here to a Naċon yᵗ Really are in a Terrible Ferment, and it is
Unaccountable how it Encreases.

Att Dumfreis They have burnt yᵉ Articles in yᵉ Market plaċe;[8] at
Glasgow They were about it but yᵉ Magistrates prevaild wᵗʰ them to
forbear On promise to sign an adress against it.[9]

It would Amaze you if I should give you The Trouble of
Repeating The Ridiculous Noċons people here have Entertaind
Against Their Own happyness. The Libells, The Absurdities and The
Insults on That head are Intollerable.

The High Com̃issioner has had Letters Sent to Threaten him wᵗʰ
Pistoll, Dagger and Variety of Assassinaċon,[10] and the[g] Unusuall
Numbers of Highlanders Makes Some people Very Uneasy here,
There being More of Them here Now[h] than has been known —
Indeed they are Formidable Fellows and I Onely Wish her Majᵗⁱᵉ
had 25000 of Them in Spain, a Naċon Equally proud and Barbarous
like Themselves.

---

[a] ships] *following letters* 'The' *(for* 'They'*) cancelled*
[b] The[i]r] *the* 'r' *is interlined;* 'i' *omitted*
[c] proporċon] *following word* 'and' *cancelled*
[d] (5)] *interlined (Defoe split the fourth item in his list to create a fifth)*
[e] be] *interlined*
[f] kno'] 'kno:' *in MS; colon omitted in this edition*
[g] the] *interlined*
[h] Now] *interlined*

DEFOE TO ROBERT HARLEY, 13 NOVEMBER 1706

They are all Gentlemen, will Take affront from No Man, and Insolent to ye last Degree. But Certainly ye Absurdity is Ridiculous, to see a Man in his Mountain habit armd[a] with a Broad sword, Targett Pistol or p[er]haps Two at his Girdle, a Dagger and staff, walking Down ye street as Upright and Haughty as if he were[b] a lord — and withall Driving a Cow. Bless us — are These ye Gentlemen! Said I —

Sr As to ye Union, Tho' I hope well and The Govornmt sticks Close to it, yet I Must Own tis yet a Dark prospect. The Difficultyes are Many and ye people Obstinately Averse, and if any Insurreccon happen wch I Must acknowlege is Not Unlikely — I Crave leav to say — The few Troops They have here are Not to be Depended Upon — I have this Confesst by Men of the best Judgement — The officers are good but Even the officers Own They Dare Not Answer for Their Men, and Some of ye Wisest and Most Disscerning Men here wish Two or Three Regiments of Horse or Dragoons were Sent but Near ye borders as Silently as might be; all ye Force This Governmt has to make a stand is Not 2000 Effective Men and of Them I Question whether 1500 Could be Drawn together.

I have More Objeccons of Trade to make but They are Not Ripe. I Wish I Might kno' what steps to Take in This affair.

Mr Bell has Sent me a farther Supply[11]

I am

sr

yor Most Obedt Servt

[monogram]

Edinb. Novembr 13.[c] 1706

Sr I am wrott to — to offer my Service to My Ld Hallifax to Accquat him wth Matters here. My Respect and Indeed Obligacon

[a] armd] interlined
[b] if he were] interlined
[c] 13] apparently amended from '14'

253

DEFOE TO ROBERT HARLEY, 13 NOVEMBER 1706

to My Ld Makes it Very Agreeable to me, and I have This post wrott to his L^dship, But as I am yo^rs s^r in Duty Abstracted from and Exclusi[ve]^a of all ye World I Thought my Self Oblig'd to Accqu^t you of it and on yor Orders shal[l]^b at any Time Desist.[12]

Text: BL Add. MS. 70291, fols. 78–9. *Address* (fol. 79^v): To The Right Honble | Robert Harley Esqr | Her Maj^ties Princ̆ipall Secret^a of State | Present | in Cover. *Endorsed by Harley* (fol. 79^v): Edenburg nov: 13 1706 R nov: 21:[13]

^a Exclusi[ve]] *obscured by MS binding*
^b shal[l]] *obscured by MS binding*

---

1   The date at the end of the letter is not perfectly legible but looks like 13 Nov. Defoe's brother-in-law, Robert Davis, delivered it to Harley in London on 21 Nov., and Harley read the date as 13 Nov., which is evident from his endorsement. However, Defoe refers to the burning of the Union articles at Dumfries, which all sources suggest occurred on 20 Nov., as given in the broadside the dissidents produced, *An Account of the Burning of the Articles of Union at Dumfries* (1706), and in Defoe's own *History of the Union, TDH*, VII, 297–8. It is possible that a smaller-scale burning than that of 20 Nov. occurred before 13 Nov. or that he says Dumfries when he means Stirling, where the articles had been burned on 4 Nov.

2   *Twopenny ... just*: 'Under English excise regulations there were two rates of tax on beer or ale, a low one levied on "small beer" (notionally defined as beer sold at 6 shillings or under per barrel), and a higher one on "strong" beer or ale. In Scotland, on the other hand, there was a single standard rate; and it was used as a great argument against Union that it might mean that Scottish so-called "Twopenny" or "Tippony" ale – the standard drink, selling at somewhat above six shillings a barrel – would be taxed at a vastly higher rate, namely the one imposed on English "strong ale"' (P. N. Furbank and W. R. Owens, 'Defoe and the "Tippony Ale"', *SHR* 72 (1993), 86–9 (at 88)). For the implications of the higher rate being applied, see Seafield's contemporaneous account in H.M.C. *Laing MSS*, II, 136–7. See Letter 71, note 4 on Defoe's 'Middle Rate of Excise'. A barrel was thirty-four English gallons or twelve Scottish gallons.

3   *Their Own ... Scotland*: In his *History*, Defoe explains that Scottish salt had proved inadequate for curing fish, so parliament required foreign salt to be used. However, parliament did not seek to have English salt counted as foreign when it came to this on 18 Dec. 1706 (*TDH*, VIII, 132).

4   *They may ... Salt*: This amendment to article eight was made by the Scottish parliament on 17 Dec. 1707 (*History, TDH*, VIII, 130).

5   *Chalder*: A dry measure of capacity. In *A Tour thro' the Whole Island of Great Britain*, Defoe says a chalder contains thirty-six bushels at London (*TDH*, II, 94). That echoes his *History*, though he discusses regional variations (*TDH*, VIII, 270). A bushel is four pecks or eight gallons.

6   *Bountyes on Corn*: A 'bounty' is a premium paid to merchants to encourage particular acts of trade, in this case a drawback on exportation of corn which originated in 1688.

7   *Grain Call'd Bear*: See *OED* noun 2.

8   *burnt ye Articles in ye Market plac̆e*: As stated above in note 1, because this letter apparently dates to 13 Nov., Defoe could be referring to an earlier burning than the large event of 20 Nov.
    On 20 Nov., a crowd of between 120 and 200 according to Defoe and 'near to two or three thousand' according to Lockhart gathered at the Market Cross at Dumfries and burned the Union articles (*Review*, III, 769 (21 Dec. 1706); *History, TDH*, VII, 297; *Lockhart Memoirs*, 177). The printed proclamation set in place of the articles on the cross, *An Account of the Burning of*

the Articles of Union at Dumfries, was according to Defoe 'full of foolish Vaunts, meer Ostentation, and other Effects of strong Delusions' (*Review*, III, 764 (19 Dec. 1706)).

9 *at Glasgow ... against it*: On 7 Nov., an anti-Union crowd formed in Glasgow following a sermon by James Clark (1660–1723), minister at the Tron Kirk. For Defoe's dispute with Clark around the time of the publication of Defoe's *History of the Union*, concerning whether or not Clark incited the mob, see F&O, *Bibliography*, 90–1, 96. In *A Seasonable Caution to the General Assembly* (1711), Defoe considers Clark the unwitting cause of the unrest (24). Though here Defoe says the magistrates promptly acceded to the demand they address parliament, his letter of 16 Nov. and his *History* say the opposite (Letter 64; *TDH*, VII, 316).

10 *High Co͠missioner ... Assassinačon*: In the *Review* for 24 Dec. 1706, Defoe mentions that 'innumerable Threats, private Letters about stabbing, pistoling, and Assassination' have not deterred Queensberry from his work (III, 774–5), echoed in his *History*, where Defoe also printed some of these 'Threatning Letters ... faithfully Transcribed from the Original' (*TDH*, VIII, 80–1).

11 *Mr Bell has Sent me a farther Supply*: Bell provided Defoe with £52.10s.6d. on 9 Nov. (H.M.C. *Portland MSS*, IV, 378).

12 *Ld Hallifax ... Desist*: For Halifax, see headnote to Letter 30. Harley approves of the correspondence (see Letter 66), but the letters are untraced.

13 *nov: 21:*: Harley received this letter a day after he received the following one.

63

To Robert Harley

14 November 1706

HEADNOTE **(Letters 63–5)**: On 12 November, parliament debated and passed the Act of Security for the Church of Scotland.[1] The Union Treaty as negotiated in London did not provide for the Church, so the act was brought about by the lobbying of its ministers, who wanted to ensure their Presbyterian ecclesiology was protected. Writing to Harley on the day the act passed, John Dalrymple, first Earl of Stair (1648–1707), said that, 'I did foresee that the want of that article [in the Treaty] might lose us the populace', but now the act has passed 'the ferment will abate and when the Ministers find themselves safe, they will soon make the people easy and quiet'.[2] The Act quelled, though did not entirely remove, the Kirk's alarms, as both camps subsequently acknowledged. John Clerk of Penicuik (1676–1755) wrote that 'in the churches, by and large, the trumpets of sedition began to fall silent', and George Lockhart reported that 'most of their zeal was cooled, and many of them quite changed their notes and preached up what not long before they had declared anathemas against'.[3] However, popular protests against the Union in Dumfries, Glasgow, and Edinburgh continued. Parliament proceeded to pass articles two and three, guaranteeing the Hanoverian succession in Scotland and a unified parliament of Great Britain, respectively.

DEFOE TO ROBERT HARLEY, 14 NOVEMBER 1706

S^r

I Sent you a Post or Two Sinće My Ld Bellhavens speech wch I presume has Diverted you; I Enclose you a short Coment Upon it⁴ wch has made Some sport here and p[er]haps Done More Serviće than a More Solid Discourse.

Sinće my last^a ye Parliam^t Voted the act for ye security of the Church and Refused ye Articles ye Church Recommended,⁵ at wch the Church are Very angry and ye Rabble at Glasgow has been Very Tumultuous upon that h[e]ad.^b

The Church has to day Voted an Adress to Cure ye suggestion to[o]^c justly Cast on them against ye succession, Viz: that the Growth of popery may be prevented, ye Open profession of it suppresst — That ye succession being Undeclard Gives ye Greatest hopes to ye party of ye prinće of Wales &c.⁶

This is a Healer but Does not fully Recompense ye folly of their last.⁷

To Day the house has Debated whether they shall go upon ye second article wth a proviso or begin at ye 4th Article and have Agreed to go upon ye second⁸ but the Majority is not^d above 25 whereas they Carryed it against ye Church affair by a Majority of 70⁹ and a good jest at ye End of it, that all the protestors and adherers — wch were 25 — were of Such as were ye known Enemies of ye Church.¹⁰

Twas Very odd and Diverting to find these Gentlemen Vote that ye Act was not a Security Suffićent for ye Church and Espećially Sr Alex^a Bruće Now E of Kincarn formerly Expelld the house for sayeing the presbyterian Church was Inconsistent with Monarchy.¹¹

I Ask your Pardon for my Brevity and am

S^r

yor Hon^rs Most Obed^t Servt

DF

The floods here are So great I question Even ye post being able to Travail.¹²

---

^a my last] 'mylast' *in MS*
^b h[e]ad] 'e' *omitted*
^c to[o]] 'o' *omitted*
^d not] *following word possibly* 'yet' *cancelled*

256

DEFOE TO ROBERT HARLEY, 14 NOVEMBER 1706

Edinb. Nov. 14. 1706

Text: BL Add. MS. 70291, fols. 80–1. *Address* (fol. 81v): To The Right Honble | Robert Harley Esqr | Princípall Secreta of State | Present. *Endorsed by Harley* (fol. 81v): Edenburg nov: 14 1706 R nov: 20. *Endorsed by an unknown hand*: Mr De Foe

1 The Act is printed with Defoe's commentary in *Review*, III, 721–4 (28 Nov. 1706). It is not to be confused with the 1704 Act of Security that threatened to terminate the union of crowns.

2 H.M.C. *Portland MSS*, IV, 348.

3 Clerk, 121; *Lockhart Memoirs*, 135.

4 *short Coment Upon it*: The enclosure is missing but was a draft or copy of Defoe's *The Vision* (see headnote to Letter 60). A manuscript copy of *The Vision* survives in the Harley family papers, which may be the one Defoe sent (Nottingham University Library, Pw V 186).

5 *Parliamt ... Recommended*: For the substance of the second address, see Letter 61, note 11. Though Defoe says that the concerns were ignored, those about the sacramental test and the coronation oath were addressed in the Act of Security; and a new overture for an act concerning the plantation of churches came to parliament (*History of the Union, TDH*, VIII, 214).

6 *Church ... Wales &c.*: The third address of the Commission, submitted to parliament on 15 Nov. 1706 (NRS PA 7/20/25; Bowie, *Addresses*, 58–61). It is included in *Review*, III, 735–8 (5 Dec. 1706). It decried the activities of Episcopalians and Jacobites, requesting parliament *'utterly to extinguish the Hopes of a Popish Successor, and to establish the Succession of the Crown in the Protestant Line'*.

7 *Healer ... last*: I.e. the third address is welcome, but does not excuse the second one. For Harley's perception of the Commission's first three addresses and conduct as a whole, see his letter to William Carstares on 7 Jan. 1707, in Joseph M'Cormick, *State-Papers and Letters, Addressed to William Carstares* (1774), 757. See Carstares to Harley, 5–7 Dec. 1706, BL Add. MS. 70039, fols. 113–14. For Carstares, see Letter 90, note 3.

8 *To Day ... second*: The second article secured the Hanoverian succession; the proviso was that it would only come into effect if the Union as a whole were approved. Bennet's diary indicates that there was a pro-Union rationale for leaving the settlement open, as it was Scotland's best bargaining chip ahead of the articles concerning trade (NRS GD 90/2/172/2/10). The fourth article gave Scots equal trading rights in England and its colonies (*History, TDH*, VIII, 60).

9 *Majority ... Majority of 70*: The vote on the Act of Security was 112 to 38; that on proceeding to vote on article two rather than skipping to article four was 112 to 84 (*APS*, XI, 321–4).

10 *good jest ... Church*: The 'jest' may be the Court party's insistence that the names of the protestors against the adequacy of the Act of Security be printed, as the Country party had done for those members voting for the first article. The protestors are duly listed in the parliamentary minutes, numbering twenty-four, not twenty-five. Defoe thought this 'opened the Eyes of many of the People, when they saw such People Voting for the Church, who never own'd the Church in their Lives', meaning Episcopalians and Jacobites (*History, TDH*, VIII, 55–6, 59). In the *Review* for 7 Dec. 1706, Defoe gives the number of protestors against the act as not sufficient as '25 or 29'; settling on the latter number, he calculates that of those '22 at least' had never entered a Presbyterian church (III, 739), which is likely an exaggeration.

11 *Sr Alexa Bruce ... Monarchy*: Sir Alexander Bruce of Broomhall, fourth Earl of Kincardine (d. 1715). See H.M.C. *Portland MSS*, VIII, 249. His expulsion was in 1702 (Andrew Lang, *A History of Scotland from the Roman Occupation*, 4 vols. (Edinburgh, 1900–7), IV, 82). Defoe alludes to this again in *Review*, III, 739 (7 Dec. 1706).

12 *floods ... Travail*: In the *Review* for 1 May 1707, Defoe recalled 'the excessive Rains and unusual wet Weather, which prevented the People, that thought and contriv'd the Mischief of Rabbles and Arms, putting any thing in Practice – The Country being unpassable, and marching or lying abroad being impracticable' (IV, 176). Cf. *Review*, IV, 68 (13 Mar. 1707).

257

DEFOE TO ROBERT HARLEY, 16 NOVEMBER 1706

64

To Robert Harley

16 November 1706

Sr

Since My Last ye Parliamt have Voted The Second Article of The Treaty, Vizt yester-Night after long struggle and Severall attempts to put it off, as First — a Moćon to Make a Recess To Accqua her Majtie what a ferment ye Naćon was in and how ye Matter was Vigorously Opposed by The wholl Country and to lay it before her Majtie in An Humble Address.[1]

This was put to ye Question and past in ye Negativ or Rather, According to ye Method here, Delay or proceed, and Carryed proceed.

Then ye Main Question was Put, Approv ye Second[a] Article or Not Aprove, and Carry'd Approv by a Majority of 58.[2]

Thus in Parliamt sr Things go Right Enough, but Really Every Where Elće ye Naćon is in strange Confusion, and The Threatnings of ye Church Party are Very high and playn.

The Rabble at Glasgow has Driven ye Provost Out of ye Town and he is fled hither; ye Reason was he would Not Address.[3] They have sent up Their Address and a great Many whose hands Are to it have Sent Up Letters to ye Ld Chancelor That They were forćed to sign it Against Their Minds.[4]

Yet The Address was Recd and Read. The Provost flyeing for his life, They have broken up his house and Plundred or Defaćt his goods. The Lenity of ye Governmt is Taken as Fear and ye Kirk is stark Mad that They have as They Say No Security and that their Articles are Rejected.[5]

The Cameronian Adress,[6] tho' of No great Moment, I Send because you should See some of ye spirit; for tho' Hepburn[7] yt Sends it is a Mad Man (that is Mad in Zeal) and has been Deposed and Disowned by The Kirk, yet, They Talk his Very Language Now Every Day in Their Comon Discourse and I Dined to Day wth a Minister[8] who Told me were ye Weather p[er]mitting They would

[a] Second] *interlined above cancelled word* 'Third'

258

DEFOE TO ROBERT HARLEY, 16 NOVEMBER 1706

have been at Edinburgh before Now wth 15000 men. They Excercise Their Men and Appear wth Arms and Drums in Glasgow,[9] and Indeed these Things Tend to a strange Conclusion.

The Next Sitting of Parliam^t will Enter On ye Main question, I Mean ye 3^d Article,[10] and If it pass we shall see whether they Dare make any Disturbance or no.

I Wish her Maj^tie would be pleased to have Some forces On ye bord^r, for if There is ye least Violence here all will be in Blood; an appearance of Some Regiments on ye Border would at least Encourage the Troops here who are not otherwise to be Depended on.[11] You will Excuse my presumtion in offring any thing that looks like^a Direcçon; No Doubt her Maj^tie will let Nothing be wanting here to Succor That Intrest wch Appears So hearty^b and wch if They are Not supported will if an Accid^t happens be Sacrifiz'd to all Manner of ye Most Barbarous Insults.

yor Most Obed^t Servt

DF

Nov. 16. 1706

Text: BL Add. MS. 70291, fols. 82–3. *Address* (fol. 83^v): To The Right Honble | Robert Harley Esqr | Prinçipall Secretary of State | Present. *Endorsed by Harley* (fol. 83^v): Edenburg nov: 16 1706 R nov: 22:

---

^a that looks like] *interlined above cancelled words* 'by way of'
^b hearty] *following word* 'here' *cancelled*

---

1 *Moçon ... Address*: On 15 Nov., an unsuccessful motion was put before parliament 'To Address Her Majesty, and to lay before Her the Condition of the Nation, and the great Aversion in many Persons to an Incorporating Union with *England*, and to acquaint Her Majesty of the Inclinations and Willingness to settle the Succession in the Protestant Line upon Limitations' (*History of the Union, TDH*, VIII, 60–2). Annandale proposed it and Hamilton was among those who seconded it. Bennet gives a detailed summary of the debates (NRS GD 90/2/172/2/10–11), as does Sir James Murray (1655–1708), Lord Philiphaugh, writing to Godolphin(?) on 16 Nov. 1706 (*Marchmont Papers*, III, 427–30).

2 *Majority of 58*: The vote was 115 to 57 (*APS*, XI, 326–7). Defoe explains in his *History* that article two divided the opposition into those willing to accept the Protestant succession instead of Union and Jacobites opposed to settling the succession against the Pretender on any terms: hence the reduction in the opposition vote (*TDH*, VIII, 67–8).

3 *Rabble ... Address*: Following the disruption of 7 Nov. 1706 (see Letter 62, note 9), on 11 Nov. a mob formed in Glasgow to protest against the Provost, John Aird the younger (1655–1730), and the town council, who opposed an address to parliament against the Union. According to Lockhart, 'great numbers betook themselves to arms, drove the magistrates out of town, insulted everybody that they thought favoured, or was so much as lukewarm in disclaiming,

DEFOE TO ROBERT HARLEY, 16 NOVEMBER 1706

the Union, mounted guards, and rambled about for two or three days together' (*Lockhart Memoirs*, 177). Defoe recounts these events in his *History*, calling Aird 'an Honest, Sober, Discreet Gentleman, one that had always been exceedingly beloved, even by the common People' (*TDH*, VII, 316–20). In his *History*, Defoe states that these events occurred on 8 Nov. – 'the next day' following his discussion of 7 Nov. (*TDH*, VII, 318). Contemporary sources indicate that it was on 11 Nov. (James Wodrow to Robert Wodrow, 13 Nov. 1706, NLS Wodrow Letters Quarto IV. fol. 157; James Brown (d. 1714), minister at St Mungo's in Glasgow, to John Stirling (1666–1738), 15 Nov. 1706, University of Glasgow Library, MS Murray 650/1/84).

4 *Address ... Minds*: The Glasgow address uses the text of the address of the Convention of Royal Burghs (NRS PA 7/28/34; Bowie, *Addresses*, 144–6). It was read in parliament on 15 Nov. 1706 and had 390 signatures. 'Many a mean Step they took to get Hands, by Threatning, Affrighting, and Hurrying People into it', Defoe said (*History*, *TDH*, VII, 319).

5 *Articles are Rejected*: See Letter 63.

6 *Cameronian Adress*: What Defoe calls the 'Cameronian Adress' was read in parliament on 12 Nov. 1706 (NRS PA 7/28/22; Bowie, *Addresses*, 206–9). It declared the impossibility of uniting with 'a Nation deeply guilty of Many National Abominations, who have openly broke and burnt their Covenant with God and league with us, entred into, in the Year 1643'. Union would require the mutual renewal of the Solemn League and Covenant. This is the one address against incorporating union received by parliament that did not come from a recognised political body. Bennet reports that it 'gave birth to much Laūghter' in parliament (NRS GD 90/2/172/2/10).

Defoe, like many contemporaries, conflates the Cameronians, followers of Richard Cameron (*c.* 1648–80), and the Hebronites (see next note), though these were distinct Covenanting groups (Presbyterians separate from the Church of Scotland). Here, then, he is discussing the Hebronite address of Nov. 1706. The Cameronians protested against the Union much later, retroactively, in Oct. 1707.

Elsewhere Defoe dismissed the address as 'against all Union whatever' but having only seven signatories in addition to that of Hepburn (*Review*, III, 723–4 (28 Nov. 1706); III, 830 (21 Jan. 1707); *History*, *TDH*, VII, 275). In 1707, Defoe challenged Charles Leslie's claim in *The Rehearsal*s for 12 and 16 July 1707 that the extremist 'Cameronian address' typified Presbyterian antipathy to the Union. Defoe argued that, far from being representative, it was merely the work of 'Mr. *John Hepburn*, and a few weak, rash People under him, *Seven at most*, who neither own the Church of *Scotland*, nor the Government of *Scotland* and whose 'Principles are Condemn'd by the Church' (*Review*, IV, 457–8 (6 Sept. 1707); IV, 538–9 (11 Oct. 1707); IV, 601 (8 Nov. 1707)).

7 *Hepburn*: John Hepburn (*c.* 1649–1723), minister of Urr in Kirkcudbrightshire from 1680 to 1705, when, after several suspensions, he was deposed, though he continued to preach there as well as being a dissident field-preacher. Hepburn led a Covenanting group called the Hebronites. W. McMillan, *John Hepburn and the Hebronites* (1934) remains useful despite some errors. See D. Stevenson, 'Hepburn, John', in *Dictionary of Scottish Church History and Theology*, ed. Nigel M. de S. Cameron (Edinburgh, 1993), 399.

8 *Minister*: Unidentified.

9 *Excercise ... Glasgow*: This appears to refer not to any activity of Hepburn but to the projected conjunction of southwestern Covenanters led by Major James Cunningham of Aiket and highlander followers of Atholl; the plan was to converge and march on Edinburgh, though Cunningham was actually Queensberry's agent (*Lockhart Papers*, I, 197–200; Clerk, 144).

10 *3d Article*: It created the parliament of Great Britain.

11 *forces ... Depended on*: Unbeknownst to Defoe, the English government had at Leven's request recently dispatched troops to the border and to northern Ireland (Leven to Godolphin, 5 Nov. 1706, *Intimate Society Letters of the Eighteenth Century*, ed. Duke of Argyll, 2 vols. (Edinburgh, 1910), I, 52, 58; H.M.C. *Ormonde MSS*, VIII, 362–8).

65

To Robert Harley

19 November 1706

S^r

I have the Satisfaccon to write yor Hon^r that ye Parliam^t has Now Voted the Third Article by a Majority of 30.^{1}

I am not willing to fill you with ye Apprehensions of people here, Nor am I Very Flegmatick on That head my Self and Therefore when I shall Tell you that ye Commission^r has been Threatned wth Daggers, pistols &c. and Now That ye last Two Sittings^2 being within Dark he was Insulted by ye Rable in ye street at his Return,^{a} Great stones Thrown at his Coach and One of ye Guards wounded^3 — I yet shall add that [I]^b am Of Opinion his Graċe will go Thoro' wth ye Matter.^{4}

I Confess I Thought it an Ill Concerted Measure that last night the Comissioner Drove thro' ye Town so hastily, The foot Guards Runing and the Horse Galloping, at wch ye Mob Hallood and ye Enemy Insults Told us The Comisse^r was Run away &c. Indeed it betray'd too Much Concern, but That is not my business.^{5}

The Church has not yet Done, and Tho' In ye Review I am Defending her proceedings, which you will Easily p[er]ciev s^r I do Not that I like them, but to Checq ye Ill use will be made of it in England, yet I doubt she will go On till no honest man Can Defend her.^{6}

Addresses are Now Comeing In from ye Respectiv presbyteries in Ord^r to Justifye the^c Comisions first address,^{7} and as by ye Enclosed, wch is ye First of them,^{8} you will see ye Nature of them, so I doubt others will be worse yet.^{9}

All ye west is full of Tumult. Glasgow is mad. I was goeing to see what I Could do there but met severall of ye honest people flying and all advised me not to Venture, so I have much against my Will playd the Coward and made my Retreat but I think to go ye Next

---

^{a} Return] *following word* 'and' *cancelled*
^{b} shall add that [I]] *interlined;* 'I' *omitted*
^{c} the] *following letters* 'Chu' *(for* 'Church's'*) cancelled*

DEFOE TO ROBERT HARLEY, 19 NOVEMBER 1706

week Incognito if it be practicable,[10] onely to Observ and be Able to giv you Exact perticulars.

The Commission[r] is Come Down from y[e] house to day by Daylight where they have Debated but not yet[a] Voted y[e] Fourth Article[11] and they[b] Came Down without any Disturbance as I yet hear of.

The Ministers are quieter here now than before but in y[e] Enclosed petition or address you have Two in p[er]ticular who were here in y[e] Commission and[c] have been in the Country to procure it, Viz: Jo Bannatyne and Linning,[12] Two Firebrands and who Merit to be Markt as Incendiaryes of whose accons I Doubt I shall have Occasion to give you farther Acco[t] and I wish they dont bring themselves to want her Majtes Mercy.

I Do my Self y[e] Honour to Congratulate yo[r] Saf[e][d] arrivall from y[e] Country[13] and Especally if y[e] Waters have been Equally Violent as here where it Exceeds all that has been known in this Age.

I am

s[r]

(Tho' Impacent[e] to hear from you)

yo[r] Obed[t] Serv[t]

DF

Edinb. Nov. 19. 1706

Text: BL Add. MS. 70291, fols. 84–5. *Address* (fol. 85v): To[f] The Right Hon[ble] | Robert Harley Esq[r] | Her Majesties Principall Secret[a] of State | Present. *Endorsed by Harley* (fol. 85v): Edenburg nov: 19 1706 R nov: 25:

[a] Debated but not yet] *interlined*
[b] they] *interlined*
[c] and] *interlined above cancelled word* 'who'
[d] Saf[e]] 'e' *omitted*
[e] (Tho' Impacent] 'Tho' (Impacent' *in MS*
[f] To] *following letter* 'M' *(perhaps for* 'Mr') *cancelled*

1   *Parliam[t] … 30*: Article three passed on 18 Nov. 1706 by 112 votes to 83 (*APS*, XI, 329–30) with the proviso that it be binding only when the Union was finalised (*History of the Union, TDH*, VIII, 68–70).
2   *last Two Sittings*: I.e. on 15 and 18 Nov. Defoe discusses the latter here.
3   *Guards wounded*: Writing to his brother George Hamilton (1666–1737), first Earl of Orkney, on 16 Nov., Hamilton mentions that a guard was hit in the face by a stone the night before (BL Add MS 70039, fols. 95–7; H.M.C. *Portland MSS*, VIII, 268).

DEFOE TO ROBERT HARLEY, 19 NOVEMBER 1706

4 *his Grace will go Thoro' wth ye Matter:* On the threats to Queensberry and his imperturbability, see *Review*, III, 774–5 (24 Dec. 1706).

5 *I Confess ... business:* See the assessment of the 18 Nov. attack on Queensberry – 'which I was an Eye Witness to', Defoe says – in his *History, TDH*, VIII, 81. He is unsure there whether the horses sped up because they had been startled or because the drivers were fearful. Bennet says that stones struck the coaches and knocked down the footmen, causing the horses to dash (NRS GD 90/2/172/2/10).

6 *The Church ... her:* In general terms, Defoe in the *Review* had stressed the shared interests of the Churches of England and Scotland since October, such as when he uses the analogy of 'two Sister Churches, ... both the same in their Nature, born of one Mother, *Religion*, begotten by one Father, *The Reformation*' (III, 664 (31 Oct. 1706)). Throughout Nov. he stressed that a shared civic interest will not negate ecclesiastical differences, and that Union is the best way of securing the Church of Scotland. However, Defoe's language here suggests that he refers to the defence of the Church of Scotland's activities undertaken in the *Review* commencing 30 Nov. 1706, rather than issues already in print. He insists that the fast called by the Church was neither incendiary nor anti-Union; he defends the Kirk's second address as more a pro forma register of protest against Episcopal elements confirmed by the Union Treaty than as an attempt to prevent the Union; and he affirms the Kirk's commitment to the Protestant succession in the Hanoverian line, as evidenced by their third address. Defoe imputes the aim of scuppering the Union not to the Kirk but to those in England who maliciously construe its actions. He is nonetheless ambivalent in his defence. For instance: 'I do not by my Exposition of things allow, that every thing done there is equally right, or with Respect to Time and Circumstances, concerted in the best Measures' (III, 725–38 (30 Nov., 3 Dec., 5 Dec. 1706); quotation at III, 735).

7 *Comissions first address:* See headnote to Letter 61. Retrospectively, Defoe called the Commission's first address 'Moderate and well Temper'd' (*History, TDH*, VII, 281).

8 *Enclosed wch is ye First of them:* The enclosure is missing from the correspondence but is identified in Defoe's next (Letter 67). On 18 Nov., parliament received the address from the Presbytery of Lanark, which had fifteen signatures (NRS PA 7/20/28; Bowie, *Addresses*, 272–4). It lamented that the Act of Security did not heed the particular concerns of the Commission of the General Assembly's second address (Letter 63).

9 *others will be worse yet:* Defoe's fears of further addresses from Scotland's presbyteries proved unfounded. The only others to come were from Dunblane and Hamilton, both read on 11 Dec., with twelve and twenty signatures, respectively (NRS PA 7/20/49; NRS PA 7/20/50; Bowie, *Addresses*, 265–71). See Letter 84 for Defoe's assessment of the Hamilton address.

10 *I think ... practicable:* Seemingly he did not go.

11 *Fourth Article:* On 19 Nov. 1706, the fourth article was read in parliament but voting delayed until the next sitting on 21 Nov. (*History, TDH*, VIII, 79).

12 *Jo Bannatyne and Linning:* John Bannatyne (see Letter 59); Thomas Linning (or Linnen) (d. 1733), minister of Lesmahagow in Lanark Presbytery, a former leader of the Cameronians. These two had proposed the Commission of the General Assembly petition the estates for a national fast (NRS Commission of the General Assembly, Scroll Minutes, CH 1/4/2, 9 Oct. 1706).

13 *yor Saf[e] arrivall from ye Country:* Presumably to London from his Herefordshire house, Brampton Bryan, for the start of the parliamentary session.

263

66

[Robert Harley] to Defoe

21 November 1706

HEADNOTE: Harley responded to Defoe's letters of 13 and 14 November, prompted by Defoe's account of his work with members of the committee looking at the calculation of the Equivalent and adjusting details of trade and commerce. Harley mentions an earlier letter he sent Defoe, which is untraced.[1] The 'Paper of Observations' that Harley sent was returned, as requested, in Defoe's reply, dated 28 Nov. This document is entitled 'Observations on a Paper Sent from Scotland in the Letters of the 7th of November Instant relateing to Severall Articles in the Treaty of Union'.[2] It impressed the need to pass the Union Treaty without amendments to the articles concerning trade and was the English response to a document sent from Scotland, described by Mar as 'a memorial of all thirr things wherein there appears a necessity of ane explanation' – which is to say, depending on one's point of view, a clarification of or an amendment to an article concerning trade or taxation.[3] On 20 November, Godolphin sent the 'Observations' to Harley along with some instructions for Defoe: 'I send you the memoriall transmitted from Scotland, by yr Lter of ye 7th wth ye paper of observations returned them since hence upon it. I believe yr Correspondent will have little more to doe, than to keep himself as near he can to ye Terms of this paper, since you will easily see by it that to allow ye explanations, in the Terms they desire them, would necessarily overturn the foundation upon which, the equivalent is Calculated.'[4] The following day, Harley transmitted the instructions to Defoe.

Novr 21. 1706.

Sir,

I recd Yesterday Your Letter of Novr 14th and this day that of the 13. from Yr Brother;[5] By last Post I wrote to You[6] the Cautions I thought necessary, Since You are intrusted in that affaire, that You may discharge Yrselfe, as becomes a lover of both Countryes. I was not then apprized of the particulars proposed for Yr consideration, but I have now obtained a Paper of Observations which were to be sent, in answer to ye Memoriall come from Scotland,[7] that will sufficiently informe You of the State of this matter, and Yr own Prudence will conduct You in it; But I must add this Caution, that You do not by any means ever suffer this Paper to be seene,

[ROBERT HARLEY] TO DEFOE, 21 NOVEMBER 1706

therefore pray transcribe the substance of it in an other forme and returne me the Originall, and be cautious, not to let the similitude of Phrases ever discover that You have seen it.

I very much approve Y^r writing to ye L^{d8} You mention; he is one I have great respect for, and have long^a <u>servd</u>; But I desire You will not by any means let him imagine, You correspond with any one here, or have any motive, beside Your selfe for Y^r going thither; and then You may continue writing to him, and I will find [a]^b way to make it usefull to You.

The Ballad[9] is the best answer to that stuff.

Text: BL Add. MS. 70277, unfoliated. [A copy in a scribe's hand.] *Address in Robert Harley's hand*: Copy | to Mr A: Goldsmith | Nov: 21: 1706:

---

^{a} long] 'longd' *in MS*
^{b} [a]] *just a dot in MS*

---

1 For an account of this letter, and its first publication, see Paula R. Backscheider, 'Robert Harley to Daniel Defoe: A New Letter', *MLR* 83 (1988), 817–19.
2 BL Add. MS. 70039, fols. 90–1.
3 H.M.C. *Mar and Kellie MSS*, 310.
4 Godolphin to Harley, 20 [Nov. 1706], Longleat House, Portland MSS Appendix 11, fol. 204.
5 *that of the 13. from Y^r Brother*: Robert Davis's letter to Harley is untraced.
6 *I wrote to You*: Untraced.
7 *Memoriall come from Scotland*: See headnote. The memorial's progress can be traced in Mar's correspondence with Nairne. It was sent to London in early Nov., and the managers in Scotland were then eager to know their latitude for adjusting the articles in response to Scottish demands. On 16 Nov., Nairne said that the English ministers were inclined to accommodate reasonable demands. However, Mar's letter to Nairne of 26 Nov. is similar in outlook to Defoe's to Harley of 28 Nov. (Letter 70): having seen the English answer to the memorial, both Mar and Defoe agree with it that alterations are undesirable but are realistic enough to see that they are inevitable and can be at best minimised. See H.M.C. *Mar and Kellie MSS*, 313, 321, 325, 333–4. For some of the particulars – duty on the twopenny ale and drawbacks on oats – see Somers to Leven, 15 Nov. 1706, Fraser, *Melvilles*, 11, 206–8.
8 *Lord*: Halifax (see Letter 62).
9 *Ballad*: Defoe's ballad *The Vision* answered Belhaven's speech; Defoe had sent it to Harley on 14 Nov. (Letter 63).

67

To [Robert Harley]

[21–3] November 1706[1]

HEADNOTE (Letters 67–70): Defoe's letters from 21 to 29 November track debates in the Scottish parliament concerning articles five and six of the Union Treaty. Article five granted Scottish-owned ships full access to English ports; article six standardised excises and trade regulations. Defoe saw his role as helping to ease the articles through parliament with a minimal number of amendments that would alarm England. As per his instructions, he maintained secrecy about his employment by the English government. Defoe also continued to work with the committee appointed to examine the Equivalent and articles of trade, where he had gained a considerable degree of trust and influenced decisions, as well as liaising with members of the Commission of the General Assembly, whose actions he continued to find self-defeating and inflammatory. Popular protests against the Union continued in Edinburgh and the country at large. In terms of his own pecuniary situation, Defoe was chary of spending too much government money but also concerned that his family at home remained in need.

Sr

In my Last I gave you the address of the Pressbytery of ......[2] and it was feared that all ye presbyterys would do the like, Nor do I question but Endeavours have been and Are still Used to procure them, tho' I hear of no more yet Come in.

The Eyes of ye people begin a little to Open and I had ye honour to hear an Assembly man tell me yesterday he was afraid some were gone too far and that they were to be onely the Cats foot,[3] and he would have no more to do in it. I do not Claim ye honour of Converting him tho' he Complimts me on that head.

But my last Essay[4] wch I Transmitted to yor honor by post has had some Effect, for Hodges's book[5] wch Indeed has done more Mischief than a thousand men is so much Exposed Now that it is grown into Contempt and a Gentleman did me the honour to Tell me to day that it has stopt Three addresses wch were Comeing Out of ye North and that a Gentleman Reading it among about 20 that had Resolvd to address they all layd it aside.[6]

DEFOE TO [ROBERT HARLEY], [21–3] NOVEMBER 1706

I am not pleading my Merit Sr but to let you see how Easily this people have been Imposed upon that a Little plain arguing would bring them to Reason again.

I hope things begin to look a little better here; they have Given some Vent in ye partyes to ye first fury and Now ye three first Articles are Over they seem to be Calmer.

At Glasgow We hear of no more Tumults tho' here was a flying Report of 15000 men[7] Got together.

Coll Areskin[8] is highly blamd, Even by his Own friends, for his Imprudencĕ; who being Provost of Sterling Drew Out the Militia to sign an adress, and wth his sword Drawn in One hand, and his pen in the Other, signd it, and made the Rest do so also; wth some Very Indecent Expressions, which in any Governmt but One so Mild and forbearing as this Would have been Otherwise Resented; but he is a Malecontent and Declining in his fortunes, tho' otherwise a Very honest Man.[9]

However these things do them no service, Nor has it been any help to them — that Fletcher of Saltoun made a speech to Tell ye parliamt the Trade to England was No advantage to them:[10] or to see 20 Members Vote against a Communication of Trade wth England in which Even Duke Hamilton himself abandon'd them,[11] and a Very pretty proposall was offred as follows, wch None of ym Could answer.

Why Gentlemen are you against ye Clause? if ye Communication of Trade be no advantage, is it Not a passive Article? Can't we let it alone, and make no use of it? the English by this Article dont bind us to Trade, they Onely lay Open their Trade to us, to Enter into or let it alone, why should we Refuse the liberty?

They go to morrow on ye 5th Article;[12] they have been Debateing it last sitting, and here is a mighty popular objeccon against on Accot of their shipping.

The Enclosed[13] will Explain it more p[er]ticularly, wch I wrot at ye Desire of the E's of Abercorn,[14] Sutherland,[15] and some[a] Members of ye Commons,[16] to prepare ym against to morrows Debate.

---

[a] some] *following letters* 'oth' *(for* 'other'*) cancelled*

DEFOE TO [ROBERT HARLEY], [21–3] NOVEMBER 1706

And thus I believ I must do, on Every article as they Come to be Debated; the Objeccons in some Cases are so Dull and so gross, and yet so puslie[17] on One side, and the honest Gentlemen So Ill informd of things here on ye Other,[a] that Really I blush for them sometimes, and am asham'd to Instruct men, who I thought I had not been Able to Informe of any thing.

They have Reprinted the book of Rates[18] here, tho' it is not yet published — but I foresee they will want an Exposition upon it, for many that have seen it, are Not One Jott ye Wiser, and honestly protest not to Understand it.[19]

They go on Calmly now — but some foresee that there will be the Greatest strugle, about ye Generall, when after all ye p[er]ticulars are Run Thoro' they shall be in Danger at last in passing the Generall[b] questions. On this some of the Lds that are Sincere friends to it, and Undr some Concern on that perticular Accot, sent to me yesterday, to Desire I would write One Essay more On ye Generalls of the Union, the Common Intrests of Trade, Governmt and Religion[20] — This as within my sphere, and ye substance of my Silent Comission hither, (pardon me that freedom) I have accepted wth Some seeming Reluctance, as haveing Raised me Enemies[21] here allready &c.

If this be finished time Enough, I hope it may be of Service, and I shall not be spareing to Disperse them, tho' I Venture putting you to Some Charge sr, and Indeed I am a Chargeable Messengr to you, but if I had been to spend my Own Money, I profess I Could not have forborn these things, and for ye sake of publick service should have Ruin'd my self.

If I am too forward, I beseech you Sr Restrain me by your Ordrs, for I have no Other Uneasiness, — I seek the service by the Directest methods, I am master of, — if[c] I Err, ye missfortune will be mine, but Indeed[d] Sr want of Instruccons, is a Mellancholly Refleccon, and makes me Frequently think my self an Unworthy Instrument.[22]

---

[a] on ye Other] *interlined*
[b] Generall] *interlined above cancelled word* 'Severall'
[c] if] *anterior word* 'but' *cancelled*
[d] Indeed] 'Indeed Indeed' *in MS*

DEFOE TO [ROBERT HARLEY], [21–3] NOVEMBER 1706

However to my Power I Resolve
to be Dilig^t and Faithfull
as becomes
yor Ob^t Servt
[*monogram*]

Edinb. Nov. 23.^a 1706

I Can Not but hint s^r my Own Missfortunes²³ to yor Remembranće and by you to her Maj^{ties} goodness as you were pleased to give me Room to Expect.

Text: BL Add. MS. 70291, fols. 88–9. *Address*: none. *Endorsed by Harley* (fol. 89ᵛ): Edenburg nov: 23: 1706 R nov: 29:

---

^a 23] *reading uncertain; see note 1*

1 Letters 67 and 68 seem to have been written and sent simultaneously. Letter 67 refers to parliament debating article 5 'to morrow', implying Defoe wrote it on 21 Nov., but the date at the end, amended by Defoe and now difficult to read, appears to be 'Nov. 23', which is how Harley read it when he endorsed the letter. Letter 68, undated and unendorsed, begins 'Since the Other part', apparently referring to Letter 67, and then refers to 'the Vote yesterday Upon ye fourth Article', dating it to 22 Nov. However, in Letter 68 Defoe also supposes that the 'next meeting of Parliament' will be on Wednesday, which points to 27 Nov., when parliament actually met on Saturday 23 and Tuesday 26 Nov. That might argue for Letter 68 having been completed on 23 Nov., reducing what is otherwise an inexplicable error. If the two were sent together, Defoe probably amended the date of Letter 67 to 23 Nov. after he had added Letter 68 to it.
2 *address of the Pressbytery of* . . . . . .: Lanark. The enclosure is missing from the correspondence (see Letter 65).
3 *Cats foot*: Alluding to the fable of a fox or a monkey using a cat's paw to remove roasted chestnuts from burning coals: hence a dupe or a tool. Defoe uses the idiom – 'a Cat's Foot to put in the Fire' – in *Greenshields Out of Prison* (1710), 13.
4 *my last Essay*: *A Fourth Essay, at Removing National Prejudices* (1706).
5 *Hodges's book*: James Hodges's *Rights and Interests of the Two British Monarchies*. See Letter 59, note 12.
6 *layd it aside*: I.e. decided not to address.
7 *15000 men*: See Letter 64.
8 *Coll Areskin*: Lt.-Col. John Erskine (1662–1743) of Carnock, Fife. He is not to be confused with Lt.-Col. John Erskine (1660–1733) of the Sand Haven, Culross, who was parliamentary commissioner in Stirling and deputy-governor of Stirling Castle. In his *A Tour thro' the Whole Island of Great Britain*, Defoe describes Erskine of Carnock as 'a very worthy and valuable Gentleman' (*TDH*, III, 211).
9 *Provost ... Man*: On 18 Nov., 'Erskine of Carnock combined mustering and petitioning by calling out the Stirling militia to sign an address from the burgh against incorporation, producing one of the largest local petitions with over 560 signatures, headed by his own' (Karin Bowie, 'A 1706 Manifesto for an Armed Rising against Incorporating Union 1706,' *SHR* 94 (2015), 237–67 (at 256)). The petition was read in parliament on 23 Nov. 1706 and then printed in *The Following Two Addresses were Presented and Read in Parliament* (NRS PA 7/28/48; Bowie, *Addresses*, 166–8). Though Defoe points to coercive tactics to gain signatures,

269

DEFOE TO [ROBERT HARLEY], [21–3] NOVEMBER 1706

the articles of Union had been burned at Stirling on 4 Nov., suggesting significant levels of dissatisfaction with it in the burgh (H.M.C. *Mar and Kellie MSS*, 347).

10 *Fletcher … them*: On 19 Nov., Fletcher spoke of the disadvantages to Scotland of the communication of trade as proposed in the fourth article, contending that because trade branched off into multiple areas each should be considered separately. Debate ran into the following sitting, after which article four passed. Mar reports that Fletcher was so angry at the article's passage on 21 Nov. that he stormed out of the House (H.M.C. *Mar and Kellie MSS*, 328, 330).

11 *20 … them*: The vote was 154 to 19; Hamilton recorded no vote but numerous opposition members voted for article four (*APS*, XI, 332–4).

12 *5th Article*: Article five, approved on 23 Nov., brought Scottish-owned ships, even ones built abroad, under the purview of the English Navigation Acts, allowing them free trade with England and her colonies.

13 *Enclosed*: Missing from the correspondence; probably Defoe's *Observations on the Fifth Article of the Treaty of Union, Humbly Offered to the Consideration of the Parliament, Relating to Foreign Ships* (1706). The debate about article five concerned when Scottish vessels should be given the freedom of English ports and what to do in case of partial ownership. Defoe's *Observations* argued that the deadline should be the signing of the Treaty, not its ratification, because a lapse would enable merchants to buy foreign ships now and have them made free. And Defoe reasoned that Scottish majority ownership of a ship should be enough to qualify it.

14 *Abercorn*: James Hamilton, sixth Earl of Abercorn (*c.* 1661–1734).

15 *Sutherland*: John Gordon, sixteenth Earl of Sutherland (*c.* 1650–1734), a Union commissioner and Squadrone member. Defoe recalls him leading a regiment of highlanders in review before William III (*Review*, III, 785 (28 Dec. 1706)).

16 *Members of yᵉ Commons*: Unidentified. Defoe means representatives of the royal burghs or shires, as opposed to the nobility: the Scottish parliament was unicameral.

17 *puslie*: Perhaps related to *pusill*: 'weak' (*OED*).

18 *book of Rates*: It listed custom duties in England. Hamilton led the request for its publication (H.M.C. *Portland MSS*, VIII, 256; BL Add. MS. 70039, fol. 78). The request that this be printed was perceived as another opposition delaying tactic (H.M.C. *Mar and Kellie MSS*, 297).

19 *they … Understand it*: See the similar statement in *History of the Union*, TDH, VIII, 15.

20 *Essay … Religion*: Defoe, *A Fifth Essay, at Removing National Prejudices* (1707), PEW, IV, 145–74.

21 *Enemies*: The main tracts (all 1706) criticising Defoe's earlier *Essays at Removing National Prejudices* to which he responds in the *Fifth* are Patrick Abercromby's (1656–*c.* 1716) *The Advantages of the Act of Security*, the anonymous *A Letter Concerning the Consequences of an Incorporating Union, in Relation to Trade*, and William Black's (d. 1745) *A Letter Concerning the Remarks upon the Considerations of Trade, by the Author of the 4th Essay, at Removing National Prejudices*.

22 *Unworthy Instrument*: Defoe refers to himself as 'an unworthy Instrument' in *A Letter to Mr. How* (1701), 6; the epithet is applied to Will Atkins in *The Farther Adventures of Robinson Crusoe* (1719), *Novels*, II, 107.

23 *Missfortunes*: Defoe later tells Harley that his wife has written to him about this time that she has been without money for ten days (Letter 69).

DEFOE TO [ROBERT HARLEY], [22 NOVEMBER 1706]

68

To [Robert Harley]

[22 November 1706]

Sr

Since the Other part[1] I have attended ye Committee;[2] The first false step I Discovred was that the Vote yesterday Upon ye fourth Article was Design'd as an alteraçon of ye Articles.[3]

I Took ye Freedom to say if they broke in Upon ye Articles to alter the Terms of them, they Unravelld ye Treaty and would Come to ye Necessity of a New Commission[4] — But that I Conciev'd all their Amendments or Regulations Might be brought into an act Explanatory of ye Articles and founded Upon them, and while these Explanations Consisted wth Equallity, proporçons and Reasonable Construcçons, they might Expect ye parliamt of England would hear Reason, whereas if they went on to Direct Alteraçons they would fall into Inextricable Difficultyes and indeed Dissolve ye Treaty or at least Endanger it — This They all adher'd to and Resolve to Call ye Vote of yesterday an Explanation in ye Minutes if they Can, tho' p[er]haps that may be too late.

Then they Desir'd my Opinion of their Demand of a Draw back on Peas,[a] Oates and Oat Meal, wch the Northern Members press for and ye people are Very Clamarous About.

I put them off from a Bounty on Oates or Peas by assureing them England will allwayes buy them and there Could be No Pretençe for a Drawback or bounty for Exporting that wch was allwayes wanted at home.[5] The justiçe of this prevaild wth the Comittee and so they have agreed to wave that.

But On Oats Ground or Oat Meal they are positive and Really the Reason of it Convinçes me — They Drive a great Trade to Norway for Deals and Timber and they purchase them and sometimes bring Silver to boot wth their Oat Meal.

On ye Other hand[b] from Ireland They do ye like and Undersell Scotland, and The Bounty will Enable ye Scots to Send larger

---

[a] Peas] interlined
[b] hand] following illegible word cancelled

DEFOE TO [ROBERT HARLEY], [22 NOVEMBER 1706]

quantityes — and I Can not but Add (to you s^r) This May Help England who Now Trades to Norway wholly for Ready Money and p[er]haps in Time May Come to Save a great Deal of it by supplyeing them wth Oatmeal —

So their Explanation On this Article is to have 2^s:6 Draw back on Oatmeal Onely p[er] Quarter.[6]

Then we had a long Debate what Price ye Oat meal must bear when y^{ea} Bounty should be Due, and ye price of Oat meal being an Uncertain thing Especally in England and hard to Determine, I Offred an Expedient, Viz^t that the price should be stated on ye wholl Corn. I proposed 12^s p[er] Quarter, My L^d presid^{t7} Demanded it at 20, m^r Paterson[8] Offred it at 13^s. 4^d, and there it^b passed, and so ye Amendment will be thus.

That a Bounty of 2^s 6^d p[er] Quarter on Oatmeal shall be Allowed when ye price of Oates in ye Port where ye S^d Oatmeal shall be Exported does not Exceed^c 13^s. 4^d p[er] Quarter.[9]

This I presume will be ye Work of ye next meeting of the parliament and if they get it pass'd as proposed and ye Amendments offred by way of Explanations I hope all will be agreeable to England and to ye Common Intrest.

The Committe then proceeded to ye Matter of ye Excise and Very great Difficultys Appear'd there.

They all Insisted that by True proporcon and the Rules of Equallity their two penny Ale here Ought to pay but as small beer — But ye people are Uneasy and affraid to be left to ye Mercy of ye Excise Office to Construe ye Law Upon them.

And Indeed ye Clamour of ye people would be Intollerable should the strong beer Duty be Demanded on their Ale wch tho' Called ale is^d little better than small beer and Really sells Under 10^s p[er] barrell.

However to Come to a Certainty they are Content that the Excise Come up to a proporcon and this they Calculate at 2^s p[er] Barrell and so ye people pay 9^s p[er] barrell Onely to be sure, and to

[a] ye] *following word* 'Duty' *cancelled*
[b] it] *following word probably* 'is' *cancelled*
[c] Exceed] *following illegible word cancelled*
[d] is] *following word probably* 'no' *cancelled*

DEFOE TO [ROBERT HARLEY], [22 NOVEMBER 1706]

bring this to be offred in ye Terms of an Explanation Their L^dships
put it Upon me to Draw it up for them against the next meeting of
Parliament which Will I Suppose be Wednesday[10] — The Rough
of ye Said Draught I herewith Enclose,[11] Your Hono^r, and wish I
had Time to have yor Opinion of it — I have done it with as Much
Indifferenĉe and Impartiallity to both Sides as I Can, and as I See
no shaddow of any Other Medium I believ it will be Approv'd here,
and I hope in England too.

The Draw back on Salt[12] will be ye Next Difficulty, and There
is a strong Demand for a Draw back on Their Pork Exported for
Sale[13] — I Menĉoned it and M^r P . . . n[14] Thought I had started
it for them, and hinted as Much after we Came Out, wch Onely
Serv'd to Convinĉe me he Converst wth but few, Sinĉe The
Merchants Concernd are Many, and Make a great Crye about it,
and I Think it Every Mans bussiness that wishes well to This work
to Allay The spirits of this Agitated people at ye Expenĉe of Every
Thing that Can be Easily parted with.

Tis true Draw Backs and Bountys will Put back ye Equivalent,[15]
but They are but Few and ye Consequenĉe of Denying y^m Very
Great; when pd They are pd by Themselves and I Dare say the
Reasons will sway England to do any Reasonable Thing to make
This people Easy.

I Wish my Ld Treasurer[16] Inform'd That a Report was spread
her[e][a] when My Ld Anandale proposed the succession w^th
Limitaĉons inste[ad][b] of the Union,[17] That There was a Letter
in Town From his L^dship to Direct the Accepting it — and That
his L^dship Wondred They should Not Close with it at the First
Offer[18] —   DF

Text: BL Add. MS. 70291, fols. 86–7. *Address*: none.

---

[a] her[e]] *obscured by MS binding*
[b] inste[ad]] *obscured by MS binding*

---

1   *Other part*: Letter 67 (see Letter 67, note 1).
2   *Committee*: I.e. the committee to calculate the Equivalent and examine articles of trade.
3   *Vote … Articles*: The fourth article was approved on 21 Nov. with a proviso 'Reserving the
    Consideration of the several Branches of Trade, till the Parliament come to the Subsequent
    Articles' (*History of the Union, TDH*, VIII, 82). Despite Defoe's fears, alterations proved minor
    and did not prevent the ratification of the Treaty at Westminster.

DEFOE TO [ROBERT HARLEY], [22 NOVEMBER 1706]

4 *New Commission*: I.e. a new negotiation of the terms of the Union, as the articles negotiated by English and Scottish commissioners in 1706 will have been nullified.

5 *I put ... home*: See *Review*, III, 809 (11 Jan. 1707).

6 *Quarter*: 8 bushels, which is approximately 291 litres.

7 *Lᵈ presidᵗ*: James Graham (1682–1742), fourth Marquess of Montrose, later first Duke of Montrose, was Lord President of the Privy Council and a member of the committee for Equivalents. Defoe praises him in *Caledonia* (1706), lines 1014–23, *PEW*, IV, 259. He belonged to the Squadrone.

8 *mr Paterson*: William Paterson (see headnote to Letter 2). From 1705, he worked as a pro-Union propagandist for Harley, producing *An Inquiry into the Reasonableness and Consequences of an Union with Scotland* (1706). He advised the committee appointed to calculate the Equivalent and adjust articles of trade (H.M.C. *Portland MSS*, VIII, 243–4; BL Add. MS. 70039, fols. 36–7). See William Deringer, *Calculated Values: Finance, Politics, and the Quantitative Age* (Cambridge, Mass., 2018), 79–114.

9 *Bounty ... Quarter*: As Defoe explains in his *History*, England allowed drawbacks on certain grains, such as corn, but not on oats, because the latter were not plentiful enough to be exported from England, unlike Scotland; the Scots therefore requested a drawback on oatmeal (*TDH*, VIII, 88). When finalised, the drawback applied when the price was below fifteen shillings per quarter.

10 *next meeting ... Wednesday*: Defoe is in error. Parliament sat on Saturday 23, Tuesday 26, and Wednesday 27 Nov. See Letter 67, note 1.

11 *Draught I herewith Enclose*: Missing. The 'Explanation and Addition' for which Defoe is claiming responsibility was entered in the parliamentary minute for 28 Nov. (*History*, *TDH*, VIII, 92).

12 *Draw back on Salt*: Article eight concerned salt duties; it was remitted to the committee that was examining articles of trade. For the outcome, see Letters 79–81.

13 *Draw back on Their Pork Exported for Sale*: This was introduced on 26 Nov. 1706 and remitted the next day to the committee. For the outcome, see Letter 81.

14 *Mr P ... n*: Presumably Paterson.

15 *Put back yᵉ Equivalent*: I.e. require its recalculation.

16 *Lᵈ Treasurer*: Godolphin.

17 *Lᵈ Anandale ... Union*: William Johnston (1664–1721), first Marquess of Annandale. Prior to the vote on article one on 4 Nov. 1706, Annandale entered a resolve proposing to settle the succession with limitations instead of Union (*APS*, XI, 312–13, 325). Mar called this 'the opposing party's last shift' to block votes (H.M.C. *Mar and Kellie MSS*, 310–11) and correctly predicted it would be unsuccessful, as it was again when Annandale renewed it on 15 Nov., prior to the vote on article two. Annandale had first proposed this in 1705 (Burnet, V, 220–1). In his *History*, Defoe observes that this 'offering the Succession in stead of the Union' came too late, as the Union's limitations on the monarchy were better than what Scotland could negotiate, and because the Jacobites who formed a large component of the opposition were unwilling to accede to the Hanoverian succession (*TDH*, VIII, 67–8).

18 *Letter ... Offer*: This 'Letter' is unidentified. On 18 Nov. 1706, Robert Wodrow (1679-1734) commented in a letter to his father that Annandale's resolve was said to have the support of Godolphin and the 'Leading Whiggs in Eng:', who 'will be satisfyed to have the succession setled on Limitations, but our coûrtiers are resolved to pûsh on this Scheme of ye union' (NLS Wodrow Letters Quarto IV, fol. 112ᵛ). However, Godolphin's correspondence concerning Scotland indicates the improbability of his support for this measure (BL Add. MS. 6420, fols. 72–7). It was likely just rumour: Godolphin had been vulnerable to attack on Scotland since 1704 for 'having advised the royall assent to the act of security, which still hangs over his head' (Lockhart to Harry Maule of Kerrie (d. 1734), 4 June 1706, *Lockhart Letters*, 34).

DEFOE TO [ROBERT HARLEY], 26 NOVEMBER 1706

69

To [Robert Harley]

26 November 1706

S[r]

I Can Not Express to yo[r] Hon[r] what a Cordial y[e] favour of yo[r]
Letter[1] was to me After Such a strange and Surpriseing Silence.
I Thank God my Faith in yo[r] Regard to me was too firmly Fix't
to suffer me to Neglect my Duty, but I Own I have been Und[r]
Perplexitys and Discouragem[ts] Inumerable. I shall Trouble you no
More with them.

My Success here I am In hopes will Answer yo[r] Expectacons, tho'
the Difficultyes have been Infinite. If No Kirk Devills More Than
we yet Meet with appear I hope all will be well and I begin to See
thoro' it.

If I Understand the Caucons you are pleasd to give me in your
Letter, they Respect England as Much as Scotland, And Indeed I
am Afraid of Erring Most that way, and Am Therefore Very Wary.

Tho I will Not Answer for Success yet I Trust in Mannagem[t]
you shall not be Uneasy at yo[r] Trusting me here. I have Compass't
my First and Main step happily Enough, in That I am Perfectly
Unsuspect[d] as Corresponding wth anybody in England.[2] I Converse
wth Presbyterian, Episcopall-Dissenter, papist and Non Juror, and
I hope wth Equall Circumspeccon. I flatter my Self you will have
no Complaints of my Conduct. I have faithfull Emissaries in
Every Comp[a] And I Talk to Every body in Their Own way; to y[e]
Merchants I am about to Settle here in Trade, Building ships &c.;
with y[e] Lawyers I want to purchase a House and Land to bring my
family & live Upon it[3] (God knows where y[e] Money is to pay for
it); to day I am Goeing into Partnership with a Memb[r] of parliam[t]
in a Glass house, to morrow wth Another in a Salt work; wth y[e]
Glasgow Mutineers I am to be a fish Merchant, wth y[e] Aberdeen
Men a woollen, and with y[e] Perth and western men a Linen
Manufacturer, and still at the End of all Discourse the Union is the[a]
Essentiall and I am all to Every one that I may Gain some.[4]

[a] the] *following letters* 'Dis' *(perhaps for* 'Discourse') *cancelled*

275

DEFOE TO [ROBERT HARLEY], 26 NOVEMBER 1706

Again I am in ye Morning at ye Committee, in ye Afternoon in the assembley; I am privy to all their folly, I wish I Could not Call it knavery, and am Entirely Confided in.

Youl Pardon me this Excursion on my self, and bear wth This allay^5 to it, that I Really have spent a great Deal of your^a Money and am like to do More — yet p[er]haps not so Much as by m^r Bells Acco^t, Since he sent me in his last more and sooner than I Expected,^{6} of wch however I am not ye Worse husband and have above £20 yet in hand, tho' ye press Dreins me and I am something behind to it.

I Assure you s^r and Entreat you to believ me I am not in anything Extravagant in this sharping Dear place, But where the Design I am in presses me, There Indeed I am not spareing — My Own Affaires I have Recommended to^b you but too often, and had not menconed y^m Now tho' severely presst there, Onely to assure you I Can not Relieve y^m from Hence, Tho' My Wife wrott me last week she had been 10 dayes without Money — I submitt it all to that providence which when he sees Good will smile & Till then I must wait —

I shall strictly Observ your Direccons and act wth ye Uttmost Caution in Every Thing.

The Regulacon of ye Clause about forreign ships has pass'd aga^t the scheme I offred,^{7} but I shall Take ye first Occasion wth my Ld President to see them to Rights in Method.

While I wrott ye Above I am Sent for by My Ld Cessnock^8 to ye Committe where I Understand m^r Paterson is to be also Tho' I Never saw him there, yet the Result I shall add to this; that Gentleman is full of Calculates, figures and Unperforming Numbers, but I see nothing he has done here nor does any body Elce speak of him but in Terms I Care not to Repeat.^{9}

> I am
> S^r
> yor Most Obed^t Servt
> D F

^{a} your] *interlined*
^{b} to] *interlined*

276

DEFOE TO [ROBERT HARLEY], 26 NOVEMBER 1706

Edinb. Nov. 26. 1706

Text: BL Add. MS. 70291, fols. 90–1. *Address*: none. *Endorsed by Harley* (fol. 91ᵛ): Edenburg Nov: 26: 1706 R Dec: 2

1   *yor Letter*: Presumably the first response Harley mentions in his 21 Nov. letter, now untraced (see Letter 66, note 6).

2   *Unsuspectᵈ as Corresponding wᵗʰ anybody in England*: John Clerk of Penicuik says Defoe 'was sent to Scotland by the prime minister of England, the Earl of Godolphin, on purpose to give a faithful account to him from time to time how everything passed here. He was therefor a Spy amongst us, but not known to be such, otherways the the Mob of Edin. had pulled him to pieces' (*Memoirs of the Life of Sir John Clerk of Penicuik* (Edinburgh, 1892), 63–4).

3   *live Upon it*: A 1706 poetic attack on Defoe remarked: 'You in each Company are pleas'd to cant, | 'Tis here to Live, and here to Dwell, you want' (*A Second Defence of the Scotish Vision*).

4   *I am all to Every one that I may Gain some*: Adapting 1 Cor. 9:22. See Letter 14, note 55.

5   *allay*: 'An undesirable element' (*OED*). Usually it would be something that tarnishes something good, like a flaw in a diamond, but that is not quite how Defoe uses it here. Compare his usage when he says 'the *French* would give us a Blow somewhere, should mingle our Joy with some Allay' (*Review*, III, 420 (9 July 1706)).

6   *more and sooner than I Expected*: Bell provided Defoe with £52. 10s. 6d. on 9 Nov. (see Letter 62, note 11).

7   *Regulaċon ... offred*: In parliament on 23 Nov. 1706, 'the Time [when Scottish-owned ships would become British] was extended from the Time of Signing the Articles, as it was agreed in *London*, to the Time of Ratification in the Parliament of *Scotland*, but not to the Time of Ratification in both Parliaments, as was proposed' (*History of the Union, TDH*, VIII, 86). Defoe preferred for this to happen at the time of signing to prevent merchants from buying foreign ships in the interim and registering them as British, undermining home manufacture (see Letter 67).

8   *Lᵈ Cessnock*: Sir Alexander Hume-Campbell, Lord Cessnock (1675–1740), MP for Berwickshire. Defoe recounts attending a meeting of the committee at Cessnock's house in his *History, TDH*, VIII, 94–6.

9   *mr Paterson ... Repeat*: Defoe challenged Paterson on economic aspects of the Union in *An Essay at Removing National Prejudices against a Union with Scotland ... Part II* (1706), *PEW*, IV, 79, and *A Fourth Essay, at Removing National Prejudices* (1706), *PEW*, IV, 116, 131.

70

To [Robert Harley]

28 November 1706

Nov. 28. 1706

S^r

I have ye hono^r of yor Second Letter wth ye Enclosed paper of Observaçons which I have Transcrib'd and here Returnd According to yor Direcçons, and shall not Fail to Observe The Caučons you were pleasd to give me.[1]

The Gentlemen kept me So late y^e last post night[2] that I Closed yor Letter in Some Confusion, y^e post being just goeing Elče I had Sent this paper back that night.

I Observ by These papers it is Expected the parliam^t here should pass the Articles Entire[3] — I fear they will Never be Able to do that, but as I wrott you in m$\ddot{y}$ last they will Onely make their Demands and Explanations in an act of parliam^t wch they will Annex to y^e Union.

It is my Dayly bussiness to Convinče them and Remove New started Difficulties in this Case, and If it had not been my Good fortune to be there that Night they had blindly Gone into Direct Modelling the Articles.

The parliam^t has been Two dayes Upon ye Sixth Article and have at last Referr'd it back to the Committee[4] where I shall have some more Opportunity to Debate it wth them.

I gave you an Account what I had Done in the severall Cases of ye Oatmeal,[5] wch I hope y^e parliam^t will Confirme, but they have Altred the Rate of Oates from 13^s 4^d to 15^s p[er] Quart^r as y^e standard of Priče.

I have also proposed a Medium by wch I put them off from layeing any Duty or prohibition on Oates from Ireland, Not that it signifyed Much but that I Avoid$^{\textbf{a}}$ Loading the Case wth Amendments — I had a Great Tug about this Triffle for they would

---

$^{\textbf{a}}$ Avoid] *following letters probably* 'Clo' *(perhaps for* 'Clogging') *cancelled*

DEFOE TO [ROBERT HARLEY], 28 NOVEMBER 1706

have 16s p[er] Quarter on their Groats or Oatmeal and 8s p[er] Quarter on the Oates, wch must then have been Altred in England.

Looking in ye book of Rates it Appeares that in England[a] there is 5s p[er] Quarter on Oates now as Imported from Ireland — this I shewd them was sufficent still and might stand for ye wholl Island, Onely wth this Addition — that Every Quarter of Groats or Oatmeal shall be Deemd as three quarter of Oates wthin ye said act.[6]

This I believ will pass; The house to day has been warm Upon ye Draw backs on Oats and Peas, but ye Gentlemen of the Comitte stood their Ground On my Notion of their being allwayes a Market in England.

I Omitted Encloseing the Draught of my proposall for ye Excise for they kept me so long I had not a Minute for the post. I Ask yor pardon for ye Ommission and have[b] sent it herewith.[7]

This Terrible people ye Church men have not yet done; they have now in Debate a protestation Against the Act of Security as Insufficent,[8] God almighty Open their Eyes.[9]

Also here is a protestation today from ye West where they burnt the Articles.[10] I shall get a Coppy of it to send p[er] next post.

I am Sorry sr to see in ye paper you Enclosed me that all the Amendments seem to be Desir'd here to be Referrd to the parliamt of Brittain.[11]

I Dare say the Gentlemen here would Come in to it but should they Attempt it the wholl Treaty will be lost. The Very word Parliamt of Brittain, is Grown Terrible here, and the people are so foolishly posest wth their haveing No justice there that tis to Say Nothing to attempt it.

On ye Other hand the Entring into these few Amendmts or Explanations mightily quiets and Eases ye minds of ye people Especally of the wiser Sort.

I Take this Liberty sr On Two Accots:

First sr that I may have yor Ordrs that if I must not go on to Lessen their Demands or put ym off from some by Granting Others and ye like, but Insist plainly that They must pass the

---

[a] that in England] *interlined*
[b] have] *following word* 'here' *cancelled*

279

DEFOE TO [ROBERT HARLEY], 28 NOVEMBER 1706

articles and Referr the Rest &c, I may know how to Obey you punctually — but then I beseech you to bear with me In saying all yᵉ Intrest here would Never Carry yᵉ Union without blood.

Secondly I offer this, That if you Encline as I hope you will in England to Grant the heads, I Dare say they shall be Triffles and I hope to put them off from a great Deal that they now Insist upon.

I am sʳ yoʳ Most Obedᵗ Servᵗ
[*monogram*]

I Could not Refrain sending you a peic̈e of my Lᵈ Beilhavens Poetry in Answer to yᵉ Ballad.¹²

I Dare say you will believ it a meer Originall¹³ and I believ he may Challenge all yᵉ World to match it or to Answer i[t].ᵃ

You will also see by it I have mannagd so in yᵉ Ballad that he does not suspect it but believs it my Lᵈ Haddington.¹⁴

The Dʳ he means is yoʳ Next Neighbour — Dʳ W . . . d.¹⁵

This morning I put abroad privately the Enclosed lines upon it;¹⁶ also the ballad is printed.¹⁷

Text: BL Add. MS. 70291, fols. 92–3. *Address*: none. *Endorsed by Harley* (fol. 93ᵛ): Edenburg nov: 28 1706 ʀ De: 4:

ᵃ i[t]] *obscured by MS binding*

---

1 *Second Letter … me*: See Letter 66.
2 *last post night*: Tuesday 26 Nov., as per the previous letter. Post nights were Tuesday, Thursday, and Saturday.
3 *Expected … Entire*: The 'Observations' states: 'It is therefore apprehended here, that the Articles of the Treaty shou'd pass Entire' (BL Add. MS. 70039, fol. 90).
4 *Sixth Article … Committee*: Article six brought England and Scotland under the same trade regulations, customs, and duties. On 27 Nov., it was referred to the Equivalents and trade committee, expanded from nine to fifteen members, following debates on that and the preceding day which Defoe believed exposed the ignorance of objectors (*History of the Union*, TDH, vɪɪɪ, 89–92). Further detail of the debate is given by Bennet (NRS GD 90/2/172/2/13).
5 *Account … Oatmeal*: See Letter 68.
6 *Every … act*: The Union would remove Scottish legislation restricting the importation of Irish oats, but Defoe proposes the English tariff on oats, multiplied for oatmeal, will be sufficient to deter imports and encourage Scottish tillage. Here he proposes oatmeal tariffs at three times those of oats; in the *History* at double (*TDH*, vɪɪɪ, 88). Compare Seafield's contemporaneous assessment, which states that the English tariff is 5s 7d per quart and fears

DEFOE TO [ROBERT HARLEY], 28 NOVEMBER 1706

that it would need to be even higher to prevent Scotland importing Irish oats (H.M.C. *Laing MSS*, II, 137–8). The Treaty's articles ultimately left the pre-Union legislation in place.

7 *Draught ... herewith*: Missing.

8 *protestation Against the Act of Security as Insufficient*: Stephen quotes this and remarks 'There is no record of any debate in the Commission at that time about protesting against the act as insufficient' (*Scottish Presbyterians*, 90).

Although Defoe was confident that the Act provided a sufficient guarantee for the Church of Scotland, in 1712 when he wrote *The Present State of the Parties in Great Britain* during the passage of the Scottish Episcopal Toleration Act, Defoe lamented: 'I wish we had not since too much reason to say these Men [who feared the Act insufficient] were too much in the Right' (128). In the *Review* for 2 Feb. 1712, he points out that the Jacobites who hoped to scupper the Union by claiming that the Act of Security did not provide against the introduction in Scotland of liturgical worship were themselves now introducing liturgical worship by supporting the Episcopal Toleration Act (VIII, 610–11).

9 *God almighty Open their Eyes*: 2 Kings 6:17. Defoe also uses this verse in *Review*, V, 170 (12 June 1708); IX, 281 (17 Mar. 1713). These usages specifically invoke God; 'open their eyes', also alluding to Acts 26:18, is extremely common in Defoe's writings. See Letters 14, 67, 71, 74, 82, 84, 134, 148, 194, 199, 204, 206, 211, 212, 216, 217, and 239.

10 *protestation ... Articles*: Probably *An Account of the Burning of the Articles of Union at Dumfries* (1706). See Letter 62. This was not a formal address presented to parliament. Defoe reprinted it as an appendix in his *History*.

11 *Referrd to the parliamt of Brittain*: The 'Observations' states: 'Whatsoever may be thought fitt further to be asked for the Ease and Benefit of the people of Scotland may be laid before the Parliament of great Britain after the Union' (BL Add. MS. 70039, fol. 90).

12 *Ld Beilhavens Poetry in Answer to ye Ballad*: Belhaven's *A Scots Answer to a British Vision* [1706], in answer to Defoe's ballad *The Vision*.

13 *meer Originall*: entirely odd or eccentric.

14 *Ld Haddington*: Thomas Hamilton, sixth Earl of Haddington (1680–1735), of the Squadrone. See *POAS*, VII, 221.

15 *Dr W ... d*: *A Scots Answer* contains the following lines:

By this the World may see
Whence the Maggot does bite,
Since a Rake and a Cullie,
A Doctor and a Bullie,
Must touch a Court's Fee,
And do their worst to Unite. (*PEW*, IV, 379)

Defoe thus identifies the doctor as James Welwood (1652–1727), personal physician to William III and Mary II, and promoter of the 1688 Revolution. He lived, as did Harley, in York Buildings. The 'Bullie' is Haddington, as Belhaven supposed he and Welwood co-wrote *The Vision*.

16 *Enclosed lines upon it*: *A Reply to the Scot's Answer, to the British Vision* (1706), *PEW*, IV, 207–8, which heaps ironic praise on Belhaven as an orator and poet. Now missing from the correspondence.

17 *the ballad is printed*: *A Reply* was probably circulating in manuscript at the time; on 7 Dec., Mar wrote to Sir David Nairne: 'I have sent you a song on Balhaven, but it's not in print which is a pittie' (H.M.C. *Mar and Kellie MSS*, 351). It is not a ballad, however, so Defoe must mean *The Vision*, strengthening the suggestion that he previously sent Harley a manuscript of that on 14 Nov.

281

71

To Robert Harley

30 November 1706

HEADNOTE (**Letters 71–4**): Defoe's earlier letters report on unrest in Glasgow, which had first flared in the protest against the refusal of the Provost John Aird the younger to address parliament on 7 November. On 23 November, a crowd protesting the imprisonment of a tobacco-spinner named Parker for his part in the earlier riots mobbed the Provost and then seized arms. For the following week, this group defied the city magistrates and guard. On 29 November, a portion of the group left Glasgow to march on Edinburgh, led by one George Finlay, 'an Abject Scondrel Wretch, that openly profess'd himself a *Jacobite*', according to Defoe.[1] The plan was to rendezvous with other companies of disaffected men. The Glasgow men abided in Hamilton from 1 to 3 December. Parliament issued a proclamation against tumults and revoked the rights of citizens to muster and exercise with arms; but ironically the public reading of these decrees in Glasgow started fresh violence. The mob disarmed a makeshift city guard and 'had the City in their full Possession, and every Bodies Life and Goods at their Mercy'.[2] Finlay's march on Edinburgh meanwhile was aborted when reinforcements from other towns did not emerge, and they returned to Glasgow and disarmed themselves just before government forces arrived there. Finlay and another man, Andrew Montgomery, were arrested on 5 December and taken to Edinburgh, upon which their followers compelled the city magistrates to sue for their release, a request that was given no truck in Edinburgh. Wodrow's assessment, given on 2 December 1706, was that 'this ill managed matter has been one of ye Best handles ever ye coūrt had under colloūr of laū and Reason to crūsh all opposite measūres to ye union, and to ye perpetuall enslaving of ye nation'.[3] The Glasgow uprising, the largest violent resistance to Union, thereafter fizzled out.

Sr

The Parliamt has Sat Three times, sinċe I wrott to you — they have passt ye 7th Article not in ye Exact Terms but on ye foot of ye[a] paper I sent in my last.[4]

I am Sorry to say it but tis Really True the Union may be Carryed on and I hope perfected on Reasonable Explanations Never wth leaving it to ye p[ar]liamt of Brittain. Tis my sphere

---

[a] ye] *following word* 'late' *cancelled*

DEFOE TO ROBERT HARLEY, 30 NOVEMBER 1706

to lessen them as much as possible and in this I think I do my Country good serviċe and this Country no Injury.

I am Sorry to Tell you the war here is begun. The Glasgo men, 100d Onely, Very well Arm'd, are Marcht and 200 are to follow;[5] the Sterling men, Hamilton Men and Galloway men are to meet them.[6]

Expresses Comeing in to day of this, the Privy Council who had yesterday Ordred a proclamation[7] against them have Dispatcht a body of Dragoons to meet ym and I must Own ye well affected people here attend ye Issue wth Great Uneasiness.

I had heard of ye west Countrymens Resolutions and purposed to have Gone among them myself but the Comittee Calling Every Day for me I thought myself able to do[a] more serviċe here — and mr Pierċe,[8] whom you kno' of, Offering himself I sent him wth my servant and horses wth some heads of Reasons if possible to Open their Eyes.

He is Very well known among them and Very Acceptable[b] to their ministers who are the firebrands and I hope may be serviċable to Cool ye people if he scapes the first fury but I Confess my self in pain for him.

He is Sincerely Zealous for the publick and will merit a pardon for what has past[9] if he p[er]forms this serviċe, whether he has success or no.

The p[ar]liamt has this Day past an act to Repeal the act of Security and Discharge the Musters and Appearing in Arms that were made lawfull before.[10] I shall not fail to give you an Accot of Every step on both sides.

I am

Sr

yor Most Obedt Servt

DF

Nov. 30. 1706

Text: BL Add. MS. 70291, fols. 94–5. *Address* (fol. 95v): To The Right Honble | Robert Harley Esqr | Prinċipall Secretary of State. *Endorsed by Harley* (fol. 95v): Edenburg nov: 30: 1706 R Dec: 6: *Endorsed by an unknown hand* (fol. 95v): Mr DeFoe

---

[a] do] 'do do' *in MS*
[b] Acceptable] 'Acc | ceptable' *across a line break in MS*

283

DEFOE TO ROBERT HARLEY, 30 NOVEMBER 1706

1 *History of the Union, TDH*, vii, 324. Defoe stated that the Glasgow uprising was 'wholly *Jacobite*', not Presbyterian (*TDH*, vii, 266).

2 *History, TDH*, vii, 327.

3 NLS Wodrow Quarto xl, fol. 29.

4 *Parliamt ... last*: Parliament sat on 28, 29, and 30 Nov. Article seven, which equalised taxes on liquor in the two nations, was passed on the last of these days after a compromise over the excise on Scottish 'Tippony Ale' had been struck: tax on it would not exceed two shillings per barrel. In his *History*, Defoe recounts his role in brokering this compromise (*TDH*, viii, 93–6). Cf. *A Fourth Essay, at Removing National Prejudices, PEW*, iv, 135–7.

5 *war ... follow*: In the *Review* of 19 Dec. 1706, Defoe says that the number of the Glasgow Men 'is variously reported, and I do not take upon me to ascertain it; but the highest Account yet receiv'd is under 100, and 200 to follow at their March' (iii, 763). Subsequently, he specifies 59 men (*Review*, iii, 790 (31 Dec. 1706)) and 45 men (*History, TDH*, vii, 324). At the time, Mar said 49 men (H.M.C. *Mar and Kellie MSS*, 339) and David Crawford (d. 1736), who saw this 'company of desperat yoŭng fellows' in Hamilton, said 'about 48 or 50 men' (Crawford to Hamilton, 1 Dec. 1706, NRS GD 406/1/5383).

6 *Sterling ... them*: The Glasgow men planned a 'Rendezvous at *Hamilton*' of armed men from Stirling, Angus, Galloway, and Lanarkshire, and with this army intended to march on Edinburgh to raise the parliament. Looking back, Defoe derided reports of a large rendezvous as 'Amusements' – that is, delusional or illusory (*History, TDH*, vii, 324).

7 *proclamation*: The 'Proclamation against all Tumultuary and Irregular Meetings and Convocations of the Liedges' was passed on 29 Nov. 1706. Defoe comments on its 'good Effect' in *History, TDH*, viii, 98.

8 *mr Pierce*: John Pierce. He likely wrote *Legion's Humble Address to the Lords* (1704), perhaps in collaboration with Defoe (see headnote to Letter 9). He was a former broker (i.e. an agent who acted as middleman between merchants) and now one of Defoe's agents in Scotland, where he went by the pseudonym 'Allan' or 'Allen' (H.M.C. *Portland MSS*, iv, 163–4). See Owens and Furbank, 'New Light on John Pierce, Defoe's Agent in Scotland', *Edinburgh Bibliographical Society Transactions* 6 (1998), 134–43. Another government spy, John Ker of Kersland (1673–1726) claimed some credit for infiltrating the Covenanters and quelling the western uprising (*The Memoirs of John Ker of Kersland*, 3 vols. (1726–7), i, 28–37). Scholars have sometimes confused and conflated the two men when in fact they acted separately but towards the same end.

9 *what has past*: Probably Pierce's role in *Legion's Humble Address to the Lords*, a pamphlet deemed seditious which had resulted in him absconding to Scotland. See *The Memorial of the Presbyterians* (1706), sig. A3r, which reflects on Pierce's mission to cajole the Covenanters. It alleges he has High Church sympathies and that he took the flak for distributing *Legion's Humble Address*, which Defoe wrote.

10 *act ... before*: This refers to the 1704 Act of Security concerning the Hanoverian succession, not the one passed just weeks earlier concerning the religious settlement. On 30 Nov., Parliament passed an Act against all Musters and Rendezvouzes during the present Session of Parliament, which suspended the right of subjects to assemble in arms, as had been granted by the 1704 Act of Security (*APS*, ix, 344; *History of the Union, TDH*, vii, 325, 332–3; viii, 99–100).

72

To [Robert Harley]

5–7 December 1706

Sr

In My last[1] I gave a p[er]ticular of ye Encreasing Rabble at Glasgow wch Grew to That hight That ye Magistrates and honest Townsmen Press't for Some Soldiers to be sent wth all speed, and Finly, One of ye Leaders of the Mob, boasted he would be at Edinburgh in Two dayes.[2]

You will please to Observ this Finly is mean scandalous scoundrell fellow, Carryed Arms in Dumbartons Regimt[3] and a profess't Jacobite, and I believ yt is One Reason the Cameronian people tho' Equally Dissaffected would not Joyn him, at least not So as to March from Glasgow or from their Other Towns.

I Think[a] I Noted In my last how the[b] prudenće of ye Dutchess Dowagr of Hamilton prevented their assembling at Hamilton,[4] and I am Sorry to Tell yor Honr that 13 Ministers of parishes in their Severll pulpits Read the paper handed about for their assembling. They Excuse it here by saying it was Onely a legall summons for ye people to Muster and Exercise as by ye Act of Security they might do and by Custome Used to do, But —— I say no More, their best Friends here are Asham'd of it — they did not Meet it seems, for ye Dss of Hamilton haveing Recd the proclamation and act of Parliamt[5] sent Ordrs to all ye places in her Country & p[er]ticularly to her Own Tenants not to Meet Upon any Terms[c] and p[er]ticularly Threatned her Own Tenants wth Disposessing them if they presumed to Appear in Arms — had his Graće the Duke behav'd like this Matters had not Come thus far.[6]

Wednsday night,[7] the Detachmt of Dragoons wch went from henće wth ye Horse Grenadiers of ye Guards and a second Detachmt who Marcht out of Fife by way of Sterling bridge were Ordred to

---

[a] I Think] *apparently inserted in the paragraph indent*
[b] the] *interlined*
[c] Upon any Terms] *interlined*

DEFOE TO [ROBERT HARLEY], 5–7 DECEMBER 1706

March all night wᵗʰ the Uttmost Expedition to Glasgow. We had sevˡˡ Reports of Accon happening between them and that yᵉ Mob haveing taken posession of yᵉ Castle at Glasgo had kill'd severall of the Dragoons, But This is Contradicted.

Tis True they have kept a Court of Guard in the Bishops house wᶜʰ is yᵉ Remain of an Old Castle, but I Can not think they will Defend themselves there; we E[x]pectᵃ yᵉ Event here with Great Impaċenċe.[8]

The Parliamᵗ have been to day on yᵉ Article of the Malt Tax,[9] and have made a Determination wᶜʰ I like yᵉ worst of any thing they have done, Not that I think it Materiall in its Nature, but that tis an Absolute breaking In Upon the Articles, and to me a breach of the Equallity wᶜʰ is the foundation of the Union.

They put it first whether Scotland should be Exempt from it for a Certain Time or for Ever,[10] and Carryed it Onely for a Certain time, by a Majority of 30; then after a long Debate it was put whether the Time should be for 7 yeares as in the Salt or <u>Dureing the war</u>, and wᵗʰ Great Difficuty itᵇ was Carry'dᶜ for the latter, and this was so niċe a Turn that the House was Equally Divided and My Lᵈ Chancellors Vote Carryed it.[11]

I Need not Tell you sʳ yᵉ long Argumᵗ to prove yᵗ Scotland Can Not bear this Tax; yᵉ Onely Argumᵗ I saw of any any forċe was this, that yᵉ Malt here is Very Ordinary and does not produċe Equall wᵗʰ the English — but when I alleag'd two things to yᵉ Gentlemen here, 1: why then do you demand Equall bounty on Exportation, and 2: that yᵉ Malt in England Used Onely for Distilling is worse than theirs and pays yᵉ full, they knew Not what to say.

I Can not help saying that these Tumults and Terrors have brought all this Mischiefs on and tis Impossible to Avoid the Amendments — I hope Some Expedient will be found in England to bear wᵗʰ them for yᵉ yet Greater benefit of the wholl, and that her Majᵗⁱᵉ will be the Great Intercessor between the

---

ᵃ E[x]pect] 'x' *omitted*
ᵇ it] *interlined*
ᶜ Carry'd] *following word* 'Onely' *cancelled*

DEFOE TO [ROBERT HARLEY], 5–7 DECEMBER 1706

Nations that these things shall not break a Treaty of so much Consequence.

I am

sr

yor Most Obedt Servt

DF

The Dutch fleet is just arriv'd and wth them near 200 men, officers and servants for Recruits,[12] wch is some help to us here.

Edinb. Dec. 7th 1706

The Above was written, but by a Misstake kept too late, for the last post, for wch I ask yor pardon but make Amends in part for it by adding that, this short war is, God be praised, at an End. The Detachment of Dragoons are Come back from Glasgow and while I am writeing This they are Marching by ye Door wth Finly and Montgomery,[13] ye Two Leaders of the Glasgow Rabble, who they seiz'd in Glasgow with out any Resistance and all Things are Restord There and by this stroke I hope all is at an End.

The Church also begin to Face about again. I wish they had been wise Enough to have done it sooner.

Last night They Concluded upon a Letter in ye Comission of ye Assembly to be written to ye severall presbyteries to Exhort Them to Use Their Endeavours in Their Severall Districts to p[er]swade ye people to peace and to prevent all Tumults and Disorders.[14]

The Draught is not finished but I hope to have a Coppy of it against Next post.

I am

sr yor Most Obedt Servt

DF

Text: BL Add. MS. 70291, fols. 99–100. *Address*: none. *Endorsed by Harley* (fol. 100v): Edenburg Dec: 7: 1706 R Dec: 15:

1 *My last*: Perhaps missing: although the previous letter, dated 30 Nov., is about the Glasgow uprising, it does not discuss the Duchess of Hamilton, as Defoe goes on to say he thinks his 'last' does.

DEFOE TO [ROBERT HARLEY], 5–7 DECEMBER 1706

2 *Magistrates … dayes*: The government in Edinburgh dispatched a detachment of dragoons under the command of Lt.-Col. James Campbell (d. before 1738) to intercept George Finlay's Glasgow army. Defoe specified its strength as 200 men in *Review*, III, 789 (31 Dec. 1706), though as 220 in *History of the Union, TDH*, VII, 328.

3 *Dumbartons Regimt*: George Douglas, first Earl of Dumbarton (*c.* 1635–92), a Jacobite. Elsewhere Defoe specifies that Finlay was 'a Sergeant in *Dumbartons* Regiment in *Flanders*', perhaps therefore in the Third Anglo-Dutch War (1672–4) (*History of the Union, TDH*, VII, 321). In *Review*, III, 763 (19 Dec. 1706), Defoe says the highest ranking member of the Glasgow men, which apparently refers to Finlay, served in the Earl of Orkney's regiment, suggesting recent service in the Nine Years' War (1689–1697) or War of the Spanish Succession (1702–14).

4 *prudence … Hamilton*: Anne Douglas (1631–1716), Dowager Duchess of Hamilton and mother of the present Duke. Writing from Hamilton to the Duke upon the arrival of the Glasgow men on 1 Dec., the Duchess's secretary David Crawford states that she was 'ill pleased that they should have come here'; she allowed them to set up quarters but convened a guard of the town's citizens to uphold order (NRS GD 406/1/5383). The Duchess's letter to her son on 3 Dec., after the company had departed to return to Glasgow, restates her displeasure (NRS GD 406/1/9735). Nonetheless it was reported that the ringleaders were 'servants or Retainers to yᵉ family of the D. of H.' (*Addison Letters*, 67).

5 *proclamation and act of Parliamt*: See Letter 71.

6 *had … far*: On 29 Nov., the Duchess wrote to her son that 'We have frequent Rendezvoūs here, and as long as we have Law for it, Lett them say what they will of me, I will encourage them' (NRS GD 406/1/9734). But on 5 Dec., after the proclamation had been issued, she detailed the measures taken to prevent an anti-Union 'rendezvoūs' in her jurisdiction (as Sheriff of Lanarkshire), sending 'express word to every parish att not to come here'. She recognised that 'this is the place That yᵉ Court seems most to levell att' in the proclamation and regrets the resentment caused by her discouraging the Glasgow men (NRS GD 406/1/9735).

7 *Wednesday night*: 4 Dec.

8 *Court … Impacence*: Finlay and his followers had established themselves in the Bishop's Castle (no longer standing) near Glasgow Cathedral, 'as it were in Opposition to the Town Guard' (*History of the Union, TDH*, VII, 324). By the time the dragoons arrived, they had disarmed and dispersed.

9 *Article of the Malt Tax*: Article fourteen, debated 5–6 Dec. 1706.

10 *whether … for Ever*: The Treaty negotiated in London exempted Scotland from the malt tax for the present year. Fletcher of Saltoun proposed the permanent exemption.

11 *Lᵈ Chancellors Vote Carryed it*: The malt tax being a temporary tax in England, Scotland was to be exempt until the end of the War of the Spanish Succession (*History of the Union, TDH*, VIII, 103–7). Seafield as Lord Chancellor broke the deadlock. *APS* has no division list for either of the votes on 5 Dec. that Defoe discusses.

 At the end of the war in 1713, parliament decided that the malt tax would continue and hence be extended to Scotland. Many Scots considered this a breach of the Union, as they regarded the wartime exemption as good as permanent. Defoe, looking back on his role in the committee appointed to examine articles of trade, agreed that the tax was regrettable but denied it amounted to a breach of the Union (*Review*, IX, 405–11 (30 May and 2 June 1713); *Union and No Union* (1713)).

12 *Dutch … Recruits*: I.e. the fleet was on a recruiting venture. James Johnstone's (1655–1737) letter to George Baillie of Jerviswood (1664–1738) on 23 Nov. 1706 mentions warships being dispatched to the Scottish coast to help quell unrest (*Jerviswood Corr.*, 170).

13 *Montgomery*: Andrew Montgomery, described by Lockhart, along with Finlay, as a 'mean artificer' (*Lockhart Memoirs*, 177) and by Defoe as 'another of the Knot, but Famous for nothing that I ever heard of' (*History of the Union, TDH*, VII, 328).

14 *Letter … Disorders*: Defoe published this letter in the *Review* of 17 Dec. 1706 (III, 758–9), giving it as evidence of the Church of Scotland's 'Aversion' to anti-Union protests such as the Glasgow riots and the burning of the articles at Dumfries.

288

73

To Robert Harley

7 December 1706

Sr

The Enclosed[1] was wrott at Three Essayes, and yet I am Obliged to add a fourth.

Since all ye proceeding of ye Forces at Glasgow, of wch you See ye Issue in ye Enclosed, The Mob has been up there Again as furious as Ever. I Confess I thought it a wrong step to let ye Dragoons quitt ye Town Again so soon.[2]

As soon as they were Come Away the Rabble Rose again and Took all ye Magistrates prisoners and Declared that if their Two men[3] were not Restored and sent home Again they would Treat ye Magistrates just in ye same Manner as they should be Treated.

They Took ye Parol of some of them[4] and let them go to Edinburgh to Sollicit and they were here as Soon as ye prisonrs; what ye Issue of their Sollicitacon will be I know not but I suppose they will Force the Govornmt to Hang these Two Men and to send the Dragoons back again; of[a] Every Thing yt Occurs you will Depend Upon an Exact Accot.

My Ld H . . . . . x[5] has not given ye Return his Ldship promisd my Bro.[6] to ye Letter I sent, so I have not wrott since, but whoever I write you may sr Depend Entirely on my Absolutely Concealing that any Thing but my Own Affaires Drov me hither.[7]

I am

Sr

yor faithfull and Obedt Servt

DF

Dec. 7. 1706

If you please to Convey to me in a Letter the Draught of yor Coat of Arms I will Onely Use it to Make you a small present of the Manufacture of this Country.[8]

---

[a] of] *interlined above cancelled word* 'for'

Text: BL Add. MS. 70291, fols. 101–2. *Address* (fol. 102ᵛ): To The Right Honble | Robert Harley Esqʳ | Her Majᵗⁱᵉˢ Prinċipall Secretᵃ of State | Present. *Endorsed by Harley* (fol. 102ᵛ): Edenburg Dec: 7: 1706 ʀ Dec: 13:

1   *Enclosed*: The preceding letter.
2   *wrong … soon*: According to the *History of the Union*, the dragoons spent about three hours in Glasgow (*TDH*, vii, 328). According to Mar, 'the troups did certainlie mistake their order in coming so soon back, but it was thought fitt to be winkt at' (H.M.C. *Mar and Kellie MSS*, 351).
3   *Two men*: Finlay and Montgomery.
4   *some of them*: Specified as 'two of the Baillies of the Town, and some of the Deacons of Trades' in *History of the Union*, *TDH*, vii, 329.
5   *Lᵈ H . . . . . x*: Halifax. See Letter 62.
6   *Bro.*: Robert Davis, Defoe's brother-in-law.
7   *Concealing … hither*: Defoe declared himself 'unsent, unemploy'd, *and then any one will grant,* not only unrewarded, but unsupported' in Scotland (*Review*, iii, 828 (21 Jan. 1707)).
8   *small present of the Manufacture of this Country*: The gift was to be a tablecloth embroidered with Harley's coat of arms, as detailed in Defoe's letter to John Bell, 18 Mar. 1707 (Letter 101).

74

To [Robert Harley]

9 December 1706

Sʳ

    I Sent you an Accoᵗ Last Post of yᵉ Takeing of Finley And Montgomery yᵉ Two Ringleaders of yᵉ Glasgow Rabble and their bringing into yᵉ Castle here.

    They had no Sooner brought them away but yᵉ Rabble Rose again there, took the Magistrates prisoners and sent some of them hither, Assuring them if they did not procure their Two men again they would burn their houses &c; yᵉ foolish men frighted wᵗʰ the Rabble were here as soon as the prisoners.

    They have been, I hear, to day before the Council who as they Very well Deserv, bid them go home and take better Care of the peaċe of yᵉ Citty, for (thatᵃ must be Ownd) had they Timely done their Duty these Rabbles had been suppresst before they Came to

---

ᵃ for (that] '(for that' *in MS*

DEFOE TO [ROBERT HARLEY], 9 DECEMBER 1706

a head;[1] I suppose these foolish people will Force the Govornm̄ᵗ to hange these Two Miserables.

Finley behaves Very Haughty and Positiv, Declares himself a Jacobite,[a] Talks of Dyeing and I believ Expects no other.[2]

The Other I hear has a pen and Ink allowd him and p[er]haps may Tell some Tales;[3] the Committee of Council have been Three times (or yᵉ Lᵈ Register[4] from them) to Examine them; what[b] has pass't there I presume you will not Expect I should be able to Accquᵃ you of.

The Committee of whom I have often hinted,[5] have been to day on the salt — The Other party Insist on haveing 10ˢ p[er] Barrˡˡ instead of[c] 8ˢ. 4ᵈ Drawback on white Herring.[6]

I was sent for, and took upon me to Oppose it. First I Convinc̈'t them Even by their Own Accoᵗˢ that 8ˢ. 4ᵈ, wᶜʰ is allowd in England, was 1ˢ. 8ᵈ more than the salt Came to wᶜʰ Cured the fish and was Clear gain to yᵉ Importer, then I Undertook to prove that on a New Demand[d] yᵉ same Drawback being allow'd in England would Encrease Our fishing so much as to make us[e] Rivall them and p[er]haps supplant them in all yᵉ streight Trade and so lessen yᵉ Encouragemᵗ of their fishery, wᶜʰ was Much of it Expected from England.

They are Come to no Conclusion yet, but I am to attend again to morrow and to give in my Reasons in writeing and my Calculation of yᵉ Duty and the Drawback.[7]

I Obtain Coppy of their Resolution or Report Rather[f] on yᵉ Customes[8] which is pretty Enough and I believ will please you; they are all Very honest hearty Gentlemen and Zealously for yᵉ Union.[9]

I am yoʳ Humble and Earnest Peticŏner not to let it be known that you have this Coppy from me.[g] It would so lessen my Esteem among them that I should be Very ill used by them and no more Consulted wᵗʰ on any Occasion.

---

[a] Jacobite] *following word* 'and' *cancelled*
[b] what] *following word* 'their' *cancelled*
[c] of] *following word* 'white' *cancelled*
[d] on a New Demand] *interlined*
[e] us] *following word* 'End' *(possibly for* 'Endeavour'*) cancelled*
[f] or Report Rather] *interlined*
[g] from me] *interlined*

DEFOE TO [ROBERT HARLEY], 9 DECEMBER 1706

I have also Estimates of ye Respectiv Customes on Goods here, to wch I am to Draw farther Replyes and to present them at ye next sitting.

These things take me up some time, and Indeed made me lose ye post for my Last Letter, for wch I again Humbly ask your Pardon.

If you will please to give me any hints in ye things Now before them, and whether you Approve my Endeavouring to lessen their Amendments, it will be Very Usefull and Encourageing In this matter to me perticularly.

I am printing a single sheet Entituled a Letter to the Glasgow men[10] but wch I presume may be usefull to all the Rest to Open their Eyes a Little; it is not out of ye press to night so shall not be able to Enclose it till next post.

Mr Bell s^r writes me[11] I must write to you for farther Ord^rs if I make any more Demand on him — I have not yet made any Demand nor shall not as long as I have any thing left — But then if you do not p[er]mitt me to do it I shall pass my Time Very ill here and be worse as to Returne. I hope you will please to approv both of my work and of the Expence when I Rend^r you my Acco^t and that in ye mean Time you will please to Recall me in Time when you do not think Fitt to subsist me any Longer.

I have I Confess spent you S^r a great Deal of Money here and tis the most Expensiv place I was Ever in But Indeed S^r that has not been my Expence. I have layd out myself and yor Money in the True Service I Came here for And I flatter my Self I have been Usefull — I Earnestly wrott to you s^r to be limited in my Expences, and I would Not^a have Exceed, and I have not been ye larger for ye liberty you have given me.

I have had £75 and a Horse of m^r Bell[12] and I have just 13 guineas left, about 6 of wch I propose to lay Out for the Effectuall spreading this letter at Glasgow and Over all the West, and therefore purpose to print about 2500 of them and send y^m to Glasgow, Lanerk, Hamilton, Sterlin and Dumfreis.

I beg s^r you will please to signifye yor mind about Expences and if you think me too forward you need but a word to Restrain me, Ile stop Immediately. Otherwise I am Every Day saying something in print that Exposes these people here and Encourages the thing.

---

^a Not] *interlined*

292

DEFOE TO [ROBERT HARLEY], 9 DECEMBER 1706

I Earnestly Entreat your Thoughts about ye salt, the draw backs I mean, and about ye Committees Report and am

S^r yor Most Obed^t Servt
DF

Edinb. Dec. 9. 1706

Text: BL Add. MS. 70291, fols. 103–4. *Address*: none. *Endorsed by Harley* (fol. 103^r): Edenburg Dec: 9: 1706

1 *Council ... head*: Defoe is more charitable in retrospect: 'Some have blam'd the Magistrates for sending to *Edinburgh*; But if such would consider Circumstances, how the Dragoons were gone, they had an Enrag'd Mob to deal with, and no strength to Defend themselves, it can not but be thought the Gentlemen were in the right to comply with the Juncture of the Time, and Gratifie rather than Exasperate them, when they were absolutely in their Power' (*History of the Union, TDH*, VII, 329).

2 *Finley ... other*: In the *Review* for 17 Dec. Defoe says Finlay, 'now a Prisoner in *Edinburgh* Castle, declar'd himself for King *James*, and his Posterity, with more particular Marks of Inveteracy, than I care to remark' (III, 758). Two weeks later, Defoe alludes to '*General Finley*, as they jestingly call him' in prison (III, 790 (31 Dec. 1706)).

3 *Other ... Tales*: Mar also indicated that Montgomery was more willing to cooperate than Finlay (H.M.C. *Mar and Kellie MSS*, 350).

4 *Ld Register*: Sir James Murray, Lord Philiphaugh, Lord Clerk Register of Scotland.

5 *Committee ... hinted*: The committee appointed to calculate the Equivalent and examine articles of trade.

6 *Barr^ll ... white Herring*: I.e. unsmoked herring. A herring-barrel was thirty-two wine gallons, holding around a thousand fish.

7 *Reasons ... Drawback*: Defoe had given these 'reasons' in *A Fourth Essay, at Removing National Prejudices, PEW*, IV, 134–5, reprinted in *Review*, III, 798–9 (4 Jan. 1707). On 17 Dec., the bounty was set at ten shillings; in his *History* Defoe seems satisfied that 'the Salt commonly used in Curing a Barrell of Herring, amounted to about Nine Shillings' (*TDH*, VIII, 129–31). The final Treaty set the bounty at 10s.5d.

8 *Resolution or Report Rather on ye Customes*: Defoe enclosed the report in this letter (see Letter 75, note 1).

9 *for ye Union*: On 24 Oct. Paterson informed Harley that the committee's members were 'all of the Union Interest' (H.M.C. *Portland MSS*, VIII, 251; BL Add. MS. 70039, fol. 70^r). Patrick Hume, first Earl of Marchmont (1641–1724) believed two members were anti-Union but noted that these seldom attended the committee (*Marchmont Papers*, III, 327). The day after Defoe was 'sent for', 10 Dec. 1706, Queensberry advised Godolphin that 'this committee of parliament ... have taken such hearty and unwearied pains to inform themselves and others' (*Marchmont Papers*, III, 442).

10 *a Letter to the Glasgow men*: *A Short Letter to the Glasgow-Men* (1706), published around 10–12 Dec. 1706 and subsequently reprinted in *Review*, III, 792–6 (2 Jan. 1707). This hectoring pamphlet aims to persuade the disaffected Glaswegians ('a handful of poor Distemper'd Lunatick People') that they are tools of the Jacobites and have no basis for protest.

11 *Mr Bell s^r writes me*: Untraced.

12 *£75 and a Horse of mr Bell*: On 4 Jan. 1707, Bell informed Harley that he had paid Defoe £40. 17s.6d on 2 Oct., £52.10s.6d in Nov., and £10 in Dec. (H.M.C. *Portland MSS*, IV, 378). The first seems to include the value of the horse Bell supplied Defoe (see Letter 54), and the last presumably came after this letter.

293

75

To Robert Harley

12 December 1706

HEADNOTE (**Letters 75 and 76**): In these letters Defoe apprised Harley of sticking points in the ongoing negotiations, including finessing the details of the separate Scottish legal system that would endure after the Union, recompensing those who would be hit by tariffs on products such as wool, and finalising details concerning products such as fish and salt. Defoe continued to update Harley on the fallout of the uprising in Glasgow. The correspondence had become one-way, and although Defoe frequently sought direction from Harley, none was forthcoming. The English parliament had reconvened on 3 December.

Sr

Since my Last Nothing Materiall has happened; the house Sitts Dilligently on ye Report wch I sent you last post.[1]

The Glasgow Magistrates Recd a Checq from ye Governmt as they Deserv'ed (for Really they have been too Accessary to all this mischief) and are sent home and there is no More done wth the prisoners yet.

The paper I menčoned in my last About ye Glasgow men I send you Enclosed;[2] tis a plain but Course[3] Expostulation and they flatter me it has done a great Deal of Service here.

I forsee sr a great Debate will Arise here about settling a Court of Appeals and I Enclose you a paper[4] on that head. I wish I Could have yor Opinion on ye subject because I fear some thing to be offred here yt may be Erroneous in fundamentalls (Viz):

A Court of Appeal in Scotland will be Insisted upon to be Establisht here.

If it be Composed of Peers they will object, for they Dare Not Trust their Own Lds. If of Commoners how will it Consist wth the Lords being the soveraign Judicature? If there is no Court of Appeals atall they will Either be forčed up to England with their Causes wch will be Intollerable, or they will have the Lds of the session be a soveraign Judicature[5] wch seems still worse.

DEFOE TO ROBERT HARLEY, 12 DECEMBER 1706

I may do much in stateing this Case, haveing some Notions of the matter wch I Digested before I thought of Comeing hither — but I Entreat your Directions in this Case as far as you think Convenient

and am
S^r
yor Most Obed^t Servt
DF

Edinb. Dec. 12. 1706

The post is Miscarryed to day; the weather is so bad and snows so great there is no Travailing.

The parliam^t have granted to day an Equivalent to the Breeders or Keepers^a of sheep for their Not Exporting wooll to France and Other parts.[6] I suppose they are to pay it themselves.[7]

Text: BL Add. MS. 70291, fols. 105–6. *Address* (fol. 106^v): To The Right Honble | Robt Harley Esqr | Her Maj^ties Principall Secret^a of State | Present. *Endorsed by an unknown hand* (fol. 106^v): Mr De Foe

---

^a or Keepers] *interlined*

---

1   *Report wch I sent you last post*: In total eight reports from the committee to which the sixth article was remitted were received by parliament from 10 to 16 Dec.; the amendments they recommended were duly approved. See Defoe's commentaries in *History of the Union, TDH*, VIII, III–28.

2   *paper … Enclosed*: Defoe's *A Short Letter to the Glasgow-Men* (see Letter 74, note 10), missing from the correspondence.

3   *Course*: I.e. coarse.

4   *paper. A Letter to a Member of Parliament, upon the 19th Article of the Treaty of Union between the Two Kingdoms of Scotland and England* (1706), attributed to George Mackenzie, first Earl of Cromarty (1630–1714). The copy remains bound with the Defoe–Harley correspondence (BL Add. MS. 70291, fols. 96–8). The *Letter* supports an incorporating union but argues for maintaining an appellate court in Scotland, composed of some or all of the forty-five Scottish commoners and sixteen Lords who were to sit in the British parliament.

5   *L^ds of the session be a sovereign Judicature*: The Lords of the Session comprised the Court of Session, the supreme civil court in Scotland. As it was finally settled, article nineteen of the Union Treaty preserved in perpetuity the Court of Session and the High Court of Justiciary (Scotland's supreme criminal court), with the same authority and privileges as before the Union (*History, TDH*, VIII, 160–1). But it did not prohibit Scottish appeals to the House of Lords, meaning that, after the Union, Scottish cases were heard in Westminster despite the separate legal systems of England and Scotland.

6   *Exporting wooll to France and Other parts*: The Scottish parliament passed an act allowing the exportation of wool in 1704, a challenge to the English embargo on trade with the enemy (*APS*, XI, 9).

DEFOE TO ROBERT HARLEY, 14 DECEMBER 1706

7 *parliamᵗ … themselves*: On 12 Dec., parliament voted to compensate the losses of Scottish sheep breeders occasioned by the Union Treaty's tariffs on exporting wool and its prohibition of their exports to France. Whereas in England, tariffs discouraged the export of wool in order to encourage domestic manufacture and consumption, there were before the Union no tariffs on exporting wool in Scotland. The allowance made was £14,000: £2,000 per year for seven years, from the Equivalent. Defoe explains the issue and debate at length in his *History*, *TDH*, VIII, 120–3. On the limited success of this economic stimulus, see Clifford Gulvin, *The Tweedmakers: A History of the Scottish Fancy Woollen Industry, 1600–1914* (Newton Abbot, 1973), 30–1.

76

To Robert Harley

14 December 1706

Sr

This post affords me Very Little Matter worth a Letter; the p[ar]liamᵗ has not Sat Since Thursdayᵗ and the Comissionʳ being Each day in yᵉ Comittee in p[er]son I have not been Sent for.

The present Close Debates² are about yᵉ Drawbacks on Salt and an Encouragemᵗ of 20ˢ p[er] last³ on Exporting fish wᶜʰ they will allow to yᵉ Merchant Out of yᵉ Money from England.

The hopes of Tumults and Noise being Over, the Designs are now if possible to Argue them into something that they think may shock England; I am as Watchfull in this as I can Upon all Occasions.

The Rabble at Glasgow are not yet quiet tho' not so Dangerously Uneasy as before. However yᵉ Govornmᵗ has thoᵗ fitt to Ordʳ a Detachmᵗ of Foot and Dragoons to March thither to protect the Magistrates.

I am

Sr

yoʳ Most Humble and Obedᵗ Servᵗ

DF

Edinb. Dec. 14. 1706

By the Enclosed⁴ you will see a little more of yᵉ Temper of yᵉ West.

DEFOE TO [ROBERT HARLEY], 16 DECEMBER 1706

Text: BL Add. MS. 70291, fols. 107–8. *Address* (fol. 108v): To The Right Honble |
Robert Harley Esqr | Her Majties Princïpall Secreta of State | Present. *Endorsed by
Harley* (fol. 108v): Edenburg Dec: 14: 1706 R Dec: 20:

1 *p[ar]liamt has not Sat Sinće Thursday*: The Scottish parliament did not sit between Thursday 12
   and Monday 16 Dec. 1706.
2 *Debates*: Within the committee appointed to examine articles of trade.
3 *last*: Twelve barrels.
4 *Enclosed*: Missing.

77

To [Robert Harley]

16 December 1706

HEADNOTE **(Letters 77–9)**: Defoe reports to Harley his conversations with
pro-Union but scrupulous Church of Scotland ministers about oaths. By the
National Covenant (1638) and Solemn League and Covenant (1643), members of
the Church of Scotland were committed to resisting religious innovations and
to working towards the religious unity of Britain under Presbyterianism. They
feared that the Union would mean Queen Anne would take a new coronation
oath, requiring them to swear a new oath of allegiance. This caused a general
concern about multiplying oaths, which they held to be sinful, as well as a particular concern about swearing loyalty to a monarch sworn to uphold the Church
of England. The second address of the Commission of the General Assembly
had requested a change to the coronation oath, so that the monarch pledged to
protect the Church of Scotland as well as the Church of England. The National
Covenant also disallowed the civic authority of churchmen, and the second address had likewise protested about bishops sitting in the House of Lords. The
abjuration oath, since the 1701 Act of Succession, required public office holders
not just to reject the right to the throne of James II's Catholic son but to resist
any successor not of the Church of England. In swearing it, Presbyterians would
be committing to resist a future monarch of their own church, unlikely as that
was. For some time in late 1706 and early 1707, Defoe endeavoured to mediate
between these ministers and the English ministry, recognising the value of their
support and seeking to ensure their consciences were respected. The abjuration
oath became a major bone of contention in 1712, in the wake of the Episcopal
Toleration Act.[1]

DEFOE TO [ROBERT HARLEY], 16 DECEMBER 1706

Sr

I have not ye honor of any from you lately. The Treaty goes on here in parliament pretty well; my Fear is ye Clogging it wth Amendments.

As I hinted in My last ye Rabbles and Noise of ye party have push't them Upon Amendments and there was no possibillity to Avoid it; Now ye Dilligence of ye party[2] is Imploy'd if possible to bring Them to Agree to Such Amendments as they know ye English Can not Complye wth. Thus ye Party would fain have Drawn ym into an Allowance for Exporting wooll.

I Told Them it was Declareing Against ye Union, and They had as good Do Nothing; Even ye Comittee, some of ym Too Much Intrested, Seemd to stagger in it but at last Came to Resolv against it and to have a Satisfaccon to ye sheep masters in ye Room of it.[3]

The 6th Article is past to day wth an addicon to[a] ye Drawback on Fish, 20s p[er] last, and a license to Salt ye provisions for ships on Inland Trade wth Their Own Salt, paying English Duty.[4]

I Confess ye Alteracons are Numerous and Confused but I Take ym hitherto to be Not Very Considerable and None of ym Fatall to the Union in Generall.

Here is a Church Dispute started in private by some Ministers to me, for they take me for Their Friend, and I am so More to their Intrest then their Mannagemt; but it is serious and Considerable and I Entreat yor private Judgemt for my Governmt, for a Committee of the assembly are to meet me privately Upon it.

Their Request is honest and if I Can have a favourable Answer they will Depend much on it and it will Reconcile a Great many to ye Union, and they believ I have Intrest Enough in England to Lay it before ye Queen and before such great people (they do not guess who) as may be of service to Them.

If The Union goes on, say they, The Queen is Declared Queen of Great Brittain, The Coronacon Oath must be altred and ye subjects must Renew their Oath.[5]

If the Oath be Imposed Upon us the Ministers half of us will be Turn'd Out of Our liveings: 1) we Can not swear to a Queen of

---

[a] to] *interlined above cancelled word* 'of'

298

DEFOE TO [ROBERT HARLEY], 16 DECEMBER 1706

Brittain as On ye foot of ye Union for that is swearing to Episcopall Magistracy and swearing to the Union — Now tho' we Can Accquiescè and be passive in a Union wth Prelacy, yet to swear to it is an Active subjeccon and we Can not do it, Our Nationall Oath is Direct upon us and we must be Undone Rather than submitt to it — we have sworn to ye Queen and we will keep it Inviolably to ye last Drop — but ye Other is^a Against Our Consciencès and we Can not do it.[6] Nay if as Queen of Scotland her Maj^tie should Require us to take the same Individual Oath of Alleigeancè Over again we Could not do it, for haveing sworn allready, to do it again would be Multiplying Oaths wch we hold sinfull and Could no more do it than Marry or baptise Twicè Over.

The Next thing is the Abjuration Oath; if this be Imposed Upon them in ye Terms as Now worded in England, there are not ten Ministers of ye Kirk will hold their placès and the Confusion will be Incredible.

The Case is This — The Oath Expressly Sayes, or ye Act for I have y^m Not here, That ye Successor must Conform to ye Church of England; Now for them to Abjure any successor but such as shall be of ye Church of England is to Joyn in Excludeing their Own Church from ye succession — wch they say is Not Reasonable, nor Can they In Consciencè Complye; but They are Content No p[er]son shall succeed that is not a protestant and they Desire the Generall Term Protestant May be Allow'd or Elcè they Can Never Abjure.[7]

Thus S^r I have stated their Questions; I assure you the p[er]sons proposeing them are Sober, wise and judicous, friends to ye Union and Sollicitous for ye Generall quiet, hearty Zealous promoters of her Maj^ties Intrest, and ye succession; But Scrupulous to a Nicety about Oaths, Episcopacy and such things as those.

I give you their Own words, and as near as I Can do not Alter — I beseech you assist me wth yor thoughts. I kno' Nothing in this Country in wch I may be able to Render her Maj^tie Equall Servicè as in this, and the Turn it will give to the Opinion of ye priests will be Unexpected — and Indeed their Mannagem^t has done Incredible Injury to the Case.

---

^a is] *following letters probably 'aga' cancelled*

299

DEFOE TO [ROBERT HARLEY], 16 DECEMBER 1706

Some Medium I hope will be found Out and I beg your thoughts whether it may not be in England Rather than here because to do it here would start such a Cloud of scruples as will allarm all yᵉ Clergy here and Espeċally in yᵉ West, and may Endanger a Reall Commotion —

The people who have broke this to me**ᵃ** are few and have promised to keep it private if possible to have it Remedyed and if it be you Gain yᵉ wholl body of Ministers at a blow.

You will pardon my warm way of Expressing it. I Confess I am Conċern'd in my thoughts that some way may be found Out to mak yᵐ Easye.

I am

Sʳ

yoʳ Most Obedᵗ Servᵗ

DF

Edinb. Dec. 16. 1706

Text: BL Add. MS. 70291, fols. 109–10. *Address*: none. *Endorsed by Harley* (fol. 110v): Edenburg Dec: 16: 1706 ʀ Dec: 23:

ᵃ to me] *interlined*

---

1 See headnote to Letter 205.
2 *party*: I.e. the opposition.
3 *Satisfacċon ... it*: Compensation from the Equivalent is the 'Satisfacċon' given to sheep breeders instead of any bounty on exporting wool.
4 *6ᵗʰ Article ... Duty*: On 16 Dec. parliament approved article six. The drawback on fish and provision on taxing salt were, in fact, within the remit of article eight, also debated on 16, 17, 18, 19, and 23 Dec., only passing on 24 Dec. (*History of the* Union, *TDH*, vɪɪɪ, 123–5).
5 *subjects must Renew their Oath*: I.e. oath of allegiance. See headnote.
6 *we Can not do it*: See headnote and Stephen, *Scottish Presbyterianism*, 55–6.
7 *Abjure*: See headnote.

78

To Robert Harley

17 December 1706

Sr

Since the Enclosed[1] we Are Inform'd ye Dragoons, who we Thot went to Lye in Glasgow to keep ye Peace there, have been to Apprehend Some Persons, who Upon ye Confessions of The Two Prisoners[2] they have here are Accused of being principalls in ye Tumults There.

We are told they have Taken Seaven; who they are I Can Not yet Learn, but a Party of Dragoons being Detach't this Day we suppose it is to Reciev the prisoners and bring them hither.

My Messenger[3] is not yet Return'd from ye West; we hear the people have been gathering a little in Galloway and the West, but Nothing Considerable.

I Again Recomend the Case Enclosed to yor Thoughts and Am

Sr

yor Most Obedt Servt

DF

Edinb. Dec. 17. 1706

Text: BL Add. MS. 70291, fols. 111–12. *Address* (fol. 112v): To The Right Honble | Robert Harley Esqr | Her Majties Principall Secreta of State | Present. *Endorsed by Harley* (fol. 112v): Edenburg Dec: 17: 1706 ℞ Dec: 23

1   *Enclosed*: The preceding letter, written on Monday 16 Dec., not a post day, and evidently sent with this letter on 17 Dec.
2   *Two Prisoners*: Finlay and Montgomery. 'Several more [Glasgow men] are taken up by the Confessions of the former two' (*Review*, 111, 800 (4 Jan. 1707)). The dragoons returned on 15 Dec. (*History of the Union, TDH*, vII, 330).
3   *Messenger*: Likely John Pierce.

79

To [Robert Harley]

19 December 1706

Sr

I wrott you a Long letter[1] last post, Relateing to the Kirk and the Uneasyness of ye Ministers. I Doubt my Accot was Something Confusd.

I have Since Convert more Closely wth Them on That head And Not to Run Out in Perticulars, The Sume of ye Matter is as Folls:

1. The Union <u>as Such</u> They are Not Against and Some of Them profess to be Very Willing to Come into it but they Complain They are Treated haughtily and at first Something Rudely.

The Overture Or Act of Security for ye Church[2] was hurryed Up Onely among a few; Large Amendments And Long Consideracons are in hand On Accots of Trade, Taxes &c, but Matters of Religion Are hurryed On too fast, the Comission Thin and the Members Not Come Up,[3] and all their Mocons or Demands, public or Private, Recd wth haughtyness and Contempt.

As to ye Bishops, they are Not Enclin'd to Any Opposicon On that Accot, Other than by ye formallity of a Protest Or[a] Declaracon, to Satisfye their Consciences as to Submitting to Episcopall Legislacon.[4]

From This short Abridgement I Crave yor Pardon for ye Freedome of giveing my Opinion.

These Are a Refractory Scrupulous and Positive people. It is in ye power of ye Govornmt to Inflame Them to ye last Degree, and were ye Design their Destruccon, they might Easly be Driven into ye Agency of their Own Ruin.

On ye Other hand if they are Mañag'd wth a Little Lenity And Tenderness, if used kindly, you may yet have Them heart and hand

---

[a] Or] *amended from* 'to'

DEFOE TO [ROBERT HARLEY], 19 DECEMBER 1706

for yᵉ Union — And I Can Not but Say it is yet worth while and Not too Late.

I know yᵉ Moderacon of yoʳ Honʳˢ Principles, and as it is Agreeable Not Onely to yᵉ Intrest but Inclinacon of her Majᵗⁱᵉ with all her people, So I Can Not but Repeat it, That a little of that Gentleness Excercised here instead of what has been a little too warm would Quench all this fire.

If it be Needfull for me to Descend to Some p[er]ticulars p[er]haps Nice Enough for yᵉ Govornmᵗ of This Matter your Ordʳ shall be Observd On yᵉ first Notice by

yoʳ Most Humble Servᵗ DF

I had this Day again yᵉ honoʳ to Dine wᵗʰ the Comittee at yᵉ Lᵈ Cessnocks.[5]

The Occasion was yᵉ Debate to Come on[a] this Day in Parliamᵗ about yᵉ Salt Tax.

The Mocon they Expect is Either a Totall Exempcon from the Duty as Insupportable to yᵉ poor, or a lengthning Out yᵉ Term of Seaven years to a longer Time.[6]

The Case I Doubt will go hard; I See no Argumᵗ has any Room on yᵉ Other Side, the people being So posesst of yᵉ Burthen that the word Insupportable is in Every Mouth[7] and they Run away wᵗʰ it wᵗʰout any Consideracon.

However I proposed to Examin what Quantity of Salt p[er] head the people Could Expend and So to Considʳ whether it was Really Insupportable or no; it happend to be a New thought to yᵐ and I was amaz'd to hear Even yᵉ Gentlemen themselves Guess yᵗ the People Consum'd 2 Bushell English Measure p[er] head p[er] Anñ and it was an Equall Surprize to Them when On a stricter Examinacon they Came all to be Convinc't that less than Two Pecks Scots Measure, wᶜʰ is not quite 1½ peck English,[8] was yᵉ Uttmost they Expended — and My Lᵈ Cessnock by Calling his Servants found his family of 24 did not Use 2 Pecks Each p[er] Anñ, Not Reckoning Children nor strangers.[b]

---

[a] on] *following illegible word cancelled*
[b] strangers] *following illegible word cancelled*

303

DEFOE TO [ROBERT HARLEY], 19 DECEMBER 1706

On this foot they Think themselves Furnisht for yᵉ Debate, at least better than they were before.

But Just as they were prepareing to go Into yᵉ house they Are all in a Surprize at an Unhappy Accident wᶜʰ happening This Morning kept yᵉ Comissionʳ back till Near One a Clock, a Duell fought in yᵉ Park this Morning between yᵉ Duke of Argyle and The E of Crawford.⁹

The Quarrell it seems was Triffling, from[a] a Bottle;¹⁰ I have Not yet yᵉ p[er]ticulars, but am Told the Duke of Queensb'ry haveing Some Notice of their Resolution[b] Took Their Parols not to fight — how they have Thoᵗ fitt to break thro' that Engagemᵗ I kno' Not yet.

They have neither Much harm; So yᵉ Hurry of it is yᵉ most. Wˡˡ Kerr, Brother to yᵉ E of Roxburgh,¹¹ Was wᵗʰ yᵉ E of Crawford, and Lᵈ Delorain¹² with yᵉ Duke.

The Dragoons have brought severall prisoners in this after noon From Glasgow and Hamilton, Among wᶜʰ Are some of the Duke of Hamiltons Servants;¹³ their Names and p[er]ticulars shall be in My Next.¹⁴

I am
Sʳ
yoʳ Most Obedᵗ Servᵗ
DF

Edinburgh
Dec. 19. 1706
The house have not gone thorow the Clause of yᵉ Salt to day.¹⁵

Text: BL Add. MS. 70291, fols. 113–14. *Address*: none. *Endorsed by Harley* (fol. 114ᵛ): Edenburg Dec: 19: 1706 ℞ Dec: 25:

[a] from] *interlined above cancelled illegible word*
[b] their Resolution] *interlined above cancelled word* 'it'

---

1 *Long letter*. I.e. Letters 77 and 78, sent together.
2 *Act of Security for yᵉ Church*: See headnote to Letters 63–5.
3 *Comission Thin and the Members Not Come Up*: The Commission comprised 222 members (143 ministers and 79 ruling elders) and letters sent before the session impressed the importance of attendance. However, its highest attendance was 98 (60 ministers, 38 elders) on 8 Nov. 1706, when it approved the second address. Ministers drifted back to their parishes, especially after the Act of Security was passed; on 24 Dec., ministers were forbidden from leaving unless relieved by another from their presbytery. Bad weather exacerbated the problem, but even many Edinburgh-based members did not attend. See Stephen, *Scottish Presbyterians*, 92–3.

DEFOE TO [ROBERT HARLEY], 19 DECEMBER 1706

4 *Bishops ... Legislaċon*: The Commission's second address objected to bishops sitting in parliament. See Letter 61, note 11.

5 *Comittee at yᵉ Lᵈ Cessnocks*: See Letter 69.

6 *Moċon ... Time*: The original Treaty granted a seven-year exemption from the salt tax; Atholl requested a permanent exemption (*History of the Union, TDH*, VIII, 141–2).

7 *the word Insupportable is in Every Mouth*: The salt duty 'was cryed out upon as Insupportable' (*History, TDH*, VIII, 142).

8 *2 Bushell ... English*: In England, a bushel was (and is) equivalent to four pecks and to eight dry gallons.

9 *Duke of Argyle and The E of Crawford*: Argyll (see Letter 56, note 32) and John Lindsey (d. 1713), nineteenth Earl of Crawford.

10 *Quarrell ... Bottle*: Addison wrote on 27 Dec. 1706: 'They are both of yᵉ same side as to yᵉ union, but yᵉ Duke of Argile's being made Captain of yᵉ Troupe of Guards over yᵉ others head who is the Lieutenant it is supposed may have produced this misunderstanding' (*Addison Letters*, 67). In *Atalantis Major* (1711), Defoe alleged that Argyll challenged Crawford but backed down, 'choosing to risk his Honour rather than his Life' (25–6).

11 *Wˡˡ Kerr Brother to yᵉ E of Roxburgh*: Lt.-Gen. William Ker (d. 1741), younger brother of Squadrone leader Roxburghe.

12 *Lᵈ Delorain*: Henry Scott (1676–1730), first Earl of Deloraine, son of the Duke of Monmouth. Defoe is saying that Ker and Deloraine acted as Crawford's and Argyll's seconds in their duel.

13 *Duke of Hamiltons Servants*: The Duchess of Hamilton's page, John Porterfield (or possibly his son), was accused of encouraging men to muster; and the Town Treasurer at Hamilton, James Weir, was accused of having given money to the Glasgow men, information the government received from Finlay (Robert Wodrow to James Wodrow, 21 Dec. 1706, NLS Wodrow Letters Quarto IV, fol. 133). Writing to her son, the Duke, on 17 Dec. the Duchess protested their innocence (NRS GD 406/1/9737). However, on 21 Dec. she wrote to him: 'If they have been such Fools as to speak idley with such a base fellow as Findlay, They have themselves to blame, For they had no allowance from me' (NRS GD 406/1/9738). Hamilton's letters indicate that Porterfield was never charged ([25 Dec. 1706?], NRS GD 406/1/7950; 14 Feb. 1707, NRS GD 406/1/7922).

14 *their Names and p[er]ticulars shall be in My Next*: But they are not.

15 *house ... to day*: The vote on the salt tax was deferred until 24 Dec. 1706.

DEFOE TO ROBERT HARLEY, 21 DECEMBER 1706

80

To Robert Harley

21 December 1706

HEADNOTE (**Letters 80 and 81**): Defoe was in his element delving into the finer details of trade as articles pertaining to commerce were debated. In the case of the Scots' request for a drawback on pork and beef exports, he was weighing the instruction to resist any adjustments to the Treaty against his sense that this concession was justified by burgeoning trade activity. He records that Paterson rebuked him for not opposing all attempts to modify the existing terms of union. Defoe considered Paterson ill-informed. The only evidence of how their masters in England saw the disagreements between Defoe and Paterson comes in a letter from Godolphin to Harley three months later, on 19 March 1707: 'I return your two letters from L and D[e] F[oe], what he says of Patterson I dare say is exactly true.'[1]

S[r]

I Doubt I Throng you wth Letters, The Variety here affording Every Day Fresh Matter.

The Debate about y[e] Salt I Wrott you in my Last is Not yet Come on, The house haveing been Embroild on Anoth[r] head, Viz[t] y[e] Draw back on Pork and Beef.[2]

This is an Article long Plotted to hamper y[e] Cause [i]f[a] Possible. The Committee had Unwarily Reported y[e][b] Beef and Pork in One Article — I must Acknowlege there Seem'd Some Reason in their Demand on pork, of w[ch] they have a large and Encreasing Trade from Aberdeen Only to Italy, Leghorn[3] and Genoa, and they Say ship't off 1000 barrells there this last year, and as the pork being fed wth Corn is a great Article of y[e] Consumtion of Corn, I the sooner Came in to it[4] w[ch] m[r] Paterson pretended[5] to give me a Caution for after wards as if I had put it into their heads.

But tis a Sign to me how little he Convert wth y[e] Gentlemen Concern'd, Since it was allwayes in their Mouths Every time I was with them from y[e] first Discourse of y[e] Salt Tax.

---

[a] [i]f] 'of' *in MS*
[b] y[e]] *following letters* 'Art' *(for* 'Article'*) cancelled*

DEFOE TO ROBERT HARLEY, 21 DECEMBER 1706

But this bringing the Beef in is a most Ridiculous thing Since tho' they have the same thing Now and a bounty paid too boot, they do not nor Can Export Ten Barrells of beef a year for Sale One year with Another.

If m^r P . . . . n Represents any branch of this thing as above in My Prejudice he does me wrong, and I beg leav to be favourably Construed and heard to it.

I must Confess I am Sometimes shock't in my Thoughts at the Multitude of Amendments here, tho' this is a most Insignificant thing in it self, neither kingdome Exporting any quantity of Beef for Sale.[6]

However, the party boast of a Victory and Say they have secur'd the Union from being Ever finished, and yet[a] they Carryed this but by One Voice, and that was <u>Seaton of Pittmeddon</u>,[7] an honest whig too, and for ye Union but byassd in this Case.

This Discovres[b] s^r what I wrott you before, that the present Design[c] was to load ye Treaty wth Such amendments As they think will Ruine it in its Consequences, and This is ye Onely Card left to play.

The affair of Crawford and Argile Made more Noise[d] Then[8] Mischief and is all Over, but the Duke has not got any Reputation by it.

I Earnestly Crave yor Tho^{ts} on My Last.

I am

S^r yor Most Obed^t Servt

DF

Edinb. Dec. 21. 1706

Text: BL Add. MS. 70291, fols. 115–16. *Address* (fol. 116v): To The Right Honble | Robert Harley Esqr | Her Maj^{ties} Princ̓ipall Secreta^a of State | Present

[a] yet] *interlined above illegible cancelled word*
[b] Discovres] *amended from* 'Discovr'd'.
[c] Design] *following word* 'and' *cancelled*
[d] Noise] *interlined*

1 H.M.C. *Bath MSS*, I, 167.
2 *Draw back on Pork and Beef*: On 19 Dec. 1706, the committee to which article eight was remitted brought a report into parliament recommending as per the original Treaty '*That there ought to be no Drawback upon the Exportation of salted Beef and Pork*' (*History of the Union*, *TDH*, VIII, 133). Whether or not it was also another attempt to thwart the Union by making

DEFOE TO ROBERT HARLEY, 24 DECEMBER 1706

adjustments England would reject, this attempt to gain drawbacks on these exports was occasioned by anxieties about total dependence on the English market (T. C. Smout, *Scottish Trade on the Eve of the Union, 1660–1707* (Edinburgh, 1963), 215).

3 *Leghorn*: Livorno.

4 *I the sooner Came in to it*: See *History*, *TDH*, VIII, 135. There, Defoe says the burgeoning export in pork from '*Aberdeen* and the Country adjacent' is to the Netherlands rather than Italy.

5 *pretended*: presumed.

6 *neither ... Sale*: See the explanation in *History*, *TDH*, VIII, 135. In short, Irish beef was superior and cheaper; as here, Defoe is frustrated by the cavilling but concludes the issue is inconsequential.

7 *Seaton of Pittmeddon*: See Letter 60, note 3.

8 *Then*: I.e. than.

81

To Robert Harley

24 December 1706

Sr

This Unhappy Debate about ye Draw back on Beef and Pork has held them here all this Week; The Case was Thus, The Comitte had Unhappily Voted it together, No Draw back on Pork or Beef Exported for Sale.

When it Came to ye house ye Draw back on Pork Appear'd So Reasonable there was no withstanding it, and The Vote being wholl ye beef went with it.

Every body Laughs at ye Demand of a Draw back for beef when Scotland Exports none for Sale to any part of ye World, but This Triffle being Carry'd made ye party Very Chearfull Thinking they had Gaind Some Ground, but all This prov'd their loss for ye Very folly of ye Vote brought this Addicon to it this Day, Vizt That This should be Subject to ye Parliamt of Brittain — wch was Carryed to ye Infinite Mortificacon of The party.[1]

I hear Nothing More About ye prisoners. There are Three more in ye Castle and Two belonging to ye Dutchess of Hamilton in ye Town.

Since my last I have had a long Accot from mr J. P.[2] whom I hinted to what purpose, and when, I Sent into ye West; he has been

308

DEFOE TO ROBERT HARLEY, 24 DECEMBER 1706

at Dumfries and in y[e] highlands, has been with John Hepburn y[e] Cameronian Minister[3] and wth Some of y[e] Most Resolute of That Party and I hope has been Very Serviċable to Cooling and Calming y[e] Minds of an Ignorant and Deluded people and I must do him that Justiċe I believ has been Very Usefull. I have a large Acco[t] from him w[ch] I had sent you this night — But I Confess myself in Some Disord[r] to night, The Acco[t] of y[e] Death of my Father[4] Comeing just as I was writeing this.

I am

S[r]

yo[r] Most Obed[t] Serv[t]

DF

Edinb

Dec. 24. 1706

Tis Very Long Sinċe I had any Acco[t] from you whether mine Come to hand.

Enclosed is y[e] Vote pass't to day about y[e] Salt.[5]

Text: BL Add. MS. 70291, fols. 117–18. *Address* (fol. 118v): To The Right Hon[ble] | Robert Harley Esq[r] | Her Maj[ties] Prinċipall Secret[a] of State | Present

1 *Every body ... party*: On 23 Dec., the Scottish Parliament voted for a drawback of '*Five Shillings* Sterling *for every Barrel of Beef or Pork Salted with Foreign Salt, and Exported for Sale, alterable by the Parliament of* Great Britain' (*History of the Union*, *TDH*, v111, 136–7).
2 *mr J. P*: John Pierce. The 'long Acco[t]' is untraced.
3 *John Hepburn y[e] Cameronian Minister*. See Letter 64.
4 *Father*. James Foe. He was buried on 21 Dec. See Frank Bastian, 'James Foe, Merchant, Father of Daniel Defoe', *N&Q* 11 (1964), 82–6.
5 *Enclosed ... Salt*. On 24 Dec. 1706, parliament finally passed the salt tax. The enclosure (BL Add. MS. 70291, fol. 119) is not in Defoe's hand:
   My Ld Registers clause (approven)
       And wth proportionall Drawbacks & allowances as in England wth this exception, That Scotland after these seven years shall remain exempted from the duety of two shills & foure pence a bushell on home salt Imposed by an act Made in England in the Ninth & tenth of K Wm the third of England And if the parlat of Great Brittain shall at or before the expireing of the said seven years substitute any other Fund in place of the said 2 sh & 4 d of excise on the Bushell of home salt Scotland shall after the said seven years beare a proportion of the sd Fund and have ane equivalent in the terms of the Treaty
   Defoe's assessment was that by this outcome 'the Burden was both lessened in the Main, and Remote in prospect, and so the General Clamour wore off' (*History*, *TDH*, v111, 142).

DEFOE TO ROBERT HARLEY, 26 DECEMBER 1706

82

To Robert Harley

26 December 1706

HEADNOTE (Letters 82 and 83): In reports written on 26, 27, and 28 December, Defoe informs Harley about potential insurgencies against the Union. First, he elaborates on the brief account given in the previous letter of his successful collaboration with John Pierce to counter an incipient insurgence by John Hepburn, leader of a Covenanting group called the Hebronites in the west of Scotland. Second, Defoe anxiously records the arrival in Edinburgh of heretors (landed proprietors holding property directly from the crown, equivalent to English freeholders) from all over Scotland, seeking responses to their addresses. Letter 83, giving details of this gathering, is probably the one that occasioned Godolphin to write to Harley on 16 January 1707: 'De Foe's letter is serious and deserves reflection. I believe it is true and it ought to guide us very much in what we are doing here, and to take care in the first place to preserve the peace of that country.'[1] Neither rumoured uprising came to anything.

Sr

I am Unhappy in all This Negotiation That yor More Important Affairs Permit you Not Sometimes to Cast an Eye This way and spare me ye Consolaċon of a Line or two.

I Accquainted you in My Last I had a Letter from Our Itinerate[2] wc^h I had Not Then Time to Abstract; I Must Acknowlege he has Succeeded there beyond Expectaċon, and has Done Such Serviċe there as No Man in Scotland but himself Could have done, Nay he has Gone where No Man but himself Durst go at this Time.

He has been at Dumfreis, in ye Mountaines of Galloway, in ye Dales, and Allmost Every where, he has been wth m^r John Hepburn The Cameronian Bishop, spent Three dayes wth him, and with his Disciples, heard him preach and pray^a without Intermission near 7 houres, to a Vast^b Congregaċon Severall of wc^h Came 24 Miles on foot to hear him,[3] he has Opened his Eyes in Severall things, and he shows us he has been Missrepresented in Severall Others, and he

^{a} and pray] *interlined*
^{b} Vast] *interlined*

310

DEFOE TO ROBERT HARLEY, 26 DECEMBER 1706

Authourizes me to assure you there is No Danger from him, Unless Some New Artifice Succeed to Inflame them.

Some p[er]sons of Quallity here, and Sincere for yᵉ Union, haveing the knowlege of his being there, have been with me for This Two or Three Dayes, pressing me to write to p[er]swade him to stay there longer, being all Convinc't of yᵉ Suitableness of The p[er]son, and yᵉ Servicablness of yᵉ Design, for tis publick here that he is in Galloway, and 'tis the Onely place from whenceᵃ any Reall Danger is Apprehended.

Indeed Sr Nothing Restraines me in this Case but yᵉ Article of Expence, and haveing Said the Needfull on that head I Can Not add, for it is Not for me to Dictate to you.

If I had of my Own to Carry me thro' this affair I would not say a word and I fear I am too plain — Tis hard Sr if the Endeavour we Use here (and shall I Say it yᵉ hazard of Our lives for in both Cases that has been Evident) in Pushing on faithfully and Sincerely a Cause of this Concern should not be supported by the Govornmt — and Nothing has more prescrib'd me than when you were pleased to say it Comes from your Self.⁴

I Earnestly Entreat your Approbation of what I am doing and a word or two about supplye, for without it 'tis Impossible for me to Render you yᵉ Service I strive for; I am and shall be as spareing as is possible — Earnestly begging a line from you I Amᵇ

Sr

yor Most Obedt Servt

DF

Dec. 26. 1706

Text: BL Add. MS. 70291, fols. 120–1. *Address* (fol. 121v): To The Right Honble | Robert Harley Esqr | Her Majties Principal Secreta of State | Present. *Endorsed by Harley* (fol. 121v): Edenburg Dec: 26: 1706 ʀ Jan: 3 1706/7 Came a post too late

ᵃ whence] *interlined above cancelled word* 'where'
ᵇ Am] *amended from* 'Remain'

---

1   H.M.C. *Portland MSS*, ɪv, 382. Backscheider posits that Godolphin refers to Defoe's reports about the Scottish clergy objecting to the abjuration oath (*Life*, 231). However, the last extant letter to mention the abjuration oath is Letter 77, written on 16 Dec. and received by Harley

on 23 Dec., about three weeks before Godolphin's remark. Godolphin's tone also suggests an uprising rather than disgruntled clergymen.

2 *Our Itinerate*: Pierce.

3 *John Hepburn ... him*: In *A Tour thro' the Whole Island of Great Britain* (1724–6), Defoe describes an occasion (maybe imaginary) in which walking with a '*Darbyshire* Gentleman' and the Duke of Queensberry near Drumlanrig: 'Here we were surpriz'd with a Sight, which is not now so frequent in *Scotland* as it has been formerly, I mean one of their Field Meetings, where one Mr. *John Hepburn*, an old Cameronian, preach'd to an Auditory of near 7000 People, all sitting in Rows on the steep Side of a green Hill, and the Preacher in a little Pulpit made under a Tent at the Foot of the Hill; he held his Auditory, with not above an Intermission of half an Hour, almost seven Hours; and many of the poor People had come fifteen or sixteen Miles to hear him, and had all the Way to go home again on Foot' (*TDH*, III, 186).

4 *it Comes from your Self*: See Letter 51. Defoe received £10 at this time (H.M.C. *Portland MSS*, IV, 377–8).

83

To Robert Harley

27–8 December 1706

S^r

My Last was ye 26°; what ye p[ar]liam^t has done in ye Salt Tax I Enclosed you and that Clause is since past.[1]

I am Very Sorry to see things Run So heavy here But I am some times afraid the worst is not past here yet.

The Court here is Very Uneasy and I Doubt not but there is some Cause for it — I have Accquainted you of ye Appearances of Mobs and Tumults and I hope they are Over — but it has been Observ'd that Unusuall Concourse of strangers and Highlanders are Resorted to Town in these few weeks: at the[a] Ferrys of Leith and Queens Ferry Unusuall Numbers of Men Armd and horses have been seen to Come Over, and some Circular Letters have been Discovred sent privately about.[2]

This makes honest people here Very Uneasye, and I must Own I am not wthout just apprehensions.

Yesterday there was a great Council at ye Abbey[3] and to day the parliam^t Met — there was no Bussiness done but to forme y^e

---

[a] at the] *interlined following illegible cancelled words*

DEFOE TO ROBERT HARLEY, 27–8 DECEMBER 1706

Enclosed Proclamation wch pass't not without Great Opposition and a protest wth a number of adherers.[4]

Tis Certain there are Some Secret Designs[5] on foot; what they are Time and providenċe alone Can Discover.

In this Criticall Juncture J P[6] is Returnd. I Can not attempt to give you the hystory of his Journey in p[er]ticular, but tis a Most Unaccountable thing to think how ye Jacobite subtillty had Imposed Upon ye Ignorant people there and brought y^m to be Ready to Joyn with allmost any body to Raise a Dissturbanċe; Hepburn ye Minister, tho' Mad man Enough, Declares against Tumult and Arms, and J P Sayes there is no fear there;[7] the worst people are about Hamilton and y^t Side of ye Country, and prinċipally because they have the worst Engines About them, and are Dayly Deluded by the party of that family.

Finly, tho' a prisoner in ye Castle, Openly Drinks King James the 8th health — and tis as good a thing as he can do. I have made m^rᵃ J P write word of it into Galloway.

And to let you kno' S^r that I leav no stone Unturnd in this work I have procur'd Letters from^b Some Dissenting Ministers in England to Mest Jno Hepburn and to some of his prinċipall Neighbours to quallifye and p[er]swade him not to peaċe Onely but to p[er]swade his people to ye like.

After all S^r I Assure you tis a Very Criticall Juncture and things are Ripening apaċe; it will be Either a Union or all Confusion in a few weeks more.

Nothing afflicts me so much as not to hear from you or have ye least hint what Measures to take; I Resolve not to stir, while I Can wth any tollerable Safety be here Either in publick or private — but if any Disturbanċe happens I shall have an ill post.

My Ld Leven[8] has appeard to day by a Friend plainly to me to Desyre the Return of m^r J P.^c [T]hey^d are Sensible he has done Serviċe there, nor is there a man in Town Dare go there but him — and they are Very Jealous of those people.

ᵃ m^r] *following letters* 'All' *(probably for* 'Allen') *cancelled. Allen was Pierce's alias; see Letter 71, note 8*

ᵇ from] *following word* 'y^e' *cancelled*

ᶜ J P] *following word* 'and' *cancelled*

ᵈ [T]hey] *MS damaged*

313

DEFOE TO ROBERT HARLEY, 27–8 DECEMBER 1706

Upon these Repeated sollicitations we have Agreed he shall go Imediately — Indeed I Expected they would have Considred that he Could not be Out a month wth himself and Two horses, for my servant goes wth him, and spend for Ought they know his Own Money — However there was not ye least Mention of it — So I have furnish't him for the Journey Out of [th]e^a little stock left — I have Said Enough of that affair — and beg your pardon for it. I am satisfyed you will do what you think Needfull. I Accquiesce and Am

S^r

yor Most Obed^t Servt

DF

Dec. 27th^b 1706

The above was wrott yesterday, the Consternation here Encreases, and I see Every honest man loaded wth Concern Even in their Countenances; they say there are above 100 strangers come in to Town to day.

ye Sherif Deput of Lanerk, y^t is Deputy Lieut^t, Issued Out Circular letters for assembling;[9] they say he sent 69 Letters.

I have Removd my Lodging, for I have been Openly Threatened to be the first Sacrifiz[e].^c

Text: BL Add. MS. 70291, fols. 122–3. *Address* (fol. 123^v): To The Right Honble | Robert Harley Esqr | Her Maj^ties Princip^ll Secreta of State | Present. *Endorsed by Harley* (fol. 123^v): Edenburg Dec: 28: 1706 R Jan 2

---

^a [th]e] *MS damaged*
^b 27th] *amended from* '28th'
^c Sacrifiz[e]] *MS torn*

---

1 *that Clause is since past*: Article eight was approved on 26 Dec., following the resolution of the salt tax on 24 Dec. (*History of the Union*, *TDH*, VIII, 142).
2 *Unusuall ... about*: Freeholders from all over Scotland were beginning to gather in Edinburgh in Dec. 1706 in order to demand answers to their petitions. Their ultimate aim was to support a national address to the Queen.
3 *Abbey*: Holyrood Abbey.
4 *Enclosed ... adherers*: The enclosure is missing but is 'A Proclamation Discharging Unwarrantable and Seditious Convocations and Meetings', passed on 27 Dec. 1706, designed to impede a national address. Opposition to the proclamation was led by Lockhart (*History*, *TDH*, VIII, 147–50).
5 *Secret Designs*: On 28 and 29 Dec., Lockhart was corralling anti-Union members to prepare the text of a national address (*Lockhart Letters*, 37).
6 *J P*: John Pierce.

DEFOE TO JOHN FRANSHAM, 28 DECEMBER 1706

7 *Hepburn ... there*: Lockhart goes further than saying that Hepburn had been subdued, affirming that he had been recruited by the Court and 'served them as a spy. And though he roared as much as any against the Union, did nevertheless oppose all [the Covenanters'] measures of appearing openly against it' (*Lockhart Memoirs*, 182). Hepburn denied this, saying 'I was always against the Union', but claimed he was loth to join only with Jacobites to oppose it (*True Copy of a Letter Sent to the Reverend Mr. William Veitch, Minister at Dumfries* (1719), 27–8). In the *Review* for 9 Jan. 1707, Defoe vouches that Hepburn will not do the Jacobites' work (III, 805) and he again declares Hepburn peaceable in *History*, *TDH*, VII, 299.

8 *L⁴ Leven*: See Letter 60, note 9. For Godolphin's letter of introduction for Defoe to Leven in 1708, see headnote to Letter 132.

9 *Sherif ... assembling*: Andrew Hay of Craignethan, Sheriff-Depute of Lanarkshire under the Hamiltons (H.M.C. *Mar and Kellie MSS*, 363; *The Diary of Andrew Hay of Craignethan*, ed. Alexander George Reid (Edinburgh, 1901), xxvi). Queensberry got wind of the plot when handed a letter by Alexander Cunningham of Harperfield (1654–1737) (*Lockhart Memoirs*, 187). He examined Craignethan in the morning on 28 Dec. (Hamilton to the Duchess of Hamilton, 28 Dec. 1706, NRS GD 406/1/8030).

84

To John Fransham

28 December 1706

HEADNOTE: Defoe's first extant letter to Fransham since 24 May 1706 recaps his experiences in Scotland. One additional detail is Defoe's assertion that he thought about returning to England when he first witnessed the violence in Edinburgh.

Sir, — I have been several times going to give you some account of my being in this part of the world and some abstract of affairs here as what I thought would be both usefull and diverting to you and our friends in your parts.

I have been here three months and in a most difficult time. The Treaty of an Union has been receiv'd here with a different gust from what we in England expected, and indeed from what any rational people might expect.

The Kirk at first seem'd very ready to comply with it, and Mr Roswell and Mr Taylor,[1] two dissenting Ministers from London who were here before me, did their endeavour to answer all scruples, and indeed I was in hopes they had effectually answer'd the end of their coming.

DEFOE TO JOHN FRANSHAM, 28 DECEMBER 1706

But we soon found an alteration, and I must acknowledge chiefly from some hot men in the Assembly who when they came to Town set all in a Flame.

The Jacobite Interest had done their best before, and possest the people with their Trade and a multitude of wild chimera's, and one Mr. Hodges wrote a Book[2] full of Invectives against the Union and the English Nation, which being sent from England was industriously spread over the whole Kingdom.

But when these discontents met with proportion'd encouragement from the Ministers a louder cry was added to it that the Church was in danger — tis hard to describe the fury of the people here. The Treaters went in danger of their Lives and Sr Patrick Johnson, late Ld Provost and till then the peoples Darling, was assaulted in his House by the Rabble and had not the Guards reliev'd him before they broke the Door I believe he had been a second De Wit.[3]

I thought myself in no danger, having offer'd nothing to any body offensive, but the name of an Englishman had been sufficient and mine much more, however some Friends here that thought me in more danger than I thought myself secur'd me and I began to think of comeing to England again.

But the Government brought the Forces into the City and took such precautions that this Tumult was appeas'd and something of peace restor'd. I call it something of peace, for really it was but a something, for the people on all occasions exprest their Inveteracy and that in a most furious manner when they durst. If the Commissioner at any time staid at the parliament House later than ordinary so as to come down in the dark he was allways insulted with Stones and Dirt and Curses, the Guards hurt wth stones from the tops of Houses and once one of his Gentlemen beaten very cruelly in the Street.

All this while Duke Hamilton was Huzza'd and followed with the Blessings and prayers of the crowd following his coach every day.

In this manner they have gone on in parliament just as Nehemiah did with the Wall of Jerusalem with the sword in one hand and the mattock in the other.[4]

316

The Country follow'd this Example and in Glascow the Rabble have excersiz'd all manner of Insolencies to their Magistrates and to every body else that appear'd for the Union till at last they carried it up to open Rebellion and a Body of men march'd to an appointed Rendezvous but the Country not being so hasty as they that Plott has miscarried and a detachment of Dragoons sent against them have taken 5 of their principals who are now safe in the Castle.

Great endeavours have been since used to inflame the presbyterians in the West and a party of them did once in arms march 24 miles to Dumfries and solemnly burn the articles at the Market-Cross there and after that posted a protest against the union up upon the Cross.

Some endeavours have been us'd to open the eies of these deluded people and perhaps I might have told you particulars but I am not writing to set out myself. I shall only tell you I have done all my share and with better success than I expected. Things are cooler now everywhere, though yet there are some apprehensions in the West, and if our Friends should be so mad as to joyn the Jacobite party the strength here is too weak to oppose them and I wish that they be not drawn in.

During these agitations the parliament and Government go on vigorously enough at least considering the Ferment of the Country, how they are every day bullyed and worried wth pamphlets, Addresses, Representations and protests; there is indeed a happy Majority in the House but it is next to miraculous that they are not . . .[5] and hurried into dispair of success and so to give up the cause.

They are now pursuing the articles and examining the particulars. The plot of the party now is if possible to push them upon some amendments in the articles such as they think England will not nor cannot comply with and so break all to pieces in England.

Indeed this project have had but too much success and having had the honour to be allways sent for to the Committee to whom these amendments were referr'd I have had the good fortune to break their measures in two particulars, vizt the Bounty on Corn and the proportion of the Excise.[6]

Thus far things are now carryed the proceedings of the Kirk are more calm and regular but the presbyteries in the Country act wth no manner of consideration and an address the other day from

DEFOE TO JOHN FRANSHAM, 28 DECEMBER 1706

the presbytery of Hamilton to the parliament narrowly escap'd in parliament being censur'd as seditious and being burnt by the Hangman and I must own it deserv'd it.[7]

I endeavour in the Review, as I suppose you will see, to put the best Face on the proceedings of the Kirk and to distinguish between their actions as a Body and the actions of their Members in order to prevent the ill use will be made of these things among our high Flyers in England.[8] Thus according to my poor Talent I endeavour to reconcile you to these people and by all possible means keep up the character of their management tho' I must own tis a very difficult task.

I cannot enlarge. I dare not prophecy the Event but tis pity the two Nations should be divided any longer; this people are a Sober, Religious and Gallant Nation, the country good, the Soil in most places capable of vast improvements and nothing wanting but English Stocks, English Art and English Trade to make us all one great people.[9]

The Court are just now in apprehensions of more Tumults, great concourse of people being observed to come arm'd to the Town.

I am S^r your Friend & Servt

D. FOE.

Edinburgh Dec. 28, 1706.

Text: MS untraced. The copytext is Norgate, 283–4. *Address*: none recorded.

1   *Mr Roswell and Mr Taylor*: Samuel Rosewell (1679–1722), minister at Old Jewry; Christopher Taylor (d. 1723), minister at Leather Lane. A newsletter of 26 Oct. 1706 announces Rosewell's departure and Taylor's continuance in Scotland (H.M.C. *Portland MSS*, viii, 253; BL Add. MS. 70039, fol. 73r). Defoe refers to these 'two eminent English Divines' in *Passion and Prejudice* (1707), ii.
2   *Mr. Hodges wrote a Book*: James Hodges's *The Rights and Interests of the Two British Monarchies*. See Letter 59, note 12.
3   *De Wit*: See Letter 56, note 25.
4   *Nehemiah ... other*: 'They which builded on the wall, and they that bare burdens, with those that laded, *every one* with one of his hands wrought in the work, and with the other *hand* held a weapon' (Nehemiah 4:17). Because of violent opposition, the men rebuilding the wall of Jerusalem are armed.
5   *not ...*: Left blank for 'mobbed', 'killed', or some such.
6   *having ... Excise*: See Letter 68.
7   *address ... deserv'd it*: The Hamilton Presbytery address, received by parliament on 11 Dec., outlined 'the woful effects and consequences of Such an Union' to 'the Liberties both civil and Religious' of the people, stating that the Union would incur 'the Guilt of National Perjury' and cause violent uprisings (Bowie, *Addresses*, 269–70).

DEFOE TO ROBERT HARLEY, 2 JANUARY 1707

8 *I endeavour ... England*: See Letter 65, note 6 on Defoe's defences of the Church of Scotland in the *Review* during Nov. and early Dec. On 17 Dec., Defoe interrupted his reprinting in the *Review* of his *Fourth Essay, at Removing National Prejudices* in order again to exonerate the Church, distinguishing the ill conduct of individuals from the Church as a collective. He also prints the Commission of the General Assembly's circular letter dissuading members from encouraging tumults (III, 757–60).

9 *Soil ... people*: On this theme, see *Review*, III, 844–5 (28 Jan. 1707), and Defoe's *Caledonia*. Six years later he wrote: '*Scotland* is the most capable Spot of Ground now in *Europe*, for the present Improvements either of Land or Trade' (*A General History of Trade ... for the Month of August* (1713), 42–3). On 'the general Improvement of *Scotland*', see also *Review*, VI, 299–300 (16 Aug. 1709).

85

To Robert Harley

2 January 1707

HEADNOTE (**Letters 85–7**): The convergence of armed men on Edinburgh, which Defoe reported in his letters to Harley and to Fransham, was an attempt by the opposition to derail the Union. The Country party had sent letters to signatories of the addresses against Union sent to parliament, requesting they come to Edinburgh to seek responses. Divisions within the opposition undermined the project: Hamilton insisted that the national address they would prepare should include a clause agreeing to settle the succession on the Hanoverians, which was unacceptable to the Jacobite contingent.[1] As the opposition argued, the government acted with a proclamation 'discharging unwarrantable and seditious convocations and meetings', and the hopes for a national address and new parliament faded, as Defoe reports. Defoe's *Two Great Questions Considered*, published in January 1707, reacted to 'the Dialect of some people here, which to me is very strange; who have been talking very Confidently, of going to ask Parliament for an Answer to their Addresses'.[2] His letters in the first week of 1707 reveal Defoe's infiltration of the resistance movement, his gleaning intelligence from participants, and his efforts to ameliorate what he deemed legitimate anxieties of the Church and to forestall their taking steps that could threaten the Union.

Sr

I wrott you at Large last post; the feares we were then in Vanish apaće. I have Incognito gotten into yᵉ Compᵃ of Some of the people who Came here on yᵉ Design I mencŏned.[3]

319

DEFOE TO ROBERT HARLEY, 2 JANUARY 1707

They Own ye Design was to have Gone in a body to ye Commissioner and Then to ye parliam^t and Demanded[a] Answers to their peticons — they do not Deny that if the people had[b] taken that Occasion to have Risen they would not have been ill pleased, Nor I suppose backward to Encourage them all they Could, But I do not find they were Very forward to venture their Own heads in ye Fray; — and this Baulks all their Designs, for I Observ they are like ye Pharisees in ye Gospell that bound heavy Burthens on Other Mens shoulders but would not Touch them &c.[4]

Some of them I Understand are gone away again, and Indeed the Dearness of this place, where people Now pay from 2^s to 5^s a night for Nasty Lodgings, will Soon Make them weary of their attendance, And their private Discourse is of addressing the Queen. I was Glad when I heard that, but Can not Imagin what they can ask of her Maj^tie or what they can have the face to say for their Cause.

The Union Mean time proceeds Apace and this day they past the 16, 17 and 18th Articles about Coin, weights and Measures.[5]

I wrott you at large About ye Kirk. I hope tho' you do not think Fitt to Replye to me you will take that Case in thought; they are now on an act to be proposed to ye house to put a Test upon all English men Enjoying places in Scotland Equivalent to that in[c] England.[6]

If nothing better Can be found Out for me I Could Wish you will please to Settle me here after ye Union;[7] p[er]haps I might do her Maj^tie a Service of One Sort while I was in an office of a Different Face, but of that hereafter.

I am

S^r

yor Most Obed^t Servt

DF

Jan. 2.^d 1706[8]

---

[a] Demanded] *following word* 'and' *cancelled*
[b] had] *following word* 'took' *cancelled*
[c] that in] *interlined*
[d] Jan. 2] *interlined above illegible cancelled words probably* 'Dec.' *and a date*

DEFOE TO ROBERT HARLEY, 2 JANUARY 1707

Text: BL Add. MS. 70291, fols. 124–5. *Address* (fol. 125ᵛ): To The Right Honᵇˡᵉ | Robert Harley Esqʳ | Her Majᵗⁱᵉˢ Prinċipall Secretᵃ of State | Present

1 Writing to his mother on 1 Jan. 1707, Hamilton states that he merely complied with Atholl in encouraging the gentlemen heretors to come to Edinburgh, and that he wanted to concede on the succession (NRS GD 406/1/8073).

2 *Two Great Questions Considered … Being a Sixth Essay at Removing National Prejudices against the Union*, *PEW*, IV, 177.

3 *people … menċoned*: The heretors who had arrived in Edinburgh to request responses from parliament to their addresses.

4 *Pharisees … them &c.*: 'For they bind heavy burdens and grievous to be borne, and lay *them* on men's shoulders; but they *themselves* will not move them with one of their fingers' (Matt. 23:4).

5 *this day … Measures*: Article sixteen regularised currency to the English standard; article seventeen standardised weights and measures; and article eighteen standardised laws of trade and excise. They were all passed on 31 Dec. 1706 rather than 2 Jan. (*History of the Union*, *TDH*, VIII, 156–9). This discrepancy might be explained by Defoe's having amended the date on this letter.

6 *act … England*: Holders of public office in England were required by the 1673 Test Act to take Anglican communion. This was one of the complaints of the Commission's second address: Scottish Presbyterians unwilling to meet this requirement would face civic restrictions in England that Anglicans would not in Scotland. Some in the Scottish parliament unsuccessfully proposed a reciprocal 'test' for Englishmen employed in Scotland, requiring they acknowledge the legality of, and pledge not to subvert, the Church of Scotland. Defoe believed these requests were 'offered only to Embarrass the present great Affair upon the Stage' (*History*, *TDH*, VIII, 159). That is perhaps true of the motion on 31 Dec., being considered here, though Bennet's account suggests it was not the intention when the idea was first mooted on 12 Nov. (NRS GD 90/2/172/2/10).

In 1712 Defoe noted that the idea of a Presbyterian 'test' in Scotland was rejected in 1706 because the Commission and parliament judged that it debased a religious ordinance to make it a civic qualification and would not keep immoral people out: they would do whatever was needed to qualify for office. Above all, the Scots trusted the English, which Defoe, in the wake of the 1712 Episcopal Toleration Act, deems an '*Unhappy Credulity*' (*Review*, VIII, 614 (5 Feb. 1712)).

7 *Settle me here after yᵉ Union*: In a 4 Jan. letter to Harley, Godolphin remarked: 'I think there is not much to be said upon your Scotch letters more than to ask you what should be given to D[e] F[oe]' (H.M.C. *Bath MSS*, I, 152). Defoe's requests for employment in Scotland would continue until summer 1707. See Letters 111, 113, and 114. Defoe was ultimately persuaded by the ministers to continue to serve in a 'Private Capascity' rather than in a salaried post (see Letters 119 and 180).

8 *1706*: 1707 new style.

321

86

To Robert Harley

4 January 1707

Sr

I wrott you last post, That ye Apprehension We were Under here began to Vanish, The Day begins to shine after all The Nights of Cloud and Darkness[1] we have had here.

The Crowd of Strangers lessens Amain. They had, as I am Informd by Some of Their Own friends, Three private Meetings and One Generall Meeting to Consult what to do.

D. Hamilton proposed to his people to wait on ye Comissr and beg him to give Them Time to adress ye Queen, but ye Difficulty was how to get to him — No Single Man would do it and to go in a body as they Designd they knew they would not be Admitted.

I am Told yt in One of Their Meetings Some Force was proposed but they found themselves too weak for ye Attempt.[2]

At their Generall Meeting it was offred to Draw up a Peticon or address to ye Queen, To Offer ye Succession and an Expedient for ye Union or at least for a Delay but the D of Athol told them his Men would not Come into the succession, so that Vanisht[3] — Then a protest was proposed In wch was to be Express't their Detestation of ye Union in Terms Bitter Enough, their being Imposed Upon in the parliamt, the Guards and power of ye Court and the Bribes of English Money haveing frighted or[a] Debaucht the Parliamt from their Duty, That they are betraid, bought and sold, and are to be Enslav'd to ye English.

I am promised a Sight of the Drafte proposed; if I Can get it I shall not fail to Transmitt it p[er] Next.

In This Little scheme of their Affaires I have Acted a True spy to you, for by an Unexpected Success I have Obtaind a Converse wth Some Gentlemen belonging to ye D of Gordon[4] who are Very Frank and I Dare say the perticulars Above are Unknown to the Commissioner himself; their Assembly broke Up without any Conclusion.

---

[a] frighted or] *interlined*

DEFOE TO ROBERT HARLEY, 4 JANUARY 1707

I Can Not help giveing you ye Satisfacçon of Letting you kno' S^r that I believ the bussiness as good as Over here and if I may yet beg a line from you S^r it should be for yor Orders when to Leave this plaçe or how to Govorn my Self.

I Confess s^r I have had an Uneasy Post here^a Under so Many frequent Feares of Murther, Tumult, Rabble &c, but I Resolv Not to be Uneasy in Any of yor Commands.

My Chief Uneasyness ha[s been the w]ant^b of Now and Then a line from you, without w[ch]^c I am in So Many Doubts whether my letters Reach your hand, whether my Measures here please you and the like that Indeed s^r It is Very Discourageing at this Distançe.

I shall Very Impaçently wait yor Direcçons About My stay here or Comeing Away; if you please to Ord^r me away my former Solliçitation for a Supply Ends wth a small Ord^r for Travailing Charge — and I Say This to Convinçe you S^r that I have Never Solliçited for any thing but ye Absolutely Necessary Dissburses, and am Very forward to put a stop to them.

I Think you will Expect me to attend yor Ord^rs for staying or Goeing and I shall do So, as a Duty to ye Serviçe, but when I See my Self Uncapable of More Serviçe I shall think Very Much of ye Charge.

The 19th Article was past yesterday wth Some Amendm^ts Relateing to their Own Courts^5 &c. wch England will not be Much Concern'd in; to day They Sitt on private bussiness^6 and I believ about 14 dayes more will End the session and I May give you Joy of the Union.

I am

S^r yor Most Obed^t Servt

DF

Edinb. Jan^a. 4. 1706^7

Text: BL Add. MS. 70291, fols. 126–7. *Address* (fol. 127^v): To The Right Honble | Robert Harley Esqr | Her Maj^ties Prinçipall Secreta of State | Present. *Endorsed by Harley* (fol. 127^v): Edenburg R Jan: 10:

---

^a here] *following letter probably* 'T' *cancelled*
^b ha[s been the w]ant] *MS torn*
^c w[ch]] *MS torn*

DEFOE TO ROBERT HARLEY, 6 JANUARY 1707

1 *Day ... Darkness*: Possibly alluding to Psalms 97:2–4.
2 *in One ... Attempt*: See *Lockhart Memoirs*, 194–5; NLS Wodrow Quarto IV, fol. 140.
3 *At their ... Vanisht*: On the disagreements among the opponents of Union at this time, see Stephen, *Scottish Presbyterians*, 199–200.
4 *D of Gordon*: George Gordon, first Duke of Gordon (b. in or before 1649, d. 1716), a Roman Catholic praised somewhat tentatively or by formula by Defoe in *Caledonia* (1706), lines 932–40, *PEW*, IV, 256–7. For the controversy caused by his wife's gift of a Jacobite medal to the Edinburgh Faculty of Advocates in 1711, see Letters 192 and 194.
5 *19th Article ... Courts*: Article nineteen provided for the continuation of Scotland's separate legal system by retaining the Court of Session and Court of Justiciary but bringing them under the administration of the British parliament. It was passed with an amendment pertaining to the qualification of judges on 3 Jan. 1707 (*History*, *TDH*, VIII, 162–4).
6 *private bussiness*: See *History*, *TDH*, VIII, 164–7.
7 *1706*: 1707 new style.

87

To Robert Harley

6 January 1707

Sr

I have little to say to Day but to Confirm what my Last hinted, That all ye feares of ye Matter is Now Over on this Side and The Angus men &c. are Most of them Dropt away as Silently as they Came.

I wrott you Earnestly sr last post for yor Ordrs about my Goeing Or staying when ye Union is Over here and I Repeat my Request on that head, but am to Accquat you They press me here to stay a few weeks^a after to Quiet peoples minds about it.

I am to leave yt Wholly to you Sr by whose breath I would Direct all my Measures on this head and therefore Again most Earnestly Entreat your thoughts on that subject.

> I am
> yor Most Obedt Servt
> DF

They have began to day on the 22th Article.[1]

---

^a weeks] *following word* 'till' *cancelled*

Edinb. Janª. 6. 1706[2]

Text: BL Add. MS. 70291, fols. 128–9. *Address* (fol. 129v): To The Right Honble | Robert Harley Esqr | Her Majties Prinċipal Secretª of State | Present.

1 *22th Article*: Article twenty-two established the Scottish representation in the British parliament as forty-five commoners and sixteen elected peers. It was read for the first time in parliament on 6 Jan. 1707 but adjourned to the next sitting (*History of the Union, TDH*, v111, 167–8).
2 *1706*: 1707 new style.

88

To Robert Harley

9 January 1707

HEADNOTE **(Letters 88–90)**: After the prospect of a national address to Queen Anne organised by the opposition faded, parliament completed the final work of ratification. Approving the proposed representation in the British parliament, and determining the selection of representatives, was expected to be a hurdle. Article twenty-two, giving Scotland sixteen peers and forty-five seats in the Commons, passed amidst acrimony.[1] But then details about how those representatives were to be selected were resolved with few problems. On 16 January 1707, parliament ratified the Union. Defoe called it 'the Famous Day to *Scotland*, in which She set Her Signal to the Union of *Great Britain*'.[2]

Defoe continued in his efforts to allay the anxieties of the ministers in the Commission of the General Assembly, and he persevered in pleading to Harley on behalf of conscientious but loyal ministers. He believed some matters were prompting disproportionate responses from the Scottish clergy, such as their abortive proposal of a Scottish equivalent to the English Test Act targeted at Anglicans, which would have required public office holders in Scotland to pledge to uphold the Church of Scotland. But he shared the ministers' qualms about the abjuration oath, which in its present form would require Scottish Presbyterians to deny the right to the throne of their own coreligionists.

Sr

I hope I may Now give you Joy of ye Union, The 22th Article haveing past last Tuesday night by a Majority of 40 Voiċes.[3]

325

DEFOE TO ROBERT HARLEY, 9 JANUARY 1707

Yesterday The house Sat But did No bussiness but Quarrell —
The Duke of Athol had made a formall protest Against ye Vote of
ye Day before, So had Severall others as you will I presume See by
The Minuts.[4]

The D of Argile Said it[5] was Indecent, Illegall and Iregular;
ye Duke of Athol Defended it and Reflected On ye D of Argile
and words Rise at last to a loss of all Decency on both sides,
giveing and Returning ye Lye in ye Open Assembly — The
house took it Up and Made them both Give Their Words to
stand by ye Decision of ye E of Marschall,[6] E of Leven, Genll,[7]
and Ld Errol, Constable,[8] or to be Committed, So I hope tis at
an End.

There is Some Expectacon of Another ill Naturd paper from
ye Church About an Oath to be Imposed Upon English men
here, and haveing ye honor to wait on the Comissionr last Night I
find[a] his grace is Something Apprehensiv of it; I have Since been
wth Some of ye Ministers and am Not Out of hopes of getting it
stop't.

Yesterday was a Day of Disaster and Scotland has Lost One of ye
best Men in ye Nacon, I mean as to Publick Matters, My Ld Stair;
he was in ye house and Made an Extraordinary speech on ye Debate
on ye 22d Article and was found Dead in his bed in ye Morning;[9] he
was Alive at 4 a Clock and spoke to his Lady,[10] Went to sleep Again
and Wak't No More in This state; he is Generally[11] Lamented, and
had he Dyed a little Sooner would ha' been Very Much Wanted
in ye house where he was One of ye Most Usefull Members in ye
Grand affair.

> I am
> yor Most Obedt Servt
> DF

Jana 9. 1707, for So they write here from New year Day.[12]

Text: BL Add. MS. 70291, fols. 130–1. *Address* (fol. 131v): To The Right Honble |
Robert Harley Esqr | Her Majties Principal Secreta of State | Present

---

[a] I find] *interlined*

326

DEFOE TO ROBERT HARLEY, 9 JANUARY 1707

1 Defoe argued that the calculations used to arrive at this representation were fair (*A Fourth Essay, at Removing National Prejudices, PEW*, IV, 131–2; *History of the Union, TDH*, VII, 208–11).

2 *History, TDH*, VIII, 190.

3 *22th Article … 40 Voices*: Article twenty-two passed in three votes on 7 and 9 Jan. 1707. The first vote, on Tuesday 7 Jan., was 113 votes to 73 (*APS*, XI, 388–96). Hamilton did not follow through on a planned protest and walk-out following the vote, and from then the opposition's unity crumbled (*Lockhart Memoirs*, 188–96).

4 *Duke … Minuts*: On 7 Jan., the following members protested against the vote on article twenty-two: Atholl; David Erskine, ninth Earl of Buchan (1672–1745); Lockhart of Carnwath; and Walter Stewart of Pardovan (1667–1719). Charles Hay (1677–1717), thirteenth Earl of Errol and Lord High Constable of Scotland, and William Keith (*c.* 1664–1712), ninth Earl Marischal and Grand Marischal of Scotland, also each protested against their heritable offices being 'weakened or prejudged' by the Union, though these were pro forma protests. On 8 Jan., the debate turned to whether these protests would be listed in the minutes or printed. The resolution reached on 9 Jan. ('after some Heat', says Defoe) was that the protests would be recorded but not inserted at length in the minutes. Defoe printed them as appendices to his *History, TDH*, VIII, 171–7.

5 *it*: I.e. the protest by Atholl, Buchan, Lockhart, and Stewart.

6 *E of Marschall*: The Earl Marischal was custodian of the royal regalia and guard of the monarch's person in parliament.

7 *E of Leven, Genll*: Leven was Commander-in-Chief in Scotland.

8 *Ld Errol, Constable*: The Earl of Erroll was the title given to the Lord High Constable.

9 *Ld Stair … Morning*: John Dalrymple (1648–1707), first Earl of Stair, former Lord Advocate and a Union commissioner. He died on 8 Jan. 1707, 'his spirits being quite exhausted by the length and vehemence of the debate' on article twenty-two the previous day (Burnet, V, 284). Defoe said that he 'was justly reputed the greatest Man of Counsel in the Kingdom of *Scotland*' and 'an Eminent Instrument in carrying on the Union' (*History, TDH*, VIII, 201). Defoe met Stair in London when he served as a Union commissioner in May 1706 (George Scott to his brother, 14 May 1706, EUL MS. Laing 11, 63).

10 *Lady*: Elizabeth Dalrymple, *née* Dundas (d. 1731).

11 *Generally*: universally.

12 *New year Day*: The convention in England was to amend the year from 25 Mar. onwards; the preceding letters use '1706', but the succeeding ones use '1707' in accordance with the Scottish convention.

89

To Robert Harley

11 January 1707

Sr

I wrott you Last post ye Accot of ye broil in the Parliamt on ye protests and of ye suddain Death of ye E of Stair.

The house have Since been Taken up Upon the proposall I hinted of an Oath &c. wch is Thrown Out.[1]

It was Hatch't in a private Cabal of parsons[a] and proposed to ye[b] Commission but ye Ministers Were prevaild on to Refuse it and I hope I may say wthout Vanity I have been Usefull in that p[ar]t.[2]

The Rejecting it there stab'd it to ye heart and tho' it was offred in p[ar]liamt it ye sooner sunk there.

The Ministers prest hard for an Explanation of ye Clause in ye Abjuration Oath binding ye successor to be in ye Communion of ye C of E — and Indeed it seems to me So Rationall that I Can not but think they Ought to have it, Not that Ever a presbyterian king is likely to Come, but it would be hard to make ye Ministers abjure a prince for being of their Own p[er]swasion, and England that Dispenses wth the Quakers takeing it atall and Accepts their Affirmation for an Oath,[3] will Never Scruple this — and if not done half the ministers in Scotland and some Sincere friends to ye Union and who have been Very Servicable in it will be Turn'd Out of their places wch will make here Intollerable Confusions.

One line sr from you to ye Commissionr here would Soften all this and I p[er]swade my Self you will be sencible of ye Necessity.

The Council are Sitting to Day on that Article of the Kirks Representation Respecting ye Encourageing papists, ye Number of popish priests &c.[4]

I am

Sr

yor Most Obedt Servt

DF

---

[a] of parsons] *interlined*
[b] ye] *following word* 'Committee' *cancelled*

DEFOE TO ROBERT HARLEY, 16 JANUARY 1707

Edinb. Jan.ᵃ 11. 1707

Text: BL Add. MS. 70291, fols. 132–3. *Address* (fol. 133ᵛ): To The Right Honᵇˡᵉ |
Robert Harley Esqʳ | Her Majᵗⁱᵉˢ Princ̓ipall Secretᵃ of State | Present

1 *house ... Out*: On 10 Jan., parliament rejected what Defoe called a 'Counter Test', an oath
   acknowledging the Church of Scotland as a precondition for civil employment in Scotland
   (*History of the Union, TDH*, vɪɪɪ, 178–80). Defoe commends the decision in *Two Great Questions Considered, PEW*, ɪv, 195–6.
2 *Hatch't ... p[ar]t*: In his *History*, Defoe explains that a majority in the Commission of the
   General Assembly either did not think it their role to interfere in civil matters, were opposed
   in principle to religious tests, or believed that the Union as it stood exempted them from the
   English sacramental test (*TDH*, vɪɪɪ, 179–80).
3 *England ... Oath*: Theologically opposed to oaths, the Quakers were permitted by a 1695 act
   to offer an affirmation where the law required an oath.
4 *Article ... popish priests &c.*: Article one of the third address of the Commission of the General Assembly (see Letter 63, note 6) blamed 'the lamentable Encrease of Popery' on the
   government's failure to clamp down on Catholic worship, education, and inter-marriage with
   Protestants (*Review*, ɪɪɪ, 736 (5 Dec. 1706)).

90

To Robert Harley

16 January 1707

Sʳ

I am Now wᵗʰ Joy to Accquaᵗ you That the Treaty of Union Recᵈ
yᵉ Touch of yᵉ scepter this dayⁱ and an Universall Joy of yᵉ Friends
of both Nations Runs thro' the Citty.

The Church has made Some Struggles² but they are faint and
Opposed by the most worthy, Learned and to be Vallued of their
Number who Deserv Regard and mʳ Carstares³ in p[er]ticular
Merits Great Consideration on that accoᵗ.

It is not my bussiness to Recomend p[er]sons. I wait now yoʳ
Instructions whether to stay or Come away and am

Sʳ

yoʳ Most Obedᵗ Servᵗ

DF

329

Edinb. Jan. 16. 1707

Text: BL Add. MS. 70291, fols. 134–5. *Address* (fol. 135ᵛ): To The Right Honble | Robert Harley Esqʳ | Princ̍ipall Secretᵃ of State | Present. *Endorsed by an unknown hand* (fol. 135ᵛ): Mr De Foe

1   *Treaty … day*: On 16 Jan. 1707, parliament ratified the Union Treaty.
2   *The Church has made Some Struggles*: On 14–15 Jan., the Commission of the General Assembly debated presenting another address to parliament but decided against it. However, an address did come. See Letter 91.
3   *mr Carstares*: William Carstares (1649–1715), minister of the Church of Scotland and Moderator of the Commission of the General Assembly. He was one of William III's main advisors on Scotland and supported the Union. See A. Ian Dunlop, *William Carstares and the Kirk by Law Established* (Edinburgh, 1964), 116 for Carstares's role in restraining this 'Second Letter to Parliament'. See also his letter to Defoe of 10 Feb. 1713 (Letter 224).

91

To Robert Harley

17 January 1707

HEADNOTE: In January Defoe published in Edinburgh *A Fifth Essay, at Removing National Prejudices*, which responded to economic arguments against the Union, and *Two Great Questions Considered … Being a Sixth Essay at Removing National Prejudices against the Union*, which considered addresses to parliament and the compatibility of Union with Scotland's national covenants. William Black (d. 1745) promptly attacked Defoe's *Fifth Essay*, saying that, in dismissing anti-Union addresses to parliament, Defoe 'endeavours to overturn the Revolution Principles, he set up for in *England*', calling him 'a Time-server' who 'Patronize[s] not the best Cause, but the wealthiest Client'.[1] As well as coming under fire for his constitutional and economic arguments for the Union, Defoe was attacked for defending its religious bases: many Scottish Presbyterians opposed a Union that approbated the Episcopal structure of the Church of England, believing this contravened the 1638 National Covenant and 1643 Solemn League and Covenant. At this time, Defoe entered into a dispute in print with the Scottish clergyman James Webster (1659–1720).

DEFOE TO ROBERT HARLEY, 17 JANUARY 1707

S#r#

Since y#e# papers I lately sent you I have printed here Two Essayes.[2] One I Enclose you here, The Other shall be sent The Next post.

The Bussiness Seems Now to be Over, But the Dissatisfaccons of y#e# kirk begin to Reviv On y#e# Two following Occasions, w#ch# I Think tis Very Needfull to Accqua#t# you with.

The kirk, Especally the Ministers, Mov'd for an Explanacon of y#e# Abjuracon Oath, y#e# Thing I formerly hinted — but no Notice was Taken of it,[3] Nor of the following.

Just at y#e# breaking Up of y#e# Parliam#t# on That Day**[a]** They Supplicated again Against y#e# Clause w#ch# leaves y#e# C of England to make any Act they shall see fitt for their Own Settlem#t# and that it shall Implicitly be passt w#th#out being Reconsidred here.[4]

Tis True, as they alleage, the Church may bring in some things Inconsistent w#th#**[b]** or Invasiv of the Church here, or y#e# Dissenters in England, and 'tis passt of Course, and This they make the people Very Uneasy about here.

Tis True also that if y#e# C of E should make an act the Most Reasonable in y#e# World And it should be brought hither to be Confirm'd, the wholl Nation would Crye Out Murther and the Clergy Roar Out prelacy and the Covenant.[5]

You will pardon my freedom S#r# of Expression; they are a Restless Uneasy people but Tender Usage and Cool Counsels may Mannage Them, and you are too Much Master of Such Measures to Need that I add any Thing on that head.

I Enclose you also a p[iece]#c#[6] like <u>a post Hume</u> birth[7] brought to light just after y#e# work was Over.

What posess't y#e# Man is hard to guess, Since he has Ever Since I have been here, and before, profess't himself for y#e# Union and often in my hearing Declared the Church Could Not be Safe without it.

But this is an Instance of y#e# Change in Temper I Mencon'd above. The Man is a worthy Good Man,**[d]** popular in Character, a

---

[a] on That Day] *interlined*
[b] w#th#] *interlined*
[c] p[iece]] *MS gives a 'special p' brevigraph followed by an 's'; 'ps' as in 'post script' is possible but 'piece' seems more probable*
[d] Man] *following illegible word cancelled*

331

DEFOE TO ROBERT HARLEY, 17 JANUARY 1707

great preacher — and wch you will think strange by his poetry[8] a Man of witt, a good judge, and of a Clear head:[a] In short s^r he is in himself ye Very Reverse of the pamphlett — what Dark Interval has posest him at such a juncture is Every mans Surprize to know.[9]

But tis most Surprizeing to see wth what Greedyness ye Town Runs wth him.

I shall Take him to task in ye best manner I Can but tis a Tender point and as I have studiously preservd[b] an Esteem wth all his friends and wch I have found Very much to ye purpose in what I have been Doeing here So I must use him wondrous Gently and shall Onely take him to task for his falling on ye English Dissenters[10] wch Indeed Everybody blames him for.

I shall by next post Transmitt you ye Coppy of what I Say to him[11] and anything Elce that Occurs Mean Time, Referring to my last.

I am

S^r

yor Most Obed^t Servt

DF

Edinb. Jan^a. 17. 1707

PS

There was a hard pull in ye Comission of ye Assembly on ye 14 and 15 to obtain a Remonstrance to ye p[ar]liam^t against the things above noted but it was Carryed in the Negativ.

Text: BL Add. MS. 70291, fols. 136–7. *Address* (fol. 137^v): To The Right Honble | Robert Harley Esqr | Her Maj^ties Principal Secret^a of State | Present

---

[a] head:] 'head:,' *in MS; comma omitted in this edition*
[b] preservd] *following word* 'my' *cancelled*

---

1 William Black, *A Reply to the Authors of the Advantages of Scotland by an Incorporate Union; and of The Fifth Essay, at Removing National Prejudices* (1706), 3, 18.
2 *Two Essayes*: Likely *A Fifth Essay, at Removing National Prejudices* and *Two Great Questions Considered ... Being a Sixth Essay at Removing National Prejudices against the Union*. See headnote. A section of the first was recycled in the *Review* for 18 Jan., and about half of the latter in the *Review* from 23 to 30 Jan. Neither of the copies Defoe enclosed remains with the letters.

DEFOE TO ROBERT HARLEY, 17 JANUARY 1707

3 *Explanaćon ... it*: By contrast, Defoe is sanguine about parliament's disinclination to address the abjuration oath in *History of the Union, TDH*, VIII, 177. He does not mention it in his observations on the parliamentary minutes of 16 Jan. 1707 in his *History*.

4 *Supplicated ... here*: The Commission of the General Assembly presented another address, its fourth, on 16 Jan. It did so because a clause was added to the Treaty allowing the English parliament to add an Act of Security for the Church of England, equivalent to that passed in Scotland, which act would not be ratified by the Scottish parliament (*History, TDH*, VIII, 190; NRS CH 1/2/5/4, 260; Bowie, *Addresses*, 62–4). On the hurried genesis and neglect of this fourth address, see the account of Walter Stewart of Pardovan, in Bowie, *Addresses*, 327–9.

5 *wholl ... Covenant*: See headnote. Answering concerns about the national covenants in *Two Great Questions Considered*, Defoe argued that the Union was a purely political measure, not a religious one (*PEW*, IV, 187–97). This is echoed in his *The Dissenters in England Vindicated* (1707), 2. In his *History*, Defoe returned to the issue of the 'Blank' left in the Treaty for a Church of England Act of Security: 'If the *Scots* may be said to have Consented to Establish Episcopacy, it is every whit as plain, That the *English* have Establish'd Presbytery in *Scotland*, with this further Distinction, That what has been done in *Scotland*, is an Act of the State only, in *England* both Church and State have given their Sanction to the Establishment of the Presbyterian Church of *Scotland*, the Bishops [in the House of Lords] being the Representatives of the Church of *England* in this Case' (*TDH*, VIII, 195).

6 *p[iece]*: The enclosure is missing from the correspondence, but it was *Lawful Prejudices against an Incorporating Union with England* (1707), by the Church of Scotland minister James Webster.

7 *a post Hume birth*: Posthumous; born after the father's death.

8 *poetry*: Webster's *Lawful Prejudices* included eight lines of poetry (5), which Defoe later mocked for 'false Measure, false Grammar, Plagiarism, want of Signification, Cadence, and Civility' in *Passion and Prejudice* (1707), 9.

9 *he ... know*: See Defoe's *The Dissenters Vindicated* (1707), sig. A 2r–v, and *Passion and Prejudice*, 4, for his account of Webster's earlier pro-Union stance and their personal acquaintance.

10 *take ... Dissenters*: As well as arguing that Union contravened Scotland's National Covenant and that the Act of Security was an inadequate safeguard for the Kirk, Webster criticised English Dissenters, 'who deserve better to be call'd *Episcopal* than *Presbyterian*' (8). Defoe called this 'a wild Attempt ... to prove, the *Dissenters* in *England* are enclin'd to Episcopacy, and therefore not to be trusted by the Kirk' (*Review*, IV, 82 (18 Mar. 1707)).

11 *what I Say to him*: Defoe responded to *Lawful Prejudices* with *The Dissenters in England Vindicated from Some Reflections in a Late Pamphlet, Entituled, Lawful Prejudices, &c.* (1707). The copy he enclosed does not remain with the letters.

DEFOE TO JAMES WEBSTER, [LATE JANUARY 1707?]

92

To James Webster

[late January 1707?][1]

HEADNOTE **(Letters 92 and 93)**: On 17 January, Defoe reported to Harley that Webster had published a pamphlet called *Lawful Prejudices against an Incorporating Union with England*, apparently a total reversal of his previous public attitude to the Union. Defoe evidently held Webster in esteem and was wary of aggravating the Church of Scotland clergy as a whole, so he wrote the first letter here to give notice of his *The Dissenters in England Vindicated*, a pamphlet that reacts to Webster's attacks on the English Presbyterians.[2] In that work, Defoe is respectful towards Webster (whom he does not name) but says Webster's '*Out-of-Season-Piece*' has 'grosly injur'd, wrong'd, and ill-treated' the English Presbyterians in charging them with trying to make accommodations with the Church of England following the Restoration.[3] Defoe says he expected a response to his 'obliging' letter and a conference, but he received none. 'The next News I heard of the Author', Defoe relates, 'was, That he was pleased to send a Messenger to my good Friend, at whose House I lodge, to borrow several Books of my Writing', which Defoe understood from his friend was to furnish materials for a rejoinder.[4]

Defoe published these two letters in *Passion and Prejudice* (1707), a response to Webster that Defoe then suppressed in favour of a more temperate response.[5] The fact that Webster could quite easily have denied the existence or accuracy of the letters suggests that they are authentic though no manuscripts are known.

Sir,

I Am heartily sorry that I find my self under an absolutely necessary Call to debate some Points with you in Print----. I am sensible, Sir, of my being a very unequal Match for you, and I'le convince you of my being unwillingly forc't to this by my taking up none of the Points you engage in, but such as concern an absent and wrongfully accused People: Pardon me that Liberty, *who I must not see injur'd, without doing them Justice.*

Indeed, Sir, I wondred much to hear, that Mr. Webster *was in Print against the Union, who, I had always heard declaring himself for it,*[6] *and there sits by me, a Reverend Brother of the same Ministry with your self, who declares you the first in his Countrey speaking for it; but of this I shall say nothing, since you ought to change your Opinion, when, and as often as you see Cause.*

334

DEFOE TO JAMES WEBSTER, [LATE JANUARY 1707?]

But what should move you to treat, with so much Contempt, your Brethren in England, *and call the Dissenters by so many hard Epithets which I hope to make appear they do not deserve. I cannot imagine, and I doubt not to convince you they have none of the Guilt on them you charge them with.*

In pursuing this, which I think my Duty and a just Defence of the injur'd and absent Strangers, I shall endeavour to preserve not the Rule of Decency only, but that sincere Respect I always had to your Personal Merit, and all possible Reverence to your Office, and the Dignity you so well, and so worthily enjoy in this City and Church.

I hope you will bear with me in all necessary Plainness, and excuse the Liberties the Argument obliges me to, who very unwillingly engage in this Cause with one, for whom no Man in Scotland *has more Respect than*

Your Humble Servant
D. F.

Text: Daniel Defoe, *Passion and Prejudice, The Support of one Another, and Both Destructive to the Happiness of this Nation, in Church and State; Being A Reply to the Vindicator of Mr. W----r's Lawful Prejudices* (Edinburgh, 1707), 5. *Address*: none recorded.

---

1 The letter as printed in Defoe's *Passion and Prejudice* is undated, but Defoe indicates it was sent to Webster before Defoe's *The Dissenters in England Vindicated* was written. Defoe was clearly planning that work when he wrote to Harley on 17 Jan., and he sent it to Harley on 27 Jan.

2 Not to be confused with Defoe's *The Dissenters Vindicated* (1707), on which see Letter 102, note 17.

3 *The Dissenters in England Vindicated*, 1, 3.

4 Defoe, *Passion and Prejudice*, 5. For Webster's rejoinder and Defoe's two responses (one of which he suppressed), see Letter 96, note 16, and Letter 102.

5 See Letter 102.

6 *Mr. Webster ... for it*: See Letter 91.

DEFOE TO JAMES WEBSTER, [LATE JANUARY 1707?]

93

To James Webster

[late January 1707?][1]

Sir,

Mr. ------[2] tells me you desire the 5th. Essay, Jure Divino, *and some other things of mine; I have not yet delivered out any of the Book* Jure Divino.[3] *However, that you may want no manner of Advantage against me, since you resolve to go on this way with me, in spite of all Peaceable Endeavours to the contrary, I have sent you* Jure Divino; *the 5th Essay I have not.*

Any thing else you want, which I can help you to, shall be at your Command, I am very sorry thus to engage with you, but not at all afraid of my Cause, only sensible, that we shall both do the Work of that Party,[4] which I hope we are sincerely against.

If I have offended you in any thing, I have by Mr. ------ offer'd you such Terms of Truce,[5] and such a Reference to your own Friends the Ministers, That if Right be on your side, *you cannot fail of as publick Amends as can be desired.*

If nothing but war will satisfy you, I take GOD and your self to Witness, you are both Aggressor, and Continuer of it; and for the rest, I am unconcern'd.

TRUTH AND I, *against all the World* AND YOU,

Your Friend and Humble Servant,

D. F.

Text: Daniel Defoe, *Passion and Prejudice, The Support of one Another, and Both Destructive to the Happiness of this Nation, in Church and State; Being A Reply to the Vindicator of Mr. W----r's Lawful Prejudices* (Edinburgh, 1707), 6. *Address:* none recorded.

1 Like its predecessor, the letter is undated in *Passion and Prejudice*. Late Jan. seems the likeliest date for two main reasons. It predates Defoe's knowledge of Webster's rejoinder to attacks on *Lawful Prejudices* in *The Author of the Lawful Prejudices against an Incorporating Union with England, Defended*, which Defoe sent to Harley on 13 Feb. (see Letter 96); and in the letter Defoe indicates that Webster sought the books to furnish materials for that response.

2 *Mr. ------*: Unidentified.

336

3 *you ... Jure Divino*: The list of Webster's request is specified as 'the fourth and fifth Essays, the first Volume of D.F. Works, *Jure Divino*, &c.' (*Passion and Prejudice*, 5). In Apr. 1707 Defoe sold copies of his *True Collection of the Writings of the Author of The True Born English-man* (1703) and *Jure Divino* (1706) to Queensberry; and he sold some of the same books to the Clerks of Penicuik in Feb. 1707. See Letter 104.

4 *Party*: The Jacobites.

5 *Terms of Truce*: 'Mr. ----- finding he [Webster] was going to write, and foreseeing a Strife of Words, which he thought at this time of day, improper, like a true Peace-maker, from his own meer Inclination, had waited on him to perswade him not to proceed by any means this way' (*Passion and Prejudice*, 6).

94

To Robert Harley

27 January 1707

HEADNOTE **(Letters 94 and 95)**: Defoe received a long-awaited letter from Harley on 21 January 1707, which is untraced. From Defoe's response we may infer that Harley expressed satisfaction with Defoe's reports, pledged to supply money, and either advised him to stay in Scotland or asked if that were necessary. Defoe's reports from the end of January to the middle of February cover the selection of Scottish representatives for the British parliament and the continued concerns of Church of Scotland ministers. In the course of creating multiple narratives for himself to justify his presence in Scotland at this time, as reported to Harley, Defoe hit on two that became reality: he went into business as a linen manufacturer and he did eventually write a history of the Union.

S[r]

I Can Not but Return my humble Acknowlegments for y[e] Hon[r] of yo[r] Letter of y[e] 21th.[1] It is my Singular Joy That y[e] Constant Acco[ts] I have Sent have been to yo[r] Satisfacćon; Indeed I have been Very Sad On y[e] Acco[t] of my haveing had No Line for Now Eight Weeks,[2] and fear'd my Self forgotten.

I Confess there seems S[r] Equall Occasion of Some body here Now as before and Indeed if a p[er]son were Constantly here, provided he had No publick Mission, it would be Very Usefull.

The Implacable parsons are Unsufferably Insolent and Now They flye in y[e] Faće of Every body, Friend and Foe, and The Coals

DEFOE TO ROBERT HARLEY, 27 JANUARY 1707

are blow'd on all Occasions by yᵉ Others; I sent you yᵉ last letter
The Attempt of One Webster, a minister, against yᵉ[a] Dissenters. I
here Send my Answer[3] to him;[b] They are Now laying their heads to
Defame yᵉ Dissenters to Rendʳ them Suspected to yᵉ people.

It is in Vain to go about to Excuse these people; they are proud,
passionate, Ignorant and Jealous. I have hitherto kept my Self
Unsuspected, have Whisprd and Caused it to be spread that I am
fled hither for Debt and Can not Return And this p[er]ticularly
that they may not suspect me. Under this Reproach,[c] tho' I get some
Scandal, yet I Effectually secure my self against Suspicon.

Now I give Out I am goeing to write yᵉ hystory of yᵉ Union in
folio[d] and have got warrants to Search yᵉ Registers and parliamᵗ
books and have begun a Subscription for it;[4] I Tell them it will Cost
me a years Time to write it.

Then I Treat wᵗʰ the Commission to Make yᵐ a New Version of
yᵉ Psalms[5] and that Ile lock my Self up in the College 2 year for the
p[er]formance — by these things sʳ I Effectually Amuse them and I
am p[er]fectly unsuspected.

Then I am Setting Weavers to work to make linen[6] and I talk of
Manufactures & Employing the poor and if that Thrives I am to
Settle here and bring my Family Down and the like, by wᶜʰ Triffles
I Serv yᵉ Great End, Viz. a Concealmᵗ.[e]

I would be Glad Sʳ you would please to Consider yᵉ Case I wrott
about yᵉ Abjuracon Oath[7] wᶜʰ is Very hard upon yᵐ.

I Humbly Thank you Sʳ for Representing Favourably my poor
Endeavours for the Service here. If her Majᵗⁱᵉ was Inform'd of
the Circumstance of my Family, from whom I have been So long
absent, & whom I Effectually stript just before by my surrendʳ,[8] I
p[er]swade myself it would Move her Royall Goodness to some
Compassion. I Need but Represent it to you sʳ, I leav yᵉ Rest to
yoʳ Self, but must Own to you I am Distress't in my Mind on their
Accoᵗ. I ask yoʳ Pardon for Runing Out on that here.

---

[a] yᵉ] *following word* 'Union' *cancelled*
[b] I here Send my Answer to him] *interlined above cancelled word* 'and'
[c] Reproach] *interlined above cancelled word* 'Suspicion'
[d] in folio] *interlined*
[e] Viz. a Concealmᵗ] *seemingly added later;* 'Concealmᵗ' *interlined*

DEFOE TO ROBERT HARLEY, 27 JANUARY 1707

The present affair S^r is about Settling the Representative here wch they have in p[ar]t agreed[9] as you will see by the Minutes — tis Now strongly Contended to keep Out ye Eldest sons of Noble men from ye house and the house are now Sitting upon it; the Barrons struggle hard for it, and ye Nobillity to get them in.[10]

I am to Thank you S^r for yor hint of a Supply. Indeed I have been Expensiv, but I Dare Say ye Money I have laid Out is Expended to ye Very Directest End you Desire it.

But I am Now attended wth a New Disaster. M^r B . . .[11] who is my Onely Resource is Gone to Lond^o & I Suppose will kiss yor hand Ere this Reaches you; he is a Capable, faithfull and Judicous Gentleman. I Suppose S^r if you Direct him he may Supply[12] as well in Lond^o as^a here, and hope he will wait on yor Ord^{rs} for that affair.

I am

S^r yor Most Obed^t Servt

DF

Edinb. Jan. 27. 1707

They have Carryed it in ye house for ye admitting ye Sons of the Nobillity — but it was by Dexterous Mannagement; they had a Majority of 14 onely[13] & ye people Rail at it abominably but that wi[ll be]^b Over —

Text: BL Add. MS. 70291, fols. 138–9. *Address* (fol. 139^v): To The Right Honble | Robert Harley Esqr | Principall Secret^a of State | Present

---

^{a} as] *following word perhaps* 'Ever' *cancelled*
^{b} wi[ll be]] *MS torn*

---

1 *Letter of ye 21th*: Untraced.
2 *No Line for Now Eight Weeks*: Harley's last letter to Defoe was dated 21 Nov. 1706 (Letter 66).
3 *my Answer*: *The Dissenters in England Vindicated* (1707).
4 *hystory ... it*: Despite here presenting this as a ploy, Defoe first raised the possibility of writing a history of the Union in *Review*, III, 775 (24 Dec. 1706). He alludes again to his intention in *Review*, III, 860 (6 Feb. 1707); IV, 69 (13 Mar. 1707); and IV, 105–6 (29 Mar. 1707). In the last of these he began advertising for subscribers (IV, 108). Further mentions come on 13 May and 7 June 1707 (IV, 197, 251). His *History of the Union* was published in late 1709 or early 1710.
5 *New Version of ye Psalms*: No new translation of the Psalms came about.
6 *Setting Weavers to work to make linen*: In the *Review* for 29 Mar. 1707, Defoe spoke about his investments in the linen trade to illustrate the commercial benefits of Union: 'I have told them of Linen Manufactures, and I have now above 100 poor Families at Work, by my Procuring and Direction, for the making such Sorts of Linen, and in such Manner as never was

339

DEFOE TO ROBERT HARLEY, 27 JANUARY 1707

made here before, and as no Person in the Trade will believe, could be made here, till they see it' (IV, 105). The claim, along with others Defoe makes alongside it about his trading activity in Scotland, was derided at the time as a fabrication (*The Review Review'd. In a Letter to the Prophet Daniel in Scotland* (1707?), 1–2). It is described by Furbank and Owens as 'not exactly the truth' but 'not pure fantasy either' (F&O, *Political Biography*, 75). Backscheider calls it 'obviously an exaggeration', though by Nov. 1710 Defoe had contracted with a partner to produce embroidered linen tablecloths (*Life*, 235, 572 n. 19). As another indicator of his probable commercial activity at this time, Defoe claimed to have suffered financial losses when a ship called *The Union* was wrecked (*Review*, IV, 599 (8 Nov. 1707)). That is uncorroborated.

7 *Abjuraċon Oath*: See headnote to Letter 77.

8 *my surrendr*: To the bankruptcy commission in summer 1706.

9 *Settling … agreed*: On 14 Jan. 1707, parliament formed a dyet to consider 'the manner of Electing the Representatives for *Scotland* to the Parliament of *Great-Britain*' (*History, TDH*, VIII, 185). After the ratification of the Treaty, debate turned to the election of the forty-five Commoners (shared between representatives of the shires and burghs) and the sixteen peers. On 21 Jan., parliament voted that the representative would be made out of the present parliament, not the constituencies. On 22 Jan., parliament voted that the Lords would be selected by open election among the peers. On 24 Jan., parliament voted that the Commoners would comprise thirty county Members ('barons' in the terminology of the Scottish parliament) and fifteen borough Members ('burgh commissioners').

10 *tis … in*: On 27 Jan., parliament debated whether the eldest sons of peers should be eligible for election to Commons seats. The matter was 'deliberately left vague in the Scottish parliament' when it voted that rights to election remain unchanged, meaning, as Defoe reports below, they were eligible (Riley, *English Ministers*, 110; Riley, *Union*, 293; *History, TDH*, VIII, 206). In Dec. 1708, the British parliament decided that eldest sons of peers could not take a seat in the Commons (*C.J.*, XVI, 27).

11 *mr B…*: John Bell.

12 *Supply*: On 13 Feb. 1707, Bell received £30 from Harley's petty accounts (BL Add. MS. 70269, misc. 6).

13 *Carryed … onely*: The vote was 85 to 72, though Queensberry – as Lord High Commissioner, a non-voter – was subsequently allowed to add his name to those in favour of allowing sons of peers to be elected to seats in the Commons (*APS*, XI, 418–20).

95

To Robert Harley

2 February 1707

S^r

I Omitted writeing ye last post p[er]fectly for Want of Subject —
being at present Entirely Taken up in Meer Cavil and Continuall
Dispute wth ye Clamorous Clergy.

If I have done any Service Since I Came hither I Think it is Now,
for These Men are Really the Boutefeus[1] of the Natiō And^a If they
Talk against ye Union Every body will do so also.

However I have Pick't Out Some who are for it, a Very Very few
I have brought Over, and I have So Sett these against the Other
That like Sathans kingdome Divided against it self the Furious
Temper Can not^b Stand.[2]

These Reconcild parsons begin to Call ye Other Mad Men,
and they Call these Apostates, and the people Divide just as their
Leaders, but Peace will prevail and I hope gets ground.

I hope ye affair shall Not Come Down again for Amendments;[3]
if it does ye Latter part will be worse than the beginning[4] and I
shall be Sincerely affraid of it, Severall of ye Best men being gone or
Goeing, Some into ye Country, some to England. Nothing Ought
therefore to be More Avoided than its Comeing back hither for
Amendm^ts. I Thought it Meet to hint this S^r because I See the party
Seem to promise themselves something of hopes in Difficultyes to
be Raised in England that shall Occasion Its being bro^t hither again
Clog'd wth Something proper to be Dislik't here.

There is Also One Criticall Day here yet, wch I Apprehend will
Put Them into Some Confusion, but as tis wisely Deferr'd to ye last,
So if ye Treaty does Not Come Down again, the breach it will Make
Can Not be fatall — and This is when They Come to Name the
p[er]sons for ye first Representativ.

The Partys here, ye Temper of ye p[ar]sons, ye Circumstances and
the forms Rend^r it Impossible to Avoid a brush when this Comes

---

^a And] *interlined*
^b not] *following illegible word beginning 'S' cancelled*

341

on ye Stage But if This should be first Entered on and Amendments from England Come after — Pardon my freedome Sr It will Endanger breaking the wholl affair.

On these and Severall Other Accots I Thought it my Duty to give This hint Tho' I question Not but yor own Judgement will agree — That it is Very Necessary To keep it if possible from a Returne hither And Indeed So Necessary that ye Sume of ye Affair will Seem to Depend Upon it —

If This Can be Avoided Sr the heat of ye Ministers will Abate and One kind thing Done for Them, I Mean that of ye Oath wch I hinted before and (wch you were pleased to Tell me in yor Last[5] you would Consider of) All would be Easy and a Little Mannagemt would Reconcile Them all or at least take off the Edge of their Discontent.

Indeed Sr would her Majtie afford ye Charge or Grant me a Very Moderate Request I kno' No way in ye World I Could Serve her Intrest More in Than Makeing Onely a Trip to London, and then[a] Come Down and spend a year at least Among a people Unaccquainted wth Peace, Moderaćon or Temper — but of That hereafter.

I ask yor Pardon for This freedome and Am

Sr

yor Most Obedt Servt

DF

Sr

Since ye Above I am Surpriz'd wth ye Accots we have here of yor Sudden Illness[6] — God almighty in Mercy to These yet Unsettled Nacons preserv a life So Necessary to Their Imediate felicity — Indeed sr I have often Thot to use ye Liberty you are pleasd to grant me On that head.

Tho' ye Vigour of yor Mind quallifyes you for Uncommon Burthens, yet sr we have all these Treasures in Earthen Vessells;[b][7] tis a New Turn[8] to ye Text but I presume it will hold — The body

---

[a] then] *interlined*
[b] Vessells] *following illegible word cancelled*

342

DEFOE TO ROBERT HARLEY, 2 FEBRUARY 1707

sᵣ is Not Made for wonders And when I hint That Denying yoᵣ
Self Needfull and Regular houres of Rest will Disorder yᵉ best
Constitućon in yᵉ world, I speak sᵣ my Own Imediate Experiençe,
who haveing Dispised sleep, houres, and Rules, have broke in Upon
a p[er]fectly Establish't health, wᶜʰ No Distresses, Disasters, Jails or
Mellancholly Could Ever hurt before — I Beseech you Sᵣ Pitty yoᵣ
Country in the spareing your Self For a work So Few but you are
able to go thorow.

Idem ut supraⁱ⁹

Edinb. Feb. 2. 1707

Text: BL Add. MS. 70291, fols. 140–1. *Address* (fol. 141ᵛ): To The Right Honᵇˡᵉ |
Robert Harley Esqᵣ | Her Majᵗⁱᵉˢ Prinćipall Secretᵃ of State | Present. *Endorsed by
Harley* (fol. 141ᵛ): Edenburg Feb: 2: 1706/7 ʀ feb: 10:

1 *Boutefeus*: French *boutefeux*: 'firebrands' or 'incendiaries'. Defoe uses the word in *Review*, I,
470 (31 Oct. 1704); II, 316 (26 June 1705); II, 474 (7 Aug. 1705); VI, 361 (15 Sept. 1709(ᴇ)).

2 *Sathans … Stand*: 'And if a kingdom be divided against itself, that kingdom cannot stand.
And if a house be divided against itself, that house cannot stand. And if Satan rise up against
himself, and be divided, he cannot stand, but hath an end' (Mark 3:24–6; cf. Matt. 12:25–6).
This was among Defoe's favourite biblical allusions. See *The Lay-Man's Sermon upon the Late
Storm* (1704), 17; *The Consolidator* (1705), *SFS*, III, 71; *Review*, II, 362 (7 July 1705); IV, 13 (15 Feb.
1707); IV, 305 (3 July 1707); IX, 242 (21 Feb. 1713); *The Secret History of the October Club* (1711),
PEW, II, 150; *Reasons against the Succession of the House of Hanover* (1713), *PEW*, I, 178; *Some
Thoughts upon the Subject of Commerce with France* (1713), 48; *The Old Whig and Modern Whig
Revived* (1717), *SFS*, IV, 199; *The Manufacturer*, no. 58 (25 Aug. 1720).

3 *Come Down again for Amendments*: I.e. that the English parliament does not make amendments to the Union Treaty requiring further consideration in Scotland.

4 *Latter part will be worse than the beginning*: Inverting Job 42:12: 'So the Lord blessed the latter
end of Job more than his beginning'. Cf. *Robinson Crusoe* (1719), *Novels*, I, 269; *Colonel Jack*
(1722), *Novels*, VIII, 32.

5 *yoᵣ Last*: Untraced but presumably that dated 21 Jan.

6 *Illness*: Harley 'estoit tombé dans espèce d'apoplexie' on the evening of 25 Jan., but three days
later dragged himself to the House of Commons to defend subsidies granted to England's
allies, the Spanish claimant Charles III and the Duke of Savoy, where he had again fallen
ill (H.M.C. *Portland MSS*, IV, 384; *Heinsius Corr.*, VI, 69). His illness clearly concerned the
Queen as St John reports to Harley on 30 Jan. 1707: 'When I waited on the Queen yesterday
she enquired after your health, and expressed her concern for your illness in such terms as
I am sure came from the bottom of her heart. She said so much of your having prejudiced
your health in her service, and showed so much trouble, that I thought it was proper for me
to tell you particularly of it' (H.M.C. *Bath MSS*, I, 157). By early 1707, Harley was Anne's firm
ally, the one amongst her leading ministers not pressing Junto demands upon her, and this
solicitude is evidence of their close relationship.

7 *we have all these Treasures in Earthen Vessells*: 'But we have this treasure in earthen vessels, that
the excellency of the power may be of God, and not of us' (2 Cor. 4:7). Defoe adapts this verse
in *The Present State of the Parties in Great Britain* (1712), 329–30. The earthen vessel in *Robinson*

343

Crusoe may be read symbolically as alluding to it (*Novels*, 1, 145–6). Defoe also alludes to it in *The Commentator*, no. 19 (4 Mar. 1720), *RDW*, IX, 91.

8 *Turn*: 'A change from the original intention; a particular construction or interpretation put upon something' (*OED*).

9 *Idem ut supra*: 'Same as above' (Latin), i.e. 'yoᵣ Most Obedᵗ Servᵗ DF'.

96

To Robert Harley

[13 February 1707][1]

HEADNOTE **(Letters 96 and 97)**: Defoe updates Harley on a range of matters, the most consequential of which is the election of the sixteen Scottish representative peers, which produced a clean sweep for the pro-Union bloc, comprising two members of the Squadrone (Tweeddale and Roxburghe) and fourteen in the Court interest.

The 13 February letters are also significant because Defoe cryptically reports to Harley an approach apparently from Charles Spencer, third Earl of Sunderland (1675–1722), one of the five Lords of the Whig Junto, who on 3 December 1706 had been appointed to replace Hedges as Secretary of State for the Southern Department. A brief excursus into English politics is necessary here because Harley's opposition to the Junto during 1706–8 would later have major ramifications for Defoe.

Sunderland's appointment was the latest concession by the duumvirs to the Lords of the Whig Junto. Godolphin felt dependent on their parliamentary support, but Anne was opposed to such concessions. She wrote to Godolphin on 30 August 1706 to protest 'that making a party man secretary of state, when there are so many of their friends in employment of all kinds already, is throwing myself into the hands of a party, which is a thing I have been desirous to avoid'.[2] Anne begrudgingly appointed Sunderland after prolonged resistance, despite her personal dislike of him.[3] Harley had been equally against the appointment, preferring government by moderate politicians of both Whig and Tory leanings, even a Whig alliance if necessary to maintain the Court's sway, rather than an exclusive dependence on the Junto that would give them power to dictate policy or demand appointments. Harley and Anne saw things similarly. Of the Whigs, Harley wrote in September: 'I am very sorry to see some sort of people Incorrigible, and endeavouring to act yᵉ same follys wᶜʰ overturned them before, and yet they are not to be obliged. ... The more they have the more they crave.'[4] On the same day Anne wrote to Godolphin, 'the making him a secretary, I can't help thinking, is throwing

DEFOE TO ROBERT HARLEY, [13 FEBRUARY 1707]

myself into the hands of a party. ... If this be complied with, you will, then, in a little time, find they must be gratified in something else, or they will not go on heartily in my business'.[5] This proved to be true.

On a personal level, Harley got on poorly with Sunderland.[6] He evidently reinforced Anne's mistrust but, like her, ultimately yielded to Godolphin and Marlborough's pressure for the appointment.[7] Defoe's communication to Harley of the approach to him, whether it was from Sunderland directly or someone on his behalf, has been interpreted by Novak as a veiled threat, showing Harley that other potential employers, more mindful of his worth than Harley, were waiting.[8] Moreover, Defoe may have been intimating that he can serve Harley by sharing knowledge about his rival. Furbank and Owens suggest that Defoe's revelation accounts for Harley's silence to Defoe for the next four months: expressly to have forbidden Defoe from corresponding with Sunderland could have aroused or confirmed suspicions, and Harley may have doubted Defoe's dependability.[9]

Sr

If I have Omitted my Constant advices to you it has been Undr ye Very Uneasy Reports spread here both of yor first illness and After of a Relapse and Severall flying Reports[10] have Allarm'd me wth ye Accot of yor being Dead.

I Will Not Trouble you wth my Concern on yt Score; The loss to ye wholl Island is what I hope God in his Mercy to ym will Not Afflict Them wth in Many yeares.

My Close Concealing my Accquaintance wth, Much less Employment from you Sr, Rendred it Impossible to kno' any Thing from Other than Common Intelligence, But haveing a Letter from mr Bell[11] this day,[a] that he had the honor to wait on you ye 8th and No Mencon of yor Indisposition, Revives my hopes of yor health and Renews my Very pleasant Labour of thus Conversing wth you.

I Wrott you a Large Letter[12] last week, but Cautious of ye Case of your health, Sent it to mr Bell who I hope will do me the honour to put it Safe into yor Own hands.

The Town Rings here wth a Report yt ye Test act is Repeal'd as far as Concerns ye Dissenters,[13] but ye Various manner of its being Told here makes me Doubtfull; I should Improve it to ye Uttmost Advantage here Against Presbyterian Jealousies, if I had ye

---

[a] this day] *interlined*

345

Certainty of Fact; however as it is I begin to make Some of them blush at their suspicons of English Sincerity.

We are Surpriz'd here wth an Acco[t] that y[e] wholl Treaty has Passt [the][a] Comittee of the house of Commons;[14] it is So Good News that I Can Not but suspend my Expectacons till a Confirmation Arrives of So Valluable a thing.

I Troubled you w[th] an Invectiv by m[r] Webster[15] here against the English Dissenters; I have had another Railing bitter[b] pamphlet[16] on y[e] same head from him, but So taken up w[th] ill language, scurillous p[er]sonall Railery, and little Sence that I Can not think it worth giveing you y[e] Trouble of it.

Raillery and ill Manners have just y[e] Same Effect here as in Other places, Viz[t] to Sink y[e] Character and Reputation of y[e] Author.

The p[ar]liam[t] have now before them the severall Requests of y[e] Commission for plantation of kirks and Valuation of Teinds[c] as they Call them here Or Tiths as w[th] us.[17]

This Very Day they are Upon Nameing the Members for y[e] first p[ar]liam[t], the Quarrellsome work I hinted in[d] my Last. The Peers as Expected are as foll,[18] but I do not yet hear they are Determined in the house:

D of Queensberry	E Rothess[26]
L[d] Chancellor[19]	E of Glasgow[27]
2 secretarys of state[20]	E of Stair[28]
Marquis of Tweedale[21]	Viscount Duplin[29]
Marq: of Montrose,	L[d] Ross[30] the others not Named[31]
L[d] Presid[t] of the Council[22]	
Marq of Louthain[23]	
E of Sutherland[24]	
E of Roxburgh[25]	

The people are strangely Irritated here and there is a spirit of Bitterness and Slander gone Out among them.

---

[a] [the]] MS torn
[b] bitter] following letters probably 'Inve' (for 'Invective') cancelled
[c] Teinds] following illegible word cancelled
[d] in] following illegible word cancelled

DEFOE TO ROBERT HARLEY, [13 FEBRUARY 1707]

The Mob are a Machine; the Jacobites have wound them up to a Pitch and Nothing but Time, Mannagem^t, Temper and success Can Reduće them to the proper Medium. They must be let Run Down Gradually or they precipitate at Onće into all Manner of Confusion.

I have had Severall Letters and Some hints I guess^a from ye Other Newly alter'd part of an offiće Near you^{32} S^r wch I long to give you ye hystory of if you please to Command it; I presume you will Suffer nothing of that to be to my prejudiće, and p[er]mit me the freedome of takeing yor honour for ye Concealm^t from all Eyes or Eares^b but yor Own.

I am Not to be pumpt or Sounded and yet would be Glad to have a hint from you where I should be wary and where not; p[er]haps here may be no Need of Caution. I believ you are all in ye True Intrest and if I may be Open I would be Glad to kno'.

I have little s^r in this world to boast of but my fidelity, and as y^t is to you before all ye world, So I Entreat a hint from you, whether I may be free in Case of Such Suggestions as — We hope he is Not Dropt — Tis hard if ye p[er]sons who say they Employ him do not stand by him. Pray let me kno' if you are in anything Uneasy, and the like.

These if Right are kind things, and to one Circumstanced like me should be Improvd, but if wrong S^r I thank God Can have No Influenće on me, who as before have neither hands to act, Mouth to speak, nor purse to Reciev favours but as you Direct. I humbly Entreat yor hints for my Conduct and as frequent Orders as your affaires will p[er]mitt.

[Your Most]^c Humble & Obedient Servt
DF

Text: BL Add. MS. 70291, fols. 146–7. *Address* (fol. 147^v): To The Right Honb^{le} | Robert Harley Esqr | Her Maj^{ties} Prinćipall Secret^a of State | Present. *Endorsed by Harley* (fol. 147^v): Edenburg Feb: 13: 1706/7 R feb: 19:

^{a} I guess] *interlined*
^{b} or Eares] *interlined*
^{c} [Your Most]] *MS torn*

1   The letter is undated, probably because it was sent with Letter 97, so the date of 13 Feb. on that one serves for both (Harley's endorsements of the two letters are identical). The selection

DEFOE TO ROBERT HARLEY, [13 FEBRUARY 1707]

of representative peers, to which Defoe refers as happening on 'This Very Day', occurred on 13 Feb. (*History of the Union, TDH*, VIII, 217–18). Healey indicates that the dating 23 Feb. 1707 given in H.M.C. *Portland MSS*, IV, 389 is erroneous (*Letters*, ed. Healey, 200 n. 1).

2 William Coxe, *The Memoirs of John, Duke of Marlborough*, 3 vols. (1818–19), II, 137.

3 Anne to Godolphin, 21 Sept. 1706, *Anne Letters*, 199–201. Sunderland's opposition to the £100,000 annual pension for Prince George should he outlive Anne, voted in 1702, was one cause of her ill-feeling.

4 Harley to Poulett, 21 Sept. 1706, BL Add. MS. 70252, section 7. See also Harley's draft memoranda in BL Add. MS. 70333, section 19; Harley to Godolphin, 15 Oct. 1706, H.M.C. *Bath MSS*, I, 109–11; Marlborough to Godolphin, 29 Oct. 1706, *Marl.–God. Corr.*, II, 725–6.

5 *Anne Letters*, 200.

6 See Harley to Sunderland (draft), 22 July 1706, University of Nottingham, Pw 2Hy 661; Harley to Newcastle, 10 Sept. 1706, H.M.C. *Portland MSS*, II, 196.

7 Henry L. Snyder, 'Godolphin and Harley: A Study of their Partnership in Politics', *HLQ* 30 (1967), 241–71 (at 260–2).

8 Novak, 320.

9 F&O, *Political Biography*, 77.

10 *flying Reports*: Untraced.

11 *Letter from mr Bell*: Untraced.

12 *Large Letter*: Untraced, unless Defoe means the previous letter, dated 2 Feb.

13 *Report ... Dissenters*: The report was false. Luttrell reports that on 11 Feb. 'a committee of lords examined several masters of coffee houses and news writers, for inserting in their letters that the house of peers had repealed the sacramental test act; and some of them will be prosecuted for the same' (VI, 137). On 18 Feb. Addison reported on the Act for securing the Church of England, the English equivalent to the Scottish Act of Security: 'The Bill for securing yᵉ Church ... is only a Confirmatⁿ of all acts yᵗ have bin already made in favor of it. Among those that are mention'd in it Lᵈ Nottingham wᵈ have had yᵉ Test Act inserted but upon a Division it was carry'd against it by 21 Voices' (*Addison Letters*, 69). This would seem to be the origin of the report.

14 *wholl ... Commons*: On 4 Feb., the committee of the whole House of Commons approved articles one to four, and on 8 Feb. they approved the rest (Cobbett, VI, 560).

Subsequently, on 28 Feb. the Treaty passed its third reading by 274 votes to 116 and went up to the House of Lords, which had already approved the articles (Luttrell, VI, 144). Defoe also expresses his surprise that the English parliament proposed no amendments in print, both in the *Review* at the time and in his *History* in retrospect (*Review*, IV, 62 (11 Mar. 1707); *TDH*, VIII, 194; cf. Defoe, *The Present State of the Parties in Great Britain* (1712), 120). Burnet reports that many thought it had been rushed through the Commons (V, 284).

15 *Invectiv by mr Webster*: Webster's *Lawful Prejudices* (see Letters 92 and 93).

16 *Railing bitter pamphlet*: Webster's *The Author of the Lawful Prejudices against an Incorporating Union with England, Defended* (1707), which answers Defoe's *The Dissenters in England Vindicated*. It charges Defoe with 'Indiscretion', 'Rudeness', lacking 'justice and ingenuity', 'want of Candor', 'ignorance', 'blunders', 'uncharitableness', 'weakness and malice', 'ignorance of Logick', 'false reasoning', being 'vacillant', and 'hectoring and bullying'. The pamphlet is presented as a defence of Webster by a friend, but as Defoe later noted, it slips from third- to first-person at the end (*The Dissenters Vindicated* (1707), sig. A3ᵛ).

The suppressed *Passion and Prejudice* was apparently written before Defoe surmised Webster was the author of its defence (7–8), unless Defoe is exploiting the defence's anonymity to attack Webster via his putative unnamed 'Answerer'. Certain sections asserting that Webster would not have handled his vindication so clumsily suggest this indirection (11, 13). If this is the case, it would be similar to how Defoe reacted to Haversham's *Vindication of his Speech in Parliament* in 1706, pretending not to be attacking Haversham or his parliamentary speech but rather some presumptuous pamphleteer (see Letter 45, note 13).

348

DEFOE TO ROBERT HARLEY, [13 FEBRUARY 1707]

17 *Requests ... us*: The contention surrounding the plantation of kirks (i.e. supplying or planting a minister in a vacant church) and that of determining teinds (tithes) led to the Act for Plantation of Kirks and Valuation of Teinds (1707). Former parliaments appointed a committee to oversee these matters, so it needed a new procedure for after the Union. An overture for the Act was made on 5 Feb.; it was read on 12 Feb.; on 17 Feb., parliament appointed the Lords of Council and Session to oversee plantation and teinds and voted the Act on 21 Feb. See Defoe's explanation in *History, TDH*, VIII, 214–15.

18 *Peers as Expected are as foll*: Defoe's list of fourteen correctly predicts eleven of the actual sixteen Scottish peers elected to the Lords. For the election manoeuvres between the Court party and the Squadrone, which involved last-minute trading to establish an approved list, see James Johnstone to George Baillie of Jerviswood, *Jerviswood Corr.*, 186–8; Mar to Nairne, 13 Feb. 1708, H.M.C. *Mar and Kellie MSS*, 374–7.

19 *Ld Chancellor*: Seafield (see Letter 60, note 6).

20 *2 secretarys of state*: Mar (see headnote to Letter 56) and Hugh Campbell, third Earl of Loudon (d. 1731).

21 *Marquis of Tweedale*: John Hay, second Marquess of Tweeddale (1645–1713) of the Squadrone; he is praised in *Caledonia*, lines 1011–13, *PEW*, IV, 259.

22 *Marq: of Montrose, Ld Presid^t of the Council*: See Letter 68, note 7.

23 *Marq of Louthain*: Lt.-Gen. William Kerr, second Marquess of Lothian (1661–1722).

24 *E of Sutherland*: See Letter 67, note 15.

25 *E of Roxburgh*: See Letter 60, note 3.

26 *E Rothess*: John Hamilton-Leslie, ninth Earl of Rothes (1679–1722), of the Squadrone. Despite being on the Court list, he was not elected, though he was in 1708.

27 *E of Glasgow*: David Boyle, first Earl of Glasgow (*c.* 1666–1733), Treasurer-Depute. Defoe praises his ancestry in *Caledonia* (1706), lines 1024–8, *PEW*, IV, 259.

28 *E of Stair*: John Dalrymple, second Earl of Stair (1673–1747). He promptly wrote to Godolphin on 22 Nov. to request a British peerage that would have obviated the need to be elected in the future (*Marchmont Papers*, III, 447–8).

29 *Viscount Duplin*: Thomas Hay, Viscount Dupplin (1660–1719), seventh Earl of Kinnoull from 1709. Not elected, though he was in 1710.

30 *Ld Ross*: William Ross, twelfth Lord Ross (*c.* 1656–1738). Not elected. Godolphin wanted Ross, but Mar explains he was laid aside because others had higher rank and stronger interest. ([Mar] to [D. Nairn], 6 Feb. 1707, NRS GD 124/15/487/9).

31 *others not Named*: The five representative peers elected in 1707 not on Defoe's list are: David Wemyss, fourth Earl of Wemyss (1678–1720), Lord High Admiral of Scotland; Archibald Campbell, first Earl of Islay, later third Duke of Argyll (1682–1761), Lord High Treasurer for Scotland; Archibald Primrose, first Earl of Rosebery (1664–1723); Leven; and Crawford (see Letter 79, note 9). The last was the only man not on the Court list who was elected (in place of Rothes).

32 *Letters ... you*: Probably from the office of the recently appointed Secretary of State, Sunderland. See headnote. The correspondence Defoe mentions is untraced.

DEFOE TO ROBERT HARLEY, 13 FEBRUARY 1707

97

To Robert Harley

13 February 1707

S^r

I had Closed ye Other letter[1] before ye Parliamt^a was Over — and gave you an Acco^t of Names but by Guess from ye Common Opinion.

Since that ye wholl is finish't and Very happily without any Broil and the True list of the Names is On ye Other Side,[2] To wch I Referr, and am

S^r

yor Most Obed^t Servt

DF

Ed. Feb. 13. 1707

Text: BL Add. MS. 70291, fols. 142–3. *Address* (fol. 143^v): To The Right Honble | Robert Harley Esqr | Her Maj^ties Princ̍ipall Secret^a of State | Present. *Endorsed by Harley* (fol. 143^v): Edenburg Feb: 13: 1706/7 R feb: 19:

---

^a Parliam^t] *following word probably* 'Rose' *cancelled*

---

1 *Other letter*: The preceding letter.
2 *True … Side*: The list of sixteen representative peers and forty-five MPs is not in Defoe's hand (BL Add. MS. 70291, fol. 142r–v). The names are given in *History of the Union, TDH*, VIII, 217.

350

98

To Sidney Godolphin, first Earl of Godolphin

22 February 1707

HEADNOTE: In December 1706, the Lord Treasurer was created first Earl of Godolphin, underscoring his place at the head of the government. Harley evidently shared with Godolphin at least some of the letters Defoe sent from Scotland,[1] but this is the first extant letter Defoe sent to the man who became his direct employer from 1707 to 1710 (albeit Defoe seems to have continued reporting primarily to Harley until February 1708). The letter serves as an advertisement of Defoe's professional abilities as he sought a post in the customs office.[2]

The occasion for Defoe's letter was the exploitation by tradesmen of the interval between the Union's parliamentary ratification and its coming into effect on 1 May. Merchants saw an opportunity to bring French goods to an English market despite England's wartime ban on commerce with France. They began importing French wine and brandy to Scotland, where the prohibition on French goods did not yet apply, intending to transport these tariff-free to England after 1 May. Lower duties on imports in Scotland before the Union also made it an attractive stopover for goods destined for England.[3] Despite Defoe's concern for the lost revenue, he offered to secure Harley some reasonably priced claret two weeks later.[4] In the coming months, the French wine and brandy to be imported to England via Scotland became a more contentious and involuted issue, as Defoe's letters starting 22 April attest.

May it Please yor Lordship

I Most Humbly Crave yor Ldships Pardon for Presuming to write to yor Ldship at This Distance, But hearing of ye Very Unhappy Illness of Mr Secretary Harley and The Subject of my writeing Concerning More Perticular yor Ldships Part in ye Govornmt, I Mean ye Revenue, I Thought it My Duty to Lay The following Case before yor Lordship.

Yor Ldship knows well That in This place There is an Open Trade with France[5] And as This Trade is Very Considerable So on ye Prospect of a Union I p[er]ciev There are Severall wheels at work to Lay schemes of Private Trade From Hence for England; Some of wch I May get Insight Enough into to Accquat yor Ldship both of Time, place and p[er]son, if yor Ldship Comands me to Search Farther into it.

DEFOE TO EARL OF GODOLPHIN, 22 FEBRUARY 1707

But ye Main Perticular I give yor L^dship This Trouble Upon is this; here Are Great Comissions from Lond^o allready for ye Buying up Wines and Brandys On ye Supposicon That They shall be Freely Convey'd to England after ye Union, and That England will Not So far Dissoblige Scotland at first as to Obstruct it — Tis true An Obstruccon of That kind would do Some harm here at first as it will be Improved[6] — But if They are Assured of a Liberty, as I find ye Merchants of Lond^o Encourage Them in it, yor L^dship will Find ye Inconvenience Very Great and ye Quantity before ye first of May Incredible: Here was Three ships Entred last week and all ye wines are bought up, and I am Informed There Are Eight More at y^e <u>Orcades</u>[7] waiting to Come in — and This place is Unusually and Prodigiously Full of English Money at This Time.

I Need Not Trouble yor L^dship wth any Notes of ye Consequence of This and how Easily 20 or 30 Thousand pounds Duty shall be avoided by The Merchants in This Case, ye best Wines being Now Sold here for 11[£] p[er] Hogs^{hd},[8] Brandys at about 13[£], and So of Other Things.

Nor shall I presume to Offer my Thoughts of Expedients in This Case Without yor L^dships Imediate Command, Onely Presume to Lay it before yor Lordship as what I Thought for her Maj^{ties} Service, for wch I Humbly Ask yor L^dships Pardon.

I am

May it Please yor L^dship

yor L^dships

Most Humble & Obedient Servt

DeFoe

Edinb. Feb. 22°. 1707
P.S.

If yor L^dships Comands Directs me to Note ye Quantities of Wines bought and by whom in Lond^o I Suppose it may Not be Difficult & p[er]haps where Lodg'd.

Text: BL Add. MS. 70291, fols. 144–5. *Address* (fol. 145v): To The Right Honble | The Ld High Treasurer of England | Humbly Present

1   Godolphin to Harley, 4 Jan. 1707, H.M.C. *Bath MSS*, 1, 152; 16 Jan. 1707, H.M.C. *Portland MSS*, IV, 382; 19 Mar. 1707, H.M.C. *Bath MSS*, 1, 167.

DEFOE TO ROBERT HARLEY, 4 MARCH 1707

2 See Letter 85, note 7.
3 The English Privy Council had considered this problem in 1705 but left it unresolved (Theodora Newton, *Commercial Relations of England and Scotland 1603–1707* (Cambridge, 1910), 201–3).
4 See Letters 100–2.
5 *Open Trade with France*: See headnote. The restrictions on English trade with France were not in force in Scotland until the Union commenced. Defoe consistently opposed the prohibition on commerce with France on the bases that the balance of trade favoured England and that other nations purchased English goods and sold them on, with a mark-up, to France. He argued this in the first vol. of the *Review* (I, 599–600 (12 Dec. 1704); 612–14 (19 Dec. 1704); 630–2 (30 Dec. 1704); 671–3 (6 Jan. 1705)) and he recommened in the wake of the Union (*Review*, IV, 270–4 (17 June 1707); 783 (24 Jan. 1708)). For his writings on the topic after 1710, see Letter 170, note 15; Letters 231, 234–6. In *Some Thoughts upon the Subject of Commerce with France* (1713), Defoe pointed out his consistency on this issue during the preceding decade (3–7).
6 *Improved*: See Letter 15, note 12.
7 *Orcades*: Orkney Islands.
8 *Hogshd*: A hogshead, equating to around 300 litres.

99

To Robert Harley

4 March 1707

HEADNOTE: The Equivalent was calculated at £398,085.10s., and conversations about how it would be disbursed were getting louder.[1] Defoe first considered the distribution of the funds in *An Enquiry into the Disposal of the Equivalent* (probably December 1706), advocating first compensating investors upon the dissolution of the Company of Scotland Trading to Africa and the Indies, and then paying private persons for reducing the Scottish coinage to the English standard.[2] Three years later, in *The History of the Union*, he spoke about others who would be compensated.[3] The process of identifying recipients and calculating their compensation was the focus for dispute well into the 1720s.

Sr

My Last[4] Represented my Feares of The Returning The Treaty hither On Accot of The Oxford Clause.[5]

Tis Very Mysterious to us why That Affair was not Included in ye Act of Security For ye Church,[6] and I fear it was kept in Petto[7] as an Ambuscade against ye Bill.

I will not Despair of Any Thing but it is a New Danger here and Some good Friends to the Affair Seem Under great Apprehensions.

DEFOE TO ROBERT HARLEY, 4 MARCH 1707

Indeed here are Disgusts and Dissatisfaccͦons among The great
Ones wᶜʰ give Room to Apprehend an ill Effect of any Thing to be
brought before yᵐ Again.

Some Are Disgusted as I wrott before That They are Not in The
Brittish List,[8] Others at Want of Plaćes, But I Can Not but Observ,
Tho' by The by The Equivalent is yᵉ Main Disgust; Many had
swallowd Large Morsells of it in Expectaćon, and I Dare say Little
Enough of it should go as Designd, if it were in yᵉ Mannagemᵗ of
Some people.

As it is, Every body Saies The Nobillity will . . . . it[9] and That
yᵉ Onely hope is, they will Fall Out about shareing it, wᶜʰ is likely
Enough.

The p[er]sons who They Say are Uneasy begin to Complain,
Loudly, and if yᵉ Temper and Moderaćon of yᵉ Comͤissioner, who
indeed is yᵉ Soul of This wholl Affair,[10] does Not help itᵃ I Doubt
least They may Come to Calling One another Some Names, wᶜʰ yᵉ
bystandʳˢᵇ may be apt to say are True on both Sides.

Tho' I write my Apprehensions of Things yet Sʳ I shall Not
be Discouragd From my small Endeavours, and wait yoʳ farther
Instruccͦons.

I am

Sʳ

yoʳ Most Obedient Servᵗ

DF

Edinb. March. 4 1707

Text: BL Add. MS. 70291, fols. 148–9. *Address* (fol. 149ᵛ): To The Right Honᵇˡᵉ |
Robert Harley Esqʳ | Prinćipall Secretary of State | Present

ᵃ does Not help it] *interlined*
ᵇ bystandʳˢ] 'by standʳˢ' *in MS*

---

1 See Riley, *English Ministers*, 207–12.
2 Defoe's pamphlet was a response to the anonymous *A Letter to a Member of Parliament, Anent
the Application of the 309885 Lib: 10 Shil: Sterl* [1706].
3 *TDH*, VIII, 152–6.
4 *My Last*: Untraced.
5 *Oxford Clause*: On 22 Feb., William Bromley, MP for Oxford University, proposed an additional clause to the Union Treaty providing that the Universities of Oxford and Cambridge
'may continue for ever, as they are now by Law established'. This would have required placing

DEFOE TO ROBERT HARLEY, 10 MARCH 1707

the Treaty again before the Scottish parliament, but Bromley's motion was defeated (*C.J.*, xv, 307).

6 *Act of Security For ye Church*: The Act of Security for the Church of England, which would be added to the Union Treaty without referring it again to Scotland's parliament.

7 *in Petto*: 'in the breast' (Italian), i.e. secret.

8 *Not in The Brittish List*: I.e. not on the Court's list of peers to be elected to the British parliament.

9 . . . . *it*: Left blank to imply rather than state 'devour' or some such word.

10 *Temper ... Affair*: 'The Prudence, Moderation and steady Conduct of his Grace the Duke of *Queensberry*, her Majesty's High Commissioner there, has been the only Support of those honest few, that stood firm for the Interest of their Country; and this I must confess, has been the more remarkable, in that his Grace has carried it on thro' the midst of all the unsufferable Insolencies of an enrag'd *High-Flying* and *Jacobite* Party' (*Review*, III, 828 (21 Jan. 1707)).

100

To Robert Harley

10 March 1707

HEADNOTE: By the start of March, Defoe was relieved that the Union had been ratified and his thoughts were on what would come next for him. He was keen to return to London. He seems to have received no encouragement in his earlier proposal to be settled in a post in Scotland.

Sr

I have Now I hope ye Satisfaccon of Seeing the fruit of all This Mischief, ye Effect of all The Labouring, Fighting, Mobbings &c., Viz: Union, and while I write This ye Guns are Fireing from ye Castle[1] and My Man brings me Up ye Queens Speech.[2]

Methinks <u>Nunc Dimitis</u> Comes Now in My head and in writing to you sr I should Say Now let me Depart from hence for My Eyes have Seen ye Conclusion.[3]

I Confess Sr I believ I might be Servicable here a long Time yet, But Sr Every body is Gone Up to Sollicit their Own Fortunes, and Some to be Rewarded for what I have Done[4] — while I Depending on yor Concern for me and her Majties Goodness am wholly Unsollicitous in yt Affair.

I wrott Earnestly to you and to my Ld Treasurer[5] about ye Import of Wine and Brandy. 3 ships More Came in yesterday

355

DEFOE TO ROBERT HARLEY, 10 MARCH 1707

and 10 more are at hand and 200 Tun[6] of Brandy is Sent for from Holland.

If it shall pass into England why shall your honor Not Permit me to buy you a Ton of Rich Claret here wch I May do as Cheap as you buy a hhd[7] and Ile Take my hazard yt it shall be Extraordina on My Own Risq.

J P[8] is This Day Gone for England; he has been at first Usefull to me but Since Some who were fond of haveing an Agent here[a] Employ'd him Out of my way,[9] of wch More hereafter, I have Not Recomended him to you.

I am Now On ye Old Doctrine of Peace and her Majties Speech is My happy Text and I please my Self in Telling yor honor it Gains Ground — I have been Invited to Glasgow where I Must[b] have been Torn to peices if I had Gone before but I Think to Venture a Round Thither and to St Andrews and spend Every Minute to ye best Issue I Can That ye Charge I have put you to sr May Not be ill laid Out, and Now I am Impacent for yor Ordrs wch way to Steer my Course wch I Entreat I may have ye honor of as Soon as possible.

yor Most Obedt Servt
DF

March. 10. 1707

Text: BL Add. MS. 70291, fols. 150–1. *Address* (fol. 151v): To The Right Honble | Robert Harley Esqr | Princìpall Secreta of State | Present

[a] here] *interlined*
[b] Must] *following word probably* 'if' *cancelled*

---

1   *Guns are Fireing from ye Castle*: In the *Review* for 29 Mar. 1707, Defoe states that the guns are firing as he writes, and he fancies they produce 'the articulate Expression of UNION, UNION' (IV, 104). Tutchin mocked Defoe for this conceit in *Observator*, 21–4 May 1707.

2   *Queens Speech*: Anne's speech to both Houses of Parliament on 6 Mar. 1707, expressing her satisfaction at the Union, reprinted in *History of the Union*, TDH, VIII, 196–7. In the *Review* for 29 Mar. 1707, Defoe was gratified by the thought that he is one of '*those, that have been instrumental to bring it to such an happy Conclusion*', echoing Anne's words (IV, 105).

3   *Nunc ... Conclusion*: Luke 2:29–32, a canticle known as the Song of Simeon, whose opening words and title (in the Latin Vulgate), *Nunc dimitis*, mean 'Now you dismiss': 'Lord, now lettest thou thy servant depart in peace according to thy word. | For mine eyes have seen thy salvation, | Which thou hast prepared before the face of all people; | A light to lighten the Gentiles and to be the glory of thy people Israel.'

DEFOE TO JOHN BELL, 18 MARCH 1707

4 *Every body ... Done*: 'I know some, that are gone to London to sollicite the Reward of what
   they have had no hand in, I might have said, are gone to claim the Merit, of what I have been
   the single Author of' (*Review*, IV, 105 (29 Mar. 1707)).
5 *I wrott ... L⁴ Treasurer*: The letter to Harley is missing; that to Godolphin is Letter 98.
6 *Tun*: Equivalent to four hogsheads.
7 *hhᵈ*: hogshead.
8 *J P*: John Pierce.
9 *Employ'd him Out of my way*: I.e. Pierce was 'suborned by another paymaster' (F&O, *Political
   Biography*, 72).

101

To John Bell

18 March 1707

HEADNOTE (**Letters 101 and 102**): Defoe's letter to Bell of 18 March is a cover
for that to Harley of the same date. Though the Union was a *fait accompli*, and
Defoe felt at something of a loose end, he continued to tussle with Presbyterian
ministers. The pamphlet warfare he waged with James Webster, for example, was
not merely a sideshow. In the *Review* for 13 March 1707, Defoe wrote that the
attempt 'to raise a Distrust between the Kirk of *Scotland*, and the Dissenters in
England' is 'the first Step' in efforts 'to raise a mutual Distrust between the two
Nations'.[1] In the build-up to the meeting of the General Assembly of the Church
of Scotland in April, Defoe thought it was his role to be placatory and to dampen
such situations.

Sʳ

Yʳ Ordring me to write no More to you at Londᵒ left me at
Some loss for a post or Two & I wrott to mʳˢ Bell[2] to Direct as
formerly by Sʳ Tho: T.[3]

I am Glad your stay in Londᵒ is Somewhat longer and
p[er]ticularly for yᵉ Conveyance of the Enclosed.[4]

When you wait on Mʳ Secr. Again, Giving My Humble Duty to
him, be pleased to Move him in The following Cases.

I have been Extremly Desirous to Choose Out One Ton of
Rare Claret here for his Own Table[5] and As we are all assured yᵗ
it will Come Free into England, & all yᵉ World are buying it up,
the Goodness and yᵉ Cheapness makes me Earnest to have his

DEFOE TO JOHN BELL, 18 MARCH 1707

Commission, Considering I may buy him a Ton as Cheap as his honor Inform'd me he gave for One hhd in London, and This Trade being my Old bussiness[6] I p[er]swade my Self my palat Can Not be Decieved in what will please him.

My Other Request is that he would be pleased to let me have a short Quartering of his Arms in Ordr to make him a small present of this Countrys Manufacture;[7] p[er]haps it may be to the Honor of Scotland and to his Own Very Good likeing.

In this Sr you will p[er]ticularly Oblige me and I shall at large Informe you of Perticulars as to ye Manufacture when I see you.

As to my Comeing up I have neither Feet to Travail Nor Toungue to say when but as I Reciev Orders from him whom you have ye honor to Converse with, and if you will make it yor p[er]ticular Request to Obtain me ye favour of a letter I shall place it to ye Accot of ye Many Favors Recd of you by

Sr

yor Most Humble Servt

DF

Edinb. Mar. 18. 1707

There Comes a packett wth this wch is said to be Enclosed[8] but it was too Large.

Text: BL Add. MS. 70291, fols. 152–3. *Address* (fol. 153v): To John Bell Esqr | At Wm Carr's Esqrs[9] Chamber | In Lincolns Inn | London

1   *Review*, IV, 67.

2   *I wrott to mrs Bell*: Letter untraced; no details on Bell's wife have been found.

3   *Sr Tho: T*: Presumably Sir Thomas Trevor (1658–1730), Chief Justice of the Common Pleas, a commissioner of the Treaty of Union, and associate of Harley.

4   *Enclosed*: The following letter.

5   *One ... Table*: See Letter 100.

6   *my Old bussiness*: 'I have sold many a Tun of as good *French Claret* as is in the World' (*Review*, VIII, 31 (3 Apr. 1711)). Defoe speaks about having switched from importing French to Portuguese wine (*Review*, IX, 386–7 (19 May 1713)). Elsewhere he stated, 'I was bred to the *French* Trade from a Youth' (*Some Thoughts upon the Subject of Commerce with France* (1713), 14; cf. 21). See the attention to the logistics of importing wine in *An Essay upon Projects* (1697), *PEW*, VIII, 49–50. Oldmixon alleged that Defoe 'never had been a Merchant, otherwise than peddling a little to *Portugal*' (Oldmixon, 519). See Bastian, 91–2.

7   *Quartering ... Countrys Manufacture*: See Letter 73, note 8. Heraldic shields are commonly divided into quarters. The Harley coat of arms is 'Or, a bend cotised sable' (i.e. a golden background with a thick black diagonal stripe downwards from left to right flanked either side by thinner black stripes).

DEFOE TO ROBERT HARLEY, 18 MARCH 1707

8 *a packett wth this wch is said to be Enclosed*: Apparently Defoe's pamphlet *A Short View of the Present State of the Protestant Religion in Britain* (1707), the 'Bulky' enclosure he mentions in the following letter.

9 *Wm Carr's Esqrs*: William Carr (1664–1720), MP for Newcastle-upon-Tyne.

102

To Robert Harley

18 March 1707

Sr

I have Not wrot So Constantly as Usuall, haveing Nothing Materiall to Communicate but private bills in parliamt, Horse Races at Leith, Fire in ye City, and Such things wch are not worth Disturbing yor Thoughts wth.

To Tell you my Ld Hoptons[1] Horse won ye plate, that a fire burnt Three or four houses and 5 people, that ye p[ar]liamt have been busy about a quarrell between ye Doctors and Surgeons[2] (<u>knaves all</u>) to Determine wch shall have ye Greatest privilege to kill people and be paid for it, These things will be so far from Informing you sr that they will Not So Much as Divert you.

Indeed should I Tell you ye story of Ecclesiastic Frenzy in these parts, and Draw a scheme of North Country Bigotry, I Could make you Merry in spight of yor Most Serious Concern for ye public peace.

I Find there is Bigotry without popery, and Gods priests Ride Upon Gods[a] people as well as ye Inferior Clergye of less Pure Churches. Certainly sr the Clergy here have More to Account for here than in Other places where ye Customary slavery of Other Nations is Inverted but is Every jot as Fatall, as there The priests lead aside Silly women; these Silly women, more Silly men. The women are ye Instructors And the Men are Meer Machins wound Up just as the Spring goes at home.

a Gods] *following word* 'priests' *cancelled*

359

DEFOE TO ROBERT HARLEY, 18 MARCH 1707

Thus as yᵉ Veloċity of Moċon Doubles and Encreases as tis
Remote from its Center, So if yᵉ priest be Chagrine at the Union
the good wife Rails at it and yᵉ Husband Grows Mad — This Sʳ
has put a Noċon into my head wᶜʰ if Ever I were to write a book
should take up a good part of it. I have heard of yᵉ Circulation of
the blood and Great Discoveries have been made of late on that
head. I think it would be Very Instructing to write an Essay Upon
the Circulation of yᵉ brain In wᶜʰ Case more wonders would be
found Out in this Clear air here than Could be hoped for Even in a
journey to the Moon.[3]

Youl pardon me Sʳ this Excursion. Indeed yᵉ Morall of it all is
Instructing; the Ministry here strangely Influenċe the people and
the Conflict between mʳ Webster and I[4] here has Discovred more of
it than I Could have Imagind was possible.

His attempt has had Two Very Fatall Designs in it tho' I
thank God I Can without Vanity Say I have Defeated him in
both.

1. To Argue yᵉ Sinfullness of yᵉ Union as a breach of yᵉ Naċonall
Covenant and Inflame yᵉ people on that Accoᵗ.

2. To Represent yᵉ Dissenters as No friends to yᵉ Kirk and Not
fit to be Depended Upon & So break yᵉ Generall Friendship of the
Nations.

Thus One design was to Inflame, yᵉ Other to Divide.

To his first[5] I printed a short peiċe to prove yᵉ Naconall
Covenant was so far from being broken that it was not at all
Concern'd in the Treaty.[6]

He Cryed fire at this, Said I had Blasphem'd yᵉ Covenant,
that Every body Ought to shun my Company, that if I Came
into his Church while he was preaching or praying he would
stop and proceed no farther till I was Removed.

But when he saw the best Ministers in yᵉ City my Constant
friends and Visitants it put him Distracted and he Goes
about Railing at my Moralls, Calls me Drunkard, Swearer,
blasphemer and I kno' not what, for wᶜʰ he has yᵉ pleasure of
Seeing himself laught at.

To his Second peiċe[7] I published Three Tracts. 1 a sheet Called yᵉ
Dissenters Vindicated &c:[8] wᶜʰ I Sent yoʳ honoʳ Long Sinċe; to this

DEFOE TO ROBERT HARLEY, 18 MARCH 1707

he Replyed[9] wth little but Ill Language wch made his Own friends Blush for him.

I had printed a Replye to him Bitter Enough,[10] But when I Considred my bussiness here was Peace, Reconciliation and Temper, I thought it was better to use him Gently, and as to his Railing it did me no harm, that wise men Would see the beauty of Moderation and bearing Reproach was better than Returning it, Especially haveing my Eye to ye work before me, So I Suppresst ye book and wrott another wch I Call <u>a short View of ye state of ye Protestant Religion in Brittain as it is professt by the Episcopall Church in England, ye Presbyterian Church in Scotland and ye Dissenters in both.</u>[11]

Here, Omitting to Mencon ye Man, I have as Clearly as I Can stated ye Case, and the Differences Among us all, how farr we Ought to Agree & how behave where we Can not.

This has gotten me a Compleat Victory[12] and ye Moderate Men of ye Clergy Come Every Day to thank me for it. I have sent it you Sr Enclosed by this post tho' tis Rather too Bulky for a Letter & I Recomend it to yor Reading, and it[s]^a Author to yor Concern when at this Distance too likely to be forgotten.

As I Told yor honor in my last my Design, if you Approve it, to stay till I see ye Issue of the Genll Assembly,[13] So I Entreat yr Orders about it; I Must Own tis too Much in ye power of the Ministers here to Ruin ye Peace of this Nacon, and this Makes me think ye Meeting of ye Generall assembly here a Thing of more Consequence than Otherwise it would be at This Time, & I Repeat my humble Mocon that their Session May be as short as May be.

I am in Nothing more Unhappy in this affair^b than that yor Extraordinary Affairs p[er]mitt you to favor me^c but Very Seldome with yor Directions, and Methinks I look too much a Voluntier in the Service; However Sr I Resolv to Omitt Nothing I Can do, and I Doubt you find I spare no Charge to Carry On ye work I am Upon in ye best Manner I Can and to push ye Great work of Reconciling the minds of this People^d to One Another and to ye Union.

^{a} it[s]] *obscured by MS binding*
^{b} affair] *interlined*
^{c} me] *interlined*
^{d} People] *interlined above cancelled word* 'kingdome'

DEFOE TO ROBERT HARLEY, 18 MARCH 1707

To This purpose I have in ye Review, wch I humbly beg you will please to Cast yor Eye on, begun a long Series of Discourse on ye Reciprocall Duties of the Two Nations One to Another after ye Union.[14]

In my Mannagem^t here I am a p[er]fect Emissary. I act ye Old part of Cardinall Richlieu.[15] I have my spyes and my Pensioners In Every plaće, and I Confess tis ye Easyest thing in the World to hire people here to betray their friends.

I have spies in ye Commission, in ye p[ar]liament and in the assembly, and Und^r pretenće of writeing my hystory[16] I have Every Thing told me.

I am in Dayly Conferenćes wth the Ministers, who are Members of ye Assembly, and hope they will Come More Moderately Enclind than was Expected.

They now Soliċit me to write to my friends in England Among the Dissenters to Assure them that they are not Concernd in ye scandal Raisd on them by Webster[17] which I shall do — In all things I labour to Reduće them to Temper and Union of affecċon, both wth England and wth One Another, and Indeed I think my work is harder and More p[er]plexing Now than it was at first, In all which I study to approve my Self to yor Judgem^t s^r, that haveing put you to a Very Great Expenće, that Expenće is faithfully Applyed and not Intrusted with an Unprofitable Servant.[18]

I am

S^r yor Most Obed^t Servt

DF

I Entreat yor Directions about a Ton of Wine.

Edinb. Mar. 18. 1707

Text: BL Add. MS. 70291, fols. 154–7. *Address* (fol. 157^v): To The Right Honble | Robert Harley Esqr | Her Maj^ties Prinċipall Secret^a of State | Present. *Endorsed by Harley* (fol. 157^v): Edenburg Mar: 18: 1706/7 R Mar: 25 1707

1 *Ld Hoptons*: Charles Hope, first Earl of Hopetoun (1681–1742).

2 *quarrell between ye Doctors and Surgeons*: On 17 Mar., an overture for an Act giving surgeons and apothecaries the right to practise medicine, hitherto the exclusive privilege of physicians, was offered in the Scottish parliament. The Royal College of Physicians submitted a petition against the Act, read along with it in parliament (*History of the Union*, *TDH*, VIII, 229). Defoe remarked that 'It would have been perhaps a contested Thing, if the House had been

DEFOE TO ROBERT HARLEY, 18 MARCH 1707

of longer Continuance, but the End of the Parliament being so near, there was no Time for it' (*TDH*, VIII, 220).

3 *book ... Moon*: Perhaps suggesting that Defoe's unrealised essay on cerebral circulation was to be a fantastical satire in the vein of his lunar voyage, *The Consolidator* (1705). See Defoe's brief 'Allegory' of the circulation of the blood to describe the Union, in *Review*, III, 64 (11 Mar. 1707).

4 *Conflict between mr Webster and I*: See Letters 92 and 93.

5 *his first*: *The Covenants of Redemption and Grace Displayed* (1707), generally attributed to James Hog (1658?–1734), but assumed by Defoe to be Webster's because its 'Address to the Reader' is signed 'Ja Webster'.

6 *short ... Treaty*: *Two Great Questions Considered* (1707), *PEW*, IV, 187–96. See headnote to Letter 85. William Adams's (1675/6–1730) *A Letter from the Country containing some Remarks concerning the National Covenant and Solemn League* (1707) supplements Defoe's response to Webster, calling Defoe 'a most ingenious Person, who gives a new and happy Turn to every Subject and Argument he handles', but also 'a Stranger, who has not applyed himself to the particular Consideration of our History' (3).

7 *his Second peice*: Webster's *Lawful Prejudices*.

8 *yᵉ Dissenters Vindicated &c:*: This is *The Dissenters in England Vindicated* (1707), which is distinct from Defoe's *The Dissenters Vindicated* (1707).

9 *he Replyed*: Webster's *The Author of the Lawful Prejudices against an Incorporating Union with England, Defended*. See Letter 96, note 16.

10 *Replye to him Bitter Enough*: Defoe's *Passion and Prejudice* (1707). Although it was suppressed, copies have survived. In it Defoe recounts Webster's *volte face* on the Union and his attack on the English Dissenters, which occasioned Defoe to write him respectful but admonitory letters (Letters 92 and 93). Defoe then recounts that he sent Webster, on request, some of his books.

11 *a short ... both*: Defoe's *A Short View of the Present State of the Protestant Religion in Britain* (1707) presents a history of the Reformation in England and Scotland, answering Webster's charges against the English Presbyterians indirectly by more fully contextualising their willingness to accept prelacy in 1661 and James II's indulgence in 1687.

12 *Compleat Victory*: *The Post-Man*'s Edinburgh correspondent wrote that 'One Mr Webster, a Minister of this City having written 2 Libels against the English Dissenters, the proceedings of that Gentleman have been very much disliked by the other Ministers of this City, and Mr Daniel de Foe being in this place, has fully vindicated the Protestant Dissenters in England against the Aspersions contained in those Pamphlets' (*Post-Man*, 25–7 Feb. 1707).

13 *Genˡˡ Assembly*: The 1707 session of the General Assembly of the Church of Scotland ran from 8 to 21 Apr.

14 *long ... Union*: In the preface to vol. III of the *Review*, published on 8 Feb. 1707, Defoe wrote, 'If it shall be my Lot to live to see this Treaty finish'd, I think to venture one Essay, at the general and reciprocal Duties of the two Nations one to another' (III, 4), which echoes III, 853 (1 Feb. 1707). He touched on this topic in the *Review* for 11 Mar., telling readers that the nations have 'one Politick Heart' (IV, 64), and on the day of this letter, 18 Mar., insisted that 'the Union is a mutual Stipulation, and Securities ought to be reciprocally given' (IV, 81). On 29 Mar., he recollects his promise of a fuller exposition (IV, 105–6), and resumes the topic on 1 Apr., continuing it through to the summer.

15 *Cardinall Richlieu*: For Defoe's interest in Richelieu as a spymaster, see Letter 14.

16 *my hystory*: See Letter 94.

17 *They ... Webster*: Defoe's *A Short View of the Present State of the Protestant Religion in Britain* was republished in England as *The Dissenters Vindicated*, first advertised in the *Review* on 25 Mar. and including a preface explaining his dispute with Webster.

18 *Unprofitable Servant*: See Letter 13, note 5. Defoe had used the phrase recently in the preface to vol. III of the *Review* (early Feb.) in one of his denials that he is employed to write: 'I have not been an unprofitable Servant to any Body but my self' (III, 3). Cf. *Review*, III, 142 (2 Mar. 1706).

363

103

To Robert Harley

25 March 1707

HEADNOTE: With the business of Union concluded, the final parliament of Scotland until 1999 was dissolved on 25 Mar. 1707. Defoe's desire for instructions and for acknowledgement of his efforts continued to intensify.

Sr

I have Now Seen ye Finishing of This happy Work. The Union has been Confirmd as they Call it here, That is, proclaim'd at ye Cross, and This Day the Parliament is at An End, and all is Over.[1]

I have wrott yor honor my Thoughts of staying to see The Assembly Meet[2] and act my part Among them, then to make a Tour to Glasgow, Aberdeen and St Andrews to preach Peace & Good Manners to ye preachers of Truth and Sedicon, for Such some of them are.

When I Signifye my Design tis allways Subjected to yor Opinion & in hopes of yor Direction, in want of wch I am Obliged to Satisfye my Self wth a Negative allowance and take yor Not forbidding me for an Order.

I Entreat you Sr to favour me wth yor Approbacon of my Measures or yor Ordrs and Withall to Signifye to me what Course I shall steer next.

I am
Sr
yor Most Obedt Servt
D Foe

I hear ye Bill for Secureing ye Right of printed Coppyes is stopt.[3] I beg of you sr in yor Respect to Encouragemt of Letters and Dilligence in Learning to give it your help.

Edinb. March 25. 1707

At ye Closeing the Parliamt ye Commissr Made a short speech[4] wch I presume you will have a Coppy of.

364

DEFOE TO ROBERT HARLEY, 25 MARCH 1707

And I Can Not but Observ y^t a Moċon was Made to Recomend Mr Paterson to her Maj^{tie}5 and if my Labour had Not been allways to Conceal my Self I might have had ye Same honour — but I have No body to Recoṁend me S^r but yor Self, to whom I leav it.[6] I am Sure he has ye Credit of a good stock in ye Faċe[7] and is Applauded for Some things I Actually did in ye Committee. I beg S^r I may not however be forgotten.

Text: BL Add. MS. 70291, fols. 158–9. *Address* (fol. 159^v): To The Right Honble | Robert Harley Esqr | Her Maj^{ties} Prinċipall Secret^a of State | Present

1   *This … Over*: As with all important civic announcements, the conclusion of Union and dissolution of parliament were publicly proclaimed at the Mercat Cross in Edinburgh.
2   *Assembly Meet*: See Letter 102, note 13.
3   *Bill … stopt*: A Bill for Securing the Rights of Owners of Printed Copies, a measure long supported by Defoe, remained in committee in the English parliament throughout the 1707 session and was not passed (*C.J.*, xv, 313, 316, 321, 327, 346). Defoe later indicated that Tory opposition forestalled it (*Review*, vi, 458 (3 Nov. 1709)). For Defoe's views, see *An Essay on the Regulation of the Press* (1704), *PEW*, viii, 143–59.
4   *Closeing … speech*: See *History of the Union, TDH*, viii, 235.
5   *Moċon … Majtie*: Paterson was recommended for his good service on 25 Mar. 1707 (*History*, *TDH*, viii, 234).
6   *No body … it*: In fact, Defoe assisted Harley with the task of recommending himself in *Review*, iv, 104–5 (29 Mar. 1707). Reacting to this issue, one enemy accused Defoe of 'making your self the Author of every good Thing, as of the *Scots Union*' (*The Review Review'd. In a Letter to the Prophet Daniel in Scotland* (1707?), 2).
7   *stock in ye Faċe*: Effrontery. Defoe uses and varies this idiom, which does not seem to be very common in the period, in numerous places. See *Review*, ii, 708 (8 Nov. 1705); iii, 415 (6 July 1706); v, 549 (28 Dec. 1708); v, 578 (11 Jan. 1709); v, 642 (12 Feb. 1709); *History, TDH*, vii, 66; *Review*, vii, 204 (29 June 1710); *An Argument Proving that the Design of Employing and Enobling Foreigners, is a Treasonable Conspiracy against the Constitution* (1717), 97; *The Anatomy of Exchange-Alley* (1719), *PEW*, vi, 130; *The Manufacturer*, no. 25 (27 Jan. 1720); *Serious Reflections, Novels*, iii, 173; *The Complete English Tradesman, Volume II* (1727), *RDW*, viii, 115; *The Compleat English Gentleman* (*c.* 1729), *RDW*, x, 86–7.

104

Receipt for the Duke of Queensberry

2 April 1707

HEADNOTE: In early April 1707, Defoe sought to foster a connection with Queensberry ahead of the High Commissioner's imminent departure for London. Defoe had written positively about Queensberry's management of parliament during the last session.[1] He dedicated *Caledonia* (1706) to Queensberry and praised him in the poem.[2] Harley subsequently encouraged Defoe to keep up the connection.[3] Later on, Queensberry and Queen Anne were the dedicatees of *The History of the Union* (1709/10), in which Defoe commended his statesmanship at length.[4] At some point, Defoe was hosted by Queensberry at his stately home, Drumlanrig.[5] He praises the house and its owner in *A Tour thro' the Whole Island of Great Britain* (1724–6), claiming to have advised on possible improvements to the estate which were never undertaken owing to Queensberry's death in 1711. Defoe also claimed that he was permitted by the Duke to read William III's and Anne's letters to him, in which they expressed 'their Satisfaction in his Fidelity and Affection of their Majesties Service, his Ability and extraordinary Judgment in the Affairs entrusted to him; his knowledge of, and Zeal for the true Interest of his Country, and their Dependance upon his Councils and Conduct'.[6]

This supposed intimacy appears to have begun when Defoe visited Queensberry in Edinburgh on 2 April, which he mentions in his letter to Harley of the following day (Letter 105). A receipt (in part in Defoe's handwriting) shows that Queensberry purchased several of Defoe's books. The same titles sold to Queensberry were also purchased in February 1707 by Sir John Clerk together with his son, Defoe's acquaintance John Clerk of Penicuik, in addition to the six *Essays at Removing National Prejudices*. Recently elected as an MP in the new British parliament, Clerk explains to his father in a letter dated 22 February 1707 that 'I have bought them & payed for them, because of their being absolutely necessary to let me knoū a Littel of the bypast transactions of the house of commons.'[7] Queensberry may also have wanted the books for the same reason.

DEFOE TO DUKE OF QUEENSBERRY, 2 APRIL 1707

Delivred To His Grace, The Duke of Queensberry, High[a]
Comission[r] to The Parliam[t] of Scotland

1.	Jure Divino folio[8] . . . . 1.	0 :	—
1.	Vol. Review Qu[a] bound & Gilt[9].	12 :	6
2.	Vol. D F Works Octa[10]	16 :	—
1.	Consol. D[o11].	3 .	6

$£2.$ 12 : —

Wm Alves[12]
Pay to Mr Daniel De Foe, two pounds twelve shi[ll], and take his
Receipt, in full of the above bill which sum shall be allowd in your
accompts.
Sign'd at Holyroodhous this 2[d] Ap[r] 1707
To Wm Alves, writer to the signet

Queensberry

Rec[d] 15 Aprill 1707 of M[r] W[m] Alves, Commiss[a], by Ord[r] of his
Grace y[e] Duke of Queensberry, Two Pounds Twelv shillings in full
of y[e] within Bill

p[ar] Dan[ll] De Foe

$£2. 12.$ —

Text: Princeton University Library, Robert H. Taylor collection, box 6, folder 2.[13]
Address: none. *Endorsed*: Receipt Mr De Foe To D: of Queensberry 2£ 12[b] 1707

[a] Queensberry, High] *interlined*
[b] 2£ 12] *illegible marks in MS*

---

1 See esp. Letters 65 and 99; *Review*, III, 828 (21 Jan. 1707); III, 857 (4 Feb. 1707); IV, 170 (29 Apr. 1707).
2 *PEW*, IV, 211–12; line 1038, IV, 259.
3 See Letter 114.
4 *TDH*, VII, 43–5; cf. VII, 257–8.
5 *Review*, VIII, 166–7 (5 June 1711).
6 *TDH*, III, 183–6.
7 NRS GD 18/3135/6; cf. Sir John to his son, 31 Dec.–4 Jan. [1706–7], NRS GD 18/3131/1.
8 *Jure Divino folio*: The original price was 15s. See Letter 49, note 10.
9 *Review Qu[a] bound & Gilt*: Probably vol. II (1705–6), assuming that these were books Defoe brought with him to Scotland in autumn 1706, but conceivably vol. III (1706–7); both were in quarto.
10 2. *D F Works Oct[a]* . . .: *A True Collection of the Writings of the Author of The True Born Englishman* (1703) and *A Second Volume of the Writings of the Author of The True-Born Englishman*

367

(1705), both in octavo. The earlier collection originally sold for 6s. (*Daily Courant*, 22 July 1703).

11 *Consol. Do . . .*: *The Consolidator* (1705), also in octavo ('Do' is 'ditto'). The book originally cost 4s. (*Flying Post*, 24–7 Mar. 1705).

12 *Wm Alves*: William Alves (d. 1722), MP for Sanquhar and Commissioner to Parliament (*The Parliaments of Scotland, Burgh and Shire Commissioners*, 2 vols., ed. Margaret D. Young (Edinburgh, 1992), I, 15).

13 The heading and price list at the top and the record of receipt at the bottom are in Defoe's hand. All but Queensberry's signature of the order to pay is in an unknown hand, probably Alves's own.

105

To Robert Harley

3 April 1707

HEADNOTE **(Letters 105 and 106):** The General Assembly of the Church of Scotland was to begin on 8 April and Defoe feared a replay of the hostility to the Union he had experienced during the past six months, especially because in that time some anti-Union ministers had insisted that the ratification of the Union should wait for the General Assembly. In the event, to Defoe's relief, the anti-Union group gained little traction in the Assembly.[1]

Sr

Mr Bell being Come from Londo has I Doubt Stopt ye Delivery of My last.[2] I have at present Nothing Materiall to write; we are prepareing for ye Genll Assembly, and tho' I hope well, yet I am Now Busyer than Ever, but it is a Nice point to Act, and the Parsons here are Unaccountable people, Humorous, Jealous, Partiall, Censorious, Haughty, Insolent and Above all Monstrously Ignorant.

I shall Omitt Nothing I Can to Influence those of them that Are <u>Come-at-able</u> and hope for a Good Issue and a short Sitting.

The Great Men are posting to London for places and Honours, Every Man full of his Own Merit, and affraid of Every One Near him: I Never Saw So Much Trick, sham, pride, Jealousy, and Cutting of Friends Throats as there is Among the Noble men; I presume Sr you will soon see the Effects of it at London, I wish some of Our Friends had Not So much hand in it.

DEFOE TO ROBERT HARLEY, 3 APRIL 1707

Last Night I Waited on yᵉ Comissionʳ to wish him a good Journey and Take my Leav;³ He Recᵈ Me Very Obligeingly. He is pleased to Say More of my small Servicés here than I have a facé to Repeat and has promised to Recommend me to yᵉ Queen and to My Lᵈ Treasurer.⁴ If his Grace be Sincére Sʳ I Can not Miss to Meet wᵗʰ Some help when tis Joyn'd wᵗʰ your prevaling Assistancé.

I shall no more afflict you wᵗʰ Sollicitations for yoʳ Ordʳˢ. I proceed by my Own Undirected judgemᵗ, Giveing you a Constant Accoᵗ, and Am forcéd to take yoʳ Long Silencé for a Tacit professing yoʳ Satisfaccon. If I Flatter my Self in a Mistake I am Doubly Unhappy.

I am spending yoʳ Money⁵ a Little Freer than Ordinary On this Occasion of the Assembly, but tis from my Sencé of yᵉ Danger if it Miscarryes and I have some Engines at work Among the Ministers — In short Money will do anything here.⁶

Some Angry Men are Chosen⁷ but yᵉ Rancor of the Temper is Abated Exceedingly and I hope shall More Abate to wᶜʰ Nothing shall be wanting in

yoʳ Most Obedᵗ Servᵗ

DF

After yᵉ Assembly I Entreat your Ordʳˢ what to do.

Edinb Aprill 3. 1707

PS

The Commissʳ Sets Out for London this Day.

Text: BL Add. MS. 70291, fols. 160–1. *Address* (fol. 161v): To The Right Honᵇˡᵉ | Robert Harley Esqʳ | Princ̔ipal Secretᵃ of State | Present. *Endorsed by Harley* (fol. 161v): Edenburg Ap: 3: 1707 ℞ Ap: 9:

1 See the assessment of D. Fearns in his letter to Harley of 15 Apr. (H.M.C. *Portland MSS*, IV, 401) and that of Mar in his letter to Carstares of 29 Apr. (*State-Papers and Letters Addressed to William Carstares*, 762).

2 *My last*: Untraced. On 18 Apr., Bell wrote to Harley, stating that the letter was returned from London to him in Newcastle, so he sent it back again to Harley in London (H.M.C. *Portland MSS*, IV, 402).

3 *Last ... Leav*: See the previous letter. Queensberry departed for London on 3 Apr. 1707, arriving on 16 Apr. See the account by John Clerk of Penicuik, who accompanied him (NRS GD 18/3134) and Clerk's letter to his father upon their arrival (17 Apr. 1707, NRS GD 18/3135/10).

4 *Recommend ... Treasurer*: No evidence that Queensberry abided by this promise has been traced.

369

DEFOE TO ROBERT HARLEY, 12 APRIL 1707

5 *Spending yor Money*: Bell told Harley on 18 April that he had provided Defoe £40 and expects he will want more (H.M.C. *Portland MSS*, IV, 402).

6 *Money will do anything here*: William Ferguson takes this to mean that Defoe bribed ministers (*Scotland's Relations with England: A Survey to 1707* (Edinburgh, 1977), 252). But Stephen deems this unlikely in the circumstances, as the opposition were a minority and the Union a *fait accompli* (*Scottish Presbyterians*, 230). Cf. Defoe's remark just a few weeks earlier that 'tis yᵉ Easyest thing in the World to hire people here to betray their friends' (Letter 102).

7 *Chosen*: I.e. as representatives to the General Assembly.

106

To Robert Harley

12 April 1707

Sʳ

    I have yᵉ Satisfacċon of writing you that yᵉ Assembly goes on here wᵗʰ all Manner of Calmness and quietness Contrary to the hopes of Some and I must Own Contrary to my Apprehensions; I have Not failed In plying them hard wᵗʰ Arguments and perswasions in Print,[1] in Discourse and by Other Instruments wᶜʰ I have Employ'd. I will not presume to Say I have been anything in the Success but I have done my Duty.

    The Hottest of yᵉ Clergy are Extreamly Coold by this Surprizeing Alteraċon, and Some of them Are Very much Asham'd of their Former behavioʳ. I Converse not much wᵗʰ them yᵗ Are for it, For they Need Not yᵉ Physitian,[2] but I Single Out the Opposers, and am Dayly and allmost Hourly in their little Clubs and Caballs. They begin to Solliċit me Now not to Represent them to their Dissadvantage In England, And Value Themselves Upon their Negativ behavioʳ, what they did Not do, to Excuse themselves from yᵉ blame of what they Did.

    And Now sʳ I Entreat yoʳ Directions how to steer my Course. I have been Long here without a word or hint how to Govern my Self But Now it Seems Absolutely Necessary to have Some Orders and I Humbly Recommend it to you Sʳ to Determine for me what Course I shall Take.

370

DEFOE TO ROBERT HARLEY, 22 APRIL 1707

I did propose a small Circle here Among the Clergy to Cultivate yᵉ Good Temper that Appeares among Them and then to Leav this Country, But I have No Satisfacċon in Undertakeing any Thing without yoʳ Ordʳˢ. I Entreat One line Sʳ for my Governmᵗ whether to go or stay here or Come for Englᵈ, for wᵗʰout yoʳ Directions I am a Meer Image wᵗʰout life, Soul or Action.

I am

yoʳ Most Obedᵗ Servᵗ

DF

Edinb Aprˡˡ 12. 1707

Text: BL Add. MS. 70291, fols. 162–3. *Address* (fol. 163ᵛ): To The Right Honᵇˡᵉ | Robert Harley Esqʳ | Prinċipall Secretᵃ of State | Present.

1 *Arguments and perswasions in Print*: Possibly referring to *A Voice from the South: or, An Address from some Protestant Dissenters in England to the Kirk of Scotland* (1707), reprinted in the *Review* for 10 and 15 May 1707.
2 *they Need Not yᵉ Physitian*: Defoe uses the phrase in *Advice to all Parties* (1705), *PEW*, 11, 104; *The Family Instructor, Volume II* (1718), *RDW*, 11, 113. The sources are Matt. 9:12, Mark 2:17, and Luke 5:31.

107

To Robert Harley

22 April 1707

HEADNOTE **(Letters 107 and 108)**: The circumstances perplexing Defoe in late April 1707 are summed up in the *Review* for 20 May:

> The Grievance in short is, That upon the Union, *Scotland* having a free Trade with *France*, was full of *French* Goods, and there being a long Interval between the Conclusion of the Treaty and the *1st* of *May*, on which Day the Union was to take Place, the Merchants crowded yet larger Quantities of *French* Goods into *Scotland*, in Prospect of a free Admission of those Goods into *England* after the Union, upon the Foot of the *4th* Article of the Treaty, *there should be a free Intercourse or Communication of Trade* between the Nations.[1]

Importing French goods to England was prohibited due to the war, and it imminently would be to Scotland too: hence the rush to capitalise on free trade by stockpiling French goods in Scotland before 1 May, then bringing them to English markets. Wine and brandy were of particular concern, as Defoe had anticipated in his February letter to Godolphin.[2] In the *Review* for 1 May Defoe imagines a London wine merchant stating his complaint: '*The* Scots *are crowding the whole Nation with* French *Goods, Wine and Brandy,* &c. *Which paying but a Trifle of Custom there, will be imported upon us here; while we having paid high Duties,* and imported from other Countries, *feel the Loss already in a general Stop of Trade, and Fall of Prices.*'[3] If England closed this loophole, as was requested by a group of merchants who petitioned the House of Commons, she risked contravening the free trade promised in the Union.[4] But not to act would be detrimental to the exchequer, to English merchants, and to the principle of proscribing trade with France.

The House of Commons on 7 April approved a bill designed to prevent the French goods from Scotland entering English ports tariff-free.[5] Unbeknownst to Defoe, Harley strongly supported this 'Drawback Bill' and even proposed to make the measure retroactive to 1 February.[6] Though it exempted Scots, it provoked an outcry from Scottish merchants who claimed it breached the articles of Union. In the *Review* for 31 May, Defoe describes in retrospect the anxious situation of late April, the time when he wrote these letters, attributing apprehensions to rumours spread by maligners of the Union.[7]

Even as Defoe was writing to Harley, the situation was being resolved in London. The Lords declined to pass the first Commons bill. Queen Anne prorogued parliament from 8 to 14 April, looking for legislators to form a proposal that would satisfy all parties and both Houses. However, a substantially similar bill was sent up on 19 April. On 22 April Godolphin wrote to Marlborough: 'The close of the best sessions of Parliament that England ever saw, has been unhappily hindred, by a wrangle between the 2 Houses which is not yett ended.'[8] The Lords engaged legal experts in consultations concerning the possibility of differentiating laws for Scottish and English subjects; but, these proving inconclusive, the Lords and the Queen allowed the bill to expire when parliament rose on 23 April.[9] John Clerk of Penicuik, who was in London, wrote: 'By this the Queen took upon her to drop the bill, not thinking it fitt that the Lords should be put upon rejecting it because of ill blood between the two houses.'[10] The loophole would not be closed.

Defoe was ultimately glad that the English parliament accepted its losses, but wished that 'some *Medium* had been found out', specifically that it had passed with the exemption for Scottish merchants.[11] Defoe gave his fullest account of this episode in his *History of the Union*.[12]

DEFOE TO ROBERT HARLEY, 22 APRIL 1707

S^r

I presume you will Now have Notice That ye assembly is Up, and all Things grow better That way Every day. The Address will Come away to Night and The E of Glasgow In ye Morning.[13]

I am much at a Loss how to Mannage My Self About ye Affair of Trade here; What ye Co^rt in England Seemd to Desire Was, as I Tho^t, to Allow Some Latitude, and Now by her Maj^ties Speech[14] it looks quite Another way — But as to ye thing it Self I Crave leav to Note:

If no Exception be Made for the Scots[15] It will make ill blood here and they Talk loudly here that ye Union is Broke before it is begun.

If an Exception be made, the End will be Defeated and all Manner of Doors are Open'd to Perjury by Transferring of Property and Inumerable frauds.[16]

And after all, ye Quantity brought in is but small Compar'd to what is Talked off — I Could Do some Service in this if I know what the Measures are — the wholl Fleet is but 42 Sail at most.[17]

The foundation laid here for Clandestine Trade is beyond all this fatall to both ye Revenue and to Trade and As I am let into Some of it I am the More Moved, Nor Do I See any possibillity of Wholly preventing it w^thout an Army of Officers.

I am too farr to offer schemes for this here. I have Said Enough to sollicit you to Think of me and shall Not press you On that head, Onely thus far, His Grace the D of Queensberry Gave me his word and his hand to Recommend me to Her Maj^tie and I p[er]swade my Self will second any Mo^con you Will please to Make for me.

I Am Inform'd, I kno' Not How true, that My L^d S .... is No Friend to me On an Occasion wch Concerns yor Self;[18] the p[er]ticulars I Referr till I have ye Hono^r to See you.

I am
S^r yor Most Humble and Obed^t Servt
DF

Edinb. Apr^ll 22. 1707

DEFOE TO ROBERT HARLEY, 22 APRIL 1707

Text: BL Add. MS. 70291, fols. 164–5. *Address* (fol. 165ᵛ): To The Right Honᵇˡᵉ | Robert Harley Esqʳ | Princîpall Secretᵃ of State | Present.

1 *Review*, IV, 211.
2 See Letter 98.
3 *Review*, IV, 177.
4 Defoe deemed the merchants' petition to the Commons a Tory tactic to create 'a mighty Stirr' against the Union. He notes that English as well as Scottish merchants have taken advantage of the situation and excuses their opportunism: 'The Knaves have done it, and the Fools, that have neglected it, complain.' He also minimises the problem by arguing that the quantities are small and so their impact on prices will be negligible (*Review*, IV, 177, 182 (1 and 3 May 1707)). This is the opposite to what he wrote to Godolphin when warning him of the problem in Feb. See Letter 98.
5 H.M.C. *House of Lords MSS*, VII, 91–4; *C.J.*, XV, 381.
6 James Brydges to William Cadogan, 10 Apr. 1707, Huntington Library Stowe MSS 57, 1, fol. 94. Harley's measure, done on principle, was opposed by the Junto, but it was a convention that the House of Lords did not alter money bills.
7 *Review*, IV, 237–8.
8 *Marl.–God. Corr.*, II, 754. See also Godolphin to Harley, 22 Apr. 1707, H.M.C. *Bath MSS*, I, 171.
9 H.M.C. *House of Lords MSS*, VII, 95–6; *Heinsius Corr.*, VI, 248–9. Defoe expresses his gladness at this outcome in *Review*, IV, 212 (20 May 1707).
10 'Memoirs of the Affairs of Scotland after the adjournment of parliament anno. 1707', NRS GD 18/3134, 19.
11 *Review*, IV, 255–64 (10 and 12 June 1707).
12 *TDH*, VIII, 237–44.
13 *Address … Morning*: In 1707 Glasgow (see Letter 96, note 21) served as Lord High Commissioner to the General Assembly, representing the monarch. The closing address to the Queen of 21 Apr. is printed in *The Principal Acts of the General Assembly, of the Church of Scotland; conveened at Edinburgh the 8th of April 1707* (1707), 47–8. Glasgow wrote to Mar on that day: 'This day I dissolved the Assembly, who parted in most calm and peaceable manner. Never was ane Assembly so well pleased with their Sovereign as this Assembly is with the Queen' (H.M.C. *Mar and Kellie MSS*, 388).
14 *her Majties Speech*: The Queen's speech on 14 Apr. encouraged parliament to act promptly 'to prevent the Inconveniencies, that may happen to our Trade by too great an Interval between the rising of the Parliament and the first of *May*' (*C.J.*, XV, 385). Defoe gives a less panicked explanation of the speech and its effects in the *Review* for 12 June 1707 (IV, 262). Anne prorogued parliament on 8 Apr. and made her speech on 14 Apr. in order to salvage the Drawback Bill, which would have hit an impasse had the Lords tried to amend a money bill (see John Mandeville to Wake, 8 Apr. 1707, Christ Church Wake MSS XVII, fol. 166). On 11 Apr., Godolphin asked Cowper to compose the speech, making it a warning to the Commons that any new bill needed to take care not to prejudice the Union (Hertfordshire Archives and Local Studies, Panshanger MSS. D/EP F54, fol. 126).
15 *If no Exception be Made for the Scots*: The act approved by the Commons did exempt Scottish merchants; see Harley's account below (Letter 114) and *History of the Union*, *TDH*, VIII, 240.
16 *Exception … frauds*: Defoe wrote that an act of parliament preventing the trade would merely require the merchants to use subterfuge, and he opposed attempts to police the trade with oaths (*Review*, IV, 181 (3 May 1707)).
17 *Quantity … most*: In the *Review* for 1 May 1707, Defoe writes: 'All this huge Fleet, that was to drown us with Wine and Brandy, are but 36 Sail, most of them Doggers and small Vessels, and one with another not above 60 to 80 Tun Burthen, and of these several are loaden with Salt' (IV, 177). In the issue for 12 June, he estimates that the totals removed from Scotland to

DEFOE TO ROBERT HARLEY, 24 APRIL 1707

England amount to '1200 Tun of Brandy' and '800 Tun of Wine', though 'a great Deal of that is a small thin Sort of Wine, which will not suit the *English* Market' (IV, 263). And later, in *History of the Union*, he says that the fleet consisted of 'about 40 Sail mostly loaded with Wine and Brandy' (*TDH*, VIII, 242).

18 *L⁴ S ... Self.* Almost certainly Sunderland. The cause has not been ascertained, though Sunderland and Harley had an acrimonious relationship throughout the time that they both served as Secretaries of State. See headnote to Letter 114.

108

To Robert Harley

24 April 1707

Sʳ

I Can Not write to you Now without Concern and I fear heartily The Unravelling all we have been Doeing.

The New Votes of yᵉ house of Commons[1] makes yᵉ most Unaccountable Fermentacon here, That if the Next News does not Cool it, I shall Need No New Orders from England about Staying Or Returning, for Really Sʳ here will be No staying here for me nor hardly any English man.

The Importation of all their Goods to England free of Dutyes is[a] they Say Expressly Capitulated in the Article of free Communication[2] and the English Ought to have known[b] the Consequence of the Intervall as well as they[3] — The Vote of yᵉ House they say is Directly Against the Union, and they talk of Meeting and Declareing yᵉ Union Broke[4] —

I Dare not write to you yᵉ Murmurs of yᵉ people, and My worst Missfortune is that I Can make no Answer to it, and tho' I thought my Reputation Establish't here, yet I must Confess this shocks it; they Come Crowding about me Reproaching me Every hour wᵗʰ what I have said of the Honour and justice of the English Parliament.

[a] is] *interlined above cancelled word* 'are'
[b] known] *following word* 'of' *cancelled*

DEFOE TO ROBERT HARLEY, 24 APRIL 1707

Ay Ay, Sayes One of them, Now you See how we are to be served! and what we Are to Expect from a Brittish Parliament! How Early they begin with us, and what Usage we are to have when Ever Our Advantage Clashes with their Intrest.

I am Exceedingly Harrass't and Fateagu'd wth them and I know Not what to Answer because I Do not know what ye Measures Are.

I Tell them (tho' I kno' nothing of it yet) that there will be an Excepçon for Scots men and have printed the Clause of the last Act wth Some Remarks,[5] shown ye Necessity of the preventing the Abuses About Tobacco and ye Drawbacks,[6] and I Endeavour to[a] Buoy them up wth hopes. But Tis a strange Hurry[7] they Are in, and if Something is Not Done to Cool and Satisfye them I acknowlege I Apprehend the Consequences.

Here's One Gentleman that shows a letter from Lond^o, as he sayes, by a p[ar]liam^t Man — wch Saies that Even those Scots who shall be Excepted shall be Obliged to Come to London to prove the property of their Goods, and the Difficultyes at ye Custome house will be Chargeable and Vexatious So that the Exception to ye Scots will signifye little.

I Entreat you S^r to Consider these things & give me a hint what I must Say to Defend the Case and make ye people Easy.

I am

yor Most Obed^t Servt

DF

Aprill 24. 1707

This Early Ferment is Very Unseasonable.

Text: BL Add. MS. 70291, fols. 166–7. *Address* (fol. 167^v): To The Right Honble | Robert Harley Esqr | Prinçipall Secret^a of State | Present.

[a] to] *following word probably a misspelling of* 'Buoy' *cancelled*

---

1   *New Votes of ye house of Commons*: The Commons approved a second bill aimed at preventing the trade on 19 Apr. 1707, which had small amendments to the bill of 7 Apr.
2   *Article of free Communication*: Article four of the Union Treaty.
3   *English ... they*: In the *Review* for 3 May 1707, Defoe says that the issue should have been anticipated when it could have been occluded (iv, 182). He was clearly alert to these issues before the ratification of the Union, as shown by his advice on article five (see Letter 67, note 13) and, touching the present matter, by his letter to Godolphin in Feb. 1707 (Letter 98).

376

DEFOE TO ROBERT HARLEY, 26 APRIL 1707

4   *Vote ... Broke*: Those in favour of prohibiting imports said the opposite. Robert Monckton (*c.* 1659–1722), MP for Aldborough and member of the board of trade, wrote to Somers that 'I am informed that Paterson declares the Scotch themselves are litle concerned & never understood it to be intended to ever to make an extravagant use of this construction of ye 4th & 6th article' (undated, Surrey History Centre, 371/14/E/34).

5   *printed ... Remarks*: *The Clause Proposed in the English Parliament to Prevent the French Goods being Imported thro' Scotland; with a Short Remark on the Same.* The clause was also reprinted as an appendix to *The History of the Union*. See Nicholas Seager, '*The Clause Proposed in the English Parliament to Prevent the French Goods being Imported thro' Scotland*: A New Defoe Attribution', *N&Q* 66 (2019), 83–6.

6   *Necessity ... Drawbacks*: A drawback on tobacco exported from England applied to tobacco exported to Scotland until the Union commenced. Merchants thus sent their product to Scotland before 1 May, drawing back most of the import duty they had paid, and waiting until duty-free trade within Britain began to bring it back (*Review*, IV, 216 (22 May 1707)). Defoe explains that this amounted to a drawback of 5d. on each pound in weight, which was all but half a penny per pound of the import duty. He says that he had been tempted to avail himself of this scam, 'and propos'd an Essay of that Nature to a Friend ... But I soon saw farther into it, and have since declined several Offers of being concern'd in it, as a thing, contrary to all Manner of Honesty and fair Trading' (*Review*, IV, 265–7 (14 June 1707)). Whereas restricting the wine and brandy trade was ticklish because it might harm Scottish merchants, Defoe would have been glad if the profiteering on tobacco drawbacks could have been prevented, especially as merchants, upon exporting it, took an oath not to re-land it in England (*The Clause Proposed in the English Parliament*; *Review*, IV, 273 (17 June 1707); *History of the Union*, TDH, VIII, 238–9).

7   *Hurry*: agitation.

109

To Robert Harley

26 April 1707

HEADNOTE: Defoe recounts the story of Robert Balfour of Burleigh (1687–1757) in *A Tour thro' the Whole Island of Great Britain* (1724–6). Balfour's attraction to Anne Robertson, a woman of a lower social rank, prompted his parents to send him abroad to travel. Before leaving, he pledged to wed her upon his return or to kill her husband if he found her already married. Upon returning, he abided by the second resolution, shooting her husband, a schoolmaster named Henry Stenhouse, on 9 April 1707 and fleeing justice.[1]

DEFOE TO ROBERT HARLEY, 26 APRIL 1707

Sr

I Write to you Now Upon a Very Odd and Unhappy Occasion. I shall Say little to ye Fact, but Referr to ye Enclosed,[2] But[a] My Appollogyes are to you Sr for giveing you the Trouble of it.

By ye Manner of ye Letter you will See I have Obtain'd Upon ye Clergy here Every whitt as Much as I have Represented to you, for This[3] was a great Opposer of the Union. I would have gladly Rac'd[4] Out his Compliments Upon me as what No way become me to be ye Messenger of, but I Could not Send you ye Letter Blotted.

You See sr what a Charge I have laid Upon me wch I knew not how to Dispense wth, and as I am Directed to Send it to you and ye Arichbishop[5] I Enclose a short Letter[6] to his Grace that you may at yor Pleasure Deliver it yor Self or Send it to his Grace wthout Accquainting[b] him that It Came thro' yor hands.

The Case is Indeed Horrid and Becomes her Majties Justice But ye Secret History of it is This. 1./ The Murtherer[7] is Grandson to ye E of Melvill[8] and a Near Relacon to ye E of Leven[9] and Tis Very Much feared My Ld Leven should Intercede for him. 2:/ Her Majties Exemplar Justice will be Very Gratefull to ye Country here who have an Exceeding Resentment of ye Fact, and ye Burgh of Innerkeithin is preparing an Address to her Majtie for a proclamation and Reward for Aprehending him.[10] 3/ He has behav'd himself So Notoriously Impudently Since ye Murther as gives a Generall Abhorrence of him, and to Pardon him will form[c] a Sad Prejudice Among the people here.[11]

I shall not Presume to give my Opinion here but have laid it before you as ye Minister has been pleased to Command me.

As to Other Matters I Refer to My Last and waiting yor Commands

I Am

Sr

yor Most Obedt Servt

DF

---

a But] *interlined; the caret indicating the insertion point precedes the comma in MS*
b Accquainting] 'ing' *interlined*
c form] *interlined above cancelled word* 'give'

DEFOE TO ROBERT HARLEY, 26 APRIL 1707

Apr^ll 26.^a 1707

I am Sorry to Tell you S^r that My Friends Write me word^12 I shall stay here till I am Forgott.

If you Think Fitt to Deliver ye Enclosed you will be pleased to Cause Coppie ye Letter and Seal ye Outer One.

Text: BL Add. MS. 70291, fols. 168–9. *Address* (fol. 169^v): To The Right Honble | Robert Harley Esqr | Principall Secretary of State | Present.

---

^a 26] *amended from* '25'

1 Stenhouse died twelve days later, not 'upon the Spot' as Defoe stated in the *Tour*.
2 *Enclosed*: Missing.
3 *This*: Not identified.
4 *Rac'd*: I.e. razed or erased.
5 *Archbishop*: Thomas Tenison (1636–1715), Archbishop of Canterbury.
6 *short Letter*: Untraced.
7 *Murtherer*: Robert Balfour of Burleigh (see headnote).
8 *E of Melvill*: George Melville, first Earl of Melville (1636–1707).
9 *E of Leven*: Melville was Leven's father; Balfour was Leven's nephew, as his parents were Leven's sister, Lady Margaret Melville (b. 1658), and Robert Balfour, fourth Lord Balfour of Burleigh (d. 1713).
10 *proclamation and Reward for Aprehending him*: In the *Tour* Defoe referred to 'Justice pursuing him, and a Proclamation being issued, with a Reward of 200*l*. for apprehending him' (*TDH*, III, 226).
11 *He ... here*: 'Nor could all the Intercession of his Family and Friends prevail with the Queen, after her Majesty had a true Account of the Fact laid before her, to pardon or reprieve him' (*Tour*, *TDH*, III, 226). In the *Review* for 1 Apr. 1708, Defoe printed a letter alleging that Balfour 'rambles, threatens, commits Rapes, &c. as he pleases, and was lately at *Edinburgh*, in the Face of Authority, without being molested' (v, 12). See Letter 124. He was eventually arrested and tried in 1709, and condemned to death, but as Defoe recounts, Balfour escaped 'disguis'd in his Sister's Clothes' (*Tour*, *TDH*, III, 226). Balfour came into his inheritance upon his father's death in 1713, but his estate was forfeited after he fought for the Jacobites in 1715.
12 *My Friends Write me word*: Letters untraced.

DEFOE TO ROBERT HARLEY, 15 MAY 1707

110

To Robert Harley
15 May 1707

HEADNOTE (**Letters 110 and 111**): The Drawback Bill had been dropped and Defoe had begun travelling around Scotland. However, as he reports in the *Review* for 3 June, as well as in these letters, rumours abounded in Scotland 'that notwithstanding the Lords have thrown out the Bill about the Wine and Brandy, yet the *Lawyers* have found out a Method wholly *to stop the Importation of it* into *England, and not break the Union*'.[1] In published works for English and Scottish readers – five *Review* essays from 3 to 12 June, the last two reprinted in Edinburgh – Defoe treats these reports as more agitation from anti-Unionists: 'There is no more in it, than a Design of ill People to amuse [i.e. deceive] us.'[2] Besides, any law that would prevent transporting goods from Scotland to England has been superseded by the Union: 'If it contravenes the Treaty, it cannot be legal; because no Law in *England*, contravening the Treaty, has any Force at all, but is dead and bury'd, and the Treaty is its Grave-stone, 'tis actually extinct, and *stands repealed by the Union*.'[3] By contrast, his letters show considerable concern that the ideal and reality of Union were about to clash. In the event, in mid-June a fleet of around forty Scottish ships transporting mainly wine and brandy had their cargo seized in London, though it was ultimately admitted without any duty being paid.[4]

Glasgow May 15. 1707

Sr

I hope yor Charity will Determine for me that Something Extraordinary has Restraind my writeing Thus Long — I found by a Suddain stop of my Letters yt Some were Opened, Some Intercepted, and three letters Currt[a] to my Wife[5] Came not to hand Till a long Time after the Course.

This sr and This Onely Interrupted my Conversing wth you in the Usuall Manner wch was my pleasure as well as my Duty Till I Saw The Course of Letters Clear and Found the stop of Letters was onely Delay tho' I knew not nor yet know where.

I stayed in Edinburgh Till ye Assembly broke up and after that the Commission and after that ye Synod of Louthain,[6] in all which

---

[a] Currt] 'Currrt' *in MS*

380

DEFOE TO ROBERT HARLEY, 15 MAY 1707

I have p[er]haps been more Jealous than Needed but I allwayes thought the Cautious[a] part yᵉ Safest in these Cases tho' it were[b] too Much; Since Over Caution may Do harm but Too little Can do no Good.

After I Saw all Clear of yᵉ priests I thought to ha' Travaild a Little as I hinted to you formerly but I am posted here to Bully a Clamarous people and as I Mention'd I think in my last if the Parliamᵗ had not Dropt the Draw back bill⁷ I must ha' fled this Country and Come away without yoʳ Commission wᶜʰ I should ha' been Very loth to ha' Done.

It is scarce possible to Describe to you the Disgust that affair gave here and what Use was made of it — and as I am posted here On the Frontiers I Could not Breath <u>hardly</u> for the Importunate Queries of the Friends to the Union what would become of yᵐ and whatᶜ the Parliamᵗ would do wᵗʰ them and the like.

I won't p[er]plex you wᵗʰ these Country Impertinences. On that head I write this Onely to Satisfye you how I have been Employed here for Some Time.

Now yᵉ Main affair is Over, Now they are frighted afresh with the Accounts they Say Come from London that Notwithstanding this the Custome house Officers will stop their Goods.⁸

Sʳ I have not had the Honoʳ of a line from you a long while. I Humbly Entreat a hint or Two in this affair what to say and what to Do, for I am at a Great loss how to Answer and Indeed in the Generall how to behave my Self, Nor Do I yet kno' whether mÿ Negotiating pleases you or Not, being to Act wholly my Own judgment in Every Case.[d]

I am Now to Offer Another thing. I am at yᵉ City of Glasgow and Unless I Reciev yoʳ Contrary Directions I Design to Take a short Tour and Come back hither and stay a week or 10 Days here.

---

[a] Cautious] *interlined above cancelled word perhaps* 'Timerous'
[b] it were] *interlined*
[c] what] *interlined*
[d] being to Act wholly my Own judgment in Every Case] *the final four words are crammed between the lines, indicating that the latter part of the sentence, probably beginning at* 'being', *was a later addition*

You will be sure Matters are Changed[a] that I Dare to show my Face here where it had been Death to have been known but a few Months Agoe.[9]

I am Acting my Part wth the Magistrates and the Ministers; for the Rest I Do not Concern my Self. I am Arguing the Great Concern England has shown for them in Letting Fall the Drawback bill, and pressing them to Suitable Returns of Duty and Moderation — and I am pleased to Tell yo[r] honour I am heard in it And that I think I am Doeing More Service Now than Ever Since I Came[b] into this Country.

And here I beg yo[r] Leav to Give One hint — There Are Officers Sent Down to y[e] Customes and Excise.[10] I make no Complaints Nor Do I Say there is yet any Cause but I Humbly Move that who Ever Are sent may be Commanded to use all y[e] Courtisye, Civillity and Calmness possible here. Nothing Elce Can Oblige This Surly, Haughty, Vain Humour of the poorest and Meanest people.

I have been often Mov'd on This head, tho' y[e] Gentlem[n] should be in y[e] Right and it Consists wth Their Duty, yet if They have any Regard to y[e] Nature and Temper of Things and Folks they Must wink, Abate and bear wth Circumstances. In short S[r] This people May be Drawn; the Contrary I Need Not Mencon.

I have Now Another Thing to Mencon s[r]. M[r] Bell is Gone Again to Lond[o] and he will Accquat you I have been No Good husband for you — Indeed I hinted the Measures I Took about y[e] Assembly, of which I was Really heartily afraid, put me to No small Expence — But I have been forced Since to supply in p[ar]t Family Demands, My Long Absence Makeing it Absolutely Necessary, and Indeed Impossible to Avoid — I shall be sorry to have yo[r] Censure in This as Invadeing yo[r] bounty but I hope yo[r] Honor will prevail to have an honest and I hope Faithfull Engine supported while Abroad — However I Thot it my Duty to Inform you of it, For I will not have (No Not bread[11]) Without yo[r] knowlege, and will Desist when Ever you summons[c] Me away.

---

[a] Changed] *following word* 'here' *cancelled*
[b] Came] *following word* 'hither' *cancelled*
[c] summons] *following illegible word cancelled*

DEFOE TO ROBERT HARLEY, 15 MAY 1707

I am to Dine On Wednesday wth The Presbytry of Dumfermling[12] and the Next week at that of St Andrews and shall then Come back hither. I Can not help Expressing my Joy at ye Visible Success of my Negotiateing here — and Tho' I am Alone too little for it yet^a I think Nothing More Needfull than this work, for this Is a Fermented and Implacable Nation.

I Am yor Most Obed^t Humble Servt
DF

Text: BL Add. MS. 70291, fols. 170–1. *Address* (fol. 171^v): To The Right Honble | Robert Harley Esqr | Princ̓ipall Secret^a of State | Present.

---

^a too little for it yet] *interlined*

---

1 *Review*, IV, 240.
2 *Review*, IV, 243 (3 June 1707).
3 *Review*, IV, 251 (7 June 1707).
4 See Defoe's account in *History of the Union*, *TDH*, VIII, 242–3. Godolphin solicited and followed the legal advice of Attorney General Sir Simon Harcourt (1661–1727) and Solicitor-General Sir James Montagu (1666–1723), who advised that the customs commissioners could legally seize French goods, as well as tobacco on which a debenture for a drawback had been gained (BL Add. MS. 70039, fols. 198–9).
5 *three letters Curr^t to my Wife*: Untraced. 'Curr^t' means 'of the current month'.
6 *Synod of Louthain*: The Synod of Lothian and Tweeddale included the Presbytery of Edinburgh. Its meeting concluded on 8 May 1707 (NRS CH 2/252/7, 236–9). The Synod's clerk, John Sandilands (1683–1716), minister at Dolphinton, wrote on 6 May 1707 to Sir John Clerk (d. 1722) to report a meeting with Defoe, at which time Sandilands alerted Defoe to a printed attack on him (NRS GD 18/4052). This was probably *The Review Reviewed. In a Letter to the Prophet Daniel in Scotland* (1707?). For discussion of this episode, see Spiro Peterson, 'Defoe in Edinburgh, 1707', *HLQ* 38 (1974), 21–33.
7 *Draw back bill*: See headnote to Letters 107 and 108. In the *Review*, Defoe spun this outcome as England's solicitous care for Scotland and zeal for fairness. 'Their Lordships being so tender in the Case of the Treaty, that they thought *England* ought rather to suffer all the other Inconveniences of Trade, than but to tread on the Confines of the Union, or give the least Shadow of Discontent on the Part of *Scotland*' (IV, 212 (20 May 1707)).
8 *Custome house Officers will Stop their Goods*: See headnote.
9 *I Dare … Agoe*: See Letter 65.
10 *Offic̓ers Sent Down to ye Customes and Excise*: In his *History of the Union*, Defoe names the five officers sent to Scotland in late April 'to put them into some manner of Order as to Exports and Imports', and he records that they were resented by some Scots as Englishmen filling places (*TDH*, VIII, 246). Hamilton complained to his mother on 1 May 1707: 'There are shoalls of English excisemen & other officers coming hither [with] the pretence to informe our people of the English methodes of exacting the Customs & the excise' (Hamilton to the Duchess, 1 May 1707, NRS GD 406/1/7892).
11 *No Not bread*: Possibly referring to Neh. 5:14.
12 *Dine … Dumfermling*: Presumably 21 May. Defoe's letter of that date does not mention it.

III

To Robert Harley
21 May 1707

Sterling May 21. 1707

S^r

My Last was from Glasgow of ye 15. I am Now at Sterling¹ in ye Circuit wch I hinted to you before; I gave you an Acco^t of my Self at Large in My last, to wch I Referr.

I Can not but think my Self Olig'd to Lay The State of Things before you as Clearly as Possible and if for want of yor Comāands Explicitly Guiding me I Err in My Conduct I hope for yor pardon Since it is Impossible for me to Judge at a Distance what is yor pleasure, being So Absolutely Destitute of your Direccons in this Affair.

The Country here was Very Easy On Acco^t of ye Union and I began to boast my Self of ye happy Success — But Two things have given So Much Disgust here that I am Amaz'd to See how Soon These people are to be turned about to Extremes.

Dyer in his Letter Sayes The Lawyers have found Out a Method to Stop the French Goods without breaking the Union and this is spread Over the wholl kingdome, being printed Again in ye Edinb. Gazette.[2]

Now S^r as to this affair I Remember I formerly hinted to you My Tho^{ts}[3] and had Some publick Notice been then Concerted, and the Court here took Some Measures to ha' Corresponding wth it Discouraged the Import, I believ much of The Mischief might have been Prevented, but that is past.

My Humble Conclusions form'd from Serious Observacon here Are, That:

1/ If a Generall stop be Made you put The wholl Nation here Distracted,

2/. with a partiall stop They will be Very well pleased.[4]

I Explain my Self Thus:

To stop or Seize Our Goods who are Scots Men is highly Injurious to us As Our Market here is Destroy'd by The Flux of Goods brought in by The English on a prospect of Trade to England, who when they shall be Obliged to Sell here will Glut ye Markett and lower ye Price and So you Ruin us for what is your Own fault wch is Not fair.

> In This part Indeed they Seem to have Reason, for if The Stop be Generall The Case will be Very Miserable here wth a Great Many and the Clamour Intollerable.

2 They Say if Their Goods are stopt The Union is Directly broken and ye Article of a Free Intercourse of Trade Destroyed.

> And Indeed this to me Seems Evident too, and the Exception in ye house of Commons[5] Imply's as Much, and This is what I am So Earnest for Direccon about.

I am Clear however That the Importacons of Forreigners and English Ought to be stop't, and tho' Concealing and Transposeing properties May be practised, yet you will find it Something Easyer to Discover properties here than in England, Especally Considering the Entries are allready Made wthout any Caution and the proprietors in Most Cases Discovred, And I have Made Some Observacons[6] that in Their Season will be Usefull that way.

I am also to Assure you Sr that if this Medium[7] be Agreed On It will Give an Universall Satisfaccon here, for rst They Can Not pretend any breach of ye Union and 2dly their pride is fully Gratifyed as well as their Purse and they all Crye Out Tis just to stop ye Encroachments of Strangers.

I Ask yor pardon for thus freely giveing my thoughts and as I kno' you put ye Stress upon the giveing just Satisfaccon to the Subject I presume it my Duty to give you ye Sence of the Country.

This is ye Scheme I have also followd in Speaking to Dyers News paper[8] and I Endeavour as rst to allow what they Claim as to their Own Goods, So to Shew ye Reasonableness of Stopping Others, In wch I hope I am Right, and Entreat a hint if I am Not, but I am Sure I am Right as to ye people here in preparing them to Accquiesce in all ye proceedings but just as farr as Touches their Seperate propertys.

I Am Inform'd Sr the Custome house is Settled for this Country;[9] is there No Room for an Absent Servant to be admitted?

DEFOE TO ROBERT HARLEY, 21 MAY 1707

I formerly hinted that a Generall Survey Such as Dr Davenant has in England¹⁰ would be of Great Service here and I am p[er]swaded if I had ye honour to Accqua^t my Ld Treasurer of the steps I formerly hinted About Clandestine Trade¹¹ wch Some have Taken and Are makeing large**ᵃ** provision for, his L^dship would find Such an Employm^t Absolutely Necessary Considering the Infinite Creeks and Coves here, in wch Frauds will be Carryed on and where tis Impossible wthout an Army of Officers to prevent it.¹²

My Brother writes me¹³ he has had the Hono^r to see you and you were pleased to Say My Ld Treasurer had Menconed Me in ye Matter of ye Settlement here¹⁴ — I have No bodÿ to Recommend me but yor Self, Save That ye D of Queensberry promised Me to Recomend Me to My Ld Treasurer & to The Queen also.

I Repeat my humble Entreaty to you to be thoughtfull of Me that I may No Longer be Thus Chargable to you.

I am yor Obed^t Servt
DF

Text: BL Add. MS. 70291, fols. 172–3. *Address* (fol. 173ᵛ): To The Right Honble | Robert Harley Esqr | Princ̈ipall Secretary of State | Present.

ᵃ large] *interlined*

---

1 *Sterling*: See Wodrow's account of Defoe hearing Robert M'Cala [MacAulay?] preach at Stirling, which probably dates to this time, given in *Analecta*, II, 305.
2 *Dyer ... Gazette*: No copy of the *Dyer's News-Letter* or of the *Edinburgh Gazette* has been located. On the question of French imports and the Union, see headnote.
3 *hinted to you My Thots*: See Letters 100, 107, and 108.
4 *If ... pleased*: These arguments are also made in the *Review*, IV, 255–64 (10 and 12 June 1707).
5 *Exception in ye house of Commons*: See Letter 107, note 15.
6 *Observac̈ons*: Untraced.
7 *Medium*: I.e. allowing Scots to bring goods to England duty-free, but not foreigners.
8 *Speaking to Dyers News paper*: Dyer is the unnamed 'News monger' challenged in the *Review* for 3 June, and attacked as 'a Firebrand, a Spye, that brings an ill Report upon the Land, a Sower of Discord, a Prophet of *evil Tidings*, and every thing that ought to be contemn'd, and abborr'd by all good Men' (IV, 241, 244 (3 and 5 June 1707)).
9 *Custome house is Settled for this Country*: Luttrell recorded on 20 May that 'Sir Alexander Rigby [*c*. 1663–1717], John Henley [d. after 1714], and James Isaacson [1660–1724], esqs., sir Robert Dixon and Mr. [William] Boile (brother to the Earl of Glasco) are appointed Commissioners of the Customes in Scotland; their salaries 400*l*. per ann. each'; Henley was subsequently replaced by Lionel Norman (VI, 173, 176). Defoe later claimed that he was offered the role of Commissioner of the Customs in Scotland (see Letter 180). In *Greenshields Out of Prison* (1710), Defoe records that Rigby is 'a zealous Church of *England*-man', though on that

386

occasion he commends his 'Vigour and Prudence' in upholding the Presbyterian settlement when employed in Scotland (13).

10 *Generall … England*: Charles Davenant (1656–1714), Inspector General of Imports and Exports since 1705.

11 *honour … Trade*: Defoe had sent such a report to Godolphin in Feb. (see Letter 98).

12 *Infinite … it*: Defoe makes similar statements about the weak condition of the Scottish customs collection, the extent of clandestine trade, amplified by the Union and exacerbated by the 'Creiks, Coves, Harbours and Bays', all of which necessitated 'a little Army of Officers' in 1707, in *History of the Union, TDH*, VIII, 247–8. In *A General History of Trade … for the Month of September* (1713), he refers to 'the innumerable Number of Creeks and Coves along that Coast, the small Number of Officers, their remote Stations from one another' (39).

13 *My Brother writes me*: Robert Davis. The letter is untraced.

14 *Ld Treasurer … here*: Godolphin wrote to Harley on 14 May: 'I have been this morning endeavouring to fix the Custom house Officers for Scotland[.] Mr Henley is named for one, & there is a blank left for the Sec^tary; I have not yett ventured to propose De Foe for fear I sh^d never gett him to goe down wth M^r [William] Lowndes, unless it bee recom͡ended from you' (BL Add. MS. 70024, fol. 72).

112

To Robert Harley

23 May 1707

HEADNOTE: Compounding the uncertainty about Scottish merchants' rights to transport French wine and brandy to England, some Scots were concerned about the delayed arrival of the Equivalent, even fearing that England might altogether bilk them.[1] In his *History of the Union*, Defoe mentions 'the Scandalous Reflections spread about, of the Delay of Payment' of the Equivalent, and he rebuts the claim that England had breached the terms of the Union Treaty by not delivering it by 1 May.[2] Although Defoe maintains in print that the complaints were merely opportunistic anti-Unionism, he recognised that the concerns were often legitimate, as people promised money now expected it.[3] The first portion of the Equivalent left London, destined for Edinburgh, on 16 June 1707.[4]

S^r

My Last to you from Sterling Gave you My Scheme of the Nac͡onall Discontents here about ye wine & Brandy. I Menc͡oned Two things but Spoke to One Onely.

387

DEFOE TO ROBERT HARLEY, 23 MAY 1707

The Next is The Affair of the Equivalent — and why is Not yᵉ Equivalent Come Down, Sayes yᵉ Country Man, you wer[e]ᵃ to pay it by the 1ˢᵗ of May, and you have broke yᵉ Union in that — and where is it all this while? Now yᵉ Treaty is finished you do what you please with us, and Thus we shall be used in Everything; this in yᵐ is Very Serious Language —

Great advantage is made Indeed of this, not So much pretending it shall not be p̄d, but that time is not kept with them, and Agreements not p[er]formed, and we have a story whispred here that D Hamilton Came the first of May in yᵉ Night and protested at yᵉ Cross of Edinb⁵ that yᵉ Union was broke. I do not I Confess believ yᵉ thing, but these Reports Joyned wᵗʰ the want of the Moneyᵇ makes a great Deal of Ill blood here and Does Unspeakable harm.⁶

The Governmᵗ knows how to Apply Suitable Remedyes to these Mischiefs, and I Doubt not will do So, but I thought it my Duty to hint my Observations.

The Apprehensions of yᵉ people here at yᵉ Stop of their Goods is Very Great, and I Confess if that matter is not Clear'd up and the property of Scots men Set Free, together wᵗʰ Some Settled Method how the property of Scots men may be ascertaind and Determind, the Discontents will Run too high and I Apprehend New Tumults Very Much.

I have spoke my mind freely in print in yᵉ Reviewᶜ and printed One here to shew yᵉ Justice of preventing Frauds,⁷ but I must wᵗʰ it Own, and Indeed my own judgemᵗ joyns in it, and I believ yours also, that yᵉ True property of Scots Men should be admitted free.

I wish I had but Two lines from you Sʳ to Direct me in this Affair; tis Really a Difficult time here, and I thinkᵈ more so than when yᵉ Union was in Agitation, for the wholl Nation is in a Ferment About the Frenchᵉ Goods and the Equivalent.

ᵃ wer[e]] *MS frayed*
ᵇ Money] *interlined above cancelled word* 'thing'
ᶜ in yᵉ Review] *interlined*
ᵈ think] *following word possibly* 'it' *cancelled*
ᵉ French] *interlined*

DEFOE TO ROBERT HARLEY, 23 MAY 1707

I might do you much more Serviċe Sr if I had but Now and then a letter of proper hints[8] from your Self — I kno' you are in a Hurry and I lament the Occasion, but Indeed Sr things here are of Consequenċe, and a little Disorder here would give things a bad Aspect and have too great an Influenċe on Credit, Trade, Funds and all these things: The Matter therefore Mourns to be Settled; I beg your Excuse for the liberty I Take wch I think my Duty.

I am

yor Most Obedt Servt

DF

At Wemyss

May. 23. 1707

Text: BL Add. MS. 70291, fols. 174–5. *Address* (fol. 175v): To The Right Honble | Robert Harley Esqr | Prinċipall Secreta of State | Present. *Endorsed by Harley* (fol. 175v): Wemys May 23: 1707 R May 30: 7 days.

1 H.M.C. *Mar and Kellie MSS*, 393.
2 *TDH*, viii, 257–9.
3 Riley, *English Ministers*, 209–10.
4 Luttrell, vi, 181.
5 *Cross of Edinb*: The Mercat Cross.
6 *Reports … harm*: Defoe made the same insinuation about Hamilton on this matter in his *History of the Union*: 'But that D.— H— was the Man, I profess not to know, and believe, that Noble Person to understand the Nature of the Treaty, and the Nature of Protesting also, better than so' (*TDH*, viii, 258).
7 *printed … Frauds*: Probably *The Trade of Britain Stated; Being the Substance of Two Papers Published in London on Occasion of the Importation of Wine and Brandy from North-Britain* [Edinburgh, 1707], a reprint of the *Review* essays for 10 and 12 June 1707.
8 *proper hints*: In the midst of a long period of financial neglect while Defoe was in Scotland, rumours persisted that he was personally collecting a pension in London, including on the day before this letter, 22 May 1707 (Hearne, ii, 14).

DEFOE TO ROBERT HARLEY, 10 [JUNE] 1707

113

To Robert Harley

10 [June] 1707

HEADNOTE: In summer 1707, Defoe continued to work on his own initiative, touring around Scotland endeavouring to persuade ministers of the Church of Scotland of the benefits of Union. He kept up his unanswered pleas for instructions or some more permanent employment.

Sr

I wrott you last post.[1] I have Nothing to Add worth your Note. The Weather haveing been favourable I am Travailing thro' ye Towns and Disputeing wth The Rigid and Refractory Clergy who are ye worst Enemies of the Union; I act all This Sr of my Own head, for haveing No Direccon From you I am loth to be Idle and live upon yor Expence wthout forwarding ye Work I Came hither About, and I hope you will believ me that I Do my uttmost not to[a] be So Expensive as I am Sensible I am, without p[er]suing the True End of the Charge.

I am Not able to Say any thing More[b] to what I have formerly Hinted[c] about my Self; I kno' absent and Forgotten are frequently Synonimous; I have no Dependence but on yor Self, but Sr while I See Such Men as <u>Rigby</u>, <u>Isaacson</u> &c. in Comission[2] I Can Not but hope you will Cause me to be Remembred.

I formerly hinted my proposall of a Survey of ye Out ports[3] and still wish for it — but if not, the Accompta or Comptr of ye Accots, things I pretend to be Master of, would be Suitable for me. I Thro' my Self wholly On yor Concern for me, and p[er]swade my Self while you are my Intercessor I Can not be Denyed.

yor Most Obedt Servt
DF

May. 10. 1707[4]

---

[a] to] *interlined*
[b] More] *interlined*
[c] Hinted] *interlined above cancelled word* 'Added'

390

Text: BL Add. MS. 70291, fols. 176–7. *Address* (fol. 177ᵛ): To The Right Honble | Robert Harley Esqʳ | Princi̇pall Secretary of State | Present. *Endorsed by Harley* (fol. 177ᵛ): D: F: dated May 10: 1707 by mistake for June 10: ʀ here 17:

1 *I wrott you last post*: Untraced.
2 *Rigby, Isaacson &c. in Coṁission*: See Letter III, note 9. In his *History of the Union*, Defoe is more complimentary, stating that the commissioners 'shewed that they wanted neither Judgment or Application' (*TDH*, vɪɪɪ, 245). The main objection to the appointees was their political rather than administrative backgrounds.
3 *Survey of yᵉ Out ports*: The letter detailing this is untraced, but see Defoe's reflections on Scottish ports and customs collection in *History of the Union*, *TDH*, vɪɪɪ, 247–9. 'Outports' are those other than Edinburgh.
4 *May. 10. 1707*: In error for 10 June 1707, as noted by Harley in his endorsement.

114

Robert Harley to Defoe

12 June 1707

HEADNOTE: Harley wrote his first response to Defoe since January. The first half of 1707 had been a challenging one for Harley and by the summer his standing within the ministry was dwindling because he stridently opposed the duumvir's tactical alliance with the Whig Junto.[1] These tensions come through more in the one known letter to Defoe from this period than in any of his other correspondence, voluminous as that is. In spring 1707, Harley had gone against the government by supporting the London merchants requesting parliament intervene to prevent duty-avoiding imports to England via Scotland after the Union. Harley specifies his reasons for this in this letter. Sunderland was outraged and complained to the duumvirs of the treachery of Harley, 'him who is the Author of all the tricks play'd here ... I will onely say no man in the service of a government ever did act such a Part'.[2] Godolphin was 'at Newmarket diverting himself with his horsematches', but his letter to Harley of 17 April indicates that, whether or not he first supported it, and whether or not he realised how far Harley had endorsed it, he now wanted it dropped: 'If it be against the sense of Scotland and contrary to the apprehension of the Treaty, I doubt it may bring a very great difficulty at this time upon the Queen.'[3] Yet Harley seemingly did not give it up.

By June, Harley was also under accusation of exacerbating the bishoprics crisis, which arose when Queen Anne's preferred choices for vacant sees clashed with the nominations the Junto were foisting on Godolphin. The Junto was threatening to embarrass the Court with a parliamentary enquiry into the navy, administered by Prince George and Marlborough's Tory brother, George Churchill (1654–1710).[4] For his disinclination to accommodate the Junto, Harley was becoming increasingly marginalised and mistrusted by his ministerial colleagues.[5]

Amidst these events, in June 1707 Defoe's relationship to Harley changed, at least in theory, as Godolphin became his direct employer. In practice, Defoe wrote mainly to Harley, and his pleas for instructions continued to receive little attention. The two ministers liaised about how his employment might continue in the future. Harley's reference to a need 'to cover yr friends in doing you justice' indicates the problem: a public reward for Defoe would expose the fact that he worked for the ministry.

June 12 — 1707

Sr

I have received yr Lers very constantly, and I cannot think that any one has miscarried;[6] I am sure I have taken care to represent yr services in the best light from time to time where it may do you service; and I hope I have not been an unprofitable Servant:[7] I Am very sorry that you or your humble servant should bear Reproach for doing what others could not, or would not do, but it has been often so, I have set up my Rest,[8] and therefore it is not[a] in their power to disappoint me; I count upon all that impotent malice, inveterate spleen can do, by misrepresentations, and notorious forgeries, to do me hurt, I am prepared for all; And the wrath is greater agt me because their Weakness as well as villanous Arts happen to be detected; And if God spares me Life; I think I shall be able to pull off the Mask from the reall Atheists & pretended Patriots[9] — but too much of this now.

You are in the right to put the D. of Queensberrie in mind of you;[10] repeat it again; It will serve to cover yr friends in doing you justice; I need give you only a hint: As to more particulars I desire you will write a Letter to Ld Treasurer (inclose it to me) proposing your own service & where you can be most usefull. He thinks surveyor of one of the Ports, if that meets with your Approbation; propose that or any other Alternative; the sooner the Better.[11]

---

[a] not] *interlined*

ROBERT HARLEY TO DEFOE, 12 JUNE 1707

I cannot let this Letter pass without a few words upon ye point
of trade: The true state of the matter is this: Upon the View[12]
of the Union, Dutch, Jews, Swedes, Danes &c struck into the
Notion of bringing in Goods before May 1,[13] which arose from one
certain Gentlemans[14] giving great Commissions, thinking to have
swallowed all ye profit; this set every body a gog to get the pence;
the Malicious World Reports & Names the Men & summs of
Money ventured by those in both Houses, but be sure you do not
believe that, for it is impossible that persons of all sorts, Colours
& pretences can be such Knaves — And what hath passed since
is only Accidental, which the Men of the world interpret to very
wrong Ends. However the House of Commons would have rescued
Us from the scandall & obliged Scotland; they had contrived to
make the Cheats do Justice, and at the same time indulged the
Scots with an Opportunity of getting clear and honestly 150000^£
to speak with the least — but Satan hindred[15] —. the Scots, but
I should more truly say one person only, solicited ag^t their Own
Nation,[16] under pretence of the Union; Whereas there is nothing
plainer can be said in words (for any Case which is contingent &
is to happen) than the words of the Union against the practice:
What is more no one Lawier, of Credit, would ever pretend to
stand by the contrary Opinion, but it was hoped that power, Faction
& Noise, which are the same, together with fear of Offending
Scotland, whom they hop'd to enrage, would bear the Cheats out
in this barefaced fraud; When they found that a middle way was
discovered, to indulge the Scots & make the others pay, then they
were surprized, and to hinder it all the tools were to be used —
Acheronta Movebo[17] — What was the present End you know, what
is to come God knows; but this is certain, if Our Scots Friends
knew what a sweet Morsel these people have taken out of their
Mouths, they would turn their rage the right way.[18]
    I will Add but two things more; those Goods (tho'[a] they should[b]
come in quickly) will come to no market, And the next thing is that
the Wine, Brandys & other Goods of the Growth & Manufacture
of ye Kingdom of France are intirely forbidden here, and can no way

---

[a] tho'] *interlined above cancelled word* 'if'
[b] should] *interlined above cancelled word* 'can'

ROBERT HARLEY TO DEFOE, 12 JUNE 1707

be brought in either before or since the Union but as Prize Goods & then the Duty is fixed high,[19] and this is as plain as A.B.C.

You will excuse me for being so large[a] upon a head which is so Copious, and as extensive as the vast Volumes of Cheat & Knavery: but you will quickly guess at the true state of Affairs relating to this matter by these short hints. I think it will be for your own service as well as y[e] public that you consider what method is the best to prevent future frauds in the Customes & to Allay the heats of Our New Friends & send it as soon as you can in writing.

I desire you will send me an Account of what Money you have received from M[r] Bell; and the times when; he being now in Town, I am clearing with him. & L. T. says it is not fit you should be longer at my Charge,[20] which I hope is for your Good.

I am most really S[r] yrs

Text: BL Add. MS. 70291, fols. 178–9. [An unsigned copy in Harley's hand.] *Address* (fol. 179[v]): Copy June 12: 1707 to D: F: inclosd to m[r] Bell.

---

[a] large] *interlined above cancelled word* 'long'

---

1   Marlborough wrote to Godolphin on 24 June 1707, '208 [Harley] does so hate and fear 5 [Somers], 6 [Sunderland] and 7 [Wharton] that he omitts no occasion of filling 42's [the Queen] head with their projects and designs'; and on 30 June that 'he continues in doing ill offices upon all occasions to 5 [Somers], 6 [Sunderland], and 7 [Halifax]' (*Marl.–God. Corr.*, 11, 831, 836).

2   Sunderland to Marlborough, 11 Apr. 1707, BL Add. MS. 61126, fol. 38[r].

3   H.M.C. *Bath MSS*, 1, 169. John Clerk of Penicuik intimated that Harley brought in the first Drawback Bill with Godolphin's encouragement (NRS GD 18/3134, 19).

4   G. V. Bennett, 'Robert Harley, the Godolphin Ministry, and the Bishoprics Crisis of 1707', *EHR* 82 (1967), 726–46.

5   Marlborough's letter to the Duchess of 23 June 1707 indicates that he thought a formal reprimand might be needed (*Marl.–God. Corr.*, 11, 829). One was eventually issued via Lord Chancellor Cowper on 9 Sept., after which both Godolphin and Harley aimed at conciliation (H.M.C. *Bath MSS*, 1, 180).

6   *miscarried*: See Letter 110 for Defoe's suspicion that his letters were being intercepted.

7   *unprofitable Servant*: See Letter 13, note 5. The phrase, or a variation on it, recurs in Harley's correspondence, as well as Defoe's, such as Harley to Godolphin, 17 Sept. 1707, H.M.C. *Bath MSS*, 1, 182; Harley to an unnamed Lord, 4 Sept. 1712, Yale Beinecke, Osborn MSS 6745.

8   *set up my Rest*: To set (up) one's rest is 'to focus all one's attention and efforts on a particular end or course of action' (*OED*).

9   *reall Atheists & pretended Patriots*: For the wider context, see Hill, 105–7.

10 *D. of Queensberrie in mind of you*: See headnote to Letter 104.

11 *I desire … Better*. In Letters 111 (21 May) and 113 (10 June), Defoe had made such proposals (Harley would not yet have received the latter). Defoe's correspondence with Godolphin from this time is untraced, but at least one letter from Defoe to Godolphin was forwarded by

394

ROBERT HARLEY TO DEFOE, 12 JUNE 1707

Harley, and that letter apparently promised further correspondence (Godolphin to Harley, 7 Aug. 1707, H.M.C. *Bath MSS*, I, 177).

12 *View*: 'Anticipation; expectation' (*OED*).

13 *Upon ... May r*: On 1 April, Harley wrote to James Dayrolles, Secretary of the Envoy to The Hague, expressing alarm at the designs of Dutch merchants (TNA SP 104/73, fols. 100v–101r). Clerk of Penicuik describes anxieties about revenue loss, as well as Tory efforts to promote the Drawback Bill so as to 'make the union go ill doūn either with Scots or English' (NRS GD 18/3134, 6–7).

14 *Gentlemans*: Jacob M. Price notes that, although the merchant Harley has in mind here cannot be identified, Thomas Johnson, Whig MP for Liverpool, was among the first to set about exploiting the tobacco loophole, and his intentions prompted the introduction of the Drawback Bill ('Glasgow, the Tobacco Trade, and the Scottish Customs, 1707–1730: Some Commercial, Administrative and Political Implications of the Union', *SHR* 63 (1984), 1–36 (at 3–7)).

15 *Satan hindred*: 1 Thess. 2:18. No examples of Defoe using the phrase before 1707 have been identified, but shortly after Harley wrote it to him, Defoe used it five times within six months, in *Review*, IV, 518 (2 Oct. 1707); 527 (7 Oct. 1707); 742 (6 Jan. 1708); 772 (20 Jan. 1708); 895 (16 Mar. 1708). His subsequent usages of the phrase include: *History of the Union* (1709/10), *TDH*, VII, 96; *Review*, IX, 114 (8 Nov. 1712); Letter 220; *Family Instructor* (1715), *RDW*, I, 43; *An Account of the Conduct of Robert Earl of Oxford* (1715), *PEW*, II, 328; *Political History of the Devil*, *SFS*, VI, 199.

16 *Scots ... Nation*: Who is meant by 'one Person' is unknown, but Scottish merchants in London petitioned the House of Lords against the Drawback Bill. Defoe printed the petition as an appendix in his *History of the Union*.

17 *Acheronta Movebo*: 'I will raise hell' (Latin). 'Flectere si nequeo superos, Acheronta movebo': 'If Heaven I cannot bend, then Hell I will arouse!' (Virgil, *Aeneid*, VII, 312, Loeb Classical Library, trans. H. Rushton Fairclough, rev. G. P. Goold (Cambridge, Mass., 2000)). Defoe uses this phrase in *A New Test of the Church of England's Honesty* (1704), *PEW*, III, 189; *Review*, VII, 505 (7 Dec. 1710); VIII, 556 (3 Jan. 1712); VIII, 923 (24 July 1712); *The Secret History of the October Club* (1711), *PEW*, II, 154; *A System of Magick* (1727), *SFS*, VII, 59.

18 *if ... way*: See Hill, 107–9, which shows how Harley had set himself up against his colleagues in the ministry on what he considered a matter of principle.

19 *Wine ... high*: French imports were prohibited, but navy ships and privateers could bring French goods from captured ships as prize-goods. They paid additional duties set by a 1696 act, in addition to which Her Majesty's ships paid 50% and privateers paid 10%. See *London Gazette*, 1–4 June 1702.

20 *L. T. ... Charge*: An undated letter from Godolphin to Harley states: 'As to De F: I should think he might bee made use of where he is without farther charge to you, but I shall bee glad to talk to you tomorrow' (BL Add. MS. 70021, fol. 358). H.M.C. *Portland MSS*, IV, 156 suggests this letter dates from 1704, but it more probably points to the conversation that led Harley to write this to Defoe.

115

To Robert Harley
8 July 1707

HEADNOTE: When Godolphin wrote to Harley on 14 August 1707, he commented, 'I don't like D[e] F[oe]'s letter, but I have often observed that he gives you the worst side of the picture.'[1] It was perhaps the letter dated 8 July, or the now-missing preceding one, that Harley had shown to the Lord Treasurer. Defoe's anxiety concerned Jacobite machinations in Scotland. Two related issues agitated Defoe: attacks on Presbyterian churches in the north, and rumours of a French-backed invasion by the Pretender.

Defoe claims that mobs attacking Presbyterian meetings were being incited by Jacobites and Episcopalians. Defoe elaborates on the example he gives Harley, of the disruption of the Synod of Ross and Sutherland on 18 June 1707, in the *Review* for 26 July 1707:

> At *Dingwall* in the North of *Scotland*, the Synod of *Ross* and *Suther-land* being Assembled, were Rabbl'd and Insulted by the Mob; and 'tis observable, that it was not a Mob of the common People, rais'd from a meer Dislike of Presbyterian Government, for that is what they Industriously strive to have believ'd, that the Common People are Episcopal — But it is made evident, that this is a Rabble rais'd by particular Persons, pushing their Servants, or Tenants, or Vassals into it; and dressing up Men in Womens Cloaths, to make the World believe it was a *Natural Tumult*, if I may be allow'd that Expression.[2]

In the issue for 14 Aug. 1707, Defoe gives a fuller account of these events. He explains that the Synod was due to appoint a minister to the vacant church at Dingwall, but that the local heretors with Episcopal and hence Jacobite sympathies, particularly John Bayne, younger of Tulloch (*c.* 1661–1731), used their authority to incite a riot which prevented the Synod meeting. In the *Review*, Defoe gives an eyewitness's narrative of the events.[3]

Secondly, rumours abounded that a French-supported Jacobite invasion was imminent. In spring 1707, Nathaniel Hooke (1664–1738), Louis XIV's emissary, had visited Scotland to buoy the hopes of the Jacobites, who were eager to capitalise on the popular dissatisfaction with the Union. In the *Review* for 26 July, Defoe reports on 'a great Meeting of the Jacobite Clergy' in the Highlands, and he mentions

DEFOE TO ROBERT HARLEY, 8 JULY 1707

Letters sent about, and Rumours spread, that King *James* VII. as they call him, was a coming; some say that he was on Board a *French* Squadron on the Coast, that all the *Northern Scotland* would Declare for him, and that there were 30000 Men ready, to take Arms and Join him.[4]

The invasion did not come to pass, though one was attempted without success in March 1708.

S[r]

I Gave you Some of my Thoughts last post[5] and Some Instances of Jacobite Insolence; I Can Not but Accquaint you of what I Think not w[th]out ground gives a Great Many Sober people a great Uneasyness and I must Acknowlege has Some Appearance of Mischief in it.

The Intollerable boldness of y[e] Jacobite party in y[e] Northern Highlands is Such Now, And in Some of y[e] Lowland provinces also in y[e] North, y[t] Unless Some Speedy Care is Taken to prevent Their Disorders The Consequences Can not but be fatall.

About 14 days Since, they Rabbled the wholl Synod of Ross and Maltreated the Ministers, and this by a Made Rabble of Men Disguised in Womens Cloths,[6] of w[ch] Complaint haveing been Made to y[e] Council I presume you have a p[er]ticular.

But y[e] Thing I Perticularly Instance Now is that The Duke of Athol who Now makes himself the head of the Discontented p[ar]ty has Appointed his Great Hunting.[7] I have not Learnt y[e] precise Day but[a] the L[d] Sinclear[8] & Sev[ll] Other of y[e] popish and Jacobite Gentlemen on Fife Side where I Now Am Are allready Gone to it who are known to be no Sports men Nor Ever Used to Go — The Jacobites Report Their K Ja. VIII will be On shore quickly. Some Report he is Arrivd Incog. but all Agree there is Some Mischief in hand — and the Forces here are So Contemptible that if any Commotion happen they Can Do Nothing.

After all S[r] the Secret Talk Among Some of their Privadoes[9] is That They have 30000 Men Ready at a word[10] — and Good people Are Very Uneasy.

---

[a] but] *following word* 'my' *cancelled*

DEFOE TO ROBERT HARLEY, 8 JULY 1707

But yᵉ p[er]ticular Reason why I write this is The Easyness of the attempt, Supposeing a party of these Desperate people should offer to Surprize the Equivalent,¹¹ and it is but this Day that I strangely had an Occasion to hear Something like it whisperd as it Comes Directly from Some that kno' more than Every body Imagin.

I Thought it my Duty to hint this Sʳ. Tis a Doubtfull Time here and [S]uchᵃ a bait would flush the wholl p[ar]ty and push them Headlong into Generall Confusion.

If you think it may Conduce to yᵉ publick Service I shall willingly hazard my Self to go North and Make my Self Master of as Much of these Mysteries of Iniquity as Can be Obtain in Order to give you Seasonable Intelligence; If you Approve it yoʳ Ordʳˢ should Come by the Very Next post.

I am

Sʳ

yoʳ Most Obedᵗ Servᵗ

DF

July 8. 1707

Text: BL Add. MS. 70291, fols. 180–1. *Address* (fol. 181ᵛ): To The Right Honᵇˡᵉ | Robert Harley Esqʳ | Her Majᵗⁱᵉˢ Principall Secretᵃ of State | Present. *Endorsed by Harley* (fol. 181ᵛ): D: F: July 8: 1707 ʀ July 16.

ᵃ [S]uch] *MS damaged*

1 H.M.C. *Bath MSS*, I, 178.
2 *Review*, IV, 361. Cf. Luttrell, VI, 195–6.
3 *Review*, IV, 399–404. The political background to the Dingwall rabble is the struggle between the Episcopalian Mackenzies and Presbyterian Rosses for control of the shire and burgh district (*HPC 1690–1715*, II, 879–86, 936–43).
4 *Review*, IV, 361. Defoe gets the Pretender's putative title correct as 'K Ja. VIII' in the letter.
5 *last post*: Untraced.
6 *About ... Cloths*: See headnote and *Review*, IV, 361 (26 July 1707); 399–404 (14 Aug. 1707).
7 *Duke ... Hunting*: Talk of such a gathering of Jacobites circulated into Aug. (Leven to Mar, 5 Aug. 1707, Fraser, *Melvilles*, II, 213). In *Review* essays for 26 and 29 July, Defoe reports on a letter from an English Jacobite read at what may be this gathering (IV, 360–1, 364–7). It advises the Scottish Jacobites to request a toleration of Episcopacy and to promulgate the idea that the British parliament may alter the terms of the Union and so undermine the Church of Scotland. Defoe vehemently opposes these positions. On 8 Sept. 1707, John Forster wrote to Harley: 'It is said that at the Duke of Athol's hunting, those that met there entered into a band of association and sent some of their number over to France' (H.M.C. *Portland MSS*, IV, 449–50).
8 *Lᵈ Sinclear*: Henry St Clair (1660–1723), tenth Lord Sinclair.
9 *Privadoes*: confidants.

398

DEFOE TO ROBERT HARLEY, 19 JULY 1707

10 *30000 Men Ready at a word*: See headnote and *Review*, IV, 361 (26 July 1707). Nathaniel
  Hooke, the Jacobite agent sent to Scotland from France in Apr. 1707, likewise projected that
  30,000 men would join an invasion (*Hooke Corr.*, II, 257).
11 *Surprize the Equivalent*: The party guarding the Equivalent as it travelled from London to
  Edinburgh comprised 120 dragoons (H.M.C. *Mar and Kellie MSS*, 404).

116

To Robert Harley

19 July 1707

HEADNOTE: The transition to English management of the Scottish economy
was fraught. Anxieties about the personnel appointed to the customs commission
persisted: as always, the English government wanted to use rewards strategically;
Scots fretted that their countrymen were overlooked in favour of English bu-
reaucrats. Defoe feared that he would be neglected too. And after the concerns
about the supposed delay to the delivery of the Equivalent, the next complaint
concerned its form: just over £100,000 was sent in ready money, the remaining
£298,000 in exchequer bills. As Defoe later explained:

> This raised a new Clamour in *Scotland*, and abundance of People run
> away with it, that the *English* Trick'd them; that they had sent them
> Paper in stead of Money, that the great Argument formerly used to
> perswade *Scotland* to the Union, to take upon them a share of the
> Burden of the *English* Debts, and to accept of an Equivalent, was the
> great Advantage that should accrue to *Scotland*, by the Circulating of
> so much ready Money in the Nation; And that now they were to be
> put off with Bills payable 300 Miles off, and which if Lost or Mislaid,
> or by Accident Burnt, were Irrecoverable.[1]

In his *History of the Union*, as in his letter to Harley of 7 August, Defoe admits that
the Bank of England made a misstep, failing to account for the lack of liquidity in
the Scottish economy, for the mistrust of paper credit there due to unfamiliarity,
and for the failure to send bills that accrued interest, which was a condition of article fifteen of the Union Treaty.

Sr

I am Sorry to Say that I look Now as One Entirly forgott,
That haveing the honour to be sent hither and Not thinking it my

Duty to Abandone my post without yor Orders have now neither
Capascity to stay Nor orders to Come Away.

The Com̃^{rs} of ye Customes are Sitting Every Day and Filling Up
the places wth p[er]sons as Usuall supplyed wth More Friends than
Merit — I have been in hopes from what you were pleased to hint
to me that I should be Thought of[2] — I Entreat you will please
to Interpose your Intrest on that Acco^t wch I Doubt not would be
Effectuall — If Nothing be to be Expected, It is a Favour I
p[er]swade my Self you will not Deny me, to let me have a hint
from you S^r and a help to Returne me to Serv you Some other way.

I Gave you an Item, of a Design to Surprize ye Equivalent; were
it Reall or not I tho^t it my Duty to Com̃unicate it to you. I believ
their heart will fail them. However I Took this Method, in wch I
believ I did not Amiss, that I Effectually spread a Report that there
was Such a Design[3] — wch I believ will make half ye Country Go
Out to Meet it, and quite make the attempt Impracticable.

Ignorance and prejudice has Raised a Clamour against y^e
Exchecq^r Bills y^t they Say are Comeing. I had wrott half a Sheet
to Explain the advantages of them and their answering Money in
their Effect on Trade but I am Run too low to print, for there is
no printing here but at an Expence. I shall Disperse Some written
Coppies[4] that I may Continue to do what Service I Can when
Straightned from Doeing what I might.

I Fear Sometimes you have tho^t me too Chargable here but if
you will p[er]mit me to give you a scheme of my way of liveing
and what I have been Doeing I p[er]swade my Self you will be
Convinced I have not missapplyed neither ye Time Nor ye Money.

I am I Confess impacent to have Some Directions what to
Do and how to Govern my Self and Entreat your pardon for my
Importunity.

It has been Reported they are Discontent here^a at ye Many
English who Come hither for places[5] but that I think is a^b
Groundles Report — But One thing I Ought to Note — It gives a
Very great Distast here that ye Officers of the Excise are Obliged to
Gauge[6] on ye Sabbath Day.

---

^a here] *interlined*
^b a] *interlined*

DEFOE TO [ROBERT HARLEY], 5 AUGUST 1707

It would be also a Caution Needfull to be given that yᵉ English Officers should not Frequent the Jacobite Conventicles[7] wᶜʰ will Soon Rendʳ not them Onely Odious but So Encourage them that they will think themselves Supported or at least Approved by the English Governmᵗ.

These hints sʳ I thought Needfull to give you yᵉ Trouble of.

I am

Sʳ

yoʳ Most Obedᵗ Servᵗ

DF

Edinb. July 19. 1707

Text: BL Add. MS. 70291, fols. 182–3. *Address* (fol. 183ᵛ): To The Right Honᵇˡᵉ | Robert Harley Esqʳ | Princíple Secretᵃ of State | Present.

1 Defoe, *History of the Union*, *TDH*, vⅠⅠⅠ, 261. Defoe's friend, John Clerk of Penicuik, anticipated payment of the Equivalent partly in specie, partly in bills, in *A Letter to a Friend* (1706), 31.
2 *hopes … of*: See Letter 114.
3 *Spread … Design*: If Defoe refers to something in print or MS, it is unidentified.
4 *I Shall Disperse Some written Coppies*: If Defoe did so, his piece is unidentified in either print or manuscript.
5 *they are … for places*: Lockhart remarked that 'vast numbers of surveyors, collectors, waiters, and, in short, all or most of the officers of the customs and excise were sent down from England, and these, generally speaking, the very scum and canalia of that country' (*Lockhart Memoirs*, 209).
6 *Gauge*: Customs officers measured the contents of containers using a gauging rod.
7 *Jacobite Conventicles*: In *An Historical Account of the Bitter Sufferings, and Melacholly Circumstances of the Episcopal Church in Scotland* (1707), Defoe claimed there were 'fourteen or sixteen' Episcopal 'Meeting-Houses' in Edinburgh (*PEW*, Ⅳ, 289).

117

To [Robert Harley]

5 August 1707

HEADNOTE: In June, a fleet of around forty ships had sailed from Scotland to England, carrying mainly wine and brandy originating in France. The ships and goods were seized as contraband in London, where French imports were prohibited. Scottish merchants petitioned the Convention of Royal Burghs, asking it to

DEFOE TO [ROBERT HARLEY], 5 AUGUST 1707

intercede, which it did in the form of an address to the Queen. The merchants were given the option of unloading their goods and giving security to abide by the judgement of parliament once it reconvened, but many were reluctant to do this. This was the situation at the time Defoe wrote this letter to Harley.

Defoe recounted the episode in his *History of the Union*. He acknowledged the traders' perspective, because the wine was at risk of spoiling while it remained on the ships, but affirms that the customs officials were required to follow the letter of the law on prohibited goods. This impasse prompted legal consultations that provided no resolution until it was agreed to allow the merchants their goods with no security, merely leaving the government the right to prosecute for debts. That right was predictably waived when parliament met and diplomatically issued a *noli prosequi* in November.[1] The protracted matter of French imports via Scotland, which Defoe first addressed in a letter to Godolphin in February 1707, was finally resolved.[2]

Sr

My Last long letter Prevented The Enclosed[3] and withall Supposeing It had been Sent you in a Public Manner — We are Told here That My Lord Marr has Suppresst yᵉ Address[4] and They Are Very Angry wᵗʰ him here for it.[a]

Noticᵉ has been Sent from Some Merchaˢ in Londᵒ to Their Prinĉipalls here That all Their Ships will be Confiscate and Their Goods spoiled and That Their Seamen Are all presst or <u>As I Tell yᵐ is More likely</u> Run Away For fear of Pressing.

The Merchᵃ here have <u>They Say</u> Sent Ordʳˢ to Their Friends in England To give No Security[5] — but to Demand Their Goods and if not Delivred to give bills of Parcels[6] to yᵉ Officᵉrs who Detain Them and to Sue Them for yᵉ Money — If This be So it Must be by procurmᵗ from Londᵒ, That Method being Unknown here — and The p[er]sons I believ are Wa. Stuart, Tho. Coots &c,[7] who are yᵉ Prinĉipall Merchants in Londᵒ Concern'd in This Affair wᵗʰ mʳ Elliot in Round Court, Laĉe Man[8] — if These Could be Made Easy This wholl Affair might be Closed.

Now They begin to be Convinĉ't here That if yᵉ First Bill[9] had past in Parliamᵗ Scotland had been Safe and Also gainers and they[b] blame yᵉ Scots Merchants for Opposeing it; a short hint Sʳ How

[a] for it] *interlined*
[b] they] *interlined*

DEFOE TO [ROBERT HARLEY], 5 AUGUST 1707

to Behave in This Affair would^a give me a great help. Indeed ye Jacobite Party make Great Use of it, and it Does an Unspeakable Injury as to ye Tempers of the people which began Very Much to Abate in Their Ill Influences but Now Encrease Again.

The Brewers are Now Goeing Mad in Their Turns.[10] I hinted ye Case in My last.[11] Severall of Them gave Over work and ye Servants, finding Others did Not, went yesterday^b in a Tumult to Those houses That were at work and Put Out Their fires and let Their Liquor Run about house and The Like Disorder today also^c — where It will End I Can Not yet foresee.

— I Entreat ye hand of ye Enclosed may Not be Seen, because I Obtain'd it by a private Correspondence wch it will be Necessary to keep up and being a known hand it would be both Unfaithfull to him and Entirely Close ye Door of my Intelligence On That Side if I should Not Conceal him.

I am

S^r

yor Most Faithfull Obedient Servt — De Foe

Edinb. Aug. 5. 1707

The Equivalent is Safely Lodg'd in ye Castle This Night.

Text: BL Add. MS. 70291, fols. 184–5. *Address*: none.

^{a} would] *following illegible word cancelled*
^{b} yesterday] *interlined*
^{c} today also] *interlined*

1 *C.J.*, xv, 438; *Review*, iv, 656 (2 Dec. 1707).
2 See *History of the Union, TDH*, viii, 242–3.
3 *Enclosed*: The printed petition from Scottish merchants requesting the Convention of Royal Burghs to intercede. The text of the Convention's address to the Queen is copied in a hand other than Defoe's on the reverse of the petition. On the printed side, Defoe has written: 'This is the Petičon of y^e ~~Royal Burghs~~ Merchants On wch ye address On ye Other Side is Founded' ('Royal Burghs' is cancelled and 'Merchants' interlined). The enclosure is no longer with the letter; it is in BL Add. MS. 70040, fols. 367–8. See H.M.C. *Portland MSS*, viii, 354. Defoe printed both the petition and the address as appendixes to his *History*.
4 *Lord Marr has Suppresst ye Address*: The address of the Convention of Royal Burghs was entrusted to the Scottish Secretaries of State, then at London, Loudon and Mar. I have found no corroboration of Defoe's allegation that Mar delayed presenting the petition.
5 *give No Security*: See headnote.
6 *bills of Parcels*: 'Note[s] of charges for goods delivered or services rendered, in which the cost of each item is separately stated' (*OED*).

7 *Wa. Stuart, Tho. Coots &c.*: Walter Stuart and Thomas Coutts were both Scottish merchants resident in London.

8 *mr Elliot in Round Court, Lace Man*: William Elliot. See Annabel Westman, 'William Elliot "the Laceman", 164?–1728', *Furniture History* 50 (2014), 89–102.

9 *First Bill*: The first Drawback Bill (headnote to Letters 107 and 108).

10 *Brewers are Now Goeing Mad in Their Turns*: Scottish brewers were in dispute with excisemen because they insisted they should be taxed at the nominal capacities of their barrels, specified as maximum two shillings per barrel in article seven of the Union Treaty, and not at the actual capacity. It had been ascertained that a twelve-Scottish-gallon barrel held more than the thirty-four English gallons stipulated as its equal in the Treaty. For the dispute and its resolution, see Riley, *English Ministers*, 70–2; Defoe, *History*, *TDH*, v III, 252–3. For other accounts of the street violence Defoe describes, see Seafield to Mar, 5 Aug. 1707, H.M.C. *Mar and Kellie MSS*, 410; Leven to Mar, 5 Aug. 1707, Fraser, *Melvilles*, II, 213.

11 *last*: Untraced.

118

To [Robert Harley]

7 August 1707

HEADNOTE: Defoe's report in early August about the view of the Equivalent coming to Scotland largely in exchequer bills is anticipated in his letter of 19 July.[1] From this crisis point, the situation was rapidly improved. First, at Seafield's request, Godolphin on 15 August ordered the treasury to send £50,000 more in gold.[2] The commissioners appointed to disburse the Equivalent were thus able to pay those who demanded cash, while 'Friends to the Government' accepted the bills, as did those happy to be paid earlier than their claim was due.[3] In October, the Bank of England empowered the commissioners for the Equivalent to draw bills from Edinburgh, 'by exchange without loss payable at three or four days sight any sums for the service of the Equivalent'.[4] Early the next year, Defoe wrote up a report for Harley on the payment of the Equivalent in exchequer bills.[5]

Sr

I wrott you in my Last yt The Equivalent was Arrived in the Castle — I think it my Duty to give you a Destinct accot of The Circumstance of That Affair here, I mean wth Respect to The Humours of ye people.

I Must Confess the ill blood Occasion'd by This is Such, and So Much has it Revived the Old Heats That were ye Union Now to be Transacted it would be Impossible —

DEFOE TO [ROBERT HARLEY], 7 AUGUST 1707

I am Never S^r you kno' for Searching an Evill to be Amazed at it, but to Applye The Remedyes.

The Capitall Quarrell is at ye Bills Come Down; were ye people here y^t are to Reciev it Men of Trade or were there any Such thing as paper Credit here or were the Bank here in hands y^t were not Secret Enemies to ye Publick good Or had the bills had a Running Intrest Upon them[6] — This Matter had been better.

But as it is, pardon me to foul my Paper wth Some of their Language.[a] Tis Necessary you should kno' it tho' you have ye happyness to be Remote from it and Out of its Reach.

First at England in Gen^{ll}, Did we not Say they would do what they pleased wth us when they had us in their power? Did not m^r Hodges Tell us they were a Tricking, faith breaking Nation,[7] and Now We have given Ourselves up, Now they Unmask, now they begin with us — Others — Ay, and they begin Early too. One would ha' Thought y^t in Policy they might ha' Dealt Smoothly wth us at first but now we see how we are to be Treated. They Contemn us So Much that they do Not Think it worth while to wheedle us.

Of The Bills — Heres ye English Money that was to Circulate Among Us and Encourage Our Trade and Now Tis Come in bitts of paper. What are their Banks and Exchecquers to us. Our Gentlemen Carry them Down to pay their[b] Heretable Debts[8] with and who Do they Think will Discharge their lands for Bitts of Paper that if they will be paid must be sent 400 mile or more to get the money where those people have neither Friend Nor Correspondent.

I Confess s^r I am Tyred wth Filling yor Eares wth these Things But Really The Gent. of the Bank have been Much in the wrong — If they had Expected their bills should have been made Currant they should have brought Sealed Notes wth Intrest and Sett up a small Cash here to Answ^r them, Something like the Subscription for Circulateing Exchecq^r Notes.[9] Credit you kno' well s^r is what Can Not be Forced.[10]

[a] Language] 'Lang | guage' *across a line break in MS*
[b] their] *interlined*

405

DEFOE TO [ROBERT HARLEY], 7 AUGUST 1707

It is a Meer Consequence of wanting No Credit. He that Can have his Money when he will will Refuse it and let it lye or Take paper for it — But he That is ask't to stay For his Money will Certainly Demand it.

If The Bank therefore has Done this They have put their Reputation On the Tenters[11] and stretched it farther than it will goe, The Prudence of which is at their Own Door.

I Write this sr On Takeing it for Granted what I suppose is True,[a] that the Bank has Thus Sent their Bills to Offer in payment And I am Glad to hear the people lay it On the Bank Rather than On ye Governmt.[12]

I am to have a Meeting in a Day or Two wth ye four Gentn who Come from Engld, sr Jna Cope &c,[13] who it Seems Desire a private Conference wth me On this head; I am Not Sencible I Can Do them Much Service but I shall Tell them heartily and Frankly what they have before them.[14]

It is most Certain if they Offer any man a Bill Till Some Other step is Taken to make ye people Easy it will be Refused and if One be Refused all the Rest Are[b] Wast paper.

In The last Letter[15] I hinted ye Arrivall of ye Carriges. It is not to be Described the Fury and Indignation of the people On ye Sight of it, Cursing Their Own Guards that brought it in, stoneing the Poor Fellows That Drew ye Waggons, Nay the Very Horses. I Saw One of the Waggon Drivers Wounded with a stone On ye Face wch if it had not Glanced On his shoulder First I believ had Certainly killed him[16] — They Call it ye Price of their Country and the poor people Are Incens'd by the Subtill Jacobites and too much by Some of the Presb. Ministers — that they go along the streets Curseing the Very English Nation.

This is a Mellancholly story sr but I Thot it was Necessary you should be Informd how it stands.

Till the Matter of the bills, and of ye Wine and brandy, is adjusted, There Can be no Temper Expected here. I hope Something may be Done after ward — It must be Time and Mannagemt which

---

[a] True] *interlined*
[b] Are] *interlined above a dash*

406

DEFOE TO [ROBERT HARLEY], 7 AUGUST 1707

must bring them to themselves again — Mean time I Omitt no Occasion of Throwing Water Upon this Flame but Can not honestly boast of any Success, I mean just Now, I hope better.

I am

S^r yor Most Obed^t Servt

DF

Augt. 7. 1707

Text: BL Add. MS. 70291, fols. 186–7. *Address*: none. *Endorsed by Harley* (fol. 187ᵛ): Edenburg Aug: 7 1707 R Aug: 18 Equivalent.

1 Letter 116.
2 TNA T 17/1, fol. 108; Seafield to Godolphin, 8 Aug. 1707, BL Add. MS. 34180, fol. 96. This arrived in about half the time it took the first payment.
3 Defoe, *History of the Union, TDH*, v111, 262.
4 Bank of England MSS, Court of Directors Minutes, E, G4/6, 178, qtd in Richard Saville, *The Bank of Scotland: A History, 1695–1995* (Edinburgh, 1996), 76.
5 See Letter 129.
6 *had the bills had a Running Intrest Upon them*: 'The Bank had Ingrossed the Interest paid on the Bills by the Government, and then sent them Naked into the World, to Run purely on the Cred-it of their Fund, without any Interest running upon them.' Article fifteen had stipulated interest at 5% was due (at least on the sizeable portion of the Equivalent destined to pay off shareholders in the Company of Scotland). Defoe also notes that the exchequer bills were promptly cashed in London by their recipients: 'So the Main End of the Bank, *viz*. The Circulation of these Bills in Trade, as a paper Credit, was quite Lost, which, had the Interest been running upon them, would have been easie, and readily complyed with' (*History, TDH*, v111, 261–2).
7 *mr Hodges … Nation*: See Letter 59, note 12.
8 *Heretable Debts*: Debts secured upon land.
9 *Exchecqr Notes*: Exchequer bills had been issued by the government since 1696, extending government credit and easing the shortage of cash in the economy. They could be issued in payment to persons willing to accept them. The 1707 issue, the first in a decade, bore interest at about 3%. A group of merchants provided funds for their encashment on demand, and 'their funds came from an annual subscription, the subscribers being given an equivalent sum in Exchequer Bills' (P. G. M. Dickson, 'War Finance, 1689–1714', in *The New Cambridge Modern History*, vol. v1: *The Rise of Great Britain and Russia, 1688–1715/25*, ed. J. S. Bromley (Cambridge, 1971), 284–315 (at 291)).
10 *Credit … Forced*: Compare *Review*, 111, 29 (10 Jan. 1706), in which 'Credit' is personified as a 'coy Lass': 'Nor is she to be won by the greatest Powers; Kings cannot bribe her; Parliaments cannot force her; as has been seen by manifold Experience, among a great Variety of Ladies.'
11 *Tenters*: A rack for stretching cloth.
12 *people … Governmt*: Be this as it may, Godolphin approved the scheme of paying the Equiv-alent in treasury bills on 8 May 1707 (Bank of England MSS, Court of Directors Minutes, E, G4/6, 155).
13 *four Gentn … Sr Jna Cope &c.*: The four commissioners of the Equivalent nominated by the Bank of England and appointed by Queen Anne on 6 June 1707, along with twenty-one Scots. In his *History*, Defoe lists all the commissioners and says of the four Englishmen, 'they were required to be present upon the Spot, in order to support the Credit of the Bank, in case any Body had scrupled their Bills' (*TDH*, v111, 257). The four were Sir John Cope,

407

Whig MP for Plympton Erle, a director of the Bank of England, who had acted as teller against the Drawback Bill on 19 Apr. 1707; Jacob Reynardson (1652–1719), also a Bank director; John Bridges, a shareholder in the Bank; and James Houblon (b. 1665), also a shareholder, whose letters from Scotland to his brother, Wynne, during this time are printed in Lady Alice Archer Houblon, *The Houblon Family: Its Story and Times*, 2 vols. (1907), 1, 349–54.

14 *what they have before them*: Apprehensions about the reception of the four English members of the commission is indicated in letters written by Queensberry, Loudon, and Mar from London to people in Scotland, asking they be treated civilly (TNA T 17/1, fols. 71–4; Riley, *English Ministers*, 209).

15 *last Letter*: Untraced.

16 *Stoning ... killed him*: A year later, in the *Review* for 10 Apr. 1708, Defoe imagines an easily misled ten-year-old boy justifying throwing stones at the wagons bringing the Equivalent: 'It was the Price of our Country, and ruin'd us all' (v, 34). In his *History*, Defoe calls this violence towards the carriages 'a Folly below Reproof, and rather deserves Pity', implicating 'a known Person, in no concealed Station', perhaps Hamilton again, in inciting the crowds (*TDH*, viii, 260). Leven, writing to Mar, played down the violence: 'Ther was a vast number of spectators, and sume of the mob threw stons at sume of those who drove the waggons, but ther was little harm done' (Fraser, *Melvilles*, ii, 213).

119

To [Robert Harley]

9 August 1707

HEADNOTE: In June 1711, four years after this letter, Defoe wrote to Harley (by then Earl of Oxford) reminding him that he and Godolphin had offered Defoe the role of Commissioner of the Customs in Scotland, a position Defoe says he did not refuse but which he passed up when the two politicians intimated that Defoe would be 'More Serviċable in a Private Capascity'. In Defoe's retrospective and regretful assessment, he forfeited a regular income with which he could have maintained his family in order to maximise his utility to the government.[1] The arrangement suited Godolphin and Harley because of unrest in Scotland owing to Presbyterian nationalism, Jacobite machinations, and traders' grievances about the interruption of free trade. Having Defoe placed in Scotland, flexible and dependent, gave them intelligence in the form of his letters and a public voice in the form of his published writings.

Sr

I am in hopes myne Come Constantly to yor hand and Therefore I Repeat Nothing of what I have wrott; My Own Case I leav wholly wth you, and Doubt not but My Ld Treasr will be pleased wth

DEFOE TO [ROBERT HARLEY], 9 AUGUST 1707

yᵉ Choice I have Made, of being Servicable Rather Than Proffiting of his Lᵈships Goodness;[2] I Referr That wholly to his Lᵈships Direction, Onely Pray the Return wᵗʰ his Lᵈships farther Ordʳˢ as Soon as may Consist wᵗʰ Convenience.

I am Not to be Discourag'd Either wᵗʰ Dangers or Difficultys in This work. I kno' That yᵉ more Disordred they are here, The more Need of what I am Upon; and Therefore when I give his Lᵈship a Very Mellancholly Accoᵗ of Things,[3] it is Neither to Enhance his Opinion of my Services nor to Suggest yᵗ I am Either weary Or Affraid of the Undertakeing; — and I speak This Now because I Really am goeing to give you a Very Mellancholly Accoᵗ of Things —

The Ferment Runs Every Day higher here, and the ill blood of This people is So much Encreased that There is No speaking among them but wᵗʰ the Uttmost Caution — Not but that I am apt Freely Enough to speak but if I should give way to Talking in Cases wᶜʰ would Move yᵉ pacentest Man On Earth to lose his Temper, I should Deprive my Self of yᵉ Opportunity of Doeing Good Another Time.

I Therefore hear all Their ill Language, and Onely Desire yᵐ to have Pacence, till they See the End of things; and to Moderate as well as I Can but 'Tis a Fitt of Lunacy Just Now and when yᵉ spirits Are Evaporated it will Cool Again.

I hinted to you a Sermon Preached at a Communion by Mʳ John Anderson of Sᵗ Andrews[4] — last Sabbath he preached Again at yᵉ Gray Fryers Kirk in this City — his Text Hosea. 7. v. 8. <u>Ephraim is a Cake Not Turn'd, Strangers have Devour'd her strength and she knew it Not;</u>[5] here he Railed atᵃ and Abused the English Nacon, Denounc't Gods Judgemᵗ Against the people for Uniteing wᵗʰ a Perjur'd and a Godless people as he Call'd them — and In short flew in yᵉ Face of The Union and of yᵉ Governmᵗ in Such a Manner as Really is Unsufferable —

He has in Conversation yᵉ Same stile and Goes up and Down Enflameing and Enrageing the people — he is a bold popular Man and thereby the more Mischievous.

ᵃ at] *interlined*

DEFOE TO [ROBERT HARLEY], 9 AUGUST 1707

I have Taken No Notice of it Other than Gently in Discourse, for Really it is not the[a] Time to Do it just Now — But if ye Governm^t here had a hint given them That her Maj^{tie} has an Acco^t of and is Displeased &c. at Such Dealing — And they Directed My Ld Advocat^6 to send for and Reprove him Gently, p[er]haps it might Give a Check to his Raillery — and as that is the Common Method here of Treating their ministers It will make No New Mocon.

This Man is Really a Fatall Instrum^t at this Time because he is Esteemd a Good Man.

I shall not Trouble you with the Artifices of ye Jacobites to Enflame these things, How Men were Employd to Go about ye streets and Crye Out Upon Scotland, and Call ye Brewers Men, Scotch Rogues, and Scots Dogs, just as^b passing in the streets,^{c} and so make the people believ it was the English Excise men — and such like Methods to Exasperate the people Against them wch makes the poor Fellows afraid to go About their bussiness.

In this Ferment We are Now and Till the affair of the ships^7 is Over it will be No Otherwise.

My Fear of it is its^d Encreaseing and Refounding a Nacon^{ll} Aversion wch is the Great thing we hoped the Union would have worne off — and wch the Ministers in p[er]ticular do now Especally strive to spread in ye Minds of the people and wch if it goes On will be past Cure.

I must Confess I Never Saw a Nacon So Universally Wild and So Readily Embraceing Everything that may Exasperate them. They Are Ripe for Every Mischief and if Some Generall step to their Satisfaccon is not Taken <u>I do not yet foresee how</u> they will Certainly Precipitate themselves into some Violent thing or Other On the first Occasion that Offers.

It Seems a p[er]fect Gang-green On the Tempers And like^e the Gen^{ll} Method of Such Exasperations it^f Reconciles smaller things to promote this Greater — Different Intrests, Differing partys

---

^{a} the] *interlined*
^{b} as] *interlined*
^{c} in the streets] *interlined*
^{d} its] *interlined*
^{e} And like] *interlined above cancelled word* 'that'
^{f} it] *interlined*

410

DEFOE TO [ROBERT HARLEY], 9 AUGUST 1707

all[a] Joyn in a Universall Clamour — and the Very whiggs Declare Openly they will Joyn wth Francè or King James or any body Rather than be Insulted as they Call it by the English — Tis ye happyest thing in the world that ye Union is finisht. Were it to act Now it would be all Confusion and Distraction.

I have nothing to Say Sr in This Relation but that it is Much short of the Fact — I wish heartily some Medium may be found Out in ye Case of ye Wines[8] — stop of the ships and p[er]ticularly the Impressing their Men — for tho' I hope things will Cool then, yet Really Such Heats as These are Dangerous in Takeing too Deep Root.

I Thot my Self Oblig'd to give you This Accot. I ask yor Pardon for its Length and

am

yor Most Obedt Servt

DF

Augt. 9. 1707

Text: BL Add. MS. 70291, fols. 188–9. *Address*: none. *Endorsed by Harley* (fol. 189v): Edenburg Aug: 9: 1707 R Aug: 15.

---

[a] all] *interlined*

---

1   See Letter 180.
2   *Choïce ... Goodness*: See headnote. Other correspondence on this arrangement is untraced.
3   *Mellancholly Accot of Things*: For Godolphin's statement to this effect regarding Defoe's letters, see H.M.C. *Bath MSS*, 178 and headnote to Letter 115.
4   *Mr John Anderson of St Andrews*: 1665–1712. See *Fasti*, v, 234. A man of the same name (1630–1708) was incumbent at St Leonard's Church in St Andrews at this time (*Fasti*, v, 243).
5   *Hosea ... Not*: Actually Hos. 7:8–9, with 'her' an error for 'him'. 'Strangers' means 'foreigners' here.
6   *Ld Advocat*: Sir James Stewart of Goodtrees (1635–1713).
7   *affair of the ships*: I.e. the refusal of English customs officials to allow Scottish ships to land the goods originating from France.
8   *Medium ... Wines*: For the outcome, see headnote to Letters 107 and 108.

120

To [Robert Harley]

19 August 1707

HEADNOTE: The large quantities of goods in Scotland, reported by Defoe, had two causes. First, merchants had imported in bulk from France before 1 May, intending to shift goods to England thereafter. The question of their duty-free admittance to England remained undetermined. Second, there were goods that English merchants had exported to Scotland before 1 May in order to gain a drawback, principally tobacco; again, the idea was to bring them back to an English market after the Union commenced. By now, Defoe believed these frauds must be tolerated.[1]

Sr

I am Glad to Tell you The Affair of ye Wines &c. wch we are Told Are Delivred Seems to Abate here — and This Clamarous Party Are Now Turning their Tongues to Other Subjects. I Can not Say they Rail less but I have ye Comfort to be able better to Defend any Case and better to Understand Any Other Case Than That.

Two Cases Now Occupy Their Gall wch I Thot it my Duty to Signifye to you. The Great Quantitys of Goods Run here as well Openly and Insolently as Secretly I hinted at before:[2] In Ordr to Make ymselves Amends Upon The Mercha and Come at a Compleat Discovery The Comissionrs have Sumon'd in Generall all ye Merchts as well those Suspected as Not, to Come in and[a] Swear whether they have not Defrauded ye Queen of her Customes and to Tell upon Oath How Much Since the 1st of May.

Now I am Not Saying This is against Their Law, for Really They have Such a Barbarous Law, being a Remnant of the Old Suppresst Tyranny.[3]

Nor Am I Debateing Sr whether ye Queen shall get Money by this Prosecucon, yea or No, for Certainly if prosecuted the Queen must get 20000£ or Multitudes Must be p[er]jured, or be[b] Undone and Unable to pay.

[a] and] *interlined*
[b] be] *interlined*

DEFOE TO [ROBERT HARLEY], 19 AUGUST 1707

But S^r I Humbly Represent to my Ld Treasurer That a Rigorous prosecuçon of this Case will be attended with Infinite Murmurs and Discontents and Serve more to y^t fatall Design[a] of Alienateing this people from ye Governm^t and ye Union Than all y^t Money Can Countervail.

1st The Kirk Exclaim and Say This is practiseing that Old Abhorr'd Custome of Multiplyeing Oaths wch Tends to perjury &c, That it is leading people to Destrucçon by forçing them to perjure themselves or be Ruind wch Multitudes Can Not Resist, That however Such a Law is in Forçe it is Against ye Law of Nations, in which it is Every where A Maxim, Nemo Tenetur Seipsū Accusare,[4] That This Law has Rarely if Ever been Practised and[b] is not Now[c] in Any Christian Country, and the like.

2. The people Say This is the First Test of ye Moderaçon of ye British Governm^t, in wch tis Apparent The Subjects of Scotland Are to Meet wth Nothing but Severity, That Tis Against ye Union, in wch all ye Subjects are to Enjoy Equallitys in Trade, Mutuall Restricçons &c, That ye Subjects of England Can Not be Thus Purged And all Laws to produçe an Inequallity are to be Repealed — That this has been a Time of as it were an Inter-regnum in Trade and Unusuall Libertys May have been Taken, That This is a Design to punish the Conscientous Offendour and let ye Hardened Sinner Escape — That This will be of no Use any Farther, for it will put y^m Upon Measures in wch the Nicest and Most Scrupulous will be Able to swear for the Future — &c.

I act in This I hope ye part My L^{ds} Means I should act, Viz^t to Accqu^a his L^dship what Measures here may work ill, and what Not; & have No Other prospect in it. I am Sençible this proceeding Makes great addiçons to ye ill Temper here wch Really S^r is too great allready[d] Not to Merit a Great Deal of Caution.

If this Matter were pusht Now to Extremety I Can Not Express ye Confusion it would Make here, For Really half ye Naçon are

---

[a] Design] *amended from* 'Designing'
[b] and] *interlined above cancelled word* 'Nor'
[c] Now] *interlined*
[d] allready] *interlined above cancelled word probably* 'here'

413

DEFOE TO [ROBERT HARLEY], 19 AUGUST 1707

in yᵉ Crime — But Measures to prevent it May better be Used to all Extremeties than Retrospects, Espećally On the foot of this Exploded Law.

The Debate by Council In yᵉ Excheqʳ Court here was Very Long and yesterday yᵉ Lordsᵃ Adjourn'd it to yᵉ Third Wednesday in November, and This Makes me lay it before you Sʳ That My Lᵈ May be judge whether it will Not, Rather be held as a Rod to Awe them, than Otherwise.

The Next Thing I Note is yᵉ Council here Settling Justićes or Comissions of yᵉ Peaće⁶ in wᶜʰ I Doubt they Distinguish too Much Such as were not for yᵉ Union, Tho' some of them being Men of Temper and Honour Are at yᵉ Same Time Well affected to the Government and being Gentlemen of Absolute Superiourity in their Severall Countryes it will be a Little too much Dishonour to yᵐ and p[er]fectly alienate yᵐ to see their Vassalls in yᵉ Comission and yᵐselves subjected andᵇ left out.

This Matter yᵉ Constitućon of Things here Makes to Differ from England⁷ and in Such Case yᵉ Law and Course of Justiće will be Obstructed Sinće those Vassalls Dare not and Will not Act wᵗʰout yᵉ Authourity of their Chiefs Tho' they were of Greater Estates Than their Chief.⁸

These Things I Humbly Offer as my Own Observaćons; if it be yoʳ pleasure I May lay before you Some Names wherein this is p[er]ticularly Mischeivous.

I should be Glad to kno' if my Answʳ to My Lᵈ T . . . . rs Letter⁹ Reach't your hands,ᶜ and if possible See my Self Delivred from yᵉ present Circumstanće I am in hereᵈ wᶜʰ I Need Not Explain to you Sʳ. I ask yoʳ Pardon and am

Sʳ

yoʳ Most Obedᵗ Servᵗ

DF

Edinb. Augᵗ 19. 1707

ᵃ Lords] *following illegible word cancelled*
ᵇ and] *interlined above cancelled words* 'to them'
ᶜ your hands,] 'hands,' *interlined;* 'your' *amended from* 'you'
ᵈ here] *interlined*

DEFOE TO [ROBERT HARLEY], 19 AUGUST 1707

Text: BL Add. MS. 70291, fols. 190–1. *Address*: none. *Endorsed by Harley* (fol. 191v): Edenburg Aug: 19: 1707 R Aug: 26.

1 See *Review*, IV, 216–18 (22 May 1707); 240–3 (3 June 1707); 265–9 (14 June 1707). On 17 June, he concludes 'we must bear it' (IV, 273).

2 *I hinted at before*: See Letter III.

3 *Barbarous ... Tyranny*: Seafield wrote to Mar on 31 July: 'By our lawes all merchants are obliged within three moneths after importation to depone if they have imported any goods to this kingdome without paying the duties, and in there oaths to condescend upon the particular goods so imported. The merchants say they are not obliged to depone because the laws of England concerning the Customes are to take place thorowout the whole kingdome, and no merchant in England is obliged to swear against himself, and they say it is most inconsistent that they should be liable both to the laws of England and Scotland which are so very different, whereas the English merchants are only liable to the laws of England' (H.M.C. *Mar and Kellie MSS*, 409).

4 *Nemo Tenetur Seipsū Accusare*: 'no man is bound to accuse himself' (Latin). See Defoe's negative view of 'Custom-House Oaths' in *A New Test of the Sence of the Nation* (1710), 10.

5 *My L^d*: Godolphin.

6 *Council ... Peaċe*: On 15 Aug. 1707, the Scottish Privy Council issued a proclamation naming justices of the peace. Defoe reprinted it, minus the names of the new JPs, as an appendix to his *History of the Union*. The main impetus was the need for judicial authority in the matter of revenue and excise (Riley, *English Ministers*, 61, 67–8).

7 *This Matter ... England*: On the system practised in Scotland from 1587 to 1707, see Charles A. Malcolm (ed.), *The Minutes of the Justices of the Peace for Lanarkshire, 1707–1723* (Edinburgh, 1931), ix–xxviii.

8 *Vassalls ... Chief*: In his *History*, Defoe states that Scotland since the Restoration 'lay as it had usually done, too much in the absolute Disposition of the Heretable Magistrates ... and such Right as the Superiorities and Usages of Places gave to the Lairds; A Constitution not at all Calculated for the Liberty of *Scotland*, or the increase of the Happiness of the People' (*TDH*, VIII, 263–4). In *The Present State of the Parties in Great Britain* (1712), Defoe called 'the *High Land* Superiorities ... the greatest Danger, and Offence to the *British Government*' (40). The heritable jurisdictions, giving primary judicial authority to their holders, were safeguarded by article twenty of the Union Treaty. As Defoe outlines in his *History*, the Scottish Privy Council, and with it the JPs it appointed in 1707, were abolished by act of parliament in 1708, with JPs subsequently appointed by the Lord Chancellor and given powers more equal to those in England (*TDH*, VIII, 254, 264, 272).

9 *Answr to My L^d T .... rs Letter*: Untraced, but Harley had received the letter and passed it to Godolphin (Godolphin to Harley, 7 Aug. 1707, H.M.C. *Bath MSS*, 177).

DEFOE TO ROBERT HARLEY, 11 SEPTEMBER 1707

121

To Robert Harley
11 September 1707

HEADNOTE (Letters 121 and 122): His long exile with scanty sustenance and instructions continued to take its toll on Defoe. The fact that he continued to correspond with Harley but considered himself employed by Godolphin exacerbated Defoe's feeling of neglect. By September, the government was increasingly concerned about Jacobite activity, and Defoe's self-appointed task was to report to Harley and Godolphin the preparations for a rising in the north. In the event, the French attempted a landing the following year.

Sr

You have Allways Allow'd me The Freedome of a plain and Direct Stateing things to you, if I Should Not do it Now I should Not be just to you, Much less Faithfull to My Self; and I Entreat yor Pardon for This from ye True and Necessary part of it.

If I were where I have had ye honor to be Sr in yor Parlour, Telling you my Own Case, and what a Posture my Affaires are in here, it would be too Moveing a Story; you Could Not, I am Perswaded <u>pardon my Vanity</u>, you have too much Concerne for me, and too much Generosity in yor Nature, you Could Not bear it — I have allwayes Sr been bred like a Man, I would Say a Gentleman[1] if Circumstances Did Not of late Alter that Denominacon, and tho' my Missfortunes and Enemies[2] have Reduced me, yet I allwayes struggled with ye world So as Never to want till Now[a] — Again Sr I had ye honour to Come hither in a Figure Suitable to yor Design, whom I have ye honor to Serv; while you Supply'd me Sr I Can Appeal to him that knows all things, I Faithfully Serv'd, I baulk't No Cases, I Appear'd in print when Others Dared not to Open Their Mouths, and without boasting I Run as Much Risq of my life, as a Grenadr in storming a Counterscarp;[3] — It is Now five Months Since you were pleased to Withdraw yor Supply;[4] — and yet I had Never yor Ordrs to Return; — I knew My Duty better Than to quitt my post without your Comand; But Really Sr if you

---

[a] till Now] *interlined*

416

DEFOE TO ROBERT HARLEY, II SEPTEMBER 1707

Supposed, I had layd up a Bank Out of yor former, It is my Great
Missfortune That Such a Mistake happens; I Depended too much
on yor Goodness to withold any Reasonable Expence, to form a
Magazine for my Last Resort.

Tis true I spent you a Large Sume, But you will Remember
how often I Entreated yor Restraint in that Case,[5] and p[er]ticular
Direccons, but as left to my liberty, I acted as I Concluded I Ought
to Do, Pushing[a] Every work as Thoro'ly as I Could, — And in stead
of Forming a Magazine for My Self, if you were to See Me Now[b]
Entertaind of Courtisy, without Subsistence, allmost Grown shabby
in Cloths,[c] Dejected &c, what I Care Not to Mencon; you would be
Mov'd to hasten My Relief, in a Manner Suitable to y^t[d] Regard you
were Allways pleased to show for me.

I was Sr Just on ye brink of Returning, and that of Meer
Necessity, when Like life From ye Dead, I Rec^d yor last, wth My L^d
Treasurers Letter;[6] But Sr Hitherto, his L^dships Goodness to Me,
Seems like Messages from an Army to a Town besieged, That Relief
is Comeing; wch heartns and Encourages ye Famished Garrison, but
Does not Feed them; and at Last They Are Obliged to Surrender
for want, when p[er]haps One week would ha' Delivred them.

What shall I farther liken my Case to? Tis like a Man hang'd,
Upon an Appeal, with the Queens Pardon in his Pocket; Tis
Really the Most Disscourageing Circumstance that Ever I was
in; I Need Not Tell you S^r y^t this is Not a place to Get Money in,
Pen and Ink and Printing will Do Nothing here.[e] Men Do Not
live here by Their Witts, — when I look on my present Condicon,
and Reflect that I am Thus, with my L^d T . . . . s Letter promiseing
Me an Allowance for Subsistence in My Pocket, and Offring me
Comfortable Things,[f] Tis a Very Mortifying Thought that I have
Not One friend in the World to Support me Till his L^dship shall
think Fitt to begin That Allowance.

The prayer of this Peticon S^r is Very Brief, That I may be helped
to wait, or that you will please S^r to Move my L^d T . . . . r That,

---

^a Pushing] *interlined*
^b Now] *interlined*
^c Cloths] *following illegible word cancelled*
^d y^t] *amended from* 'yor'
^e here.] *interlined*
^f Things] *following words* 'I think' *cancelled*

DEFOE TO ROBERT HARLEY, II SEPTEMBER 1707

Since his L^dship has thought Fitt to Encourage Me, to Expect Assistance in Order to Serve the Govemm^t in this place; — his L^dship will be pleased to Make Such steps Towards it, as may prevent My being Oblig'd to abandone, an Employ of Such Consequence, to My Own Ruine and the loss of the Capascity I am Now in of Doeing his L^dship Service.

I Need Say No More to Move you to This S^r. I Entreat a speedy Reply and Supply to

S^r yor Faithfull Tho' Discouragd Servt.
DF

Sept^a 11. 1707

Text: BL Add. MS. 70291, fols. 192–3 (Figure 6). *Address* (fol. 193v): To The Right Honble | Robert Harley Esqr | Princ̓ipall Secret^a of State | Present. *Endorsed by Harley* (fol. 193v): Edenburg Sept: 11: 1707 R Sept: 17:

---

^a Sept] *following word probably* 'Aug^t' *cancelled*

---

1 *Gentleman*: See Letter 1, note 19.
2 *Enemies*: Probably meaning his creditors.
3 *Counterscarp*: In military fortifications, a slope or wall in front of the ditch before the defensive wall.
4 *Supply*: Defoe last received £40 in April via Bell (H.M.C. *Portland MSS*, IV, 402). In June, Harley had told Defoe he was no longer to be at his charge (Letter 114).
5 *Large … Case*: Defoe's earlier letters frequently mention his expenditure and ask Harley for guidance, though that was unforthcoming (see Letters 51, 54, 69, 74, 82, 94, 102, 105, 110, and 113).
6 *yor last, wth My Ld Treasurers Letter*: Both untraced.

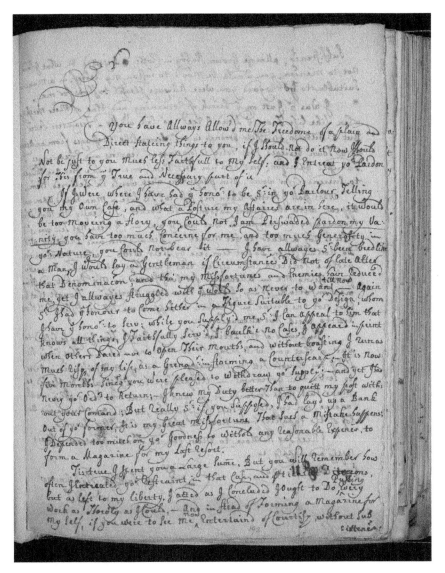

Figure 6 Daniel Defoe to Robert Harley, 11 September 1707, BL Add. MS. 70291, fol. 192r–v

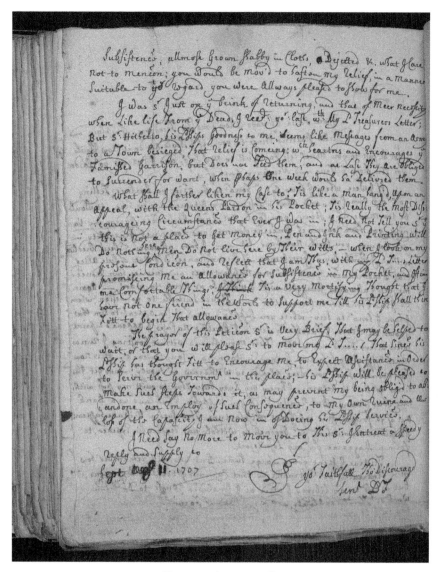

Figure 6 (continued)

To Robert Harley

18 September 1707

S^r

My Impaćenće Urged me to Write a Long and Importunate Letter Two Posts Agoe; I Would Not be Construed that I Doubt yor Concern for me, but fear you Are Not Senćible of my Incapaćity of Waiting, As I am Circumstanć'd in This Remote plaće.

I Do Not in ye Least Doubt but^a you will So far Carry On what in your Meer Goodness to Me you have begun, As to^b Move My L^d T . . . . r to Rememb^r me, and I will be Easy in Depending On it, That I shall Not be Obliged to Make a Dishon^{ble} Retreat from a plaće where I have work't my Self Into a Capasćity of Serving both Countryes; I Therefore Give you No More Trouble of That Sort Tho' hard press't &c. —

It would be of Serviće if I Could kno' p[er]ticularly how ye Affair of the Wines stands that I might Mannage ye Clamo^{rs} of ye people here as Much to Advantage as possible; you will Depend Safely On its being Caućously Used.

We are Taken Up wth a Discourse of Sever^{ll} people Landed in ye West of Scotland From Franće and Capt Murray is Apprehended.[1] The Council Are Sitting On it to Day and I Doubt not you Will be Rightly Accquainted wth the p[er]ticulars; I hope There is Nothing Dangerous in Agitaćon yet, But I Must Own and have Often Thought to hint it; The humo^{rs} of That party Are at present Und^r Such fermentaćon, So Encouraged by the successes of The French[2] and So Unhappily Back'd by the Common Disgusts, that should the K of Franće but support them Not wth Men for they Need y^m Not but should he send About 200 Offićers, Arms and Amunition, Artillery &c. to furnish y^m & about 100000 Crowns[3] in Money he might soon Get Together 12 or 15000 stout fellows & Do a great Deal of Mischief. Nor is it so Much ye Inclination of ye Men as y^e

---

^{a} but] *interlined*
^{b} As to] *interlined above cancelled word* 'and'

DEFOE TO ROBERT HARLEY, 18 SEPTEMBER 1707

Money Disperst am⁰ the Landlords, the Lairds & Jacobite Gentry That would bring them in and The Men Follow of Course.

I Confess this would be a Very Fatall Diversion As things stand here Now and I hint it because tis a juncture in wᶜʰ it would be of Worse Consequenće than Ever wᵗʰ Respect to other parts of yᵉ World.[4]

I am
Sʳ
yoʳ Most Obedᵗ Servᵗ DF

Sept. 18. 1707

Text: BL Add. MS. 70291, fols. 194–5. *Address* (fol. 195ᵛ): To The Right Honᵇˡᵉ | Robert Harley Esqʳ | Prinćipal Secretᵃ of State | Present.

1   *Capᵗ Murray is Apprehended*: Robert Murray of Abercairney was arrested on 13 Sept. and brought to Edinburgh Castle on 20 Sept. (*CTP 1702–1707*, LXXXIV, 536). His undercover visit to France earlier in the year, in the company of his brother Lt.-Col. John Murray (d. 1710), was a Jacobite reconnaisance mission (*Hooke Corr.*, 11, 121, 173, 176, 179, 181, 199, 500, 504–5, 512). On 25 Aug. Seafield advised Godolphin of the Murrays' rumoured presence in Scotland (BL Add. MS. 34180, fol. 98). Godolphin wrote to Leven and Seafield on 30 Aug. to command the arrest of John (Fraser, *Melvilles*, 11, 214; H.M.C. *Seafield MSS*, 208). Jean Gassion wrote to Harley on 18 Oct. 1707 to report that no papers had been taken with Robert and that his brother had got away (H.M.C. *Portland MSS*, IV, 456–7). Godolphin felt John 'to be much the more obnoxious man' of the brothers (to Harley, 18 Oct. 1707, H.M.C. *Bath MSS*, I, 182). Robert Murray was released in Dec. For the Murrays' perspective on their intriguing with France and Robert's arrest and release, see the family memoir written up by their younger brother Maurice, 'Memoirs of the Morays' (*c.* 1731), NRS GD 24/1/872/1/3, fols. 199–215.
2   *Successes of The French*: In Spain, France and Philip V defeated the allies at the Battle of Almansa on 25 Apr. 1707. In May, the French army captured the Bühl-Stollhofen Line of defensive entrenchments in southwestern Germany, 'so that the fruits of the victory of Blenheim were lost in one night without opposition' (Luttrell, VI, 179). In August, the allied siege of Toulon failed. A stalemate in Flanders also favoured France. Defoe had been commenting closely on the war in the *Review* since July 1707.
3   *100000 Crowns*: £25,000.
4   *Worse ... World*: I.e. troops from abroad, namely Flanders, would need to be recalled to Scotland to fight Jacobites.

DEFOE TO ROBERT HARLEY, 29 SEPTEMBER 1707

123

To Robert Harley

29 September 1707

HEADNOTE (Letters 123–5): Defoe languished in Scotland in autumn 1707. He had fallen between paymasters; Godolphin had taken over, but funds that would enable Defoe's return to London were not forthcoming. On 20 September, Defoe's brother-in-law Robert Davis wrote to Harley:

> I Crave leave to remind y^r Honor of y^r Promise, That y^o would not onely take care that my Brother D: F: should be supply'd but alsoe spurr my L^d T - - - er to settell that afaire on him before y^r honor goes in the Countery.
>
> I hope That Neither y^r honor nor my L^d T - - - er will not Now Neglect him, while all the world sayeth he hath been very servicable – and will soe continue both to private and publicke (if he be not too much Neglected), wch wth submission, my L^d T - - - er he may stand in need off before hes aware &c.
>
> I beg y^r honor^s pardon for this trouble, and hope his condition wth his sickely, large & needy famely here may be sufficient motives to move y^r honor and my L^d T - - - er to a speedy Resolution; not onely to fix that afaire on him; but order him a supply – That he may not be put to such straights, as I am Informed he is in a strainge place. I shall be very glad to Receive y^r honor^s commands, in order to Releive him a littell.[1]

In the meantime, Defoe continued to aid the ministry's agendas, pacifying Presbyterian ministers ambivalent about the Union, allaying the concerns of traders, and rallying behind the government despite the year's military defeats. Funds to bring him back to England eventually arrived in late November.

S^r

When I Read Over Sometimes My L^d Tr . . . s Letter wch I Carry in My Pocket I Think 'tis Impossible I should be in ye Case I am; Since Therein his L^dship Mencons That he knows my Necessitys.

I Can not but Think it hard to be left So in a Strange place, and where, I speak wth Out Vanity, I had Made my Self Capable of Doing Ten Times More Service than I or any Ten Can do by New

DEFOE TO ROBERT HARLEY, 29 SEPTEMBER 1707

Measures; why the Service as well as yᵉ Man is So forgotten is Not for me to Enquire.

I Bless God Sʳ I have Never been Driven to Importunitys wᵗʰ My Friends, and were I in England, tho' I have Missfortunes yᵗ Crush me, yet I shall Never be So Reduc't as to sollicit Bread, and Sue for Subsistence.

I kno' Sʳ it is yoʳ Supposition that They will Supply me, for you Never would have left me to This. I have too much Experience of your Concern for me; I Humbly Entreat But This Last Favour As yᵉ <u>Coup de Grace</u>, to Send me Out of This Torture; Give me your Ordʳ to Come Away; Ile Ever be your faithfull and Sincere Servᵗᵃ whether Subsisted Or Not; Ile be yᵉ Constant Friend of yoʳ Family And Intrest, in Meer Remembrance of yoʳ past Care of me; It is Sʳ my Aversion to quit a post I am plac't in by yoʳ Ordʳ and wᶜʰ without yoʳ Ordʳ I Ought not to abandonne; but Sʳ yᵉ Bravest Garrison May be starv'd Out, and It is my Duty to Tell you when I Am Not able to hold out Any Longer.

I had a letter from my Bro:[2] who Tells me you Ordred him to write to me I should be Supply'd and I had Resolved to Come Away yᵉ last Week but for That letter; I will make hard shift Till, if you please, I may have a line in Answer to this; I kno' My Lᵈ T . . . r will be at New Markett and if I am left to his Return T is Impossible for me to wait.

If I Do not Come away this Month The Roads will be Impassable and to Subsist here of my Self the winter is not for me to pretend to.

Besids Sʳ If My Lᵈ had Answᵈ his Own Letter and I had Gone[b] On here I would ha' proposed my Makeing a Trip up tho I had Come post back Again and ha' Convinc't you of what Use it had been for me to ha' been Among Our Scots Members at yᵉ Meeting of yᵉ p[ar]liamt.[3]

I beseech you Sʳ to Believ me that Nothing but Necessity Can Oblige me to This; had I been in a Condition I would have Conquer'd all Delays with a pacence should ha' forc't My Lᵈ to

---

ᵃ Servᵗ] *seemingly amended from* 'Servic'
ᵇ Gone] *following letters possibly* 'exp' *cancelled*

DEFOE TO ROBERT HARLEY, 29 SEPTEMBER 1707

Remember — But it is Not wth me as it has been And I Can hold Out No Longer, And tis a Double Affliction to me to Tell you so.

I am S^r
yor Most Obed^t Servt
DeFoe

Wemyss
Sept. 29. 1707

To morrow The Synod of Fi[fe me]ets.^a I have been Very busye Among the Ministers there for 14 Dayes past^b — for This I have found to be a Maxim for Mannageing here, If you will form any Thing here it must be by The Ministers — I am Invited to Dine wth The Presbytry of <u>Kircaldy</u> to day, being^c the Day before the Synod,^d And shall have ye hono^r to Sit in The Synod the Next Day and Hear all their proceedings;⁴ and wch is More Than Ever was allow'd to a stranger have Liberty to give my Opinion in any Case tho' Not to Vote, That Can not be; But you may Judge S^r by This whether I am Not Come a length to Render me Capable to Serve ye Intrest & Tis Great Pity it should be all blasted at Once.

Text: BL Add. MS. 70291, fols. 196–7. *Address* (fol. 197^v): To The Right Honble | Robert Harley Esqr | Principall Secret^a of State | Present.

---

^a Fi[fe me]ets] *MS torn*
^b past] *interlined*
^c to day, being] *interlined*
^d the Synod] *interlined*

---

1 BL Add. MS. 70024, fol. 221.
2 *letter from my Bro:*: Untraced. See headnote for Davis's letter to Harley of 20 Sept., to which Harley presumably replied giving Davis the assurance in turn sent to Defoe.
3 *Meeting of ye p[ar]liam^t*: The new British parliament first met on 23 Oct. 1707.
4 *Invited ... proceedings*: The Synod's minutes record the business Defoe would have heard and list the ministers from Kirkcaldy with whom he apparently dined (NRS CH 2/154/6, fols. 146–54).

425

DEFOE TO ROBERT HARLEY, 31 OCTOBER 1707

124

To Robert Harley

31 October 1707

Sr

According to yor Ordr & Direccons I wrott to my Ld Treasurer and This Day I had ye honor of a Letter From his Ldshipr in wch his Ldship, Not Thinking proper to Ordr any p[er]son On whom I May Draw, proposes my Bro: whom I Sent wth my Letter.

Still Sr My Lord Neither Directs Me when to Draw or how Much. I had Sollicited his Ldship That in Consideracon of my Circumstances, family &c.² and That I had No Subsistence ye Last half year, that his Ldship would give me leav to Draw Something, Leaving ye Sume and Time to his Ldship.

Now his Ldship Ordrs me to Draw by my Brother but Gives Me No Ordr Either as to Sume or Time, Trying My Modesty in a manner I Dare Not Venture On.

I am Sr yor Humble Peticoner that you will please to Move in My Favour for The advance of That half year — I have Not Dissembled when I have Wrott you of ye Difficulties I have been in And have gotten into Some Debt both here and On Family Accot and if my Ld please to give his Allowance that Retrospect he shall Never find Me Craveing — I have been all ye While Upon ye spott and Sincerely Dilligent in the Grand work. I leav it to you[r]ᵃ Goodnessᵇ and hope you will prevail by yor powerfull Intercession.

What my Ld is pleased to give my Brother I have Ordred him to bring forthwith to you, Entreating you will please to give him yor Letter to Mr Bell to Answr it to me, for ye Exchecqr bills have So Supplyed all Exchas from Londo Hither it is Impossible to Remitt hither, by wch you will Observe Sr That ye project of bringing Those bills hither has Answerd No End here, Not One of Them passing in paymt but being Imediately Sent for England and Even for that Are Now Sold at 2 and 3 p[er] Ct Discount. But of This hereafter.

ᵃ you[r]] *MS frayed*
ᵇ Goodness] *interlined*

426

DEFOE TO ROBERT HARLEY, 31 OCTOBER 1707

It is my Humble Opinion That ye best way to Make me Truly Usefull in The Affair I am Upon is to have me be 8 Month here and 3 Months in London Each year, And the One Month Travailing between, Goeing Various Roads I shall p[er]haps do More Service in Than in all the Rest.

I have hinted ye Same Thing to his L^dship and if yor Opinion Concurrs I Could wish to be Comeing forward Ere ye wayes Are too Deep and That I may be here Again before The Assembly Sitts wch is in March.[3]

I Humbly Referr all This to yor favour and Am

Yo^r Most Obedient Thankfull Servt
DF

Octo. 31. 1707

I formerly gave you The Trouble of a Letter About ye Mast^r of Burleigh[4] who barbarously Murthered an Inocent poor Man w^thout Any. Tis a Surprizeing Thing to See That Mad Man Come home again and Goes Unmolested about ye Country Insulting and Threatning the people & boast he has ye Queens Remission or pardon in his pockett.

Text: BL Add. MS. 70291, fols. 198–9. *Address* (fol. 199^v): To The Right Honble | Robert Harley Esqr | Princ̈ipall Secret^a of State | Present. *Endorsed by Harley* (fol. 199^v): Edenb[urg]^a Oct 31 1707 ℞ nov: 7:

---

^a Edenb[urg]] *obscured by residue of wax seal*

---

1 *I wrott ... L^dship*: Both letters are untraced.
2 *my Circumstances, family &c.*: See Davis's account of Defoe's family on 20 Sept. (headnote to Letter 123). Defoe's infant daughter, Martha, died in mid-Oct. 1707 (Backscheider, *Life*, 246).
3 *Assembly Sitts, wch is in March*: In fact, the 1708 General Assembly commenced on 15 Apr.
4 *Mast^r of Burleigh*: See Letter 109.

DEFOE TO ROBERT HARLEY, 28 NOVEMBER 1707

125

To Robert Harley

28 November 1707

Sr

I have Not ye honor of any from you Since My Last, But I have an Accot from mr Bell That he has yor Ordr to Furnish me wth One hundred pounds[1] and This post has Accordingly Remitted it hither — And as This gives New life to my Affaires So Sr in Three or Four Dayes I Purpose to Set Out for Londo[2] and hope to Kiss yor hand, and Acknowlege My Engagemts to yor Constant Goodness in a Few Dayes, Tho' The shortness of ye Dayes and badness of ye Way will Make me Longer On The Road Than I would be.

I have little to advise of here. The Vote of Takeing off ye Noli prosequi from ye Scots Merchats[3] pleases Very well, and My Ld Havershams Speech is Laught at by Every body; I am Sorry My being So far off will make me late in gieving my Ld his Due praise but I shall be Out of his Debt This post.[4]

I am yor Most Humble Peticoner to give My Sincerest Acknowlegemt and The Fullest Expressions of Duty and Gratitude That a Mind Deeply Sencible of his bounty Can Imagin to My Ld Treasurer.

As I Come forward I shall Continue to Accquat my Self of ye Circumstances of Every place & The state of Things, and shall do my Self ye honor to Write[5] On all Occasions.

I am

Sr

yor Most Obedt Servt

DF

Edinb. Novemb. 28. 1707

Text: BL Add. MS. 70291, fols. 200–1. *Address* (fol. 201v): To The Right Honble | Robert Harley Esqr | Principall Secreta of State | Present.

DEFOE TO ROBERT HARLEY, 28 NOVEMBER 1707

1   *Acco^t ... pounds*: Letter untraced. On this £100, see Letter 136.

2   *in Three ... Lond^o*: In a work probably published in Oct., Defoe had announced his intention 'to go to *England* in about 14 days' (*De Foe's Answer, To Dyer's Scandalous News Letter*, 3). Carstares wrote to Harley on 18 Nov.: 'Mr De Foe is now returning to England and really Sir I cannot but say that he seems to have a pretty good knowledge of our affairs and just enough notions of them and he represents himself S^r with great honour of you' (H.M.C. *Portland MSS*, VIII, 298; BL Add. MS. 70039, fols. 261v–262r). On 25 Dec. 1707, another of Harley's spies, John Ogilvie [*alias* Jean Gassion], gives an image of Defoe in his last days in Edinburgh in 1707: 'Mr. Defoe was in town but nobody would suffer him in their company except the anti-monarchial men, for they believe he is sent down to be a spy over them and that his flight is only a pretence; he hath tried to insinuate himself in several companies but none will admit him' (H.M.C. *Portland*, IV, 466).

3   *Vote ... Merchat^s*: On 22 Nov. 1707, parliament agreed not to prosecute merchants who transported French goods from Scotland to England during the summer (*C.J.*, XV, 438).

4   *Ld Havershams ... post*: The Tory Haversham (see Letter 45, note 13) was 'a convert from Whiggery and a political eccentric', several of whose speeches against the increasingly Whig-allied Godolphin ministry were published (Holmes, 273). On 19 Nov. 1707 he delivered a scathing attack on the ministry in the House of Lords, occasioned by the decline in trade and reversals in the war: '*I take the Root of all our Misfortunes to be in the Ministry*, and without *a change of Ministry* in my Opinion, no other *Remedy* will be *effectual*' (*Ld. Haversham's Speech in the Committee of the Whole House of Peers* [1707]). Defoe replied with derision in the *Review*s for 6, 9, and 11 Dec. 1707, and subsequent issues, ironically concurring that Godolphin, Marlborough, Harley, and Sunderland were responsible for things actually beyond their control (IV, 664–81).

In his responses to *Haversham's Speech* in Dec., Defoe also looks back at Haversham's anti-Union speech of 15 Feb. 1707, which in the *Review* at that time he had labelled 'a Rhapsody of wayward Expression, calculated for the frowning Malecontent Genius of a Party' (IV, 84, 20 Mar. 1707). Defoe continued to mock the Nov. 1707 speech in *Review*, V, 28 (8 Apr. 1708); 118 (18 May 1707); 487 (27 Nov. 1707); VII, 17 (3 Apr. 1710). Eventually Haversham furnished him with fresher material with another anti-ministerial speech on 12 Jan. 1709 (*Review*, V, 603–5 (25 Jan. 1709)). In 1711, after Haversham's death, Defoe referred to his 'Annual Speeches ... making the Clamour against the Ministry become Popular' (*The Secret History of the October Club*, PEW, II, 147).

5   *Write*: Any letters Defoe sent to Harley while travelling south are untraced.

126

To John Fransham

20 December 1707

HEADNOTE: Defoe's final known letter to Fransham, written en route to London, alludes to battles in print with English antagonists that Defoe engaged in in late 1707.

In September 1707, *Dyer's News-Letter* reported that, following a formal complaint to the British government by the Swedish ambassador Christoffer Leijoncrona (1662–1710), Defoe had been taken into custody for his criticisms of Charles XII in the *Review*.[1] On 21 October, Defoe reacted in the *Review*, denying any slight on Charles but offering to return to England should the government require it.[2] He wrote two pamphlets in self-defence in October: *Dyers News Examined as to His Sweddish Memorial against the Review* and *De Foe's Answer, To Dyer's Scandalous News Letter*. In these, Defoe congratulates himself that he is subject to British laws and so will not be handed over to a foreign power. Moreover, Defoe has reviewed what he said about Charles and finds it entirely inoffensive. It amounts to saying that he is leaving his subjects in Livonia undefended against the Russians by keeping his army in Saxony; and that his threats to the Holy Roman Emperor, seeking the relief of oppressed Protestants in Silesia, undermine the allies fighting France, a confederacy Charles is actually bound by treaty to furnish with soldiers.[3] As for Dyer: 'He often takes Liberty to Forge Stories that have not the least ground of Truth in them, and this is not the first time he has done so by me in particular.'[4] Defoe points out that Dyer has himself been in hot water for abusing the government, and that he is either ignored or caned by those he abuses in England. Defoe states that he has only stooped to contradict Dyer 'at the Importunity of my Friends, who think I am wanting in my own Defence'.[5]

A second antagonist was the non-juror Charles Leslie. Leslie's *Rehearsal* attacked Defoe during July 1707, especially for *The Dissenters Vindicated*. Leslie called Defoe 'a remarkable *agent* of the *presbyterians* in *England*, who has long been employed by them as their publick *Vindicator* here, which he still continues; and he was sent down by them last winter into *Scotland*, to manage their concerns as to the *union* there; where he stayed a long time, and performed the part of their *Vindicator* to their brethren in *Scotland* ... And this *Vindicator's* work now is, to clear the *English presbyterians* to their brethren in *Scotland*.[6] (Defoe's employment by the ministry was not yet widely known.) Defoe responded to Leslie in the *Review*, having, he says on 13 Dec. 1707, only recently seen the paper in Scotland by accident, as it does not circulate there.[7] The dispute, concerning the status of Episcopalian Dissenters in Scotland, continued into 1708.[8]

DEFOE TO JOHN FRANSHAM, 20 DECEMBER 1707

Mr. Fransham, — It is a long time since I had the least hint from any body that you or any of my Friends in Norwich were in the Land of the Living.

I take this occasion to let you know that your old Friend and humble Serv[t] is yet alive in Spite of Scotch Mobs, Swedish Monarchs[9] or Bullying Jacobites[10] and is going to London to shew his Face to the worst of his Enemies and bid them defiance.

I took the freedom to write to you[11] from the antient Kingdome and suppose you receiv'd it but never had the favour of a return w[ch] made me suppose you thought the charge of that correspondence not worth while.

I should be glad to hear you are well and if it pleases you now and then to exchange a Scribble as usual with

Your very humble Serv[t]

D. FOE.

Gainsbro' Dec. 20, 1707.

Text: MS untraced. The copytext is Norgate, 284. *Address*: none recorded.

1 No copy of the *Dyer's News-Letter* has been traced; Defoe acknowledges but dismisses it in *Review*, IV, 472 (13 Sept. 1707). Luttrell appears to follow Dyer in reporting on 23 Sept. that 'the Suedish envoy has complained against D'Foe for reflecting on his master in his reviews of 9th and 28th of August, and 2 of September', then that 'an order was sent to Scotland to take into custody Daniel D'Foe, for reflecting on the king of Sueden in his reviews' (VI, 215–16). Hearne does likewise on 27 Sept., saying that 'Dan. de Foe is under the Hands of Justice by complaint of y[e] Swedish Embassador for abuse of his Master' (II, 53). The following month, the Russian ambassador complained against Defoe too (Luttrell, VI, 224).

2 *Review*, IV, 555–6.

3 The offensive statements were probably Defoe saying that Charles must have a deep design, and if he does not he is an 'Impolitick nothing-doing Prince' (*Review*, IV, 388 (9 Aug. 1707)), and questioning whether he acted honourably in his diplomatic dealings with Austria (IV, 454 (6 Sept. 1707)).

4 *Dyers News Examined as to His Sweddish Memorial against the Review* (1707), 4. For the previous occurrence to which Defoe alludes, see Letter 21. Several paragraphs are common to *Dyers News Examined* and the 21 Oct. *Review*.

5 *De Foe's Answer, To Dyer's Scandalous News Letter* (1707), 1. Defoe recalls Dyer's allegation that Marlborough bribed a Swedish general, Count Piper (1647–1716). See *Review*, IV, 226–9 (27 May 1707).

6 *Rehearsal*, 16 July 1707 (and subsequent issues for 19, 23, 26, 30 July, 2 Aug., and 17 Sept. 1707).

7 *Review*, IV, 442–53 (2 and 4 Sept. 1707); 534–9 (9 and 11 Oct. 1707); 599–607 (8 and 11 Nov. 1707); 685–7 (13 Dec. 1707).

8 See *Review*, IV, 810–13 (7 Feb. 1708).

9 *Swedish Monarchs*: See headnote.

10 *Bullying Jacobites*: As well as Jacobites in Scotland, Defoe may mean Leslie. See headnote.

11 *write to you*: See Letter 84.

DEFOE TO [ROBERT HARLEY], 5 JANUARY 1708

127

To [Robert Harley]

5 January 1708

HEADNOTE: Having arrived in London on 31 December 1707, Defoe awaited contact from Harley or Godolphin. His asking the former to arrange a meeting with the latter indicates that Defoe considered the Lord Treasurer his employer despite, as yet, having had little to do with him.

Sr

I have been in Town five Days, but have kept my Self Incognito,[1] being willing to have My Ld Treasurrs Commands how to Dispose my Self before I Took any Step of My Own — In Ordr to This I Sent by my Bro:[2] as I Thot it my Duty to Accqua his Ldpp That I attended his Ldpps Pleasure but have Not yet had ye Honor of his Ldpps Answer.[3]

I Give you This Trouble to Entreat yor Intercession wth his Ldpp for an Audience, Since I shall Not be Able to Continue Long Conceald And I have No hand to Act or Tongue to speak Now but by his Ldpps Direccons,[a] to whom I Resolv to be Not Onely a Faithfull but a punctuall Servt. I Ask yor Pardon for This and Am

Sr

yor Most Obedt Servt
DeFoe

Kingsland[4] Jan. 5. 1707[5]

Text: BL Add. MS. 70291, fols. 202–3. *Address*: none.

[a] Direccons] 'Dir | reccons' *across a line break in MS*

1 *Incognito*: In the *Review* Defoe declared himself still 'remote' on 8 Jan., then still 'at a distance' on 15 Jan., though those issues may have been written before his arrival in London. He first intimates that he is in London on 24 Jan., and states on 9 Mar. that he has been there 'above two Months' (IV, 646, 658, 680, 882).
2 *Bro.*: Robert Davis.
3 *Answer*: Defoe's letter to Godolphin and any response are untraced.
4 *Kingsland*: In the area now known as Dalston, in Hackney. See Arthur W. Secord, 'Defoe in Stoke Newington', *PMLA* 66 (1951), 211–25 (at 212).
5 *1707*: 1708 new style.

128

To Robert Harley

10 February 1708

HEADNOTE: Harley resigned as Secretary of State on 11 February 1708, following a chain of events that both fascinated and mystified contemporaries. As one said: 'The Spring of his Disgrace at Court (tho' not with Her Majesty) has so many intricate Pipes which lead up to it, that we must at present lodge it amongst the Mysteries of State.'[1] The complex political manoeuvres that led to this event have continued to divide historians.[2] Godolphin's and Harley's respective approaches to maintaining the Court's control of parliament had increasingly diverged for some time before the rupture, and there were flare-ups during summer 1707: the end to the drawback affair, the bishoprics crisis, and the formal reprimand to Harley in September.[3] Once parliament reconvened in October, the ministry was attacked from both sides. Boyer wrote that 'many of the *Whig Lords*, and most of the *Tories*, were by this Time equally disgusted' with the ministry.[4] The Almansa debate[5] and the Greg affair[6] offered further grounds for the estrangement between Harley and the duumvirs, on the basis of the Secretary's carelessness rather than his perfidy.

However, events starting in January 1708 account for Harley's exit, namely his plan to reconstitute the ministry along Tory lines, checking the rising power of the Junto. He had broached the idea to the duumvirs throughout the autumn; by January he planned to implement it even if that meant sacrificing Godolphin.[7] The plan failed, despite the support of Queen Anne. It did so, first, because (as Addison said) it 'came to Light before its time': that is, before Harley had gained support among either the Tory rank and file or the moderate Whigs.[8] Harley's hand was forced because the Junto was clamouring for his removal as a condition of their continued support of the ministry. Second, it failed because the indispensable Marlborough resolved to adhere to Godolphin.[9]

Defoe's letter was written just after the crisis point, what he later called the 'fatal Breach'.[10] On 8 February, prior to a meeting of the cabinet, Godolphin offered to resign the white staff to the Queen, and Marlborough offered the sword. According to a witness, the Lord Treasurer told Anne 'that serving her longer with one so perfidious as Mr H was impossible', and Marlborough 'lament[ed] he came into competition with so vile a creature as H'. 'If you do my Lord resign your sword let me tel you you run it through my heart', Anne replied.[11] The cabinet meeting proceeded without the Treasurer and Captain-General, but during its transactions the Duke of Somerset ostentatiously walked out, stating 'if her Majesty suffered that fellow (Pointing to Harley), to treat affairs of the war without advice of the General, he could not serve her'.[12] Several others echoed his sentiment. The next day, the Lords dealt a final blow to Harley's plot:

433

In the House, after a warm Report that the Queen was not to be prevailed on by the Duke of Marlborough and Lord Treasurer's united Requests to part with Secretary Harley, Lord Wharton made a motion to enquire into the matter of Gregg's Condemnation.[13]

The Lords appointed a packed jury of the Junto and its friends, clearly a threat 'to bring in Harley as a party in that business, and to carry it as far as an impeachment'.[14] 'So in the heat after the Lord[s] had begun the Q[ueen] sent for the Duke and told him she would comply.'[15] On 10 February, Harley had his final interview with the Queen as Secretary.[16] The next day, he resigned, soon followed by his allies, Comptroller of the Household Thomas Mansel (1667–1723), Attorney General Sir Simon Harcourt, and Secretary at War Henry St John.

Sr

The Report wch fills ye Mouths of yor Enemies of yor being No Longer Sec. of State Allarm'd me a Little I Confess, And Perticularly Brot me to Wait Upon you this Night. Others Sr Complimt you On The Accession of yor Good fortune; I Sr Desire to be The Servant of yor worst Dayes, And yet Upon My word Sr I kno' Not whether to Congratulate or Condole. I Think Verily you are Delivred From a Fateague wch Never Answer'd ye Harrassing you in Such a Manner and ye Wasting yor Houres in ye Service of Those That Understand Not how to Vallue or Reward in proporcon to Merit.

Perticularly you Are Delivred from Envy and I p[er]swade my Self you Are Removed from a Tottering Party That you may Not share in Their Fall.

My Bussiness Sr was Onely in Duty and Gratitude to Offer my Self to you Against all yor Enemies. My sphere is Low, but I Distinguish No body when I am speaking of The ill Treatmt of One I am Engag'd to as to you in The Bonds of an Inveiolable Duty. I Entreat you Sr to Use me in Any Thing in wch I may Serve you and that More Freely Than when I might be Supposed following yor Riseing Fortunes;[17] Tis also my Opinion you are still Riseing — I Wish you as Successfull as I Believ you Unshaken by This storm.

I am

yor Most Obedit faithfull Servt

[   ][a]

---

[a] [   ]] *MS torn: signature torn out*

DEFOE TO ROBERT HARLEY, 10 FEBRUARY 1708

Feb. 10. 1707[18]
I shall wait On you To Morro' Evening as by yo[r] Ord[r].

Text: BL Add. MS. 70291, fols. 204–5. *Address* (fol. 205[v]): To The [R]ight[a] Hon[ble] |
Robert Harley Esq[r] | Principall Secret[a] of State | Present. *Endorsed by Harley* (fol.
205[v]): Mr De Foe

[a] R[ight] *MS torn*

---

1 P. H., *An Impartial View of the Two Last Parliaments* (1711), 117.
2 The account given by G. S. Holmes and W. A. Speck carries by far the greatest authority ('The
  Fall of Harley in 1708 Reconsidered', *EHR* 80 (1965), 673–98). This may be supplemented by
  Henry L. Snyder, 'Godolphin and Harley: A Study of Their Partnership in Politics', *HLQ* 30
  (1967), 241–71 (at 263–71). Some details are corrected in W. A. Speck, *The Birth of Britain: A
  New Nation, 1700–10* (Oxford, 1994), 131–8, which distils the evidence I draw on here.
3 On the Drawback Bill, see headnote to Letters 107 and 108. Harley seems to have stuck to his
  principled support of the legislation even when Godolphin thought it should be dropped. On
  the bishoprics crisis, see headnote to Letter 114. Harley encouraged the Queen to adhere to
  her own nominations for the vacant sees, not to yield to the Junto demands that the duumvirs thought worth accommodating. Harley's brother Edward later dated Marlborough and
  Godolphin's fallout with Harley even earlier, to when Harley urged an end to the war after
  Ramillies in 1706 (H.M.C. *Portland MSS*, v, 647).
4 Boyer, 309.
5 From Dec. 1707 onwards, the ministry was interrogated in parliament by Tories for a large
  discrepancy between the soldiers voted for the previous year's Spanish campaign and the
  number on the field at the Battle of Almansa. The Whigs used the debate to exert further
  pressure on Godolphin. Defoe defended the ministry on this issue in the *Review* from 24
  Feb. to 4 Mar. 1708 (IV, 848–71).
6 William Greg was a clerk in Harley's office who in Dec. 1707 was discovered to have sold
  military information to France; he was convicted in Jan. 1708 but died without implicating
  Harley in his treason, as his interrogators wished. See Hill, 113–14. The affair indicated poor
  security in Harley's office, of the sort Defoe warned him about three years earlier (see Letter
  14).
7 Godolphin got wind of this plan at the end of Jan., ending his letter to Harley of 30 Jan. 'I
  am very far from having deserved it from you. God forgive you!' (H.M.C. *Bath MSS*, I, 190).
8 *Addison Letters*, 95.
9 The evidence suggests Harley aimed to retain Marlborough, at least until he learned on 6 or
  7 Feb. of the Duke's resolution not to come into his scheme, at which time he perhaps contemplated installing Ormond as Commander-in-Chief, as is reflected in the poem *Abigail's
  Lamentation for the Loss of Mr. Harley*, by the Junto Whig William Walsh (1662–1708). See
  POAS, VII, 297–305.
10 *Appeal*, 14. Cf. *The Present State of the Parties in Great Britain* (1712), 26, 38.
11 Cropley to Shaftesbury, undated [19 Feb. 1708], TNA PRO 30/24/21/150, qtd in Holmes and
  Speck, 'Fall of Harley', 695. Cf. Addison to Charles Montagu, Earl of Manchester, 13 and 27
  Feb. 1708, *Addison Letters*, 91–2, 95.
12 Jonathan Swift to [Deane Stearne], 12 Feb. 1708, *Swift Corr.*, I, 175. Previous editors and
  commentators assumed this letter was addressed to William King (1650–1729), Archbishop
  of Dublin, but Woolley proves Stearne is the addressee.
13 Nicolson, 449–50. Thomas Wharton (1648–1715), first Marquess of Wharton, Malmesbury
  and Catherlough, member of the Whig Junto. He became Lord Lieutenant of Ireland in
  Nov. 1708. See Letter 142.

435

DEFOE TO ROBERT HARLEY, 20 FEBRUARY 1708

14 *Swift Corr.*, I, 175.
15 TNA PRO 30/24/21/148, qtd in Holmes and Speck, 'Fall of Harley', 697.
16 Harley's notes for this meeting are cryptic: 'concurr for your sake ... ready to serve you ... leave for Controler, Attorney, Mr St Johns ... stay a day or two ... The Prince' (qtd in Holmes and Speck, 'Fall of Harley', 697).
17 *Riseing Fortunes: The Welsh-Monster* [1708], a poem that attacks Harley in the wake of his fall, aims to make Defoe collateral, giving a colourful and extensive account of Harley and Defoe's relationship, variable in its accuracy (26–40): 'Now, link'd in Friendship, *Bob* and *Dan*, | Became as great as Cup and Can' (30).
18 *1707:* 1708 new style.

129

To Robert Harley

20 February 1708

HEADNOTE: Defoe's final letter to Harley for over two years – not quite 'above three years', as he later advertised in *An Appeal to Honour and Justice* (1715)[1] – encloses a report on the problems caused the previous year by the payment of a large proportion of the Equivalent in exchequer bills.

The letter has a valedictory tone that indicates their farewell meeting had already occurred. In the *Appeal*, Defoe recalls that meeting:

> I look'd upon my self as lost, it being a general Rule in such Cases, when a great Officer falls, that all who came in by his Interest fall with him. And resolving never to abandon the Fortunes of the Man to whom I ow'd so much of my own, I quitted the usual Applications which I had made to my Lord Treasurer.
>
> But my generous Benefactor, when he understood it, frankly told me, That I should by no means do so; for, said he, in the most engaging terms, My Lord Treasurer will employ you in nothing but what is for the publick Service, and agreeable to your own Sentiments of Things: And besides, it is the Queen you are serving, who has been very good to you. Pray apply your self as you used to do; I shall not take it ill from you in the least.[2]

Defoe reports his kind reception by Godolphin, his presentation to the Queen, and the continuation of his employment by the ministry.

Unlike most of his writing on Scotland, Defoe's enclosure is entirely critical of the English management of Scotland in the early months after the Union.

436

DEFOE TO ROBERT HARLEY, 20 FEBRUARY 1708

He probably produced it to give Harley ammunition for a counterstrike against
Godolphin.

S^r

In Obedience to yor Comm^{as} I Send you Enclosed The state of y^e
Case in Scotland Between ye Bank and The People in ye Payment of
The Equivalent.[3]
I shall allwayes be Glad of an Opportunity to Rend^r you
Service[4] in This or any Thing in My Power. Sincerely Wishing you
Deliverance from all yor Enemyes

I am
yor Most Oblig'd Humble Servt
DF

Feb. 20. 1707[5]

Of The Paying The Eqivalent in Excheq Bills[6]

By The Treaty The Scots were to be paid The Equivalent
in Money and The Affrican Debt in Perticular was to have
Intrest Till it was paid.
In all Our Discourses For ye Union, Prints without Doores[7]
and^a speeches within, it was an Argum^t Used to Inforce y^e
Union, Viz^t the Great Advantage Scotland would Reap by
400000£ Sterl Imediately bro^t to them Circulateing in specie
and Encourageing Commerce &c.

When it Came to be paid, 100000£ Onely was bro^t in Money &
the Rest in Bills; it is True they Sent for 50000 more,[8] because they
Saw plainly they Could not do without it.

It is True They^b did not Force any body to take them But
the Methods used to put them off were a force in Effect and
Inconsistent wth the Nature of ye Union and farr from that Study
& Care for ye Good of Scotland wch was So Much promised and
pretended to.

^a and] *interlined*
^b They] *following word 'But' interlined and cancelled*

437

DEFOE TO ROBERT HARLEY, 20 FEBRUARY 1708

1. Those whose Money was Due were as Much as they Durst Delayd to bring them to take bills while those that Would Accept them were paid before They were Due.

2. Every One was askt to Take them and prest as far as possible where any p[er]son had power or Influence Upon them.

But ye Sending them was Unjust, and the bills in themselves a Fraud put upon ye[a] Nation by the Bank.

1st. Because they were payable no where but in London, Nor was there any Such thing as a Runing Cash Set up to Circulate ym, wch at first might Easily ha' been Done.

2. Because They had no Intrest upon them to ye person Recieveing them, whereas by the Treaty Intrest was Due till the money was Recd.

3. The Bank Engrosst ye Intrest plac't on ye bills by p[ar]liamt and put their Credit upon the Scots wch to them was Good for nothing.

4. Whereas Every man that Recd them Could neither have his money in Scotland nor Intrest till paid, for they were of no Use to any but such as Wanted to Remitt to London, wch to be sure they would not do with out a Consideration & So they Came to a discount Imediately.[9]

5 No man Could send them Safely to Londo, for neither Coppying them or Wittness of Sending them Could secure them, but if they miscarryed by post the Money was lost, No second or third bill being to be had as in the Case of bills of Exchange.

Thus ye Reciever was Imposed Upon — Scotland Cheated, being Supplyed wth paper not Cash and the Articles broke in Not giveing Intrest Till paid as by the Treaty.

And after all, the End was not Answerd here, neither (Viz)[b] of Makeing the bills Circulate in Scotland and Extending the Credit of the Bank, Since they Imediately Dissappeared in Scotland and not One of them is now to be Seen, whereas had the Intrest been

---

[a] ye] *following letters* 'Ba' *(for 'Bank') cancelled*
[b] (Viz)] 'Viz)' *in MS*

DEFOE TO THOMAS BOWREY, [9 MARCH 1708?]

Running On Upon them One half of them had Remaind there, both to the advantage of[a] Scotland and also of the Bank.

Text (letter): BL Add. MS. 70291, fols. 206–7. *Text (enclosure)*: BL Add. MS. 70039, fols. 350–1. *Address for letter* (fol. 207v): To The Right Honble | Robert Harley Esqr | Present. *Letter endorsed by an unknown hand* (fol. 207v): Mr De Foe.

1 *Appeal*, 16.
2 *Appeal*, 14–15.
3 *Equivalent*: See Letter 60, note 11.
4 *Service*: See the poem by Joseph Browne, written in Defoe's voice and addressed to Harley, that prefaces a pamphlet which exalts over the Secretary's fall, *A Dialogue between Louis le Petite, and Harlequin le Grand* [1708], v–vii; cf. *POAS*, VII, 322–9. It exposes aspects of Defoe and Harley's collaboration over the past few years and suggests that Defoe will not hesitate to betray Harley if it suits his own interest.
5 *1707*: 1708 new style.
6 *Paying The Eqivalent in Excheq Bills*: See Defoe, *History of the Union*, *TDH*, VIII, 260–2.
7 *without Doores*: Outside of parliament.
8 *50000 more*: Seafield made the request, which Godolphin accommodated (see headnote to Letter 118).
9 *discount Imediately*: See headnotes to Letters 116 and 118.

130

To Thomas Bowrey
[9 March 1708?][1]

HEADNOTE **(Letters 130 and 131):** The reason that Thomas Bowrey (*c.* 1650–1713) contacted Defoe in 1708 remains unclear. Bowrey, best known for compiling the first English–Malay dictionary in 1701, spent nineteen years as a merchant seaman in the East Indies, from 1669 when he first set sail to Fort St George in Madras. In 1691 Bowrey was sworn a younger brother of Trinity House, a maritime fraternity. Based on some separate notes found among the Bowrey papers, R. C. Temple, who first published these letters in 1931, supposed that Bowrey wished to consult Defoe about Juan Fernandez Island, which is plausible but must be considered as conjecture.[2]

A roundabout connection to Defoe is the fact that Bowrey owned part of the cargo of the *Worcester*, the East India merchant vessel seized in Edinburgh in 1704.

[a] of] *following word* 'the' *cancelled*

439

DEFOE TO THOMAS BOWREY, [9 MARCH 1708?]

Defoe commented on this affair in several places; there is no evidence he knew Bowrey at that time, but he likely knew of him. Bowrey was among those who alleged that the seizure of the ship and arrest of Captain Thomas Green and two other crew members on trumped-up piracy charges was a reprisal for the East India Company's seizure of a Scottish ship.[3] Despite Bowrey's vigorous campaign, Green was executed. The owners of the freight, including Bowrey, pursued their losses but were never fully compensated.[4] In 1705 Defoe lamented the execution of Green in the *Review*, but he was on the whole diplomatic about the *Worcester* affair: he was prepared to call it a miscarriage of justice but, in the build-up to the Union, refused to make it a national quarrel.[5] He recounted the story of the *Worcester* in the *History of the Union*, identifying it as one of the crises that convinced both sides that Union was imperative.[6]

In 1711, independently of one another, Bowrey and Defoe advised Harley on establishing South American colonies at the time the South Sea Company was established; Bowrey's 'Proposal for takeing Baldivia in ye So Seas' is similar to Defoe's proposals and resembles action depicted in Defoe's *A New Voyage Round the World* (1724).[7]

Tuesday night

Sr

I have yors of ye 8th Instt[8] in wch you Desire a Meeting with me to Advise &c. On Something you have to propose.

You Can Not Take it ill Sr That being wholly a stranger to you And My Self a Person Not without Enemyes, I make Some little stipulations before hand, after wch I shall show all Readyness to give you The best advice or Assistance I Can.

If Sr you please to Communicate in writing Anything of the bussiness you Design to propose to me by wch I may judge whether I am able to Render you any Service or not.

Or If you please to Call as you Come to ye Exchange at Waits Coffee house in Bell yard in Grace Church street[9] and let ye Misstress^a of ye House know when and Where you would meet and but in ye least give^b a knowlege of yor p[er]son[10] I will wait on you as you shall Direct.

---

^a Misstress] *interlined above illegible cancelled word*
^b give] *interlined*

DEFOE TO THOMAS BOWREY, [9 MARCH 1708?]

You will Excuse my being thus Cautious, for wch I shall give you Very Sufficent Reasons when I See you. Interim I am

Sr yor Most Humble Servt
DeFoe

Text: MS untraced. The copytext is a facsimile copy, Cornell University, Kroch Library, Archives 4630.[11] *Address*: To | Mr Tho: Bowrey | In Marine Square Near | Goodmans fields

1 Arthur W. Secord's logic for assuming that these two letters to Bowrey date from 1708 rather than 1709 is sound. The following letter, which refers to this 'Tuesday night' one as having been written 'last week', is dated 14 Mar. 1708, which could suggest 1709 new style. However, in 1709, the Tuesday previous to 14 Mar. was 8 Mar., and Defoe states in the first letter that he has received Bowrey's letter of 'ye 8th Instr', which would be an unusual expression applied to the same day. In 1708, however, 9 Mar. was a Tuesday. 1709 cannot be discounted, but 1708 is more probable. See Secord, 'Defoe in Stoke Newington', *PMLA* 66 (1951), 211–25 (at 212–15); *Letters*, ed. Healey, 253 n. 2.
2 R. C. Temple, 'Daniel Defoe and Thomas Bowrey', *N&Q* 160 (1931), 139–40. Bowrey's notes on Juan Fernandez remain with the autograph letters, being auctioned with them in 2007 (see note 11, below).
3 H.M.C. *Portland MSS*, VIII, 320.
4 TNA SP 34/8, fols. 42–3; H.M.C. *Portland MSS*, VIII, 278.
5 *Review*, II, 134–6 (26 Apr. 1705); cf. V, 507 (7 Dec. 1708). James Kelly also attributes *Observations Made in England, on the Trial of Captain Green* (1705) to Defoe. See 'The Worcester Affair', *RES* 51 (2000), 1–23.
6 *TDH*, VII, 126–31.
7 BL Add. MS. 28140, fols. 31–2, dated 10 Sept. 1711. See Letters 187 and 188. On Bowrey's life, see Sue Paul, *Jeopardy of Every Wind: The Biography of Captain Thomas Bowrey* (Melton Mowbray, 2020).
8 *yors of ye 8th Instr*: Untraced.
9 *Waits ... street*: This letter is the only record of the coffee house offered in Lillywhite, 630 (erroneously stating the letter is addressed to Harley).
10 *p[er]son*: appearance.
11 The two letters to Bowrey were discovered with Bowrey's papers in 1913, fetched £115 at auction in 1949, and were subsequently purchased by Henry Clinton Hutchins (Secord, 'Defoe in Stoke Newington', 212). They were auctioned again in 1985 and in 2007, fetching £15,600 the final time.

131

To Thomas Bowrey

14 March [1708?]¹

Sr

I Wrott you a line Or Two last week in Answer to yoᵣˢ and being wholly a stranger to you Desir'd a word Or Two of yoʳ affair.

But I Am So well Satisfyed Since in yoʳ Character, That Hearing you have been Indisposed I give you This trouble to Let you kno', I shall be Very Ready to Meet you where you please, in Ordʳ to do you Any Service I am Capable of, — and if yoʳ Illness Continues So as to Make yoʳ Comeing Abroad Inconvenient, Tho' I have not a great Deal of Time to Spare, yet Rather Than yoʳ bussiness you have to propose should Suffer by Delay, I'l make No Difficulty to Wait on you at yoʳ House.

I am

Sr

yoʳ Very Humble Servᵗ

DeFoe

Newington² March 14. 1708

Text: MS untraced. The copytext is a facsimile copy, Cornell University, Kroch Library, Archives 4630. *Address*: none.

1   See Letter 130, note 1 for dating.
2   *Newington*: Arthur Secord notes that this is the earliest record of Defoe having moved to Stoke Newington ('Defoe in Stoke Newington', 212).

132

To [Sidney Godolphin, first Earl of Godolphin]
20 April 1708

HEADNOTE: Godolphin had been Defoe's main employer since summer 1707.[1] In practice, however, Defoe had principally corresponded with Harley until his exit from the ministry in February 1708. In *An Appeal to Honour and Justice* (1715), Defoe recounts that upon Harley's fall he 'quitted the usual Applications which I had made to my Lord Treasurer' until Harley gave his blessing for Defoe to continue working for the ministry. In this version, Defoe was effectively passed on from Harley to Godolphin with a reminder that he truly served the Queen; he was graciously received by his new master and presented to Anne. Thereafter, Defoe's first assignment was a secretive trip to Scotland. In the *Appeal* he gives no details of his mission except for saying that 'my Errand was such as was far from being unfit for a Sovereign to direct, or an honest Man to perform'.[2] He arrived in Edinburgh on 17 April 1708. In his pocket was a letter dated 22 March addressed from Godolphin to Leven: 'I give your lordship the trouble of this letter by the bearer, Mr. De Foe, only to recommend him to your protection as a person employed for the queens service in Scotland relating to the revenue, etc.'[3] Defoe had resumed his work as an intelligence agent, which was especially timely in the wake of a failed attempt in March 1708 to land a French force in Scotland to support a Jacobite rising and an impending general election in June.

My Lord

I forbear to Trouble your Ldpp with any Account of the Severest Journey That Ever man had, Onely as it will I hope be my Most Just Excuse to your Ldpp For being So long On the Road; The Continued Rains for the First Eight dayes, and the Depth of The Wayes all the length, Made it Almost Impossible for me to Come faster, Rideing my Own horse, One of which I have been Oblig'd to Leave behind Me.[4] I am the More Concern'd at it because I do Not Use to be a slow Messenger, And hope your Ldpp shall Not find me a slothfull Servt.

The Assembly had been Sat Down Two days[5] when I Came, So I Need Not Accquaint your Ldpp That Mr Carstares was Chosen Moderator.[6] But I May Note That it may be Taken by your Ldpp as a Signall of The Good Temper here, That people are pleased Generally with the Election of That Gentleman, Tho' they Never

DEFOE TO [EARL OF GODOLPHIN], 20 APRIL 1708

liked him before; His Moderate principles, his Temper and Caution, were allways offensiv to Those that Could Not Imitate him.

I Need Not give your Ldpp his Character, But Crave leav to add Her Majtie has in him a Faithfull and Above most Men here a Capable subject.

I Have Made but Few Observations yet, but I Think by what I have Observ'd I find The Ministers in better Temper Than Formerly, and the forbearing to Offer the Abjuration Oath to them[7] has this Good Effect, That it Deprives those That would ha' Clamour'd, and Love it, of their Expected Occasion.

I am pressed by a private Message to Visit my Ld Beilhaven in the Castle.[8] I have been in Doubt whether I should go or No, but as I Can Not Tell the Occasion, and am sure I shall Either Make a Right Use of it, or no Use at all, I Purpose to see his Ldpp, And shall Not fail to let your Ldpp kno', if it be worth while, what his Mighty bussiness Can be. I shall not fail on all Occasions to Accquaint your Ldpp with Every Thing that Appeares worth your Ldpps Note.

> I am, May it Please your Ldpp
> Your Ldpps Most Obedt Servt
> De Foe

Edinb. Aprll 20th 1708

Text: MS untraced. The copytext is *Letters*, ed. Healey, 254–6. *Address*: none.[9]

1 See Letter 114.

2 *Appeal*, 15–17.

3 Fraser, *Melvilles*, II, 217. Defoe had met Leven in 1706.

4 *horse ... Me*: Defoe's horse became lame at Coventry. This incident was later used to asperse Defoe's honesty in *A Hue and Cry after Daniel Foe and His Coventry Beast* (1711). The pamphlet charged that Defoe never returned the horse he hired in Coventry. Defoe responded to this charge in the *Review* for 10 May 1711, labelling it a 'Senseless Slander', claiming that it was actually a companion who hired the horse rather than himself, and that the agreed upon sum to purchase the horse was offered to the owner but had been refused (VIII, 118).

5 *Assembly had been Sat Down Two days*: The General Assembly of the Church of Scotland convened on 15 Apr. 1708.

6 *Mr Carstares was Chosen Moderator*: William Carstares (see Letter 90, note 3). Glasgow told Mar after the first session on 15 Apr. that Carstares was 'very unanimously chosen moderator of the session, so your Lordship may judge they were all in a good temper and disposition' (H.M.C. *Mar and Kellie MSS*, 437).

7 *forbearing to Offer the Abjuration Oath to them*: Many Presbyterians were reluctant to take the oath of abjuration because they considered it an acknowledgement of the supremacy of

the Church of England. The Solemn League and Covenant committed them to labour for Presbyterian uniformity in Britain, but the abjuration oath would commit them to countenance only a monarch sworn to uphold Episcopacy. An Act for the Better Security of Her Majesty's Person and Government, passed in Mar. 1708 amid the invasion scare, made it an offence to refuse the oath, but it was not yet insisted upon for Scottish ministers (the 1712 Episcopal Toleration Act created more severe penalties). See the *Review* for 1 Apr. 1708, in which Defoe prints a letter he has received from a Presbyterian acquaintance at Inverkeithing stating that they are against multiplying oaths and furthermore wary of swearing allegiance to the monarch in a way that infringes on the right of parliament to limit and even resist the monarch (v, 12–13).

8   *Visit my Ld Beilhaven in the Castle*: See Letter 133.

9   Healey records that in 1955 the MS was in the possession of Lt.-Col. F. D. E. Fremantle, Bedwell Lodge, Hartfield, Hertfordshire (*Letters*, ed. Healey, 256). Healey records no address.

133

John Hamilton, Lord Belhaven to Defoe (extracts)

[April–May 1708]

HEADNOTE: Defoe's correspondence with his antagonist during the Union debates, Lord Belhaven, is known only from excerpts Defoe published in the *Review*.[1] In March 1708, Belhaven was imprisoned in Edinburgh Castle under suspicion of conspiring for the Pretender in the invasion attempt of that month. In April and May, the Godolphin ministry actively sought alliances with Country party peers ahead of the general election, so in cultivating the connection Defoe may have been an intermediary to this end.[2] Defoe visited Belhaven before he was transferred to London, where Belhaven died on 21 June 1708.[3] Defoe wrote a fulsome eulogy of Belhaven in the *Review* for 10 July 1708, reporting on their meetings in Edinburgh Castle. Defoe wholly rejects the suspicion against Belhaven of operating for the Pretender. It was not widely known, but in the wake of the Darien crisis and James II's death, Belhaven in 1701–2 had travelled to France to explore the possibility of the Pretender converting to Protestantism and becoming King of Scotland.[4] However, there is no evidence that Belhaven conspired in the 1708 attempt.

Defoe concludes the *Review* essay: 'He was a Person of Nobility, of Disposition as well as Title, of Sence, Manners and Vertue, of Honesty, Sobriety and Religion, of Courage, Learning and Loyalty; besides being Master of a great many good Qualities, he had an excellent Temper, Goodness of Disposition, and Clearness of Judgment above most Men; he had an easie Conception, a Beauty of Thought, and a Readiness of Expression.'[5] It is in that *Review* essay that Defoe also presents segments of his correspondence with Belhaven from this time. Like the letters from Defoe to James Webster, a printed work by Defoe is our only source for these letters.[6] But whereas Defoe had a strong deterrent from misrepresenting the Webster letters, because the recipient could presumably have produced the originals, that is not the case with these Belhaven extracts, so they should be handled with a tad more caution.

I cannot but repeat two Passages, in the first Letters I had the Honour to receive from, and write to this noble Person, after our Difference about the Union; in which his generous Temper will very much appear.

His Lordship's Words are these.

— I confess, I thought you gave your self too much Liberty in bantering Me and my Speech in your Writings, especially in your Introduction to that of my Lord *H——ms*;[7] yet by what I have seen of your other Writings, you are of the same Sentiments with me as to Government, *&c.* and, *except in the Matter of Uriah*,[8] you are a Man after my own Heart.

And I am so well pleased with some of your late *Reviews*, with Relation to the Affairs of *Scotland*, and particularly your *Ænigma* or Allegory of the Widow,[9] that I freely forgive you all your former Sins of Ignorance. —

In my Answer I told his Lordship among other Things,

That I should not enter upon any Defence of the former Disputes I had with his Lordship, because I would not lessen the Value I put upon his Lordship's Remission[10] — And so our short Debates entirely ended. [...]

In another of his Lordship's Letters to me before I came to *Scotland*, his Lordship has this Expression, *'Tis now 27 Years since I had the Honour to be Prisoner in this very Place for opposing a Popish Successor in the Parliament* 1681, *when the Successor himself was upon the Throne representing his Brother.*[11] This made it seem very hard to his Lordship to be mix'd with a Sort of People he had always appear'd against, and stuck a little too close to him. [...]

His Lordship readily acknowledg'd the Necessity, Prudence and Justice of the Government, in securing the Persons of all that were suspected,[12] only regretted that he was number'd among the Persons suspected — *I am here*, says his Lordship in the last quoted Letter to me, *in Custody with* Three *Papists,* Five *Non-Jurants, and* One *who*

LORD BELHAVEN TO DEFOE, [APRIL–MAY 1708]

*may be reckoned worse than any of the other, because of his Treachery in
King* William's *Service;*[13] *I meet with the same Measure and the same
Treatment, and am the only Person who having been always faithful to
the present Government, am to have my Fame and Reputation blasted,
by being number'd amongst the Transgressors* — [...]

And *how then,* says his Lordship, *comes the Lord* Beilhaven *to
be secured, who never could be thought of in any of these, who was all
the Winter preceding the Revolution in* Holland *with the Prince of*
Orange, *was with the first in the Revolution* — *And one of the first
entrusted with Military Command after it, being especially honour'd
with the Command of the Horse against the Viscount of* Dundee,[14] *who
has had the Honour to serve her Majesty and her Royal Predeccessor
in Council, in Treasury, in Exchequer, and in several other Offices;*[15]
*who had the Honour not only to be the Taker, but among the Number
of the Makers of such Oaths and Acts from time to time, as were judg'd
necessary for the Security of the present Settlement, and not the least
forward to make them* — *Where then, says his Lordship, does the
Suspicion lie?* [...]

[H]is Lordship concluded another Letter to me on that Head;
thus,

— *Tho I am able to answer all my Accusers, and know that no Man
can lay any thing to my Charge, yet as many will hear of my Accusation,
that will not hear of my Exoneration, I should be content you would,
as Occasion offers, say what you think proper and true for my Personal
Vindication.* — [...]

Again in a Letter I have by me from his Lordship, there is this
Expression — *I am not,* says my Lord, *going to perswade you to be an
ANTI-UNIONER* — *since the thing being done I my Self am become
an* Unioner,[16] *as all peaceable Subjects ought to be.*

Text: Daniel Defoe, *A Review of the State of the British Nation*, IV, no. 45, Saturday
10 July 1708. *Address*: none recorded.

---

1   For the exchanges between Defoe and Belhaven in 1706, see Letters 67 and 70.
2   For the Court's overtures to the 'Cavalier party', including Belhaven, see Glasgow to Mar,
    1 May 1708, H.M.C. *Mar and Kellie MSS*, 438–9. Belhaven ultimately sided with the Ham-
    ilton–Squadrone interest against the Court (Hamilton to Sunderland, 22 May 1708, *Duch.
    Marl. Corr.*, 11, 252–5), though his death made the point moot.

447

LORD BELHAVEN TO DEFOE, [APRIL–MAY 1708]

3 Defoe later criticised the handling of the arrests and transportations to London of Scottish nobles suspected of Jacobitism in 1708, as the government made a show without then presenting charges (*The Secret History of the White-Staff, Part III* (1715), 18).

4 Daniel Szechi, *Britain's Lost Revolution? Jacobite Scotland and French Grand Strategy, 1701–1708* (Manchester, 2015), 117. At the height of the Union debates on 30 Nov. 1706, Belhaven pledged to Godolphin that 'Her Majesty shall never find me a rebel' (*Marchmont Papers*, III, 437).

5 *Review*, v, 224–8 (10 July 1708). In his *History of the Union*, Defoe calls Belhaven 'a Person of extraordinary Parts and Capacity' (*TDH*, VIII, 44).

6 See Letters 92 and 93.

7 *bantering ... Lord H—ms*: In the *Review* for 6 Dec. 1707, Defoe attacked one of Haversham's anti-ministerial speeches in part by comparing it to Belhaven's famous anti-Union speech of 2 Nov. 1706 (IV, 664).

8 *except in the Matter of Uriah*: 1 Kings 15:5 declares that King David has behaved exemplarily 'save only in the matter of Uriah the Hittite'. David has sex with his faithful soldier Uriah's wife, Bathsheba, and then orchestrates Uriah's death in battle. Defoe refers to the story in *Review*, VII, 247 (20 July 1710).

9 *Ænigma or Allegory of the Widow*: *Review*, IV, 905–6 (20 Mar. 1708).

10 *Remission*: Forgiveness.

11 *27 ... Brother*: In 1681, the Catholic James Duke of York, the future James II, acted as Lord High Commissioner in the Scottish parliament, representing his brother Charles II. During a debate, Belhaven lamented that no law secured the Protestant religion against a popish successor to the crown. Parliament voted to commit him to Edinburgh Castle and he faced the threat of a treason charge; but he was released and readmitted to parliament when he begged pardon.

12 *all that were suspected*: I.e. those arrested in the wake of the attempted invasion in 1708.

13 *One ... Service*: Probably alluding to Hamilton, who opposed William III throughout his reign.

14 *in Holland ... Dundee*: Belhaven supported the 1688–9 Revolution and commanded the Haddingtonshire troop of horse at the Battle of Killicrankie (1689), in which the Jacobite commander John Graham, Viscount Dundee (1647–89) was killed.

15 *Offices*: Belhaven was a Privy Councillor under William and Anne, and he held many offices. He had been alienated from William during the Darien crisis, when the English government failed to support Scotland's colony in Central America. The scheme, in which Belhaven had invested, failed.

16 *Unioner*: In his *History of the Union*, Defoe states that Belhaven 'acquiesced in the Union freely enough when it was made' (*TDH*, VIII, 67).

As well as the passages given here from the *Review* for 10 July 1708, Defoe quotes one other passage from Belhaven's letters in the issue for 15 July: '[I]n one of his Lordship's Letters I find this Expression — *I think fit to assure you, that the Body of the* Presbyterians *of this Nation, who were against the Union, however they may be,* as you say, *surly and angry too, will yet generally oppose any* French *Invasion, and are honest and true to the present Settlement*' (*Review*, v, 237 (15 July 1708)).

134

To [Charles Spencer, third Earl of Sunderland]

20 May 1708

HEADNOTE (Letters 134 and 135): In 1718, Defoe referred to 'My Ld Sunderland to whose Goodness I had Many yeares agoe been Obliged when I was in a Secret Commission Sent to Scotland'.[1] Of Defoe's only two letters to Sunderland, Furbank and Owens observe that 'the Earl evidently took a self-important and *de haut en bas* line towards him, ... causing him to write more than usually humbly and self-abasingly'.[2] Back in 1707, Sunderland appears to have wooed Defoe while he was still under Harley's wing.[3] Signing on to the Junto cause may have appealed to Defoe in early 1708, as he had experienced Godolphin's patchy patronage since the previous summer and shared fewer political principles with the pragmatic Lord Treasurer than with men like Somers and Halifax.

Defoe insists in his second letter that he requested Sunderland in the first to conceal their correspondence from Godolphin merely because he feared the Lord Treasurer might abate his financial support if he thought Sunderland was also maintaining Defoe. Either Defoe was ignorant of the situation between his two correspondents or he pretended to be so. The truth was that at this time the Junto aimed to undermine and ultimately displace Godolphin, with Sunderland leading the enterprise during the first all-British general election that followed parliament's dissolution on 15 April 1708.[4] The Junto scented the chance to strengthen the Whigs in both Houses of Parliament, bolstering their demands for more places, pursuant to ousting Godolphin. Against Anne's wishes, they pressed for Somers and Wharton to be brought into government, and they spread rumours of Godolphin's wilful neglect of Scotland's defence during the invasion scare.[5] In the Scottish elections the Junto maintained its alliance with the Squadrone to oppose candidates backed by the Court party, thus severing the conjunction of Whigs that had ensured the passage of the Act of Union.[6] The Junto even struck a deal with the Duke of Hamilton, securing his release from prison, notwithstanding his probable complicity in the 1708 French invasion, on condition that he would wield his considerable influence to support Squadrone Whigs.[7] Finally, to offset the obvious royal support for Court candidates, the Squadrone leaked a letter from Sunderland to Roxburghe implying that a Whig parliament would enquire into election irregularities and that the Queen had no hopes of supporting the Godolphin ministry for much longer and so was inclining to the Junto.[8]

When Defoe arrived in Scotland, therefore, he was perplexed by the campaigning for the election. In a *Review* essay published on 22 June but written earlier, he wrote:

DEFOE TO [EARL OF SUNDERLAND], 20 MAY 1708

The Outside is very mysterious, both sides set up *Whigs*, and both sides set up *Tories*; they that would be call'd the *Whig* Party vote for profess'd *Jacobites*, *Whigs* set up *Tories* against *Whigs*, and *Jacobites* take the Oaths to quallifie themselves to vote for *Whigs*, and *Tories* set up *Whigs* against *Tories*. In short, it is all a Game of Parties, the Squadrons jostle in Politicks where they joyn in Principle, and joyn in the Means where they are Opposites in the End.[9]

As subsequent letters to Godolphin indicate, Defoe did not approve of Whigs fighting Whigs when Jacobites were around.

The two Defoe–Sunderland letters, written five days apart, were sent together on 25 May, and the latter is the last known direct contact between Defoe and Sunderland. But as Downie surmises, 'although there are only two extant letters between the two men, it would seem reasonable to assume that there were more'.[10] When Sunderland was removed as Secretary of State in 1710, Defoe eulogised him in the *Review*.[11]

My Lord

According to yor L^{dpps} Ord^r to me to Apply my Self to yor L^{dpp} by m^r Shute,[12] I did the first post after my Arriv^{ll} here write at Large to him to wch I humbly Referr.

But my L^d, According to ye Liberty I humbly Crav'd of yor L^{dpp}, and wch I had yor L^{dpps} p[er]mission^a in, I Intreat yor L^{dpps} Pardon and Paċenċe, while I Lay before yor L^{dpp} Impartially, and in a Manner I Care not to Trust but wth yor L^{dpp}, the p[er]ticular Observaċons I have Made On ye State of this Miserable Naċon I am in.

I Cease Troubling yor L^{dpp} wth Appologyes and Circumlocutions. I kno' Nothing Can be More Agreeable to yor L^{dpp} or More Usefull to ye Publick Serviċe, than plain, Naked and Unbyass't Acco^{ts} both of Persons and of Things, and yor L^{dpp} shall allways find me Endeavouring to act the honest Rather than ye Artfull part in My Acco^{ts}.

I kno' My L^d all the Acco^{ts} from henċe Are full of the^b Steadyness of ye People here, Espeċally the presbyterians; and of them More p[er]ticularly the west;[13] And it is Very True in ye Gross

---

^{a} p[er]mission] *following word probably* 'I' *cancelled*
^{b} the] *interlined*

450

DEFOE TO [EARL OF SUNDERLAND], 20 MAY 1708

that it is So, Nor is it without its Uses to Magnifye those Reports, and Much Noise I have Made About it my Self; and Much More praise I give them for it here, wᶜʰ I find they are fondest to hear who are Most Conscious they do not Merit it.

But My Lord, when I View More Narrowly the past Circumstance of the Invasion, when I See how Much of the present principle has its foundacon in the Success, how it was procur'd, how shallow it Lyes in the affeccons of the people, how Little of yᵉ Out-of-humour principle is Remov'd by it, how blind, how prejudic't and how much Averse to English Governmᵗ A large party Even of our Friends Are here, I Can Not but Say, the Bauk yᵉ French have Recᵈ here is a Double Deliverance, and it is yet Unknown to the Greatest part of Brittain what in this Success we are Delivred from.¹⁴

I am Not Treating Now My Lᵈ of yᵉ Jacobite Intrest here, for tho' it be in its Turn formidable yet it is Visible, it is known and is to be provided Against by Open Measures, Viz: force, and yᵉ Iron hands of yᵉ Law.

But My Lᵈ These poor, honest, but ill Natur'd, Imposed Upon people, are to be Mannag'd Another Way. They Really Merit the Compassion of yᵉ Governmᵗ, as they are Ignorant, Abused by Others, and Led by a Certain Je ne scay Quoy¹⁵ of Temper, into Violent Extremes; yet I Must Acknowlege they Merit Some Concern from yᵉ Governmᵗ, I Mean as to keeping them within bounds, and this wᵗʰ Respect to Publick**ᵃ** Safety.

It is Most Certain My Lᵈ that there are a party here, who have allwayes Served themselves of the Infirmity of these people, and the Governmᵗ haveing No Agents Among them, have wheedled them into Severall Excesses, of wᶜʰ The Tumult at Glasgow¹⁶ was a Manifest Example. The Dilligence of this p[ar]ty my Lord is but too Successfull and has but too Much Matter to work upon.

In the affair of yᵉ Union they Inflam'd them by**ᵇ** a Great Varyety of Suggestions, Needless to Repeat to yoʳ Lᵈᵖᵖ; the Radicated Aversion to Episcopacy, and to yᵉ English, were the Toppicks then,

---

ᵃ Publick] *interlined*
ᵇ by] *interlined*

451

DEFOE TO [EARL OF SUNDERLAND], 20 MAY 1708

The like Aversions to the Union are the foundačon Now, and I am Sorry to Say My Lord, this Aversion to yᵉ Union had politickly Enough been^a Improv'd¹⁷ by That party, till it had wrought the poor people up to a kind of Neutrallity, a thing^b as Fatall in it Self as a Direct Opposičon, and It began to be yᵉ Generall Answer in yᵉ Case of yᵉ Invasion, That it was the Effect of the Union, that it Lay between the English and the French and Let them Fight it Out. There was Nothing for the honest people as they called themselves to do in it.

While They were Encreasing in this Temper of Neutrallity, and p[er]haps were Come to a greater hight in it than yoʳ Ldᵖᵖ would Imagin possible, the French Appear'd.

What Temper then began to shew it Self, there was So little Time between the Appearing of yᵉ French and Sʳ Geo: Bing,¹⁸ being but One after noon that Little judgement Can be Made and^c yet here are honest people to be found who Speak of it with Con̆cern Enough.

Now My Lᵈ as I am farr from Accuseing this people, So I think yoʳ Ldᵖᵖ, who I kno' will make a prudent Use of it, Ought to be Informed of the Most Exact and Nicest part of this Affair and to kno' who are The Friends of her Majᵗⁱᵉˢ Intrest and who yᵉ Friends of her prosperity Onely.

Two Things have Effectually turned yᵉ Scale here, Success Princ̆ipally, and yᵉ Dilligenc̆e of the Ministers, And I Take the liberty to assure yoʳ Ldᵖᵖ that yᵉ Strength of her Majᵗⁱᵉˢ Intrest in this Country Depends Upon yᵉ Ministers, of wᶜʰ I shall have Opportunity to give yoʳ Ldᵖᵖ Other Instanc̆es hereafter. But in this Case it is Remarkable what Dilligenc̆e they Used to Awaken yᵉ Abused people, goeing from house to house Engageing them under their hands, and Opening their Eyes to yᵉ Delusions they had been Under, till in Some parishes where before They were Ready to stone their Ministers for prayeing for the queen they became yᵉ Most forward Against yᵉ Enemy.

And yet my Lord these are of yᵉ Men who will Refuse The Abjurac̆on, and tho' firm in her Majᵗⁱᵉˢ Intrest yet Can Not Get

^a been] *interlined*
^b a thing] *interlined*
^c and] *following word probably* 'how' *(for* 'however'*) cancelled*

DEFOE TO [EARL OF SUNDERLAND], 20 MAY 1708

Over their Scruples On that Account, from whence and My
Observaćon of the Jacobites Complyeing wth ye Abjuraćon I
humbly Offer yor L^{dpp} this Northern Paradox, That her Maj^{tie} is in
Danger from those that Take ye Abjuraćon, and Safe in those That
Refuse it.[19]

I am Not pleading Merit when I take ye Freedom to Assure yor
Lordship I am Not Idle and I hope Not Unsuccessfull in Clearing
Up the Doubts, and Opening the Eyes of these good but^a Out-of-
Humour people.

Here is Now a New Scene of Aff[a]ires^b Opened, Viz: of
Eleccons of Members for ye p[ar]liament and in This there Are
Some p[er]fect Novelties in Conduct <u>Mysteria Politica</u>[20] that Are
hard to Understand, The Squadrone and as they Call them here y^e
Court party acting Aga^t One Another.[21]

My Lord I Own I may at this Distance take wrong Aim,
but if the Gentlemen called the Squadrone^c here Act from a
Right prinćiple Then the best Meaning people here are quite
wrong, for There is Certainly an Error in Design or in Conduct,
that Party Now Setting Up Tories On ye foot of their Party in
Sever^{ll} places Against ye honestest Gentlemen and Truest whigs in
the Nacon.

I am Caućous of Enlargeing On This head, till if possible yor
L^{dpp} will be pleased to Signifye Either Directly if I may Obtain that
Hon^r, or by any hand yor L^{dpp} thinks fitt that this Reaches yor L^{dpps}
hands.[22]

According to what I hinted to yor L^{dpp} I have wrott of this
to My L^d T . . . . r,[23] yet I Humbly Referr to yor L^{dpp} My former
Entreaty That yor L^{dpp} will be pleased Not to Comunicate to My
L^d the favours I have Rec^d from yor L^{dpp}, least p[er]haps it May
Cool ye Inclinaćon My L^d T . . . r has been pleased to Express of
Doeing Something for me.

I presume her Maj^{ties} Intrest is ye Same in ye hands of My L^d
T . . . r and yor L^{dpp} and that it Can Not be Offensiv to Either that
I give Equall hints of things of this Nature Nor have I Any Reason

---

^a but] *inserted in lefthand margin*
^b Aff[a]ires] 'a' *omitted*
^c Squadrone] *the* 'a' *is interlined*

DEFOE TO [EARL OF SUNDERLAND], 20 MAY 1708

for yᵉ Caution, but what I Nakedly and honestly give yoʳ Lᵈᵖᵖ, for wᶜʰ I beg yoʳ Lᵈᵖᵖˢ Pardon and

Am

May it Please yoʳ Lᵈᵖᵖ

yoʳ Lᵈᵖᵖˢ Most Humble and Obedient Servᵗ

DeFoe

Edinb. May 20. 1708

Text: Beinecke Library, Yale University, Gen. MSS. File 495.[24] *Address*: none.

1 Letter 259.

2 F&O, *Political Biography*, 91.

3 Letter 96.

4 See Defoe's retrospective account in *The Conduct of Parties in England* (1712), *PEW*, 11, 249–54. The election represented a chance to alter the balance of the House of Lords as well as the Commons, because of the votes on Scottish representative peers.

5 *The Memoirs of John Ker, of Kersland* (1726), 1, 54–8. For further evidence of Sunderland undermining Godolphin by hinting at his Jacobitism, see Roy A. Sundstrom, *Sidney Godolphin: Servant of the State* (Newark, Del., 1992), 302 n. 39.

6 The Whig alliance of Squadrone and Junto against Queensberry's Court party, and therefore against Godolphin, had solidified in 1707 when they successfully campaigned for the dissolution of the Court-dominated Scottish Privy Council, thereby reducing the English ministry's ability to manage Scotland (Riley, *English Ministers*, 90–9).

7 Roxburghe to Baillie, 25 and 27 Apr. 1708, *Jerviswood Corr.*, 192; Sunderland to Montrose, 7 May 1708, NRS GD 220/5/172/1; Hamilton to Sunderland, 8/12 May 1708, *Duch. Marl. Corr.*, 11, 256–63; Mar to Queen Anne, 14 June 1708, H.M.C. *Mar and Kellie MSS*, 445–7.

8 Riley, *English Ministers*, 105–9; H.M.C. *Mar and Kellie MSS*, 448; Sunderland to Montrose, 7 June 1708, NRS GD 220/5/172/2.

9 *Review*, v, 186–7.

10 J. A. Downie, 'Daniel Defoe and the General Election of 1708 in Scotland', *ECS* 8 (1975), 315–28 (at 321).

11 *Review*, vii, 176–90 (17, 20, and 22 June 1710).

12 *mr Shute*: Sunderland's intermediary was probably John Shut, a councillor of Lincoln's Inn, sent to Scotland by Wharton in 1706 (H.M.C. *Portland MSS*, viii, 253, 255). This may or may not be John Shute (1678–1734), from 1710 first Viscount Barrington, who also went to Scotland in 1706 to win Presbyterian support for the Union and was made one of the Commissioners of the Customs, a position held until 1711, when he was removed by the Tory government (F&O, *Political Biography*, 246 n. 52). Defoe quotes Barrington's *A Dissuasive from Jacobitism* (1713) in *Review*, ix, 289 (21 Mar. 1713).

13 *Steadyness ... west*: In the *Review* for 27 Mar. 1708, Defoe prints a letter from Edinburgh designed 'to undeceive you and all good Men, as to your Fears about the *West*-Country'; the strict Presbyterians there were indeed against the Union 'yet when it comes to a foreign Invasion, and a *Popish* Pretender, they will match the best of us for Loyalty to their QUEEN' (v, 8). On 6 May, Defoe recounts a story of 'an honest Minister in the *West*' who is immune to Jacobite blandishments (v, 91). See *History of the Union* (1709/10), *TDH*, vii, 58.

14 *Bauk ... from*: Defoe's fullest account of the 1708 attempted invasion is in his *History*, *TDH*, vii, 48–62. In the *History*, and in the *Review* at the time, Defoe consistently rebuts those who would play down the dangerousness of the invasion (*Review*, v, 59 (22 Apr. 1708); 149 (3 June

DEFOE TO [EARL OF SUNDERLAND], 25 MAY 1708

1708); 195–6 (26 June 1708)). Quoting from his *History*, Defoe restates his rejection of the idea that it would have been better for the French to have landed so that the Jacobites could be defeated, in *The Present State of the Parties in Great Britain* (1712), 39–47.

15 *Je ne scay Quoy*: 'Je ne sais quoi' (French): 'I do not know what'.

16 *Tumult at Glasgow*: During the Union debates in Nov. 1706. See Letters 71–4.

17 *Improv'd*: See Letter 15, note 12.

18 *sr Geo: Bing*: Sir George Byng (1663–1733) commanded the squadron in the North Sea that pursued the French invasion fleet and prevented its landing in Scotland. See Defoe's praise of Byng in *Tour*, TDH, 11, 17.

19 *Northern ... it*: Defoe emphasised this paradox in the *Review*. In the issue for 20 Apr. 1708, he wrote: 'In the *North* the *Presbyterian* scruples the Abjuration, and yet abhors the *Jacobite* Cause, the Episcopal Man takes it, and yet adheres to *James* VIII' (v, 55).

Four and a half years later, when an abjuration oath was being imposed on Church of Scotland ministers as a consequence of the Episcopal Toleration Act, Defoe seems obliquely to give himself credit for putting that measure off while the Whigs were in power: 'But for one weak and contemptible Instrument, who never was thank'd for it, and who you would be loth to give the Honour of it, this had been done in the late *Ministry*' (*Review*, IX, 120 (15 Nov. 1712)). He was probably thinking of the advice on the subject he gave to Godolphin and Sunderland.

20 *Mysteria Politica*: 'mysteries of politics' (Latin).

21 *Squadrone ... Another*: See headnote.

22 *yor Ldpp ... Ldpps hands*: No such response has been traced. Defoe repeats the request in the following letter.

23 *I have wrott of this to My Ld T .... r*: Untraced.

24 The letter bears the notation 'D1-22' made by William Coxe when he arranged the Blenheim Papers in the nineteenth century. See J. P. Hudson, 'The Blenheim Papers', *BLJ* 8 (1982), 1–6; H.M.C. *Eighth Report MSS*, 48–9. Healey reports the MS untraced (*Letters*, ed. Healey, 259). It was sold from the Blenheim estate in 1920, and it was gifted to Yale by Arthur M. Rosenbloom in 1956.

135

To [Charles Spencer, Earl of Sunderland]

25 May 1708

My Lord

I have Endeavord to Pay the Debt of Correspondence to yor Ldpp by ye Method yor Ldpp Directed, Viz: by mr Shute, but have not ye favor of a line from him, to Signifye The Rect of it, wch Makes me fear it is Not Come to his hand.

Yet I Could Not Satisfye my Self wth Neglecting My Duty to yor Ldpp, on So Weak an Excuse, and therefore Resolv'd to write

DEFOE TO [EARL OF SUNDERLAND], 25 MAY 1708

Directly to yor Ldpp; And^a On This head I wrott yor Ldpp the Enclosed.[1]

Now you will Pardon My Weakness my Ld in This. Were I keeping a Foul, and False Correspondence between this part, and England; or Serving Two Masters,[2] wch would in Effect be betraying One, I should want to Engage Either Side to Secresie; But my Ld, My strait is of Another kind, and I find No Remedy for it but in An Open, Candid, and honest stateing the Case to your Ldpp, and Depending On yor Ldpps Generous Care for me, of wch I have had Sufficent Testimoney.

I have Since my Comeing hither, from Time to Time, Given My Ld Treasurr an Accot of affaires here,[3] in Such a Manner, as I p[er]swade my Self shall be, Exact as to Truth of Fact, usefull to His Ldpp, and For ye Good and Advantage Even of this Country too; and I have ye honour and Satisfaccon of his Ldpps Approveing my thots on those things.

I have No Reason to Doubt but his Ldpp Finding me faithfull, and Capable, will as he shall Think I Merit, Considr Either my Services, or Circumstances; and I leav yt Entirely to God and his Ldpps Goodness.

But when I write to yor Ldpp as p[er] ye Enclosed, and Sollicit yor Ldpp not to Comunicate ye Secret of my writeing to^b yor Ldpp, wch looks as if Something Clandestine was acting, a thing wch in all my life I Thank God I have abhorrd, it has shock't my Sending it without this Explanation, and that has kept me from forwarding it for Some Dayes.

I Doubt not but my Ld T . . . r may have Comunicated to yor Ldpp what I have wrott, and^c I kno' yor Ldpp and my Ld T . . . r are in One Intrest,[4] and both Entirely in ye Intrest of England, the Same Intrest of Truth, Liberty, & Peace, wch all Good Men love, and Equally Honour yor Ldpps for; and Therefore all my Caucon my Ld in this Case (shall I acknowledge it) has been my Own^d Intrest; a Thing Till Now I Confess I Never Persued, and My Distress has

^a And] *interlined*
^b to] *following letter probably* 'h' *(for* '*him*'*) cancelled*
^c and] *following word probably* 'as' *cancelled*
^d Own] *interlined*

456

DEFOE TO [EARL OF SUNDERLAND], 25 MAY 1708

been here, I hope yor L^{dpp} will not Let it be Said I Speak it^a wth more Ingenuity than Discretion; That My L^d T . . . r Supposeing yor L^{dpp} Supports me, should Decline what otherwise his L^{dpp} may Design to Do for me, Or yor L^{dpp} Supposeing my L^d T . . . . r — &c. Viċe Versa. I need Say no More, but begging yor L^{dpp} Pardon I Venture ye Enclosed, and layeing my Self at yor L^{dpps} Feet, Recomend me Onely for So Much Tenderness in this Case, as yor L^{dpp} shall Think^b I Merit.

I have but One humble Petiċon to Close This Matter wth, that if it be Acceptable to yor L^{dpp} that I should Continue to Represent the Affaires of this Country to yor L^{dpp}, in the best Manner I Can, yor L^{dpp} will be pleased, Either by a Servant, <u>if Not doeing me the Hono^r of a Line from yor L^{dpp}</u>, Directed to Robt Davis⁵ at ye post house in Edinb, to Signifye in two Words the Rec^t of this and what Elċe yor L^{dpp} pleases to Command

> yor L^{dpps}
> Most Obliged Humble and Obedient Servt
> DeFoe

Edinb. May. 25. 1708

PS

I have Some Other things of Consequenċe to Comunicate to yor L^{dpp} after I have ye hono^r to kno' that this Comes Safe to yor L^{dpps} hands.

Text: Princeton University Library, Robert H. Taylor Collection, box 6, folder 2.[6]
Address: none.

^a I Speak it] *interlined*
^b Think] *amended from* 'Thing'

---

1 *Enclosed*: The preceding letter.
2 *Serving Two Masters*: Alluding to Matt. 6:24.
3 *Given My Ld Treasur^r an Acco^t of affaires here*: Up to this point, only the letter of 20 Apr. 1708 has survived.
4 *yor L^{dpp} and my L^d T . . . r are in One Intrest*: But see headnote.
5 *Robt Davis*: Defoe's brother-in-law.
6 Like the previous letter, this one has Coxe's notation 'D1-22'. See Letter 134, note 24; H.M.C. *Eighth Report MSS*, 49. The MS was sold from the Blenheim estate in 1920 and Robert H. Taylor (1909–85) donated it to Princeton.

136

To [Sidney Godolphin, first Earl of Godolphin]

26 June 1708

HEADNOTE (**Letters 136 and 137**): If Defoe was ignorant of the Junto–Squadrone machinations against Godolphin when he wrote to Sunderland in May, he understood the situation by late June, following the election of representative peers on the 17th. The Scottish nobles who elected the sixteen Scottish peers for the British parliament largely adhered to a small number of dominant interest groups. Queensberry had become a British Secretary of State after the Union and led the Court party, directed by Godolphin's ministry in England. Rather than acting in conjunction with the Court, the Junto resumed its association with the Squadrone, but it also established a surprising new alliance with the Duke of Hamilton. Each side prepared a list of sixteen peers they wished elected. In the event, eleven peers from the Court list were returned and six from the opposition list (only Orkney appeared on both lists). Considering the Court's mighty influence over the election, due to the patronage at its disposal, it is unsurprising that Hamilton regarded this a 'Glorious victorie', and Godolphin as a defeat.[1]

The election of Scotland's forty-five MPs to sit in the House of Commons was ongoing when Defoe wrote to Godolphin in late June. While in Edinburgh, Defoe published pro-ministry propaganda. The eventual result was that nineteen Squadrone or Cavalier MPs were chosen along with the Court's twenty-six.[2] Defoe's letters would not have been especially welcomed by Godolphin, judging by his exasperation in a letter to Marlborough on 18 June: 'The letters wee have to-day from Scotland are full of the heats and animosity of that country about the election of the peers. I have no mind to trouble you with the particulars, (for they could bee endless).'[3]

My Lord,

It is really work enough, and requires some Applicacon and Time also, to heal and Allay the Ferment that This late Affaire[4] has raised here, Or indeed my L^d but to lay it asleep for a while, for Once in Three yeares it must revive, and p[er]haps Encrease, for mischief Seldome Declines.

Tis hard <u>my L^d</u> That Medicine should Thus turn to Poison, and what was Contrived to secure a Nacon Should Expose it: The Trienniall Bill has This irreparable Mischief in it, That it Keeps alive

458

DEFOE TO [EARL OF GODOLPHIN], 26 JUNE 1708

Our Divisions, and Sets us Triennially[5] together by the Eares all Over the Nacon.

The remainder of Strife wch my Ld had its beginning in ye Center, is Now Diffused into The Circle; The Intrest makeing, Heaving, and Struggling, tho' it be now Spread in ye Countrys remote from hence, is yet as Eagerly Pusht, and has in proporcon as mischievous Causes, and as ill Effects, as here; Nay as if They were a sport (tho' I look on ym I Confess wth another view) and That ye Gentlemen Could Divert Themselves with the Distraccons of their Country. The D. of Argile[6] and The E of Marr,[7] have been as it were Playing a Game at Eleccons in Kinross and Clackmannon, two shires united by the Treaty.[8] Both ye Gentlemen They set up were of One Side, and both right,[9] and both ye Gentn Setting Them up are So also, But whether it were private respect to ye p[er]sons, or relacon or Humour, or Triall of Skill, I Kno' not, but They made the Eleccon a meer Farce; Lieut Genll Ross[10] and . . . Dalrymple of Glenmuir[11] are ye Candidates. The Earl of Marr setts up ye last his Estate lying in The place there;[12] there are but 15 or 16 Voters in all. Of These Dalrymple has 13. Ross however makes up Eight — and Then both fall to protesting. Ross protests against Dalrymple's Voters, yt is Severall of them, Enough to bring him to a Majority. Mr Dalrymple Protests That of Rosses Eight Freeholders, Seavin of Them are Fagots,[13] Made Barons[14] but for ye Day, a Sad Scandalous Method now taken up here, and wch must I hope receiv some Checq in Parliamt.

From This Strife in the Country they Come to Town, and Fall to a Pen and Ink Scuffle, Scandalous Enough. Dalrymple puts it into ye Town News paper,[15] That he is Chosen. Ross Puts it in next day that he protests against the Eleccon, and resolves to Dispute it, haveing protested against his Voters; Dalrymple Puts it in again, That Ross had but Eight votes, and he protested against Seaven of them, and Thus they go on Exposeing themselves, a la Mob, and Serve for nothing but to make Their Enemyes Laugh at both.

In the North my Ld the Eleccons Go very well, and if ye Ld Strathnaver[16] be right, There is none wrong; he is son to ye E of Sutherland,[17] who it seems is revolted to ye Squadr., and is one of those they call the Squadruche or little Squadroni[18] — but he married the Daughter of Morrison of Prestongrange,[19] and by

DEFOE TO [EARL OF GODOLPHIN], 26 JUNE 1708

whom and yᵉ E of Glasgow²⁰ he is Chiefly guided, besides That he has a regimᵗ of Foot in yᵉ Forces here, without wᶜʰ he is hardly able to subsist, and ought by that to be Taught his Duty.

The Country Elecc̈ons²¹ My Lᵈ Are not yet all Over, and Therefore I can not Draw yoʳ Lᵈpp The Table I menc̈oned and wᶜʰ I purpose to do, as soon as all yᵉ Names are known —

In my Last²² my Lord I Lay'd before yoʳ Lᵈpp an Humble request on my own Accoᵗ about yᵉ Audit of yᵉ Customs, founded on yoʳ Lᵈpps former Goodness to me, and the Assurᶜᵉ I had from yoʳ Lᵈpps Letter,²³ that if any Patent Place offred in yᵉ Customes here,²⁴ yoʳ Lᵈpp would reserve one for me.

When I look Farther into This Case here, and See how Easily I may Enjoy this place Under yoʳ Lᵈpps Favour, and be Entirely Concealed from yᵉ wholl world, How it will Enable me to be allwayes Serving her Majᵗⁱᵉ both in Public, and private: — Nay how I might even offic̈iat Myself, and give very Little Umbrage here, but by a Deputy might have it entirely Concealed in England,²⁵ and so be Free to be Disposed as her Majᵗⁱᵉˢ Pleasure should think fitt, when I see this, and look back on yᵉ many Occasions in wᶜʰ yoʳ Lᵈpp has done me Good, I Flatter My Self, yᵗ yoʳ Lᵈpp will Think of me in this affair.

I have now no Intercessors wᵗʰ yoʳ Lᵈpp.²⁶ I have nothing but yoʳ Lᵈpps Meer Goodness, and the Favours of That Promise to Depend upon, And my Lᵈ this puts me upon filling my Letters with This unwellcom Importunity — Nor my Lord do I plead any Merit; I have been willing to Merit, but I am none of those that put a great Vallue on their own Performances; My Chief Merit, My Lᵈ, is yᵉ suffring part, by wᶜʰ I am reduc't to a Circumstance I was ever unaccquainted wᵗʰ, and have little but my Integrity to recommend me to yoʳ Lᵈpp.

Yet my Lᵈ according to yᵉ Common rate of Merit, I have some Merit too, <u>for Men now Think they Merit when they do Their Duty</u> — In yᵉ Affair of yᵉ Union My Lᵈ I was placed here with assurance of Support — I did here my Uttmost, I had my Share of yᵉ Hazard of yᵉ Union More Than any man; — Every man more or less (but I) reaped some share of her Majᵗⁱᵉˢ Bounty on yᵗ Occasion,²⁷ But, <u>had not your Lᵈpp Took me up</u> I was left 8 months wᵗʰ out Subsistence, Nay out of what your Lᵈpps Bounty remitted me, vizᵗ £100 to bring

460

DEFOE TO [EARL OF GODOLPHIN], 26 JUNE 1708

me away[28] £18: - : - was stopt upon me at NCastle, in yᵉ hands of The Person it was remitted to for Postage of Letters;[29] wᶜʰ Letters had been Frank't[30] as I Thought upon yᵉ publick Accoᵗ, — So That upon yᵉ wholl, I can safely assure yoʳ Lᵈᵖᵖ I had not subsistence while I was here, Till yoʳ Lᵈᵖᵖˢ Goodness relieved me, wᶜʰ I can never Omit letting yoʳ Lᵈᵖᵖ know, it is Impossible I can forgett.

Now My Lᵈ an occasion offers to restore a Man Crusht by Inumerable Disasters, and to Make a Life Easy, that will for Ever be a Volunteer in yoʳ Lᵈᵖᵖˢ Intrest, whether Private or Publick, That Dares be faithfull, and Can not be unthankfull; If yoʳ Lᵈᵖᵖ shall Think fitt to bestow This Favoʳ on me, and I may have a hint from yoʳ Lᵈᵖᵖ of yᵉ method yoʳ Lᵈᵖᵖ will be pleased to Direct it in, I shall then Trouble yoʳ Lᵈᵖᵖ with my Farther Thoughts about it.

I kno' yoʳ Lᵈᵖᵖ will be sollicited by Mʳ Tilson, but my Lᵈ, That Gentⁿ Enjoys Two very Good Things allready;[31] other Powerfull Sollicitàcons yoʳ Lᵈᵖᵖ may have, whereas I have nothing to move your Lᵈᵖᵖ wᵗʰ but the same Bounty, and Goodness, That moved yoʳ Lᵈᵖᵖ to Think on me in a prison,[32] and to Fetch me back from a deserted Case in This Country, and to Honoʳ me Sinċe that wᵗʰ a Confidence which I am Endeavouring Faithfully to Improve to yoʳ Lᵈᵖᵖˢ Service, — I lay Therefore my request at yoʳ Lᵈᵖᵖˢ Feet and am

> May it please yoʳ Lᵈᵖᵖ
> yoʳ Lᵈᵖᵖˢ Most Humble & Obedᵗ Servᵗ
> De Foe.

Edinb. June 26. 1708.

Text: MS untraced. The copytext is a modern handwritten copy: Lincolnshire County Archives, ʏᴀʀʙ/16/7/1.[33] *Address*: none present.

1 Hamilton to [Sunderland], 20 July 1708, BL Add. MS. 61628, fol. 132; Godolphin to Conings-by, 2 July 1708, BL Add. MS. 57861, fols. 100–1.
2 Defoe stated that 'of 45 Members chosen for the *North* by *Tweed* Part of *Britain*, there are not six that will think themselves scandalized at the Name of a *Whig*', thus combining the Court and Squadrone Whigs (*Review*, v, 186 (22 June 1708)).
3 *Marl.–God. Corr.*, ɪɪ, 1016.
4 *Affaire*: The 1708 general election.
5 *Triennially*: The 1694 Triennial Act mandated elections at least every three years. Defoe had just discussed the Act in the *Review* for 19 June 1708, calling it 'a very good thing', which he would not alter, but with 'this fatal Consequence in it, which all *England* feels, and *Scotland*,

461

DEFOE TO [EARL OF GODOLPHIN], 26 JUNE 1708

I doubt, will feel it; *Viz.* That the Certainty of a new Election in three Years is an unhappy Occasion of keeping alive the Divisions and Party-Strife among the People, which would otherwise have dy'd of Course.' In the article, Defoe employs a similar image to the poisoned medicine here to express his ambivalence: 'This Honey has its Poison with it' (v, 182). Defoe made similar comments about the Triennial Act during the 1705 election (*Review*, 11, 642–3 (9 Oct. 1705)). The Act was repealed in 1716, following the Jacobite uprising, and in *Some Considerations on a Law for Triennial Parliaments* (1716), Defoe argued for its temporary suspension, offering among his reasons that it maintains faction (*PEW*, 11, 359).

6 *D. of Argile*: See Letter 56, note 32.

7 *E of Marr*: See headnote to Letters 56 and 57.

8 *Eleccons ... Treaty*: In the post-Union parliament Scotland had fifteen burgh and thirty-three county constituencies but forty-five seats; there were therefore three pairs of alternating county constituencies, including Clackmannanshire and Kinross-shire. For a full account of the 1708 Clackmannanshire election, see *HPC 1690–1715*, 11, 840–2.

9 *right*: I.e. Whigs.

10 *Lieut. Genll Ross*: Charles Ross (1667–1732), cavalry officer, made a general in 1712, and MP for Ross-shire from 1710 after a by-election.

11 *... Dalrymple of Glenmuir*: William Dalrymple of Glenmuir (1678–1744), second son of the first Earl of Stair (see headnote to Letter 63), MP for Clackmannanshire 1708–10, for Wigtown Burghs 1722–7, and Wigtownshire 1727–41.

12 *his Estate ... there*: Mar's estate at Alloa in Clackmannanshire.

13 *Fagots*: 'A vote for a particular candidate or party fraudulently contrived by nominally transferring sufficient property to a person who would not otherwise be qualified' (*OED*). Defoe decried duplicitous conduct in the election in the *Review* for 15 June 1708 (v, 172).

14 *Made Barons*: Used in Scotland to signify any freeholder. For election purposes those holding land directly of the sovereign, worth 40s. of 'old extent' or rated for taxation purposes at £400 Scots. In this case 'made Barons' refers to men infeft with a qualifying freehold for the duration of the election.

15 *Town News paper*: Edinburgh *Courant*, 16–18, 21–3 June 1708 (Owens and Furbank, 'Secret Agent'). I have been unable to trace copies of these issues.

16 *Ld Strathnaver*: William Gordon, Lord Strathnaver (1683–1720), MP for Tain Burghs 26 May–3 Dec. 1708, a 'Revolution Whig'. Strathnaver served only seven months before he was disqualified from parliament by a ruling that the eldest sons of Scottish peers could not sit in the House of Commons (*C.J.*, xvi, 27).

17 *E of Sutherland*: See Letter 67, note 15.

18 *Squadruche or little Squadroni*: During the 1707–8 session, some Court magnates broke their alliance with Queensberry and went into opposition. Of this number, Sutherland and the two members loyal to him – Strathnaver and William Gordon (d. 1742) – were referred to derisively as the Squadruche (*HPC 1690–1715*, 1, 229; iv, 44–5; v, 597–8).

19 *Daughter of Morrison of Prestongrange*: In 1705 Strathnaver married Katharine (d. 1765), daughter of William Morison (1663–1739) of Prestongrange, Haddingtonshire.

20 *E of Glasgow*: See Letter 96, note 21.

21 *Country Eleccons*: The election of Scotland's forty-five MPs.

22 *my Last*: Untraced.

23 *yor Làpps Letter*: Untraced.

24 *Patent Place offred in ye Customes here*: The patent office issued documents conferring rights and privileges. Defoe had requested of Harley such a post in Scotland the previous year; in Aug. 1707, Godolphin apparently offered him the post of Commissioner of the Customs, but Defoe was persuaded to continue to serve the ministry in an unofficial capacity (see Letters 114 and 180). See Backscheider, *Life*, 227–8.

25 *Deputy ... England*: The appointment of a deputy would help conceal Defoe's presence in Scotland, as it was common for postholders in the Scottish administration to work remotely.

26 *no Intercessors wth yor Làpp*: Alluding to Harley.

462

DEFOE TO [EARL OF GODOLPHIN], 29 JUNE 1708

27 *Every ... Occasion*: In the *Review* for 12 Feb. 1709, Defoe recounts some of his work in support of the Union but complained that '*the Reward for those Services is yet behind*' (V, 641). See Letter 103.

28 *Bounty ... away*: See Letter 125.

29 *Person ... Letters*: John Bell. Cf. Bell to Harley, 2 Dec. 1707, H.M.C. *Portland*, IV, 465.

30 *Frank't*: Franking was when MPs or clerks of the post office signed the address leaf or envelope of a letter so that it could be sent without postal charge.

31 *Mr Tilson ... allready*: George Tilson (*c*. 1672–1738), appointed Auditor of the Scottish Excise by Godolphin in July 1707 and made Undersecretary of State to Boyle in Feb. 1708 (Luttrell, VI, 193, 267).

32 *Bounty ... prison*: In 1703 (see headnote to Letters 4 and 5).

33 Letters 136, 137, and 138 were first published in Owens and Furbank, 'Secret Agent'. The annotations here draw on Furbank and Owens's article, which also provides a possible provenance for the copies.

137

To [Sidney Godolphin, first Earl of Godolphin]

29 June 1708

My Lord,

I have little of moment to Trouble yor Ldpp wth this Post; I am Applying as I hinted to yor Ldpp in my Last to healing as much as Possible The breaches of This last Combustion,[1] wch I assure yor Ldpp are not Small: This City My Ld seems to me like the City of Naples after a Vesuvian Erruption,[2] when The people are Clearing Their streets and Cleaning their houses, of the Cinders, ye Ashes, and Bituminous stuff ye Emblem of Hell has Thrown out upon Them: The people here Universally Censure The Conduct of The nobillity and foresee that The Visible persuit of Private Intrest among Them gives Them very little Hopes of any Public Good from Them.

I have been in Confce wth some of The Gentlemen Sinċe ye Eleċċon, and Find they are not a little anxious least her Majtie resenting Their behaviour should use them as They Deserv.

But I must not forget to remind yor Ldpp how ye party boast here, That ye E of Orkney is gone Directly to Harwch in Ordr for Flanders; and that as he Influence'd severall of ye officers of ye Army here, so he is to Cultivate The same Intrest in ye Army, and to form

463

DEFOE TO [EARL OF GODOLPHIN], 29 JUNE 1708

his Party there.³ It is Enough for mee to Accquaᵗ yoʳ Lᵈpp of this; yoʳ Lᵈpp knows well who it is proper should be made Sencible of this Design,⁴ wᶜʰ I believe is really their next Thing in View.

Enclosed I send yoʳ Lᵈpp the printed paper⁵ I promised (in my Last but one⁶) should Come last Post, but Could not be ready; yoʳ Lᵈpp will see by it The steps I am Taking. It would be a most usefull Encouragemᵗ to kno' if yoʳ Lᵈpp approves This, and my Design of Dispersing it over yᵉ wholl Island, in a Method I noted to yoʳ Lᵈpp was formerly Done in yᵉ Case of yᵉ reply to yᵉ Memoriall.⁷

It is but a short piece, but I am p[er]swaded it may be Usefull, and I shall Follow it wᵗʰ Another, and p[er]haps a Third, to expose yᵉ Conjuncċon of These men wᵗʰ yᵉ Enemies of yᵉ Governmᵗ.⁸ I have sent this up this post to be printed in England; yoʳ Lᵈpp will p[er]ceive I have Disguised the Stile,⁹ and I am p[er]swaded no body will so much as guess it is mine.

I proposed to yoʳ Lᵈpp Spending Some Time among The Towns, and Gentlemen, &c. in Ordʳ to propagate the work I am alwayes Upon, Viz. of reconcileing People here to Their Own Intrest and to yᵉ Governmᵗ, and fortifying them against Such Noċons as are now spread about to poison their Principles; I am waiting yoʳ Lᵈpps Approbaċon of That Design, or what other Commands yoʳ Lᵈpp May have for me, being ready to Obey yoʳ Lᵈpps Orders.

> I am, May it Please yoʳ Lᵈpp
> yoʳ Lᵈpps Most Humble & obedᵗ Servᵗ
> De Foe.

Edinb. June 29. 1708.

I am oblig'd to ask yoʳ Lᵈpps pardon for not sending this last post; yᵉ Press kept yᵉ sheet so long I lost¹⁰ yᵉ Post.

Text: MS untraced. The copytext is a modern handwritten copy: Lincolnshire County Archives, YARB/16/7/1. *Address*: none present.

1 *last Combustion*: The election of Scottish peers.
2 *Vesuvian Erruption*: Mount Vesuvius had erupted most recently in 1707.
3 *E of Orkney ... there*: Orkney (see Letter 65, note 3) was Lieutenant-General under Marlborough and was elected as a representative peer in 1708. For his activity in the election in support of his brother Hamilton and the Squadrone, see Riley, *English Ministers*, 104–9. Seafield advised Godolphin on 20 June that Orkney would nonetheless cooperate with the ministry (H.M.C. *Laing MSS*, 11, 147).

464

DEFOE TO [EARL OF GODOLPHIN], 3 JULY 1708

4 *who ... Design*: Marlborough. See Defoe's *The Conduct of Parties in England* (1712) for the allegation that Orkney was being lined up by the opposition to replace Marlborough (*PEW*, II, 255), as well as *Review*, IX, 52 (14 Sept. 1712).

5 *printed paper*: Probably *A Memorial to the Nobility of Scotland* (1708), as Furbank and Owens suggest (F&O, *Bibliography*, 91). It implores the Scottish nobles to lay aside party divisions in the election of representative peers, aiming to heal the breach between the Court and the Squadrone.

6 *Last but one*: Untraced.

7 *reply to yᵉ Memoriall*: Defoe could be referring to *The High-Church Legion: or, The Memorial Examin'd* (1705), a reply to James Drake's *Memorial of the Church of England* (1705) that Defoe had dedicated to Godolphin (see Letter 35). He could also mean his *Remarks on the Letter to the Author of the State-Memorial* (1706), a later contribution to the extended debate occasioned by Drake's *Memorial*. Letter 46 is Defoe's distribution network showing how in 1706 he dispersed the *Remarks* over Britain and Ireland.

8 *short piece ... Governmᵗ*: One of these publications was likely *Scotland in Danger* (1708), which adapts for Scottish readers the *Review*s of 1, 3, and 5 June 1708. See the close parallel between the *Review* for 5 June and *A Memorial to the Nobility of Scotland*, 15, when Defoe laments that 'Here *Whigs* put up *Tories*, and vote against *Whigs*; there *Tories* put up *Whigs*, and vote against *Tories*' (v, 152).

9 *printed ... Stile*: *A Memorial to the Nobility of Scotland* is written as though by a Scot. No edition published in England is known of.

10 *lost*: missed.

138

To [Sidney Godolphin, first Earl of Godolphin]

3 July 1708

HEADNOTE: In early July, the dust was settling from the 1708 Scottish elections, and Defoe had a fuller grasp of the situation, an understanding almost as full as when he looked back on these elections in the *Review* in September 1712. There, he decried the Junto's break from the ministry. The '*Old Whigs* ... whom others knew by the Name of the *Juncto* at that Time ... Separated from the Court, *or New Whigs*, as they called them — And particularly in *Scotland*, the *Squadroni* then, and still being, United to them [the Junto], join'd openly with Duke *Ha—ton's* Party, and Voted for the most open, profess'd *Jacobites*, against the honestest *Whigs* in the Nation, who were for the Ministry.' Of his own participation, Defoe says:

> What I say of these Things, I do not speak *by hearsay*; I was on the Spot, I saw it all acted, and was Concern'd in the Particulars; and I bless God, as I always thought it my Duty to oppose *Jacobites*, and all that join'd in their Interest, I oppos'd them with all my might, altho' I knew them to be *Whigs*, and in other Cases, very honest Gentlemen;

DEFOE TO [EARL OF GODOLPHIN], 3 JULY 1708

and I did it with good Success, and thereby incurr'd the Displeasure of those, whom, if I had been guided by my Interest against my Judgment, I ought to have acted for, *being under Obligations enough to have them expect it of me.*[1]

The final reference is to Sunderland, whose brazen and continuing undermining of his ministerial colleagues, Godolphin and Marlborough, exasperated the Queen to the point that she wanted to dismiss him. The duumvirs realised that they had to lie in the bed they had made, as removing Sunderland would alienate the Junto, on whom they were more dependent than ever after the 1708 election produced a clear Whig majority in parliament.[2] Defoe was proud of having supported the ministry, but he was troubled by the fissures within it that were becoming more pronounced.

My Lord,

I enclosed yor Ldpp in my Last a Printed sheet Chiefly to show yor Ldpp a Specimen of ye Steps I am Takeing to Illuminate ye Darkness of an Imposed-upon people, and to kno' if yor Ldpp Approves my Thots upon That Subject.

I am Spending my Time here, as I formerly Noted, to heal ye wide breaches this Party makeing Season has made among the people, wch are indeed too large, and may not be without Very Unhappy Consequences in ye Course of Time — I Can not but say This Affair has serv'd to highten ye aversion to ye Union, which I was in hopes had begun to lessen apace; But as ye Uneasy people here, are fond of Laying Every Thing to ye charge of ye Union, so now they say, and p[er]haps with too much Truth, That The Squadroni receiv all Their Support from England,[3] and that all this Division is from the Union.[4]

It were Therefore to be Wished that while The Squadroni really sink in Intrest here as They have done by These Eleccons They might be resolutely Discountenanced in England and above all if Possible Divided. That as There is a Visible Inclinacon in This Nacon against them it may be Encouraged from England, For my Ld ye present Division here is Onely kept up on Two Accots: Hope in Their Own Party that they will support them and be able by Their Influence above to do mighty Things for Them, and but for This some who fawned upon Them would not Dare'd to have appeared, I mean Such of ye Queens Servts as are Gone over to

466

Them[5] — and <u>Secondly Fear</u> in ye other Party Least they should prevail and That then Their resentm^t should affect Them here. My Ld Forbess,[6] a Poor Depending Gentleman wth whom I had a Conversaċon on This head, is an Emin^t Instance; yor L^{dpp} will Take his Own words to me in a Confidence to wch I hope yor L^{dpp} will Conceal his name.

— "What can such a man as I do? They pretend they are sure of Kings, They show me Lett^{rs} from Noblemen,[7] That I kno' ye Queen Trusts — I kno' my own Circumstances, if I appear against Them, and they prevail I am undone, If I oppose ye present Ministry I am in Danger — I Kno' no better way Than to Vote for Some of both Those that I think are most in ye Gen^{ll} Intrest"[8] —

This My Lord was ye Principle That really Chose The <u>Six</u>[9] and wth out wch They had never been Elected, and if Their projects in England[10] Fail, Their Intrest here will Entirely Sink wth a very little good Mannagem^t.

I have had some farther occasion to hint Letters[11] sent hither, and am onely Cautious Least yor L^{dpp} find it necessary to use These hints, where p[er]haps those Gentlemen May obtain some Guess, that they Come by my hand, or may See my writeing; I Entreat one word from yor L^{dpp} if I may be assured that my letters are secured in yor L^{dpp's} own hands and no hints of my Intelligence Comes near those p[er]sons, Since I shall be Utterly Unable to make the steps I am Takeing <u>another way</u> in ye least Effectuall, if either My P. s. . . . [12] or any of ye Noble men formerly Menċoned Can Come to ye Knowledge of it — Besides my L^d it would sacrifice my Character as to Integrity, wch I do not Think I Injure at all in Serving yor L^{dpp}; but should seem to blott by Maintaining a Counter Correspondence &c. tho' at ye same Time <u>as yor L^{dpp} noted</u> it is in ye Main for those Gentlemens Services.

I Entreat yor L^{dpp} for This Caution. I doubt not but yor L^{dpp} will be Carefull <u>Even of Me</u> while I am Thus Engaged in yor Service, but I also humbly Suggest, that it will be for yor L^{dpps} Service to Keep me perfectly Concealed; Especially My L^d while I am Insinuateing my Self into ye Cabinet of ye Party, that are Acting Against yor L^{dpps} Intrest[13] — and My L^d if I am but preserved from being Suspected on the Subject of These Letters to yor L^{dpp} I dare

DEFOE TO [EARL OF GODOLPHIN], 3 JULY 1708

assure yor L^{dpp} I shall be in ye very Cabinet of yor L^{dpps} Enemyes, where I shall never fail to promote yor L^{dpps} Intrest.

This is a most Serious request, and I do not presume to make it to yor L^{dpp} without Some little Ground of Apprehension that Some hints have been obtain'd of my Corresponding wth yor L^{dpp} — If I may have ye Hono^r of one line from yor L^{dpp} On This Affair, I shall be larger in Explaining p[er]ticulars to yor L^{dpp} in my next.

I am

May it please yor L^{dpp}

yor L^{dpps} Most obedient Humble and Faithfull Servt

De Foe.

Edinb. July 3. 1708.
I enclose to yor L^{dpp} another of ye prints[14] Least ye former be not arrived.

Text: Manuscript untraced. The copytext is a modern handwritten copy: Lincolnshire County Archives, YARB/16/7/1. *Address*: none present.

1   *Review*, IX, 52–3 (14 Sept. 1712). Defoe adds: 'As to the Truth of Fact, I am sure I may Appeal to his Grace the Duke of *Marl—gh*, and to the late Lord Treasurer, who were the Persons then Insulted, and who know what I write is Truth.' See also *The Conduct of Parties in England* (1712), *PEW*, 11, 249–54; *The Secret History of the White-Staff, Part II* (1714), 7–8; *The Old Whig and Modern Whig Revived* (1717), *SFS*, IV, 190.

2   Marlborough to Queen Anne, 2 Aug. 1708, William Coxe, *The Memoirs of John, Duke of Marlborough*, 3 vols. (1818–19), 11, 505–6. The election returned 268 Whigs, 225 Tories, and 20 unclassifiable by party (*HPC 1690–1715*, 1, 227).

3   *Squadroni ... England*: From the Whig Junto.

4   *Division ... Union*: In the *Review* for 24 June 1708, Defoe states that 'The Mouths of those that formerly exclaim'd against the Union, *are kept open by*' the factiousness of the election (v, 191).

5   *Queens ... Them*: Amongst the defectors from the Court party to the Squadrone were Crawford (see Letter 79, note 9); Buchan (see Letter 88, note 4); Archibald Douglas, first Earl of Forfar (1653–1712); William Cunningham, twelfth Earl of Glencairn (*c.* 1676–1734); Alexander Montgomerie, ninth Earl of Eglinton (1660–1729); and William Ramsay, sixth Earl of Dalhousie (*c.* 1660–1739). See Riley, *English Ministers*, 108; Hamilton to Sunderland, 19–21 June 1708, BL Add. MS. 61628, fols. 102–6; Montrose to Sunderland, 22 June 1708, NRS GD 220/5/172/3.

6   *Ld Forbess*: William Forbes (*c.* 1656–1716), thirteenth Earl of Forbes. In the preface to *Caledonia* (1706), Defoe refers to his 'extraordinary Obligations' to the Forbes family (*PEW*, IV, 215).

7   *Lett^{rs} from Noblemen*: Letters written by Sunderland, widely circulated, including the one to Roxburghe hinting that Queen Anne was leaning towards the Junto (headnote to Letter 134) and one to Dalhousie promising better military patronage for Scots army peers if they elected Squadrone candidates (Mar to Queen Anne, 14 June 1708, H.M.C. *Mar and Kellie MSS*, 445). Four years later, Defoe mentioned 'that famous Letter written by a Person of Honour here,

468

DEFOE TO [EARL OF GODOLPHIN], 3 JULY 1708

to the D— of R— in *Scotland*, and of which a Thousand Copies are yet to be had in *Scotland*, wherein, among other Things, are Words like these; *I would not have you be bullied by the Court Party, for the Queen herself cannot support that Faction long*' (*Review*, IX, 52–3 (14 Sept. 1712)).

8 *Vote … Intrest*: On 21 June Mar told Nairne that Forbes was 'mad to be chosen' but neither side could make room for him, and that he 'voted them all [i.e. the Squadrone list] save one or tuo of us who were sure of it without him' (H.M.C. *Mar and Kellie MSS*, 453). Writing to Sunderland, Hamilton commended Forbes for his support, saying he has 'considerable merite concidering his circumstances' (19–21 June 1708, BL Add. MS. 61628, fols. 102–6), and Montrose counted him as a gain from the Court (Montrose to Sunderland, 22 June 1708, NRS GD 220/5/172/3). Ultimately, Forbes split his vote between the Court and Squadrone lists (Shin Matsuzono, 'The House of Lords and the Godolphin Ministry, 1702–1710' (University of Leeds PhD, 1990), 404).

9 *Six*: The six peers elected in 1708 from the Hamilton–Squadrone list. They comprised the Squadrone's Montrose, Roxburghe, and Rothes; the Cavaliers Hamilton and Orkney; and Crawford, who had opportunistically switched from the Court to secure election (H.M.C. *Mar and Kellie MSS*, 452–3). Orkney also appeared on the Court list, apparently at Marlborough's request (Marlborough to Godolphin, 27 Apr. 1708, *Marl.–God. Corr.*, 11, 967). The other ten elected peers – those from the Court list – were Mar, Seafield, Loudon, Leven, Wemyss, Rosebery, Northesk, Islay, Glasgow, and Lothian. Queensberry had been made a British peer earlier in 1708, and Argyll had an English peerage, so they did not need to seek election.

10 *projects in England*: Probably referring to the Junto–Squadrone intention to dispute election results once parliament convened. Upon petition, Lothian for the Court was unseated in favour of Annandale of the Squadrone, which fell short of the Squadrone's hopes to overturn four Court peers. See Hamilton to Sunderland, 19–21 June 1708, BL Add. MS. 61628, fols. 102–6; Sunderland to Montrose, 24 July 1708, NRS GD 220/5/172/6; Riley, *English Ministers*, 115; Clyve Jones, 'Godolphin, the Whig Junto, and the Scots: A New Lords' Division List from 1709', *SHR* 58 (1979), 158–74.

11 *hint Letters*: Seemingly meaning 'pass on extracts from'. Any such documents are untraced.

12 *My P. s. . . .*: Furbank and Owens convincingly suggest this is an error in the transcription for 'L. S.', meaning Lord Sunderland (F&O, *Political Biography*, 257 n. 34).

13 *Party … Intrest*: Defoe could merely mean the Squadrone and its allies in Scotland or the Junto as a whole. See Letters 134 and 135 for Defoe's letters to Sunderland. For Defoe's efforts to win the favour of Wharton see Letter 142. In Nov. 1708, in the wake of Prince George's death, the Queen's resistance broke and Somers was appointed the Lord President and Wharton the Lord Lieutenant of Ireland (Gregg, *Queen Anne*, 283).

14 *prints*: See Letter 137.

DEFOE TO [EARL OF GODOLPHIN], 3 AUGUST 1708

139

To [Sidney Godolphin, first Earl of Godolphin]

3 August 1708

HEADNOTE: Defoe continued to report to Godolphin on the ministry's Scottish opponents. He supported the ministry by counteracting criticism of Marlborough in the *Review*. Defoe was back in London by December 1708. This is the final known letter he wrote to Godolphin, though Defoe continued to support his ministry for two more years, principally in the *Review*. We do not have much information about their relationship, but Defoe's own claims imply he was highly trusted by the Lord Treasurer. For instance, in 1713, Defoe claimed that Godolphin had sought and approved his advice on the (abortive) peace negotiations during 1709 and 1710.[1] He also returned to Scotland in August 1709 and seems to have stayed there until early 1710.[2] However, no Defoe letters survive after this one until March 1710.

My Lord

In My Last[a3] I Noted to yor Ldpp ye good Use I hope I have been Makeing[b] of ye humour of ye people, here Raised by the Two public Acts of ye Governmt, <u>One</u> ye Proclamacon for a Thanksgiving,[4] <u>the Other</u> ye letter to ye Royal Burghs, Expressing the Care Taken of their ships, p[er]suant to wch the ship <u>Norwich</u> is Come in From ye Bar of Tinmo[5] to Convoy their ships thither for Londo or the Baltick.[6]

I Think Verily Such Small things as these will in Time bring This People to Much better Temper, than they have Ever yet shown, & I shall not Cease to Improve it all I Can to Their Conviccon.

I Have Often Hinted to yor Ldpp that ye Squadr. have Really Little or no Intrest here. I think tis Discovred More Evidently in this, than in Any thing, that One May Perciev A kind of Uneasyness Among the best Sort of People here, least they should carry their Point in England; wch Apprehensions Chiefly Rise from ye Generall Nocon they Spread Among the people here, that All ye Whigs in England are With Them; and that The queen must Come undr <u>their Mannagemt</u>, as they Rudely Call it; and wch they gather

---

[a] Last] *following illegible word cancelled*
[b] Making] *following word* 'here' *cancelled*

470

DEFOE TO [EARL OF GODOLPHIN], 3 AUGUST 1708

from Letters, wch they basely shew'd About here, of wch I formerly hinted Something to yor Ldpp both of things and Persons.[7]

Now They Talk Loudly of a Letter from[a] the Earl of Orkeney From ye Army wch Reflects Upon ye D of Marlbro'[b] wth Respect to Delays Since the Battail;[8] and in wch They Say, there is an Expression to This Purpose, That at last there is a Detachmt Sent to ye Frontiers, of About 15000 Men, but if it had been 5000 More, he Could have gone to ye Gates of Paris wth them, But Complains they Are both too few, and Sent too late; I am in hope to Obtain all ye p[er]ticulars of the Letter, for they Make Nothing a Secret here, and this Insolence, My Ld, Makes ye people here Apprehensiv; for while I have assur'd yor Ldpp they have no Intrest, and Are Not beloved here, it is a Very just Consequence, that while Their Success is in prospect, they will be feared in proporcon, and Indeed ye honestest and best and Most Sencible people here, Are affraid of them, and Very Uneasy About them.

On ye Other hand, it is Not Very Easy to Express to yor Ldpp, what Use They Make of this Letter, and How they Vallue themselves Upon it; And I am Confident (According to what I formerly Noted to yor Ldpp of that Gent. Upon whom[c] They Depend Very Much for[d] Makeing a Party by him in ye Army) — I Say I am Confident they shall Never want a Missrepresenter of his Graces[9] proceedings On Every Occasion, — This I thot Very Proper to Lay before yor Ldpps, for his Graces p[er]ticular Service.

They Made Their Cavils at ye Victory[10] a Great while Their shift, and Now that grows stale, Now they Are Raiseing Excepcons to ye Conduct of ye Duke, and both Carry On ye Same Cause.

And here My Ld I Crave Leav to Offer yor Ldpp Another Observacon Purely My Own, and yor Ldpp will be judge whether it be just or Not. It Seems at This Time My Lord Very prejudicall, that The public News Men, Perticularly ye Dayly Courant, and ye Post boye, and a post script by the flyeing post,[11] Are Suffred to Translate ye Blusters and Form'd storys, wch the Paris Gazette, the Mercure Gallant, and Gazette a la Main, spread Over the world.[12]

---

[a] from] *following illegible word cancelled*
[b] Marlbro'] 'Marlbro:' *in MS; colon omitted in this edition*
[c] Upon whom] *interlined; the caret indicating the insertion point precedes the full stop in MS*
[d] for] *interlined above cancelled word* 'Upon'

DEFOE TO [EARL OF GODOLPHIN], 3 AUGUST 1708

Without Question My Lord, it would be of No little Use, if a True Accot of Things as we have them, Could be allowed to be printed in Paris, and it is Most Certainly of Use to them, that ye Glosses they put on their Accons, and wch Serve to Delude and Hoodwink their Own people, should be spread Among us; where they want Not Emissarys to Make a Use of them, Pernicous Enough to ye publick peace.

I Remember Some yeares ago an Attempt was Made to Translate ye Paris Gazette, and I was Offred an Annuall Sume to do it, but it was Suppresst by the Governmt;[13] Now My Ld yor Ldpp will allow, that ye Governmt in Vain Suppresst the publicacon of that paper, if ye Dayly Courant shall in Every paper Translate Such paragraphs as Serv their Cause; — for ye Author and proprietors of that paper Are known to be of that Party.[14]

If it be Objected that those papers Can Not be Suppresst, I shall presume to Say of my Own knowledge — They are a Club of 20 Booksellers, who are Concern'd in that paper, and whose Aim is ye Gain of it, and if mr Secretary[15] does but Send for ye Author, and Reprimand him for ye printing the French News, and Threatn him,[16] Tho' they will not Refrain in Respect to ye Governmt, they will for Fear of prosecucon, which would both Ruine their paper, and Sink ye proffit of it: — and if Once ye Messengr of the press leaves word at ye publishers, that ye Governmt has Ordred him to prevent the publicacon,[a] to prosecute &c, tho' that prosecucon would Not do Much, they would Imediately Submit, from ye Apprehension, and if they did Not it would Ruin their paper.

In One of ye last Flyeing Posts[17] wch I Saw here, They have News from Ghent That all things were Very plentifull and Cheap[b] in ye French Camp, and that their Army Encreased Every Day; — when Our Advices from ye Army at ye Same Time, published, that the Enemy were Very Much streightned, in their quarters & Found it hard to Subsist.

At least my Ld, this makes ye people believ, that ye Governmt, According to The French Mode, Orders wrong Accounts of Things to be spread abroad, and that these are ye Onely True Accots. I Need Not Observe to yor Ldpp what Irreparable Mischiefs this brings

[a] publicacon] *following letter 'w' cancelled*
[b] and Cheap] *interlined*

DEFOE TO [EARL OF GODOLPHIN], 3 AUGUST 1708

Among us here,[a] And how Usefull it is to them,[b] Especally at This Time while a Party Among ye people are So busy Endeavouring to put false Representacons Upon Every public Accon. — I Submitt this Thought to yor L^dpps Observacon and Am

May it Please yor L^dpp
yor L^dpps Most Obed^t
And Faithfull Servt
DeFoe

Edinb. Augt 3. 1708

May it please yor L^dpp

I Humbly Ask yor L^dpps pardon for Offering to Remind yor L^dpp of My former Request; I Confess I Ought Not to be Impacent But ye just Concern wch I have layd before yor L^dpp for a Desolate family, and Considering I have No Advocate but yor L^dpps Meer Goodness to me, these Are powerfull Motives.

I have layn My L^d at ye Pool for Deliverance a long Time,[18] But have Ever wanted the Help Needfull when ye Moment for Cure happend; I Most Humbly Seek yor L^dpps Help: wch with the breath of yor Mouth Can Restore the Disstresses of your faithfull Servant,[19] who shall Ever Dedicate his life, and strength, to yor L^dpps Intrest and Service.

I Am ut supra[20]
DF

Text: Beinecke Library, Yale University Gen. MSS. File 496.[21] *Address*: none. *Endorsed by an unknown hand*: De Foe to the Lord Treasurer Aug: 3: 1708.

[a] here] *interlined; following superfluous semi-colon omitted in this edition*
[b] to them] *interlined*

---

1   *Review*, IX, 319 (7 Apr. 1713). A government press spy's brief report on the *Review* in Nov. 1708 suggests that the ministry's direct links to Defoe were kept secret (William Borrett (d. after 1715) to George Tilson, 16 Nov. 1708, TNA SP 34/10, fol. 143).
2   *Review*, VI, 392 (4 Oct. 1709); 638 (28 Jan. 1710).
3   *My Last*: Untraced.
4   *Proclamacon for a Thanksgiving*: The royal proclamation issued on 20 July 1708 appointed a public thanksgiving for 19 Aug. to celebrate the failure of the French invasion and Marlborough's victory at the Battle of Oudenarde in July. See *Review*, V, 278 (7 Aug. 1708).

DEFOE TO [EARL OF GODOLPHIN], 3 AUGUST 1708

5 *Bar of Tinm͟ᵒ*: Tynemouth. A bar is 'a bank of sand, silt, etc., across the mouth of a river or harbour, which obstructs navigation' (*OED*).

6 *letter ... Baltick*: The details of this letter have not been traced. The Cruisers and Convoys Act of 1708 appointed forty-three ships to protect merchant ships around Britain, including twelve for Scotland. Defoe apparently refers to the Norwich 54, a fourth-rate, 50-gun Baltic convoy (John Hely Owen, *War at Sea under Queen Anne* (Cambridge, 1938), 60; Rif Winfield, *British Warships in the Age of Sail, 1603–1714* (Barnsley, 2010), 307).

7 *Letters ... Persons*: See headnote to Letter 134.

8 *Letter ... Battail*: This letter is untraced. After the Battle of Oudenarde, Orkney voted for an immediate march on Paris. In fact, this was also Marlborough's preference, but he accepted the Austrian and Dutch plan of besieging Lille instead (Marlborough to Godolphin, 15 July 1708, *Marl.–God. Corr.*, 11, 1038). Four years later, in the *Review* for 14 Sept. 1712, Defoe re-called that at this time the ministry's opponents 'made the lightest Things in the World, of the Merit and Services of the Duke of *Mar—gh*, and of the Danger of Removing him, and openly nam'd the Earl of *O—y* for his Successor in the Command, who for Experience, for Conduct, and especially, for the Love of the Army, they cry'd up for his Superiour' (1x, 52).

9 *his Graćes*: Marlborough's.

10 *Cavils at yᵉ Victory*: Defoe criticises those who talked down Marlborough's victory at Oude-naarde in *Review*, v, 261–8 (29 and 31 July 1708); 658 (19 Feb. 1709).

11 *public ... flyeing post*: Defoe had recently tussled with each of these newspapers in the pages of the *Review*. The *Daily Courant* was edited by Samuel Buckley (*c.* 1673–1741), *The Post Boy* by Abel Roper, and *The Flying Post* by George Ridpath (d. 1726). The last two papers were thrice-weekly, appearing like Defoe's *Review* on post days: Tuesday, Thursday, and Saturday mornings. *The Flying Post* issued a supplementary *Postscript* in the evenings on publication days, giving the latest news from foreign mails.

12 *Blusters ... world*: See Marlborough's excoriation of the *Paris Gazette*'s coverage of the Battle of Oudenaarde in his letter to Godolphin of 15 July (*Marl.–God. Corr.*, 11, 1037).

13 *Offred ... Governmᵗ*: No corroborative evidence is known for these claims.

14 *Party*: Buckley was a Whig. For his career, see Michael Treadwell, 'London Printers and Printing Houses in 1705', *Publishing History* 7 (1980), 5–43 (at 17–18). Defoe mocked *The Daily Courant*'s translation of French news in *Review*, 1, 114 (2 May 1704) and 1v, 528 (7 Oct. 1707), and he decried its 'false Reports and Shams' in reporting on France using French sources on 11 Nov. 1708 (v, 455). Defoe and Buckley later cooperated in support of Townsend's ministry (see Letters 259 and 262).

15 *mr Secretary*: Sunderland.

16 *Reprimand ... him*: In 1706 Harley as Secretary had forced Buckley to produce originals of the 'States' letter to the Emperor in Latin, Mr Stepney's speech to the Emperor, and Prince Ragotski's letter to the State in French', all of which had appeared in translation in *The Daily Courant* that year (Samuel Buckley to Harley, 6 Sept. 1706, H.M.C. *Portland MSS*, v111, 245). No evidence has been found to show Sunderland acted against the paper in 1708.

17 *One of yᵉ last Flyeing Posts*: Not seen: probably a *Postscript* to *The Flying Post*, of which issues are more scarce than the actual paper.

18 *layn ... Time*: Alluding to the cripple at the pool in John 5:1–15. Defoe had applied this scrip-ture to himself earlier, in Letter 30.

19 *breath ... Servant*: See John 20:19–22.

20 *ut supra*: 'as above' (Latin).

21 The letter bears the notation 'B2-33' made by William Coxe when he arranged the Blenheim Papers in the nineteenth century. See Letter 134, note 24; H.M.C. *Eighth Report MSS*, 44–5. The MS was sold from the Blenheim estate in 1920 and was purchased by Yale from Charles Boesen in 1947.

140

To Lieutenant-General James Stanhope
8 March 1710

HEADNOTE: James Stanhope, later first Earl Stanhope (1673–1721), was an army officer, diplomat, and Whig MP for Cockermouth. He was made Commander in Chief of the British forces in Spain in 1708 and promoted to Lieutenant-General in January 1709.

Stanhope returned to England in January 1710 and was appointed shortly thereafter as one of the managers in the impeachment of the High Church clergyman Henry Sacheverell.[1] On 5 November 1709, Sacheverell had preached a sermon at St Paul's Cathedral, published later that month as *The Perils of False Brethren, both in Church, and State*. In the sermon, Sacheverell used the occasion of the anniversary of the 1605 gunpowder plot and of William III's 1688 arrival in England to deny that the Revolution was an act of resistance and to allege that the Church remained in danger under politicians who were at best lukewarm in its service and under siege from Dissenters who were actively plotting to subvert it.[2] The sermon sold in phenomenal numbers and its publication gave rise to an extensive pamphlet war.[3] In December, the government resolved to impeach Sacheverell for sedition. The trial, before both Houses of Parliament and two thousand spectators, was conducted in Westminster Hall from 27 February to 23 March 1710. On 28 February, during the trial, Stanhope countered Sacheverell's advocacy of passive resistance by arguing that consent was the basis for government.[4]

From December 1709 to April 1710, Defoe followed these events in the *Review*, which since March 1709 had been appearing in Edinburgh as well as London (that stopped in 1710). He initially argued that Sacheverell's sermons were so obviously noxious they were their own best remedy and could safely be ignored.[5] The impeachment, however, made Sacheverell a *cause célèbre*, and Defoe turned to framing the trial as the definitive contest on the 'Validity of the Revolution' and the 'present Constitution', a chance to have parliament unequivocally endorse the legal limitation of the succession, reject divine right theory, and affirm the toleration of Nonconformity.[6] Defoe had by February come to the position that the prosecution was essential to prevent subversive ideas from prevailing.[7] He also saw the charges against Sacheverell as a belated vindication of *The Shortest Way with the Dissenters*: parliament was finally penalising the incendiary language which Defoe had been pilloried for having mimicked.[8]

With hindsight, Defoe realised that the impeachment backfired spectacularly, turning from a charge against one 'worthless Man' to a fruitless fight against 'a popular Cause' that made it seem like the ministry was acting 'against the Church Interest'.[9] Eventually, the backlash against the Whig ministry for prosecuting

475

Sacheverell turned public opinion in favour of the Tories, as reflected by the ministerial changes and the general election outcome later in 1710.

At the time Defoe wrote to Stanhope, hoping to bolster his evidence for the trial, pro-Sacheverell mobs had terrorised London, tearing down meeting houses in particular, incited by Sacheverell's diatribe against Nonconformists as '*Miscreants Begot* in *Rebellion, Born* in *Sedition, and Nurs'd up in Faction*'.[10] Defoe probably wrote *A Letter from Captain Tom to the Mobb* (March 1710), which chastises this crowd as the first mob to oppose the cause of liberty.[11] Defoe continued to attack Sacheverell in the *Review* after parliament had found him guilty. Defoe took pains to deny the High Tories' claims that Sacheverell's punishment – a three-year ban from preaching and his two offending sermons to be burnt by the common hangman – was moderate and represented a moral victory for the Doctor. He insisted on the symbolic significance of the guilty verdict and ridiculed Tories for celebrating it.[12] Defoe jibed in the *Review* for 1 April 1710 that banning him from preaching the gospel is immaterial because Sacheverell only preaches sedition.[13]

Stanhope appears to have made no use of Defoe's information and not to have cultivated any association. The following January, Defoe defended 'gallant *Stanhope*' after the allies' defeat in Spain.[14] After the Whigs returned to power in 1715, Defoe worked for Stanhope as a double agent, infiltrating the Tory press on behalf of the Whig government.[15]

Sr

As it is My missfortune Not to have The honor to be known to you, So at This Time it May be Some Loss to ye Public Intrest in ye Affair of Sacheverell, which you Are Mannageing, (Pardon me ye Word) With So Much Applause.

I was Moved to Give you This Trouble Sr Upon My being Informed you had Sent for Some Reviews to furnish Something of The Drs Character,[16] But, as I will Not Deceiv you Sr in what I am writeing, So Neither will I in ye p[er]son writeing, and Therefore after asking yor Pardon for ye Rudeness of This I have plainly Subscrib'd my Name.

Nothing Sr has witheld me From blackning and Exposeing This Insolent Priest but A[a] Nicety of honour, That I Thought it Disshonourable to strike him when he was Down, or to fall on, when he had Other Enemyes to Engage;[17] But Since his Defence is Made up of false Suggestions as to his being for the Revolucon,

---

[a] A] *interlined above cancelled word* 'That'

DEFOE TO LT.-GEN. JAMES STANHOPE, 8 MARCH 1710

and his Character is part of his Applause Among the Rabble, and
Perticularly Since you find it Necessary to Represent him Right, to
Those who Are his judges, I Chose Rather to be Impertinent, wch
I ask yor Pardon for, Than That you should Not be let a little way
into his Character, to The Truth of wch I will at any Time Appear
and produce Sufficent Testimoney; at ye Same Time Ruñing the
Venture of The Indignacon both of ye Dr and his Rabble wth which
I am Severely and Openly Threatned.[18]

First Sr as to his Morralls, I do Not Say There Are
Members in yor house[19] who have been Drunk with him
a Hundred Times, And Can Say Enough of That to you;
because I kno' it would be hard to press Gentn to betray
Conversacon, but if you please to Converse wth Mr Duckett[20]
a Member of yor house, Or wth Coll. Oughton[21] of ye Guards
They will (Especally The First) Furnish you Abundantly On
That head, (or at least Can).

Then Sr as to his Favouring the Revolucon, That he has
Drank King James's Health Upon his knees,[22] That he has
spoken So Scandalously of the Government That Some
Strangers have Asked him if he had Taken The Oaths to
ye Queen, and being Answerd by him, That he had, have
Expostulated wth him how it was possible Either That Talking
in That Manner he Could Take ye Oaths, Or That Takeing the
Oaths he Could Talk in that Manner.

And lastly (as to The Revolucon also) I shall Name you Two
persons (Vizt)[a] Samll Eberall of Birmingham[23] and The Minister
of Birmingham, I Think his Name is Smith,[24] but can Come to a
Certain knowlege of the Name. These Can Make[b] proof Even to
Conviccon, That in Their Hearing, He Said wth an Oath in the late
king Williams Reign — He (Sachevrell) Believed that He (The
king) would Come to be De-Witted and that he hoped he should
live to See it.[25]

These words Mr Eberall Affirms he heard him Speak, and will
justifye the fact in his Teeth; And These Things I Thought it My
Duty to Accquaint you of, That you May Make Such Use of Them

[a] (Vizt)] 'Vizt' in MS
[b] knowlege of the Name. These Can Make] interlined

477

as you shall See Cause; If I had the Honor to kno' you Sr I Might Give you larger Accots and if you Think it for yor Service I shall do it when Ever you please.

Asking you Pardon Again for This Freedome

I am

Sr

yor Most Humble
and Obedient Servt
DeFoe

Newington Near Hackney
March. 8. 1709[26]

Text: Kent Archives and Local History Centre, U1590/0140/17 (Figure 7). *Address*: none. *Endorsed probably by Stanhope*: 1709 from England defoe

1 Stanhope was one of six 'managers', along with Spencer Compton (1674?–1743), Sir Peter King (1669–1734), Sir James Montagu, Sir Thomas Parker, and Treasurer of the Navy Robert Walpole (1676–1745).

2 On the Sacheverell affair, see Geoffrey Holmes, *The Trial of Doctor Sacheverell* (1973); Brian Cowan (ed.), *The State Trial of Doctor Henry Sacheverell* (Oxford, 2012); Mark Knights (ed.), *Faction Displayed: Reconsidering the Impeachment of Dr Henry Sacheverell* (Oxford, 2012). Sacheverell's sermon preached at the Derby assizes on 15 Aug. 1709, published in Oct. as *The Communication of Sin*, was also cited as a cause for his impeachment.

3 F. F. Madan, *A Critical Bibliography of Dr. Henry Sacheverell*, ed. W. A. Speck (Lawrence, Kan., 1978).

4 Basil Williams, *Stanhope: A Study in Eighteenth-Century War and Diplomacy* (Oxford, 1932), 123–5.

5 *Review*, VI, 525 (3 Dec. 1709); 533–4 (8 Dec. 1709); 538–9 (10 Dec. 1709). In his ironical *A Letter to Mr. Bisset … In Answer to his Remarks on Dr. Sacheverell's Sermon*, published on 22 Dec. 1709, Defoe rejected Rev. William Bissett's (1669?–1747) criticism of Sacheverell's sermon as pernicious, suggesting that he weakened the highflying cause with his vitriol, so should be thanked by adherents to the Revolution settlement and Hanoverian succession. For Defoe's authorship, see Nicholas Seager, 'Defoe, the Sacheverell Affair, and *A Letter to Mr. Bisset* (1709)', *PBSA* 115 (2021), 79–86.

6 *Review*, VI, 683 (18 Feb. 1710); 652 (4 Feb. 1709).

7 *Review*, VI, 675 (14 Feb. 1710).

8 *A Letter to Mr. Bisset*, 5, 7, 11; *Review*, VI, 574–5 (27 Dec. 1709). Defoe called Sacheverell 'the Foundation of my Destruction' (*Review*, VI, 580 (29 Dec. 1709(E))).

9 *The Secret History of the White-Staff* (1714), *PEW*, II, 266. Having initially thought 'that it was a bad sermon, and that he deserved well to be punished for it', by late Mar. Queen Anne believed 'there ought to be a punishment but a mild one, least the mobb appearing of his side, should occasion great commotions and that his Impeachment had been better left alone' (Burnet, V, 446; Hamilton, *Diary*, 6).

10 *The Perils of False Brethren, both in Church, and State* (1709), 19.

11 *A Letter from Captain Tom to the Mobb, Now Rais'd for Dr. Sacheverel* (1710), 3; cf. *Review*, VI, 705 (2 Mar. 1710); 710 (4 Mar. 1710).

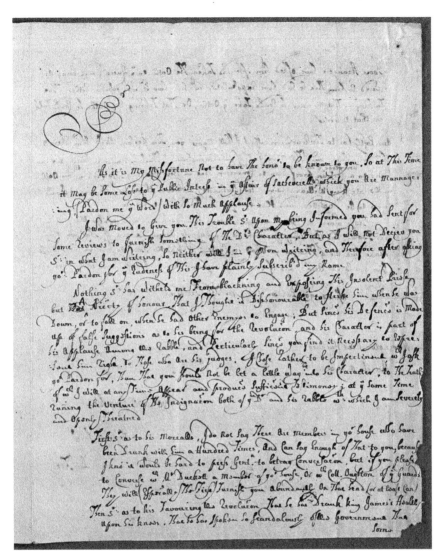

Figure 7 Daniel Defoe to Lieutenant-General James Stanhope, 8 March 1710, Kent History Centre, Maidstone, U1590/0140/17. Reproduced by kind permission of The Board of Trustees of the Chevening Estate

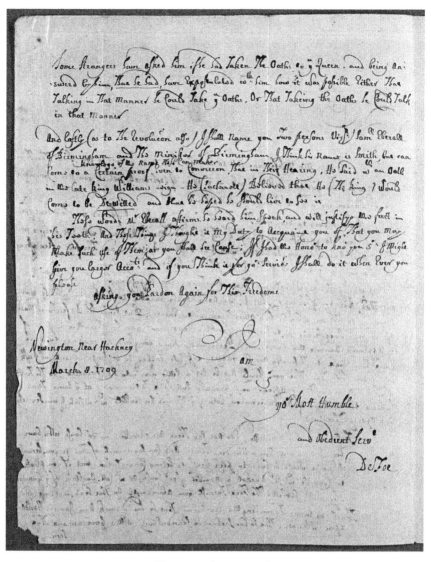

Figure 7 (continued)

DEFOE TO LT.-GEN. JAMES STANHOPE, 8 MARCH 1710

12 *Review*, VII, 7–10 (28 Mar. 1710); 13–16 (30 Mar. 1710).

13 *Review*, VII, 18.

14 *Review*, VII, 587 (25 Jan. 1711).

15 See Letters 258–63.

16 *Sent ... Character*: Sacheverell had cited the *Review* in his defence, aiming to prove the Church remained in danger while such publications attacked its ministers. See Abigail Harley to Edward Harley, 7 Mar. 1710, H.M.C. *Portland MSS*, IV, 534; *Review*, VI, 720–3 (9 Mar. 1710).

17 *Disshonourable ... to Engage*: See Defoe's comment on Sacheverell to this effect in *Review*, VI, 579 (29 Dec. 1710(E)): 'It is against my Temper, and contrary to my known Practice, to beat a Man when he is down'. He said the same of Leslie in *Review*, VI, 269 (2 Aug. 1709). In the *Review* for 9 Mar., one day after this letter to one of Sacheverell's prosecutors, Defoe again claims that he has forborn doing anything to harm his cause. The disjunction between Defoe's public denial of vindictiveness and how he offers to supply Stanhope with evidence leads Backscheider to call this 'a petty, smarmy letter' (*Life*, 266–7).

18 *Threatned*: Defoe comments on threats against his person by the Sacheverell mob, and the precautions he takes when walking the streets, in *Review*, VI, 651 (4 Feb. 1710); VI, 2–4 (preface, late Mar. 1710).

19 *yor house*: the House of Commons.

20 *Mr Duckett*: George Duckett (see Letter 44, note 37).

21 *Coll. Oughton*: Adolphus Oughton (1684?–1736), Lieutenant-Colonel in the first foot guards (*Army Lists*, V, 43), later MP for Coventry, 1715–36.

22 *Drank King James's Health Upon his knees*: 'He has, in his more private Conversation, Drank on his Knees to the Prosperity of a Popish Pretender' (Defoe, *A Word against a New Election*, 6).

23 *Samll Eberall of Birmingham*: Possibly Samuel Eborall (1676–1737) of Balsall, near Solihull.

24 *Smith*: Unidentified.

25 *He ... it*: Defoe explains this in his Oct. 1710 pamphlet *A Word against a New Election*, 9: 'Dr. *Sacheverell* publickly said at *Birmingham*, *as has been proved upon Oath*, that he hoped to see King *William De Witted*, That is, *Torn in pieces, by the Mob.*' It refers to Johan and Cornelis De Witt (see Letter 56). Defoe made the claim against Sacheverell in *Review*, VI, 723 (9 Mar. 1710), in which he named Eborall. In the *Review* for 13 Apr. 1710, Defoe responds to an advertisement taken out in *The Daily Courant* for 8 Apr. 1710 by three men who rebutted Defoe's allegation by denying having heard Eborall say this (VII, 42–3). Sacheverell's defenders countered the accusation, as in [William King], *A Vindication of the Reverend Henry Sacheverell* (1711), 69–72. Defoe repeated the charge in *Review*, IX, 117 (11 Nov. 1712), claiming he has a signed affadavit from the witnesses. Defoe then reproduced Eborall's oath, dated to 6 May 1710, averring that Sacheverell spoke the words '*twelve or thirteen years ago*', in *A Sharp Rebuke from One of the People Call'd Quakers to Henry Sacheverell* (1715), 15–16.

26 *1709*: 1710 new style.

481

141

John Russell to Defoe
14 March 1710

HEADNOTE: The lawyer John Russell of Braidshaw (1672–1759) acted as Defoe's factor in Edinburgh. Fifteen letters addressed from him to Defoe survive in Russell's copybook, in the hand of several scribes, the latest dated 30 October 1712.[1] This, the first, indicates his work on Defoe's behalf in securing the privilege of printing *The Edinburgh Courant*, following the death in January of that newspaper's proprietor, Adam Boig. On 1 February 1710, the Edinburgh town council granted Defoe exclusive rights to the name of the newspaper, setting aside three days of the week on which Defoe's paper would be the only one published.[2] Defoe was already publishing a Scottish edition of the *Review* (since spring 1709) and he later secured the rights to publish another Scottish newspaper.[3] However, only two issues of the *Courant* are extant, those for 20 and 23 Mar. 1710, and the paper seems to have died out at a time when Defoe became immersed in London politics during the Sacheverell trial and its fallout.

Ed^b 14 March <u>1710</u>

Dr Sir

Yoūrs of ye 3^d currant[4] is befor me which indeed wes[5] very acceptable, for I wes affray'd you had met wth unkind treatment^a from Mr Mob:[6] I have been wth the Magistrates anent[7] what you propose & they tell me they cannot^b Grant ane exclusive privilledges as you desyre but if you will choice any three dayes in the week to publish your paper upon^c they will disscharge any others to be printed on these dayes.[8] I refer you to Mr Goodale[9] who will wryte you more fully, all I shall say is^d had ye affair been my oūn I wuld not have presst it more warmly. I have payed Mrs Goodale[10] £5 Ster[11] as you desired me & she brought me her brothers receipt of it; You may forward Any thing you buy for my wife either by land or sea as you think fitt, And if you have occasion

---

^a treatment] *interlined above cancelled word* 'usage'
^b cannot] *following illegible word ending* 'res' *cancelled*
^c upon] *interlined*
^d is] *following word* 'that' *cancelled*

JOHN RUSSELL TO DEFOE, 14 MARCH 1710

of a sure hand by sea I wish you woūld send me two good Canarie barrels[12] of your oūn choiceing And place the price of them wth y[r] cargos to my accompt. You will oblidge me mūch to let me hear from you. My wife gives your lady, you & daughters[13] her service, as I lykewayes doe & when I can serve you have comand with all freedom.

S[r]

Yoūr assured freind and very hūmble

Servant

Text: NLS MS. 25.3.9, fol. 60r–v [scribe's copy]. *Address* (fol. 60v): To Daniell Defoe <u>Esq</u> | att John Mathewes[14] printer in | Little Brittain | London

---

1 For the letters' first printing and discussion, see Backscheider, 'John Russell'. For further biographical information on Russell, see Janet Starkey, *The Scottish Enlightenment Abroad: The Russells of Braidshaw in Aleppo and on the Coast of Coromandel* (Leiden, 2018).

2 W. J. Couper, *The Edinburgh Periodical Press*, 2 vols. (Stirling, 1908), I, 244–6.

3 On 13 Dec. 1710, Defoe contracted with the proprietor of *The Scots Postman*, David Fearne, to publish the newspaper for a year commencing 27 Dec. On 9 Jan. 1711, the Edinburgh town council transferred Fearne's rights to Defoe (NRS RD 4/107, fols. 1129–30, no. 1817).

4 *Yoūrs of ye 3d currant*: Untraced.

5 *wes*: 'was' (Scots).

6 *Mr Mob*: The Sacheverell riots had begun on 1 Mar. 1710. The mob targeted the homes and meeting houses of Dissenters in particular. See Geoffrey Holmes, 'The Sacheverell Riots: The Crowd and the Church in Early Eighteenth-Century London', *Past and Present* 72 (1976), 55–85. Defoe chastised the Sacheverell mob in *A Letter from Captain Tom to the Mobb*, as well as in the *Review* during Mar. 1710.

7 *anent*: 'about' (Scots).

8 *exclusive … dayes*: See headnote. Charles Eaton Burch argues that Defoe had been a frequent contributor to this paper before becoming its proprietor ('Defoe's Connections with the *Edinburgh Courant*', *RES* 5 (1929), 437–40; cf. Backscheider, *Life*, 302, 584 n. 41), but Furbank and Owens conclude this is unproven (F&O, 'Periodicals', 86–7).

9 *Mr Goodale*: Backscheider suggests John Goodale (d. after 1720), professor of Hebrew at the University of Edinburgh, and brother to Hanna Goodale (*Life*, 304).

10 *Mrs Goodale*: Hanna (or Anna) Goodale in the following year became Defoe's factor in Edinburgh (NRS RD 4/109, fols. 462–3). Defoe's son Benjamin boarded with her while a student at the University of Edinburgh (Backscheider, *Life*, 301, 304).

11 *Ster*: Sterling as opposed to Scots; the Scots pound continued as a unit of account after the Union.

12 *Canarie Barrels*: Wine produced on the Canary Islands.

13 *lady … daughters*: See Letter 1, note 16.

14 *John Mathewes*: John Matthews, printer of the 1707 London edition of Defoe's *Caledonia* (1706). See Plomer, 200. In the *Review* for 22 July 1710, Defoe specified that letters for the author could be 'left at Mr. *Matthews's* in *Pilkington Court* in *Little Britain*' (VII, 253).

142

To Thomas Wharton, first Earl of Wharton

7 April 1710

HEADNOTE: Wharton of the Whig Junto, Lord Lieutenant of Ireland, played a prominent role in the prosecution of Sacheverell, leading the Lords' impeachment committee and pressing for the most whiggish interpretation of the Revolution as a lawful resistance of a monarch.[1] He enjoyed the distinction of being the first gentleman in England to raise a troop of soldiers to join William's force in 1688. When in January 1710 Marlborough had asked him 'how far they should proceed' with Sacheverell, Wharton 'answerd in a very high manner, do wth him, my lord? Quash him and damn Him'.[2] Wharton was regularly insulted in the street during the trial.[3]

Wharton is mentioned briefly as '*Whartsky*' in Defoe's *The Dyet of Poland* (1705): he was an opponent of the bills to prevent occasional conformity, so lines up against Nottingham ('*Finksky*') in Defoe's satire.[4] Defoe then praised his statesmanship at greater length in *Jure Divino* (1706) as

> *Vig'rous* in Counsel, and in State-Dispute
> *Swift* to resolve, and *bold* to execute;
> *Fearless* of Parties, *steady* to the Laws,
> With Courage always equal to the Cause;
> *Unbrib'd, unbyass'd*, is his Country's Friend,
> *Enjoys* their Love, and will that Love *defend*.[5]

However, Wharton subsequently came in for a sizeable share of Defoe's criticism for how the Junto undermined the Godolphin–Marlborough ministry in its later years.[6] Like many contemporaries, Defoe considered Wharton irreligious.[7] In *The Compleat English Gentleman*, Defoe lamented the decline of certain 'famous' and 'antient' families including the Whartons, likely because he thought the current Earl (and his brothers) had betrayed their religious heritage from the Puritan movement, and because Wharton's son Philip (1698–1731) became a Jacobite.[8]

Defoe's overture in this letter does not appear to have had much of an immediate result, and Wharton was out of power before the end of the year. During 1709 Defoe stigmatised several Anglican clergymen for ungodliness in a similar manner to his report to Wharton on Cooper of Leeds, including another Yorkshireman, Rev. George Plaxton.[9]

DEFOE TO EARL OF WHARTON, 7 APRIL 1710

My Lord

As This is written from a Sincére Prinćiple of Duty, and Respect to yoᵣ Lᵈpp and a just Conćern for that honest Cause yoᵣ Lᵈpp is So heartily Embark'd in, I hope yoᵣ Lᵈpp will Pardon The forwardness and presumćon of The attempt, tho' you Should Not Accept of yᵉ Hint.

I am Not goeing to Offer to yoᵣ Lᵈpp any Thing that wants Proof or that shuns Suffićent Enquiry. I would Not have Insulted a Person of yoᵣ Lᵈpps Character in that Manner. The Design is Not to Speak in yᵉ Dark, but to assist Truth to Come into yᵉ Light,[10] and Offer Something to yoᵣ Lᵈpp, for yoᵣ Lᵈpps farther and More p[er]ticular Enquiry, and Serviće, and Therefore My Lord I shall Neither Conceal from yoᵣ Lᵈpp the Story, Nor who it is That writes it.

I have My Lord Repeated Importunitys from Some people in yᵉ North, Men of Honesty and Friends to yoᵣ Lᵈpps Intrest, to Accquat yoᵣ Lᵈpp of The following Affair. Their Onely Mistake is that they Suppose I have yᵉ honoᵣ to be known to yoᵣ Lᵈpp, wᶜʰ is Their Error as it is my Missfortune and My Not haveing that honour is yᵉ Occasion of My Makeing So Much preamble to yoᵣ Lᵈpp Contrary to My Custome in yᵉ World, and for wᶜʰ I ask yoᵣ Lᵈpps Pardon.

The Story is This:

There is One Cooper, a Clergye Man of oᵣ Near Leeds,[11] who if Fame Sayes True, is Now or has been Lately, Applying himself to yoᵣ Lᵈpp Either to be Entertaind in yoᵣ Lᵈpps Serviće, or to Obtain yoᵣ Lᵈpps Favour, and Recomendaćon to Some Liveing, Or Some Other Way to be Employ'd or advanćed by, yoᵣ Lᵈpp; And p[er]ticularly it is alleaged that he gets himself Recomended to yoᵣ Lᵈpp as a Low Church Man or a Moderate Man, and as persecuted and Turn'd Out by The Vicar On Accoᵗ of his Moderaćon &c. —

Now My Lord The bussiness of This Letter is To give yoᵣ Lᵈpp a True Accoᵗ of yᵉ Moralls and Manners of This Man, That yoᵣ Lᵈpp May be Inform'd from Unquestioned Authourityes what kind of Person he is; And No body Then questions but yoᵣ Lᵈpp knows what Measures to Take, Either That yᵉ Church May Not be ill Serv'd and Further Reproach't, or yoᵣ Lᵈpps Recomendaćon Dishonour'd, by the Most Scandalous p[er]son alive.

485

DEFOE TO EARL OF WHARTON, 7 APRIL 1710

And My Lord That yor L^{dpp} May Not Depend Upon My Single Authourity I shall Give yor L^{dpp} his Brief Character in ye Wor[l]d:^a I Rec^d it and the p[er]sons shall at any Time be produc̓ed for yor L^{dpps} Farther Satisfacc̓on.

  From Leeds March. 22.

This Scandalous priest, his Name is Cooper, he was Seen in ye Very Act, Debauching a woman On a Sunday Morning, and p[er]ticularly being to Administer ye Sacrament the Same Day, and Did also Actually administer ye Sacram^t in Our Church That Same day (call'd ye Old Church in Leeds). Perjury in Severall Cases can be proved Against him, and that in Severall plac̓es he has been Discarded as a Common Drunkard, and for his being a Common Swearer Our wholl Town will wittness it.¹²

  For these Crymes Our Vicar¹³ Turnd him Out, and Deny'd him his pulpit, Upon wch he is fled to My Ld Wharton for preferm^t, and We are told my Lord has given him hopes of a liveing &c.

  Thus far my Authors. There is More in My Letters, but I presume This is Enough to prevent yor L^{dpps} being Imposed Upon — and This I Thought it My Duty to Lay before yor L^{dpp}. If yor L^{dpp} pleases to hear any More, or that I should Make farther Enquiry about it, in That, or Any Thing El̓ce for yor L^{dpps} Servic̓e I shall Esteem it My Hono^r to Reciev yor L^{dpps} Com̄ands.

    I am May it Please yor L^{dpp}
     yor L^{dpps} Most Humble and Obedient Servt
        DeFoe

From Newington Near Hackney
Apr^{ll}^b 7th 1710

Text: Harvard University Library, Houghton bMS Hyde 10.¹⁴ *Address*: none.

^a Wor[l]d] 'l' *omitted*
^b Apr^{ll}] *anterior word* 'Mar' *cancelled*

1 John Oldmixon, *Memoirs of the Life of the Most Noble Thomas, Late Marquess of Wharton* (1715), 70. See Christopher Robbins, *The Earl of Wharton and Whig Party Politics, 1679–1715* (Lampeter, 1992), 241–3; Geoffrey Holmes, 'Tom Wharton and the Whig Junto', in *British Politics in the Age of Holmes*, ed. Clyve Jones (Oxford, 2009), 100–14.
2 Ralph Bridges to Sir William Trumbull, 9 Jan. 1710, BL Add. MS. 72494, fol. 150v.

486

JOHN RUSSELL TO DEFOE, 8 JUNE 1710

3 Abigail Harley to Edward Harley, 2 Mar. 1710, H.M.C. *Portland MSS*, IV, 532.
4 Line 1019, *SFS*, I, 372.
5 Book XII, lines 336–45, *SFS*, II, 354.
6 *The Conduct of Parties in England* (1712), *PEW*, II, 254.
7 See Letter 217.
8 *RDW*, X, 72, 255–6.
9 For Defoe's satire 'Par—n Pl—ton in ye County of York turned inside out' [1709?], see Spiro Peterson, 'Defoe's Yorkshire Quarrel', *HLQ* 19 (1955), 57–79.
10 *Not ... Light*: Matt. 10:27.
11 *Cooper, a Clergye Man of or Near Leeds*: Unidentified. See next note.
12 *Scandalous ... it*: In the *Review* for 1 Dec. 1709, Defoe printed a letter from Yorkshire dated 18 July 1709, which echoes and elaborates on this account of the debauched clergyman (VI, 520). He alludes to the episode in *Review*, VIII, 14 (27 Mar. 1711). In *The Secret History of the October-Club ... Part II* (1711), Defoe discusses a 'Dr. Short A—se of *Leeds*' who hates Dissenters for 'reproaching him with Incest and other Lewdness' but 'pretends to be a Whigg himself, and got himself recommended to my Lord *W——n* for such a one' (38–9). This must be Cooper too.
13 *Vicar*: John Killingbeck (1650–1716), Vicar of Leeds from 1690 to 1715.
14 First published by Wilson in 1830, this letter was auctioned in 1928, at which time it was inserted in a run of the newspaper *The Original London Post, or Heathcote's Intelligence* which carried a serialisation of *Robinson Crusoe* (*Times Literary Supplement*, 16 Feb. 1928, 116).

143

John Russell to Defoe

8 June 1710

HEADNOTE: Russell and the Goodales had successfully secured Defoe's privileges in printing Edinburgh newspapers, mentioned in the 14 March letter. This letter refers to personal and business transactions, as well as payments made and received, indicating 'a Defoe deeply immersed in Edinburgh life'.[1]

Edb 8th June 1710

Sr

I am debter to severall of yours[2] and partilcularlie your last of the [ ].[a] I give you thanks for your care in executing my wifes[3] Comission and doubts not both the China & plate you have sent her[b] will please when they arive here. I have given Mrs Goodale

---

[a] last of the [ ]] *blank in MS*
[b] sent her] *interlined above cancelled words* 'forward by sea & land'

487

JOHN RUSSELL TO DEFOE, 8 JUNE 1710

other[4] £5 as[a] you ordered & taken her recept on your accompt. As for y[e] project anent y[e] copar[5] money I wish it may Succeed & doubts not but it will answer your expectancies[b] but I am inteerly a stranger to that affair.[6] Coūld I doe any thing to forward your design, I would doe it very willingly; I can advyse nothing certain anent y[e] invasion.[7] You doubtles have got accompt of our late false alarm here but it is very probable[c] that pairty are still designing which I hop the wisdome & vigillance of y[e] government will prevent. I have frequently been with the Magistrates anent y[e] newes papers as M[r] Goodale will advise you & parti[cul]arly[d] last week Baillie Broūn[8] came to my chamber and promised befor me to M[r] Goodale if he would get 4 boyes to disperse y[e] printes imediatly as they shall be printed[e] he would authorize & protect them which indeed I thought the most propre way for your advantadge. I wes in y[e] Country Sometyme which prevented my wryteing to you befor this. Pray give M[rs] Defoe & the young Ladyes my wifes and my service which with dutyfull regards to you is all at present from

S[r]

Your very humble serv[t]

Text: NLS MS. 25.3.9, fol. 62[v] [scribe's copy]. *Address*: To Daniell Defoe | <u>Esq</u> London

---

[a] as] *interlined*
[b] expectancies] *reading uncertain*
[c] it is very probable] *interlined above cancelled words* 'no doubt'.
[d] parti[cul]arly] *abbreviation expanded*
[e] shall be printed] *interlined above cancelled words* 'come out'

---

1 Backscheider, 'John Russell', 163.
2 *severall of yours*: All untraced.
3 *wifes*: Russell's second wife, Ursulla Russell, *née* Alexander (1688–1717), whom he married in 1706 (Janet Starkey, *The Scottish Enlightenment Abroad: The Russells of Braidshaw in Aleppo and on the Coast of Coromandel* (Leiden, 2018), 379).
4 *other*: I.e. another.
5 *copar*: An abbreviation of 'copairtnery', Scots for 'co-partnership'.
6 *affair*: Not identified.
7 *invasion*: Defoe alludes to ongoing rumours of an invasion of Scotland in *Review*, VII, 152 (6 June 1710).
8 *Baillie Broūn*: Adam Brown of Blackford (d. 1711), who became Lord Provost of Edinburgh later in 1710 (see Letter 156). He was a member of the Merchant's Company, as was Russell. See Letter 166.

144

To John Dyer

17 June 1710

HEADNOTE: Defoe's proposed truce with the Tory journalist Dyer, whose manuscript newsletter had frequently attacked Defoe in the past six years, came after unrelenting assaults on this rival in the *Review*. On 27 September 1709, Defoe called Dyer 'that unsufferable Traducer of the Government'.[1] He criticised Dyer's coverage of Sacheverell's impeachment and of the supposed persecution of Episcopalians in Scotland.[2] On 9 February 1710, Defoe wrote:

> There is a Gentleman, whom they call Mr. *Dyer* — I have no particular aim at his Person, I neither am acquainted with him, nor design him any Injury: Nor do I think it worth while to say this by way of Retaliation of many Insolencies received from him; he is a Person who has often receiv'd Personal Correction from Gentlemen that he has abus'd, and he knows very well how to take a Dish of Coffee in his Face, or a Cane upon his Surface, decently and like a Gentleman; and of that part of the Gentleman's Character, I need say no more.[3]

Defoe goes on to allege that Dyer panders to people's partisan biases, offering to shape the news to fit the prejudices of its recipients:

> Not that Mr. *Dyer* delights in Lying; No, no, he may be a very honest Gentleman — but he writes such News as will fit the Company; he writes to suit the People he Writes to; and he knows what you like, and as you like it, whether it be true or false, so he writes it, whether it be true or false — And certainly the Man, meerly as a News-Writer, is in the right, for he Sells such Ware as will please his Customers — and if you will be pleas'd with shams you must have them.[4]

Defoe evidently thought this a good time to try to nullify his opponent with a truce, the aim of this letter. Dyer is not mentioned in the *Review* after this point, though Defoe gives an account of his 'small Acquaintance with the famous Mr. Dyer' in his periodical *The Commentator* ten years later that seems to relate to this *détente*. 'Knowing the Man to be a *Whig* in his Heart, and bred a Dissenter', Defoe's Commentator persona asks Dyer why he produces 'a Tory News-Letter', to which Dyer replies that he inherited the newsletter from his master, has a right to sell what his customers demand, and a change of style would alienate his readers. In Defoe's account, Dyer said that he clears £800 a year but would happily write for the Whigs if they would pay him just £600.[5]

Mr Dyer

I have yor Letter.[6] I am Rather glad to find you put it upon ye Tryall who was Aggressor, than justifye a Thing wch I am Sure you can Not Approve, and in this I assure you I am farr from Injuring you, and Referr you to The Time when long Since you wrott I was fled from Justice, One Samon being Taken up for printing a libell, and I being Then on a Journey, Nor ye least Charge Against me for being Concern'd in it, by any body but yor Letter:[7] — Also Many Unkind p[er]sonall Refleccons[a] on me in yor Letter, when I was in Scotland, On ye Affair of ye Union,[8] and I Assure you when My papers had Not in ye Least Menconed you, and These I Referr to Time and Date for ye proof of.

I mencon This Onely in Defence of My Last Letter,[9] in wch I Said no More of it than to let you See I did Not Merit Such Treatment, and Could Nevertheless be Content to Render any Service to you Tho' I Thot my Self hardly Used.

But[b] to State ye Matter fairly between you and I, as writeing for Differing Intrests,[c] and So possibly Comeing Under an Unavoidable Necessity of Jarring in Severall Cases; I am Ready to Make a fair Truce of Honour wth you, (Viz) That if what Either party are doeing, or Sayeing, that May Clash with ye party we are for, and Urge us to Speak, it shall be done without Nameing Eithers Name and[d] without p[er]sonall Refleccons; and Thus we May Differ Still, and yet preserv both the Christian and The Gentleman.

This I Think is an Offer, may Satisfye you I have not been Desirous of giveing just Offence to you, Neither would I to any Man, however I may Differ from him; and I See no Reason why I should Affront a Mans p[er]son because I do Not Joyn wth him in princiiple. I please my Self wth being ye first proposer of So fair a Treaty wth you, because I believ as you can Not Denye its being Very Honble, So it is not ye less So, in Comeing first from me, who I[e] believ Could Convince you of My haveing been ye first, and ye Most ill Treated — for Farther proof of wch I Referr you to

---

[a] Refleccons] 'Reflecc | tions' *across a line break in MS*
[b] But] *interlined above cancelled word* 'And'
[c] Intrests] *interlined*
[d] and] *interlined above cancelled word* 'or'
[e] I] *interlined*

DEFOE TO JOHN DYER, 17 JUNE 1710

yoᵣ letters, at yᵉ Time I was Threatned by The Envoy of yᵉ king of Sweden.[10]

However Mᵣ Dyer, This is aᵃ Method Which may End what is past, and prevent what is future; and if Refused, the future part I am Sure can Not Lye at my Door.

As to yoᵣ Letter, yoᵣ proposall is So agreeable to me, That Truly wᵗʰout it I Could Not have Taken yᵉ Thing attall, for it would ha' been a Trouble Intollerable both to you as well as me, to Take yoᵣ Letter[11] Every post, first From you and then Send it to yᵉ post house.

Yoᵣ Method of Sending to yᵉ black box,[12] is just what I Design'd to propose, and mᵣ Shaw[13] will Doubtless Take it of you; if you Think it Needfull for me to Speak to him, it shall be Done — What I want to kno', is Onely, the Charge, and that you will ordᵣ it Constantly to be sent, Upon hinting whereof I shall Send you The Names — Wishing you Success inᵇ all things (your Opinions of yᵉ Governmᵗ Excepted)

I am

yoᵣ Humble Servᵗ

DeFoe

Newington June. 17.ᶜ 1710.

Text: BL Harley MS. 7001, fols. 460–1. *Address* (fol. 461ᵛ): To Mᵣ | J Dyer | in | Shoe Lane

ᵃ is a] *interlined*
ᵇ in] *anterior open parenthesis cancelled*
ᶜ 17] *amended from* '16'

---

1 *Review*, VI, 377.
2 *Review*, VI, 574 (27 Dec. 1709); 650 (4 Feb. 1710); 678–9 (16 Feb. 1710).
3 *Review*, VI, 665.
4 *Review*, VI, 666.
5 Defoe, *The Commentator*, no. 13 (12 Feb. 1720), *RDW*, IX, 67.
6 *yoᵣ Letter*. Untraced.
7 *yoᵣ Letter*. Dyer's *News-Letter*. For this episode in 1704, see Letters 21 and 23.
8 *Unkind ... Union*: See Letter 57, note 13.
9 *Last Letter*. Untraced.
10 *yoᵣ letters ... Sweden*: See headnote to Letter 126.
11 *yoᵣ Letter*. I.e. Dyer's *News-Letter*.
12 *black box*: Unidentified.
13 *mr Shaw*: Unidentified.

145

To [Robert Harley]

17 July 1710

HEADNOTE: Defoe's resumption of his correspondence with Harley after a hiatus of almost two and a half years was a momentous step, as it led to four years of his supporting a Tory government, alienating him from the Whigs.

By spring 1710, Queen Anne had long been dissatisfied with her leading ministers. She had no political sympathy with the Junto Whig Lords, and she blamed Godolphin and Marlborough for persuading her to conciliate the Junto with offices, which was hateful to a Queen who treasured her prerogative of appointments.[1] The Junto's leverage was the Whig majority in the House of Commons. However, a groundswell of public opinion favouring the Tories in 1709–10 shifted the power balance. There were several interrelated causes. First, war-weariness caused by taxation levels and a swelling national debt was exacerbated by what Defoe called the 'dear-bought Victory' at Malplaquet in September 1709.[2] Second, the Whigs had pursued a divisive pro-immigration policy towards Protestant refugees from the Rhenish Palatinate.[3] Finally, following their prosecution of Sacheverell, the Whigs' commitment to the Church could be cast in doubt. A spate of 'loyal' Tory addresses to Queen Anne came in from constituencies across the nation.[4] With the Whigs vulnerable, Anne could threaten a dissolution of parliament and call an election, though one was not legally due until 1711. She exercised her new-found freedom nine days after parliament rose on 5 April, replacing the Whig Marquess of Kent as Lord Chamberlain with the Duke of Shrewsbury.[5] Harley worked behind the scenes to secure this appointment. Historians have found it difficult precisely to ascertain Harley's and Anne's ultimate intentions, whether he was to rejoin the existing ministry in some capacity or (as came to pass) form a new ministry to replace it.[6] But there is no doubt the next victim was in both their sights. The 'obnoxious' Sunderland was removed as Secretary of State on 14 June, a measure delayed for so long only while Harley and Anne contemplated his replacement.[7] The choice was William Legge, first Earl of Dartmouth (1672–1750), a Church Tory but 'known to be no zealous party man'.[8] Anne seems to have wanted to rest with this last change, but Harley promptly urged her to remove Godolphin too.[9]

Defoe remained publicly supportive of the ministry. Even in the wake of Sunderland's removal, when he fulminated against 'the Folly, the Divisions, the selfish Principles, the Pride, and the Security of the Party that have had it to Defend', his motivation was to bring about Whig unity rather than their downfall.[10] A month after that, he was back in contact with Harley.

DEFOE TO [ROBERT HARLEY], 17 JULY 1710

Sr

I can Not but Think that Now is The Time to find Out and Improve Those blessed Mediums of This Naçons happyness, which lye between The wild Extremes of all Partys, and which I know you have long Wisht for.

I kno' sr you are blest wth Prinçiples of Peaçe, and Concern for yor Country and a True Tast of its Liberty, and Intrest, which are Now Sadly Embarrast.

My Lot (in wch yor Favour was My Introducçon) has been So Much abroad,[11] That I have had but a Small View of Things; yet I have Room Enough to See and Lament Preposterous Conduct On Every Side;[12] I can Not but hope That Heaven has yet Reserv'd you to be ye Restorer of yor Country by yet bringing Exasperated Parties and ye[a] Respective Mad-Men to Their Politick Sençes, And Healing the Breaches on both Sides which have Thus wounded The Naçon.[13]

If I can be Usefull to So Good a Work without ye Least View of private advantage I Should be Very Glad, and for This Reason I presume to Renew the Liberty of Writeing to you which was Onçe My honour and Advantage and wch I hope I have done Nothing to forfeit.

My Personall Obligaçons to you are Very Great, and Can Not be forgotten by me. It would be a Double honour to Me to have my Gratitude Mixt wth the Serviçe of My Country.

If you please to Admitt a short Conferençe On These heads, That honour to me May at Least Issue in My being Rendred More Able to Guide My Self to ye publick advantage, which is what I Sinçerely Desire to Make The End of all my Accons, and shall[b] Esteem it My Singular advantage to Take Right Measures by yor Direccon.

I am

Sr

yor Very Much Obliged

Faithfull and Obedient Servt

DeFoe

July. 17. 1710.

---

[a] ye] *following words* 'Mad Men' *cancelled*
[b] shall] *following word* 'shall' *cancelled (accidentally repeated)*

DEFOE TO [ROBERT HARLEY], 17 JULY 1710

PS.

If I May have ye hono^r of a line or any Ord^r by yor Servt The bearer shall attend for it as you Shall please to Direct.

Be pleased S^r to Direct it To A Goldsmith as Usuall.

Text: BL Add. MS. 70291, fols. 208–9. *Address*: none.

1 Anne and the Duchess of Marlborough had had a particularly acrimonious quarrel in Oct. 1709, and Marlborough and Anne had clashed over the disposal of the Earl of Essex's regiment in Jan. 1710 (Gregg, *Queen Anne*, 289–96, 300–5).
2 *Review*, VI, 366 (17 Sept. 1709(E)).
3 Daniel Statt, 'Daniel Defoe and Immigration', *ECS* 24 (1991), 293–313.
4 Defoe attacks this addressing campaign in *Review*, VII, 117–20 (20 May 1710); *A New Test of the Sence of the Nation* (1710); and retrospectively in *The Present State of the Parties in Great Britain* (1712), 59–60. *The Modern Addresses Vindicated* (1710) tried to embarrass Defoe by publishing extracts from his *Original Power of the Collective Body of the People of England* (1701) to legitimate the right to petition.
5 Luttrell, VI, 570. Henry Grey (1671–1740) was made Duke of Kent in 1710 as compensation. For Shrewsbury, see Letter 146, note 3.
6 See Geoffrey Holmes, 'Robert Harley and the Ministerial Revolution of 1710', ed. W. A. Speck, *PH* 29 (2010), 275–307; Geoffrey Holmes, 'The Great Ministry' (unpublished typescript, Institute for Historical Research, University of London).
7 Luttrell, VI, 594; *Anne Letters*, 303–4. Defoe praises the outgoing Sunderland in the *Review* for 17 June 1710: he does not offer to dispute the propriety of his removal but insists there is no 'Objection against his Conduct' (VII, 177).
8 Holmes, 254; Burnet, VI, 9.
9 Harley's memorandum for a meeting with Anne on 3 July 1710 said 'you must preserve yr character & spirit and speak to Ld Treasurer. Get quit of him' (BL Add. MS. 70333, section 19).
10 *Review*, VII, 176 (17 June 1710). Two years later, when he was writing in support of Harley's new ministry and being vilified by the Whigs, Defoe wrote that in 1710 he had 'opposed the Change [of ministry] as much, and as long as I could' (*Review*, VIII, 915 (22 July 1712)).
11 *abroad*: I.e. in Scotland during 1708–10.
12 *Preposterous Conduct On Every Side*: Defoe's criticisms of the High Tories – 'a desperate Party … who are in themselves Implacable' – was unrelenting; but he criticised the Whigs for their 'hasty Prosecution' of Sacheverell that 'made him Popular', their internal divisions, and their pride (*An Essay upon Publick Credit* (1710), *PEW*, VI, 60; *Review*, VII, 176 (17 June 1710); *The Present State of the Parties in Great Britain*, 54–7).
13 *Healing … Naćon*: On 8 July 1710, the *Review* stated: 'The Wisest and most Understanding, even of these warm Gentlemen, begin already to Talk of Moderation; and a Third Party that must carry the Balance between the Extreams on both sides; *and there it will go at last*' (*Review*, VII, 223).

494

146

To [Robert Harley]

28 July 1710

HEADNOTE: By late July, Defoe was again writing the *Review* in alignment with Harley's interests. This meant reassuring Whigs that the nation was not about to move to an entirely Tory administration and concomitantly urging that upholding public credit was in the national interest, not merely a party concern. The latter campaign was necessitated by concerns over credit initiated when, after Sunderland's dismissal, 'a group of directors of the Bank of England approached the Queen to request that the existing ministers should be retained, on the grounds that a Tory ministry would not be able to command financial credit for her government'.[1] On top of this, there were rumours of a Whig plan to 'sink the credit of the Government', particularly by refusing to lend to the government as a means of forestalling further changes at Court.[2] Defoe started on his theme in early July by insisting on the stability of the government, including Anne's reassurance to the Bank directors that no further changes were planned.

Sr

Since I had ye honor of Seeing you, I can Assure you by Experience, I find, That Accquainting Some people They are Not all to be Devoured, and Eaten up — will have all ye Effect upon Them Could be Wish't for; Assureing Them That Moderate Councils are at ye Bottom of all These Things, That ye Old Mad Party are Not Comeing in; That his Grace the D of S . . . . . . y[3] and yor Self &c. Are[a] at ye head of This Managemt and That Neither have been Mov'd, however ill Treated, to forsake The Principles you allways Own'd, That Tolleracon, Succession or Union are Not Struck at and They May be Easy as to ye Nacons Libertys. These Things Make Strong Impressions, and Well Improved[4] May bring all to Rights again.

I Wish for an Occasion to Discourse Farther on These heads when yor Leisure will Permitt me That Favour, when I have Also Something to Offer about Ways and Means to prevent ye Ruine of the public Credit; and Raise Things Again in Spight of Some peoples Endeavor to Run them Down; In which if I can do any

---

[a] Are] *interlined*

495

DEFOE TO [ROBERT HARLEY], 28 JULY 1710

Service I shall Think my Self happy. I should Enlarge but Rather Referr it to Discourse, and shall call on yor Servt my Self to Reciev yor Comands as to Time, promiseing My Self when I have That Hono^r Again I shall Not break away So Rudely as I did last.

I am

S^r yor Most Obed^t Servt

DF

July. 28. 1710

Text: BL Add. MS. 70291, fols. 210–11. *Address*: none.

1 Brian W. Hill, 'The Change of Government and the "Loss of the City", 1710–1711', *Economic History Review* 24 (1971), 395–413 (at 395).
2 H.M.C. *Portland MSS*, v, 650.
3 *D of S . . . . . . y*: Charles Talbot, first Duke of Shrewsbury (1660–1718). Like Harley, his background was as an independent Whig but by this point he can best be described as a moderate Tory; he had spoken and voted for Sacheverell. He was appointed Lord Chamberlain in Apr. 1710. He was among the architects of the 1688 Revolution and served as Secretary of State under William III until his retirement on health grounds in 1700. He spent the next six years in Italy but became friendly with Harley upon his return; they shared a conviction that peace with France was necessary (Shrewsbury to Harley, 3 Nov. 1709, H.M.C. *Bath MSS*, I, 197). Shrewsbury remained alienated from the Junto and his appointment alarmed the Whigs (Burnet, v, 454).

In the *Review* for 29 Apr. 1704, Defoe spoke of the Talbots as 'one of the most Gallant, and Antient Families of the *English* Nobility' (I, 107). Shortly after his return to government in 1710, Defoe praised 'the known Honour and Virtue of that Noble Person, his Zeal for his Country, Early Appearing for the Revolution, and Steady Adhering to Her Majesty's Interest, and the Protestant Succession' (*A New Test of the Sence of the Nation* (1710), 55).

However, Defoe's most extensive treatments of Shrewsbury, which are ambivalent or downright hostile, came after Queen Anne's death. In *Minutes of the Negotiations of Monsr. Mesnager* (1717), Defoe depicts Shrewsbury's chicanery in dealing with the French plenipotentiary, Nicolas Mesnager (1658–1714), during the 1711 peace negotiations. In *Secret Memoirs of a Treasonable Conference at S—— House* (1717), Defoe depicts Shrewsbury as 'Monoculus' (he had lost an eye and wore an eye-patch), a well-intentioned but timid politician who conspires with the disaffected Jacobite High Tories after the 1715 uprising: 'Over rating his own Merit ... he rather was thought wise, than was really so'; he is unable to lead the nation, 'not for want of Capacity, so much for want of Application', being characterised by 'Indolence' and 'excessive Love of his own Quiet' (*SFS*, IV, 158).
4 *Improved*: See Letter 15, note 12.

496

JOHN RUSSELL TO DEFOE, 8 AUGUST 1710

147

John Russell to Defoe

8 August 1710

HEADNOTE: Russell reports on various business dealings but also reflects the
Whigs' anxiety that parliament was about to be dissolved and a general election
called. The dissolution became inevitable after Godolphin's dismissal on the very
day of this letter, 8 August, though parliament was not dissolved until 21 September,
by which time Defoe was firmly in Harley's camp.

Ed^b 8th August 1710

Dear Sir

Yours of the 29th past[1] is before me And the bill on M̄r William
Balliaguell[2] for 12..8.. is accepted And when payed shall advysed
you. I ask pardon for my not wryting^a on receipt of the plate^b but
the hurry of the session pleads my excuse. However According
to your desyre I payed to M̄rs Hamiltoun[3] upon her receipt the
ballance of the accompt due by me to you, being £8..5..5 ster; I
return many thanks for your care in my small affairs and shall
be Glade of any opportunity to serve you here. My wife kindly
Remembers madam and you I doubt not but the Kinnary birrels[4]
are weell Chosen. I wish them a safe arrivall here as soon the ale^c
can be shipt of Conveniently. I hop youll mind it as you^d expect a
bottle here when the h. Cch.[5] shall make home too warm for you.
Your reviews on the present state of affaires please exceedingly but
if that party prevaill expect no quarter. I shall be glade to heare from
you anent the disolution of the parl:[6] if your tyme can allow, for we
are mad[e]^e to hope by last post that M̄r Dyers[7] may yet be mistaken.
Pray Remember me kyndly to madam and the young Lady
quhilk, wth my tender respects to you, is all at present from

---

^a wryting] *following words* 'to you' *cancelled*
^b plate] *following word probably* '&c:' *cancelled*
^c the ale] *amended from* 'they all'
^d you] *interlined above illegible cancelled words*
^e mad[e]] 'mad' *in MS*

DEFOE TO [ROBERT HARLEY], 12 AUGUST 1710

S^r

Your assured freind and very

humble serv^t

Text: NLS MS. 25.3.9, fol. 64^r [scribe's copy]. *Address*: To Daniell Defoe <u>Esq</u> | at his house at Newingtoūn

1 *Yours of the 29th past*: Untraced.
2 *Mr William Balliaguell*: Unidentified but mentioned again in Letter 149 and presumably the same man mentioned in Letter 176. He was probably a member of the Ballingall family in Glasgow.
3 *M̄rs Hamiltoun*: Unidentified.
4 *Kinnary birrels*: Canary barrels (see Letter 141, note 12).
5 *h. Cch.*: High Church.
6 *reviews ... parl*: To Defoe's horror, rumours of the impending dissolution grew during July. In the *Review* during July and early Aug., Defoe defended the ministry, opposed the dissolution, and attacked High Flyers. See *Review*, VII, 215 (4 July 1710); 232–3 (13 July 1710); 277 (3 Aug. 1710).
   The Edinburgh *Review* ceased publication in June 1710.
7 *M̄r Dyers*: Copy not seen. Defoe had entered a truce with Dyer (Letter 144), but his discussion of those who spread the rumour of a dissolution in order to help bring it about might reflect on Dyer (*Review*, VII, 232 (13 July 1710)).

148

To [Robert Harley]

12 August 1710

HEADNOTE: Godolphin's dismissal completed what Defoe called 'the greatest Revolution of Affairs' since 1688.[1] Anne had been reluctant to discard Godolphin, but her attempts to reconcile him and Harley proved unsuccessful.[2] Harley had continued to press for the Lord Treasurer's removal.[3] Anne requested Godolphin to break his white staff on 8 August.[4] Defoe praised Godolphin's management of the Treasury even on that day.[5] Defoe later wrote of the ministerial revolution: 'The *Coup de Grace* was given; by dismissing the great Treasurer at once *without the Favour of a hearing*; sending him an Order by the Master of the Horse, that he should break *his Staff*; and with him fell the Administration of the *Whigs* for that Reign.'[6] On 10 August Harley was appointed Chancellor of the Exchequer and the Treasury was put into commission. Harley's fellow Commissioners of the Treasury were all moderate Tories like him: Poulett (as First Lord of the Treasury), Robert Benson (1676–1731), Sir Thomas Mansel, and Henry Paget (1663–1743).

DEFOE TO [ROBERT HARLEY], 12 AUGUST 1710

S^r

I can Not but heartily Congratulate you On ye happy Recovery of yor Hono^{rs} and Trusts in The Governm^t. Her Maj^{tie} is Perticularly just in placeing you in This Staċon, where you had been So Coursly Treated.[7]

It is with a Satisfacċon Sr That I can Not Express, That I See you Thus Establish'd Again; And it was Allways wth Regret That when you Met with ill Treatment I found My Self left and Oblig'd by Circumstanċes to Continue in The[a] Serviċe of yor Enemyes.[8]

And Now Sr Tho' I am Sunk by The Change,[9] And kno' Not yet whether I shall find help in it or No, yet I not Onely Rejoyċe in the Thing, but shall Convinċe you I do So, by Publickly Appearing to Defend and Reconċile Things if possible, to Open the Eys of a wilfully blind and prejudiċ't Party.

In Ord^r to This S^r I shall wait on you in The Evening wth those sheets[10] I shewed you, finished from ye press, and to Lay before you Some Measures I am Takeing to Serve That Honest Prinċiple, wch I kno' you Espouse, at a Time So Niċe, and when Every Man Thinks 'tis in his Power to wound the Government, Thro' the Sides of The Treasury, and to Run Down Their Masters by Running Down The Public Credit.

I Have Two or Three Times Set Pen to Paper to Move you S^r in My Own Case, yet Can Not put on Assuranċe Enough to do it, Believing Also yor Own Generosity, and The former Goodness I have had Such Experienċe of, will Move you in My behalf.

Providenċe Sr Seems to Cast me back Upon you (I write that wth Joy) and Layes me at yor Door, at ye Very Juncture when She blesses you with The Means, of doeing For me, what yor Bounty shall prompt to.

But S^r in Recomending My Self to you, I Would fain have an Eye to yor Serviċe. I would Not be an <u>Invalid</u>,[11] and My hope is, That as you were pleased to Recomēnd Me to Another,[12] As One That Could be Made Usefull, and who it was worth while to Encourage; The Same Argum^t will Move you to Entertain The Man yor Self, Sinċe yor Merit, and The Voiċe of the Naċon, plaċes you in The Same Point, in wch you were pleased to present me to Another.

---

[a] The] *following letters* 'han' *(for* 'hands'*) cancelled*

DEFOE TO [ROBERT HARLEY], 12 AUGUST 1710

I Cease to press you Upon This head — I shall Study to Make my Self Usefull, and Leav The Rest wholly to yor Goodness.

I am

S^r

yor Most Humble & Faithfull Servt

DeFoe

Augt. 12. 1710

Text: BL Add. MS. 70291, fols. 212–13. *Address*: none. *Endorsed by Harley* (fol. 213^v): M^r D: F: Augu: 12: 1710

1 *The Present State of the Parties in Great Britain* (1712), 54.
2 Godolphin to Marlborough, 21 July 1710, *Marl.–God. Corr.*, III, 1575: 'Yesterday 28 [Shrewsbury] told 4 [Halifax] that 42 [the Queen] was resolved to make 38 [Godolphin] and 199 [Harley] agree.'
3 On 5 Aug., Harley wrote to Newcastle that he was about to meet the Queen and that he intended to persuade her that 'it is impracticable 32 (the Queen) and 37 (Lord Godolphin) can live together. He every day grows sourer and indeed ruder to 32 (the Queen), which is unaccountable, and will hear of no accommodation, so that it is impossible he can continue many days' (H.M.C. *Portland MSS*, II, 213).
4 *Marl.–God. Corr.*, III, 1596; *Anne Letters*, 305.
5 *Review*, VII, 284–7 (8 Aug. 1710). See Oldmixon's dubious allegation, purportedly derived from Arthur Maynwaring, that Defoe continued to take money from Godolphin after he switched his allegiance to Harley, and that Defoe wrote an unconvincing excuse to Godolphin for turning against his ministry (Oldmixon, 476).
6 *Minutes of the Negotiations of Monsr. Mesnager* (1717), *SFS*, IV, 45. Like most modern historians, Defoe believed that Harley wanted no further ministerial changes after Godolphin's removal, so the High Tory resurgence was an unintended consequence of the ministerial revolution. His picture of Harley craftily wheedling the Tories rather than making concessions to them is obviously partial (*The Secret History of the October Club* (1711), *PEW*, II, 152–3, 159–62).
7 *Coursly Treated*: Referring to Harley's removal in 1708 (see headnote to Letter 128).
8 *Continue in The Service of yor Enemyes*: Sunderland was Harley's biggest enemy when they shared the Secretaryship of State from Dec. 1706 to Feb. 1708 (see headnote to Letter 96), but Harley's alienation from Godolphin by Feb. 1708 was total (see headnote to Letter 128).
9 *I am Sunk by The Change*: The *Review* for 12 Aug. 1710 makes this point: 'If I have had any Friends, Gentlemen, it is among them you have turn'd out' (VII, 293). Charles Leslie gleefully expected the *Review* to be suppressed and Defoe held to account for sedition now that Tories were in charge (*Now or Never: or, a Project under God, to Secure the Church and Monarchy of England* (1710), 3, 6). In the wake of the election, Defoe was depicted trying to revive a dying man who represents the Whig party in the Tory satirical print 'The Funeral of the Low Church or the Whig's last Will and Testament' (1710). By the end of the year, Defoe was using his Whig credentials to insist upon his integrity while he supported a Tory administration: 'All Men know I serv'd the Old, *now turn'd-out Party*, and, had the Power to dismiss them attended my Suffrage, not a Tory in the Nation had come in their Places, I believ'd the General Security was Establish'd, and dreaded the Change; *what I was, I am*, and shall die, till Truth appears on another Side' (*Review*, VII, 532 (23 Dec. 1710)).
Aside from the politics of the change of government, Defoe later told Harley that Godolphin 'On ye Change left me Desolate w^{t}hout ye Arrear' of his pension (Letter 184).

JOHN RUSSELL TO DEFOE, 22 AUGUST 1710

10 *sheets*: Probably *An Essay upon Publick Credit* (1710).
11 *I would Not be an Invalid*: Perhaps alluding to John 5:1–15 (see Letter 30, note 9; Letter 139, note 19).
12 *you were pleased to Recomend Me to Another*: Godolphin in 1708 (see headnote to Letter 132; *Appeal*, 14–15).

149

John Russell to Defoe

22 August 1710

HEADNOTE: As well as managing Defoe's business affairs, Russell was entrusted with keeping an eye on Defoe's eldest son, Benjamin, now enrolled in the University of Edinburgh, and he increasingly became an intermediary between Defoe and religious and military personnel.

Edb 22 Augt 1710

Sir

My Last the 8th Currant, to which refers this, serves chiefly to advyse of the payt of yoūr bill on Mr Ballianquell mentioned in my last. My servant received ye money last week but I being oūt of toūn coūld not then wryte to you. I wait your orders how to dispose of ye money And if I shall clear wth Mrs Hamiltoūn as you ordereda in your last.[1] My wife kindly remembers Madam and you. Yoūr Son[2] is very well. I am

Sr

Yoūr very humble servt

Mr Blackwell[3] desired me to put you in mind to recomend his bookes lately sent to Lond to any of your freinds

Text: NLS MS. 25.3.9, fol. 64v [scribe's copy]. *Address*: To Dan: defoe | Esq at his hoūse | att Newingtoūn

a ordered] *interlined above cancelled word* 'advys'

501

DEFOE TO [ROBERT HARLEY], 2 SEPTEMBER 1710

1 *your last*: Untraced.
2 *Son*: Benjamin: see headnote.
3 *Mr Blackwell*: Thomas Blackwell (1660?–1728), professor at the University of Aberdeen, author of *Schema Sacrum, or a Sacred Scheme of Natural and Revealed Religion* (1710) and *Ratio Sacra, or An Appeal unto the Rational World, about the Reasonableness of Revealed Religion* (1710). He was one of the ministers appointed by the Church of Scotland to lobby against the 1712 Episcopal Toleration Act. Defoe mentions him as one of the ministers assaulted at the rabble at Old Deer in 1711 (*Review*, VIII, 109 (8 May 1711)). On that event, see Letter 179.

150

To [Robert Harley]

2 September 1710

HEADNOTE: In the *Review* for 26 August 1710, Defoe issued a lengthy personal plea, attesting to his disinterestedness, distase for flattery, public service, and unrewarded deserving: 'I have been now seven Years, under what we call a *Whig* Government; I have not been a Stranger to Men in Power; to Men in Management; I have had the Honour to have it told me, I have serv'd the Government; the Fury of an enrag'd Party, has given their Testimony to it; and I could produce yet greater, but the Man is not alive of whom I have sought Preferment, or Reward.'[1] He states that in urging the nation 'to uphold the publick Credit, notwithstanding the remove of my Lord T—r—', by lending to the government, he is not seeking a place, nor even appealing to the recently appointed Treasury Commissioners: 'It is no court to them or their Office.'[2] This letter indicates that regular payment was being set up for Defoe.

Sr

What you were pleased to Say to me Relateing to my Own Perticular, The last time I had the honour to wait on you, has So much goodness in it, and Especially So Much concern for me, that it Extorts my Acknowlegments, tho' I am a man Entirely Void of Ceremoney; That you will be pleased to Move her Majtie on My behalf Sr I must look upon as an Assurance, That it shall be done; knowing The Queen will Denye Nothing to yor Intercession, Especlly when back't wth Such Argumts as I hope My Case Affords, Such as a Man Entirely Given up to, and I had almost Said Ruin'd in her Majties Service.[3]

DEFOE TO [ROBERT HARLEY], 2 SEPTEMBER 1710

I will Say Nothing of being Capable of Serving, willing, faithfull, and in ye Affair of ye Union Successfull; I leav That Sr to yor kindness in Recomending; If I would Move her Majtie in Any Part of it, Twould be of a wife, and Six Children allmost Grown up, and Perfectly Unprovided for, After haveing been Stript Naked, in That Jayl[4] from whence you Sr were Once pleased to Redeem Me.

What I have Enjoy'd, (And that too had its Originall in yor kindness) has Constantly gone in Expensiv Travelling,[a] Maintaining Usefull Intelligences abroad, family Subsistence, and a little Clearing of Encumbring Circumstances Tho' far from finishing that Unhappy work.[5]

This Sr Makes The Step[6] wch I Menconed to you of Almost half a year past Distress me, More Than I am Willing to Mencon, And Really These Things too Much Dissable ye Very Capascity of Serving Usefully, and is a great Reason why I Move in This Matter wth More Assurance, haveing No Reason Sr to Expect from you any Thing but as it May Render me Servicable to you. Tis wth too Much Experience Sr That I Express to you That ye Anxieties and Impacence of Perplext Circumstances lessen[b] ye Very Capascity of Service, Sink[c] ye Spirits, and leave[d] Neither ye hands Free, or The head Clear, for any Valluable Performance.

I Entreat yor Pardon for This Importunate Writeing; you May Judge Sr of The Importuneing Circumstance, by the Importunity it Self, which you will Easily believ is too Irksome to me, if The Occasion did Not Urge it.

And yet sr, what Ever was ye Necessity, I would Not Press upon yor Goodness, wch has hitherto Allways Prevented me, If I did Not Perswade My Self, That being Once Made Easy, I Might have Some little Merit, to Render ye Queens bounty to Me, and yors Also, Rationall; I would Not be an Invalid,[7] and hope still I May Render you Some Service, That may Save me from ye Scandall of an Unprofitable Servant;[e][8] yet I forbear to promise for my Self, Onely This Sr, That I shall Serv both wth Principle, and Inclinacon; which

---

[a] Travelling] *amended from* 'Travalling'
[b] lessen] *amended from* 'lessens'
[c] Sink] *amended from* 'Sinks'
[d] leave] *amended from* 'leaves'
[e] Servant] *amended from* 'Service'

DEFOE TO [ROBERT HARLEY], 2 SEPTEMBER 1710

I can Not Say has been So Clear to me, Since I have been Out of yoᵣ Service, as it was before, and is Now.

I am Convinc't And Thorowly Assur'd, you Sʳ have in View yᵉ True Intrest of your Country, and Think it an Unaccountable blindness, That hides it From Some, who Ought to See it as well as I; This Made me Apply my Self to you, before I Saw yoᵣ present happy Restoracon in View, or indeed Expected it; which Cleares me of Worshiping yoᵣ Fortunes Rather Than yoᵣ Person; I Perswade my Self Sʳ it shall be in My Power to Assist yᵉ honest, but prejudiced people of both Kingdomes, to kno' Their Intrest, and Their Friends, better Than Hitherto They have done: This I Applye My Self to, wᵗʰ all my Might, and begin to Meet with Unexpected Success; But shall Ever be backward in Magnifying My Own Merit, and therefore I Refrain to Say any More of That.

I have sʳ Since I have Serv'd (as you kno') Established a Generall Correspondence, and at Some Charge Maintain'd it, by which I have a Fixt Intelligence (I May Say) all Over Brittain, But Especally in yᵉ North.⁹ I Confess it Grievs me to Think of Letting it Fall, Because I can Not fail of Rendring it Very Usefull to yoᵣ Service, On Every Occasion, and shall the Next Time I have yᵉ honoᵣ to wait on you, show you a Proof of it.

I Humbly Ask your Pardon for This Long and Pressing Letter. I will No More be Importunate, but Resolving to have my Entire Dependence Upon you, Endeavoᵣ to Convince you That I am Entirely

Sʳ

yoᵣ Faithfull Obedient
and Greatly Obliged Servᵗ
DeFoe

Sept. 2. 1710.

Text: BL Add. MS. 70291, fols. 214–15. *Address*: none. *Endorsed by Harley* (fol. 215ᵛ): Mr Goldsmith Sept: 2: 1710

1 *Review*, VII, 318.
2 *Review*, VII, 319.
3 *Ruin'd in her Majties Service*: Alluding to his precarity while in Scotland in 1707.
4 *Jayl*: Newgate in 1703 (see Letters 4 and 5).
5 *far from finishing that Unhappy work*: I.e. some of his financial debts remain.

DEFOE TO [ROBERT HARLEY], 5 SEPTEMBER 1710

6 *Step*: Not identified.
7 *Invalid*: See Letter 148 for the same phrase.
8 *Unprofitable Servant*: See Letter 13, note 5.
9 *Intelligence ... North*: In the *Review* for 13 Apr. 1710, Defoe refers to his 'Intelligence through-out *England* and *Scotland*' (VII, 40). The 1706 list of intelligence agents (Letter 46) is stronger for the south than the north, but Defoe had since then spent much time in the north and especially Scotland.

151

To [Robert Harley]

5 September 1710

HEADNOTE: During August and September, Defoe continued to support the government's solvency. *An Essay upon Publick Credit* was published around 17 August. It sought to raise public confidence in the nation's finances following Godolphin's removal by disabusing those who believed credit depends on one man alone – 'as if Credit was pinn'd to the Girdle of a Man, or waited at the Door of the House of Commons'. As capably as Godolphin had managed the Treasury, the new ministry would be equally punctilious and honourable: otherwise the Queen would not have appointed them.[1] Godolphin actually expressed similar sentiments.[2] In the *Review* for 15 July 1710, Defoe had, albeit with characteristic equivocation and qualification, stated the opposite: '*CREDIT* ... is AT PRESENT (without Flattery) absolutely Dependant upon the Person of the said Treasurer, tho' at another Time it may not be so.'[3]

Defoe's follow-up, *An Essay upon Loans*, argued that politically motivated boycotts of loans to the government would be pointless as long as the House of Commons continued to vote supplies: 'Keep up but the Credit of Parliament, and let that Parliament find Funds, it is not in the Power of any Party of Men to Stop the Current of Loans, any more than they can Stop the Tide at *London-Bridge*.' People needed the interest from their investments just as much as the government needed the loans.[4] Defoe disguised his authorship of both *Essays* by tussling in them with the *Review*, which remained a decidedly Whig paper.[5]

Backscheider explains that the enclosure to the present letter is an example of Defoe 'acting disingenuously toward Harley'.[6] In it, he opposes the Corporation of Edinburgh's petition to the Queen (April 1710) to construct wet and dry docks at Leith for the purpose of building, fitting, and careening naval and trading vessels. The proposal was met with initial approval.[7] However, Defoe's brother-in-law, Robert Davis, had established himself as a shipbuilder at Leith and the

505

DEFOE TO [ROBERT HARLEY], 5 SEPTEMBER 1710

proposed new facilities would have presented him with stiff competition. As often, Defoe's arguments admit of selfish and public-spirited explanations. No docks were begun at Leith until 1717.

The enclosure has five sections. The first three – 'Of Improvemts in Scotland', 'The Proposall', and 'Of the Advantages of this to Scotland' – are not in Defoe's hand. The last two, on a sheet he labelled 'The Generall Proposall', are in his hand: they are headed 'The State of The Case of Docks &c. at Leith' and 'The advantages of The Firth for Laying Up The ships'.

Sr

I would fain be Rendring you Some Service in Returne for yᵉ favours I dayly Reciev from you, and This Makes me give you Frequent Troubles of This Nature.

I am Not Insensible That to bring a Certain Party of People[8] to a Sence of Things, (Viz)[a] to be Sensible of Their Need of Friends, and to kno' them, as also to kno' how to Use Them, is a Materiall Work, and a Thing which by Degrees May be brought to pass, Tho' it must Not be attempted abruptly and hastily; The people are Out of humour, and Allarm'd, and to speak to Them in yᵉ Public Paper I write, would be to do no good atall,[9] Yet They should be Spoken to; Even just as Solomon Directs of a Certain kind of People, to whom we should <u>Answer</u> and <u>Answer Not</u>.[10]

I am Vain of Saying Sr The first Step I Took, has been Successfull and has done More Service Than I Expected, in wᶜʰ The Town does me too much Honour, in Supposeing it well Enough done to be your Own, I Mean yᵉ Essay Upon Credit.[11]

If you Think it proper I would Offer Another Piece of The Same kind; wᶜʰ I would Call an Essay Upon Loans;[12] in which I Think it May be of Some Service, to Take a Certain people a little off of a Noçon, That They can bring The governmt to do what They please, by Refuseing to Advance Their Money; Layeing No Weight Upon The Advantage The lenders Make, and what Need They stand in of Funds. This Sr I promise My Self shall Tend to lessen yᵉ Vanity of Some people, who still[b] fancy The Governmt Must be obliged to

---

[a] (Viz)] *interlined above cancelled word* 'and'
[b] still] *following letters perhaps* 'pre' *(for* 'presume'*) cancelled*

Change hands Again, Meerly to Oblige Them, if They do but Exert Themselves by keeping back Their Money.

After This S^r I Would Offer <u>an Essay upon Banks</u>[13] in which I would attempt to bring Those Men of Paper, to kno' Themselves a little, by shewing how well ye Government can do without The Bank, and how ill The Bank can do without ye Government. These Things S^r are ye Effects of My Constant Study to Render my Self Usefull, in the Low Sphere in wch I act; and I Humbly Offer y^m for your Approbacon.

Enclosed I Give you The papers I Menconed formerly About Edinburgh, and The proposall as I formerly Layd it before ye Late Lord Treasurer; I Lay Them before you Sr That you May be Rightly Apprised of That Matter, when ye Pick-Poket proposall of a Dock at Leith shall Come to be Debated, and Doubt not you will be Convinc't That my Scheme is Equally of Service to Scotland, and Onely Saves her Maj^{tie} Thirty Thousand Pound in her Pocket; I shall give you farther hints of This kind, when Ever you shall judge it Seasonable.

<blockquote>
I am

S^r

yor Most Humble and Obedient Servt

DeFoe
</blockquote>

Sept. 5. 1710.

Anoth^r paper of Insolent Queries[14] Appears about To day, and a Most Impud^t Ballad[15] — Sure There are printers[16] of These Things and I Fancy I kno' Them too.

Of Improvem^{ts} in Scotland

I Lay it down as a foundation Principle upon wch all the following Proposals will Depend That it is the great Interest of England to study & Promote the Prosperity and Encrease of Scotland.

By the Encrease of Scotland I mean Encrease of wealth and People.

And that is Only to be brought about by Encrease of Trade wch brings home wealth and Encrease of Employment for the People to keep them at home.

The People of Scotland do not fly abroad and help to People all Europe because this Country is not Equally Fruitfull and Habitable wth other Places but because want of employment at home for the People makes it more difficult for them to Subsist and therefore they fly abroad.

If employment for the Poor may be found out and encouragem^t given by raising the Price of Labour and encreaseing Wages, the People will Stay at home, Nay People will flock thither from foreign Parts & Scotland may be made as populous as other Nations.

If the Number of People Encreased, the Consumption of Provissions would Increase, and as the Value of Labour and rate of Labour shall rise the Price of Provissions would Rise and by Consequence land will be Improved and the Estates of Landed men will rise in Proportion.

Improvements Then being Confin'd to these Heads may be Farther Considered:

Improvem^{ts} of Trade	By Navigation and foreign Commerce
	By Manufacturing and Employing the Poor
of Land	By altering the methods of Husbandry in Scotland
	By planting Encloseing & mending the Lands
	By Grafting[17] & Dary keeping a method wch would soon bring Scotland to Plenty & Quite alter the Miserable Lives of the Poor Tenantry

Of all these I have Some thing to offer but in my Present Proposal I Confine my Self to Navall Improvem^{ts}, in which I take upon me to Say Scotland is as Capable of being Improved as any Nation in the world notwithstanding he[r]^a present Deficiency of Materialls.

And wch is still more to the Present Purpose I^b alledge that in this one affair of Navigation The Governm^t of Britain have the

---

^a he[r]] 'r' *omitted*
^b I] *following word* 'allege' *cancelled*

DEFOE TO [ROBERT HARLEY], 5 SEPTEMBER 1710

Greatest opportunity Imaginable to make a Present Immediate advance in the Improveing & encourageing Scotland (viz):[a]

First In Building and Repairing Ships, and Here I cannot but observe that it[b] was a very great mistake in the Commissioners of the Customs in Scotland when they Obtain'd my Lord Treasurers Order to Build Three Small Frigates[18] to Cruise upon the Coast to preserve the Trade, That they should Send for an English builder to Contract for them and then give him leave to goe back into England & build them at New Castle, whereas by a Workman[19] (I carryed down there and) who has Since built them Severall Smaller Boats, it Has appeared it May even Under the Present Discouragem[ts] and Scarcity of Materials be very well Perform'd in Scotland.

Again the Encrease of Building would encourage the Importing Materialls and in Time the Produceing them in Scotland, Particularly Hemp for Cordage & planting Timber for the Work & So make the work Cheap.

But all men kno' that in Holland They have neither Timber nor Iron, Hemp or Plank or Pitch or Tar or any Materialls and Yet that they are the greatest Builders in the World.

And all men kno' That whether it be from Archangell or from the east Country,[20] From Swedeland or from[c] Norway, Scotland Lyes nearer & more Convenient For the Importing Navall Stores Then Holland, Nor do they want the most proper things to export for the Purchase of those Stores, I mean Herrings, and which in its Course would be a Considerable advance to the fishery of Scotland which otherwise I confess I never promised much from. But of these things Hereafter.

In Order to Push This advantageous proposall of Encourageing Scotland to build, fitt out and repair Her Own Shipping, it seems the Government have an Oppertunity to Give an Introduction to it and that wth such Force as shall (tho' it may be Some Charge at First) most Infallibly put Scotland in such a Posture as for ever after to be able to Do it without Help and Perhaps not Build for

---

[a] (viz)] 'viz' in MS
[b] it] following illegible word cancelled
[c] from] following letters 'Scot' (for 'Scotland') cancelled

Her Self only but for Her Neighbours also, and this is most the Substance of my proposall.

The Proposall

The Short of my Proposall is to erect a Yard wth Docks, Store houses, Launches, Wayes and the Like, for building, Laying up, Fitting and repairing of Ships in Scotland, Such as is now at Plymmouth, Portsmouth &c, For the Use of the Navy, and then to appoint a certain Squadron of Her Maj[ties] Ships to have their winter Station and be Laid up there.

It Seem[s][a] Proper Here to examine Three Things:

1 The Occasion of it to England[b] and its advantages Here in Order to make it please the English.

2/ The Practicableness and Charge and in that a further explaining the Particulars.

3 The Advantages to Scotland.

As to England Two Things prove the Occasion or indeed the Necessity of this Proposall:

1) That Since this War with France, The Navall Power of our Enemy Lying to the west of us,[21] it was found So Dangerous to our Trade to have no Port in the west &c, where our Ships might winter, that the Governm[t] was oblig'd at[c] Prodigious expence to erect a Dock and Yards at Plymouth, Tho the place was So[d] improper that the Dock is Cut by force out of a Firm Solid Rock,[22] But without it Our Navall affairs were Perfectly impotent. And if the French were powerfull in the Channell, as Sometimes they were, and Lay between Our Ships and their winter Ports, Our Squadrons Could not come Home but were oblig'd to Lye in the Roads of Falmouth, Plymouth &c and not to be repair'd or refitted and So became Useless for the Next Summer, or if they waited till the Enemy was Retired they Came Home in the Winter and were exposed to Storms and Tempests by which they were Lost and Destroyed, all which is now remydyed by the Yards and Stores being

---

[a] Seem[s]] 's' *omitted*
[b] England] *following words* 'to Please th' *cancelled*
[c] at] 'at at' *in MS*
[d] So] *following letters possibly* 'inc' *(for* 'inconvenient) *cancelled*

DEFOE TO [ROBERT HARLEY], 5 SEPTEMBER 1710

Placed at Plymouth by which we have alwayes a Number of men of war there ready to Protect our Trade and to Join on occasion with the Grand fleet who alwayes come that way.

2/ There was the like want of a Dock &c to the Northward in the Late wars wth the Dutch[23] and for the very Same Reason King Charles the 2nd was So Sencible of it, that Haveing no Port capable of receiveing the men of war farther North than the Humber the King built the Cittadell of Hull and Design'd a Station there for Layeing up a Squadron[24] and we found a Prodigious Disadvantage in the want of it, the Dutch getting frequently between us and our Northern Trade in Such a manner That our Commerce with the Baltique was almost wholly Cut off & our Coal Trade So Stopt that no Ships dared to Stir but wth very Strong Squadrons for Convoy, whereas Had we then Had a Squadron of men of war in the Firth there had been a Retreat for our East Land Fleets and Norway and Russia Fleets, where they would have been protected and at Convenient Times brought Home wth a Strong Convoy.

These are I Humbly Suppose Sufficient precedents to prove the necessity and usefulness of the thing; it is true we all Hope there[a] is no Probability of a Dutch war But we are always to Provide and be in Ready posture for all Events.

The Explaining the Proposall is next wch would require a long Discourse but I shall contract it, reserving a farther explication to a farther Occasion.

By a Station of Men of War in Scotland I mean:

That Such a Certain number of men of [war][b] as the Government Shall think needfull for the Security of our[c] Northern Trade in Time of war Should be appointed to winter in Scotland in Time of peace.

That at Some Proper place in the Firth of Forth (and I am not to Seek for the place) a yard may be Erected wth Dry Docks for repairing, Launches for building and wayes for Graveing and Washing the men of War.

That Offices and Store Houses be built for Layeing up and Secureing the Sails, rigging, ammunition &c for the Said Ships

---

[a] there] *following word* 'there' *cancelled (accidentally repeated)*
[b] [war]] 'men' *in MS*
[c] our] *following word* 'Children' *cancelled*

DEFOE TO [ROBERT HARLEY], 5 SEPTEMBER 1710

with Victualling Offices for provissions that they may be entirely Fitted Out to Sea.

2/ That Navall Stores be furnish'd from the Proper Countryes & Sufficient Quantityes Laid in for all Occasions.

That Rope Walks[25] and all Necessaryes be built and Provided for makeing all Sorts of Cables and Cordage wth Encouragemts for Planting Timber and Hemp Flax &c for Supplyes.

In Short that all things be modell'd according to the Usage of the Navy for the Effectuall furnishing and Supplying about 14 men of war of the[a] fourth and fifth Rate[26] or as many as the Governmt shall appoint and for building or rebuilding as occasion may require.

And above all that it may be in Such a Place in the Firth as if Possible may be Secured from the Insults of an Enemy and in Particular as Cannot be bombarded, for which proposalls Shall be offered when needfull.

Of the Advantages of this to Scotland

It would be very Long to Enter into all the Particular[b] advantages But wthout Enlarging on the Heads they will be Such as these:

1) The Expending and Circulateing a very great Sum̃[c] of money every[d] year in Scotland an[d][e] especially in the first erecting the Yards.

2) The Employing a great number of people in the Necessary[f] Works, Constantly attending an Undertakeing of Such Consequence, Such as Carpenters, Caulkers, Labourers &c about the repairing and building Ships; Carvers, Painters, Joyners, blockmakers, anchor smiths, rope makers and a Multitude of Trades which depend upon the fitting out Ships.

3/ The breeding Seamen and Encourageing them to Stay at Home in Scotland, of which a Certain Number would be always Entertain'd in Pay and the youth of Scotland would have a kind of School to Initiate them into the needfull Arts of Building and

---

[a] the] *following words* '4 &' *cancelled*
[b] Particular] *amended from* 'Particulars'
[c] Sum̃] *anterior word* 'Sume' *cancelled (accidentally repeated)*
[d] every] *anterior word* 'every' *cancelled (accidentally repeated)*
[e] an[d]] 'd' *omitted*
[f] Necessary] *amended from* 'Necessaryes'

DEFOE TO [ROBERT HARLEY], 5 SEPTEMBER 1710

Navigating Ships, The Said men of War being alwayes Mann'd from Scotland.

4) Encrease of Shipping and Trade for Importing the navall Stores for these things and Encrease of business for goods to export.

5/ Consumption of Provissions, encrease of wages to the Poor, encrease of Labour and by Consequence detaining the people at Home, and by all these Improveing the Land.

6./ Security to the Trade of Scotland in Time of War, Such a Strength being kept at their Own door[a] as will be always able to Protect them from Pyrates and Sea Robbers, whereas at this time there is not a Gun Can be fired at an Enemy in all the Firth But all the Shipping there Lyes exposed to every rover and it Seems Something Wonderfull that in all this War the French Have not Swept the whole firth and even burnt the Very Town of Leith which they might Frequently Have done but with 2 men of war and a Bomb Ketch.[27]

The Generall Proposall[b]

The State of The Case of Docks &c. at Leith

The First Proposall Being Made for Docks, yards &c, and The Town of Edinburgh projecting Great Advantages to Themselves, without any View of the public profitt — They Peticon the Queen and Council for Docks, yards &c. in the River or Haven of Leith.

Which Proposall of Theirs being Enquir'd into will be found:

1. Deficent to ye Main proposall of Layeing Up a Squadron of Men of war.
2. Impracticable in its Nature by The Scituacon and Other Circumstances of The place.
3. Calculated Onely for ye private Advantage of ye City of Edinburgh without any View of ye Public Good.

Their Proposall Consists of a Projected wet Dock and Enlargeing The Harbour and Peir of Leith, by which They propose to bring in any of The Men of war to Refitt &c.

---

[a] door] *amended from* 'doors'
[b] The Generall Proposall] *these words, in Defoe's hand, are upside down on the reverse of fol. 221v*

513

DEFOE TO [ROBERT HARLEY], 5 SEPTEMBER 1710

Objeccon:

1. Tis Humbly Suggested That if all This were done, The Port of Leith can Not be Capable of Bringing in a Squadron, and of all The Necessary yards, Buildings, &c. wch are Required to That Purpose; They do Not propose it, Nor is There Room for The work on the spot they Lay out for it.

2. The Expence wch They propose, being at Least 40 or 50 Thousand pound, will Seem to be ill Lay'd Out, Onely for bringing in Now and Then a ship to Refitt, Seeing There is allready Room Enough for all The shipping The place does or Can be Expected to Employ.

3 The few ships of war Requisit to Guard ye Trade in Time of This war can Not be Worth while to Expend So large Sums for Refitting Them; in Time of peace None Are Required And for Layeing Them up, Their proposall is Not Calculated for it.

But Supposeing They would Lay up a Squadron in Scotland, The Port of Leith Can Not be Capable On Sundry Accounts:

1. The Hazard of Bringing Men of war into a Peir, or Narrow Haven, which has allways been Avoided in ye Navy, Upon any Accot whatsoever; and The Perticular Difficulties of The Pier of Leith, with Respect to a[a] Dangerous Bar,[28] shoal water, and Storms of wind &c. Make it On all Accounts too great a hazard for ye Queens ships.

2 All The while They are within ye Harbour and Out of ye Wett Dock They Must Lye a ground at Low Water, wch has on all Occasions been judg'd Inconvenient, and Carefully Avoided in The Navy.

3. The Onely Piece of Ground Practicable for a Wett dock and where it is proposed has These Inconveniences:

1. That being just on ye Edge of ye shore, wch is all a Sand, it is Not probable it can Retaine ye Water But it will Drayn Out with ye Ebb and leave ye ships a ground Every Tide.

2. That Lyeing just on ye Edge of The Firth it is Exposed to an Enemy and May be bombarded at Pleasure.

3. It is believed That it is Impracticable to have a Depth of water to Bring The Queens ships into it.

---

[a] a] *following words* 'Bar and' *cancelled*

DEFOE TO [ROBERT HARLEY], 5 SEPTEMBER 1710

4.[a] But Suppose all These Things Could be Answer'd, This Seems Meerly Calculated for y[e] Advantage of The City of Edinb without any View of y[e] Public Good Since Nature has allready Made a wet Dock of The Firth it Self, above The Queens Ferry; and There can be None Made like it, So That to Make one at Leith, can have no pretence, but to help y[e] City of Edinburgh;[b] which if her Maj[tie] Thinks Fitt to do by Giveing Them fourty Thousand pounds Out of her Pocket, and Letting The Dock Alone, it shall be Much More to y[e] Publick Advantage.

The advantages of The Firth[29] for Laying Up The ships

1. For at Least Eight Mile in Length, From y[e] Narrow Passage as high as Alloway, The Seat of The Earle of Marr,[30] The Channel is Safe, The[c] Ground Good, Land'lockt From Storms and Safe for Rideing The ships.

2. There is a Full Depth of water From Six fathoms to Eighteen fathom at Low water For The breadth in Most places of a Mile, So That y[e] ships have Roome to Wind[31] Upon y[e] flood and Ebb and Ride Clear of One Another in Case of Fire.

3. A Small Charge will Fortifye The Mouth of y[e] Passage at y[e] Queensferry, The Island of Inch Garve[32] Lyeing in The Middle and The Main Channell Not half a Mile Broad On Either Side yet Deep and Safe, in Some places 30 to 40 Fathom water, So That No ships can pass but Must Come Under The Command of The Batterys on both Sides.

4. No Enemy Can Come Near to Bombard Them or to Burn y[e] Storehouses and yards Unless They Bring a land Force to Go on shore and March Round.

Thus The work will be better done and all y[e] Charges Saved.

Text: BL Add. MS. 70291, fols. 216–25. [The letter is fols. 216–17; the enclosure is fols. 218–25.] *Address*: none. *Endorsed by Harley* (fol. 225v): The Perticular[d] Proposall of y[e] Town of Edinburgh stated

[a] 4.] '3.' *in MS*
[b] Edinburgh] *following illegible word cancelled*
[c] The] *following letters possibly* 'Are' *(for* 'Area'*) cancelled*
[d] Perticular] *interlined above cancelled word* 'Generall'

1 *PEW*, VI, 55.
2 Hamilton, *Diary*, 13 (25 July 1710).
3 *Review*, VII, 237.
4 *PEW*, VI, 75.

515

DEFOE TO [ROBERT HARLEY], 5 SEPTEMBER 1710

5 *PEW*, VI, 51, 72. In turn the *Review* pretended to be ambivalent about *An Essay upon Publick Credit* (VII, 529 (21 Dec. 1710)).

6 Backscheider, *Life*, 277–9.

7 James Campbell Irons, *Leith and its Antiquities, from the Earliest Times to the Close of the Nineteenth Century*, 2 vols. (Edinburgh, 1898), II, 146–7.

8 *a Certain Party of People*: Whigs.

9 *to speak ... good atall*: Nonetheless, during Aug. and Sept. the *Review* did aim to reconcile Whigs to the ministerial revolution, assuring them that 'Whig' principles swayed the government whichever party held power.

10 *Solomon ... Answer Not*: Prov. 26:4–5. A favourite allusion of Defoe's, which he often adapts in this idiosyncratic way: *Review*, IV, 249 (7 June 1707); VII, 305 (19 Aug. 1710); VII, 350 (12 Sept. 1710); VII, 514 (14 Dec. 1710); VIII, 925 (26 July 1712); *Moll Flanders, Novels*, VI, 61.

11 *Town ... Credit*: In sending a copy to Wharton in Ireland, Addison wrote on 24 Aug. 1710 that 'the "Essay upon Credit" is said to be written by Mr. Harley' (*Addison Letters*, 232). This idea endured during the eighteenth century (F&O, *Bibliography*, 99). Charles Davenant and Shrewsbury were also suspected of writing it (Downie, *Robert Harley*, 167; F&O, *De-attributions*, 114–15; Hamilton, *Diary*, 17). Defoe himself perpetuated the rumour of Harley's authorship in *The Secret History of the White-Staff, Part III* (1715), 32.

12 *an Essay Upon Loans*: This pamphlet was published on 24 Sept. 1710, its title page advertising it as by the author of *An Essay upon Publick Credit*.

13 *an Essay upon Banks*: No such publication is known, which is also the case for an essay on '*FUNDS*' mooted at the end of *An Essay upon Loans* (*PEW*, VI, 76).

14 *Insolent Queries*: The half-sheet pamphlet named *Queries* (1710), possibly by Arthur Maynwaring, reprinted in *Somers Tracts*, posed a series of questions about how Anne's ministerial changes pleased France, perturbed the allies, and had been engineered by a 'certain person', meaning Harley (*A Collection of Scarce and Valuable Tracts ... of the Late Lord Somers*, 13 vols., ed. Walter Scott (1809–15), XII, 667–70). The Queen saw a copy on 16 Aug. (Hamilton, *Diary*, 14–15). Among the numerous replies, one called *Counter Queries* (1710) is very likely Defoe's. Its questions defend the Queen's right to change ministers, the fiscal capability of the new ministers, and the necessity of upholding public credit. *Counter Queries* is the best candidate for the '100 Queries at 1d½ each' for which the printer John Barber billed Harley 12s.6d., indicating that it was distributed at the new ministry's charge (J. A. Downie, 'Swift and the Oxford Ministry: New Evidence', *Swift Studies* 1 (1986), 1–8).

15 *Impudt Ballad*: Not identified with certainty. Frank H. Ellis assumes it is *The Age of Wonders* (1710), a ballad which lampoons the voice of a Sacheverellite celebrating the recent ministerial changes: hence, Defoe is veiling his authorship of the ballad from Harley (*POAS*, VII, 463). In their de-attribution of that work, Furbank and Owens acknowledge Ellis's points about suggestive parallels between *The Age of Wonders* and Defoe's known writings, as well as the fact that Defoe quoted it twice in the *Review* (F&O, *De-attributions*, 36). However, their objection to the ascription, that the ballad insults Harley, is false, as Ellis subsequently observed, though Ellis also missteps in claiming that Defoe mentions it in this letter as part of a list of his own writings (review of Furbank and Owens, *Defoe De-attributions*, *RES* 47 (1996), 263–6). *The Age of Wonders* may or may not be the ballad referred to here, and either way is or may not be by Defoe.

16 *printers*: On 25 Aug. 1710, Arthur Maynwaring wrote to the Duchess of Marlborough that '[Erasmus] Lewis the undersecretary has taken up the woman that sells pamphlets at Charing-Cross for selling the *Queries*: examined her about the printer and author. She said she knew neither: she sold them in the way of her trade' (quoted in Hamilton, *Diary*, 76 n. 54).

17 *Grafting*: planting.

18 *Lord Treasurers Order to Build Three Small Frigates*: In Jan. 1708, the Godolphin administration approved the proposal of the Scottish Commissioners of the Customs for three sloops for coast patrols (TNA T 17/1, fols. 219–23; Riley, *English Ministers*, 127).

19 *Workman*: Perhaps Robert Davis, Defoe's brother-in-law (Backscheider, *Life*, 278). See headnote.

DEFOE TO [ROBERT HARLEY], 12 SEPTEMBER 1710

20 *east Country*: The Baltic ports of Danzig (now Gdańsk), Elbing (Elblag), and Königsberg (Kaliningrad).

21 *west of us*: At Brest.

22 *Governmt ... Rock*: Defoe describes the construction of the docks at Plymouth in the 1690s in his *Tour thro' the Whole Island of Great Britain* (*TDH*, 1, 260). The expense was calculated at over £67,000 in 1698 (BL Kings MS 43, fol. 143ᵛ). See further John Ehrman, *The Navy in the War of William III* (Cambridge, 1953), 416–27.

23 *Late wars wth the Dutch*: The three Anglo-Dutch Wars (1652–4, 1665–7, 1672–4).

24 *Station there for Layeing up a Squadron*: Defoe mentions this project in his *Tour*, noting that the station was never completed (*TDH*, 111, 111).

25 *Rope Walks*: Rope-making yards, in which horses pulled the rope taut as it was twisted.

26 *fourth and fifth Rate*: Fourth rate ships had fifty to sixty guns on two decks; fifth rates from thirty-two to forty-four guns. These were towards the smaller end of the naval rating system.

27 *Bomb Ketch*: A specialised ship for bombarding a fixed location on land with mortar shot.

28 *Bar*: See Letter 139, note 5.

29 *Firth*: See Defoe's account of the Firth of Forth in his *Tour, TDH*, 111, 176–9.

30 *Alloway, The Seat of The Earle of Marr*: Now Alloa. Fifteen years later, Defoe wrote in the *Tour* about the 'setting up a Wharf and Conveniencies at *Alloway* in the *Forth*' (*TDH*, 111, 203). He records visiting Mar's Wark in Stirling and describes the route from there to Mar's house, Alloa Tower (*TDH*, 111, 208–9). His hope then was that a canal could join the Clyde to the Forth, a project which had to wait until 1790.

31 *Wind*: 'Of a ship: to turn in some direction; e.g. to swing round when at anchor; to lie with her head towards a particular point of the compass' (*OED*).

32 *Inch Garve*: Inchgarvie.

152

To [Robert Harley]

12 September 1710

HEADNOTE: The ministerial changes caused concern in Scotland, because the Church of Scotland mistrusted the English Tories. From London, Defoe worked to allay the concerns of Scottish ministers. He felt the importance of keeping the Kirk easy, especially as he feared other English Dissenters were inclined to foment discontent there. Defoe broached to Harley the idea of his returning to Scotland.

Sʳ

Since I waited On you last I have farther Enquir'd into yᵉ Scots Mission, I hinted to you; and Find it goes forward. yᵉ Gentleman has Signify'd his Goeing to his Congregaċon. The Occasion as I Noted is Purely (So farrᵃ as Appeares) yᵉ affair of yᵉ College.¹

ᵃ farr] *following opening parenthesis cancelled (moved back to before* 'So'*)*

517

DEFOE TO [ROBERT HARLEY], 12 SEPTEMBER 1710

I am sr Very well Assur'd of ye Good Disposicon of ye Ministers of Scotland to ye Queen, and to a quiet peacible behavior, and am Very Sorry to See any Attempts to Infuse Groundless Jealousys into Their heads, Wherefore sr as ye best Service I can Render her Majtie on This Occasion, I shall (if you Approve of it) Apply my Self, to Weaken ye Councils of Achitophell,[2] and preposess the Ministers There, with whom my Intrest[3] I believ is So good, That he shall be able to do Little Mischief.

This I did before in ye Case of mr Callamy, and wth Such Success[a] That to This day, he has Not been able to Maintain a Correspondence There,[4] And This I do, Not to prejudice Them on Either hand, But I have a Double View in it, and both I hope Very honest, and Very Usefull.

First I would prevent Them Makeing the honest poor people in Scotland Uneasy to Themselves, As I Think Our Dissenters here now are, without any Cause.

Secondly, I would prevent Their being Uneasy to ye Government, wch Now God be praisd They are Not, but if Fermented From Hence May be.

I am Really Concern'd, to See Our people Dilligently spread, and Others Eagerly Reciev, ye Grossest Absurdities, by wch They would Make Their Disgusts at ye late Changes appear Rationall; Such as the favouring a French Intrest, and Countenancing The pretender, — Terrifying the poor Ignorant People wth Notions of Popery, and of Persecucon, as if Our Safety was Not in her Majtie, but in her Servants; and The Queen Could Not Govern us, but by Such hands as we lik'd of.

This sr I Apply my Self to Expose, as Ridiculous; and in all ye Correspondence I keep up, wch is Now all Over Brittain, I Dilligently Counter act this folly.[5]

I Relate This Sr Not to Vallue my Self Upon my Service, but to have yor Approbacon of it, That I may Not Ignorantly Or Officously Take Much pains and do No Service.

I kno' ye Gentlemen are busye, Spreading Jealousies Among all the Country People, and I may Trace Some of their Methods too; if to Set ye people Right in Their Nocons, if to prevent The Malignity

---

[a] and wth Such Success] *interlined*

518

DEFOE TO [ROBERT HARLEY], 12 SEPTEMBER 1710

of Naçonall Jealousy, if to keep up in yᵉ Minds of her Majᵗⁱᵉˢ Subjects, Their Zeal and Affecçon to yᵉ person as well as to yᵉ Government of Their Soveraign, be any Serviçe to her Majᵗⁱᵉ, be ofᵃ any Moment,ᵇ I flatter my Self I shall be Made usefull Espeçally in Scotland, and yᵉ North of England.

Matters of Credit, and Oppressing the public affairs, by Refuseing to lend Money and withdrawing the Assistançe Their Duty, as well as Intrest, Demands is the Great Consequençe of These Discontents, and No Doubt is The Great Design in propogateing This Uneasy Temper. To This Sʳ I shall not fail to Applye yᵉ best Remedy I can by Exposing first yᵉ Malliçe, and Then the folly of it.

You See Sʳ in This a Speçimen of Party Fury, and how Difficult it is to Struggle wᵗʰ the follys of Men, but I hope Time and a little Experiençe will Make Our people wiser. I ask yoʳ Pardon for The length of This and am

Sʳ

yoʳ Most Humble and Obedᵗ Servant
DeFoe

Sept. 12. 1710

Text: BL Add. MS. 70291, fols. 226–7. *Address*: none. *Endorsed by Harley* (fol. 227ᵛ): Mʳ Goldsmith Sept: 12: 1710 ʀ Sept: 13:

ᵃ of] *interlined*
ᵇ Moment] *interlined above cancelled word* 'Service'

---

1 *Gentleman ... College*: Probably Joshua Oldfield (1656–1729), Presbyterian minister at Globe Alley, Southwark. His sermon celebrating the Union was published as *Israel and Judah made One Kingdom* (1707). The University of Edinburgh had conferred a Doctor of Divinity degree on him *in absentia* in 1709. He travelled to Scotland in Sept. 1710 with a letter of introduction from the London Presbyterian Daniel Williams (1643–1716) to the University of Glasgow's Principal, John Stirling. Glasgow conferred a degree on him *in eundem* with Edinburgh (Williams to Stirling, 7 Sept. 1710, University of Glasgow Library, MS Gen. 206/104, 206/105).
   There is a legend that Defoe and Oldfield together set up a Presbyterian church in Tooting, Surrey, around 1686 (Backscheider, *Life*, 41).
2 *Achitophell*: The counsellor who deserted David and supported Absalom's rebellion; the undercover Hushai sabotaged Absalom by countering Achitophel's advice. Achitophel ultimately hanged himself (2 Sam. 15–17). It is unclear whether or not Defoe means someone in particular, such as Oldfield. See the comparisons to Achitophel of Robert Spencer, second Earl of Sunderland (1641–1702) in Defoe's *The Consolidator* (1705), *SFS*, III, 83, 86; and see his account of the biblical story in *The Political History of the Devil*, *SFS*, VI, 148.
3 *Intrest*: An anonymous report on the state of religion in Scotland, compiled on 29 Dec. 1710, which was sympathetic to the Episcopalians, alleged that 'Daniel De-Foe, for his good Services

519

DEFOE TO [ROBERT HARLEY], 21 SEPTEMBER 1710

by the Review, has ten shillings Sterling p[er] Annum at least from every Presbyterian Minister, and many Gifts from the Communion and otherwise' (Bodl. MS North a.3, fol. 107ᵛ).

4   *mr Callamy ... There*: Edmund Calamy (1671–1732), Presbyterian minister at Westminster. In 1709, at the invitation of Carstares and with a pass from Secretary of State Sunderland, he had travelled to Scotland for his health but also to establish a 'friendly correspondence' between English Dissenters and the Church of Scotland. Calamy was well received by the most eminent ministers across Scotland and received degrees from several universities, but he confessed to finding some of the Kirk's practices tantamount to 'the Inquisition revived'. See Calamy, *Historical Account of My Own Life*, 2 vols. (1830), 11, 144–219. How Defoe undermined Calamy's influence in Scotland is not clear, but William Dunlop wrote to Carstares on 18 Oct. 1710 telling him that people preferred Oldfield to Calamy, 'thinking him less given to ostentation & vanity' (EUL DK. 1.1⅛, qtd in Anthony David Garland Steers, '"New Light" Thinking and Non-Subscription amongst Protestant Dissenters in England and Ireland in the Early 18th Century and their Relationship with Glasgow University and Scotland' (University of Glasgow PhD, 2006), 100).

5   *I Dilligently Counter act this folly*: See Defoe's *Counter Queries* (1710).

153

To [Robert Harley]

21 September 1710

HEADNOTE: Parliament was dissolved on this day, 21 September. In his aim 'to graft the Whiggs on the bulk of the Church Party', Harley had tried but failed to gain the support of a number of leading Whigs who wanted to keep the old parliament until the following year when an election was mandatory.[1] 'Mr. Harley himself would not let the Tories be too numerous, for fear they should be insolent, and kick against him', Swift noted in early October, 'and for that reason they have kept several Whigs in employments, who expected to be turned out every day.'[2] Many not turned out resigned nonetheless. Defoe always criticised the Whigs for opposing Harley; he believed this gave Harley no choice but to accommodate more High Tories in government.[3] Now employed by the government with a regular, though secret, pension, Defoe prepared to produce propaganda promoting Harley's moderation, designed to create a political balance in parliament; and he proposed touring the nation ahead of the elections.

Sʳ

The Joy I Conciev'd, When you were Pleas'd to Signifye to me That Her Majᵗⁱᵉ has Directed yᵉ Affair in My Favour,[4] Moves Me Sʳ in yᵉ Humblest Manner to Applye my Self to you in Two Cases.

520

DEFOE TO [ROBERT HARLEY], 21 SEPTEMBER 1710

First Sr That ye Sence I have of her Majties Goodness May be Represented in ye best Manner Possible to her Majtie, So, as becomes a Subject, Under ye Strongest Tyes of Duty, and Gratitude.

And Secondly Sr, That you would be pleased to Furnish ye Occasion how I May[a] Render her Majtie Such Services, as May at least Testifye for me That This Bounty is Not wrong Plac't.

I do Not pretend to be Able to Merit So Much Favor yet ye Meanest Capacity can allways do Something. There is a Difference between Not being Worthy, and being Unworthy. I hope I Need Not assure you Sr That I will slip no Opportunity of Service, but Sr It is wholly in yor Self to make me [U]sefull,[b] and as ye Favor Comes by yor Intercession, So ye Power of Serving Depends Upon yor Assistance in Directing.

I Remembr yor Discourse About ye Approaching Dissolucon. I would Humbly Offer it to yor Consideracon Whether you Think I may Not do Some Service in ye Country for a Month or Two, I Mean in ye North, to Argue with, p[er]swade and bring to Their Temper and Eye-Sight a Certain people who are but too Apt to Reciev Impressions from Some here who want both.

I do Not propose it as Matter of Charge. I shall Submitt that to you. I shall Endeavour Rather to be too backward Than too forward on That Account But I humbly Offer it as my Opinion Onely That at This Juncture It May be[c] of More Service Than p[er]haps it would be possible at another Time; I Can Not but Remembr Sr, The Journey I Once went on Such an Occasion, I Mean at ye Last Eleccon, By yor Ordr,[5] In which I had Such Success That I can hardly Wish More upon like Occasion. I Submit it wholly to you Sr and shall Chearfully Obey yor Ordrs in it One way Or Other.

I am

Sr

yor Most Humble and Ob[edt Servt]

[   ][d]

Sept. 21. 1710

---

[a] how I May] *the 'a' interlined and 'I' probably inserted, so* 'how My' *became* 'how I May'
[b] [U]sefull] *MS torn*
[c] be] *interlined*
[d] Ob[edt Servt] [   ]] *MS torn; signature torn out, affecting words above*

JOHN RUSSELL TO DEFOE, 21 SEPTEMBER 1710

Text: BL Add. MS. 70291, fols. 228–9. *Address*: none. *Endorsed by Harley* (fol. 229ᵛ): Mr Goldsmith Sept: 21: 1710

1 BL Add. MS. 70333, section 19. Harley had hoped that allegiance to the Court might persuade Halifax, Somers, Orford, and Cowper to part from Sunderland and Wharton. He told Cowper that 'a Whig Game [was] intended at bottom', but to no avail (*The Private Diary of William, First Earl Cowper, Lord Chancellor of England* (Eton, 1833), 43).
2 *Swift Journal*, 29; cf. Swift to King, 10 Oct. 1710, *Swift Corr.*, 1, 305.
3 See Defoe's reproach for the Old Whigs in *Eleven Opinions about Mr. H——y* (1711), *PEW*, 11, 192; see his account of Harley's desire for no further administrative changes after Godolphin's removal in *The Secret History of the White-Staff* (1714), *PEW*, 11, 268; and see his depiction of the Whigs resolving to hold together and resist Harley's overtures in *Minutes of the Negotiations of Monsr. Mesnager* (1717), *SFS*, 1v, 50.
4 *Her Majᵗⁱᵉ has Directed yᵉ Affair in My Favour.* The first known payment, of £100, to Claude Guilot from secret service accounts followed on 27 Sept. 1710 (TNA T 48/16, fol. 1).
5 *Journey … Ordr.* His tour of England after the 1705 general election (the last election was actually 1708, when Defoe was in Scotland and when Harley was out of office).

154

John Russell to Defoe

21 September 1710

HEADNOTE: This is the last known letter from Russell to Defoe for about seven months, the correspondence resuming on 19 April 1711. Defoe returned to Edinburgh in November 1710 to report on the election and the mood of the nation in light of the political changes in England and renewed rumours of Jacobite activity. He returned to London in early February 1711.

Edᵇ 21 7ber 1710

Sir

Yours of yᵉ 30th past¹ I receav'd at Glasgow, providence haveing call'd me to yᵉ Country upon a very melancholly ocasion, I mean the death & funerall of my dear litle daughᵗ² who dyed of yᵉ Small pox at Pasly;³ since I came to toun I complyd wᵗʰ your orders in paying Mʳˢ Goodale £5ˢᵗᵉ upon her receipt And to Mʳˢ Davies⁴ £5 which I saw mark'd upon yᵉ back of yoʳ Note for £20 as you desir'd us. I return thanks for your care anent yᵉ ale as for yᵉ pickles;⁵ my wife tells me she has latly had occasion to provyd her self of all

522

DEFOE TO [ROBERT HARLEY], 29 SEPTEMBER 1710

these litle things she wants. I notice by yours that on[e]ᵃ of myne, when I writt you fully on receipt of yᵉ china has been misscaryd, which seems strange to me, however I return my hearty thanks for your care in that affair but have no tyme now to send you yᵉ copy of yᵗ letter. My wife gives Mdᵐ & you her Service as doe I.

Dʳ Sir yours

Text: NLS MS. 25.3.9, fol. 65ᵛ [scribe's copy]. *Address*: To Daniell Defoe Esq at his | house at Newingtoun London

ᵃ on[e]] 'e' *omitted*

1 *Yours of yᵉ 30th past*: Untraced.
2 daught: Unidentified, but Russell had nine children by his second wife, three of whom, all male, reached adulthood. All of his children by his first wife died in infancy; he had several further children by a third marriage (Janet Starkey, *The Scottish Enlightenment Abroad: The Russells of Braidshaw in Aleppo and on the Coast of Coromandel* (Leiden, 2018), 379–80).
3 *Pasly*: Paisley.
4 *Mrs Davies*: Probably Mary Davis, *née* Foe (b. 1657), Defoe's sister, married to Robert Davis.
5 *as for yᵉ pickles*: Joseph Button wrote to Defoe in Dec. 1710 that the 'pickles' have been shipped to '[yʳ] Brother Davis' (Letter 166).

155

To [Robert Harley]

29 September 1710

HEADNOTE: In the *Review* for 19 October 1710, Defoe gives short shrift to 'Rumours of Plots, and Contrivances of bringing in the Pretender upon us; landing *French* Troops to Support him, and having a great Party here, to join him'. In differentiating real from 'imaginary Dangers', Defoe talks about letters passed around the street hinting at Jacobite machinations:

> We have several Letters, *the Copies of which are* industriously spread about, and are said to be *found in the Street*, which all tend to Allarm us in this Matter — They are full of Cyphers, and *half Sentences* — Pointing at Persons, and suggesting Dangers — From abroad, and from at home.

Defoe is sceptical of the authenticity of such documents: the plots they reveal are too general, their ciphers fail to conceal salient details, they seem too tentative for

DEFOE TO [ROBERT HARLEY], 29 SEPTEMBER 1710

people truly involved in such conspiracies, and they are mostly concerned with implicating random persons in Jacobite schemes by encouraging the interception of their letters. Defoe does not doubt that there is a plot to bring in the Pretender, but he doubts the Jacobites will show their hand at this time, just as the Tories are gaining the ascendancy. 'For these Reasons, I cannot lay any stress upon these Street-Letters, but look, upon them to be weak, empty Things — And whether design'd to do Mischief, or to do Good, are perfectly uncapable of either.'[1]

Sr

Tho' This is Sooner Than ye Time I had yor Ordrs to attend, I Could Not but give you This Trouble to Cover The Enclosed.[2]

This is Another Street Letter, Said to be Taken up in ye Night. I will not presume to Anticipate yor Thoughts of These Things; To me They Appear Very Naked, and Undresst. The design Appeares Villainous (Viz) To Draw Innocent Persons into Suggested Plots &c. 'Tis the Easyest thing in ye World to Cause Trayterous Letters, to be written to any p[er]son and Then prompt ye Intercepting Them, — The Thing therefore, as it is a Vile and Most Abhorrd Method, So 'tis Withall So foolish, and So ill Set Out, That ye Mischief Seems Taken away, and The Mischievous Design Onely left; — For Surely in Vain is ye Net spread in The Sight of Any Bird.[3]

As to ye Comeing of ye Pretender, The Vain Scarecrow is too Visible: I kno' Not whether if Ever we should wish for him, it should Not be Now; and That an Invasion Might Set us to Rights — Then we should See the falsity of The Clamours, and Noise of a Party, And Many of Those who are Reproacht wth being for him, would have an Opportunity to Wipe off That Scandall, by Discovering The p[er]sons who Really are So: It is True the Experiment Might be Costly, but a knave Discoverd is Cheap bought, Almost at any price.[4]

If This Method be Used wth Success, I Expect Next, Counterfeit Letters and Treasonable papers to be Convey'd into houses, and Then be Searcht for, Letters Sent and Then Intercepted, Innocent Men to be Suspected, and Then to be falsly Accused; and all ye wicked Things That can be, past for Current Law Among us — I hope her Majtie will Take a Right View of these Things, and will protect her faithfull Servants from The Snares Thus Laid for Their Honour and Safety.

524

DEFOE TO [ROBERT HARLEY], 29 SEPTEMBER 1710

There May be other Ends in Spreading These Letters wch without Doors[5] a man can Not See. I must Confess I See nothing in Them to be Apprehensiv of. They Tend indeed to Encrease Jealousys Among The people and Make Them Affraid of One Another, but They are So Weak, So Much Malice wth So little Witt, That I Think There is Not Much to fear from Them.

I kno' Sr you will abate me The Ceremony of Thanks, For ye Favour done Me.[6] The best Acknowlegemts I can Make Either to her Majtie The Originall, or yor Self ye Means, of My Support, is a Vigrous Applicacon to what is ye Duty of Every honest Man (Viz) To promote The Generall Peace, and Upon all Occasions to Persue The best Intrest both of her Majtie and her People, which is The Union of all Their hearts in her Service; This I Take to be the best Method to oblige you and the best Way to shew The Sence I have both of My Duty and Obligacon, and in This I shall Not be wanting.

This is a day of City Hurry. I Could ha' been Very Glad to have Seen A Haughty, Proud, and (I must Own I Think) Empty Man, Defeated; and a Man of Peace, Temper, and Modesty in his Room,[7] but I foresee Right Measures are Not Taken[8] for it, So if it should happen I must Acknowlege my Self Deciev'd.

This is a day when Men of Peace and Pacence, are The Onely Usefull people Either for themselves or ye Governmt; But how few Such are to be found! The Zeal of Parties has Eaten Them up, and Men Seem heated for Their Countries Mischief, as if They were to Feel no share of her Ruin, when it should Come to pass.

I am Prepareing Sr to Reciev yor Commands, and p[er]swade My Self you will Agree in This, that ye Sooner I am There[9] The More Service I May do: The Gentleman of Letters and Degrees[10] who I formerly hinted to you Sr was Goeing Northward is Sett Out.

I am
Sr
yor Most Humble
And Most Obedt Servt
[ ][a]

---

[a] [ ]] *MS torn; signature torn out*

DEFOE TO [ROBERT HARLEY], 29 SEPTEMBER 1710

Sept 29°. 1710.

Text: BL Add. MS. 70291, fols. 230–1. *Address*: none.

1 *Review*, VII, 415–18 (19 Oct. 1710).
2 *Enclosed*: Missing and untraced.
3 *Surely … Bird*: Prov. 1:17. Defoe also alludes to this verse in *Review*, II, 555 (30 Aug. 1705); VII, 123 (23 May 1710); VIII, 782 (6 May 1712); IX, 105 (28 Oct. 1712); *A New Family Instructor* (1727), *RDW*, III, 131.
4 *Experiment … price*: See the *Review* for 19 Oct. 1710, in which Defoe says that from the High Flyers' perspective the Pretender's coming now would be premature and ruin their schemes by uniting loyalists who are currently divided: 'Alas! should *the Pretender come just now*, he would be undone; we are not gone so far yet, but that his Name would reconcile us all — His coming would set us all to Rights, and we should lay aside the Snarling at one another, and fall Unanimously upon him' (VII, 417).
5 *without Doors*: outside of parliament.
6 *Favour done Me*: See Letter 153.
7 *Haughty … Room*: Sir Gilbert Heathcote (1652–1733), Whig MP for London and Governor of the Bank of England, was campaigning to become London Lord Mayor, but the Tories vigorously supported his opponent, also a Whig, Sir Robert Beachcroft (d. 1721). They resented that, after Sunderland's dismissal, Heathcote was one of the four Directors of the Bank who lobbied Queen Anne to make no further ministerial changes, an action considered a gross overstep (Holmes, 174). Harley himself thought it 'a matter of a very extraordinary nature, that private gentlemen … should have the presumption to take upon them to direct the sovereign. If this be so let us swear allegiance to these four men and give them a right to our passive obedience without reserve' (Harley draft to Arthur Moore (*c.* 1666–1730), 19 June 1710, H.M.C. *Portland MSS*, IV, 545). Heathcote felt the backlash but tried to justify the Directors' approach to the Queen in a letter to Newcastle of 30 Sept. 1710 (H.M.C. *Portland MSS*, II, 222). In the event, Beachcroft gained more votes than Heathcote, but the Court of Aldermen disregarded this result and followed tradition in choosing Heathcote, the senior alderman, as Lord Mayor (Luttrell, VI, 635, 637). Within a few weeks, in the parliamentary election, Heathcote lost his seat to Tory candidates.
   When he was defending Godolphin's Whig administration earlier in the year, Defoe had allegorised the Sacheverellites and the ministry as opposed armies with Spanish-sounding names, ranking Heathcote in the latter camp as '*Don Gilberto de Cabaretta Coronna*, a good Officer of try'd Fidelity' (*Review*, VII, 58 (20 Apr. 1710)). His opinion of Heathcote, then, had changed considerably in the last six months.
8 *Right Measures are Not Taken*: Possibly referring to the Tories' belated remodelling of the London lieutenancy to try further to undermine Heathcote. See *HPC 1690–1715*, IV, 315.
9 *There*: In Scotland.
10 *Gentleman of Letters and Degrees*: Probably Joshua Oldfield (see Letter 152, note 1).

526

DEFOE TO [ROBERT HARLEY], 10 OCTOBER 1710

156

To [Robert Harley]

10 October 1710

HEADNOTE: Defoe was confident that he could influence the newly elected Edinburgh city magistrates because he had met most of them in his earlier trips to Scotland. From March to November 1707, he had been a member of the Edinburgh Society for the Reformation of Manners, and he knew Adam Brown and John Duncan well. Duncan had proposed Defoe's membership and in March 1707 worked with him on establishing a correspondence between the London and Edinburgh branches.[1]

Sr

Tho' I am to Attend in ye Evening According to yor Ordr yet I Could not Delay Sending you an Accot (wch I Recd Last Night after I had ye honor of Seeing you), of the Eleccons of Magistrats for ye City of Edinburgh.[2]

Adam Brown[3] Ld Provost Lord Mayor

William Hutchinson
Archibald Cockbourn
John Hay   } Bailies[4]
Thomas Dundass

John Duncan[5] Lord Dean of Guild   { Le Mesme Avec Le Provost
                                      de Merchands au Paris[6]
William Dundass[7] Treasurer or Chamberlain
   I Referr Their Characters Till Evening, Onely hint to you Sr, That they are all but Two My Very Perticular Accquaintances, wch will I believ give Me Occasion of Influencing Them Very Much for her Majties Service.

I am
Sr
yor Most Humble and Obedt [Servt]
[ ]a

Octob.b 10. 1710.

---

a [Servt] [   ]] *MS torn; signature torn out, affecting word above*
b Octob.] *anterior letters* 'Sep' *cancelled*

527

DEFOE TO [ROBERT HARLEY], 10 OCTOBER 1710

Text: BL Add. MS. 70291, fols. 232–3. *Address*: none. *Endorsed by Harley* (fol. 233ᵛ): Edenburgh Octo: 10: 1710

1 C. E. Burch, 'Defoe and the Edinburgh Society for the Reformation of Manners', *RES* 15 (1940), 306–12; EUL MS. Laing III, 339.
2 *Eleccons of Magistrats for yᵉ City of Edinburgh*: It occurred on 3 Oct. 1710 (*Extracts from the Records of the Burgh of Edinburgh, 1701 to 1718*, ed. Helen Armet (Edinburgh, 1967), 201).
3 *Adam Brown*: See Letter 143.
4 *Bailies*: Defoe mentions Cockburn (1692–1735) and Duncan (see below, now the Dean of Guild) as bailies in *Review*, v, 330 (31 Aug. 1708). For Cockburn, see Sir Robert Cockburn and Harry A. Cockburn, *The Records of the Cockburn Family* (1913), 58. For Thomas Dundas (1681?–1762), a woollen draper, see M. I. Dundas, *Dundas of Fingask: Some Memorials of the Family* (Edinburgh, 1891), 40–51; R. P. Fereday, 'Dundas Family of Fingask and Kerse', *ODNB*. John Hay and William Hutchison were merchants.
5 *John Duncan*: See headnote.
6 *Le Mesme Avec Le Provost de Merchands au Paris*: The prévôt des marchands de Paris had charge of the city's supply, taxes, and trade.
7 *William Dundass*: William Dundas (b. 1681, d. after 1737), a merchant.

157

To [Robert Harley]

10 October 1710

HEADNOTE: The cipher list Defoe drew up for Harley in October 1710 indicates that, rather than undertaking an English election tour as Defoe proposed on 21 September, he was destined for Scotland, where elections would take place in November.

Factions in Scottish politics had been complicated by the ministerial revolution in England, although there had as yet been no significant alterations to placeholders in Scotland. At this moment, there were essentially four groups within the Scottish peerage: the Squadrone, allied to the Whig Junto since before the Union; the 'Old Court' interest led by Queensberry, through which Godolphin had administrated Scotland prior to and since the Union; the Episcopalian Jacobites, led by Hamilton, most compatible with the High Tories in England, though they had opportunistically allied with the Whigs in 1708; and finally a motley alliance of politicians from across the spectrum who had come into Harley's interest during 1709 and 1710, ranging from Presbyterian Whigs enticed from the 'Old Court'

DEFOE TO [ROBERT HARLEY], 10 OCTOBER 1710

interest through to Episcopalian Jacobites. Harley's aim was to ensure the return of Scottish peers who would reliably vote with Tories, offsetting the Whig majority in the Lords. The Court produced a list of its preferred sixteen peers and pressurised all peers to vote accordingly.

Defoe's cipher is used in the letters dated 18 and 25 November and 6 December 1710 (Letters 160, 162, and 164). J. A. Downie notes that just nineteen numbers of its 247 are used in the extant letters and that 'the cipher is absurdly easy to crack'. For Downie, it indicates 'that Defoe loved the outward trappings of an intelligence agent and he tended to dramatise his role in Scotland'.[1]

52 America	79 Chancelor	106 Dissenters
53 Admirall	80 Church	107 Douglass[19]
54 Army	81 Common Prayer	108 Duplin[20]
55 Arms	82 College	109 Dunglass[21]
56 Assembly	83 Council	110 Dunbar[22]
57 Abjuraćon	84 Commissionʳ	111 Devill
58 Archbishop	85 Custome house	112 Dublin
59 Aberdeen[2]	86 Castle	113 Dartmouth[23]
60 Argyle[3]	87 Crown	114 Dunkirk
61 Amsterdam	88 Clan	115 DeFoe
62 Annuity	89 Court	
63 Athol[4]	90 Country	116 England
64 Agreement	91 Covenant	117 Edinburgh
65 Absolute	92 Cameronian[12]	118 Equivalent
66 Arbitrary	93 Carstaires[13]	119 Episcopaćy
	94 Callamy[14]	120 Excise
67 Books	95 Campbell[15]	121 Exchequer
68 Bank	96 Cornwarth[16]	122 Eleccon
69 Bishops	97 Carr[17]	123 Ereskin[24]
70 Berwick[5]	98 Crawford[18]	124 Elliot[25]
71 Buckingham[6]	99 Coast	125 Erroll[26]
72 Buchan[7]	100 Clergy	
73 Boyl[8]	101 Correspondeńce	126 Fleet
74 Bruće[9]	102 Conformity	127 Flanders
75 Burleigh[10]		128 Firth
76 Balmerino[11]	103 Dutch	129 Funds
77 Baily	104 Duke	130 Franće
78 Bayliff	105 Dutchess	131 French king

529

DEFOE TO [ROBERT HARLEY], 10 OCTOBER 1710

132 Frazier[27]
133 Forfar[28]
134 Fullerton[29]
135 Faction
136 Fool

137 Generall
138 Glasgow[30]
139 Godolphin[31]
140 Gordon[32]
141 Gazette[33]
142 Guard
143 Germany

144 Harley
145 History
146 Hannover
147 Hamilton[34]
148 Highlander
149 High Church
150 Haversham[35]
151 Huntley[36]
152 Halifax[37]
153 Hopton[38]
154 Haddington[39]
155 Holland

156 Juncto
157 Invasion
158 Inverness
159 Inverlocky
160 Jersey[40]
161 Jacobite
162 Ireland
163 Isla[41]
164 Innerkethin
165 Indies
166 Intelligençe

167 Kirk
168 Kirkubright[42]
169 Kerr[43]
170 Kent[44]
171 Kinoul[45]
172 Knight
173 Knight Errant

174 London
174 Leith
176 Leeds[46]
177 Laws
178 Lords
179 Lieut Generll
180 Loudon[47]
181 Lothain[48]
182 Leven[49]
183 Lockart[50]
184 Lisbone
185 Loan

186 Mint
187 Money
188 Magistrates
189 Ministry
190 Mobb
191 Members
192 Montrose[51]
193 Marlbro'[52]
194 Marr[53]
195 Marchmont[54]
196 Maitland[55]
197 Marshall[56]
198 Madrid
199 Mistress
200 Moderaçon

201 Newcastle[57]

202 Northesk[58]
203 Nottingham[59]
204 News
205 Norman[60]

206 Orkeney[61]
207 Orford[62]
208 Oxford[63]
209 Oaths
210 Offices
211 Oldfield[64]

212 Parliamt
213 Peers
214 Pretender
215 Presbyterian
216 Peaçe
217 Petiçon
218 Party
219 Provost[65]
220 Protestant
221 Printing
222 Press
223 Pulpit
224 Pembrook[66]
225 Portugall
226 Persecuçon
227 Peterboro'[67]
228 Projector
229 Pamphlet
230 Paris
231 Pension
232 Poor

233 Queen
234 Queensberry[68]
235 Query
236 Question

530

DEFOE TO [ROBERT HARLEY], 10 OCTOBER 1710

237 Rabble[69]

238 Rebellion

239 Rogue

240 Roxboro'[70]

241 Rialton[71]

242 Rugland[72]

243 Rochester[73]

244 Rothes[74]

245 Roseberry[75]

246 Rutland[76]

247 Rigby[77]

248 Spain

249 Secret Service

250 Synod

251 Session

252 Supply

253 Succession

254 Sea

255 Son

256 Somers[78]

257 Simple

258 Semple[79]

259 Sunderland[80]

260 Stairs[81]

261 Stuart[82]

262 Sterling

263 Stock Jobber

264 Severity

265 Scotland

266 Tory

267 Treaty

268 Truce

269 Treasury

270 Treasurer

271 Tally

272 Tiveot[83]

273 Tweedale[84]

274 Trimmer

275 Thousand

276 Tumult

277 Union

278 Upperhouse

279 Under Officers

280 Underhand

281 Understanding

282 Urquhar[85]

283 University

284 Uniformity

285 Votes

286 Valiant

287 Vitious

288 Whiggs

289 War

290 Weemyss[86]

291 Wharton[87]

292 Weymouth[88]

293 Window Tax[89]

294 Wiely[90]

295 Webster[91]

296 Williams[92]

297 Watch

298 Yester[93]

299 Yaremouth[94]

Text: BL Add. MS. 70314, section 7. *Endorsed by Harley*: Cipher. D: F: Octo: 10 1710

1 'Defoe the Spy', *British Society for Eighteenth-Century Studies Newsletter* 9 (1976), 17–18. Downie notes that the code was evidently available to the editor of H.M.C. *Portland MSS*, IV, but not to Healey. Defoe also makes several errors in his employment of the code.

2 *Aberdeen*: George Gordon, first Earl of Aberdeen (1637–1720), Lord Chancellor of Scotland in Charles II's reign, was moderately anti-Union but not actively Jacobite.

3 *Argyle*: Argyll came into Harley's interest in 1710, not least because of his rivalries with Marlborough, under whose command he served, and the Squadrone. In Sept. he replaced Marlborough's brother Charles Churchill (1656–1714) as General of the English Infantry in Flanders (Luttrell, VI, 633). His part in the English Court's management of the election of Scottish representative peers in Nov. 1710 provoked Defoe's censure (see Letters 160 and 162, and *Atalantis Major* (1711)). Defoe's dislike of Argyll continued beyond the election. In *The Secret History of the October Club* (1711), Argyll is among a small number of Whigs sufficiently Jacobite to be admissable to the eponymous High Tory group (*PEW*, 11, 175). In the voice of a French emissary, Defoe acknowledged Argyll's military abilities but criticised his politicking and ambition, in *Minutes of the Negotiations of Monsr. Mesnager* (1717), *SFS*, IV, 61.

4 *Athol*: Atholl was collaborating with Harley ahead of the election (Atholl to Harley, 19 Sept. 1710; Kinnoull to Harley, 26 Sept. 1710, H.M.C. *Portland MSS*, IV, 597, 601).

531

DEFOE TO [ROBERT HARLEY], 10 OCTOBER 1710

5 *Berwick*: If not merely the town, then James FitzJames, first Duke of Berwick (1670–1734), illegitimate son of James II by Marlborough's sister, Arabella Churchill (1648–1730). Berwick was a commander in the French army.

6 *Buckingham*: Buckingham was back in government, appointed Lord Steward in 1710, having set aside his personal hostility to Harley (*Wentworth Papers*, 136). Defoe later wrote that Harley turned to Buckingham and Rochester during the ministerial revolution when Whigs rejected his overtures (*The Secret History of the White-Staff, Part III* (1715), 26).

7 *Buchan*: Buchan had been turned out of all offices in 1707 due to his opposition to the Union but was restored as Governor of Blackness Castle in 1710. For Defoe's appraisal of him, see Letters 171 and 178.

8 *Boyl*: Either the Scottish customs commissioner, Glasgow's brother, William Boyle, or the moderate Whig Henry Boyle (1669–1725), who resigned as Secretary of State on 20 Sept. 1710 despite Harley's efforts to recruit him to the reconstituted ministry (Harley to Newcastle, 23 Sept. 1710, H.M.C. *Portland MSS*, 11, 220; Hamilton, *Diary*, 16–17). St John replaced him.

9 *Bruce*: Perhaps John Bruce, whose removal as Customs Collector at Kirkcaldy in July 1710 was currently under investigation by Harley's agents (Riley, *English Ministers*, 196; H.M.C. *Portland MSS*, x, 464); or possibly Sir John Bruce (d. 1711), MP 1707–8, and a Commissioner of the Equivalent (*HPC 1690–1715*, 111, 370–1).

10 *Burleigh*: See Letters 109 and 124.

11 *Balmerino*: John Elphinstone, fourth Lord Balmerino (1652–1736), a Harley ally promised a place or pension for his support in 1710 (H.M.C. *Portland MSS*, x, 329).

12 *Cameronian*: See Letter 64, note 6.

13 *Carstaires*: Probably the most influential minister in the Church of Scotland, Carstares remained a close associate of Harley (see Harley to Carstares, 12 Sept. 1709, *State-Papers and Letters Addressed to William Carstares* (1774), 774–6). See Letter 224.

14 *Callamy*: See Letter 152.

15 *Campbell*: If referring to a particular Campbell (Argyll's clan), probably James Campbell of Ardkinglas (*c.* 1666–1752), MP for Argyllshire, returned in 1710, the most prominent and closely allied to the Duke. Other possibilities include Daniel Campbell of Saltmarket (*c.* 1672–1753), who agreed not to stand in 1710; Sir James Campbell of Auchinbreck (*c.* 1679–1756), who emerged as a rebel against Argyll; Col. James Campbell (1660?–1713), Argyll's uncle, MP for Ayr Burghs but not returned in 1710; and John Campbell (*c.* 1660–1729), MP for Dumbartonshire, returned in 1710. See *HPC 1690–1715*, 111, 444–52.

16 *Cornwarth*: The Jacobite Robert Dalzell (1687–1737), fifth Earl of Carnwath.

17 *Carr*: Perhaps William Carr (see Letter 101, note 9), Whig MP for Newcastle-upon-Tyne from 1690 to 1710, when he was defeated, two Tory candidates being returned for the city (*HPC 1690–1715*, 111, 477).

18 *Crawford*: Crawford of the Squadrone was currently a representative peer. He is praised (as 'Crawlinfordsay') in Defoe's *Atalantis Major*, 16.

19 *Douglass*: Archibald Douglas, first Duke of Douglas (1694–1761), Queensberry's kinsman, seems unlikely on account of age; possibly Hon. George Douglas (1662–1738), MP for Linlithgow Burghs.

20 *Duplin*: George Henry Hay (1689–1758), Viscount Dupplin, 1709–19, and eighth Earl of Kinnoull after 1719. He came under Harley's wing in 1708 and became his son-in-law the following year.

21 *Dunglass*: Apparently the Episcopalian Alexander Home, seventh Earl of Home (d. 1720); Lord Dunglass was a subsidiary title. Defoe classed him among the 'Declar'd profest Jacobites' (Letter 160).

22 *Dunbar*: Robert Constable, third Viscount Dunbar (*c.* 1651–1714), or Sir James Dunbar (after 1676–1724), MP for Caithness-shire (1710–13).

23 *Dartmouth*: The moderate Tory Dartmouth had replaced Sunderland as Secretary of State in June 1710 (see headnote to Letter 145).

532

DEFOE TO [ROBERT HARLEY], 10 OCTOBER 1710

24 *Ereskin*: There are several possibilities. The Episcopalian Sir Alexander Areskine of Cambo (*c.* 1663–1727), Lord Lyon, was a follower of Mar; the Court successfully supported his candidacy for Fifeshire in the 1710 election (Dupplin to Harley, 8 Aug. 1710, H.M.C. *Portland MSS*, IV, 558). James Erskine, Lord Grange (1679–1754), became Lord Justice Clerk in July 1710, second most senior judge in Scotland; he assisted his brother, Mar, in managing the election (Erskine to Mar, 19 Sept. 1710, H.M.C. *Portland MSS*, X, 342–4).

25 *Elliot*: Perhaps Sir Gilbert Elliot, Lord Minto (1650/1–1718), Scottish judge and politician, who had voted against the Union in 1707. In Nov. 1706, he was added to the committee of parliament that examined articles 6 and 8 of the Union Treaty, so Defoe, who advised that committee, may have encountered him then.

26 *Erroll*: Erroll continued as Lord High Constable; he opposed the Union in 1707 and was implicated in the Jacobite invasion in 1708.

27 *Frazier*: The Jacobite Charles Fraser, fourth Lord Fraser (d. 1720).

28 *Forfar*: See Letter 138, note 5. Forfar was in Harley's interest.

29 *Fullerton*: Thomas Fullerton or Foulerton, a Commissioner of the Customs in Scotland, appointed in 1709, whose views on customs Harley gained via Wemyss (Riley, *English Ministers*, 190; Foulerton to Wemyss, 6 Oct. 1710, H.M.C. *Portland MSS*, X, 182).

30 *Glasgow*: Glasgow adhered to Queensberry and the 'Old Court' interest; he continued as Lord Clerk Register but was excluded from the ministry's list of peers in the upcoming election (Mar to Harley, 7 Nov. 1710, H.M.C. *Portland MSS*, X, 349–50). See Letter 160 for Defoe's assessment of Glasgow's political position in the 1710 election.

31 *Godolphin*: For Godolphin's continued support of Whig causes after his dismissal, see Roy A. Sundstrom, *Sidney Godolphin: Servant of the State* (Newark, Del., 1992), 258–60. Defoe continued to praise Godolphin, for example in *Atalantis Major*, 13–14. In *Appeal*, 14 Defoe wrote that he always honoured Godolphin's memory.

32 *Gordon*: A Jacobite conspirator, arrested following the abortive invasion of 1708. See Letter 86, note 4.

33 *Gazette*: *The Edinburgh Gazette*, the official newspaper, published since 1699.

34 *Hamilton*: As early as 8 Aug. 1710, Kinnoull via Dupplin advised Harley that Hamilton was 'not entirely Tory as yet', urging Harley to 'make him of your interest, as being the Scotchman that is by far most capable to do service in the elections' (H.M.C. *Portland MSS*, IV, 558). Harley's first offer of the Lord Lieutenancy of Ireland did not gain him (Mar to Harley, 21 Aug. 1710, H.M.C. *Portland MSS*, X, 331). On 5 Sept., Sir Michael Warton (*c.* 1648–1725), MP for Beverley, warned Harley that Hamilton was angling for a British dukedom in return for his support, and Godolphin realised he was keeping open his options in pursuit of this (H.M.C. *Portland MSS*, IV, 590; Godolphin to Seafield, 13 Sept. 1710, H.M.C. *Seafield MSS*, 210). Though the British dukedom was not given, Hamilton committed to Harley by 24 Sept. 1710 (Hamilton to Harley, H.M.C. *Portland MSS*, IV, 600). Szechi explains that Hamilton was acting in accordance with a concerted Jacobite strategy (64–6).

35 *Haversham*: Haversham came into Harley's interest during 1709 (Haversham to Harley, 5 and 15 Sept. 1709, H.M.C. *Portland MSS*, IV, 524–6).

36 *Huntley*: The Jacobite Alexander Gordon, Marquess of Huntley, second Duke of Gordon after 1716 (*c.* 1678–1728).

37 *Halifax*: Halifax, the one Junto lord still out of office prior to the ministerial revolution, had resumed correspondence with Harley. However, his appointment as envoy at the Hague came to nothing because peace negotiations broke down.

38 *Hopton*: Hopetoun (see Letter 102, note 1).

39 *Haddington*: A Squadrone politician. See Letter 70, note 14.

40 *Jersey*: Edward Villiers, first Earl of Jersey (*c.* 1655–1711), a Tory and Jacobite dismissed as Lord Chamberlain in Apr. 1704. The Queen's hostility toward him prevented Jersey re-entering government in 1710, though Harley used Jersey to enter secret peace negotiations with France during 1710 and 1711 (Gregg, *Queen Anne*, 334–6; Holmes, 201–2; Shrewsbury to Harley, 10 Nov. 1710, H.M.C. *Bath MSS*, I, 200).

533

DEFOE TO [ROBERT HARLEY], 10 OCTOBER 1710

41 *Isla*: Islay entered Harley's interest with his brother, Argyll, and assisted the English Court's management of the 1710 election of Scottish representative peers. For Defoe's hostility towards Islay, see Letter 160.

42 *Kirkubright*: James Maclellan, sixth Lord Kirkcudbright (1661–1730).

43 *Kerr*: See Letter 79, note 11.

44 *Kent*: See headnote to Letter 145.

45 *Kinoul*: See Letter 96, note 25. Viscount Dupplin until 1709, Kinnoull joined Harley's interest in 1709, around the time their children married. Queenberry's confidence that Kinnoull remained loyal to Godolphin and Marlborough was misplaced (Maynwaring to the Duchess of Marlborough, Aug./Sept. 1709, *Duch. Marl. Corr.*, 1, 208–10).

46 *Leeds*: The Tory Thomas Osborne, first Duke of Leeds (1632–1712), was rumoured for a return to frontline politics during the ministerial revolution of 1710, but it did not occur.

47 *Loudon*: Former Secretary of State in Scotland, Loudon was in Harley's interest. See Letter 96, note 22.

48 *Lothain*: See Letter 96, note 29. Lothian, like his nephew and political ally, Argyll, seems to have assisted Harley's interest in the 1710 election.

49 *Leven*: Leven adhered to Queensberry and the 'Old Court' interest; he remained as Commander in Chief in Scotland but was excluded from the ministry's list of peers for the upcoming election (Mar to Harley, 7 Nov. 1710, H.M.C. *Portland MSS*, x, 349–50). See Defoe's assessment of his conduct during the election in Letter 160. Defoe supported Leven's retention of the command in Scotland (*The Secret History of the October-Club ... Part II* (1711), 86), but his removal was inevitable, albeit deferred until 1712 (see Letter 197).

50 *Lockart*: George Lockhart of Carnwarth. Defoe attacked Lockhart, after his election to parliament in 1710, in *The Secret History of the October-Club ... Part II*, 6–7, 68–73. Lockhart criticised Defoe for his pro-Union work (see Letter 60, note 8).

51 *Montrose*: See Letter 68, note 7. Montrose is singled out, as 'the Prince of *Rosymonte*', for extensive praise by Defoe in *Atalantis Major*, 34–6.

52 *Marlbro'*: Marlborough was in the midst of the 1710 military campaign in Flanders when the ministerial revolution took place, and he acceded to the advice of Godolphin and Britain's allies, especially the Dutch, in not resigning as Captain General. The breakdown of peace negotiations in July 1710 precluded Harley and the Queen from replacing him at the head of the Flanders army with the Elector of Hanover. Marlborough was eventually dismissed at the end of 1711. Defoe's positions on Marlborough from the time of Harley's return to the aftermath of his removal are mixed (see headnote to Letter 204).

53 *Marr*: Mar 'was very intimate with Mr. Harley', as Lockhart put it, certainly by the end of 1709 (*Lockhart Papers*, 1, 315; H.M.C. *Portland MSS*, x, 326). He helped coordinate the ministry's management of the Scottish elections in 1710, incurring Defoe's criticism (see Letter 160). After the Hanoverian succession, Mar joined the Jacobites and raised the Pretender's standard at Sheriffmuir to initiate the 1715 uprising. Defoe rebuked him then in one of his pamphlets written in Quaker voice, *A Trumpet Blown in the North* (1715).

54 *Marchmont*: See Letter 74, note 9.

55 *Maitland*: Lt.-Gen. James Maitland (d. 1716), Commander of Fort William. See Defoe's allusion to Maitland's endorsement of Harley in Letter 164 and Defoe's positive assessment of Maitland in Letter 197.

56 *Marshall*: Marischal was classed by Defoe as one of the 'Declar'd profest Jacobites' (Letter 160); he was included on the Court list for the representative peers thanks to Hamilton's influence (Szechi, 204).

57 *Newcastle*: Newcastle was Lord Privy Seal and among Harley's principal collaborators in reforming the ministry in autumn 1710. 'The Duke of Newcastle is very well with Mr. Harley, for whom, they say he had formerly a great friendship and esteem' (Addison to Wharton, [25 Aug. 1710], *Addison Letters*, 233).

58 *Northesk*: David Carnegie, fourth Earl of Northesk (1675–1729). A follower of Mar, he also joined Harley's interest.

DEFOE TO [ROBERT HARLEY], 10 OCTOBER 1710

59 *Nottingham*: Nottingham was pointedly excluded from the re-entry of leading Tories – Rochester, Buckingham, and Bromley – to government in 1710. For Defoe's steady attacks on him since 1703, see Letter 3, note 20. Defoe's most recent jibe had been to draw attention to Nottingham's relationship with the opera singer Francesca Margherita de L'Epine (d. 1746) (*Review*, VII, 285 (8 Aug. 1710)). For Defoe's later attacks on Nottingham, see headnote to Letter 203.

60 *Norman*: Lionel Norman, Commissioner of the Customs in Scotland. See Letter III, note 9.

61 *Orkeney*: Defoe had warned Godolphin about Orkney's attempts to supplant Marlborough in 1708 (Letter 137); his suggestion of Orkney as Commander in Chief in Scotland in 1711 seems motivated by a desire to avoid Argyll's appointment to that post (Letter 197).

62 *Orford*: Edward Russell, first Earl of Orford (1653–1727), of the Whig Junto, resigned as First Lord of the Admiralty on 22 Sept. 1710, the day after the dissolution of parliament. This was despite Harley's efforts, via emissaries, to persuade him to remain (Harley to Newcastle, 10 Aug. and 23 Sept. 1710; Halifax to Newcastle, 26 Sept. 1710, H.M.C. *Portland MSS*, II, 214, 220–1). Quite apart from the desirability of the Whig alliance, Harley knew that Orford was the most able lord to manage the admiralty.

63 *Oxford*: Perhaps David Makgill, third Viscount of Oxfuird (d. 1717), a Jacobite.

64 *Oldfield*: See Letter 152, note 1.

65 *Provost*: Adam Brown, Lord Provost in Edinburgh. See Letters 143 and 156.

66 *Pembrook*: The moderate Tory, Thomas Herbert, eighth Earl of Pembroke (*c.* 1656–1733).

67 *Peterboro'*: See Letter 43, note 17. In 1710 he was appointed General of the Marines; the Queen's dislike kept him from the admiralty (Holmes, 202).

68 *Queensberry*: Comparing the four most powerful Scottish dukes – Hamilton, Queensberry, Argyll, and Atholl – Dupplin told Harley on 8 Aug. that Queensberry, 'except in so far as he is supported by the Queen's favour, is of the smallest interest' (H.M.C. *Portland MSS*, IV, 558). Though his 'Old Court' comrades were excluded from the ministerial list for the upcoming election, he was retained as Secretary of State for Scotland until his death in 1711. Defoe consistently praised Queensberry, such as in the personage of 'the Duke of *Sanquarius*' (his home was in Sanquhar) in *Atalantis Major*, 14–15; cf. headnote to Letter 104.

69 *Rabble*: As well as meaning a mob in general, the word refers to the forcible displacement of Episcopalian ministers by Presbyterians after the 1688 Revolution, and latterly to resisting the settling of a (Presbyterian) minister in his living by Episcopalian crowds.

70 *Roxboro'*: See Letter 60, note 3.

71 *Rialton*: Godolphin's son, Francis, Viscount Rialton from 1706 to 1712, second Earl of Godolphin from 1712. See Letter 39, note 14.

72 *Rugland*: John Douglas-Hamilton, first Earl of Ruglen (1664–1744).

73 *Rochester*: See Letter 15, note 13. Rochester, the Queen's uncle, came back into government as part of the ministerial revolution, replacing Godolphin as Lord Lieutenant of Cornwall on 2 Sept. 1710 (Luttrell, VI, 625) and replacing Somers as Lord President of the Council on 21 Sept. See note 6 to the present Letter. Geoffrey Holmes argues that Rochester's 'forcing tactics' in 1710 compelled Harley to tack to the Tories ('Robert Harley and the Ministerial Revolution of 1710', ed. W. A. Speck, *PH* 29 (2010), 275–307 (at 295–6, 304)).

74 *Rothes*: See Letter 96.

75 *Roseberry*: See Letter 96, note 27. Rosebery was in Harley's interest by 1710.

76 *Rutland*: The Whig John Manners, first Duke of Rutland (1638–1711).

77 *Rigby*: See Letter III, note 9, and Letter 113.

78 *Somers*: Somers was dismissed as Lord President of the Council on 21 Sept. 1710; he and Harley had not managed to come to an agreement to work together (see Holmes, 112).

79 *Semple*: Francis Sempill, tenth Lord Sempill (*c.* 1685–1716).

80 *Sunderland*: See headnote to Letter 145. After his removal as Secretary of State, Sunderland was one of the most prominent Whig leaders in the Lords in opposition during the last four years of Anne's reign. For Defoe's connections to Sunderland in the next reign, see Letters 258–9.

535

DEFOE TO [ROBERT HARLEY], 10 OCTOBER 1710

81 *Stairs*: Stair adhered to Queensberry and the 'Old Court' interest; he was excluded from the ministry's list of peers in the upcoming election (Mar to Harley, 7 Nov. 1710, H.M.C. *Portland MSS*, x, 349–50). See Defoe's assessment of his actions during the 1710 election in Letter 160.

82 *Stuart*: Sir James Stewart, the former Lord Advocate. See Letter 119, note 6. Possible alternative or additional people include: Lt.-Col. James Steuart (*c.* 1652–1722), Deputy Governor of Edinburgh Castle, whose honourable conduct during the attempted Jacobite invasion of 1708 Defoe praised (*Review*, v, 237 (15 July 1708)); Sir James Steuart (1681–1727), Solicitor General for Scotland; William Stuart (d. 1729), minister at Kilterne, who was rabbled and threatened at gunpoint when he preached at Dingwall, which Defoe used to illustrate Episcopalian trespasses (*Review*, v, 446–52 (6 and 9 Nov. 1708); 513 (9 Dec. 1708)).

83 *Tiveot*: The Scottish nobleman Sir Thomas Livingstone, Viscount Teviot (1651–1711), resident in England, was evidently in Harley's interest, as he gave his proxy vote to Mar (Mar to Harley, 1 Nov. 1710, H.M.C. *Portland MSS*, x, 346; William Robertson, *Proceedings Relating to the Peerage of Scotland* (Edinburgh, 1790), 51).

84 *Tweedale*: See Letter 96, note 24.

85 *Urquhar*: Perhaps Capt. Robert Urquhart of Burdysyards (d. 1741), MP for Elginshire, 1708–10, but who did not contest the seat in 1710 (*HPC 1690–1715*, v, 715); or Col. James Urquhart of Cromarty (1680–1741), a Jacobite. See Henrietta Tayler, *The History of the Family of Urquhart* (Aberdeen, 1946), 126–9.

86 *Weemyss*: See Letter 96, note 27. Wemyss, a follower of Mar, also joined Harley's interest in 1710.

87 *Wharton*: Wharton resigned as Lord Lieutenant of Ireland on 22 Sept. 1710, the day after the dissolution of parliament, though he continued until his successor was appointed. Wharton's denunciation of Harley and his proposed 'motley ministry' in the preceding weeks was the cause of other leading Whigs such as Somers and Lord Chancellor Cowper resisting Harley's blandishments (Burnet, VI, 13). He was soon after traduced in Swift's *Short Character of His Ex. T. E. of W., L. L. of I.* (*Swift Journal*, 83).

88 *Weymouth*: Thomas Thynne, first Viscount Weymouth (1640–1714), a longstanding ally of Harley.

89 *Window Tax*: Scotland's exemption from the window tax which had been in force in England since 1696 expired on 1 Aug. 1710.

90 *Wiely*: Probably Robert Wylie or Wyllie (1650–1715), minister at Hamilton who had opposed the Union.

91 *Webster*: Probably Defoe's antagonist of 1707, James Webster. See Letters 92 and 93.

92 *Williams*: Daniel Williams (see Letter 152, note 1).

93 *Yester*: Charles Hay (1670–1715), Lord Yester, eldest son of Tweeddale whom he succeeded as the third Marquess in 1713.

94 *Yaremouth*: William Paston, second Earl of Yarmouth (1654–1732), a Jacobite Tory.

DEFOE TO [ROBERT HARLEY], [21 OCTOBER 1710]

158

To [Robert Harley]

[21 October 1710]

HEADNOTE (Letters 158 and 159): Defoe's list of objectives for his journey to Scotland (Letter 158) reflects his own perception of his mission rather than anything expressly from Harley. In some ways it parallels the election advice Defoe produced for the English, in the *Review* and in pamphlets he likely wrote in early October, including *A Word against a New Election, A New Test of the Sence of the Nation*, and *Queries to the New Hereditary Right-Men*.[1] Whereas in England he warned the electorate to avoid High Flyers and trust the new ministry's commitment to Revolution principles, in Scotland his task was to reassure people that the Union and Kirk would remain inviolate even under a Tory government. Defoe arrived in Edinburgh on 9 November and set about allaying the concerns of his Presbyterian acquaintances. He arrived just in time to see the election of sixteen Tory peers, including, to Defoe's consternation, some Jacobites. Unbeknownst to Defoe, a list of the peers had been compiled by Harley and his allies, who threatened and bribed the Scots to vote accordingly.[2]

Queries for Mannagem^t

1/ Whether ye Generall Design be not, to Inform and advise The people of her Maj^{ties} Resoluçons as well in These Changes of Things as any Other that shall happen, to Continue to Maintain —
    1 The Union in all its Parts.
    2 The Church in all its Just Rights and Established priveleges And to Discourage and Disscountenançe Intrusions and Innovaçons.[3]
    That her Maj^{tie} will protect and Defend Their Revoluçon Establishment and Take all Occasions to Encourage And protect Their Commerçe and the Improvem^t of their Country.

2/ Whether I am Not to Apply my Self on all Occasions to Calm and Make Easy The Minds of people there, Filld with Jealousies and Feares, and On Every Opportunity to Detect the false Accounts Imposed Upon Them from Hençe, whether by writeing, Printing or Conversaçon, That ye Poison of a Facçous spirit May Not Spread Among them Nor ye people be Irritated and Exasperated Against

DEFOE TO [ROBERT HARLEY], [21 OCTOBER 1710]

ye Public Administraċon of Affaires here, as if Calculated for Their Destruction.^a

3/ In Matters of Eleċċon, whether of ye Commons or Peers, by all Such Methods as shall Offer (for tis Impossible to prescribe Them here) to forward the Intrest and Choiċe of Such Men whose Tempers are Most Moderate and best Enclind &c. and as plainly as Circumstanċes will admitt, to Discourage The Contrary.

4/ From Time to Time to give Such Intelligenċe of Things and Persons as May be for her Maj^ties Serviċe.

5/ To Settle and Continue Such Correspondenċe in Every Part, whether ye Same allready Settled or Such as May be proper for an Exact Intelligenċe in all parts after this Journey May be Over.

Text: BL Add. MS. 70291, fols. 234–5. *Address*: none. *Endorsed by Harley* (fol. 235^v): Queries Mr Goldsmith Octo: 21 1710

---

^a Destruction] *the word* 'I' *cancelled in the following space between paragraphs*

---

1 F&O, *Bibliography*, 101–3. See the *Review* for 24 Oct. 1710, in which Defoe promotes the election of 'Men or Temper, and Moderate Principles ... let them be of which Side they will' (VII, 424).

2 On Harley's manoeuvres ahead of the election of the Scottish representative peers, see Riley, *English Ministers*, 149–57, which draws on letters to Harley dated 1–10 Nov. from Mar, the ministry's principal manager during the election of the peers (H.M.C. *Portland MSS*, x, 346–51). Szechi explains that Harley's initial plan in Aug. to secure the elections of exclusively moderate peers in Scotland gave way, as he realised the necessity of following Kinnoull's advice of 'go[ing] in entirely to the Tories' (Szechi, 62–6; Kinnoull to Harley, 27 Sept. 1710, H.M.C. *Portland MSS*, IV, 602).

3 *Intrusions and Innovaċons*: An intrusion is 'the settlement of a minister of the Church of Scotland contrary to the will or without the consent of the congregation' (*OED*). Defoe discusses such intrusions since the death of William III in *The Present State of the Parties in Great Britain* (1712), 162–70. In this context, an innovation is an alteration to the form of worship in the Church of Scotland.

538

DEFOE TO [ROBERT HARLEY], 16 NOVEMBER 1710

159

To [Robert Harley]

16 November 1710

Sr

The stop I Met wth at Newcastle prevented My Arriveing here
Till ye Day before The Eleccon of Peers.[1] I kno' I Need Not give you
a List of Their Names.[2] Some Observations on ye Conduct of ye
Parties on both Sides[a] I shall Comunicate in My Next, being Not
Sufficiently furnish'd for That work at So short Notice.

I find ye people here Allarm'd Very Much, but willing to hope
Every Thing shall not Isue So bad, as The Embassador of a Certain
Party[3] whom you kno' was here before Me had Suggested. They
Seem Surpriz'd when They hear that Moderate Thoughts Remain
Among Those of whose Mannagement They had Recd Such
formidable Ideas. I flatter my Self her Majtie shall be Successfully as
well as Faithfully Serv'd in The Great work of quieting The Minds of
her Subjects in This Part of Britain, and Really I find a Disposicon
here, Especally Among the Most Judicous both of Ministers and
people, to Rest Upon ye Assurances of her Majties preserving Their
libertys, and to leav all Other Things to her Royall Justice; The
Church here is Their Great Concern. This being Untouch'd They will
be The Easyest part of ye Nacon in Other Cases.

This is ye foundacon I am building Upon, and Indeed Srb[b] I find
as Many Endeavours to Embroil Them here and Disorder ye heads
of ye people[c] as I did in ye Time of ye Treaty,[4] Tho' I hope Easyer
to be Defeated — I presume Confuteing these and Informing the
people here of Their True Intrest and a little of Their Duty May be
Acceptable Service to her Majtie and May Answer ye End of My
stay here, and in this I shall Not fail and shall More Constantly
Now Inform you of what Occurs.

I presume you have an Accot of what I Did at N Castle in
Answer to Mine. I am Very Sorry to write That ye Gentleman[5] I

---

[a] on both Sides] *interlined*
[b] Sr] *following word* 'Tho' *cancelled*
[c] people] *following word* 'here' *cancelled*

539

DEFOE TO [ROBERT HARLEY], 18 NOVEMBER 1710

Sent My Last by From Thence is No More to be Confided in, of wch I shall Give a Larger Acco^t Among Other Things in My Next.

I am

S^r

yor Most Obedient Servt

&c

Edinb. Nov. 16. 1710

Text: BL Add. MS. 70291, fols. 236–7. *Address*: none. *Endorsed by Harley* (fol. 237^v): Eden Mr Guilot Nov: 16 1710

1 *Elecćon of Peers*: On 10 Nov.
2 *Names*: The sixteen elected Lords represented a clean sweep for the English ministry. They were Hamilton, Atholl, Annandale, Eglinton, Orkney, Mar, Loudon, Marischal, Islay, Rosebery, Kinnoull, Northesk, Balmerino, Home, Kilsyth, and Blantyre. Englishmen divided them into 'Episcopalian' and 'Court' Tories. See Daniel Szechi, 'Some Insights on the Scottish MPs and Peers Returned in the 1710 Election', *SHR* 60 (1981), 61–8, which assesses the contemporary analysis given by Richard Dongworth to Wake on 11 Nov. 1710 (Christ Church Oxford Wake MS. xvii, fols. 268–9). Some of these peers had been arrested for Jacobitism in 1708 (Bodl. Carte MS. 129, fol. 445v).
3 *Embassador of a Certain Party*: Probably Joshua Oldfield and the English Dissenters.
4 *Treaty*: The Union Treaty.
5 *Gentleman*: John Bell, Harley's agent and the postmaster at Newcastle-upon-Tyne. See Letter 51, note 20, and headnote to Letters 53–5.

160

To [Robert Harley]

18 November 1710

HEADNOTE **(Letters 160–3)**: Throughout late November, Defoe warned Harley – using a disguised handwriting, a code to conceal names, and the pseudonym Claude Guillot – about the Tory skulduggery done in the Queen and ministry's name during the election of the sixteen representative peers for Scotland. Mar, Argyll, and Islay managed that election, ensuring the return of Scottish peers preferred by the Court in England.[1] Harley's aim was to secure peers who would support him in the House of Lords, but Defoe feared opening the door to Jacobitism. Defoe's indignation at the whole experience did not evaporate, and he eventually published *Atalantis Major* (1711), a thinly veiled allegory recounting the events and

DEFOE TO [ROBERT HARLEY], 18 NOVEMBER 1710

attacking the three Scottish noblemen, Argyll especially.[2] He kept his authorship of this work secret from Harley.

In *Atalantis Major*, Defoe describes the 'Farce' of the election of peers at 'Olreeky'. '*Greeniccio*', '*Marereskine*', and '*Bellcampo*' (Argyll, Mar, and Islay) 'called themselves the Queen's Managers' and set about demanding their fellow peers vote for the Queen's list. They blustered about the impending impeachment of '*Dolphinus*' and '*Heymuthius*' (Godolphin and Marlborough). 'This new-fashioned Way of Proceeding' – rigging a supposedly free election – resulted in the return of some peers in the 'Tartarian' (Jacobite) interest. The Tartarians were, however, disappointed when they arrived to take their seats in parliament and had to take oaths for 'the Queen of the Island' and against the Tartarian pretender to her throne.[3] Greeniccio was promptly dispatched for undistinguished service in Japan (Spain).[4]

Aside from bemoaning the management of the election, Defoe requested money and fretted about his letters safely reaching Harley. It could be said that the patterns of his service while in Scotland in 1706 and 1707 had resumed.

Sr

I Wrot you breifly last Post but One.[5] I have been in Close Conference Since that with men of all Parties; indeed the Scenes here have as great a Variety as can be Imagin'd, differing not Onely from themselves but from things of the like Nature in England in a most Extraordinary Manner. This Moves me to be the more Perticular, believing it Very Much for her Majties Service to give you a Succinct Account of the humours of men and Parties, and of their Conduct in the present juncture.

The Whigs here are Bauk'd in their Elecctions of the Peers of whom I Need Not Give you the Names tho' they are in ye Enclosed list.[6] How Unhappily the Severall Parties behave in this Case shall be my first Remark.

The Torys (as we call ym in England) are here a Differing kind of People from Ours of that Denomination, being Universally Jacobite,[7] and so above-board as to Own it, in ye last of which they Certainly Show more honesty than Discretion; it is so Open[a] a thing and So much the Mode of the Place to Own the pretender, Drink his health and Talk most Insolently of his being Restored

---

[a] Open] *letter 'l' cancelled at the end of this word (for 'Openly')*

541

DEFOE TO [ROBERT HARLEY], 18 NOVEMBER 1710

that I think it my Duty to Represent this to you S^r for her Maj^{ties} Service and that wth the greatest Concern.

You will wonder when I shall Repeat to you an absurdity of a Nature — wch One Would think Uncapable of Deludeing any body (Viz) that the 233 [Queen] should have been privately Resolved to dissolve the 253 [succession] and to Restore 214 [the Pretender], being Chagrin, Pensiv and in Consĉiencĕ Uneasy at his being So long and so much Injur'd — and Not Onely So but that 233 [the Queen] will Resign In favour of the said 214 [Pretender].[8]

I had not Mencon'd this, for I would not Trouble you with Triffles, if I did not see a Strange Use made of it here to Encourage the profest Jacobite and to Impose upon the poor highlanders and Other People in the Country who do not look for their Saviours Comeing wth half ye Assuranĉe as they do for that of the 214 [Pretender]. I doubt not S^r but you will Think it proper in its Season to represent this to her Maj^{tie} Since the Encouragem^t of the Jacobites in the New Turn of Affaires is the great Argument wch the other people make Use of to Make their Quarell at ye late Changes become Popular.

In the late Eleccon the Conduct of the D of 60 [Argyll], the E of 163[a] [Islay] and the Earle of 194 [Mar] is Very Perticular,[9] and Either their Instructions were to use no Temper[10] or they discovred most Impolitick Openess — Many that were Willing to Come into Measures Exclaim'd Openly Upon the Imprudence of those Gentlemen — who Treated them wth Mennaĉes and Contempt on the One hand[b] and Declared Openly the Quallification of those to be Chosen, wch is Now called the Test upon wch the[c] Peers were Closeted by those two above[d] (Viz) their agreeing to Impeach 140 [Godolphin][11] and 193 [Marlborough] — Nor did the Imprudence End there but On all Occasions to Say in So Many words[e] They had her Maj^{ties} Orders to Choose Such and Such and it must be don: This was So abandonning all Reservs, that it has disgusted the Generallity, and has Put them Upon Measures of Uniteing, which

---

[a] the E of 163] *interlined*
[b] hand] *amended from* 'End'
[c] the] *following illegible word cancelled*
[d] above] *interlined*
[e] in So Many words] *interlined*

DEFOE TO [ROBERT HARLEY], 18 NOVEMBER 1710

may Shut yᵉ door upon all future Measures, what Ever yᵉ Occasion may be; Prudence Will never let a Wise man Play a game So as he can Never play it again, but these Gentlemen have not onely don So, but Exposed their Measures So Openly that had a Proposall 260 [Stair] made been Closed with, all the Mannage of 60 [Argyll] and 194 [Mar] had been Dissappointed,[12] and the Success of this Eleccon, is Oweing to the Cowardice not good will of 182 [Leven],[13] 138 [Glasgow],[14] withᵃ Seafield,[15] Hyndford[16] and [ ][17] and not atall to the Wisdom and Conduct of 60 [Argyll] and 194 [Mar], who Certainly lost themselves More in this than Any man would have thoᵗ Possible for men of their Character, Especially 194 [Mar] to have done, and was within a Triffle of Spoiling all their Work.

Now they have Returnd their Number, it were to be Wished they Could have Avoided a few who are Declar'd profest Jacobites Such asᵇ 197 [Marischal],[18] Kilsyth,[19] Blantyre,[20] Humeᶜ[21] &c, who are known to aim in all they do at the Pretender and whose being Now Chosen has many ill Effects here, what Ever may be as to Over-ruleing them in England, I mean as to Encreasing the Insolence of Jacobitisme in the North where its Strength is far from being Contemptible and the Rendring the work of Makeing the other people Easy far more difficult than itᵈ might Otherwise have been.

It was Very Remarkable that when My Lᵈ 163 [Islay] attempted Some of the 100 [clergy] of this City to assure them of the good Intentions of the 233 [Queen] and Resolutions not to Invade their Church, the Circumstance of Nameing Jacobite Peers as the Express order from 233 [the Queen] to be Chosen was Retorted as a bad token for them to Rest upon, and the famous Tale of the Hangman of Edinb. was Told him by One Mʳ Miller of Kirkliston (Viz) How he used when he had any man to Excecute to Encourage them and bid them not fear, not fear, Till he Got them Up the ladder and So Turnd them off.[22]

I hint this sʳ to Confirm my Censure of the Conduct aforesaid as Imprudent and as what has rendred the quieting these people wᶜʰ was Easy before Very Difficult now.

ᵃ with] *interlined above cancelled word* 'and'
ᵇ as] *following illegible word cancelled*
ᶜ Hume] *interlined; the caret indicating the insertion point follows* '&c.' *in MS*
ᵈ it] *following words* 'must be' *cancelled*

DEFOE TO [ROBERT HARLEY], 18 NOVEMBER 1710

I would not lay down my Opinion of things too Positively, therefore
I Cease to Enlarge on the affair of this Mannagement — How
the whig lords behave, how the Squadroni and old Court Unite,[23]
what Measures they took then and are Takeing Now wth Some
Observations on both shall be y[e] Subject of my Next[24] — Mean
Time S[r] I should be Made Easy if I had the Honour to know if
these Accounts Come Safe to hand, being Unexpectedly Depriv'd of
the Opportunity of Conveying by M[r] Bell whom I can not think of
Trusting in this affair Unless I have again your Commands to do so.

I am
S[r]
yo[r] Most Humble, faithfull and Obedient Serv[t]
C. Guilot[25]

Nov. 18. 1710

Text: BL Add. MS. 70291, fols. 238–9 (Figure 8). [Disguised handwriting.] *Address*:
none. *Endorsed by Harley* (fol. 239[v]): Eden Claude Guilot Nov: 18[a] 1710 R nov: 27:

[a] 18] *amended from* '28'

---

1 Argyll himself was not among the sixteen peers on the Court list because he sat in the House
   of Lords as Earl of Greenwich.
2 Cf. Defoe, *The Present State of the Parties in Great Britain* (1712), 138.
3 The point is echoed in *The Secret History of the October Club* (1711), *PEW*, 11, 163. Defoe ex-
   pands on this version in *The Secret History of the White-Staff, Part II* (1714), 14–23, in which he
   manages simultaneously to credit Harley with outmanoeuvring the Scottish Jacobite peers by
   taking them into parliament so as to nullify them, and to cast doubt on whether Harley was
   ever responsible for their election.
4 *Atalantis Major*, 19, 23, 26, 33, 40, 42.
5 *last Post but One*: Apparently an error, as the preceding letter seems to have gone by the last
   post.
6 *Enclosed list*: Missing. For the elected peers, see Letter 159, note 2.
7 *Torys … Jacobite*: In *An Historical Account of the Bitter Sufferings, and Melacholly Circumstances
   of the Episcopal Church in Scotland* (1707), Defoe says that Scottish Episcopalians 'are universally declar'd Jacobites, and professed Enemies to the Protestant Succession' (*PEW*, IV, 287).
   In the *Review* for 7 Dec. 1710, he says that 'in the North Parts of *Britain* … Tory and Jacobite
   is the same Thing' (VII, 503); on 28 Nov. 1710, he reported a Scot telling him '*if you see a TORY
   in our Country, you always see a JACOBITE*' (VII, 486).
8 *233 … 214 [Pretender]*: Defoe began confuting this rumour in the *Review* for 26 Sept. 1710
   and did so again on 21 Oct. and 5 Dec. (VII, 374–5, 422, 499–500). In the last of these he even
   argues that Anne, should she abdicate, would not be able to name her successor: parliament
   would decide. He reflects derisively on these rumours in *The Secret History of the October Club*,
   PEW, 11, 153, 163; he indicates their lack of foundation in *The Present State of the Parties in
   Great Britain*, 63; and he denied 'this foolish Notion' retrospectively in *The Secret History of
   the White-Staff, Part II*, 21.

544

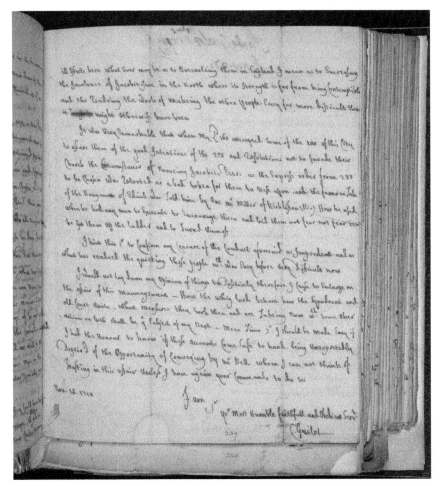

Figure 8 Daniel Defoe [Claude Guilot] to [Robert Harley], 18 November 1710, BL Add. MS. 70291, fol. 239ʳ

9 *Perticular*: peculiar.
10 *Temper*: restraint.
11 *140 [Godolphin]*: Apparently in error for '139' (see Letter 157).
12 *Proposall ... Dissappointed*: In *Atalantis Major*, Defoe indicates that Stair ('the Earl of *Stairdale*' in the narrative) saw through Argyll's scheme, scorning to come into his list, and accusing him of betraying his country. 'Had the other Lords been advised by this gallant Gentleman, they had broke all their [i.e. Argyll and Mar's] Schemes; but they were not all united in their Resolutions, or equally determined in their Measures' (27–8; cf. 15–16). So, Defoe regrets that prominent members of the 'Old Court' interest, Leven, Glasgow, Seafield, and Hyndford, did not defy the Court list and seek their own elections. Dongworth informed Wake that they complied with the Court's demands in order to keep their places (Christ Church Oxford Wake MS xvii, fol. 269ᵛ).
13 *182 [Leven]*: '*Lesleynus*' in *Atalantis Major*, 24.
14 *138 [Glasgow]*: '*Boislio*' in *Atalantis Major*, 24.

DEFOE TO [ROBERT HARLEY], 21 NOVEMBER 1710

15 *Seafield*: See Letter 60, note 6.
16 *Hyndford*: John Carmichael, first Earl of Hyndford (1638–1710) died in Sept., succeeded by his son James, the second Earl (b. before 1671, d. 1737).
17 *[ ]*: Left blank and perhaps meaning Queensberry, though reluctant to rebuke him explicitly. However, Queensberry is on the code list.
18 *197 [Marischal]*: Marischal was arrested as a Jacobite conspirator in 1708.
19 *Kilsyth*: William Livingston, third Viscount Kilsyth (1650–1733), included on the Court list thanks to Hamilton's influence (Szechi, 204); he was arrested as a Jacobite conspirator in 1708. He took part in the 1715 Rising, was captured, escaped, and joined the Pretender in Rome.
20 *Blantyre*: Walter Stuart, sixth Lord Blantyre (1683–1713).
21 *Hume*: I.e. Home. See Letter 157, note 21. He was arrested as a Jacobite conspirator in 1708.
22 *famous ... off*: Defoe gives this account of John White, an Edinburgh hangman, in the *Review* for 30 Nov. 1710 (VII, 491) and in *Atalantis Major*, 22–3. In *Atalantis Major*, Defoe claims that White beheaded Argyll's grandfather, a Monmouth rebel, in 1685. The minister was Thomas Miller (*c.* 1649–1716) of Kirkliston.
23 *Squadroni and old Court Unite*: In 1711, in *The Secret History of the October Club*, Defoe praised the Squadrone for their 'unanimous Conjunction in the last Election against their Enemies, *the Jacobites, but it was too late*' (*PEW*, II, 151).
24 *my Next*: The subject is not taken up in the next extant letter; one may be untraced.
25 *C. Guilot*: Defoe's first known use of the pseudonym 'Claude Guilot', though Harley endorsed the previous letter with this. It became the main alias under which Defoe operated in Harley's service from 1710 to 1714. Long after he had stopped being a spy, Defoe included 'Claude Guilote' in an illustrative shopkeeper's account of income and expenses in one of his conduct books (*A Supplement to the Complete English Tradesman* (1726), *RDW*, VII, 309, 311, 313).

161

To [Robert Harley]

21 November 1710

Sr

I am Unhappily in Some Perplexity about the Conveying my letters as well as my other Circumstances in this Place and this Causes me giveing you this Trouble by the Ordin^a Post.[a] I Subjoyn my humble Request that I may Reciev a line or Two Signifyeing that my letters Arriv: and also that my proceedings are to yor Satisfaccon if according to my hopes I have the hono^r to Answer yor Expectation.

I had the Hono^r of yor Credit to m^r J Bell Restricting me to Twenty Pound which he Readily Complyed wth but Imediately

[a] Post] *following word* 'and' *cancelled*

546

DEFOE TO [ROBERT HARLEY], 21 NOVEMBER 1710

made my haveing that Credit and Waiting there for it Public all Over the Town, Haveing himself Espoused a Contrary Intrest to what he Supposed me Acting for, of wch I shall add more largely when I Am assured my letters Arriv Safe to your hand.

This Causes me (However straightned) to offer no farther desire of Supply that way, Chooseing Rather to struggle with my Own Circumstances than to hazard the Service.

I kno' s^r If you think fitt to Continue me here any Time, you will not Abbandonne me in yor,a Service; and as for Methods of Supply, if you please to Order me any Support here I may Draw it in this hand and Name[1] Safely and Entirely Conceal'd on yor Self or any Person you shall please to Appoint.

If you do me the Hono^r,b to leav me to judge whether I am More Usefull in staying here or not, I must Confess I think I can in no Spot of Ground in Britain Render her Maj^tie like Service (tho' in this I Speak against my Own Intrest and affairs), I Mean for a Month or two yet longer, Since these people are Infinitely prejudiced and alarm'd and yet not So Tenatious and ill Temperd as I Expected and will be Soon Restored and Recovred to their Temper.

I Humbly lay my Own Circumstance before you, but Submitt it Entirely to yor goodness whose Concern for me has allwayes been beyond my Merit. I Most Humbly and Earnestly Entreat for a line signifying the Receipt of my letters, Since I can not write wth Equall freedome while I am Uncertain whether what I write Comes Safe to your hands.

I am

S^r

yor Most Humble

and most Obedient Servt

C Guilot.

Novemb. 21. 1710

PS

I have written at large last Post, directed to m^r Bateman.[2]

---

a yor] *following letters probably* 'Sev' *or* 'Ser' *cancelled*
b Hono^r] *following illegible word cancelled*

Text: BL Add. MS. 70291, fols. 240–1. [Disguised handwriting.] *Address*: none. *Endorsed by Harley* (fol. 241v): Eden C. Guilot Nov: 21: 1710 R Nov: 27:

1 *this hand* and *Name*: The disguised handwriting of this letter and Defoe's pseudonym, Claude Guilot.
2 *mr Bateman*: Thomas Bateman (d. 1719) was Deputy Surveyor and Comptroller of Duty on Coals for St Paul's Cathedral. He had received letters for Harley as early as 1705 (H.M.C. *Portland MSS*, IV, 182).

162

To [Robert Harley]

25 November 1710

Sr

I wrott you at large the Observations I had made on the Conduct of Our Great men here. I am not the best judge of the reasons of things, but the Consequences Seem Obvious, and any Man may determine of them.

On this Accot Sr I Presume to assure you, that the Unwary Openess, wch I Gave you my thoughts about in My last, has done a great deal of hurt here, in Raiseing the jealousies and Uneasinesses of this people, who[a] were Very much Enclined to accquiesce, before, in her Majties prudence, and Relye on the assurances Given of the Royall Protection.

The Queen (they Say) has allways adhered to the Law, and Never Carryed it with a High hand, But the D of 60 [Argyll] Destroy'd the Very appearance of Liberty in producing a list, and Openly telling the Peers, The Queen Would have those Men Chosen — It is not my bussiness Sr to make Coments — Her Majtie will judge whether this was her pleasure, — The best I can Say to them is, that they can not Suppose her Majtie gave his Grace Instructions to treat the Peers, in that Mañer, but that the 60 [Duke of Argyll] might be a little Warm: That[b] Perhaps her Majtie might have Seen Such a

a who] *illegible word interlined and cancelled*
b That] *interlined*

list, and appear Satisfyed in the persons, but that her Maj^tie would Command them to Choose Such, and no Other, was not Probable.[1] In this S^r, If I do wrong I shall be Very Unhappy, Since I do it as the Onely Means of quieting the Uneasy People, wch I take to be Very Much her Maj^ties Intrest.

I Shall go on to Accquaint you with this part as the Perticulars Offer But for ye Present I can not Avoid Representing One thing to you, which as it Concerns the Public Peace Here, I believ it my Duty to Lay before her Maj^tie.

The Uneasyness the people are Under here on the Affair above Said is not little, Espe̱cally att the Returning four of the Number Profestly 161 [Jacobite], But they are now farther allarmd at the Confident assurances given them, of a Change in the Great Officers here, Perticularly the Military Government.[2]

I perswade my Self you will believ me S^r, that I have No Intrest to make or Persons to Serv. I am No biggot to a Party, Much less to Persons, But when her Maj^tie Shall be Inform'd of the Temper of her people here, and of the Imediate Consequen̯ces of a Change, I Doubt not my Notion of that Matter, will appear to have Some Weight in it, at least Enough to Excuse Me in the Men̯coning it.

1st/ S^r be it that Some (Worthless Enough) May have the Cheif hand in the affair — yet to Take it from them and leave it to the Next in Course May not Mend the Matter or^a to put it into the hand of any of the Same Party, May not be Worth the broil Such a Remove will make among them.

2dly/ To Give the millitary Power here wch indeed is the Supreme (till ye Country is a little more Accquainted with the Civill) to the New Party,[3] who the people by the Needless and Unseasonable Conduct aforesaid are So Jealous of, is to put them into Infinite Confusions and make the Uneasinesses past any Private Mans Remedy.

3/ To let in the Tory Party or indeed those who would be called the Episcopall Party into the Millitary Command, is to put the Pretender in Actuall Posession of this Part of the Island.

I humbly ask yor Pardon for Representing this So Positively yet I am not Able to See any Medium. I Would not Refflect on any of

---

^a or] *following words* 'at least' *cancelled*

DEFOE TO [ROBERT HARLEY], 25 NOVEMBER 1710

her Majties Episcopall Subjects But Certainely if they are in her Intrest they act the most Impolitic Part in the world, for they will not So Much as Say it themselves, nor in all my knowlege of things and persons in this Part of Brittain did I Ever See or know or find any Other man that has Seen or known any One Man who was Purely Episcopall and not also Jacobite avowedly So,[4] Except a Very few under the Ministry of Some of ye Episcopall Ministers who are continued in their Churches by the Presbyterian Government.[5]

I Cease sr to go on wth my Notes on this till I See how the disposition of the people Shall hold, for these things Vary as Every New Notion Comes on But I must Offer you One farther hint sr of my Own wch I Submit to yor Charity because I think it Acting beyond my Sphere — I do not love to be officious But if you would please to give me leave I could Name Two or three Persons who while they are in are Rendred Suspected[a] to the New Juncto here, and who Perhaps may be kept off from them whereas their being Displac't will make them Popular and place them at th[e][b] head of a Party which it is Very Much her Majties Intrest to keep down and which can Never be better kept Down than by Rendring them Suspected to One Another — I shall Explain my Self farther If I May Obtain yor Commands and Som hint that my letters Come to yor hands.[6]

I am

Sr

yor Most Obedient Servt

C Guilot

Edinb.
Novembr 25. 1710

Any letter Directed to Mr Wm Cliff at Mr Walter Ross's to be left at Mr David Monroe[7] in Edinb will come to my hand.
The Number of Such Names is to make it Secure.

Text: BL Add. MS. 70291, fols. 242–3. [Disguised handwriting.] *Address*: none. *Endorsed by Harley* (fol. 243v): Edenburg Mr Guillot Nov: 25: 1710 R Dec: 1

[a] Suspected] *following illegible word cancelled*
[b] th[e]] *obscured by MS binding*

DEFOE TO [ROBERT HARLEY], 3 DECEMBER 1710

1 *Perhaps ... Probable*: A 9 Nov. 1710 letter from Islay indicates that the Queen did command adherence to the English list of Scottish peers (H.M.C. *Portland MSS*, IV, 625–6).

2 *Confident ... Government*: Despite the election outcome, 'Old Court' politicians remained in their posts: Queensberry as Secretary of State for Scotland, Leven as Commander in Chief, Glasgow as Lord Clerk Register, and Seafield as Lord Chief Baron of the Exchequer. For Harley's motivations for leaving Scottish posts alone at this time, see Riley, *English Ministers*, 158–62.

3 *New Party*: I.e. the Tories who had swept the election of peers, not the Squadrone, which was sometimes referred to as the new party.

4 *nor ... So*: See Letter 160, note 7.

5 *Episcopall ... Government*: Some parishes in Scotland still had Episcopalian ministers despite not swearing oaths to William or Anne, because the support of local landowners allowed them to ignore sentences of deprivation.

6 *hint that my letters Come to yor hands*: No reply giving Defoe this reassurance has been traced.

7 *Mr Wm Cliff at Mr Walter Ross's ... Mr David Monroe*: These three men are unidentified, but 'Wm Cliff' witnessed a deed Defoe signed in Dec. 1709 (NRS RD 4/107, fol. 1130).

163

To [Robert Harley]

3 December 1710

Sr

I have been So Anxious About the Safe Conveying of My Letters, haveing Not had the honor of ye Least hint from yor Self, That I Convey This Enclosed[a] by a Trusty Friend as well That I May be Sure of its Comeing to yor hand, as That I may Reciev if you please One line for my Direccon whether to Stay here or Returne, and whether what I am doeing here, is for yor Service and to yor Satisfaccon.

It is a Dissaster to me That I lost ye Occasion of writeing by mr Bell whose Conduct I Observ'd to you Renders him[b] Suspected to me.

What Ever you please sr to do me The Honor to Direct Either by Word or by writeing will be faithfully Convey'd to me by Mr Young[1] the bearer, a faithfull and honest Man, and On whom I can So farr Depend or I would Not have Entrusted him.

---

[a] Enclosed] *interlined*
[b] him] *interlined above cancelled word* 'me'

551

DEFOE TO [ROBERT HARLEY], 6 DECEMBER 1710

                                    I am
                                    Sʳ
                        yoʳ Most Humble and Obedᵗ Servᵗ
                                    DF

Edinb. Decembʳ 3. 1710

I wrot a long Letter[2] this Night Directed to mʳ Tho: Bateman to wᶜʰ
I Humbly Referr.

Text: BL Add. MS. 70291, fols. 244–5. *Address*: none. *Endorsed by Harley* (fol. 245ᵛ):
Edenburg Dece: 3 1710 ʀ Dec: 13

1   *Mʳ Young*: Unidentified.
2   *long Letter*: Untraced.

164

To [Robert Harley]

6 December 1710

HEADNOTE: The new parliament sat down at the end of November 1710. Harley
had led the Tories to a landslide: of clearly identifiable party-men, there were
332 Tories to 181 Whigs.[1] Harley recognised the need for care in 'conducting this
majority', as he put it, because the Country Tories had never forgiven him for
splitting the party in 1705. Harley knew that 'the Affair of the House of Hanover'
was a weak point because many Country Tories were outright Jacobites.[2] They
would demand a thorough investigation of the former Whig ministry with a view
to impeachments, as well as a purge of all Whig officeholders. Harley knew that
compliance would make him as dependent on the Tories as Godolphin had become on the Whigs. Moreover, the Whigs continued to enjoy a majority in the
House of Lords notwithstanding the successful management of the election of
Scottish representative peers. As Defoe had warned, the encouragement given to
Jacobites in those elections risked alienating the moderate Presbyterian majority in Scotland. Harley realised he would be pulled between competing interest
groups during this session, opposed by both the party he had displaced and many
of his own backbenchers. Defoe was willing to put his trust in Harley as the 'Prop
to the Constitution' despite the election of a Tory parliament.

552

DEFOE TO [ROBERT HARLEY], 6 DECEMBER 1710

Sr

I Wrott you Two letters the last Post, One to Mr Bateman and One in Cover to a faithfull friend to Convey if possible to yor Self and Reciv Some Notice of yor haveing Recd Mine, for wch I have been Indeed Very Anxious, and also to Reciev yor further Commands.

The Notice here Sr that in 212 [Parliament] you have Personally Spoken Against 214 [the Pretender][3] has fixed the Character I have had the Honor to Spread here of yor Steddy Zeal for the Revolution[4] and Confirm'd what I hinted in My last,[5] that Lieutt Generall Maitland had Avouch'd Publickly in yor just Defence (Vizt), that No Man in Britain was a Greater Prop to the Constitution than yor Self.

I was Very Glad to have So Good an Assistant in So great a piece of Justice to you sr who I think have Recd So Much Injury from Some, from whom[a] you have Merited much better and the rather because it directly Contradicted what Dr Oldfield had been bussye here in Spreading both of yor Self and Even of[b] yor Great Mistress the Queen her Self.

How the joy begins to be Visible among the honest people who were and Still are firm to her Majties Person as Well as Governmt but were Terrifyed wth the Absurd Notions of all being to be Given up to the 214 [Pretender] Even by 233 [the Queen] her Self; it is not strange that a Thing So Ridiculous Should prevail if the assurance of those who Reported it were Considred and that they had Obtaind to be Sent up to 212 [Parliament] where they had peremptorily Said it Should be don.

This sr will Satisfye her Majtie That the Intrest of the Pretender is too great here to be Slighted and that Nothing but Discouragements of it from her Self can keep them in bounds but if her Majtie Pleases on any Occasion to Express her being pleased wth the Zeal of her Subjects Against the Pretender it Would strike them here as wth a blast from Heaven[6] and Weaken his Intrest More than an army of 10000 Men Could do.

---

[a] whom] *interlined*
[b] Even of] *interlined*

553

DEFOE TO [ROBERT HARLEY], 6 DECEMBER 1710

As to the people here, I mean the presbyterians, they Come heartily into Her Maj^ties Intrest, Neither do they Relish the Chagrin of Our^a 288 [Whigs] in 116 [England]. The Ambassador[7] who has Resided here from the 106 [Dissenters] and who has left his Mission here for 249 [secret service] is gone back re Infecta[8] and his Negotiations have Made less Impression than indeed I Expected; in short s^r Nothing but the 214 [Pretender] and Encroachments of 109 [Clergy][9] can make them Uneasy. I Endeavour to Assure them and Shall hereafter Give you Some acco^ts of Mediums to preserv her Maj^ties Intrest here and yet make all but the 161 [Jacobites] Easy also.

I am
S^r
yor Most Obliged Obedient Servt
C Guilot

117 [Edinburgh] Decemb. 6. 1710

Text: BL Add. MS. 70291, fols. 246–7. [Disguised handwriting.] *Address*: none. *Endorsed by Harley* (fol. 247^v): Edenburg Dece: 6 1710 R Dece: 15^b

---

^a Our] *following word possibly* 'Originall' *cancelled*
^b 15] *amended from* '16'

---

1 Speck, *Tory and Whig*, 123.
2 Harley's plan of administration, dated 30 Oct. 1710 (TNA SP 34/13, fols. 136–9), published in *Miscellaneous State Papers: From 1501 to 1726*, 2 vols. (1778), 11, 485–8.
3 *in 212 [Parliament] … 214 [the Pretender]*: At the opening of parliament on 25 Nov., Harley supported a motion to include a reference to the Hanoverian succession in the House of Commons's address to the Queen (Cobbett, VI, 930).
4 *Character … Revolution*: Representing a moderate Presbyterian perspective, Wodrow wrote in Dec. 1710: 'They say that Harley … is stanch for the Revolution and Succession' (*Analecta*, I, 311).
5 *My last*: Untraced. Presumably this is the letter referred to in the postscript to the previous letter.
6 *blast from Heaven*: This was a favourite phrase of Defoe's for an immediate providential consequence. See *The Farther Adventures of Robinson Crusoe, Novels*, 11, 50; *Serious Reflections, Novels*, 111, 110; *The Commentator*, no. 53 (4 July 1720), *RDW*, IX, 226; *The Fortunate Mistress, Novels*, IX, 262; *The Political History of the Devil, SFS*, VI, 42.
7 *Ambassador*: Oldfield (see Letter 152, note 1).
8 *re Infecta*: 'the thing unfinished' (Latin). Defoe uses this expression in *The Consolidator, SFS*, III, 144; *Review*, V, 56 (20 Apr. 1708); *The Political History of the Devil, SFS*, VI, 40.
9 *109 [Clergy]*: Apparently in error for '100' (see Letter 157). '119' (Episcopacy) is also possible.

554

165

To [Robert Harley]
18 December 1710

HEADNOTE: In Scotland, Presbyterians were alarmed at the increasing use of the English liturgy by Episcopalian congregations, in particular the Book of Common Prayer, an 'innovation' that Defoe noted had been 'expressly articled against in the Act of Security for the Church of *Scotland*'.[1] In September 1709, Rev. James Greenshields (1669–1741?) was arrested at the behest of the Edinburgh Presbytery after ostentatiously conducting such services right across the street from St Giles's Church, the bastion of Scottish Presbyterianism. When the Court of Session, Scotland's highest civil appeals court, refused to release him, Greenshields appealed to the House of Lords. It was unclear whether the Lords had jurisdiction, because the independence of Scottish courts had been guaranteed by the Union. Many Scots resented the idea that a House of Lords that included Anglican bishops should determine a matter relating to the religious settlement in Scotland. As Defoe wrote this letter, Greenshields's appeal was depending. On that appeal seemed to hinge the prospect of a legal toleration for Scottish Episcopalians issued from London.

In the *Review* in October and November 1709, Defoe defended the punishment of Greenshields, whom he labelled a 'Tool' of the Jacobites, who hoped to make him a martyr in order to promote a divisive toleration act.[2] Greenshields, Defoe claimed, was 'a poor Vicar of 15*l.* a Year Revenue in *Ireland*', promised '80*l.* per annum' for setting up Common Prayer in Scotland with the objective of provoking the magistrates to act.[3] Defoe denied that the Book of Common Prayer was widely used in Scotland before 1688, and he insisted, as he had done in *The Scot's Narrative Examin'd* (February 1709), that Episcopalians were not being persecuted: they were only barred from preaching if they were Jacobites who refused to swear allegiance to Anne, so the disqualification was civic, not religious.[4] Besides, Defoe continued, Greenshields's arrest was not for using the Book of Common Prayer but for unlicensed preaching, as his ordination was invalid, conducted as it was by a 'Depos'd *Non-Jurant* Bishop' – that is, by a deprived Scottish bishop after the abolition of Episcopacy.[5] In Defoe's view the whole affair was orchestrated to undermine Scottish Presbyterianism and the Union in favour of the Pretender.[6] In *Greenshields Out of Prison and Toleration Settled in Scotland* (April 1710), he restated his case, arguing that setting up Greenshields and Common Prayer was a cleft stick for the authorities, who stood to be attacked whether they ignored or punished him.[7]

DEFOE TO [ROBERT HARLEY], 18 DECEMBER 1710

S[r]

I have wrott Frequently Since My Comeing hither. I hope they
are all Arrived. I had Determin'd to leave this Place Some days
Since Unless yo[r] Commands had prevented me, believing it more
Usefull to Tender my Service Nearer yo[r] hand, But y[e] Unusuall
Tempests, Storms and floods have Made the Country Impracticable
So that there is No Passing the Country without Iminent Danger.

The Acco[ts] last Post from England Seem to Make my Stay here,
tho' Otherwise Accidentall, Very Usefull. Some Private letters have
Alarm'd the Poor people here wth a Story That an Attempt is to be
Made Upon their Church in the Case of Greenshields and in the
Article of Patronages.[8] The first Tends to a Tolleration, the other[a] a
Direct[b] Invasion of the Constitution of the Church and as they Say
The Union.

Whether This be fact or no I can Give them No Answer as
to that, but as I have all along perswaded them that No Evill is
Designd Against them in all these alteraçons, and have Satisfyed
them So Well that they began to be Very Easy; So I Assure them
Now, that her Maj[tie] is So Tender of the Union that they May
be assured Nothing will be done of any kind that shall any Way
Encroach Upon it.

I would Vallue my Self upon my haveing Some Influence[c] upon
things and p[er]sons here if I was pleading My Own Merit but
when I have an Argum[t] So well founded as this of her Maj[ties]
Royall Promise[d] I think it Very Much more to my advantage to Say
I rather Improve that forcible Argum[t] than p[er]swade them by my
Influence. The Queens promise in her late Speech,[9] This I Insist
upon and the people Depend upon it Very Much.

It is Not my bussiness S[r] to Debate here y[e] Reasons for or
against A Tolleracon here. I Presume from What you were pleased
to Say to me, that you agree w[th] Me in this, that this is not a proper
Season[10] and I Crave leav to add that what Ever Some people may
pretend it is Not the Aim of the Dissenters here,[11] Nor do they
Desire it.

[a] other] *following word probably* 'is' *cancelled*
[b] Direct] *following word* 'in' *cancelled*
[c] Influence] *following illegible word cancelled*
[d] of her Maj[ties] Royall Promise] *interlined*

556

DEFOE TO [ROBERT HARLEY], 18 DECEMBER 1710

However I wave This Now. I Conciev my proper Worke here is to Calm and quiet the minds of the people here, Reconcile them to her Maj^ties Measures and keep them Easy — of this I hope I can Give you a good Acco^t and am Very Thankfull for my Success.

I Fear indeed their Uneasyness from these New Allarms and Wish I knew what Answer to Give, but it is My Misfortune to act wholly by my Own judgement. If I am Defficent I Shall ye Rather hope for yor Pardon but if I had the Honor of your Instructions I Should act wth More Effect as well as wth More Courage.

I am
S^r your Most Obedient faithfull Servant
C Guilot

Edinb. Decemb. 18. 1710

Text: BL Add. MS. 70291, fols. 248–9. [Disguised handwriting.] *Address*: none. *Endorsed by Harley* (fol. 249^v): Cl. Guilot Dece: 18 1710 R Dece: 25:

1 *Review*, VI, 393 (4 Oct. 1709). But cf. Defoe, *The Present State of the Parties in Great Britain* (1712), 127–35, where he laments the lack of a more explicit safeguard.
2 *Review*, VI, 392 (4 Oct. 1709); 395 (6 Oct. 1709).
3 *Review*, VI, 399 (8 Oct. 1709).
4 *Review*, VI, 404 (8 Oct. 1709(E)). Cf. *Review*, VI, 270 (2 Aug. 1709).
5 *Review*, VI, 490 (19 Nov. 1709); 596–7 (5 Jan. 1710(E)). Cf. Defoe's account of Greenshields in *History of the Union*, published in late 1709 or early 1710 (*TDH*, VII, 66–70).
6 For the successful outcome of Greenshields's appeal to the Lords, and Defoe's reaction, see Letters 173 and 174. Defoe gives a retrospective account of events in *The Present State of the Parties in Great Britain*, 193–233.
7 *Greenshields Out of Prison*, 19.
8 *Patronages*: See headnote to Letter 175.
9 *Queens promise in her late Speech*: In her speech to both Houses of Parliament on 29 Nov. 1710 Anne pledged 'to preserve the *British* Constitution according to the Union', and to 'employ none, but such, as are heartily for the Protestant Succession in the House of Hanover; the Interest of which Family no Person can be more truly concerned for, than myself' (*C.J.*, XVI, 403).
10 *not a proper Season*: The issue of Episcopal toleration was a nuisance to Harley in his attempts to conciliate moderate Presbyterians in Scotland and restrain hardline Anglican Tories in England: he could not oppose a toleration but would have been content to see it fail. See Szechi, 87. Lockhart recorded Harley's opposition: he 'seem'd much displeas'd and wou'd once more have perswaded us to wait for a better season' (*Lockhart Papers*, I, 378). In a letter dated one day after this one, 19 Dec. 1710, Carstares warned Harley about what he euphemistically calls the 'inconvenience' of an Episcopal Toleration Act in Scotland (H.M.C. *Portland MSS*, X, 351–2). For the passage of the Act in Mar. 1712, and Defoe's reaction, see headnote to Letter 205.
11 *Dissenters here*: I.e. Episcopalians, dissenters from the Church of Scotland.

557

JOSEPH BUTTON TO DEFOE, [*C.* 25 DECEMBER] 1710

166

Joseph Button to Defoe

[*c.* 25 December] 1710

HEADNOTE: Joseph Button (d. 1735) was a bookseller on Tyne Bridge, Newcastle-upon-Tyne. He was the publisher of *The New-castle Gazette: or, The Northern Courant.*[1] He and Defoe had a longstanding relationship, though its extent and nature remains largely unknown. In 1706 Defoe listed him as his distribution agent in the city.[2] In 1715, Button printed Defoe's *The Family Instructor* in Newcastle, albeit not to a very satisfactory standard.[3]

In April 1711, Defoe's *The British Visions: or, Isaac Bickerstaff, Sen. Being Twelve Prophesies for the Year 1711* was published in London under the pretence that it had been printed at Newcastle in January.[4] The book was in the vein of the Bickerstaff hoaxes of Jonathan Swift (1667–1745), such as *Predictions for the Year 1708*; it appeared to have foretold recent events in advance of their occurrence, such as the death of Emperor Joseph on 17 April 1711. In the *Review* for 5 May 1711, Defoe wrote: 'The Book was Printed in *Newcastle* at a Publick Printing-House — Where Mr. *Button*, the Master of the said Work, a Man known in this City, and of good Reputation here as well as there, may be enquir'd of.'[5] Though this was a ruse, Defoe and Button were evidently corresponding about it as far back as December 1710.

Sr

Yors of ye 23 Inst[6] I recd, but had Sent you before 400 Pa[ ]**a** prophesies.[7] I knew there were Severall Errata's in't but did [not] think it worth while to amend; however when I've Sold these [yt]**b** I've already done, & do more, shall both correct & print [ye] addenda's; if you don't Sell those Sent pray return 'em. In the Gazette of Thursday xbr 21. there is Something of Sr [J.] Cunningham.[8] I suppose yt is it you wou'd ha' printed; there is [ ]**c** in yt you Sent last & you Say it is in yt paper —

As to ye Man & boy I can't tell wt to Say in the**d** Matter if you can get a boy; p[er]haps now this Saywell[9] is bad & lo[w] in Pockett & in debt, wou'd be willing for ye Money to Instruct him.

---

a Pa[ ]] *the righthand edge of the entire MS is frayed; inferred text is supplied in square brackets*
b [yt]] *or possibly no word*
c [ ]] *or possibly no word*
d in the] *reading uncertain*

JOSEPH BUTTON TO DEFOE, [C. 25 DECEMBER] 1710

But than Who must he be bound to, it must be to yorselfe, [for] I can neither make him free of London nor Edinburgh — & another [of] these fellows have So disgusted & tired my wife yt I don't know how I Sha[ll] please her in bringing Any More. I'm for haveing these two fell[ows] out of ye house as soon as possible, & in order to it have desired [ym] to look out Lodgeings &c.

When you do Bickerstaff,[10] I wou'd not ha' you fright all peopl[e] as you Say you will; p[er]haps ye Governt may call us in question fo[r] intimidateing her Majesties good Subjects.

Who woud ha' thought but ye Provost[11] who I heard you Say was [yr] very good friend, wou'd ha' given you ye advertiset, else it Shou'd [ha'] been Sent.

Mr Moody[12] hase yr stell[13] & 3d p[er] pound & he pay Carriage. 5[ ]a are shipt aboard ye Same old wife[14] yor pickles are in & directed for [yr] Brother Davis.[15] Yr specticles hase been mended many daies ago & [are] lyeing by me if you'll ha'em Sent they Shall.

I hear nothing of ye paper[16] you Say you orderd from London. A happy Xmas.

I am

yor friend & Servt

Jos: Button

[ ]b 1710

Text: NLS MS. 1707, fol. 16.[17] *Address* (fol. 16v): To | Daniel Dfoe Esqr | in | Edinburgh. *Notation*: post pd 3d but one Sheet

---

a 5[ ]] *or possibly no unit of measure or word*
b [ ]] *date cut out*

---

1   Furbank and Owens note that the present letter is the only evidence for the assumption that Defoe was involved in the production of this newspaper, and that this is by no means conclusive (F&O, 'Periodicals', 88).
2   See Letter 46.
3   See *RDW*, I, 331–3.
4   The advertisement for the tract in *The Post Boy* for 21–4 Apr. 1711 said that *The British Visions* had been in print for six months.
5   *Review*, VIII, 101 (5 May 1711). See the puffs for the book in the *Review*, VIII, 70–3, 79–82 (21 and 26 Apr. and 17 May 1711).
6   *Yors of ye 23 Inst*: Untraced.
7   *Pa[ ] prophesies*: Unidentified.

DEFOE TO [ROBERT HARLEY], 26 DECEMBER 1710

8 *Gazette ... Cunningham*: No copy of *The New-castle Gazette* for 21 Dec. 1710 has been traced. Cunningham cannot be identified with certainty, but what can be seen of the obliterated initial suggests a 'J', and so Sir James Cunynghame (*c.* 1685–1747) is possible, though what Defoe asked Button to print in the *Gazette* remains unknown. See *Letters*, ed. Healey, 304 n. 4 for a convincing argument against this referring to the jurist and classicist Sir Alexander Cunningham (1655–1730).

9 *Saywell*: Joseph Saywell, sometimes referred to as John. *The New-castle Gazette* was printed in Gateshead by J. Saywell for J. Button. In the *Review* for 5 May 1711, Defoe perpetuates his hoax concerning the printing of *The British Visions* in Newcastle, saying 'Three Servants, whose names are *J. Saywell*, ... *Kid*, and *James Goodall*, are all Witnesses and Workmen, in the setting or Composing and Printing it off' (VIII, 101).

10 *Bickerstaff*: Defoe's *The British Vision: or, Isaac Bickerstaff, Sen. Being Twelve Prophesies for the Year 1711* (1711). See headnote.

11 *Provost*: Adam Brown (see Letter 143). The allusion here is unidentified.

12 *Mr Moody*: Unidentified.

13 *stell*: A vat for distilling whiskey, and by extension the whiskey itself.

14 *wife*: I.e. boat.

15 *Davis*: The nature and extent of Defoe and his brother-in-law Robert Davis's business relationship with Button has not come to light. On the pickles, see John Russell's letter to Defoe of 21 Sept. 1710 (Letter 154).

16 *paper*: Unidentified.

17 An archivist's note explains: 'Found in <u>Newcastle Gazette</u>, no. 65 (23–5. xii. 1710) in Printed Books Dept in July, 1935'. There are sums on the reverse in an eighteenth-century hand. The letter was known to scholars before 1935 because a not-too-accurate version was published in *Analecta Scotica: Collections Illustrative of the Civil, Ecclesiastical, and Literary History of Scotland*, ed. James Maidment (Edinburgh, 1837), 79–80.

167

To [Robert Harley]

26 December 1710

HEADNOTE: Defoe's principal task in Scotland during the winter of 1710–11 was to reconcile Scottish Presbyterians to the political changes in England in favour of the Tories, and to alleviate mistrust caused by the Court and ministry's support for Country and Jacobite peers in the Scottish elections. His own grave misgivings over the latter events, expressed in earlier letters, led him to write *Atalantis Major*, keeping his authorship secret from Harley. That pamphlet denounced the coercion Argyll and Mar, acting for the Court, placed on Scottish peers in the election. Defoe claims to have suppressed *Atalantis Major*, as well as another satire; there is no evidence to suggest that Harley detected Defoe's deceit.

560

DEFOE TO [ROBERT HARLEY], 26 DECEMBER 1710

S[r]

I have Constantly written to you by the Same Convey[a][r] as this and have given you an Exact Acco[t] of Every thing Materiall in this Part. I am Perticularly Unhappy in Not haveing the least hint Any way whether mine Come to hand or no, w[ch] Restrains me Very much in my writeing, fearing what hands it may fall[a] into and knowing the jealousy and temper of the people I have to do w[th].

I think s[r] I may boast to you of my little mannagem[t] in this Place, where the people are brought to be perfectly Easy in her Maj[ties] Measures and have a full Confidenĉe in her Maj[ties] Concern for y[e] Generall Good. I might assume y[e] Words <u>I have brought them to this</u>[2] but I leave that to yo[r] Charity.

I have done my Self y[e] honour On all Occasions to do justiĉe to her Maj[ties] Measures in the late Changes in Answer to the Clamour of Some Certain people which had Reached thus far, and w[ch] began to Spread here both Against yo[r] Self and against Other of her Maj[ties] faithfull Servants, and in this I have the happyness to assure you S[r] there is none of that Nois heard here; but the Dependanĉe of y[e] Honestest[b] people here, is On yo[r] Zeal for the libertys of yo[r] Country and her Maj[ties] justice to y[e] Constitution, and when They hear of Some let in to posts of Trust and Power whose former Measures they have Reason to Apprehend[3] They Frequently Conclude Their Safety Depends upon Her Maj[tie] and the Councils of m[r] H . . . .

This is y[e] Plain and True state of y[e] Temper here. I hope you will not Suspect I flatter My Self in it; if it were Otherwise I know my Duty better than to Conceal it.

Here have been Two Vile Ill Natur'd Pamphlets prepared, both of w[ch] have fallen into my hands in Manuscript and I think I have prevented both[c] their Printing. The first was advertised in the Gazette here and Called y[e] Scots atalantis.[4] The Printer being My Accquaintance I got a Sight of it but Could not get a Coppie; however I Warnd him Against Venturing to print it, upon his Refuseing which y[e] Author Sent for it Again and he knows not

---

[a] fall] *amended from* 'falling'
[b] Honestest] 'est' *interlined*
[c] both] *interlined*

561

DEFOE TO [ROBERT HARLEY], 26 DECEMBER 1710

the Messenger — it was full of Invectives Against the Queen and Governm^t, the Parliam^t and Especally the Members Sent from hence to ye Peers; it had Some Banter on the Lord Glennochy^5 and Some Satyr upon familys wch Appeard meer Scotish but Otherwise it Seemd to be done in England or at least by Some hand that had been lately there; the Messeng^r Said he that Sent the advertisem^t was a Lord and Gave the Printer 2. 6^d for putting it in ye first Time and paid him for a Second, but on My Warning the Printer he Refused to put in the Second and they have never yet Sent to kno' the Reason, but I Suppose on his Returning the Coppy they care not to be So Much known as to Reciev the Money back.

The Other Pamphlet is called <u>Atalantis Major</u>:^{6} and is a Bitter Invective against the D of Argyle, the E of Mar and the Eleccon of the Peers; it is Certainly written by Some English man and I have Some Guess at the Man, but dare not be positive. I have hitherto kept this also^a from the Press,^{7} and believ it will be Impossible for them to get it printed here after the Measures I have Taken. The Party I Got it of pretends ye Coppy Came from England but I am of Another Opinion. I Shall Trouble you no farther about it because if possible I can get it Coppyed I will Transmit ye Coppy by Next post, for I have the Originall in My hand; they Expect I Shall Encourage and assist them in the Mannageing it and Till I can Take a Coppy I Shall not Undeciev them.

I beg yor favourable Construction of My Conduct in an Age So Nice as this and hope On all Occasions to Approve my Self to be.

S^r yor faithfull Humble and Obedient Servt
C Guilot

Edinb. Decemb. 26. 1710

Text: BL Add. MS. 70291, fols. 250–1. [Disguised handwriting.] *Address*: none. *Endorsed by Harley* (fol. 251^v): Mr Guilot Dec: 26 1710

---

^{a} also] *interlined*

---

1 *Same Convey^a*: Unidentified.
2 *I have brought them to this*: The phrase resonates with God's references to the Exodus (e.g. Exodus 20:2) but does not match any particular biblical verse.
3 *Some ... Apprehend*: Including Rochester as Lord President of the Council and Buckingham as Lord Steward.

DEFOE TO [ROBERT HARLEY], 1 JANUARY 1711

4 *Two … Scots atalantis*: The advertisement is untraced, and the pamphlet, if it was ever published, is unidentified (as are the printer and author).
5 *Lord Glennochy*: John Campbell, Lord Glenorchy (1662–1752), second Earl of Breadalbane and Holland after 1717.
6 *Atalantis Major*: See headnote to Letters 160–3.
7 *I have hitherto kept this also from the Press*: *Atalantis Major* was apparently not published until June 1711. See P. N. Furbank and W. R. Owens, 'The Dating of Defoe's *Atalantis Major*', *N&Q* 44 (1997), 189–90.

168

To [Robert Harley]

1 January 1711

HEADNOTE: As well as ongoing anxieties about Episcopal toleration in Scotland, at the start of 1711 Defoe's *Review* addressed the anticipated difficulty the ministry faced in raising funds for the war. Even though the Whig opposition did not oppose supply bills, taxation was unpopular among Country Tories.[1]

Sr

I am humbly to Ask yor Pardon that I have not been Able to Send you yet the Coppy of the Book[2] wch in my last I Gave you Notice of, yet I have with Some Difficulty and meerly by force prevented its goeing to the press. I Shall yet in a few days Compass an Opportunity to get it Coppyed.

I am Very Anxious About my letters yet I presume to give you hints of what Occurrs here. The Concern of ye people here has been quieted as I formerly Noted but a New Suggestion Rises Now of Some Mischief awaiting them from ye Case of Greenshields whose Peticon and Appeal lyes Now before ye house of Lords and whose wholl Case has from its beginning threatned them here wth that formidable Creature a Tolleration.[3]

I have sr wth yor license allways Taken So Much freedome in My Layeing these things before you as to State Rather ye Intrest of ye Governmt than the Merits of ye Cause, but here I think both Argue Against Countenancing this attempt — I am No biggot and farther yet from a friend to Coertions of any kind But sr The

563

DEFOE TO [ROBERT HARLEY], 1 JANUARY 1711

Liberty Obtaind here by Connivance is So great, the people that will Accept of a Tolleration Except without Oaths[4] to ye Governmt So few,[a] the Design of Seeking it So Manifestly a plot upon the public peace, and the Consequences apparently So Distracting to the people here, who are Now So happily Easy Under all her Majties Measures, that I Can not but in Duty to her Majtie, and in Obedience to ye Orders you were pleased to give me, Accquat you of the Case,[b] And humbly Offer it to yor Consideration whether at Least this may be a Time for it.

There is Another Affair Relateing to Justices Imposeing the Oaths to ye Ministers which Requires a little yor Thots when[c] at Leisure, and wch I shall be better[d] quallifyed to lay before you in a post or Two.

I have been So long here wthout yor Commands Either to stay or to Remove, That Indeed I had presum'd to Come Away, had the Roads been Passable,[5] my Circumstances also[e] Unhappily Dissableing me to Subsist longer, without yor Goodness had been Extended as Usuall for my Support.

I[f] Can Not but presume to hint,[g] (however Remote to My present Sphere)[h] the Time for Ways and Means being at hand, That[i] a Contrivance of Some people in England,[j] to prevent ye Governmt in the Article of Funds,[6] has Gone that length, as they are Very Sure of Success.

I am at a loss how to Express My Self on this head, but I humbly Lay it before you, whether it Shall be Expedient for her Majties Service, to Lay funds and Venture their filling <u>by loan</u>, or Rather, to think of Means to Raise the Sums within the Time, which No Doubt Notwithstanding pretences of Poverty, bad News abroad, and Divisions at home,[k] May be Effected: My Anxiety on this head

---

[a] few] *following word* 'and' *cancelled*
[b] of the Case] *interlined; the caret indicating the insertion point follows the comma in MS*
[c] when] *interlined*
[d] better] *following words* 'at Leis' *cancelled*
[e] also] *interlined*
[f] I] *anterior word* 'But' *cancelled*
[g] to hint] *interlined*
[h] Sphere)] *following word* 'That' *cancelled*
[i] That] *interlined*
[j] in England] *interlined; the caret indicating the insertion point follows the comma in MS*
[k] at home,] *interlined*

564

DEFOE TO [ROBERT HARLEY], 1 JANUARY 1711

proceeds from My knowledge of ye Design above, to bauk ye funds and My Senće of ye Consequenće of Such a Dissappointment.

I am

S^r

yor Most Humble and Obedient Servt

DeF^a

Edinb Jan. 1. 1710^7

Text: BL Add. MS. 70291, fols. 252–3. [Disguised handwriting.] *Address*: none. *Endorsed by Harley* (fol. 253^v): Cl. Guilot Janu: 1: 1710/11 R Janu: 8:

---

^{a} DeF] *this signature is not certainly written by Defoe*

---

1 Szechi, 83.

2 *Book*: *Atalantis Major*.

3 *Case … Tolleration*: On 24 Dec. Mar wrote to Harley acknowledging that if Greenshields's appeal succeeded in the House of Lords, an Episcopal Toleration Act would follow; Mar expresses his support in principle for such a toleration but thinks the timing is bad and advises trying to pay off Greenshields (H.M.C. *Portland MSS*, x, 352–3). The toleration was not passed in the 1710–11 session because Harley prevented its introduction by promising Court support for it in the next session. Hence it passed in 1712 (Szechi, 110–11).

4 *people that will Accept of a Tolleration Except without Oaths*: 'As to Toleration of *Episcopacy* by Law, the *Episcopal* People in *Scotland* neither desire it, nor would accept it, unless you would give it them without the Incumbrances of Oaths, or obliging them to Pray for Queen *Anne*, which they will not do; and if they wou'd, their People would not hear them; to Tolerate them, would be to Divide and Destroy them' (Defoe, *Greenshields Out of Prison* (1710), 11). Wodrow also believed the ministers did not desire a toleration 'clogged with the Oaths' of abjuration and allegiance (*Analecta*, 1, 312). Defoe put it succinctly: 'Toleration with Oaths would ruin the Party, if they accepted it, for it would immediately expose them as *Jacobites*' (*Review*, VI, 483 (12 Nov. 1709)). See Jeffrey Stephen, *Defending the Revolution: The Church of Scotland, 1689–1716* (Farnham, 2013), 186–96.

5 *had the Roads been Passable*: In Dec., Wodrow wrote: 'This moneth and the last, yes, almost these ten weeks, we have had the most excessive rains and tempestouse winds that I ever was witness to' (*Analecta*, 1, 313).

6 *Article of Funds*: Defoe had kept up his advice to Whigs not to undermine public credit since Godolphin's fall in Aug. 1710. See for example *Review*, VII, 293–304 (12, 15, 17 Aug. 1710); 465–81 (16, 18, 21, 23 Nov. 1710); 531–3 (23 Dec. 1710).

7 *1710*: 1711 new style.

565

DEFOE TO [ROBERT HARLEY], 9 JANUARY 1711

169

To [Robert Harley]

9 January 1711

HEADNOTE: Defoe was relieved to be able to report to Harley that, notwithstanding Greenshields's case coming before the Lords and instances of local
violence against Presbyterians, the recently gathered Commission of the General
Assembly of the Church of Scotland was being conducted in a way that should
cause no alarm to the ministry.

Sr

I have Since My last had Occasion of doeing I hope Some
little Service here, The Commission of the assembly haveing been
Sitting for this Week past; I have been forward to Accquaint you
Every Time I write of the Good Disposition of the people here
and Especally how Well the Ministers behave, yet at this time the
Numbers Met being Great they were not without Some hot Spirits
who had Diverse projects and made Severall Essays to bring the
Meeting into Some Heats: first they were for an Address to the
queen in which they would have been Glad to Introduce Some
Uneasy things about Greenshields, about Tolleration and about
Invasion of Churches in the North. But with Some help they have
been put off from this.

Then they were for appointing a fast and had that design Gone
On, it Might have been hard to have kept them from bringing in
Some Odd reasons for a fast, for fear of haveing No Good Reasons
to Give, but the News of Our loss in Spain[1] falling in, Some Moved
for a fast upon that Accot which had Some Reall foundation; but
then[a] the Gentlemen that had a worse Design in it Dropt their
Motion and So the wholl fell to the ground for that Time.[2]

There fell an Unhappy Jarr in their Way of a rabble upon a
Number of their Ministers in a Presbytry Meeting in Angus;[3] in[b]
which Many of the Ministers were Stoned and Beaten. This is put
in a way of process in the Criminall Court[4] and at that they are

[a] then] *interlined*
[b] in] *interlined*

DEFOE TO [ROBERT HARLEY], 9 JANUARY 1711

Something Pacifyed;[a] the Gentlemen of that Country have Really Acted too Imprudently in it and thereby given them advantages Against them which they Need Not have done.

Last night the Commission Rose again and the Ministers are Most of them Disperst; and I am Glad to Write in this Time of Uneasyness that they parted So Well.

I am

S^r yor Most Humble & Obedient Servt

C Guilot

Edinb. Jan. 9. 1710[5]

Text: BL Add. MS. 70291, fols. 254–5. [Disguised handwriting.] *Address*: none. *Endorsed by Harley* (fol. 255v): Mr Guilot Eden: Janu: 9 1710/11 R Janu: 18:

---

[a] Pacifyed] *following word* 'But' *cancelled*

---

1 *loss in Spain*: On 8–9 Dec. 1710, the British forces commanded by Stanhope were defeated and taken prisoner at Brihuega by a Franco-Spanish army commanded by Louis Joseph, duc de Vendôme (1654–1712). On 11 Dec., Britain's Habsburg allies, commanded by Guido Starhemberg (1657–1737), were forced to retreat after battling Vendôme's army at Villaviciosa. These were the last major battles in Spain in the Grand Alliance's efforts to dispossess King Philip and install Archduke Charles by force of arms. Defoe reacted by suggesting that it would be better to stop fighting in Spain and instead attack Spain's American colonies to arrest the flow of gold that enabled France to sustain the war (*Review*, VII, 574–7 (18 Jan. 1711)).

2 *fast ... Time*: Wodrow records that the Commission agreed against asking the Queen to appoint a national fast, and so left appointing regional fasts to the discretion of individual presbyteries (*Analecta*, I, 315).

3 *rabble ... Angus*: See Letter 157, note 69. There is some evidence that Defoe was asked to write on the rabblings of ministers by his associates in the Church of Scotland. On 7 Dec. 1710, David Archer (*c.* 1679–1726), minister at Laurencekirk, wrote to Nicol Spence (d. 1743), an agent of the Church, offering to send an account of an incident at Benholm 'to some trustee in England, such as M^r De Foe y^t so he may represent ye matter as he has occasion even in print' (NLS MS 3430, fol. 164r; Alasdair Raffe, *The Culture of Controversy: Religious Arguments in Scotland, 1660–1714* (Woodbridge, 2012), 20 n. 80). Spence was known to Defoe through the Edinburgh Society for the Reformation of Manners and supported Defoe's joining in 1706 (EUL MS. Laing III, 339). Archer gathered two reports (NRS CH 1/2/30/4, fols. 370–4) but there is no evidence they were sent to Defoe: Defoe does not mention Benholm in his known writings, and anyway Benholm is in Aberdeenshire rather than Angus.

4 *Criminall Court*: Wodrow writes that on 8 Jan., the Commission 'had a bussiness of a ryot committed on a Presbitry near Angus before them, and the matter was referred to the Justiciary' (*Analecta*, I, 315).

5 *1710*: 1711 new style.

DEFOE TO [ROBERT HARLEY], 13 FEBRUARY 1711

170

To [Robert Harley]

13 February 1711

HEADNOTE: Now back in London, Defoe outlined a broad range of challenges, English and Scottish, faced by Harley and the ministry as it proceeded in the parliamentary session, negotiating the demands of an increasingly vociferous High Tory backbench pressure group known as the October Club.[1]

Sr

Tho' I Confess ye honour you are Pleased to do me in Frequent and long Audience is Very Great, yet sr Considering The weight of Public Affaires wch Lyes on yor hands, and The Sevll Things which after so long Absence[2] I have to Give you an Accot of, Some of wch if Not all May be of Importance; I thought it my Duty to Save as Much as possible yor Time and Trouble by Minuting Down Thus the heads of Things That you May please to call for Such first as you find Most proper and Such as you please may be after lay'd before you in writing.

1st   Of The Temper of ye People in Scotland, Their Temper when I came There, Their Temper when I left Them, what Uneasynesses They have left, and how they May be kept Easy. Of The Affaires of ye Church, Greenshields, Tolleracon, Common prayer, Intrusion and ye Rabbles upon their Presbytrys in ye North.[3]
Of The Mission of Dr O,[4] The Breaking up of all Correspondence between Them and The Dissenters in Londo and of Their New Agent, The Commissions Mocon for a Correspondence[5] &c.
The State of ye Civill and Millitary administracon There wth Characters of Persons And Conduct as They Respect The late Changes.
Of The State of ye Debate between Johnston and Hamilton or Between ye Merchats and The Trades in The Eleccon for Edinb.[6]

568

DEFOE TO [ROBERT HARLEY], 13 FEBRUARY 1711

Of The Project Pushing on by s^r Pat. Johnston at ye Expence
of ye City of Edinb. for a Dock &c. at Leith[7] —
Of The Raiseing Men in The Highlands and The Directing
Gen^{ll} Maitland to That Work.[8]
Of The Assembly, Their last Division and How Cool'd, about
a Medium for quieting Them in ye Nicety of Appointing Fasts
&c, about a Comissioner[9] and about her Maj' letter to Their
Next Meeting.
Of all These Perticulars I May have Severall Things to lay
before you, Usefull and proper^a for yor Observacon in yor
Mannageing That Difficult people in ye North.

In Matters Relateing to England I Humbly Crave leave to Offer
That if you^b Think it proper I should Turn My Thoughts That way I
May have Something to Say On ye following Subjects:

Credit and of Proper Means for Filling The Lottery[10] wch I
hear Allready Some people please Themselves wth Expectacon
of Seeing Dissappointed.
Funds, and Therein of a Clause in ye Coal Duty wch Very
Much Sinks ye Revenue.[11]
Post Office and Some Circumstances wch May Enlarge That
Duty.[12]
Stamp Office and Some Perticulars of Encreasing That Duty[13]
wth Some brief hints of Other Funds wch if you Approve of
May be Enlarg'd Upon afterward.
Affrican Company and How to Make Them Usefull to
advance a Sum of Money on Their New proposall wch is Now
prepareing.[14]
French Trade and how it May be Opened Most to advantage
both of ye Nacon and of ye Revenue.[15]

I ask yor Pardon for ye Length of This, and hope it is Not
Impertinent. I shall wait yor Comands On which of These Things to

---

^{a} proper] *following illegible word cancelled*
^{b} you] 'your' *in MS*

DEFOE TO [ROBERT HARLEY], 13 FEBRUARY 1711

begin, That I May be as little Troublesome[a] and as Much usefull, as possible.

I am

Sr

yor Most Humble and Obedient Servt

DeFoe

Feb. 13. 1710[16]

Sr

Haveing Given you So long a Diversion Allready I Should have forborne Sayeing any Thing of ye Unpleasant Part, but a Long and Expensive Journey, Family Importunitys, and all the <u>et Cetera's</u> that Make a Dependant allways Importunate; These sr force me, in spight of Blushes, to Remind you of The Usuall Period being past, of That Relief,[17] wch by what Ever hand I Recd it, was Originally Owing to yor Goodness.

I shall Venture to Say Nothing of Merit but This, That as I Resolve to have an Entire Dependance On yor hand sr, So I would Gladly be made Usefull, That I May Not be an Unprofitable Servant.[18]

I am

Sr and Ever Shall be

yor Most faithfull and Obedt Servt

DeFoe

Text: BL Add. MS. 70291, fols. 256–7. *Address*: none. *Endorsed by Harley* (fol. 257v): Msr Claude Guilot Febr: 13: 1710/11 R Febr: 14

---

[a] Troublesome] 'some' *interlined*

---

1 Holmes, 342–4.

2 *long Absence*: Defoe had recently returned to London, having been in Scotland since Nov. 1710.

3 *Rabbles upon their Presbytrys in ye North*: Defoe refers to such an attack on a presbytery at Angus in the previous letter. 'Blood and Murther Rages in *Scotland* against *Presbyterians*', he wrote in the *Review*, VII, 568 (13 Jan. 1711).

4 *Dr O*: Oldfield (see Letter 152, note 1).

5 *New Agent ... Correspondence*: In Jan. 1711, Wodrow had written: 'The bussiness of sending up some to agent the Churche's business at London is yet delayed as unfitt, and soe I think

DEFOE TO [ROBERT HARLEY], 13 FEBRUARY 1711

it will be delayed till the nixt Assembly' (*Analecta*, 1, 315). Defoe himself apparently acted as a London correspondent to several presbyteries in the coming months: in Letter 173 (2 Mar. 1711), he mentions corresponding with seven or eight places; Letter 193 (24 Aug. 1711) indicates that Harley enjoined him to cultivate this network; and Defoe refers to it again in Letter 206 (14 Feb. 1712). Letters 175 and 192 – respectively, a formal memorial and a familiar letter – are probably examples of this correspondence.

6 *Debate ... Edinb*: The Burgh of Edinburgh was represented in Scotland's pre-Union parliament by two members, traditionally one merchant and one tradesman. The Union reduced its representation to one, and in 1710 the incumbent Patrick Johnston (see Letter 56, note 19) contended with Henry Hamilton (b. *c.* 1670, d. after 1712). The former Provost Johnston was Commissioner for the Merchants, pro-Union, and a Court supporter, whereas Hamilton was the Deacon of the Surgeons and the anti-Union younger brother of the late Lord Belhaven. Johnston was elected, but Hamilton petitioned on the grounds that the single seat was to go to merchants and tradesmen by turns. The petition was ultimately unsuccessful. See *HPC 1690–1715*, 1, 176–7; 11, 911–12.

7 *Project ... Leith*: See Letter 151. Johnston, now MP for Edinburgh, was active in seeking funds for the projected docks.

8 *Raiseing ... Work*: For Maitland, see Letter 157. In Sept. 1710, Cromarty sent Harley a report on the strength of loyal forces in the Highlands in case of an invasion (H.M.C. *Portland MSS*, x, 338). Parliament voted funds for three companies of troops comprising 232 men (Mar to Harley, [1710], H.M.C. *Portland MSS*, x, 353; John Ogilvie to Harley, May 1711, H.M.C. *Portland MSS*, x, 374).

9 *Commissioner*: Defoe lists and evaluates candidates for Commissioner of the General Assembly in Letter 171.

10 *Lottery*: See Letter 172.

11 *Clause ... Revenue*: Possibly referring to the clause providing an exemption from duty for coal carried from Stirling Bridge to Dunbar at the mouth of the Firth of Forth. See *A Memorial: Shewing the Import, Extent, and Limits, of the Last Clause of an Act made in the 2d Session of the 3d Parliament of Her present Majesty, intitl'd, An Act for continuing Part of the Duties upon Coal, Culm, and Cynders* [1711].

12 *Post Office ... Duty*: The new parliament had passed the Post Office Revenues Act (1710), settling charges for conveying letters and parcels to and within Britain's colonies. Defoe's ideas about how to increase revenue from postage have not come to light.

13 *Stamp Office ... Duty*: In the preface to vol. VII of the *Review* (late Mar. 1711), Defoe wrote: 'I have Calculated it, above two Hundred Thousand single Papers publish'd every Week in this Nation, and a light Tax would raise a considerable Summ.' He was however wary of taxation as 'a Design to suppress the Papers' (VII, 4). See also *Review*, VIII, 19 (29 Mar. 1711). For Defoe's writings on press regulation in 1704, see headnote to Letters 7 and 8. The Stamp Act of 1712 applied such a tax to periodicals and pamphlets (see Letter 207, note 5).

14 *Affrican Company ... prepareing*: In the dispute between the Royal African Company and independent merchants, Defoe sided with the Company against opening up the trade. The Company, founded in 1672, lost its exclusive trading rights in 1698, after which 'interlopers' to the trade paid it a 10% levy on exports. These separate traders were now lobbying parliament to dissolve the heavily indebted Company; Defoe supported the Company's objective to re-incorporate through a new subscription, satisfying creditors with stock in a new company.

Defoe first intervened in the debate in the *Review* in Feb. 1709, maintaining over the coming years that private traders could not be depended on to sustain a trade of such national importance through lean as well as prosperous times. Defoe treated the subject in the *Review* during Feb.–Mar. 1709, Jan.–Feb. 1710, June–Aug. 1710, and (following this letter) from 24 Feb.–24 Apr. 1711. In June 1711, he published *An Essay upon the Trade to Africa* to restate his position. A payment to Defoe of £12.10s.6d. by the Company on 12 Apr. 1711 was probably his reward, maybe with Harley's approval (Tim Keirn, 'Daniel Defoe and the Royal African Company', *Historical Research* 61 (1988), 243–7). Defoe denied having been paid by

571

the Company to defend it (*Review*, VII, 200 (27 June 1710)). His claim to have lost most of an £800 investment in the Company (*Review*, VII, 268 (29 July 1710)) could have been a ruse to enhance his supposedly disinterested position, as Keirn records that Defoe is absent from the Company's extant stock ledgers between 1704 and 1719.

In the event, the 1698 legislation expired in 1712, leaving trade unregulated. Defoe continued to press for the African trade to be settled in a company with exclusive privileges (*Review*, IX, 147–78 (20 Dec. 1712–13 Jan. 1713); *A Brief Account of the Present State of the African Trade* (1713), *PEW*, VII, 57–82) and generally decried missed opportunities in maximising the African trade (e.g. *Mercator*, no. 134 (30 Mar.–1 Apr. 1714); *The Advantages of Peace and Commerce* (1729), 10–15).

15 *French Trade ... Revenue*: For Defoe's longstanding opposition to England's (now Britain's) wartime prohibition of trade with France, see Letter 98. In the *Review* from 24 Feb. to 17 Apr. 1711, he continuously argued that the balance of trade favoured Britain, and he contended that its prohibition had not pinched France during the war (*Review*, VII, 636 (24 Feb. 1711)). After parliament had lifted the prohibition on importing French wine in Mar. 1711, Defoe advocated keeping high tariffs on them as a revenue-raising measure (*Review*, VIII, 62 (17 Apr. 1711)). For his promotion of the abortive Commercial Treaty with France in 1713–14, see Letters 231 and 234–6.

16 *1710*: 1711 new style.

17 *Relief*: Defoe presumably had not received any payment since £50 on 27 Dec. (TNA T 48/16, fol. 9). This was transmitted to Claude Guilot via James Turner, presumably Defoe's Weymouth associate of 1705 (see Letter 40), and in Letter 180 (19 June 1711) Defoe indicates that this payment was directly from Harley.

18 *Unprofitable Servant*: See Letter 13, note 5.

171

To [Robert Harley]

19 February 1711

HEADNOTE: Harley had evidently asked for Defoe's advice concerning the appointment of a Commissioner to the General Assembly, ahead of its reconvening in May 1711. Harley and Defoe recognised the importance of the upcoming General Assembly. In the *Review*, Defoe expressed his apprehensions about an Episcopalian plot to 'kindle a Flame in the next Assembly'.[1] In the event the Marquess of Annandale, a candidate Defoe advises against, was selected.

S^r

In Obedience to yor Comands, I have Applyed My Self More Perticularly to Think of a Proper Person to Serve her Maj^{tie} as Commission^r to ye Gen^{ll} Assembly, and in Ord^r S^r to Represent

DEFOE TO [ROBERT HARLEY], 19 FEBRUARY 1711

Things wth More Clearness, I have wth y[e] best of My Judgment, Drawn Out short Descripćons, or Characters of y[e] Persons, That Seem proper for That Charge; w[ch] I beg Leave to[a] Lay before you for Observaćon, w[th] This Excepćon Onely, That These Characters are more Perticularly Confind to Their Conduct in y[e] Affair before you,[b] Their Temper, Intrest, and Acceptableness w[th] y[e] people There, and The Governm[t] here, Sinće as I Conciev a p[er]son May be fitt and Acceptable on One Side, and Not On y[e] Other. But That y[e] present Case is to find One if possible That May be So to both.

From Henće S[r] I Conclude The wholl Squadroni Utterly Unquallifyed, as a Set of Men Tho' Otherwise Well Enough w[th] y[e] kirk, yet Unfitt for y[e] Queens Intrest to Consist w[th];[2] and This s[r] is y[e] Onely Objecćon I have to My Lord Polwarth,[3] who would Otherwise be a Man w[th]out Excepćon, both for Senće, Moderaćon, and Agreeablness to both Sides, and p[er]haps were Some Method Used w[th] him, Might be Seperated From Them: — This Also Removes My L[d] Yester[4] from My Thoughts, Tho' he has also No Intrest among y[e] Ministers, w[ch] is an adićonall Excepćon.

I Come Next to y[e] Persons you were Pleased to Name, and w[ch] I humbly Objected Against, as First y[e] Marquiss of Annandale, and (Sec[o]) y[e] Marquis of Louthain. The first is of No Reputacon on Either Side, because Steady to None,[5] Nor would y[e] Ministers have any Confidenće in him, Or Come into any Thing he should propose, — The Second has Made himself Odious by Scandalous Vićes, and Imorrallitys, Sordid Covetousness, and Some Things So Offensive, That it Might be Some question, whether They would Not Rather Think of Delateing[6] him for Scandal, Than Recieving him as a Commissioner.[7]

If I did Not Think it my Duty S[r] to Lay Every Thing Nakedly before you, I should Not go Such a length in Characters, Espećally of Men you were pleased to Name, But I hope The Necessity of Giveing you a Clear View of Things, will Excuse Me.

It is Really Not y[e] Easyest Thing, in a plaće where a Church is So Generally Abandonn'd of her Nobillity, to find a Man who will Suit

---

[a] Leave to] *interlined above illegible cancelled word*
[b] you] *following word* 'and' *cancelled*

DEFOE TO [ROBERT HARLEY], 19 FEBRUARY 1711

both Sides of The present Circumstance; yet I shall Name a few of Such, as I Think May be Depended Upon.

The Earle of Polewarth	(Except as before Excepted).
The Earle of Loudon.[8]	I do Not Take his Character to be So Clear wth ye Church, as I Take him to have a True View of her Maj^{ties} Intrest, and yet to be without any Visible Objecċon on the Side of ye kirk also.
The Earl of Hyndford[9]	I Think a p[er]son wthout Excepċon, but Doubt if he would Serve.
The Earle of Buchan[10]	Think without Excepċon also Perfectly Agreeable to ye Ministers, and yet to be Mannag'd; He parted From The Squadroni in ye Affair of ye Union, and was Dissoblig'd by The last Ministry in ye Voteing Against ye Court, for wch My Lord Marr quarrelled him; and he lost ye Governm^t of Blackness Castle. They Report him to be Hott — but I Think I Could Answer for him on That head; he is a p[er]son of Great Integrity and Understanding, and I believ Can do More wth ye Ministers Than Any Noble Man in Scotland.
The Earl of Weymiss[11]	I can Not Say for his Steadyness So Much, but he stands well Enough with ye Ministers, and is Generally Belov'd.

There is another Person wch for Ought I kno' Might be able to Mannage both Sides Very Well, if Other Circumstances will admitt. This is The Old Lord Advocate;[12] But I Doubt his being Tractable to Measures, and is Imoderately Politick.

DEFOE TO [ROBERT HARLEY], 19 FEBRUARY 1711

The Onely Person I Think Remaining That both Sides would Trust is ye Earle of Staires, of whom There is Onely This Objecċon, his late Engagemt with The Squadroni.[13]

I Humbly lay These Thoughts before you in Ordr to be farther Discours't of Tomorrow when I shall attend According to yor Commands.

Sr

I Can Not Close wthout Some Acknowlegemt (Tho' Small in Proporċon) of yor Constant Bounty to me; The Small Return I can Make Sr, is a Steady adhering to yor Intrest, and Serviċe, and a Dependenċe On yor Goodness; That her Majties Bounty to me and yor Perticular Favors May Not be ill plaċed.

It is allways wth Regrett That I Menċon My Own Case to you, and yor Goodness has been allways Perticular in Preventing My Blushes, on That Accot. This Makes me Remembr with Thankfullness, How you were pleased to Anticipate my feares, by Telling Me yor Last bounty[14] (wch I am Now Acknowleging) was Not Part of her Majties Appointment; This Sr Doubles my Thanks and Makes me Earnest to Merit (as Much as Possible) So Much Goodness. I Most Humbly beg The Continuanċe of yor Favour and Goodness wch I shall Study Never to forfeit.

I am

Sr

yor Most faithfull Obedt Servt
DeFoe

Feb. 19. 1710[15]

Text: BL Add. MS. 70291, fols. 258–9. *Address*: none. *Endorsed by Harley* (fol. 259v): Cl: Guilot Febr: 19: 1710/11

1   *Review*, VIII, 153–6 (29 May 1711); *The Secret History of the October-Club ... Part II* (1711), 59–61. In the event, the General Assembly did not cause Defoe great alarm.

2   *Squadroni ... Consist wth*: Defoe believed the Squadrone had behaved reprehensibly since the Union, opposing the Court in both the 1707–8 session and forming an alliance with Jacobites in the 1708 election (see Letters 134–8). Though they had redeemed themselves somewhat in the 1710 election, Defoe had them pegged as self-interested.

575

DEFOE TO [ROBERT HARLEY], 19 FEBRUARY 1711

3 *Lord Polwarth*: Sir Alexander Hume-Campbell, Lord Polwarth, the former Lord Cessnock, with whom Defoe had worked on the Equivalents committee in 1706 (see Letters 69 and 79). He was styled Lord Polwarth following the death of his elder brother, Patrick, in 1710. He would succeed his father as second Earl of Marchmont in 1724.

4 *Ld Yester*: See Letter 157, note 93.

5 *first ... None*: See Letter 68, note 17. The anti-Union Annandale was elected a representative peer in 1708 (working in conjunction with the English Whigs and Squadrone) and again in 1710 (working with the English Tory ministry). Defoe points to the changeability he evinced in 1708 in *The Secret History of the October Club* (1711), *PEW*, II, 150. 'Opposition to Queensberry was almost the only consistent factor in Annandale's politics' (Riley, *English Ministers*, 93–4). Despite Defoe's advice, Annandale was chosen Commissioner of the General Assembly (*Review*, VIII, 153–6 (29 May 1711)).

6 *Delateing*: To delate is 'to accuse, bring a charge against, impeach; to inform against; to denounce to a judicial tribunal, *esp.* that of the Scotch ecclesiastical courts' (*OED*).

7 *Second ... Commissioner*: See Letter 96, note 29. Lothian 'Laughs at all *Revealed Religion*, yet sets up for a Pillar of *Presbytery*, and proves the surest *Card* in their *Pack*, being very zealous, though not devout. ... [he] loves his Country and his Bottle; a *thorough Libertine*' (*Memoirs of the Secret Services of John Macky* (1733), 197–8).

8 *Earle of Loudon*: See Letter 96, note 22. The former Secretary of State for Scotland, Loudon was elected as a representative peer in 1707, 1708, and 1710; in 1708 he became Keeper of the Great Seal of Scotland.

9 *Earl of Hyndford*: See Letter 160, note 16. Hyndford later commissioned Defoe to supply him with horses (see Letters 181 and 183). Paula R. Backscheider refers to a record of the correspondence between Defoe and Hyndford, but no letters have been traced ('Accounts of an Eyewitness: Defoe's Dispatches from the Vale of Trade and the Edinburgh Parliament House', in *Sent as a Gift: Eight Correspondences from the Eighteenth Century*, ed. Alan T. McKenzie (Athens, Ga., 1993), 21–47 (at 33).

10 *Earle of Buchan*: See Letter 88, note 4. For Buchan's acknowledgement of Defoe's recommendation, see Letter 178.

11 *Earl of Weymiss*: See Letter 96, note 27.

12 *Old Lord Advocate*: Sir James Stewart (see Letter 119, note 6), Lord Advocate from 1692 to 1709 and again from 1711 until his death two years later.

13 *Earle of Staires ... Squadroni*: See Letter 160. Later in 1711, Stair sought office via Mar, angling for a British peerage and offering his service to Oxford (Stair to Mar, 25 May 1711, H.M.C. *Portland MSS*, x, 366–7).

14 *Last bounty*: No record of a payment since 27 Dec. 1710 (see Letter 170, note 17) has been traced.

15 *1710*: 1711 new style.

172

To [Robert Harley]

26 February 1711

HEADNOTE: Back in London by mid-February, Defoe turned from Scottish to English matters, where revenue was a priority. Raising funds through lotteries proved crucial to Harley's ministry in satisfying immediate debts and allaying the Bank of England's concerns during the credit crunch of 1710–11. State lotteries were first operated in England in 1694 but had been disused for more than a decade when Godolphin's ministry ran one in 1710. The first of the two 1711 lotteries raised £1.5 million through sales of 150,000 £10 tickets. Lotteries in Anne's reigns were loans as well as prize draws: for the first of 1711, ticketholders received six per cent per annum on their investment for up to 32 years.[1] The lottery managers reduced the risk of undersubscription by having corporations buy large numbers of tickets. So, despite the Whig attempts to undermine the lottery, to which Defoe alludes, it was filled by 13 March 1711.[2]

Defoe reflected on this lottery in the *Review* for 10 February 1711. He felt the top prize (£12,000) was too high and that instead the yield for blanks should have been better.[3] Defoe disliked the liquidity of the tickets, which resulted in them being 'Stock-Jobb'd' by 'Hucksters' – brokers who speculated in them like any other bond.[4] Defoe alleged that those very people who cried down the lottery engrossed the tickets to sell them at second hand, and he disapproved of that practice.[5] Despite reservations over finer details, Defoe generally supported Harley's scheme; however, we must be open to the idea that what he presents in this letter as the opposition's criticisms may reflect his own views in an attempt to steer policies.[6]

Sr

Tho' ye Other Accots I am prepareing[7] Seem Interrupted by This, yet I Thought it my Duty to have my Eyes About me here also as well as my Thoughts Intent Upon Scotland.

I have had but Little Time Since My Return to look among Our old Friends The Whigs and Therefore Could Say but Little when you were pleased to ask me of Them.

I am Sorry to be Witness to So Much of The weakness of Those I Thought would have before Now have been wiser. When I came Among Some of My Oldest Accquaintance They would hardly Converse wth me Because as They Said I had fallen Upon Them

DEFOE TO [ROBERT HARLEY], 26 FEBRUARY 1711

in My Review for Runing Down Credit,[8] yet I had Not Discourst half an hour before They Discovred themselves. One Said he Used to Pay Six Thousand Pounds in Upon Every Land Tax but Now had Not Paid in a farthing, Another had Constantly Discounted Navy bills[9] but would Meddle wth No More of Them, a Third would keep his Money by him Seaven year before he would Trust The Governm^t wth a Farthing, And ye like, and yet These Gentlemen would Not have it Said That They Run Down ye Public Credit.

They Now Set up to Run Down and Discourage The Lottery and Say Tis a Cheat That The prizes Carry a shew of Smaller Odds Than ye last but are but Triffles Except a Few and They Inferiour to ye Other,[10] That ye Fund is Confused and Uncertain, and The Sume Suppositious, That ye Sume Appropriated[11] in Perticular is Defficent by a great Deal besides ye Charge of Mannagem^t,[12] of which No Notice is Taken.

By This Last I p[er]ciev the Calculator[13] I gave you Notice of Comes From Them and has been Among Them — I am Sorry to See The Weakness of These people and indeed Not[a] More So That I am Apprehensive of The Mischief They Can do, as That[b] No Men Are So Inconsiderable but They May do Some Hurt.[c] S^r if you Think it May be of any Service, I Humbly Offer my Thoughts, That a Small Tract[14] may be written About the Size of The Essay Upon Credit;[15] and wth The Same Secresie; to Explain The Lottery it Self, and Answer a little The Coffee house Clamour[16] of ill Men, and Make Some of Them blush — it May be So ordred as to be Disposed all Over England, and Into Scotland, principally Among Those people who are Most Influenced by These people, and I am Verily Perswaded will be Mighty Usefull at This Time.

I hope yor Charity will prevent any Suspicon That I do This to Make a Charge; you are too Generous to me S^r, to have any Such Thought, Enter into My heart; My wholl Design is to Render Some Good Service, if Possible[d] to Merit, and Make Raconall, The Bounty I do Reciev; and if it Cost Me Twenty Pound Out of My

---

[a] Not] *interlined*
[b] as That] *interlined above cancelled words* 'and yet as'
[c] Hurt] *following letter possibly* 'B' *(for 'But') cancelled*
[d] if Possible] *interlined*

578

DEFOE TO [ROBERT HARLEY], 26 FEBRUARY 1711

Pocket, I shall Rejoyce to have done any Thing if possible to Restore These wild People to yᵉ Governments Intrest, and The Rest (as well I May) I Referr to yoʳ Self.

I am
Sʳ
yoʳ Most Humble and Obedᵗ Servᵗ
DeFoe

Feb. 26. 1710¹⁷

Text: BL Add. MS. 70291, fols. 260–1. *Address*: none. *Endorsed by Harley* (fol. 261ᵛ): Mʳ DF: Febr: 26: 1710/11 R Febr: 27.

1 Dickson, 72–4.
2 Luttrell, VI, 701.
3 *Review*, VII, 615.
4 *Review*, VIII, 59, 66–8 (14 and 19 Apr. 1711).
5 *Review*, VIII, 117 (10 May 1711). Defoe enjoys pointing out that the Whigs who sought to frustrate public credit clamoured for lottery tickets when they realised the profits available (*Eleven Opinions about Mr. H——y* (1711), *PEW*, II, 197).
6 Defoe later praised Harley's management of the lotteries at this time in *The Secret History of the White-Staff, Part III* (1715), 31–5.
7 *Other Accots I am prepareing*: See the list of topics in Letter 170.
8 *Runing Down Credit*: In the *Review* for 6 Jan. 1711, Defoe lamented that he is labelled a High Flyer 'if I tell the Whigs they have been in the wrong, to talk of running down Credit; that they Ruin'd their own Estates, and gratify'd *France*, Encourag'd Jacobitism, and laid the Foundation, to lessen their own Figure' (VII, 554). For Defoe's correspondence with Harley on public credit, and his wider writings on the matter, during 1710, see Letters 146, 148, and 151.
9 *Discounted Navy bills*: To discount a bill of exchange is to pay its value before its maturity date with a deduction based on an interest rate applied to the length of time it has to run. The navy ran in part on credit, issuing bills of exchequer yielding 6% annual interest, but the debt was unsecured by any parliamentary funds and had risen to above £5 million (*C.J.*, XV, 416, 423). By early 1711 navy bills were being discounted at over 30% (Dickson, 362). Defoe discusses the rise of this debt under Godolphin in *The Secret History of the White-Staff, Part III*, 17, 36; in *Minutes of the Negotiations of Monsr. Mesnager* (1717), the eponymous Frenchman says 'these were, it seems, the Debts which afterward grew very Clamorous against the said *Treasurer*, and which, as we are told in *France*, were laid to the Charge of his Mismanagement' (*SFS*, IV, 31; cf. Hamilton, *Diary*, 20–1).
10 *Lottery ... Other*: 'In 1710, prize tickets constituted *c*. 2.6 per cent of the total number; in the £10 lotteries of 1711 and 1712 this figure rose to 20 per cent' (Bob Harris, 'Lottery Adventuring in Britain, c.1710–1760', *EHR* 133 (2018), 284–322 (at 289 n. 24)). See Cecil L'Estrange Ewen, *Lotteries and Sweepstakes: An Historical, Legal, and Ethical Survey of Their Introduction, Suppression and Re-establishment in the British Isles* (1932), 163.
11 *Suṁe Appropriated*: The government's liability over 32 years was £1,928,570 (Dickson, 72).
12 *Charge of Mannagemᵗ*: accusation of manipulation. 'Management' here means 'cunning, manipulation, trickery; the use of scheming, intrigue, prudence, etc., to achieve something' (*OED*).

579

DEFOE TO [ROBERT HARLEY], 2 MARCH 1711

13 *Calculator*: Not identified.

14 *Tract*: The tract Defoe proposes is not known to have been written.

15 *The Essay Upon Credit*: Defoe's *An Essay upon Publick Credit*, published in Aug. 1710. See headnote to Letter 151.

16 *Coffee house Clamour*: Defoe uses the same phrase in *Review*, III, 19 (5 Jan. 1706); there are numerous instances of his using 'coffee-house' as a derisive adjective, as in 'Coffee-House Chat' (*Review*, VI, 378 (27 Sept. 1709)) and 'Coffee-House Politicks' (*Review*, IX, 418 (6 June 1713)).

17 *1710*: 1711 new style.

173

To [Robert Harley]

2 March 1711

HEADNOTE **(Letters 173 and 174)**: On 1 March 1711, the House of Lords upheld Greenshields's appeal, and he was released in April. He had successfully argued before the Lords that no statute of conformity required attendance at Church of Scotland services or prohibited other religious meetings. Attendance in the House of Lords was particularly strong that day, and twenty of twenty-six bishops were present, which confirmed Presbyterian Scots in their distrust of prelates holding civil office. The House of Lords had asserted its right to determine the limits of ecclesiastical jurisdiction in Scotland.

In the *Review* for 8 March Defoe barely suppresses his despair, coming close to criticising the Lords' decision: 'I will not say of them or any other Assembly in the World, that there are not Times, Junctures, and Circumstances apter than others, to lead their fallible Lordships into Mistakes.'[1] On 17 March Defoe turned his ire against Swift's *Examiner*, correcting its assumption that Greenshields had been punished merely for using the English liturgy; Defoe insisted, as he had done elsewhere, that Greenshields's ordination was invalid and he refused the oaths.[2] Anticipating a flood of arguments for a legal toleration of Episcopal services, Defoe pointed out that such services were already allowed.[3]

Greenshields's case became important in the eventual passage of the Scottish Episcopal Toleration Act in March 1712. The Act allowed the use of the English liturgy by Episcopalian clergy without Presbyterian interference. Harley made Greenshields a client to lobby for the delay of this Act, but it was Greenshields's case that made Episcopal toleration inevitable.[4]

580

DEFOE TO [ROBERT HARLEY], 2 MARCH 1711

Sr

I am Very Sorry to write to you On This Occasion, And
Indeed Never Thought ye affair Could ha' been Carryed This
Length — Especally Considering what Assurances were given by
her Majties Express Direccon, at ye Time of The Union. —
I am ye More Concern'd, because of ye Quiet, and Good Temper
Things were brought to There, and The Difficulty There has been
Ever Since, as well as at ye Treaty, to bring it to That pass; which
had Never been, had Not her Majtie been Very Faithfully Serv'd, by
Some who p[er]haps have not themselves been heard of.5
But it is Not a Time to look back. The bussiness isa how to
prevent ye Mischief That will Otherwise Follow, which According
to yor Order sr I have been Applying My Self to.
The First step I have Thought of is, to Let Them6 kno', and Make
Them if possible Satisfy'd in ye Belief of it, That This part has not
been Concerted by The Court, That her Majtie was Surpris'd at
it, and Very Much Concern'd, to hear, how it was Carryed; That
all ye Queens Servts (Except &c.) were Ordred to Oppose it, and
That her Majtie will do any Reasonable Thing to prevent The Evill
Consequences of it.
This Sr I Hint, because I have for These Three yeares past,
Given Them Repeated assurances (and I presume by her
Majties Especall Direccon) That The Queen would upon all
Such Occasions, Take Them into her Proteccon; and prevent,
as farr as possible, The Encroachments and Invasions wch
The Heat of That Party might push Them Upon,7 And This
was Confirm'd by Letters, From ye Ministers of State, at That
Time and by Her Majties Express Command, Approveing of
ye proceedings of ye Magistrates Against This Greenshiels,8
whose behavior was Not Insolent Onely to ye kirk-men,
and Ecclesiastic judicatories, wch he Contemn'd; but Even
to theb Magistrates and Indeed to Magistracy it Self; and
This Sr is Indeed One of ye worst Things I Apprehend as
the Consequence of This,c That if The Magistrates of ye

---

a is] *interlined*
b the] *interlined*
c This] *following word* 'Reason' *cancelled; following superfluous comma omitted in this edition*

581

DEFOE TO [ROBERT HARLEY], 2 MARCH 1711

Capitall City May be Insulted, as They were Then, and I fear
will be again on This Occasion; The Little Civil Governm^t
There is in Scotland will be Lost, and The Matter will be
Decided in Every place by Tumults, and Rabbles; — which
Tho' Mischievous Every where, will be worse There, and will
Never End without blood, to ye Destruccon of her Maj^ties
Authourity, and bringing all Things into Confusion.
For This Reason S^r I Most Humbly propose, That if her Maj^tie
Thinks Fitt, These Two steps, or Such Other as Shall Appear
Reasonable, May be Taken.

 1st as before, to quiet Them Gradually, wth Assurances That y^e
 Queen will Protect Their Church, in all its just Rights, and
 Encourage No Innovacons &c. and let Them have (as before)
 private hints, That ye Queen was Not pleased wth or Concern'd
 in the past Transaccon of the Peers, And This if you please
 May be My Province.
 2. To Restrain (by Managem^t on ye Other hand) The
 Insolence of Those, who Think themselves Let loose by This
 Victory, to Offer New Affronts, to ye people There; and to
 Invade Either Their Civill, or Religious Rights.

These Two Things I Humbly Offer my Thoughts in, in Obedience
to yor Commands; As what I Conciev to be The Onely^a Method
to quiet Them, Under ye First Surprises, and I Doubt Not but
Time and Application May Reconcile Things better; But if the
Other Side Gentlemen go on to Renew Their Insulting of The
Magistrates, and of ye kirk; and Set up ye Common prayer book, as
it were by Authourity, I Dread The Consequences, and am allmost
assured The Rabble will Tear y^m to peices, The Consequence of w^ch
I Need Not Insist on to you s^r.

 And yet s^r I Dare Say, were quiet Calm Steps Taken, Even
That formidable Creature ye Liturgy, would in Time, Come to be a
Native of Scotland; But by Violence The Aversions will Encrease.

 The proposall s^r I Humbly offer here, I Make ye Rather, because
The Ministers There, in whom you kno' Much of ye peoples
Conduct is Resolved, have been Ever Since the Union p[er]swaded,
That Their Safety Depends, More Upon her Maj^ties Personall

---

 a Onely] *following letter perhaps 'p' cancelled*

582

DEFOE TO [ROBERT HARLEY], 2 MARCH 1711

Veracity, and Pious adhereing to her Royall word in The Assurances Given Them of her Gracous proteccon, Than in any Security by The Constitucon of The Treaty — and This will Not Onely Confirm That Opinion, which I have allways Cultivated Among Them, But farther Endear her Maj^{tie} to Them.

At ye Same Time, Her Maj^{tie} May So Hold the Ballance Between Them, That They May No More Oppress The Episcopall men, Than They May Invade The Establishm^t, and I shall lay before her Maj^{tie} A Scheme of Such a Temperament[9] when Ever you please to Command it.

I Shall Omit Nothing in This juncture, That May Contribute to heal This Breach, and to Restore Things There; And if you Think s^r, My Goeing May Contribute any Thing to Makeing Them Easy, I am allways at yor Disposall: — Tho' if you please to Accept my Thoughts upon That, I humbly Suggest, It May Not be So^a Usefull just Now, as Some Time hence; least on My Suddain Return, They May Think They want a Correspondent here, and Return to ye Nocon of Settling Some Other Agent, By which I May loose the Opportunity (Not ye Office, for That is of Not a penney Advantage) of Serving her Maj^{ties} Intrest with Them.

I Shall attend in ye Evening, According to your Commands, in Ord^r to Reciev what Instruccons you please to Give in This Affair; and beg, if you please, That I May Reciev Them This Night, because, as you were pleased to Say you would Not have it Delay'd Longer Than Next post, I would have Time Enough to write to all ye parts where I Correspond, which is Seaven or Eight;[10] That if possible The Antidote May Spread as far as The Poison, and as fast.

I am
Sr
yor Most Humble Faithfull And Obedient Servt
[ ]^b

March. 2. 1710.[11]

Text: BL Add. MS. 70291, fols. 262–3. *Address*: none. *Endorsed by Harley* (fol. 263v):
Scotland Mr Guilot March: 2: 1710/11

^a So] *interlined*
^b [ ]] *signature torn out*

DEFOE TO [ROBERT HARLEY], 3 MARCH 1711

1 *Review*, VII, 654 (8 Mar. 1711).
2 *Review*, VII, 674–7 (17 Mar. 1711). For Swift's emergence as the ministry's chief propagandist after the 1710 election, see J. A. Downie, *Jonathan Swift: Political Writer* (1984); David Oakleaf, *A Political Biography of Jonathan Swift* (2008), 95–140.
3 *Review*, VII, 683–6 (22 Mar. 1711).
4 Szechi, 110; Richard S. Tompson, 'James Greenshields and the House of Lords: A Reappraisal', in *Legal History in the Making: Proceedings of the Ninth British Legal History Conference*, ed. W. M. Gordon and T. D. Fergus (1991), 109–24. In some odd and inaccurate statements in *Memoirs of the Church of Scotland* (1717), Defoe says that after his appeal to the House of Lords Greenshields was given some money to go away and the case was quietly dropped (*TDH*, VI, 278–9).
5 *Some ... heard of*: Defoe included himself in this category. See Letters 103 and 136.
6 *Them*: The ministers with whom Defoe corresponded.
7 *The Queen ... Upon*: As Defoe wrote elsewhere: 'We have her Majesty's Sacred Promise to protect the Church of *Scotland*, in all her Rights and Priviledges, *According to the Union*' (*A Seasonable Caution to the General Assembly* (1711), 20).
8 *Letters ... Greenshiels*: In *The Present State of the Parties in Great Britain* (1712), Defoe claimed that 'the said Magistrates ... had receiv'd Letters from his Grace the Duke of *Queensberry* and the Earl of *Sund——d*, by Her Majesties special Command, approving of their Proceedings, and assuring them, That Her Majesty was resolved to give no Encouragement to those Innovations' (208). Cf. *A Seasonable Caution to the General Assembly*, 17–18.
9 *A Scheme of Such a Temperament*: If Defoe produced this, it is untraced. 'Temperament' seems to be used in the sense of 'compromise' (*OED*).
10 *parts where I Correspond, which is Seaven or Eight*: With whom Defoe corresponded and in what places remain unidentified.
11 *1710*: 1711 new style.

174

To [Robert Harley]

3 March 1711

Sr

I am Really Perplexing you wth Letters on The Occasion of This New Affair of Scotland,[a] But hope My Zeal for The Service, will Excuse My Impertinence.

I have had My Thoughts Very Intent Upon The Thing it Self, and have been up all Night writeing Letters Upon ye Subject,[1] According to My Proposall and yor Commands; But a New

[a] of Scotland] *interlined*

584

DEFOE TO [ROBERT HARLEY], 3 MARCH 1711

Thought Offring it Self, I Could Not but Lay it before you Sʳ, for yoʳ Approbacon, and This is whether if a Small pamphlett² of 2 or 3 sheets at Most, were written to Allay the feares, and Lessen yᵉ Surprize of the people There, to Dispose Them to Consider Calmly of Things, and a Little Encourage Them, — whether you may not Think it Usefull at Such a juncture as This, and follow it wᵗʰ a Second at Some Distance of Time, to Improve and Applye the first.

This sʳ I Can Send from Hence**ᵃ** in Manuscript, and print it at Edinb: and privately Convey Them Among The Ministers all Over Scotland, and I am p[er]swaded Submitting it at yᵉ Same Time to yoʳ Commands, That it May do a Very Great Service.

I am Sorry to Mencon The Expence, and should not if My Unhappy Craveing Circumstances would bear it,**ᵇ** But as I Entirely Submitt that to yoʳ Self, So Sʳ I shall go yᵉ Uttmost Length I Can wᵗʰout a Demand; But if I Speak my Own Sence, I Think if it Came to 30 or**ᶜ** 40 or 50 pound it would be well plac't, and May do More Service just Now, Than Modesty will let me Name — But I forbear to Urge my Own Opinion. I shall attend in yᵉ Evening According to yoʳ Command.

I am

Sʳ yoʳ Most Obedᵗ Servᵗ

DeFoe

March 3. 1710³

Text: BL Add. MS. 70291, fols. 264–5. *Address*: none. *Endorsed by Harley* (fol. 265v): Edenburg March: 3: 1710/11

ᵃ Hence] *following words* 'and print' *cancelled*
ᵇ would bear it] *interlined*
ᶜ 30 or] *interlined*

---

1 *Letters Upon yᵉ Subject*: Presumably to the Presbyterian ministers in Scotland with whom he was corresponding; none of the letters have been traced.

2 *pamphlett*: Probably Defoe's *A Seasonable Caution to the General Assembly*, published before 10 May 1711 (F&O, *Bibliography*, 108–9). Written from the perspective of a Scottish MP, this pamphlet sought to reassure Scots that the Lords had not overruled the Presbytery of Edinburgh: upholding Greenshields's appeal was a civil, not ecclesiastical, ruling. (Defoe echoes this in *Review*, VIII, 94 (3 May 1711)). Actually, Defoe says, the ruling tacitly acknowledges

that Scotland's Church authorities are *not* subject to British civil power and that the case does *not* necessarily have a wider implication about the legality of using the Book of Common Prayer. To resort to street violence would be to imitate the Sacheverell mob, playing into the Episcopalians' hands. The pamphlet is not a total whitewash: Defoe urges that Scots 'wisely distinguish between a Party busie to invade you, and the Governments Concurring to their Endeavours' (29).

3   *1710*: 1711 new style.

175

[Author unknown] to Defoe

24 March 1711

HEADNOTE: The presentation of ministers of the Church of Scotland to livings by lay patrons had ended in 1690, following the Revolution. Since then, congregations had had the authority to accept ministers nominated by synods. The Union pledged to leave the Church settlement untouched but also to maintain heritable rights and jurisdictions. Lay patronage put those two commitments at odds: lay patrons with Episcopalian sympathies were arguing that they had been denied a purely civil right. The Tories sided with them, so pressure mounted for legislation restoring this privilege. The established Church wanted to maintain its independence, again resenting the prospect of interference from a British parliament in which bishops sat; of course they did not want Episcopalian lairds presenting ministers. Defoe wrote that restoring patronages 'was effectually opening a door to Episcopacy, as it took from the People the right of *Choosing their own Ministers*, which was essential to Presbytery'.[1]

An unknown Scottish writer, perhaps one of the ministers with whom Defoe corresponded, sent this summary history of Scottish Church patronage to Defoe ahead of the anticipated battle to restore lay patronage in the 1711–12 parliamentary session.[2] Defoe used some of it in the *Review* for 22 May 1711.[3]

Like Episcopal toleration in Scotland, lay patronage was a battle with Tory backbenchers that Harley could not afford to fight. He fudged the truth with Carstares, Moderator of the General Assembly, when on 8 May 1711 he wrote that restoring lay patronage 'was never movd nor in the least countenanced or entertaind' in the 1710–11 session.[4] In fact, he had managed to have it deferred only on condition of not opposing it in the 1711–12 session.[5]

Lay patronage was restored by the Church Patronage (Scotland) Act in May 1712. In the *Review* for 6 May 1712, Defoe indicated his disappointment with the Toleration and Patronage Acts but insisted they would not serve the ends of the

586

[AUTHOR UNKNOWN] TO DEFOE, 24 MARCH 1711

Episcopalians and Jacobites who promoted them.[6] In *The Present State of the Parties in Great Britain*, written at the time that Act was depending, Defoe gave a detailed history of lay patronage in Scotland, which marries with but goes beyond the account he was provided in this anonymous letter.[7]

24th March 1711

Memoriall Anent the power and priviledge of presenting ministers in Scotland

Before the reformation[8] the power of presentation of ministers belonged to the Patrons who were bound to present a fitt qualified person upon any vacancy in the Church, with this distinction, That the Laick patron was bound to present Such a fitt person to the Bishop within four months of the Vacancy, And if ane Ecclesiastick Patron within Six months, which time was computed from their knowledge of the vacancy, and the reason of the distinction of the time was because if the Laick Patron did present ane ūnfitt person he had liberty to present ane other, but if the Ecclesiastick Patron to whom the qualifications of the person were presumed to have been knowen did present ane ūnfitt person he did forfaūlt his priviledge for that time Lib. 1 Reg. Maj. cap. 2. parag. 3d and 4th.[9]

The Patron's right did arryse either from the donation of the Subject which was the Subsistence of the Ecclesiastick person or from building[a] the Church, or from the donation of the ground wherūpon the Church was built, conform to the knowen rūle Patronūm faciunt dos,[b] edificatio fundūs.[10] And before the reformation where no Patron was knowen the Pope claimed the right as universall Patron though many of our Kings of Scotland did both question and deney them that priviledge.

Though the Patrons had allwayes this power of presentation, yet the institution and collation or admission[11] was allwayes lodged in the hands of Churchmen to whom also the power of presentation belonged jure devoluto[12] when the Patrons did not present a fitt person within the Space[13] appointed by Law.

---

[a] building] *following word* 'and' *cancelled*
[b] dos] *following word probably* 'in' *cancelled*

[AUTHOR UNKNOWN] TO DEFOE, 24 MARCH 1711

Before the reformation the power and priviledge of institution, collation or admission[a] and priviledge of presentation jure devoluto was lodged in the hands of the Bishop or Arch Bishop as Sd is, But after the reformation Scotland haveing reformed by Presbiters, and the Church government then consisting of Presbiters divided into Presbitries Provinciall[b] and Generall assemblies, and each Presbitrie and Provinciall assemblie haveing a Superintendant, and there being ane appeall from the Presbitry to the[c] Provinciall, and from the Provinciall to the Generall assembly, By the 7th act 1 parl James the 6[14] the examination and admission of Ministers in Scotland was lodged in the hands of these Church men, And the Patrons bound to present a qualified person within Six moneths from their knowledge of the Vacancy to the Superintendent of the bounds or those haveing commission from the Presbiters[d] within that bounds, And in case of refusall to admitt the person So presented[15] there was ane appeall to the Superintendant and[e] the Provinciall assembly and from them to the Nationall Assembly, And in case the Patron did not present a fitt person wthin the Space forsaid, the power of presentation as well[f] as admission did belong to the Superintendant and Presbiters within the bounds where the benefice lay.

The Patrons had the power of retaining and disposeing of the whole fruits of the benefice dureing the Vacancy by the act 115 parl. 12 James 6,[16] yea even after Episcopacy was restored by K. James the 6th anno 1606,[17] As appears by the 1st act parl. 21 James 6.[18]

By the introduction[g] of Episcopacy the time forsaid the power of admission of ministers and presentation jure devoluto was lodged in the hands of the Bishops and Archbishops from the act forsaid and other acts of parliament James the 6th.[19]

After the reformation the Abbacies and Priories were erected into temporall Lordships and the Lords of erection[20] had the right to the tyths and were Patrons of the Churches within these Benefices, whereby and with the Patronages that belonged to Laick

---

[a] admission] *following words* 'was lodged in the' *cancelled*
[b] Provinciall] *following word* 'Synods' *cancelled*
[c] the] *following word* 'assembly' *cancelled*
[d] Presbiters] *interlined above cancelled word* 'Churchmen'
[e] and] *interlined above cancelled word* 'of'
[f] well] *following word* 'of' *cancelled*
[g] introduction] *interlined above cancelled word* 'institution'

[AUTHOR UNKNOWN] TO DEFOE, 24 MARCH 1711

Patrons before the reformation very few patronages were reserved to the Croūn, and of these few a pairt did accress[21] to the Bishops from the[a] establishing of Episcopacy by K. Ja. 6th.

King Charles the 1st upon his accession to the Croūn from the information of the prejudice to the Croūn by these erections of Church lands, teynds[22] and patronages did make a revocation of all alienations of the Croūn in order to resūme the Same, whereupon ensūed four Submissions and Surrenders, ane by the Lords of Erection, Another by the Titulars of the teynds,[23] a third by the Clergy and a fourth by the Royall Burrows and decreets arbitrall[24] when ratified in the parliament 1633,[25] And by which decreets the Lords of erection were to get ten years purchase for the rents,[b] fewdueties,[c] Superiorities[26] and patronages[d] and to retain the Same, ay and while they be redeemed, but this reversion of Kirklands is rescinded by the 11th act Q. Anne anno[e] 1707[27] and the reversion renuncd & discharged for ever, but prejudice of her majesties right of Superiority of the erections and services and casūalties[f] arryseing therefrom.

This revocation made a great noyse in Scotland and was the first thing that gave ryse to those troubles that ensued dureing that good King's life, Presbyterian Government haveing been restored in anno 40.[g][28]

By the 20th act anno[h] 1644 Charles the 1st[29] Patrons are ordained to apply the rents and fruits of the benefices dureing the vacancy for pioūs ūses within the paroch by the advice and consent of the Severall Presbitries, and where the Presbitries have the power of planting kirks in place of the Patrons they are to apply the Same for pioūs uses wthin the paroch by the advice and consent of the Heritors and Parochiners, and by the 39th act anno 1649 Charles the 1st[30] all presentations by Patrons are made void, and the Patrons to have the heritable right to the Superplūs tyths over and above the

---

[a] the] *following illegible word cancelled*
[b] rents] *following word* 'and' *cancelled*
[c] fewdueties] *following word* 'and' *cancelled*
[d] and patronages] *interlined*
[e] anno] *interlined*
[f] services and casūalties] *interlined above cancelled word* 'causes'
[g] Presbyterian Government haveing been restored in anno 40] *inserted in margin*
[h] anno] *interlined above cancelled word* 'parl'

provisions to the Minister and wᵗʰout prejudice to the Titulars or tacksmen of their prior rights thereto.

These acts were repealled ūpon King Charles the 2ᵈs restaūration, and the restauration of Episcopacy anno 1661, but by the 52 act parl. 1ˢᵗ Charles the 2ᵈ³¹ and the 23ᵈ act 3ᵈ sess. of the same parliament³² the Vacand stipends are to be applyed for pioūs ūses.³³

Upon the late Happy revolution Episcopacy was abolished, and the Presbiterian church government reestablished in Scotland upon the foot of the claim of right and grievances and by the 23ᵈ act anno 1690 K. Wᵐ & Q. Mary³⁴ the power of presentation is taken from the Patrons And lodged in the hands of the Heritors and Elders except as to the Royall Burrows where it is lodged in the Magistrates, Toūn Councill and Kirk session of the burgh, and in the hands of the Presbitry jure devoluto, And for ane equivalent of this right of presentation the Patrons are to be payed 600 mks³⁵ by the Heritors andᵃ have a right to the Superplus teynds over and above the provisions to the Ministers where the teynds were not heritably disponed, and wᵗʰ a priviledge to the Heritors to buy those teynds which did So accress to the Patron at the rate of Six years pūrchase, And by the 26ᵗʰ act anno 1693 parl. K. Wᵐ & Q. Mary³⁶ this right to the Superplūs teynds in favoūrs of Patrons in lieū of their right of presentation is extended to personages and other benefices, And by the 6ᵗʰ act of her Majestie Q. Anne anno 1707³⁷ The Presbiterian Church goverment in Scotland in it's doctrine, discipline and worshipᵇ and whoseᶜ acts relative thereto are ratifiedᵈ and to be held and observed in all time comeing as a fundamentall and essentiall condition of the Union.³⁸

From what is Said it's manifest: 1°/ thatᵉ while Presbitry obtained in Scotland, the power of admission of Ministers was allwayes lodged in the hands of the Presbitry, and even the power of presentation conform to their book of discipline³⁹ and the laws dureing Presbiterian government to be lodged in the hands of the

---

ᵃ are to be payed 600 mks by the Heritors and] *interlined*
ᵇ in it's doctrine, discipline and worship] *inserted in margin*
ᶜ whose] *interlined above illegible cancelled word*
ᵈ ratified] *following illegible character cancelled, possibly the 'X' signalling where the above marginal insertion was first placed, before the author moved it several words earlier*
ᵉ 1°/ that] '1°' *interlined*

[AUTHOR UNKNOWN] TO DEFOE, 24 MARCH 1711

Heritors and Elders, which Seems also more equitable and conform to the practise of the Primative Church, That those who are to reap the benefit and Success of the Gosple ministry should have the choyse and call of the Minister than one Single person who probably neither is to reside in the p[aroch]^a nor injoy the fruits of his Ministry.

2°/ This point Seems now to be established by the Union as being a pairt of the disciplin, form and practise of Presbiterian Church government ratified and made ane essentiall pairt of the Treaty of Union as Sd is.^{40}

3°/ The Patrons have ane equivalent by their right to the Superplūs tyths in manner forsaid & all Heritors and proprietars of teyths have the priviledge of purchaseing yᵐ at ane easie rate in manner above exprest.^{41}

4°/ By these acts all the teynds are with the burden of Suteable provisions to the Ministers^b and ūpon application to the Lords of the Commission they accordingly get Suteable provisions and Aūgmentations forth of the teynds which prevents those Simoniacall^c pactions^{42} which were in use to be interposed and ad hibit^{43} betwixt the Patron and the person he presented.

From what is premised in Sum it's manifest that the resumption of patronages and repealling the former acts must necessar[i]ly^d infer a great prejūdice to all the pairties concerned above exprest, and Seems inconsistant with the Presbiterian Church Government in Scotland ratified and made ane essentiall pairt of the Treaty of Union as Said is.

As to the [Cit]y^e of Edr the teynds pertaining to them were by K. Charles [the]^f first's letter ordained to continūe in the same^g state they were in before his revocation and which was ratified in the parliament 1633.^{44} And the Mag[ist]rates,^{h} Toun Councill and

---

^{a} p[aroch]] *MS torn*
^{b} Ministers] *following letters* 'wh' *cancelled*
^{c} Simoniacall] *following word* 'practises' *cancelled*
^{d} necessar[i]ly] 'i' *omitted*
^{e} [Cit]y] *hole in MS*
^{f} [the]] *hole in MS*
^{g} same] *following letter* 'p' *cancelled*
^{h} Mag[ist]rates] *abbreviated* 'Magrates' *in MS*

591

[AUTHOR UNKNOWN] TO DEFOE, 24 MARCH 1711

Kirk sessions were allwayes in use [to]ᵃ present their Ministers and the Mag[ist]ratesᵇ and Toūn Coūncill even in time of Episcopacy had right of presentation by the payment of the Stipends, the building and repairing the Churches and all the tittles that constitut a patron, And Since Episcopacy and patronages were abolished the power of presentation lodged in manne[r]ᶜ forsaid.

Text: BL Add. MS. 70048, fols. 183–5. *Address* (fol. 185v): Daniel Defoe Esquire | at Newington | near London. *Notation in same hand as document* (fol. 185v): Memoriall Anent The power and priviledge of presenting Ministers in Scotland 1711

ᵃ [to]] *hole in MS*
ᵇ Mag[ist]rates] *abbreviated* 'Magrates' *in MS*
ᶜ manne[r]] *hole in MS*

---

1 *The Secret History of the October-Club ... Part II* (1711), 60.
2 See Laurence A. B. Whitley, *A Great Grievance: Ecclesiastical Lay Patronage in Scotland until 1750* (Eugene, Oreg., 2013).
3 *Review*, VIII, 140.
4 H.M.C. *Laing MSS*, II, 161.
5 Riley, *English Ministers*, 254; Szechi, III–12.
6 *Review*, VIII, 780–3.
7 Defoe, *The Present State of the Parties in Great Britain* (1712), 260–82. Cf. Defoe, *Memoirs of the Church of Scotland* (1717), *TDH*, VI, 279–82.
8 *reformation*: In *Memoirs of the Church of Scotland*, Defoe wrote that the Scottish Reformation commenced in 1557, was fully acknowledged in 1560, and was recognised by an act of the General Assembly in 1582 (*TDH*, VI, 26, 49, 79).
9 *Lib. I Reg. Maj. cap. 2. parag. 3ᵈ and 4ᵗʰ*: Citing book I, chapter II, paragraphs 3 and 4 of *Regiam Majestatem: The Auld Lawes and Constitutions of Scotland* (Edinburgh, 1609), 6–7. This digest of Scottish statutes originated in the early fourteenth century and was edited in 1609 by Sir John Skene, Lord Curriehill (*c.* 1543–1617).
10 *Patronūm faciunt dos, edificatio fundūs*: 'The gift, estate, building, make the patron' (Latin). This is a maxim of canon law. In *The Present State of the Parties in Great Britain*, 264–5, Defoe says that it barely pertained in Scotland even before the Reformation.
11 *collation or admission*: 'The appointment of a clergyman to a benefice' (*OED*).
12 *jure devoluto*: 'by devolving right' (Latin).
13 *Space*: I.e. time.
14 *7ᵗʰ act 1 parl James the 6*: *APS*, III, 23. This was passed in 1567. In numbering acts of the Scottish parliament, Defoe's correspondent appears to follow *The Lawes and Acts of Parliament made by ... Kings of Scotland* (1681), which Defoe himself used in *Memoirs of the Church of Scotland* (*TDH*, VI, 315 n. 98) and which is in *Defoe–Farewell Catalogue* (item 184a). These differ sometimes from *APS*, which is used in explanatory notes to this edition.
15 *refusall to admit the person So presented*: In *The Present State of the Parties in Great Britain*, 270, Defoe specifies that the qualifications for admission are 'That he should agree with the *Church* in Doctrine, and the Administration of the Sacraments, according to the *Confession of Faith*'.
16 *act 115 parl. 12 James 6*: 'Anent depositioun of unqualifiet personis frome thair functionis and Beneficis', passed in 1592 (*APS*, III, 542–3).

592

[AUTHOR UNKNOWN] TO DEFOE, 24 MARCH 1711

17 *K. James the 6th anno 1606*: 'Act Anent the restitution of the estate of Bischoppis' (*APS*, IV, 281–4).

18 *1st act parl. 21 James 6*: 'Ratification of the acts set downe … in the [1610] generall assemblie of the kirk' in the 1612 parliament (*APS*, IV, 469).

19 *other acts of parliament James the 6th*: Defoe offers a critical account of James VI and I's dealings with the Kirk in *Memoirs of the Church of Scotland*. He says that James 'mortally hated the Kirk' and was its 'open and declared Enemy' (*TDH*, VI, 87, 86). He details 'the Fraud, the Artifice, and hypocritical Fawnings, the arbitrary and outragious Dealings, which were practised with the Ministers' in the build up to the 1606 '*Act for Restitution of Bishops*' (112, 114). Defoe also discusses James I's impiety in *The Representation Examined* (June 1711), 8–9. For a modern account of James's religious policies, see W. B. Patterson, *James VI and I and the Reunion of Christendom* (Cambridge, 1997).

20 *Lords of erection*: In Scottish law, men 'possessing a temporal lordship erected or derived from a spiritual benefice after the Reformation' (*OED*).

21 *access*: accrue.

22 *teynds*: tithes; again, a particularly Scottish term.

23 *Titulars of the teynds*: Laymen to whom the Crown in Scotland transferred the tithes of church benefices after the Reformation.

24 *decreets arbitrall*: A judgement by arbitration.

25 *revocation … 1633*: Charles I's Revocation Act (1625) resumed for the Crown all grants of land made in Scotland since the death of James V in 1542 and compensated those dispossessed. This prerogative act was ratified by the Scottish parliament in 1633 (*APS*, V, 23–7).

26 *fewdueties, Superiorities*: Periodic payments to a feudal superior. For Defoe's negative assessment of superiorities, see Letter 120, note 8. This system was abolished in Scotland in 2004.

27 *11th act Q. Anne anno 1707*: 'Act renouncing the reversion of Kirklands' (*APS*, XI, 482–3).

28 *This revocation … anno 40*: See Allan I. MacInnes, *Charles I and the Making of the Covenanting Movement, 1625–1641* (Edinburgh, 1991). Defoe narrates Charles's relationship with the Kirk prior to the Civil War, in *Memoirs of the Church of Scotland*, *TDH*, VI, 124–34.

29 *20th act anno 1644 Charles the 1st*: 'Act declaring vacant stipends should be imployed upon pious uses' (*APS*, VI, 128–9).

30 *39th act anno 1649 Charles the 1st*: 'Act abolishing the patronages of kirks' (*APS*, VI, 411–13).

31 *52 act parl. 1st Charles the 2d*: 'Act enent the disposall of vacand stipends' (*APS*, VII, 18–19). An act of the following year turned Presbyterian ministers out of their livings (*APS*, VII, 376).

32 *23d act 3d sess. of the same parliament*: 'An Act for Additional Provision in Favours of the Universities', passed in 1663, suspended the 1661 act for the period 1664 to 1668; during this time a tax on clerical benefices was levied to fund Scotland's universities (*APS*, VII, 491). ('23d' seems to be an error, as the 1681 *Lawes and Acts of Parliament* gives this as the twenty-fourth act.)

33 *Vacand stipends are to be applyed for pioŭs ŭses*: Defoe discusses the re-establishment of Episcopacy, including the depriving the Church of the power to call its own ministers, in *Memoirs of the Church of Scotland*, *TDH*, VI, 161–6.

34 *23d act anno 1690 K. Wm & Q. Mary*: *APS*, IX, 196–7. Defoe glosses this Act in *The Present State of the Parties in Great Britain*, 261. See his account of the Kirk immediately after the 1688 Revolution in *Memoirs of the Church of Scotland*, *TDH*, VI, 255–62. See also Defoe's citation of the '22d Act, the first Parliament of *WILLIAM* and *MARY*, which Ordain'd, *That all those* Episcopal *Ministers, who would take the Oaths, should continue in their Churches*' (*Review*, VI, 488 (17 Nov. 1709)).

35 *600 mks*: The Scots merk or mark was worth around 13 shillings sterling, making this around £390.

36 *26th act anno 1693 parl. K. Wm & Q. Mary*: *APS*, IX, 304–5.

37 *6th act of her Majestie Q. Anne anno 1707*: The Act of Security (*APS*, XI, 402–3), approved in Scotland in 1706 and ratified with the Union in Jan. 1707. See headnote to Letters 63–5.

38 *a fundamentall and essentiall condition of the Union*: The wording of Defoe's correspondent exactly matches Defoe's in *The Present State of the Parties in Great Britain* 277, where he says

that Presbyterian church government in Scotland is 'a Fundamental and Essential Condition of the Treaty of Union'.

39 *book of discipline*: The first *Book of Discipline* (1560) outlined a Presbyterian system for the reformed Church of Scotland. It was drawn up by a committee of 'six Johns', including John Knox (1513–72). A second *Book* (1578) was produced by Andrew Melville (1545–1622). Defoe recounts the genesis and gradual adoption of the Book of Discipline in *Memoirs of the Church of Scotland, TDH*, VI, 52–3, 65–6, 69, 94.

40 *essentiall pairt of the Treaty of Union as Sd is*: The Church's petition to parliament ahead of the 1712 Scottish Patronage Act, which restored lay patronage, argued this point; it is given in *Memoirs of the Church of Scotland, TDH*, VI, 280. Defoe expressed it himself in *Review*, VIII, 38 (5 Apr. 1711); *The Present State of the Parties in Great Britain*, 276.

41 *Patrons … exprest*: Again, see the argument in the Church's petition, which claims 'this Bill takes back from the Church the Power of Presentation of Ministers, without restoring the Tythes which formerly belong'd to her, by which the Patrons come to enjoy both the Purchase and the Price' (*Memoirs of the Church of Scotland, TDH*, VI, 281).

42 *Simoniacall pactions*: In *The Present State of the Parties in Great Britain*, 273, Defoe explains this as 'a direct Bargain betwixt the *Patron* and the *Minister* to be presented, for obtaining a Spiritual Charge in the *Church*'. He goes on: 'The *Patrons*, by these *Simoniacal* Contracts, inverted the Tythes to their own private Use, and no Minister was Presented, till he had given a Lease to his *Patron* of the Tythes of his Parish.'

43 *ad hibit*: 'held' (Latin).

44 *[Cit]y of Edr … 1633*: *APS*, V, 25.

176

John Russell to Defoe

19 April 1711

HEADNOTE: Having departed from Edinburgh in February, Defoe had again left his business affairs there in Russell's hands.

Ed^b 19th Aprill 1711

Dr Sir

After beging your pardon for my long silence[1] please know that I receaved yours after you pairted from this[2] with my accompt which is very right except the od 8 sh: on Mr Ballianquiells[3] bill which you have omitted to charge me with, For ye bill wes for £12..8 sh that ye ballance in my hand of yours ought to be £9..8 which you may order as you please. I charge you wth nothing for port of lers,[4] haveing given you much more trouble. I wes indeed uneasie at my not seeing

JOHN RUSSELL TO DEFOE, 19 APRIL 1711

you befor you left this but you know my goeing to yᵉ country[a] that tyme wes very unexpected, being occasion'd by my brothers[5] death.[b] I wes very fond[6] of yours of yᵉ 13th of March[7] — and got the boy[8] as you desired and shall be much obleidged to you if your time can allow to let me hear frequently from you And how you pairted with our freind My Ld L:[9] who I hear is now on yᵉ road thither; my wife kindly remembers Madam, the young Ladyes & your self as I likewayes doe who am

Sir

yʳ Servt

Text: NLS MS. 25.3.9, fol. 69ᵛ [scribe's copy]. *Address*: To Mr Dan: Defoe | London

---

[a] country] *following illegible word cancelled*
[b] death] *amended from* 'dead'

---

1 *long silence*: If Russell had written any letters to Defoe since Sept. 1710 (Letter 154) they are untraced.
2 *this*: I.e. 'this place', Edinburgh.
3 *Mr Ballianquiells*: See Letter 147, note 2.
4 *port of lers*: I.e. postage of letters.
5 *brothers*: Unidentified.
6 *fond*: 'glad' (Scots).
7 *yours of yᵉ 13th of March*: Untraced.
8 *boy*: Presumably an apprentice or servant.
9 *Ld L.:*: Leven.

DEFOE TO [ROBERT HARLEY], 25 APRIL 1711

177

To [Robert Harley]

25 April 1711

HEADNOTE: On 8 March 1711, Antoine, Marquis de Guiscard (1658–1711), while being interviewed by a Committee of Council on suspicion of spying for France, attempted to assassinate Harley by stabbing him with a penknife.[1] His grudge was apparently an unsettled pension. Harley was incapacitated for over six weeks.

On 13 March in the *Review*, Defoe reacted to the attack as 'Brutal' and 'Barbarous', identifying it as an assault on the nation, stating that the public affairs would have been thrown into crisis had it succeeded.[2] Defoe promptly used the event to attack Harley's critics at both ends of the political spectrum. In *A Letter to the Whigs* and *A Spectators Address to the Whigs* (1711), he reproached that party for doubting Harley's loyalty: a French assassination attempt is plain demonstration that Louis XIV and the Pretender recognise Harley as their greatest enemy in Britain. In the *Review*, Defoe began his sustained criticism of the October Club, a group of backbench Tory extremists frustrated by Harley's 'moderate' measures. In April he published *The Secret History of the October Club*; a second part came out in June. In this work the Club's members denounce Guiscard not for the attempt but for its failure.[3] Defoe described the October Club as 'a Faction of the hot exasperated Part of the People called *Tories*, composed of Swearing, Oath-taking, abjuring *Jacobites*, self-contradicting, Moon-blind *High-Flyers*'.[4] This comes in *Eleven Opinions about Mr. H——y*, an apologia for the Chancellor published in May, which portrays Harley as the embodiment of political harmony.[5] Harley returned to public business the day after this letter, 26 April.

Sr

Tho' I am Comforted wth ye Sight of yor Personall Safety,[a] which No Man has More Reason to be Thankfull for Than my Self, yet when I See ye wonders of Providence in yor Preservacon, and Reflect Upon what Depends Upon yor life, I Confess I am Silent with Astonishment.

These Sr are Some of The wayes God is Pleased to Take to Vindicate The being and Power of his Governing Attribute in The world, and[b] by Invincible Demonstracons[6] to[c] Conquer

[a] Safety] *following word* 'yet' *cancelled*
[b] and] *following word* 'to' *cancelled*
[c] to] *interlined*

596

The Influences of The Devill in ye hearts of Men[7] — when The Endeavours They use to blott Out ye Prints of his being, wch Nature left on That blank leaf The Soul,[8] Grow strong^a and they^b Perswade Themselves There Either is no God Or That he is Not ye Agent of his Own produccͦons. This Secret wittness[9] whispers <u>Thou Fool</u>[10] in Their hearts; and The^c Conviccͦon can Not be withstood.

The Same Testimony Sr That he is Pleas'd to Give of himself in Thus Directing The Accͦons of Men, as it is a wittness to his Providence, Prescience and his Descending to The Governm^t of his Creacͦon, So it can Not w^thout gross absurdity but Argue That an Eternall Wisdome and Goodness is Concern'd in That Governm^t; From This I Inferr to ye present Case That ye Singular Discoveries of That wisdom <u>for Example</u> in Eminent Deliverances,[11] prove That there is Some End and Design in Every One of Those Deliverances, as well as in the Other Events of his Providence.

It can Not be, That (in yor Case in Perticul^r) wise and Righteous Providence should Distinguish its Self, in Sacrifizeing One life, and preserving Another,[12] Abandoning a wretch[13] to Rage and Desperacͦon, Directing him to Reach Out a Murthering hand pointed at That life, it was forbidden to Touch, and which it should Onely hurt, but Not Destroy.

Why was he Permitted to Assault, and Not Permitted to Effect his Design — what Armour Guarded The Precous Part, what Restrain'd The point — why Directed^d just to The Onely Little Solid part That was in The wounded place,[14] But to bear wittness to This Glorious Truth That Verily There is a God That Governs The Earth, That The Hairs of Our head are Numbred, and Not a Sparrow falls to ye Ground[15] &c.

Yet This is Not all, nor is it ye End of my Goeing Thus Out of My way S^r in this Manner of Discourse — But <u>The Why</u> — is The Thing I Dwell upon, why a life Thus Cloth'd with Wonders, and Cover'd with Mercy — But because The Same hand That Thus Guarded yor life Sr From Evill by its Imediate power, has Some Great work for you to do, wch Must be done; Must be done by you,

---

a Grow Strong] *interlined*
b they] *interlined*
c The] *following word* 'Secret' *cancelled*
d Directed] *interlined*

DEFOE TO [ROBERT HARLEY], 25 APRIL 1711

and For w^{ch}, as he has Furnish'd you Above Others,[a] So he will preserv you till it be Compleatly Finished,[b] Nor can it be Doubted, But as yor preservaćon beares a proporćon to The greatness of The worke you have to do, So The work beares a due proporćon to ye Greatness of The Deliverance.

May The Same hand Still Guard you, The Same Goodness protect you, May you be fill'd with Wisdome[16] and Counsell For The great Things Heaven has Reserv'd you for, and as I Doubt Not yor Eyes are up to him, who has bid us if we want wisdome to ask it of him;[17] So I am Perswaded, he has Not plaćed The Weight of This Great Naćons affaires, on yor Shoulders, and Thus Miraculously Preserv'd yor life, But he will (for his Works like himself are all Perfect[18]), He will Compleat, what he has Purposed to Do For us, by yor hand; to his Own Glory, and The Great Honour of The Instrum^t also[19] — and Great is your happyness That They are Joyn'd together.

The Subject S^r is So Moveing, My weakness Betrays it Self, and I am Forćed to break off; Onely Prayeing That The life Thus Sav'd by wonders, May be Dedicated to him That has preserv'd it, That it may be Employ'd for, blesst by, and Directed From himself, That Heaven May have ye Praise, This Naćon The Benefit, and yor Self The Open, Comfortable Reward from him That Sees in Secret[20] — Amen.

Yo^r Most faithfull Sinćere
Humble and Obedient Servt
[ ][c]

Aprill 25. 1711

P.S.

I began this Letter s^r wth a Design of bussiness but My Thoughts are too full So that I am forć't to adjourn it, for wch I ask yor Pardon; if yor Leisure p[er]mits I would Gladly wait on Thursday

---

[a] Others] *following words* 'for it' *cancelled; superfluous comma omitted in this edition*
[b] till it be Compleatly Finished] *interlined above cancelled words* 'for That work'
[c] [ ]] *signature torn out*

DEFOE TO [ROBERT HARLEY], 25 APRIL 1711

Evening²¹ for half an hours Audience or any Other Time you please to Direct.

Text: BL Add. MS. 70291, fols. 266–7.²² *Address*: none. *Endorsed by Harley* (fol. 267ᵛ): Mʳ Goldsmith Apr: 25 1711

1 There are numerous contemporaneous accounts, private and public, of the incident, on which see Peter Jones, 'Antoine de Guiscard, "Abbé de la Bourlie", "Marquis de Guiscard"', *BLJ* 8 (1982), 94–113; Clyve Jones, 'Robert Harley and the Myth of the Golden Thread: Family Piety, Journalism and the History of the Assassination Attempt of 8 March 1711', *Electronic BLJ* (2010), art. 11, 1–15, www.bl.uk/eblj/2010articles/article11.html. For its political consequences, see H. T. Dickinson, 'The Attempt to Assassinate Harley, 1711', *History Today* 15 (1965), 788–95.
2 *Review*, VII, 664.
3 *PEW*, II, 172. On 19 May, Elizabeth Lyttleton wrote of Harley to the Countess of Buchan: ''tis Thought he writ or orderd to be writ yᵉ Secret history of yᵉ October Club, tho it pretends to be a Whig' (Yale Beinecke, Osborne MSS Files 17846).
4 *Eleven Opinions about Mr. H——y, PEW*, II, 203.
5 Unknown to Defoe but necessary to be recorded is the growing hostility at this time between Harley and St John, the origin of which Harley dated to Feb. 1711, suspecting St John of conniving with the October Club. St John's attempt to claim he was Guiscard's true target and his opportunistic use of Harley's incapacitation to put into execution an invasion of Quebec which Harley opposed exacerbated a rivalry that simmered for the next two years and climaxed in 1713–14. See Geoffrey Holmes, 'Harley, St John and the Death of the Tory Party', in *Britain after the Glorious Revolution, 1689–1714*, ed. Geoffrey Holmes (1969), 216–37.
6 *Invincible Demonstraċons*: Defoe uses the phrase in *The Poor Man's Plea* (1698), *RDW*, VI, 27; *Jure Divino* (1706), *SFS*, II, 331.
7 *The Devill in yᵉ hearts of Men*: Crusoe instructs Friday that 'the Devil was God's Enemy in the Hearts of Men' (*Novels*, I, 218). Defoe elsewhere wrote: 'Because Judgment is not speedily Executed against Evil Doers, therefore the Hearts of Men are bent within them to do Wickedly' (*Review*, VIII, 860 (21 June 1712)). The expression perhaps glances at Mark 7:21.
8 *blank leaf The Soul*: In *The Compleat English Gentleman*, Defoe wrote: 'Nature's production is a Charte Blanch, and the soul is plac'd in him like a piece of clean paper, upon which the precepts of life are to be written by his instructors' (*RDW*, X, 28).
9 *Secret wittness*: Defoe also uses this phrase in *Mercator*, no. 101 (12–14 Jan. 1714).
10 *Thou Fool*: The biblical source for the fool who denies God is Psalm 14:1; Defoe perhaps also glances at Luke 12:20 and 1 Cor. 15:36. Compare Defoe, *More Reformation* (1703), lines 474–5, also concerning one who would deny God: 'The secret Trepedation racks his Soul, | And when he says, *No God*, replies, *Thou Fool*' (*SFS*, I, 227). Defoe quoted these lines in 'The Storm. An Essay' (1704), lines 242–3, *SFS*, I, 289; *Review*, I, 555 (Nov. 1704 supp.); *Serious Reflections* (1720), *Novels*, III, 116; and *A System of Magick* (1727), *SFS*, VII, 179. He adapts the lines into prose in *A Continuation of Letters written by a Turkish Spy* (1718): 'When [atheists] suggest No God, [conscience] replies, *THOU FOOL*' (*SFS*, V, 118).
11 *Eminent Deliverances*: 'Eminent Deliverances in sudden Dangers are of the most significant kind of Providences, and which accordingly have a loud Voice in them, calling upon us to be thankful, to that blessed Hand, that has been pleased to spare and protect us' (*Serious Reflections, Novels*, III, 190).
12 *Providence … Another*: I.e. Guiscard died and Harley survived. Guiscard was stabbed by other members of the Council and died on 17 Mar.
13 *wretch*: This word, as well as 'Miscreant', is applied to Guiscard in Defoe's account of the assassination in *Minutes of the Negotiations of Monsr. Mesnager* (1717), *SFS*, IV, 60.

599

DEFOE TO [EARL OF BUCHAN], 26–9 MAY 1711

14 *Onely Little Solid part That was in The wounded place*: Guiscard 'stabbed him just under the Breast, a little to the Right side; but, it pleased God, that the Point stopped at one of the Ribs, and broke short half an Inch' (Swift to King, 8 Mar. 1711, *Swift Corr.*, I, 337; cf. *Swift Journal*, 201). Delarivier Manley says 'the Blow was struck exactly upon his Breast-bone, which broke the Knife' (*A True Narrative of what Pass'd at the Examination of the Marquis De Guiscard* (1711), 25). On providentialism in accounts of the attempted assassination, see Jones, 'Robert Harley and the Myth of the Golden Thread'.

15 *The Hairs ... Ground*: Matt. 10:29–30.

16 *fill'd with Wisdome*: Scriptural verses using this phrase that Defoe may have in mind include Exodus 35:35 (Bezalel and Oholiab), 1 Kings 7:14 (Hiram of Tyre), and Luke 2:40 (Christ).

17 *bid us if we want wisdome to ask it of him*: James 1:5.

18 *his Works like himself are all Perfect*: Deut. 32:4.

19 *Great Honour of The Instrumt also*: Perhaps glancing at 2 Tim. 2:21.

20 *him That Sees in Secret*: Defoe uses the phrase in *Serious Reflections* (*Novels*, III, 169). In the *Review* for 7 Feb. 1712, he wrote: 'He that sees in secret will Reward me, if he approves the Service' (VIII, 619). The source is the Sermon on the Mount: Matthew 6:4–6.

21 *Thursday Evening*: 26 Apr., the following day.

22 This letter was overlooked and not printed in H.M.C. *Portland MSS*, IV.

178

To [David Erskine, ninth Earl of Buchan]

26–9 May 1711

HEADNOTE: Buchan had evidently learned that Defoe recommended him for the role of Commissioner of the General Assembly and had written to thank him.[1] There is no evidence that the correspondence was maintained, but several years later Defoe's son-in-law Henry Baker (1698–1774), a teacher of the deaf, was tutor to Buchan's son. In correspondence with Baker, Buchan on several occasions sent his regards to Defoe.[2] Baker's son and Defoe's grandson, David Lionel Erskine Baker (1730–67?), was honoured with the Earl's surname.

In politics, in May 1711, Harley, riding the wave of popularity that swelled in the wake of the assassination attempt, was elevated to the peerage and appointed Lord High Treasurer, effectively becoming prime minister.[3]

My Lord

I have had the honour of yor Ldpps Letter of ye 12° ultimo[4] so long that indeed I blush to Date my answer ye 26° May. I could indeed make some excuses, but I choose to own it a Fault, because I will not lessen the vallue of yor Ldpps remission.[5]

DEFOE TO [EARL OF BUCHAN], 26–9 MAY 1711

Yo[r] L[dpp] does me too much honor in acknowleging good wishes instead of Services, and bestowing on a Late and Unsuccessfull proposall of mine,[6] the weight due to a reall and effectuall Piece of Service; this generous Principle of yo[r] L[dpps] however Lays an obligacon on me, to watch for any opportunity that may offer, of Layeing reall obligacons on a hand so bountifull in accepting. And yo[r] L[dpp] may be assur'd I shall Lose no occasion.

The Person wth whom I endeavoured to Plant yo[r] intrest has been strangely taken up since I had that occasion (viz.) First in suffering the operacon of the Surgeons to heal the wound of the assassine and since in accumulateing Honours from Parliam[t], Queen and People.

On Thursday[7] evening her Maj[tie] created him Earl Mortimer, Earle of Oxford and Lord Harley of Wigmore and we expect that to-morrow in Council he will have the white staff[8] given him by the Queen herself and be Declar'd L[d] High Treasurer.

I writ this yesterday and this Day May 29 he is made L[d] High Treasurer of Britain and Carryed the white staff before the queen this morning to y[e] Chappell.

Yo[r] L[dpp] will easily believ the hurry there too great to make any Mocons at this time. But you may assure yo[r]self (my Lord) nothing shall be wanting to represent either yo[r]self or y[r] affaires to y[r] L[dpps] greatest advantage, and I hint by the way that no man is Fitter to move in such a case than the Duke of Newcastle[9] whom yo[r] L[dpp] mencon[d]. When ever y[r] L[dpp] resolves to attempt y[e] thing I shall be glad to have notice that I may take a proper season to mencon it to advantage.

I am,
　　May it Please yo[r] L[dpp],
　　　　yo[r] L[dpps] most Humble & obedient servant,
　　　　　　De Foe

Newington, May 29, 1711

Text: MS untraced. The copytext is Fred. W. Joy, 'Autograph Letter of Daniel de Foe', *N&Q*, 6th ser., 9 (1884), 65.[10] *Address*: none recorded.

DEFOE TO [EARL OF BUCHAN], 26–9 MAY 1711

1 See Letter 171.

2 Buchan to Henry Baker, 13 July 1727, 3 July 1729, John Rylands Library, University of Manchester, Eng MS 19, fols. 73, 90.

3 'Prime minister' was a term that roused suspicion, but Defoe applies it to Harley, such as in *Review*, IX, 60 (20 Sept. 1712). On the defensive in 1715, Defoe wrote that Oxford considered himself as 'delivering the Government from the Grievance of a *PRIME MINISTER*' (*An Account of the Conduct of Robert Earl of Oxford*, *PEW*, II, 330).

4 *yor Ldpps Letter of ye 12° ultimo*: I.e. of 12 Apr. Untraced.

5 *remission*: forgiveness.

6 *Late and Unsuccessfull proposall of mine*: See headnote and Letter 171.

7 *Thursday*: Defoe's error for Wednesday 23 May, the date of Harley's elevation. The *Reviews* for Tuesday 22 and Thursday 24 May are misdated 21 and 23 May respectively (*Review*, VIII, 139, 144).

8 *white staff*: The Lord Treasurer's staff of office.

9 *Duke of Newcastle*: Newcastle died just a few weeks later on 15 July following a fall from his horse.

10 Joy was unaware of the addressee, though it was established as Buchan when an extract of the letter – paragraphs three, four, and five, from 'The Person...' to '...ye Chappell' – was published in George Chalmers, *The Life of Daniel De Foe* (1790), 33. One significant variation between Joy and Chalmers is that Joy's 'Plant yor intrest' had been rendered '*plant the interest of your Lordship's friend*' by Chalmers. Joy's text is more authoritative: he was purportedly transcribing first-hand the complete MS, whereas Chalmers had the text second-hand from David Stewart Erskine, eleventh Earl of Buchan (1742–1829), who may deliberately have concealed his grandfather's pursuit of Oxford's patronage by making it seem he was soliciting on behalf of a friend.

The letter was also transcribed, with minor variations from Joy, in *The Collection of Autograph Letters and Historical Documents formed by Alfred Morrison, Second Series, 1882–1893: A–D*, 3 vols., ed. Alphonse Wyatt Thibaudeau (1893–6), III, 62–3. This text notes that the MS is endorsed in Sir Walter Scott's handwriting, 'Daniel De Foe, author of *The Trueborn Englishman, The Adventures of Robinson Crusoe*, and *The History of the Union*, 1706, &c., and various other works'.

In 1918, the letter was auctioned as part of the Morrison collection, fetching £195 (*Catalogue of the Renowned Collection of Autograph Letters and Historical Manuscripts, formed by the Late Alfred Morrison, Esq. of Fonthill ... The First Portion* (1917), 248; *Times Literary Supplement*, 25 Apr. 1918, 200).

DEFOE TO [EARL OF OXFORD], 7 JUNE 1711

179

To [Robert Harley, Earl of Oxford]

7 June 1711

HEADNOTE (**Letters 179 and 180**): There is no evidence that Defoe had met with Harley, now Lord Oxford, since early March.[1] His pension was in arrears and in his letters he lists headings of affairs, mostly pertaining to Scotland, that he would be willing to write about.

My Lord

In Obedience to yor L^{dpps} Commands I have here Enclosed an Abstract[2] of ye Papers I Recieved From Scotland wch Relate to The Late Tumult in ye City and ye B[r]each^a between The Magistrates of Edinb. and ye Custome house Officers.[3]

It is Not for me to Offer any Thoughts on This Affair But to Lay before your L^{dpp} The Matter of Fact in Generall; yor L^{dpp} will Easily See whether ye Custome house Officers have been in The Right. My Accot has Sev^{ll} Little aggravacons in it and Recriminacons on ye Characters of ye Officers, (wch Indeed are Not Very Good) But These as Less Materiall and Comeing From but One party, I Omit.

My Lord

As I am big wth Severall Things of This kind to Lay before yor L^{dpp} wch ye happy Hurryes[4] you have been Taken up wth have Deprived Me of the Opportunity of, and as I kno' ye Inconvenience of Troubling yor L^{dpp} wth Tedious preambles wch Come from that Country, I beg leave to Lay Things Down in heads That yor L^{dpp} May Command The Perticulars of Such first as are Most Usefull.

1. The Composicon Made by The Heretors of <u>Old Deer</u>[5] (where The Great Rable[6] Now und^r prosecucon before ye Justicary in Scotland was begun) As ye First Fruits of The happy Conclusion of the Gener^{ll} Assembly.[7]

---

^{a} B[r]each] *MS damaged*

603

DEFOE TO [EARL OF OXFORD], 7 JUNE 1711

2. A great Uneasyness of yᵉ Ministers for Fear of The Printing The Bible being given Exclusively to a Sett of Men, who They Say are Not Enemy's Onely to Their Church, But not Orthodox in yᵉ prinćiples of Religion,[8] by which They judge Erroneous and Clandestine Coppys of yᵉ Bible May be Dispersed in The Higlands and Disputes about yᵉ Translaćon of yᵉ Scriptures be Com̃enćed among the Com̃on people.

3. A Dispute Between yᵉ Commissʳˢ of Excise and The Garrison of Innerlochy[9] which will be Brought before yoʳ Lᵈᵖᵖ and of wᶜʰ I have all yᵉ Perticulars to Apprise yoʳ Lᵈᵖᵖ of before hand.

4. A Case of yᵉ Earle of Hyndfords Dragoons.[10]

5. The Case of Dalziel yᵉ Privateer and yᵉ Merchants of Aberdeen.[11]

6. A proposall of Improvemᵗ of yᵉ Duty of Excise.

These and Sevˡˡ Other Cases, as yoʳ Lᵈᵖᵖ pleases to Command, Shall be Lay'd before yoʳ Lᵈᵖᵖ More at Large. I Shall attend On Monday[12] Evening According to yoʳ Lᵈᵖᵖˢ Ordʳ.

I am

May it Please yoʳ Lᵈᵖᵖ

yoʳ Lᵈᵖᵖˢ Most Humble & Obedᵗ Servᵗ

DFᵃ

June. 7. 1711

Text: BL Add. MS. 70291, fols. ²1–2. *Address*: none. *Endorsed by Oxford* (fol. ²2v): Claude Guilot June 7: 1711

ᵃ DF] *signature torn out but the tops of the letters remain visible*

---

1 Letter 174.

2 *Abstract*: Missing.

3 *Late ... Officers*: Baron of the Scottish Exchequer Court John Scrope (1662–1752) informed Oxford on 13 July that customs officers were struggling in the detention of illegal imports, especially of French wines and brandies, because locals, perhaps with the connivance of the Scottish military officers, were stealing them (H.M.C. *Portland MSS*, x, 386). The matter rumbled on for several months; at a cabinet meeting on 21 Sept., Dartmouth was instructed to write to Lord Provost Adam Brown that 'no ship should be discharged of their Quarantine but by an Order of Councill' (Staffordshire Record Office, D742/U/1/37).

4 *happy Hurryes*: See Letter 178.

5 *Composićon Made by The Heretors of Old Deer*: At Old Deer in the Presbytery of Deer, Aberdeenshire, the minister George Keith (*c.* 1642–1710), an Episcopalian, died in July 1710,

604

DEFOE TO [EARL OF OXFORD], 7 JUNE 1711

whereupon John Keith (1649–1735) began preaching without the Presbytery's sanction (*Scottish Episcopal Clergy, 1689–2000*, ed. David Bertie (Edinburgh, 2000), 73–4). The Presbytery selected John Gordon (1685–1718) to fill the vacancy, the first minister in that parish appointed by the elders rather than the local heretors (NRS CH 1/2/30/4, fols. 340–59; *Fasti*, VII, 216). But on 22 Mar. 1711 the delegation that arrived to ordain Gordon met with violent opposition from an Episcopalian crowd. In the *Review* for 8 May 1711, Defoe printed the indictment issued against the perpetrators, and that document gives a detailed account of events: Defoe actually doubled the length of the *Review* for this issue to accommodate the document (VIII, 103–13). See Wodrow's accounts of Old Deer (*Wodrow Corr.*, I, 218; *Analecta*, I, 328).

Then in the *Review* for 9 June, Defoe printed the terms on which the heretors submitted to the law (their 'Composición'), amounting to full acceptance of Gordon's appointment and support for the prosecution of the ringleaders of the rabble (VIII, 174–5). In the *Review* for 4 Aug. 1711, Defoe called this 'the meanest and most servile Capitulation possible' (VIII, 277). Defoe reflected on the Old Deer episode in *The Secret History of the October-Club ... Part II* (1711), 61 and (borrowing sections of his 9 June *Review*) in *The Present State of the Parties in Great Britain* (1712), 179–92.

6 *Rable*: See Letter 157, note 69.

7 *happy Conclusion of the Gener^{ll} Assembly*: The General Assembly concluded on 23 May 1711. For the first time, its letter to the Queen expressed hope for the succession of 'the Illustrious Family of *Hanover*', and it passed an act recommending that public prayers mention the Electress Sophia as well as Anne (*The Principal Acts of the General Assembly, of the Church of Scotland ... 1711* (Edinburgh, 1711), 6–7; Seafield to Carstares, 24 May 1711, *State-Papers and Letters Addressed to William Carstares* (1774), 792–3; *Review*, VIII, 154 (29 May 1711)).

8 *Printing ... Religion*: See Letter 186.

9 *Dispute ... Innerlochy*: Details of this matter have not been traced. The garrison at Inverlochy was provided with stone barracks, replacing wooden ones, in 1711 (Victoria Henshaw, *Scotland and the British Army, 1700–1750: Defending the Union* (2014), 152). That could have been the source of tension with customs officials. Another possible cause is the fact that the Jacobite Duke of Gordon claimed ownership of the garrison. See Lord Advocate Sir James Steuart to Oxford, 26 Aug. 1712, H.M.C. *Portland MSS*, x, 280. Commander in Chief Leven reported to Oxford a short-lived mutiny there on 12 July 1711 (H.M.C. *Portland MSS*, v, 42).

10 *Earle of Hyndfords Dragoons*: The death of a Captain Denham had left a vacancy in this regiment, and Oxford was receiving nominations for filling it (H.M.C. *Portland MSS*, x, 193, 376, 438).

11 *Dalziel ye Privateer and ye Merchants of Aberdeen*: Alexander Dalziel (*c.* 1673–1715), a Scottish-born, French-naturalised Jacobite who commanded the French privateer *Agrippa*, captured in the Forth in 1710. The Earl of Mar intervened to secure his acquittal, and Dalziel returned to France, but he was arrested again for piracy and executed in 1715. See Dartmouth's cabinet minutes for 23 June 1712, Staffordshire Record Office, D742/U/2/4; *Weekly Journal*, 11 June 1715; Paul Lorrain, *The Ordinary of Newgate His Account of the Behaviour, Confession, and Last Speech of Capt. Alexander Dolzell, a Pirate, who was Hang'd at Execution-Dock in Wapping, on Monday the 5th of December, 1715* (1715); *Weekly Journal, or British Gazette*, 10 Dec. 1715. The connection with the merchants of Aberdeen remains unexplained.

12 *Monday*: 11 June. The following letter may indicate Defoe did not gain this interview.

DEFOE TO [EARL OF OXFORD], 19 JUNE 1711

180

To [Robert Harley, Earl of Oxford]

19 June 1711

My Lord

I am Very Unhappy Not in My Private Affaires Onely, wᶜʰ are Mellancholly, and Ruinous, from yᵉ Discontinuanċe of yoʳ Favoʳ But in Not haveing The Occasion and Honoʳ of Layeing before yoʳ Lᵈᵖᵖ Severall Matters of Importanċe Relateing to yᵉ Publick.[1]

I had Onċe My Lord The honoʳ of yoʳ Promise That if I did any Thing Offensive you would be yoʳ Self my Reprover, and would not be Dissobliged Till I had first yoʳ Mind for my Governmᵗ. God is My wittness if I knew any Thing in which I Should Dissplease your Lᵈᵖᵖ I would Avoid it Dilligently. If my Lord I am Not So Usefull a Servant as I would be, I hope I have been Usefull, and still May be So, and it must be want of Opportunity Not fidellity or Dilligenċe if it is Otherwise.

I Humbly Lay my Case at yoʳ Lᵈᵖᵖˢ Feet. Yoʳ Lᵈᵖᵖ knows and I Presume Remembers That when yoʳ Lᵈᵖᵖ Honoʳᵈ me wᵗʰ yoʳ Recoᵐendaċon to The Late Lᵈ Treasurer My Lord Offred Me a Very Good Post in Scotland and afterward Offred me to be Coᵐissionʳ of The Customes There, and That I did Not Refuse Those Offers but it being yoʳ Opinion as well as his Lᵈᵖᵖˢ That I Might be More Serviċable in a Private Capascity I Chose Rather to Depend Upon her Majᵗⁱᵉˢ Goodness That I Might be Most Serviċable Than to Secure My Family a Maintenanċe and be Rendred Uncapable to Serve her Majᵗⁱᵉˢ Intrest.[2]

Sinċe My Lord I had The honoʳ of Returning into yoʳ Lᵈᵖᵖˢ Serviċe and Proteċċon yoʳ Lᵈᵖᵖ was pleased to Speak for me to her Majᵗⁱᵉ and to Assure me her Majᵗⁱᵉ had been pleased to Appoint yᵉ Paymᵗ of My Pension, and yoʳ Lᵈᵖᵖ had yᵉ Goodness to Supply me The first quarter;[3] had I Not My Lord The Importuneing Circumstanċe of a Large Family, a Wife and Six Children, I could Serve yoʳ Lᵈᵖᵖ Twenty year wᵗʰout yᵉ Least Supply Rather Than Thus press upon yoʳ Goodness. But my Lord . . . My Weakness Permits me to Say No More; a Family Often Ruin'd and Now

DEFOE TO [EARL OF OXFORD], 19 JUNE 1711

Depending Upon yor L^{dpps} Goodness presses me beyond Measure. I humbly Ask yor L^{dpps} Pardon for it.

May it Please yor L^{dpp}

I am yor Dayly Peticŏner for an Opportunity in but Six words to Lay before yor L^{dpp} Some Things Relateing to New Uneasynesses in Scotland.

Something Relateing to The Trade to ye South Seas[4] wch abundančě Speak Evill of because They do Not Understand.

And Something Relateing to The Poor keel men at Newcastle[5] whose Oppressions Seem Reserved for yor L^{dpps} hand to put an End to — I beg a few Minutes at yor Leisure and Am

My Lord yor L^{dpps} Most Humble & Obedient Servt

[   ]^a

June. 19. 1711

Text: BL Add. MS. 70291, fols. ²3–4. *Address*: none. *Endorsed by Oxford* (fol. ²4^v): Claude Guilot June 19: 1711

^a [   ]] *signature torn out*

---

1 *Severall Matters of Importančě Relateing to ye Publick*: See the list of topics in Letter 179.
2 *Late Ld Treasurer … Intrest*: See Letter 119.
3 *first quarter*: See Letter 153 for the first payment of Defoe's quarterly pension of £100 on 27 Sept. 1710; see Letter 170, note 17 for a payment of £50 on 27 Dec., which Defoe indicates was paid by Harley himself. See Letter 184 for the next payment to Defoe.
4 *Trade to ye South Seas*: The Act incorporating the South Sea Company was brought before the House of Commons on 17 May and given the royal assent on 12 June. See Letters 185, 187, and 188. Defoe's first, brief mention of the South Sea trade in print came in the *Review* for 21 June 1711, nearly echoing this letter in describing it as 'a Trade … few People Understand, and some for that very Reason, *viz*. Because they Understand it not, speak Evil of it' (VIII, 193). John Robert Moore argues that, given the lack of communication Defoe complains about, it is unlikely Defoe influenced Oxford in the formation of the Company, as other commentators had suggested ('Defoe and the South Sea Company', *Boston Public Library Quarterly* 5 (1953), 175–88; Sutherland, 181).
5 *Poor keel men at Newcastle*: 'The Keel Men are those who manage the Lighters, which they call Keels [shallow-draught boats], by which the Coals are taken from the Steaths or Wharfs [in the Tyne], and carryed on board the Ships, to load them for *London*' (*A Tour thro' the Whole Island of Great Britain, TDH*, III, 118). The Newcastle keelmen were in dispute with their employers, the 'hostmen' who held a monopoly on transporting coal between its producers and shippers. Since spending time in Newcastle in 1710, Defoe had opposed the hostmen's monopoly and supported the keelmen's bid for a charter of incorporation that would give them control of a hospital they had set up at their own expense in 1699. Defoe intervened more directly in the dispute in 1712: see Letter 206.

JOHN RUSSELL TO DEFOE, 21 JUNE 1711

181

John Russell to Defoe

21 June 1711

HEADNOTE (Letters 181–3): In late June, Defoe received letters from Russell that show the extent to which he had become involved in supplying horses to the Earl of Hyndford. His letters from Russell and that to Oxford indicate that Defoe undertook to support Leven's retention of the position of Commander in Chief in Scotland, which was especially important amidst fears of a French invasion. The letter to Oxford shows a range of other Scottish disputes in which Defoe was engaged.

Edb June 21 1711

Sr

Yours of ye 16th instant[1] is befor me. I wes this morning with the Earle of Hyndfoord[2] who told me he would Pay your bill of £78..15 sent me wth the £6..4..6 you mention in yours which his Ldp desired me to let you have and said he would write to you himself; He wes with our freind[3] this morning when I went in and after he wes gon I tooke occasion to comunicat ye hint you gave me which wes very kindly taken and I wes ordered to return you many thanks and to tell you he would have writt to you but that he had nothing worth while to advyse you of, only ye prospect of haveing no comander in cheif[4] here would certainly be prejudiciall to her Maties interest, for besides ye difficultyes might occure anent the eldest officers haveing ye comand, if any disput shoūld hapen anent ye Security what is every bodyes bussines is no bodyes bussines.[5] I only hint at things that doubtless youll improve to ye best advantadge. I had on[e]ᵃ from you to him by Sundayes post[6] which I delivred. I hop to hear from you and I shall advyse you [that]ᵇ ye bill is payed. My wife remembers you and Madam as doe [I].ᶜ

Servt

ᵃ on[e]]: 'e' *omitted*
ᵇ [that]] *MS torn*
ᶜ [I]] *MS torn*

608

DEFOE TO [EARL OF OXFORD], 26 JUNE 1711

Text: NLS MS. 25.3.9, fol. 71ᵛ [scribe's copy]. *Address*: To Daniell Defoe Esq̲ | at his house in Newingtoūn | near London

1 *Yours of yᵉ 16th instant*: Untraced.
2 *Earle of Hyndfoord*: See Letter 160, note 16. Backscheider notes that Hyndford was a prominent and shrewd horse trader ('John Russell', 173 n. 32). As Letter 183 details, Defoe acted as his intermediary, taking a commission for his role in buying horses on the Earl's behalf.
3 *Our friend*: Probably Leven (see Letter 176).
4 *haveing no comander in chief*: Leven had served as Commander in Chief for Scotland since 1706; his long-expected dismissal from this and all offices came in 1712. The position was not dissolved: Argyll succeeded to it.
5 *every bodyes bussines is no bodyes bussines*: Defoe would publish a pamphlet called *Every-Body's Business, is No-Body's Business* under the pseudonym Andrew Morton in 1725. It deals with the rising wages and lowering morals of servants.
6 *on[e] from you to him by Sundayes post*: Untraced; 24 June.

182

To [Robert Harley, Earl of Oxford]

26 June 1711

My Lord

I am backward to Trouble yoͬ Lᵈpp at Such a Time of Hurry as This, yet I Thought it my Duty to Lay before you in Generalls Onely what Seems Necessary for yoͬ Lᵈpp to be Inform'd of Since My Last.

As 1ˢᵗ The Affair of yᵉ Provost,¹ and Magistrates of Edinb., wᵗʰ The Custome house Officͅers; of wᶜʰ I Enclosed an Abstract² According to yoͬ Lᵈpps Commands; The Magistrates Say They have Recᵈ Some Threatning Message or letter On That Occasion, Telling Them they Shall be Sent forᵃ up to answer before yᵉ Council for Their behavioͬ to yᵉ Custome house Men. This They Believ Neither yoͬ Lᵈpp or Her Majᵗⁱᵉ has been Made Accquainted wᵗʰ and Desire yoͬ Lᵈpps Proteccͅon, of wᶜʰ I shall Give yoͬ Lᵈpp a Farther Accoᵗ when I may have yᵉ honoͬ to wait on you.

The Next is The Constant feares of The Good people of yᵉ North, about The Pretender and The French Squadron, Occasioned Rather

ᵃ for] *interlined*

609

DEFOE TO [EARL OF OXFORD], 26 JUNE 1711

by The Insults and Openess[a] of[b] ye Jacobite Party There Than any Intelligence of The Thing, which Feares are Encreased They Say by The Naked Condicon of Scotland as to Troops, haveing No Troops[3] That Can be Drawn into ye Field but One Battalion of Foot and Three Regimts of Dragoons, One of wch is but half a Regimt.

I hinted Something Also About ye Millitary Governmt in Scotland and ye affair of Superiourities,[4] wch however Weighty at This Time I adjourn Till I have yor Ldpps Commands.

I would Gladly have Spoken Six words to yor Ldpp on ye Subject of ye South-Sea Affaire in which I Perswade My Self I May do Some Service in print.[5]

I am May it Please yor Ldpp
yor Most Humble & Obedt Servt
DeFoe

June. 26. 1711

Text: BL Add. MS. 70291, fols. [2]5–6. *Address*: none.

---

[a] Openess] *following illegible word cancelled*
[b] of] 'off' *in MS*

---

1 *Provost*: Adam Brown. See Letter 143.
2 *Abstract*: Missing. On this 'Affair', see Letter 179, note 3.
3 *No Troops*: In the *Review* for 26 May 1711, Defoe lamented the lack of a military presence in the Highlands (VIII, 149).
4 *Superiourities*: Article twenty of the Union Treaty preserved superiorities, which Defoe defined as 'the Rights of Vassalage which the Gentry of *Scotland* have over the People, which, as it is Extended, gives the Chiefs and Heads of Clans, Lairds and Heretors, such an absolute Dominion over both the Persons and Goods of the poor Subjected People, as seems perfectly inconsistent both with the Peace and the Improvement of *Scotland*' (*History of the Union*, *TDH*, VIII, 169). In the *Review* for 26 May 1711, Defoe fretted that the Scottish people's first loyalty was to their laird, not the Queen, and he urged the government 'to put a Stop to the Mischiefs that lie hid under those *Highland Superiorities* – For if ever the present Establishment receives any fatal Blow, it must be from hence; if ever *Jacobitism* comes to any formidable Power in *Britain*, it must be from this Part – Nor is it impossible to find out Ways and Means to bring this legally to pass, though this is not a proper Subject for a Printed Paper' (VIII, 151). See *Review*, VIII, 709 (27 Mar. 1712); 749 (19 Apr. 1712). The superiorities were removed by act of parliament in 1746.
5 *Subject … print*: Five days earlier, on 21 June, Defoe's *Review* introduced the South Sea trade: 'I shall endeavour to turn it round, and shew you its dark and its bright Sides, with all possible Clearness and Impartiality' (VIII, 193). However, he did not immediately move to the finer details, perhaps awaiting Oxford's approbation. Whether or not at Oxford's bidding, Defoe then discussed the South Sea Company in the *Review* from 28 June to 26 July 1711, and intermittently thereafter. On the Company and Defoe's writings, see Letters 185, 187, and 188.

JOHN RUSSELL TO DEFOE, 30 JUNE 1711

183

John Russell to Defoe

30 June 1711

Ed^b June 30th 1711

S^r

My Last the 21 Currant to which refers, the Earle of Hyndfoord
payed your bill and the £6..4..6 mention'd in yoūrs and I discharged
the bill & that money in full of all demands for horses as you
advysed. My Ldp desired me to put you in mind of ye two horses
which he yet wants And to tell you^a that he had spoak to his
officers that they would give you Comission to buy horses for^b them
which youll no doubt hear of. I'l wait your orders for disposeing of
your money. Our freind[1] is well & very senceable of your concern
anent him; pray be so kind to advyse me how maters goe with you.
My duty to Madam & the young Ladyes. I saw your Son in good
health this day. My wife remembers you as doe I.

Servt

Text: NLS MS. 25.3.9, fol. 71^v [scribe's copy]. *Address*: To Daniell Defoe <u>Esq</u> at his
house | in Newingtoun near London

---

^a to tell you] *interlined*
^b to buy horses for] 'to buy horses' *interlined above cancelled words* 'horses to' *following* 'for'

---

1   *Our friend*: Probably Leven again.

DEFOE TO [EARL OF OXFORD], 13 JULY 1711

184

To [Robert Harley, Earl of Oxford]

13 July 1711

HEADNOTE: Defoe's pension was resumed. The Secretary of State for Scotland, the Duke of Queensberry, died on 6 July. This was a headache for Oxford, because several associates including Mar, Hamilton, and Islay wanted the position. Any Tory appointment risked alienating Presbyterians in Scotland; a Whig one would seem like betraying the Tories in England. Oxford apparently solicited advice on what to do with the position, seemingly minded to appoint a Keeper of the Signet, as Mar had been appointed in 1708, rather than a Secretary of State, having the legal function of that office discharged without bestowing the prestige and influence that attached to a secretaryship.[1] For Riley 'the most significant point in his advice' is Defoe's insistence that having a Scottish Secretary maintains faction in that nation: Oxford intended to rule Scotland as a mediator with all parties looking to him, not to a subordinate Scottish ministry, for support.[2] Accordingly, the post was not immediately filled, but Mar was appointed in September 1713.[3]

My Lord

I can No way Express My humble Thankfullness to yo[r] L[dpp] for The Relief, w[ch] The Return of yo[r] Goodness and Bounty[4] has been to Me, Unless I should give you The Trouble of a Sad Acco[t] of The Anxietys and p[er]plexitys w[ch] The Late Interrup[con] of her Maj[ties] Appointm[t] had brought me to,[a] first by The late L[d] T .... r who On y[e] Change left me Desolate w[th]out y[e] Arrear;[5] and Next by The Dissaster on yo[r] L[dpp],[6] w[ch] for a long Time gave me a Dark View of y[e] Na[con]s Ruine, as well as my Own: These Things (My Lord) had brought me Very Low, and as a Sinking Family is Thus Raised Again (Espe[c]ally in hope) by yo[r] hand, in Propor[con] to That Deliveran[c]e, is My Sen[c]e of yo[r] Bounty.

But my Lord as words can Not Describe This, I Extreamly wish for an Occasion to Render my Self Usefull, as The best Method to shew my Self Gratefull, and According to The Freedome yo[r]

---

[a] brought me to] 'to' *cancelled following* 'brought' *and interlined following* 'me'

612

DEFOE TO [EARL OF OXFORD], 13 JULY 1711

L^{dpp} was allways pleased to allow me, I Shall Endeavour to shew my fidellity to yor Intrest, and Zeal for ye Public Service, as The best way to Serve, and Oblige yor L^{dpp} — In Ord^r to This — and in Obedience to yor L^{dpps} Commands of Putting My Thoughts into writeing, I am Now Applying My Self to State to yor L^{dpp} Some heads of Observacon, wch I hope May be Usefull, on Some Transaccons More Imediately before yor L^{dpp} — I shall Sett down The heads here, and Enlarge on Them in Their Ord^r, as I Think They May be Seasonable and Servicable.

Yet I am yor L^{dpps} Humble Peticoner, That you will be pleased, Some-times, when Leisure May admitt, to Continue Me the Liberty of a p[er]sonall Conference as Usuall, as well to Explain my Self on Such Things as are Needfull, as to Reciev Such Hints From yor L^{dpp} in Public Matters, as yor L^{dpp} shall See Meet to Comunicate for my Direccon.

The Heads I Crave Leave first to Lay before yor L^{dpp} as More Imediately for yor Service Are:

1. The Affair of a Third Secretary for Public Affaires, wth Some Remarks[a] Upon ye State of The Civil Governm^t[b] in Scotland.
2. The New Undertaking of ye Trade to ye South-Seas and How it May be put in Terms not to Give The Spaniards any Umbrage and yet carry as good a Face and be as Effectuall at home as if it were otherwise.
3. Some Observacons On The Miscarriage of The Customes in Scotl^d and Schemes of a Better Mannagem^t.
4. Some Proposalls (if yor L^{dpp} pleases to allow me That Liberty) for Improvem^t of The Revenue and Raiseing Money in England Against The Next year.

I forbear to Trouble yor L^{dpp} wth a Multitude of heads. Other Things Remain in Petto,[7] but I begin wth These, as well because I Think Them Most Usefull as because I gather From yor hints to me

---

a Remarks] *following word* 'of' *cancelled*
b Governmt] *following word* 'There' *cancelled*

DEFOE TO [EARL OF OXFORD], 13 JULY 1711

in yor Last Discourse That These Things will be Acceptable to yor L^{dpp}, I Mean the Three First.

I am
May it Please yor L^{dpp}
yor L^{dpps} Most Humble & Obed^t Servt
[ ]^a

July. 13. 1711.

May it Please yor L^{dpp}

On The affair of a Third Secretary &c. I Need Say The less Because I Observ My Thoughts on That head happily Agree with yor L^{dpps} Judgem^t.

As a Third Offiċe was Erected Upon The Union wth Scotland, and fill'd wth a Native of that Country,⁸ It became Insensibly to Seem an Offiċe Peculiar to Scottland and for Scottish affaires, wch has allready been^b attended wth Sev^{ll} Inconvenienċes and is^c Threatned wth More.

1. It became The Center of The Hungry Solliċitaċons Naturall to That Country, and Mightily Encreased and Encouraged Them, by which Her Maj^{tie} would in Time be Under a Constant Painfull Opperaċon From a poor, Craveing, and Importunate people; who had So Easy a Method of Obtaining Requests, That it Made Them Invite One Another to be Allways Requesting; and Every Desire Granted, procured a Multiplicaċon of Petiċons; Till in Time That Offiċe would have been a True Court of Requests; — a Certain Clark⁹ in That Offiċe who has Resided in Scotland, and is There still, has Made his Market of prepareing, Solliċiting, and handing forward bussiness of This Nature, has his Offiċe in Edinb. and Gives Methods, Instrucċons and Recomendaċons to the Offiċe here, As if it were his Bussiness to prompt people On Every Triffle to Seek Redress and Supply from ye Queen.

---

^a [ ]] *signature torn out*
^b been] *interlined*
^c is] *interlined*

DEFOE TO [EARL OF OXFORD], 13 JULY 1711

Her Maj^ties Goodness and Bounty (Tho' Great) Must be
at Last Exhausted by Continued Craveings and Cases
Really Moveing will Suffer by The Constant Clamour and
Sollicitation of a Multitude.

2. What Ever Secretary Succeeds must be a Scots man. They
Seem to Claim it as a Right — This (first) keeps up a kind of
a Form of Seperate Mannagem^t, wch being Destroy'd by the
Union, all Vestiges of The Seperate State of Things Ought
to Dye wth it, and ye Very Remembrance if possible be^a
Taken away;^b Scotland No More Requires a Secretary Than
Yorkshire or Wales, Nor (ye Clamour of Petitions Excepted)
can it Supply bussiness for an Office wth Two Clarks. As to
Needfull Peticons her Maj^ties Eares will allwayes be Open to
her Subjects just Requests and private Persons may Sollicit
Their Own Cases as ye English did before, whereas a Scotish
Secreatary is No Other Than a Scottish Sollicitor. This I kno'
The D of Queensberry^10 allways Complain'd of and I^c have
heard his Grace^d Say it was The Burthen of his Office, yet he
Could Deny No body.^e

If a New Scots Secretary Succeeds he has a New Throng of
Dependents wh[o]^f hang about him as if he had ye wholl kingdome
to Give, and I kno' The Names of Some who have Entertain'd
Thoughts of This Very Office Some Time passt and have kept back
Their Craveing Friends from Pushing Their Requests till They
should be in power to act for them, when They hav[e]^g promised to
do^h Mighty Things for Them.

If a Third Secretary Should be put in (and Not a Scots man)
They themselves would be The First who would Crye Out There
was No Occasion for the Office.

---

^a be] *interlined*
^b away] *following word* 'and' *cancelled*
^c I] *interlined*
^d Grace] 'ace' *interlined*
^e yet he Could Deny No body] *these words are crammed in, suggesting they are a later addition*
^f wh[o]] *obscured by MS binding*
^g hav[e]] *MS torn*
^h to do] *interlined*

DEFOE TO [EARL OF OXFORD], 13 JULY 1711

The addicͨon of Bussiness from Scotland (Peticͨons Onely Excepted as before) Seems to be No Argument at all Sinͨce That Bussiness Seems So little as that it can Not be an Employ for any One Clark in yᵉ Other Officͤes and when it is promiscuously Mannaged Among them all will not be felt at all.

The Signet[11] May have a little Officͤe for it in Either of yᵉ Other Officͤes, or in The Signet Officͤe here, or by it Self, of wᶜʰ a proposall[12] may be Lay'd down by its Self.

3. The Very Appointing A Scots Secretary has Severall Inconvenienͨces in it 1./ It keeps up a Faccͨon in Scotland, and Forms a Party To Support yᵉ Intrest of That Person, as also another to Supplant him, So That Instead of his Secureing the quiet of The people he is Ipso facto[13] The Mean of Disquieting and Dividing them. (2) he Constitutes himself a kind of a Governour of Scotland Sinͨce he becomes quietly and Gradually (Whether wᵗʰ or without Design) yᵉ Medium of all Transaccͨons between her Majᵗⁱᵉ and The people of Scotland and Makes those people More Depending on him than p[er]haps is fit for any p[er]ticular p[er]son on That Side to boast of.
4. It Seems to Lay a foundacͨon of a Custome which in Time will plead prescripcͨon and be Claim'd by Posterity as a Right and No Time can be So proper to Crush it as while (The Thing being young) No Suchᵃ Claim can be made.
5. It Layes The Crown Under a Constant and Needless Expenͨce.[14]

There might be Many Other Reasons Given for This, But These Seem Sufficͤent — There Seems to be No Objeccͨon but yᵉ Discontenting The Scots, to wᶜʰ I Answer:

The People will Soon be Easy, Sinͨce They can Assign No Injury They Reciev as aᵇ Reason why They should be Dissatisfyed.

The Clamour will be Onely Among those Who Expect yᵉ Officͤe, wᶜʰ Requires No Other Answer Than This — They

---

ᵃ Such] *interlined*
ᵇ a] *interlined*

DEFOE TO [EARL OF OXFORD], 13 JULY 1711

can Not Desire the queen should do it Onely to find them an Employment — a Pension if her Maj^tie Sees it Reasonable is an Equivalent to that.

As to ye Power They want by The Office, The Very Reason why They Desire it is a strong Argument against Her Maj^ties bestowing it.

All wch is Humbly Submitted to yor L^dpp
By yor L^dpps Most Obed^t Servt
[ ]^a

Text: BL Add. MS. 70291, fols. ²11–14. [The letter is fols. ²13–14; the enclosure is fols. ²11–12.] *Address*: none. *Letter endorsed by Oxford* (fol. ²14v): Mr Goldsmith July 13 1711 R July 14: *Enclosure endorsed by Oxford* (fol. ²12v): Mr Goldsmith July 13 R July 14 1711 3 Secretary &c:

---

^a [ ]] *signature torn out*

---

1 See John Scrope to Oxford, 7 July 1711, BL Add. MS. 70256; anon. to Oxford, [July 1711], BL Add. MS. 70050, fol. 54.
2 Riley, *English Ministers*, 167.
3 This was in the wake of the crisis of 1713, when the Scottish representative peers and MPs united to try to dissolve the Union. See headnote to Letter 231; Riley, *English Ministers*, 246–7.
4 *Bounty*: A receipt made out by Oxford and signed by C. Guilot reads: 'Receiv'd July 10. 1711. of Wm Lowndes Esqre of her Maties Secret service the sum of one hundred pounds of her ma^ties secret service 100^£'. Unlike the other payments to Guilot during the Oxford ministry, but like an undated receipt for the same amount, this one does not appear in Lowndes's secret service accounts (BL Add. MS. 70152, fol. 271). See J. A. Downie, 'Secret Service Payments to Daniel Defoe, 1710–1714', *RES* 30 (1979), 437–41.
5 *wthout ye Arrear*: See Letter 148.
6 *Dissaster on yor L^dpp*: The assassination attempt on Harley on 8 Mar. 1711.
7 *in Petto*: See Letter 99, note 7.
8 *Native of that Country*: Queensberry.
9 *Clark*: I.e. clerk, but unidentified.
10 *D of Queensberry*: For Defoe and Queensberry's acquaintance, see headnote to Letter 104.
11 *Signet*: Following the Union, the office of Keeper of the Signet had been shared between Queensberry and Sunderland, then Dartmouth after Sunderland's dismissal. Oxford removed the Signet from the Secretaries, appointing separate Keepers, which spread patronage and achieved greater efficiency in the office. The appointees were Court Tories: John Pringle of Haining (*c.* 1674–1754), MP for Selkirkshire, and William Cochrane of Kilmaronock (after 1659–1717), MP for Wigtown Burghs. See Riley, *English Ministers*, 169.
12 *proposall*: No such proposal has been traced.
13 *Ipso facto*: 'by the fact itself' (Latin); a fact that is a direct consequence of a given action.
14 *Needless Expence*: 'It was thought my Lord Marr would have succeeded as Secretary upon the Duke of Queensberry's Death; but the Court seems now disposed to have no third Secretary, which was a useless Charge' (Swift to King, 12 July 1711, *Swift Corr.*, 1, 361).

DEFOE TO [EARL OF OXFORD], 17 JULY 1711

185

To [Robert Harley, Earl of Oxford]

17 July 1711

HEADNOTE: Since Defoe proposed to Oxford that he should write publicly on the South Sea Company on 21 June – reiterated on 26 June and 13 July – he had done just that in the *Review*. Whether or not Oxford encouraged the *Review* essays, he requested private memoranda on the scheme from Defoe: the enclosure that follows this letter.

The Company was Oxford's solution to the floating debt: that is, the nation's immediately payable debt not backed by parliamentary security, as opposed to its long-term borrowing. The floating debt had increased to almost £9 million: there was no prospect of paying it in cash, and the decline in lenders' confidence was signalled by the heavy discounting of bills of exchange. By the Act establishing the South Sea Company, the government's creditors were incorporated, their debts were converted to stock (yielding six per cent interest as well as dividends from future profits), and the Company was granted exclusive trading rights in the Spanish dominions in South and Central America.[1] How exactly the Company would overcome Spain's determination to exclude foreigners from their territory was up for debate.

In the *Review*, starting on 28 June, Defoe explained the history and extent of the South Sea trade to his readers. He lamented that France's influence over Spain during the present war gave them unprecedented access to that trade; he insisted that the Grand Alliance of 1689 allowed England to commandeer territory from Spain; and he was wary of promising a free trade between the Company and Spain's colonies, whatever the outcome of the war as regards the Spanish monarchy. Defoe positioned himself between the extremes of unrealistic enthusiasm ('wild Expectations') and misplaced pessimism ('Phlegmatick Discouraging Notions').[2]

My Lord

In Persuance of yor L^{dpps} Orders of Putting My Thoughts in writeing on ye Subject of The Trade to ye South-Seas, I have Enclosed to yor L^{dpp} a Short General wch I humbly Offer to yor L^{dpp}. I have put a Stop to what I was Saying in Print[3] Till I may kno' if my Thoughts are of any Consideracon in yor L^{dpps} Judgem^t, and because I would Not by Distinguishing too Nicely, Discourage ye Thing in Gener^{ll}; I Shall go on to draw up my Nocons as Succinct as possible, and Then attend yor L^{dpp} if I may have The Honr to know how far my scheme May be agreeable.

618

DEFOE TO [EARL OF OXFORD], 17 JULY 1711

I kno' well how Much is at stake upon This Affair, and how well pleased Some would be, (Meerly on yor L^{dpps} Perticular Acco^t) to have it Misscarry;[4] I Perswade My Self what I have Offred here, is ye best way to Dissapoint Them; as it Shall leave Least possibillity of a Misscarrige, and Lay Less Weight on That p[er]ticular Than Now Seems to Lye Upon it. I Shall be glad to Make This So Clear as That yor L^{dpp} May have ye Same Opinion of it.

> I am May it Please yor L^{dpp}
> yor L^{dpps} Most Humble and Obed^t Servt
> [ ]^a

July. 17. 1711.

May it Please yor L^{dpp}

The Present Difficulty in ye Affair of The South-Sea-Trade Seems to Consist in The Noćon of what we call <u>a Free-Trade</u>[5] and The Dissatisfaccons That Some people are Industrious to Spread, Arise from ye Differing Construccon wch people put upon The Thing called a Free-Trade and The Insuperable Difficulties wch Seem to attend it.

All our Merchants kno' That ye Spaniards (I mean by Spaniards ye Governm^t of Old Spain) in whatsoever Circumstanće Considred, whether in Peaće, or war, Und^r Philip of Bourbon, or Cha: of Austria,[6] will Never be brought to Consent to a Generall liberty of Comerće, wth any Collony, or Settlement ye English may Make on ye Coast of America.

By <u>a Liberty of Comerce</u> I Mean, just as yor Ldpp was pleased to Explain it to Me, (Viz) That Such Collony, or Settlement, should be as The Magasin, or warehouse, of English goods <u>which</u> instead of being Landed in Old Spain, (paying 23 p[er] C^t Customes There, Then Registring in The Contractaćon house at Sevill,[7] and payeing Duty again There, and The Effects of ye Galleons wch is The Return, paying an Indulto[8] of 4 to 8 p[er] C^t to ye king), shall Come Directly from England Custome Free, and be admitted into all ye Spanish dominions in America.

^a [ ]] *signature torn out*

DEFOE TO [EARL OF OXFORD], 17 JULY 1711

This My Lord is what I Grant, and what Every body in Town who knows yᵉ Trade Say, The Spaniards will Not be brought to; — I Need Not Trouble yoʳ Lᵈpp wᵗʰ Other Reasons Than This, That Really <u>Old Spain</u> is Ruined if They do, and The Indies (Farther Than barely The Revenue of Them to yᵉ Public) Areᵃ Lost, And of no Vallue to Them (Comparitively speaking) if They Should.

On The Other hand, The Very Pretence of This Undertakeing will Make a handle to yᵉ French Intrest, will Speak Loud in Spain, in Favour of king Philip; Since king Charles, has by Contract Given Them away to The English,⁹ who <u>as They Say</u> are to Enjoy The America Trade for Ever, whereas yᵉ French wᵗʰ Specious pretences of Protecting The Indies Now, from The Enemies of Spain, Promise to quit all pretensions to yᵉ Trade, in Time of peace; and Entirely to withdraw and Recall all Their Merchants, and all Their people from Thence.¹⁰

I Need not hint to yoʳ Lᵈpp, That yᵉ people who Are Enemies to yᵉ project, On Accoᵗ of yoʳ Lᵈpps Concern in Proposeing it,¹¹ Think They have Gain'd a great Point in haveing So Specious and as they Think Unanswerable Argumᵗˢ Against yᵉ probabillity and Practicablness of yᵉ Design and how They give Out boldly That it is an Inconsistency in it Self and Must Therefore of Meer Necessity Misscarry and Come to Nothing.

But My Lord if My Thoughts of this Affair Are Agreeable to yoʳ Lᵈpp I am of Opinion I Might State This Undertakeing So That it Might Neither Give Umbrage to yᵉ Spaniards Abroad, Or appear Impracticable or Inconsiderable to Our people at home. I shall Onely Lay it Down in Generalls here but Shall Enlarge on it in Perticular and in Print when first the heads of it have passed your Lᵈpps Opinion.

1. There Seems to be No Necessity of Putting This Term <u>A Free Trade</u> into yᵉ Proposall for yᵉ Reasons following.

1ˢᵗ It is This Onely can Give any Pretence to yᵉ French and Jealousie to yᵉ Spaniards.

ᵃ Are] *interlined above cancelled word* 'is'

DEFOE TO [EARL OF OXFORD], 17 JULY 1711

2. It is This Onely wch Creates Difficulties and Raises Suspiċons and Doubts of the Success in England to ye Discredit of The Design.

2 The Thing will in Some Degree be a^a Consequencė wthout a Public Claim to it, in wch Lyes The greatest part of The Inconveniencė, And The Assiento[12] will be Naturally the Companys.

3 Tho' we Should have no Such Thing as a Freedome of Commercė wth ye Spaniards yet will a Settlement on ye Spanish Continent of America,[13] Espeċally in Such placės as May be Named be of Suffiċent Consequencė to justifye The prudencė of ye wholl Undertakeing, Give a Credit to ye Design and Answer all the Ends of a <u>South-Sea</u> Company Tho' Their Stock was to Contain ye Capitall of The wholl Subscripċon.

A Scheme of which Shall be Lay'd before yor L^{dpp} when Ever you please to Direct it.

I Presume Two Great Ends Must be Answerd in The Proposall:

1st Respecting The Governm^t, That a Debt of Nine Millions[14] be at Oncė Satisfyed and y^{eb} Governm^t Eased of So Great a Demand.

2°. That ye Creditors for That Debt may Reciev Some advantage above Their Six p[er] Cent[15] That may be So Considerable as to Raise Their Actions, and Make them gainers by Their Subscripċon.

This I presume Shall better be done, by Setting Forth what The Comp^a May, and Shall do, wch is Feizible, and probable, Than by Pretending to Something Impracticable or at Least Improbable wch Opens ye Mouths of Male contents, and Gives The Enemies of The Design an advantage — Especally Considering That the Probable adventure Shall be Suffiċent both to Encourage The Undertakeing and Answer The greatest Reasonable Expectaċon.

All which is Humbly Submitted to yor L^{dpp} &c.

---

^a a] *interlined*
^b y^e] *following word* 'Demand' *cancelled*

DEFOE TO [EARL OF OXFORD], 17 JULY 1711

Text: BL Add. MS. 70291, fols. ²7–10. [The letter is fols. ²7–8; the enclosure is fols. ²9–10.] *Address*: none.

1 Dickson, 65–70.

2 *Review*, VIII, 245 (17 July 1711). For the development of Defoe's attitude to the South Sea Company, see Letters 187–8.

3 *a Stop to what I was Saying in Print*: After the *Review* for 19 July 1711, Defoe left the South Sea Company alone for the following two issues. He returned to it on 26 July, which suggests that Oxford did not dissuade him from pursuing the topic following this letter.

4 *how … Misscarry*: Whigs were talking down the South Sea Company. They had sought to have its directors elected by shareholders, but parliament voted on 25 May 1711 to vest the right to appoint directors in the Queen (*C.J.*, XVI, 278). Oxford then selected Tories.

5 *a Free-Trade*: In the *Review* for this day, 17 July, Defoe wrote: 'To think of the *Spaniards* giving Consent to a Peace, upon Condition that the *English* shall have a FREE TRADE to *New Spain*; is just as if *England* should make Peace with *France*, upon Condition that the *French* should come over hither, and lie with our Wives' (VIII, 242).

6 *Philip of Bourbon, or Cha: of Austria*: Since the allies' defeats in Spain in 1710, it seemed increasingly probable that France's candidate, Philip V (1683–1746), rather than the allies' candidate, Archduke Charles of Austria (1685–1740), would win the Spanish crown. Moreover, Charles's brother Joseph (1678–1711) had died in Apr. and it was expected, as came to pass, that Charles would succeed him as Holy Roman Emperor. As Defoe spelled out in the *Review* for 28 Apr. 1711 (VIII, 84–7) and *The Succession of Spain Consider'd* (May 1711), the allies did not want to reunite the Spanish and Holy Roman empires.

7 *Contractaċon house at Sevill*: The *Casa de Contratación* in Seville regulated Spain's colonial trade.

8 *Indulto*: Literally 'exemption' or 'privilege' (Spanish). It was a duty paid to the King of Spain on commodities imported from Spanish America.

9 *king Charles … English*: In May 1709, the British commander in Spain, James Stanhope, directed by Sunderland, negotiated an advantageous commercial treaty with 'Charles III' which would have excluded France from trading with the Spanish West Indies (BL Add. MS. 61500, fols. 5r, 70r). The Barrier Treaty signed with the Dutch in Oct. 1709 gave them equal trading privileges in South America (Trevelyan, III, 30). In the *Review* for 12 July 1711, Defoe argued that if Charles were to win the Spanish crown and make concessions to Britain of trading privileges in the Americas, 'it would occasion a general Revolt among his Subjects' (VIII, 233).

10 *French … Thence*: Defoe gives an account of France's insinuating itself into the Spanish American trade in *Review*, VIII, 219–20 (5 July 1711). And in the issue for 7 July, he records Spain's qualms on this account, as well as Louis XIV's insincere promise to evacuate the continent and discontinue trade once the war is over (VIII, 224–5).

11 *Enemies … Proposeing it*: Six years later, in *Minutes of the Negotiations of Monsr. Mesnager* (1717), Defoe wrote that opponents of the South Sea Company 'opposed it at first rather because they envied [Oxford] the Success of it, than that they did not think it the best Scheme of its Kind that ever was laid in that Nation' (*SFS*, IV, 42). Cf. *The Secret History of the White-Staff, Part III* (1715), 41.

12 *Assiento*: The contract to provide African slaves to Spain's American colonies, currently held by France. In 1711 Defoe lamented that England had not secured it (*Review*, VIII, 218 (3 July 1711)) and hoped the Royal African Company eventually would (*An Essay on the South-Sea Trade, PEW*, VII, 52). Britain gained the *asiento* at the conclusion of the war in 1713.

13 *Settlement on ye Spanish Continent of America*: Defoe proposed a British colony in South America for the first time in *Review*, VIII, 248 (19 July 1711).

14 *Debt of Nine Millions*: The floating debt stood at £9 million (see headnote). In *A Brief Deduction of the Original, Progress, and Immense Greatness of the British Woollen Manufacture*

DEFOE TO [EARL OF OXFORD], 20 JULY 1711

(1727), Defoe recalled parliament's ability to vote such an immense sum to satisfy the debt, saying that it utterly cowed Louis XIV and made him resolved to seek peace on any terms (31–2).

15 *advantage above Their Six p[er] Cent:* Shareholders in the South Sea Company were paid 6% interest on their debt until the principal was repaid; the advantage beyond that was a dividend of the profits.

186

To [Robert Harley, Earl of Oxford]

20 July 1711

HEADNOTE: Mrs Agnes Campbell, Lady Roseburn (1637–1716) was Defoe's printer in Edinburgh, who printed his *Caledonia, History of the Union,* and the Edinburgh edition of the *Review,* as well as some pamphlets. In 1671 her first husband, Andrew Anderson (1635–76), had been appointed King's Printer for Scotland and granted a 41-year patent allowing him the exclusive privilege of printing the Bible in Scotland. She inherited this monopoly, continuing Anderson's business as 'Heirs of Andrew Anderson', becoming very wealthy.[1] The patent was due to expire on 12 May 1712. A syndicate was trying to prevent its renewal and gain the reversion for themselves. Agnes Campbell Anderson petitioned Oxford.[2] Defoe first broached the issue with him on 7 June, expressing concern about the religious orthodoxy of the men challenging Campbell. Those men were John Baskett (1664/5–1742), James Watson (*c.* 1664–1722), and Robert Freebairn (d. 1747). Baskett was the Queen's Printer for England. Watson was a suspected Roman Catholic and Jacobite. Freebairn was openly Jacobite and gained notoriety as the 'Pretender's printer' during the 1715 Jacobite invasion. Watson, the leader of this syndicate, alleged that Campbell's Bibles were badly printed and that she was mercenary and oppressive in her business practice.[3] He also folded into his complaints against her the fact that Campbell 'printed the seditious Reviews of Defoe (in the very time she was soliciting for the renewing of her gift of Sovereign's printer) containing unparalleled reproaches against the Queen and her present ministers'.[4] Campbell duly defended her printing the *Review,* pointing out it appeared first in London and the government did not object to it.[5] As Defoe wrote this, the outcome was uncertain, but the grant was eventually awarded to the syndicate on 11 August; Defoe made one final appeal to Oxford on 7 September 1711 but to no avail.[6]

623

DEFOE TO [EARL OF OXFORD], 20 JULY 1711

My Lord

Among Severall Other Things wch wth yor Ldpps Approbacon
I have had The Honor to Lay before yor Ldpp, I have Taken ye
Freedome to Mencon a Dispute wch I fear is Now wthout yor Ldpps
Interposicon Comeing to a Very Unhappy Period; This is My Lord
The Changeing The Authourity of Printing The Bible in Scotland,
From ye hands who have Now with Generall Approbacon been
Entrusted wth it for Many yeares.

My Lord, if it were The Intrests of ye Persons Onely, who were
Concern'd, Tho' I See The Ruine of Many Families Lyes in it also,
yet it were No bussiness of Mine to Mencon it to yor Ldpp, who are
better judge Than to Need any hints from Me, and I better kno' My
Duty Than to Meddle with it.[a]

But (My Lord) as I have ye honor of yor Commands, to
Represent Such Things to yor Ldpp as May, or May Not be, for
ye Public Good, and for her Majties Service in Scotland, and as I
have had Frequent Letters[7] from ye Ministers there,[b] Expressing
Their Apprehensions, and Uneasyness at the Mischiefs, wch May,
(and I doubt indeed will) follow, Putting the Printing of The Bible
into hands who (as They Say) Are Professt Enemies to ye Church
of Scotland, and Contrary in Principle to Orthodox Religion in
Generall — I Thought it My Duty humbly to Move yor Ldpp, That
if possible a Stop May be put in ye Secretas Office,[8] to Such grant,
Till yor Ldpp May have from better hands Than Mine, a True Accot
of The Disorders wch May attend it.

I Doubt Not but mr Carstaires and Those Other Ministers[9]
whom yor Ldpp knows to be Judicous, as well as Zealous for ye Peace
of her Majties Subjects, will all give yor Ldpp the Same Account,[10]
and also That when yor Ldpp shall Examine The Merits of ye Cause,
I Mean as to ye Public Peace, This Ordr (wch I hear has just Now[c]
been Obtain'd, without any address to yor Ldpp) will pass a farther
Test from yor judgemt, Than has yet been Thought Needfull: I
Humbly ask yor Ldpps Pardon, for This Representacon, wch I do

[a] and I better kno' My Duty Than to Meddle with it] *seemingly a later addition;* 'with it' *inter-lined*
[b] there] *interlined*
[c] just Now] *interlined*

624

DEFOE TO [EARL OF OXFORD], 20 JULY 1711

purely on Acco^t of ye Satisfacçon of That Unhappy People, who I foresee will be Most Uneasy on this Acco^t; in Any Other Respect I am Perfectly Dissintrested,[11] On One Side or Other.

I am

May it Please yor L^dpp

yor L^dpps Most Humble and Obed^t Servt

DeFoe

July 20. 1711

Text: BL Add. MS. 70291, fols. ²15–16. *Address*: none.

1 W. J. Couper, 'Mrs. Anderson and the Royal Prerogative in Printing', *Proceedings of the Royal Philosophical Society of Glasgow* 48 (1918), 79–102; John A. Fairley, *Agnes Campbell, Lady Roseburn, Relict of Andrew Anderson the King's Printer: A Contribution to the History of Printing in Scotland* (Aberdeen, 1925); Jane Rendall, 'Agnes Campbell (Lady Roseburn)', in *The Biographical Dictionary of Scottish Women*, ed. Elizabeth Ewan *et al.* (Edinburgh, 2006), 61–2. She is variously referred to as Campbell or Anderson.
2 BL Add. MS. 70051, fols. 204–6.
3 James Watson, 'Publisher's Preface', in Jean de la Caille, *The History of the Art of Printing* (Edinburgh, 1713), 12–20.
4 James Watson, 'The Case of James Watson, one of Her Majesty's Printers' (1713), in *Watson's Preface to the 'History of Printing', 1713*, ed. W. J. Couper (Edinburgh, 1913), 76.
5 *A Brief Reply to the Letter from Edinburgh, Relating to the Case of Mrs. Anderson, Her Majesty's Printer in Scotland* (1710). Cf. C. E. Burch, 'Defoe and his Northern Printers', *PMLA* 60 (1945), 121–8.
6 See Letter 196.
7 *Letters*: None traced.
8 *stop May be put in ye Secretas Office*: Lord Advocate Sir James Stewart notified William Carstares that 'Secretary St. John is positive that Freebairn's gift must be maintained' (H.M.C. *Portland MSS*, v, 123). Since Queensberry's death, Scottish affairs were handled by St John in his capacity as Secretary of State for the Northern Department.
9 *Ministers*: Thomas Blackwell (*c.* 1660–1728) and Robert Baillie (*c.* 1672–1726) along with Carstares formed the deputation of the General Assembly that in late 1711 travelled to London and lobbied the ministry, without avail, against a legal toleration of Episcopacy and the restoration of lay patronage (Nicolson, 585–6).
10 *Same Account*: Carstares sent Oxford the letter from Stewart quoted in note 8 above, but no other intervention from him is known.
11 *I am Perfectly Dissintrested*: This is debatable given Defoe's connections with Anderson.

187

To [Robert Harley, Earl of Oxford]
[*c.* 20 July 1711][1]

HEADNOTE **(Letters 187 and 188)**: Defoe had a longstanding plan to take the war to Spanish America, believing that cutting off the flow of bullion into Spain and France would incapacitate them more surely than the land campaign on the Iberian peninsula.[2] The South Sea Company established in June 1711 presented a new prospect – or perhaps rather the revival of an old one. Defoe advocated establishing British colonies on the Spanish-controlled mainland of South America in the *Review* for 19 July 1711.[3] In the *Review* for 7 August he argued for the legitimacy of annexing territory there: it would represent some repayment of the vast sums Britain had expended trying to secure the Spanish throne for the Habsburgs, and it had been agreed in the articles of the Grand Alliance at the outset of the war that conquests in the Americas would remain Britain's.[4] Defoe's *An Essay on the South-Sea Trade*, published in September 1711, reiterated the case for a South American British colony that would trade with or without Spanish consent.[5]

Defoe claimed in numerous places to have laid a similar plan before William III towards the end of his reign, immediately prior to the present war.[6] The King was keen, Defoe says, but his death put paid to the plan. Defoe himself is the only authority for his repeated claim to have advised William, so this must be treated with caution.[7] It is true, however, that copies of letters addressed to William dating from 1701 outlining a version of this plan were kept with Defoe family letters down to the 1950s. Scholars agree that these are the work of William Paterson, an architect of the abortive Darien scheme to settle a Scottish colony on the isthmus of Panama.[8] When he mentions plans presented to William, Defoe could be referring to these documents, if he had them in his possession, though he also claimed to have destroyed his own plans.[9]

Another probable influence on Defoe as he developed his scheme was Thomas Bowrey, who also advised Oxford on the South Sea Company and had some acquaintance with Defoe.[10] In 1711 Bowrey sent Oxford a 'Proposal for takeing Baldivia in yᵉ Sᵒ Seas'.[11] Like Defoe, Bowrey advocated a refreshment harbour on the east coast and like Defoe he stressed that the indigenous peoples would be friendly and the few Spaniards in that area either amenable to or impotent to prevent a British presence.[12] Defoe's ideas evidently came from his reading too. The main geographic and ethnographic ideas informing Defoe's plans for South America – the salubrious climate, the tractable natives hostile to their Spanish overlords, and the prospect of a trade route overland across the Andes – appear to be Alonso de Ovalle's *Historical Relation of the Kingdom of Chile* (1649; trans. 1703),

DEFOE TO [EARL OF OXFORD], [C. 20 JULY 1711]

John Narbrough's *An Account of Several Late Voyages & Discoveries to the South and North* (1694), and Herman Moll's map of South America in *A View of the Coasts, Countrys, & Islands within the Limits of the South–Sea Company* (1711).[13]

In mid-1711 ambitions for new colonies in South America were part of Britain's diplomatic efforts as well as colonial ambitions. Secret peace preliminaries offered to France in late July 1711, almost exactly as Defoe was writing his memoranda on the South Seas, included a demand for four colonies, two on each coast.[14] In his own writings on the peace later in 1711, Defoe again advocated 'putting the Queen of *Great Britain* in possession of a Part of the *Spanish* Dominions in *America, to wit*, In the Kingdoms of *Chili* and *Peru*'.[15] Oxford contemplated a naval expedition in 1712, but it was not executed.[16] These plans came to nought when peace was eventually settled, and the South Sea Company did not pursue the project in anything like the terms Defoe set out.[17] But Defoe did not let it go, and in numerous publications, down to the 1720s, he promoted a plan to establish colonies in South America, favouring the plan to have one on the east and one on the west coast of the continent, envisaging an overland route that would join them.[18] This idea received fullest expression in his novel, *A New Voyage Round the World* (1724). The narrator's adventures in this part of the world lead him 'to recommend that Part of *America*, as the best, and most advantageous Part of the whole Globe for an *English* Colony'.[19]

May it Please yor Ldpp

What is allready Offred[20] to yor Ldpp on Accot of The Trade to The South-Seas being on ye Supposiċon of The Impossibillity of Obtaining a Free-Trade with The Spaniards in America, It Remaines to Enquire whether[a] The Proposall of ye Said Trade May Not be Made, On a foundaċon as Effectuall, and a Prospect Every way as advantageous and Encourageing, yet at ye Same Time Not Lyable to Those Objecċons wch Some people So Dilligently Improve to make ye world[b] Uneasy, and to lessen ye Vallue of The Undertakeing.

If This can be done, The Reputaċon of The proposall And by consequenċe of ye Proposer wch is what Those people aim at, Seems to be better Secured, and any Uncertainty wch may afterwards appear in Circumstanċes will not be placed to The Accot of ye Undertakeing in Generall.

---

[a] whether] *following word* 'if' *cancelled*
[b] world] *following letters perhaps* 'Ass' *(perhaps for* 'Assume') *cancelled*

DEFOE TO [EARL OF OXFORD], [C. 20 JULY 1711]

I beg leave to Explain My Self Thus:

That all proposalls for ye Carrying On a Trade To The South-Seas Should be made So That ye Substance or Main Stress of The Design, May Turn Upon Makeing a Settlement or Colloney, (or Severall Such) On ye Continent of America; and Supporting it by The Governm^t for Improvement — Not Laying any, (or Not So great) weight on an Imediate Comerce Thro' ye Spanish Dominions (wch people have allready a Nocon can not be Obtained) as On ye Reall advantages of haveing an English Collony on ye Continent of America, and in ye Midst of The Gold, Silver and Other produccons, wth which The Spaniards have So Enrich't Themselves, and wch The English are Much more capable to Improve Than They.

On This Foundacon, So Much May be Said, and The Objeccons against it will be So Few, So weak, and So Easily Confuted, That it is humbly Conciev'd it will Soon gain an Universall Approbacon.

No Man can Object against The advantages of a Collony, provided The place be well Chosen; and Even Those places in wch ye Spaniards Could Make little or no advantage, Shall be Infinitely profitable to us, Since England is quallifyed to Grow Rich Even, where A Spanish Settlement would Perish, and Starv, Because we Are posest of So many Other Collonys wch would be Their Support.[21]

Thus we have Improved Barbadoes,[22] Upon wch There Now Subsists So Many Souls wch if it were in The Governm^t of ye Spaniards would Eat up one Another, The place being in No Capascity to Support and Feed Them, whereas by Constant Supplys from Our plantacons on The Main land Provisions of all Sorts are often as Cheap as in NewEngland, New York &c. From whence They Come.

That a Settlement Made in America would be Infinitely advantageous to England Tho' there were to be no Free Trade wth the Spaniards, is Easy to prove, Nor will The people be hard to Take in ye Nocon of it and Understand it. The advantages are Manifest and May be handsomely Enlarg'd on; if New England, N York &c. and Our Collonys on ye North where The Spaniards Thought it Not worth while to plant and where meer husbandry and labour has

628

DEFOE TO [EARL OF OXFORD], [C. 20 JULY 1711]

brought The Inhabitants to Such a Degree of wealth and Strength, have Brought So great a Trade; Planting On ye South and West of America where ye Soil and Country is So Naturally Rich and Gold and Silver is the Imediate Return will Much Sooner and wth Much More Ease Make The Trade Great and The plantaçon flourish.

The advantage of Private Trade wth the Spaniards will also be a Constant Addiçon as it is Now at Jamaica[23] and Much More,[a] Since Tho' The Spaniards will Not Open Their Ports and Markets for us to Sell,[b] we Shall allways have an Open Port and Market for Them to buy.

To Carry on Such a proposall and Make it More Intelligible I Humbly Suggest That Schemes of Proper Plaçes, for Such Settlements, wth Their Respective Advantages of Trade, May be Lay'd before yor L^dpp and if Approved by yor L^dpp May be Made Public — That people may be Taken off From Amuseing Themselves about Difficultys and Impossibillitys and May be Led to a probable View of The Thing wch May be Intelligible and Encourageing, which Schemes I Shall Humbly Lay before yor L^dpp when Ever yor L^dpp shall please to Command Me.

All which is Humbly Submitted to yor L^dpp
By yor L^dpps Most Humble & Obed^t Servt
DF

Text: BL Add. MS. 70291, fols. ²23–4. *Address*: none.

---

[a] and Much More] *interlined*
[b] to Sell] *interlined; following superfluous semi-colon omitted in this edition*

---

1 Internal evidence shows that this undated letter comes between Letter 185 (17 July) and Letter 188 (23 July).
2 *Review*, VII, 574–7 (18 Jan. 1711). In *The Secret History of the White-Staff, Part III* (1715), he identified the Godolphin ministry's decision not to pursue this tack one of its key mistakes (18).
3 *Review*, VIII, 248.
4 *Review*, VIII, 281–3.
5 *PEW*, VII, 50–5.
6 *Review*, VIII, 206 (28 June 1711); 246 (19 July 1711); *An Essay on the South-Sea Trade*, *PEW*, VII, 56.
7 See headnote to Letter 2.
8 G. H. Healey's correspondence with John Robert Moore establishes Paterson rather than Defoe as the author. See his letters of 8 Feb. 1948, 14 Nov. 1949, 13 Jan. 1950, and especially 21 Mar. 1951, in Indiana University Archives, H140.

DEFOE TO [EARL OF OXFORD], [*C.* 20 JULY 1711]

9 Letter 188.

10 The only known contact is in Mar. 1708. See Letters 130–1.

11 BL Add. MS. 28140, fols. 31–2.

12 For other proposals to settle a South American colony sent to Oxford at this time, see BL Add. MS. 70163. These include (fols. 26–33) a MS in Abel Boyer's hand of part of *A True Account of the Design, and Advantages of the South-Sea Trade* (1711), a publication until recently attributed to Defoe (F&O, *De-attributions*, 49; Arne Bialuschewski, '*A True Account of the Design, and Advantages of the South-Sea Trade*: Profits, Propaganda, and the Peace Preliminaries of 1711', *HLQ* 73 (2010), 273–85).

13 *Novels*, x, 12–18; Burton J. Fishman, 'Defoe, Herman Moll, and the Geography of South America', *HLQ* 36 (1973), 227–38. For discussion of Moll and the South Sea Company, with a reproduction of his maps, see Glyndwr Williams, *The Great South Sea: English Voyages and Encounters, 1570–1750* (New Haven, Conn., 1997), 161–74. For the longer tradition of South Sea voyaging that would have shaped Defoe's thinking, see Helen Wallis, 'English Enterprise in the Region of the Strait of Magellan', in *Merchants and Scholars: Essays in the History of Exploration and Trade*, ed. John Parker (Minneapolis, Minn., 1965), 193–220.

14 L. G. Wickham Legg, 'Torcy's Account of Matthew Prior's Negotiations at Fontainebleau in July 1711', *EHR* 29 (1914), 525–32 (at 526).

15 *Reasons why this Nation Ought to put a Speedy End to this Expensive War*, PEW, ii, 239.

16 Shinsuke Satsuma, 'The South Sea Company and its Plan for a Naval Expedition in 1712', *Historical Journal* 85 (2012), 410–29.

17 Steven Pincus, 'Empire and the Treaty of Utrecht (1713)', in *New Worlds?: Transformations in the Culture of International Relations Around the Peace of Utrecht*, ed. Inken Schmidt-Voges and Ana Crespo Solana (Oxford, 2017), 153–75.

18 *A Secret History of One Year* (1714), 40; *A General History of Discoveries and Improvements* (1725–6), *TDH*, iv, 211–17; *A Plan of the English Commerce* (1728), PEW, vii, 318–20; *An Humble Proposal to the People of England, for the Encrease of their Trade, and Encouragement of their Manufactures* (1729), 44.

19 *Novels*, x, 258. See Jane Jack, '*A New Voyage round the World*: Defoe's *Roman à Thèse*', *HLQ* 24 (1961), 323–36.

20 *allready Offred*: See Letter 185.

21 *we … Support*: Defoe wrote that, compared to the Spanish, 'the *English* Nation … are so much better qualified every Way, both by their Manufactures to Trade *with*, Islands to Trade *from*, and Naval Strength to manage and protect that Trade' (*An Essay on the South Sea Trade*, PEW, vii, 32). A friendly Spaniard tells the hero of *New Voyage*, 'the *Spaniards* seemed already to have more Dominions in *America*, than they were able to reap the Benefit of, and still more infinitely than they could improve, and especially in those Parts called *South America*' (*Novels*, x, 209).

22 *we have Improved Barbadoes*: Defoe reflects on the English 'improvement' of Barbados in *Review*, viii, 89 (1 May 1711), estimating the slave population at 60,000, and in *A Plan of the English Commerce*, PEW, vii, 287, putting the total population above 100,000.

23 *Jamaica*: Again, Defoe gives an account of the English 'improvement' of Jamaica after it had been taken from Spain in 1655, and he discusses the clandestine trading (euphemistically here called 'Private Trade') between Jamaica and the Spanish American territories, in *A Plan of the English Commerce*, PEW, vii, 287–8, 296.

DEFOE TO [EARL OF OXFORD], 23 JULY 1711

188

To [Robert Harley, Earl of Oxford]

23 July 1711

My Lord

The Two Papers[1] I have allready Sent yor L^dpp were Onely
The Thoughts in Gener^ll wch in Obedience to yor Commands I
have Reduc'd to form on ye South Sea Expedicon. I here Offer
to yor L^dpp a Scheme for The Practise. I hope it May Not be less
acceptable to yor L^dpp for That it has been formerly proposed, Since
I can Assure yor L^dpp No Eye Ever Saw The Drafft Except his
Late Maj^tie and The Earle of Portland,[2] and The Originalls were
allways in My Own hand, Till my Lord Nottinghams fury forced
me to Burn Them[3] with Other papers to keep Them Out of his
hands.

They are here Rough and Indigested But if yor L^dpp Approves
any of Them in The Gross I shall Single it Out to put it in a Dress
more Suitable for yor Service; Mean Time I Shall go On to Lay The
Remaining Schemes before yor L^dpp.

> I am May it Please yor L^dpp
> yor L^dpps Most Humble and Obedient [Servt]
> [   ]^a

July. 23. 1711

May it Please yor L^dpp

In Persuance of a Proposall for a Settlement Upon The Coast
of America as well in y^e <u>North</u> as in y^e <u>South Seas</u>,[4] which May
be Effectuall for ye Establishing a Trade whether wth ye Spaniards
or no, and Every way Suitable to ye present Undertakeing and
Encourageing to ye Subscribers,[5] I Humbly Lay before yor
Lordshipp The Severall Schemes Following, Some of Them being
The Same which I had the Hono^r by his Maj^ties p[er]ticular Order
to Lay before him at ye begiñning of This war, And which The Said

---

^a [Servt] [   ]: *signature torn out, affecting word above*

631

DEFOE TO [EARL OF OXFORD], 23 JULY 1711

king Approved Very well and had Not Death prevented him, had been Then Put in Practiċe.[6] I present yor L^{dpp} Onely The Heads, and Shall Enlarge on any of The Perticulars as you Shall please to Direct.

> 1.° A Proposall for Seizing, Posessing, and forming an English Collony on The kingdome of Chili in ye South Part of America.

The Kingdome of Chili is Perticularly Proper for an English Collony, Because by The Sċituaċon And Other Properties it is More Adapted For Commerċe, Planting, and Inhabiting, wch are The Three Articles Espeċally to be Considred.

> 1. It Lyes between The Latitude of 27 and 45 Degrees, in a Climate So Tempered both for ye Constituċon of English bodyes[7] and The produccon of Necessary Fruits for life That all Sorts of provisions, Corn, Cattle and Fruits may be Raised by Themselves Espeċally in The Southern parts, and ye wholl Country Lyeing Upon ye Coast Such Things are with Ease Carryed to ye More Northern parts wch are Hotter and More Unfruitfull, The want of which[a] Fruitfullness and Temper of Clime was Evidently The Ruine of The Design at Darien[8] —
> 2 The Collonys of ye Spaniards being So Remote[9] and The Countries between Them and Chili being Part[b] under The Line it Self, and all The way between The Tropicks,[10] it will be Impracticable for Them to March by Land to Attack Our Collony, and by Sea it is Supposed we may be allways too strong For any attempt They can Make, in That Part of The world.
> 3 This Country as being too Remote, The Spaniards as if They had been Sated and Glutted wth the Wealth of Peru, Never Entirely[c] Conquerd, by wch Means tho' They did posess The Coast, yet ye Natives Remain, and Are Very Numerous, Hateing The Spaniards, and willing to Reciev any Naċon That are likely to Deliver Them from The Slavery They are Und^r to ye Cruell and Tyrannic Temper of the Said Spaniards.[11]

---

[a] which] *interlined above cancelled word* 'This'
[b] Part] *interlined*
[c] Entirely] *interlined*

DEFOE TO [EARL OF OXFORD], 23 JULY 1711

4 These Natives are a foundaċon of Commerċe, because They
Go Cloathed, and would Generally Cloth Themselves, if
They Could Obtain Manufactures; They Inhabite Chiefly The
Hill Countrys and the^a Sierra-Cordilliera or Mountains of
Andes,[12] From whenċe They bring Gold and Skins of Beasts
for Exchange of Goods.

5 By Means of These Natives a Correspondenċe of Comerċe
will of Course be Carryed on with The people of Peru, and
by Consequenċe wth ye Spaniards, On ye other^b Side of the
Mountains, From whenċe They have a Navigaċon to ye Rio
de la Plata and The Cityes Le Concepċon, and de Beuenos
Ayres,[13] and which Country The Spaniards call^c <u>des Valegas</u> or
The Valleys, From whenċe to ye North, They have a Clear plain
Country to The Cityes of Potosi and La Plata in The Country
of Peru[14] — This will be a Private Trade am[on]g^d The Natives

—

6 The Plenty of Gold in Chili Exceeds That on ye Coast
of Guinea in Affrick, and The Spaniards who bring Great
Quantitys From Thenċe, would have much more if Their
Improvident Pride,[15] would Permit Them to Encourage The
Natives to bring it in, But The Treachery and Cruelty wth
which They Treat the <u>Chileans</u> has Ruin'd That Trade.

The Best Plaċe for a Capitall City and Collony in This kingdome
of Chili, is at ye Port of <u>Baldavia</u> as we call it, But More Properly
<u>Valdivia</u>, called So by The Spanish Gener^{ll} of That Name[16] who
Planted Here — Being an Excellent Port, a good Harbour, and
Three fresh Rivers[17] falling into it, haveing a Navigaċon allmost^e up
to <u>St Iago</u> North, and <u>Villa-Rica</u> East,[18] a Considerable way into y^e
Country.

Here The Climate is good, The Country Fruitfull, The Natives
Courteous and Tractable, and The Wealth of ye Plaċe in Gold
Incredible.

---

^a the] *interlined*
^b other] *interlined*
^c call] *interlined*
^d am[on]g] *hole in MS*
^e allmost] *interlined*

DEFOE TO [EARL OF OXFORD], 23 JULY 1711

The Soil here will Encourage The Industry of Our People, who will Settle and plant, produceing Rice, Cocoa, Wine, Exceeding Rich and Pleasant, and on yᵉ North Side Sugar, and Spices in Abundance, but Especally Gold and Salt peter.[19]

The Air[a] here is pleasant, Agreeable, and Healthy. The Mountaines of Andes being Exceeding high, The winds from Their Tops keep The air Cool; and on yᵉ Other side The breezes from the Sea, keep it Moist, and Moderate; and being in yᵉ Latitude of 39 to 40 Degrees it Answers to Our Collony of Carolina, wᶜʰ is Esteemed the Most Healthy of all Our Collonys in yᵉ North Parts of America.

Both to yᵉ North, and South of This, are Severall Other Ports Very Proper for Settling Smaller Collonys, preserving The Center of Strength, and Commerce at Valdivia, Both for Safety and Strength, of Shipping.

2 To Secure Our Passage to This Collony, as well as to Supply the Collony it Self wᵗʰ Corne and Cattle in Case of Need, and Also For yᵉ Refreshment and p[er]haps wintering[b] of Our Men and Ships in Their passage to or from[c] yᵉ Collony both Goeing and Comeing, The passage thro' The Straights of Magellan being Sometimes Found Impracticable.[20]

It is Next[d] Humbly Proposed That a Previous Settlement be made on yᵉ South East Coast of America, Between The Rio-de-La-Plata and The Mouth of The Straights of Magellan,[21] where Our Ships may all Touch In Their Passage, Out and home; whither Convoys may Go wᵗʰ Them, and Meet Others Comeing home and bring them back.

It is Observed That by The Accoᵗˢ of all That have gone on shore[e] here The Country is adapted For Corn and Pasture in Especall Manner, being a plain Country Covered wel[l][f] wᵗʰ good Grass, Vast Downs, and Valleys for Feeding, and Rich Marly Ground for plowing, Very Little Wood, And Very Good Rivers, So That This

---

ᵃ Air] *interlined above cancelled word* 'Climate'
ᵇ and p[er]haps wintering] *interlined*
ᶜ or from] *interlined*
ᵈ Next] *interlined*
ᵉ on shore] 'on' *interlined;* 'shore' *amended from* 'Ashore'
ᶠ wel[l]] *obscured by MS binding*

634

DEFOE TO [EARL OF OXFORD], 23 JULY 1711

Country may be a Magasin for Supplying The <u>Chilean</u> Collony, wth all Manner of Provisions, and For Supporting The Navigaćon against The Length of The Voiage.

Also a Comunicaćon May be Made by Land From This Collony to Chili[a] wch will not be Above 360 Miles, which[b] (Especally For Intelligenće) May be Easily p[er]formed, The Voiage by Sea being at ye Same Time Near 2000 Miles.

This Collony I Propose to be on ye Coast Between The River <u>De la Plata</u> and The Fretum Magellanicum[22] but Especally from Cape Redondo to St Julien[23] and Near ye Mouth of <u>Rio:Camarones</u>[24] wch River is Navigable wthin 200 Miles of Valdivia and Rises Out of y^e <u>Andes</u> aforesaid.

All The Sea Coast here and The Banks of This River have been Discovred and Appear to be Excellent Land to breed and Feed Cattle, Sow Corn and Establish a Collony.

It Seems That a Collony on The Coast of Chili Could not be So well Maintaind as by The Assistanće of Such a Sister Collony in The North Seas.

But Especally This Northern Collony[c] may be Usefull to The Navigaćon, The Voiage[d] to The Other Coast being So Very Long and in Time Barks[25] being Built There for ye Currenćy of The Trade Between Them, The European Navigaćon May End here and The Goods be Respectively Carryed and Fetch't in sloops and Barqs of Their Own.

If any Ships Lose Their Passage in The Straights They may[e] Come back and winter here, Or Unlade here and Return, wch is Most proper by Reason of The Exchange of The Seasons, Their Winter being Our Summer, So That ye Season Most Improper to pass The straights in is ye Most proper to Come to England in.

A Post being Established From Henće to Chili in 7 or 8 dayes,[26] advićes May Come to England in about four Months One Time wth another Very often in Three Months or Ten weeks.

---

[a] Chili] *following words* 'by land' *cancelled*
[b] which] *interlined above cancelled word* 'and'
[c] Collony] *amended from* 'Colloney'
[d] Voiage] *the* 'a' *interlined*
[e] may] *the* 'a' *interlined*

DEFOE TO [EARL OF OXFORD], 23 JULY 1711

The Collony on yᵉ North Side[27] is Not Appointed Nearer The Mouth of yᵉ Straights because The Climate is Reckoned Too Cold,[a] The Air Inclement and The Country Not atall Fruitfull or capable of Improvemᵗ.

All which is Humbly Submitted to yoʳ Lᵈᵖᵖˢ judgemᵗ
By yoʳ Lᵈᵖᵖˢ Most Humble and Obedient Se[rvᵗ]
[ ][b]

Text: BL Add. MS. 70291, fols. ²17–22. [The letter is fols. ²17–18; the enclosure is fols. ²19–22.] *Address*: none. *Endorsed by Oxford*: Mˢʳ Guilot July 23: 1711 ʀ July 24: South Sea

---

[a] Cold] *following word* 'and' *cancelled*
[b] Se[rvᵗ] [ ]] *signature torn out, affecting word above*

---

1   *Two Papers*: Letters 185 and 187.
2   *Earle of Portland*: Hans William Bentinck, first Earl of Portland, one of William III's favourites. In *The True-Born Englishman* (1700/1), Defoe praised Portland for his part in the Revolution, the Battle of the Boyne, and the negotiations for the 1697 Treaty of Ryswick (lines 984–1010, *SFS*, I, 112). On Portland and the Treaty of Ryswick, see also *Review*, VIII, 747 (17 Apr. 1712). In *The Felonious Treaty* (1711), Defoe decried Portland's 1701 impeachment for his role in the Treaties of Partition (*PEW*, V, 162).
3   *Lord Nottinghams fury forced me to Burn Them*: Defoe is recalling his prosecution by Nottingham for *The Shortest Way with the Dissenters* in 1703.
4   yᵉ *North* ... yᵉ *South Seas*: Respectively, the Atlantic and Pacific Oceans in the vicinity of South and Central America.
5   *Encourageing to* yᵉ *Subscribers*: Some shareholders in the South Sea Company were disgruntled because they had had no say in the conversion of their debts to Company stock and had to subscribe 10% to the Company. Defoe addressed these concerns, by pointing out the likelihood of large profits, in *Review*, VIII, 321–3 (30 Aug. 1711); 330 (4 Sept. 1711); *An Essay on the South-Sea Trade*, *PEW*, VII, 46; and at greatest length in *The True State of the Case between the Government and the Creditors of the Navy* (Sept. 1711). When he recounted the origins of the Company in *The Secret History of the White-Staff, Part III* (1715), Defoe commended Oxford's will to honour unsecured debts, though he believed subscriptions to the Company should have been sought independently of the government creditors (35–46).
6   *king ... Practice*: See headnote.
7   *Climate So Tempered both for* yᵉ *Constitucon of English bodyes*: Defoe makes identical points about English settlers and the climate of this part of South America in several places, from the *Review* for 7 Aug. 1711 (VIII, 283) to *New Voyage* in 1724 (*Novels*, X, 190). On Defoe's distorted ideas about the South American climate, see Robert Markley, 'Defoe and the Imagined Ecologies of Patagonia', *PQ* 93 (2014), 295–313.
8   *Ruine of The Design at Darien*: In the *Reviews* for 3 and 5 July, Defoe laments the failure of the Scottish colony on the isthmus of Panama because it would have been a good footing for the South Sea Company (VIII, 216, 219). Cf. *The Manufacturer*, no. 19 (1 Jan. 1720).
9   *Collonys of* yᵉ *Spaniards being So Remote*: La Frontera, a system of Spanish fortifications developed during the seventeenth century to defend against Araucanian revolts from the south,

636

DEFOE TO [EARL OF OXFORD], 23 JULY 1711

was near the Bío Bío river, around 200 miles north of Valdivia where Defoe hoped for an English colony; Spain's larger settlements were yet further north.

10 *Line ... Tropicks*: The Equator and the Tropics of Cancer and Capricorn.

11 *Natives ... Spaniards*: On Araucanian resistance to Spanish rule, see David J. Weber, *Bárbaros: Spaniards and Their Savages in the Age of Enlightenment* (New Haven, Conn., 2005), 54–68. Defoe discusses 'the Cruelty and Barbarity with which the *Spaniards* Treated the poor Natives' in *Review*, VIII, 207 (28 June 1711).

12 *They Inhabite ... Andes*: 'Many of the Nations of the *Chilians*, had been driven to live in the Hills, and some even beyond them, to avoid the Cruelty and Tyranny of the *Spaniards*' (*New Voyage, Novels*, x, 153).

13 *Le Concepçon ... de Beuenos Ayres*: Buenos Aires is on the Rio de la Plata estuary; Concepçion is on the coast of Chile.

14 *Potosi and La Plata in The Country of Peru*: The silver mining areas north of Chile. Potosí is in modern Bolivia.

15 *Improvident Pride*: Speaking of his compatriots, the friendly Spaniard in *New Voyage* tells the narrator that 'we have so much Pride, that we have no Avarice, and we do not covet enough to make us work for it', suggesting the Spaniards are too lazy to stoop to pick up the gold they see lying around (*Novels*, x, 173).

16 *Spanish General of That Name*: Pedro Gutiérrez de Valdivia (1497–1553) founded Valdivia (sometimes Baldivia) in 1552.

17 *Three fresh Rivers*: The Caucau, Calle-Calle, and Cruces rivers join, forming the larger Valdivia River.

18 *St Iago North, and Villa-Rica East*: Villarica is seventy miles north-east of Valdivia at the foot of the Andes, connected to Valdivia by the Cruces river. Santiago is around 460 miles north, and Defoe means that it is possible to sail up the western coast of the continent and up the Maipo and then Mapocho rivers to Santiago. The mariners in *New Voyage* do this, though merchants come from Santiago to the Pacific coast to trade (*Novels*, x, 154).

19 *Salt peter*: potassium nitrate, used mainly in gunpowder.

20 *straights of Magellan being Sometimes Found Impracticable*: Defoe describes the Straits of Magellan, named for the Spanish explorer Ferdinand Magellan (1480–1521), and the difficulties of navigating through them, in *New Voyage, Novels*, x, 38.

21 *South ... Magellan*: This coast's suitability for English colonisation is outlined in *New Voyage*. The narrator extols its agricultural, climatological, and geographical advantages, and he learns of Spain's incapacity or unwillingness to settle in these regions (*Novels*, x, 37, 209–13).

22 *Fretum Magellanicum*: Defoe also gives the Latin name in *New Voyage, Novels*, x, 211.

23 *Cape Redondo to St Julien*: Puerto San Julián, founded and named by Magellan in 1520, was the last stopping point before the Straits. 'Cabo Ridondo', marked on Moll's map, is about halfway between Rio de la Plata and San Julián, around what is now the mouth of the Rio Negro.

24 *Rio:Camarones*: This river does not exist: Defoe may have been misled by Moll's map (see headnote).

25 *Barks*: small ships.

26 *Chili in 7 or 8 dayes*: Compare the advice given the narrator in *New Voyage*, that crossing 'the whole Ridge of the Andes' is possible in 'Eight or Nine Days', but a safer and easier route was available, taking 'Sixteen or Seventeen Days' (*Novels*, x, 175–6).

27 *North Side*: I.e. the east coast, on the Atlantic.

189

John Russell to Defoe

26 July 1711

HEADNOTE (**Letters 189 and 190**): In summer 1711, Defoe lobbied on behalf of Major James Coult (d. 1714), who was the brother-in-law of William Carstares, having married his sister Margaret in 1706. Coult was Lieutenant at Edinburgh Castle, serving under its Governor, the Earl of Leven.[1] Defoe campaigned to have Coult and Leven retain their commands when the Tories came to power in 1710.[2] Defoe knew Coult through the Edinburgh Society for the Reformation of Manners.[3]

Ed^b Jully <u>1711</u>

Dear Sir

I receaved yoūrs[4] ye last post with the two you mention; in dūe time I delivered y^m to our Freind.[a] I wroat to you ye 21 & 30th of June Last[5] which you doe not[b] notice to have receaved; I payed Mrs Goodale[6] £8 as you ordered me and shall observe what you wryte anent your son tho I have not had oportunity yet to doe it, Nor can I till the few dayes of ye Session be over.[7] I Spoak to Major Coult[8] who in a post or two will give me a bill for £60 as you desire. Mrs Hamiltoūn[9] pretends more then which you order me to pay her; but adjust that matter between you and I shall doe as you direct; Our freind gave you his service & desired me to show you that he thought Sinking of ye Secretaryes post[10] might be a loss to North Brittain but more of this afterward, As also of what you allowed me to comunicat to ye Major; tyme so straitens me at present that I cannot enlarge; Mrs Flint sent for me & told me a long story about her Son[11] which I told her I wūld not medle in and wished you might adjust maters betwixt your selfes. My Service to Madam & familly. I am

S^r

Yours

---

^a you mention; in dūe time I delivered y^m to our Friend] *interlined above cancelled words* 'for me direct to our freind which I delivered'
^b not] *following word* 'like' *cancelled*

· 638

JOHN RUSSELL TO DEFOE, 4 AUGUST 1711

Text: NLS MS. 25.3.9, fol. 72ʳ [scribe's copy]. *Address*: To Daniell Defoe Esq | at his house in Newingtoūn | near London

1 *Army Lists*, v, 226.
2 See Backscheider, *Life*, 211, 303. See Letters 192 and 224.
3 EUL MS. Laing III, 339.
4 *yoūrs*: Untraced.
5 *I wroat to you yᵉ 21 & 30th of June Last*: Letters 181 and 183.
6 *Mrs Goodale:* See Letter 141, note 10.
7 *yᵉ Session be over*: In 1711 the Scottish legal session ended on 27 July and resumed on 6 Nov. (Sir John Lauder of Fountainhall, *The Decisions of the Lords of Council and Session, from June 6th, 1678, to July 30th, 1712*, 2 vols. (Edinburgh, 1759–61), II, 667).
8 *Major Coult:* See headnote.
9 *Mʳˢ Hamiltoūn*: Unidentified.
10 *Sinking of yᵉ Secretaryes post*: See Letter 184.
11 *Mʳˢ Flint … her Son*: Unidentified with certainty. Backscheider notes that Benjamin Defoe had a classmate called David Flint ('John Russell', 176 n. 41). Otherwise, the allusion could be to the minister John Flint (1659–1730), minister of West St Giles in Edinburgh, an acquaintance of Defoe's, with whom he had financial dealings (*Fasti*, I, 143; Backscheider, *Life*, 240). See Letter 218.

190

John Russell to Defoe

4 August 1711

Edᵇ 4ᵗʰ August 1711

Dear Sir

My Last the 26ᵗʰ past, since which none from you. According to your desire I herewith send you a bill on Mʳ John Campell, goldsmith in yᵉ Strand,¹ for £60 ster which I hop you'll credeit me for in my accoᵗ. I give you yᵉ trouble of yᵉ inclosed Memoriall for our good freind Major Coult² And earnestly recomends it to your care. What Service you doe him in that mater I am sure will be gratefully remembered. Principal Carstairs³ parted from this⁴ on Wedn Last⁵ boūnd for London whom I doubt not youll have occasion to see, And he will commūne with you anent yᵉ affair.⁶ I am sure I need say nothing to you in yᵉ Majors favour for his knowen Zeall & affection for yᵉ govemment (which no man can

639

JOHN RUSSELL TO DEFOE, 4 AUGUST 1711

better represent yⁿ your self)[a] pleads more than ordinary favoūr. I shall rest upon your freindship & hopes to hear from you as[b] soon as conveniently you can. I Saw your Son Some dayes since And told him I wanted to talk a litle wᵗʰ him which you may be sure I shall doe Monday or Tuesday next[7] And treat the affair you recomend with all yᵉ tenderness I can And give you account of yᵉ issue. I gave him no accoᵗ yᵗ I had your allowance to give him any money, Not thinking it convenient till I shoūld have tyme to desscourse wᵗʰ him fully. Now that oūr Session is over I shall wryte you more frequently. The Major gave a litle hint to oūr great freind[8] of yᵉ Service you have done him which I am to speak to him anent lykewayes yᵉ first oportunity I can get, And I doubt not but the return will be aggreable, And you shall hear from me more particullarly. My humble duty to Madam &c:

Text: NLS MS. 25.3.9, fol. 72ᵛ [scribe's copy]. *Address*: To Daniell Defoe <u>Esq</u> | at his house at Newingtoūn

---

[a] self)] 'self' *in MS*
[b] as] 'als' *in MS*

---

1 *Mr John Campell, goldsmith in yᵉ Strand*: John Campbell of Lundie, active from 1691 until his death in 1712, whose operation became Coutts Bank in the 1760s. He operated at the sign of the Three Crowns near Hungerford Market in The Strand (Coutts retains three crowns in its logo). See Sir Ambrose Heal, *The London Goldsmiths, 1200–1800* (Cambridge, 1935), 119; Edna Healey, *Coutts and Co., 1692–1992: The Portrait of a Private Bank* (1992), 1–24.
2 *inclosed Memoriall for our good freind Major Coult*: Possibly the 'Memorial for Major James Coūlt in her Majties Castle of Edinburgh' (NRS GD 26/9/79), though Oxford received this over a year later, in Sept. 1712 (H.M.C. *Portland MSS*, x, 473–4). In 1711 and 1712, Carstares wrote several times to Oxford asking that a 'Lieut.-Colonel's Act' be procured for Coult (H.M.C. *Portland MSS*, x, 411, 419); Coult petitioned Mar to the same effect in 1712, as well as for the resumption of pay that had been mistakenly withdrawn at the Union (NRS GD 26/9/468).
3 *principal Carstairs*: Carstares was Principal of Edinburgh University, 1703–15.
4 *this*: I.e. this place, Edinburgh.
5 *Wedn Last*: 1 Aug.
6 *he will commūne with you anent yᵉ affair*: Carstares wrote to Defoe in February 1713 asking him to intercede with Oxford on Coult's behalf (Letter 224) but any earlier correspondence is untraced.
7 *Monday or Tuesday next*: 6 or 7 Aug.
8 *Our great friend*: Leven.

640

191

John Russell to Defoe

10 August 1711

HEADNOTE: Defoe's son Benjamin was enrolled at the University of Edinburgh; he boarded with Hanna Goodale, and Russell evidently remitted him money from his father and reported to Defoe on his welfare. Concerns about his dissolute life-style resulted in Benjamin being called home by Defoe at the start of September 1711.[1]

Ed[b] 10 August 1711

Dir Sir

My last y[e] 4th currant wth a bill on M[r] John Campbell for £60 Ster which I am glade to know by your last to me[a] is come safe to hand & accepted.[b] I have tūo from you[2] since; I hope your fears anent Mr H[3] are removed.[c] I sent for your Son and wes very plain with him anent several things I had heard; Tis needless to repeat what arguments I us'd wth him to change his way of liveing, both from y[e] advantadges woūld redoūnd to himself & y[e] Satisefaction it woūld be to you; He seem'd to take all I sd very well and promis'd to gūard ag[t] those things I Lay'd to his charge; But indeed I must be so free as to tell you that I belive it will tend to his advantadge to be ūnder yoūr oūn inspection; And therefor I cannot but aprove of your designe to call him hom, which M[rs] Goodale[4] tells me of. I have at several tymes given him thirtie shillings Ster: which he told me he necessarily wanted to pay for washing his linings & to buy[d] Shoes & Stockings & other Small occasiones;[e] if you inclyn I shall give him any more let me know; I hop all goes well wth our freind.[5]

---

[a] am glade to know by your last to me] *interlined above cancelled word* 'hop'
[b] & accepted] *interlined*
[c] I hope your fears anent Mr H are removed] *interlined above cancelled words* 'by mine of ye sd date you'll See yoūre fears groūndless'
[d] to buy] *interlined*
[e] occasiones] *interlined above cancelled word* 'things'

T. P. TO DEFOE, 15 AUGUST [1711]

I Expect to hear from you this post. My wife remembers Mad^m & you and ye yoūng Ladyes, as I doe who is in all duty

Servt

I am glade ye mind ye Major.

Text: NLS MS. 25.3.9, fol. 73^r [scribe's copy]. *Address*: To Daniell defoe <u>Esq</u> | att his house in Newingtoūn

1 Letter 198. For a contemporaneous account of Benjamin's predilection for drink, see *The Diary of Dudley Ryder, 1715–1716* (1939), 39.
2 *your last … tūo from you*: All untraced.
3 *Mr H*: Possibly Harley, as Backscheider supposes, whether this is connected to immediate concerns like the South Sea Company or, as the phrasing might suggest, Oxford's health (Backscheider, 'John Russell', 176 n. 45). However, because Harley was now a Lord and because the MS cancellation suggests Russell is giving Defoe the news rather than vice versa, it probably refers to someone else. Letter 189 refers to a Mrs Hamilton, and this could be her husband.
4 *Mrs Goodale*: Three days earlier, Defoe and Hanna Goodale had signed a contract making Goodale Defoe's factor in Scotland (NRS RD 4/109, fols. 462–3).
5 *friend*: Probably Coult.

192

T. P. to Defoe

15 August [1711]^1

HEADNOTE: This unidentified Scottish ally of Defoe gives an upbeat assessment of affairs. Parliament had risen on 12 June and Scottish Tory members felt they had gained little either by way of legislation or places. The present letter is among the Harley papers, suggesting Defoe passed it to Oxford. One matter with which Defoe was concerned was the backlash against the Edinburgh Faculty of Advocates for having accepted on 30 June the gift of a Jacobite medal by Elizabeth, Duchess of Gordon (*c.* 1658–1732). Defoe recounted the events in the *Review* for 31 July and 4 August 1711.^2

T. P. TO DEFOE, 15 AUGUST [1711]

Edb Aūg. 15.

My Dear D Foe

Yoū revivd me by your last[3] when ye tell me that our Scots Tories are sent doūne with disgrace and have scarce gott a footmans wages for their blind service.[4] I am also glad to hear that my freind R: Cūninghame[5] has the greatest interest of any S[c]ots[a] man with the Treasūrer. I desyre no other Scots Secretary;[6] we'll feed the better when he rūles the roast.[7]

I hope worthy Mr Carstairs is at London by this time; his cheife errand as I am told is to preserve Montrose and Levin.[8] God grant him Sūccess. Be sure to keep up the alarm about the medal.[9] Rippeth hath done us Knights Service in England.[10]

I hear Mr Dūndass will be at the press againe aboūt the medal;[11] that may affoord you some work for your happy pen.[12] I hope in a short time to see all matters at rights againe. I See a letter from R: Cuninghame wherein he tells that there are great differences arisen among our great men, and that the Duke of Salsbury (as I remember) has left the Coūrt[13] and that the Tories will In a short time rūin themselves. It were no Smal misfortune if our great man were as good at keeping in himself as he is in turning out others;[14] let heaven never bestow upon him that blessing. Pray let me hear from you freqūently, by which ye'll much oblige

Yr affecᵒnate Comrade T: P:

Text: BL Add. MS. 70028, fol. 127. *Address*: none.

---

[a] S[c]ots] 'c' *omitted*

---

1 The topical references within the letter place it clearly in 1711.
2 *Review*, VIII, 270, 277–8.
3 *your last*: Untraced, as is any other correspondence between Defoe and 'T.P.'
4 *Scots Tories ... service*: At the start of Sept., Wodrow wrote: 'I hear a generall dissatisfaction our Nobility, that wer at last Parliament, have at their treatment at London. They complean they are only made use of as tools among the English, and cast by when their party designs are over' (*Analecta*, I, 348).
5 *R: Cūninghame*: Robert Cunningham, one of Oxford's agents in Scotland (see Godolphin to Harley, 17 Aug. 1703, H.M.C. *Portland MSS*, IV, 64–5). On 19 Nov. 1711, an anonymous letter to Oxford advised him that some of his agents ('some little wretches whom you allow to be about you') betray him: Defoe to the City Whigs, but also Toland, Boyer, and Cunningham.

643

T. P. TO DEFOE, 15 AUGUST [1711]

'Have a care of such Wretches, My Lord, for they may run you into Inconveniences. Remember the case of Gregg' (BL Add. MS. 70267, misc. 41l).

6 *Scots Secretary*: See Letter 184.

7 *roast*: I.e. roost.

8 *Montrose and Levin*: The Whigs Leven as Commander in Chief and Montrose as Keeper of the Privy Seal of Scotland were at risk of removal; Leven was eventually dropped in 1712, Montrose in 1713.

9 *medal*: See headnote.

10 *Rippeth … England*: In the Whig paper *The Flying Post* for 31 July–2 Aug. 1711, George Ridpath (d. 1726) printed the purported minutes of the Faculty of Advocates from 30 June 1711 when they agreed to accept the medal. The issue for 16–18 Aug. 1711 responds to accusations of falsification.

11 *Mr Dŭndass … medal*: The medal had been gratefully acknowledged in a speech by James Dundas of Arniston (d. before 1726), whom the advocates deputed to accept it (they subsequently disavowed it, and apologised). In Aug. Dundas wrote *The Faculty of Advocats Loyalty In a Letter to the Queen's Most Excellent Majesty*, which resulted in his prosecution for attacking the Revolution, Union, and Hanoverian succession. Secretary of State Henry St John posited that Dundas's pamphlet had a whiggish design akin to Defoe's *The Shortest Way with the Dissenters* (1702), trying to force Tories to less equivocal expressions of loyalty to Anne (St John to John Drummond, 4 Sept. 1711, in *Letters and Correspondence, Public and Private*, ed. Gilbert Parke, 4 vols. (1798), I, 343–4). For a detailed account of the medal controversy, Dundas's *Letter*, and the aftermath, see *POAS*, VII, 491–503; Adrian Lashmore-Davies, 'The Misuse of Loyalty? James Dundas and the Faculty of Advocates' Letter to Queen Anne of 1711', *Historical Research* 87 (2013), 94–115.

12 *work for your happy pen*: Defoe could be the author of *A Speech for Mr. D[unda]sse Younger of Arnistown* (Aug. 1711), but the absence of clinching evidence led Furbank and Owens to reject it (F&O, *De-attributions*, 48–9).

13 *Duke of Salsbury … Coūrt*: Seemingly an error for the Duke of Somerset, Master of the Horse. His wife had replaced the Duchess of Marlborough as Groom of the Stole, but the Whig Somerset was increasingly at odds with Oxford and especially St John. On 12 Aug. 1711, he had been denied his seat in the cabinet when St John refused to sit with him, believing Somerset to be conniving with the Whigs (Swift to King, 26 Aug. 1711, *Swift Corr.*, I, 371; *Swift Journal*, 257). Somerset was subsequently kept away from Court and then dismissed in Jan. 1712.

14 *great man … others*: Perhaps a reflection on the Earl of Mar who had orchestrated the 1710 election in Scotland and was keen to replace the deceased Queensberry as Secretary of State.

DEFOE TO [EARL OF OXFORD], 24 AUGUST 1711

193

To [Robert Harley, Earl of Oxford]

24 August 1711

HEADNOTE **(Letters 193 and 194)**: Defoe evidently believed he would be most serviceable to Oxford in Scotland. His correspondents there were painting a bleak picture of administrative neglect and Jacobite encroachments, typified by the affair of the Jacobite medal. Oxford was aware that a firmer administration of Scotland was needed. It had ticked over in the old way, with Queensberry Whigs holding major offices.

My Lord

It was my great Missfortune to Miss ye Moment of yor Ldpps Leisure when I had ye honour of yor Last Appointment, and as what I Offred in My Last,[1] was as I Thought Very Much for ye public Serviće, I Mean my goeing Northward, So I have wisht Earnestly for yor Ldpps Opinion, According to wch I Desire to govern all my Steps in these Affairs. I have been Interrupted by Indisposićon in My Attendanće on yor Ldpp, wch I hope[a] I Shall Now be able to Retriev. I Humbly beg yor Ldpp to believ I have no End in My proposall, but to preserv ye Intrest and Correspondenće[2] wch I First Fixed there by yor Command, and wch I hope allways to Improve, and Employ wth yor Approbaćon for her Majties Serviće, and Indeed for ye Serviće and Intrest of That people, who want Nothing So Much, as to kno' what is Their True Intrest, and How much Their Intrest and Their Duty to her Majtie Are Twisted together, and built upon One Foundaćon, And a little to be warned From Joyning in wth Some honest but weak people here, whom yor Ldpp[b] Needs not to have me Describe.

I can not Close This wthout Sending yor Ldpp a Printed paper[3] wch is a Test of ye Forwardness and boldness of a Party Among us. I make no Coments on ye Subject but Shall Accquat yor Ldpp of ye

---

[a] hope] *following word* 'is' *cancelled*
[b] Ldpp] 'Ldpps' *in MS*

645

DEFOE TO [EARL OF OXFORD], 27 AUGUST 1711

Manner how I obtain'd it when I shall have ye hono^r to wait on you, wch I Shall attend for as usuall Every Evening.

I am May it Please yor L^dpp
yor L^dpps Most Humble & Obed^t Servt
DeFoe

Augt 24. 1711

Text: BL Add. MS. 70291, fols. ²25–6. *Address*: none.

1 *My Last*: Untraced.
2 *Correspondence*: See Letter 170, note 5.
3 *Printed paper*: Missing and unidentified.

194

To [Robert Harley, Earl of Oxford]

27 August 1711

My Lord

I had Not Given yor L^dpp This Trouble, being So Near ye Appointment I have of attending yor L^dpp; but On ye Occasion of what you were pleased to Observe to me of The Magistrates of Edinb. Not doeing Their Duty in The Case of The Virulent Pamphlets published There by Dundass and Others.[1]
My Lord, I Humbly Take this Occasion to Represent to yor L^dpp That ye Madness and Insolence of The Jacobites in Scotland is come to That hight That The Magistrates are Dispirited and Aw'd by them, and in Generall This has been Obtained by those people asserting on all Occasions y^t The Governm^t is wth them and Supports Them allows and Countenances them.
I Doubt not but They will go on till they^a Force ye Governm^t to Resent, But (My Lord) it wants but Little of Their believing Not Onely That they will not but That they Dare Not Strike.

---

^a till they] *interlined above cancelled word* 'to'

646

DEFOE TO [EARL OF OXFORD], 27 AUGUST 1711

On ye Other hand My Lord The Magistrates are Intimidated.
The Provost and Bailys[2] are honest but They want Some
Encouragem^t from yor L^{dpp} or ye Queen That They Shall be
protected and Countenanc'd by her Maj^{tie} in ye Discharge of Their
Duty; I Need Not Trouble yor L^{dpp} wth the Acco^{ts} I have From
Severall hands of this, and how The Jacobite Party boast themselves
of it, yet[a] I can Not but wth A plaineness wch I hope yor L^{dpp} will
allow to be my Duty, Observ to yor L^{dpp}, That there are Unhappily
a Party Among us, who I Need Not Name, both There as well as
here, who Take great pains from These Things to posess ye Minds of
The People That ye Ministry Are Not in the Revolu^{c}on Intrest; That
ye Ends of all These Things are The Dissolu^{c}on of ye Establishm^t,
and The Bringing in the pretender; That ye Ministry aim at
Overturning the Union, The Succession, and the Constitution; It
is not Needfull to hint to yor L^{dpp} who these Things are pointed at;
Nor is it Sufficent to Render it Doubtfull, to Say, tis aim'd at Their
Benefactor, and They can not be So Ingrate; There are people had
Rather ye Vessell Should Sink, Tho' they Run ye Risq of Shipwreck
in it, Than That their Own Pilots should Not Steer;[3] These are y^e
Men yor L^{dpp} Must Save against Their wills, and (like Heaven to us
all) Must do Good to, while They do Evill to you.[4]
But (my Lord) There are Some Honest Men yet, whose Eyes
are Open; who abhorr the Facćon, and Ingratitude of the Other;
and who being True and Firm to yor L^{dpp}, and to ye Government,
should (Pardon me That Arrogance my Lord) be Cherished and
Encouraged; I Mean <u>Should</u>, in Order to keep up The Governm^{ts}
Intrest, and Ballance the Mad Men on both Sides: One of My
Letters from Scotland from a Man True to ye Queens Intrest and
to ye best Measures of Preserving it, has the following Expressions
which I beg Leav to Quote in This Case.
"The Narrativ of ye Act of ye Faculty,[5] a Coppy of wch was
Sent to ye Queen, if Narrowly Enquir'd into, will be found Not
to Give a full or True acco^t of Matter of Fact; but it passes, —
<u>cum Cæteris Erroribus</u>.[6] If the Governm^t shall let this Affair
of ye Medall drop thro' their Fingers, what ye Jacobites on One
hand Give Out, That the Government is on Their Side, and

---

[a] yet] *interlined above cancelled word* 'But'

647

DEFOE TO [EARL OF OXFORD], 27 AUGUST 1711

what yᵉ Squad. gives Out on yᵉ Other hand, That yᵉ Ministry Are for The Pretender, will be So farr Confirm'd to yᵉ people, That all honest Men and Friends to yᵉ Queen, and the present Ministry, will be Silenc'd; and all That you or any Man can Say, Will Never be able to Remove yᵉ Jealousies of it Out of the peoples thoughts." — Thus far my Letter.

My Unfeigned Zeal for yoʳ Ldᵖᵖˢ Person and Intrest, and yᵉ Senće of Many Obligaćons I Lye Under to Espouse both, Makes me Importunate wᵗʰ yoʳ Ldᵖᵖ That both These Sorts of people, whose Aims point One at yᵉ Person, Crown and Governmᵗ of The Queen**ᵃ** and The Other at yoʳ Ldᵖᵖˢ Person and Administraćon, may Reciev Their Respective Dissappointments, and This is One Reason why I Moved to yoʳ Ldᵖᵖ my goeing North, Neither yᵉ plaće or people**ᵇ** makeing it Desirable; but That I might be where I may Render you Most Serviće.

I Humbly Lay This Matter before yoʳ Ldᵖᵖ, That yᵉ Insolenće of a Party in Scotland May be Suppresst, her Majᵗⁱᵉˢ Faithfull Friends and Servants Encouraged, and a weak foolish Out-of-Temper Party here, and There also, be Effectually Dissappointed.

I am

May it Please yoʳ Ldᵖᵖ

yoʳ Ldᵖᵖˢ Most Humble and Obedᵗ Servᵗ

[   ]**ᶜ**

Augᵗ. 27. 1711

Text: BL Add. MS. 70291, fols. ²27–8. *Address*: none.

ᵃ Queen] *interlined above cancelled word* 'Governmᵗ'
ᵇ people] *following illegible word cancelled*
ᶜ [   ]] *signature torn out*

---

1 *Magistrates ... Others*: See Letter 192. In Sept., the Lord Advocate, Sir David Dalrymple (1665–1721), was dismissed from office for his failure to deal with the medal affair.
2 *Provost and Bailys*: See Letter 156. The Provost Adam Brown died in Oct. and was succeeded by Sir Robert Blackwood of Pitreaves (1624–1720).
3 *Vessell ... steer*: Defoe often used this imagery elsewhere, such as to blame displaced Whigs for running down public credit in late 1710: for example, he says the Whigs 'had rather sink the Ship, than not have their own Pilots steer' (*Review*, VII, 442 (2 Nov. 1710)). In the anonymously published *Reasons why this Nation Ought to put a Speedy End to this Expensive War* (Oct. 1711), Defoe discusses his own writings on public credit (as a way of disguising his authorship) and refers to his use of 'the apposite Simily of sinking the Ship' (*PEW*, 11, 230).

DEFOE TO [EARL OF OXFORD], 3 SEPTEMBER 1711

4 *do Good to, while They do Evill to you*: See Luke 6:27.
5 *Act of ye Faculty*: The Faculty's act drawn up on 18 July 1711 insisted on the advocates' loyalty to
   Anne and the Hanoverian succession, claiming that they had rejected the medal (*The Minute
   Book of the Faculty of Advocates*, vol. 1: *1661–1712*, ed. J. Macpherson Pinkerton (Edinburgh,
   1976), 294). The government published it in *The London Gazette*, 14–16 Aug. 1711.
6 *cum Cæteris Erroribus*: 'along with the rest of the mistakes' (Latin).

195

To [Robert Harley, Earl of Oxford]

3 September 1711

HEADNOTE: The absence of a Privy Council in Scotland and a dedicated Secretary of State led Oxford to plan to resurrect the powers of the Lord High
Chamberlain of Scotland, a defunct office that once exercised wide jurisdiction in
financial matters, in particular acting as a check on burgh magistrates and stim-
ulating trade.[1] Plans for this had first been presented to Harley in February 1711.
In appointing a commission, he saw a way to fill the vacuum in proximate government in Scotland and to gratify the representative peers who expected rewards
for supporting the ministry. The Commission of Chamberlainry and Trade was
enacted on 15 November 1711. Its membership was predominantly Tory: impatient
allies whose votes were sorely needed in the 1711–12 session were rewarded. Defoe's
suggestion that fresh overtures be made to moderate Presbyterians were ignored.[2]

My Lord

   Seeing yor Ldpp was pleased to Approve My goeing North,
I Thought it My Duty to Lay before yor Ldpp Some Thoughts
of Mine Relateing to Affaires There as They Occurr from My
Constant advices from p[er]sons of Probity and judgement On ye
place as well as From My Own Observačon.
   The Erecting a Form of Governmt Among Them as an
Equivalent for ye Loss of ye Privy Council[3] (The Dissolving
of which was no Token of the Skill of Our late Mannagers) is
Doubtless My Lord a Thought calculated for ye health of That place.
The Choice of Persons and the Conduct of Those Persons when
Chosen Seems to be Now The Onely Nicety in ye Case.

DEFOE TO [EARL OF OXFORD], 3 SEPTEMBER 1711

There are Three Partys in Scotland wch yor Ldpp will Observ Influence affaires and who will come under yor Consideracon:

1st The Jacobite Party, whether Popish or Episcopall it Matters Little. These Fancy they have Now a Crisis to Push Their Intrest in That the juncture is Favourable to Them, and That ye Governmt (at least) has Some Need of Them.[a] They act Now barefaced, Furious, and Insolent, Even to ye Amazemt of ye honest people, who are Terrifyed, and Discouraged at The Insolence of The Jacobites; These I presume are to be a little Check'd or Elce The Governmt it Self will be Insulted.

2 The Hot Presbyterians called The Squadroni — These Are by a kind of Principle allwayes against ye Court, Right or wrong. They were So in king Williams Time, And were So in The Last Ministry, and Are So Still, and Are indeed worthy to be lay'd Aside by Every Party that purpose to keep ye Governmt in bounds.[4]

3 There are a Third kind wch indeed Are ye Generallity of The people who Tho' they are Presbyterian yet go upon Right principles of Government,[b] are Entirely in the present Intrest, hearty to ye Queen and Easy undr her administracon;[c] Onely Jealous of The Great Favour ye Jacobite Party Meet wth Least Sometime or Other They get The Power into Their hand in Scotland to pull Down The kirk.

It is Observable The Squadroni Never had any Ruleing Intrest wth these Nor indeed Are Many of The Nobillity wth Them, who are Rather Divided between ye Jacobite and The Squadroni, But The Ministers are Generally of These and by The Ministers They are kept Right. These are The people who indeed are The Stay of her Majties Intrest in Scotland. The Little Intrest ye Squadroni have wth them Appeared in ye Great struggle at ye last Eleccon[5] but One when These stuck all to ye Court whigs against The Other and Threw Them Out Every where.

These are The people wch I humbly Move it is her Majties Intrest to preserv to keep Them Easy and Safe, for These May be Depended Upon in all Extremeties whether of Invasion from

[a] Them] *following word* 'and' *cancelled*
[b] of Government,] *interlined*
[c] administracon] *following word* 'and' *cancelled*

650

DEFOE TO [EARL OF OXFORD], 3 SEPTEMBER 1711

Abroad or Partys at home. They will allways Appear on her Majties Part against all Sides — These My Lord Are The people I allways Acted by, These Made The Union and These keep ye Ballance in Their hands So as you will Never find any hot Measures or Furious Moćons while They are Encouraged.

If I go Thither I shall give yor Ldpp a View of who Among the Nobillity are well with These people and who Not, That in ye Scheme yor Ldpp is Layeing Such Regard May be had to These people as May Consist wth her Majties Serviće, and That all Such steps May if possible be Avoided as May Tend to Make these Jealous or Uneasye.

The Nobillity of Scotland My Lord are an Odd kind of People to Say no More of Them. There are Some of Them May Deserv Favour who Should hardly be admitted to any Power. Others (wch is Very Strange), it^a May be Requisite to Entrust wth Power who yet hardly Merit The Governmts Favour and Others yet Merit to be Entirly Neglected and are Neither proper for Favour or Power, and Most of This Varyety Arises From The posture these people stand in wth Respect to ye kirk, wch I Explain to yor Ldpp Thus.

Some of ye Nobillity are Men of worth, honour and Prinćiples and as Such Merit her Majties Favour. But to put Them in Power would put all in Confusion as They onely Are Episcopall in judgement and can not bear wth ye Establishmt wch is Presbyterian So That Neither would They be Easy to the Presbyterians nor The Presbyterians be Easy under them.

Some of The Nobillity, however worthless in Themselves and hardly worth any of her Majties Favour, yet as They Are in ye Intrest of The well Enclyn'd people above namd and of Prinćiples Conforming to ye public Serviće and withall have Som Considerable Intrest in and Influenće upon The best people, are The best Objects for ye Trust of Power.

Some of The Nobillity again for Many and known Reasons are Dangerous to her Majtie and The administraćon and are Neither Quallifyed for Favour or Power but to be Continually Forming Squadrons of Malecontents and Disquieting ye Governmt.

---

^a it] *interlined*

651

DEFOE TO [EARL OF OXFORD], 3 SEPTEMBER 1711

If it May be for yoʳ Lᵈpps Serviċe I shall Give you lists of Names to These Classes and The just Characters of The Persons.⁶ However Thus Much I Thought it My Duty to Represent to yoʳ Lᵈpp while yoʳ Scheme for Governmᵗ May be young and in Embrio and while p[er]haps The Persons are not fix't upon in yoʳ Thoughts —

I am

May it Please yoʳ Lᵈpp

yoʳ Most Humble and Obedᵗ Servᵗ

[ ]ᵃ

Septembʳ 3. 1711

PS

I shall attend Wednsday⁷ Evening According to yoʳ Lᵈpps Command.

Text: BL Add. MS. 70291, fols. ²29–30. *Address*: none. *Endorsed by Oxford* (fol. ²30ᵛ): Mʳ Goldsmith Sept: 3 1711

ᵃ [ ]] *signature torn out*

---

1 For a full account, see Riley, *English Ministers*, 174–83.

2 Annandale was first-named commissioner, joined by fellow representative peers Eglinton, Northesk, and Balmerino. Another Tory nobleman was appointed: William Gordon (*c.* 1679–1745), Lord Haddo, later second Earl of Aberdeen (Riley, *English Ministers*, 178). And three commoners completed the commission. Sir Hugh Paterson (*c.* 1685–1777), MP for Stirlingshire, was about to become Mar's son-in-law (*HPC 1690–1715*, v, 112). Alexander Murray of Stanhope (after 1684–1743) was an ally of Oxford's son-in-law, Viscount Dupplin (*HPC 1690–1715*, IV, 957–8); he later joined the 1715 Rising. Sir Patrick Murray of Ochtertyre had connections with Highland chieftains (Riley, *English Ministers*, 178).

3 *Loss of yᵉ Privy Council*: In *History of the Union*, Defoe reflected on the inconveniences in the immediate wake of the 1708 abolition of the Scottish Privy Council but did not criticise the measure, as he does here (*TDH*, vIII, 254, 264–5).

4 *Squadroni ... bounds*: In contrast, Lord Yester advised Oxford on 28 Aug. 1711 that the Squadrone could prove troublesome if denied places, claiming that the Presbyterians as a whole would join with them if the ministry backed them (H.M.C. *Portland MSS*, v, 76).

5 *Great struggle at yᵉ last Elecċon*: See Letters 160 and 162.

6 *lists ... Persons*: No such inventories have been traced.

7 *Wednsday*: I.e. 5 Sept.

652

DEFOE TO [EARL OF OXFORD], 7 SEPTEMBER 1711

196

To [Robert Harley, Earl of Oxford]

7 September 1711

HEADNOTE: The dispute over the lucrative right to publish the Bible in Scotland had been settled in favour of the Watson–Freebairn–Baskett syndicate. Defoe outlined why he believed Agnes Campbell and her heirs should be continued in the patent in his letter to Oxford of 20 July.[1] Years of litigation concerning the right to print Bibles followed, including Baskett and Freebairn changing to Campbell's side; but two years after Campbell's death Watson's right was confirmed by the House of Lords in 1718.[2]

My Lord

It is wth Concern That I give yor Ldpp Frequent Trouble of Letters on The affair of Scotland. My Last was Long and I hope Acceptable to yor Ldpp; I had Not given yor Ldpp This farther Trouble But on Recieving advices from Thence of a Grant wch it Seems is Come down Thither And passed The Seals — (One Letter Says Stopped at The Seals,) to Take away The Privelege of Printing the Bible From ye present Posessor mrs Anderson and Give it to Others.

I formerly hinted Much of This by Letter to yor Ldpp; I did Not Say More, least yor Ldpp Should think me Solliciting Private Intrests, and Cases;[3] But I hope yor Ldpp will believ me to Regard, as well as to know My Duty better; My Study, and ye Reason of My pleading wth yor Ldpp in these or Such Cases is, to Remove or prevent as Much as possible, all Grounds of Jealousy, Discontent, and Uneasyness from those people, who are True Friends to ye Governmt, and to yor Ldpps administracon; and wch I Take it to be good Service to both to keep Right; — and This My Lord The More, by how much ye Friends of the Pretender, go on wth too much Success, to Divide, Disturb and Intimidate Them, Rendring Them Jealous and Fearfull of Designs to Overthrow Their Kirk and Constitucon.

653

DEFOE TO [EARL OF OXFORD], 7 SEPTEMBER 1711

In This Case My Lord They are Made Very Uneasy and I have a long Representaċon or adress to her Maj^tie From ye Printers against this Grant to be presented to her Maj^tie. The Coppy [is]^a in My hands. The Originall^4 is to be brought me and wch I shall Lay before yor L^dpp also.

The Uneasyness of ye Other people is Expresst Or Rather Abridgd into Two heads:

1. They Say The Printing of The Bible is put into ye Hands Of One Papist,^5 One Nonjuror^6 and a wholl Scoċyety of Men Declared Enemyes to The Church of Scotland and to ye Revoluċon.

2. That ye Grant is Illegall^7 in its Nature, Inconsistent wth The Union, Invades private Right and The known Liberty of The Subject.

These being heads on wch Loud Clamours may be Raised I Thought it My Duty to Lay before yor L^dpp; Not presumeing to Say any thing of My Own thoughts One way or Other, But humbly to Recomend to yor L^dpp as I have done all along the Occasion There is to keep those honest weak people as Easy as possible by Such Methods as yor L^dpp shall Think proper.

I have Persuant to yor L^dpps Commands Put my Self in a Posture for Travailling into Scotland; If yor L^dpp pleases to Suffer me to go while The Weather and Roads are Tollerable, it will be a great^b Favour, The year Declining Appaċe.

I have One Humble Request to Subjoyn to This Relateing to My attending yor L^dpp in ye Morning as by yor L^dpps Appointment for tomorrow —^c It is my Hono^r and a Privelege no Man Vallues more That yor L^dpp admitts me to wait on you at any Time, and if yor L^dpp Commands my Attendanċe in Public I shall Thankfully Obey. But as my being able to Serve yor L^dpp and Her Maj^ties Intrest Consists Much On My being Concealed I Humbly Submit it to yor L^dpp^d whether I should Not Rather Attend in an Evening; — I Say no More, Leaving the Rest Entirely to your L^dpps Wisdome and

---

^a [is]] *MS torn*
^b great] *interlined*
^c tomorrow —] *following word perhaps* 'when' *cancelled*
^d I Humbly Submit it to yor L^dpp] *interlined*

654

DEFOE TO [EARL OF OXFORD], 15 SEPTEMBER 1711

Direccon, Onely begging leav to Attend this Evening Rather Than to morrow Morning till I have yor farther Commands.

I am May it please yor L^{dpp}
yor Most Humble and Obed^t Servan^t
[ ]^a

Sept. 7. 1711

Text: BL Add. MS. 70291, fols. ²31–2. *Address*: none. *Endorsed by Oxford* (fol. ²32ᵛ): Mr Goldsmith Sept: 7: 1711

1 Letter 186.
2 W. J. Couper, 'James Watson, King's Printer', *SHR* 7 (1910), 244–62; W. J. Couper, 'The Pretender's Printer', *SHR* 15 (1918), 106–23.
3 *Solliciting Private Intrests, and Cases*: Agnes Campbell Anderson was Defoe's principal publisher in Scotland. However, they were in dispute with one another in September 1712 (see Letter 219).
4 *Originall*: Oxford received two petitions on Campbell Anderson's behalf (BL Add. MS. 70051, fols. 204–5, 206).
5 *Papist*: James Watson (see headnote to Letter 186). Probably unauthorised, Watson published extracts from Defoe's *The Consolidator* as *A Journey to the World in the Moon* [1705] and republished *Reasons why this Nation Ought to put a Speedy End to this Expensive War* (1711).
6 *Nonjuror*: Robert Freebairn (see headnote to Letter 186).
7 *Grant is Illegall*: Couper notes that the patent was alleged to be illegal because 'it had been obtained while the Anderson patent was still running, that Freebairn had never qualified according to law for holding it, and that it transgressed certain Scottish Acts. An unfavourable opinion of Sir James Stewart, the Lord Advocate, had declared it null and void' ('James Watson', 256).

197

To [Robert Harley, Earl of Oxford]

15 September 1711

HEADNOTE: Leven remained as Commander in Chief in Scotland. As a Whig, he had been vulnerable since the previous year's election. In the event, he remained in post until the summer of 1712 when Argyll was appointed in his stead.

^a [ ]] *signature torn out*

655

DEFOE TO [EARL OF OXFORD], 15 SEPTEMBER 1711

My Lord

In Obedience to yor L^{dpps} Comand I have Applyed My Thoughts Seriously to The Affair of a Commander in Chief in Scotland. Yo^r L^{dpps} proposicon is, what Person May be Thought of who May be Easy to ye Kirk, or Rather, who ye Kirk Party May be Easy with,[a] who is Untainted wth Jacobitisme.

It is Not for me my Lord to Give Characters here. The question Principally Lyes on The Character The Kirk Gives of The Person, Or how ye Person Stands wth the Kirk &c.

I have Rumaged The wholl List of The Nobillity for a Man, and it is hard to Find Them, But Either They are Tainted wth Jacobitisme, or Embarkt wth the Squadroni, Or Uncapable and Improper for The Employ, And Therefore before I Mencon Perticular Men, I ask yor L^{dpps} Leave to Make Two Proposalls for yor[b] Consideracon as an Alternative.

1. That a Person May have The Title of The Employ, who is, Or is Likely to be allways Abroad, and May be Especally kept abroad; And the Queen[c] Appoint a Person Under him to Command — This I Humbly Offer For two Reasons 1.) Because Appointing Either The E of Orkney[1] or Some Such Experienc'd Officer to be Command^r, The Strife of Competitours would Cease, and 2.) Then her Maj^{tie} May Give The Sub-Command to Lieu^t Generall Maitland,[2] a Man Acceptable to all Partyes, A Hearty Friend to ye Present Establishm^t, both Governm^t, and Ministry; No Bigot, yet Perfectly well with The Kirk, and who None would Object Against, Nor ye Oldest Souldier in ye Army Think it below him to Serve Under him.

Or, if (wthout ye Ceremony of a Comm^a in Chief abroad) he had The wholl Trust I am Perswaded Not a Man in Scotland would be Uneasy Tho' he be not a Noble man.

2. My Second Proposall is, to have no Commander in Chief atall — Any More Than a Third Secretary, or a Privy Council,

[a] with] *following word* 'and' *cancelled*
[b] yor] *following word perhaps* 'L^{dpps}' *cancelled*
[c] the Queen] *interlined*

656

DEFOE TO [EARL OF OXFORD], 15 SEPTEMBER 1711

or a Com̃ander in Chief for Yorkshire, But to[a] Let yᵉ Eldest Officer Command, Takeing it as it happens, and The Custome and Usage of The Army Directs.

I am Not Now Giveing My Reasons, but Barely Proposeing to yᵒʳ Lᵈᵖᵖˢ Consideraċon, Onely I Crave Leav to Offer This, as what I aim at all along[b] in Every Thing I propose (Viz) The Takeing Away Every Thing, That keeps up a Facċon, or a strife of Partys Among Them. This is what I have my Eye Upon in both These. I Referr My Explanaċons till yᵒʳ Lᵈᵖᵖ shall have Perused The Generall proposall.

I am

May it Please yᵒʳ Lᵈᵖᵖ

yᵒʳ Lᵈᵖᵖˢ Most Humble and Obedᵗ Servᵗ

[*monogram*]

Sept. 15. 1711

Text: BL Add. MS. 70291, fols. ²33–4. *Address*: none. *Endorsed by Oxford* (fol. ²34ᵛ): Mʳ Goldsmith ʀ Sept: 18:ᶜ 1711

---

[a] to] *interlined*

[b] along] *following word probably '(Viz)' cancelled*

[c] 18] *reading uncertain due to amendment*

---

1 *E of Orkney*: See Letter 65, note 3. Orkney was mostly deployed in Flanders during the war.

2 *Lieut Generall Maitland*: See Letter 157, note 55. In *A Tour thro' the Whole Island of Great Britain*, Defoe calls Maitland 'a Gentleman of great merit, and who rais'd himself by the Sword', recounting his loss of a hand at the Battle of Treves (1675) and his being nicknamed '*Handy Maitland*' because he 'supply'd the Want of his Hand with one of Steel' (*TDH*, III, 223). He compliments Maitland's ability to keep the Highlanders in check 'by his winning and obliging behaviour' rather than force, especially at the time of the Union, when Defoe apparently met him (*TDH*, III, 279). In *Memoirs of the Church of Scotland* (1717), Defoe reports having personally heard Maitland decry the enormities he witnessed enacted by his military superiors against the Scottish Covenanters after the Battle of Bothwell Bridge in 1679, as well as his efforts to prevent them (*TDH*, VI, 224–5).

JOHN RUSSELL TO DEFOE, 29 SEPTEMBER 1711

198

John Russell to Defoe

29 September 1711

HEADNOTE: As well as the ongoing lobbying efforts on behalf of his and Defoe's Scottish acquaintances, Russell reports on Benjamin Defoe's departure from Edinburgh at the start of September.[1]

Edb 29th 7ber 1711

Dear Sr

I receaved your blyth letter[2] And wes glade to find you & those Gentlemen you mentiond so much in humor And especiallie to observ yt my good freind [   ][3][a] stands yet firm in his post. I delivered yours to oūr great Freind[4] who ordered me to return you his hearty thanks for yoūr many services & hopes youll continue ye Same. I hop your Son is Safe ariv'd to you by this tyme. I payed Mrs Goodale £3 as you ordered & some dayes since gave her £3 more Upon your accott which she said she necessarily wanted. I gave your Sevt £3..10 for which your Son gave receipt because the Sevt coūld[b] not wryte. I gave your son lykewayes £1..5 just befor he went to his house which he necessarily wanted as the deabt Mrs Goodale hes advised you. I gave him St 10..9 Sch on ye first 7ber to buy some things he sd he wanted for his joūrnay, All this besides £2.. I gave him at severall tymes after you ordered me to speak to him, all which I have charg'd to yoūr accompt. I hop he will doe much better under your own care then he woūld have don at a distance from you. I Indeed wes more plain then pleasant when I pairted with him but I hop he will make good use of what I said, being nothing but what I judg'd my duty to you & ye allowance you had given me call'd me to, But I hop youll wiselie consider his youth leads him to many things now that his reaper[5] years will amend. I doubt not of yoūr minding ye Major[6] who is a hearty well wisher

---

[a] [   ]] *illegible word or words*
[b] coūld] 'wūld' *is a possible reading*

658

DEFOE TO [EARL OF OXFORD], 16 OCTOBER 1711

of yours. I wish you coūld[a] end with Mr Flint,[7] for the mater is not worth your while. My wife remembers you & your familly as doe I.

Y[r] Serv[t]

Pray give my service to those honest Gentlemen you drunk y[e] punch with.

Text: NLS MS. 25.3.9, fol. 75[r] [scribe's copy]. *Address*: To Daniell defoe Esq at his house | in Newingtoun near London

---

[a] coūld] 'wūld' *is a possible reading*

---

1   See Letter 191.
2   *letter*. Untraced.
3   [   ]: The first of perhaps two illegible words appears to begin 'leve', so this could be a refer-ence to Leven, as Backscheider proposes ('John Russell', 176 n. 48). Leven was under fire as Commander in Chief in Scotland. But it could also be 'leve' as an abbreviation of 'lieutenant', with a surname that may be 'McLearie' or similar.
4   *oūr great Freind*: Possibly Hyndford.
5   *reaper*. I.e. riper.
6   *Major*. Major James Coult. See headnote to Letters 189 and 190.
7   *Mr Flint*. Possibly John Flint. See Letter 189, note 10.

199

To [Robert Harley, Earl of Oxford]

16 October 1711

HEADNOTE: Defoe's requests to be serviceable to Oxford concern the peace ne-gotiations with France. These had started in secret in July, resulting in 'preliminar-ies' that were leaked to the press in September, causing anxiety in Britain at the prospect of Spain remaining in Philip V's possession and consternation among the allies that Britain seemed willing to treat unilaterally with France. Defoe had expressed doubts about the suitability of peace in the *Review* as recently as 8 September.[1] On 8 October the peace preliminaries were signed by Britain and France, and the following day Defoe turned wholeheartedly to promoting the ministry's peace campaign in the *Review*, with no real intermission until 20 De-cember (when the bill against occasional conformity became Defoe's focus).

Defoe had already written *Reasons why this Nation Ought to put a Speedy End to this Expensive War*, published anonymously on 6 October 1711. As in the *Review*,

659

in this pamphlet he argues that the war has cost many lives for relatively modest gains, has hampered British trade, and has brought about unmanageable levels of taxation. Moreover, he notes that the international situation has changed: renewed fighting in the Great Northern War will distract several allies, and Archduke Charles's imminent election as Holy Roman Emperor makes a diplomatic partition of Spain's territories preferable to securing them all for Charles through further campaigns.[2] Better trade concessions might even be available from Philip than from Charles.[3]

Defoe followed up with *An Essay at a Plain Exposition of that Difficult Phrase a Good Peace*, published on 16 October. A 'good peace', he insisted, would adhere to the terms of the Grand Alliance, focusing on preserving a balance of power in Europe. Keeping the entirety of Spain's possessions out of Bourbon hands is nowhere specified and may be inimical to that aim. In short, partition is necessary.[4] Defoe vindicates the negotiation of preliminaries between Britain and France: listening to proposals is no betrayal of the allies.[5] Defoe's position on the ministry's peace negotiations drew repeated attacks, mainly from Whigs.[6]

My Lord

As it has allways been my Study to be where, and be doeing what may Render me most Usefull, So I allways think it my Duty to Signifye it to yoᵣ Lᵈpp when, and where I May be capable of doeing any Serviċe; This Occasions me humbly to Move yoᵣ Lᵈpp at This Time: I acknowledge it is But little my Low Staċon is Capable of; But if Ever I was, or Ever Shall be capable of Rendring your Lᵈpp any Serviċe, If I have any foresight into Things, Now is yᵉ juncture; when The Minds of The People Fluctuating and Stormy like The Sea Listen to Every wicked Inflamer and would Listen also to Calm and Cool admoniċons if Given wᵗʰ Temper and Sinċerity.

I have My Lord Humbly addressed yoᵣ Lᵈpp and Constantly attended in Order to Obtain yoᵣ Approbaċon of my thoughts on This head, being Affraid to be Officous, yet hitherto I go Unsent; yoᵣ Lᵈpps Leisure Not Permitting My Audienċe: This however is a great Missfortune to me, and My Enemies who Reproach me (as they think) wᵗʰ being Under yoᵣ Lᵈpps Direcċon, Labour to Suppress Me for what I do Not Enjoy The Honoᵣ of.[7]

My Lord I am Perswaded, and This makes me bold to Move yoᵣ Lᵈpp, That I am yet able to Conquer yᵉ Obstinaċy of a hot but Deluded Party and at least to take off yᵉ Edge of That Venemous Spirit that has Infected Them.[8] I Onely Humbly Entreat yoᵣ Lᵈpps

DEFOE TO [EARL OF OXFORD], 16 OCTOBER 1711

Approbačon and Protecčon So far as I do my Duty Therein. I have Represented My Case to yoᵣ Lᵈpp; I add Nothing to it but [that I]ᵃ have Irritated and Exasperated The Party So Much by butᵇ Gently Refuseing to Declare for [their refr]actoryᶜ and Unpeačable Measures; That Unless yoᵣ Lᵈpp pleases to Take me into yoᵣ Protecčon, and Afford me The Usuall Support yoᵣ Own Goodness Lay'd yᵉ Foundačon of, I shall One day Fall by The hand of This Saul.⁹ Pardon me My Lord The Allusion But The Case is So farr gone That I Could Not Refrain This hint.

The present Case I beg of yoᵣ Lᵈpp is Onely whether a warm Applicačon to The Opening the peoples Eyes in The Affair of Peače in wᶜʰ They are goeing Mad will be Acceptable to yoᵣ Lᵈpp in wᶜʰ as my Own prinčiple agrees, andᵈ The Public Service Requires, So I Humbly Suggest yoᵣ Lᵈpps Serviče also Very Much Consists.

There are Some Measures for This wᶜʰ I would lay before yoᵣ Lᵈpp also if I had yᵉ honour of half an hour of yoᵣ Leisure. I Shall attend This Evening as yoᵣ Lᵈpp was pleased to Ordᵣ me, in hopes of Admittanče.¹⁰

> I am
> May it Please yoᵣ Lᵈpp
> yoᵣ Lᵈpps Most Humble and Obedᵗ Servᵗ
> [De]Foeᵉ

Octo. 16. 1711

PS.
I hope yoᵣ Lᵈpp does not forget that I had Success inᶠ as hard a Case in Scotland.¹¹

Text: BL Add. MS. 70291, fols. ²35–6. *Address*: none. *Endorsed by Oxford* (fol. ²36v): Mᵣ Goldsmith Octo: 16 1711

ᵃ [that I] *MS torn; the supplied text is Healey's suggestion (Letters, ed. Healey, 361)*
ᵇ but] *interlined*
ᶜ [their refr]actory] *MS torn; the supplied text is Healey's suggestion (Letters, ed. Healey, 361)*
ᵈ and] *interlined*
ᵉ [De]Foe] *signature partially torn out*
ᶠ in] *following illegible word cancelled*

---

1 *Review*, VIII, 338.

JOHN RUSSELL TO DEFOE, 13 NOVEMBER 1711

2 Defoe made similar points in *Review*, VIII, 84–7 (28 Apr. 1711) and *The Succession of Spain Consider'd* (May 1711). See below, note 6. For the Whig perspective on Defoe's arguments against establishing Charles on the Spanish throne, with the usual accusations of venality and ignorance, see John Oldmixon, *The Life and Posthumous Works of Arthur Maynwaring* (1715), 269.

3 *PEW*, II, 227, 232, 233, 238.

4 Unfortunately for Defoe, on 1 Sept. 1711 he had written against giving Spain to Philip. See headnote to Letter 201.

5 *PEW*, V, 141, 146, 151. Defoe acknowledges his authorship of this work ('by the Author of the *Review*') and indicates he is writing it on 7 Oct. 1711 (137).

6 [Francis Hare], *A Caveat to the Treaters; or, the Modern Schemes of Partition Examin'd* (1711), 84–8; *Queries A-propos, About the Review's Question, No. 92. Who shall the Monarchy of Spain be given to?* (1711).

7 *Enemies ... of*: In the *Review* for 6 Oct. 1711, Defoe denies writing for the ministry, insisting that he is merely able to distinguish a change of administration from one of constitution. 'He that tells me of Bribery, and Writing to please, is, *first*, A Knave, in charging me with what he cannot prove; and, *secondly*, A Fool, in putting more Value upon the *Review*, and its Author also, than he pretends to, and suggesting, that his Pen is of such Consequence to the present Ministry, as to make it worth their while' (VIII, 387). On 11 Oct. he quotes an attack accusing him of being '*under the Directing of a much greater Man than himself*' and he defies his enemies 'to prove I write under the Direction of any Man alive, or ever would submit to do so, were he the Greatest Man alive' (VIII, 393).

8 *Obstinacy ... Them*: On 21 Sept., Swift wrote that 'the pamphleteers begin to be very busy against the ministry ... They are very bold and abusive' (*Swift Journal*, 283).

9 *I shall One day Fall by The hand of This Saul*: 1 Sam. 27:1. Defoe alludes to it in *The Commentator*, no. 50 (24 June 1720), *RDW*, IX, 216.

10 *hopes of Admittance*: Oxford was ill in the second half of October (*Swift Journal*, 301–11).

11 *I had Success in as hard a Case in Scotland*: I.e. overcoming opposition to the Union in 1706 and 1707.

200

John Russell to Defoe

13 November 1711

HEADNOTE: Russell's postscript to his businesslike letter refers to Thomas Blackwell, whose journey to London was for the purpose of lobbying against the reintroduction of lay patronage to the Church of Scotland and against the Episcopal Toleration Act. Defoe had written against these two policies as infringements on the Scottish religious settlement guaranteed in the Union.[1] Whether Defoe and Blackwell met in 1711–12 is unknown.

JOHN RUSSELL TO DEFOE, 13 NOVEMBER 1711

Edinr Nover 13th <u>1711</u>

Dear Sir

Upon my return from the Country I had yours[2] ordering me to pay 18 Guineas to Mr John Campbell on accompt of Mr Archibald Campbell of Rochain[3] but by Mr John Campbells letter from Rochain he required only seven Guineas which I accordingly payed him upon his receipt whereof no doubt Rochain is advysed by his Freind; this very near ballances Our Accompt whereof you shall have ane Coppy if you desire it. By yours to the Major[4] this day I observe your care anent our great Freind which I doubt not youll continue. I wish you would end w̄ Mr [   ],[a][5] for a law Suit may have Many inconveniency's. My wife remembers you and yours as doeth

Sir

Your very humble Servant

Subservitur[6] John Russell

I had almost forgot to recomend to you my very Good Freind Mr Tho: Blackwell, minr at Abd',[7] who was on the road to Lond: and will resyde at Lond: for some time. I desyred him to wait upon you and doubts not youll give him your best advice.

Text: NLS MS. 25.3.9, fol. 76r [scribe's copy]. *Address*: none.

---

[a] Mr [   ]] *blank in MS*

---

1   See headnotes to Letters 165, 175, and 205.
2   *yours*: Untraced.
3   *Mr John Campbell ... Mr Archibald Campbell of Rochain*: Archibald Campbell of Rachean, a writer (lawyer) in Edinburgh. His kinsman John Campbell was Commissioner of Supply for Dumbartonshire in 1715.
4   *yours to the Major*: Untraced.
5   *Mr [   ]*: Presumably Flint, mentioned in Letter 198.
6   *Subservitur*: 'Your servant' (Latin).
7   *Mr Tho: Blackwell, minr at Abd'*: See Letter 186, note 9. He was Professor of Divinity at Marischal College at the University of Aberdeen, and author of several theological works.

663

201

To [Robert Harley, Earl of Oxford]

30 November 1711

HEADNOTE: Defoe's support for the peace preliminaries drew the ire of Whig journalists including George Ridpath in the *Observator*.[1] Whereas Defoe advocated a partition of the Spanish dominions, Ridpath insisted that the allies could not go back on their commitment to installing Charles in Madrid regardless of his becoming Emperor. Ridpath alleged that Defoe overestimated the extent of the Emperor's forces, meaning that Defoe's vision of a Habsburg superstate was phantasmal: the Franco-Spanish conjunction that would exist were Philip to remain in Madrid was a far greater threat. Ridpath countered Defoe's argument that the same logic for choosing Charles for Spain in 1701 – that he was unlikely to become Emperor with a father and elder brother still alive – offered a good reason *not* to give him all the Spanish dominions now: it was always intended to keep Spain and the Empire separate.[2] Ridpath also enjoyed pointing out that in the *Review* for 1 September 1711, Defoe had argued against leaving a Bourbon king in possession of Spain, against which Defoe could only claim unconvincingly that he had meant its full territory, including Italian and the American territories.[3]

The dispute inevitably became personal. Ridpath taunted Defoe by doubting that he could afford to see the expensive books that detailed the Imperial realm, or understand the Latin in which they were written.[4] He also mocked Defoe's style: 'I always own'd him to be a Man of Words, and now give it him under my hand, that I believe him to be the most *Verbose* Author in the Island, and the best skill'd in that part of Grammar call'd *Tautology* of any Man I ever knew.'[5] Ridpath pointed out a fact of which Defoe was increasingly aware: that these days he sided more often with Tories than Whigs. 'If the *Review* would not be ranked with Jacobites and Madmen, he should not use their Arguments', Ridpath cautioned; 'the profess'd Jacobites are now become his Admirers'.[6] He portrays Defoe as a turncoat, 'a Tool, who has so far bankrupt his Credit in every Respect, that his Name is not to be mention'd without a *Honos sit Auribus*'.[7] These attacks rankled Defoe, and his calm expostulation gave way to invective in the *Review* for 4 December 1711, in which he labelled Ridpath 'a meer Bully or Buffoon; a Man of Arrogance and meer Insolence, abandoned by the Civillity and Courtisie his own Country is Valuable for, and given up to the Vice of it; *furieux comme un Ecosse*'.[8] Ridpath laughed at 'the paultry Eruptions of his Choler, and the Weakness of his Arguments'.[9]

Defoe's arguments for peace based on a Spanish partition were unstinting. At the start of December he published *The Felonious Treaty*, an extended justification and revival of the Partition Treaties William III negotiated with Louis XIV

DEFOE TO [EARL OF OXFORD], 30 NOVEMBER 1711

before the dying Carlos II of Spain bequeathed his domains to Philip duc d'Anjou in 1700.[10] Underscoring Defoe's distance from the Whigs, on 11 Dec. 1711 the Whig-majority House of Lords voted that any peace that left Spain in Philip V's hands was dishonourable.

My Lord

In Obedience to yor L^{dpps} Command I here Enclose The Rect¹¹ wch I had to Signe and have Filled Up ye blank wth the Date. I do not Exactly Remember whether yor L^{dpps} Order was to Send The Same Signed or a Coppy written by me but if I have Mistaken I Shall not Fail to Rectify it on yor first Comand; Suitable My Lord to ye Extremetys My Last[12] gave yor L^{dpp} an Acco^t I am Reduced to, is My Humble Thankfull Return to yor L^{dpps} goodness and Her Maj^{ties} Bounty.

I Believ My Lord I Need not give yor L^{dpp} an Acco^t how I am Treated in Print by The Observator[13] for Espouseing The just article of Peace, and how he is (and I have been Offred to be) Supported and by who.^a I am Far from Menconing it as Merit;[14] but to Let yor L^{dpp} kno' yor Enemyes and The Fury They Act wth; The assurance They pretend to of Breaking all her Maj^{ties} Measures abroad Makes Their Friends Perfectly Insolent, and The Feares Least They should Terrifyes on ye Other hand.

I have my Lord Openly Declared against and Opposed Them, my Own Principle Concurring wth my Duty to yor L^{dpp} Therein; and as my Entire Dependence is That I Shall not be left Unsupported in The prosecucon of That Duty; This gives Me Confidence wth all humillity to Represent my Condicon to yor L^{dpp} and^b How if Ever This Party Prevail I am to Expect No Quarter Or Favour, and in ye Mean Time am Onely Supported by This Bounty of her Maj^{tie} wch is all Owing to yor L^{dpps} Goodness and The Arrear whereof has So Much Reduced me.

I Long for an Occasion to Lay before yor L^{dpp} The Madness and Rage of yor Enemies And Something Also of The Feares of yor Friends; God Give yor L^{dpp} wisdome and Courage, Faithfullness to himself and Success to Dissappoint Them all.

^a and by who] *interlined*
^b and] *interlined*

DEFOE TO [EARL OF OXFORD], 30 NOVEMBER 1711

I shall go on to Discharge My Duty in Opposiçon to all The Madness of The Age, Recomending Onely My Self and Family to yor Goodness, which I can Not but hope will not Decrease to me for my steady adhereing however weakly to yor L^dpps and The Naçons Intrest.

I am
May it Please yor L^dpp
yor L^dpps Most Humble and Obedient Servt
DeFoe

Novemb^r 30. 1711.

Text: BL Add. MS. 70291, fols. ²37–8. *Address*: none.

1 Defoe preferred to consider the preliminaries as 'proposals', therefore less binding and so no betrayal of the allies (*Review*, VIII, 407–8 (18 Oct. 1711)).
2 *Observator*, 7–10 Nov. 1711.
3 *Review*, VIII, 499 (4 Dec. 1711). Whigs attacked Defoe for this self-contradiction for some time, at least as late as *The Flying Post*, 19–21 Feb. 1713.
4 *Observator*, 7–10 Nov. 1711.
5 *Observator*, 28 Nov.–1 Dec. 1711.
6 *Observator*, 1–5 Dec. 1711.
7 *Observator*, 5–8 Dec. 1711. The Latin means 'pardon the expression'.
8 *Review*, VIII, 498.
9 *Observator*, 1–5 Dec. 1711.
10 *PEW*, V, 155–77. Defoe also acknowledges his authorship of this work.
11 *Rec^t*: Untraced.
12 *My Last*: Untraced.
13 *how I am Treated in Print by The Observator*: See headnote.
14 *I have … Supported … Merit*: It is not clear to whom Defoe refers as the financial supporter of the *Observator*. As regards the offers Defoe had received, in the fictitious *Minutes of the Negotiations of Monsr. Mesnager* (1717), Defoe wrote in the voice of the French plenipotentiary, Nicolas Mesnager, who came to London in 1711, and he inserts an account of Mesnager unsuccessfully endeavouring to recruit Defoe, having read and approved of *Reasons why this Nation Ought to put a Speedy End to this Expensive War* (*SFS*, IV, 64–5).

JOHN RUSSELL TO DEFOE, 13 DECEMBER 1711

202

John Russell to Defoe

13 December 1711

HEADNOTE: Defoe continued to campaign on behalf of both Leven and Coult, and he was rewarded financially by the former.

Edb 13th decb 1711

Dr Sir

I have only tyme to desire you to charge my accompt wth 20 guineas, a Memerandy[1] from yor great freind which I desire you to order as you please, And if you think fitt You may in yours to ye Major let him know that I have writt you this, for ye person you know is very senceable of your favours and as maters ocur doūtes not of your concern, and gieving due warning I am

Yr Servt

Text: NLS MS. 25.3.9, fol. 76v [scribe's copy]. *Address*: To Danell defoe Esq | at his house in Newingtoūn | near London

1 *Memerandy*: I.e. memorandi (Latin), meaning 'reminded', hence memorandum.

203

To [Robert Harley, Earl of Oxford]

20 December 1711

HEADNOTE: Early in the 1711–12 parliamentary session, the House of Lords passed an Act to Prevent the Occasional Conformity of Dissenters. It was now before the Commons, a formality given its Tory majority. The Act was the result of the unlikely alliance of Defoe's old nemesis the Earl of Nottingham and the Whig Lords, which Defoe called an 'unnatural Conjunction' and 'the Greatest Mystery of Politicks that this Age has been acquainted with'.[1] Nottingham, who had been pointedly excluded from the Tory restoration to government, had agreed

667

DEFOE TO [EARL OF OXFORD], 20 DECEMBER 1711

to support the Whigs' opposition to any peace that did not reclaim the Spanish monarchy from Philip V in exchange for Whig backing for his cherished Occasional Conformity Act.

Defoe was outraged at this betrayal of the Dissenters by the Whigs. In the *Review* on the same day as this letter, he reminded readers that:

> I am, and have always been, a declar'd Enemy to the *Occasional Conformity of Dissenters*, as it is Calculated meerly for a Qualification to Temporal Interest, and that I take it to be of the worst kind of Hypocrisie – That it has been the Scandal of the *Dissenters* in *England*, and that it is, at this Day, the Ruin of their Interest.

However, he felt that legislation against it would be dangerous, betokening a diminution of Dissenters' civic rights that contravened the Toleration Act, employing penal laws designed to exclude Catholics to renew the persecution of Protestant Dissent.[2] (He was, however, careful to avoid direct reflections on parliament's proceedings.) Defoe's relationship with the main body of Dissenters had been fraught since his writings against occasional conformity in the late 1690s and especially since *The Shortest Way with the Dissenters*, for which Defoe in his own view had been punished for bravely defending Dissent, then abandoned by his coreligionists:

> Nor do I know, whether what I am now going to say, may not be a second Sacrifize of myself and Family, for a Body of People, some of whom would not pull me from under a Cart-Wheel, if they saw me in the Danger of it; and this only, for telling them Truth and their own Interest.[3]

Defoe had hard words for Nottingham. He wrote that the Whigs, by joining the 'N—nhamian Brigade', had 'sold the Dissenters for a Groaning-Board, a Speaking-Trumpet, an Empty Tinkling Cymbal, or a long, tall piece of sounding Brass'.[4] The Whig Lords who had reversed their stance did not escape Defoe's opprobrium: 'The same worthy *Patriots* that formerly threw it out, now bring it in; the same People that rejoyc'd in the Disappointment of the High-Church Men, acquiesce now in the Ruin of the *Dissenters*.'[5]

As well as trying to influence opinion in the *Review*, Defoe published *An Essay on the History of Parties and Persecution in Britain*, in which he recounts the failure of the attempted occasional bills in Anne's first parliament, from 1702 to 1705. He was exasperated at the Dissenters' quiescence, that they are 'less Allarm'd at their approaching Bondage, than they us'd to be', and that they retain trust in a Whig party that has betrayed them.[6] The Occasional Conformity Act passed into law on 22 December. On 25 December Defoe published in the *Review* an imagined

668

DEFOE TO [EARL OF OXFORD], 20 DECEMBER 1711

speech by a chimney-piece from the House of Lords: though made of stone, its heart is not as hard as the Lords who passed this act.[7]

Oxford did not favour an Occasional Conformity Bill, and he tried to limit its penalties; but opposing it would have been impolitic and futile. It is even possible that he offered it himself to secure Tory support for the peace.[8] On the day after Defoe's letter, 21 Dec. 1711, Oxford wrote to Daniel Williams to say that, though he was powerless to prevent the bill, he remained an ally: 'The Dissenters must be sav'd whether they wil or no … All they have done or can do, shall never make me their enemy.' Like Defoe he laments their ill-judged political alliances and hopes that they can 'recover their Reputation of sobriety, integrity & love of their country'.[9]

My Lord

I confess my Self So much Surprized wth ye Perticulars which yor L^{dpp} did me ye hono^r to Comunicate to Me On Tuesday of ye Conduct of a Set of Men with Respect to ye Dissenters That I could not Express my Self on Severall Things Needfull to be Observ'd to yor L^{dpp} on ye Occasion, wch Defect According to ye Freedome yor L^{dpp} is pleased to Allow me I Supply in This Manner.

And first My Lord in ye Midst of My Real and just Concern for The Intrest of ye Dissenters wch I look upon as Ruind; I can Not but look up wth Thankfullness in yor L^{dpps} behalf That The Mouths of yor Enemies Are Most Effectually Stopt in Offring to Lay ye Reproach of Their Dissaster Upon your L^{dpp},^{a} which is Most Aparently the Effect of an Implacable but I hope Impotent Aversion to yor L^{dpp} and of a Manifest Resolucon to Injure and Insult you:

Had it Not been too late to Retriev The Injury I Should have Rejoyc't Also^{b} in behalf of The Dissenters; That The Idols They adored have Appear'd capable of So Mean a Step, as to Sell The Party That Ventur'd Their Safety on The Leaky bottom of a Supposed Zeal, into Perpetuall Tory bondage, to form a New Interest for The Supporting Their Party Designs; but my Lord This Joy is like Singing a Psalm at a Funerall, too Sad to be Sonorous.[10]

---

^{a} Upon your L^{dpp}] *interlined*
^{b} Also] *interlined*

669

DEFOE TO [EARL OF OXFORD], 20 DECEMBER 1711

May it Please yor L^{dpp}

As yor L^{dpp} has for ye Sake of a Little Sincerity, borne wth a great Deal of Course[11] and Unpolish't plaiñess from me, Indulgeing a Freedome wch I have No Title to but from yor Own Goodness, So I beg yor L^{dpp} to bear wth One humble Moċon in behalf of an Intrest, which I kno' yor L^{dpp} has been a Patron of, which has been Vallued[a] by you, and wch Tho' ye Usage of Some of The People to yor L^{dpp} has been Inexcusable, yet I am Fully Perswaded yor L^{dpp} has still at Heart; I Mean that of The Dissenters.

There Remains but One Point between Them and The Fate of Their wholl Cause (Viz) her Maj^{ties} Passing Or Not Passing The bill; I kno' The Negativ is Not wthout its hazard, and Many watch The advantage; But My Lord Her Maj^{tie} has Sollemnly Pass't her Royall Promise to ye Dissenters, to Preserv The Tolleraċon Inveiolable.[12] I kno' My Duty too well to Enter On any Argum^t on ye Consistency of Passing This bill, wth The keeping this Promise; yet I could not Satisfye my Self, Neither in Duty to ye Dissenters Intrest, or The Imediate Intrest of yor L^{dpp}, without Humbly Moveing yor L^{dpp} in This Case (Viz) How Effectually it would bind to yor Intrest, and to her Maj^{ties} Person and Governm^t, and to all yor just Measures, The wholl body of The Dissenters, and Low Church men also, who are as ill Pleased as any; How Effectually it would bring in Those Very People who have Suffred This Chicane of a Party to be pass't upon them;[b] and Are Rageing wth shame and Confusion at what They have done; How Effectually it would Rivet yor L^{dpp} in ye hearts of all Good Men, Silenċe passt Unjust Clamours, and Powerfully Establish yor L^{dpp} as The protector of Liberty, The Patron of justiċe, and The true Refuge of an Injur'd people: All This I firmly believ, wth a blessing From Heaven, would be The Consequenċe, if her Maj^{tie} in Maintenanċe of her Sacred Promise aforesaid, May be advised to Refuse This Bill.[13]

God Allmighty give yor L^{dpp} Wisdome, and Council from himself, to Direct in an Affair of So Niċe but Important

---

[a] Vallued] *the* 'u' *interlined*
[b] them;] *interlined*

670

DEFOE TO [EARL OF OXFORD], 20 DECEMBER 1711

Consequence, So as May Issue in his Glory, yor Own blessing, and an Innocent Peoples Deliverance, asking Pardon for This freedom.

I am

May it Please yor L^{dpp}

yor L^{dpps} Most Humble and Obed^t Servt

DeFoe

Decemb. 20. 1711

Text: BL Add. MS. 70291, fols. ²39–40. *Address*: none.

1 *Review*, VIII, 558 (3 Jan. 1712); 539 (25 Dec. 1711).
2 As in 1704–5, Defoe was accused in 1711–12 of contradicting himself on occasional conformity, because he criticised the practice and opposed the legislation against it. See *A Long Ramble, Or Several Years Travels, In … O-Brazil* (1712), 22–3.
3 *Review*, VIII, 529 (20 Dec. 1711).
4 *Review*, IX, 61 (20 Sept. 1712); VIII, 668 (4 Mar. 1712). See also *Review*, IX, 344 (21 Apr. 1713); *The Weakest Go to the Wall* (1714), *PEW*, III, 349; *The Conduct of Robert Earl of Oxford* (1715), *PEW*, II, 335.
    Defoe's attacks on Nottingham continued in the following years. Several issues of the *Review* in 1713 were devoted to opposing *Observations Upon the State of the Nation, in January 1712/13* (*Review*, IX, 240–50 (21, 24, 26 Feb. 1713)), a pamphlet Defoe supposed Nottingham had written. *Observations* suggested that the Hanoverian succession was imperilled due to Scottish divisions. Defoe blasted Nottingham as a 'romancing L…d' (*Review*, IX, 295 (24 Mar. 1713)). In *And What if the Pretender should come?* (1713), Defoe attacked Nottingham for his opposition to the Anglo-Scottish Union (*PEW*, I, 199); cf. *Review*, VIII, 705 (25 Mar. 1712). 'Sir *Politick Falshood*', a fictitious opponent of the Anglo-French Commercial Treaty in *Memoirs of Count Tariff* (1713), is probably a portrait of Nottingham (*SFS*, III, 187); and Defoe attacked Nottingham more directly for his opposition to the Treaty in *Some Thoughts upon the Subject of Commerce with France* (1713), 26. Defoe enjoyed reporting that Nottingham's son, Daniel, Lord Finch (1689–1769), misspoke during a Lords debate in calling his father 'the FIRST Man in this Nation that would be for bringing in the Pretender', when he meant to say 'last' (*The Monitor*, no. 2 (24 Apr. 1714)). *Secret Memoirs of a Treasonable Conference at S—— House* (1716) satirises Nottingham as '*Nigroque*', 'an old discarded Statesman, … noble by Birth, rather than Disposition'. '*Nigroque*' unscrupulously plots how to gain the Tories greater influence after the Hanoverian succession and 1715 election (*SFS*, IV, 159). The name refers to Nottingham's saturnine features. In short, Defoe did not pass up any opportunities to criticise Nottingham.
5 *Review*, VIII, 534 (22 Dec. 1711).
6 *An Essay on the History of Parties and Persecution in Britain* (1711), 24.
7 *Review*, VIII, 539–40.
8 Szechi, 106–7.
9 BL Add. MS. 70263.
10 *This Joy … Sonorous*: In the *Review* for 22 Dec. 1711 Defoe wrote: 'One would make pleasant Remarks enough here; but this is too serious to jest with, the Sacrifice is too great, to make Pastime of the Practice' (VIII, 534).
11 *Course*: coarse.

671

DEFOE TO [EARL OF OXFORD], 10 JANUARY 1712

12 *Her Maj*^{tie} *... Inveiolable*: Defoe recalls the Queen's promise in identical terms in *Review*,
VIII, 531 (20 Dec. 1711) and in *An Essay on the History of Parties and Persecution in Britain*
(1711), 23.

13 *her Maj*^{tie} *... Bill*: Defoe took the bold step of addressing the Queen directly in the *Review*
for 22 Dec., and again at the very end of *An Essay on the History of Parties and Persecution in
Britain*, imploring her to refuse royal assent to the Act.

204

To [Robert Harley, Earl of Oxford]

10 January 1712

HEADNOTE: Defoe continued to defend Oxford and the ministry against vehe-
ment Whig attacks, intensified by Oxford's creation *en bloc* at the end of December 1711 of twelve new Tory peers to gain control of the Upper House. Defoe's
compunction about defending the ministry had been allayed by what he considered the Whigs' unreasonable position on treating for peace (refusing to realise
that Holy Roman Emperor Charles VI's installation in Madrid as Charles III
would unbalance power just as much as would leaving Philip V there) and their
unconscionable concession to High Tories on an Occasional Conformity Act.

On 31 December 1711, prompted by Oxford and St John, Queen Anne finally
dismissed Marlborough, whose military brilliance was no longer needed and who
had joined the Whigs in opposing the government on the peace. The pretext was
a peculation charge. Swift had traduced Marlborough without restraint in *The
Conduct of the Allies* (November 1711), alleging he had prolonged the war for his
personal enrichment.[1] Defoe offers a more moderate assessment in the *Review* for
22 January 1712, criticising both the Tory attempts to blacken his character and the
Whig alternative of 'Bullying the Queen in every Coffee-House with the History
of the Duke's Merit'. Defoe gives a characteristically subtle equivocation: 'If there
is no Occasion for Displacing the Duke, I am sorry it is done, for the Nation's
sake; and if there is an Occasion for it, I am doubly sorry for it, for his sake.'[2]

Defoe's *The Conduct of Parties in England*, published around 23 January 1712,
took the Whigs to task by examining their conduct since gradually attaining political offices from 1706 onwards, all of which amounted to a self-interested pursuit
of power. Recognising that Harley, then Secretary of State, saw their unpatriotic
ends, the Junto had rounded on him, resulting in his break with the duumvirs in
1708. The Whigs then undermined the very ministry to which they were supposedly allied, plotting Godolphin and Marlborough's downfalls. Their unscrupulous
tactics included an alliance with Haversham in 1708 (a harbinger of that with Not-

DEFOE TO [EARL OF OXFORD], 10 JANUARY 1712

tingham now), backing opponents to the Court in the 1708 election of Scottish representative peers, and fending for themselves and not their dependents when in office (anticipating their treatment of Dissenters now). The Whigs had themselves lined up Orkney to replace Marlborough in 1708, so their complaints about his dismissal rang false: 'These very Whig Lords, this very Juncto, that now stickle and struggle for the D— of M—, are the same who laid the Foundation of his Fall.'[3] According to Defoe, it was remarkable not just that the Dissenters continued to put their trust in the Whigs but that they had ever done so. Though Defoe supported Marlborough's removal, he never forgot his glorious actions or allowed Tory attacks to go unanswered.[4] *The Conduct of Parties in England* manages to set out the case against Marlborough without quite arguing it, illustrating Defoe's efforts to serve the ministry without altogether reneging on his principles.[5]

My Lord

When I am Thanking yor Ldpp for ye Continuance of a Bounty I can Not Merit, I Blame My Self for ye Importunities I have Used. But I hope for yor Ldpps Pardon when I Consider, That Really The Treatmt I meet wth from a poor Enraged People,[6] whose True Intrest I believ I Serv, Seems to Recomend Me to yor Ldpps Compassion — God Grant yor Ldpp Victory Over This New Posession, for however I May Fare while yor Ldpp holds ye Reins; I am Sure to Sink if any Thing happen to The prejudice of yor Intrest.

I have Not ye Fewest yeares Over my head of any Man That Observes these Things, And I have Seen Many of these Court Revolucons, But of all The Outed Parties That Ever were Seen at least[a] in the Last 50 yeares, None Ever[b] push't wth So much Fury at The Governmt who have Dissmiss't them, as These have done, Nothing but down Right Takeing Arms can be like This, and I am Perswaded Onely want of Power Restrains from ye worst Sort of Violence.

God That Directs yor Ldpp I hope in all Things, has Moved you No doubt to Take This Most Necessary step, of Deposeing The Idol Man,[7] who Coveted to Set himself up as The head of a Party, and by whom They pretended to Make Themselves Formidable; all wise men Own ye Necessity, and Applaud The wisdome of This step, and if it be Needfull for her Majties Safety to go on, I believ no Man can

[a] at least] *interlined*
[b] Ever] *amended from* 'Every'

673

DEFOE TO [EARL OF OXFORD], 10 JANUARY 1712

Think Amiss That those who Eat her Maj^ties Bread, should (when a Threatning behaviour Demands Such a Course) be left to kno' the want of it.

The Small Tract[8] which I hinted to yor Ld^pp in My Last[9] I Send herew^th and as yor Ld^pp was pleased to ask me if no way Might be found Out to Open The Eyes of These poor Deluded people The Dissenters; I doubt Not My Lord but ye Fury and Precipitaćon of Their Old Supporters[10] will be a proper Means, and The Exposeing it for That purpose I make my bussiness in Ord^r to help on Their Convicćon, Nor Shall all Their Fury at me Cause me to Cease This Method wch I Take to be The best Serviće to yor Ld^pp wch lyes in My Power.

I am

May it Please yor Ld^pp

&c. — [*monogram*]

I Omit my Name by yor Ld^pps Ord^r.

Jan. 10. 1711[11]

Text: BL Add. MS. 70291, fols. ²41–2. *Address*: none.

1 Swift, *EPW 1711–14*, 62, 76, 83. It is in *Defoe–Farewell Catalogue* (item 247b). The Queen told David Hamilton that 'the Duke of Marlborough was out; for he had not carry'd himself Well to her Majesty since he came home. That she did not mean to her Personally, but in her business' (Hamilton, *Diary*, 37).

2 *Review*, VIII, 589, 588. Defoe defends Marlborough again from Tory attacks in *Review*, VIII, 802 (17 May 1712); IX, 9–10 (9 Aug. 1712).

3 *The Conduct of Parties in England* (1712), *PEW*, II, 261. Cf. *Review*, IX, 46–54 (9 and 14 Sept. 1712).

4 See Defoe's recent comments in *Atalantis Major* (1711), 13–14.

5 In *The Secret History of the White-Staff, Part III* (1715), Defoe indicated that Oxford did not want to remove Marlborough, and he puts the action on the Queen. This is an extension of his argument that Oxford would gladly have continued the war but Anne wanted it ended (47).

6 *a poor Enraged People*: The Dissenters.

7 *Idol Man*: Defoe describes Marlborough as 'the Nation's Idol' in *The Conduct of Parties in England*, *PEW*, II, 255. In the *Review* for 22 Jan. 1711, he says in reference to Marlborough: 'I was never for making Man an Idol' (VIII, 588). For Defoe's later treatments of Marlborough, see Letter 248, note 30.

8 *Small Tract*: Probably either *An Essay on the History of Parties and Persecution in Britain*, published in Dec. 1711, or *The Conduct of Parties in England*, published later in Jan. 1712.

9 *My Last*: Untraced. By 'hinted' Defoe means 'conveyed' rather than merely 'alluded to'.

10 *Their Old Supporters*: The Whigs.

11 *1711*: 1712 new style.

DEFOE TO [EARL OF OXFORD], 24 JANUARY 1712

205

To [Robert Harley, Earl of Oxford]

24 January 1712

HEADNOTE: To Defoe's dismay, on 23 January 1712 the Episcopal Toleration Act for Scotland was introduced in the House of Commons.[1] It gave legal protections for liturgical worship. Oxford had only managed to prevent its introduction in the previous session, in the wake of the Lords' verdict on Greenshields, by promising Tory backbenchers that the Court would not oppose it the following year. However, the measure ran against his aim of appeasing Presbyterians in Scotland, so he sought to limit the damage.[2]

To Defoe's mind this legislation was a betrayal of the Union which had pledged to maintain the Kirk's establishment inviolably. He had previously declared Episcopal toleration constitutionally impossible on the grounds that the Union Treaty occluded a British parliament's authority to alter either nation's religious settlement.[3] In the *Review* for 29 January he recalled his role in bringing about the Union, which he considered to his honour as long as England stuck to its commitments:

> But if ever that wretched Day shall come, that *England* should break Faith with their Brethren, and do any Thing in Contravention *to this Union*, what others may do I know not, *but I shall for my part*, be asham'd, Repent, and count it my Reproach that I was any way Instrumental to bring that Treaty to so fatal a Conclusion, and desire to forget the Day that I was sent thither.[4]

The bill advanced through parliament and on 2 February Defoe reflected with an ounce more circumspection on British laws that affect the Kirk: 'Whether they entirely break the Union or no, is not for me to say here, but [they] go so near the Brink of the Union, as makes many Hearts that wish well to their Country, in pain for the Event – While this is doing, who can be silent?'[5]

The unpopularity of toleration among Presbyterians was compounded by the Lords' addition requiring all clergy to swear the oath of abjuration. Though Defoe could briefly triumph that 'the *Jacobites* are fallen in their own Snare', he realised that scrupulous Presbyterians were equally opposed to the oath.[6] Though they were happy to abjure the Catholic Pretender, Scottish ministers believed that swearing to uphold prelacy, which the oath required, would be perjury against the national covenants that committed them to seek religious unity in Britain under a Presbyterian structure.[7] And they believed this requirement infringed further on the Act of Security written into the Union that had promised no new oaths against conscience would be mandated by the British parliament. On 4 March, the day after the Episcopal Toleration Act became law, Defoe lamented that 'the Union,

675

DEFOE TO [EARL OF OXFORD], 24 JANUARY 1712

which is the Hold we have taken of the Civil Power which *Scotland* had to help itself, and which ought therefore to be the Protection of their Ecclesiastick Liberties, is now to be made the Instrument of their Destruction'.[8] In *The Present State of the Parties in Great Britain*, published in May 1712, Defoe gave a detailed account of events leading from the Union to the Episcopal Toleration Act, 'to leave upon Record for our Posterity to see how notoriously we broke F—th with our United Brethren, and how soon we made Infractions into that Treaty'.[9] Ultimately Defoe absolved the ministry on this score, claiming that Episcopal toleration and the imposition of the abjuration oath 'was a Storm upon the Ministry, and over the Bellies of those, who some would have charg'd with it' – meaning Lord Oxford.[10]

My Lord

In My Last[11] I hinted to yor Ldpp Something I would Lay before yor Ldpp wch I Thot Transacting Against her Majties Intrest in Scotland, but I confess to yor Ldpp I did not Suppose So Near breaking Out, and in This Manner.

In Duty to yor Ldpp I can Not but humbly Represent That This Step wch Amounts to no less Than a Setting up The Common Prayer book on One hand and a Tolleraċon of Episcopaċy on The Other will besides The Unhappy Consequenċes wch are Easy to foresee Effectually Lose The wholl body of The presbyterians From her Majties Intrest in That Kingdome who till now have kept Steady and have not Mingled wth the Common Discontents of ye Dissenters here Or of ye whigs on Either part,[12] And I Humbly beseech yor Ldpp to Think Whether on ye Other hand The Episcopal Party (not jacobite) in That plaċe are Able to Stand her Majtie in Any Stead in ye Room of it.

I Am Not Arguing The affair of Religion One way or Other but Nothing Seems More Evident Than that her Majties Intrest There is founded Onely on The Presbytea Party and she has Very Few Other Friends There.[13]

Farther My Ld I beg Leav to Suggest That ye Snare Lay'd in This bill to Involv in Ruin a Poor hot and Furious but well Meaning people is Very Visible; and ye Gentlemen who kno' that No Act of Parliamt can Restrain the Zealous people in This Case Depend upon Embroiling Them as Formerly wth the Governmt and bringing Them into blood wch I fear will be Unavoidable Nor will The Liturgy Ever be Set up in Scotland (The poor Subjected Clans

DEFOE TO [EARL OF OXFORD], 24 JANUARY 1712

of highland Slaves[14] Excepted) but by Force, Persecucon, and all y^e
Unhappy Consequences of Arms; I Entreat in ye humblest Manner
yor L^{dpps} Leave to Remind yor L^{dpp} of This Very Objeccon Made
by the poor jealous people at ye Time of ye Union, wch I did my Self
ye hono^r frequently to Signifye to yor L^{dpp} at That Time,[15] and w^{ch}
I had yor L^{dpps} License then to Assure Them They Should not have
Need to fear.

I have frequently Recomended The poor warm people There,
as on Many Acco^{ts} to be borne wth and Pityed, and Capable on
Many Occasions to Render her Maj^{tie} Good Service, and Their
Steddyness in the last affair of The Invasion[16] Testifyes for Them,
and Recomends Them to her Maj^{ties} Compassion; When These
Episcopall people who Appear Now So Zealous for ye English
Liturgy, (and My Ld Lyon[17] more Especally) Openly shew'd
Themselves Ready to Embrace a popish Pretender.

I pray God This be not a Plot to Deprive her Maj^{tie} of The
Assistance, and Service of So Considerable a part of her faithfull
Subjects; and to make Them a constant Uneasyness to ye Governm^t,
and The Governm^t to Them.

I can Not but Apprehend The Fatal Consequence of This to
ye Peace of Scotland, and as yor L^{dpp} has been pleased to give me
Leave wth Freedome, and Faithfullness to Lay Such Things at yor
Feet, I could not Omit it; I Lament ye Obstinacy of a Party Among
us which Make Such Things Necessary, But My Lord The Poor
people of Scotland have had no share in Them, and Resolv'd to
adhere to her Maj^{tie} in all her Just Measures.

I kno' if any help be for Them wth Man, it is in yor L^{dpp}; I pray
God Make yor L^{dpp} The happy Instrum^t to Save Them from the
Ruine Evidently before Them.

I have Much of This Affair to add but I am loth to Offend yor
L^{dpp} wth My Importunities; I Shall attend yor L^{dpps} Leisure to
Mencon it More Fully. I Humbly ask yor L^{dpp} Pardon for So Much
Freedome and Am

> May it Please yor L^{dpp}
> yor L^{dpps} Most Humble and Obedient Servt
> [*monogram*]

Jan^a. 24. 1711[18]

677

Text: BL Add. MS. 70291, fols. ²43–4. *Address*: none. *Endorsed by Oxford* (fol. ²44ᵛ): Scotland Goldsmith Janu: 24: 1711/12

1 *C.J.*, XVII, 35.
2 Szechi, 110–11. See Greenshields to Oxford, 28 Jan. 1712, H.M.C. *Portland MSS*, X, 379.
3 *Review*, VII, 524 (19 Dec. 1710). Cf. *Review*, VII, 584–5 (23 Jan. 1711).
4 *Review*, VIII, 601.
5 *Review*, VIII, 610.
6 *Review*, VIII, 654 (26 Feb. 1712); 750 (19 Apr. 1712).
7 Hugh Clark (d. 1724), *The Oath of Abjuration Displayed* (Edinburgh, 1712); Robert Wodrow, *The Oath of Abjuration, Considered* (Edinburgh, 1712).
8 *Review*, VIII, 669.
9 Defoe, *The Present State of the Parties in Great Britain* (1712), 114.
10 *Review*, IX, 120 (15 Nov. 1712). Cf. *An Answer to a Question that No Body thinks of, viz. But What if the Queen Should Die?* (1713), in which Defoe mentions the 'little Encroachments' on the Kirk and Union but sees minor infractions as evidence that there is no comprehensive plan to overturn the religious settlement in Scotland (*PEW*, I, 218).
11 *My Last*: Untraced.
12 *whigs on Either part*: I.e. the English Whigs and the Scottish Squadrone.
13 *she has Very Few Other Friends There*: 'It is plain, the Queen has no Friends in *Scotland* but the Presbyterians, no willing Subjects but them; none that pray for Her, and will fight for Her but them' (*Review*, VIII, 157 (31 May 1711)). Cf. *Review*, IX, 19 (16 Aug. 1712) and Letter 195.
14 *poor Subjected Clans of highland Slaves*: See Letter 120, note 8. Defoe continued to rail at the 'Absolute Command' and 'Arbitrary Government' that the '*Highland* and other Gentlemen of *Scotland* exercise over 'their Tenants and Vassals' who behave as 'abject Slaves' in paying them 'Submissive Obedience' (*Review*, VIII, 710 (26 Mar. 1712)).
15 *Objecćon … Time*: See Defoe's letters to Harley from Scotland during late 1706 and early 1707.
16 *Invasion*: The failed 1708 invasion of Scotland by the Pretender with French backing.
17 *Lᵈ Lyon*: Sir Alexander Areskine of Cambo, MP for Fifeshire (see Letter 157, note 24). He was one of the three politicians who prepared the Episcopal Toleration Bill. See *HPC 1690–1715*, III, 49–52.
18 *1711*: 1712 new style.

206

To [Robert Harley, Earl of Oxford]

14 February 1712

HEADNOTE: Defoe had defended the cause of the Newcastle keelmen since 1710 and first raised it with Oxford in June 1711.[1] The keelmen wanted control of a charitable hospital paid for by voluntary contributions from their wages, which their oppressive employers (hostmen) and the town magistrates controlled, allegedly embezzling or detaining the funds. Defoe believed that the keelmen's greater independence would curb the high prices on coal caused by the current monopoly.

DEFOE TO [EARL OF OXFORD], 14 FEBRUARY 1712

In the *Review* for 27 June 1710, he had decried 'the Arbitrary and Tyrannical Usage of the Masters and Keelmen, by the Coal-Owners at *New-castle*'.[2] He defended them again in the *Review*s for 6 and 11 July 1710, reporting their strike and their having been misrepresented to the government as troublemakers.[3] The Newcastle coal magnate Henry Liddell (*c.* 1673–1717) complained in private correspondence that Defoe's writings encouraged 'refractoriness among that sort of people'.[4] In 1711, Defoe supported the keelmen in their petitioning the Crown asking to be incorporated so that they could collect and apply the charity money; but the hostmen and magistrates produced a counter-petition of keelmen asking for the magistrates to continue controlling the fund.

The issue was just about to come before the Commons when, in February 1712, Defoe wrote *The Case of the Poor Skippers and Keel-Men of Newcastle* and *A Farther Case Relating to the Poor Keel-Men of Newcastle*, defending their right to incorporate and take control of the hospital. The bill before parliament would settle the charity and hospital under the magistrates' management and make their contributions a compulsory tax.[5] Defoe also took up the issue in the *Review*, alleging that the magistrates had extorted signatures for their petition through a combination of force and fraud.[6] Opponents alleged that Defoe had been paid £100 out of the charitable fund to help the keelmen pursue their cause.[7] Defoe countered in the *Review* that he stood not to gain.[8] He reportedly said that he had accepted £40, but that left him out of pocket in supporting the petition.[9] The bill passed the Commons on 29 March.[10] It was rejected by the Lords, but the keelmen's plan to incorporate did not come about.[11] Defoe's promise to write further on the matter on 22 April was unfulfilled, but years later he bemoaned the discouragement given to the keelmen's hospital in *A Tour thro' the Whole Island of Great Britain*.[12]

Besides the Newcastle keelmen, Defoe's letter offers help to Oxford on revenue-generating schemes, communicates his anxiety that the impending tax on print will weaken his ability to support the ministry, bemoans his treatment by the Whigs on account of his support for the government, and offers to go to Scotland to help allay concerns about the recent Episcopal Toleration Act.

My Lord

I Reproach my Self wth The Answer I gave yor L^dpp when you were pleased to Ask me if I had any Thing Perticular to Offer, Because I Fully purposed to have Represented a Perticular Case of ye Poor keel men of New Castle, wch I Once offred formerly to yor L^dpp[13] and who are Now like to have ye Governm^t and Mannagem^t of Their Own Charity Subjected to The Fitters[14] and Magistrates; by wch a New foundaćon also will be Lay'd to Influenće and Enslave

The poor Men, and Thereby Again Make a Monopoly of the Coal Trade.

There is So Much Justiċe and Charity in The Case, That I Perswade my Self your Ldpp will be pleased with Appearing in behalf of a Thousand Families of poor and Injured Men,[15] who None but God and yoͬ Ldpp can Now Deliver; If yoͬ Ldpp pleases to give me Leav I would Gladly Lay an Abstract[16] of The Case before you; It being in a Few days to pass yͤ house of Commons.

I have had Severall People Frequently comeing to me for adviċe in Little projects wᶜʰ They offer afterwards to yoͬ Ldpp as I Suppose in The Treasury offiċe, and I have not Troubled yoͬ Ldpp wᵗʰ any of Them because I have Thought Few of Them worth yoͬ Notiċe But There is One who offers a proposall for Raiseing The Revenue of Excise as he Sayes about 60000ᶫ p[er] Ann̄ wᵗʰout any Addiconall Charge — I Confess I Thought his design well Lay'd, and Encouraged him for That Reason to proceed. The Mans Name is Finch,[17] an honest man and of Good Character, by Trade a Brewer; If yoͬ Ldpp pleases to call for Such a Name, I believ his Peticon or Memoriall is in yͤ Offiċe; or if it May be for yoͬ Ldpps Serviċe, I Shall Lay his scheme before yoͬ Ldpp, First Assureing yoͬ Ldpp I have No Concern or Intrest Directly or Indirectly in it Onely as I Thought it my Duty to Lay any Thing before yoͬ Ldpp which I Thought Might be for yͤ public good.

May it Please yoͬ Ldpp

I would on My Own Accoᵗ Gladly have Represented Some Things Relateing to yͤ Press.[18] I have allways Expresst my Self Ready to Lay down My pen when it shall Cease to be any Longer Usefull to yoͬ Ldpp yet I would humbly hope yoͬ Ldpp will not look upon me as an Invalid, If I should be Lay'd by as to printing, Believing That Generall Intrest and Correspondenċe I have Settled Especially in The North shall allways be Capable of being Improved for yoͬ Serviċe.

Indeed My Lᵈ as I am Used by the whigs and Dissenters[19] for writeing & Printing because I can not go Their Length, and Dare to write what does not please Them, It can be Nothing but The hopes I have That I am Some way Usefull To yoͬ Ldpp That Supports me; and tho' I forbear to Trouble yoͬ Ldpp wᵗʰ it, as Not worth yoͬ

680

DEFOE TO [EARL OF OXFORD], 14 FEBRUARY 1712

Notice, yet in The Generall it may Suffize to Say, The Persecucon and Reproach I Meet wth from Them is Turn'd to Personall Mischief,^a Raiseing Creditors, Reviveing old prosecucons, and Open Endeavo^rs to Ruine and Disstress me.

But My Lord as This Drives me the More into yor Proteccon, and yor Goodness has been pleased to Support me, I have not failed, With ye Uttmost Force I have had to Detect The Arts and shifts of a Party, and Open The Eyes of Those who would Otherwise be blinded by Their^b popular Clamour, and it is My happyness That this is Perfectly Agreeable to My judgem^t and Principle as I hope it is to yor L^dpps Service. I Therefore Lay My Self att yor L^dpps Feet Entirely Depending On yor Goodness for my Support and I Openly Defye and Contemn ye fury of a Party Baffled by Their Own Ungovernd Heat.

I Sincerely Lament The Case of Scotland.[20] I See The Necessity of Giveing way to ye Current and can heartily blame those who have Driven Things to Such Extremeties; But I Dread The Consequences in Scotland; I do not fail to Temper and Perswade The warm people There to Calm Their Thoughts and keep Themselves quiet; and were There to be no Aggressors More might be done But I fear The Fury of ye Jacobite party will Drive ye Other into Excesses.

If my health would Permit me I should Tender my Service to Spend ye Summer Now at hand Among Them, And if yor L^dpp shall Think me Usefull Nothing but Utter Dissabillity shall Detain me, for I Perswade my Self I may do Something among Them wch Every One can Not — But all That and My Self, my Fortunes and hopes Are at yor L^dpps absolute Command and Direction.

> I am May it Please yor L^dpp
> yor L^dpps Most Humble and Obedient Servt
> [*monogram*]

Feb. 14. 1711[21]

---

^a Mischief] *following word* 'and' *cancelled*
^b Their] *amended from* 'The'

DEFOE TO [EARL OF OXFORD], 14 FEBRUARY 1712

P.S.

I Shall attend on Saturday[22] Morning According to yor L^dpps Command.

Text: BL Add. MS. 70291, fols. ²45–6. *Address*: none. *Endorsed by Oxford* (fol. ²46ᵛ): Mr Goldsmith Febr: 14: 1711/12

1 See Letter 180.
2 *Review*, VII, 202.
3 *Review*, VII, 219–20.
4 Liddell to William Cotesworth (*c*. 1668–1725), 21 Nov. and 4 Dec. 1710, in *The Letters of Henry Liddell to William Cotesworth*, ed. J. M. Ellis (Durham, 1987), II, 13.
5 *Review*, VIII, 676 (8 Mar. 1712).
6 *Review*, VIII, 628–38 (12, 14, 16 and Feb. 1712).
7 Draft affidavit of David Gibson and William Ormiston, 11 Nov. 1711, Tyne and Wear Archives 394/3. A reply to Defoe, *The Case of the Poor Skippers and Keel-men of New-Castle, Truly Stated* (1712) appears to refer to him as 'a Mercinary Writer well acquainted with some Instances of the Wasting and Misapplying [the keelmen's] Money'. In the *Review* for 26 July 1712, Defoe denied being paid by the ministry for writing on politics in the *Review*, but indicates that he has been 'Rewarded' for writing on trade, which could refer to this (VIII, 926).
8 *Review*, VIII, 629 (12 Feb. 1712).
9 Neville Ridley to Matthew Fetherstonhaugh (*c*. 1659/60–1762), 27 Mar. 1712, Tyne and Wear Archives 394/4. Fetherstonhaugh was the Mayor.
10 *C.J.*, XVII, 160.
11 See Joseph M. Fewster, *The Keelmen of Tyneside: Labour Organisation and Conflict in the North-east Coal Industry, 1600–1830* (Woodbridge, 2011), 21–38.
12 *Review*, VIII, 753; *TDH*, III, 118.
13 *Case … yor Ldpp*: See Letter 180.
14 *Fitters*: coal vendors or brokers.
15 *a Thousand Families of poor and Injured Men*: Defoe overestimated when numbering the keelmen 'above 4000' in *Review*, VIII, 219 (6 June 1710). He says their numbers are 'about 1600' and 'within 1600' in (respectively) *The Case of the Poor Skippers and Keel-Men of Newcastle* and *A Farther Case Relating to the Poor Keel-Men of Newcastle*, and 'near two Thousand' in *Review*, VIII, 629–30 (12 Feb. 1712).
16 *Abstract*: If Defoe did produce this, it remains untraced.
17 *Finch*: Probably Robert Finch (b. *c*. 1655), who had made a similar proposal in 1704 which was rejected. Finch had a 'proposal for the better securing and advancing the duty on malt, upwards of 50,000*l*. per ann. … To prevent frauds his principal proposal was to make all maltsters steep their barley only twice a week' (*CTP 1702–7*, 302). As a member of the Brewer's Company, Finch voted for Tories in parliamentary elections for the City of London. In 1718 he stood for the post of bridgemaster, stating he had been a member of the livery for more than thirty years and giving his age as 63 (*Post Man*, 29 Apr. 1718).
18 *Things Relateing to ye Press*: In a message to parliament on 17 Jan. 1712, the Queen observed 'how great a Licence is taken in publishing false and scandalous Libels; such as are a Reproach to any Government: The Evil seems to be grown too strong for the Laws now in force: It is therefore recommended to you to find a Remedy equal to the Mischief.' The House promised to act against such 'false and seditious Libels' (*C.J.*, XVII, 28). Commenting on the Queen's address, Defoe expressed his wariness of censorship: 'I cannot but say there may be

DEFOE TO [EARL OF OXFORD], 5 APRIL 1712

some Difficulties in this Article of Regulating the Press – The Hateful, Scandalous Way of a Licenser has been so exploded by former Parliaments, and appears such an Entrenchment on the Liberty of the Subject, besides the Scandal of saying that this is to Argue by Force, and taking care to have nothing said but on one Side, and indeed is liable to so many Partialities, and so many Difficulties, that I do not see how it is practicable' (*Review*, VIII, 594 (24 Jan. 1712)). See headnote to Letter 7 and Letter 170, note 13.

19 *Used by the whigs and Dissenters*: In the *Review* for 7 Feb. 1712, Defoe responded to Whig accusations that he was betraying their cause by insisting that he expressed his own views on the peace and was not directed to write (VIII, 618–19).

20 *Case of Scotland*: See Letter 205. The Episcopal Toleration Bill had passed the House of Commons and was before the Lords; it became law on 3 Mar. 1712.

21 *1711*: 1712 new style.

22 *Saturday*: 16 Feb.

207

To [Robert Harley, Earl of Oxford]

5 April 1712

HEADNOTE: In the *Review* Defoe continued to defend the ministry's peace policy, arguing that it made sense to listen to France's proposals while continuing to prepare for a fresh campaign.[1] In *Imperial Gratitude* (February) he attacked Charles VI of Austria for his refusal to send representatives to Utrecht where negotiations were taking place, which Defoe considered an ungrateful way of treating Britain, who had contributed so much to Charles's campaigns in Spain.[2] In March and April Defoe expressed his frustration at the slowness of the negotiations at Utrecht, satirically comparing it to a 'Horse-Fair' and then bemoaning the diplomatic punctilios and ceremony observed.[3] Time was of the essence because the time for a fresh campaign was approaching.

My Lord

My last[4] Seems to Make this Necessary. The Evill I Then hinted at about ye Stamp Office[5] I wait an Opportunity to Lay before yor Ldpp.

I could not but Represent to yor Ldpp how The party Among us, who are So Famous for pushing their Own dissasters, as well as those of their Country, please Themselves wth the hope of haveing broke all ye Ministry's Measures; and that they have as they think

683

DEFOE TO [EARL OF OXFORD], 5 APRIL 1712

put an End to the Treaty of Peace:[6] were They alone to Suffer by a war it were Pity but They Should be Fill'd wth Their Own ways;[7] It is Evedent They desire ye war Onely as They Envy yor Ldpp the Glory of The peace, and as they think it Gratifyes The Party They foolishly call Their Friends: Honest Men hope Still, yor Ldpps prudence will[a] Baffle all the plots they carry on Against ye Generall good, and That ye Peace So Needfull to a bleeding Nacon[8] Shall not be So slightly Rejected.

It is a Sort of pleasant tho' Mellancholly Contradiccon to hear These Men Rail at ye peace in One breath and at ye New[b] Taxes wth the Next, as if we were to Carry On the war without Money; as if they could have a War Renewed and a Stop put to The Raiseing Money at the Same Time. The Contrary must be One of the ways to Convince them who are Their Friends, Those who would Take off the burthen or those who would bind it On and Encrease it till the Nacon Sinks undr it.

These[c] Things p[er]swades us all to peace if Our Eyes were Open, but who shall cure[d] a Nacon born blind![9]

I long Impatiently to Represent to yor Ldpp Some Very Materiall things Relateing to Scotland; I am full of Feares for The public peace on That Side, and as I kno' The hardships put Upon Them there, Are Against yor Ldpps Mind;[10] and Against The Queens Intrest, I am Studious to find out Mediums to keep both sides Easy, and if you[r][e] Ldpp pleases at Leisure to Enter on Some Measures for That good work, I Shall hope it may not be too late, Especally if Something May be done before The assembly meets.[11]

I Apply my Self with constant and Dilligent Endeavour to stem ye Torrent of Clamour and Dissaffeccon both here and [There],[f] and Tho' the[g] Success may Not Answer, I hope The Labour, and the

---

[a] will] *following word* 'Still' *cancelled*
[b] New] *interlined*
[c] These] *anterior illegible word cancelled*
[d] cure] *inserted in lefthand margin and anterior illegible word cancelled*
[e] you[r]] 'r' *omitted in MS*
[f] [There]] *obscured by an engrafted piece of paper*
[g] the] *interlined*

DEFOE TO [EARL OF OXFORD], 5 APRIL 1712

Labourer Shall be Accepted by yor L^dpp, and This Supports me Under The worst Treatment (Among them) That Ever man Met with.

I am

May it Please yor L^dpp

yor L^dpp^s Most Obed^t &c.

[*monogram*]

Aprill 5. 1712

Text: BL Add. MS. 70291, fols. ²47–8. *Address*: none. *Endorsed by Oxford* (fol. ²48^v): Mr Defoe

1 *Review*, VIII, 645 (21 Feb. 1712).
2 *PEW*, V, 179–220. Cf. *Review*, VIII, 726 (5 Apr. 1712).
3 *Review*, VIII, 662–4 (1 Mar. 1712); 716 (1 Apr. 1712).
4 *My last*: Untraced.
5 *stamp Office*: Defoe had already expressed to Oxford his apprehensions about press repression through taxation (see Letter 206, note 18). In the *Review* during Apr. and May 1712, he outlined his reservations about the Stamp Act that was passing through parliament at this time. The Act, which became law on 1 Aug. 1712, was more prohibitive for periodicals than pamphlets: it placed a halfpenny duty on every copy sold of a half-sheet periodical, two shillings per sheet in a single copy for longer pamphlets. Defoe argued that the proposed taxation would prove ineffectual at raising funds because it would make the industry unviable. The welcome removal of antagonistic political writing would be at the cost of destroying beneficial writing aimed at poor consumers and putting 3,000 people out of work (*Review*, VIII, 763–9 (26 and 29 Apr. 1712); 778 (3 May 1712)). He argues for a moderate tax on printed works and specific laws directed against seditious publications, because a prohibitive tax on printed works would revive the manuscript satires of the Restoration, which are even harder to regulate or prosecute (*Review*, VIII, 786–7 (8 May 1712); 793–5 (13 May 1712)).
6 *Treaty of Peace*: On 15 Feb. 1712, the House of Lords 'voted an Adres to te Qu, to tell her they are not satisfyed with th K. of France's Offers. Th Whigs brought it in of a sudden, and te Court could not prevent it, and therefore did not oppose it. Th H of L^ds is too strong in Whigs notwithstanding th new Creations' (*Swift Journal*, 389). See *L.J.*, XIX, 379–80. The 'new Creations' were the twelve new peerages created by Queen Anne at the beginning of 1712 to overturn Whig control of the House of Lords.
7 *Fill'd wth Their Own ways*: 'The backslider in heart shall be filled with his own ways: and a good man *shall be satisfied* from himself' (Prov. 14:14).
8 *bleeding Nacon*: Defoe uses this phrase in *A Hymn to Peace* (1706), line 667, *SFS*, I, 401; *Review*, VI, 362 (15 Sept. 1709(E)); and (if he was its author) *The Age of Wonders* (1710), line 14, *POAS*, VII, 466.
9 *who shall cure a Nacon born blind!*: Alluding to Jesus' restoring the sight of a blind man (John 9:1–12).
10 *hardships … Mind*: Defoe was correct that Oxford opposed the Scottish Episcopal Toleration Act, but he was unable to prevent it. See headnote to Letter 213.
11 *assembly meets*: The General Assembly of the Church of Scotland was to convene on 1 May 1712. Defoe anticipated that 'the Wisdom, the Moderation, the Temper, and Prudence of the Ministers of the Church of *Scotland* will have a full Tryal' at the Assembly, in light of the Episcopal Toleration Act, the likely restoration of lay patronages, and the rabbling of ministers (*Review*, VIII, 796 (15 May 1712)).

DEFOE TO [EARL OF OXFORD], 17 APRIL 1712

208

To [Robert Harley, Earl of Oxford]
17 April 1712

HEADNOTE (Letters 208 and 209): Following the Occasional Conformity Act, passed the previous December, Defoe was eager to take stock of the state of the Dissenters at what he considered a crossroad. Rather than despairing and deploring the situation, he explored 'how the Dissenters shall bring Good out of Evil'.[1] He did so in the *Review* for 1 and 10 May 1712, in a pamphlet called *Wise as Serpents*, and in a substantial tract called *The Present State of the Parties in Great Britain*. As in his earlier polemics on the subject of Dissent, Defoe in these writings presented himself as a teller of hard truths, a critical friend, unjustifiably mistrusted and vilified by his coreligionists: 'I, that have learn'd to meet their Contempt of me with a Compassionate Sincere Desire to serve their Interest, will not refrain from speaking.'[2] In 1712, he wished to impress upon Dissenters the dangerousness of the Occasional Conformity Act. He thought too many deemed it innocuous, whereas Defoe considered it a tightening of the Test Act that presaged further erosions of the Toleration.[3] Looking at the Dissenters' fortunes since the Toleration Act, Defoe lamented the rise of the practice of occasional conformity, because it sacrificed a religious principle to a secular interest and so typified the decline of Dissent from its heroic survival under Stuart persecution.[4] He regretted that the Dissenters did not press for the repeal of the sacramental test following the Revolution, and considered this symptomatic of their short-sighted trust in the Whigs, who betrayed them in 1711. Defoe's solution, echoing some earlier publications, was for Dissenters to close ranks, to trade and fraternise exclusively with one another as much as possible, and to rediscover their religious integrity, putting 'meer Conscientious Nonconformity' above worldly affairs. Defoe was particularly exercised by the parlous condition of the Dissenting ministry and called for better funding for training pastors and preachers.[5] In the *Review* for 15 May, Defoe signalled that he did not blame the government: 'It was done over the Belly of the publick Schemes, pointed and Calculated to Cement an Interest against the present Administration.'[6]

My Lord

I am to ask Pardon for a Mistake I thought my Self Uncapable of (Viz:) That haveing written to yor L^{dpp} last Night, for Cover of The Enclosed, and Given The letter to a Servt to Carry, I Found The Receipt[7] on My Table left Out. I have left it without Date because

DEFOE TO [EARL OF OXFORD], 29 APRIL 1712

yoᵣ Lᵈᵖᵖ So Ordred before I Humbly Ask yoᵣ Lᵈᵖᵖˢ pardon for yᵉ
Mistake And am

May it Please yoᵣ Lᵈᵖᵖ
yoᵣ Most Humble and Obedᵗ Servᵗ
[*monogram*]

Aprill. 17. 1712.

Text: BL Add. MS. 70291, fols. ²49–50. *Address*: none.

1 *Review*, VIII, 789 (10 May 1712).
2 *Review*, VIII, 771 (1 May 1712).
3 *Wise as Serpents*, *PEW*, III, 299.
4 *Wise as Serpents*, *PEW*, III, 288–91.
5 *The Present State of the Parties in Great Britain* (1712), 283–352.
6 *Review*, VIII, 797.
7 *Receipt*: Untraced. Healey refers to two payments to Defoe in early 1712 (*Letters*, ed. Healey, 373 n. 1). However, J. A. Downie demonstrates that the records of these payments are old style dates, so they are actually 1713 payments ('Secret Service Payments to Daniel Defoe', *RES* 30 (1979), 437–41).

209

To [Robert Harley, Earl of Oxford]

29 April 1712

My Lord

I can Not Pay The Debt I owe to yoᵣ Lᵈᵖᵖˢ goodness a better way
Then by faithfully and Impartially Representing things to as well as
from yoᵣ Lᵈᵖᵖ in This Nice and Difficult Time.

It was wisely Observ'd by yoᵣ Lᵈᵖᵖ the Last Time I had the honoᵣ
to wait on you That There might Come a Time when yᵉ Dissenters
Might better be Talked to Than They can Now; It is an Unhappy
Truth, that The Temper of those honest men is yet So Ruffled at yᵉ
Loss of their Politick Intrest, That it Threatns their Religious, and
I find too Many of them willing Enough to Sacrifize the Latter, to
Retriev the former.

687

DEFOE TO [EARL OF OXFORD], 29 APRIL 1712

This Makes me I Confess not atall Regrett that they Are Ruin'd
in their Politick Intrest, hopeing Still that Their Religious Intrest
Shall be Established by it,[1] and when all yᵉ Dissenters in Masq
are Drop't from Them, and Nothing but meer Conscientious
Nonconformity Remains, I Doubt not yoʳ Lᵈpp will become their
protector as you have allways been of Honest prínciples and Honest
Men.

Mean Time God Deliver yoʳ Lᵈpp from a New Doctrine in
Politicks which I Suppose is Taught them by their Old Masters
(Viz) that The Ministry Ought to be prompted and push't On to
all Immoderate Councils That They May be Overthrown by Them;[2]
if this be Borrowd from The practise of the Late Lᵈ Sunderland,[3]
wᵗʰ King James, to which they Say we Owe the Revolućon,[4] I can
Onely Say to Them — We like the Treason But &c.[5]

I Apply my Self to Represent to yᵉ Dissenters the ground they
have lost[6] and the Injury they have done Themselves by joyning
into Parties and Meddling wᵗʰ Politicks, and to let them See, that
being beaten off from these Things with loss, and much wounded
in yᵉ Scuffle The Onely way they have left to Retriev their Figure
in the world is to become a Religious body as they were at first,
and by Layeing Aside Politicall Views and Party makeing, Remove
Effectually from Their Enemys the pretencé, and From others the
Reall Apprehensions, of their being Dangerous to yᵉ Church.

Perhaps yoʳ Lᵈpp, Than whom None knows The Temper of the
Men better, May believ my Success Improbable; But I hope yet a
Time for their Illuminaćon May Come; And I p[er]swade my Self
yoʳ Lᵈpp is So Much their Friend Still, Tho' Amidst a Thousand
provocations, as that you would be Glad to See it.

I Trouble yoʳ Lᵈpp wᵗʰ Nothing Relateing to Scotland because
The Success of the assembly is So Near.[7]

> I am
> May it Please yoʳ Lᵈpp
> yoʳ Lᵈpps Most Humble and Obedient Servᵗ
> [*monogram*]

Aprill 29. 1712

Text: BL Add. MS. 70291, fols. ²51–2. *Address*: none.

DEFOE TO [EARL OF OXFORD], 27 MAY 1712

1   *Ruin'd … by it*: In the *Review* for 1 May 1712, Defoe wrote that the Occasional Conformity Act was 'a Blow to their Politick Interest, but none at all to their Religious Interest' (VIII, 774).
2   *Ministry … Them*: In *Eleven Opinions about Mr. H——y* (1711), Defoe says that this is the Whigs' hope for Oxford and the Tories (*PEW*, II, 192).
3   *Ld Sunderland*: Robert Spencer (1641–1702), second Earl of Sunderland, Secretary of State under James II.
4   *we Owe the Revolucon*: In *Reasons against the Succession of the House of Hanover* (1713), Defoe wrote: 'This Famous Politician, if Fame lyes not, turn'd Papist himself, went publickly to Mass, advised and directed all the forward rash Steps that King *James* afterwards took, towards the introducing of Popery into the Nation … and many more of the Arbitrary Steps which that Monarch took for the Ruin of the Protestant Religion, as he thought, were brought about by this Politick Earl, purely with Design, and as the only effectual Means, to ruin the Popish Schemes, and bring about the Establishment of the Protestant Religion by the Revolution' (*PEW*, I, 179–80). Defoe gave an allegorical account of Sunderland's undermining James II in *The Consolidator* (1705), *SFS*, III, 83–90.
5   *We like the Treason But &c.*: The proverb is given by Defoe in the *Review* for 1 Sept. 1705 as 'they will hate the Traitors, tho' they love the Treason' (II, 561), and in the *Review* for 26 Oct. 1708 as 'you love the Treason, but abhor the Traytors' (V, 429).
6   *ground they have lost*: See similar phrasing in *Wise as Serpents*, *PEW*, III, 290, 297.
7   *The Successs of the assembly is So Near*: See Letter 207, note 11. 'Success' means 'outcome'.

210

To [Robert Harley, Earl of Oxford]

27 May 1712

HEADNOTE **(Letters 210 and 211)**: On 26 May the infamous restraining orders issued to the British commander James Butler (1665–1745), second Duke of Ormond, became public knowledge. With peace negotiations in an advanced state, Ormond was commanded not to attack the French in Flanders without permission from home. Defoe defended the restraining orders in the *Review* for 31 May and then in *Reasons against Fighting*, published around 7 June. Here Defoe seeks Oxford's permission to publish *Reasons against Fighting*. Defoe took the position that the Queen is within her rights and is manifesting an admirable regard for life by not engaging in unnecessary battles and sieges.[1]

Published around the same time, *A Further Search into the Conduct of the Allies, and the Late Ministry, as to Peace and War* responded to the controversial Dutch memorials delivered to the British government early in 1712. The memorials were the United Provinces' response to the House of Commons's review of the Dutch failure to meet their quotas for the army and navy. A memorial presented to the ministry on 3 April was leaked and published by Samuel Buckley in *The Daily*

689

DEFOE TO [EARL OF OXFORD], 27 MAY 1712

Courant on 7 and 8 April. In his pamphlet, which presents itself as a sequel to Swift's *The Conduct of the Allies*, published the previous November, Defoe approvingly writes that 'the *British* Court entering into a more narrow Inspection of Things, have not thought fit so calmly to suffer the Weight of the War to lye heavier upon one Shoulder than another'.[2] Defoe indicates that the Dutch response, assuming it is not a fabrication, actually concedes the fact that they provided fewer ships and soldiers than had been agreed and it resorts to extenuating factors which Defoe argues are specious.[3]

My Lord

Tho' my Observaçons in This Letter Should not be just yet My Zeal for yor L[dpp]s Intrest and ye public Good Shall plead I hope wth yor L[dpp] if it Should Not be According to knowlege.

The Article published yesterday in The post-Script to y[e] flying Post ((Viz) <u>y[t] when y[e] Gen[lls] of The Confederates were Resolv'd to Attack The Enemy The British Generall pull'd Out y[e] Queens Ord[r] Not to fight Or Undertake a Siege</u>) Occasions This.[4]

This My Lord is told in Such a Manner and Rec[d] wth Such a Temper as Raises a Mighty popular Clamour, and does Much Mischief Thro' the Naçon.

If The Fact is Not True,[5] I Need Not hint to yo[r] L[dpp] what Resentm[t] The publishing it calls for from y[e] Governm[t], for tho'[a] I am None of Those who prompt y[e] Missfortunes of My Neighbours, yet Governm[ts] as well as private Men, Sometimes find it Necessary to do themselves justiçe.

On The Other hand if The Thing be Fact, I can Not but Think it Recieves Such a Compleat Justificaçon in practise, from ye Constant Conduct of the Dutch, of The Imperialists, and Other Confederates; and There Are Such justifyable Reasons to be given for Such a Conduct, at This Time; That Might I Reciev The least Remote hint from yor L[dpp], Something Might Easily be Said without doores, that would Take off all ye Edge of The popular Surprize Some people Think They have Raised in ye Naçon and Turn all the Mischief Against Themselves. If yor L[dpp] please but to hint yor Comands to m[r] Read[6] by a Single <u>yes</u> or <u>No</u> it is Enough

---

[a] tho'] *interlined*

690

DEFOE TO [EARL OF OXFORD], 27 MAY 1712

to be Understood by me,^a and shall be Imediately Obey'd, I hope to yor L^{dpps} Satisfacćon. I Mean by <u>yes</u> or <u>No</u> Onely whether <u>yea</u> or <u>No</u> Such a Historicall Deduction of practise From Our Idolised Allies[7] May be Tho^t Usefull at this Time to do her Maj^{tie} Justiće and to Checq The Loud Clamours of a Party who watch for all Occasions to Enflame us; I Humbly Ask yor L^{dpps} pardon for This Moćon and Am

May it Please yor L^{dpp}**^b**
yor L^{dpps} Most Humble and Obedient Servt
[*monogram*]

May 27. 1712

Text: BL Add. MS. 70291, fol. ²53. *Address*: none.

---

^a me,] *interlined*
^b L^{dpp}] 'L^{dpps}' *in MS*

---

1 *Review*, VIII, 826–9 (31 May 1712); *Reasons against Fighting* (1712), 9.
2 *A Further Search into the Conduct of the Allies* (1712), 15.
3 For the ministry and its propagandists' reactions to the memorial, see Holmes, 69–71; Coombs, 314–16. Defoe discusses the Dutch failure to meet its obligations, and the Whig propaganda that excused them, in *Memoirs of Count Tariff* (1713), *SFS*, III, 171.
4 *The Article … This*: The *Postscript to The Flying Post* for 26 May 1712. It says 'one of the Generals' rather than 'The British Generall'. The *Flying Post* was at the vanguard of Whig anti-ministerial propaganda. In *Reasons against Fighting*, Defoe wrote that Ridpath's *Postscript* 'is calculated to lay as much Reproach on the *British* Nation, and on Her Majesty, as is possible' (1) and he labelled its author a 'Scandalous Scribler of false News' (17). The previous Sept., the paper had reported with malice on a duel between Defoe's brother-in-law Samuel Tuffley and a Captain Silk (W. P. Trent, 'New Light on Defoe's Life', *The Nation*, no. 2255, 17 Sept. 1908, 261–3).
5 *Not True*: In *Reasons against Fighting* Defoe assumes the truth of Ridpath's report only for the sake of the argument, noting that it is 'believed to be a meer Forgery of the *Scotchman* who writes that Paper, whose Talent of Lying is so well known to Mankind' (2).
6 *mr Read*: Probably Michael Read, Oxford's porter (see Letter 55, note 4).
7 *Idolised Allies*: *Reasons against Fighting* points out that the Dutch vetoed numerous offences during both the Nine Years' War and the War of the Spanish Succession to the point that they think 'the States alone should have a Negative Voice in the Field' (8).

691

DEFOE TO [EARL OF OXFORD], 5 JUNE 1712

211

To [Robert Harley, Earl of Oxford]

5 June 1712

My Lord

I am humbly to Ask yor L^{dpp} Pardon That the Enclosed books have been So long Comeing Out; But ye Case proves Longer Than I Expected to Make it.

The Sincerity of My Design is my Appology to yor L^{dpp} for ye Performance;[1] it is written without Doores, and for The Use of Those Cheifly, who kno' Nothing but without Doores. I hope it May be Usefull to Undeciev an abused people, and Let Them see How The wholl Nacon was Forming into One Tribe of Issachar,[2] and Taught to Couch Under The Tyranny of Our Neighbours, to bear what Burthen was Imposed Upon them, by Those who allways took care by Loading us to Ease Themselves.

I Send also another book to yor L^{dpp} in Answer to The Dutch Memorialls,[3] in all wch yor L^{dpp} will p[er]ciev, an[a] Honest but Artless Design, of Opening ye Eyes of a people So Imposed Upon, and So Tenacous of Their Own Mistakes, as Leads Them to a world of Troublesome and Dangerous Excesses.

Yo^r L^{dpps} Goodness will pass The Errors of p[er]formance; it is My Satisfaccon to be Serving yor Intrest, and doeing the people good together; I am farr from Exciting ye people against The Dutch, and believ it is not ye Governments View to Injure, or to Break with The Dutch; but it Seems Necessary, and I believ it is yor L^{dpps} Aim, to have the Dutch Friends, and Not Masters; Confederates not Governours; and to keep us from a Dutch as well as a French Mannagement.[4]

[a] an] *amended from* 'and'

DEFOE TO [EARL OF OXFORD], 16 JUNE 1712

I Shall go on to Open ye Eyes of The Injur'd people in These The More Chearfully if My Service in it is Approved and Accepted by your L^dpp —

I am May it Please yor L^dpp
yor faithfull obed^t Servt
[*monogram*]

June. 5. 1712^a

Text: BL Add. MS. 70291, fols. ²54–5. *Address*: none.

---

^a June. 5. 1712] *written vertically up the lefthand margin*

---

1 *Performance: Reasons against Fighting.*
2 *Tribe of Issachar*: Gen. 49:14–15. This is among Defoe's favourite biblical allusions, which he had recently used in *Reasons against Fighting*, 22. He also used it in *Jure Divino* (1706), *SFS*, 11, 36, 39 (preface), 335 (book XI, lines 443–4); *Dyers News Examined* (1707), 3; *Review*, 11, 785 (8 Dec. 1705); IV, 558 (21 Oct. 1707); IV, 593 (6 Nov. 1707); VI, 293 (13 Aug. 1709); VII, 365 (21 Sept. 1710).
3 *another book ... Memorialls*: Probably *A Further Search into the Conduct of the Allies, and the Late Ministry, as to Peace and War*, published around 7 June. See headnote. The Dutch memorial (see headnote) had been published in *The Daily Courant* on 7 and 8 Apr., which is perhaps why Defoe apologises for the delay in publication of his response. In *Memoirs of Count Tariff* (1713), Defoe points to Whig collaboration with the Dutch in their memorials (*SFS*, III, 171).
4 *I am farr ... Mannagement*: In the *Review*, Defoe consistently attempted to suppress the public appetite for a war with the Dutch during 1712. See *Review*, VIII, 643 (21 Feb. 1712). Two days before this letter, he expressed a position similar to this one, that 'it is our Undisputed Interest to maintain a constant, steady Union with the Dutch', but Britain should not sacrifice its commercial interests to this end (VIII, 831 (3 June 1712)). In *Reasons against Fighting*, he said that the British risked being 'made Tools and Engines to the *Dutch* Avarice' (20). For Defoe's writings on the subject during June and July, see headnote to Letter 212.

212

To [Robert Harley, Earl of Oxford]

16 June 1712

HEADNOTE: On 6 June 1712 Queen Anne announced to parliament the terms of the peace her government was negotiating with France. Both Houses promptly approved an address expressing their satisfaction. Defoe defended the peace terms in the *Review* during June and July. He also wrote *The Validity of the Renunciations*

DEFOE TO [EARL OF OXFORD], 16 JUNE 1712

of Former Powers (*c.* 10 July), a pamphlet defending leaving Philip V as Spanish monarch on the basis of his renouncing any claim to the French throne. Defoe continued the argument he first articulated in the *Review* for 21 February 1712 that a war with the Dutch, undesirable as it was, risked becoming inevitable.[1] He pursued this line in the *Review*, *An Enquiry into the Danger and Consequences of a War with the Dutch* (16 July), and *The Justice and Necessity of a War with Holland* (26 July).[2] In doing so, Defoe incurred the ire of the Whigs.[3] Defoe also continued to advise Oxford on Scottish matters: a coming by-election for a representative peer, and the risk of having Argyll as Commander-in-Chief.

My Lord

My Attending The Other day was Principally to Congratulate yoʳ Lᵈpp On yᵉ Successes of yoʳ Late Mannagemᵗ On Accoᵗ of yᵉ Peaċe, and to have given yoʳ Lᵈpp an Accoᵗ of The Influenċe it has Among The partys; How Many of The Wisest begin to Open Their Eyes, and be Easy; while The Rest Rather Rage that they can do noᵃ Mischief, Than hope to Obstruct yoʳ Lᵈpps Measures.

Withall I purposed to have Accquainted yoʳ Lᵈpp with an Extraordinary Congress of The Squadroni, just Now at Edinburgh;[4] whether the affair they Meet about be worth yoʳ Lᵈpps Notiċe Or not, is Not My provinċe. The avow'd Occasion is (as I hear but do not Assert) to Consult The Advocate,[5] and Other Lawyers, About The form of An Associaċon &c. and also to Consider how to Act, at yᵉ Ensueing Eleccon of a Peer, in the Room of Lᵈ Mareschall;[6] This I Thought it my Duty to Lay before yoʳ Lᵈpp, and Shall be able to Send More p[er]ticulars as they go On.

If your Lᵈpp would be pleased to Allow me So Much Freedome, I would Express My Apprehensions from yᵉ Warmth of his graċe of Argyle in his New Command,[7] Unless he be Restraind by yoʳ Lᵈpps Authourity: — A Middle way, wᵗʰ Temper, and Prudenċe, May yet preserv the Peaċe of That Country, and Cultivate her Majᵗⁱᵉˢ Intrest There; But Alas it is No slander On his graċe to Suggest, That These are Not the Greatest part of his Graċes Character: The Onely Security of that Uneasy people, is in yoʳ Lᵈpps Wisdome, and This

---

ᵃ no] *interlined*

694

DEFOE TO [EARL OF OXFORD], 16 JUNE 1712

Makes me Officously Lay these things So Often before you, for which I Humbly Ask yor Ld^{pps} Pardon, and Am May it please yor Ld^{pp}

yor Ld^{pps} Most Humble and Obed^t Servt
[*monogram*]

June. 16. 1712

Text: BL Add. MS. 70291, fol. ²56. *Address*: none.

1 *Review*, VIII, 643–6. Coombs, 338–54 gives a detailed account of debates about an Anglo-Dutch war, which developed during 1712. However, Defoe's own positions are clarified by W. R. Owens and P. N. Furbank, 'Defoe and the Dutch Alliance: Some Attributions Examined', *BJECS* 9 (1986), 169–82.

2 *Review*, VIII, 842 (10 June 1712); 880–2 (3 July 1712); 908 (17 July 1712). *The Justice and Necessity of a War with Holland* was de-attributed in F&O, *De-attributions*, 57–8. They argued that the pamphlet's arguments being similar to those of the *Review* are outweighed by the absence of external evidence for Defoe and its 'laboured prose'. However, external evidence for the attribution to Defoe comes from L'Hermitage (*Heinsius Corr.*, XIII, 628).

3 *The Medley* for 14–18 July 1712 alleged that Defoe 'is against a War with the *Dutch*, yet writes with all the Rancour and Malice that his Natural Talents can furnish against them'. The author of *A Letter from a Tory Freeholder to his Representative in Parliament upon Her Majesty's speech to Both Houses … June 6. 1712* claims he is informed by the Whigs that 'it was evident that since the Change of Ministry, that Scribler had chang'd his Conduct, and was visibly retain'd on our side [i.e. Tories]; adding, that he was always a Tool, that they could prove he had taken Mony on both sides, and that the Whigs did now universally disown him' (15).

4 *Congress of The Squadroni, just Now at Edinburgh*: Balmerino mentioned this meeting to Mar on 11 June (H.M.C. *Portland MSS*, v, 183).

5 *Advocate*: Sir James Stewart, Lord Advocate (see Letter 119, note 6; Letter 157, note 82).

6 *Eleccon of a Peer, in the Room of Ld Mareschall*: Marischal (see Letter 88, note 4) had died on 27 May 1712. Mar wrote to Oxford on 3 June anxious about an alliance between Argyll and Hamilton to return a successor against the Court (H.M.C. *Portland MSS*, x, 270). In Aug., Seafield was elected by the Scottish peers as Marischal's successor.

7 *Argyle in his New Command*: Argyll had recently replaced Leven as Commander in Chief in Scotland.

DEFOE TO [EARL OF OXFORD], 18 AUGUST 1712

213

To [Robert Harley, Earl of Oxford]

18 August 1712

HEADNOTE: In the recent preface to volume VIII of the *Review*, published at the end of July 1712, Defoe hit back at his critics, defending his conduct as a political writer and vowing to continue to tell harsh truths, particularly to the Dissenters who considered him an apostate. He complained that he had been 'Condemn'd by common Clamour, as Writing for Money, Writing for particular Persons, Writing by great Men's Direction, being Dictated to, *and the like*; every tittle of which, I have the Testimony of my own Conscience, is abominably false'.[1] The accusation that he was Oxford's hireling, a lackey to the Tory government, and a traitor to Whig principles had been intensive, especially since he started to support the peace campaign in autumn 1711.[2] Defoe wrote:

> The narrowest search I can make of my own Thoughts, Desires, and Designs, I find a clear untainted Principle, and consequently an entire calm of Conscience, founded upon the satisfying Sense, that I neither am touch'd with Bribes, guided or influenc'd by Fear, Favour, Hope, Dependance or Reward, of, upon, or from any Person or Party under Heaven: And that I have written and do write nothing, but what is my Native, Free, Undirected Opinion and Judgment.[3]

Defoe professes to draw his comfort from a trust in divine providence that keeps him tranquil despite a lifetime of turmoil which he lays out in a manner that anticipates his fuller autobiographical self-justification in *An Appeal to Honour and Justice* (1715).

The evidence is against Defoe's public and personal account of his integrity while writing under Oxford during Queen Anne's last ministry. The secret service payments, albeit frequently missed, indicate he was indeed paid, though he notes in this letter that this commenced under the previous Whig administration. Moreover, Defoe was engaged in reconnaissance work on behalf of the government, as well as journalism.[4] His letters going all the way back to the start of his association with Oxford contain requests for steers in his writing: at best, Defoe asks for information to furnish writing already planned; at worst, he directly asks how he should treat a topic. On occasion Defoe asks for permission to publish a given piece. On the other hand, the initiation often comes from Defoe, not Oxford, whether this was because the Lord Treasurer was negligent or that he 'Scorns the Service of a Mercenary Conscience', or even just the fact that many more letters from Defoe to Oxford exist than the other way round. We know that Defoe deceived his employer concerning what he wrote, *Atalantis Major* (1711)

696

DEFOE TO [EARL OF OXFORD], 18 AUGUST 1712

being the most notorious example. And it must be said that Defoe can hardly ever be seen writing something flagrantly against his principles. It would hardly have suited Oxford's ministry to have Defoe writing against the Occasional Conformity Act or the Scottish Episcopal Toleration Act, but he did. Oxford personally disagreed with such measures, imposed on him by a large Tory majority that had to be appeased, but publicly he had to support these acts.[5] In 1711 and 1712, Defoe publicly expressed reservations about topics including the Stamp Act, the terms on which the South Sea Company was established, and even aspects of the peace treaty. At such times, he clearly felt that he had great freedom from Oxford, and that their shared principles nullified the fact that he was being funded to write in support of the ministry.

My Lord

The Notice yor L^{dpp} was pleased to take of My Mellancholly Case, Stated in The preface to ye Review, and The goodness wherewith you were pleased to^a Express it to Me, Make Deep Impressions On a Mind fixt to yor L^{dpp}, by So Many Obligacons.

At The Same time (My Lord) That I profess Not to plead it as Merit, I acknowlege it is^b to My Honour, That The Indignity and Reproach cast on me by These Unhappy People, is Levell'd at yor L^{dpp};[6] and Providence Haveing placed you out of Their Reach (May it Ever be So!) They fall upon him They can hurt, to Shew Their Rage at yor L^{dpp} who They Can not; as The Dog Bites The stone Flung at him, Not Dareing Or not able to Touch The Hand That throws it.[7]

I Endeavo^r to practise The great work of Resignacon,[8] Under The Injurious Treatm^t I Reciev, Submitting it to his Disposall who in a like Occasion (Tho' of higher Moment) Bad Shimei Curse, But left him Not Unrewarded.[9]

It is My Satisfaccon, that as Their Rage is a Testimoney to The weight, and to the^c Conviccon of what I Say, So yor L^{dpp} is pleased to Approve my Service, and thereby add a Weight to it, wch I have not Modesty Little Enough to Think it Deserves.

God and yor L^{dpp} are witnesses for me Against This Generacon, in That yor Goodness to me was founded On No Principles of

---

^a to] *interlined*
^b is] *interlined*
^c weight, and to the] *interlined*

697

DEFOE TO [EARL OF OXFORD], 18 AUGUST 1712

Bribery, and Corrupčon, but a generous Compassion to a Man Oppressed by Power without a Crime, and Abandon'd, <u>Even Then</u>, by Those he Sacrifized himself to Serve.[10]

The[a] Same witnesses Are a Testemony for me, that[b] My Servičes (However Small) are founded Rather <u>and indeed Entirely</u> on a Deep Senče of Duty, and Gratitude for That Early goodness,[11] Than on any View, That I can Merit what may be to Come.

Yor Ldpp has allways acted wth Me[c] On Such foundačons of Meer abstracted Bounty and Goodness, That it has Not So Much as Suggested The Least Expectačon on yor part, That I Should act This way, or That, Leaving[d] me at full Liberty to Persue My Own Reason, and Prinčiple; And above all Enableing Me to Declare my Innočenče In the Black Charge of Bribery.

What Ever yor Ldpp has done for me, you Never yet So much as Intimated, (tho' Ever So Remotely) That you Expected from me The Least Byass in what I should write, or That her Majties Bounty to me was Intended to Guide my Opinion; yor Ldpp has too Much Honour in yor principle, to look That way, Or to Think me worth yor Notiče, if I Could ha' been So Moved; and How would These people blush Should I Own to Them, That Her Majties Bounty, wch I Now Enjoy, was procur'd for me by yor Ldpps Intercession, Even Under The Administračon of yor Ldpps worst Enemyes.[12]

This Fills me with Peače Under all Their Clamour, That I Serv a Master who Scorns the Serviče of a Mercenary Conscienče; and who at ye Same Time That he does me good, leaves me full Liberty to Obey the Dictates of My Own principles; This My Lord Gives Me Room to Declare, as I do in Print Every day, That I am Neither Employ'd, Dictated to, or Rewarded for, or in, what I write by any Person Undr Heaven; And I Make This Acknowlegement wth Thankfullness to yor Ldpp, and as a Testimony to yor great Goodness to me, That yor Ldpp Never lay'd The least Injunccon on Me, of One kind or Other, To write or Not to write, This, or That, in any Case whatsoever.

---

[a] The] *anterior word* 'And' *cancelled*
[b] that] *interlined*
[c] Me] *amended from* 'Meer'
[d] That, Leaving] *amended from* 'This Leaves'

698

DEFOE TO [EARL OF OXFORD], 18 AUGUST 1712

It is However my great Satisfaccon, That what first is founded on principle, and Reason, agreeable to Conscience, Equity, and The good of my Country, (aÿ, and to These Unhappy peoples[13] Intrest too, if They Understood their Intrest)[a] is at ye Same Time Agreeable to yor Ldpp, and That while I am Rendring yor Ldpp Service, I am Dischargeing The Debt of justice to Truth, and Liberty,[14] The great Principle on wch I hope I shall Never Cease to Act; and which while I persue I am allwayes Sure to please and Oblige yor Ldpp.

I Most Humbly Ask yor Ldpps Pardon for This Excursion, a Heart Oppress't as Mine, by Publick Reproach (without Guilt) must Needs be Full; and as I am Driven by The Torrent, Upon a More Entire Dependance On yor Ldpp, So have I No Humane Appeal But to yor Self; However I Cease to Enlarge on This Unpleasant Subject, haveing yet a farther Humble applicacon to Make, for wch I have Still More Reason to ask Pardon.

May it Please yor Ldpp

I Hinted to yor Ldpp My Desire to Take a Journey North.[15] I will not Dissemble So farr with yor Ldpp,[b] as Not to Own, That a Little Bussiness[16] part of the way, and withall The Direccon of Physitians for my goeing to The Bath in Derbyshire,[17] Joyn in to Make me Desirous of goeing — But I am perswaded also I may be More Usefull to yor Ldpp in a small Circuit On That Side, at This Time; as well for Counteracting the Measures taken to Distract the Country, as for Calming and quieting the Minds of ye poor preposess't people, Than Ever I was yet; and as The Juncture for Such a bussiness Seems proper, and Leisure at home agrees, I am yor Ldpps Humble Peticoner for Leave.

But my Ld I am yet Straightn'd in The Rest of My Peticon. Yor Ldpps Goodness to Me is too great to allow me the Least Sollicitacon for farther Favours than I Enjoy; Nor My Lord Am I Representing the Expence of My Journey, (For wch yor Ldpp had allways the Goodness to make me Large Allowance); But I am forced by Importuneing Circumstances to Remind yor Ldpp That of That Allowance Or Appointment wch by yor Ldpps Intercession,

---

[a] Intrest)] 'Intrest;' *in MS*
[b] Ldpp] *following words* 'So farr' *cancelled*

DEFOE TO [EARL OF OXFORD], 18 AUGUST 1712

and Her Maj^ties Goodness, I Enjoy, There are Two quarters behind wch Insensibly (Except to me) Elapsed, Dureing The Mellancholly Intervall, when^a yor Ld^pp was Hurt,[18] and Things Unsettled. —

I Say no More! I am a Very Mean Advocate in My Own Case, and had Rather My Circumstances Should Silently^b Move yor Tenderness and Compassion, Than That by Importunity I should be forward and Craveing; God has Cast me on yor Ld^pps Goodness So Entirely, That he Seems to Direct me Thereby to a More close Applicacon than Ever to yor Intrest, and Service; for Sure, when Ever I shall be Depriv'd Of yor Ld^pps favour, or assistance, if This party can Make me Miserable, They will No[t]^c fail to do it to ye Uttmost.

I am

May it please yor Ld^pp

yor Most Humble Obed^t Servt

[*monogram*]

Augt 18.^d 1712

Text: BL Add. MS. 70291, fols. ^2 57–8. *Address*: none. *Endorsed by Oxford* (fol. ^2 58v): M^sr Guilot Augu: 19: 1712

<hr>

^a when] *following word* 'The' *cancelled*
^b Silently] *interlined*
^c No[t]] *MS frayed*
^d 18] *amended; Oxford endorsed the letter 19 Aug.*

<hr>

1   *Review*, VIII, 2 (preface, 24 Mar. 1711). See also VIII, 894 (10 July 1712); 915 (22 July 1712).
2   *Remarks on a False, Scandalous, and Seditious Libel, Entitled, The Conduct of the Allies* (1711), 2; *A Letter from a Tory Freeholder to his Representative in Parliament* (1712), 15; *The Medley*, 11–14 July 1712. *The Medley* kept up its attacks in subsequent issues, but its last one, for 1–4 Aug. 1712, following Defoe's defiant preface, admits that the accusation is based on 'Common Fame' and concedes, 'I have no sort of Evidence, that he has ever received any Mony of any one; but *this* I shall venture to say of him, that no Man ever better deserved to be rewarded by those Men that call themselves *Tories*, because no one has said so much to vindicate the Proceedings of that Party'.
3   *Review*, VIII, 3 (preface).
4   See *Review*, VIII, 925 (26 July 1712), in which Defoe makes a point of rebutting allegations that he has '*taken Money* FOR WRITING REVIEWS', so does not entirely deny having been paid by the ministry.
5   See *Review*, VIII, 853 (17 June 1712).
6   *Indignity and Reproach ... yor Ldpp*: 'Certainly what this *Review* writes, must have some strange Force in it, some unusual Energy, that they will not allow me to be the Author of it myself – But I must have the Materials from the greatest Head in the Nation; they do me an

700

DEFOE TO [EARL OF OXFORD], 27 AUGUST 1712

Honour that I do not deserve, and which they do not design for an Honour, but will for ever be so in spight of them' (*Review*, VIII, 926 (26 July 1712)).

7 *Dog ... throws it*: 'So Dogs, provok'd by something thrown, | That cannot bite the Hand, will bite the Stone' (Defoe, *A Hymn to the Mob* (1715), lines 400–1, *SFS*, I, 428–9).

8 *great work of Resignaĉon*: In the preface to vol. VIII of the *Review*, Defoe refers to his 'constant serious Application to the great, solemn and weighty Work of Resignation to the Will of Heaven' (VIII, 8). There, Defoe also revised his poem on the theme of 'Resignaĉon'. See Frank H. Ellis, 'Defoe's "Resignaĉon" and the Limitations of Mathematical Plainness', *RES* 36 (1985), 338–54.

9 *his Disposall ... Shimei ... Unrewarded*: 2 Sam. 16:5–13. Defoe compares himself to David. He perhaps makes explicit a covert allusion in the preface to vol. VIII of the *Review*, in which he says that the Whigs 'shall have leave to throw Stones at me as long as I live', which is how Shimei treats David at 16:13. See *Jure Divino*, book XI, line 665, *SFS*, II, 344.

10 *Abandon'd ... Serve*: Defoe felt abandoned by his Whig and Dissenter allies following his prosecution for *The Shortest Way with the Dissenters* in 1703, before his release from prison was arranged by Harley. He alludes to this in the preface to vol. VIII of the *Review* (4).

11 *Gratitude for That Early goodness*: Defoe speaks of his gratitude to Oxford in similar terms in *Appeal*, 15–16.

12 *Intercession ... Enemyes*: Apparently referring to Harley's securing the continuation of Defoe's employment under Godolphin after Harley's fall in Feb. 1708 (*Appeal*, 15).

13 *Unhappy peoples*: The Dissenters.

14 *Truth, and Liberty*: In the preface to vol. VIII of the *Review*, Defoe wrote: 'From the beginning of this Undertaking, which I have now carryed on almost Ten Years, I have always, according to the best of my Judgment, Calculated it for the Support and Defence of TRUTH and LIBERTY' (2).

15 *I Hinted ... North*: I.e. to Scotland. Defoe hinted his desire to go there in Feb. 1712 (Letter 206) and presumably had renewed the offer more recently.

16 *Bussiness*: Not identified.

17 *Bath in Derbyshire*: Matlock or Buxton. Defoe writes about the baths in these towns in *A Tour thro' the Whole Island of Great Britain*, giving detailed attention to the 'medicinal Virtues' of the warm springs at Buxton (*TDH*, III, 39).

18 *when yor Ldp was Hurt*: At the time Harley was recuperating from Guiscard's assassination attempt in Mar. 1711. See Letter 177.

214

To [Robert Harley, Earl of Oxford]

27 August 1712

HEADNOTE (**Letters 214 and 215**): The Cameronian gathering Defoe reports on to Oxford occurred at the end of July 1712 at Auchensaugh Hill, near Douglas, in Lanarkshire. Wodrow suspected Jacobite involvement in this renewal of the 1638 National Covenant and 1643 Solemn League and Covenant, and he feared that it could lead the government in London to pass an act compelling Scots to renounce their national oaths.[1]

In September, Wodrow wrote: 'I hear some private letters from London bear, that the end of the last moneth, or beginning of this, the Treasurer called for De Foe, and told him he heard of ane insurrection in Scotland, meaning Mr M'millan's meeting at Douglasse, and ordered him to write to Scotland, and inform himself about it, and write some revues upon it. I'le be fond to see them, when they come out.'[2] Defoe addressed the Cameronian meeting in the *Review* for 30 August 1712, seeking to pre-empt aggravating accounts of this 'poor Rash People' in the English press by stating that 'they seem to merit the Compassion and Pity of the Government, rather than their Resentment'.[3] A clampdown would exacerbate the situation, whereas lenience would eventually lead to the end of the Covenanting movement.

My Lord

According to yor Ldpps Order I have Enclosed an Exact Coppie of The Letter[4] wch I Recd from Scotland So farr as Relates to ye Thing I Menćoned to yor Ldpp.

As (my Lord) I Accquainted yor Ldpp wth The Name of The Person, From whom I Recd The Said Accot, I Take This Occasion to Assure yor Ldpp, That The Character of That Gentlemn is Such, as May Recomend him Upon all Occasions to yor Intrest and Favour, and as may Render him perticularly Usefull to yor Ldpp in Case The Squadroni Take any Measures against ye Governmt; of all wch by This Means a Constant True account of Every step may be Obtaind: — More is not proper to Say Till Occasion makes it for yor Ldpps Serviće. But This I Thought perticularly Needfull, That yor Ldpp May allways kno' who may be Depended Upon, and who not.

> I am
> May it Please yor Ldpp
> yor Ldpps Most Humble & Obedt Servt
> [*monogram*]

Augt 27. 1712

Sr

— We have had in This Country a great Confluenće of people about 5 Miles from the Earl of Hyndfords Seat of Caermichell,[5] who on Thursday the 25th of July[6] to ye Number of about 8 or 9000

DEFOE TO [EARL OF OXFORD], 27 AUGUST 1712

people[7] met in the fields on Occasion of Recieving the Sacrament the Sabbath following. Preparatory to ye Sacramt, The Sd Thursday was their fast, when in the first plaće They Sollemnly Renew'd the Covenant, tho' they thot fitt to Exclude that part of it wch Menćons the Governmt and Establish't Church;[8] They then went On publickly Confessing their Sins, Tho' I believ they Confessed not the Greatest of them. Among Other Sins they Insisted on ye Crime of hearing and Joyning wth the present Ministers and the Kirk.

At This Rate They Spent Three whole dayes, Most of them[a] lyeing all night in the Hills and on ye Ground, Till the Sabbath following when the Sacrament was administred to them, Before wch, pronouncing as is Usuall The Comination,[9] They publickly Excomunicated Her Majtie by Name,[10] The wholl British Parliament, and all the Establish't Kirk Ministers. One mr McMillan[11] is their Leader, being an Ordaind Minister but Deposed by the Assembly, and he has One Mc Neil[12] for his assistant who was Never Ordaind; what Carryes off these poor people So much at this Time is the Apprehensions They are Under that their Ministers will take the Abjuration.[13]

They had no Arms, nor do I See that they have any thoughts of Disturbing the peaće; but you kno' Some people who May in Time Make Some use of Such a Thing, Especally if their Numbers Encrease; and it would be well if The Governmt would please to post Some Troops at hand, to be Some Awe to Those who hope for Some advantage from The poor peoples folly —

Text: BL Add. MS. 70291, fols. ²59–61. [The letter is fol. ²59; the enclosure is fols. ²60–1.] *Address*: none. *Endorsed by Oxford* (fol. ²61v): Guilot Scotland R Augu: 28: 1712

---

[a] Most of them] *interlined*

---

1   *Analecta*, 11, 76–8.
2   *Analecta*, 11, 88–9.
3   *Review*, IX, 35–7.
4   *Letter*. Original untraced; the correspondent is unidentified.
5   *Caermichell*: The house was rebuilt on the same site later in the eighteenth century; it is in South Lanarkshire, about thirty miles southwest of Edinburgh.
6   *Thursday the 25th of July*: Actually Thursday 24 July.

DEFOE TO [EARL OF OXFORD], 3 SEPTEMBER 1712

7 *8 or 9000 people*: Probably an overestimate. Wodrow wrote: 'Some say one thousand, some say seventeen hundred' (*Analecta*, 11, 76). In the *Review*, Defoe echoed '8 or 9000' but stressed that 'there is nothing Formidable in the Power or Numbers of the People' (ix, 37 (30 Aug. 1712)).

8 *Covenant … Church*: Both covenants uphold the civic power of parliament and the government.

9 *Comīnation*: 'Denunciation of punishment or vengeance' (*OED*), reciting God's anger against sinners.

10 *Excomūnicated Her Majtie by Name*: Defoe alludes to this in *Review*, ix, 64 (23 Sept. 1712).

11 *mr McMillan*: John Macmillan of Balmaghie (1669–1753), ordained in 1701 but deposed in 1703 when he complained to the Presbytery of Kirkcudbright that the Revolution settlement failed to establish Presbyterianism on a *jus divinum* basis in Scotland. His local support meant that Macmillan continued to preach in his church, but he also joined the United Societies (Covenanters). His followers were called 'Macmillanites' or 'the Remnant'. After 1743, they were the Reformed Presbyterians. See H. M. B. Reid, *A Cameronian Apostle: Being some Account of John Macmillan of Balmaghie* (Paisley, 1896). See 175–83 for the Auchensaugh gathering.

12 *Mc Neil*: John M'Kneilly or MacNeil. In the *Review*, Defoe echoes these details of '*Mac-Mellan*' and '*Mac-Neil*', 'neither of them of any Character or Capacity, other than is peculiar to the unhappy People themselves' (ix, 36).

13 *Abjuration*: Defoe considered this requirement of the Scottish Episcopal Toleration Act 'expressly against the late Union' (*Review*, ix, 36 (30 Aug. 1712)).

215

To [Robert Harley, Earl of Oxford]

3 September 1712

My Lord

Since I had ye honor to Accquat yor Ldpp of The affair in Scotland I have had Sevll Concurring Accotsˡ both of ye fact, and Subsequent Circumstances But do not find There has been any More Assemblyes of ye Nature of That I formerly gave accot of.

But (My Lord) as The Encrease of That Party to ye Degree Menćoned was Not Without Some Extraordinary Applicaćon of Emessaries and bussy people who Dilligently foment The Popular Noćons of That poor Distracted people, So if Those Leaders are Not in Some Manner Discouraged Or Removed From Them, There May be Many ill Consequences to be Apprehended.

I believ yor Ldpp Knows I am an Enemy to all Coerćons in Matters of Religion or (and indeed more Espećally) of

704

DEFOE TO [EARL OF OXFORD], 3 SEPTEMBER 1712

Enthusiasme, and am Convinc't That there is No way So Effectuall to Confirm and Encrease This Disorder, Than to fall upon Them with Force and put ye Laws in Execuçon Severely Upon Them. But Some Method May in yor L^dpps Wisdome be p[er]haps thought of to Take from Them That Poor Ignorant Incendiary[2] who Now Leads Them into all These wild Things.

This (my Lord) I Say The Rather, because all my Accounts agree That he goes about Increasing The Evill, and Confirming The poor people in Their Noçons wth Too Much Success and will Certainly at Last precipitate Them into Some Mischeivous Thing to Their Own Ruine, and To The Injury of The public.

If yor L^dpp Thinks Fit to Approve The Design I had of a private Tour to The border, I would have gone Incognito Among Some of these people, and have Given your L^dpp a More Exact and Impartiall Acco^t both of ye people and of The Reasons of Their New Appearance; and p[er]haps have found out Some of The Persons also, whom I can not but Think it is Very Much for ye Service of The Governm^t to Discover.

I hope yor L^dpp is Fully Satisfyed That I have no Other View in This part Than The public Service; as for my p[er]ticular Journey wch I am und^r a little Necessity of Takeing into Darby Shire, if yor L^dpp does not Approve of ye Other I Shall Onely beg leav for about a Fortnight and Shall not fail, God willing, to be here again in That Time.

I do Confess it has been Upon my Mind That I might be Usefull in The Country Upon Many Acco^ts but I Submit That and My Self wholly to your L^dpps Direcçon Onely beg Again yor License for the Small Step above

And Am
yor L^dpps Most Humble and Obedient Servant
[*monogram*]

Septemb^r 3. 1712

I Send here One of Their Distracted papers[3] On Occasion of The public Fast —

DEFOE TO [EARL OF OXFORD], 20 SEPTEMBER 1712

Text: BL Add. MS. 70291, fols. ²62–3. *Address*: none. *Endorsed by Oxford* (fol. ²63ᵛ): Guilot Sept: 4: 1712

1 *Accots*: None traced.
2 *Incendiary*: Macmillan.
3 *One of Their Distracted papers*: Missing. Possibly it was *The National Covenant, and Solemn League and Covenant with the Acknowledgement of Sins, and Engagement to Duties: as they were Renewed at Douglas July 24th 1712 … Together with an Introductory Preface* (Edinburgh, 1712).

216

To [Robert Harley, Earl of Oxford]

20 September 1712

HEADNOTE: Defoe was travelling north when he wrote to Oxford in September 1712. He reports on political unease among Whigs and Dissenters in East Anglia. In the *Review* during September and into October, Defoe targeted Whig readers to defend the ministry. His case was that it had no Jacobite intentions despite making use of Jacobite instruments. He pointed out that even Whigs had '*join'd with the Jacobites*' in the recent past, that Whig disunity had let the Tories back in, and that working for the Pretender was against the self-interest of the current managers, especially 'the Person now at the Helm of Affairs', Lord Oxford.[1]

My Lord

I had Not been So long before I paid my Duty to yoʳ Ldᵖᵖ, but That I have been for Some Time Out of yᵉ Reach of yᵉ post. But as I Shall Now Continue to give yoʳ Ldᵖᵖ a full accoᵗ of what Ever Occurrs Worth yoʳ Ldᵖᵖˢ Notice,ᵃ So I can Not Omit a few hints of what is allready passt.

Meeting wᵗʰ an Accidentall Invitacon, and My Curiosity joyning in, I went from Sturbrige Fair (which I had Made My first Stage)ᵇ Towards Lyn,[2] where Resolveing to be Incognito, I found I had Room for Many Speculacons. Here My Lᵈ (Asking yoʳ License to jest a little wᵗʰ what is indeed yᵉ Nacons Dissaster) I found my

ᵃ Notice,] *interlined*
ᵇ I went from Sturbrige Fair (which] '(I went from Sturbrige Fair which' *in MS*

706

DEFOE TO [EARL OF OXFORD], 20 SEPTEMBER 1712

Self Out of her Maj^ties Dominions, and in ye Capital City of ye Terretorys of king Walpole.³

Here I have Seen what I confess it is Difficult to Express, and what I could not have thought had been in The Nature Much less in The practise of protestants or English Subjects. Here I have Seen wth Some Horrour^a The Spirit of Parties in its highest Extraccon. How her Maj^tie is Treated Among them, would fill any Man who Makes Loyalty and Duty to his^b Soveraign a Principle with Indignacon, any Man who Vallues ye peace and Tranquillity of his Country wth abhorrence and Any Man that has his Sences in Excercise with Contempt and Aversion.

If They do This in The Green Tree what Shall They do in The Drye!⁴ The Deciple is Not Above his Lord;⁵ if her Maj^tie is Thus Treated Among Them, yor L^dpp and all That Serve her Maj^tie and Their Country faithfully Share most Plentifully of Their Rage, in a Manner I blush for Them too Much to Relate. But yor L^dpp has Learnt from a Superiour Pattern, To Pity and Contemn the Madness of The people. God Almighty who has placed her Maj^tie and all her faithfull Servants Out of The Reach of Their hands Be praised for the Safety Enjoy'd by it.

Yo^r L^dpp Can Not doubt, But where A Party wth Such a Temper Seem to prevail, and have what they call a Leading Intrest, The people, Smothered wth the Smoke or Mist of Their Delusions, Suffer a generall Inflamacon, and are Made Lunatick wth the Madness of their Leaders; what Strange Things they are Made to believ, what wild Inconsistent Nocons they have Infused into ye Minds of^c One Another, what preposterous Ridiculous Incongruous things Take up their heads, is Incredible, and but for the Novelty of Them Are not worth Repeating, Such as, That The queen is For The Pretender, The Ministry Under The Proteccon of France, That Popery is to be Tollerated, That as Soon as a Peace is Declared The War with ye Dutch will be proclaimed, That The French are to keep their Trade to the South Seas;⁶ That ye people will be brought to address the Queen Not to Interrupt ye Heredetary Right of

---

ᵃ Horrour] *interlined above cancelled letters probably* 'Horro'
ᵇ his] *following letters probably* 'pri' *(for* 'prince'*) cancelled*
ᶜ of] *following letters probably* 'ye p' *(for* 'people'*) cancelled*

707

DEFOE TO [EARL OF OXFORD], 20 SEPTEMBER 1712

The Royall Line, Since The Heir is willing to Abjure popery;[7] and The like.

As far (my Lord) as Consisted w[th][8] my Resolucon of keeping Incognito, which[a] I have Effectually Done, and w[ch] I Thought Necessary on Many Acco[ts] I have Layd the foundacon of Undecieving the poor people in these things[b] and have Effectually Convinc't The Dissenting Minister,[9] and Two Leading Men Among the Dissenters,[10] who wth Astonishment look back upon The Delusions they[c] have been Under, and who I doubt not will in A Short Time Undeciev Many More.

I Find my Lord The Countrys Every where Share of The Generall Distemper, Tho' not with the Same warmth; An Inclinacon to Moderacon Appeares Among The best men Every where, but The poison is Unhappily Spread from London, and Especally Among the Dissenters, who are made Every where to Believ That the Ministry is for The pretender, and That French Governm[t] and Popery is y[e] Design; wherever I Converse wth Them, I find Them posest wth The Very Same Nocons, w[ch] is an Evedence that it is a Concerted Measure of The party, to Spread Such Things thro' the Country.[11]

I also find it less Difficult than I Expected, to Open The Eyes of The Honest and well Meaning, and that They are Eager and Forward to be better Inform'd, and hope I may not be an Unprofitable Servant[12] That way, So farr as This Short Journey will Extend; I wish proper p[er]sons were on y[e] like Occasion in Other parts. I am Perswaded yo[r] L[dpp] would Soon find a good Effect from it.

I am
May it please yo[r] L[dpp]
[*monogram*]

Lincoln Sept. 20. 1712

Text: BL Add. MS. 70291, fols. ²64–5. *Address*: none. *Endorsed by Oxford* (fol. ²65v): Claude Guilot Sept: 20: 1712 R octo: 1

---

[a] which] *interlined*
[b] these things] *interlined*
[c] they] *interlined*

DEFOE TO [EARL OF OXFORD], 20 SEPTEMBER 1712

1 *Review*, IX, 63 (23 Sept. 1712); 67 (27 Sept. 1712).

2 *Sturbrige Fair ... Lyn*: Stourbridge Fair, near Cambridge; King's Lynn.

3 *king Walpole*: Robert Walpole, at this time the unseated MP for King's Lynn, later First Lord of the Treasury and Chancellor of the Exchequer (1715–17, 1721–42). He had served as Secretary of War (1708–10) under the Whigs and Treasurer for the Navy (1710–11) even after the 1710 ministerial revolution; but he eventually resisted Harley's overtures and became, in Swift's words, 'one of the Whigs chief speakers' in opposition to the ministry (*Swift Journal*, 349). In the 1711–12 session the Tories 'resolved to put [him] out of the way of disturbing them in the house' (Burnet, VI, 93). He was found guilty of corruption in Jan. 1712, unseated, and committed to the Tower. This turned him into a Whig martyr: he comfortably won the ensuing by-election, but the Commons declared the election void. Walpole was released from prison in July 1712, was returned unopposed for King's Lynn in 1713, and continued to attack the ministry in the Commons thereafter. See *HPC 1690–1715*, V, 780–3. Defoe criticised Walpole's victory speech (printed as *The Speech of R— W--p-le; at his Election at Lynn-Regis, Norfolk, August 31, 1713* (1713)) in *A Letter to the Whigs* (1714) and *The Monitor*, no. 5 (1 May 1714), pointing out that it attacked the ministry with generalities without identifying particular measures that were objectionable. Defoe alleged that it was seditious libel.

Defoe's later attitude to Walpole and his policies when the Whigs were back in government is generally negative. In *The Danger of Court Differences* and *The Quarrel of the School-Boys at Athens* (both Jan. 1717), Defoe looked askance on both sides of the Whig split that resulted in the resignation from government in Apr. 1717 of Walpole and Charles Townshend, second Viscount Townshend (1674–1738). *The Quarrel* alludes to Walpole's expulsion from parliament in 1712, as well as his 'implacable' and perhaps unjust treatment of his opponents at that time, as Walpole had been appointed to the committee to investigate the impeached Oxford and Bolingbroke in 1715 (*SFS*, III, 207). In *The Old Whig and Modern Whig Revived* (Aug. 1717), Defoe comes down on the side of Sunderland and Stanhope against the Walpolite opposition, noting that Walpole's zeal for prosecuting Oxford abated when he saw a chance to bolster his faction. However, in *Fair Payment No Spunge* (Mar. 1717), Defoe defended Walpole's plan to repay the national debt. Defoe's writings in the wake of the bursting of the South Sea Bubble in 1720 are indirect in their criticism of Walpole's role. Defoe's *Due Preparations for the Plague* (1722) is arguably a reaction to the 1721 Quarantine Act that Walpole introduced.

4 *If ... Drye!*: Luke 23:31. Defoe also uses the expression in *Review*, II, 757 (27 Nov. 1705) and in Letter 230.

5 *The Deciple is Not Above his Lord*: Luke 6:40; Matt. 10:24.

6 *French are to keep their Trade to the South Seas*: See Letter 185, note 10.

7 *Heir is willing to Abjure popery*: In the *Review*, Defoe countered reports that the Pretender 'is a *Papist* indeed, because his Father made him so, but that he is a Protestant in his Heart, and will declare himself so, as soon as it is convenient and safe for him' (IX, 92 (18 Oct. 1712)). He thought those who believed they could have the Stuarts and Protestantism were delusional.

8 *Consisted wth*: Used in the archaic sense of 'was compatible with'.

9 *Dissenting Minister*: Probably John Rastrick (1650–1727), Presbyterian minister in Spinner Lane, King's Lynn (*ODNB*).

10 *Two Leading Men Among the Dissenters*: Unidentified.

11 *Spread Such Things thro' the Country*: In the *Review* Defoe notes that he is 'in the Country, very remote', and shocked at 'how the People are Debauch'd, by *Popish* and *Jacobite* Agents, from their Foundation Principles, in Matters of Government and Constitution'. He mentions that 'Printed Papers are dispers'd cunningly among the Country People, which you in *London* never see, and written ones yet more' (IX, 101–2 (25 Oct. 1712); 92 (18 Oct. 1712)).

12 *Unprofitable Servant*: See Letter 13, note 5.

DEFOE TO [EARL OF OXFORD], 3 OCTOBER 1712

217

To [Robert Harley, Earl of Oxford]

3 October 1712

HEADNOTE: Defoe wrote from Newcastle with another account of the delusions he was encountering among Whigs and Dissenters outside of London. Defoe's *A Seasonable Warning and Caution against the Insinuations of Papists and Jacobites in Favour of the Pretender*, published around this time, was written to 'undeceive the Good People of *Britain*' regarding rumours that 'the Generality of the People are inclin'd to receive the *Pretender*'. These reports are fabrications 'calculated and prepar'd to deceive the Ignorant People in the Country'. Notably, the pamphlet does not simply insist on the integrity of the ministry, indicating Defoe's doubts about prominent figures such as Bolingbroke; but it does insist that the ministry is publicly acting on the basis of a Hanoverian succession and would be strengthened in that cause were the will of the people more overtly Hanoverian. 'There is a manifest Difference between the Fears of Honest Men, as that the Measures of the Ministry may encourage the Friends of the *Pretender*, and on the other Hand, the insolent Way of the *Jacobites* claiming the Ministry to be acting in their Behalf.' Defoe feared that the Jacobite agents were playing the ministry and the people against one another, trying to persuade each that the other favoured the Pretender. His advice to the people was to show a united front against Jacobitism: 'Is it not Evident that the Unanimous Appearance of the People of *Great-Britain* against the *Pretender* would at once render all the Party desperate, and make them look upon the Design as utterly Impracticable. As their only Hope is in the Breaches they are making in your Resolutions, so if they should see they gain no Ground there, they would despair, and give it over.'[1] Defoe made identical points in the *Review* at this time, such as when he argues that the Pretender can only be a threat if he captures 'the Affections ... of the People of *Britain*'.[2] In *An Appeal to Honour and Justice* (1715), Defoe speaks of *Seasonable Warning* as 'a Book sincerely written to open the Eyes of the poor ignorant Country People, and to warn them against the subtle Insinuations of the Emissaries of the *Pretender*, and that it might be effectual to that Purpose, I prevail'd with several of my Friends to give them away among the poor People all over *England*, especially in the *North*; and several thousands were actually given away, the Price being reduced so low, that the bare Expence of Paper and Press was only preserv'd, that every one might be convinc'd, that nothing of Gain was design'd, but a sincere Endeavour to do a publick Good, and assist to keep the People entirely in the Interest of the Protestant Succession'.[3]

DEFOE TO [EARL OF OXFORD], 3 OCTOBER 1712

My Lord

Mr Milton in his Paradise lost in the [   ]th[a] Book (it is I think) brings in Adam Listening with wonder and Astonishmt at ye Accot The Angell Gives him of The Great and strang[e][b] Things wch Shall happen in The world; and of The attempts Sathan Shall make to Ruine and Delude his posterity[4] — Comparing Those Great Things wth these Small I Could not but Think of That Description, when I found The poor Country people here, Wondring and Astonished, when they look back into The Noćons and falsities They had been[c] posess't with, and find That It was all Delusion and a[d] Ridiculous Cheat put upon them by a Party.

How did an honest Country Minister[5] stand Amazed when I would Not Agree That my Ld Wharton[6] was a Most Pious Devote Christian; <u>Sure I have liv'd in a wood</u> Said a Very Sensible and Considerable Man[7] at Gainsbro', when he heard That The late Juncto, had Ever push'd at ye Lord Treasurer Godolphin and The Duke of Marlboro'; and Said all the wicked Things of Them That have been Said Since, and That they Joyn'd wth Jacobites to Throw them Out;[8] If I Ventur'd to Say The queen was Not a Jacobite,[9] or That ye Ministry were protestants, That The Pretender was not Just comeing ashore and The like, tis hardly Possible to Tell yor Ldpp how ye people Lissen with a kind of Amazemt wch Testifyes, (1) how glad they are to hear it is So, and (2)[e] how they wonder at The Delusions They have been Undr before.

I am Now My Lord Reach't to Newcastle, wher (Except Lyn) I find the posessions I have hinted at The most Riveted of any plaće I have been at, and prinćipally Occasioned by Two Dissenting Ministers[10] who have been at London, and Convers't at ye Amsterdam and Hamlins Coffee houses[11] and who Came down with[f] Such a fraight of the Ridiculous Things Menćoned in My Last, That I Confess I am Amaz'd to See good Men Satisfye themselves in Drinking in Such Delusions and Spreading Them Among Others.

---

[a] [   ]th] *blank in MS*
[b] strang[e]]: *MS frayed*
[c] been] *interlined*
[d] a] *interlined*
[e] (2)] *interlined*
[f] with] *interlined*

DEFOE TO [EARL OF OXFORD], 3 OCTOBER 1712

There are (My Lord) besides These, Inumerable Storys Spread Among the Common people in Prejudiĉe of the Queen and of the present Mannagem^t as to ye Peaĉe^a and p[er]ticularly That The queen will have The Dutch give up their Barrier in Flanders,^{12} That ye French are to Carry On their Trade to ye South Seas and the like, and Tho' the Nature and the public Accounts of things plainly Contradict this yet it is hard to Open their Eyes.

The Jacobite party on the Other hand,^{b} behave wth So Much Imprudent Assuranĉe that Terrefyes the poor people wth the Apprehensions of the pretender and tho' they Ought to See^c That ye queen and the Ministry Are the Onely Security they have left against the Jacobite Faction, yet ye Other party blindly perswade Them, that The Queen and The Ministry are Their Enemies and That their Onely Danger is where Their Safety Indeed can Onely be.

Ile Trouble yor L^{dpp} No More wth these Follies. My Stay Among them is So Small as can not go farr, in Turning Such a Stream, but I Endeavour to Undeciev the most Reasonable and Moderate and leave Them to work upon ye Rest.

The great floods^{13} have hindred my Travelling for Some Time, The like Rains Especally on the border haveing not been known a long Time.

God Direct yor L^{dpp} to Heal the breaches Made Among us by a wretched party who however They Rage Against yor Person, have nothing to hope for, but from yor Wisdome and prudenĉe; and who like Children must be Saved against ye Struggles of their Own passions; Surely if yor L^{dpp} is Onĉe Made ye Instrument to Save Them from Their Feares, and From ye Pretender, and to Secure Their Religion, and Libertys, <u>As I hope</u> Even Their Deliveranĉe Must be a Burthen, it will load them wth So Many Blushes, and Self Reproaches at what is past.

I am

May it please yor L^{dpp}

yor Most Humble & Obedient

[*monogram*]

^{a} as to ye Peaĉe] *interlined*
^{b} hand,] *interlined*
^{c} See] 'See)' *in MS*

DEFOE TO [EARL OF OXFORD], 3 OCTOBER 1712

Newcastle Octob. 3. 1712[a]

Text: BL Add. MS. 70291, fols. ²66–7. *Address*: none. *Endorsed by Oxford* (fol. ²67ᵛ): Cl. Guilot Newcastle octo: 3 1712

---

[a] Newcastle Octob. 3. 1712] *written vertically down lefthand margin*

---

1 Defoe, *A Seasonable Warning and Caution against the Insinuations of Papists and Jacobites in Favour of the Pretender* (1712), 13, 14, 15, 13, 23.

2 *Review*, IX, 108 (1 Nov. 1712).

3 *Appeal*, 26.

4 *Mr Milton ... posterity*: In books XI and XII of John Milton's *Paradise Lost* (1667–74), Michael foretells events from Genesis down to Christ's crucifixion. Defoe refers to the same section of *Paradise Lost* in *Christianity Not as Old as the Creation* (1730), ed. G. A. Starr (2012), 27. See Defoe's similar attempt to recall which book of the poem a particular image comes from, in *Review*, V, 173–4 (15 June 1708).

  Defoe engaged with *Paradise Lost* in numerous places. His most sustained treatment of it is in *The Political History of the Devil* (1726), in which he praises the poetry but faults the theology and its relation to biblical history (see John Mullan, 'Introduction', *SFS*, VI, 23–4). This ambivalence is typical. Defoe praised the sublimity of *Paradise Lost* in *Reformation of Manners* (1702), lines 1159–63, *SFS*, I, 188; *Review*, II, 784 (8 Dec. 1705); *Review*, VIII, 302 (18 Aug. 1711); and *Christianity Not as Old as the Creation*, 39. However, Crusoe complains that Milton's imagination took him too far (*Serious Reflections* (1720), *Novels*, III, 245). And, responding to Addison's commentary on *Paradise Lost*, Defoe challenged Milton on whether Adam and Eve had sex before the Fall (*Review*, VIII, 712–14 (29 Mar. 1711)).

5 *Minister*: Unidentified.

6 *Lᵈ Wharton*: See Letter 142. Wharton's irreligion was notorious.

7 *Man*: Unidentified.

8 *they Joyn'd wᵗʰ Jacobites to Throw them Out*: See headnotes to Letters 134–8. Defoe described these 1708 events in *The Conduct of Parties in England*. He had more recently discussed them in *Review*, IX, 52 (14 Sept. 1712).

9 *queen was Not a Jacobite*: The idea that the Queen is a Jacobite is one of the contradictions in politics Defoe exposed in *Review*, IX, 20 (16 Aug. 1712).

10 *Two Dissenting Ministers*: Possibly Benjamin Bennett (d. 1726) and his assistant Nathaniel Fancourt (d. 1720), who shared duties at the Church of the Divine Unity in Newcastle-up-on-Tyne (Eneas Mackenzie, *A Descriptive and Historical Account of the Town and County of Newcastle-upon-Tyne* (Newcastle, 1827), 371–2).

11 *Amsterdam and Hamlins Coffee houses*: On Bartholomew Lane and Swithin's Alley, respectively, both near to the Royal Exchange (Lillywhite, 261, 80–1). Colonel Jack hangs around the coffee house doors there (*Novels*, VIII, 63–5).

12 *Dutch give up their Barrier in Flanders*: The primary Dutch objective in the war was to secure a defensive barrier of fortresses as protection from French incursions and for their trade. In Oct. 1709, the Whig ministry and the Dutch States General agreed the first Treaty of Succession and Barrier. This was a dear bargain for Britain, keeping the Dutch in the war by granting them a series of fortresses that amounted to permanent control of the Spanish Netherlands. Unsurprisingly, the Tory government now considered it too generous in terms of both the fortress towns it accorded the Dutch and the trade privileges they would retain; they demanded its renegotiation. In a context of anti-Dutch feeling exemplified by Swift's *Some Remarks on the Barrier Treaty* (Feb. 1712), Defoe emphasised that the Dutch barrier was also Britain's barrier against French aggression (*Review*, IX, 7 (5 Aug. 1712); 96 (21 Oct. 1712)). For the second Treaty of Succession and Barrier, agreed in 1713, see Letter 225. For discussion,

713

DEFOE TO [EARL OF OXFORD], OCTOBER 1712

see Roderick Geikie and Isabel A. Montgomery, *The Dutch Barrier, 1705–1719* (Cambridge, 1930).

13 *floods*: On 24 Sept. 1712, Wodrow described 'the greatest land-flood that has been for ane age in Scotland, or in the memory of man at least' (*Analecta*, 11, 90).

218

To [Robert Harley, Earl of Oxford]

October 1712

HEADNOTE: Defoe spent a portion of October 1712 in Scotland where he found Church of Scotland ministers averse to the abjuration oath imposed on them by the Episcopal Toleration Act passed earlier that year. Ministers who failed to take the oath by 1 November faced deprivation. In the *Review* for 15 November 1712, Defoe defended the ministers who scrupled at taking it, reiterating that they were not hesitant about abjuring the Pretender but rather did not wish to pledge to reject any monarch not belonging to the Church of England, which amounted to a voluntary rather than passive submission to Episcopacy, hence a breach of the national covenants.[1] Defoe feared that a conjunction of the Whig interests in Scotland – the Squadrone which was actively opposing the government and the remnant of the Old Court party that had wielded influence in the days of Queensberry – could be a problem for the ministry, so he encouraged Oxford to sustain the current division. After this letter, no correspondence between Defoe and Oxford is known of until January 1713.

My Lord

Since My Last I have been Out of yᵉ Reach of any post Road wᶜʰ has hindred my writeing to yoʳ Lᵈpp. I am Now Return'd From a land of Distraccion and Confusion[2] and Indeed am at a loss how to Describe it to yoʳ Lᵈpp. The best Thing I can Say of it is That I hope it is an Uneasyness That will not Imediately Give yᵉ Governmᵗ any Disturbance. I Say Imediately Onely because I fear it will hereafter.

I find in yᵉ West and South part Many of the Ministers would Take yᵉ Oath but The people are So Enraged at Them That They Dare not, and This puts yᵉ poor Men to an Inextricable Difficulty, So That They are like to be Martyrs for a principle which they do

714

DEFOE TO [EARL OF OXFORD], OCTOBER 1712

not hold. I perswaded Some of Them to quallifye privately, and Continue preaching as if They had not quallifyed.

In Edinburgh There are Onely Four Ministers who will Refuse. These are Mr Webster of The Tol-booth Kirk,[3] mr Flint of The Old Kirk,[4] mr Hart of ye Grey Fryers[5] and mr Miller (an English man) of Lady yesters Kirk.[6] mr Hart I am in hopes will Complye.

I find The Squadroni Exceeding bussy in prompting Every[a] thing which Appeares Malecontent, and They Seem pleased at ye Breach This Makes, as They Think it prepares The Minds of the people for Something worse; and I can Not Say They Endeavour to Reconcile The people to ye Oath but Rather The Contrary, Tho' they Take it themselves.

There is a Manifest Distrust and Division between Those they call The last Court whiggs and The Squadroni,[7] and it were to be Wished Some Measures were Thought On to keep Them from Joyning, and I Menĉon it ye Rather because I See it is So Easie to be done (Viz) by Takeing off but One Man,[8] who yor Ldpp May have with a Word. I Referr The Rest Till I have ye honor to attend yor Ldpp.

It is for me Onely to Represent Dangers to yor Ldpp, Not to presume to prescribe Remedies, and Therefore I do not Descend to any Methods to be Taken wth those poor Distressed people. If They Merit any thing it is The Governmts Pity; but I fear They Shall Some Time or Other put Themselves out of The way of her Majties Clemenĉy; They are Entirely Naked and Defenĉeless, and yet So provokeing, That I See not how ye Governmt can long preserv its Authourity without Some[b] Method of Restraint Upon them.

I am allarm'd at my Comeing into ye Conversible part of ye World Again wth an Accot of yor Ldpps Indisposiĉon:[9] God preserv a life on wch So Much of ye Naĉons Safety Depends. Yor Ldpp Might have ye Satisfacĉon here of Seeing those people who are poisoned with Prejudiĉes from ye City Tremble at The Thoughts of That Persons being Removed who they kno' not how to Vallue when alive. They acknowlege That when They look beyond yor Ldpp They See Nothing but Confusion yet it is Not Among Their Mercys to See The hand That does Them good.

---

a Every] *the 'r' is interlined*
b Some] *interlined above cancelled illegible word*

DEFOE TO [EARL OF OXFORD], OCTOBER 1712

I Struggle in My Mean staċon with This Delusion But[a] in Some plaċes wth more Success than in Others.

I am

May it Please yo[r] L[dpp]

yo[r] Most Humble and Obed[t] Serv[t]

[*monogram*]

Newcastle Octob. [ ][b] 1712

Text: BL Add. MS. 70291, fols. [2]68–9. *Address*: none. *Endorsed by Oxford* (fol. [2]69[v]): Newcastle R nov: 10: 1712

---

[a] But] *interlined above cancelled word* 'and'
[b] Octob. [ ]] *blank in MS*

---

1 *Review*, IX, 120–2.
2 *land of Distracċon and Confusion*: Scotland.
3 *Mr Webster of The Tol-booth Kirk*: James Webster, with whom Defoe had argued about the Union in 1707 (see Letters 92 and 93).
4 *mr Flint of The Old Kirk*: John Flint (see Letter 189, note 11). Formerly a Cameronian, he was ordained in 1688 and became minister of West St Giles (or New North Church) in Edinburgh in 1710. The pulpit at the Old Kirk was temporarily vacant, so Flint may have preached there too (*Fasti*, I, 71, 143). He took the abjuration oath in 1719 when the reference in that oath to the monarchy remaining Anglican was removed (Thomas Boston, *Memoirs of the Life, Time, and Writings, of … Thomas Boston* (Edinburgh, 1776), 357–8). On 30 Oct. 1712, Flint wrote to Wodrow, listing eleven ministers in Edinburgh who had refused the oath (including all four Defoe names), and seventeen who had taken it (*Wodrow Corr.*, I, 321–33).
5 *mr Hart of y[e] Grey Fryers*: James Hart (1663–1729), minister at Old Greyfriars since 1702 (*Fasti*, I, 40). Despite Defoe's hopes, he did not take the oath. For evidence of Defoe's correspondence with Hart, see Letter 219. In Dec. 1714, while in London, Hart drew bills on Defoe on Flint's behalf. See John Robert Moore, 'Defoe and the Rev. James Hart: A Chapter in High Finance', *PQ* 19 (1940), 404–9.
6 *mr Miller (an English man) of Lady yesters Kirk*: William Miller or Millar (d. 1732), minister at Lady Yester's since 1708 (*Fasti*, I, 81). Like Flint, he took the oath in 1719.
7 *Distrust … Squadroni*: In the *Review* for 14 Sept. 1712, Defoe recounts again the 1708 division between '*Old Whig*' and *New Whig*'. 'New Whig' signified the Court Whigs or ministry led by Godolphin and Marlborough, along with its Scottish allies led by Queensberry. 'Old Whig' signified the Junto Lords, who allied with the Squadrone in Scotland (as well as Hamilton and the Jacobites) to try to bring down the ministry (IX, 52).
8 *One Man*: Unidentified.
9 *yo[r] L[dpp]s Indisposiċon*: On 9 Oct. Swift wrote: 'Ld Treas[r] has hd an ugly fit of th Rheumatism, but is now near quite well' (*Swift Journal*, 449).

716

John Russell to Defoe

30 October 1712

HEADNOTE: This final extant letter from Russell shows Defoe, now back in London, closing his account with Russell. Paula Backscheider surmises that 'this letter suggests that some of Defoe's affairs were in disarray … becoming tangled as they often had in England'.[1]

Edn[b] October 30 1712

Dear Sir

I intended to have writt by your Son[2] when he parted but not haveing then time to draw out your acco[t] delay'd it till next post And bussiness falling then ūnexpectedly in prevented my wryting; however I Send you now inclosed the acco[t] betwixt you & me, the ballance whereof is £289: 6 sh Scots[3] which I shall pay to Mr Flint[4] as you direct, only it is fit you send a bill upon me for the forsaid £289: 6 sh payable to Mr. Flint & let your draught upon me bear to hem full of all accots betwixt us preceeding the date of the bill. Mr Grierson[5] hes already my note as I formerly advysed you which will prevent what you feared from M[r] C:[6] And it is fit when ye draw upon me to Mr Flint that ye Send the bill to Mr Grierson who upon pay[t] will delyver up my note. Some days since M[rs] Anderson[a][7] came to my house wth a heavy complaint of you anent not paying these bills and your serving a subpena ag[st] her. I told her very frankly y[t] if it wes fact y[t] I wes informed of anent y[t] matter you had been very unkindly used. She told me M[r] Campbell positively refuised the aggreement you mention, as indeed he did at a communeing betwixt him and your son at which I was present. I Indeavoured, as your son no doubt hes told you, all that was in my power to have the matter setled but Since you both diffred So much in matter of fact it was impossible that I could give my Judgement in the affair; however I told her my mind freely And

---

[a] Anderson] *following illegible word cancelled*

JOHN RUSSELL TO DEFOE, 30 OCTOBER 1712

how much I thought She was out of the way to break wth you.
She at last took my promise to write to you & tell you y^t if your
conveniency could allow you to come any place within 12 or 20
miles of this She would wait upon[8] her Self and doubted not but
ye wou'd come to ane aggreement, but if your conveniency could
not admitt of y^t She was content to refer the affair to arbiters,
you chooseing one and she another, and begd ye would give me a
return. Our great freind hes been in ye country these two months
so y^t I have not Seen him; if any thing hes occurred for his Service
you may freely advyse me and Shall lay it befor him when he comes
to toun which I expect in a Short time. The oath of abjuration is
like to make a great rent in our Church, there being not above two
thirds of the whole ministry of Scotland that will qualify. I pray
God may prevent the lamentable effects of this breack; knowing
ye will be desireous to be informed of what hes passed anent^a y^t
matter in the place I referr you to ye Instrument inclosed[9] which
you may depend upon to be fact, I my self being one of the nottars
Sub[scrib]ing^b to it. I wysh the penalties of the law may not be
inflicted ag^t those who are non:jurants. I mean upon our side; None
of the Episcopall party will take it, And I am informed they will be
so [w]ise^c to forbear to preach. I saw your kind letter to Mr Heart[10]
& heartily [   ]^d wish he could take your advyce. I forgot to tell you
y^t ye other night I saw your bill upon Mr Herdman[11] which I had
left wth his wife to get recepted & had fallen by her hand and could
not be got when your Son was here, and I find the sume in it is 12
lib: Stl & you'l see by your acco^t she hes only payd 10 lib: for which
I would give her no receit unless she would pay the whole as She
had promised to me. She still insists upon some botles of wine you
got when here and refuses to pay the remainder. I desyre you may
write to her & tell her y^t ye depended upon the money according
to her promise to me. My wife is recovered & my children are well

---

^a anent] *interlined above cancelled word* 'in'
^b Sub[scrib]ing] *brevigraph expanded in this edition*
^c [w]ise] *MS torn*
^d [   ]] *MS torn*

DEFOE TO [EARL OF OXFORD], 7 JANUARY 1713

and give their humble service to you and your Son as doth Sir your
humble Servant.

Subserv^t

Jo Russell

Text: NLS MS. 25.3.9, fol. 80 [scribe's copy]. *Address*: To Daniell Defoe Esq: |
London

1 Backscheider, 'John Russell', 170.
2 *Son*: Benjamin Defoe. Benjamin settled in London and was enrolled in the Inner Temple in
   Aug. 1712 (Moore, 331).
3 *£289: 6sh Scots*: Less than £25 sterling. Where specified, amounts in Russell's earlier letters
   are in sterling.
4 *Mr Flint*: See Letter 189, note 11.
5 *Mr Grierson*: Possibly James Grierson (1662–1732), minister at Trinity parish in Edinburgh
   (*Fasti*, 1, 133), a close associate of Carstares. In 1719 he was Moderator of the General Assembly of the Church of Scotland.
6 *Mr C.*: Unidentified with certainty, but Backscheider's suggestion that it was John Campbell,
   Mrs Anderson's grandson-in-law, is plausible ('John Russell', 177 n. 56).
7 *Mrs Anderson*: Agnes Campbell Anderson. See Letter 186.
8 *wait upon*: I.e. 'wait upon you'.
9 *Instrument inclosed*: Untraced.
10 *Mr Heart*: James Hart. See Letter 218, note 5. Defoe's letter to Hart is untraced.
11 *Mr Herdman*: Unidentified.

220

To [Robert Harley, Earl of Oxford]

7 January 1713

HEADNOTE **(Letters 220 and 221)**: The first of these two letters is Defoe's first
known letter to Oxford in perhaps ten weeks. In the first half of January 1713,
he was evidently despondent, feeling neglected by Oxford, financially precarious,
assailed by enemy journalists, and ill.[1] Nonetheless, ever eager to be a good advisor, Defoe wrote to support a brass company's proposals to supply the Mint with
wrought brass rather than copper for coinage.

DEFOE TO [EARL OF OXFORD], 7 JANUARY 1713

My Lord

Yo^r L^dpps Indisposi̇con[2] is Not Onely My Missfortune But ye Nȧcons And I yet believ The Time will come when yor Enemyes will Acknowlege it, Tho' for So long as Heaven Permits, Sathan Hinders.[3]

The Earnest Desire I had to have Lay'd before yor L^dpp a brief Acco^t of My long Journey[4] has Made Me too Importunate; and My Own Circumstaṅces wch I can Not hide from yor L^dpp On whom Provideṅce and a Cruel Party have Made me More Than Ever Entirly Depending, have Concurr'd, and I Most Humbly ask yor L^dpps Pardon.

But a Perticular Spėcall Affair Moves me Now to Applye to yor L^dpp in a Case From ye Comp^a of Brass Manufacturers;[5] who have been wth me to State Their Affair, and wch I may Lay before yor L^dpp, previous to Their Public Applicȧcon.

They Say They Are Able to Serv ye Governm^t So, as to Save a Great Sum̄ in ye Vallue of Copper, for ye Coinage of Farthings, wch they hear is Now Und^r Dirėccon; They do not Offer at ye Coining Part, but at Furnishing Copper Ready Wrought for ye Work.

It is My Zeal for her Maj^ties Intrest wch I kno' yor L^dpp Makes yor Own, which Makes me Meṅcon This; and Shall be Very glad to have been So Offi̇cous, if yor L^dpp finds it as They alleage, Fitt to be Accepted; Assureing yor L^dpp I have no Other Intrest in it.

I am May it Please yor L^dpp

yor L^dpps Most Humble & Obed^t Servt

[*monogram*]

Jan. 7th 1712[6]

Text: BL Add. MS. 70291, fols. ^270–1. *Address*: none.

1 *Review*, IX, 158 (3 Jan. 1713).
2 *Yor L^dpps Indisposi̇con*: On 30 Dec. 1712 Swift wrote: 'I calld this Evening at Ld Treas^rs, and sate with him 2 hours; he has been cupped for a cold, & has been very ill' (*Swift Journal*, 474).
3 *Sathan Hinders*: 1 Thess. 2:18. See Letter 114, note 15.
4 *My long Journey*: His trip to Scotland and back.
5 *a Case From ye Comp^a of Brass Manufacturers*: The proposal of Charles Tunnah and William Dale to coin a thousand tonnes of halfpence and farthings was rejected. See the Master of the Royal Mint Sir Isaac Newton's (1643–1727) report to Oxford on the scheme (TNA MINT

720

DEFOE TO [EARL OF OXFORD], 15 JANUARY 1713

19/2/435), as well as John Craig, *The Mint: A History of the London Mint from A.D. 287 to 1948* (Cambridge, 1953), 220–1.

6 *1712*: 1713 new style.

221

To [Robert Harley, Earl of Oxford]

15 January 1713

My Lord

The Afflicċon it is to me to have Lost yᵉ Favour of being Admitted to yoʳ Lᵈpp as Usuall,[a] I can Not Express; If I were Consċious of haveing Dishonourd That favour, Or done Any thing willingly to Offend yoʳ Lᵈpp, I Should kno', that I Ought to Expect it as a just Punishment.

I Humbly Ask leav to Claim yoʳ Lᵈpps Promise to Me, Made long Agoe, That if in any thing I Incurr'd yoʳ Dislike, or Displeased you, I should kno' it first from yoʳ Self: No Man Alive would if Occasion p[er]mitted, Serv yoʳ Lᵈpp wᵗʰ a More Dissintrested Zeal, at More hazard, or p[er]haps So Much, from a Sinċere Prinċiple of affecċon to yoʳ Intrest, Shall I Say (My Lord) No Man has been Used like me by this Furious Age,[1] For Openly Avowing My Self in yoʳ Intrest tho' My Serviċes are but small.

I am not Saying (My Lord) what I have been able to do. I am not Either Vain to boast, Or Reflecting; But What I have a will and Inclinaċon to do, I may; and wᵗʰ the Greatest Humillity I Say, <u>No Man has More</u>, But when I Speake of yᵉ Treatment I Meet with in yᵉ world; for Even but a Will to Render My Self Usefull to yoʳ Intrest, There my Lord I Suffer, as if I had been More yoʳ Lᵈpps Instrument Than I have Vanity to Suppose I was Ever Capable of.

The Disstresses I am Reduċʹt to by This, tho' they plead Nothing wᵗʰ yoʳ Lᵈpp by way of Demand, yet They Claim yoʳ Pity and Compassion, Because They Oppress me on a Supposiċon of My haveing The honour of Serving yoʳ Lᵈpp.

[a] as Usuall,] *interlined*

721

DEFOE TO [EARL OF OXFORD], 15 JANUARY 1713

At Least my Lord, I would Humbly hope, The Popular Hatred Incur'd by Me, for Opposeing This Enrag'd Party, Shall[a] not be a ground to Lose me your Favour, which would Cause Them to Triumph Over My Disstress.

I kno' yoʳ Lᵈᵖᵖˢ Goodness, and have had long Experience of it. I kno' yᵉ being Ruin'd for adhereing to princíple, and The True Entrest of yᵉ Nacon, which yoʳ Lᵈᵖᵖ Allways made yoʳ Own, Can Not Dissoblige you, Nor does any Man Suffer (My Unhappy Case Excepted) for Faithfully Espouseing her Majᵗⁱᵉˢ Intrest without being Otherwise Comforted.

While yoʳ Lᵈᵖᵖ was pleased to be The Instrument of her Majᵗⁱᵉˢ Bounty to me I Chearfully Fac't Them all; But if I lose That Relief I must Fall Under Their hands who have no Mercy and be as Miserable as they can Wish.

Nothing but an Extremety of this kind Could Oblige me to Expose my Case So Much, But were it possible to Describe The Treatment I have from These people, and yᵉ Circumstances I am Reduc't to[b] by it, Unless yoʳ Lᵈᵖᵖ on whom Under God I Depend Deliver and Support me,[c] It would Move yoʳ Compassion beyond what I can hope for.

I most Humbly Entreat yoʳ Lᵈᵖᵖˢ Favour, That her Majᵗⁱᵉˢ Bounty wᶜʰ I have Enjoy'd by yoʳ Goodness and Intercession May not be stopped,[2] Since being Malitiously Depriv'd of all bussiness and Other[d] Subsistance by the Party fury of yoʳ Lᵈᵖᵖˢ as well as my Enemyes, I Shall be Reduct to yᵉ Uttmost Distress if I am Depriv'd of yoʳ Lᵈᵖᵖˢ assistance.[3]

I am

> yoʳ Lᵈᵖᵖˢ Most Humble and Most Obedᵗ Servᵗ
>
> [*monogram*]

Jan. 15. 1712[4]

Text: BL Add. MS. 70291, fols. ²72–3. *Address*: none.

---

[a] Shall] *amended perhaps from* 'Should'
[b] to] *interlined*
[c] me;] *interlined*
[d] Other] *interlined*

722

DEFOE TO [EARL OF OXFORD], 19 JANUARY 1713

1 *No Man has been Used like me by this Furious Age*: Defoe had been decrying and defying his critics in the *Review* for several months. On 2 Sept. 1712, he wrote that 'he that will speak plain Truth on both Sides, pleases neither' (IX, 39). On 4 Oct. he pledged, 'however unkindly I think myself Treated', to continue his public-spirited work (IX, 73). And on 11 Nov., he indicated that the righteousness of his cause is confirmed by the invective he provokes: 'With such Manners shall all those be Treated, who Sacrifice themselves for a Cause, *tho' never so honest*' (IX, 118).

2 *Bounty ... stopped*: Claude Guilot was paid £100 the next day, 16 Jan. (TNA T 48/16, fol. 86).

3 *Depriv'd of all bussiness ... assistance*: The allusion to being deprived of business is obscure and unexplained; for payments to Defoe in the following months, see headnote to Letter 225.

4 *1712*: 1713 new style.

222

To [Robert Harley, Earl of Oxford]

19 January 1713

HEADNOTE (**Letters 222 and 223**): Defoe's plaintive letter of 15 January seems to have prompted a response from Oxford, as well as payment. Defoe's responses in turn urge legal action against Whig journalists (especially Ridpath), which became his constant counsel to Oxford during the remainder of the reign.[1] He also presented the recoinage proposal of the brass company.

My Lord

What yor L^{dpp} was pleased to Say to Me,^{a} about ye Distracćon of a Party is Nothing but what I have Seen wth great Regret, and what I have Long waited an Occasion to Lay before yor L^{dpp}.

It is This (My Lord) which I have Lamented in My Own Case; That haveing No Assuranće of Support, Or of yor L^{dpps} Favour, I have Not Dared to Tell Them So plainly, as I would do, and as They Deserv, how They Prevent her Maj^{tie} and yor L^{dpp} doeing Even Themselves ye Good^b you would do Them and as far as in Them lyes do The Naćon all The Mischief They Are able.

It is my Missfortune to be what I Never was, Espećally in a just Cause (Viz) a Coward,[2] and Affraid to be at ye Merćy of Furious

^{a} Me] *following word* 'Me' *cancelled (accidentally repeated)*
^{b} ye Good] *interlined above cancelled word* 'they'

723

DEFOE TO [EARL OF OXFORD], 19 JANUARY 1713

and Foolish Party-Men, Meerly For want of That Capascity of Standing, which My Confidencĕ in yoᵣ Lᵈᵖᵖˢ Goodness Ought to Furnish me with; I Humbly Lay My Self at yoᵣ Lᵈᵖᵖ[s] Feet**ᵃ** with This Resoluc̆on, That These wicked Designs shall Never want a due Reproof and For My Self I will Still Depend Upon yoᵣ Goodness, That you will not Suffer a Mean Servant to Perish in The Defencĕ of his Country, And yoᵣ Lᵈᵖᵖ.

The attempt if possible to Raise a Mob to Insult The French Ambassador,[3] On pretencĕ of Importing wrought Silks, French Wines, &c. Custome Free, This I purposed to Accquaint yoᵣ Lᵈᵖᵖ of, and how bussy They have been in Spittle Fields[4] to That purpose — As to his Exellᶜᵉ Importing a great Many Bales of Jesuits and Priests a Sort of Goods Contraband[5] — This however Ridiculous here, They Make great Use of in yᵉ Country, and print Libells[6] about it Stuff't with all The Simple and Absurd Stuff in yᵉ world, yet it Takes with Their Party.

The Distracćon Runs Now (My Lord) to Such a hight That They are not Backward to Own That Horrid Princ̆iple of <u>The worse The Better</u> and That all Our Safety Now Lyes in bringing All Things into Confusion. They Say Openly They Desire The Ministry would bring in The Pretender, and That Enflameing the Naćon is The Onely way to Deliver Them.

To This End Their Incendiary The Flyeing post goes on with Such a kind of Unsufferable Insolencĕ, and They Triumph So in The Ministrys Forbearancĕ,[7] That Really he does a Very great Deal of Mischief. They Openly Boast The Governmᵗ Can Not Touch him, That Four Informaćons Are Layd[8] indeed but The Ministry Dare Not Trye Them, That They Are Ready for Them Let Them begin when They will, and The like. This My Lord No Government Can bear, and I am Sure The Late Ministry did Not bear it.

There is No Doubt my Lord Any jury in England would bring in That paper a libell Inumerable passages are to be found in it which They blush at Themselves, and I could give yoᵣ Lᵈᵖᵖ abundant Assurancĕ That if The Fellow were push't he will Never

---

ᵃ Lᵈᵖᵖ[s] Feet] 's' *omitted;* 'Feet' *interlined*

724

DEFOE TO [EARL OF OXFORD], 19 JANUARY 1713

Screen the Author[9] long. I kno' him to be No Man of Senĉe or Principle.

I Never was forward to prompt any Mans Fate or Dissaster. I believ yor L^dpp knows it is Not My Temper. But Never Governm^t was Insulted in Such a Manner, and Never Cause was So kept alive by The Scandall and Ribaldry of So Insolent an Author.

I have Many Other Things to Lay before yor L^dpp but I wait The Time when yor L^dpp will admitt me, and shall attend to Morrow According to yor Commands.

I am

yor L^dpp^s Most Humble & Obed^t Servt

[*monogram*]

Jan. 19. 1712[10]

Text: BL Add. MS. 70291, fols. ²74–5. *Address*: none.

1 Defoe looked back on Oxford's restrained treatment of the Whig press in *The Secret History of the White-Staff, Part III* (1715), 65–6. As is typical of Defoe's defence of his patron after his fall, Oxford's lenience is portrayed as simultaneously commendable and blameworthy.

2 *Coward*: See the preface to vol. VIII of the *Review*, published 31 July 1712, in which Defoe avers that the truth and a just cause prevent him from being a coward (VIII, 7).

3 *Mob to Insult The French Ambassador*: Louis d'Aumont de Rochebaron, duc d'Aumont (1666–1723), who arrived in London on 2 Jan. 1713, a source of anxiety for those who saw him as a Jacobite emissary proximate to the British Court. Whether by accident or arson, his house was burned down on 26 Jan. (*Evening Post*, 24–7 Jan. 1713; *Swift Journal*, 488–9).

4 *Spittle Fields*: The centre of London's weaving industry, home to many Protestant refugees from France; its denizens were hostile to the prospect of imported French cloths (hence the joke about 'Bales of Jesuits').

5 *Bales of Jesuits and Priests a Sort of Goods Contraband*: Defoe ridicules the clamour against the ambassador, based on allegations he had illicitly brought French goods to sell in Britain. The same joke about d'Aumont not importing French comestibles but rather a train of Catholic attendants appears in *Review*, IX, 191–3, 195 (22 and 24 Jan. 1713).

6 *Libells*: Trading on anxieties about the prospect of a renewal of trade with France, broadside ballads in 1712, such as *The French Pedlar* and *The Merchant A-la-Mode*, portrayed d'Aumont as a huckster. *The Merchant* also insinuated that Oxford was a Jacobite. Defoe criticised this Whig campaign in *Memoirs of Count Tariff* (1713), *SFS*, III, 183.

7 *Flyeing post ... Ministrys Forbearanĉe*: The *Flying Post* attacked the Tory ministry through its column, 'The Present State of Fairy Land' during summer 1712. In the *Review* for 25 Nov. and 27 Dec. 1712, Defoe grumbled about the 'Impunity' with which it proceeded. Ridpath's paper also lashed Defoe. Its 21–3 Oct. issue criticised him for saying that the rise in popular Jacobitism was the Whigs' as much as the Tories' fault.

8 *Four Informaĉons Are Layd*: Both arrested in early Sept., *The Flying Post*'s publisher, William Hurt, faced one charge of sedition and its author, George Ridpath, faced three. They had been on bail since 23 Oct. 'We have the dog under prosecution, but Bolingbroke is not active

DEFOE TO [EARL OF OXFORD], 23 JANUARY 1713

enough', wrote Swift (*Swift Journal*, 455). Ridpath was tried and convicted of two counts on 19 Feb. 1713; his sentencing was deferred and he fled justice in May 1713, first to Scotland and then to the Netherlands. For a detailed account, see *Miscellany of the Abbotsford Club, Volume First* (Edinburgh, 1837), 374–8. Defoe attacked Ridpath as an exiled fugitive in *Memoirs of Count Tariff, SFS*, III, 174, 191.

9 *Fellow ... Author*: Hurt and Ridpath, respectively.

10 *1712*: 1713 new style.

223

To [Robert Harley, Earl of Oxford]

23 January 1713

My Lord

I had Not given yor L^dpp The Trouble of my^a calling last Night, but (as I Understood yor Servant) by yor L^dpps Command and Ask Pardon For The Mistake.

At ye Severall Times I have had ye hono^r to See yor L^dpp (yor Leisure Not Admitting Me to Give you The Trouble) I have forborn Offring The Enclosed proposal^1 — I Thought it Might be Improper to Delay it Longer, Least as The people alleage, it be of Reall Service to ye Government That benefitt Should be also Delay'd: It Relates to a petición which I Enclosed Some Dayes Ago From ye Brass Comp^a to Supply wth Copper Plates for Coinage. If it be of Public Use, I Shall be glad to have Comunicated it, if Not I hope for yor L^dpps Pardon; They will Applye in The Ordin^a way by Petición to yor L^dpp, and My Laying it before yor L^dpp Thus, was in Ord^r to have stated The Thing for yor Immed[i]ate^b Informatión in Case yor L^dpp had found it Needfull.

I am May it please yor L^dpp
yor Most Obed^t Humble and Faithfull Servt
[*monogram*]

Jan. 23. 1712.^2

---

^a my] *interlined*

^b Immed[i]ate] 'i' *omitted*

726

Text: BL Add. MS. 70291, fols. ²76–7. *Address*: none.

1   *Enclosed proposal*: Missing.
2   *1712*: 1713 new style.

224

William Carstares to Defoe

10 February 1713

HEADNOTE: Though only one letter survives between Defoe and Carstares, one of the most influential ministers of the Church of Scotland, it attests, like several references in each man's letters to Oxford, to a mutual respect and friendship of several years' duration.[1] Defoe evidently passed the letter to Oxford.

Edʳ Feb: 10. 1713.

Sir

I am heartilie glad to hear that you are safe at London, and shall be glad to hear too that you find the heat of parties so farr at least abated, as that they will allow themselves calmlie to consider what may be for the publick safetie and quiet.

As for us here, our matters are in such a posture as it is hard to frame a Judgment of them; they seem to be in a suspence till it be seen what course the Parˡᵗᵗ will steer, but our Jacobits are unaccountable in their bold and foolish actings in some places, and as I am informed they seem to be much displeased with our great friend,[2] which I must say doeth not much grieve me; I only wish he might have more of support and encouragement from men of another kidney, for I have a great honour and true concern for him and doe allways attend him with my best wishes.

My great design Sʳ in troubling you with these lines is earnestlie to desire that when at any time you see our noble friend, you would take occasion to putt him in mind of my brother in law Major Coult,[3] who you know hath been long an Officer, is a gentleman of true merit and worth and Justlie esteemed as such here, and

WILLIAM CARSTARES TO DEFOE, 10 FEBRUARY 1713

is of untainted integritie. He had an Act to be Major of the Castle of Edr, and additional pay before the Union which is of late retranched, though her Matie hath been pleased to continue[a] to some others the advantages they had before the Union though they were not allowed by the English establishment. That noble person when I was at London did shew an inclination to doe some kindnesse to Major Coult, and I hope he may yet doe something for him, both as to renewing his Commission as Major and restoreing his additional pay, if seasonablie putt in mind of him. I know Sr I may with confidence leave this affair to your discreet mannagement. I trouble you with my heartie respects to your Lady and the young Ladies your daughters, not forgetting your sons; believe me to be without complement

Sir
your most faithfull
humble servant
W Carstares

Text: BL Add. MS. 70049, fol. 76. *Address* (fol. 76r): To | Daniel De Foe Esqr

---

[a] continue] *interlined above cancelled word* 'allow'

---

1 See Letter 90 and Letter 125, note 2.
   Charles Eaton Burch attributed to Defoe a proposal sent to Carstares for encouraging English Dissenters to send their sons to the University of Edinburgh, of which Carstares was the Principal ('Benjamin Defoe at Edinburgh University, 1710–11', *PQ* 19 (1940), 343–8). Backscheider supports the attribution (*Life*, 309–10), but there is no concrete evidence (Novak, 375 n. 32).
2 *our great friend*: Oxford.
3 *Major Coult*: See headnote to Letter 189. For Carstares's earlier appeals to Oxford on Coult's behalf, see Letter 190, note 2. Upon Coult's death in 1714, Carstares appealed again to Oxford for an allowance for Coult's widow (Carstares's sister) and children (H.M.C. *Portland MSS*, x, 313).

DEFOE TO [EARL OF OXFORD], 14 FEBRUARY 1713

225

To [Robert Harley, Earl of Oxford]

14 February 1713

HEADNOTE: By February 1713, with the peace treaty imminent but as yet unannounced, the barrage of Whig propaganda accusing the ministry of covert Jacobitism had reached an apogee. In this letter Defoe reports on some of the rumours, tending to paint the bleakest picture. He was himself anxious about the true motives of the ministry, so may have wanted to jolt Oxford out of complacency or gauge his intentions. The record of payments to Defoe suggests that he was being well rewarded at this time.[1] He also felt vindictive towards journalists who had attacked him as an apostate Whig and hireling of the Tories. Ridpath of *The Flying Post* was particularly in his sights.

My Lord

In My last[2] I Menčoned The Usefullness and Serviče Severall wayes of Some Measures for Seperateing The Squadroni in Scotland. I could not Refrain (tho' I hope to Attend yor Ldpp on Monday[3] According to yor Command) Gieveing a Short Accot to yor Ldpp of The Restless attempts of The Disstracted people here to Carry on Their professt Aversion to her Majties Measures.

More Espečally That Their present View is to allarm and Amuse The Common people wth Terrible Dismall Apprehensions Of Popery and The Pretender.

Under The first head They are Now Spreading it Over ye Countrys That The papists Are Arming and Prepareing for a Generall Massacre, That Inumerable Numbers of Priests and Irish Papists are Come Over <u>and The like</u> with which They Really Amuse The poor people and Render Them Very Uneasie Especally in The Country.

Of Their Suggestions About The Pretender I Shall give yor Ldpp a Farther Accot but for ye present Humbly Lay before yor Ldpp a Paragraph or Two Coppyed Out of a letter[4] I Recd Last post Out of Lincoln Shire wch I Thought Very Nečessary to Accquaint yor Ldpp of — and is as folls:

"We Are Very Much Disturb'd here wth the News Our friends write us from London and with The Paper called The flying Post, wch Has been Sent Enclosed like a Circular

729

DEFOE TO [EARL OF OXFORD], 14 FEBRUARY 1713

letter Over all This Country, Suggesting Very strange and
Unaccountable Things, which allmost Sink us, and had we not
Some hopes That These Things are not True in Fact but Meer
Entities of his Own Brain, it would quite Overwhelm us.

"The first is the Affair of m^r Lewis^5 wch has made So much
Noise in Town and Country. The Substance of The story he
Takes Out of the Dayly Courant.^{6} I wish you would Explain
That affair to us, for he Insinuates a Direct Correspondence by
it between Our Court and That of St Germans.

"The Next Relates to y^e New$^{\mathbf{a}}$ Treaty of Barrier and
Succession, Concerning which The Flying-Post Tells us,
That what Ever Our Danger Shall be The Dutch are Come
Under Obligacon Never to come to Our Assistance Till The
Government Or Ministry That Shall then be Shall Send
for Them, and this they Represent as Effectually Tyeing Up
the hands of the Dutch to leav us to y^e Mercy of a Jacobite
Ministry.^{7}

"Another Story he Tells us is of a Design in The Next
Parliam^t to Settle the Succession So as The Queen Shall leav
it by will to whom She Pleases^8 and This is Much Magnifyed
by private letters From . . . . &c$^{\mathbf{b}}$

"Another Story by the S^d letters is That The Ministry
Design to Complim^t The Freeholders and Landed Men by
Takeing off The Land Tax Entirely and Laying a Settled and
Excessiv load Upon stock and That a Vast Loan to The Queen
is to be Made Upon That Fund, The Ministry Designing for
Their Secret purposes to get all the Money in The Nacon into
Their hand.

"These Are Dismall stories I must Own but what Very
Much Supports me is That I believ Them to be Most if not all
of Them False — If these Men have no grounds for what they
write I Think They are Very ill Suffred^9 Not Onely as Causing
Very Unreasonable but Very Anxious p[er]plexing Thoughts
in the breasts of the best people, but as Endeavouring thus
to Support a Cause That Never till Now wanted Lyes and

$^{\mathbf{a}}$ New] *interlined*

$^{\mathbf{b}}$ &c] *MS contains an asterisk at the end of this paragraph and a corresponding one in the left margin, indicating an intended insertion, but no text has been added*

730

DEFOE TO [EARL OF OXFORD], 14 FEBRUARY 1713

Chimericall Contrivances for a Refuge and also putting those Things into The heads of Our Enemyes which p[er]haps They Never thot of before."

I Could not But Lay These Things before yor Ldpp who Alone is able to Correct The Insolence of These people who are Justly called Incendiaries. I Do Not fail to Use My Uttmost Endeavours in all places to Undeciev The people and Expose These wicked Designs. But what is The Uttmost So Mean a hand can do! Yor Ldpp can Applye The More Imediate Cure.[10] My Author is a Dissenting Minister but One of Differing Nocons and Temper from these people. I Humbly Lay this Matter at yor Ldpps feet and am

> May it please yor Ldpp
> yor Most Humble & Obedt Servt
> [*monogram*]

Feb 14. 1712[11]

Text: BL Add. MS. 70291, fols. [2]78–9. *Address*: none. *Endorsed by Oxford* (fol. [2]79v): Cl: Guilot febr: 14: 1712/13 **R** febr: 15

1 Guilot received £100 on both 24 Feb. and 6 Mar. 1713 (TNA T 48/16, fols. 67, 68).
2 *My last*: Untraced.
3 *Monday*: 16 Feb.
4 *letter*: Untraced, and the author unidentified.
5 *Affair of mr Lewis*: The Whigs sought to brand Erasmus Lewis, Undersecretary to the Earl of Dartmouth, a Jacobite and thereby tarnish the ministry. An officer in the French service named Charles Skelton wished to call on Lewis to thank him for granting a pass to visit England, but he mistakenly called on Henry Lewis (or Levi), a merchant. A rumour then spread of secretive correspondence between the Secretary of State's office and the Pretender's Court at St Germains. See *Wentworth Papers*, 316, 318.
6 *Dayly Courant*: On 29 Jan. *The Daily Courant* reported that Henry Lewis had sworn before the Lords of the Cabinet Council that the story was false; but on 31 Jan. Lewis responded with a counter-advertisement clarifying that Skelton's misunderstanding did occur, which reignited the rumours. Erasmus Lewis's friend Swift vilified Henry Lewis for contradicting himself (*Swift Journal*, 488–9; *Examiner*, vol. III, no. 21 (30 Jan.–2 Feb. 1713), *EPW 1711–14*, 205–10). The Whig *Flying Post* for 31 Jan.–3 Feb. printed a series of queries aiming to stoke the scandal, such as claiming that Tories like Swift were falsely making out Lewis was a Jew, and hence untrustworthy, by naming him Levi.
7 *Treaty of Barrier and Succession ... Jacobite Ministry*: As well as specifying the fortresses that would comprise the Dutch barrier, the 1709 Treaty of Succession and Barrier (see Letter 217, note 12) committed the Dutch to lend forces to ensure the Protestant succession occurred in Britain following Anne's death. The 1713 Treaty of Succession and Barrier replaced that of 1709. Signed at the end of Jan., it stated that the Dutch would intervene in the British succession only upon request. See Coombs, 362–72; Roderick Geikie and Isabel A. Montgomery, *The Dutch Barrier, 1705–1719* (Cambridge, 1930), 284–98. Here, Defoe exaggerates about *The*

731

Flying Post's reports on article fourteen of the Treaty. See *Flying Post*, 3–6 Jan. 1713, and the following issues. Defoe defended the 1713 barrier on the basis that it was still stronger than older Dutch demands, and that it would have been even better had the Dutch and Austrians not lost ground to the French by recklessly engaging in the Battle of Denain in July 1712, where they were defeated (*Review*, IX, 298–301 (26 Mar. 1713)). Defoe also dismissed Swift's claim in *The Conduct of the Allies* (Feb. 1712) that a strong Dutch barrier would enable the Dutch to overtake Britain in woollen manufacture (*Review*, IX, 350–3 (25 Apr. 1713)). In *Memoirs of Count Tariff* (1713), Defoe indicates that the Dutch guarantee of the Hanoverian succession in Britain is needless.

8 *Design ... Pleases*: Wodrow comments on this report too (*Analecta*, II, 160).
9 *They are Very ill Suffred*: I.e. it is dangerous to tolerate what they are doing.
10 *Iṁediate Cure*: Ridpath's trial was five days later, and he was found guilty.
11 *1712*: 1713 new style.

226

To [Robert Harley, Earl of Oxford]

1 April 1713

HEADNOTE: On 23 March Defoe was arrested for a £1,500 debt dating from before his 1706 bankruptcy and spent eleven days in debtors' jail, from where he wrote to Oxford. He managed to persuade the creditor to accept £150, and just £25 in ready money. Defoe believed that the creditor had been put up to reviving the old debt, which Defoe believed settled, by political enemies of the ministry. Nine months later, in response to Henry Martin's misrepresentation of the episode, Defoe gave his version in his periodical *Mercator*.[1]

My Lord

The last Time I had yᵉ honour to See yoʳ Lᵈᵖᵖ, was Upon[a] The Case wᶜʰ I had Lay'd before yoʳ Lᵈᵖᵖ of Clark of Darby Shire,[2] and the Clamours of The foolish People on That Occasion: Had Not yᵉ Accident of wᶜʰ I Shall Speak presently Interven'd, I had waited on yoʳ Lᵈᵖᵖ to Relate The Victory I Gain'd Upon that Occasion; when I came to Talk with those people Again, How Mute and Asham'd they stood, when I ask'd them, If they Could Name Me any One Man to whom yoʳ Lᵈᵖᵖ had allow'd the Liberty of Selling a Civil Employmᵗ? and when they Could not Say they could Name

---

[a] was Upon] *interlined*

DEFOE TO [EARL OF OXFORD], 1 APRIL 1713

any, I ask'd, how then they could Say this was a Singling Out a Dissenter? and where ye Dissenter was who <u>Even Since the late act</u>[3] had been Prosecuted, tho' I Nam'd them Severall, who kept Posts in the Publick Offices and Were Seen at The Meeting houses Every day, and Some who went Railing about in Coffee houses all The Week at That Very Governm^t whose bread they Eat.

After That, I Saw the Man himself. I Convinc't him that his friends, as he tho^t them, were far from doeing him any Service in the Noise They Made; and That if those Things were prompted by his Complaints; I could liken his Case to Nothing So Readily, as that of Adonijah, in the Text, who Not Content wth haveing been Spar'd by Solomon, Ask'd a foolish Favour against his Own life;[4] I Told him if these things Came to ye Governments Eares, he Ought to Think it an Unusuall Clemency, if he was Permited to Enjoy what he had. The Man I believ was Satisfyed he was in ye wrong, and as I Hear is Since Gone home, and I Suppose yor L^{dpp} will be Troubled No More with him.

I had Lay'd Some Other Things before yor Lord^{pp} but am Oblig'd to Excuse my Self On The Following Occasion — I have Often Troubled yor L^{dpp} wth long Complaints of ye hardships I Meet wth from an Angry Party Upon their Nocons of My being in the Intrest of the Ministry and Entertain'd by yor L^{dpp}, and Tho' I have not ye Merit of Rendring yor L^{dpp} Any Services Worth Nameing, yet the Fury wth which These Men Treat me[5] is proporcon'd to the greatest, and Indeed they hono^r Me in their Malice as if I was Capable to Serv yor L^{dpp} More Than I can pretend to, tho' I Rather Judge They Show by it what Treatment Not yor L^{dpp} Onely but all Her Maj^{ties} faithfull Servants and best friends should Meet with if This party had the Power.

However My Lord I Never Thought that Party Resentment could have stoopt So low as to Persue it to private Injury till I was Surprised, as I was Comeing from home to have attended Upon yor L^{dpp} last Monday Seven night,[6] and Was^a Taken up by an Escape Warrant.

This sleeping Lyon, had been Retired, into the Country where the Creditor liv'd (at Yaremouth) Ever Since the year That by yor

---

^a Was] *interlined*

DEFOE TO [EARL OF OXFORD], 1 APRIL 1713

L^dpps Favour And Appointm^t I Travelled a journey into The West,[7] and when (which I Ought Never to forget) yor L^dpp was pleased to Concern yor Self for my preservacon from it.

It had Never More stirr'd had not a private Set of Men here, in Meer Revenge prompted and Even Sollicited the p[er]son to stirr Now, Assureing him That I had Great Favours &c. wch I am Satisfyed they knew Nothing of,[a] but believing that Such a process would Effectually Ruine and Destroy Me.

May it please yor L^dpp

Tho' I do Humbly Complain in this Manner, and am Indeed in Great Danger of being Quite Overwhelm'd by this Dissaster, yet I am Not Representing it to yor L^dpp to Plead for Unusuall Favo^rs; yor L^dpps Goodness to me has allways called for my Thankfullness, and left no Room for Encroachments Unless wth ye Uttmost breach of Modesty wch I hope is not in My Nature.

However Unhappy this May Render me, I Struggle to Submit to it, wth That Resignacon that becomes me. I have yet kept it from Comeing Abroad,[8] and am Striveing to bring it to Some Accomodacon if possible.

If yor L^dpp will allow me, in a Case of Such Extremety Humbly to^b Mencon, That ye Usuall Period of her Maj^ties Bounty[9] being a few days past, and wch yor L^dpps goodness would have allow'd me to Move (tho' this had not happend), If I Say yor L^dpp will be pleased to grant me that help at This Time, I shall hope to Dissentangle my Self without a public blow to My affaires.

I Would have Conceald this Dissaster from yor L^dpp, haveing too often Spoke of My Own Circumstances, but I fear'd My being So long Absent, might cause yor L^dpp to Think me Defficent in My Duty.

The youth that brings This is My Son,[10] and Shall attend if yor L^dpp please to Permit it, to bring Any Return yor L^dpp pleases to grant me to This Request —

With ye Humblest Submission to yor L^dpps pleasure, I Ask Pardon for this Mocon, and Tho' Now Distress't by a Faction,

---

[a] of] '*off*' *in MS*
[b] to] *interlined*

734

DEFOE TO [EARL OF OXFORD], 1 APRIL 1713

Rather than a Creditor; I shall allways Endeavour to Approve my Self, at what Ever hazard

yor L^{dpps} Most Humble faithfull and Obed^t Servt
[*monogram*]

p^{mo}. Apr^l 1713

Text: BL Add. MS. 70291, fols. ²80–1. *Address*: none.

---

1 *The British Merchant; or, Commerce Preserv'd*, no. 46 (8–12 Jan. 1714); *Mercator*, no. 101 (12–14 Jan. 1714).
2 *Clark of Darby Shire*: The individual and the circumstances are unidentified. It seems to refer to a Dissenter denied the liberty of selling his patent to some civil office.
3 *late act*: The 1711 Occasional Conformity Act.
4 *Adonijah … life*: 1 Kings 2:23. Adonijah was pardoned for his unsuccessful challenge to his half-brother Solomon's accession to the throne of Israel. But Adonijah's request to marry Abishag, their father David's concubine, was interpreted by Solomon as another attempt at usurpation, and Adonijah was killed. See 1 Kings 1:5–53, 2:13–25. Defoe makes the same allusion in *Review*, III, 794 (2 Jan. 1707); VII, 232 (13 July 1710); VIII, 183 (14 June 1711); 287 (9 Aug. 1711); *A Seasonable Expostulation with, and Friendly Reproof unto James Butler, … Duke of O——d* (1715), 15; *Political History of the Devil*, SFS, VI, 148.
5 *Fury wth which These Men Treat me*: Defoe had most recently complained about printed attacks on him in *Review*, IX, 228–9 (14 Feb. 1713).
6 *last Monday Seven night*: 23 Mar.
7 *journey into The West*: In 1705. In spring 1706, Defoe and John Fransham had corresponded about these unidentified creditors in Yarmouth. See Letters 45 and 49.
8 *Comeing Abroad*: I.e. being made public.
9 *her Maj^{ties} Bounty*: Claude Guilot had received £100 on both 24 Feb. and 6 Mar. 1713 (TNA T 48/16, fols. 67, 68).
10 *Son*: Depositions against Defoe in the matter of his three succession pamphlets (see headnote to Letter 228) indicate that both of Defoe's sons, Benjamin and Daniel, were running errands for him at this time (TNA SP 34/21, fols. 28–32).

DEFOE TO [EARL OF OXFORD], 11 APRIL 1713

227

To [Robert Harley, Earl of Oxford]
11 April 1713

HEADNOTE: The abjuration oath imposed as part of the Episcopal Toleration Act threatened to cause a schism in the Church of Scotland between jurants and non-jurants, and potentially an exodus of ministers into nonconformity.[1] Defoe and Oxford anticipated that the upcoming General Assembly would bring tensions into the open. Defoe addressed the abjuration oath in the *Review* during March 1713, impressing on readers its solemnity: whereas an oath of allegiance is contingent because monarchs can act in ways that forfeit their subjects' obedience, an abjuration is 'Indissolvible', making Jacobite jurants especially pernicious.[2] Defoe still advocated ministers taking the oath, but he refused to condemn those whose scruples caused them to refuse it.

My Lord

It was to pay the Duty of My Acknowlegem[t] to yo[r] great goodness to Me in My Late afflicc̆on[3] that I waited y[e] Other day On yo[r] L[dpp] tho indeed Not in Condic̆on to have come Abroad, And being still indisposed I beg leav to Lay Some Thoughts before yo[r] L[dpp] w[ch] [I] believ[a] of Moment Enough to Merit Som Considerac̆on.

The Affaires in Scotland, tho' yet quiet, Stand Very Tottering, and The Public peac̆e Seems to Turn upon Very Nic̆e and Criticall Points; The Division of The Ministers Among themselves I mean as <u>Jurant</u> And <u>Non jurant</u> Tends to a Wide Breach, and in The Approaching Assembly[4] may probably appear ill Enough stated. The <u>Non jurant</u> behave wth Rage and want of Charity to y[e] <u>Jurant</u>, and Are back't by The people who Especally in the West Treat y[e] last wth Insolenc̆e, Contempt, and Scarc̆ely keep the Peac̆e wth them, Universally forsakeing the Churches where They preach, and Refuseing to hear Them.

Hitherto y[e] Clemenc̆y of the governm[t] in forbearing to prosecute y[e] Penal part of the act[5] keeps them quiet as to Outrage and Violenc̆e. What Medium to find Out to keep them So Still Deserves the Governm[ts] Im̆ediate Care.

---

[a] [I] believ] 'believ' *in MS*

736

DEFOE TO [EARL OF OXFORD], 11 APRIL 1713

I kno' Some will Offer to yor L^{dpp} a proposall to bring in a Clause or bill to grant longer Time &c. for the Takeing the Oaths; I Confess My Lord I do not See that will be any Expedient because They will Naturally Contemn a grace that They do not Seek. That longer Time Must Some time or Other Expire; if <u>when it Expires</u> the Law is not prosecuted they will Conclude ye Government Either Approves their Contempt of it or is Not in a Condicon to Resent it.

If The Last The Ministers who have shown Their Wisdome and Loyalty to ye Government by Complyeing Will Really want her Maj^{ties} proteccon from ye Rabbles and Those poor wild people will bring her Maj^{tie} to a Necessity of useing Rough Means with Them On That Acco^t.

If On ye Other hand when the given Time <u>Expires</u>, Those who Refuse The Oath Now Refuse it Still As it is Certain They will, and The government allows or Commands ye putting the Law in Excecucon; those Ministers go Imediately to ye Hills as they call it, Set up Field Conventicles, and all the people Run after Them: If They are not Suppresst <u>then</u>, They will grow formidable to ye Peace, Insolent to ye Governm^t and Upon Occasion Dangerous. If They are <u>Then</u> Follows a Crye of Persecucon and They'l all Run to Arms as if on Purpose to Dye for Religion.

Pardon me (My Lord) The freedom of Thus Stateing the affair of those people wch I do with a True Zeal both for Their good and Her Maj^{ties} Intrest, Humbly adding My Thoughts Thus:

That Tho' it is True the Governm^t Seems Obliged to protect and as much as possible to Encourage Those who have Complyed wth the Laws, yet Since it is Many wayes Inconvenient to press too Warmly the Excecucon of Those Laws, It Seems better That those Ministers May yet labour Under Some Dissadvantages Than that ye Public Peace be Endangerd.

On ye Other hand My Lord, it May not be forgotten that if the Non jurant Ministers (I Mean Presbyterian all the Way[6]) are prosecuted, to a Dissposessing them of their liveing, a great Many of Them will Flock into England and Up to London, and what flames they will blow up Among a poor Distracted Sett of people here[7] yor L^{dpp} knows Very Well.

DEFOE TO [EARL OF OXFORD], 11 APRIL 1713

Upon The whole My Lord The affair Seems to Turn Upon this Single point which yor L^{dpps} wisdom will Determine, whether The proposall of a longer Time wth the Hazard of ye Inconveniences above Named is best Or whether keeping the Law as a Rod Over Their heads. The Excecucon May not be Delay'd Meerly as an act of Clemency and Forbearance, ye Certainty of its being Excecuted as well as the Reasons being Not known.

I am &c.

[*monogram*]

Aprill 11. 1713

I was goeing on wth this My Lord when ye Occasion Expresst in ye Cover to This[8] broke me off and I was fearfull They would have Taken this from me.

Text: BL Add. MS. 70291, fols. ²82–3. *Address*: none.

---

1 For the non-jurant perspective, see headnote to Letter 205. The jurant perspective was that the Act of Security that formed part of the Union Treaty limited the abjuration oath, making it a singular not perpetual pledge to uphold Episcopacy (*The Oath of Abjuration Considered, Both as to the Lawfulness and Expediency of it's being taken by the Ministers of the Church of Scotland* (1712)).

2 *Review*, IX, 281–90 (17 and 19 Mar. 1713).

3 *Late afflicton*: The exact nature of Oxford's intervention is not clear but presumably he supplied Defoe with what he paid to the creditor (see headnote to Letter 226). Novak suggests that the delay between the arrest and this letter, as well as Defoe's embarrassed tone, indicate that 'he was unwilling to involve Harley if he could help it' (425).

4 *Approaching Assembly*: The General Assembly of the Church of Scotland met from 30 Apr. to 11 May 1713.

5 *forbearing to prosecute ye Penal part of the act*: In 1708, parliament had amended the wording of the abjuration oath to remove phrases that Scottish Presbyterians found objectionable. No such latitude was given in 1712, but as yet no ministers had been fined or evicted from their livings for failing to take it. See Defoe's reference to 'Laws wch it will be Necessary to Break' in Letter 250.

6 *Presbyterian all the Way*: I.e. not the Episcopal refusers of the oath, who refused it because they were Jacobites.

7 *poor Distracted Sett of people here*: The Dissenters in England.

8 *ye Cover to This*: The following letter. Defoe was interrupted by arresting officers.

DEFOE TO [EARL OF OXFORD], 12 APRIL 1713

228

To [Robert Harley, Earl of Oxford]

12 April 1713

HEADNOTE (Letters 228 and 229): On 11 April, Defoe was arrested at his home in Stoke Newington after three Whig writers filed a complaint against him before the Lord Chief Justice Thomas Parker (1666–1732). Defoe was accused of writing against the Hanoverian succession. In fact, he had anonymously written three pamphlets with titles that suggested a Jacobite stance but truly undercut it through irony.

Reasons against the Succession of the House of Hanover, published in February, presents patently specious arguments for rejecting Hanover after the Queen's death. Importing a foreign king caused such fuss with William III, and crowning a Protestant in contravention of the divine, hereditary right of a Catholic had such dismal consequences for Lady Jane Gray, it argues, that the Elector of Hanover is better off left in peace in Germany. Besides, political strife will only persist or get worse under the Hanoverians, whereas the Pretender's tyranny would spell an end to partisanship. Defoe continues in this vein in *And What if the Pretender should come?*, published in March, laying out the benefits of receiving James III. France will be transformed from a threatening enemy to a constant ally, one whose conquest of Europe Britain can dutifully abet. Domestic strife will cease, as James will not trouble voters with elections, or burden MPs with the expense of bribing electors, preferring to rule without parliament, putting revenue into building a standing army rather than honouring the public debts contracted to fight a war with the purpose of keeping him out. The Union can be dissolved at once. Finally, in *An Answer to a Question that No Body thinks of, viz. But What if the Queen Should Die?*, published in April, Defoe drops the obvious irony, arguing that their self-interest currently keep the ministry, Louis XIV, and Pretender quiescent as long as the Queen lives, but her death would cause a constitutional crisis potentially fatal to the Protestant cause and rule of law.

His arrest was a surprise to Defoe; he could not imagine how anyone could interpret these pamphlets as anything but pro-Hanoverian or how such a disingenuous view of them could be countenanced.[1] The arrest was contrived and reported on with a view to maximising the damage against him and the ministry. First, the information against Defoe was obtained through subterfuge. Defoe's printer Richard Janeway (*c.* 1670–1713) was tricked into selling copies of *Reasons against the Succession of the House of Hanover*; the purchaser then intimidated Janeway into revealing Defoe's authorship by threatening him with a charge of treason. Janeway, Defoe's publisher John Baker, and members of their staff were deposed by Parker to confirm Defoe's authorship of the pamphlets.[2] The arrest was delayed from Friday 10 to Saturday 11 April, preventing Defoe appearing in court to tender bail

739

DEFOE TO [EARL OF OXFORD], 12 APRIL 1713

until Monday 13 April.[3] Next, *The Flying Post* reported that Defoe had fortified his house to resist the arresting officers, an allegation Defoe vehemently denied.[4] And a pamphlet was produced to shame Defoe yet further, accusing him of political apostasy, characterising him as 'an *High-Church Man* one Day, and a *Rank Whig* the Next', who was now writing for the Pretender. It summarised *Reasons* to make its ironic arguments sound sincerely anti-Hanoverian, and falsely stated that bail was refused because the pamphlet was treasonous.[5]

Defoe was in prison until Tuesday 14 April when he tendered £1,600 bail. He then published three issues of the *Review* – 16, 18, and 21 April – decrying the wilful misconstrual of his pamphlets by the Whigs.[6] He was appointed to appear before the court on 22 April.

My Lord

I am Really Asham'd to Lay before yor L^{d}pp So Scandalous an Acco^t of a party of Men (who Ought to know better), as I must do in Stateing my Affair to yor L^{d}pp.

The Persons, ye Pretencés and the Design are Equally foolish and Malitious.

The Persons, Are Benson,[7] Burnet,[8] and Redpath; all Three Under prosecucón from the Governm^t for Scandalous pamphlets, the first for ye Letter to Sr Jac. Banks,[9] The Second for a Book called <u>a Certain Discourse</u>,[10] The last for his flyeing Post.[11]

The Pretences Are Sev^{ll}, Some too Simple to Name, But they were heard to Say that they had all been prosecuted and the Review had a full Liberty but They would bring him in whether the Ministry would or no.[12]

The book wch Angers Them, is Entituled Reasons Against ye Hannover Succession where There[13] Own Topicks of the Allyes being Disobliged by the Peacé and Francé being a Power Irresistible and Our fatall Heats at home are Ironically Lay'd Down as Reasons why We Should think no More of the Succession &c. But all the Rest of ye book are Clear and professt Banters upon The Pretender.[14]

The perticular in all most grievous is That in all I Say,^{a} I Never would Allow that ye Queen and The Ministry were in the Intrest of the Pretender, wch however I Think Now her Maj^{ties} Speech[15] must make them Asham'd of.

---

^{a} I Say,] *interlined*

740

DEFOE TO [EARL OF OXFORD], 12 APRIL 1713

As to Their Design, I Find their first Noćon is, That The book is Treason, and That therefore My Ld Chief Justiće[16] should Refuse Bail, and Commit me to Newgate; which I am Some times Apprehensiv, my Lord May be Weak and warm Enough to do, and In that I Can not but beg yor L^dpps Interposition.

Their Next Design is Visibly an Insult upon ye Ministry, Pretending that ye Governm^t Neglecting to prosecute for an affront upon the House of Hannover They would Officously shew their Zeal and also to let the Ministry see they will prosecute who they please^a in the Governm^ts Name whether The Ministry will or no.

I forbear to Trouble yor L^dpp wth ye Contradicćons in this attempt. The Town begins to be Asham'd of it allready, for ye Whiggs (not Seeing the Satyr upon themselves in it) were all pleased with the book,[17] and Now they give Out that ye prosecution was for ye Scurrillous paper called The Ambassadress's Speech.[18]

I Think I Need Say no More to yor L^dpp, than give ye Names of the Persons and the Manner of their goeing to work, as a Test of the Design, Onely Hinting Again to yor L^dpp as a Reason for The Manner of writeing[19] in all these books, the Necessity There has been to give a Turn in all I Wrot, which should gratifye Some of the Weaknesses of those poor people, to Detect the Rest.

I Believ the greatest Injury they can do me is the Expenće and the Surprise:

the first the wound[20] wch yor L^dpp knows I had So lately makes me ill able to bear;

The last I hope will wear off.

I Humbly beg yor L^dpps Protection and Such Direcćons from the Secretarys Offiće, as may be tho^t proper by yor L^dpp, to make my Ld Chief Justiće Easye tomorrow, when I am brought before him: The Rest I Referr to Such Measures as The Nature of the Thing shall Direct afterwards; and as yor L^dpp shall think proper.

> I am
> yor L^dpps Most Obed^t Humble & Faithfull Servt
> [*monogram*]

Apr^ll 12. 1713

---

^a who they please] *interlined*

DEFOE TO [EARL OF OXFORD], 12 APRIL 1713

Text: BL Add. MS. 70291, fol. ²84–84 *bis*. [The consecutive leaves of this letter have mistakenly both been numbered '84'.] *Address*: none.

1   A reference to Defoe in a letter to Jean de Robethon (d. 1722), the Elector of Hanover's private secretary, also portrayed him as an enemy to the Hanoverian succession on the basis of these pamphlets (Geoffrey M. Sill, 'A Report to Hanover on the "Insolent De Foe"', *N&Q* 28 (1981), 224–5).

2   TNA SP 34/21, fols. 28–32. Baker's deposition indicates that Defoe had an established agreement of two guineas in payment 'for every six penny pamphlet ... upon the Sale of every Five hundred'. This probably dates back to 1710, when Baker started to print and sell the *Review* (and he went on to issue a number of Defoe pamphlets in the following years). Janeway deposed that for *Reasons against the Succession of the House of Hanover* he paid Defoe 'the usuall Price for a Pamphlet of that size', four guineas plus twenty-five copies per thousand. Defoe professed to send his own copies to Newcastle and Scotland, though Janeway suspected he sold them in London, contrary to their agreement.

3   *Review*, IX, 340 (18 Apr. 1713).

4   *Flying Post*, 14–16 Apr. 1713; *Review*, IX, 339 (18 Apr. 1713). *The Post Boy* for 14–16 Apr. 1713 reported that Defoe, Baker, and Janeway had all been arrested.

5   *Judas Discuver'd, and Catch'd at Last: Or, Daniel de Foe in Lob's Pound* (1713), 3. The claim that the charge was treason rather than libel seems to have been widely reported. See Folger Shakespeare Library, Newdigate Newsletters, L.c. 3601, 14 Apr. 1713.

6   Defoe recapitulated the events with unabated indignation two years later in *Appeal*, 28–37. See the Whig version written by Defoe's enemy John Oldmixon in his *History*, 509–10.

7   *Benson*: William Benson (1682–1756), architect and Whig polemicist. He was High Sheriff of Wiltshire in 1710 and MP for Shaftesbury, 1715–19.

8   *Burnet*: Thomas Burnet (1694–1753), son of the Bishop of Salisbury, later Consul of Lisbon, lawyer, and judge, knighted in 1745.

9   *Letter to Sr Jac. Banks*: Benson's *A Letter to Sir J—— B——*, originally published as *The History, or Present State of Sweden* (1711). Sir Jacob Banks was a Swedish-born naval officer, naturalised as British, and Tory MP for Minehead. During the 1710 election campaign he expressed support for Sacheverell by promoting the doctrine of passive obedience. In the pamphlet, Benson compared Banks's views to Swedish arbitrary government; he was prosecuted for seditious libel, bailed for £4,000, but not convicted. Benson unsuccessfully challenged Banks at Minehead in the 1713 general election.

10 *a Certain Discourse*: Burnet's *A Certain Information of a Certain Discourse. That happen'd at a Certain Gentlemans House, in a Certain County. Written by a Certain Person then Present, to a Certain Friend now at London. From whence you may Collect the Great Certainty of the Account* (1712). It was an attack on the ministry's peace policy and led to his arrest in Jan. 1713. It names Defoe among those who fabricated lies about Marlborough at the time of his removal (43). Burnet was also prosecuted for *Some New Proofs by which it Appears the Pretender is Truly James III* (1713).

11 *flyeing Post*: For the legal action against *The Flying Post*, see Letter 222, note 8. *The Flying Post* had continued to attack Defoe in the early months of 1713. After it jabbed at Defoe in the issue for 10–12 Feb., Defoe responded in the *Review* for 14 Feb., calling *The Flying Post* an 'enflaming *Incendiar[y]*' (IX, 229). Thereafter, *The Flying Post* for 19–21 Feb. accused Defoe of self-contradiction concerning the peace; that for 5–7 Mar. criticised his implication that the Whigs' attacks on the ministry were allowing the Jacobites to gain ground; and that for 11–14 Apr. reprinted part of the *Review* for 18 May 1708, when Defoe had argued against electing Tories. This was also printed separately. Defoe had most recently attacked Ridpath in *An Answer to a Question that No Body thinks of, viz. But What if the Queen Should Die?* (*PEW*, I, 209).

742

DEFOE TO [EARL OF OXFORD], 12 APRIL 1713

12 *They would bring him in whether the Ministry would or no*: See the similar phrasing in *Review*, IX, 335 (16 Apr. 1713).

13 *There*: I.e. 'their'.

14 *Clear and professt Banters upon The Pretender. The Post Boy* seems to recognise the irony, stating that *Reasons against the Succession of the House of Hanover* 'is a silly, malicious, Whiggish Book, and publish'd with Design to raise Jealousies in the Minds of Her Majesty's Subjects. Several other Books which have been printed, with Titles of the same Tendency, have come from the same Quarter, and with the same villainous Intention' (26–8 Feb. 1713).

15 *her Majties Speech*: In her speech to parliament on 9 Apr. 1713, announcing the signing of the Treaty of Utrecht, Anne said that 'the *Perfect Friendship* there is between Me and the House of *HANOVER* may convince such who wish well to both ... how vain all Attempts are to divide Us; and those who would make a Merit by separating our Interests, will never attain their ill Ends' (Boyer, 628). In the *Reviews* for 14 and 16 Apr. 1713, Defoe used the speech to rebut those who believed the peace was a Jacobite plot (IX, 329, 336).

16 *Ld Chief Justice*: Thomas Parker, later first Earl of Macclesfield, a Whig, who held the post from 1710 to 1718, when he became Lord Chancellor. In 1720, Richard Steele, who emerged as a champion of the Whig cause in 1713, wrote to Parker: 'That you were Lord Cheif Justice was a Consideration which gave me much Resolution in the last Reign' (*Steele Corr.*, 150).

17 *Whiggs ... book*: See Defoe's account of the positive reception of *Reasons* and *Answer* in *Appeal*, 27.

18 *The Ambassadress's Speech*: The Br[iti]sh Embassadress's Speech to the French King (1713), a broadside poem attacking the peace, clearly not by Defoe (*POAS*, VII, 590–6). The ambassadress is Adelhida Talbot (1660–1726), the Italian wife of the Duke of Shrewsbury, now English ambassador to France. The Duchess advises Louis XIV that Anne is laying the foundations for the Pretender's restoration by securing a ruinous peace and selecting traitorous ministers, particularly Oxford. The poem was widely disseminated in manuscript and print. On 23 Mar. Swift wrote: 'Here is the cursedest Libel in Verse come out, that ever was seen, called th Ambassadress; it is very dull too. It has been printed in 3 or 4 different ways, & is handed about, but not sold; it abuses th Qu— horribly' (*Swift Journal*, 517). Oxford received a copy on 25 Mar. (H.M.C. *Dartmouth MSS*, I, 315).

Several people were arrested for their part in the poem (*Post Boy*, 24–6 Mar. 1713). William Hurt was convicted, pilloried three times, and imprisoned for two years (Bolingbroke to Sir Edward Northey (1652–1723), 7 Apr. 1713, TNA SP 44/114, fol. 124; *Post Boy*, 23 Apr. 1713; *Political State* for July 1713, VI, 57). Defoe took notice of the poem in the *Reviews* for 28 Mar., 4 Apr., and 21 Apr., calling it 'Virulent', '*Witless*', 'Scurrilous', and 'Treasonable', 'an infamous and abominable Libel', and part of 'a Project to enflame the Nation, and set us all together by the Ears' (IX, 314, 345, 316). On 7 May, Defoe wrote: 'It has been very maliciously reported, *written in News Letters*, and even printed in the North of *Britain*, that the Trouble I have been lately in, was for being the Author of that insolent and unmannerly Libel, call'd *The Ambassadress Speech*, &c. To which my Answer is in short this, *viz*. That it not only is *false*, but not *rational*; and that it is not possible that I can be either such a Villain to Her Majesty, or such a Fool to my self' (IX, 369). In *Memoirs of Count Tariff* (1713), Defoe implies that Ridpath either wrote it or helped distribute it (*SFS*, III, 183). Defoe criticised it again in *A Letter to the Whigs* (1714), 13.

19 *Manner of writeing*: I.e. irony. In the *Review*, Defoe said that he resorted to 'ironical, Satyrical Methods' in the pamphlets in order to state his antipathy to a Jacobite succession more strongly than he had yet (IX, 336 (16 Apr. 1713)). In his petition to the Queen (Letter 240) and his *Appeal*, he suggests that compelling readers to infer meaning enhances the efficacy of polemic.

20 *wound*: Presumably his arrest earlier in the spring (see Letter 226).

DEFOE TO [EARL OF OXFORD], 14 APRIL 1713

229

To [Robert Harley, Earl of Oxford]

14 April 1713

My Lord

I had Not gone home to My Family before I had come like yᵉ Tenth Leper[1] to pay my Duty and acknowlegemᵗˢ to yoʳ Lᵈᵖᴾ, had not my[a] Case made me Unfitt to See yoʳ Lᵈᵖᴾ; Harrass'd by The Treatment I Recᵈ; So Hoarse wᵗʰ[b] Cold Taken in Their hands That I can Not Speak, to be heard; But however, Effectually Cheer'd, and Reviv'd, by yoʳ Lᵈᵖᴾˢ Most Seasonable, and happy Deliverance.

This My Lord is The Third Time, I am Rescued from Misery, and A[c] jail, by yoʳ Lᵈᵖᴾˢ Generous and Uncomon Goodness;[2] and This is the goodness for wᶜʰ yᵉ Gratitude of This Age, would have me, Against principle, Conscience, Honour, and Gratitude,[3] Maltreat and Abuse you, and for Refuseing wᶜʰ They fall upon me in This Manner.

But I am bound to your Lᵈᵖᴾ in bonds[d] too strong, and Am Sure, Unless God and Nature Abandone me together, it is Impossible I can forbear to Serv yoʳ Lᵈᵖᴾˢ p[er]son, and Intrest, while I live; at what Hazard Soever.

I Should be Unjust (my Lord) to mʳ Borrett[4] if I did not Accquaint yoʳ Lᵈᵖᴾ, That he Excecuted yoʳ Lᵈᵖᴾˢ Orders, So wisely, wᵗʰ So Much Caucon, So Much Indifference, and yet wᵗʰ So just an Authority, That no Suggestion Could be made of his being Directed, and yet The End was Imediately Answerd; and I was Set Free, Giveing Two Sufficent Bail[5] for 800ᵉ and my Self £800.

I Shall Take up no Room in This Letter wᵗʰ any Thing but[e] my humble Thanks, and Acknowlegemᵗ of So Seasonable a Deliverance; Except it be Humbly to beg yoʳ Lᵈᵖᴾ, That mʳ Borrett may watch,

---

ᵃ my] 'my My' *in MS*
ᵇ wth] *following word* 'a' *cancelled*
ᶜ A: *following illegible word cancelled*
ᵈ bonds] *amended from* 'bands'
ᵉ but] *following illegible word cancelled*

744

DEFOE TO [EARL OF OXFORD], 14 APRIL 1713

what progress They may pretend to Make in The prosecution of This foolish attempt (to Say no worse of it).

> I am with yᵉ Uttmost Duty and Humillity
> My Lord yoʳ Ldᵖᵖˢ Most Obedient Servᵗ
> [*monogram*]

Newington Aprill 14. 1713.ᵃ

Text: BL Add. MS. 70291, fols. ²85–6. *Address*: none. *Endorsed by Oxford* (fol. ²86ᵛ): mʳ Goldsmith Apri: 14: 1713

ᵃ Newington Aprill 14. 1713.] *written vertically down lefthand margin*

---

1 *Tenth Leper*: Luke 17:11–19. Defoe also alludes to this scripture in Letter 5.
2 *Third Time ... Goodness*: Oxford secured Defoe's release from Newgate in Nov. 1703 and apparently assisted him with funds following his arrest for debt earlier in Apr. 1713.
3 *Gratitude*: Defoe talks about his 'indelible Bond of Gratitude' to Oxford in *Appeal*, 13.
4 *mʳ Borrett*: William Borrett, Solicitor to the Treasury, 1700–15. He was involved in Defoe's prosecution in 1703 (*CTB*, XIX, 408–9) and investigated the *Review* on the government's behalf in Nov. 1708, evidently unaware of Defoe's employment by the Godolphin ministry at that time (TNA SP 34/10, fol. 143; cf. Letter 139, note 1).
5 *Two Sufficent Bail*: John Grantham (*c.* 1650–1723?) and Thomas Warner (d. 1733) stood surety for £400 each for Defoe's bail (*Flying Post*, 14–16 Apr. 1713). On the master printer, Grantham, including his association with Warner, see Michael Treadwell, 'London Printers and Printing Houses in 1705', *Publishing History* 7 (1980), 5–43 (at 22–3). Warner entered into partnership with John Baker in 1716 (Michael Treadwell, 'London Trade Publishers, 1675–1750', *The Library* 4 (1982), 99–134). He published a number of Defoe's books starting in 1716, including lengthy, major works such as *Memoirs of the Church of Scotland* (1717), *Captain Singleton* (1720), *Memoirs of a Cavalier* (1720), *The Fortunate Mistress* (1724), *The Political History of the Devil* (1726), *Conjugal Lewdness* (1727), and *A New Family Instructor* (1727). He testified against Defoe concerning contributions to Mist's *Weekly Journal* in 1718 (TNA SP 35/13, fols. 85–6). See headnote to Letter 263.

DEFOE TO [EARL OF OXFORD], 19 APRIL 1713

230

To [Robert Harley, Earl of Oxford]

19 April 1713

HEADNOTE: Defoe had the ingenious idea of having the government appear to take up the prosecution against him, in order to give him an opportunity to decry his treatment and thereby silence critics who portrayed him as the ministry's hireling.

On 15 April, the day after Defoe's release on bail, Parker wrote to Bolingbroke, the Secretary of State responsible for prosecuting libels, enclosing the depositions and the pamphlets, and advising 'that directions be given to the Attorny Generall to prosequute at her Maties charge and that the reason why it has not been done already, is that such Scribbles have not faln within Your Lordships notice'. This was an implicit accusation that Bolingbroke was turning a blind eye. Parker continued: 'The very Titles of two of them are libellous and seditious, and neare Treason; And the third sawcy.' Parker acknowledges Defoe's 'banter' but professed to believe it the screen for genuinely seditious intentions; anyway, he concludes, 'these are not subjects to be play'd with'.[1] Bolingbroke's reply on 20 April was no less pointed, hinting at Parker's adjournment of Ridpath's sentencing, which had allowed that author's escape: 'Your Ldp judges very right that these Pamphlets had not come to my knowledge, and I must confess I have been very much discourag'd by the success [outcome] of some late Tryalls of Libellers, and by what has followed thereupon, from searching so diligently into things of this Nature.' Bolingbroke advised Parker that the Queen had already ordered the other Secretary, Dartmouth, to prosecute Defoe, which is recorded in Dartmouth's minutes of the cabinet meeting on 19 and 20 April.[2] If this was Oxford putting Defoe's scheme into motion, the ploy was overtaken by events. When Defoe appeared in court on 22 April, as *The Flying Post* gleefully reported, 'he was continued upon his Recognizance; but before he went out of Court, my Lord Chief Justice caused the 2 Reviews of Thursday and Saturday last to be shewn to him, and asked him whether he was the Author of them, which, after some Hessitation, he confess'd; whereupon his Lordship declar'd, that those 2 Papers were insolent Libels against him in particular, and also against the Laws of England'. Defoe had imprudently complained in print about his treatment. Parker referred the matter to his fellow judges, who 'concurred in Opinion, that they were highly insolent to the Lord Chief Justice, and a notorious Contempt to that Court'. Defoe's three pamphlets were likewise adjudged '*Scandalous, Wicked*, and *Treasonable* Libels', and Defoe's defence that they were 'writ Ironically' was dismissed as an 'Absurdity'.[3] Defoe was again committed to the Queen's Bench prison. After Oxford's intervention, Defoe was excused from this charge but required to pay a nominal fine of 3s.6d.

746

DEFOE TO [EARL OF OXFORD], 19 APRIL 1713

and, more damagingly, to print an apology in the *Reviews* for 28 April and 5 May.[4] The charge against the three pamphlets remained.

My Lord

I attended on Saturday[5] and also yᵉ Evening before to have Layd before yoʳ Lᵈpp Some farther Perticulars of This Affair of Mine wᶜʰ has given yoʳ Lᵈpp So Much Trouble and Made So Much Noise in The world.[6]

Tho' My Lord, by yoʳ Lᵈpps Assistanće I believ The Mischief of This attempt will be Effectually prevented yet The Perticulars of it Every day discover Themselves More and More, and let us into a View of the Originall Design, wᶜʰ Design, least my present Indisposićon should prevent My attendanće tomorrow Morning According to yoʳ Lᵈpps Command I beg leav to Give Some View of, together with a Method wᶜʰ I Humbly Offer, to Render Their Dissappointment More Effectuall, and More Mortifying to Them, Than Ordinᵃ.

The Design My Lᵈ has Many branches, and if I may Use So much freedome I think they are all weak, foolish, and yet Malicous to a Degree.

1. Their Design is Aim'd at yoʳ Lᵈpp and Her Majᵗⁱᵉˢ Intrest, to let yᵉ Naćon See how formidable Their Faction is, and That They Could Overthro' any Man who dared Oppose Them, in Spight of her Majᵗⁱᵉˢ Favour or protection.

2. They Aim at makeing a Discovery to yᵉ Naćon, who are or are not in yoʳ Lᵈpps Serviće, So that Their falling upon me Must as They Thought Infallibly Answer Their End One way or Other; for That, if yᵉ Ministry <u>did not</u> protect me They knew they Should Oppress and Sink me by The Partiallity and Favour of my Lᵈ Chief justiće, (whose Conduct has been Really wonderfull[7] in it), And if yoʳ Lᵈpp <u>Did</u> protect me Then They Gaind yᵉ Other point by publishing First That I was Secretly Entertaind and Employd by yoʳ Lᵈpp, wᶜʰ hitherto They have made Much Noise of, but Could Never prove;[a] and <u>Secondly</u> That yoʳ Lᵈpp should Oppose a prosecution wᶜʰ Seemd to be in behalf of the House of Hannover.[8]

They have a Third End in all This (Viz) Meerly to shew an Insult upon the Ministry of wᶜʰ I Need Say no More here.

---

[a] prove] *following word cancelled probably* 'it'

DEFOE TO [EARL OF OXFORD], 19 APRIL 1713

In all These things I Think I may Venture to Say They shall be Effectually Dissappointed if my Following proposall be Approv'd by yor L^{dpp}; and yet they shall Never know that yor L^{dpp} has any way Thought it worth yor Notiċe, or any way in ye least Concern'd yor Self in it —

Mr Borret My Lord Mannag'd himself wth So Much Prudenċe and good Conduct, That they are Perfectly Amused,[9] and make no Guess upon what foundation he acted: And this because he Came, (not as Concerning himself in haveing Me delivred or in Giveing Bail but) As haveing good Satisfaccon That ye Bail wch I had Ready, were Suffiċent, (as They Really were) Tho' had he not Appeared the best Bail I Could have produced, would have been Rejected.

After I was Bailed, My Ld Chief justiċe call'd m^r Borret aside, and Asked him if the Governm^t would prosecute This De Foe; m^r Borret answerd he knew Nothing of that atall, Upon wch his L^{dpp} Said he would write to my Lord Bollingbrook[10] to kno', as I Suppose he has done.

The Design of This my Lord is, That if The Secretarys[11] Decline it, This m^r Benson will bring an Informaċon On purpose to Trye if I can obtain a Stop to be put to Their Proceedings by <u>Noli Pros.</u>[12] wch will give Them an Occasion of Plentifull Railing, wch is what They Desire.

Now My Lord The Governm^t May Effectually prevent this if a Seeming prosecution be actually begun (Onely I must Depend upon yor L^{dpp} That it be not pushed On) and an Informaċon Ordred against me.

   1. This prevents Their stirring in any Separate^a prosecution
     Effectually.
   2. The True Reason for not prosecuting it, may be want of
     good Evedenċe, which Really will be wanting.
   3. They have no Reason to Examin why the Governm^t does or
     does not prosecute, after an Information is layd.

All This while, Ile Complain Loudly of ye Oppression, Ile Petition (I mean in Print) to be brought to Tryall; And shall have abundant Room to Expose Them for attacking me in a Thing they can not

---

^a Separate] *interlined*

748

DEFOE TO [EARL OF OXFORD], 19 APRIL 1713

make Out; and Thus^a ye preten̊ce of being protected by yor L^dpp or the Ministry will be quite Taken away.

May it please yor L^dpp

If There is any Defect in This scheme wch I can not foresee I Humbly Referr it to yor L^dpp^s Wisdome; The Reason of My proposeing it, is purely to Dissappoint Them in That Part of Their Malitious Design, which is Pointed at yor L^dpp^s Person and Administration; For There is no Doubt but haveing a Full stop Put to Their Rage by yor L^dpp^s Authourity, would be much more for my Safety, as well as Reputåcon; Perticularly as it would Make Them Cautious of Falling Upon me Again; But My Lord I See who This Bullet is shot at, and if They do This in The green Tree, what would They do in The Drye?[13] May yor L^dpp be Ever Preserv'd from Their Rage: Myne be The wounds, and The hazard, of whatever kind; and May^b My ståcon be, between yor L^dpp, and all yor Dangers, in The worst attempts of yor Enemies, Even to a <u>Guiscards Knife</u>.[14]

I am Sorry My Lord This foolish Affair has Interrupted me, in Those Things of Much greater Consequen̊ce, wch I had just begun to Lay before yor L^dpp, of ye affaires of Scotland; where The assembly Approaches;[15] and where The Establishing ye Troops and The Approaching Elec̊con,[16] Offred me Many Things Very Needfull for yor L^dpp to kno'; The first of wch I was writeing, when ye Furies[17] Came upon me, and wch I Sent away to yor L^dpp Unfinished, and without Takeing a Coppie.[18]

I shall Endeavour (being a little Composed Now) to begin where I broke off, and go on to Those Things I Conciev are for yor Servi̊ce. As to This Affair, I leave my Self Entirely in yor L^dpp^s Disposall, wth ye Greatest Tranquillity Immaginable, Resting on That Goodness for my protection, of wch I have had Such Constant Experien̊ce.

I am

May it Please yor L^dpp

yor L^dpp^s Most Obed^t &c

[*monogram*]

---

^a Thus] *interlined*
^b May] *interlined*

DEFOE TO [EARL OF OXFORD], 19 APRIL 1713

Aprill 19. 1713

P S

If I am able to Come Out of Doors I will not fail to attend according to yor L^dpps Command.

Text: BL Add. MS. 70291, fols. ²87–8. *Address*: none. *Endorsed by Oxford* (fol. ²88ᵛ): Mr Goldsmith. Apri 19 1713

1 TNA SP 34/21, fol. 33.
2 TNA SP 44/114, fol. 126; Staffordshire Record Office, D742/U/3/26–7.
3 *Flying Post*, 21–3 Apr. 1713. The charge was still reported as treason by some (Folger Shakespeare Library, Newdigate Newsletters, L.c. 3605, 23 Apr. 1713). For sources on Defoe's court appearances, see Backscheider, *Life*, 588 n. 25.
4 *The Weekly Packet*, no. 44 (2–9 May 1713).
5 *Saturday*: 18 Apr.
6 *Affair ... world*: See headnote to Letter 228.
7 *wonderfull*: to be wondered at; bemusing.
8 *Secondly ... Hannover*: Defoe elaborated on how the prosecution was intended to put Oxford in a bind in *Review*, IX, 335 (16 Apr. 1713).
9 *Amused*: deceived.
10 *Lord Bollingbrook*: See headnote. St John had been elevated to the peerage as Viscount Bolingbroke in July 1712.
11 *Secretarys*: The other Secretary of State was Dartmouth, until Aug. 1713 when Bromley took over the Northern Department and Bolingbroke moved to the Southern.
12 *Noli Pros.*: Noli prosequi: a dismissal of legal proceedings.
13 *if They ... Drye?*: Luke 23:31. See Letter 216.
14 *Guiscards Knife*: See Letter 177.
15 *assembly Approaches*: The General Assembly was to convene on 30 Apr.
16 *Approaching Eleccon*: The general election was held between 22 Aug. and 12 Nov. 1713.
17 *Furies*: The three goddesses of vengeance in Greek mythology.
18 *first ... Coppie*: Letter 227.

231

To [Robert Harley, Earl of Oxford]

18 July 1713

HEADNOTE: The brief 1713 parliament, the opening of which was delayed until 9 April by the completion of the Treaty of Utrecht, saw the ministry attacked from multiple angles. Oxford later reflected that 'a confederation was made against the Treasurer'.[1] The Whigs continued to do all they could to oppose the government, but ruptures in the Tory party were more worrying. Hanoverian Tories occasionally allied with the Whig opposition to pressure the ministry to firmer commitments to the Protestant succession. High Tories were exasperated by Oxford's continued commitment to 'moderation'. Oxford's long-running rivalry with Bolingbroke turned into a direct struggle for leadership of the party.[2] Defoe answered the critics of the peace in *A View of the Real Dangers of the Succession, from the Peace with France* (June 1713), arguing that its protections for the Hanoverian succession and against the Pretender were as good as could be wished for.

An embarrassment to the ministry came from the Scottish members and representative peers in an attempt to dissolve the Union after parliament voted that the malt tax would be extended to Scotland. Scots considered the exemption until the end of the war negotiated in 1707 as effectively permanent, that taxation being understood as a wartime measure. Besides, though peace was signed with France, Britain was still technically at war with Spain. Now, they felt Scotland could not bear this new tax. Encouraged by Whigs and anti-Union Tories, and united for once as a bloc actuated by a national sense of grievance, the Scots addressed the Queen and introduced to the House of Lords a bill to terminate the Union, which was narrowly defeated.[3] In the *Review* and in a pamphlet called *Union and No Union*, Defoe sought to placate the Scots. He agreed the extension of the malt tax was regrettable but demonstrated that it did not technically breach article fourteen of the Union Treaty.[4]

A yet larger embarrassment to the ministry came when enough Tories rebelled and joined the Whig opposition to the bill for implementing a Treaty of Commerce with France that the government was defeated. The Treaty would have eased trade between Britain and France after fifty years of protectionist tariff-escalation and wartime prohibitions. However, articles eight and nine of the Treaty entailed adjustments to custom duties in Britain, so required parliamentary ratification, providing the opposition with a chance to assail the ministry, and exposing ideological differences within the Tories concerning trade and alignment with France.[5] Opponents of the Treaty of Commerce feared that it would not advance British overseas commerce but rather jeopardise the domestic cloth

DEFOE TO [EARL OF OXFORD], 18 JULY 1713

industry, expose Britain to French commercial penetration, and in the longer run create a vested interest in trade with France that could lead to a Jacobite restoration. Defoe did not share these fears and promoted the Treaty in several anonymous pamphlets and the *Review*, before that paper closed in June.[6] In the final *Review*, Defoe wrote that 'Writing upon Trade was the Whore I really doated upon, and design'd to have taken up with, but she is ravish'd out of my hands by the *Mercator*.'[7] This was a new, triweekly periodical which commenced on 26 May specifically to promote the Treaty of Commerce. In fact, whether or not he founded *Mercator*, Defoe was contributing to it by June and was probably its sole author either by then or soon afterwards.[8] Defoe's mercantilist line on the Treaty was that the balance of trade favoured Britain, so it should be implemented.[9] However, as one observer put it, 'it hath so long been a receiv'd opinion that a trade with France is prejudicial to this kingdom that it is noe easie task to beat them out of it'.[10] Opposition to the Treaty came from politicians, tradesmen, and pamphleteers, who either mistrusted the ministry's pursuit of closer ties with France, believed (unlike Defoe) that the trade balance favoured France, or feared the Treaty jeopardised existing alliances with the Portuguese or Dutch. The Bill was surprisingly defeated in the Commons on 18 June, indicating Oxford's limited control over the Tory party and exacerbating his growing rivalry with the Treaty's architect, Secretary of State Bolingbroke.[11]

My Lord

I am Among Those who look on The Times wth Grief and Indignacon, to See the Violence and Rage of a Party, Drive men who at ye Same time Make a profession of Religion and call Themselves Christians to Such Dreadfull Extreams, That ye Ruine of Their Country, and Of all That Should be Dear to honest Men, is of No Vallue when in Competition wth their Party-Designs.

To See These men^a Act The Same Injurious Extravagant Things, which They allways condemn'd in Others, and while They Reproach The Ministry For Joyning wth Jacobites to keep Them Out,[12] They Plainly Confess They would Joyn with any Men and in Any Measures to^b get in.

The Scots,[13] however Weak and Missled, are honester Then these, Even in That folly of Rejecting the Thanksgiveing;[14] for These Mock

---

^a men] *amended from* 'mean'
^b to] *following word* 'keep' *cancelled*

752

DEFOE TO [EARL OF OXFORD], 18 JULY 1713

men in keeping The day while They Insult those who Appointed it; and Mock God in Meeting to Give him thanks for The Peaċe, while They Curse The Peaċe in their Hearts wᶜʰ they Seem to give Thanks for.

It is wᵗʰ Horror I Menċon to yoʳ Lᵈᵖᵖ Their Treatment of The Queen, How Visibly they discover in Their Very Faċes a Secret Satisfacċon at any Indisposition Her Majᵗⁱᵉ may Suffer,¹⁵ Eagerly Enlarge The Account, and Report Every Triffle of That kind to be Fatall;ᵃ as if her Majᵗⁱᵉˢ Dangers, wᶜʰ makes an honest Mans Heart Sink at the Very Thought of them,ᵇ were Their Pleasure. They Appear Dissappointed when They find The Hellish hopes are but Imaginary and The Confusions they Expect Are Delay'd.¹⁶

God Allmighty for Ever Dissappoint Them and Grant Her Majᵗⁱᵉ may Out live Not So Much the Men, but The Temper; and May See The Spirit of Faction and Fury allay'd and all Our Storms Calm'd in a generall Peaċe both at home and Abroad.

I hope yoʳ Lᵈᵖᵖ will believ I am not an Idle Spectator of These Things, and Tho' I was backward to Trouble yoʳ Lᵈᵖᵖ, while The Hurry of the house lasted,¹⁷ I can Not but Renew My humble Petiċon to yoʳ Lᵈᵖᵖ, That I may be Directed in My Opposeing these Things, in Such Manner and plaċe as Iᶜ May be Most Usefull.

I am

May it Please yoʳ Lᵈᵖᵖ

yoʳ Most Humble and Obedᵗ Servᵗ

[*monogram*]

July. 18. 1713

Text: BL Add. MS. 70291, fols. ²89–90. *Address*: none. *Endorsed by Oxford* (fol. ²90ᵛ): Mʳ Goldsmith July 18 1713 faction

---

ᵃ to be Fatall;] *interlined; superfluous comma omitted in this edition*
ᵇ them] *interlined*
ᶜ I] *interlined*

---

1 H.M.C. *Portland MSS*, v, 466.
2 Sheila Biddle, *Bolingbroke and Harley* (New York, 1974), 219–94.
3 Geoffrey Holmes and Clyve Jones, 'Trade, the Scots, and the Parliamentary Crisis of 1713', *PH* 1 (1982), 47–77; Szechi, 130–5.
4 *Review*, IX, 405–14 (30 May, 2 June, 4 June 1713).

DEFOE TO [EARL OF OXFORD], 18 JULY 1713

5 D. C. Coleman, 'Politics and Economics in the Age of Anne: The Case of the Anglo-French Trade Treaty of 1713', in *Trade, Government, and Economy in Pre-Industrial England*, ed. D. C. Coleman and A. H. John (1976), 187–211; Perry Gauci, *The Politics of Trade: The Overseas Merchant in State and Society, 1660–1720* (Oxford, 2001), 234–70.

6 *An Essay on the Treaty of Commerce with France* (May 1713); *Considerations upon the Eighth and Ninth Articles of the Treaty of Commerce and Navigation* (June 1713). The *Review* turned to the Treaty of Commerce on 14 May (IX, 378) and concentrated on it until turning to the Union on 30 May.

7 *Review*, IX, 425–6 (11 June 1713).

The cessation of the *Review* may be attributed to political, commercial, and personal factors. Its sales were down, it was less financially viable in the wake of the duties imposed by the Stamp Act, and its recent legal troubles had discredited it (see headnote to Letter 230). Defoe was professedly weary with the strife, as he explained in *Some Thoughts upon the Subject of Commerce with France* (1713), 46. He was ill during 1712 and 1713 and missed deadlines resulting in the non-appearance of some issues; on 3 Jan. 1713 the *Review* apologised for '*the frequent Interruptions of this Paper, of late ... occasioned by a Dangerous Illness the Author has been under for some time*' (IX, 158).

8 In *The Political State* for May 1713, Boyer stated of *Mercator* that 'this Paper was at first generally father'd upon *Arthur Moore*, assisted by Dr. *D'Avenant*; but the latter solemnly disown'd it, with the utmost Indignation; and indeed it soon appear'd to be the *Production of Daniel De Foe*, an Ambidextrous Hireling, who for this *Dirty Work* receiv'd a large Weekly Allowance from the *Treasury*' (v, 323). Oldmixon amplifies Boyer's statements in his *History* (518–19). An attack on 'the false and trifling Arguments of The Mercator' shortly after the defeat of the bill concerning the Treaty of Commerce called it '*a Paper which is now certainly known to be written by* Daniel Foe, *a Fellow who has prostituted his Pen in the vilest manner to all Partys, and to all Persons; who has formerly suffer'd the most ignominious Punishment, and is at present under Prosecution, by her Majesty's Order, for Three infamous and treasonable Libels ...*; so that *this Author*, notwithstanding his fair Pretences, is *a Snake in the Grass*' (*A Letter to a West-Country Clothier and Freeholder* (1713), 5–6). Another blistering attack on *Mercator* at this time attributed it to Defoe, stating that he was 'under the Protection of a *Foot-man*', which alludes to Arthur Moore (*Remarks on a Scandalous Libel, Entitil'd A Letter from A Member of Parliament*, 3rd ed. (1713), 5). For Moore, see Letter 233, note 4. The *Flying Post* for 25–8 July 1713 mentions '*my old Acquaintance* Daniel Foe, *lately turn'd French Merchant, with a Latin Title*'. The *British Merchant; or, Commerce Preserv'd*, no. 4 (14–18 Aug. 1713) names Defoe as author of *Mercator*. See Letters 232 and 250, which indicate Defoe's involvement in *Mercator*; see *Appeal*, 47–50 for his equivocal and partial denial; and see the following note for his qualified acknowledgement, in 1719, that he wrote it.

9 In a 'Supplement' to *The Manufacturer*, no. 10 (2 Dec. 1719), Defoe seems to acknowledge authorship of *Mercator* but to distance himself from its arguments: 'If I had a bad Cause to handle, I did the best for my Clients.' Given the vehemence of his support for the Treaty of Commerce in 1713–14, his advocacy of renewing trade with France in the decade before that, and his restatement of the view in 1715 (*Appeal*, 47), it is hard not to see Defoe's 1719 statement as a *post facto* exigency designed to distance himself from Tory policies. However, for the view that Defoe had major reservations about the Treaty, see Maximillian E. Novak, *Economics and the Fiction of Daniel Defoe* (Berkeley, Cal., 1962), 24–8.

10 William Berkeley, fourth Baron Berkeley of Stratton (d. 1741) to Thomas Wentworth, first Earl of Strafford, 2 May 1713, *Wentworth Papers*, 331.

11 There were suggestions at the time that Oxford connived at the defeat of the bill ratifying articles eight and nine of the Treaty of Commerce. The logic is either that he sought to undermine the Treaty's architect, Bolingbroke, as their rivalry intensified, or that he worked in conjunction with Bolingbroke to this end, the objective being to extract better trade concessions from France. Peter J. Schaepel cites contemporaneous French sources which reflect the

DEFOE TO [EARL OF OXFORD], 18 JULY 1713

latter idea ('French and English Trade after the Treaty of Utrecht: The Missions of Anisson and Fénellon in London, 1713–1714', *BJECS* 9 (1986), 1–18). Strafford and Swift allege that Oxford was indifferent to the bill's fortunes (*Wentworth Papers*, 338; Swift to Charles Ford, 9 July 1713, *Swift Corr.*, 1, 516). These are not especially likely explanations for the bill's defeat, particularly as most Court dependants voted for it and any defeat was bad for the government; it is better explained by Tory members' reluctance to harm the economic interests of their constituents (Boyer, 638; Holmes and Jones, 'Trade, the Scots, and the Parliamentary Crisis of 1713'). If there was some elaborate masterplan, Defoe's letters to Oxford indicate he was not privy to it.

The reformation of the ministry in autumn 1713 consolidated Oxford's strength, particularly the appointment of his ally Bromley as Secretary of State in place of Dartmouth and Mar's appointment as Secretary of State for Scotland. 'These things make Lord Bol—stare', Lewis wrote to Dartmouth (H.M.C. *Dartmouth MSS*, 1, 318). Bromley was a highly respected High Churchman, and thus his appointment was a concession to the hotter Tories, a stroke which undermined Bolingbroke's exploitation of October Club dissatisfaction with Oxford.

12 *They Reproach … Out*: Whig propaganda ahead of the 1713 election, like that during the parliament as a whole, accused the ministry of Jacobitism, including in the matter of its commercial policy. See James O. Richards, *Party Propaganda Under Queen Anne: The General Elections of 1702–1713* (Athens, Ga., 1972), 133–6, 140–2.

13 *Scots*: See headnote.

14 *Rejecting the Thanksgiveing*: Public thanksgiving for the peace was appointed for 16 June in Scotland, but dissatisfaction with the malt tax led to it being boycotted (*Wodrow Corr.*, 1, 468, 476–9). The public thanksgiving held at St Paul's Cathedral in London and across the nation on 7 July 1713, postponed from 16 June because of the Queen's illness, was also snubbed by many Whigs. See Julie Farguson, 'Promoting the Peace: Queen Anne and the Public Thanksgiving at St Paul's Cathedral', in *Performances of Peace: Utrecht 1713*, ed. Renger de Bruin *et al.* (Leiden, 2015), 207–22.

15 *any Indisposition Her Majtie may Suffer*: Anne was too unwell to attend the public thanksgiving even after the delay.

16 *They Appear Dissappointed … Delay'd*: Defoe says much the same five months later (Letter 245).

17 *while The Hurry of the house lasted*: Parliament rose on 16 July. 'Hurry' means 'commotion'.

DEFOE TO [EARL OF OXFORD], I AUGUST 1713

232

To [Robert Harley, Earl of Oxford]

I August 1713

HEADNOTE: The 1713 general election was to start on 22 August, though election-
eering commenced well before the formal dissolution of parliament on 8 August.
Defoe's focus was the promotion of the Treaty of Commerce, the revival of which
was anticipated after its shock defeat in the Commons in June, making it a central
concern in the election campaign. Defoe's *Mercator* continued to advocate for a
trade agreement with France; a rival Whig periodical called *The British Merchant*,
initiated on 7 August, opposed *Mercator*.[1] Its first issue alleged that, ahead of the
elections, *Mercator* was disseminated 'throughout the Country for the Instruction
of the Ignorant' and 'his Readers have him *gratis*'.[2] On the whole, the peace was
popular and Whig criticisms of its terms reinforced their association with the
long, expensive war. Therefore the unpopularity of the French trade caused little damage to the Tories. Anyway, a Tory parliament had rejected the Treaty of
Commerce, so the ministry's support for it barely damaged the party's electoral
fortunes, and the Tories won the election handily.[3]

My Lord

As no Man That has any Sencé of Duty to her Maj^tie or Regard
to his Country Can look on The Conduct of Some People Among
us without Just Indignacón So (My Lord) I That have all my Life
been brought up among and Conversant wth Those People[4] profess
my Self Amazed at Them.

I allwayes Tho^t <u>However Mistaken</u> They Meant well, acted From
Principle, and lookt up, as well as about Them in The Measures They
Took; But I am Astonished to See Them Implacable, Outrageous,
and Flying to all Those abhorr'd Methods of Compassing Their
Own Designs, which They allways Censur'd and Condemn'd in
Others.

This and The Indefatigable Applicacón with wch They are just
Now working at Their Scheme for a New Eleccón, and what They
promise Themselves, and Good Men fear in Case of Their Success,
Makes me Renew My address to yor Ld^pp with This Humble
Question (Viz) <u>Can I Render yor Ld^pp and Her Maj^ties Intrest No
Servicé On This Nicé Occasion?</u>

756

DEFOE TO [EARL OF OXFORD], I AUGUST 1713

Yo^r L^{dpps} Indisposicon[5] is Not an Afflicċon to yor Faithfull Servants Onely, but to all Honest Men and a loss to ye whole Naċon; My Loss in it is not worth Naming, tho' to Me Very Heavy; but I Omit Troubling yor L^{dpp} with my Missfortunes.

I Hope I have not been an Unprofitable Servant[6] in ye New Undertakeing[7] wch I am Embarkt in, But I would willingly be Farther Usefull According to My Duty, and For This Reason I attend The First Occasion I may have to Lay before yor L^{dpp}, Such Thoughts as I hope^a May be for yor Serviċe, On This Occasion.

I am
May it Please yor L^{dpp}^b
yor L^{dpps} Most Humble and Obed^t Servt
[*monogram*]

Augt 1. 1713.

Text: BL Add. MS. 70291, fols. ²91–2. *Address*: none.

---

^a as I hope] *interlined above cancelled word probably* 'I'
^b L^{dpp}] 'L^{dpps}' *in MS*

---

1 On the rival Whig–Tory conceptions of the balance of trade, see William Deringer, *Calculated Values: Finance, Politics, and the Quantitative Age* (Cambridge, Mass., 2018), 115–52. Deringer's assumption that Defoe took the lead of *Mercator* only in late 1713 is conjectural (145) – see Letter 231, note 8.
2 *The British Merchant; or, Commerce Preserv'd*, no. 1 (7 Aug. 1713).
3 *HPC 1690–1715*, I, 232–5.
4 *Those People*: Whigs.
5 *Indisposicon*: Erasmus Lewis wrote to Swift on 30 July that 'Lord Treasurer was abroad this evening for ye 1st time, after a fortnights illness' (*Swift Corr.*, I, 519). Cf. Frances, Viscountess Bolingbroke (1679–1718) to Oxford's son, Edward, Lord Harley (1689–1741), 25 July 1713, H.M.C. *Portland MSS*, v, 310.
6 *Unprofitable Servant*: See Letter 13, note 5.
7 *New Undertakeing*: *Mercator*. See headnote to Letter 231 and note 8 there.

DEFOE TO [EARL OF OXFORD], 9 OCTOBER 1713

233

To [Robert Harley, Earl of Oxford]

9 October 1713

HEADNOTE: Defoe was surprised that his prosecution for the three succession pamphlets rumbled on; he believed it had been swept away by Oxford, so when summoned to appear he set about trying to secure a pardon.

My Lord

I had Not Sent again So Soon to yor Ldpp haveing yor Orders to Attend to Morrow but on This Extraorda Occasion.

I am Surprized My Lord wth Notice given Me From mr Borret That Notwithstanding all That has been Said and yor Ldpps Orders to him They are proceeding Formally Against me On Accot of The Old affair of the Three Pamphlets and That if^a yor Ldpp is Not pleased to Interpose I shall be Made a Sacrifize to a Party who would Sacrifize yor Ldpp and The queen also if it Lay in Their Power.

I can Not forget That yor Ldpp was pleased to assure me of yor Protection and That I should Reciev No Prejudice by This affair. Indeed my Lord I have no Other Guilt Than is Included in My Zeal for yor Ldpps Intrest and her Majties Service and Their Rage at Me^1 is founded Purely on my Serving the publick And it would be Very hard if I Should fall by The hand of That Very Government I am Serving.

The Attorney Genll^2 Sends me Word I must Peticon The Queen and That there is No Other way to be Effectually Safe but to Obtain her Majties Pardon and Sayes This Must be Lay'd before yor Ldpp Imediately.

I have no Other Method but to doe as Directed, and have Therefore Sent a Peticon,^{3} which I Humbly beg yor Ldpps help in, Haveing No Other^b Protection Against These Furious Men, Than yor Ldpps Intercession and her Majties Clemency. Mr Moore^4 has promised to be The bearer of my Peticon^5 to yor Ldpp.

---

^{a} if] *interlined*
^{b} Other] *interlined*

DEFOE TO [EARL OF OXFORD], 9 OCTOBER 1713

They have Sent to me to day to Take out a Coppie of The Informacon wch is a Charge together wth the Following wch I am no way able to Support.

I am

May it Please yor L^{dpp}

yor L^{dpps} Most Humble & Obed^t Servt

[*monogram*]

Octob. 9. 1713

Text: BL Add. MS. 70291, fols. ²95–6.⁶ *Address*: none.

---

1 *Their Rage at Me*: The Whig 'Rage' at Defoe is illustrated in *Remarks on a Scandalous Libel, Entitil'd A Letter from A Member of Parliament*, 3rd ed. (1713), probably by Oldmixon. It states that Defoe 'has had Principles indeed, but never had any Morals; these Principles he has basely Sold for a precarious Subsistance, and while he pretends to *Liberty* and *Fanaticism*, he labours with equal Industry in the Service of *Popery* and *France*'. Defoe's pretensions to worldly mercantile knowledge are the fantasies of a man who has merely grubbed with 'Owlers, Bankrupts, Projectors, State-Quacks, Lighter-Men, and Bailiffs'. Defoe is a '*Hireling*' who 'will write any thing, do any thing, *Pro* or *Con*, according to the *Cue* that's given him.' The ministry is to be pitied for having to depend on 'so foul and prostituted a Pen' to support its policies (1–3).

2 *Attorney Gen^{ll}*: Sir Edward Northey, a moderate Tory; Attorney General from 1701 to 1708 and 1710 to 1718, also MP for Tiverton. See Holmes, 257. He had helped to draft the bill to confirm articles eight and nine of the Anglo-French Treaty of Commerce (*HPC 1690–1715*, IV, 1048).

3 *Peti¿on*: See Letter 240.

4 *Mr Moore*: Arthur Moore (*c.* 1666–1730), Tory MP for Great Grimsby, a Commissioner for Trade, and the ministry's main advisor on financial policies. In collaboration with Bolingbroke, he was central to the commercial policy concerning the peace. Burnet's character sketch indicates his prominence during the last Tory ministry of Queen Anne: 'He had a confidence with the ministers in their most secret measures; first with the treasurer, then with the lord Bolingbroke, and always with the chancellor (Harcourt,) and mediated between them in their quarrels; but when he found them irreconcilable, took his part with the lord Bolingbroke' (Burnet, VI, 151). See *HPC 1690–1715*, IV, 905–15.

   Moore evidently set Defoe on to write *Mercator* (see Letter 231, note 8), and he employed him in other pro-ministerial writings in the following year (see Letter 255).

5 *Peti¿on*: See Letter 240.

6 The text of the letter is on fols. ²95v–²96r, the inner two pages when folded, which is unusual, as Defoe usually started with the front page.

759

DEFOE TO [EARL OF OXFORD], 16 OCTOBER 1713

234

To [Robert Harley, Earl of Oxford]
16 October 1713

HEADNOTE: Trade was keenly debated during the 1713 general election, nowhere more so than in the City of London election, a test of the ministry's credibility that it narrowly passed when all four Tories were returned. This could be seen less as an endorsement of the ministry than a reflection of the fact that three of them had voted against the bill to ratify the Treaty of Commerce. Defoe continued to promote that Treaty in *Mercator* and other publications. His *Memoirs of Count Tariff* (August) is an allegorical secret history of the Whig and Dutch machinations against the Treaty. It adopts the conceit of personifying French trade from Joseph Addison's *The Late Tryal and Conviction of Count Tariff* (1713), a pamphlet which attacked *Mercator* as 'a False, Shuffling, Prevaricating Rascal'.[1] Defoe's *Memoirs* recounts how the Frenchman, Count Tariff, establishes an agreement with Alderman Traffick and Sir Harry Woolpack to import into France British woollen goods in exchange for lower British duties on French products. However, their plan is ruined by the manouevres of Sir Politick Falshood and Mynheer van Coopmanschap, 'a cunning, tricking, circumventing, sharping *Dutch* Broker'.[2] *A General History of Trade*, published in monthly instalments from June to September 1713, has the broader purpose of aligning commerce, divine providence, and societal progress, but it also promotes the Treaty, especially in the final issue. *Some Thoughts upon the Subject of Commerce with France. By the Author of the Review* (October) is presented as Defoe's re-entry to the debate (the other contributions were anonymous). It emphasises his own consistency on the French trade being profitable to Britain and ends with a complaint about his treatment by rival journalists, including for unspecified publications he claims not to have written.[3]

My Lord

If a Stranger were to Make a Judgement from The Hurry the Town is in at this juncture, and from The Rage and Elevačon of a Set of Deluded People on yᵉ Success they promise themselves in the City Elecčon,[4] He would Conclude The Sume of Affaires Depended upon These Four Members, and That The[a] Fate of The Governmᵗ was Determined By The City Elecčon.

---

[a] The] *following word* 'whole' *cancelled*

760

DEFOE TO [EARL OF OXFORD], 16 OCTOBER 1713

Altho' My Lord The Victory if they Should gain it, May be of Much less Consequence Than they Imagine, yet I hope it will Assist her Maj^ties Friends to Apply themselves to the giveing Some Needfull Check to This Insolence, wch is Really Come to Such a hight That it Calls aloud for The just Resentment of the Governm^t.

Were^a The House of Hannover to kno', how They are Thrown in The Face of Every Honest Man, Upon all Disputes of This Nature, They would Easily See that Nothing Can Weaken Their True Intrest More Than to make Them a Terrour to ye People who^b They are to Govern;^c To have English Liberty Aw'd wth the Apprehension of The Successor, is to Make That Successor Odious as well as Terrible and Arm Mens Minds wth Aversions to Them; and by Consequence put Them upon Considering whether They Ought to admit or Oppose Them.[5]

I kno' yor L^dpp is Sensible what These Men drive at, and I hope are Sufficently Prepared to dissappoint Them: The Shibboleth of Trade[6] is Now artfully put into ye Mouths of the people, and The Parliament will be Throng'd with Clamarous Petitions[7] on The Subject; if Some Vigorous and Speedy Resolution does not Repulse Them at first, They promise Themselves to put The whole Nacon in ye Same Ferment They have don The City.

I have Many Expedients to Offer yor L^dpp on This Affair if yor L^dpp would be pleased to Admit me at Proper Times to attend for That purpose; No question but Some Wayes May be proposed to put a stop to This Fury.

I Shall Attend in ye Evening as by yor L^dpps Command, and Humbly Acknowlege in the Mean Time yor L^dpps Goodness in Delivering Me From The Danger I was in,[8] by which I hope I shall with greater Composure Applye my Self to yor Service.

> I Am
> May it Please yor L^dpp
> yor L^dpps Most Humble and Obed^t Servt
> [*monogram*]

Octob. 16. 1713.

---

a Were] *amended from* 'Where'
b who] *interlined*
c Govern] *following word* 'and' *cancelled*

DEFOE TO [EARL OF OXFORD], 16 OCTOBER 1713

Text: BL Add. MS. 70291, fols. ²93–4. *Address*: none.

1 Joseph Addison, *The Late Tryal and Conviction of Count Tariff* (1713), 12. It is in *Defoe–Farewell Catalogue* (item 1441h).

2 *SFS*, III, 163. For the identification of Sir Politick with the Earl of Nottingham, see Letter 203, note 4.

3 *Some Thoughts upon the Subject of Commerce with France* (1713), 46–8.

4 *City Election*: In a tempestuous London election in 1713, four incumbent Tories were challenged by four eminent overseas merchants set up by the Whigs. The Tories were Sir John Cass (1661–1718), Lord Mayor Sir Richard Hoare (1649–1719), Sir George Newland (*c*. 1646–1714), and Sir William Withers (*c*. 1654–1721). The Whig candidates were Peter Godfrey (1665–1724), Robert Heysham (1663–1723), Thomas Scawen (*c*. 1649–1730), and John Ward (*c*. 1650–1726). Cass, Hoare, and Newland had voted against the bill to ratify the Treaty of Commerce, so were able to portray themselves as patriotic defenders of British trade. Voting closed on 24 Oct. In a very close contest, the Tories took all four seats (*HPC 1690–1715*, II, 393–4; Gary Stuart De Krey, *A Fractured Society: The Politics of London in the First Age of Party, 1688–1715* (Oxford, 1985), 244–7).

5 *To have English Liberty ... Oppose Them*: 'These People injure the House of *Hanover*, and the Succession it self, in their Conduct, by Threats of what shall be done to Persons and Parties, when the *Hanover* Succession takes place: ... Were the Princes of the House of *Hanover* to see how they are, on the most frivolous Occasions, thrown in the Faces of the most Loyal Subjects the QUEEN has; how the aforesaid *Faction* Bullies the People with the *Hanover* Succession; and threatens the Ministry and all their Friends with the Resentment of the Successor: They would shew their Displeasure at it, and tell them plainly that this is weakning, not strengthening, their Interest, by making them Terrible to the Nation they are to Govern; filling the Minds of the People with the Apprehensions of what Treatment they shall meet with from the House of *Hanover*, which tends to arm their Minds with Fear of, and consequently an Aversion to the Person of the Successor, and, by the same Rule, to the Succession it self' (Defoe, *A Letter to the Dissenters, PEW*, III, 322–3).

6 *Shibboleth of Trade*: See *Mercator*, no. 45 (3–5 Sept. 1713), in which Defoe says the bill ratifying the Treaty of Commerce is made 'a Shibboleth for our Elections'.

7 *Parliament will be Throng'd with Clamarous Petitions*: Parliament had received a large number of petitions opposing the bill as it proceeded through the Commons in May and June (*C.J.*, XVII, 377–80, 385–6, 391–4). Defoe spoke of 'Clamouring Petitions' in *An Essay on the Treaty of Commerce with France* (1713), 37.

8 *The Danger I was in*: See Letter 233. Presumably Oxford had assured Defoe that a pardon could be procured.

DEFOE TO [EARL OF OXFORD], 19 OCTOBER 1713

235

To [Robert Harley, Earl of Oxford]

19 October 1713

HEADNOTE **(Letters 235 and 236)**: Defoe strategised with Oxford on how the reintroduction of the bill ratifying the Anglo-French Treaty of Commerce might be managed in the next parliament. The crux of the opposition was that manufacturers and tradesmen feared they would lose out to French imports. Defoe advocated deferring the bill and instead increasing import duties on wine and woollen products from other nations. The Treaty only committed Britain to giving France duties equal to or lower than those applied to other nations, and a system of high duties across the board, Defoe thought, would give the Treaty a more favourable reception among merchants trading to Portugal and the Mediterranean. He also continued to present the government's economic arguments in favour of renewed trade with France in *Mercator*. However, the bill never was reintroduced, which Defoe lamented in *An Appeal to Honour and Justice* (1715).[1] French and British trade remained highly circumscribed until the late eighteenth century.

My Lord

Haveing yor L^{dpps} Commands[2] to Think on ye Expedients I Mencŏned in My Last wth Relacŏn to The French Trade wch Occasions Such a Hurry in ye Nacŏn at This Time, I presume to Offer a Few Gener^{lls} preliminary to farther Thoughts on That affair, wch if yor L^{dpp} Gives me Leave to attend at yor Leisure I would Gladly Explain My Self upon.

It is Most Certain The Party[3] are fallen into This Clamour about Trade Not from Their Zeal for Our Commerce but for a Handle, and to Raise a Party Against ye Ministry.

Suppose Then (Tho' it is hoped it May be Otherwise[a]) There Should be Some Difficulty in or Room to Doubt of Carrying The Bill[4] against Them, or of doeing it So Easily as might be desired.

Q. May Not The Ministry proceed by Another Method, and if The bill can not be brought down to ye Trade, Bring the Trade up to The Bill?

---

[a] Otherwise] 'wise' *interlined*

763

DEFOE TO [EARL OF OXFORD], 19 OCTOBER 1713

By This Means the Treaty Shall be Made Effectuall without bringing the Bill in atall, and in One Sessions More, or p[er]haps The Same Session, The Very Portugall Merchants[5] Themselves Shall beg to have the bill brought in, and The Ministry in the Mean Time Not[a] Run yᵉ Risq of Recieving any Affront From The Party, <u>to Their Eternall Mortification</u> and Dissappointmᵗ.

My Lord I was Loth to Communicate This to Any Till yoʳ Lᵈpp had Given Me yoʳ Leave to do So, and had Determined whether it has Weight in it or no. I am Perswaded it will be an Effectuall step to put a check to This Broil, and if yoʳ Lᵈpp Approves it I Shall Endeavour to give yoʳ Lᵈpp a full Satisfacċon in The Methods,[6] and Shall attend to morrow in the Evening According to yoʳ Lᵈpps Command.

I beg yoʳ Lᵈpps leave to Menċon Onċe More My Own Affair, mʳ Borret Giveing me still Reason to fear, That if it be not Effectually done before The Term[7] I may be still Insulted by This Enraged party: If yoʳ Lᵈpp was to kno' how I am Treated by Them, yoʳ Own known Generous Principles would Move you to Pity and to[b] Protect a faithfull Servant from a Generaċon of Men who have Neither Justiċe or Compassion.

I Humbly also Lay before yoʳ Lᵈpp my Other Circumstanċe, The quarter being Expired Some Time and haveing No Subsistenċe[8] but in yoʳ Goodness and her Majᵗⁱᵉˢ Bounty, haveing also Recᵈ Not One Penny On the Other affair[9] wᶜʰ yoʳ Lᵈpp knows of, which Encreases my Importunityes, for wᶜʰ I Humbly ask yoʳ Lᵈpps Pardon.

> I am
>> May it please yoʳ Lᵈpp
>>> yoʳ Lᵈpps Most faithfull Humble and Obedᵗ Servᵗ
>>> [*monogram*]

Octob. 19. 1713

Text: BL Add. MS. 70291, fols. ²97–8. *Address*: none.

---

[a] Not] *interlined*
[b] to] *interlined*

DEFOE TO [EARL OF OXFORD], [C. 22 OCTOBER 1713]

1   *Appeal*, 48–50.
2   *Commands*: Presumably issued in the meeting on 16 Oct. mentioned at the end of the previous letter.
3   *Party*: Whigs. See Defoe's statements about trade being dragged into 'Politick Squabbles' in *Some Thoughts upon the Subject of Commerce with France* (1713), 10–12; *Mercator*, no. 32 (20–2 Aug. 1713); no. 59 (6–8 Oct. 1713).
4   *Bill*: The bill to confirm articles eight and nine of the Treaty of Commerce was never reintroduced. Peter J. Schaepel indicates that this was as much to do with French second thoughts as opposition in Britain ('French and English Trade after the Treaty of Utrecht', *BJECS* 9 (1986), 1–18).
5   *Portugall Merchants*: Traders to Portugal. The Methuen Treaty (1703) lowered England's import duties on Portuguese goods, especially wines, in exchange for removal of Portuguese prohibition on English woollens; and Portugal entered the alliance against France. British merchants trading with Portugal anticipated a decline in their trade if duties were lowered on French goods, especially wine.
6   *Methods*: He sets them out in Letter 236.
7   *Term*: The first day of Michaelmas term, when Defoe was due to plead.
8   *Subsistence*: No payments to Defoe are known since that of 6 Mar. 1713. See Letter 226, note 9.
9   *Other affair*: Probably the costs associated with *Mercator*.

236

To [Robert Harley, Earl of Oxford]

[22 October 1713][1]

My Lord

Nothing is More plain than that The Disputes upon ye Subject of ye Commerce with France, are Carryed on, Not Meerly as a Dispute about Trade, wch Most of The people Now So hot about it Understand little of, But as an Arrow Shot at The present administraçon, a handle taken hold of, and an Opportunity wch They think is given Them, to Raise a Tumult against ye Ministry, and Enflame The People.

It had been to be wish't That The Ministry had Layed less Stress or at least Seemed to do So, upon This affair at First; But Rather Lay'd it before Them as a Thing Indifferent to The Ministry, whether it was accepted or Refused; Then There[a] is Reason to

---

a   There] *interlined above cancelled illegible word*

believ, they would Soon have Desired the Trade, because Those who Understood Trade would have Seen The loss of it, and Those who did Not would have been left Out of The Question.

It May So happen Still, that The Clamour of the Rabbles They have Raised May Prevail to preposess the Members and Make it doubtfull.

If The Ministry are Not Certain to Carry it Thro' both houses,[2] The better Way Seems to be to Lay it Aside at First and Not bring it to The question till Some Other Steps may be Taken which May Let Men See Their Mistake and bring those Very Men to Seek it who Now Oppose it.

Two Sorts of Men began The Opposicon against The Bill; all That have followed are come into it as a Party Question not as a Tradeing Question:

> 1. The Portugall Merchants, On The Accot of The Trade They Drive in Portugall Wine in which their Argumts are Specious wth Respect to our woolln Manufactures[3] but Not of any Weight in The Generll Argumt of Commerce.
>
> 2. The Dutch, of whom This is to be Said in few words, They are Very Desirous that we Should be Excluded the French Trade That they may Carry it On themselves.[4]

That The Dutch are against Our Trade wth France is in it Self a Reason why We Ought to Open that Trade and More Need Not be Said to it.

That ye Portugall Merchants are against it is plainly Opposeing a Private Intrest to a public Good.[5]

Supposeing Then That ye Ministry Find it Reasonable to Lay aside The Debate for a Few dayes and be pleased to let Them Suppose it was quite Lay'd aside and look't Upon by The Ministry as a Thing Indifferent to Them whether it pass't or No.

In The Mean Time as The house of Course Comes to Consider of Wayes and Means For Raiseing Money, Silently Among Other Things Some of the Following Dutyes May be proposed.

> A Duty on all Forreign wrought Silks Except French, The Duty of wch is high Enough allready.[6]
>
> A Duty On Wines of Galitia,[7] Leghorne called Florence,[8] Portugall, and Mallaga.

DEFOE TO [EARL OF OXFORD], [C. 22 OCTOBER 1713]

All The Weavers, Turkey[9] and East India Merchants will Come into ye First and The Opposiċon to The Last will be but from a Few Private[a] Merchants.

This is what I call bringing ye Trade up to The Bill,[10] For as I Conciev The Treaty does not Oblige The English to Take off, Or not to Lay[b] any Dutyes on French Goods Provided That Our Dutyes on Other Goods[c] of The like quallity are The Same.[11]

When The Portugall Merchants Shall See The house Resolved to Lay higher Dutyes on Their Trade They will Choose The Bill of Commerce Rather than The high Dutyes for Many Reasons.

First because Such Addiċonall Dutyes Streighten Them in Their Trade, Requiring Greater stocks to Carry it On. (2). Lessen The Consumption in Generall and (3). The French wines will out Sell them Much More, in proporcon when both are at a high Priċe, Than when both were Lower.

It will at The Same Time be Easie to bring in a Clause, to Take Off the Eight Pounds p[er] Ton, upon French Wine formerly Spoken of;[12] and The French and Portugall Wines Shall be Brought Very Near a <u>Par</u>.

Thus The Portugall Merchants will be put to a Full stand, and The Letter of ye Treaty of Commerce be Exactly Complyed w^th, in Makeing The Dutyes Equall.

I am perswaded Makeing a Moċon Towards it, Or but passing a Vote for it in the House, first, before The bill of Commerċe is proposed, would Effectually bring all The Portugall and Italian Merchants Over to The bill, and bring them to beg For One, to Avoid the Other.

The Objections From ye Portugall Treaty, and The Threats of prohibiting Our Trade in Portugall,[13] Are all to be Answerd another Way; Her Maj^tie is Not without Means in her Own hands to keep the king of Portugall[14] in Temper, or to bring him to Reason, if he Should pretend to Resent it; and if Not, The Merchants have themselves to blame, for the Consequenċes, who would Make The Portugall Wine trade a Monopoly, and Oblige The Governm^t to

---

[a] Private] 'rivate' *interlined above cancelled letters* 'ortugall'
[b] Lay] *following word* 'On' *cancelled*
[c] Goods] *following word* 'are' *cancelled*

767

DEFOE TO [EARL OF OXFORD], [C. 22 OCTOBER 1713]

Support an Exclusive Trade to Some of her Maj^ties^a Subjects, to The Injury of The Rest.

By The Same Method The Dutyes on Wrought Silks will be brought to An Equallity, So That The Dutch who Now Enjoy a great Trade wth us, by ye Excludeing The French[15] will Either Come to an Equallity wth the French, or Not Import any Silks atall, wch Our weavers will have No Reason to Repine at.

> Note, The Dutch have great Reason to desire ye Dutyes on French alamodes and Lustrings^b[16] Should Remaine, because They have all That Trade Now in their Own hands; and Run them on shore[17] here in Such quantities, as has quite Overthrown The English Manufacture of Alamodes and Lustrings.

The Linen, and Paper, Canvas, Sail-Cloth, Dowlasses[18] &c. will all admit ye Same Method, and wth This advantage, That The Manufacturing The like Goods in Scotland, Ireland, and The North of England, will be Thereby Encouraged.[19]

But There is great Reason to believ, That a quietly begiñing the Method abov[e]^c with The Silk, and The^d Wine; will at Onċe allay all the Clamours at the Bill of Commerċe, and bring all The Merchants Over to Submit to it.

The question of how Much The Said Dutyes should be is Reserved^e to a Callculation of the proporċon between the Dutyes allready^f Charg'd on both Sides.

All wch is Humbly Submitted &c.

Text: BL Add. MS. 70291, fols. ²99–102.²⁰ *Address*: none. *Endorsed by Oxford* (fol. ²102ᵛ): Commerce Proposal of an Accomodation R octo: 22: 1713

---

a Maj^ties] *interlined*
b Lustrings] *amended from* 'Lutestrings'
c abov[e]] *MS frayed*
d The] *following word* 'linen' *cancelled*
e Reserved] *the* 'r' *is interlined*
f allready] *following word* 'Laid' *cancelled*

---

1 The date is that of Oxford's endorsement.
2 *Ministry ... houses*: The opposition in the last parliament had been more hopeful of defeating the bill ratifying the Treaty of Commerce in the House of Lords than in the House of

DEFOE TO [EARL OF OXFORD], [*C.* 22 OCTOBER 1713]

Commons, before its surprise defeat in the lower House on 18 June. See Geoffrey Holmes and Clyve Jones, 'Trade, the Scots, and the Parliamentary Crisis of 1713', *PH* 1 (1982), 47–77.

3 *Portugall Merchants ... woolln Manufactures*: Defoe thought Portugal's threat to prohibit British woollen imports an empty one, first because Portugal was threatened by war with Spain, so needed its British alliance, and secondly because its increased trade with its Brazilian colonies required woollen goods that none but Britain could supply. See *Mercator*, no. 10 (13–16 June 1713); no. 39 (20–2 Aug. 1713); *Memoirs of Count Tariff* (1713), *SFS*, III, 192; *Some Thoughts upon the Subject of Commerce with France* (1713), 21–7.

4 *Dutch ... themselves*: The Dutch had continued to trade with France during the war, and ministerial propaganda emphasised their opposition to the Anglo-French Treaty of Commerce on the basis of avarice and aversion to competition. In 1712, the Inspector General of Imports and Exports, Charles Davenant, wrote *A Report to the Honourable the Commissioners for Putting in Execution ... An Act, for the Taking, Examining, and Stating the Publick Accounts of the Kingdom* and *A Second Report*, effectively the ministry's first propaganda to support renewing trade with France. Davenant argued that the Dutch gained at Britain's expense, capitalising on anti-Dutch feeling at that time (Coombs, 350–1). This is the main theme of Defoe's *Memoirs of Count Tariff*. Cf. *Mercator*, no. 30 (30 July–1 Aug. 1713); no. 33 (6–8 Aug. 1713); no. 92 (22–4 Dec. 1713).

5 *That ... Good*: In *An Essay on the Treaty of Commerce with France* (1713), Defoe acknowledged that 'some particular Persons and Interests in Trade may be touch'd' by the passage of the Treaty but that 'the Interest of Trade in General' took precedence (37). See also Defoe, *Considerations upon the Eighth and Ninth Articles of the Treaty of Commerce and Navigation* (1713), 31.

6 *Duty ... high Enough allready*: As opposed to raw silks, wrought silks are those that have been manufactured for use. British production of wrought silks rapidly increased in the late seventeenth century with high duties on foreign imports encouraging domestic production. Defoe supported maintaining high duties on French wine, brandy, and fine linens (*An Essay on the Treaty of Commerce with France*, 17; *Considerations upon the Eighth and Ninth Articles of the Treaty of Commerce and Navigation*, 34, 40). In 1729, Defoe wrote that tariffs had effectually excluded French wrought silks from Britain (*An Humble Proposal to the People of England, for the Encrease of their Trade, and Encouragement of their Manufactures* (1729), 24–5).

7 *Galitia*: Galicia, a region of northwestern Spain.

8 *Leghorne called Florence*: Leghorn is modern Livorno, fifty miles west of Florence; the wine imported from there was called 'Florence'.

9 *Turkey*: Turkey was a major market for British linen exports, so merchants trading to Turkey would support duties against importing linens to Britain.

10 *bringing ye Trade up to The Bill*: See Letter 235.

11 *The Treaty ... Same*: Defoe pointed out that the Treaty of Commerce committed France to lowering duties on British goods, whereas Britain is 'only obliged to provide by a Law that their Goods pay no more than the Goods of other Nations: So that if we please to Charge the *Spanish* Brandy, the *Portugal* Reds; *Malaga* Whites, *Florence, Galitia*, &c. at 100*l. per* Ton, the *French* must pay the same' (*An Essay on the Treaty of Commerce with France*, 34). As he later put it, '*the* French [are] *bound,* Britain *left free*' (*Mercator*, no. 45 (3–5 Sept. 1713)). He echoes the idea, and some of the phrasing, two years later in *Appeal*, 49.

12 *Eight Pounds ... Spoken of*: In Dec. 1692 parliament added a duty of £8 per tun on the importation of French wines (*C.J.*, X, 743).

13 *prohibiting Our Trade in Portugall*: See Letter 235, note 5. The Portuguese envoy in London delivered a memorial threatening an embargo on the import of British woollens if Portuguese wines lost the preferential treatment they currently received. Defoe argued that the Methuen Treaty had to be set aside, as pacts made by envoys should not bind the British parliament. See *Mercator*, no. 40 (22–5 Aug. 1713); no. 45 (3–5 Sept. 1713); *Some Thoughts*, 22–4; *A General History of Trade ... for the Month of September* (1713), 21–33.

DEFOE TO [EARL OF OXFORD], 26 OCTOBER 1713

In *The Evident Approach of a War* (1727), Defoe gives a very different assessment, recalling the disputes of 1713 and stating that the duties could not be taken off French wines 'because *England* was under Express Conditions to the contrary in the Treaty of Peace and Commerce then subsisting with *Portugal*', which 'was admitted as a sufficient Reason why the Commerce of *France* could not be opened as was proposed' (31).

14 *king of Portugall*: João V (1689–1750), who succeeded to the throne in 1706. Defoe judged Portugal 'a Power who is in no manner of Condition to quarrel with us' even if João did resent the Anglo-French trade agreement (*Some Thoughts*, 26). In *Mercator*, he wrote derisively of 'the formidable Monarch of our Trade, the King of P——l' (no. 59 (6–8 Oct. 1713)). Cf. *Memoirs of Count Tariff*, *SFS*, III, 192.

15 *Dutch ... French*: In *Some Thoughts*, Defoe noted that the duties on French alamodes and lustrings were 'so great as utterly Destroys the Trade; not a Piece can be Imported to any Advantage' (31).

16 *French alamodes and Lustrings*: Both silk fabrics.

17 *Run them on shore*: I.e. smuggled. See Defoe, *Some Thoughts*, 31.

18 *Dowlasses*: A coarse linen.

19 *Manufacturing ... Encouraged*: Defoe discusses the proportionate decline of French imports and British and Irish production of these coarse linens in *Some Thoughts*, 32–3.

20 The text of this memorandum is on fols. ^{2}99^r, ^{2}100^r, ^{2}101^r, and ^{2}102^r; it is possible that ink bleedthrough averted Defoe from writing on the verso pages.

237

To [Robert Harley, Earl of Oxford]

26 October 1713

HEADNOTE **(Letters 237 and 238)**: The urgency of securing his pardon was pressing because Defoe was obliged to plead on the first day of the term. The delay may be related to the fact that another legal threat was levelled at Defoe when on 15 October Baron Schack (1659–1728), the Russian Envoy Extraordinary in London, pressed Queen Anne to abide by her earlier personal promise to prosecute Defoe for libelling Peter the Great (1672–1725) in the *Review* back in April.[1] A charge had been filed but it was buried, again through Borrett, whose 5 November note cites 'want of Evedence'.[2]

My Lord

If I had not Enemyes who have Neither Justice or Compassion I Should Not Importune yor L^{dpp} in this Manner.

It was my great Dissaster That I had not ye honor to See yor L^{dpp} when I Attended This Evening, Mr Borret giveing Me Notice That The Attor. Gen^{ll}, Timerous and Caucous to a Fault, has Ordred a

770

DEFOE TO [EARL OF OXFORD], 26 OCTOBER 1713

Rule[3] for me to plead and That if The Pardon be not Obtain'd before I am Obliged to plead, I Shall still be brought upon The Stage.[4]

This Makes me Apply my Self Again to yo[r] L[dpp], begging yo[r] Protecćon, and That Such dispatch may be Used as That my Enemyes May Not Triumph, and yo[r] L[dpp]s good Design for my Delivrance be Frustrated by The Delay; M[r] Borret will attend to[a] Give yo[r] L[dpp] an Acco[t] of y[e] Danger if yo[r] L[dpp] pleases when at the Treasury to[b] call for him, to That purpose.

I Am May it please yo[r] L[dpp] yo[r] Most Humble & Obed[t] Serv[t]
[monogram]
Octob. 26. 1713[c]

Text: BL Add. MS. 70291, fols. [2]103–4. *Address*: none.

[a] attend to] *interlined*
[b] when at the Treasury to] *interlined following cancelled word* 'to' *on previous line*
[c] Octob. 26. 1713] *written vertically down lefthand margin*

1   Schack wrote that 'the emperor of Great Russia hopes that Your Majesty will have the goodness to punish the infamous Daniel Defoe, who has written in so shameful a manner against his Czarish Majesty in his paper printed on 2 April 1713. Your Majesty promised Sr. de Lith [von der Lieth], then the czar's envoy to her court, that this Defoe would be prosecuted and punished according to the enormity of his crime. But as until now this shameful man has not suffered the penalty for his felony, His Czarish Majesty, being fully persuaded that Your Majesty will see justice done to a criminal who has spoken so atrociously of the Sacred Majesty of crowned heads, has ordered me to insist to Your Majesty that proceedings be brought against the criminal as soon as possible and carried to a conclusion' (TNA SP 100/51, fols. 331–2, trans. from French in *Britain and Russia in the Age of Peter the Great: Historical Documents*, ed. Simon Dixon *et al.* (1998), 124–5). In the offending *Review* essay Defoe decried Russian war atrocities and compared Peter to a Siberian bear (IX, 312–13). Cf. *Heinsius Corr.*, XV, 337.
      For assessments of Defoe's writings on Petrine Russia, see Paula R. Backscheider, 'Daniel Defoe's Russia', *Literaturnoe nasledstvo* (Leningrad, 1998), 1–16; Anthony Cross, *Peter the Great through British Eyes: Perceptions and Representations of the Tsar since 1698* (Cambridge, 2000), 52–5.
2   TNA SP 34/22, fol. 80; *CTB*, XXVII, cdvii.
3   *Rule*: I.e. a rule of court, which is a judge's order in a particular case.
4   *Stage*: scaffold, figuratively.

238

To [Robert Harley, Earl of Oxford]

28 October 1713

My Lord

I had yor L^{dpps} Command to Attend This Evening and Considering of what Importanće it is To me to Lay my Case before yor L^{dpp} Nothing could have hindred me but an Indisposicon So Violent as has Obliged me to be Carryed home and lay all bussiness aside.

Yet my Lord I can not go, without Humbly Repeating my Importunitys to yor L^{dpp} in The affair of my deliveranće, Mr Borret[1] again assureing me That if it be Delayed a Very little longer It will be my Ruine. I have no hope but in yor Lo^{dpps} Goodness and Humbly Entreat yor L^{dpp} I may not be forgotten till it may be too late to help me.

I am May it please yor L^{dpp}
yor Most Humble & Obed^t but Distresst Servt
[*monogram*]

Octob. 28. 1713

Text: BL Add. MS. 70291, fols. ²105–6. *Address*: none.

---

1 *Mr Borret*: For the record of Borret's expenditure in the prosecution of Defoe, amounting to £7.19s., see *CTB*, XXIX, 450.

DEFOE TO [EARL OF OXFORD], 31 OCTOBER 1713

239

To [Robert Harley, Earl of Oxford]

31 October 1713

HEADNOTE: Defoe's polemics in late 1713 focused, first, on promoting the Treaty of Commerce, in which matter he recognised that a unified stance from the Tories would ensure success; second, on trying to loosen the alliance of the Dissenters and the Whigs. To the latter end, he wrote the incendiary *A Letter to the Dissenters*, published in December, of which he gives Oxford advance notice in this letter. In the *Letter* Defoe takes a tough line with his coreligionists, warning that if they continue to take the part of the discontented Whigs against the government they risk sharing in the inevitable repercussions when the clemency of the Queen and ministry is exhausted. In the Dissenters' case this could include further legislation weakening their status, of which they have had a taste with the Occasional Conformity Act in 1711. Now, the Dissenters are living up to the worst stereotypes levelled at them, of being 'Factious and Seditious'; their cleaving to the Whigs even after the Occasional Conformity Act indicates 'that they were more zealous for carrying on a Faction in the Civil Government, than for enjoying or preserving their Religious Liberties'.[1] Despite Defoe's insistence that the *Letter* offered '*friendly Cautions*' and was 'designed meekly to admonish and persuade' the Dissenters, it was inevitably received as a series of threats.[2] This tract indicates Defoe's impatience with the Dissenters but also his pragmatic understanding of what another Tory-dominated Commons could do in the next three years: the Dissenters would be better off allied to the ministry than to the Whigs.

My Lord

It is Time that I Should Mençon Something to yor L^dpp besides my Own affaires and Let My fate Rest upon yor L^dpps pleasure, as my Prosperity does on yor Goodness and Bounty.

I Gave yor L^dpp Some hints[3] for a Method to Reduce These Clamours aga^t The bill of Commerçe Supposeing Those Clamours Should grow So Loud as to Make it Reasonable not to hazard the debate in Parliament.

But as Things Seem to look wth a better Façe, and The Case appeares wth its True Shape[a] on, It Occurrs to me, and This I thought worth yor L^dpps Notiçe That it is Very Needfull to apply

---

[a] Shape] *interlined above cancelled word* 'Face'

773

DEFOE TO [EARL OF OXFORD], 31 OCTOBER 1713

by all possible Means to Open ye Eyes of all The Governments
Friends[4] to This Perticular, wch Indeed too Many have been
Perswaded not to See (Viz) That The dispute about Trade is but a
Circumstanče, An Excressenče grown Out of The Generall Party
Broil, Taken hold of, as They would have done of Any thing Elče
That had Offred, as Men Drowning Take hold of One Another
and Drown the Faster,[5] But That the Quarrell is Individually the
Same as before, and They who will be Amused wth the Clamour of
a Party without Enquireing into The True design, Really Make that
Design Effectuall, and Assist that Party to Destroy themselves And
the government together; And^a Those (I Say) who will be Amused,
wth this Artifiče, Ought to Remember, it is Not^b Trade, That they
are Voteing For, but The Queen and Ministry, against Rage, and
Disorder.

This My Lord is what, if yor L^{dpp} Approves my thoughts, I Shall
Applye my Self to; and wish that all Men who have any Zeal for
her Maj^{ties} Serviče would do The Same; and I The Rather Menčon
it, because I See There is Room for the Arguments on This head;
and People do begin to See it allready, tho' Not Sufficently.

I have also Compil'd a Letter to The Dissenters,[6] of wch I had
a hint from yor L^{dpp}, and Tho' I may Not Reach The Scheme of
yor L^{dpps} Thoughts; yet I am hopefull it May have Some Effect
upon Them; Onely I would hint a Thing to yor L^{dpp} without
ye Least View to my Own Intrest (Viz) They have Taken of
Late Such Measures to stiffle Every thing that is not for their
Turn by Clamouring at it in their flyeing Post and by their New
Corresponding Letters[7] that Nothing Can be Spread into the
Country but by Forče of Mannagem^t and Indeed No printer will
now print at his Own Charge[8] wch is the Reason The World is
Over-Run wth their Pamphletts wch they disperse privately Two
or three Editions at a Time and No Man stirrs a hand to Oppose
Them because They Must do it at Their Own hazard and Expenče.

I have done what Lay in My Power But yor L^{dpp} knows by
Other ways the Extent of My strength is too Small. However I
Lay this before yor L^{dpp} without any Respect to My Self, Humbly

---

^a And] *interlined*
^b Not] *interlined*

DEFOE TO [EARL OF OXFORD], 31 OCTOBER 1713

Recomending it to yor L^{dpp} because Tho' the thing it Self is Small The Mischief they do is not Inconsiderable.

I am

May it Please yor L^{dpp}

yor L^{dpps} Most Humble and Obedient Servt

[*monogram*]

Octob. 31. 1713

Text: BL Add. MS. 70291, fols. ^{2}107–8. *Address*: none.

1 *A Letter to the Dissenters, PEW*, III, 313, 316.

2 *A Letter to the Dissenters, PEW*, III, 310, 315.

3 *hints*: See Letter 236.

4 *Governments Friends*: Defoe alludes to the so-called 'whimsical' Tories, led in the House of Commons by Sir Thomas Hanmer (1677–1746), who had voted against the Treaty of Commerce in June. As late as *The Compleat English Gentleman* (*c.* 1729), Defoe animadverted on 'Sir T. Ha—r's 50' MPs who 'blindly voted after him', calling them 'the *dead weight* of the House' (*RDW*, x, 138, 176).

5 *Men Drowning ... Faster*: On the Spanish wreck Crusoe discovers 'two Men drown'd in the Cookroom, or Forecastle of the Ship, with their Arms fast about one another' (*Novels*, I, 197). See Defoe's challenge to his readers in the *Review* for 15 Sept. 1711: 'Will the honestest Man of you all, if ye were drowning in the *Thames*, refuse to lay hold of your Neighbour who is in the same Condition, for fear he drown with you? Nay, will you not pull him down by the Hair of his Head, tread on him with your Feet, tho' you sink him to the Bottom, to get your self out?' (VIII, 352).

6 *Letter to The Dissenters*: It was published in early Dec. 1713. See headnote.

7 *New Corresponding Letters*: Not identified with certainty, but see Letter 243, note 7.

8 *No printer will now print at his Own Charge*: On the increasing occurrence in this period of authors bearing the costs of printing, see J. A. Downie, 'Printing for the Author in the Long Eighteenth Century', in *British Literature and Print Culture*, ed. Sandro Jung (Woodbridge, 2013), 58–77.

DEFOE TO QUEEN ANNE, [OCTOBER/NOVEMBER 1713]

240

Petition to Queen Anne
[October/November 1713]

HEADNOTE (**Letters 240 and 241**): Defoe was pardoned on 3 December. Attorney General Northey's draft of the pardon is dated 17 November, meaning Defoe produced his petition addressed to Queen Anne, first mentioned on 9 October, before that date, perhaps after his 28 October letter to Oxford.[1] On 20 November Bolingbroke signed a copy of the pardon at Windsor and sent it to Northey with directions it be dated 27 November.[2]

In *An Appeal to Honour and Justice* (1715), Defoe claims that 'I was inform'd, her Majesty was pleas'd to express it in the Council, *She saw nothing but private Pique in the first Prosecution.*' Defoe remained bemused by his treatment: 'I was *the first Man* that ever was oblig'd to seek a Pardon for writing for the *Hanover* Succession; and *the first Man* that these People ever sought to Ruin for writing against the *Pretender.*'[3]

To The Queens Most Excellent Majesty

The Humble Peticon of Daniel De Foe

Sheweth

That yor Peticoner wth a Sincere design to Propogate The Intrest of The Hannover Succession and to Animate The people against The designs of The Pretender, who he Allways look'd on as an Enemy to yor Maj^ties Sacred Person and Government, did Publish Severall Pamphlets, Perticularly One Entituled Reasons against The Hannover Succession, One^a What if The Pretender Should Come, and Others.[4]

In all which books Altho' The Titles[5] Seemed to look as if written in Favour of the Pretender and Sundry Expressions, as in all Ironicall writeing it Must be, May be Wrested Against the True Design of the whole, and Turned to a Meaning quite different From ye Intencon of the Author: yet yor Peticoner Humbly Assures yor Maj^tie in The Solemnest Manner Possible, That his True and

---

^a One] *interlined*

DEFOE TO QUEEN ANNE, [OCTOBER/NOVEMBER 1713]

Onely Design in all yᵉ Said books, was by An Ironicall Discourse of Recomending The Pretender; In The strongest and Most Forcible Manner to Expose his designs, and The Ruinous Consequences of his Succeeding Therein.

And yoʳ Peticoner Humbly hopes The Truth of this will appear to yoʳ Majᵗⁱᵉˢ Satisfaction, by The books Themselves, where The Following Expressions are Very plain (Viz) That The Pretender is Recomended as a Person proper to Amass The English libertys into his Own Soveraignty; Supply Them wᵗʰ The priveleges of Wearing Wooden shoes,⁶ Easing Them of The Trouble of Chooseing Parliaments, and The Gentry and Nobillity of The hazard and Expence of Winter Journeys;⁷ By Governing them in that More Righteous Method of his Absolute will, and Enforcing his Laws by a Glorious standing Army, Paying all the Nacons Debts at Once, by stopping the Funds, and Shutting up the Excheqʳ, Easing and quieting Their Differences in Religion, by bring[ing]ᵃ them to The Union of Popery Or leaving Them at Liberty to have no Religion at all; and The like.

These May it Please yoʳ Majᵗⁱᵉ are Some of the Very Expressions in yᵉ Said Books, wᶜʰ yoʳ Peticonʳ Sincerely designed to Expose and Oppose, as far as in him Lyes, The Intrest of the Pretendʳ, and with No Other Intencon; Nevertheless yoʳ Peticoner to his great Surprize has been Missrepresented, and yᵉ Said Books Missconstrued, as if written in Favoʳ of the Pretender, and yoʳ Peticoner is Now Under Prosecucon for The Same, wᶜʰ Prosecution if farther Carryed On will be The Utter Ruine of your Peticoner, and his Numerous Family.

Wherefore yoʳ Peticoner Humbly Assureing yoʳ Majᵗⁱᵉ of the Innocence of his Design, as Aforesaid, Flyes to yoʳ Majᵗⁱᵉˢ Clemency, and Most Humbly Implores yoʳ Majᵗⁱᵉˢ Most Gracous, and Free Pardon.

And yoʳ Peticonʳ Shall Ever Pray &c.

Text: TNA SP 34/37, fol. 205. *Address*: none.

ᵃ bring[ing]] 'bring' *in MS*

DEFOE TO [EARL OF OXFORD], 18 NOVEMBER 1713

1 TNA SP 34/37, fols. 206–7.
2 TNA SP 44/356, fols. 435–8; *Post Boy*, 5–8 Dec. 1713. For other documentation relating to the pardon, see Backscheider, *Life*, 588 n. 29.
3 *Appeal*, 32, 35.
4 *Others*: 'Tactfully, Defoe focuses on the Hanover and Pretender pamphlets, and neglects to name *But What if the Queen Should Die?*, though this was the question now dominating the minds of all actors and observers' (Thomas Keymer, *Poetics of the Pillory: English Literature and Seditious Libel, 1660–1820* (Oxford, 2019), 146).
5 *Titles*: 'Nothing can be more plain, than that the Titles of these Books were Amusements, in order to put the Books into the Hands of those People who the *Jacobites* had deluded, and to bring the Books to be read by them' (*Appeal*, 27).
6 *Wooden shoes*: A metonym for French poverty as a consequence of tyranny, as used for example in *Reasons against the Succession of the House of Hanover*, PEW, 1, 175.
7 *Winter Journeys*: I.e. to London for parliamentary sessions.

241

To [Robert Harley, Earl of Oxford]

18 November 1713

My Lord

My Senċe of yoͬ Lᵈpps Goodness to me in This Unhappy Affair is too great for me to Express; it must be Testifyed in Duty Rather Than words.

But my Lord It still leaves me in A Difficulty too Great for me, without The farther help of yoͬ Lᵈpp as to The Expenċe of The Pardon¹ wᶜʰ is too great for me; yoͬ Lᵈpp was pleased to Say That mͬ Borret Should do that part and I humbly beg he may have yoͬ Lᵈpps Ordͬˢ on That Accoᵗ because he Seems to Say he is Not Empowred.

I Fear also Mͬ Attorney² May So Contract and limit yᵉ Pardon as to leave Room to a Mallitious Party to Fall on me Again; I was in hopes, Like a Recᵗ in Full, it Should have Ballanċᵗ all accoᵗˢ and I doubt not If yoͬ Lᵈpp Sees fit it May be So still.

I am May it Please yoͬ Lᵈpp
yoͬ Lᵈpps Most Obedᵗ Servᵗ
[*monogram*]

Novemb. 18. 1713

DEFOE TO [EARL OF OXFORD], 26 NOVEMBER 1713

Text: BL Add. MS. 70291, fols. ²109–10. *Address*: none.

1 *Expen̄ce of The Pardon*: I have been unable to ascertain the costs involved.
2 *Mr Attorney*: Attorney General Northey.

242

To [Robert Harley, Earl of Oxford]

26 November 1713

HEADNOTE: Oxford's oldest and favourite daughter, Lady Elizabeth Osborne (1686–1713), Duchess of Leeds, died on 19 November 1713. She had given birth to a son two weeks earlier. Oxford also received letters of condolence from Bolingbroke, Swift, the Duke of Leeds (her father-in-law), Dartmouth, and Abigail Masham.[1] The event has a political as well as personal significance because the bereavement contributed to Oxford's depression and in turn his loss of control of the party and alienation from the Queen.

My Lord

No Man That has a Reall Concern in yor Prosperity but Must Condole wth you in This Second Stab So Near yor heart.[2]

But you (My Lord)^a That have allways made The publick Cares So Much Superiour to yor Private Intrests, will wth ye More Ease heal all The wounds of This Kind, wth That Soveraign Specifick, That Truly Noble and Sublime Remedy I Mean <u>Resignac̄on</u>.[3]

I know I Need but Name it to^b yor L^dpp, who have long Sin̄ce Made it yor Guide, and by wch you have been Led thro' The Various Changes of Life to That Eminent Greatness, for wch wicked Men Envy you.

^a (My Lord)] *interlined*
^b to] *interlined*

DEFOE TO [EARL OF OXFORD], 7 DECEMBER 1713

Yet I Thought it My Duty, and The Duty of Respect, to Make Such a*a* Hint, in ye stead of a Complim^t of Condoleanc̆e, which I hope yor Ld^pp will accept and Pardon The Offic̆ous forwardness of

May it Please yor Ld^pp

yor Ld^pps Faithfull and Obed^t Servt

[*monogram*]

Novemb. 26. 1713

Text: BL Add. MS. 70291, fols. ²111–12. *Address*: none.

1 H.M.C. *Portland MSS*, v, 360, 367; *Swift Corr.*, 1, 549–51.
2 *Second Stab So Near yor heart*: Alluding to Guiscard's assassination attempt in May 1711. See Letter 177.
3 *Resignac̆on*: Defoe's fullest treatment of the theme is in his poem, 'Resignation', on which see Letter 213, note 8.

243

To [Robert Harley, Earl of Oxford]

7 December 1713

HEADNOTE (**Letters 243 and 244**): Defoe's *Letter to the Dissenters* was published at the start of December and caused a strong reaction from those who considered it a threat of government retribution. Ridpath said 'it seems to be the Second Part of *The Shortest Way with the Dissenters*'.[1] In a preface to the second edition (May 1714), purportedly contributed by a different writer, Defoe insisted that its reception had been generally good, that it was having beneficial effects in leading Dissenters away from factious '*Hot Whigs*', and that '*the frivolous Cavils*' against it only confirmed its charges against that party.[2]

My Lord

I have forborn Troubling yor Ld^pp as much as possible, being Very Senc̆ible I Ought to do So.[3]

---

a a] *following word* 'hint' *cancelled (squeezed by the end of the page, so rewritten on the next line)*

DEFOE TO [EARL OF OXFORD], 7 DECEMBER 1713

I presented yor L^{dpp} a Small tract about ye Dissenters;[4] ye hint is yor L^{dpps} Own, But^a Ought to have had a better workman, for So good a foundaćon deserv'd a Compleat Building; yet I have ye Satisfaccon of Seeing Some good Effects from it allready and Some men begin to be Convinc't.[5]

I Never Sollicited yor L^{dpp} for any thing in My life, however great my pressures have been, with So much Earnestness as I would beg yor L^{dpp} to Enable me to Make This Little book Extensive That in Spight of The arts used here to check and Stiffle it[6] I might make it be Seen Among the Country Dissenters. I am Verily Perswaded it would do more Serviće Than any Single Thing of its kind at least That I Ever Perform'd.

I am not Seeking private advantage and will be Contented to Reap None by it, but I See The Contrivanće of a Set of Men Among us, if possible to Suppress it and Especally to Send None into The Country.

It Seems hard That the most Virulent Inflameing Writeings Such as are not fit to be Read in a Civiliz'd Naćon are privately Sent all Over ye Nation at a public Contributed Charge[7] thereby to poison^b and posess the People.

But my Lord if a Word is written in behalf of ye Governm^t it is not Onely left upon the Authors hands at his Own loss, but ye Serviće honestly Intended is Rendred abortive and The True End not Answered.

Would yor L^{dpp} give me leav There are Very Few dissenters in England but Should See This little Tract,[8] and should also be Told who have Endeavourd to keep it From them and why.

Pardon me my Lord That I Seem to put So much Value upon this Small piece. I do hope it is a Word in Season,[9] and am Sure There is Need of Something to be done to allay the Spirits of an honest but Missguided people.

Were it in my Power My Lord, my Zeal for The public good would make me do this and More, But my Case is Such, as I can Neither bear to Relate, Or forbear to Lament. I Cease my Complaint however Now, because I am Moveing yor L^{dpp} in an

---

^a But] *interlined above cancelled word* 'and'
^b poison] *following word* 'the' *cancelled*

DEFOE TO [EARL OF OXFORD], 25 DECEMBER 1713

Affair That I flatter my Self is an Opportunity of doeing Good to a body of Men who May yet be made Usefull both to The governmt and Themselves and Tis on that Accot I am bold to Importune yor Ldpp and No Other.

I am May it please yor Ldpp
yor Ldpps Most Humble & Obedt Servt
[*monogram*]

Decemb. 7. 1713

Text: BL Add. MS. 70291, fols. ²113–14. *Address*: none.

1 *Flying Post*, 8–10 Dec. 1713.
2 *PEW*, III, 312.
3 *forborn Troubling ... do So*: Due to the recent death of Oxford's daughter. See Letter 242.
4 *Small tract about ye Dissenters*: *A Letter to the Dissenters*. See headnote to Letter 239.
5 *good Effects ... Convinc't*: In *A Letter to the Whigs* (1714), Defoe wrote optimistically that the Dissenters were beginning to see they had been imposed on by the Whigs (22).
6 *arts used here to check and Stiffle it*: See Letter 239.
7 *public Contributed Charge*: Perhaps a suggestion that Whig MPs were using their franking privileges to disperse newsletters or packages of pamphlets.
8 *Very Few dissenters in England but Should See This little Tract*: I.e. very few would not see it.
9 *Word in Season*: Defoe uses this phrase in *Review*, II, 108 (17 Apr. 1705); v, 145 (1 June 1708).

244

To [Robert Harley, Earl of Oxford]

25 December 1713

My Lord

I hope yor Servts accquainted yor Ldpp That I attended last Night and The Evening before according to yor Command.

I Mencŏn it That yor Ldpp May Not Think me wanting in duty in Not attending This Evening, being Confin'd by a Violent Cold.

I assure yor Ldpp I have Imediately apply'd good part of yor Ldpps Last bounty¹ to ye Use I proposed it.² I am Vain of The honor They

DEFOE TO [EARL OF OXFORD], 25 DECEMBER 1713

do ye letter to ye Dissenters in[a] Nameing yor Ldpp to be ye Author of it,[3] But More yet am I Vain with ye Success I hope That Little work has among The wisest and best of The Dissenters. I have Caused it[b] to be Reprinted in Little[4] to be Convey'd as proposed Over The West and have Ordred it to be printed at New Castle and Edinburgh;[5] p[er]haps it may Mutatis Mutandis[6] be Many Wayes usefull in Scotland as well as here.

Either My Lord These Men Must alter Their Conduct to ye Governmt or ye Governmt Must alter its Conduct to Them. There is a Time when Clemency becomes Criminall and when Justice Must Exert it Self or Suffer a Contempt Dangerous Even to Governmt it Self.[7]

I am May it please yor Ldpp
yor Ldpps Most Humble & Obedt Servt
[*monogram*]

Decemb. 25. 1713

Text: BL Add. MS. 70291, fols. ²115–16. *Address*: none.

---

[a] in] *interlined above cancelled word* 'and'
[b] it] *interlined*

---

1 *bounty*: No record of this payment has been traced. In early 1714, 'Guilot' was paid £100 three times from secret service funds, on 16 Jan., 1 Feb., and 10 Feb. (TNA T 48/16, fols. 86–7).

2 *Use I proposed it*: Presumably the dispersal of *A Letter to the Dissenters*, as proposed in Letter 243.

3 *Nameing yor Ldpp to be ye Author of it*: Edmund Calamy wrote: 'This letter was generally reckoned to have come from my Lord Treasurer Harley, or at least to have been published under his direction' (*An Historical Account of My Own Life*, 2 vols. (1830), II, 277). There were contemporaneous attributions that point to Defoe, such as *Remarks on the Letter to the Dissenters* (1714), probably by John Oldmixon: 'The Author of the *Letter* to the *Dissenters*, is some inconsiderable Wretch that has sold both his Principles and Pen to a *Faction*', a writer 'render'd *infamous* by *Law*' (1–2).

4 *Reprinted in Little*: This refers to the size of the type rather than the format: the first edition was a 48-page octavo; the second added a preface but used smaller type to condense the tract to a 16-page octavo, making it cheaper. In a similar manner, Swift alluded to the fifth edition of *The Conduct of the Allies* printed 'in small, and sold for six-pence', half its original cost (*Swift Journal*, 338, 348). The second edition of *A Letter to the Dissenters* was advertised in *Mercator*, no. 159 (27–9 May 1714) as available at John Morphew's shop 'Where may be had the said Book in smaller Character, Price 3d'. The first edition cost 6d., as advertised in *Mercator*, no. 84 (3–5 Dec. 1713).

5 *printed at New Castle and Edinburgh*: Janeway's deposition to Parker on Defoe's three succession pamphlets indicates that the same dissemination strategy was employed for them (TNA SP 34/21, fol. 30). No Newcastle or Edinburgh edition of *A Letter to the Dissenters* is known.

783

DEFOE TO [EARL OF OXFORD], 30 DECEMBER 1713

6 *Mutatis Mutandis*: 'once the necessary changes have been made' (Latin). The phrase is used to compare situations with circumstantial differences but the same essential point at stake.

7 *These Men ... it Self*: 'It cannot then be imagined that the Government will always sit still and suffer the Indignities, the Reproaches, and the scandalous Treatment which it now bears with. The Clemency of the QUEEN, and the Forbearance and Moderation of a Ministry, are a Blessing to the Nation, when practised in their due Measure, but become Criminal to themselves, and Injurious to the Publick Safety, when they suffer themselves to be so Insulted, as to bring Authority it self into Contempt' (*A Letter to the Dissenters*, PEW, III, 317). 'Had Her Majesty but abated that Excess of Clemency, which is become almost a Crime in Government, such Invectives had never been suffered to appear' (Defoe, *The Monitor*, no. 9, (11 May 1714)).

245

To [Robert Harley, Earl of Oxford]

30 December 1713

HEADNOTE: Queen Anne was taken ill over Christmas 1713, amplifying anxieties over the Protestant succession.

My Lord

In my Last I hinted Something of The Necessity There was for The Governm^t to Exert it Self, So far as May Tend to^a Checq of The Fury of a Party who grow Insolent, by The Indulgence of their Superiours.

It is No New Temper; <u>These Things^b thou didst and I kept Silence</u> &c.[1] was a Complaint mov'd Even from Heaven it Self, by The Insolence of Men.

God knows My Lord I would be The last in This Nacon, who Should prompt Justice, Especally On The Men I Mean; But We Restrain Our Children From playing with Gunpowder, Least They blast Themselves and blow up The house.

It has been wth Amazem^t That I have Observ'd These Men On ye late Surprise of Her Maj^ties Indisposition,[2] and it Fills Every honest faithfull Subject of her Maj^tie with Indignation to See These

^a to] *following word* 'The' *cancelled*
^b Things] *following word* 'I' *cancelled*

784

DEFOE TO [EARL OF OXFORD], 30 DECEMBER 1713

men Brighten Their Faces and Betray a Secret Satisfaction at The appearance of That Danger wᶜʰ Every Good Man Trembled at, and Now How Do they feign a joy at her Majᵗⁱᵉˢ Recovery wᶜʰ any One May See is Rather a Visible dissappointment to yᵐ.³

In like Manner My Lord Upon yᵉ Little Disorder at Canterbury Among the Marines,⁴ How did They Magnifye it to Such a Degree as if half yᵉ kingdome had been in Arms! what Joy did They Express at The hopes of Seeing Some blood Shed among us! and how do they appear disspleased at yᵉ Dissappointment.

I Need Say No more Than this to prove to yoʳ Lᵈᵖᵖ, That This Spirit of Rage and Fury is gone too Far for The Clemency and Moderacon of the Administracon to have any Effect upon, And The Mercy of yᵉ Governmᵗ to them, is but like a little water Castᵃ on a great fire wᶜʰ makes it Burn with the More Fury.⁵

It is True My Lord when we call Forᵇ Fire From Heaven &c., We kno' not what Spirit We are of,⁶ But my Lord Resentmᵗ in an Injur'd Insulted Governmᵗ is as Necessary to The publick Safety as Correccon is in a Family.

What I Say proceeds from what I See dayly in That Conduct of a party who have Vowed the Destruccon of The present administracon and who Own Themselves not to be Obliged or Won by The Tenderest Usage in The World.

God Deliver Her Majᵗⁱᵉ and all her faithfull Servants Out of their hands.

I am May it please yoʳ Lᵈᵖᵖ

yoʳ Lᵈᵖᵖˢ Most Humble & Obedᵗ Servᵗ

[*monogram*]

Dec. 30. 1713

Text: BL Add. MS. 70291, fols. ²117–18. *Address*: none.

ᵃ Cast] *interlined*
ᵇ For] *following illegible word cancelled*

---

1 *These Things thou didst and I kept Silence &c.*: 'These things hast thou done, and I kept silence; thou thoughtest that I was altogether such an one as thyself: but I will reprove thee, and set them in order before thine eyes' (Psalm 50:21).
2 *Her Majᵗⁱᵉˢ Indisposition*: On the Queen's illness at Christmas, see the letters to Oxford from Lewis, Bolingbroke, and Bromley (H.M.C. *Portland MSS*, v, 374–5); for the reactions of her ministers and the Whigs, see Gregg, *Queen Anne*, 374–5.

DEFOE TO EARL OF OXFORD, 19 FEBRUARY 1714

3 *These men ... dissappointment to y^m*: Defoe had said much the same five months earlier (Letter 231). See the anonymous *A Modest Enquiry into the Reasons of the Joy Expressed by a Certain Sett of People, upon the Spreading of a Report of Her Majesty's Death* (1714).
4 *Disorder at Canterbury Among the Marines*: *The British Mercury*, 23–30 Dec. 1713, and *The Post Boy*, 29 Dec. 1713, have reports of a mutiny of disbanded marines at Canterbury, who marched on London, with their arms, in order to represent their grievance, not having received their due. A detachment of guards was sent against them, but before these arrived the mutineers had handed in their weapons to the Governor of the Royal Naval Hospital at Greenwich, declaring that their sole intention was 'to make their case known' and procure redress.
5 *little water ... More Fury*: In the *Review* for 14 Feb. 1713, Defoe recalls witnessing attempts to put out conflagrations during the Great Fire of London (1666): 'The Water they cast upon it, made it rage with the more Fury' (IX, 228).
6 *when we call ... Spirit We are of*: Luke 9:51–6. For Defoe's cluster of uses of this allusion in 1714, see Letter 254, note 15. Earlier uses include: *More Short-Ways with the Dissenters* (1704), 18; *Eleven Opinions about Mr. H——y* (1711), *PEW*, II, 198.

246

To [Robert Harley, Earl of Oxford]

19 February 1714

HEADNOTE: Parliament sat down on 16 February. One of its first matters was the expulsion of the Whig member Richard Steele, the celebrated co-author of *The Tatler* (1709–11) and *The Spectator* (1711–12).[1] His contributions to *The Guardian* (12 March–1 October 1713) had criticised the government during the election campaign, focusing on the fact that France had taken no steps to demolish the harbour at Dunkirk, as was stipulated in the Treaty of Utrecht, despite a British expeditionary force having taken possession of that port in July 1712.[2] Dunkirk was strategically important because privateers issuing from there disrupted British commerce, and it was the departure point of the French fleet that tried to land the Pretender in Scotland in 1708.[3] Dunkirk carried historical significance too because England had captured the port under Cromwell in 1658, only for Charles II to sell it back to France in 1662.[4] Steele insinuated that the ministry was deferring Dunkirk's demolition because it planned to allow the Pretender to succeed Queen Anne, with French assistance. It was a gauge not only of France's intention to adhere to the terms of the peace but of the ministry's willingness to make them.

Steele's essay provoked a wave of attacks which focused on his insistence 'that the *British* Nation expect the immediate Demolition' of Dunkirk.[5] Defoe's *Reasons Concerning the Immediate Demolishing of Dunkirk* (September 1713) argued that, as Dunkirk had been placed in British hands as a pledge for the observance of Treaty provisions, demolishing it before these were fulfilled would be irrational: 'We have

786

DEFOE TO EARL OF OXFORD, 19 FEBRUARY 1714

the Town in Possession: If it were never Demolished, what can the Hurt be on our side?'[6] Steele and the Whigs of course trusted the Tories neither to destroy nor to keep Dunkirk. Above all, Defoe argues, Steele's presumption in dictating measures to the Queen and parliament is an overstep, and 'it is not doubted but that Honorable House [of Commons] will do Justice in the Case when it comes before them'.[7] Defoe also wrote against Steele's *Guardian* in *Mercator* concerning the Treaty of Commerce.[8]

Steele defended his position in *The Importance of Dunkirk Consider'd*, prompting Swift's *ad hominem* attack in *The Importance of the Guardian Consider'd*. In October, *The Guardian* had ceased and Steele had started a new Whig periodical, *The Englishman* (6 October–15 February 1714), attacking the ministry as Jacobite up to the very eve of the new parliamentary session. Steele also published *The Crisis* in January, which alleged that the Protestant succession was endangered under the present ministry. His expulsion from parliament once it met was considered inevitable. On 10 March, Defoe presented Oxford with an analysis of Steele's seditious writings on which an indictment could be based (Letter 248).[9]

My Lord

It is Impossible but wth The Uttmost Indignation to hear and Converse among the Constant Indecencys and Furious Excursions[10] of The people here, who Set Themselves in Opposition to her Maj[tie] and all That are Faithfull to her Intrest, and Sometimes I Suspect my Self whether I do not Really Complain to yo[r] L[dpp] Rather to give Room to The Resentment Than to Inform yo[r] L[dpp] of The Fact.

Sure My Lord, Justice Vested with Legall Power will not allwayes Suffer; If The Governm[t] Never Exerts it Self The Friends of The Government will not be Protected.

The New Champion of The Party M[r] Steel is Now to Trye an Experim[t] Upon The Ministry[11] and Shall Set up to make Speeches in The house and Print them,[12] That y[e] Mallice of the Party may be Gratifyed and The Ministry be Bullyed in as Publick a Manner as possible.

If my Lord The Virulent writeings of this Man May Not be Voted Seditious, None Ever May; and if Thereupon he May be Expell'd, it would Suppress and Discourage The Party and break all Their New Measures, But if not The Mischiefs w[ch] will follow will be Inumerable: They are prepard for his Loseing his Election

DEFOE TO [EARL OF OXFORD], 19 FEBRUARY 1714

of Stock-bridge[13] and mr Hampden has the Town of Wendover Or Berwick to put him into,[14] But if he may be Expell'd it would break all Their projects at Once.

My Ld It is far from me to Move yor Ldpp to p[er]sonall Resentmts. It is The party Not the Man, and I See Such black Designs in Their View That if possible They will Run things up to blood and Confusion.

Mr Steel (as they Say) is to Move for Calling Over The D. of Cambrige[15] and if they Could Draw that young Gentleman into Their Measures They would show themselves quickly, for they are not asham'd to Say They want Onely a head to Make a begining.[16]

I have No Excuse to Make for This Freedom My Ld but my Zeal for her Majties Safety and The Nations peace. The Ferment is So Great that they want Nothing but power and Believ [they]ᵃ do not want That; and This Makes them Unsufferably Insolent. God Deliver yor Ldpp and all her Majties faithfull Servants Out of their hands.

I Am May it please yor Ldpp

yor Ldpps Most Obedient Servt

[*monogram*]

Feb. 19. 1713[17]

Text: BL Add. MS. 70291, fols. ²119–20. *Address*: none.

ᵃ [they]] 'that' *in MS*

---

1 Defoe had written admiringly of Steele's earlier periodicals, referring to 'the Immortal *Tattler*' (*Review*, VII, 93 (9 May 1710)) and calling him a '*compleat Author* (*Review*, VII, 514 (14 Dec. 1710)).

2 *Guardian*, no. 128 (7 Aug. 1713). In June, Steele resigned as Commissioner of the Stamp Office in order to seek election to parliament (Steele to Oxford, 4 June 1713, *Steele Corr.*, 79–81). He had remained as Stamp Commissioner, probably thanks to Oxford, after having been forced to resign as Gazetteer in Oct. 1710, when *The Tatler* engaged in party-political commentary.

3 Recognising its importance, Defoe had advocated besieging Dunkirk in *Review*, IV, 259–60 (27 July 1708). Four years later he surmises it never happened because the allies would never have agreed on whether the British, Dutch, or Austrians should then possess it (*Review*, VIII, 648 (23 Feb. 1712)).

4 Paul Hyland, 'A Breach of the Peace: The Controversy over the Ninth Article of the Treaty of Utrecht', *BJECS* 22 (1999), 51–66. Defoe periodically criticised the 1662 sale of Dunkirk in the *Review*, for example in I, 601 (12 Dec. 1704); III, 585 (24 Sept. 1706); VIII, 460 (15 Nov. 1711). The first of these praised the refusal of its then governor, Sir Edward Harley (1624–1700) – Oxford's father – to comply with the shameful sale of Dunkirk.

DEFOE TO [EARL OF OXFORD], 19 FEBRUARY 1714

5 *Examiner*, vol. IV, nos. 27 and 28 (21 and 24 Aug. 1713). See Charles A. Knight, *The Literature of Satire* (Cambridge, 2004), 233–50.

6 *PEW*, v, 293. Defoe wrote effusively when Britain took possession of Dunkirk in July 1712: 'The King of *France* has put the Balance into the Queen's Hands, and the Peace may, for the future, be of her own making' (*Review*, VIII, 897 (12 July 1712)). Defoe had supported the demolition of Dunkirk as a condition of peace in *Review*, v, 718 (19 Mar. 1709), but his position in *Reasons Concerning the Immediate Demolishing of Dunkirk* (1713), that it is in Britain's interest to hold it as a pledge, is compatible with that of *Review*, IX, 7–8 (5 Aug. 1712). In *A General History of Trade ... for the Month of July* (1713), Defoe proposes that Dunkirk's fortifications be destroyed but its harbour be left intact as a neutral trading port, even suggesting a demilitarised Dunkirk could be kept in British possession in perpetuity (36–44). In *The Secret History of the White-Staff, Part III* (1715), Defoe lamented that Britain had not insisted on 'having *Dunkirk* in *PROPERTY*, and not as a Pledge only, to be given up again demolished' (51); in that work he of course defends again the ministry's good faith (50–3). Defoe imaginatively recounts the negotiations that led to the concession of Dunkirk, emphasising it as a great coup for Oxford, in *Minutes of the Negotiations of Monsr. Mesnager* (1717), *SFS*, IV, 78–83.

7 *PEW*, v, 305. *The Honour and Prerogative of the Queen's Majesty Vindicated and Defended Against the Unexampled Insolence of the Author of the Guardian* (1713) was formerly assumed to be Defoe's but has been de-attributed (F&O, *De-attributions*, 61).

8 *Mercator*, nos. 55–8 (26–9 Sept. to 3–6 Oct. 1713), in which Defoe responds to *Guardian*, no. 170 (25 Sept. 1713).

9 See *Steele Corr.*, 85–7. *The Political Writings of Sir Richard Steele* (1715) is in *Defoe–Farewell Catalogue* (item 1028), as is a 1723 edition of Steele's periodicals *The Reader* and *The Lover* (item 1127).

10 *Excursions*: 'Overstepping of the bounds of propriety or custom' (*OED*).

11 *Experim' Upon The Ministry*: Charles Knight discusses what was perceived as experimental about Steele's intentions upon entering parliament, effectively to combine the roles of pamphleteer-journalist and MP, acting as an 'embedded reporter' (*A Political Biography of Richard Steele* (2009), 124–33).

12 *make Speeches in The house and Print them*: On the 'embarrassing fiasco' of Steele's maiden speech, in support of the 'whimsical' Tory Hanmer's candidacy as Speaker, see *HPC 1690–1715*, v, 562. It was printed as *Mr. Steele's Speech upon the Proposal of Sir Thomas Hanmer for Speaker of the House of Commons* (1714) but with Tory 'Remarks' appended. The speech was then printed and parodied in *A Speech Suppos'd to be Spoke by R---- St---l, Esq; at the Opening this Present Parliament, with Some Remarks in a Letter to the Bailiff of St---dge, Very Proper to be Bound up with the Crisis* (1714).

13 *Loseing his Election of Stock-bridge*: The inevitable petition of Steele's Tory opponents for Stockbridge (in Hampshire) – James Barry, fourth Earl of Barrymore (1667–1748) and Sir Richard Vernon (1678–1725) – came on 3 Mar. 1714, by which time his expulsion was already planned by the ministry. Barrymore was subsequently seated for Stockbridge after Steele's expulsion.

14 *mr Hampden has the Town of Wendover Or Berwick to put him into*: The Whig landowner and Lord of the Manor Richard Hampden (after 1674–1728) controlled the constituency of Wendover, Buckinghamshire; in 1713 he unsuccessfully contested the county election but successfully contested those of Wendover and Berwick-upon-Tweed. He chose to sit for the latter and facilitated the unopposed return of Stanhope for Wendover.

15 *Move for Calling Over The D. of Cambridge*: George August, Duke of Cambridge (1683–1760), son of the Elector of Hanover, and from 1727 King George II. He was naturalised in 1705 and given his British title in 1706. 'Invitation schemes', by which High Tories in parliament would attempt to embarrass the Godolphin–Marlborough ministry by raising a motion for one of the Hanoverians to come and reside in Britain, a prospect Queen Anne abhorred,

DEFOE TO [EARL OF OXFORD], 2 MARCH 1714

were threatened but never executed on several occasions earlier in the reign (Holmes, 113–14; Gregg, *Queen Anne*, 183–4, 210–13, 268–9; Szechi, 135). The Whigs now saw an opportunity to embarrass the Tory ministry by reviving the proposal. In Apr. they persuaded the Hanoverian envoy, Baron Augustus Schütz (1689–1757), to request of the Queen a writ inviting George to take his seat in the Lords (H.M.C. *Portland MSS*, v, 417–19; Cobbett, vi, 1341–3; Gregg, *Queen Anne*, 381–2; Szechi, 166). Trying to prop up the ailing ministry, Oxford persuaded her to comply, anticipating that the Elector would hold to his position of refusing for his son to come to Britain; when the Elector issued a memorial requesting the invitation, Oxford had to retract. This all caused the Queen considerable distress (Hamilton, *Diary*, 60–1), worsening her trust in Oxford, and it further embittered the Hanoverians, already dissatisfied with Oxford's peace policy. The Duke of Cambridge, by then Prince of Wales, came to Britain with his father in Sept. 1714, after Anne's death.

16 *They want Onely a head to Make a begining*: In *The Monitor*, no. 6 (4 May 1714), Defoe decried Whig attempts 'to make the Presence of that Prince, if he should come here, a Foundation of Tumult and Rebellion', insisting that George would hate 'to be made the Head of a Faction against the Queen'. He continued this message in *The Monitor* throughout May and June.

17 *1713*: 1714 new style.

247

To [Robert Harley, Earl of Oxford]

2 March 1714

HEADNOTE: Steele's pamphlet *The Crisis*, published on 19 January 1714, insinuated that the leading ministers were undermining the Hanoverian succession, a message Steele had pressed in his periodical *The Englishman* since October 1713. Swift responded in *The Publick Spirit of the Whigs*, published on 23 February, with a section-by-section dismissal of *The Crisis*'s alarmism and a personal denigration of its author. However, Swift's adverse reflections on the Scots and the Union resulted in his prosecution by the House of Lords. Though ostensibly they were on the same side, Defoe inevitably took issue with Swift's remarks on Scotland, and he reacted in *The Scots Nation and Union Vindicated*, published on 23 March, calling for Swift to be punished and pointing out that English complaints against the Union are absurd: England was the keener partner, and the Scots had been eager to dissolve it less than a year earlier.

Defoe wrote a more general remonstrance to the '*Hot Whigs*' in *A Letter to the Whigs*, also published on 23 February, warning that their actions 'Legitimate the utmost Severity which your Enemies can return upon you, as a just Retaliation of your own Measures'.[1] Defoe had of course been counselling Oxford to take punitive measures against Whig writers for more than a year. In the tract, he alleges

DEFOE TO [EARL OF OXFORD], 2 MARCH 1714

that the Whigs truly fear not that the ministry is for the Pretender but that it is for the House of Hanover, and so will take the credit for bringing in the Protestant successor.

My Lord

I believ yor L^{dpp} is Not atall Surpris'd at The Unexampled Fury of the Party. Their public Conduct has Threatn'd This a^a Long While. As ye Justice of yor L^{dpps} Cause will Not Suffer any discouragem^t Either from ye Growing Enemies or wch is worse Unsteaddy Friends of the^b Administracon, So it Puts me in Mind of The words of Henry ye IIII of France to his Predecessor Hen III when he Seem'd Amaz'd at The Rage of The Guises and of The Parisians and ask'd him what Course was left to Take; But One S^r, Said ye king of Navarr; what's That Cousin S^d Hen. III. <u>To Conquer</u> Reply'd The Great Henry, and Accordingly he attack't The Enemy, and Delivred him.[2]

Yo^r L^{dpp} has but One way left wth These Men, They Must be Conquer'd; Or The Nation is Undone, The Queen Undone, and all her Maj^{ties} Faithfull Friends and Servants Sacrifiz'd to a Rageing and Mercyless Party.

I Presume yor L^{dpp} is Not destitute Either of Means or Council. You have The Fountain of Honour, The strength and The Right on yor Side; all Legall steps are justifyable in Such a Case. If a slack Rein is held Now, They will Run down all before Them. Clemency and Kindness will prevail No More^c wth Men that Can be Ingratefull, or justice and Reason with Men who Resolv to play the Bully. They Openly Declare That They have Thrown away the Scabbard[3] and as They Expect So They will Give no Quarter.

They have begun their attack where they found an advantage. I am Sorry That Gentleman layd himself So Open to them;[4] But my Lord They have by this step pointed the way^d Out and Told what Ought to be done to The most Insolent Pamphlet writer[5] that Ever was p[er]mitted to go Unpunishd. I hope the Occasion will appear

---

^{a} a] *interlined*
^{b} the] *amended from* 'their'
^{c} No More] *interlined*
^{d} way] *following word* 'Ought' *cancelled*

DEFOE TO [EARL OF OXFORD], 2 MARCH 1714

of Too Much Moment to be Overslippd Tho' they pretend to Give no Time for it. God Deliver y[or] L[dpp] From the hands of these Violent and Unreasonable Men.

I am

May it please y[or] L[dpp]

y[or] L[dpps] Most Humble and Obed[t] Serv[t]

[*monogram*]

March. 2. 1713[a], [6]

Text: BL Add. MS. 70291, fols. [2]121–2. *Address*: none

---

[a] March. 2. 1713] *written below cancelled words* 'Feb. 28'

1   *A Letter to the Whigs* (1714), 3, 8.
2   *words of Henry y[e] IIII … Delivred him*: Henri III (1551–89) and Henri IV (1553–1610). The latter was King of Navarre from 1572, succeeded the former as King of France in 1589, and was styled Henry the Great. They fought together against the Catholic League established by the Duke of Guise and supported by the Pope and Spain, which sought to eradicate Protestantism from France during the Wars of Religion (1562–98). Defoe gives a brief account of the Guise revolt in *Review*, I, 86–7 (18 Apr. 1704). He gives this same anecdote about Henri IV's martial advice to 'conquer' in *Review*, II, 576 (8 Sept. 1705); III, 302 (14 May 1706). Defoe's source is Arrigo Caterino Davila's *Historie of the Civill Warres of France* (1630), translated into English by William Aylesbury and Charles Cotterell in 1647. The 1678 English edition and 1630 Italian appear in *Defoe–Farewell Catalogue* (items 131 and 514); Defoe cites the 1678 edition in *Review*, I, 68 (8 Apr. 1704); this story comes on p. 402 of the 1678 edition. Defoe also uses Davila in *The Monitor*, no. 3 (27 Apr. 1714).
    Defoe admired Henri IV, attributing to him the beginning of French domination in Europe (*Review*, I, 13–15 (26 Feb. 1704); IV, 385–6 (7 Aug. 1707)). He commended Henri for bringing an end to the Wars of Religion (*Review*, VI, 39 (12 Apr. 1709)). However, he regretted that Henri was forced by his nobles to convert to Catholicism (*Review*, I, 67–8 (8 Apr. 1704); *Political History of the Devil*, *SFS*, VI, 181) but praised his passing the Edict of Nantes (1598), which secured religious toleration for French Protestants (*The Danger of the Protestant Religion Consider'd, from the Prospect of a Religious War in Europe* (1701), *PEW*, V, 64; *Review*, IV, 465 (9 Sept. 1707)).
3   *Thrown away the Scabbard*: The same image is used in *A Letter to the Whigs* (1714), 5. Defoe uses it elsewhere, for example in *Review*, I, 523 (14 Nov. 1704); VI, 158 (9 June 1709); IX, 60 (20 Sept. 1712); *Memoirs of a Cavalier* (1720), *Novels*, IV, 155.
4   *That Gentleman layd himself So Open to them*: Swift had laid himself open to the Whigs by heedlessly animadverting on Scotland and the Union in *The Publick Spirit of the Whigs* (*EPW* 1711–14, 262–5), to which Defoe responded in *The Scots Nation and Union Vindicated*. See headnote.
    On 2 Mar., the Queen's speech to both Houses of Parliament (delayed due to her health) included instructions 'to suppress … seditious Papers', particularly those that 'insinuate, that the House of *Hanover* is in Danger under my Government' (*C.J.*, XVII, 474). Defoe wrote in praise of the sentiment in *The Monitor*, no. 11 (15 May 1714). Swift had assisted Oxford in finalising the speech, and the target of this part was clearly Steele (J. A. Downie and David Woolley, 'Swift, Oxford, and the Composition of Queen's Speeches, 1710–1714', *BLJ* 8

DEFOE TO [EARL OF OXFORD], [*C.* 10 MARCH 1714]

(1982), 121–46). It was therefore ironic that Wharton immediately used the Queen's message to complain about Swift's own *Publick Spirit* in the House of Lords. The offensive passages (cut from later editions) were read and the House resolved that it was a 'false, malicious, and factious Libel, highly dishonourable and scandalous to the *Scotch* Nation' and therefore to the Queen (*L.J.*, XIX, 627–8). During the following days the Tory bookseller John Morphew (d. after 1720) and printer John Barber (*c.* 1675–1741) were interrogated, which did not reveal the author but did reveal that Secretary of State Mar had begun investigating the pamphlet even before Wharton's complaint. Oxford sent Swift £100 to assist Barber on 3 Mar. (*Swift Corr.*, I, 589). On 11 Mar., an address to the Queen asked that she issue a reward of £300 for details of the author. The proposal to insert in the proclamation the words 'because the Author ... pretends to know the Secrets of Your Majesty's Administration', which would have implicated and embarrassed the ministry, was defeated (*L.J.*, XIX, 631–4). However it came about, the ministry made the matter go away. In *The Political State* for Mar. 1714, Boyer complained that 'JONATHAN, the most *scandalous* and *flagitious* of all *Libellers*, being under the Wings of some great Men escaped *Discovery* and *Punishment*, at least, for the present' (VII, 215–23). But Swift was made nervous and was irked by the affair: 'The fault was, calling the Scots a fierce poor northern people. So well protected are those who scribble for the Government', he sarcastically wrote to Peterborough on 18 May 1714 (*Swift Corr.*, I, 602). See John Irwin Fischer, 'The Legal Response to Swift's *The Public Spirit of the Whigs*', in *Swift and His Contexts*, ed. John Irwin Fischer, Hermann J. Real, and James Woolley (New York, 1989), 21–38.

5   *Insolent Pamphlet writer.* Steele.
6   *1713*: 1714 new style.

248

To [Robert Harley, Earl of Oxford]
[*c.* 10 March 1714]

HEADNOTE: As the ministry prepared to pursue Steele's expulsion from the House of Commons, Defoe drew up an account of Steele's supposedly seditious writings since the previous summer, focusing on the non-demolition of Dunkirk. In *Mercator*, Defoe had recently reaffirmed his position that 'a particular Sett of People here' are wrong to demand 'it rashly Demolished now'.[1] Now, he tried to arm Oxford with a charge-sheet against Steele that has been called everything from 'near-hysterical' to an instance of Defoe's 'political integrity', these extremes coming from scholars focused on Steele and on Defoe, respectively.[2] In his *Apology for Himself and His Writings*, published after the Hanoverian succession in October 1714, Steele complained of his expulsion: 'If an Author's Words, in the obvious and natural Interpretation of them, have a Meaning which is Innocent, they cannot without great Injustice be condemned of another Meaning which is Criminal.'[3] Defoe's construal of the quotation from p. 17 of Steele's final *Englishman*

793

essay is perhaps most guilty of this wresting of meaning, of which Defoe had of course complained regarding his 1713 pamphlets on the succession.

On 11 March, John Hungerford (*c.* 1658–1729), MP for Scarborough, complained in the House of Commons about Steele's writings, but Steele was tactically absent, so the matter was deferred. The following day Oxford's cousin, MP for Hereford and one of the Auditors of the Imprest, Thomas Foley (1670?–1737), complained about Steele's *The Crisis* and two *Englishman* essays (nos. 46 and 57). These were censured by the House and Steele was ordered to appear on the 13th, when he was given until the 18th to prepare his defence. Steele counterstruck on 15 March when he moved that the works at Dunkirk be inspected; that motion was of course defeated. Steele and his collaborators – including Walpole, Halifax, and Stanhope – presented what is considered a robust defence.[4] But his writings were deemed seditious, as implying the Hanoverian succession was in danger, and Steele was expelled, becoming a Whig martyr.[5] Steele returned to lampooning Oxford in his new periodicals, *The Lover* (2 February–27 May 1714) and *The Reader* (22 April–10 May 1714), trading blows with *The Monitor*, a Tory paper to which Defoe contributed. Steele continued to press on Dunkirk in his pamphlet *The French Faith Represented in the Present State of Dunkirk* (July 1714). After the Hanoverian succession, Steele was returned to parliament for Boroughbridge (Yorkshire) in 1715 and was knighted that year. Defoe's *An Essay upon Buying and Selling of Speeches* (May 1716) gives a malicious summary of Steele's career. And Defoe criticised Steele again during 1720 in his periodical *The Commentator*.

Colleccon of Scandal

In The Late Guardian[6]

Many Repetitions of That Insolence Upon The Queen in Three Guardians Successively (Viz) <u>The People of Britain Expect Dunkirk to be Imediately Demolished</u>.[7]

This Repeated Severall Times and wickedly Paraphrased in The flying Post.[8]

The First English-Man

In The Letter Signed Richard Steel where he Falls upon The Examiner There are Diverse Threatning Speeches to The Ministers of state but Concealed Under The Generall Head of a Certain Lord.[9]

DEFOE TO [EARL OF OXFORD], [C. 10 MARCH 1714]

In The last English Man[10]

Pa 3.   The following words.
"That the Honour and Intrest of the Queen and her Love of her people hath been Sacrifiz'd to a Scandal"[11]
The Examples he Gives of these are as follows ibid:
   1. The Blackning and Ridiculeing the Noblest Parts of her Reign
   2. Inhumane Usage of her Old Servants[12]
   3. The life of The Queen doubtfull.[a][13]

In The Same page he Subjoyns The following Question as foll^s:
   Whether it be for The Queens Honour to have One half of her peoples affecċons alienated From her by studyed provocations.
      1 This Insinuates That ye Queen has alienated half[b] her peoples affections By studyed Provocaċons, for if Those Provocacons were from any One Elċe why should it alienate our affeccons From The Queen.
      2 This Supposes half The peoples affeccons alienated from her Maj^{tie} which is Malitious and Scandalous to the highest Degree and God be praised is False also.
      3 It is a Charge upon The administraċon as studying to Provoke The People and Consequently is a Reall stirring up and provokeing the people Against The Governm^t which is Sedition and of the worst kind.

Page. 17   he has These words:
   One might Very Lately[c] have Said — The Dignity and Authourity of Parliaments Could not be better strengthened Than by plaċeing a Despotick power in the Soveraign.[14]
      This he has warily Express'd but he Ought to have proved That Such a Prinċiple has been allowed and Encouraged by the Government, for he Sayes Expressly a Man would be Thought to Argue Very well who Said So.

---

[a] doubtfull] *following numeral '4' cancelled on the next line*
[b] half] *interlined*
[c] *Lately*] *interlined above cancelled word* 'well'

795

DEFOE TO [EARL OF OXFORD], [*C.* 10 MARCH 1714]

Pa. 18 and also Page 10   The Following Expressions Concerning
The Demolishing Dunkirk:

"The Queens Garrison is Exposed by Levelling the Works to
yᵉ Mercy of The French And The Mole[15] and Harbour wᶜʰ were
first to be demolished stand as They did, The Terrour[a] of Great
Britain."[16]

Before this, Page 10,[17] He Sayes "at This Day it (Dunkirk)
is in a More Dangerous Condiċon as to England Than it was
when I wrot about yᵉ Importanċe of it,[18] for I Insisted on yᵉ
Demolition of the Mole and Harbour, and Instead of That
They have Exactly, as if Mʳ Tugghe's Memorial[19] had been the
Direccon in This Case, Demolished The Works, and left The
Harbour, its sluices, and all its Accesses, that Concern us, Our
Trade, and Our Safety, in Good Condicon."

The Seditious Design of this is Evedent, and The
Falshood of it is Manifesst; in That The Accesses as he
Calls Them, to The Mole, were The Risbank,[20] and Forts;
wᶜʰ Guarded The Access to The Said Harbour From us;
which[b] are all Demolished and The Harbour till it is filled
up is left Open, and Defenceless, Except by The Citadelle,
wᶜʰ was in her Majᵗⁱᵉˢ posession.

To Say The Mole and Harbour stand as they did, when
they are stript of Their Defence wᶜʰ Rendred them Safe, is
Very absurd.[21]

Pa. 22.   He has The Following abominable Refleccon upon The
Queen:

"I Wish[c] Thirdly[22] That his Electorall highness of Hannover
would be So Gratefull to Signifye to all The World The perfect
Good Understanding he has with The Court of England in as
plain Terms as her Majᵗⁱᵉ was pleased to Declare She had with
That house on her part."

---

[a] Terrour] *the* 'u' *is interlined*
[b] which] *interlined*
[c] Wish] *following word perhaps* 'hear' *cancelled*

DEFOE TO [EARL OF OXFORD], [C. 10 MARCH 1714]

This is The Most Malicous, Undutifull and
Reproachfull Thing he Could possibly Say of the Queen,
Suggesting That her Maj^ties haveing Declar'd it was
of No Weight, nor Ought not to be Depended upon
by her people without a Voucher From The Elector of
Hannover.[23]

In The Crisis[24]

Pa 1   of The Dedicacon to The Clergy:

He Endeavours to perswade The Clergy to preach Sedition
and uses Arguments to press the Necessity, Dictateing
Arrogantly and Scandalously to The Ministers of the Church
of England to Recomend what he has Collected both in Their
Sermons and writeings.[25]
    The body of his book Consists Onely of Quotacons
    and Reciteings of Acts of Parliament,[26] But —
In his Seasonable Remarks on The Said Quotacons he has
The following Expressions:

Pa 27.
    "One can not but Think that Our Popish and Jacobite
Party who have been of Late So bold both in Writing and
Speaking Against ye Settlement of ye Crown of Great Britain
in The Protestant line[27] Must have Some Unaccountable
Encouragement for their Support."
    Here is a plain Insinuacon of The Danger of y^e
    Succession under her Maj^ties administracon.

In The Same Page he Sayes:
    "Let me Inform Every Briton That Loves his Queen,
Religion, laws and Liberties it is his Duty to Appear boldly
in Their Defence, and Detect and <u>Seize</u> Those (Jacobites)[28]
Enemies to his Country wherever he Finds Them."
    Here he puts The Civil Justice into The hands of y^e
    Rabble and Empowers them to fall upon who They please
    under The pretence of Their being Jacobites.

DEFOE TO [EARL OF OXFORD], [*C.* 10 MARCH 1714]

Pa. 29   He asks a question Relateing to The Settlem^t of Our
          Peace which Implyes a Strong Negacon (Viz):
     "Where are The Marks of a Lasting Security?"
          Insinuating That Our Settlement is without any Visible
          Security for Our posterity.

Pa. 31   After a fulsome Harangue upon The Conduct of The
          Duke of Marlbro'[29] he Sayes:
     "The Reputacon of The Duke of Marlebro'[30] Could not Well
be Impair'd without Sullying The Glory of Great Britain it
Self.
     "The Minds of the Common People Against all Comon
Sence are Debauched with Impressions of The Dukes
Affectacon of Prolonging the War for his Own Glory."
     "That The Duke of Marlbro' was not permitted to Enjoy the
Fruits of his Glorious Labour."
          Here he acknowleges Takeing Away his Employm^t as
          an Injury to The Duke; and That prolonging The War was
          the Fruit of his Glorious Labour, wch he Expected but was
          not Permitted to Enjoy.

Pa. 31   Speaking of The Peace he Sayes:
     "The house of Bourbon is at This Juncture become More
Formidable and bids Fairer for an Universall Monarchy^a and to
Engross ye whole Trade of Europe Than it did before The war."
          This a Most False and Therefore Scandalous Suggestion
          and Inconsistent wth what he had been Saying before^b of
          The Glories and Conquests of The D of Marlbro' and w^th
          what he had printed of the Importance of Dunkirk and
          of France being Removd 2 or 300 Miles From us by The
          Demolishing Dunkirk.[31]

Ibid
     "The Brittish in the Midst of The Enemies Garrisons
withdraw themselves from The[32] Confederates."

---

^a Monarchy] *following word* 'Than' *cancelled*
^b before] *following word* 'and' *cancelled*

798

DEFOE TO [EARL OF OXFORD], [C. 10 MARCH 1714]

This was False in Fact, for when The D of Ormond
Withdrew, The Confederates had not advanc't from Their
First Encampment and had all Their Own Garrisons
in Their Reer, and were Superiour to The Enemy as
Appear'd by Their Attacking Quesnoy, and Might have
Continued So if by a Fatal Arrogance They had not in
Contempt of Their Enemy Exposed Themselves in ye
Most Unsoldierlike Manner in The World wch was their
Ruin at^a Landrecy.[33]

P 31. and 32 Speaking of Dunkirk he Sayes Thus:
"Which They have begun Contemptuously and Arbitrarily
(to Demolish) Their Own Way.[34] The Mole and Harbour which
Onely are Dreadfull to us are yet Untouch't and just Suspicons
Given That They Will Ever be."
   This Needs No Comment. It is in Every Sentence
Most Scandalous, false and Seditious.[35]

P 32 Speaking of Portugall he Says:
"Portugall has Onely^b at Present a Suspencon of Arms for its
Security."[36]
   This is upon The Queen also who has Engaged to Get
Reasonable Satisfaccon for Portugall as Well as for the Rest
of her Allyes, wch Engagemt he here Calls No Security.

Pa. 33 Speaking of The Catalognians[37] He Sayes:
"Drawn into The war by The Encouragemt of The Maritime
Powers — Now abandon'd and Exposed."
   Insinuateing That her Majtie both Drew the
Catalans into The Snare of the war and has basely and
Unrighteously abandon'd and Exposed Them.[38]

P. 33 Speaking of The present state of The French kings
affaires he adds:
"What have Great Britain[39] to hope From But The Mercy of
France."

^a at] *interlined*
^b has Onely] 'has Onely has Onely' *in MS*

799

DEFOE TO [EARL OF OXFORD], [*c*. 10 MARCH 1714]

Here he Represents his Country as Given up to France and bound hand and Foot lyeing at The Mercy of The French king.

The Remainder of The whole book is an In[c]ongruous[a] un adapted discourse On The Danger of The Pretender, Insinuating That we have no present Security Against him but in[b] the Severall Laws and acts of Parliament which he had Recited, Never once Suggesting what Farther Security humane Wit Can Invent or proposeing any Thing To that End; But[c] allowing That her Majties Zeal for The Safety of her Subjects is No[d] Manner of Security &c.

The Next book Observable is The <u>Neck or Nothing</u>, of wch They have printed Six Thousand and Many whereof are Sent down into Scotland, The Author John Dunton.[40]

But The whole book is Such a Continued Rhapsody of Scandal and Raillery That it Seems Enough to Name it and to Collect from it would be to Transcribe it, from One End to the Other, for it is but One Continued Breath of Slander and Scurrillity on The administracon, Calling The Ministry Vile Names and Charging The Queens faithfull Servants with Treason, Robbery, Drunkness and all Manner of Crimes.

This it is hardly worth while to Lay before The Ministry Except Onely to Observe how pleasing Such Scandalous Things are Among us.

Text: BL Add. MS. 70291, fols. ²123–32.[41] *Address*: none. *Endorsed by Oxford* (fol. 130ᵛ): Heads of Scandal – R march: 10: 1713/14

a In[c]ongruous] 'c' *omitted in MS*
b in] *interlined*
c To that End; But] *interlined above cancelled word* 'Nor'; *superfluous semi-colon omitted in this edition*
d No] *interlined above cancelled word* 'any'

---

1 *Mercator*, no. III (4–6 Feb. 1714).
2 Paul Hyland, 'A Breach of the Peace: The Controversy over the Ninth Article of the Treaty of Utrecht', *BJECS* 22 (1999), 51–66 (at 59); John Robert Moore, 'Defoe, Steele, and the Demolition of Dunkirk', *HLQ* 13 (1950), 279–302 (at 300).

DEFOE TO [EARL OF OXFORD], [*C.* 10 MARCH 1714]

3 *Mr. Steele's Apology for Himself and His Writings; Occasioned by His Expulsion from the House of Commons* (1714), 54.

4 His speech was published in *Mr. Steele's Apology*.

5 See Charles A. Knight, *A Political Biography of Richard Steele* (2009), 154–7; *Steele Corr.*, 89–92. Defoe quotes the House's censure of Steele in *The Monitor*, no. 4 (29 Apr. 1714).

6 *Late Guardian*: *The Guardian* ceased publication on 1 Oct. 1713, succeeded by *The Englishman* five days later. *The Englishman* is in *Defoe–Farewell Catalogue* (item 1459b).

7 *Three Guardians … Demolished*: Defoe is apparently misremembering. *The Guardian*, no. 128 (7 Aug. 1713), states 'That the British Nation expect the immediate Demolition of *Dunkirk*', but no three successive issues focus on Dunkirk.

8 *Paraphrased in The flying Post*: Throughout Sept. 1713, perhaps most flagrantly in *The Flying Post* for 15–17 Sept., which justifies the controversial use of 'expects'.

9 *Letter … Lord*: *Englishman*, no. 1 (6 Oct. 1713), contains a letter signed by Steele that encloses a letter 'from the Servant of a Man of Quality'; it is directed to the master ('whom every Body supposes to be some great Lord') of the author of *The Examiner* who has assaulted the letter-writer (see *Examiner*, vol. IV, no. 35 (25 Sept.–2 Oct. 1713)). The conceit is that the *Examiner* is the unruly servant of the ministry in general (it was well known that the ministry subsidised it) but of Oxford in particular (the letter alludes to the creation of new peers, a common Whig criticism of Oxford since the creation of twelve peers to ensure the passage of the peace preliminaries). See Steele, *The Englishman*, ed. Rae Blanchard (Oxford, 1955), 6–10.

10 *last English Man*: *The Englishman: Being the Close of the Paper so Called* was *Englishman*, no. 57 (15 Feb. 1714); it was a longer final issue, published as a quarto pamphlet, whereas nos. 1–56 were each single folio half-sheets (*Englishman*, ed. Blanchard, 227–49).

11 *That the Honour … Scandal*: Defoe's quotations from Steele are not always verbatim. For example, the original here reads: 'her Honour, and Interest, and Love of her People, hath been sacrific'd to a Scandal'.

12 *Old Servants*: Godolphin, Marlborough, and the Junto Whig Lords.

13 *life of The Queen doubtfull*: Steele is actually attacking the *Examiner's* disrespectful partisanship and levity 'while the Life of the Queen was yet doubtful', meaning at Christmas.

14 *The Dignity … Soveraign*: Steele is exposing a fallacy: it is as sensible to say that giving both France and Spain to the Bourbons is the best way to secure British commerce as it is to argue that placing a despot on the throne will secure our liberties. In suggesting that what Steele says 'Expressly' is actionable, despite his meaning clearly being the opposite, Defoe commits the kind of wilful misreading he decried in the case of his 1713 succession pamphlets.

15 *Mole*: Structure serving as a pier or breakwater.

16 *"The Queens Garrison … Great Britain."*: The quotation, actually 18–19, is within a letter Steele states he wrote to a friend who challenged his writings.

17 *Page 10*: Actually 10–11.

18 *when I wrot about ye Importance of it*: See headnote to Letter 246. This passage follows a substantial quotation from Defoe's *Reasons Concerning the Immediate Demolishing of Dunkirk*, though Steele does not identify Defoe as the author.

19 *Mr Tugghe's Memorial*: Ignace Tugghe (d. after 1721), Deputy to the Magistrates of Dunkirk, came to London to attempt to persuade the Queen to spare the mole and dikes that served the harbour, claiming these had no military function. When his pleas were ignored, he printed his *Memorial* in French and English: *Très-humble adresse présentée à la Reine de la Grande Bretagne, par le Deputé du Magistrat de Dunkerkerque auprès de sa Majesté / A Most Humble Address or Memorial presented to Her Majesty the Queen of Great Britain, by the Deputy of the Magistrates of Dunkirk* (1713). The Whigs took this as evidence of the ministry's perfidy, and Steele reprinted it in *The Importance of Dunkirk Consider'd* (1713).

20 *Risbank*: The risbanc was a fort erected by Vauban (1633–1707) to defend the western jetty at Dunkirk. See *A Particular Description of the Famous Town and Cittadel of Dunkirk* (1712), 6–7. In *Englishman*, no. 31 (15 Dec. 1713), Steele printed a letter that dismissed the idea that the risbanc's destruction indicated compliance with the Treaty of Utrecht's stipulations for

DEFOE TO [EARL OF OXFORD], [C. 10 MARCH 1714]

demolishing Dunkirk. Defoe gave a substantial account of the Dunkirk fortifications, including the risbanc, in *A Continuation of Letters written by a Turkish Spy* (1718), *SFS*, v, 188–91.

21 *To Say ... Very absurd*: In *The Monitor*, no. 5 (1 May 1714), Defoe cites the same passage from Steele – 'an Author famous for recommending those Vertues which he never practis'd' – and comments on it as follows:

> The Risbank and the Fort de Reserve, Fort Verd, and, in brief, all the Forts to the Sea-ward, which guarded the Entrance into *the Harbour*, and made it inaccessible ... were all demolished, blown up, and torn in pieces, before this was written; not a Gun was left standing to the Sea-side, that could command the Entrance into *the Harbour*, except the Citadel, which the *English* were possess'd of.

> If then all those things which render'd *the Harbour* strong, and difficult of access, were actually demolished and destroy'd, how could this Author, who says he is a Gentleman, have the assurance to print such a Manifest Falshood[?]

22 *Thirdly*: The first two wishes in Steele's original are for the demolition of the harbour at Dunkirk and for the Pretender's removal from Lorraine (the Treaty of Utrecht required France to expel the Pretender but Whigs pointed out that he had so far only removed from St Germain to Lorraine).

23 *Voucher From The Elector of Hannover*: This was a sore point for the Queen, jealous of being undermined by her successor. As Knight notes, this specific sentence 'became one of the points of attack when Steele was expelled from the House of Commons' (*Political Biography of Richard Steele*, 144).

24 *The Crisis*: See headnotes to Letters 246 and 247. It is in *Defoe–Farewell Catalogue* (item 1459a).

25 *He Endeavours ... writeings*: Steele begins his dedication to the clergy by offering 'the following Comment upon the Laws which regard the Settlement of the Imperial Crown of Great Britain' and conjures the clergymen 'to recommend them, in Your Writings and Discourses, to Your Fellow-Subjects' (*The Crisis* (1714), i). Swift was the first wilfully to distort Steele's meaning by alleging that Steele was recommending his own comment on the laws rather than the laws themselves (*The Publick Spirit of the Whigs, EPW 1711–14*, 247–8).

26 *The body ... Parliament*: Steele was mocked for his extensive recital and reproduction of twenty years of legislation that bolstered the Protestant succession. Swift jeered: 'Whoever is Patentee for Printing Acts of Parliament, may have a very fair Action against him, for Invasion of Property' (*EPW 1711–14*, 261).

27 *Protestant line*: Defoe elides the following words, after 'line' and surrounded by commas, in Steele's original: 'and cannot possibly plead Ignorance of these Things'.

28 *Seize Those (Jacobites)*: 'seize' is not underlined in Steele's original; '(Jacobite)' is Defoe's insertion.

29 *Harangue ... Duke of Marlbro'*: See *The Crisis*, 29–31. The three quotations that follow are in reverse order of their appearance in *The Crisis*.

30 *Reputaćon of The Duke of Marlebro'*: Marlborough's reputation had bifurcated across party lines. The division is epitomised by *The Crisis* on the laudatory Whig side, and by Steele's Tory respondents, Marlborough's detractors, including Swift's latest diatribe in *The Public Spirit of the Whigs, EPW 1711–14*, 267–72, and B. R., *Remarks on Mr. Steele's Crisis* (1714), 14–17. Tories decried Marlborough's pride, ambition, philistinism, and haughtiness to the Queen; they considered him careless of the lives of the common soldiery, eager to engross their glory to himself, and willing to protract a war that enhanced his personal glory and wealth. Marlborough's alleged avarice was central to the Tory attacks. They imagined him either uxuriously submissive to a termagent wife or plotting in concert with her for greater power. Whigs viewed Marlborough as the great military figure of the age, who won every battle he fought and took every town he besieged; but his victories were betrayed by a grubby peace, and the Duke was treated with ingratitude and ignominy. See Frances Marjorie

DEFOE TO [EARL OF OXFORD], [C. 10 MARCH 1714]

Harris, 'A Study of the Paper War Relating to the Career of the 1st Duke of Marlborough, 1710–1712' (Westfield College PhD, 1975).

Defoe's position is arguably more complex. He preferred to point out to the Whigs now decrying Marlborough's treatment that they had attempted to oust Marlborough and Godolphin, so have no basis for charging the Tories with mistreatment of a hero (*A Letter to the Dissenters* (1713), *PEW*, III, 330). But he distanced himself from the strongest Tory attacks. 'I am not justifying the *Examiner* in his Treatment of the Duke of M——gh', Defoe insists (*A Letter to the Whigs* (1714), 12). But Defoe did join in the sniping, such as in his reference to 'Families enriched out of the publick Spoils' in *A Letter to the Dissenters*, *PEW*, III, 320; and Defoe had referred to the 'selfish Principles in some of the Persons concern'd, who for Reasons of their own, were unwilling the War should End' in 1709 (*Reasons why this Nation Ought to put a Speedy End to this Expensive War* (1711), *PEW*, II, 226). The depiction of Marlborough in Defoe's *Minutes of the Negotiations of Monsr. Mesnager* (1717), written from the perspective of an enemy French emissary, is characteristically ambivalent, doing justice to the Duke's military and diplomatic abilities but invoking the idea that he was haughty and dictatorial; Mesnager acknowledges that Tory efforts to blacken Marlborough's name were party quarrels, making him a victim, not proponent, of partisanship (*SFS*, IV, 28–9, 64, 91–2, 110).

31 *what he had printed … Dunkirk*: In *The Importance of Dunkirk Consider'd* (1713), Steele wrote that, after Dunkirk's demolition, the French fleet would be closest to Britain at Brest, 200 miles west (26–7).

32 *The*: 'Their' in Steele's original.

33 *Landrecy*: Fighting on without Britain after Ormond obeyed the restraining orders, the Austrians and Dutch captured Le Quesnoy in June 1712, then laid siege to Landrecies, but were defeated at Denain on 24 July.

34 *Contemptuously and Arbitrarily (to Demolish) Their Own Way*: The parenthetical part is Defoe's insertion to clarify the meaning.

There are numerous and evolving factors for the limited, not total, demolition of Dunkirk almost a year after the Treaty of Utrecht. If Bolingbroke wavered, that can be interpreted in several ways. In his favour, it can be said that he thought British possession of Dunkirk would be valuable leverage in trade discussions with the Dutch should they emerge from negotiations with the Holy Roman Empire in possession of Ostend (Bolingbroke to Oxford, 25 Aug. 1713, H.M.C. *Portland MSS*, v, 325; Bolingbroke to Prior, 15 Sept. 1713, TNA SP 104/28, fols. 14ʳ–19ᵛ). By contrast, it can be construed unfavourably, as it was after his flight to the Pretender in 1715, as evidence of Bolingbroke's collusion with the Jacobites (Steele, *Englishman*, 2nd series, no. 4 (22 July 1715); Thomas Burnet, *Grumbler*, nos. 29 and 30 (28 June and 1 July 1715)). There were logistical difficulties to demolishing such strong fortifications and the French set about frustrating the work, as Bolingbroke complained in late 1713 (Bolingbroke to Prior, 2 Dec. and 29 Dec. 1713, *British Diplomatic Instructions, 1689–1789, Vol. II: France, 1689–1721*, ed. L. G. Wickham Legg (1925), 54–6, 59–61). Steele went on to decry the inactivity in his subsequent periodical, *The Reader*, no. 5 (30 Apr. 1714), and in *The French Faith Represented in the Present State of Dunkirk* (July 1714).

In Nov. 1716, France and Britain signed an alliance against Spain – later joined by the Dutch to form the Triple Alliance – that obviated the issue of Dunkirk's demolition.

35 *Scandalous, false and Seditious*: Defoe cited and rebutted the preceding passage from *The Crisis* in *The Monitor*, no. 5 (1 May 1714).

36 *"Portugall … Security."*: Spain and Portugal remained at war until 1715; Steele and other Whigs portrayed the peace as an abandonment of Portugal – 'and who knows but the old Pretensions of *Spain* to *Portugal* may be then revived' (*The Crisis*, 32).

37 *Catalognians*: The Catalans continued to oppose Philip V and Castilian rule; they capitulated after the prolonged siege of Barcelona succeeded in Sept. 1714. Again, Steele portrays the peace as a betrayal of allies.

DEFOE TO [EARL OF OXFORD], [c. 10 MARCH 1714]

38 *Catalans ... abandon'd and Exposed Them*: In *The Secret History of the White-Staff* (1714), Defoe insisted that the Queen and her ministers had done all for the Catalans that could reasonably be expected (*PEW*, II, 270–1). By the time Defoe wrote that, an English fleet was blockading Barcelona to help Spain and France bring the Catalans to heel; 'English opinion was shocked and shamed' and the Whigs attacked the ministry for this betrayal of former allies (Trevelyan, III, 227).

39 *Britain*: Defoe omits 'and *Holland*' after '*Britain*' in Steele's original.

40 *Neck or Nothing ... John Dunton*: Dunton (1659–1732) was a Whig bookseller and author; in his autobiographical *Life and Errors*, Dunton stated that his tract *Neck or Nothing* (1713) contained 'early discoveries of Oxford's and Bolingbroke's treason' (*Life and Errors*, II, 733). It accused those ministers of Jacobitism. A warrant was issued for his arrest. Defoe attacked *Neck or Nothing* in *A Letter to the Whigs* (1714), 13.

Defoe and Dunton were well acquainted. Dunton had often cited Defoe as a bold defender of truth – such as in *Dunton's Whipping-Post: or, A Satyr upon Every Body* (1706), 91 – and he quotes Defoe's *Some Thoughts upon the Subject of Commerce with France* on p. 59. Dunton called Defoe 'a man of good parts, and very clear sense' (*Life and Errors*, I, 180). Defoe's work for the ministry, especially after the peace, undid much of Dunton's good will. His *The Impeachment, or Great Britain's Charge Against the Present M—y* (1714) attacks Defoe's ironically titled *Reasons for Im— the L—d H— T—r, and Some Others of the P— M—* (Apr. 1714). For further attacks in 1714, see headnote to Letter 256.

The two men's connection goes back to the 1690s, when Dunton, according to his account, commissioned Defoe to write the poems 'To the Athenian Society' (1692) and *The Character of the Late Dr. Samuel Annesley* (1697). Dunton was the son-in-law of the Defoe family's pastor, Annesley (*c.* 1620–96), so that may be how the two first met. Aside from their political differences, Dunton resented Defoe for separately printing the Annesley poem (*Life and Errors*, I, 180; Dunton, *The Preaching Weathercock* (1712), 79). Dunton had another gripe, believing that the *Review* among others took the idea of answering readers' letters on cases of conscience from his own *Athenian Mercury* (1690–7). See Dunton, *Stinking Fish* (1708), sig. B2v; *Athenianism* (1710), 113; *Life and Errors*, I, 423. On Dunton, see Stephen Parks, *John Dunton and the English Book Trade: A Study of His Career with a Checklist of His Publications* (New York, 1976).

41 Defoe writes on recto pages and he numbers the sheets 1–5, so '1' is written in the top left corner on fol. ²123r, '2' on fol. ²125r, '3' on fol. ²127r, '4' on fol. ²129r, and '5' on fol. ²131r.

DEFOE TO [EARL OF OXFORD], 11 MARCH 1714

249

To [Robert Harley, Earl of Oxford]
11 March 1714

HEADNOTE: The passage in this day's *Flying Post* that Defoe complains about is in a letter to the newspaper, and it reflects on the Queen's speech opening parliament on 2 March:

> Since we were lately told from the Throne, that those who represent the Hanover Succession to be *in Danger under her Majesty's Administration*, are a Faction, and no Friends either to her Majesty or to that Succession; 'tis not to be presum'd that a Man of Foresight will so far hazard his own Ease and Safety, to assert the Contrary. What tho the Duke of Lorrain, who still harbours the Pretender, is raising great Levys of Men, at a time when a Peace seems almost concluded between the Empire and France? What tho the Pretender's Friends here dare publickly to drink his Health and his *Secretarys* to assert his pretended Hereditary *Jure Divino* Title; and all this with an Air of Authority, and in Defiance of the many solemn Oaths, Acts of Parliament, and Treatys, by which (as the Commons observe) the Hanover Succession stands secured? Yet a Man of profound Duty and Loyalty will, whatever he thinks, for the future never open his Lips about the Danger of the Protestant Succession, till he hears that the Pretender is come again with a French Fleet into the Frith of Edinburg, or into the Mouth of the Thames, and till he actually lands his Men and disperses his Treasonable Manifestos to seduce her Majesty's loving Subjects from their Obligations to God and their lawful Sovereign.

The letter goes on to present a declaration purportedly from the Pretender, 'not only to divert your Readers, but to give them a Sample of what are like to be the Pretender's *Manifestos*, if ever he should presume, upon her Majesty's most gracious Clemency to some of his Friends, to make another formal Invasion upon these Protestant Realms'.[1] This was a sign of what Oxford would face in the House of Lords. On 5 April 1714, the Whigs introduced a motion there, patently levelled at Oxford, declaring that the Succession was in danger, which was narrowly defeated in a vote by 76 to 64 but not before members had accused the Treasurer of Jacobitism.[2] On 22 April Defoe began a new pro-ministry journal, *The Monitor*.[3]

805

DEFOE TO [EARL OF OXFORD], 11 MARCH 1714

My Lord

After what is printed This day in The Flying Post[4] I Think Nothing[a] can be So Insolent, but her Maj^tie May Expect it From These Men; And if The house does not Think Fit to Resent it, They will neither do justice to her Maj^tie or to her Subjects who They Represent.

The Supposition That ye Printer[5] is in Prison, Tho' in Reallity he is at full Liberty, is it Seems The Encouragem^t to This Offenče, as if a Man Under Convicčon of One Crime Could not Committ Another;[6] But Neither is The Man Concern'd but ye Party who Insultingly Say The Printer has ye Protecčon of a jail and That The Government can not Come at it Nor Suppress it.

I am far From Prompting justiče but No faithfull Subject can be Satisfyed to See justiče Thus affronted and I Move yor Ld^pp The Rather because I See This as a forerunner of Greater Insults under ye Same protecčon.

I Hear ye whole Town Crye out of this Insolenče as ye Most Unparalelld affront to The Person and Honour of her Maj^tie That Ever Subject was permitted Unpunished to be Guilty of; My Zeal Carrys me too Far. I Humbly ask yor Ld^pp Pardon.

The words I Speak of and wch I Humbly Referr yor Ld^pp to are in The first 26 lines of The Third Paragraph The Second Col. Flying Post N° 3462, March 11. I presume I Need not Send The paper, haveing it not at hand.

I am
May it please yor Ld^pp
yor Ld^pps Most Humble & Obed^t Servt
[*monogram*]

Ma: 11. 1713[7]

Text: BL Add. MS. 70291, fols. ²133–4. *Address*: none.

---

[a] Nothing] *interlined*

---

1 *The Flying Post*, 9–11 Mar. 1714.
2 Cobbett, vi, 1335–7.
3 Defoe is identified as author of *The Monitor* in *The Flying Post* for 26–9 June, which snipes at his fondness for irony, and the attribution is repeated in the same paper for 4–7 Dec. 1714,

DEFOE TO [EARL OF OXFORD], 21 MAY 1714

which alleges Defoe skimped on his sons' educations. In *The Reader*, no. 9 (10 May 1714), Steele prints a letter that associates Defoe with *The Monitor*, alluding to his pillorying in 1703 and royal pardon in 1713 (Steele, *Periodical Journalism, 1714–1716*, ed. Rae Blanchard (Oxford, 1959), 179). *The Monitor* speaks of its own authorship as plural, and some issues do not sound like Defoe (Novak, 447 n. 14). Furbank and Owens treat the attribution to Defoe as 'probable' (F&O, *Bibliography*, 251–3). This edition draws on *The Monitor* only where the coincidence of ideas or expressions between the periodical and the correspondence inspires confidence that Defoe was the contributor.

4   *what is printed This day in The Flying Post*: See headnote.
5   *Printer*: Hurt.
6   *as if a Man ... Another*: These words are similar to those in *The Monitor*, no. 6 (4 May 1714): 'They seem to behave themselves now, as if the Law had done with them, and that Men under Sentence for one Crime, could not commit another.'
7   *1713*: 1714 new style.

250

To [Robert Harley, Earl of Oxford]

21 May 1714

HEADNOTE **(Letters 250 and 251)**: The Schism Bill initiated by Bolingbroke was introduced into the Commons by his associate Sir William Wyndham (*c.* 1688–1740) on the day of this letter. It was part of Bolingbroke's effort to position himself as the Church of England's defender, garnering the support of the backbenchers and the Queen in his plan to replace Oxford at the helm of the Tory party. It targeted Dissenters' schools by requiring all teachers to be licensed by the diocesan bishop and to be Anglican communicants. So as not to seem antipathetic to the Church, further alienate the Queen, and expose the weakness of his handle on parliament, Oxford was compelled to support it against both his inclination and his policy of seeking the support of Whigs and Dissenters. Defoe later called it 'a Mine dug to blow up the *White-Staff*'; he says Dissenters blamed him for it at first but soon realised he was not its author.[1]

In March 1712, following the Occasional Conformity Act, Defoe had warned the Dissenters that their schools were not protected by law and were vulnerable.[2] He decried the state of Dissenting educational establishments in *The Present State of the Parties in Great Britain* (1712). Defoe published two pamphlets in June that attacked the Schism Bill while it was depending. *A Brief Survey of the Legal Liberties of the Dissenters* argues that it encroached on the Toleration Act.[3] *The Weakest Go to the Wall* tries to show the Dissenters that the Whigs had never truly espoused their interests. They reneged on a promise to exempt the Dissenters from

DEFOE TO [EARL OF OXFORD], 21 MAY 1714

the sacramental test in the immediate wake of the 1673 Test Act, thwarted William III's aims to do the same in 1689, and disregarded the issue when in power from 1705 to 1710. Their betrayal of the Dissenters over the 1711 Occasional Conformity Act was hardly a *volte face*, as even the defeats of Occasional Conformity Bills early in Anne's reign owed little to the Whigs. Defoe reiterates advice from his earlier publications, especially *A Letter to the Dissenters*:

> [The Dissenters] are a great body of Men, but not a united Body, not a concerted cemented Body; he that is a true Friend to the Dissenters, will advise them never to expect any thing from the Quarrels of Parties, and the Heats and Feuds of the State, except it be to be destroyed.[4]

He laments the Dissenters' failure to distinguish between the High Tories, who swept the election, and the ministry, which remained committed to moderation. The fervour of the Whig opposition to the ministry, to which the Dissenters had contributed, had made the ministry yet more dependent on the High Tories, less able to resist their demands for persecutory legislation. The Schism Act therefore was at least in part self-inflicted. In his 23 June letter Defoe was eager to prevent over-reactions from Dissenters that risked exacerbating the situation.

The Bill passed the Commons on 1 June, the Lords on 15 June, and would come into force on 1 August. In the event, the Queen's death and the Whig victory in the 1715 general election meant it was never enforced and was repealed in 1719. Because the Act was 'a Warm Admonition to the *Dissenters* to Revive the Ancient Family Discipline and Instruction, which was the original Method by which the Reformation was begun in this Nation', Defoe's conduct book *The Family Instructor* (1715) may be interpreted as a response to the Schism Act.[5]

My Lord

Last Nights Conversaćon Could not but afford Many Usefull Remarks to Me and[a] I Thought it[b] My Duty to Menćon to yo[r] L[d]pp again my[c] Observaćons on that part of it which Relates To The Dissenters.[d]

First The Bill depending about The dissenters Schools,[6] w[ch] I fear will pass; It is True My Lord The Conduct of The Dissenters has call'd for More Than this, and This may Remind them of a hint I

---

[a] and] *interlined above cancelled word* 'w[ch]'
[b] it] *interlined*
[c] my] *interlined above cancelled letter possibly* 'w'
[d] which Relates To The Dissenters] *squeezed between lines, indicating that the end of the paragraph was inserted later*

DEFOE TO [EARL OF OXFORD], 21 MAY 1714

gave Them in <u>The Letter</u>,[7] whether They Enjoy'd No Favours from her Maj[ties] Bounty which They might not Forfeit by Their present behaviour.

I doubt not but Their Pretended Friends the Whigs, will give them up in this, as they did in y[e] Occasionall Bill;[8] and which is Worse, They will Give Themselves up too, Rather Than not Carry On Their Party Mischief; I Pity Them, but I can not but Recommend The Intrest of Posterity to yo[r] L[dpps] Compassion; As to Their Accademies, if there had Never been any, I kno' not but Theyr Intrest had been as Good, and Fewer beggars and Drones had been bred up for Ministers Among Them;[9] But for The Schooles for Common Introduction of Children, I think Their Loss will be Irreparable. It is True, That They will have schooles still; They will be No More Illegall Than before,[10] but it Seems hard upon y[e] Naćon in Gener[ll], to make Laws w[ch] it will be Necessary to Break, Like That of y[e] late Abjuraćon[a] act in Scotland.[11]

The Dissenters have Now Leisure to Reflect upon Their Indolenće, and Supine Negligenće, who at y[e] Revolućon when They Obtain'd the Tolleraćon, Took no Thought for The Educaćon of their Posterity, or a Succession of Ministers to Preach to Them, Neither of which would Then have been denyed them at That Time.[12]

I am Prepareing to put Them in Mind of Their Duty, and Intrest in y[e] Present juncture,[13] and if (as I hope) I have Room to Morrow when According to yo[r] Command I shall attend yo[r] L[dpp] I purpose to Give yo[r] L[dpp] Some Acco[t] of it: I am in Great want also to Lay before you Something about y[e] Mercator, and if it May[b] Please yo[r] L[dpp] to have That Paper Made More usefull, I Mean to More Purposes Than its Single Originall design.[14] I have Some Thoughts to Lay before yo[r] L[dpp] on That head.

I Hope yo[r] L[dpp] is made Accquainted That M[r] M . . .[15] who first Set me upon that work, and Undertook The Support of it, has Declined any Consideraćon for it Ever Sinće Lady day Last;[16] So That I perform it wholly without any Appointm[t] for it, or benefit by it;[17] which I do Singly, as I hope it is of Serviće, and That it may be

---

[a] Abjuraćon] *following word* 'Oath' *cancelled*
[b] May] *following illegible word cancelled*

809

DEFOE TO [EARL OF OXFORD], 21 MAY 1714

agreeable to yor Ldpp to have it Continued; Tho' my Circumstances render it hard to me to do So because it is Expensive to me. But I Lay it all, and my Self at yor Ldpps Feet.

I am

May it Please yor Ldpp

yor Ldpps Most Humble and Obedt Servt

[*monogram*]

May. 21. 1714

Text: BL Add. MS. 70291, fols. ²135–6. *Address*: none. *Endorsed by Oxford* (fol. ²136v): mr Goldsmith may 21: 1714

1 *The Secret History of the White-Staff* (1714), *PEW*, II, 277; cf. Trevelyan, III, 280–3; Angus McInnes, *Robert Harley, Puritan Politician* (1970), 164–5.

2 *Review*, VIII, 668–9 (4 Mar. 1712).

3 He argued the same point in *Review*, III, 235–6 (16 Apr. 1706), stating that the Tories in Anne's first parliament wished to bring in such an act.

4 *The Weakest Go to the Wall*, *PEW*, III, 349. Defoe blamed the Whigs for embroiling the Dissenters with the government in *The Monitor*, no. 22 (10 June 1714).

5 *A Brief Survey of the Legal Liberties of the Dissenters*, 14; Irving N. Rothman, 'Defoe's *The Family Instructor*: A Response to the Schism Act', *PBSA* 74 (1980), 201–20.

6 *Bill depending about The dissenters Schools*: The Schism Bill. See headnote.

7 *The Letter*: *A Letter to the Dissenters*.

8 *Occasionall Bill*: See headnote to Letter 203.

9 *As to Their Accademies ... Among Them*: Defoe criticised the current state of the Dissenters' academies in *The Present State of the Parties in Great Britain* (1712), 296–305, 315–19; he proposes some reforms at 334–7. For his own education at Newington Green Academy under Charles Morton (1627–98), see Lew Girdler, 'Defoe's Education at Newington Green Academy', *SP* 50 (1953), 573–91; Backscheider, *Life*, 13–21; Ilse Vickers, *Defoe and the New Sciences* (Cambridge, 1996), 32–51.

10 *No More Illegall Than before*: Technically Dissenters could be punished for teaching without an Episcopal licence. Defoe wrote in *A Letter to the Dissenters* that Nonconformists' 'Schools and Seminaries [are] allow'd them, though by Law they may and ought to be suppressed' (*PEW*, III, 321).

11 *Laws ... Scotland*: See Defoe's discussion in *A Brief Survey of the Legal Liberties of the Dissenters*, in which he says that Dissenters 'must offend against this Law, because they are bound to *obey God rather than Man*' (7). On the abjuration oath requirement as a law the breach of which was expected, see Letter 227, note 5.

12 *The Dissenters ... That Time*: Defoe regretted the Dissenters' failure in 1689 to gain legislation for 'the allowance of Schools and Tutors, as well as for the common Instruction of their Children, as for preserving the Succession of their Ministers' (*The Weakest Go to the Wall*, *PEW*, III, 344; cf. *Review*, VIII, 668 (4 Mar. 1712)).

13 *I am Prepareing ... Present juncture*: He published *A Brief Survey of the Legal Liberties of the Dissenters* and *The Weakest Go to the Wall* in June.

14 *Single Originall design*: The promotion of the Anglo-French Treaty of Commerce in 1713, which remained *Mercator*'s focus despite the increasing improbability of the Bill being revived. The idea of giving *Mercator* a more general topical focus may be why no. 159, for 27–9

810

DEFOE TO [EARL OF OXFORD], 23 JUNE 1714

May 1714, reflects on the Schism Bill, blaming the Whigs for embroiling the Dissenters with the government.

15 *Mr M . . .*: Arthur Moore. See Letter 233, note 4.

16 *Lady day Last*: 25 Mar. 1714.

17 *I perform ... by it*: See Letter 231, notes 8 and 9. In *Mercator*, no. 159 (27–9 May 1714), Defoe pointedly asserted that his Whig opponents are 'Employed, and Supported, and Paid; which is what cannot be said with Truth of those who write the *Mercator*'. The final issue avers that 'no Fee, or Payment, or Reward has been the Motive, nor have the Persons who have been concerned in it received any' (*Mercator*, no. 181 (17–20 July 1714)).

251

To [Robert Harley, Earl of Oxford]

23 June 1714

My Lord

Tho' I have Not been able to pay my Duty to yor L^{dpp} as Usuall by Reason of a lameness wch has long Confin'd me, yet I Could not Refrain writeing on ye following Occasions.

Tho' I go not abroad yet I find Ever Since the Depending bill against ye Dissenters[1] There has been a Certain Set of Men, Appointed no doubt, who make it their bussiness Among the Dissenters to Talk in a New Dialect (Viz) That Things are Now Comeing to a Crisis; That Men had as Good lose Their Lives as their Libertyes and Their Religion; That these Were The Onely Two Things which made The Revolucon; That There is a Time when Men Can bear No Longer; That we Ought to Resist Such Violence; That Our Children will be Taken from us Next and put to Charity Schooles;[2] That we had better begin at first while we^a have Some Friends and Means to help Our Selves Than stay till we are quite Ruin'd and till Matters become Irretrievable —

There is Much More in The discourses of these men. I hope and Believ My Lord That ye Main body of the dissenters are wiser Than to be Influenced by Such Speeches to any thing Undutifull and

^{a} we] *interlined*

811

DEFOE TO [EARL OF OXFORD], 23 JUNE 1714

Unquiet and if they should, wᶜʰ I should be Very Sorry For, I know it would End in Their Ruine.³

But That there are Some who would Gladly bring them into Some Such Snare, Nay tho' it were to Their Ruine, So it might but Give Some shock to yᵉ Public Tranquillity, This I Make no Doubt of and Therefore I Thoᵗ it might not be Improper to Represent it to yoʳ Lᵈpp.

I am

May it Please yoʳ Lᵈpp

yoʳ Lᵈpps Most Obedᵗ Servᵗ

[*monogram*]

June. 23.ᵃ 1714

Text: BL Add. MS. 70291, fols. ²137–8. *Address*: none.

ᵃ 23] *amended from* '24'

---

1 *Depending bill against yᵉ Dissenters*: The Schism Bill passed the Lords on 15 June and was due to come into effect on 1 Aug.

2 *Charity Schooles*: These were established and maintained by local parishes to teach poor children to read and write; they were of course Anglican. Defoe praised the charity school movement in *A Fourth Essay, at Removing National Prejudices* (1706), *PEW*, IV, 126. See M. G. Jones, *The Charity School Movement: A Study of Eighteenth-Century Puritanism in Action* (Cambridge, 1938); Craig Rose, 'Evangelical Philanthropy and Anglican Revival: The Charity Schools of Augustan London, 1698–1740', *London Journal* 16 (1991), 35–65.

3 *Ruine*: Having spent many years encouraging the Dissenters to bear with their legal disabilities, including up to the Schism Act, after the Hanoverian succession Defoe published pamphlets urging that the time was right to remove penal laws such as the Test Act. *The Layman's Vindication of the Church of England* (1716) insisted that the Dissenters were loyalists, and Defoe urged that that loyalty be rewarded with greater civic enfranchisement in *The Question Fairly Stated* (1717).

DEFOE TO [EARL OF OXFORD], 26 JULY 1714

252

To [Robert Harley, Earl of Oxford]

26 July 1714

HEADNOTE: By 26 July, Oxford was on the brink of dismissal and Bolingbroke on the verge of power.[1] Oxford's relationship with the Queen had deteriorated since summer 1713, partly stemming from what he called his 'never enough to be lamented folly' in requesting the defunct dukedom of Newcastle for his son, Edward (1689–1741),[2] and partly due to his personal conduct to the Queen, who accused him of being negligent, cryptic, quarrelsome, and too often inebriated.[3] Although his grip on power was weakening, Oxford attempted a last-ditch alliance with Whigs, mainly with the aim of securing the Protestant succession, mistrusting Bolingbroke's intentions.

My Lord

I humbly Thank yor L^{d}pp for yor Order to me to Send a Reciept for ye Usuall Sum^4 on my p[er]ticular Acco^t which I have done Enclosed^a and Shall attend my Self in ye Evening.

I am My Lord Capable of Judgeing but by Outsides of Things, and of knowing Little but without doores, but my Lord when I See Those who Owe Their Fortunes to yor L^{d}pp,[5] and who have pretended So Much, faće About upon Their Benefactor, It can Not but Move me to Lay Their Conduct before you.

When I See with^b what assurance They Tell the world how Capable they are to act without yor help; when I kno' The Time They Could not^c have stood an hour without you, This Tells me Their Folly, and Treachery at ye Same Time.

But My Lord, when They Speak of their haveing Power wth the Queen to disposess and Succeed yor L^{d}pp, I must Confess it Amazes me, as well to Think whether Such a thing Can be, as what Ruine The Naćon will be Exposed to if it should.

I hope still yor L^{d}pp, who has been Victorious Over worse Enemyes than These, will Easily Baffle their projects; if Not I Think it my Duty to Repeat my assuranćes of my following yor worst

---

^{a} Enclosed] *interlined above cancelled words* 'by the Bearer'
^{b} with] *amended from* 'without'
^{c} not] *interlined*

813

DEFOE TO [EARL OF OXFORD], 26 JULY 1714

Fortunes, and of being, fall it foul or fair, yor Constant faithfull and Steddy as well as Humble and Obed^t Servt.

[monogram]

July. 26. 1714^a

Text: BL Add. MS. 70291, fols. ^{2}139–40. *Address*: none.

---

^{a} July. 26. 1714] *written vertically down lefthand margin*

1 Matthew Decker (1679–1749) to [Oxford], 26 July 1714, H.M.C. *Portland MSS*, v, 476.

2 H.M.C. *Portland MSS*, v, 466. See Holmes, 206. The request in Sept. 1713 still rankled now, nine months later; on 23 July 1714, Anne said Oxford 'had never Acted Right in the Queens Affairs since his being refus'd the Title of Duke of Newcastle' (Hamilton, *Diary*, 64). In Aug. 1713, Edward Harley, second Earl of Oxford from 1724, had married the only child of the recently deceased Duke, Lady Henrietta Cavendish Holles (1694–1755).

3 Erasmus Lewis to Swift, 27 July 1714, *Swift Corr.*, II, 31.

4 *Usuall Sum̄*: 'Guilot' received the standard £100 from secret service accounts on both 2 and 26 July 1714 (TNA T 48/16, fols. 92, 95). Cf. Oxford's memoranda for 24 July in which he records a payment to Guilot and crosses out the beginning of a reference to 'Alexander Goldsmith' (BL Add. MS. 70331, fols. 120, 122).

5 *Those who Owe Their Fortunes to yor Ldpp*: The main conspirators against Oxford were all past recipients of his patronage and mentoring: Bolingbroke; Abigail, Baroness Masham (*c.* 1670–1734), Keeper of the Privy Purse; Francis Atterbury, Bishop of Rochester; and Simon Harcourt, first Viscount Harcourt (1661–1728), Lord High Chancellor. Defoe emphasises that each owed their position to Oxford in *The Secret History of the White-Staff*, *PEW*, II, 282–3, and *Part II* (1714), 39–44.

Oxford was Lady Masham's second cousin and she helped him to confer with the Queen while he was out of power from 1708 to 1710; after Oxford began to quarrel with the Queen in 1713, she worked with Bolingbroke.

Oxford secured for Atterbury the Deanery of Carlisle in 1704 and trusted him as an ecclesiastical lieutenant until 1708; after 1710, Atterbury worked with Oxford's ministry and was appointed Dean of Christ Church, Oxford, in 1711 and to his bishopric in 1713. But he sympathised more with Bolingbroke's plan to strengthen the Church party than Oxford's moderating scheme and conspired against Oxford in 1713–14. See G. V. Bennett, *The Tory Crisis in Church and State: The Career of Francis Atterbury, Bishop of Rochester* (Oxford, 1975), esp. 75–97, 139–44, 161–82.

Harcourt and Bolingbroke both resigned with Oxford in 1708 and returned with him in 1710. Though Harcourt sided with Bolingbroke in 1713–14, he was instrumental in ensuring the dying Queen gave the white staff to Shrewsbury rather than Bolingbroke, and he helped to organise Oxford's legal defence against impeachment charges in 1717. As Attorney General in 1703, Harcourt conducted the prosecution of *The Shortest Way with the Dissenters*, Defoe having called him '*Socinian H—t*' in *Reformation of Manners* (1702), line 573, *SFS*, I, 172.

DEFOE TO [EARL OF OXFORD], 3 AUGUST 1714

253

To [Robert Harley, Earl of Oxford]

3 August 1714

HEADNOTE: On 27 July, the dying Queen Anne dismissed Oxford as Lord Treasurer.[1] But rather than bestowing the white staff on Bolingbroke, at the Privy Council's urging she gave it to Shrewsbury. Shrewsbury's appointment as Lord Treasurer signalled that the Act of Settlement would certainly be honoured.[2] Bolingbroke had failed to win either the Queen's confidence or a commanding share of the Tory party. The other iron he had in the fire had not paid off either: he had maintained correspondence with the Pretender's Court but had not managed to persuade James to convert to Protestantism. His strategy for beyond Anne's death, then, seems to have been to strengthen the Tories to the extent that even the Hanoverian Elector would have to come to terms with them, though even he sought an amnesty or rapprochement with the Whigs to strengthen his position in the new reign.[3] On 1 August, Anne died, and George I was immediately proclaimed king.

My Lord

The Surpriseing Turn given by The Imediate hand of Providence[4] to the State of things Since my Last has been the Reason why I have not Persued what I was upon[5] for Vindicateing yor L^dpps p[er]son and Conduct and Exposeing yor Enemyes as I had proposed to yor L^dpp and wch was actually in the Press and p[ar]t of it Printed off.

The Change of affaires Necessarily working a Change in The judgement Men Make of things, I tho^t It my duty to Take my Measures from yor L^dpp, and from ye farther Turns in The publick administra͡con wch a Little Time may produce.

I Give yor L^dpp the Trouble of This Onely to Let yor L^dpp See that I am Not Unmindfull of my duty, and that yor Service^a and Intrest wch was allways at My heart is still So as much as Ever, and will Remain So at all Times.

I can not Omitt My humble and Thankfull Men͡con of yor L^dpps Goodness to me, when I had last ye hono^r to attend you, and^b when you were^c pleased to give me Assurance of ye Continuance of

---

^a Service] *following letter* 'w' *cancelled*
^b and] *interlined*
^c were] *interlined*

DEFOE TO [EARL OF OXFORD], 26 AUGUST 1714

yor favour and Bounty. It Remains that I Endeavour to Merit yor goodness, or at Least to Convince yor L^dpp That I am willing to do So, by a Constant adhereing to yor Intrest and Service to ye Uttmost.

I am, May it Please yor L^dpp

yor L^dpps Most Obliged Humble & Obed^t Servant

[*monogram*]

August. 3. 1714

Text: BL Add. MS. 70291, fols. ²141–2. *Address*: none.

1   See the contemporary accounts quoted in Henry L. Snyder, 'The Last Days of Queen Anne: The Account of Sir John Evelyn Examined', *HLQ* 34 (1971), 261–76.
2   Robin Eagles, '"I Have Neither Interest nor Eloquence Sufficient to Prevaile": The Duke of Shrewsbury and the Politics of Succession during the Reign of Anne', *Electronic BLJ* (2015), art. 11, 1–14, www.bl.uk/eblj/2015articles/article11.html.
3   Geoffrey Holmes, 'Harley, St John and the Death of the Tory Party', in *Britain after the Glorious Revolution*, ed. Geoffrey Holmes (1969), 216–37; H. T. Dickinson, *Bolingbroke* (1970), 111–33; W. A. Speck, *Stability and Strife, England 1714–1760* (1977), 169–70; Szechi, 161–3.
4   *Imediate hand of Providence*: This expression is common in Defoe's writing, with variations on the adjective. For instances with 'immediate', see *Review*, III, 571 (17 Sept. 1706); IV, 623 (18 Nov. 1707); VII, 345 (9 Sept. 1710); *History of the Union, TDH*, VII, 90.
5   *what I was upon*: Probably what became *The Secret History of the White-Staff*, published in Sept.

254

To [Robert Harley, Earl of Oxford]

26 August 1714

HEADNOTE: As he promises in this letter, during the following five months, Defoe produced a succession of defences of Oxford.[1] *The Secret History of the White-Staff*, published towards the end of September, recounts the later stages of Queen Anne's reign, personifying Oxford as the emblem of his office: the White Staff. Defoe defends Oxford's record, his acting 'in a medium between all the extreams of Parties' gaining him the opprobrium of both Whig and Tory zealots.[2] Through it all, Oxford remained 'immoveably attach'd to the Interest of the Protestant Succession, and inseparably engaged to that of the illustrious House of *Hanover*'.[3] His Jacobite enemies managed finally to displace him but not before he had 'Effectually disconcerted all their Measures', ensuring the staff was given not to one of their number but to the loyal Duke of Shrewsbury.[4]

816

DEFOE TO [EARL OF OXFORD], 26 AUGUST 1714

In late October, Defoe published *Part II*, focusing on Oxford's rivals. He dismisses 'that Calumny raised on the *White Staff, viz.* that he was in the Interest of the Pretender, because he made use of the Assistance of *Jacobite* Instruments'. By contrast, 'nothing less than the effectual Ruine of their whole Party, would have been the Consequence of the Measures the [Staff] was engaged in'.5 Oxford is depicted outmanoeuvring his enemies within the Tory party, even factoring for his own dismissal. Despite Atterbury ('the Mitre'), Harcourt ('the Purse'), and Masham favouring the Pretender, they are unable to do anything in the wake of Anne's death but follow the advice of Bolingbroke ('John Bull') in declaring for the House of Hanover.6 In *Advice to the People of Great Britain*, published in September, Defoe urged for national conciliation rather than vindictiveness now that the Hanoverian succession had come to pass.

Defoe's *White-Staff* tracts provoked numerous immediate responses from Whigs eager to rebut their defence of Oxford's loyalty to the Hanoverian succession and Tories denying that Oxford was opposed by a Jacobite element within the party.7 In early January 1715, Defoe published *The Secret History of the Secret History of the White-Staff*, which takes the remarkable step of dismissing the two earlier pamphlets as 'Romances' produced by hack writers to earn a few pence and foment discord; to the same ends, it alleges, the producers of the originals also churned out the retorts to enhance sales.8 Accusations that Oxford himself or Defoe wrote them are false: it says that Oxford had repudiated them (which was true9); and Defoe was too ill to do anything more than look at some of the sheets and correct errors.

Defoe did not rest there. *Part III* of *The Secret History*, published at the end of January 1715, concentrated on Oxford's political management while in office, his desire to govern with a moderate ministry using Court influence to attain 'an equilibrium or ballance of Parties' by alternately rewarding men of each party. This stands in contrast to his rivals, the Tory conspirators, who aimed at '*making the Ministry absolute*' by incrementally strengthening the royal prerogative, thus undermining the constitution and thereby laying the foundations for the Pretender whether by design or not.10 *Part III* emphasises that Oxford was only following Queen Anne's wishes in securing a peace, it being her prerogative to make war and peace, but that he did so transparently. Also in January, Defoe produced *Memoirs of the Conduct of Her Late Majesty and Her Last Ministry* to underscore this point.11

Thus, Defoe developed his main lines of defence of Oxford. He was a Hanoverian loyalist who strung along the Jacobites to nullify them. His moderation ensured both Whigs and Tories were dissatisfied. He clung to office in apparently desultory fashion for the final six months though he was already powerless because he needed to thwart the Tory extremists. The fact that Anne handed the white staff to Shrewsbury and that the Protestant succession came to pass without

DEFOE TO [EARL OF OXFORD], 26 AUGUST 1714

a hitch showed his tactics worked, but recent measures frowned on by Hanover were not of his doing. The peace was at Anne's urging; Oxford went along out of duty to the Queen and ensured the Treaty safeguarded the Hanoverian succession. As well as these defences of Oxford's ministry, Defoe published tracts to enjoin the new regime to act in a conciliatory spirit, seeking to resist the inevitable government through the Whig party that George I would almost certainly implement.[12]

My Lord

It is not That I have been Either Negligent Or Unmindfull Either of yor Ldpps Intrest or my Own Obligaċon, That I have not Sooner offred to yor Ldpp what I formerly Proposed for yor Serviċe, But I hope in a Few dayes by Convinċeing proofs to shew yor Ldpp what my Zeal for yor Intrest will allwayes dictate to me. Indeed my Lord, the juncture has been So Niċe[13] I hardly could Tell which way to direct words So to Suit ye Fluctuating Tempers of the people, as Not to do harm instead of Good; If I press'd Moderaċon and a Return to Charity and Temper, Our Outrageous people presently call it fear of punishmt and The Law[14] and They begin to be calling for Fire from Heaven allready Not knowing what Spirit they are of;[15] Alas how Sick will They be of their New king if he will not Gratifye their Revenge and make war upon half his people.

In this difficulty My Lord I find the way to Talk wth them, is by Little and Little gaining upon their Furious Tempers by Inches. This[16] therefore is but an Introduction and Speaks all upon Generalls, and will be followed wth Another and Another as things present, and as the Distinċċon between yor Ldpps administraċon and That wch would have follow'd is absolutely Necessary. My Next[17] will state That part more Clearly Than any thing Seems to have done yet,[a] I mean within the Reach of Common Observaċon.

I Humbly Referr ye Tract herewth Lay'd before yor Ldpp to yor Charity; on Accot of ye Goodness of the design I shall go on to do Every thing that I Can See the least Room to Suppose may be of Serviċe, haveing Neither Thought or Judgemt but what is fully Employed to find out Methods how I may[b] Render my Self

[a] yet,] *interlined*
[b] may] *following illegible word cancelled*

818

Usefull and Servicable to yor L^{dpp} to whom I am bound by So many Obligaćons.

              I am
                  May it please yor L^{dpp}
                      yor Most Humble & Obedient Servt
                                  [*monogram*]

Augt. 26. 1714

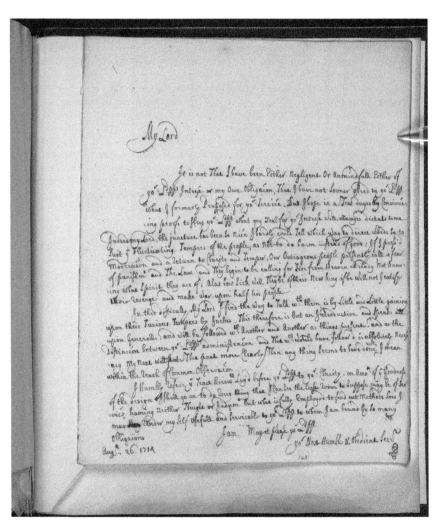

Figure 9 Daniel Defoe to [the Earl of Oxford], 26 August 1714, BL Add. MS. 70291, fol. ²143ʳ

819

DEFOE TO [EARL OF OXFORD], 26 AUGUST 1714

Text: BL Add. MS. 70291, fols. ²143–4 (Figure 9). *Address*: none.

1 For clarification of Defoe's authorship of the many defences of Oxford at this time, and the de-attribution of some attacks on Oxford, see P. N. Furbank and W. R. Owens, 'The Lost Property Office: Some Defoe Attributions Reconsidered', *PBSA* 86 (1992), 245–67.

2 *The Secret History of the White-Staff* (1714), *PEW*, II, 274.

3 *PEW*, II, 279.

4 *PEW*, II, 291.

5 *The Secret History of the White-Staff, Part II* (1714), 9.

6 *Part II* defends Bolingbroke, who has become 'the *Butt* for the Populace to shoot Scandal at', distinguishing him from Harcourt, Atterbury, and Masham: 'The Measures which the *Three* drove at, would no more have consisted with the Captain [Bolingbroke] than it had done with the Colonel [Oxford]' (64, 47). 'John Bull' delivers a speech on the necessity and propriety of executing the requirements of the 1705 Regency Act (57–60), though Defoe arguably undercuts this with a suggestion that he is presenting as much what 'for his Lordships sake he Wishes were true … until it shall by a better Authority be contradicted' (61). Bolingbroke fled to France and the Pretender's Court in Mar. 1715.

    'John Bull' was a personification of Englishness popularised in Tory pro-peace pamphlets written in 1712 by John Arbuthnot (1667–1735), possibly to some degree playing on Bolingbroke's full name or even written in conjunction with him. See John Arbuthnot, *The History of John Bull*, ed. Alan W. Bower and Robert A. Erickson (Oxford, 1976), xxviii, lxiv.

7 John Oldmixon, *A Detection of the Sophistry and Falsities of the Pamphlet entitul'd the Secret History of the White-Staff* (1714); Francis Atterbury, *Considerations upon The Secret History of the White Staff, Humbly Addressed to the E— of O—* (1714); William Pittis, *The History of the Mitre and Purse* (1714); Pittis, *The History of the Mitre and Purse Continued, Wherein the Villainies of the Staff are Further Detected* (1714); Oldmixon, *The Secret History of the White-Staff … With a Detection of the Sophistry and Falsities of the said Pamphlet* (1714). The Pittis book is in *Defoe-Farewell Catalogue* (item 973b).

8 *The Secret History of the Secret History of the White-Staff* (1715), *PEW*, II, 298.

9 Oxford told Stratford on 23 Nov. 1714 that 'the Whigs brag in print they caused the two books of the White Staff to be written; and the policy is plain. He ought to be treated as a fool who had the staff, if he ever encouraged a vindication.' Stratford replied the following day: 'The report about the author of the "White Staff," though industriously propagated, begins like others that have such a foundation to die of itself. But though your old enemies contrived it, I am afraid your Lordship's old friends had the greatest share in spreading it' (H.M.C. *Portland MSS*, v, 501). On 12 Mar. 1715, Oxford again complained that enemies 'pretend to father libels upon me, which I was so far from knowing of them, that I never to this day read them' (BL Add. MS. 70419, qtd in Downie, *Robert Harley*, 187). After Defoe, in response to Oxford's impeachment in July 1715, published *An Account of the Conduct of Robert Earl of Oxford* (1715), Oxford placed a notice in *The London Gazette* for 5–9 July 1715, disavowing Defoe's vindications:

> Whereas some Months since a Pamphlet, Entituled, *The Secret History of the White Staff*, and lately another Pamphlet, Entituled, *An Account of the Conduct of* Robert *Earl of* Oxford, have been Printed and Published; these are to informe the Publick that neither of the said Pamphlets have been written by the said Earl, or with his Knowledge, or by his Direction or Encouragement; but on the contrary he has reason to believe from several Passages therein contained, that it was the Intention of the Author or Authors to do him a Prejudice; and that the last of the said Pamphlets is Published at this Juncture to that end.

Oldmixon maintained that Defoe wrote *The Secret History of the White-Staff* 'by the Earl of *Oxford*'s Direction, and that the most natural Hints for it came from him, because the whole Treatise is calculated for his Vindication; and *Foe* depended upon him too much to dare to publish any such thing without his Participation and Consent' (Oldmixon, 537).

DEFOE TO [EARL OF OXFORD], 31 AUGUST 1714

10 *The Secret History of the White-Staff, Part III* (1715), 23, 60.

11 *The Secret History of the White-Staff, Part III*, 47–9, 54–8. For the attribution to Defoe of *Memoirs of the Conduct of Her Late Majesty and Her Last Ministry*, see Nicholas Seager, 'Literary Evaluation and Authorship Attribution, or Defoe's Politics at the Hanoverian Succession', *HLQ* 80 (2017), 47–69. Pittis attacked this work and *The Secret History of the Secret History of the White-Staff* in *Queen Anne Vindicated* (1715). See also Nicholas Seager, '"She Will Not Be That Tyrant They Desire": Daniel Defoe and Queen Anne', in *Queen Anne and the Arts*, ed. Cedric D. Reverand III (Lewisburg, Penn., 2014), 41–55.

12 *Advice to the People of Great Britain* (1714); *A Secret History of One Year* (1714). The latter was a response to Oldmixon's *The False Steps of the Ministry after the Revolution* (1714). For the attribution of *A Secret History of One Year* to Defoe, see Seager, 'Literary Evaluation and Authorship Attribution'.

13 *the juncture has been So Nice*: See the similar phrasing in *The Secret History of the White-Staff, Part II*, 60.

14 *If I press'd Moderaċon ... Law*: In *Advice to the People of Great Britain*, Defoe anticipates his call for reconciliation being taken as an attempt 'to skreen Criminals from Justice' and 'prevent Punishment' (15, 35).

15 *calling for Fire ... Spirit they are of*: Luke 9:51–6. See Letter 245, note 6. These verses were much in Defoe's head in 1713–14 as he contemplated Whig repercussions against the ministry and its agents. See *A Letter to the Whigs* (1714), 40; *Advice to the People of Great Britain*, 15, 33.

16 *This*: Probably *The Secret History of the White-Staff*.

17 *Next*: Apparently *The Secret History of the White-Staff, Part II*.

255

To [Robert Harley, Earl of Oxford]

31 August 1714

HEADNOTE: From Holland, where he remained a fugitive from British justice, Ridpath continued to direct *The Flying Post, Or, The Post-Master* through agents including his sub-editor Stephen Whately. William Hurt, though still imprisoned, managed to continue to produce the paper.[1] But in summer 1714, Ridpath or his agents replaced Hurt as printer with Robert Tookey, that being announced in the 22–4 July issue.[2] Hurt reacted by printing a rival, *The Flying Post and Medley*, starting on 27 July, and he employed Defoe to supply news. On 14 August, Hurt's *Flying Post* published a letter implying that Arthur Annesley, fifth Earl of Anglesey (*c.* 1678–1737), one of the regents appointed to govern prior to the arrival of George I, was a Jacobite. Hurt, Defoe, and the publisher John Baker were arrested and interrogated; a search of Hurt's premises produced a copy of the letter in Defoe's handwriting.[3] Defoe was charged, brought to trial in summer 1715, and found guilty.[4] The prosecution was apparently not pursued, as Defoe came to an agreement to serve the government.[5] Hyland, Backscheider, and Furbank and Owens

821

DEFOE TO [EARL OF OXFORD], 31 AUGUST 1714

cast doubt on Defoe's account in this letter that he merely edited and re-copied the objectionable letter, removing its worst aspersions on Anglesey.[6]

My Lord

I had not given yo[r] L[d]pp The trouble of any of the Little Ruffles I meet wth in The world, if it were not That I See allwayes Som little Stroaks of Malice (in Every Thing that pushes at me) pointing at yo[r] L[d]pp who they would fain Think they affront when they fall upon me.

This makes it Necessary for me to Lay before yo[r] L[d]pp a brief hystory of Fact in a Broil w[ch] I have just Now upon my hands, w[ch] would not be Otherwise worth your hearing.

It has been long That I have been Endeavouring to Take off the Virulence and Rage of the Flying Post. M[r] Moore has been wittness to y[e] Design and to Some of the Measures[7] I took for it, w[ch] were Unsuccessfull.

After Some Time an Occasion Offred me w[ch] I Thought might be Improv'd Effectually to Overthrow it; The Old Author Ridpath Quarrell'd with his Printer Hurt[8] and Takes the Paper From him; Hurt, Sets up for himself and applyes himself to a Certain Author[9] to write it for him, but[a] being Not Able to get any One to Publish it he lost ground.

It Occurr'd to me That To Support Hurt would be the Onely Way to bring the paper it Self Out of Redpaths hand, and to this Intent I frequently at his Request Sent him paragraphs of forreign News but Declin'd Medling with home Matters.[10]

The publisher[11] Rec[d] a letter[12] Very Unhappily for me and finding it full of Reflections desir'd it to be Softn'd as he calld it, and Sends it to me. I left out indeed a great Deal of Scandalous Stuff that was in it but added Nothing and Sent it back. This they have printed from[b] my hand, and I am Charg'd as y[e] Author of the Letter, am Sent for by a warrant and held to Bail.[13]

The use They make of this is that I have Insulted my L[d] Anglesey[14] and that yo[r] L[d]pp has Employd me to do So.

---

[a] but] *following word* 'it' *cancelled*
[b] from] *interlined above cancelled word* 'in'

DEFOE TO [EARL OF OXFORD], 31 AUGUST 1714

God knows that all I did in it was to prevent their Printing Severall Scandalous Refleccons on his L^dpp wch I therefore struck quite out and Wrot the Rest Over again;[15] I Humbly beg yor L^dpps Intercession wth my Ld Anglesey in this Matter, assureing his L^dpp I Never knew any thing in this Matter Other than the Above, and did nothing in it^a but with Design to Serve his L^dpp.

I am May it Please yor L^dpp
yor L^dpps Most Humble and Obed^t Servt
[*monogram*]

Augt 31.

Text: BL Add. MS. 70291, fols. ²145–6. *Address*: none.

---

^a it] *interlined above cancelled words* 'This Matter'

---

1 P. B. J. Hyland, 'Liberty and Libel: Government and the Press during the Succession Crisis in Britain, 1712–1716', *EHR* 101 (1986), 863–88 (at 867–8).
2 *The Flying Post; Or, The Post-Master*, 22–4 July 1714.
3 TNA SP 44/79A, fols. 12–13. Anglesey had recently proposed an amendment to the Schism Bill to extend it to Ireland, which would help explain Defoe's animosity.
4 *Evening Post*, 12–14 July.
5 In Nov. came reports of his non-appearance in court: 'Mr. Daniel De Foe having forfeited his Recognizance by not appearing last Week at the Court of King's Bench, a Process is order'd against him and his Bail' (*British Weekly Merchant*, 16 Nov. 1715). It was apparently dropped.
6 Hyland, 'Liberty and Libel', 871; Backscheider, *Life*, 379; P. N. Furbank and W. R. Owens, 'Defoe and the Sham *Flying-Post*', *Publishing History* 43 (1998), 5–15. As Furbank and Owens state, it is hard to know how much of Hurt's *Flying Post* can be attributed to Defoe, and Hyland notes an attack on Lord Oxford as just one item among several it is unlikely Defoe wrote.
7 *Mr Moore ... Measures*: Arthur Moore, who directed Defoe in writing *Mercator*. An attack of May 1714 on 'the *Mercator*, and his Dictator', Defoe and Moore, suggested that Defoe and Moore were in daily collaboration (*A Letter to the Honourable A——r M——re* (1714), 25). Unless Defoe means vilifying Ridpath and Hurt in print, as he did for example in *The Monitor*, no. 6 (4 May 1714), his 'Measures' are unidentified.
8 *Ridpath Quarrell'd with his Printer Hurt*: In his notice in the first issue of his rival paper, *The Flying Post and Medley*, for 27 July 1714, Hurt states that he does not know '*the Reason of the real or pretended Difference between the former Author and him*', blaming those who were managing *The Flying Post* in Ridpath's absence. They reacted in *The Flying Post; Or, The Post-Master* for 27–9 July stating that Hurt in his '*Sham-Paper*' is disingenuous to plead ignorance: '*Tho we have a Copy of the* Proprietor's [Ridpath's] *Letter to Mr.* Hurt, *and consequently are privy to his Reasons; and tho they are own'd by all who have seen them to be strictly just; yet as the* Proprietor *has hitherto thought fit to conceal them, we don't think it convenient for us to publish them, till we have his express Orders for so doing*'. As Furbank and Owens state, there is no evidence for earlier biographers' assertions that Defoe was the cause of Ridpath and Hurt's quarrel.

DEFOE TO [EARL OF OXFORD], 31 AUGUST 1714

9 *Certain Author*: Either unidentified or an oblique reference to Defoe himself.

10 *paragraphs ... home Matters*: An anecdote about perceptions of Defoe's contributions given half a century later in the *St. James's Chronicle or the British Evening Post* for 25–7 June 1761 is probably apocryphal, reflecting views of his mercenary journalism that persisted long after his death: 'When the famous Daniel de Foe had the Conduct of a ministerial News Paper, called the FLYING POST, so little Credit was given to its Intelligence, that a Wag at a Coffee-House cut out the initial F, which converted it into what he thought a more proper Title, the LYING POST.'

11 *publisher*: John Baker was the publisher of Hurt's *Flying Post* by no. 5 (3 Aug. 1714); it also dropped its subtitle. The last known issue is no. 25 (21 Sept. 1714).

12 *letter*: The letter, signed 'Dublin', published in Hurt's *Flying Post*, no. 11 (19 Aug. 1714) runs:

> You cannot be ignorant of the late Journey of a No. Pe-r to Ireland, being dispatch'd thither by the new modelled Juncto of the last Ministry; part of the Design of which we are assur'd was, to new model the Forces there, and particularly to break no less than 70 of the honest Forces there, and to fill up their Places with the Tools and Creatures of Con-Ph---ps [Constantine Phipps (1656–1723), Tory Lord Chancellor of Ireland], and such a Rabble of Cut-throats as were fit for the Work that they had for them to do.
>
> Among these, I am assured Capt. Tho. Hales was to be one to be disbanded, the same who commanded at the Tolsey in Dublin at the time of the Election for that City, and at the late great Tumult there, when the honest Recorder and a great many Protestant Gentlemen, had been made a Sacrifice to a Popish Rabble, if the said Captain Hales had not sent his Guard to their Relief.
>
> But Heaven has defeated this wicked Contrivance, and now the Wretches who had swallowed up the Protestant Interest in Ireland in the hopes of their Party, and who were resolved in a short time to have betraid that Kingdom into the Hands of Popery and the Pretender, are in the greatest Confusion imaginable, and have little to expect but the Punishment they have deserved.
>
> The said Capt. Hales, with Col. Windervis, Col. Fane, Capt. Walker and several other Protestant Officers are now going to their Post; and no question it will be a Satisfaction to the City of Dublin to see that worthy Officer, who so timely rescued that City from the Fury of a Popish Tumult, be again at the Head of the same brave Troops, with which he perform'd it, and this notwithstanding the arbitrary Scheme of some People lately in Power.

With a commission to remodel the army in Ireland to purge it of Whigs, Anglesey had set out for Ireland on 27 July but came straight back to take his place on the Council of Regency for the new King when the news of the Queen's death reached him. D. W. Hayton surmises that it is unlikely the commission was part of a Jacobite conspiracy, viewing it instead as part of Bolingbroke's plans to tighten the Tories' grip on the institutions of government and the armed forces to strengthen the party's negotiating position with George I (*Ruling Ireland, 1685–1742: Politics, Politicians, and Parties* (Woodbridge, 2004), 176–85).

13 *I am Charg'd ... Bail*: Hurt and Baker were arraigned and examined on 23 Aug. (newsletter, 24 Aug. 1714, BL Add. MS. 70070). Hurt's premises were searched. On 27 Aug. Secretary of State William Bromley advised Attorney General Sir Edward Northey that the messengers had discovered 'a Manuscript Letter signed Dublin, from which Part of the Pamphlet was printed'. Defoe was suspected but, Bromley continued, 'there is no positive Proof who writ the Manuscript, nor is De Foe yet apprehended, tho' a Messenger has been employ'd to make diligent Search for him'. He issued a warrant. The regents ordered Northey to 'lay before them an Account of the last Prosecution against Defoe' (TNA SP 44/115, fols. 278–9; SP 44/79A, fol. 13 – the latter refers to an offensive paragraph by Defoe appearing in 'ye Post boy of 19 Augt 1714 No 3010', which appears to be in error but could conceivably be a concurrent prosecution). The next day, Northey informed Bromley that evidence against Hurt and Baker

824

DEFOE TO [EARL OF OXFORD], 28 SEPTEMBER 1714

was strong but, 'as to Deffoe, there is no Evidence against him, but Hurt's saying he believes the Letter mentioned in the Flyeing Post to be his hand writing, which I doubt is an Evidence not to be depended upon' (TNA SP 35/1, fol. 93). By 3 Sept. Bromley was satisfied the manuscript was in Defoe's hand (TNA, SP 44/115, fol. 282).

14 *Ld Anglesey*: The Hanoverian Tory Anglesey was frustrated in his ambition to become Lord Lieutenant of Ireland in 1713 by the appointment of the Duke of Shrewsbury. Thereafter he oscillated between support for and opposition to Oxford, and between attachment to Oxford and Bolingbroke. He joined the opposition to the Anglo-French Treaty of Commerce, went against the government in the succession in danger debate in 1714, and supported the Schism Bill, the last illustrating his hostility to Dissenters. He had emerged as a leader of the Hanoverian Tories in the Lords in the 1714 parliament but in the new reign the taint of Jacobitism stuck to him, and Anglesey was removed from office in Jan. 1716. See Holmes, 278–9; *HPC 1690–1715*, III, 27–34; Szechi, 153–6.

15 *Scandalous … again*: The apology Hurt issued in the paper on 26 Aug. stuck to this story, claiming that '*the Proprietor of this Paper got several of the harshest Paragraphs of the original Letter left out*'.

256

To [Robert Harley, Earl of Oxford]

28 September 1714

HEADNOTE: Defoe's final letter to Oxford came ten days after George I landed in Britain.[1] Despite Oxford's letter of congratulation, which emphasised his 'promoting what is now come to pass, your Majesty's succession to the crowns of these kingdoms', George conspicuously snubbed the former Lord Treasurer.[2] Defoe's campaign to exonerate Oxford in print started at this time.[3] In the early months of the new reign, Defoe was widely attacked in pamphlets by both Tories like Pittis and Atterbury and Whigs like Oldmixon and Dunton. The attacks lumped Defoe with the '*Tools* of the *Jacobite* Party', stating he was a pen for hire who reneged on his principles in supporting such a ministry.[4] Oldmixon pointed to his prolixity, 'his abundance of Words, his false Thoughts, and false *English*', and Pittis said Defoe is 'perfectly versed in the Art and Mistery of *spoiling Paper*'.[5] Under fire, Defoe in February 1715 published *An Appeal to Honour and Justice*, attempting to vindicate his career as a political writer, denying the imputation that he was a mercenary, pointing out his not-infrequent dissensions from ministerial policy, his consistency during the reign, and the basis of his loyalty to the Queen, as well as to Oxford and Godolphin, neither of whom dictated to him what he should write.

825

DEFOE TO [EARL OF OXFORD], 28 SEPTEMBER 1714

On 11 April 1715 a secret committee was appointed to investigate Oxford's ministry, resulting in his impeachment on 10 June. The articles of impeachment were brought against him on 7 July and two days later he was confined to the Tower of London. After two years, Oxford was discharged by the Lords and released on 1 July 1717. No Defoe letters survive for more than two years following this.

My Lord

It is not want of Duty or of a Sençe of Duty that I have Layn Still[6] at a Time when Others take Such an Unbounded Liberty, but in Such a juncture who can direct his Own steps?

I presume The Artifiçe of the present Politiçans is Now to have it believed That all who acted under The late administraçon were Enemies to the Succession of the Present King, and in Such a Stream as Now Runs Such Absurdityes may go down, how Evedent So Ever the Contrary May be; Honest Men then must Reserv themselves for better Fortunes, and For times when Truth May be more quietly heard.

In the Mean Time as I am and[a] shall be Ever Watchfull for yor L^{dpps} Intrest I Could not but Send the Enclosed[7] to yor L^{dpp} wch came to my hand Very Odly, But is the Originall and as Directed was Sent to ye writer of Dyers News[8] to Publish; That it was written in Town is most probable, because There is a Frank on ye Outside and yet no Post Mark on ye back and The Frank I Suppose is a Counterfeit also.

Yo^r L^{dpp} will kno' what use to make of it, without shewing the Superscripçon; mean time I have Obtained that it shall not be put into ye News Letter, if they keep their Word with me.

I Can not but humbly Remind yor L^{dpp} of the Case between my Ld Anglesey &c.[9] I hope yor L^{dpp} will prevail wth him to drop a prosecuçon wch None but his Enemyes Prompt him to and Against a Man that did Nothing but with a Sincere Design to Serv him, haveing done Nothing towards ye Letter published but Taken Out what was Most[b] Injurious to his L^{dpp}.

---

[a] am and] *interlined; illegible word within insertion cancelled*
[b] Most] *interlined*

DEFOE TO [EARL OF OXFORD], 28 SEPTEMBER 1714

God Preserv yor L^{dpp} From the Rage of those who haveing Long had a will Now think they have power to hurt you.

I am

May it Please yor L^{dpp}

yor L^{dpps} Ever faithfull and Obed^t Servt

[*monogram*]

Septemb^r 28. 1714

Text: BL Add. MS. 70291, fols. ²147–8. *Address*: none.

1 In Feb. 1715, Defoe stated that 'I have not seen or spoken to my Lord of *Oxford* but once since the King's Landing, nor receiv'd the least Message, Order, or Writing from his Lordship, or any other Way Corresponded with him' (*Appeal*, 56).

2 Oxford to the King, 6 Aug. 1714, H.M.C. *Portland MSS*, v, 484. For political manoeuvring in the wake of the Queen's death, see Stuart Handley, 'The Members of the House of Lords and the Hanoverian Succession', *PH* 39 (2020), 126–42. See Oxford to Dartmouth, late Aug. 1714, for the former Lord Treasurer's hope to re-establish himself within a mixed ministry (H.M.C. *Dartmouth MSS*, 1, 321). For Oxford's snub by George, and an anticipation of his impeachment, see James Brydges (1673–1744) to Bolingbroke, 23 Sept. 1714, in Godfrey Davies and Marion Tinling, 'Letters from James Brydges, Created Duke of Chandos, to Henry St. John, Created Viscount Bolingbroke', *Huntington Library Bulletin* 9 (1936), 119–66 (at 135–6).

3 See headnote to Letter 254.

4 Dunton, *The Golden Age* (1714), sig. AA4^v; Oldmixon, *The Life and Posthumous Works of Arthur Maynwaring* (1715), 269, 276.

5 Oldmixon, *A Detection of the Sophistry and Falsities of the Pamphlet entitul'd The Secret History of the White-Staff* (1714), 6; Pittis, *Queen Anne Vindicated* (1715), 5.

6 *Layn Still*: Defoe had apparently published nothing since the cessation of *The Monitor* on 7 Aug., unless he still wrote for Hurt's *Flying Post*, which ceased on 21 Sept.

7 *Enclosed*: Unidentified and missing.

8 *ye writer of Dyers News*: Dyer died in Sept. 1713, but his manuscript newsletter continued in the hands of George Dormer (d. 1718). For Defoe's involvement in the newsletter, see Letter 259.

9 *Case between my Ld Anglesey &c.*: See Letter 255.

257

To Samuel Keimer

[1717?]

HEADNOTE: Samuel Keimer (1689–1742) was a printer who, around 1707, became associated with a millenarian group called the French Prophets.[1] Conspicuous in appearance (he followed Leviticus in wearing his beard untrimmed and adorned himself with several long green ribbons), Keimer ran his own print office between 1713 and 1716, during which time he was regularly in trouble with the authorities.[2] He published Defoe's *Secret History of the Secret History of the White Staff* and *Memoirs of the Conduct of Her Late Majesty and Her Last Ministry* (both January 1715), as well as Defoe's four tracts written as though by a Quaker. Keimer himself had a long and tumultuous relationship with the Society of Friends and was generally called a Quaker. Defoe and Keimer appear to have collaborated on a newspaper early in 1716 called *The London Post*.[3] In *Queen Anne Vindicated*, Pittis attacked Defoe and 'the Wretch that sets his Enthusiastical Name to the *Imprimitur*' of his works, pointing to their close association.[4] In the wake of the 1715 Jacobite rising Keimer was imprisoned for printing seditious materials and went into bankruptcy the following year.

In an autobiographical narrative published in October 1718, *A Brand Pluck'd from the Burning*, Keimer describes a further period of imprisonment after 1716 and reproduces a letter of condolence he received from an unnamed friend while in prison.[5] The letter's author is, says Keimer, 'one who had known the different Stations of Life, from the Closet Conversation of a KING and QUEEN, to the fatiguing Difficulties of a Dungeon', which points towards Defoe.[6] The letter was first attributed to Defoe, without evidence, by James Crossley in 1851.[7] The attribution is supported by the appearance of the letter's verse prayer in *Colonel Jack* (1722). There is no known evidence for any further contact between Defoe and Keimer after 1717. Keimer emigrated to Philadelphia in the early 1720s and is best remembered for unflattering appearances in Benjamin Franklin's *Autobiography* (1793). Keimer died in Barbados in 1742.

Mr. Keimer,

I Have your Letter:[8] The Account you give of your Hardships[9] is indeed very moving; the Relief[10] I have been able to give you, has been very small; however I have repeated it by the same kind Messenger.

DEFOE TO SAMUEL KEIMER, [1717?]

Of all your Letter, nothing pleases me so much as to find you hint something of your being touch'd with a Sense of breaking in[11] upon Principle and Conscience; God grant the Motion may be sincere. Afflictions do not rise out of the Dust:[12] They seem to leave God himself no other room but that of Vengeance to deal with them, who are neither better'd by Mercies or Afflictions. The Time of Sorrow is a Time to reflect, and to look and see wherefore he that is righteous is contending with you. Only remember that he is not mocked. Nothing but a deep, thorough, unfeigned, sincere Humiliation is accepted by him. God restore you to your Health, Liberty and Prosperity; and last of all to his Blessing and Favour.

Shall I recommend a sincere Prayer put up to Heaven, tho' in Verse, by one I knew under deep and dreadful Afflictions? I'll write you but a few of them;

> Lord, whatsoever Troubles wrack my Breast,
> Till Sin removes too, let me take no Rest;
> How dark soe'er my Case, or sharp my Pain,
> O let not Sorrows cease, and Sin remain!
> For JESUS Sake, remove not my Distress
> Till thy Almighty Grace shall repossess
> The vacant Throne, from whence my Crimes depart,
> And makes a willing Captive of my Heart.[13]

These are serious Lines, tho' Poetical. Its a Prayer, I doubt few can make: But the Moral is excellent; if Afflictions cease, and Cause of Afflictions remain, the Joy of your Deliverance will be short.[14]

I have sent you the printed Paper[15] you wrote for. ———— I should be glad to render you any Service within my Power, having been always perhaps more than you imagin'd,

Your sincere Friend and Servant.

Text: MS untraced. The copytext is Samuel Keimer, *A Brand Pluck'd from the Burning: Exemplify'd in the Unparallel'd Case of Samuel Keimer* (1718), 98–9. *Address*: none recorded.

1   See Hillel Schwartz, *The French Prophets: The History of a Millenarian Group in Eighteenth-Century England* (Berkeley, Cal., 1980). Defoe makes a brief negative comment about the group in *The Commentator*, no. 7 (22 Jan. 1720), *RDW*, IX, 42.

DEFOE TO SAMUEL KEIMER, [1717?]

2 Arrest warrants for Keimer: TNA SP 44/79A, fol. 8 (20 Nov. 1713); TNA SP 44/77, fol. 161 (29 Dec. 1714); TNA SP 44/79A, fol. 21 (30 May 1715).

3 The Quaker pamphlets are *A Friendly Epistle by Way of Reproof ... to Thomas Bradbury*, *A Seasonable Expostulation with, and Friendly Reproof unto James Butler, ... Duke of O[rmon]d*, *A Sharp Rebuke from One of the People Call'd Quakers to Henry Sacheverell*, and *A Trumpet Blown in the North, and Sounded in the Ears of John Eriskine, ... Duke of Mar* (all 1715). On the *London Post*, see F&O, *Bibliography*, 148.

4 Pittis, *Queen Anne Vindicated* (1715), 9.

5 It was advertised as published 'this day' in *The Post Boy* for 2–4 Oct. 1718. It was also advertised in *The White-Hall Evening Post*, a paper Defoe was at that time editing and writing for.

6 *A Brand Pluck'd from the Burning: Exemplify'd in the Unparallel'd Case of Samuel Keimer* (1718), 98.

7 James Crossley, 'Warnings to Scotland', *N&Q* 4 (1851), 283; Crossley, 'Defoe's Letter to Keimer,' *N&Q* 3 (1869), 422.

8 *your Letter*. Untraced. Keimer explains that, while imprisoned, he wrote to 'several of my former Acquaintance for Relief' but that only one responded (*Brand*, 98).

9 *Hardships*: In addition to the hardships of prison, Keimer had come to recognise the 'very dangerous and strong Delusions' of the French Prophets, who had abandoned him, and he consequently suffered a spiritual crisis (*Brand*, 98).

10 *Relief*. Financial aid.

11 *breaking in*: 'Burst or flash upon' (*OED*).

12 *Afflictions do not rise out of the Dust*. Job 5:6.

13 *Lord ... Heart*: Probably Defoe's own verse. The lines recur in *Colonel Jack* (1722). Jack states that his tutor in Virginia 'pull'd out a little Dirty Paper Book, in which he had wrote down such a Prayer in Verse, as I doubt few Christians in the World could Subscribe to'. There are several variations in the *Colonel Jack* version: 'Sorrows' for 'Troubles' (line 1); 'Crime' for 'Sin' (line 2); 'State' for 'Case' (line 3); 'Troubles' for 'Sorrows' (line 4); 'free Triumphant' for 'thy Almighty' (line 6); and 'Sins' for 'Crimes' (line 7). An extra couplet appears in the novel at the end: 'Till Grace Completely shall my Soul Subdue, | Thy Conquest full, and my Subjection True'. Jack states: 'There were more Lines on the same Subject, but these were the beginning; and these touching me sensibly, I have remember'd them distinctly ever since, and have I believe repeated them to my self a Thousand times' (*Novels*, VIII, 154–5). The tone and theme of the verse resemble Defoe's early meditative poetry. See Andreas K. E. Mueller, *A Critical Study of Daniel Defoe's Verse: Recovering the Neglected Corpus of his Poetic Work* (Lampeter, 2010), 251–71. Wright, 200, considered the lines a Christian paraphrase of Pliny's *Epistles*, book 7, letter 26; cf. Peterson, *Reference Guide*, 183.

14 *if Afflictions ... short*: Compare *Moll Flanders*: 'When ever sincere Repentance succeeds such a Crime as this, there never fails to attend a Hatred of the Object; ... there cannot be a true and sincere Abhorrence of the Offence, and the Love to the Cause of it remain' (*Novels*, VI, 113).

15 *printed Paper*. Unidentified. Keimer apparently liked to entertain his fellow prisoners with Quaker sermons during this period of imprisonment (*Brand*, 96).

DEFOE TO [CHARLES DELAFAYE], 12 APRIL 1718

258

To [Charles Delafaye]

12 April 1718

HEADNOTE (Letters 258 and 259): The following series of letters gives evidence of Defoe's covert work to infiltrate Tory newspapers on behalf of the Whig ministry during 1717 and 1718. His contact was the Undersecretary of State, Charles Delafaye (1677–1762).

As part of the ministerial reshuffle caused by the Whig schism of April 1717, Delafaye was appointed Undersecretary by the returning Secretary of State for the Northern Department, the Earl of Sunderland.[1] Over the previous two decades Delafaye had gained extensive clerical experience in a variety of civil service positions and, for several years after 1702, acted as a writer for the government's official paper, *The London Gazette*.[2] Delafaye's main task as Undersecretary was to manage the press on behalf of the newly constituted government, which included Stanhope as the First Lord of the Treasury, effectively the prime minister. When Sunderland and Stanhope exchanged ministerial posts in March 1718, Delafaye continued as Northern Undersecretary under Stanhope and around this time his correspondence with Defoe apparently commenced.[3]

Since Defoe's letters to Delafaye were discovered and published in 1864, they have been taken as the clue to his journalistic activity in the period from 1716 to 1720, with major implications for assessments of his integrity and political beliefs. In Defoe's version, sometime in 1716, the then Northern Secretary Charles, second Viscount Townshend tasked Defoe with infiltrating the opposition Tory press, under the cover of his ongoing disaffection from the government, to take the sting out of its attacks on the ministry. Defoe explains that his main project was to write for the pseudo-Tory monthly periodical *Mercurius Politicus*, which commenced in May 1716 as a rival to Boyer's Whig paper, *The Political State*. Defoe acted as editor and writer for this journal which, 'despite its professed impartiality, was malicious towards the Government'.[4]

After succeeding Townshend as Northern Secretary in December 1716, Sunderland was apparently content to retain Defoe's services as an undercover government writer and Defoe was tasked with tempering Nathaniel Mist's High Church, crypto-Jacobite newspaper, *The Weekly Journal: or, Saturday's Post*. Defoe professed that he was mainly responsible for translating foreign news letters, though at the very least he contributed a series of letters from 'Sir Andrew Politick', and editorials thereon, between February and October 1718.[5]

Furbank and Owens's reassessment of this stage of Defoe's career overturns the accounts of his motivations offered by biographers since the discovery of the Delafaye letters in 1864. Rather than covertly infiltrating Tory papers as a Whig

831

DEFOE TO [CHARLES DELAFAYE], 12 APRIL 1718

agent, Defoe may have been deceiving Delafaye and his superiors about his press work, covering up his writing against the current Whig administration.[6] This interpretation is a reasonable inference from the available evidence, but nothing categorically confutes Defoe's own account and much would seem to support it.

Sr

I could Not Read wthout Pain to day in The Publick Prints Some thing of An Accot of that Traiterous Pamphlet[7] being Printed, I Mean that wch I Shewed you and which I[a] Sent to my Lord Sunderland.[8]

I beg you will Please to Assure his Ldpp From me, That the Originall wch I Shewed you is still in my hand, and has Never been Out of my keeping, Nor has any Eye[b] Seen it, or any Coppy been taken of it, that One Excepted wch I Sent to his Ldpp.

I here Enclose a Letter[9] wch I have stopt wch I Think is Worth his Ldpps Notice. I dare not yet Come Abroad but hope to See you in three or four dayes if ye Cold Weather abates.

I am
Sr
yor Most Humble Servt
DeFoe

Newington Aprll 12. 1718

Text: TNA SP 35/11, fol. 162. *Address*: none.

---

[a] I] *following word probably* 'she' *(perhaps for* 'shewed'*?) cancelled*
[b] Eye] *interlined*

---

1   The Whig split saw Townshend dismissed first as Secretary of State in Dec. 1716 and then from the post he had been shunted into, Lord Lieutenant of Ireland, in Apr. 1717, whereupon Walpole and his followers resigned and went into opposition to Sunderland and Stanhope. See John J. Murray, *George I, the Baltic, and the Whig Split of 1717* (1969), and W. A. Speck, 'The Whig Schism Under George I', *HLQ* 40 (1977), 171–9. Defoe contributed two tracts to the debates on the evolving schism in Jan. 1717 – *The Danger of Court Differences* and *The Quarrel of the School-Boys at Athens* – as well as commenting on it in *Mercurius Politicus*. The thrust of his contributions is that Jacobites have falsely propagated rumours of Whig turmoil, that both sides are at fault, but that it has been resolved. The rupture in Apr. disproved his optimistic take on events, and his *The Old Whig and Modern Whig Revived* (1717) was critical of both sides.
2   For Delafaye's career and his intelligence work for the early Hanoverian government, see J. C. Sainty, 'A Huguenot Civil Servant: The Career of Charles Delafaye', *Proceedings of the Huguenot Society* 22 (1975), 398–413; Michael Harris, 'Newspaper Distribution during Queen

DEFOE TO [CHARLES DELAFAYE], 26 APRIL 1718

Anne's Reign: Charles Delafaye and the Secretary of State's Office', in *Studies in the Book Trade in Honour of Graham Pollard*, ed. R. W. Hunt *et al.* (Oxford, 1975), 139–51; R. J. Goulden, '*Vox Populi, Vox Dei*: Charles Delafaye's Paperchase', *The Book Collector* 28 (1979), 368–90; Ric Berman, *Espionage, Diplomacy and the Lodge: Charles Delafaye and the Secret Department of the Post Office* (Goring Heath, 2017).

3 Letter 259, dated 26 Apr. 1718, in which Defoe offers an extensive overview of his press work since 1714, suggests that the two men had not yet corresponded about Defoe's role as a clandestine government writer. Berman notes that Delafaye's centrality to the ministry's intelligence operations and his constancy amidst shuffles helps explain why Defoe was corresponding with him (*Espionage*, 64).

4 F&O, *Political Biography*, 159–60.

5 P. N. Furbank and W. R. Owens, 'Defoe and "Sir Andrew Politick"', *BJECS* 17 (1994), 27–39.

6 F&O, *Political Biography*, 159–71; cf. Novak, 502.

7 *Traiterous Pamphlet*: Probably *Sultan Galga*. See Letter 259, note 25.

8 *Lord Sunderland*: The previous month, Sunderland was appointed First Lord of the Treasury and Lord President of the Council. Stanhope was now Northern Secretary and Delafaye's direct superior.

9 *Letter*: Untraced and unidentified.

259

To [Charles Delafaye]

26 April 1718

Sr

Tho' I doubt Not but you have Accquainted My Ld Stanhope[1] with what Humble Sence of his Ldpps goodness I Recd The Accot you were Pleased to Give me That My Little Services are Accepted, and That his Ldpp is Satisfyed to go on Upon the Foot of Former Capitulacons[2] &c. yet I Confess Sr I have been Anxious On Many Accots, wth Respect as well to ye Service it Self, as to my Own Safety, Least My Lord May Think himself ill Served by me,[a] Even when I may have best Perform'd My Duty.

I Thought it therefore Not Onely a Debt to my Self, But a Duty to his Ldpp that I should give his Ldpp a Short Accot as Clear as I can, How far my former Instruccons Empowred me to Act, and in a Word what this Little Peice of Secret Service is for which I am So much a Subject of his Ldpps Present Favour and Bounty.

[a] by me] *interlined*

833

DEFOE TO [CHARLES DELAFAYE], 26 APRIL 1718

It was in ye Ministry of My Lord Townshend,[3] When My Ld Chief Justice Parker,[4] to whom I stand Obliged for ye favour, Was pleased So farr to state my Case, That Notwithstanding ye Missrepresentacons Under wch I had Suffred, and Notwithstanding Some Mistakes which I was the first to Acknowlege,[5] I was So happy as to be believ'd in the Professions I made of a Sincere attachm^t to The Intrest of ye Present Governm^t and speaking with all Possible Humillity, I hope I Have not Dishonourd My Ld Parkers Recomendacon.[6]

In Considring after this^a which way I might be Rendred Most usefull to ye Government It was proposed By My Lord Townshend That I should still appear as if I were as before under the Displeasure of the Governm^t, and Seperated From the Whiggs;[7] and That I might be more Servicable in a kind of Disguise, Than If I appeard openly; and Upon this foot a Weekly Paper wch I was at first Directed to Write, in Opposicon^b to a Scandalous paper called the Shif shifted,[8] was Lay'd aside;^c[9] and The first thing I Engaged in was a Monthly Book called Mercurius Politicus,[10] of wch Presently.

In the Intervall of This, Dyer The News Letter writer haveing been Dead, and Dormer[11] his Successor being Unable by his Troubles[12] to Carry on that Work, I had an Offer of a share in The Property as Well as in ye Mannagem^t of that work.[13]

I Imediately Accquainted my Ld Townshend of it, who by m^r Buckley[14] let me know, it would be a Very Acceptable P[iece]^d of Service; for that Letter Was Really Very Prejudicall to ye Public, and the most Difficult to Come at in a judiciall way^e in Case of Offence Given; My L^d was pleased to Add by m^r Buckley that he would Consider[15] my Service in that Case as he afterwards did.

Upon This I Engaged in it, and That So far, that Tho' the Property was not wholly my Own, yet the Conduct, and Governm^t of the stile and News, was So Entirely in Me, that I Ventur'd to assure his L^dpp the sting of that Mischeivous Paper should

---

^a after this] *interlined*
^b Opposicon] *the second 'p' is interlined*
^c aside] *interlined above cancelled word* 'Down'
^d P[iece]] 'Ps' *in MS; abbreviation expanded in this edition*
^e in a judiciall way] *interlined*

DEFOE TO [CHARLES DELAFAYE], 26 APRIL 1718

be Entirely Taken out, Tho' it was Granted that ye stile should Continue Tory, as it was, that ye Party might be Amused,[16] and Not Set up another, which would have destroy'd the Design, and This Part I therefore Take Entirely on my Self still.

This Went on for a year, before My Ld Townshend went Out of The Office;[a,17] and his L^dpp in Consideracon of This Service, Made me the Appointment which[b] m^r Buckley knows of, with Promise of a Further allowance[18] as Service Presented.

My Ld Sunderland, to whose Goodness I had Many yeares agoe been Obliged when I was in a Secret Commission Sent to Scotland,[19] was pleased to approve and Continue this Service, and the Appointm^t Annexed; And with his L^dpps Approbation, I Introduced my Self in ye Disguise of a Translator of the Forreign News, to be So farr Concernd in This Weekly Paper of <u>Mists</u>,[20] as to be able to keep it within the Circle of a Secret Mannagement also,[c] prevent ye Mischievous Part of it, and yet Neither Mist or any of those Concernd with him have ye least Guess or Suspicon By whose Direccon I do it.[21]

But here it becomes Necessary to Accquaint My Lord (as I hinted to you S^r) Tha[t][d] This paper called the journall, is not in My Self in Property, as ye Other,[22] Onely in Mannagem^t, wth this Express Difference, that if any thing happens to be put in without my knowlege, which may Give Offence, Or if any thing slips my Observacon which may be ill Taken, His L^dpp shall be Sure Allways to kno', whether he has a Servant to Reprove, or a stranger to Correct.

Upon the whole However, this is the Consequence, that by this Mannagem^t The Weekly Journall and Dormers Letter, as Also ye Mercurius Politicus wch is in ye Same Nature of Mannagem^t as The journall, Will be allwayes kept (mistakes Excepted) To Pass as Tory Papers, and yet be[e] Dissabled, and Ennervated, So as to do no Mischief[f] or give any Offence to ye Governm^t.

---

[a] Office] *following illegible word cancelled*
[b] which] *interlined*
[c] also] *interlined*
[d] Tha[t]] *MS frayed*
[e] be] *interlined*
[f] Mischief] *following illegible word cancelled*

DEFOE TO [CHARLES DELAFAYE], 26 APRIL 1718

I Beg leav to Observ S^r one Thing More to his L^{dpp} in my Own behalf, And without which Indeed I May^a one Time Or Other Run ye hazard of fatall Missconstructions: I am S^r for This Service, Posted among Papists, Jacobites, and Enraged High Torys, a Generaçon who^b I Profess My Very Soul abhorrs; I am Oblig'd to hear Trayterous Expressions, and Outrageous Words against his Maj^{ties} Person, and Governm^t, and his Most^c faithfull Servants; and Smile at it all as if I Approv'd it; I am Oblig'd to take all the Scandalous and Indeed Villainous papers that Come, and keep them by Me as if I would gather Materialls from them to Put them into ye News; Nay I often Venture to Let things pass wch are a little shocking that I may not Render my Self Suspected.

Thus I bow in The House of <u>Rimmon</u>;[23] and must Humbly Recommend my Self to his Lord^{pps} Protecçon, or I may be Undone the Sooner, by how much the more faithfully I Excecute The Commands I am Under.

I forbear to Enlarge. I beg you S^r to Represent these Circumstances to his L^{dpp} in Behalf of a faithfull Servant That Shall allways Endeavour to approve his fidellity by acçons Rather Than Words.

I am

S^r

yor Most Humble Servt

DeFoe

Newington Apr^{ll} 26. 1718

P.S.

I Send you here One of the Letters stopt at ye Press[24] as I Mençon'd to you. As to ye Manuscript of Sultan Galga,[25] another Villainous Paper, I Sent ye Coppie to my Ld Sunderland, if the Originall be of any Service it is Ready at yor first orders.

Text: TNA SP 35/11, fol. 218. *Address*: none.

^a May] *interlined above cancelled word perhaps* 'Should'
^b who] *interlined*
^c Most] *inserted in margin*

---

1   *Ld Stanhope*: See Letter 140. Stanhope's earldom was given him on 18 Apr. 1718, by which point he was effectively prime minister. His ministerial career had started only recently, after

DEFOE TO [CHARLES DELAFAYE], 26 APRIL 1718

the Hanoverian succession, when he was appointed Secretary of State for the Southern Department, in which office he presided over the preparations for Oxford's trial, though charges were dropped in summer 1717.

2 *Former Capitulaĉons*: Defoe refers to a succession of Whig politicians with whom he claims to have had an agreement to work as an undercover journalist: first Townshend, then Sunderland, and now Stanhope.

3 *Lord Townshend*: Townshend was Northern Secretary from Sept. 1714 to Dec. 1716. Defoe's reference to *The Shift Shifted* suggests that he was hired by Townshend some time after 5 May 1716, the date when that journal's title changed from *Robin's Last Shift*.

Defoe praised Townshend in a catalogue of Whig peers in *Jure Divino* (1706), book XII, line 313, *SFS*, 11, 353, and he seems to be included among the 'honest and loyal Patriots, who yet remain in the Administration', in *An Argument Proving that the Design of Employing and Enobling Foreigners, is a Treasonable Conspiracy against the Constitution* (Feb. 1717), 6. But later in 1717 Defoe was critical of Townshend, his brother-in-law Walpole, and those Whigs they led into opposition (*The Old Whig and Modern Whig Revived* (Aug. 1717), *SFS*, IV, 200–1).

4 *Lᵈ Chief Justiĉe Parker*: Parker was the judge in the prosecution of Defoe for his three succession pamphlets in 1713 (see Letters 228–30).

5 *Mistakes which I was the first to Acknowlege*: Defoe's reflections on his prosecution in the *Review* resulted in a fine and the requirement to issue an apology in the issues for 28 Apr. and 5 May 1713 (see headnote to Letter 230). Defoe may also be alluding to his prosecution in 1714 for a letter in the 'sham' *Flying Post* that satirised Anglesey (see Letter 255).

6 *Lᵈ Parkers Recomĕndaĉon*: In 'A Vision of the Angelick World' in *Serious Reflections* (1720), Defoe appears to give an account of his winning Parker's favour with a letter written while he awaited sentencing. This is presented as the experience of one of Crusoe's friends, who faces a ruinous prosecution and so writes to the judge. 'The Letter was so stren[u]ous in its Argument, so pathetick in its Eloquence, and so moving and perswasive, that as soon as the Judge read it, he sent him Word he should be easie, for he would Endeavour to make that Matter light to him, and in a Word, never left, till he obtained to stop Prosecution, and restore him to his Liberty and to his Family' (*Novels*, 111, 250).

7 *Seperated From the Whiggs*: See headnote.

8 *Shif shifted*: *The Shift Shifted* was an overtly Jacobite weekly periodical written principally by the Roman Catholic George Flint (d. after 1720), which first appeared as *Robin's Last Shift* on 18 Feb. 1716, changed its name to this on 5 May 1716, and apparently wound up as *Shift's Last Shift*, as it tried to avoid government censorship, before apparently terminating in Feb. 1717. Flint, members of his family including his wife and sister, his collaborator and printer Isaac Dalton (d. after 1723), and numerous hawkers were frequently imprisoned for their part in the paper. Defoe describes a government raid on Flint's printing-house in *Mercurius Politicus*, Sept. 1716, 298.

9 *Lay'd aside*: Commenting on this, Furbank and Owens state: 'One tends to assume he means by this that it never reached the stage of publication; but the words could almost equally well mean "laid aside after one or two issues". This possibility might be worth exploring' ('Defoe, the De la Faye Letters and *Mercurius Politicus*', *BJECS* 23 (2000), 13–19 (at 13)). Defoe's textual emendation here – the substitution of 'aside' for 'Down' – supports that possibility, but no contender for any such paper has been identified.

10 *Engaged in … Mercurius Politicus*: *Mercurius Politicus: Being Monthly Observations on the Affairs of Great Britain* (May 1716–Dec. 1720). Furbank and Owens note the ambiguity, asking: 'Is to "engage in" the same as to launch or to found?' ('Defoe, the De la Faye Letters and *Mercurius Politicus*', 15). They understandably question why the Whig ministry would sponsor the launching of a new Tory paper, as opposed to funding the infiltration of an existing one, leading them to surmise that if, as seems likely, Defoe initiated *Mercurius Politicus*, it was his own idea and not Townshend's. Either way, Defoe's contributions appear to extend from its inception to at least summer 1718, but as Furbank and Owens state, 'it is not possible to specify exactly what he himself wrote for it' (F&O, 'Periodicals', 91).

837

DEFOE TO [CHARLES DELAFAYE], 26 APRIL 1718

11 *Dormer*: Dyer's successor, the Catholic George Dormer, who had just died in Mar. 1718, and was succeeded on the newsletter by his brother. Pastiching the divine right theory of the newsletter, *The Flying Post* for 24 June 1714 dubbed Dormer 'the undoubted Hereditary indefeasible heir to Mr. Dyer's pen'.

12 *Troubles*: Dormer was arrested amidst the Jacobite uprising in Oct. 1715 (*Evening Post*, 20–2 Oct. 1715).

13 *share ... work*: No copies of Dormer's *News-letter* for the relevant period have been traced.

14 *mr Buckley*: See Letter 139, notes 11, 14, and 16. Buckley's work on *The Daily Courant* during Anne's reign was rewarded after the Hanoverian succession with his appointment as Gazetteer, writer of the official government paper, *The London Gazette*, in Sept. 1714, a position given to him for life in 1719. In this office 'he served as unofficial surveyor of the press' for the Whig government (Michael Treadwell, 'London Printers and Printing Houses in 1705', *Publishing History* 7 (1980), 5–43 (at 17–18)).

15 *Consider*: remunerate.

16 *Amused*: deceived.

17 *Ld Townshend went Out of The Office*: Townshend was Northern Secretary between 17 Sept. 1714 and 12 Dec. 1716.

18 *allowance*: We have details of one payment of £25 to Defoe during Sunderland's time in office. Defoe made out and signed a receipt that runs: 'Recd Dec̀ 13. 1717 of the Rt Honble The Earl of Sunderld By The hands of Mr Samll Buckley Esqr The Sume of Twenty Five Pounds Being To ye 17th Novembr last.' To maintain secrecy, the funds were channelled through Sunderland's chief clerk, John Wace (d. 1745) – who incidentally was Delafaye's brother-in-law – as well as Buckley, and paid to a 'Mr. Amy', as Buckley's notation indicates: 'This Money I had of Mr Wace, and gave him a Recт for it as paid by my Lord's Order to Mr. Amy' (BL Add. MS. 61597, fol. 73; cf. fols. 52, 71). 'Mr Amy' is either a now-unidentified intermediary or, which is more probable, a pseudonym of Defoe. See J. D. Alsop, 'Defoe and his Whig Paymasters', *N&Q* 28 (1981), 225–6. Letter 261 indicates that £25 was a half-yearly salary.

19 *Ld Sunderland ... Scotland*: See Letters 134 and 135.

20 *Weekly Paper of Mists*: The *Weekly Journal, or Saturday's Post*, which commenced on 15 Dec. 1716, under the proprietorship of the Jacobite Nathaniel Mist (d. 1737).

Again, Furbank and Owens write that 'it is not possible to identify many of his contributions with any certainty' (F&O, 'Periodicals', 91). For a valuable discussion of the likely extent of Defoe's contributions to *The Weekly Journal*, see Maximillian E. Novak, 'Defoe's Role in the *Weekly Journal*: Gesture and Rhetoric, Archive and Canon, and the Uses of Literary History in Attribution', *SP* 113 (2016), 694–711. The earliest known external evidence is an attack on Defoe as 'Daniel Turncoat', 'Author of the Weekly-Journal' and 'Corrector-General' of all the News-Papers', in a Whig paper that frequently opposed Mist's (Read's *Weekly Journal*, 24 Aug. 1717). Mist's *Weekly Journal* for 21 Dec. 1717 denied that Defoe was author of the paper, though the very next issue, for 28 Dec. 1717, contained a letter on imprisonment for debt signed 'D.D.F.' As late as 1720, *The Humorist: Being Essays upon Several Subjects*, no. 2, 76, alludes to 'the ingenious Lucubrations of Mist and De Foe', implying an ongoing connection.

21 *Neither Mist ... do it*: Much of J. D. Alsop's account of Defoe's infiltration of Mist's *Weekly Journal* having been facilitated by Sunderland's tactical arrest of Mist in order to coerce him is predicated on Defoe's involvement starting with the issue for 3 Aug. 1717, because Mist was then in custody on Sunderland's orders. For the origin of the argument that Defoe's work commenced on 3 Aug. 1717, see G. A. Aitken, 'Defoe and Mist's "Weekly Journal"', *The Athenæum*, 26 Aug. 1893, 287–8. However, the evidence that Defoe began working on Mist's paper at that particular moment is far from definitive. Nonetheless, Alsop's suggestion that Mist had a deal with the Whig government to moderate his newspaper, remains plausible. See Alsop, 'New Light on Nathaniel Mist and Daniel Defoe', *PBSA* 75 (1981), 57–60.

22 *Other*: Dormer's *News-letter*.

23 *bow in The House of Rimmon*: 2 Kings 5:18. Naaman obtained Elisha's permission to worship Rimmon when with his master. It means outwardly to conform against one's conscience.

DEFOE TO CHARLES DELAFAYE, 10 MAY 1718

Defoe gives a brief exegesis on the verse in *An Enquiry into the Occasional Conformity of Dissenters, in Cases of Preferment* (1698), *PEW*, 111, 47; he also uses the allusion in *Serious Reflections, Novels*, 111, 154. See Paula R. Backscheider, 'Personality and Biblical Allusion in Defoe's Letters', *South Atlantic Review* 47 (1982), 1–20 (at 13–14).

24 *Letters stopt at yᵉ Press*: Untraced.

25 *Sultan Galga: The Character of Sultan Galga, the Present Cham of Tartary*, a broadside describing a despotic sultan, is a barely veiled attack on George I. It focused on his engrossment of British wealth for exportation to Germany and his tyrannical treatment of his family (George and the Prince of Wales got on badly, and George's repudiated wife was confined in Hanover).

260

To Charles Delafaye

10 May 1718

HEADNOTE: Defoe's involvement in Mist's *Weekly Journal* repeatedly placed him in awkward positions with his Whig employers. Reporting the death on 26 April of Mary of Modena (1658–1718), *The Weekly Journal* for 10 May listed her children including 'James Francis-Edward, born at St. James's the 10th of June 1688, the Person who is now stiled the Pretender', thereby endorsing his legitimacy and potentially his *de jure* right to the throne. Defoe thus sought to dissociate himself from that report.

Sr

I am Extreamly Concern'd That yᵉ Journall of this day has Coppyed from yᵉ Post boy That Ridiculous Paragraph of The Pretenders being in the List of The Queen Dowagers Legitimate Children,[1] and I have Spoken my Mind Very Freely to him of it.

But Sr I think in Consequence of what I wrote last to you it is my Duty to assure My Lᵈ That I have no Part in this slip, but that Mr Mist did it after I had lookt Over what he had Gotten Together, wᶜʰ it Seems was not Sufficent; and Tho' I Would If I may Presume So far Intercede for him, yet My Lᵈ May be assured I have no Concern in it Directly or Indirectly; This Sr I Say I thoᵗ my Self Obligd to Notice to you, to make good

839

DEFOE TO [CHARLES DELAFAYE], 23 MAY 1718

what I Said in my Last (Viz) that if any mistake happend my L^d should allwayes kno' whether he had a Servant to Reprove, or a stranger to Punish.

I am

S^r

yor Most Humble Servt

DeFoe

May. 10. 1718

PS

He has Renew'd his Promise to me that he will be more wary and I do think Verily it was not done Malitiously But that I leave as I find it.

Text: TNA SP 35/12, fol. 19. *Address*: To .... De La faye Esqr | Present

1   *Journall ... Post boy ... Children*: *Post Boy*, 6–8 May 1718; Mist's *Weekly Journal*, 10 May 1718. The other journal whose anti-government rhetoric Defoe was supposedly tempering, *Mercurius Politicus*, also printed the list to which Defoe refers (May 1718, 301).

261

To [Charles Delafaye]

23 May 1718

HEADNOTE: Defoe was on alert due to the prosecution of John Morphew, the Tory trade publisher of *Mercurius Politicus*, for a report published in the September 1716 issue. The story concerned the executions of two men in York, Thomas Barron and Edward Bourn, for a theft on the highway of three halfpence from a Mr King and Mr Jackson, which the defendants pleaded was only begged for and not received.

S^r

When I had ye Favour of Seeing you last, you were pleased to Mencōn to me My Perticular Cončern, and That you Would intrest yor Self in That Part for me; The Exceeding kindness of that Offer

840

DEFOE TO [CHARLES DELAFAYE], 23 MAY 1718

Sr Encourages me to give you This Trouble and [to]ᵃ Observe to you That yᵉ half year Expire'd The 17ᵗʰ Instt.[1]

I Need Say no More but to Ask you Pardon for this Freedome and Leave yᵉ Rest to yoʳ Own Time and Methods, and shall attend at what Time you please to Appoint.

I hope I have kept yᵉ Difficult people I have to do wᵗʰ within yᵉ bounds of Duty and am in hopes to Draw yᵐ Gradually into yet Narrower Limits of Respect; It is a hard Matter to please yᵉ Tory Party as their present Temper Opperates,ᵇ without Abuseing not Onely The Government but yᵉ Persons of Our Governours in Every thing they Write. But to the best of my skill I Cause all letters and Paragraphs which look that Way to be intercepted and stop't at yᵉ press.

I am a Little Allarm'd at a prosecution against Morphew[2] in yᵉ kings Bench Court for a passage in The Mercurius Politicus,[3] which began in a Private Person Sueing Morphew on Pretence of Damages on a Paragraph printed from another printed paper[4] of a Person Hang'd at York for Three half pence But it Seems yᵉ Court Resenting a line or Two in it as a Reflection on the Judges have Made it a public Cause and have Comitted Morphew till sentençe wᶜʰ it is Fear'd will be Severe.

But Sr I think my Self oblig'd to Lay before my Lᵈ Stanhope the following perticulars in Case they should Offer to Conçern me in it; first That it is Two year or More Since this wasᶜ done, and Consequently before yᵉ Capitulaçon made in My Lᵈ Townshendsᵈ time[5] when all former Mistakes of Mine we[re]ᵉ forgiven; Secondly, That The Thing it Self was not Myne, neither can any One Pretend to Charge it o[n]ᶠ me, Otherwise than It might be Said I Saw or Overlookt yᵉ book, nor indeed can they prove So Much as th[at,]ᵍ So that I can in No wise be Said to have faild in my Duty on accoᵗ of this Latent affair wᶜʰ indeed Seems to me to be but Triffling in it Self.

ᵃ [to]] *hole in MS*
ᵇ Opperates] *the second* 'p' *is interlined*
ᶜ was] *interlined*
ᵈ Townshends] 'S' *amended to* 'T'; *Defoe perhaps started to write* 'Sunderland' *or* 'Stanhope'
ᵉ we[re]] *MS frayed*
ᶠ o[n]] *MS frayed*
ᵍ th[at]] *MS frayed*

DEFOE TO [CHARLES DELAFAYE], 23 MAY 1718

I have an Entire Dependenċe on my L^{ds} Justiċe and Goodness That no Offence formerly Com̃itted (were this Really So) Shall be Remembred to my Prejudiċe; However I thought it my Duty to give his L^{dpp} this Acco^t That my Enemyes, may not Antiċipate me by giveing wrong and injurious Acco^{ts} of it before me.

I am

S^r

yor Most Humble Servt

DeFoe

May. 23. 1718

N.B.

The words as I hear y^m wch the Judges take Offence at are in ye Introduceing ye story of ye Fellow y^t was Execcuted Saying, it was a peiċe of Justice Unmix'd with Merċy.[6]

Text: TNA SP 35/12, fol. 64.[7] *Address*: none.

---

1 *ye half year Expire'd The 17th Inst^t*: See Letter 259, note 18.
2 *Morphew*: See Letter 247, note 4.
3 *passage in The Mercurius Politicus*: Sept. 1716, 261–3.
4 *Paragraph printed from another printed paper*: The report of the execution of Barron and Bourn reprinted in part by *Mercurius Politicus* was published in *The St. James's Evening Post*, 11–13 Sept. 1716, among other places.
5 *Capitulaċon made in My Ld Townshends time*: See Letter 259.
6 *it was a peiċe of Justice Unmix'd with Merċy*: Before replicating the story from *The St. James's Evening Post*, *Mercurius Politicus* introduces it as 'an Example of Justice, unmix'd with Mercy …, as the like has not happen'd in our Memory, or scarce in History, at least that we can give any Account of' (261). It ends the report stating 'Three Half-pence is a very small Sum to be hang'd for, and he must be a very hard-mouth'd Fellow that swore it a Robbery' (263).
7 '23 May 1718' is written on the back in a hand other than Defoe's.

DEFOE TO [CHARLES DELAFAYE], 4 JUNE 1718

262

To [Charles Delafaye]

4 June 1718

HEADNOTE: Defoe's claim to have successfully enervated the Tory press's attacks on the ministry, including those of *The Weekly Journal*, was thrown into question by the fact that Mist's paper continued to be troublesome to the government. Mist was arrested in April, May, and December 1717 for Jacobite pieces in his paper, and he was being accused now of having confessed that his paper was Jacobite. Defoe feared being implicated if that charge stuck.

Sr

Since Our last Conference I have Entred into a New Treaty wth mr Mist.[1] I need not Trouble you with ye Perticulars But in a Word he Professes himself Convinc't that he has been Wrong, that ye Governmt has Treated him with Lenety and Forbearance and he Sollemnly Engages to me to give no more Offence.

The Libertys mr Buckley Menconed (Viz) to Seem on ye Same Side as before <u>to Rally the Flying Post</u>,[2] ye whig writers and Even ye Word Whig &c. and to admit foolish and Triffling things in Favour of the Tories. This as I Represented it to him he Agrees is liberty Enough and Resolves his Paper Shall For ye Future Amuse the Tories But not affront ye Governmt.

I have Freely Told him That this is ye Onely Way to preserv his paper, to keep himself from a Jail and to Secure The Advantages which Now Rise to him From it, for that he might be assured the Complaint against him Was So Generall that ye Governmt could bear it No longer.

I Said Sr all that Could be Said on that head, Onely Reserving the Secret of who I spoke from, and Concluded that Unless he Would keep Measures with me and be Punctuall in these things I Could not Serve him any farther Or be Concern'd any More.

Thus far Sr I have acted I hope in a Right Method, in Persuance of wch, in his Next paper he is to make a kind of a Declaracon in Answer to Two letters printed in his Last wherein he shall Publish

DEFOE TO [CHARLES DELAFAYE], 4 JUNE 1718

his Resoluċon Not[a] to Meddle wth or write any thing Offensiv to ye Governmt.[3]

In Prosecuċon also of this[b] Reformaċon he Brought me this Morning the Enclosed Letter,[4] which Indeed I was glad to See, because Tho' it Seems Couch'd in Terms which might have been made publick, yet has a Secret Gall in it, and a Manifest Tendenċy to Reproach ye Governmt wth Partiallity and Injustice, and (as it acknowleges Expressly) was written to Serv a Present Turn; As This is an Earnest of his just Intenċon I hope he will Go on to yor Satisfacċon.

Give me Leave sr to Menċon here a Circumstanċe which Conċerns my Self and wch Indeed is a little hardship upon me (Viz) That I Seem to Merit less when I Interċept a p[iece][c] of Barefaċ'd flagrant Treason at ye Press than when I stop[d] Such a letter as this Enclosed, Because One Seems to be of a kind which no Man Would Dare to Meddle wth, But I would Perswade my Self Sr that stopping Such Notorious things is not without its good Effect, perticularly because as[e] it is True that Some people are generally found who do Venture to print anything that Offers, So stopping them here, is Some Discouragemt and Dissappointmt to them, and they Often Dye in our hands.

I speak this Sr as well on Occasion of what you were pleasd to Say upon that letter which I Sent you formerly about Killing No Murther[f] as upon Another wth Verses in it[5] wch mr Mist Gave me yesterday, which Upon my Word is So Villainous and scandalous that I scarse Dare to Send it without yor Order and an assuranċe That my doeing So Shall be Taken Well. For I confess, it has a Peculiar Insolenċe in it Against his Majties Person wch (as Blasphemous Words agat God) are scarse fit to be Repeated.

I am the More Conċern'd you should know this also, because if I Guess Right and mr Mist is of that Opinion too, it is the

---

[a] Not] *interlined*
[b] this] *following illegible word cancelled*
[c] *p[iece]*: 'ps' in MS, using the 'special p' brevigraph.
[d] stop] *following letter probably* 'a' *cancelled*
[e] as] *interlined above cancelled word* 'tho"
[f] about Killing No Murther] *interlined*

844

DEFOE TO [CHARLES DELAFAYE], 4 JUNE 1718

Same hand that ye Manuscript wch I shewed m^r Buckley of Sultan Galga^6 was Writen in, and I Suppose Comes From ye Same Quarter.

If you please to ord^r my Sending it I shall Obey, and in ye Mean time assure you No Eye Shall See it.

Here has been a Very Barbarous attempt made by Curl ye Bookseller upon m^r Mist (Viz) to Trepann him into words Against ye Governm^t with a Design to Inform against him;^{7} I think Mist has Escaped him but if he brings it into yor Office I shall Lay a Clear state of the Matter before you. I kno' the Government is Sufficent to it Self for punishing Offendors, and is Above Employing Trepanns to Draw Men into Offences On Purpose to Resent them.

I am

S^r

yor Most Humble and Obed^t Servt

DeFoe

Newington June. 4th 1718

Text: TNA SP 35/12, fol. 80. *Address*: none.

1 *a New Treaty wth m^r Mist*: Novak states that 'Mist must have understood that Defoe was speaking for the government in warning him about the extent of his offences and in getting them pardoned', even though Defoe states that he conceals the identity of those from whom he issues the warning. 'To some extent, then, Defoe was enlisting Mist for the government as well' (Novak, 503).

2 *Rally the Flying Post*: A non-authorial marginal comment – 'not true' – appears here; the annotator may be responsible for the underscoring. This annotation predates 1864, when the letter was first published (*London Review of Politics, Society, Literature, Art, and Science*, 11 June 1864, 618).

3 *Next paper ... Governm^t*: Mist's *Weekly Journal* for 7 June includes an article in which, after a long harangue against the Whig journalists, Mist capitulates to the Hanoverian regime: 'We quietly and willingly submit to the Government of King George, are his Majesty's peaceable Subjects, far from desiring or intending to make any Reflections upon either his Person or his Administration; much farther are we from raising any Disturbances, Rebellions, or Uneasinesses whatsoever. We have no Views to the Pretender, we know not, nor are we Favourers of, any Designs for his Interest, and we should be very ill Friends to his Party here, if we prompted them to any kind of Violence against the present Government, in which they have already had such ill Success.' This is couched in a way that would not alienate his core Jacobite readership, as an expedient submission calling for greater circumspection in future issues, rather than a sincere expression of loyalty. 'We shall be more watchful hereafter than perhaps we have been, of giving our Enemies any Advantage against us for Words capable of their ill natur'd Constructions', Mist continues.

4 *Enclosed Letter*: Untraced.

DEFOE TO [CHARLES DELAFAYE], 4 JUNE 1718

5   *letter ... Killing No Murther ... Another wth Verses in it*: *Killing No Murder* (1657) is a pamphlet probably by Silius Titus (1623–1704) and Edward Sexby (1616–58), encouraging the assassination of Lord Protector Oliver Cromwell (1599–1658). It was republished to a Jacobite agenda against three successive monarchs in 1689, 1708, and 1715. Mist's *Weekly Journal* for 29 Mar. 1718 reports having received 'two treasonable Papers', which it refused to publish, from a Mr. Paul Fogg, one of which relates to 'the Cause of Murther and Assassination of Kings', so these could be the ones passed to Delafaye.

6   *Sultan Galga*: See Letter 259, note 25.

7   *Curl ... against him*: In *Curlicism Display'd*, published on 26 May 1718, the prolific, disreputable bookseller Edmund Curll (*c.* 1683–1747) had accused Mist of confessing to writing his *Weekly Journal* in support of the Jacobite cause.

This quite involved episode started in Apr. with Defoe's accusation in a letter in the *Journal* that Curll was publishing little better than pornography with recent titles like *Eunuchism Display'd* and *Onanism Display'd* (both 1718). Defoe labelled this '*Curlicism*', after that 'Manufacturer of Sodomy': 'The Fellow is a contemptible Wretch a thousand Ways; he is odious in his Person, scandalous in his Fame, he is mark'd by Nature, for he has a bawdy Countenance, and a debauch'd Mein; his Tongue is an Ecchoe of all the beastly Language his Shop is fill'd with, and Filthiness drivels in the very Tone of his Voice' (Mist's *Weekly Journal*, 5 Apr. 1718). A piece the following week, perhaps again Defoe's, follows up the attack but blames the authors more than the publisher: 'If a Book be Bawdy or Blasphemy, pray what is that to the Bookseller; he is a Tradesman, his Shop is like that of a Butcher's Shambles, where you may buy wholsom Food or Carrion, or like that of an Apothecary, where he equally deals in Physick or Poison' (Mist's *Weekly Journal*, 12 Apr. 1718). Defoe held Curll in contempt: in 1715 he referred ironically to 'that Conscientious Bookseller, so celebrated for his Honesty, Mr. *Edmund Curll*' (*The Secret History of the Secret History of the White-Staff*, *PEW*, 11, 305). Curll had pirated the English edition of Defoe's *History of the Union* in 1712.

In late May 1718, Curll hit back with *Curlicism Display'd*, composed as a letter to Mist, defending Curll's portfolio and thanking Mist for the free publicity. Curll derides the '*formal gravity*' of Mist's 'super-annuated *Letter-Writer*', and certain allusions indicate he thinks it was Defoe (27, 2). But Curll also says that Mist's '*Journal* is now become the *Oracle* of a discontended Party', the Jacobites, spewing 'MISTICISM and POPERYCISM' (1, 27). More specifically, Curll writes: '*Whereas you publickly declar'd, in my Presence, before several Witnesses ... that the first Letter against me was inserted designedly to reflect on His* MAJESTY *under my Cover; and likewise, that as for any Passages in your* JOURNAL, *whether they should be* True *or* False, *they equally conduc'd to the Interest of the* CAUSE *in which you are embark'd, and to the Reputation of your* PAPER, *amongst the* PARTY, *your only constant* READERS' (29). Defoe feared being implicated.

Subsequently, Mist published letters in his rival Read's *Weekly Journal* demanding Curll retract his allegations and challenging him to a duel (14 June 1718). That never happened, but Curll issued Charles Gildon's attack on *Robinson Crusoe* and Defoe two years later, *The Life and Strange Surprizing Adventures of D--- de F--* (1719). See Paul Baines and Pat Rogers, *Edmund Curll, Bookseller* (Oxford, 2007), 112–20.

846

DEFOE TO [CHARLES DELAFAYE], 13 JUNE 1718

263

To [Charles Delafaye]

13 June 1718

HEADNOTE: Defoe's assurance in this letter that he had persuaded Mist to be more circumspect came while *The Weekly Journal* continued to publish criticisms of the ministry. With respect to Defoe, this came to a head at the end of the year when a letter in the *Journal* on 25 October signed 'Sir Andrew Politick' landed Mist in fresh trouble. Letters from 'Politick' critical of the government had appeared in the paper since February; the October one was 'calculated to give the people the worst Impressions of the proceedings in relation to Spain', as it objected to the ministry's policy of involving Britain in the War of the Quadruple Alliance (1718–20).[1] When arrested, Mist told the authorities that Defoe was the author of the letter and of the *Journal*'s response.[2] Defoe's associate, the bookseller Thomas Warner, corroborated this when he was deposed; Warner stated that Defoe 'appear[ed] much concerned at the proceedings against M[r] Mist, saying that he, Defoe, would not on any account be known to be the Author, for if He thought he should be proved the Author he would quit the Nation, and that he was under an Obligation from above not to meddle with the Paper above-mentioned & desired the Examinant [Warner] to exhort M[r] Mist to stand by it, & not declare the Author, promising in such case to stand by him & to use all his Interest in his favour'.[3] As Furbank and Owens state, this affair casts doubt on Defoe's claim that he was enervating Mist's paper, suggesting rather that 'Defoe and Mist were in collusion *against* the Government.'[4] No substantive correspondence between Defoe and Delafaye survives between June 1718 and a letter of 7 June 1720. That final letter was occasioned by another accusation by Mist that Defoe had written something the government was charging to Mist.

S[r]

 I gave you y[e] Trouble of a Letter a few days agoe. The acco[t] I Gave you There of the Conditions I had Engag'd M[r] M . . . . t to will I hope be Satisfactory and Perticularly in his Performance of those Conditions.

 I Suppose you will Remember I Hinted when I had last y[e] favour of waiting on you that there was a Book Printing at his house Scandalously Reflecting on My L[d] Sund . . .[5] and that M . . . . was willing as a Testimoney of his Sincerity to Consent to a method how to put it into his L[dpps] hands.

DEFOE TO [CHARLES DELAFAYE], 13 JUNE 1718

I have gotten yᵉ sheets into my hands in Performanċe of this Promise, and Would Gladly Reciev yoʳ Commands about them.

I believ yᵉ Time is Come when yᵉ Journall instead of affronting and Offending the Governmᵗ may many ways be made Serviceable to yᵉ Governmᵗ, and I have mʳ M . . . . So absolutely Resign'd to proper Measures for it That I am p[er]swaded I may answer for it.

I am

Sʳ

yoʳ Most Humble and Obedᵗ Servant

DeFoe

June. 13. 1718

Text: TNA SP 35/12, fol. 106. *Address*: none.

1   TNA SP 35/13, fol. 77.
2   TNA SP 35/13, fols. 52, 79.
3   TNA SP 35/13, fols. 85–6. Read's *Weekly Journal* for 18 Oct. 1718 alleged that 'the Press Pad *Daniel Foe*' was the author of the 'scandalous and treasonable' *Weekly Post*. Mist's *Weekly Journal* for 8 Nov. 1718 denied Defoe was the 'Author', 'nor has he any concern at all in it, or ever had, except that formerly he has sometimes translated some Foreign Letters, in the absence of the Person who was more constantly employed for that part'. Mist likewise called it a 'forgery' to assert, as Read's paper had, that he had given a bond to Defoe, 'obliging himself in the penalty of 500l., not to discover his being the writer of his Paper'. There was also an advertisement in another paper to which Defoe was contributing, *The White-Hall Evening Post* for 15 November, signed 'DE FOE', making a similar denial. For Defoe's treatment in Read's *Weekly Journal* in late 1718, see Novak, 503–4. For his role as editor of *The White-Hall Evening Post*, see F&O, 'Periodicals', 93–4.
4   P. N. Furbank and W. R. Owens, 'Defoe and "Sir Andrew Politick"', *BJECS* 17 (1994), 27–39.
5   *Book . . . Lᵈ Sund . . .*: Unidentified.

DEFOE TO CHARLES DELAFAYE, [SEPTEMBER 1719?]

264

To Charles Delafaye
[September 1719?]

HEADNOTE **(Letters 264 and 265):** The following two notes, in which Defoe makes appointments with Charles Delafaye, are undated. They possibly date from September 1719 but could have been written any time from 1718 to 1720.[1]

Sr

I was just goeing home this Morning Very ill[2] when I Met my Son[3] wth whom your Messengr left an Order to attend you, wch tho' it was for to morrow I Chose to Come up to day least I should not be able to Come Out to morrow for I have not till yesterday been out of Doors these 5 Weeks past.

I shall wait yor ordrs but If I might be admitted to See you it will be a Singular favour to

Sr

yor Most Obedt Servt

DeFoe

One a Clock at yor own house

Text: TNA SP 35/66/2, fol. 90. *Address*: To | Mr Delafaye | Present. *Endorsed in an unknown hand*: D.F.

1 They were first published in J. P. W. Rogers, 'Two Unrecorded Letters by Daniel Defoe', *Papers on Language and Literature* 7 (1971), 298–9. Rogers states that the notes are bound with other items that suggests a date of 1719 or 1720, and that the first has an illegible endorsement that could be '1st Sept'. This fact and the report cited below about Defoe's illness in Sept. 1719 suggest that date, though periods of illness are reported in 1718 and 1720 too.
2 *The Jesuite*, no. 6, for 12 Sept. 1719, reported that 'Daniel de Foe lies very Ill at his House at Newington.'
3 *Son*: Benjamin seems more likely than Daniel Jr. For his dealings with the ministry see head-note to Letter 266.

849

DEFOE TO [CHARLES DELAFAYE], [SEPTEMBER 1719?]

265

To [Charles Delafaye]

[September 1719?]

Sr

I have yᵉ Favour of yoʳˢ This Moment, and send back the Bearer to Accquaint you I will attend Exactly at Eight and Send him then[a] again to Reciev yoʳ Commands as to yᵉ place where I shall have yᵉ favour to wait on you.

I am
Sr
yoʳ Most Obliged Humble Servᵗ
DeFoe

Text: TNA SP 35/66/2, fol. 110. *Address*: none.

ᵃ then] *interlined*

266

To [Charles Delafaye]

7 June 1720

HEADNOTE: The fallout of the government's investigation of the 'Sir Andrew Politick' letter in late 1718 was a rupture between Mist and Defoe.[1] Some time in 1719 Defoe resumed his work for Mist, who continued to be watched carefully by the government. In June 1720 Mist was again in trouble: the Bishop of Gloucester, Richard Willis (1664–1734), a Whig supporter of the ministry, laid a complaint in the House of Lords concerning some numbers of *The Weekly Journal* published earlier that year. Mist's paper had criticised Britain's lack of effort to support the persecuted Protestants of the Palatine. On 2 June, the Lords resolved that 'these Papers are scandalous, injurious to the poor Protestants in The Palatinate, and highly reflecting on the Conduct and Interposition of His Majesty and other Protestant Powers in their Favour'.[2] Mist was promptly imprisoned and examined

850

DEFOE TO [CHARLES DELAFAYE], 7 JUNE 1720

on 7 June. He implicated Defoe, which occasioned this, Defoe's final known letter to Delafaye. Defoe was taken up and bailed on 13 June for £400, the same amount as Mist; he denied the allegation and no prosecution against him seems to have been pursued.[3]

By contrast, the following February, Mist was sentenced to stand twice in the pillory, pay a £50 fine, spend three months in prison, and give security for his good behaviour for seven years. Mob violence between groups setting out respectively to defend and attack Mist in the pillory gave rise to a further paper war. Mist was repeatedly arrested in subsequent years.[4]

By then, Defoe had ceased to play a major role in the *Journal*. At the time of this letter, he was writing a periodical called *The Commentator*, which praised the current administration and often attacked Mist. However, Delafaye could not yet forget the name 'Defoe', because in August 1721 he investigated Defoe's son, Benjamin, who was arrested at Townshend's instigation for reporting on parliamentary committees in *The London Journal*. Benjamin followed his father's footsteps in agreeing to work for the government he was accused of having subverted, with Delafaye as his contact.[5]

No letters to or from Defoe have been traced for almost eight years after the last to Delafaye.

Sr

If I was not Very ill and in no Condicon to Come abroad I should have waited on you imediately, and I acknowlege wth all possible Thankfullness yor Kindness in Sending in So Obligeing a Manner.

The Small share I had in mr Mists journall at That Time gives him no ground to Say I had the Direccon of it, Nor indeed did I Some times See what was or was not Put in, There being Severall people Employ'd by him at The Same time who I had no knowlege of.

I am Very Well assur'd I had no Concern in ye Paragraph in question,[6] and he can not Lay it justly to my Charge unless he has my Coppie[7] to produce: It is indeed hard to be Certain at This distance of Time, But I hope I shall be Treated wth Clemency as Well as justice in a Case where my whole study was to keep things Out of the paper which might give Offence, and Especally after I had by Inadvertancy given Offence[8] before as you kno' Sr, for wch I am a Sincere Penitent and a Great Sufferer, and after wch I Endeavod by[a] all ways possible to be Servisable in The paper.

---

[a] by] *interlined*

DEFOE TO [CHARLES DELAFAYE], 7 JUNE 1720

If my attendance be absolutely necessary, wch I hope it may not, I Will not fail to wait on you in a Few dayes if I am able to Come Abroad.

I am

S^r

yor Most Humble And Obedient Servt

DeFoe

June. 7. 1720

Text: Historical Society of Pennsylvania, Philadelphia, Simon Gratz Autograph Collection (Figure 10).⁹ *Address*: To | Cha: De la Faye Esqr | Present

1 See headnote to Letter 263. Read's *Weekly Journal* for 6 Dec. 1718 included a poem 'On *Daniel Foe*'s turning *Whig* again', which includes these lines: '*What strange Adventures cou'd untwist | Such true-born Knaves as* Foe *and* Mist? | *They quarrel'd sure about the Pelf,* | *For* Dan's *a needy greedy Elf* | ... | *As Rats do run from falling Houses,* | *So* Dan *another Cause espouses:* | *Leaves poor* Nat *sinking in the Mire,* | *Writes* White-Hall Evening-Post *for Hire* | *Deserts his Tory-Rory Prigs,* | *And finds new Fools among the Whigs.* | *We wish the Gentlemen much Joy;* | *And since they're Fond of a Decoy,* | *May* Daniel *dive into their Pockets* | *And laugh to think he found such Blockheads.*'

2 *L.J.*, XXI, 344.

3 TNA SP 44/79A, fol. 339.

4 Pat Rogers, 'Nathaniel Mist, Daniel Defoe, and the Perils of Publishing', *The Library* 10 (2009), 298–313.

5 Charles Bechdolt Realey, '*The London Journal* and its Authors, 1720–1723', *Bulletin of the University of Kansas* 5 (1935), 1–38 (at 13–20). For the government's investigation, see TNA SP 35/28, fols. 12–26; *Daily Courant*, 16 and 17 Aug. 1721; *Daily Post*, 17 Aug. 1721. *The Daily Journal*, 18 Aug. 1721, erroneously reported it was Defoe himself who had been arrested. *Applebee's Original Weekly Journal* for 26 Aug. 1721 intimated that Benjamin was the 'Stalking Horse', not responsible for the offending paragraph.
   It is plausible but not certain that Defoe contributed to *Applebee's* in the 1720s. See P. N. Furbank and W. R. Owens, 'The Myth of Defoe as Applebee's Man', *RES* 48 (1997), 198–204; Maximillian Novak, 'Daniel Defoe and *Applebee's Original Weekly Journal*: An Attempt at Re-Attribution', *ECS* 45 (2012), 585–608.

6 *Paragraph in question*: Not identified precisely. Willis cited excerpts from Mist's *Weekly Journal* for 2 Jan. and 2, 9, and 16 Apr. 1720. Boyer reprinted the latter three, as well as similar material from other issues, in the *Political State* for June 1720, XIX, 632–40.

7 *my Coppie*: In Nov. 1718 Mist deposed to Secretary of State Stanhope that Defoe usually destroyed his copy, so that 'it should not be known who was the author' (TNA SP 35/13, fol. 79).

8 *I had by Inadvertancy given Offence*: Perhaps referring to the 'Sir Andrew Politick' letter of 25 Oct. 1718. See headnote to Letter 263. In *The Manufacturer*, no. 44 (18 May 1720), Defoe says 'the Author ... being now in the Hands of his Friends again', 'tis hoped former Prejudices shall not obstruct a good Design', suggesting his Tory pose was over.

9 This letter was sold by Sotheby's in July 1891. See G. A. Aitken, 'Defoe and Mist's "Weekly Journal"', *The Athenæum*, 26 Aug. 1893, 287–8, which is the letter's first printing. The Philadelphia lawyer and collector Simon Gratz (1840–1925) donated it to the Historical Society of Pennsylvania.

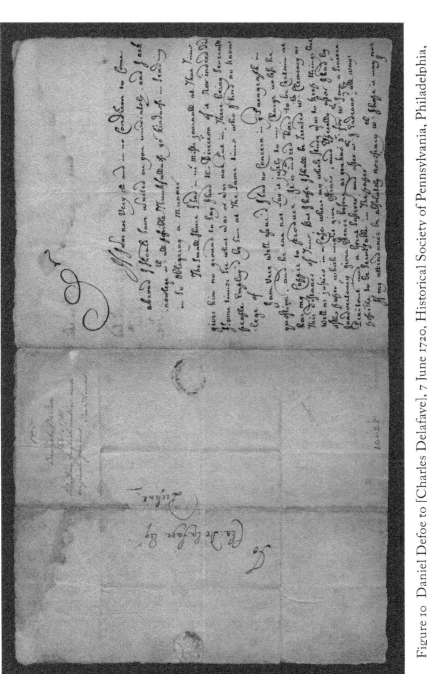

Figure 10 Daniel Defoe to [Charles Delafaye], 7 June 1720, Historical Society of Pennsylvania, Philadelphia, Simon Gratz Autograph Collection

267

To Henry Baker

23 August 1728

HEADNOTE (Letters 267 and 268): Henry Baker (1698–1774) was a poet, natural philosopher, and teacher of deaf children.[1] He resided in Enfield but met Defoe in 1724 while teaching a child in Stoke Newington. Defoe praised Baker effusively in *Mere Nature Delineated* (1726), a work in which Defoe addressed language acquisition by the 'deaf and dumb'.[2] Baker's 'Autobiographical Memorandum', written in the third person, gives one of the fullest descriptions of Defoe in his final decade:[3]

> Amongst the first who desired his acquaintance at Newington was Mr D—, a Gentleman well known by his Writings, who had newly built there a very handsom House, as a Retirement from London, and amused his Time either in the Cultivation of a large and pleasant Garden, or in the Pursuit of his Studies, which he found means of making very profitable. He was now at least sixty years of age, afflicted with the Gout and Stone, but retained all his mental Faculties intire.[4]

The emphasis on Defoe's affluence is not innocuous. Baker began to court Defoe's youngest daughter, Sophia. He proposed to her in August 1727 and was accepted 'some Months' later.[5] Thereafter Defoe and Baker entered protracted financial negotiations regarding the marriage. This had been going on for a year before the first extant letter, with Baker the impatient lover growing increasingly frustrated.

Baker did not want to wait until Defoe's death for his dowry, as Defoe had proposed. He describes his own financial situation as follows, again in the third person: 'His own Fortune was not sufficient to maintain a Family in the Manner he should desire, and he had long before determined never to think of marrying without a reasonable Assurance of living comfortably … His expenses were so triffling that he had already out of the Profits of his Employment laid by one thousand Pounds, and there was little Doubt but a few years would procure him an easy Competency, provided he did not prevent it by an imprudent Match.'[6] He recounts that when he requested permission to address Sophia, Defoe had told him: 'I cannot pretend to give her a Portion equal to Mr B—'s Merit, but he shall not take her like a Charity Girl with nothing, I hope she will bring him at least [expunged in MS] Pounds, which added to as much of his, if properly secured will be some Provision for her and her Children (if God sends them) in case of Accident [i.e. Baker's death].'[7] Baker states that after he had been accepted by Sophia, Defoe admitted 'that when they talked before he did not know the true State of his own affairs: that on due Consideration he found he could not part with any Money

854

DEFOE TO HENRY BAKER, 23 AUGUST 1728

at present, but at his Death his Daughter Sophy's Share would be more than he had promised'.[8] The offer was £500 at Defoe's death. Baker declined this proposal until the sum was secured with property and interest was paid in the meantime.

The couple eventually married on 30 April 1729. Baker put the worst construction on Defoe's dealings during the negotiations:

> Mr D seems to have imagined that by creating these Difficulties and Delays, the Impatience of the young People would have induced them to marry without any previous Agreement with him, and that afterwards he should have had it in his Power to treat them as he thought fit. But they had both resolved not to come together till every thing was set.[9]

Paula Backscheider aptly states that Defoe's and Baker's 'letters are careful exercises in barely suppressed dislike and resentment'.[10]

I cannot but say I am concerned on many Accounts, to see an Affair of this Nature hang thus in suspence; and you will not take it ill that I add, It is more than I expected, and that it is highly reasonable it should be brought to an Issue.

As I said to you at first, that if you design'd to ask my Daughter, you must take her as I could give her,[11] so I think it is far from being out of the Way to repeat it: adding with it that I also think I have endeavoured to shew the Respect I profess'd for you, by making as good proposals as my affairs[12] will admit.

The first Proposal you have rejected, and also a second;[13] You and I will no more debate the Reasons of it, because whether I think it fair or kind or otherwise, Yet as I resolve to take nothing ill from You, so I choose to say no more of it, I think my Offer was fully consistent with my first proposal as it is with my Ability.

You have since plac'd the Affair in another Situation demanding [ ]ᵃ down,[14] which I said I would consider of. Many intervening Accidents[15] have made the Time much longer than I intended to take in giving my Answer. I have now drawn it up and sent it herewith to my Daughter, to show you: I have only to add, that as this is my *Ultimatum*, not that I shall but that I can make an Offer of, I intreat, that you will consider of it so effectually, that your answer may put an end to the whole affair, one way or other; which

ᵃ demanding [ ]] 'word or sum scratched out' (Wright, 399)

855

I think highly necessary, as well for yourself, who have much trouble in it, as for my child, who I am too heartily concerned for to think it proper to leave it longer in Suspence.

I am (and shall be which way soever this matter may issue) always

Your sincere Friend and Servant.

London, August 23rd, 1728.

Mr. B—r's last Demand as of [ ]^a down, and my Return is thus—

My Affairs do not permit me to advance the money presently, but I offer this as Equivalent.

1. That I will pay [ ]^b at a certain Term, or sooner if it may be.

2. That till it be paid I will pay the Interest annually at £4 per cent., which is the ordinary Interest of Money.[16]

3. That in Case of Mortality, Hannah will oblige herself to pay the [ ]^c out of the Essex Estate,[17] which shall be legally vested in her to enable her to perform it, and to come immediately upon my Decease into her Hands.

This I take to be paying the Money down, seeing Mr. B—r does not pretend to want the Money otherwise than to put it out to Interest.

August 23rd, 1728

Text: MS untraced. The copytext is Wright, 399–400. *Address*: none recorded.

^a of [ ]] *'scratched out' (Wright, 399)*
^b pay [ ]] *'scratched out'. Wright, 400*
^c the [ ]] *'scratched out'. Wright, 400*

1 On Baker, see John Nichols, *Literary Anecdotes of the Eighteenth Century*, 9 vols. (1812), v, 272–8; G. L'E. Turner, 'Henry Baker, F. R. S.: Founder of the Bakerian Lecture', *Notes and Records of the Royal Society of London* 29 (1974), 53–79; Savile Bradbury, *The Evolution of the Microscope* (Oxford, 1967), 113–15.

2 For Defoe's writings on educating deaf people, see Letter 31, note 9; *Mere Nature Delineated*, *TDH*, v, 178, 192, 204.

3 Defoe's words in the voice of '*an over officious* Old Man', Andrew Moreton, in the preface to *The Protestant Monastery* (1726), may be autobiographical: '*I have but small Health ... being now in my 67th Year, almost worn out with Age and Sickness*' (*PEW*, viii, 239–40).

856

DEFOE TO HENRY BAKER, 23 AUGUST 1728

4 Baker, fol. 1. Baker's 'Autobiographical Memorandum' is transcribed in George Reuben Potter, 'Henry Baker, F. R. S. (1698–1774)', *MP* 29 (1932), 301–21 (at 310–17). The 'Memorandum' was previously prefaced to Baker's letters to Sophia Defoe, but those letters are now untraced, known only from the extracts published in Wright, 355–74, which is also the only source for parts of the Defoe–Baker correspondence. Wright does not appear to have seen Baker's 'Memorandum'. It was in the possession of John Forster (1812–76) by 1860, and he describes it in *Oliver Cromwell. Daniel De Foe. Sir Richard Steele. Charles Churchill. Samuel Foote. Biographical Essays*, 3rd ed. (1860), 149–54. William Lee had seen and described the 'Memorandum' and the Sophia–Henry letters in his 1869 biography of Defoe, but he had not seen the Defoe–Baker letters other than the very last one (Letter 278), which had been published by Wilson in 1830 (Lee, 1, 440; Wilson, 111, 605–8).

In addition to the 'Autobiographical Memorandum', Baker left another manuscript biography covering the 1720s, called 'Memoranda, Principally Relating to Pecuniary Affairs, Interspersed with Anecdotes of Himself & Family', now in the History of Science Museum Archive, Oxford.

5 Baker, fol. 12.

6 Baker, fol. 4. Turner calculates that Baker's annual income at this time was around £308 and his expenditure averages £217.10s. ('Henry Baker', 58).

7 Baker, fol. 8.

8 Baker, fols. 12–13.

9 Baker, fol. 15.

10 Backscheider, *Life*, 502.

11 *you must take her as I could give her*: Baker reports this as Defoe's 'final Reply': 'Sir, if you will take my Daughter, you must take her as I can give her' (Baker, fol. 13).

In *The Protestant Monastery*, Defoe relates the story of an elderly man who gives his wealth in marriage to his daughter and lives with the couple, but soon finds himself mistreated and powerless, a warning to parents to reserve enough for their own independence (*PEW*, VIII, 243–7).

12 *my affairs*: Baker's letters to Sophia suggest that Defoe was chary of disclosing his financial affairs, which Baker calls 'an imaginary evil' (Wright, 359). Two Chancery cases in 1728 are part of the reason Defoe's affairs were unsettled. First, his manager and business partner on his Colchester farm, John Ward, alleged that Defoe owed him around £253 because Defoe had not paid his share of an investment towards a pantile factory on the estate; Defoe took out a suit in Chancery claiming that Ward owed him upwards of £750 in unpaid rent and loans (TNA C 11/2578/31; Backscheider, *Life*, 470, 496–9). Second, and more worryingly, Mary Brooke was pursuing an alleged debt dating back to 1691. See headnote to Letter 278.

13 *first Proposal ... second*: Defoe had apparently offered a £500 dowry to be pledged in his will.

14 *down*: up front.

15 *Accidents*: events.

16 *£4 per cent., which is the ordinary Interest of Money*: Recent examples of Defoe writing on the basis of 5% interest (and higher) on investments and loans include *The Fortunate Mistress, Novels*, IX, 146; *The Protestant Monastery, PEW*, VIII, 252.

17 *Hannah ... Essex Estate*: Defoe held a 99-year lease on Kingswood Heath in Mile End, Colchester. He acquired it on 6 Aug. 1722, paying £120 per year rent, having paid a £1,000 'fine' (a single payment that secured a lower rent) in two instalments (Essex Record Office, D/DC 5/18; Philip Morant, *The History and Antiquities of the Most Ancient Town and Borough of Colchester* (1748), book 11, 26; Backscheider, *Life*, 467–8). Defoe leased the estate, the value of which Sutherland states was about £300 a year, for the benefit of his daughter Hannah, who was co-signatory on the lease. Hannah owned £706.13s.6d. of South Sea stock at that time, which may have been sold to fund the Colchester investment. See Wilson, 111, 644; Wright, 296–8; James R. Sutherland, 'A Note on the Last Years of Defoe', *MLR* 29 (1934), 137–41.

857

DEFOE TO HENRY BAKER, 27 AUGUST 1728

268

To Henry Baker

27 August 1728

Sr

I am Sorry there Should be any Manner of Room for an Objecċon when we are So Near a Conclusion of an Affair like This. I Should be Very Uneasie when I give you a Gift I So much Value (and I hope I do not Over Rate her Neither) There Should be any Reserv among us, that Should leav yᵉ least Room for Unkindness, or So much as thinking of Unkindness, no not so Much as of[a] the Word.

But there is a Family Reason why I am Tyed down to yᵉ Words of Four p[er] Cent, and[b] I can not Think mr Baker Should Dispute So Small a Matter wᵗʰ me, after I Tell him So (Viz) that I am So Tyed Down; I can I believ many Wayes make him up the Little Sum̄ of five pound a year,[1] and when I Tell you Thus under my hand, that I shall Think my Self Obligd to do it Durante Vita[2] I shall add that, I shall Think my Self more Obligd to do So, than if you had it Under Hand and Seal.

But if you are not willing to Trust me on my Parole, for So Small a [sum],[c] and that According To the Great Treatys abroad, there must be a [secr]et[d] Article in Our Negotiaċon; I Say if it must be So, I Would fain put my Self in a Condiċon to Deny you Nothing, wᶜʰ you can ask, believing you Will ask nothing of me wᶜʰ I ought to Denye.

When you Speak of a childs Fortune, wᶜʰ I Own you do Very Modestly, you Must giv me leave to Say Onely this, you must accept of this in Bar of any Claim from the City Customes;[3] and I doubt you will have but Too much Reason, Seeing I can[e] hardly hope to do Equally[f] for all yᵉ Rest, as I shall for my Dear Sophie;

---

[a] of] *interlined*
[b] and] *interlined*
[c] [sum]] *MS damaged; text supplied from the Rylands copy of the letter*
[d] [secr]et] *MS damaged*
[e] can] *interlined*
[f] Equally] *following illegible word cancelled*

858

DEFOE TO HENRY BAKER, 27 AUGUST 1728

But after that, you shall Onely allow me to Say, and that you shall
Depend upon, what Ever it shall please God to bless me with, None
Shall have a Deeper share in it, and you Need do no more Than
Remember, That she is, Ever was and Ever Will be My Dearest and
Best Beloved; and let me add again I hope you will Take it for a
Mark of my Singular and affectionate Concern for you, That I Thus
giv her you, and That I Say too If I could giv her much More it
should be to you, wth the Same affecċon.

Yo^rs Without Flattery
D F

Augt 27th 1728

Text: National Art Gallery, Victoria and Albert Museum, Forster Collection MS
142M S L/1876/Forster/142.[4] *Address*: To | Mr Baker | Present

---

1 *Four p[er] Cent ... five pound a year.* Baker had requested 5% per annum of a £500 dowry (£25)
   rather than the 4% (£20) Defoe offered.
2 *Durante Vita*: 'during lifetime' (Latin).
3 *City Customes*: Spiro Peterson explains that Defoe refers to the 'Custom of *London*', a limit
   on testamentary liberty that took precedence over a will and dictated that surviving children
   shared a third part of the estate. Defoe seems to have received from Baker written confirmation that Sophia forfeited her claim to a share of this. See Peterson, 'Daniel Defoe and "City
   Customes"', *N&Q* 203 (1958), 400–1. Frank Bastian explained it earlier in correspondence
   with John Robert Moore, 18 Dec. 1956, Indiana University Archives, H140; Moore, 327–8. See
   Letter 276, note 8.
4 The letter was bequeathed to the V&A by Eliza Forster (1819–94), widow of John Forster;
   it was previously sold as part of the estate of Dawson Turner (1775–1858) (*Catalogue of the
   Manuscript Library of the Late Dawson Turner, Esq* (1859), 274). Forster published it in *Oliver
   Cromwell. Daniel De Foe. Sir Richard Steele. Charles Churchill. Samuel Foote. Biographical Essays*, 3rd ed. (1860), 153–4. A copy of the letter made by Harriet Defoe Baker (1798–1865), wife
   of Defoe's great grandson Henry De Foe Baker (1789–1845), who gifted it to Turner, is now
   in John Rylands Library, University of Manchester, Eng MS 19, vol. 1, fol. 85. See Shipley,
   325 n. 1.

DEFOE TO HENRY BAKER, 9 SEPTEMBER 1728

269

To Henry Baker

9 September 1728

HEADNOTE: Baker proposed that Defoe mortgage his Colchester property or Stoke Newington house to pay Sophia's dowry, but Defoe professed 'these were already settled for Family purposes, which he could not break through'. Baker stated that he 'would no longer place any Confidence in Mr D— which created such a Coldness that they seldom saw each other, tho' Mr B. constantly visited his dear Sophia'.[1] Despite their disagreement, Defoe contributed an essay to the first number of Baker's periodical *The Universal Spectator and Weekly Journal* in October 1728.[2]

Sr

I am Very Sorry to Hear that mr Forster[3] should Say I have not acted[a] with Honour in this affair. I must ask your leav to think quite otherwise, and that I am not well used atall.

From the begining I Said both to you and to mr Forster that I would not Mortgage the Triffle I have in Essex[4] for ye Security of this affair. I did not speak ambiguously in it atall, but in words at length and Explicit, Such as were Capabl[e][b] of no other Meaning, So as an Honest Man Ought allways to speak.

Mr Forster Concludes from Hence that It is allready Mortgagd wch is Something hard. I told him it was indeed at first Engagd for 200£ which is Since paid off.[5]

But that I may more fully Explain it If it must be So the Case [is][c] this and nothing Elce, Viz, that being arrivd to an age when if Ever it is Needfull to Settle what little I have among my Children, This is So Settled and So Engagd and no otherwise, and I can not think it a Breach of Honour that I do not think it proper to Expose, no not to my Own Children, all the Perticulars of my Family Settlement while I am still living, and as this is [the][d] Onely Reason and that no Mortgage or other Engagemt is made on ye Estate but this and yet that this binds me not to make any other Disposition of

---

[a] acted] *following word* 'like' *cancelled*
[b] Capabl[e]] *MS frayed*
[c] [is]] *MS damaged by broken wax seal*
[d] [the]] *just a dot in MS*

860

HENRY BAKER TO DEFOE, 7 JANUARY [1729?]

it, I can not see how I act Dishonourably and I think ought not to be told so.

I am Sorry I am Obligd to Say this, but Since this is Truth and that yᵉ Circumstances Oblige me to speak it I hope you will Excuse my freedom. I shall still be wᵗʰ Respect as before,

yoʳ Humble Servᵗ
DeFoe

Newington Monday Sept. 9ᵗʰ 1728 —

Text: BL Add. MS. 88618A, fol. 1.[6] *Address*: To | Mʳ Henry Baker | at mʳ Forsters on Baker [Street]ᵃ | in | Enfield

---

ᵃ [Street]] *MS smudged; rewritten below in a different hand*

---

1 Baker, fol. 14.
2 F&O, *Bibliography*, 260.
3 *mr Forster*: John Forster, attorney in Enfield, related to Baker by marriage. Baker had resided with Forster since 1720 and was tutor to Forster's two deaf daughters (John Nichols, *Literary Anecdotes of the Eighteenth Century*, 9 vols. (1812), v, 273).
4 *Triffle I have in Essex*: The Colchester property. See Letter 267, note 17.
5 *Engagd for 200ᵏ which is Since paid off*: Defoe mortgaged the Essex land to Mary Norton for £200 in 1723, apparently to raise money to pay the second instalment of the 'fine'; but he redeemed this in Nov. 1727 (Wright, 298; Backscheider, *Life*, 468).
6 There is a post stamp.

270

Henry Baker to Defoe

7 January [1729?]

HEADNOTE: As Baker and Defoe neared an agreement, Defoe tried to provide for his remaining daughters by requesting Sophia's dowry revert to his estate should she die without child by Baker. This excerpt of a letter is known from Wright's biography; Wright places it in 1728, but Healey seems justified in thinking Wright took old style dates at face value, so 1729 seems more probable.[1]

I can't help objecting to that part of your paper[2] which provides that in case your daughter dies without issue her portion[3] shall revert to

DEFOE TO HENRY BAKER, 9 JANUARY [1729?]

your executors. Will you consent if I die childless that what I leave shall go among my relations. I know you won't. And is not your negative a good argument for my objection?

Text: MS untraced. The copytext is Wright, 359. *Address*: none recorded.

1 Wright, 360; *Letters*, ed. Healey, 466 n. 1.
2 *paper*. Untraced.
3 *portion*: dowry.

271

To Henry Baker

9 January [1729?][1]

HEADNOTE: On 9 January, the same day as this letter, Sophia wrote to Baker with reference to the previous letter: 'Your letter, sir, to my father seems to have much of the air of barter and sale. My fortune, though not great, fully answers yours, which is less than I need accept of, and which I think does not justify such nice demands.'[2] Sophia evidently defended Defoe as 'a most indulgent father' and undertook to plead with him.[3]

Sir,—I must acknowledge I am very Sorry we should break at last upon a Point so very nice and yet so important as This, and I am the more concerned because I think we have been both wrong in omitting a more early Debate about it.

After the Frankness with which I at first treated your proposal, and the Kindness with which I always treated you personally, I should be very sorry to offer anything now that should seem less kind than at first. Nor can I see the least room to have it thought so; but at the same time that I desire to be thought kind, you will not, I hope, offer anything that shall look like unkind.

The Thing proposed, I confess, is in my Opinion consistent not wth kindness only, but with Justice. And, indeed, Justice to the rest of my little Family commands it from Me: It is a little hard to put a Father to express himself upon it, but at the same time that You argue your Case as an Husband, with what

862

DEFOE TO HENRY BAKER, 9 JANUARY [1729?]

Horror (excuse the Word) must I suppose the case before I can argue upon it as a Father. I must suppose My Child lost, dead, childless. Mr. Baker, who now I value and shall (before that) say I value and love, lost to me; the Relation sunk out of Nature and embarked perhaps in another Family, how can I look on the rest of my Children disinherited and impoverisht by the double Loss of their Sister and their Fortune! Make the Case your own if that be possible.

I can say no more! 'tis my Weakness: I would hope for long Life and a Family between you. God in his mercy grant it if you come together: but how can You (and I much less) enter upon the melancholy and mornful Negative and suppose me deprived doubly and made miserable, and yourself supported at the expence of the Family.

Besides what Necessity as well as what Justice to lay such a dead weight[4] always on a Father's Thoughts ready to sink with but the mention of it.

If you live and encrease,[5] the Thing is at an end; if not, the Occasion is at least lessened. I hope the odds is in your Favour: may it be to you and yours for ever; and if there is so apparent Hopes, why should you lay so much more weight on the melancholy part: I run the Risque Equally and indeed much more than you, for upon the whole you run no Risque at all. If you lose your Wife you have all your own with its encrease, and I can not call it a maintaining her in the mean time; if she will not more than merit her maintenance, She will be a worse Wife than I would wish Mr. Baker to have, and much worse than I hope she will make.

I am very sorry my Family circumstances make it needful to me to say this, but as it is nothing but what is consistent with my first offer, and with the Nature of the Thing customary in like Cases, and which I yielded to myself on the like occasion, I can not be chargeable with taking the least step aside, from what I proposed and what you had accepted.

I am, with the same kindness and sincerity as before,

Yr Friend affectionately,

D. F.

DEFOE TO HENRY BAKER, 21 JANUARY [1729?]

Newington, January 9th, 1728.[6]

P.S.—Pray reflect on the risque on my Side if my Child should drop off in a year or two or less, as often happens. The very Thought afflicts me so I cannot go on writing upon it. Suppose again you should be taken from her in a few Years before you had encreased sufficiently for the support of a Family which may be left: Where would that dead weight lye?

God avert these melancholy Things! but they are all possible.

Text: MS untraced. The copytext is Wright, 397–8. *Address*: none recorded.

1　See headnote to Letter 270.
2　Wright, 360.
3　Baker, fol. 13; John Forster, *Oliver Cromwell. Daniel De Foe. Sir Richard Steele. Charles Churchill. Samuel Foote. Biographical Essays*, 3rd ed. (1860), 152.
4　*dead weight*: Defoe uses this phrase in *The Six Distinguishing Characters of a Parliament-Man* (1701), *PEW*, 11, 34; *Memoirs of a Cavalier* (1720), *Novels*, IV, 209; *The Complete English Tradesman* (1725–7), *RDW*, VII, 32.
5　*encrease*: Taken in either a financial or a familial sense, the Bakers did increase. Their two children were David Lionel Erskine Baker (1730–67?) and Henry Baker (1734–66); and Henry's wealth at his death was £20,000 (Moore, 330).
6　*1728*: Probably 1729 new style; see headnote to Letter 270.

272

To Henry Baker

21 January [1729?]

HEADNOTE **(Letters 272 and 273)**: Defoe had finally agreed to use his house in Stoke Newington as security for the payment of Sophia's dowry, though Baker evidently had reservations about his ownership of the lease, causing another disagreement. Baker's draft response (Letter 273) is very rough and is written on the reverse of Defoe's letter, so it may or may not reflect what he actually sent to his future father-in-law.[1]

Sʳ

I believ you will now be Convinc'd that what I Suggested in this affair Was Right Judg'd, Tho' as I was not Sure you might then think me Mistaken.

864

DEFOE TO HENRY BAKER, 21 JANUARY [1729?]

The Sending me to Sutton[2] to Mend a Title[3] wch I have not t[he least Re]ason[a] to think Precarious has had the Effect I Expected (Viz)[b] to put Vain Conciets in his head, of his power, wch however I Se[e][c] no Weight in yet puffs him up to Refuse, what I have Really no Occasion to ask and you will See if you please to judge Impartially that I was not Wrong when I Said it Was Harassing me and without Cause too.

However Nothing shall Move me to have any Disputes wth mr Baker or to lessen my Respect for him, and for that Reason,[d] if my Circumstances allow me not to offer any thing that He thinks fit to accept, (I can Onely Say I am Sorry for it), I[e] shall make no Remarks upon it here.[f]

If you please to let my Lease be Returnd Either to my Daughter or to my Son in Finch Lane[4] I shall leav yor Receipt wth Either of them as you Shall Direct.

I am

Sr yor Very Humble Servt

DeFoe

Jan. 21th 1728[5]

Text: BL Add. MS. 88618A, fol. 2.[6] *Address* (fol. 2v): To | Mr Baker | Present

[a] t[he least Re]ason] *MS damaged by wax seal and a tear*
[b] (Viz)] *MS torn*
[c] Se[e]] 'e' *omitted*
[d] and for that Reason] *interlined*
[e] I] *anterior word* 'and' *cancelled*
[f] here] *following words* 'for that Rea' *cancelled*

---

1 In the heavily revised draft, 'we can see [Baker] in the throes of composition, trying to control his anger and to put his remonstrance to his future father-in-law in the best form' (Secord, 49).
2 *Sutton*: Timothy Sutton owned the copyhold on which Defoe's house in Stoke Newington stood. Secord conjectures that when on 6 Aug. 1714 a George Willcocks leased the house for fifty years from Anne Sutton, probably Timothy's mother, it was done on behalf of Defoe to protect him against creditors. Defoe purchased the basic lease from Willcocks's heir, Jarvis Willcocks, on 22 Nov. 1727 but immediately assigned it to George Virgoe, a London merchant, again presumably to protect himself from creditors. Thus, Defoe did not possess the basic lease that he used as security for his bond to Baker (Arthur Secord, 'Defoe in Stoke Newington', *PMLA* 66 (1951), 211–26 (at 216–17)).
3 *Mend a Title*: Baker had evidently doubted Defoe's lease.
4 *my Son in Finch Lane*: Daniel Defoe Jr, now a merchant.
5 *1728*: 1729 new style. See headnote to Letter 270.
6 Letter 273, Baker's draft reply, is also on fol. 2v.

865

273

Henry Baker to Defoe

[21–5 January 1729?][1]

S^r

I never suppos'd you could[a] force Sutton, but[b] presum'd I might without Offence[c] desire your Endeavours[d] towards another Lease.

You have try'd it seems in vain:[e] if then it can't be done, we must make the best of things without it. I never shall exact Impossibilities; but indeed wonder'd at your unwillingness to attempt it. But I never intended it as the sine qua non.[2]

To have the House is not[f] my Wish,[g] & if You please as yourself propos'd[h] to secure the[i] Yearly payments[j] I shall not only rest[k] well contented,[l] but[m] be in the Sincerest Manner

Your most Obliged humble Servt

Text: BL Add. MS. 88618A, fol. 2v. [A very rough draft.[3]] *Address*: none.

---

[a] suppos'd you could] *interlined above cancelled words* 'expected from [illegible word] you should'; *the illegible word may be a cancellation within the cancellation*

[b] but] *following words cancelled (cancelled alternatives within the cancellation are indicated here by forward slashes)* 'I wonder'd you should call that a Hardship & / I presum'd I might // expect // reasonably desire // it was not unreasonable to desire / you would attempt gaining what so evidently was for / your own advantage / the Security of us both / Advantage of us both. It seems you went, but without Success'

[c] without Offence] *interlined*

[d] Endeavours] *following word perhaps* 'to' *cancelled*

[e] vain] *following illegible word cancelled*

[f] not] *interlined above cancelled words* 'in no wis'

[g] Wish] *following words* 'otherwise than' *cancelled*

[h] as yourself propos'd] *interlined above cancelled words possibly* 'any way I'

[i] the] *interlined above cancelled word* 'those'

[j] payments] *following words* 'yourself propos'd' *cancelled*

[k] rest] *interlined above cancelled word* 'be'

[l] contented] *interlined above cancelled word* 'Satisfy'd'

[m] but] *following word* 'in' *cancelled*

---

1 The date range is ascertained from the fact that Baker wrote this on the reverse of the preceding letter and Letter 274 is a response to whatever Baker actually sent to Defoe.

2 *sine qua non*: An essential condition, literally 'without which, not' (Latin).

3 Wright's transcription (399) is possibly from Baker's own copy and therefore may better reflect what was actually sent than this scribbled draft. Wright standardises punctuation, orthography, and typography, and his version of this letter is just one paragraph; therefore, and also because Wright's version is substantially the same as the MS draft, I have used the draft as the copytext. Wright's text restores material cancelled in the MS draft. Indeed, Healey silently adopts these, though he states his copytext was the MS (*Letters*, ed. Healey, 469).

See also the transcription in Backscheider, *Life*, 610 n. 27, which shows some of the more substantial cancellations within the text, providing a helpful visualisation of the state of the MS (there are minor differences in our readings of some cancelled parts). Secord summarises: '[Baker] starts the first sentence and then lines out and rephrases the opening clause. In the second clause he first wondered "you should call that a hardship" and then lined it all out; next, he presumed he might expect, and changed that successively to "reasonably desire," "not unreasonably desire," etc., before he finally got the sentence finished. The rest goes more easily, though some passages are hard to read' (49).

274

To Henry Baker

25 January [1729?]

HEADNOTE: Baker's letters to Sophia indicate the mounting mutual hostility between him and Defoe.[1] Considering that he was writing to Defoe's daughter, Baker uses some colourful language, making himself the Ferdinand to Defoe's Prospero and Sophia's Miranda:

> You … are my good genius, and your father is my evil one. He like a curst infernal, continually torments, betrays, and overturns my quiet; you, like a divinity, allay the storm he raises and hush my soul to peace. Ruin and wild destruction sport around him and exercise their fury on all he has to do with, but joy and happiness are your attendants and bless where'er you come.

On 1 February 1729, Baker proposed to Sophia that they both drink poison and die in one another's arms. When that did not happen, he continued his complaints to her against Defoe's conduct as 'deceit and baseness', 'dark and hideous', 'crafty, ungenerous, dishonest'. Sophia wrote that 'Your suspicions of my father … I think wholly unjust and groundless, He has not one thought I am assured of, that you so rashly charge him with.'[2]

DEFOE TO HENRY BAKER, 25 JANUARY [1729?]

S^r

I am Very much Surpris'd that Now you^a plainly see the Difficulty, which I foresaw Would Occur in this Affair^b have happend accordingly, you Now Drop them as things wch may be let alone, after they had been Insisted upon before, as Absolutely Necessary, and after^c [you]^d have by this brought me into a Labirinth, wch I do not see [any]^e Way out of, and like Some other people Ventur'd to Raise a W[ork]^f they can not help^g to finish;[3] had you done it before ye thing had been [   ].^h

What you Expect Nextⁱ I kno' not, or what after having been so Handled^j you can desire me to do next, and Therefore must Desire you will please to let the Lease be left wth my Son[4] in Finch Lane, where I will also leav your Reciept for it: I am Sorry my poor Child has ye Missfortune to have no better Treatment after So long being Exposd.[5] But I hope God will Provide for her his Own Way.

I am

S^r

yor Fr^d and Humble Servt

DeFoe

Fryday Jan 25th 1728[6]

Text: MS untraced. The copytext is a tracing of Defoe's autograph original, BL Add. MS. 88618A, fol. 3.[7] *Address* (fol. 3^r at the foot): To Mr Baker

---

^a you] *interlined*
^b in this Affair] *interlined*
^c and after] *interlined*
^d [you]] *for four lines the tracing seems to stop at an arc on the right edge, presumably the wax seal*
^e [any]] *lost on the tracing*
^f W[ork]] *lost on the tracing*
^g help] *following illegible word cancelled*
^h been [   ]] *lost on the tracing*
ⁱ Next] *possibly cancelled*
^j Handled] *following illegible word cancelled*

---

1 Wright, 362.
2 Wright, 369–70.
3 *Raise a W[ork] they can not help to finish*: See Luke 14:28–30.
4 *Son*: Daniel Defoe Jr.
5 *Exposd*: That is, having been engaged.

DEFOE TO HENRY BAKER, [APRIL 1729?]

6 *Fryday Jan 25ᵗʰ 1728*: 1729 new style. See headnote to Letter 270. As Healey notes, there must be an error in the day or the date, as 25 Jan. was a Saturday in 1729 and a Thursday in 1728 (*Letters*, ed. Healey, 470 n. 2).

7 '(copy)' is written at the top in an unidentified hand. As with the previous letter, Wright's transcription (361), possibly based on a separate Baker copy, varies from the tracing used as the copytext in this edition. See Letter 273, note 3. Wright's text is in one paragraph, not two, and he clearly standardised punctuation, orthography, and typography. In this case, the editor disagrees with Secord, who suggests that the Wright version may be more authoritative than the tracing. The MS for Letter 273 is a very rough draft which Wright's version supplements without much changing; hence in that case this edition adopts some readings from Wright. The tracing used here as the copytext for Letter 274, by contrast, is a substantial tracing of Defoe's autograph apparently in its final form, which contains more text than appears in Wright, as well as some significant variations:

> Difficulty] difficulties *Wright*
> you Now Drop] you drop *Wright*
> [any]] my *Wright*
> Raise a W[ork]] rouse a devil *Wright*
> can not help to finish; had you done it before yᵉ thing had been [   ].] cannot lay. *Wright*
> what after having] what, from having *Wright*
> you can desire] you desire *Wright*
> to do next] to do *Wright*
> Therefore must Desire] therefore desire *Wright*

275

To Henry Baker

[April 1729?]

HEADNOTE: Baker says in his autobiographical memorandum that 'after almost two years, Mʳ D consented to engage his House at Newington as a Security, and Articles being accordingly executed, the Marriage was celebrated April 30ᵗʰ 1729'.[1] Sophia's health had declined, to which Defoe alludes in the letter. This apparently persuaded Defoe to yield.[2] On 3 April 1729, Defoe had again purchased the basic lease of the Stoke Newington house and made the property security for the payment of Sophia's £500 dowry at his death, paying 5% per annum in the meantime. On 5 April, he gave Baker a bond confirming these details, along with a 34½-year mortgage on the house at a 'peppercorn rent'. In 1741, a decade after Defoe's death, Baker purchased the house from Sutton.[3]

Sʳ

I have Perused the writing and See nothing amiss in it, if you Think the Security against yᵉ Lost Writings is Sufficent: but I Thoᵗ

DEFOE TO HENRY BAKER, [APRIL 1729?]

m^r Curryer[4] in whose Posession they were left, and by whom they are lost (or by p[er]sons Entrusted by him) should have^a given Something under his^b hand, Obliging him to Deliver up the Old Deed and Assignm^t to be Cancelld, if it should Come to his hand; and should have Indemnifyed D F from all Claims or Pretensions wch might hereafter be made by any person on ye foot of those writings: nothing of which is Mencond in this Deed.[5]

There is a Small Objeccon wch Occurrs to me against a Clause in the Dra^t of ye Marriage Contract wch I perusd but Hastily and in Disorder that night on Acco^t of o^r family^c being So Disstemperd. I Suppose 'tis not too late.

The paym^t of the^d 200^£ is made to take place within a Month after my Decease wch is Sooner than it can be Supposed Excecutors can be in Readyness after such a Revolution in the family. Such things have usually Twelv months time allowed and as my Effects will lye much abroad I think it can not be Expected in less; this is a matter So Reasonble that I hope you can not Scruple the alteracon.

I am yor Friend & Servt
De Foe

Fryday night

Text: BL Add. MS. 88618A, fol. 4. *Address*: To | Mr Baker | Present

---

a have] *following word* 'been' *cancelled*
b his] *interlined above cancelled word* 'their'
c family] *following letters* 'Dis' *cancelled*
d the] *following letters probably* 'bon' *(for* 'bond') *cancelled*

---

1 Baker, fols. 14–15.
2 Wright, 370.
3 *The Gentleman's Magazine* 82 (1812), 529; Arthur Secord, 'Defoe in Stoke Newington', *PMLA* 66 (1951), 211–26 (at 216–17, 219–20).
4 *m^r Curryer*: Unidentified.
5 *Deed*: See headnote.

870

DEFOE TO SOPHIA BAKER, 9 JUNE [1729]

276

To Sophia Baker

9 June [1729]

HEADNOTE: Defoe's undated letter to his daughter is his only surviving letter to a woman, coming about six weeks after her marriage.

My Dearest Sophia

Allow me to begin wth a Little Phylosophy. Where Affecčons are strongest they are allways most Sencible of a shock, and Unkindnesses (Nay tho'but Seeming Such) make ye Deepest Impressions:[1] Henče Cæsar Tho' of a Spirit Invincible Gave up to Death, when he felt a stroke From his Adopted Brutus, and Said no More But (et tuo quoq mi fili! Tue Brute!)[2] What! and Thou too Brutus! my Son! Nay Henče ye wise man Says, a Brother Offended, is harder to be Won, than ye Barrs of a Castle:[3] Love is of So Niče a Nature, That like ye heart, it faints wth ye least Touch. Where it is not So, it must be because Such kno'not how to Love.

If I have been more Sencibly Grievd at what I tho^t Unkind in my Sophi (Say it was Onely that I tho^t So), if I Took Fire more Than another would have done, it was because I Lov'd you More Than Ever any lovd, or will or can love you^a (he that has you Excepted). Had Deb.[4] The Hasty, the Rash and So far Weak, Said Ten Times as much to me, it had Made no Impression atall: But From Sophi, Thee Sophi! whose Image Sits close to my affecčons, and who I Lov beyond the Power of Expressing: I acknowlege it Wounded my Very Soul; and my Weakness is So much ye more, as that Affecčon is strong; So that I can as ill Express The Satisfacčon I have from yor Letter,[5] as I could the grief of what I tho^t an Unkindness.

Perhaps I do not write like a Father. But p[er]haps I do too, if it be Considred That Love is the Same, let ye Relačon be what it will; besides as a father, I hope I may be allowd not to Love in a less Exalted^b Sublime Manner, but a greater; and From thenče I still Inferr, as my affecčon made my Grief the greater, So the Same

---

^a love you] *interlined*
^b Exalted] *following dash omitted in this edition*

871

DEFOE TO SOPHIA BAKER, 9 JUNE [1729]

Affecćon Doubles yᵉ Satisfaccon I have at my Dear Sophys Return: I Reciev yoʳ Letter my Dear, wᵗʰ a joy not to be Describ'd, but in yᵉ Deepest Silenće,ᵃ or Expressd but in Teares.

From Henće I Forbear to Enter upon the Subject of this Irrupcon, & shall Onely hint, That you mistake it; and be it That you mistake it, yet as on that mistake you Are So Generous as to make this Reparaćon, I will believ you would wᵗʰ yᵉ Same filial goodness have made The like <u>and</u> more, if ᵇ you had been Sencible in what Tender part you gave yᵉ Wound.

But you have heald it. One word can Wound where Love is Niće, and One Word can Heal where Sincerity Joyns the Affeccon: you have heald it at Once; and Since you do not yetᶜ See where yᵉ hurt was, I choose to leav it Conceald, because what Ever I had, I would have you feel no grief.

I would Say more, but hope I need not. Let this Tell you, I am Satisfyd, and Rejoyce That you Think yoʳ fathers Affeccon, worth preserving; I am perswaded I shall Never giv you Room to Lessen yoʳ Value for it, humane Frailty Excepted: I shall Conclude Onely with letting you See, with what a Sinćere heart, I was acting when this happened, and how little I thought of Dissobliging you, or mʳ Forster:⁶ and This I can not do better, than in Sending you the letter⁷ (Unopend) wᶜʰ I had written to mʳ Baker, and had in my hand to giv you.ᵈ Let this Speak for me, and believ it to be yᵉ Very Meaning and Intent of my heart, and I am Sure you will Continue your affeccon to yoʳ Father upon the Very Conviccon of it.

All the Pennance I shall Enjoyn you, on this whole affair, is that you Will give mʳ Baker yᵉ Letter, let him kno' when I wrote it, and Desire him to Lend me a kiss of Peaće to his Sophi, and I'll pay it him in Kind.

My Dearest Sophi I am and Ever Shall be
yoʳ Most Affecconate Father
DF
(But Very much Tormented With Pain Ever Sinće)

ᵃ Silenće] *following word* 'and' *cancelled*
ᵇ like <u>and</u> more, if] 'if' *cancelled following* 'like' *and interlined*
ᶜ yet] *interlined*
ᵈ you] *top edge of the MS apparently cut; a caret follows* 'you' *but anything interlined is lost*

DEFOE TO JOHN WATTS, 10 SEPTEMBER 1729

Newington Monday June. 9ᵗʰ

Thank mʳ Baker for his Enclosd paper about theᵃ Customs.[8]

Text: BL Add. MS. 88618A, fols. 5–6. *Address* (fol. 6ᵛ): To | My Daughter

---

ᵃ the] *just a dot in MS*

---

1 *Where Affecĉons ... Impressions*: See Defoe's similar discussion of a tender father's resentment of his daughter's defiance in the *Review* for 2 Oct. 1711: 'Proportion'd to the Greatness of his Affection, may be the Depth of his Resentment' (vIII, 378). See Letter 278, note 9.
2 *et tuo quoq mi fili! Tue Brute!*: Defoe uses or else adapts the Latin phrase in *The Vision* (1706), line 111, *PEW*, IV, 204; *Review*, IV, 801 (3 Feb. 1708); vIII, 539 (25 Dec. 1711); *Political History of the Devil* (1726), *SFS*, vI, 213; and Letter 278.
3 *wise man ... Castle*: Solomon in Prov. 18:19.
4 *Deb.*: Given that he is comparing Sophia's conduct to Deb's, this is probably a nickname for one of Defoe's other daughters, most obviously Henrietta or Hannah. Possibly it is a domestic servant of Defoe's. Otherwise, she is unidentified.
5 *Letter*. Untraced.
6 *mr Forster*. See Letter 269, note 3.
7 *letter*. Untraced.
8 *Enclosd paper about Customs*: Untraced, but perhaps confirmation that Sophia would not claim on Defoe's estate, as the customs of London entitled her to. See Letter 268, note 3.

277

To John Watts

10 September 1729

HEADNOTE: John Watts (d. 1763) was the proprietor of one of the most important printing houses in London. Like Samuel Keimer, he employed a young Benjamin Franklin, who left in his *Autobiography* 'a description of Watts's office that remains the most vivid surviving account of life as a printer in the eighteenth century'.[1] Watts was printing Defoe's *The Compleat English Gentleman*, but as far as we know only the first proof sheet was printed, the work was left in manuscript, and it went unpublished until 1890. Why the work did not progress is not known, but it could be because Defoe was being hounded by creditors. As far as we know, Watts printed no other Defoe title in the author's lifetime, but in 1735 he printed a 'second edition' of *The Secrets of the Invisible World Disclos'd*, the title assigned in early reprints to Defoe's *An Essay on the History and Reality of Apparitions* (1727).

873

DEFOE TO JOHN WATTS, 10 SEPTEMBER 1729

S^r

I am to ask yor Pardon for keeping the Enclosed[2] so long, Mr Baker having told me yor Resolution of taking it in hand and Working it off But I have been Exceeding ill.

I have Revisd it again and Contracted it Very Much and hope to bring it wthin the Bulk you Desire or as Near it as Possible.

But this and Some Needfull alterations will Oblige you to much Trouble in the first sheet, p[er]haps allmost as bad as Setting it over again wch Can not be avoided.

I will Endeavour to send the Rest of [the][a] Coppy So Well Corrected as to giv you Very little Trouble.

I here Return the first sheet and as much Coppy as will make near 3 sheets more; you shall have all [the][b] Remainder So as not to let you stand still atall.

> I am
> S^r
> yor Most Humble Servt
> DeFoe

Sept. 10. 1729.

Text: Bodl. MS. Montagu d. 17, fol. 76.[3] *Address*: To | Mr J Watts | in | Wild Court[4] | Present

^a [the]] *just a dot in MS*
^b [the]] *just a dot in MS*

---

1 Hazel Wilkinson, 'Benjamin Franklin's London Printing 1725–26', *PBSA* 110 (2016), 139–80 (at 140).

2 *Enclosed*: The first printed proof sheet, comprising sixteen pages, of Defoe's *The Compleat English Gentleman*. The proof sheet, with some corrections not in Defoe's hand, survives with Defoe's holograph MS (BL Add. MS. 32555). In 1830, it was in the possession of Rev. Henry De Foe Baker (Wilson, III, 599).

3 This letter was apparently the one that William Upcott (1779–1845) allowed Walter Wilson to use for his biography of Defoe in 1830 (Wilson, I, xx). On 19 June 1822, William Hone (1780–1842) wrote to Upcott asking him to look out for Defoe autograph letters and stated that Upcott possessed two Defoe letters. What the other one was is unknown (Yale Beinecke, Osborne MSS Files 7524). The letter passed into Wilson's possession, and it was purchased along with the traced copy of Letter 278 at the sale of Wilson's estate in 1847 by Captain Montagu Montagu (1787–1863). John Forster evidently saw it, stating that 'even in its signature the bold upright hand is broken down' (*Oliver Cromwell. Daniel De Foe. Sir Richard Steele. Charles Churchill. Samuel Foote. Biographical Essays*, 3rd ed. (1860), 154–5). Montagu left it to the Bodleian at his death. See Secord, 48; Shipley, 324 n. 3.

874

DEFOE TO HENRY BAKER, 12 AUGUST 1730

4 *Wild Court*. In Holborn; Watts moved to premises there in 1718 (Wilkinson, 'Benjamin Franklin's London Printing', 141).

278

To Henry Baker

12 August 1730

HEADNOTE: Defoe's final surviving letter was written while he was in hiding from a creditor. Mary Brooke first brought a bill of complaint against Defoe on 18 January 1728 and an amended version of that was lodged in April 1730. The alleged debt went back to Defoe's partnership with Samuel and James Stancliffe in the 1690s but was one he understood had been included in his composition with creditors when James Stancliffe acted as trustee for Defoe's 1706 bankruptcy. When Stancliffe died intestate in 1727, a weaver named Samuel Brooke took out administration to his estate. According to Defoe, Brooke concurred that Defoe's debts were settled, but then he died. His widow Mary, along with Elizabeth Stancliffe (Samuel's widow) and Aaron Lambe, claimed Defoe still owed £800. The creditors commenced several actions in King's Bench and Exchequer; Defoe had recourse to Chancery to attempt to stop those proceedings. He insisted that any bonds to the Stancliffes were in trust for other creditors, not private debts.[1] But he was unable to prevent the suit proceeding.[2] James Sutherland justifiably calls this 'a strangely distracted letter'.[3]

Defoe died in Rope Maker's Alley in London on 24 or 25 April 1731.[4]

Dear Mr Baker

I have yor Very kind and Affecċonate Letter[5] of ye 1st But not come to my hand till ye 10th; where it had been Delayd I kno' not.

As ye kind Manner and ye kinder Thought from wch it Flows (for I take all you Say to be as I allways believ'd you to be Sincere and Nathaniel like, without Guile[6]) was a Perticular Satisfaccon to me, So The stop of ye letter, however it happend, Depriv'd me of that Cordial too many Days, Considring how Much I stood in Need of it to Support a Mind Sinking under the Weight of an Afflicċon too heavy for my strength and looking on my Self as Abandon'd of Every Comfort, Every Friend and Every Relativ, Except Such only as are Able to give me no Assistanċe.

I was Sorry you Should Say at ye beginning of yor Letter you were Debarr'd Seeing me. Depend upon my Sincerity for this, I am far from Debarring you, On ye Contrary it would be a greater comfort to me than any I Now Enjoy, that I could have yor Agreeable Visits wth Safety and could See both you and my Dearest Sophia, could it be without giving her ye Grief of Seeing her Father in Tenebris[7] and Under ye Load of Insupportable Sorrows.

I am Sorry I must Open my Griefs So Far as to Tell her it is not ye Blow I Rec^d from a Wicked Perjur'd and Contemptible Enemy[8] That has Broken in upon my Spirit, wch as she well knows has Carryed me on thro' Greater Dissasters than these; But it has been ye Injustice, Unkindness and I must Say Inhuman Dealing of my Own Son[9] wch has both Ruind my family and in a Word has broken my heart, and as I am at this time Under a Weight of Very heavy Illness wch I think will be a Fever I take this Occasion to Vent my Grief in yor Breasts who I kno' will make a prudent use of it and Tell you That Nothing but this has Conquerd or could Conquer me.^a Et tu! Brute.[10] I Depended upon him, I Trusted him, I gave up my Two Dear unprovided Child^r unto his hands;[11] But he has no Compassion, and Suffres them and their poor Dying Mother[12] to Beg their Bread at his door, and to crave, as if it were an Alms, What he is bound under Hand and^b Seal Beside the most sacred promises to Supply them with, himself at ye Same time living in a Profusion of Plenty.[13]

It is too much for me. Excuse my Infirmity I can Say no More; my heart is too full. I Onely ask One thing of you as a Dying Request, Stand by them when I am Gone, and let them not be wrongd, while he is able to do them Right; Stand by them as a Bro: and if you have any thing within you Owing to my Memory who have bestowd On you the Best Gift I had to give[14] Let y^m not be Injurd, and Trampled on^c by False pretences, and Unnaturall Reflections: I hope they will want no help but that of Comfort and Council, But that they will indeed want, being too Easie to be Mannagd by Words and promises.

---

  ^a me] *interlined*
  ^b and] *interlined*
  ^c on] *interlined*

DEFOE TO HENRY BAKER, 12 AUGUST 1730

It adds to my Grief that It is So Difficult to me to See you. I am at a Distance from Lond^n in Kent, Nor have I^a a Lodging in London, nor have been at that place in ye Old Baily, Since I wrote you I was Remov'd from it; at p[re]sent I am Weak, having had Some fitts of a Fever that have left me Low, But these things much more.

I have not Seen Son or Daughter, Wife or Child, Many Weeks and kno' not which Way to See them. They Dare not Come by Water and by Land here is no Coach and I kno' not what to do.

It is not possible for me to Come to Enfield, Unless you could find a Retir'd Lodging for me, where I might not be known, and might have ye Comfort of Seeing you both Now and Then; upon Such a Circumstance I could gladly giv the Days to Solitude to have ye Comfort of half an hour now and then wth you Both; for Two or three Weeks But just to come and look at you, and Retire Imediately, tis a Burthen too Heavy, The Parting Will be a price beyond the Enjoym^t.

I Would Say (I hope) wth Comfort That tis yet well I am So Near my Journeys End, and am Hastening to ye place where ye Weary are at Rest, and where the Wicked Cease to Trouble; be it that ye Passage is Rough, and the Day Stormy, by what way So ever he please to Bring me to the End of^b it, I desire to Finish life with this Temper of Soul in all Cases. Te Deum laudamus[15] —

I Congratulate you on ye Occasion of yor happy advance in yor Employm^ts.[16] May all you do be prosperous and all you Meet with Pleasant, and May you both Escape the Tortures and Troubles of Uneasie life.

May you Sail ye Dang'rous^c Voiage of Life <u>a' fore ye Wind</u>, and Make the Port of Heaven <u>Without a storm</u>.

It adds to my Grief that I must Never See The pledge of yor Mutual love my Little Grandson.[17] Give him my Blessing, and May he Be to you both, yor Joy in youth, and yor Comfort in age, and never add a Sigh to yor Sorrows, But alas! that is not to be Expected:^d kiss my Dear Sophy Once more for me, and if I must

---

^a I] *interlined*
^b of] *following illegible word cancelled*
^c Dang'rous] *interlined*
^d Expected] *following superfluous comma omitted in this edition*

DEFOE TO HENRY BAKER, 12 AUGUST 1730

See her no more Tell her, This is from a Father That lovd her above
all his Comforts, to his last Breath.

yor Unhappy
DF

about Two mile from Greenw^{ch} in Kent
Tuesday Augt 12. 1730

P.S.

I wrote you a Letter Some Months ago in Answer to one From
you[18] About Selling ye house[19] But you Never Signifyd to me
whether you Rec^d it.

I have not ye Policy of Assurance.[20] I Suppose my Wife or
Hannah may hav it.

Idem
DF

Text: Bodl. MS. Montagu d. 12, fols. 203v–204r (Figure 11). [A traced copy in
Defoe's hand.][21] *Address*: none present.

1 TNA C 11/679/2; TNA C 11/1473/18. See James R. Sutherland, 'A Note on the Last Years of
Defoe', *MLR* 29 (1934), 137–41; Backscheider, *Life*, 503.
2 The Chancery cases concerning Brooke and Defoe beginning in 1727, but extending to 1733,
after Defoe's death, are TNA C 11/2601/26; TNA C 11/1473/18; TNA C 11/366/72; TNA C
11/1502/5; TNA C 11/1700/24; TNA C 11/679/2.
3 Sutherland, 269.
4 For early obituaries, see Peterson, *Reference Guide*, 1–2.
5 *Letter*: Untraced.
6 *Nathaniel like, without Guile*: John 1:47.
7 *in Tenebris*: 'in darkness' (Latin).
8 *Enemy*: Almost certainly Defoe's creditor Mary Brooke. See headnote.
9 *Injustice ... Son*: Daniel Defoe Jr. By now, he was a 'fairly well-to-do' merchant in Cornhill;
Defoe had assigned the Essex property to him as a precaution against its being involved in
prosecutions for debts (Moore, 334–5; Backscheider, *Life*, 503–4, 611 n. 30).
  In a discussion of the Christian duty of forgiveness in the *Review* for 2 Oct. 1711, Defoe
makes an exception for filial rebellion: 'The Disobedience of Children to Parents, like
that of Subjects to a Prince, remain to be judicially Resented; neither does the Command
of Forgiveness take Place here, at least the Obligation to it cannot be the same' (*Review*,
VIII, 378).
10 *Et tu! Brute*: See Letter 276, note 2.
11 *Two Dear unprovided Childr unto his hands*: See Matt. 19:13–14. Defoe refers to his unmarried
daughters Henrietta and Hannah. Moore's suggestion that Sophia and Henrietta are intended is unwarranted, an attempt to exonerate Defoe from what seems to be an exaggeration
about Hannah's financial dependence (329).

878

DEFOE TO HENRY BAKER, 12 AUGUST 1730

12 *poor Dying Mother*: In fact, Mary had been left 'financially independent' by an inheritance from her brother, Samuel Tuffley, who died in 1725. Tuffley's estate was valued at £5,000 to £6,000 (TNA PROB 11/604/383; Backscheider, *Life*, 497–8). Mary died in 1732 (TNA PROB 11/655/282).

13 *living in a Profusion of Plenty*: Daniel Defoe Jr's financial circumstances may cautiously be inferred from his dealings with Freame and Gould, the goldsmith bank that later became Barclays. A surviving ledger from this period shows his borrowing against bills of exchange received from a number of individuals, mostly merchants (Barclays Group Archives, Freame and Gould Loan and Discount Ledger, 1729–31). In this month, Aug. 1730, just over £500 passed through his hands, though turnover is of course different from income. The Daniel Defoe importing anchovies in 1730 could be Daniel Jr. See G. A. Starr, '"Sauces to whet our gorg'd Appetites": Defoe at Seventy in the Anchovy Trade', *PQ* 54 (1975), 531–3.

14 *Best Gift I had to give*: Baker wrote that when he requested permission to propose, Defoe called Sophia 'the dearest Jewel I possess; Sophy is my best beloved Child' (Baker, fol. 8).

15 *Te Deum laudamus*: 'Thee, O God, we praise' (Latin).

16 *advance in yor Employmts*: The details of Baker's professional success are unidentified.

17 *Grandson*: David Lionel Erskine Baker, born 30 Jan. 1730. He became a dramatist and theatre historian. Defoe's other son, Benjamin, eking out an impecunious living as a pamphleteer for Walpole's government, had at least three children at this point.

18 *Letter ... one From you*: Both untraced.

19 *house*: Defoe's Stoke Newington house.

20 *Policy of Assurance*: On 2 Aug. 1721, Daniel Defoe Jr took out a fire insurance policy, paying £1. 10s., but he seems not to have subsequently renewed (LMA CLC/B/192/MS08740A, fol. 4; Bernard Drew, *The London Assurance: A Second Chronicle* (1949), 136).

21 On the tracing's provenance and publication history, see Shipley. Montagu purchased the tracing from the sale of Walter Wilson's estate in 1847, as well as the holograph of Letter 277. Wilson had obtained it from Baker's descendants and published it in 1830 (Wilson, III, 605–8). For the Montagu bequest to the Bodleian, see Letter 277, note 3. A copy of the letter, again made by Harriet De Foe Baker, is now in John Rylands Library, University of Manchester, Eng MS 19, vol. 1, fol. 93 (see Letter 268, note 4).

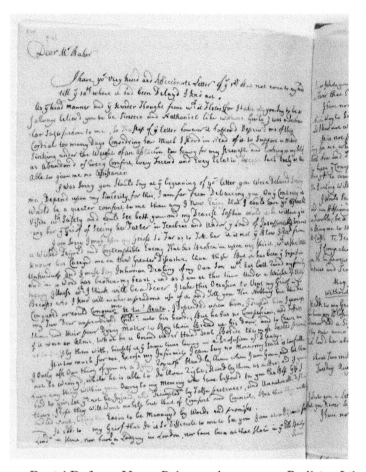

Figure 11 Daniel Defoe to Henry Baker, 12 August 1730, Bodleian Library, University of Oxford, MS. Montagu d. 12, fols. 203ᵛ–204ʳ

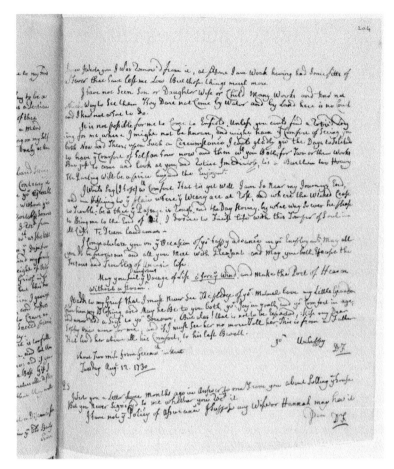

Figure 11 (continued)

SELECT BIBLIOGRAPHY

Primary Sources

Defoe's Writings

Individual titles in collections of Defoe's works (*Novels, PEW, RDW, SFS, TDH*) are not listed.

The Advantages of Peace and Commerce, London, 1729
Advice to the People of Great Britain, London, 1714
An Answer to the L—d H—sham's Speech. By Daniel D'Foe, 1706
An Appeal to Honour and Justice, London, 1715
An Argument Proving that the Design of Employing and Enobling Foreigners, is a Treasonable Conspiracy against the Constitution, London, 1717
Atalantis Major, [Edinburgh?], 1711
A Brief Deduction of the Original, Progress, and Immense Greatness of the British Woollen Manufacture, London, 1727
A Brief Survey of the Legal Liberties of the Dissenters, London, 1714
The British Visions: or, Isaac Bickerstaff, Sen. Being Twelve Prophesies for the Year 1711, [London?], 1711
The Case of the Poor Skippers and Keel-Men of Newcastle, [London, 1712]
A Challenge of Peace, Address'd to the Whole Nation, London, 1703
The Character of the Late Dr. Samuel Annesley, London, 1697
Christianity Not as Old as the Creation, ed. G. A. Starr, London, 2012
The Clause Proposed in the English Parliament to Prevent the French Goods being Imported thro' Scotland; with a Short Remark on the Same, Edinburgh, 1707
The Compleat English Gentleman, ed. Karl D. Bülbring, London, 1890
Considerations upon the Eighth and Ninth Articles of the Treaty of Commerce and Navigation, London, 1713
Counter Queries, [London, 1710]
The Danger of Court Differences, London, 1717
De Foe's Answer, To Dyer's Scandalous News Letter, [Edinburgh, 1707]
The Dissenters in England Vindicated from Some Reflections in a Late Pamphlet, Entituled, Lawful Prejudices, &c. [Edinburgh, 1707]
The Dissenters Vindicated; or, a Short View of the Present State of the Protestant Religion in Britain, London, 1707
Dyers News Examined as to His Sweddish Memorial against the Review, [Edinburgh, 1707]
An Enquiry into the Disposal of the Equivalent, [Edinburgh, 1706?]

882

SELECT BIBLIOGRAPHY

An Essay upon Buying and Selling of Speeches, London, 1716
An Essay on the History of Parties and Persecution in Britain, London, 1711
An Essay upon the Trade to Africa, London, 1711
An Essay on the Treaty of Commerce with France, London, 1713
The Evident Approach of a War, London, 1727
The Experiment: or, The Shortest Way with the Dissenters Exemplified. Being the Case of Mr. Abraham Gill, a Dissenting Minister in the Isle of Ely, London, 1705
A Farther Case Relating to the Poor Keel-Men of Newcastle, [London, 1712]
A Friendly Epistle by Way of Reproof ... to Thomas Bradbury, London, 1715
A Further Search into the Conduct of the Allies, and the Late Ministry, as to Peace and War, London, 1712
A General History of Trade ... for the Month of July, London, 1713
A General History of Trade ... for the Month of August, London, 1713
A General History of Trade ... for the Month of September, London, 1713
Greenshields Out of Prison and Toleration Settled in Scotland, London, 1710
An Humble Proposal to the People of England, for the Encrease of their Trade, and Encouragement of their Manufactures, London, 1729
The Justice and Necessity of a War with Holland, London, 1712
The Lay-Man's Sermon upon the Late Storm, London, 1704
The Layman's Vindication of the Church of England, London, 1716
Legion's Humble Address to the Lords, London, 1704
A Letter from Captain Tom to the Mobb, Now Rais'd for Dr. Sacheverel, London, 1710
A Letter to Mr. Bisset ... In Answer to his Remarks on Dr. Sacheverell's Sermon, London, 1709
A Letter to Mr. How, London, 1701
A Letter to the Whigs, Expostulating with them upon their Present Conduct, London, 1714
A Letter to the Whigs, being an Enquiry into the Particular Resentments of the Times, at the Assassination of Mr. Harley by the Marquis de Guiscard, [London], 1711
The Letters of Daniel Defoe, ed. G. H. Healey, Oxford, 1955
Lex Talionis, London, 1698
The Manufacturer (1719–21), intro. Robert N. Gosselink, Delmar, N.Y., 1978
The Master Mercury, intro. Frank H. Ellis and Henry L. Snyder, Augustan Reprint Society no. 184, Los Angeles, Cal., 1977
Memoirs of the Conduct of Her Late Majesty and Her Last Ministry, London, 1715
A Memorial to the Nobility of Scotland, Edinburgh, 1708
Mercator: or, Commerce Retriev'd, London, 1713–14
Mercurius Politicus: Being Monthly Observations on the Affairs of Great Britain, London, 1716–20
The Monitor, London, 1714
More Short-Ways with the Dissenters, London, 1704
A New Test of the Sence of the Nation, London, 1710
The Novels of Daniel Defoe, 10 vols., ed. P. N. Furbank and W. R. Owens, London, 2007–8
Observations on the Fifth Article of the Treaty of Union, Humbly Offered to the Consideration of the Parliament, Relating to Foreign Ships, London, 1706

883

SELECT BIBLIOGRAPHY

The Paralel: or, Persecution of Protestants the Shortest Way to Prevent the Growth of Popery in Ireland, Dublin, 1705

Passion and Prejudice, The Support of one Another, and Both Destructive to the Happiness of this Nation, in Church and State; Being A Reply to the Vindicator of Mr. W----r's Lawful Prejudices, Edinburgh, 1707

Peace without Union, London, 1703

Political and Economic Writings of Daniel Defoe, 8 vols., ed. P. N. Furbank and W. R. Owens, London, 2000

The Present State of the Parties in Great Britain, London, 1712

Queries upon the Bill against Occasional Conformity, London, 1704

Queries to the New Hereditary Right-Men, London, 1710

The Question Fairly Stated, London, 1717

Reasons against Fighting, London, 1712

Reasons for Im— the L—d H— T—r, and Some Others of the P— M—, London, 1714

Religious and Didactic Writings by Daniel Defoe, 10 vols., ed. P. N. Furbank and W. R. Owens, London, 2005–6

Remarks on the Bill to Prevent Frauds Committed by Bankrupts, London, 1706

Remarks on the Letter to the Author of the State-Memorial, London, 1706

A Reply to a Pamphlet entituled, The L[or]d H[aversham]'s Vindication of his Speech, London, 1706

The Representation Examined, London, 1711

Review, 9 vols., ed. John McVeagh, London, 2004–11

Royal Religion, London, 1704

Satire, Fantasy and Writings on the Supernatural by Daniel Defoe, 8 vols., ed. P. N. Furbank and W. R. Owens, London, 2003–4

Scotland in Danger, Edinburgh, 1708

The Scot's Narrative Examin'd; or, the Case of the Episcopal Ministers in Scotland Stated, London, 1709

The Scots Nation and Union Vindicated, London, 1714

A Seasonable Caution to the General Assembly, London, 1711

A Seasonable Expostulation with, and Friendly Reproof unto James Butler, ... Duke of O——d, London, 1715

A Seasonable Warning and Caution against the Insinuations of Papists and Jacobites in Favour of the Pretender, London, 1712

A Second Volume of the Writings of the Author of The True-Born Englishman, London, 1705

The Secret History of the October-Club ... Part II, London, 1711

A Secret History of One Year, London, 1714

The Secret History of the White-Staff, Part II, London, 1714

The Secret History of the White-Staff, Part III, London, 1715

A Serious Inquiry into this Grand Question; whether a Law to Prevent the Occasional Conformity of Dissenters, would not be Inconsistent with the Act of Toleration, London, 1704

A Sharp Rebuke from One of the People Call'd Quakers to Henry Sacheverell, London, 1715

A Short Letter to the Glasgow-Men, [Edinburgh, 1706]

SELECT BIBLIOGRAPHY

A Short View of the Present State of the Protestant Religion in Britain, Edinburgh, 1707
The Sincerity of the Dissenters Vindicated, from the Scandal of Occasional Conformity,
  London, 1703
*Some Considerations on the Reasonableness and Necessity of Encreasing and Encouraging the
  Seamen*, London, 1728
Some Thoughts of an Honest Tory in the Country, London, 1716
Some Thoughts upon the Subject of Commerce with France. By the Author of the Review,
  London, 1713
A Spectators Address to the Whigs, [London], 1711
The Storm, ed. Richard Hamblyn, London, 2005
The Succession to the Crown of England, Consider'd, London, 1701
*The Trade of Britain Stated; Being the Substance of Two Papers Published in London on
  Occasion of the Importation of Wine and Brandy from North-Britain*, [Edinburgh,
  1707]
A True Collection of the Writings of the Author of The True Born English-man, London, 1703
The True State of the Case between the Government and the Creditors of the Navy, London,
  1711
A Trumpet Blown in the North, and Sounded in the Ears of John Eriskine, … Duke of Mar,
  London, 1715
Union and No Union, London, 1713
*A Voice from the South: or, An Address from some Protestant Dissenters in England to the Kirk
  of Scotland*, Edinburgh, 1707
A Word Against a New Election, [London], 1710
Writings on Travel, Discovery and History, 8 vols., ed. P. N. Furbank and W. R. Owens,
  London, 2001–2

Other Primary Sources

The Acts of the Parliaments of Scotland, 1124–1707, 11 vols., ed. Thomas Thomson, Edinburgh,
  1814–24
Addison, Joseph, *The Letters of Joseph Addison*, ed. Walter Graham, Oxford, 1941
Addresses against Incorporating Union, 1706–1707, ed. Karin Bowie, Aberdeen, 2018
*Analecta Scotica: Collections Illustrative of the Civil, Ecclesiastical, and Literary History of
  Scotland*, 2 vols., ed. James Maidment, Edinburgh, 1834–7
Anne, Queen, *The Letters and Diplomatic Instructions of Queen Anne*, ed. Beatrice Curtis
  Brown, London, 1935
Atterbury, Francis, *Considerations upon The Secret History of the White Staff, Humbly
  Addressed to the E— of O—*, London, 1714
Baillie of Jerviswood, George, *Correspondence of George Baillie of Jerviswood, 1702–1708*, ed.
  G. E. M. Kynynmond, Earl of Minto, Edinburgh, 1842
Black, William, *A Reply to the Authors of the Advantages of Scotland by an Incorporate Union;
  and of The Fifth Essay, at Removing National Prejudices*, Edinburgh, 1706
Bolingbroke, Henry St John, Viscount, *Letters and Correspondence, Public and Private*, ed.
  Gilbert Parke, 4 vols., London, 1798

SELECT BIBLIOGRAPHY

Boyer, Abel, *The History of the Life and Reign of Queen Anne*, London, 1722

Browne, Joseph, *A Dialogue between Church and No-Church: Or, A Rehearsal of the Review*, London, 1706

Burnet, Gilbert, *Bishop Burnet's History of his Own Time*, 6 vols., Oxford, 1823

Burnett, Thomas, *The Letters of Thomas Burnet to George Duckett*, ed. David Nichol Smith, Oxford, 1914

Calamy, Edmund, *An Historical Account of My Own Life*, 2 vols., London, 1830

Churchill, Sarah, Duchess of Marlborough, *Private Correspondence of Sarah, Duchess of Marlborough*, 2 vols., London, 1838

Clerk of Penicuik, Sir John, *History of the Union of Scotland and England*, abr., trans., and ed. Douglas Duncan, Edinburgh, 1993

Memoirs of the Life of Sir John Clerk of Penicuik, Edinburgh, 1892

Cocks, Sir Richard, *The Parliamentary Diary of Sir Richard Cocks, 1698–1702*, ed. D. W. Hayton, Oxford, 1996

Cowper, William, *The Private Diary of William, First Earl Cowper, Lord Chancellor of England*, Eton, 1833

[Drake, James], *The Memorial of the Church of England*, London, 1705

Dunton, John, *Dunton's Whipping-Post: or, A Satyr upon Every Body*, London, 1706

The Life and Errors of John Dunton, 2 vols., London, 1818

The Fox with his Fire-brand Unkennell'd and Insnar'd: Or, A Short Answer to Mr Daniel Foe's Shortest Way with the Dissenters, London, 1703

The Gates of Hell Opend, in a Dialogue between the Observator and the Review, London, 1711

Gildon, Charles, *The Life and Strange Surprizing Adventures of D--- de F--*, London, 1719

Goodman, Thomas, *The Experienc'd Secretary: or, Citizen and Countryman's Companion*, London, 1699

Hamilton, Sir David, *The Diary of Sir David Hamilton*, ed. Philip Roberts, Oxford, 1975

Have a Care What You Say, [London, 1707]

Hearne, Thomas, *Remarks and Collections of Thomas Hearne*, 11 vols., ed. Charles Doble *et al.*, Oxford, 1885–1921

Heinsius, Anthonie, *De Briefwisseling van Anthonie Heinsius*, 19 vols., ed. A. J. Veernendaal, The Hague, 1976–94

Hill, John, *The Young Secretary's Guide, Or Speedy Help to Learning*, London, 1691

Hooke, Nathaniel, *Correspondence of Colonel N. Hooke, Agent from the Court of France to the Scottish Jacobites, in the Years 1703 to 1707*, 2 vols., ed. William Dunn Macray, London, 1870–1

A Hue and Cry after Daniel Foe and His Coventry Beast, London, 1711

Intimate Society Letters of the Eighteenth Century, ed. Duke of Argyll, 2 vols., Edinburgh, 1910

Judas Discuver'd, and Catch'd at Last: Or, Daniel de Foe in Lob's Pound, London, 1713

Keimer, Samuel, *A Brand Pluck'd from the Burning: Exemplify'd in the Unparallel'd Case of Samuel Keimer*, London, 1718

Ker, John, *The Memoirs of John Ker of Kersland*, 3 vols., London, 1726–7

Letters relating to Scotland in the Reign of Queen Anne by James Ogilvy, First Earl of Seafield and Others, ed. P. Hume Brown, Edinburgh, 1915

SELECT BIBLIOGRAPHY

Liddell, Henry, *The Letters of Henry Liddell to William Cotesworth*, ed. J. M. Ellis, Durham, 1987

Locke, John, *Some Thoughts concerning Education* (1693), ed. John W. and Jean S. Yolton, Oxford, 1989

Lockhart of Carnwath, George, *Letters of George Lockhart of Carnwath, 1698–1732*, ed. Daniel Szechi, Edinburgh, 1989

    Lockhart Papers: Containing Memoirs and Commentaries upon the Affairs of Scotland from 1702 to 1715, by George Lockhart, Esq. of Carnwath, 2 vols., London, 1817

    'Scotland's Ruine': Lockhart of Carnwath's Memoirs of the Union, ed. Daniel Szechi, Aberdeen, 1989

Lowther, Sir John, *The Correspondence of Sir John Lowther of Whitehaven, 1693–1698: A Provincial Community in Wartime*, ed. D. R. Hainsworth, London, 1983

Luttrell, Narcissus, *A Brief Historical Relation of State Affairs from September 1678 to April 1714*, 6 vols., Oxford, 1857

Macky, John, *Memoirs of the Secret Services of John Macky*, London, 1733

The Marlborough–Godolphin Correspondence, 3 vols., ed. Henry L. Snyder, Oxford, 1975

Melmoth, William, Jr, *Memoirs of a Late Eminent Advocate, and Member of the Honourable Society of Lincoln's Inn*, London, 1796

New Letters to the Tatler and Spectator, ed. Richmond P. Bond, Austin, Tex., 1959

Nichols, John, *Literary Anecdotes of the Eighteenth Century*, 9 vols., London, 1812

Nicolson, William, *The London Diaries of William Nicolson Bishop of Carlisle, 1702–1718*, ed. Clyve Jones and Geoffrey Holmes, Oxford, 1985

Oldmixon, John, *A Detection of the Sophistry and Falsities of the Pamphlet entitul'd the Secret History of the White-Staff*, London, 1714

    The False Steps of the Ministry after the Revolution, London, 1714

    The History of England from the Earliest Accounts of Time, to the Death of the Late Queen Anne, London, 1735

    The Life and Posthumous Works of Arthur Maynwaring, London, 1715

    Remarks on the Letter to the Dissenters, London, 1714

    The Secret History of the White-Staff … With a Detection of the Sophistry and Falsities of the said Pamphlet, London, 1714

Owen, James, *Moderation a Virtue*, London, 1703

A Paper concerning Daniel DeFoe, London, 1708

Pittis, William, *The History of the Mitre and Purse*, London, 1714

    The History of the Mitre and Purse Continued, Wherein the Villainies of the Staff are Further Detected, London, 1714

    Queen Anne Vindicated, London, 1715

    The True-Born-Hugonot: or, Daniel de Foe, London, 1703

Poems on Affairs of State: Augustan Satirical Verse, 1660–1714, 7 vols., ed. George deForest Lord *et al.*, New Haven, Conn., 1963–75

The Proceedings at the Tryal Examination, and Condemnation Of a Certain Scribling, Rhyming, Versifying, Poeteering Hosier, and True-born Englishman, London, 1705

SELECT BIBLIOGRAPHY

Queries A-propos, About the Review's Question, No. 92. Who shall the Monarchy of Spain be given to?, London, 1711

The Reformer Reform'd: or, The Shortest Way with Daniel D' Fooe, London, 1703

Remarks on the Review, Numb. 74. Concerning the New Chappel in Russel-Court, Covent-Garden, London, 1706

The Republican Bullies, London, 1705

The Review and Observator Reviewed, London, 1706

The Review Review'd. In a Letter to the Prophet Daniel in Scotland, London, 1707

A Second Defence of the Scotish Vision, [Edinburgh, 1706]

A Selection from the Papers of the Earls of Marchmont, 3 vols., ed. Sir George Henry Rose, London, 1831

The Shortest Way with the Dissenters … With its Author's Brief Explication Consider'd, his Name Expos'd, his Practices Detected, and his Hellish Designs set in a True Light, London, 1703

Steele, Sir Richard, *The Correspondence of Richard Steele*, ed. Rae Blanchard, Oxford, 1941

 The Englishman, ed. Rae Blanchard, Oxford, 1955

 Mr. Steele's Apology for Himself and His Writings; Occasioned by His Expulsion from the House of Commons, London, 1714

 Periodical Journalism, 1714–1716, ed. Rae Blanchard, Oxford, 1959

[Stephens, William?], *A Letter to the Author of the Memorial of the State of England*, London, 1705

Swift, Jonathan, *The Correspondence of Jonathan Swift, D. D.*, 5 vols., ed. David Woolley, Frankfurt am Main, 1999–2014

 English Political Writings, 1711–1714, ed. Bertrand A. Goldgar and Ian Gadd, Cambridge, 2008

 Journal to Stella: Letters to Esther Johnson and Rebecca Dingley, 1710–1713, ed. Abigail Williams, Cambridge, 2013

 The Prose Writings of Jonathan Swift, ed. Herbert Davis *et al.*, 16 vols., Oxford, 1939–74

Symson, Joseph, *An Exact and Industrious Tradesman: The Letter Book of Joseph Symson of Kendal, 1711–1720*, ed. S. D. Smith, London, 2002

A True State of the Case of the Election at Coventry, shewing the Misrepresentations of a Scandalous Paper, calld, The Review of the Affairs of France, London, 1705

A True State of the Difference between Sir George Rook, Knt and William Colepeper, Esq, London, 1704

Vernon, James, *Letters Illustrative of the Reign of William III. From 1696 to 1708. Addressed to the Duke of Shrewsbury, by James Vernon, Esq., Secretary of State*, 3 vols., London, 1841

Ward, Ned, *In Imitation of Hudibras. The Dissenting Hypocrite*, London, 1703

Watson, James, *Watson's Preface to the 'History of Printing', 1713*, ed. W. J. Couper, Edinburgh, 1913

Webster, James, *The Author of the Lawful Prejudices against an Incorporating Union with England, Defended*, Edinburgh, 1707

 Lawful Prejudices against an Incorporating Union with England, Edinburgh, 1707

The Welsh-Monster: or, The Rise and Downfal of That Late Upstart, the R—t H—ble Innuendo Scribble, London, [1708?]

SELECT BIBLIOGRAPHY

Wentworth, Thomas, *The Wentworth Papers 1705–1739: Selected from the Private and Family Correspondence of Thomas Wentworth, Lord Raby*, ed. J. J. Cartwright, London, 1883

Wodrow, Robert, *Analecta: Or, Materials for a History of Remarkable Providences; Mostly Relating to Scotch Ministers and Christians*, 2 vols., Edinburgh, 1842

The Correspondence of the Rev. Robert Wodrow, ed. Rev. Thomas M'Crie, 3 vols., Edinburgh, 1842

Secondary Sources

Aitken, G. A., 'Defoe and Mist's "Weekly Journal"', *The Athenæum*, 26 Aug. 1893, 287–8

'Defoe in Trouble: 1703', *The Athenæum*, 22 Dec. 1894, 862

'Defoe's Brick-Kilns', *The Athenæum*, 13 Apr. 1889, 472–3

Alsop, J. D., 'Defoe, Toland, and *The Shortest Way with the Dissenters*', *RES* 43 (1992), 245–7

'Defoe and his Whig Paymasters', *N&Q* 28 (1981), 225–6

'New Light on Nathaniel Mist and Daniel Defoe', *PBSA* 75 (1981), 57–60

Backscheider, Paula R., 'Accounts of an Eyewitness: Defoe's Dispatches from the Vale of Trade and the Edinburgh Parliament House', in *Sent as a Gift: Eight Correspondences from the Eighteenth Century*, ed. Alan T. McKenzie, Athens, Ga., 1993, 21–47

Daniel Defoe: His Life, Baltimore, Md., 1989

'Daniel Defoe and Early Modern Intelligence', *Intelligence and National Security* 11 (1996), 1–21

'Daniel Defoe's Russia', *Literaturnoe nasledstvo*, Leningrad, 1998, 1–16

'Defoe: The Man in the Works', in *The Cambridge Companion to Daniel Defoe*, ed. John Richetti, Cambridge, 2009, 5–24

'Defoe and the Clerks of Penicuik', *MP* 84 (1987), 372–81

'John Russell to Daniel Defoe: Fifteen Unpublished Letters from Scotland', *PQ* 61 (1982), 161–77

'Personality and Biblical Allusion in Defoe's Letters', *South Atlantic Review* 47 (1982), 1–20

'Robert Harley to Daniel Defoe: A New Letter', *MLR* 83 (1988), 817–19

Baine, Rodney M., 'Chalmers' First Bibliography of Daniel Defoe', *Texas Studies in Language and Literature* 10 (1969), 547–68

Baines, Paul, and Pat Rogers, *Edmund Curll, Bookseller*, Oxford, 2007

Bastian, Frank, *Defoe's Early Life*, London, 1981

'James Foe, Merchant, Father of Daniel Defoe', *N&Q* 11 (1964), 82–6

Bateson, Thomas, 'The Relations of Defoe and Harley', *EHR* 15 (1900), 238–50

Bennett, G. V., 'Robert Harley, the Godolphin Ministry, and the Bishoprics Crisis of 1707', *EHR* 82 (1967), 726–46

The Tory Crisis in Church and State: The Career of Francis Atterbury, Bishop of Rochester, Oxford, 1975

Berman, Ric, *Espionage, Diplomacy and the Lodge: Charles Delafaye and the Secret Department of the Post Office*, Goring Heath, 2017

Bialuschewski, Arne, '*A True Account of the Design, and Advantages of the South-Sea Trade*: Profits, Propaganda, and the Peace Preliminaries of 1711', *HLQ* 73 (2010), 273–85

SELECT BIBLIOGRAPHY

Biddle, Sheila, *Bolingbroke and Harley*, New York, 1974

Bowie, Karin, *Scottish Public Opinion and the Anglo-Scottish Union, 1699–1707*, Woodbridge, 2007

Burch, Charles Eaton, 'Benjamin Defoe at Edinburgh University, 1710–11', *PQ* 19 (1940), 343–8

    'Defoe and the Edinburgh Society for the Reformation of Manners', *RES* 15 (1940), 306–12

    'Defoe and his Northern Printers', *PMLA* 60 (1945), 121–8

    'Defoe's Connections with the *Edinburgh Courant*', *RES* 5 (1929), 437–40

Chadwick, William, *The Life and Times of Daniel De Foe*, London, 1859

Chalmers, George, *The Life of Daniel De Foe*, London, 1790

Cockburn, James D., 'Daniel Defoe in Scotland', *Scottish Review* 36 (1900), 250–69

Coleman, D. C., 'Politics and Economics in the Age of Anne: The Case of the Anglo-French Trade Treaty of 1713', in *Trade, Government, and Economy in Pre-Industrial England*, ed. D. C. Coleman and A. H. John, London, 1976, 187–211

Coombs, Douglas, *The Conduct of the Dutch: British Opinion and the Dutch Alliance during the War of the Spanish Succession*, The Hague, 1958

    'William Stephens and the *Letter to the Author of the Memorial of the State of England* (1705)', *BIHR* 32 (1959), 24–37

Cowan, Brian, ed., *The State Trial of Doctor Henry Sacheverell*, Oxford, 2012

Coxe, William, *The Memoirs of John, Duke of Marlborough*, 3 vols., London, 1818–19

Cruickshanks, Eveline, '*Ashby v. White*: The Case of the Men of Aylesbury', in *Party and Management in Parliament, 1660–1784*, ed. Clyve Jones, Leicester, 1984, 87–106

Cruickshanks, Eveline, Stuart Handley, and D. W. Hayton, ed., *The History of Parliament: The House of Commons, 1690–1715*, 5 vols., Cambridge, 2002

Curtis, Laura A., 'A Rhetorical Approach to the Prose of Daniel Defoe', *Rhetorica* 11 (1993), 293–319

Dalton, Charles, ed., *English Army Lists and Commission Registers, 1661–1714*, 6 vols., London, 1892–1904

Davis, Leith, *Acts of Union: Scotland and the Literary Negotiation of the British Nation, 1707–1830*, Stanford, Cal., 1998

De Krey, Gary Stuart, *A Fractured Society: The Politics of London in the First Age of Party, 1688–1715*, Oxford, 1985

Deringer, William, *Calculated Values: Finance, Politics, and the Quantitative Age*, Cambridge, Mass., 2018

Dickinson, H. T., 'The Attempt to Assassinate Harley, 1711', *History Today* 15 (1965), 788–95

    Bolingbroke, London, 1970

Dickson, P. G. M., *The Financial Revolution in England: A Study in the Development of Public Credit 1688–1756*, London, 1967

    'War Finance, 1689–1714', in *The New Cambridge Modern History, Volume VI: The Rise of Great Britain and Russia, 1688–1715/25*, ed. J. S. Bromley, Cambridge, 1971, 284–315

Dobrée, Bonamy, 'Some Aspects of Defoe's Prose', in *Pope and His Contemporaries: Essays Presented to George Sherburn*, ed. James L. Clifford and Louis A. Landa, Oxford, 1949, 171–84

890

SELECT BIBLIOGRAPHY

Downie, J. A., 'Daniel Defoe: King William's Pamphleteer?', *ECL* 12 (1988), 105–17

'Daniel Defoe and the General Election of 1708 in Scotland', *ECS* 8 (1975), 315–28

'Defoe in the Fleet Prison', *N&Q* 22 (1975), 343–5

'Defoe the Spy', *British Society for Eighteenth-Century Studies Newsletter* 9 (1976), 17–18

'Defoe's *Review*, the Theatre, and Anti-High Church Propaganda', *Restoration and 18th-Century Theatre Research* 15 (1976), 24–32

Jonathan Swift: Political Writer, London, 1984

'"Mistakes on all Sides": A New Defoe Manuscript', *RES* 27 (1976), 431–7

'Mr. Review and his Scribbling Friends: Defoe and the Critics, 1705–1706', *HLQ* 41 (1978), 345–66

Robert Harley and the Press: Propaganda and Public Opinion in the Age of Swift and Defoe, Cambridge, 1979

'Secret Service Payments to Daniel Defoe, 1710–1714', *RES* 30 (1979), 437–41

'An Unknown Defoe Broadsheet on the Regulation of the Press?', *The Library* 33 (1978), 51–8

'William Stephens and the *Letter to the Author of the Memorial of the State of England* Reconsidered', *BIHR* 50 (1977), 253–9

Downie, J. A., and David Woolley, 'Swift, Oxford, and the Composition of Queen's Speeches, 1710–1714', *BLJ* 8 (1982), 121–46

Dunlop, A. Ian, *William Carstares and the Kirk by Law Established*, Edinburgh, 1964

Eagles, Robin, '"I Have Neither Interest nor Eloquence Sufficient to Prevaile": The Duke of Shrewsbury and the Politics of Succession during the Reign of Anne', *Electronic BLJ* (2015), art. 11, 1–14, www.bl.uk/eblj/2015articles/article11.html

Ellis, E. L., 'The Whig Junto in Relation to the Development of Party Politics and Party Organization, from its Inception to 1714', University of Oxford PhD, 1962

Ellis, Frank H., 'Defoe's "Resignaĉon" and the Limitations of Mathematical Plainness', *RES* 36 (1985), 338–54

Ellis, Sir Henry, *Original Letters of Eminent Literary Men of the Sixteenth, Seventeenth, and Eighteenth Centuries*, London, 1843

Fasti Ecclesiæ Scoticanæ, 11 vols., Edinburgh, 1866–2000

Ferguson, William, *Scotland's Relations with England: A Survey to 1707*, Edinburgh, 1977

Fewster, Joseph M., *The Keelmen of Tyneside: Labour Organisation and Conflict in the North-east Coal Industry, 1600–1830*, Woodbridge, 2011

Fischer, John Irwin, 'The Legal Response to Swift's *The Public Spirit of the Whigs*', in *Swift and His Contexts*, ed. John Irwin Fischer, Hermann J. Real, and James Woolley, New York, 1989, 21–38

Fishman, Burton J., 'Defoe, Herman Moll, and the Geography of South America', *HLQ* 36 (1973), 227–38

Fitzmaurice, Susan M., 'Epistolary Identity: Convention and Idiosyncrasy in Late Modern English Letters', in *Studies in Late Modern English Correspondence: Methodology and Data*, ed. Marina Dossena and Ingrid Tieken-Boon van Ostade, Bern, 2008, 77–112

Fletcher, Edward G., 'Defoe and the Theatre', *PQ* 13 (1934), 382–9

Forster, John, *Oliver Cromwell. Daniel De Foe. Sir Richard Steele. Charles Churchill. Samuel Foote. Biographical Essays*, 3rd ed., London, 1860

SELECT BIBLIOGRAPHY

Fraser, Sir William, *The Melvilles, Earls of Melville, and the Leslies, Earls of Leslie*, 3 vols., Edinburgh, 1890

Furbank, P. N. and W. R. Owens, *The Canonisation of Daniel Defoe*, New Haven, Conn., 1988

    A Critical Bibliography of Daniel Defoe, London, 1998

    'The Dating of Defoe's *Atalantis Major*', *N&Q* 44 (1997), 189–90

    'Defoe, the De la Faye Letters and *Mercurius Politicus*', *BJECS* 23 (2000), 13–19

    Defoe De-attributions: A Critique of J. R. Moore's 'Checklist', London, 1994

    'Defoe and the "Improvisatory" Sentence', *English Studies* 67 (1986), 157–66

    'Defoe and the Sham *Flying-Post*', *Publishing History* 43 (1998), 5–15

    'Defoe and "Sir Andrew Politick"', *BJECS* 17 (1994), 27–39

    'The Myth of Defoe as Applebee's Man', *RES* 48 (1997), 198–204

    'On the Attribution of Periodicals and Newspapers to Daniel Defoe', *Publishing History* 40 (1996), 83–98

    A Political Biography of Daniel Defoe, London, 2006

Gauci, Perry, *The Politics of Trade: The Overseas Merchant in State and Society, 1660–1720*, Oxford, 2001

Geikie, Roderick, and Isabel A. Montgomery, *The Dutch Barrier, 1705–1719*, Cambridge, 1930

Girdler, Lew, 'Defoe's Education at Newington Green Academy', *SP* 50 (1953), 573–91

Glassey, Lionel K. J., *Politics and the Appointment of Justices of the Peace, 1675–1720*, Oxford, 1979

Gregg, Edward, *Queen Anne*, New Haven, Conn., 1980

Halliday, Paul D., *Dismembering the Body Politic: Partisan Politics in England's Towns, 1650–1730*, Cambridge, 1998

Hayton, D. W., 'Robert Harley's "Middle Way": The Puritan Heritage in Augustan Politics', *BLJ* 15 (1989), 158–72

    Ruling Ireland, 1685–1742: Politics, Politicians, and Parties, Woodbridge, 2004

Healey, G. H., 'The Earlier Correspondence of Daniel Defoe (1703–1707)', Cornell University PhD, 1947

Hill, Brian W., 'The Change of Government and the "Loss of the City", 1710–1711', *Economic History Review* 24 (1971), 395–413

    Robert Harley: Speaker, Secretary of State and Premier Minister, New Haven, Conn., 1988

Holmes, Geoffrey, *British Politics in the Age of Anne*, London, 1967

    'The Great Ministry', unpublished typescript, Institute for Historical Research, University of London

    'Harley, St John and the Death of the Tory Party', in *Britain after the Glorious Revolution, 1689–1714*, ed. Geoffrey Holmes, London, 1969, 216–37

    'Robert Harley and the Ministerial Revolution of 1710', ed. W. A. Speck, *PH* 29 (2010), 275–307

    'The Sacheverell Riots: The Crowd and the Church in Early Eighteenth-Century London', *Past and Present* 72 (1976), 55–85

    'Tom Wharton and the Whig Junto', in *British Politics in the Age of Holmes*, ed. Clyve Jones, Oxford, 2009, 100–14

SELECT BIBLIOGRAPHY

The Trial of Doctor Sacheverell, London, 1973

Holmes, Geoffrey, and Clyve Jones, 'Trade, the Scots, and the Parliamentary Crisis of 1713', *PH* 1 (1982), 47–77

Holmes, G. S., and W. A. Speck, 'The Fall of Harley in 1708 Reconsidered', *EHR* 80 (1965), 673–98

Hone, Joseph, *The Paper Chase: The Printer, the Spymaster, and the Hunt for the Rebel Pamphleteers*, London, 2020

Horsley, Lee Sonsteng, 'The Trial of John Tutchin, Author of the *Observator*', *Yearbook of English Studies* 3 (1973), 124–40

Horwitz, Henry, *Parliament, Policy and Politics in the Reign of William III*, Manchester, 1977

Revolution Politics: The Career of Daniel Finch, Second Earl of Nottingham, 1647–1730, Cambridge, 1968

Hyland, Paul, 'A Breach of the Peace: The Controversy over the Ninth Article of the Treaty of Utrecht', *BJECS* 22 (1999), 51–66

'Liberty and Libel: Government and the Press during the Succession Crisis in Britain, 1712–1716', *EHR* 101 (1986), 863–88

Jack, Jane, '*A New Voyage round the World*: Defoe's *Roman à Thèse*', *HLQ* 24 (1961), 323–36

Jones, Clyve, 'Godolphin, the Whig Junto, and the Scots: A New Lords' Division List from 1709', *SHR* 58 (1979), 158–74

'Robert Harley and the Myth of the Golden Thread: Family Piety, Journalism and the History of the Assassination Attempt of 8 March 1711', *Electronic BLJ* (2010), art. 11, 1–15, www.bl.uk/eblj/2010articles/article11.html

Joy, Fred W., 'Autograph Letter of Daniel de Foe', *N&Q*, 6th ser., 9 (1884), 65

Keirn, Tim, 'Daniel Defoe and the Royal African Company', *Historical Research* 61 (1988), 243–7

Keymer, Thomas, *Poetics of the Pillory: English Literature and Seditious Libel, 1660–1820*, Oxford, 2019

Knight, Charles A., *A Political Biography of Richard Steele*, London, 2009

Knights, Mark, ed., *Faction Displayed: Reconsidering the Impeachment of Dr Henry Sacheverell*, Oxford, 2012

Lee, William, *Daniel Defoe: His Life, and Recently Discovered Writings*, 3 vols,. London, 1869

The Libraries of Daniel Defoe and Phillips Farewell: Olive Payne's Sales Catalogue (1731), ed. Helmut Heidenreich, Berlin, 1970

Lillywhite, Bryant, *London Coffee Houses: A Reference Book of Coffee Houses of the Seventeenth, Eighteenth, and Nineteenth Centuries*, London, 1963

Madan, F. F., *A Critical Bibliography of Dr. Henry Sacheverell*, ed. W. A. Speck, Lawrence, Kan., 1978

Marshall, Ashley, 'Fabricating Defoes: From Anonymous Hack to Master of Fictions', *ECL* 36 (2012), 1–35

McInnes, Angus, 'The Appointment of Harley in 1704', *Historical Journal* 11 (1968), 255–71

Robert Harley, Puritan Politician, London, 1970

SELECT BIBLIOGRAPHY

Minto, William, *Daniel Defoe*, London, 1879

Moore, John Robert, *Daniel Defoe: Citizen of the World*, Chicago, Ill., 1958

Mueller, Andreas K. E. *A Critical Study of Daniel Defoe's Verse: Recovering the Neglected Corpus of his Poetic Work*, Lampeter, 2010

Murray, John J., *George I, the Baltic, and the Whig Split of 1717*, London, 1969

Norgate, Francis, 'Correspondence between De Foe and John Fransham, of Norwich (1704–1707)', *N&Q*, 5th ser., 66 (1875), 261–3

'Correspondence between De Foe and John Fransham, of Norwich (1704–1707)', *N&Q*, 5th ser., 67 (1875), 282–4

Novak, Maximillian E., 'Daniel Defoe and *Applebee's Original Weekly Journal*: An Attempt at Re-Attribution', *ECS* 45 (2012), 585–608

Daniel Defoe, Master of Fictions: His Life and Ideas, Oxford, 2001

'Defoe as a Biographical Subject', *Literature Compass* 3 (2006), 1218–36

Defoe and the Nature of Man, Oxford, 1963

'Defoe's Role in the *Weekly Journal*: Gesture and Rhetoric, Archive and Canon, and the Uses of Literary History in Attribution', *SP* 113 (2016), 694–711

Economics and the Fiction of Daniel Defoe, Berkeley, Cal., 1962

'Humanum Est Errare', *The Clark Newsletter* 4 (1983), 1–3

Oakleaf, David, *A Political Biography of Jonathan Swift*, London, 2008

Osselton, N. E., 'Informal Spelling Systems in Early Modern Europe: 1500–1800', in *English Historical Linguistics: Studies in Development*, ed. N. F. Blake and Charles Jones, Sheffield, 1984, 123–37

'Spelling Book Rules and the Capitalization of Nouns in the Seventeenth and Eighteenth Centuries', in *Historical and Editorial Studies in Medieval and Modern English: For Johan Gerritsen*, ed. Mary-Jo Arn, Hanneke Wirtjes, and Hans Jansen Wolters-Noordhoff, Groningen, 1985, 49–61

Owens, W. R. and P. N. Furbank, 'Defoe and the Dutch Alliance: Some Attributions Examined', *BJECS* 9 (1986), 169–82

'Defoe and Imprisonment for Debt: Some Attributions Reviewed', *RES* 37 (1986), 495–502

'Defoe as Secret Agent: Three Unpublished Letters', *The Scriblerian* 25 (1993), 145–53

'New Light on John Pierce, Defoe's Agent in Scotland', *Edinburgh Bibliographical Society Transactions* 6 (1998), 134–43

Paley, Ruth, ed., *The History of Parliament: The House of Lords, 1660–1715*, 5 vols., Cambridge, 2016

Peterson, Spiro, *Daniel Defoe: A Reference Guide, 1731–1924*, Boston, Mass., 1987

'Defoe in Edinburgh, 1707', *HLQ* 38 (1974), 21–33

Plomer, Henry R., *A Dictionary of the Printers and Booksellers who were at Work in England, Ireland and Scotland from 1668 to 1725*, Oxford, 1922

Raffe, Alasdair, *The Culture of Controversy: Religious Arguments in Scotland, 1660–1714*, Woodbridge, 2012

Richards, James O., *Party Propaganda Under Queen Anne: The General Elections of 1702–1713*, Athens, Ga., 1972

SELECT BIBLIOGRAPHY

Richetti, John, *The Life of Daniel Defoe: A Critical Biography*, Oxford, 2005
'Writing About Defoe: What is a Critical Biography?', *Literature Compass* 3 (2006), 65–79
Riley, P. W. J., *The English Ministers and Scotland, 1707–1727*, London, 1964
The Union of England and Scotland: A Study in Anglo-Scottish Politics of the Eighteenth Century, Manchester, 1978
Rogers, J. P. W. 'Two Unrecorded Letters by Daniel Defoe', *Papers on Language and Literature* 7 (1971), 298–9
Rogers, Pat, 'Defoe's Distribution Agents and Robert Harley', *EHR* 121 (2006), 146–61
'An Eighteenth-Century Alarm: Defoe, Sir Justinian Isham and the Secretaries of State', *Northamptonshire Past and Present* 4 (1966–71), 383–7
'Nathaniel Mist, Daniel Defoe, and the Perils of Publishing', *The Library* 10 (2009), 298–313
Roosen, William, *Daniel Defoe and Diplomacy*, Selingsgrove, Penn., 1986
Sachse, William L., *Lord Somers: A Political Portrait*, Manchester, 1986
Sainty, J. C., 'A Huguenot Civil Servant: The Career of Charles Delafaye', *Proceedings of the Huguenot Society* 22 (1975), 398–413
Schonhorn, Manuel, *Defoe's Politics: Parliament, Power, Kingship, and 'Robinson Crusoe'*, Cambridge, 1991
Seager, Nicholas, '*The Clause Proposed in the English Parliament to Prevent the French Goods being Imported thro' Scotland*: A New Defoe Attribution', *N&Q* 66 (2019), 83–6
'Daniel Defoe's *Some Thoughts of an Honest Tory in the Country* (1716): A Critical Edition', *Digital Defoe* 7 (2015), 1–33
'Defoe, the Sacheverell Affair, and *A Letter to Mr. Bisset* (1709)', *PBSA* 115 (2021), 79–86
'Literary Evaluation and Authorship Attribution, or Defoe's Politics at the Hanoverian Succession', *HLQ* 80 (2017), 47–69
'Party Politics', in *Daniel Defoe in Context*, ed. George Justice and Albert Rivero, Cambridge, forthcoming
'"She Will Not Be That Tyrant They Desire": Daniel Defoe and Queen Anne', in *Queen Anne and the Arts*, ed. Cedric D. Reverand III, Lewisburg, Penn., 2014, 41–55
Secord, Arthur W., 'The Correspondence of Daniel Defoe', *MP* 54 (1956), 45–52
'Defoe in Stoke Newington', *PMLA* 66 (1951), 211–25
Shipley, John B., 'Daniel Defoe and Henry Baker: Some of their Correspondence Again and its Provenance', *Bodleian Library Record* 7 (1967), 317–29
Sill, Geoffrey M., 'A Report to Hanover on the "Insolent De Foe"', *N&Q* 28 (1981), 224–5
Snyder, Henry L., 'The Defeat of the Occasional Conformity Bill and the Tack: A Study in the Techniques of Parliamentary Management in the Reign of Queen Anne', *BIHR* 41 (1968), 172–86
'Godolphin and Harley: A Study of their Partnership in Politics', *HLQ* 30 (1967), 241–71
'The Last Days of Queen Anne: The Account of Sir John Evelyn Examined', *HLQ* 34 (1971), 261–76
'Newsletters in England, 1689–1715, with Special Reference to John Dyer: A Byway in the History of England', in *Newsletters to Newspapers: Eighteenth-Century Journalism*, ed. D. H. Bond and W. R. McLeod, Morgantown, W. Va., 1977, 3–19

SELECT BIBLIOGRAPHY

Speck, W. A., *The Birth of Britain: A New Nation, 1700–10*, Oxford, 1994
    'The Choice of a Speaker in 1705', *BIHR* 37 (1964), 20–46
    Stability and Strife, England 1714–1760, London, 1977
    Tory and Whig: The Struggle in the Constituencies, 1701–1715, New York, 1970
    'The Whig Schism Under George I', *HLQ* 40 (1977), 171–9
Starr, G. A., 'Defoe's Prose Style: 1. The Language of Interpretation', *MP* 71 (1974), 277–94
Statt, Daniel, 'Daniel Defoe and Immigration', *ECS* 24 (1991), 293–313
Stephen, Jeffrey, *Defending the Revolution: The Church of Scotland, 1689–1716*, Farnham, 2013
    Scottish Presbyterians and the Act of Union 1707, Edinburgh, 2007
Stevens, David, *Party Politics and English Journalism, 1702–1742*, Menasha, Wisc., 1916
Sundstrom, Roy A., *Sidney Godolphin: Servant of the State*, Newark, Del., 1992
Sutherland, James R., 'A Note on the Last Years of Defoe', *MLR* 29 (1934), 137–41
    Defoe, London, 1937
Szechi, Daniel, *Britain's Lost Revolution? Jacobite Scotland and French Grand Strategy,*
    1701–1708, Manchester, 2015
    Jacobitism and Tory Politics, 1710–1714, Edinburgh, 1984
Thomson, Mark A., *The Secretaries of State, 1681–1782*, Oxford, 1932
Treadwell, Michael, 'London Printers and Printing Houses in 1705', *Publishing History* 7
    (1980), 5–43
    'London Trade Publishers, 1675–1750', *The Library* 4 (1982), 99–134
Trent, W. P., *Daniel Defoe: How to Know Him*, Indianapolis, Ind., 1916
    'New Light on Defoe's Life', *The Nation*, no. 2255, 17 Sept. 1908, 261–3
Trevelyan, George Macaulay, *England Under Queen Anne, Vol. I: Blenheim*, London, 1930
    England Under Queen Anne, Vol. II: Ramillies and the Union with Scotland, London, 1930
    England Under Queen Anne, Vol. III: The Peace and the Protestant Succession, London, 1930
Vickers, Ilse, *Defoe and the New Sciences*, Cambridge, 1996
Warner, G. F., 'An Unpublished Political Paper by Daniel Defoe', *EHR* 22 (1907), 130–43
Wilson, Walter, *Memoirs of the Life and Times of Daniel De Foe*, 3 vols., London, 1830
Winn, James Anderson, *Queen Anne: Patroness of Arts*, Oxford, 2014
Wright, Thomas, 'The Letters of Daniel Defoe', *The Leisure Hour*, November 1901, 29–32
    The Life of Daniel Defoe, London, 1894, rev. 1931

INDEX

'D' refers to Defoe. Bold italic page numbers denote correspondence between D and the given person. Nobles and clergy are included by the name or rank they most commonly appear as in the edition. Mere citations are not usually indexed.

Abercorn, John Hamilton, sixth Earl of, 267
Abercromby, Patrick, *The Advantages of the Act of Security*, 270
Aberdeen, George Gordon, first Earl of, 529, 531
Aberdeen, University of, 502, 663
Abjuration Oath, *see under* Oaths
Academies, Dissenters', *see* Dissenting Academies
Acton, Sir Edward, 183, 188
Acton, Whitmore, 188
Acts and Bills of Parliament
of England (to 1707)
Alien Act (1705), 213, 217
Bankruptcy Act (1706), 190–2, 201, 205, 210–12
Copyright Bill (1707), 364, 365
Cruisers and Convoys Act (1708), 474
Disbanding Bill (1699), 172
Drawback Bills (1707), 372–7, 380–3, 394, 395, 402, 408, 435
Occasional Conformity Bills (1702, 1703), 17, 29, 68, 82–3, 85, 88, 98, 178–9, 484
Promissory Notes Act (1704), 136
Recruiting Acts (1703–11), 128
Security for the Church of England, Act of, 348, 353, 355
Tack of Occasional Bill to Land Tax (1704), 98, 111, 117–18, 120–1
Test Act (1673), 321, 325, 345, 348, 686, 808, 812
Toleration, Act of (1689), lxix, 16, 82, 94, 668, 686, 807
Triennial Act (1694), 94, 458–9, 461–2
of Great Britain (after 1707)
Act for the Better Security of Her Majesty's Person (1708), 445
Act incorporating the South Sea Company (1711), 607

Church Patronage (Scotland) Act (1712), *see under* Church of Scotland
Episcopal Toleration Act (1712), *see under* Church of Scotland
Occasional Conformity Act (1711), lxx, 179, 659, 667–71, 672, 686, 689, 697, 733, 773, 807–8
Schism Act (1714), lxx, 807–12, 823, 825
Stamp Act (1712), 571, 685, 697, 754
of Scotland (to 1707)
Plantation of Kirks, Act for (1707), *see under* Church of Scotland
Security, Act of (1704), 25, 82, 111, 116, 213, 217, 257, 274, 283–4, 285
Security, Act of (1706), *see under* Church of Scotland
Adams, William, *A Letter from the Country*, 363
Addison, Joseph, 288, 305, 348, 433, 435, 516, 534, 713
Late Tryal and Conviction of Count Tariff, 760, 762
Spectator, 786
Tatler, 786, 788
Advocates, Faculty of, see under Edinburgh
Age of Wonders, 516, 685
Aird, John, the younger, 259–60, 282
Aitken, George A., lxxxvi
Allen, Henry, 3
Allestree, Charles, 184, 189
Alliance, Grand, 55, 618, 626, 660
Almansa, Battle of, *see under* War of the Spanish Succession
Alsop, J. D., 838
Alves, William, 367–8
Anderson, Agnes Campbell, 623–5, 653–5, 717, 719
Anderson, Andrew, 623
Anderson, John, 409

897

INDEX

Anglesey, Arthur Annesley, fifth Earl of, 821–5, 826–7, 837

Anglo-Dutch Wars, 288, 511, 517

Annandale, William Johnston, first Marquess of, 259, 274, 469, 540, 572–3, 576, 652

Anne, Queen of England,
appointments made by, 43, 47, 81, 391, 407, 435, 494, 495, 505, 516, 526, 656, 685, 815, 817–18

D, 'bounty' and 'goodness' to, 36–7, 51, 203, 216, 269, 338, 355, 502, 520–1, 575, 606, 665, 698, 700, 722, 734, 764

D, prosecutes and pardons, 4–6, 16–17, 21, 24, 25, 50–1, 746, 758, 770, 776–8

D commended to, 369, 386, 443

D's correspondence with, xii, xci, 36, **776–8**

D's published addresses to, 26, 366, 672

death of, 808, 815, 824, 827

favourites of, 143–4, 494, 814

Hanoverians and, 193, 739, 743, 789–90, 796–7, 802, 805

Harley's relationship with, l, 68, 112, 343, 344–5, 492, 494, 498, 502–3, 807, 814, 815, 825

illnesses, 753, 755, 784–5, 792, 795, 801

Jacobitism of (rumoured), 542, 544, 707–8, 711, 713, 730, 740, 743

peace and, 674, 689–90, 693, 712, 804, 817–18

relationship to Church of England, 87, 89, 92, 93, 145, 391–2, 478

relationship to Dissenters, 4, 29, 68, 70–1, 82, 88, 90, 92, 94, 670, 672, 773

Scottish Union promoted by, 213–14, 225, 249, 297–9, 320, 322, 325, 355–6, 372, 374, 402–3, 537, 556–7, 581, 647–8, 650, 751

seditious/libellous writings denounced by, 682–3, 784, 792–3

succession to crown of, 86, 93, 174

Tory party, view of, lxv, 20, 85, 93, 433, 492, 644

theatre, view of the, 239

Whig party, view of, lxix, 117, 159, 344–5, 449, 468–9, 492, 672

Annesley, Samuel, 804

Applebee's Original Weekly Journal, lxxxii, 852

Arbuthnot, John, *The History of John Bull*, 820

Archer, David, 567

Argyll, John Campbell, second Earl of, 230, 233, 304, 305, 469, 529, 531, 534, 535, 540–5, 548, 560, 562, 609, 655, 694, 695

Arundell, Francis, 189

Ashby, Matthew, 33, 132

asiento, 621–2

Atholl, John Murray, first Duke of, 228, 232, 260, 305, 321, 322, 326–7, 397–8, 529, 531, 535, 540

Atterbury, Francis, Bishop of Rochester, 150–1, 814, 817, 820, 825

Augustus II, King of Poland, 52, 55–6, 74, 77, 83, 84

Aumont de Rochebaron, Louis, duc d', 724–5

Austin, Benjamin, 132

Aylesbury case, 33, 98, 132, 149

Backscheider, Paula R., lviii, lxi, lxxii, xcii, 25, 199, 311, 340, 481, 483, 505, 576, 609, 639, 642, 659, 717, 719, 728, 821–2, 855

Baillie, Robert, 625

Baillie of Jerviswood, George, 288, 349, 454

Baker, David Lionel Erskine, 600, 864, 877, 881

Baker, Harriett Defoe, 859, 881

Baker, Henry, lxxix, lxxxi, lxxxii, lxxxiv, lxxxvi, xciii, 600, **854–70, 875–81**
Universal Spectator and Weekly Journal, 860

Baker, Henry, Jr, 864

Baker, Henry De Foe, 859, 874

Baker, John, 739, 742, 745, 821, 822, 824–5, 874

Baker, Sophia, *see* Defoe, Sophia

Balch, George, 187

Balfour of Burleigh, Robert, 377–9, 427, 529

Balfour of Burleigh, Robert, fourth Lord, 379

Balliaguell (Ballianquell), William, 497–8, 501

Balmerino, John Elphinstone, fourth Lord, 529, 532, 540, 652, 695

Bank of England, 399, 404–8, 437–9, 495, 507, 526, 529, 577

Banks, Sir Jacob, 16, 740, 742

Bannatyne, John, 262, 263
Some Queries ... Relative to the Union, 241, 243

Barber, John, 516, 793

Barcelona, *see under* War of the Spanish Succession

Baron, Peter, 194, 197

Barrier Treaties, 622, 712–14, 730, 731–2

Barrington, John Shute, first Viscount, xcii, 450, 454, 455

Barron, Thomas, 840, 842

Barrymore, James Barry, fourth Earl of, 789

898

INDEX

Baskett, John, 623, 653
Bateman, Thomas, lxxx, xcii, 547–8, 552, 553
Bateson, Thomas, lxxxvi–lxxxvii
Bathurst, Allen, 187
Baxter, Richard, 199
Bayne of Tulloch, John, 396
Beachcroft, Sir Robert, 526
Beaumont, Sir George, 188
Bedford, Arthur, 238
    Evil and Danger of Stage-Plays, 239
    Evil and Mischief of Stage-Playing, 239
    Serious Remonstrance in Behalf of the
        Christian Religion, 239
Belhaven, John Hamilton, second Lord, lxxi,
    244, 246, 256, 265, 280–1, 444, ***445–8***,
    571
Bell, John, xcii, 216, 218, 219, 221–4, 242,
    253, 255, 276, 277, 290, 292, 293, 339,
    340, 345, ***357–9***, 368, 369–70, 382,
    394, 418, 426, 428, 461, 539, 540, 544,
    546, 551
Bellamy, Edward, 3, 7
Bennet of Grubbet, William, 233, 257, 259,
    260, 263, 280, 321
Bennett, Benjamin, 713
Benson, Robert, 498
Benson, William, 740, 742, 748
    Letter to Sir J—— B——, 742
Bere, Francis, lxxx, 157, 160, 194
Bere, Thomas, 160, 187
Berg, Albert, 243
Berkeley of Stratton, William, fourth Baron,
    754
Berman, Ric, 833
Bertie, Henry, 187
Bertie, Robert, 187
Berwick, James FitzJames, first Duke of, 529,
    532
Bissett, William, 478
Bishoprics Crisis, 391, 433
Black, William,
    Letter Concerning the Remarks upon the
        Considerations of Trade, 270
    Reply to the Authors of the Advantages of
        Scotland by an Incorporate Union, 330
Blackburne, Lancelot, 160
Blackwell, Thomas, 501–2, 625
Blantyre, Walter Stuart, sixth Lord, 540, 543
Blathwayt, William, 172, 187
Blenheim, Battle of, *see under* War of the
    Spanish Succession
Blythe, William, 131, 132, 140
Boig, Adam, 482

Bolingbroke, Henry St John, first Viscount,
    750, 779
    Commercial Treaty written by, 754–5, 759
    Dunkirk's demolition, 803
    Jacobitism of, 710, 803, 817, 820, 824
    partnership with Harley, 54–5, 343, 434,
        436, 672, 785, 804, 814
    rivalry with Harley, 599, 751–2, 754–5,
        759, 807, 813, 814, 815, 825
    Schism Act promoted by, 807
    Secretary of State, 532, 625, 644, 725–6,
        746, 776
    impeachment of, 709
Below, Mr, 195
Bolton Charles Powlett, second Duke of, 122,
    128–9, 157
Borrett, William, 473, 744–5, 748, 758, 764,
    770–1, 772, 778
Bothwell Bridge, Battle of, 83, 657
Bourn, Edward, 840, 842
Bowen, Icabod, 183, 188
Bowie, Karin, 261
Bowrey, Thomas, ***439–42***, 626
Boyer, Abel, 26, 118, 433, 643, 743
    History of the Life and Reign of Queen Anne,
        754
    Political State, 754, 793, 831, 852
    True Account … of the South-Sea Trade, 630
Boyle, Henry, 463, 532
Boyle, William, 386, 532
Boyne, Battle of the, *see under* Nine Years'
    War
Brabant, Lines of, *see under* War of the
    Spanish Succession
Bradgate, Jarvis or Gervase, 184, 189
Bray, Edmund, 173
Bridgeman, Sir Orlando, 159
Bridges, Brook, 35–6
Bridges, John, 408
Bridges, William, 187
Brihuega, Battle of, *see under* War of the
    Spanish Succession
Br[iti]sh Embassadress's Speech to the French
    King, 741, 743
British Merchant, 205, 732, 754, 756
Britton, Col. William, 163
Bromley, William, 173, 176, 178–9, 186, 187,
    220, 535, 750, 755, 785, 824–5
    Remarkes in the Grande Tour of France and
        Italy, 179
Brooke, Mary, lxxxiv, 212, 857, 875, 878
Brooke, Samuel, 212, 875
Brown, James, 260

INDEX

Brown of Blackford, Adam, 488, 527, 535, 559, 604, 609, 648
Browne, Joseph,
  Dialogue between Church and No-Church, lvi
  Dialogue between Louis le Petite, and Harlequin le Grand, 439
Bruce, Charles, Lord, 180, 186
Bruce, James, 180, 186
Bruce, John, 532
Bruce, Sir John, 532
Brutus, 871, 876
Buchan, David Erskine, ninth Earl of, lxxxi, xcii, 327, 468, 529, 532, 574, 576, **600–2**
Buchan, David Stewart Erskine, eleventh Earl of, 602
Buckingham, George Villiers, first Duke of, 57, 79
Buckingham, John Sheffield, first Duke of, 16–17, 19, 23, 117, 153, 529, 532, 535, 562
Buckley, Samuel, 474, 689, 834–5, 838, 843, 845
Buller, James, 187
Bullock, Edward, 189
Burch, Charles Eaton, 483, 728
Burnet, Gilbert, Bishop of Salisbury, 159, 172, 348, 759
Burnet, Thomas, 740, 742
  Certain Information of a Certain Discourse, 742
  Grumbler, 803
  Some New Proofs by which it Appears the Pretender is Truly James III, 742
Burridge, John, 186
Burridge, Robert, 187
Button, Joseph, lxxxii, xcii, 195, 199, 523, **558–60**
Byng, Sir George, 186, 187, 455

Caesar, Julius, 11, 14, 61, 871
Calamy, Edmund, 518, 520, 529, 783
Cambridge, George, Duke of, *see* George II, King of England
Cambridge, University of, 160, 185, 354
Cameronians, *see under* Covenanters
Camisards, 43, 48–9
Campbell, Agnes, *see* Anderson, Agnes Campbell
Campbell, Col. James, 532
Campbell, Lt.-Col. James, 288
Campbell, John (D's associate), 717
Campbell, John (Dumbartonshire), 663

Campbell, John (politician), 532
Campbell of Ardkinglas, James, 532
Campbell of Auchinbreck, Sir James, 532
Campbell of Lundie, John, 639–41
Campbell of Rachean, Archibald, 663
Campbell of Saltmarket, Daniel, 532
Carlos II, King of Spain, 665
Carnwath, Robert Dalzell, fifth Earl of, 529, 532
Carr, William, 358, 529, 532
Carstares, William, lxxxvii, 257, 329–30, 369, 429, 443, 444, 520, 529, 532, 557, 586, 624, 625, 638–40, 643, 719, *727–8*
Carswell, John, xc
Carter, Lawrence, 188–9
Cartwright, J. J., lxxxvi, 31
Cary, William, 187
Casca, Servilius, 11, 14
Case of the Poor Skippers and Keel-men of New-Castle, Truly Stated, 682
Cass, Sir John, 762
Castelnaudary, Battle of, 80
Cater, Joseph, *173–9*, 217
Cato the Elder, 84
Cavendish, James, Lord, 188
Cavendish Holles, Lady Henrietta, 814
Cessnock, Sir Alexander Hume-Campbell, Lord, 276, 277, 303, 576
Chadwick, William, lxxxi–lxxxii
Chalmers, George, lxxxi, xci, 602
Chambers, Abraham, 195
Charles, Archduke, *see* Charles VI, Holy Roman Emperor
Charles I, King of England, 97, 589, 591, 593
Charles II, King of England, lxiv, 83, 93, 97, 446, 448, 511, 531, 590, 786
Charles VI, Holy Roman Emperor, 49, 178, 343, 567, 619, 620, 622, 660, 662, 664, 672, 683
Charles XII, King of Sweden, 52, 54, 55, 74, 77–8, 83, 84, 430, 431, 491
Charlton, Nicholas, 180, 186
Childs, Sir Francis, 171, 173
Childs, John, 171, 173
Chivers, Col. Henry, 170–2, 182
Civil Wars, English, 93, 593
Chorlton, John, 218
Church of England,
  'danger of', 140, 149, 154–5, 179, 475, 481
  D's views of, lxxxiii, 18–19, 86–92
  High Church party, li, lxvi, 26, 29, 85, 89–93, 98, 102, 114, 138, 144, 174–6, 190, 197, 220, 497, 530, 668, 807, 814

900

INDEX

Scottish ministers' views of, 248–9, 297, 299, 330–1, 334, 444–5, 714

Security for the Church of England, Act of, *see under* Acts and Bills of Parliament

Church of Scotland,

Church Patronage (Scotland) Act (1712), 556, 586–7, 594, 625, 662, 685

concerns about Union of, lxii, 214–15, 226–7, 240, 247–8, 250, 255, 258, 297, 315, 331, 333, 337

D's communications with ministers of, lxx, xcii, 214, 325, 390, 517

D's support for, lxii, 227, 248, 263, 281, 288, 318–19, 347, 360, 624, 650–3, 654, 685

Episcopal Toleration Act (1712), 281, 297, 321, 398, 445, 455, 502, 555, 557, 565, 580, 586–7, 625, 662, 675–6, 678, 679, 683, 685, 697, 704, 714, 736

General Assembly of (and Commission of), 226–7, 231–2, 236, 240, 247, 249, 263, 276, 287, 297, 319, 329, 332, 333, 357, 361–3, 364, 368–70, 373–4, 380, 382, 427, 443–4, 529, 566, 569, 572–5, 586, 600, 603, 605, 625, 684–5, 688, 719, 736, 738, 749–50

history of, 587–94

intrusions and rabbles upon, 396–8, 502, 531, 535, 536, 537–8, 567, 568, 570, 582, 603, 605

Plantation of Kirks, Act for (1707), 349

post-Union status, lxviii, lxix–lxx, 255, 321, 325, 398, 517, 584, 656, 675, 703, 714

Security, Act of (1706), 247, 255, 256–7, 263, 279, 281, 302, 304, 333, 348, 355, 555, 583, 590, 593, 675, 738

Churchill, Arabella, 532

Churchill, Awnsham, 159, 181

Churchill, Charles, 531

Churchill, George, 392

Clark, Mr, of Derbyshire, 732

Clark, Hugh, *The Oath of Abjuration Displayed*, 678

Clark, James, 255

Clarke, Edward, 187

Clarke, Thomas, 200

Clayton, William, 188

Clerk of Penicuik, Sir John, 337, 366, 367, 369, 383

Clerk of Penicuik, John, 246, 255, 277, 337, 366, 367, 369, 372, 394, 395, 401

Cliff, William, 550, 551

Coates, John, 195, 199

Cochrane of Kilmarnock, William, 617

Cockburn, Archibald, 527–8

Cockburn, James D., lxii–lxiii, lxxxvii

Cocks, Sir Richard, 183, 188

Codrington, Samuel, 194, 197

Colbert, Jean Baptiste, 57, 79

Colepeper, William, 16, 19, 28, 29, 40, 48

Collins, Mrs, 225–6

Collins, Gabriel, 225

Combalet, Marie de, 67, 82

Commerce, Anglo-French Treaty of, 189–90, 572, 671, 751–2, 754, 756, 759, 760–9, 773, 775, 787, 810, 825

Compton, Spencer, 478

Coningham, Rev. James, 195, 198–9, 217, 218

Critical Essay on Modern Medals, 198

Coningsby, Thomas, 188

Connell, Matthew, 242

Cooke, Sir Thomas, 189

Cooke, William, 173

Coole, Benjamin, 194, 197

Coombs, Douglas, 695

Cooper, Mr, 484–7

Cope, Sir John, 187, 407–8

Coronation Oath, *see under* Oaths

Cotton, Sir John, 189

Cotton, Sir John (second Bt.), 189

Coulson, Thomas, 186

Coult, Maj. James, xcii, 638–42, 659, 667, 727–8

Couper, W. J., 655

Coutts, Thomas, 402, 404

Covenanters, lxiv, 83, 244, 260, 284, 315, 657, 701–4

Cameronians, 258–60, 263, 285, 309, 310–12, 529, 701–4, 716

Hebronites, 260, 310

National Covenant, 246, 297, 330–3, 360, 529, 675, 701, 703, 704, 714

Solemn League and Covenant, 260, 297, 330–3, 445, 675, 701, 704, 714

Cowper, William, 200, 374, 394, 522, 536

Coxe, Charles, 183, 185, 187–8

Coxe, William, 455, 457, 474

Crawford, David, 284, 288

Crawford, John Lindsey, nineteenth Earl of, 304, 305, 307, 349, 468, 469, 529, 532

Cromarty, George Mackenzie, first Earl of, 571

A Letter to a Member of Parliament, 295

Crompton, John, 199

Crompton, Joseph, 199

901

INDEX

Cromwell, Oliver, 786, 846
Cromwell, Thomas, 58, 79–80
Croome, George, 3, 7
Crossley, James, 828
Crowe, Eyre, *Defoe in the Pillory*, lxxxii–lxxxiii
Cullum, Sir Dudley, 185, 189
Cunningham, Sir Alexander, 560
Cunningham, Robert, 643
Cunningham of Aiket, Maj. James, 260
Cunningham of Harperfield, Alexander, 315
Cunynghame, Sir James, 560
Curll, Edmund, 845–6
Curriehill, John Skene, Lord, *Regiam Majestatem*, 592
Curryer, Mr, 870

Daily Courant, 220, 471–4, 481, 689–90, 693, 730–1, 838
Daines, Sir William, 172
Dale, William, 720–1
Dalhousie, William Ramsay, sixth Earl of, 468
Dalrymple, Sir David, 648
Dalrymple, Sir John, xciii
Dalrymple of Glenmuir, William, 459, 462
Dalton, Charles, 10
Dalton, Isaac, 837
Dalziel, Alexander, 604, 605
Darien project, 81–2, 217, 445, 448, 626, 632, 636
Darracott, John, 163, 167, 168
Dartmouth, William Legge, first Earl of, 492, 529, 532, 604, 605, 617, 731, 746, 750, 755, 779
Dashwood, George (Bath candidate), 187
Dashwood, George (Sudbury candidate), 189
Davenant, Charles, 386, 516
  Report to the Honourable the Commissioners, 769
  Second Report, 769
Davers, Sir Robert, 100, 105, 189
Davila, Arrigo Caterino, *Historie of the Civill Warres of France*, 792
Davis, Mary, 21, 523
Davis, Robert, lxxx, 10, 21, 26, 134, 151, 153, 165, 170–1, 210, 212, 254, 264–5, 289, 386, 423, 425, 432, 457, 505–6, 516, 523, 559–60
Daybell, James, lxxvi
Dayrolles, James, 395
Defoe, Benjamin, 7, 34, 483, 501, 639, 641–2, 658, 717, 719, 734, 849, 851, 852, 881

Defoe, Daniel, life of,
  Accomptant to the Commissioners of the Glass Duty, 36
  Alexander Goldsmith alias, lxxx, 39, 104–5, 157, 172, 197, 212, 217, 218, 221, 494, 814
  arrests for debt, 7, 12, 193, 208, 732, 734–5
  bankruptcies, lxxix, 7, 25, 39, 178, 190, 192, 202, 208, 210–12, 216, 732, 875
  business career, 25, 185, 208, 337, 339–40, 358, 560
  Claude Guilot alias, lxxx, 522, 544, 546, 547, 548, 550, 554, 557, 562, 567, 572, 583, 617, 723, 731, 735, 783, 814
  customs commissionership offered to, 386, 408, 460, 462
  death of, 875
  Dissenters' treatment of, lxx, 11, 14, 15, 22, 680, 696, 698, 701
  Edinburgh newspapers operated by, 482–3
  education of, liv–lv, 198, 810
  emotions of, lix–lxi, lxxvi–lxxix, lxxxiv, lxxxix, 37–8, 416, 598
  epistolary habits, xlix–liii, lvii–lxiv, lxxiii
  family, *see entries under* Baker, Foe, *and* Defoe
  gentility, claim to, l, 5, 10
  handwriting of, lxxiv–lxxv, lxxix–lxxx, 97, 540, 547, 821, 825, 847
  Harley, loyalty to, lxvi–lxvii, lxxii, lxxv, lxxvii, 492, 497, 552, 816–18, 825
  hiding, xlix, 3–4, 10–11, 201, 873, 875–81
  intelligence agent and spy, li, lvi, lxviii, lxxii–lxxiii, lxxx, lxxxii, xci, 41, 54, 56–84, 203, 215, 223, 225, 277, 322, 362, 403, 429, 443, 503–5, 528–9, 538, 546
  ironic writing, lxxi, 3, 55, 84, 104, 179, 281, 429, 478, 739, 740, 743, 746, 804, 806, 846
  later life, lxxix, 197, 212, 854–81
  library catalogue, 49, 239, 243, 247, 592, 674, 762, 789, 792, 801, 820
  marriage, xlix, 39
  materiality of letters, lxxiii–lxxx
  ministerial writer, lxvi–lxxii, 51, 142, 443, 458, 492
  Monmouth rebel, lxiv, 10, 83
  pantile factory, 4, 22, 37, 38, 39, 857
  political thought, lxv, lxvii–lxix, lxxxviii, 56–84, 174
  press censor, 831–53

902

INDEX

prose style, liv–lv, lxi–lxiv, lxxvi
prosecutions and punishment for sedition, lviii, 3–29, 38, 50, 82, 110, 153, 178, 179, 197, 213, 475, 631, 739–50, 745, 764, 770–2, 776–8, 837
published attacks on, x, lii, lxv, lxx, lxxvi, xc, 14, 29, 31, 153, 277, 330, 346, 348, 365, 389, 436, 439, 444, 481, 500, 664, 671, 691, 696, 739–40, 742, 759, 760, 846, 848
religiosity of, li, lxi, lxx, 82, 596–600, 686, 779–80, 828–30
Royal African Company, writes for, 571–2
Scottish sojourns of, lxviii, lxxvi, xci–xcii, 10, 213–429, 443–74, 522, 537–67, 714
secret service payments, lxx, lxxviii, 166, 205, 255, 277, 293, 370, 418, 502, 572, 607, 612, 617, 687, 723, 838
sells his books, 366–8
South American colony, D promotes, 621–2, 626–37
tours England in 1704–5, lxviii, lxxx, xci, 52, 95–106, 144–6, 156–73, 180–90, 193–200, 213
Whig party, relationship with, lviii, lxv–lxxi, lxxxiii, lxxviii, 129, 492, 494, 660, 664–5, 679–80, 694–6, 741, 759, 790–1, 834, 852
William III, career under, lxv–lxvi, lxxvi, 7, 11, 17, 38, 80, 82, 117, 270, 626, 631–2
Defoe, Daniel, works of,
Account of the Conduct of Robert Earl of Oxford, 395, 602, 820
Address, 33, 40, 109, 110
Advantages of Peace and Commerce, 572
Advice to all Parties, 19, 20, 48, 371
Advice to the People of Great Britain, 817, 821
Anatomy of Exchange-Alley, 365
Answer to the L—d H—sham's Speech, 193
Answer to a Question that No Body thinks of, viz. But What if the Queen Should Die?, 678, 739, 742, 778
Appeal to Honour and Justice, lxi, lxxii, lxxxii, lxxxiii, lxxxviii, 14, 22, 25, 84, 436, 443, 533, 696, 701, 710, 742, 743, 745, 754, 763, 769, 776, 778, 825, 827
Argument … Employing and Enobling Foreigners, 365, 837

Argument Shewing, That a Standing Army … is not Inconsistent with a Free Government, lxv, 79, 232–3
Atalantis Major, 305, 531, 532, 533, 534, 535, 540–1, 545, 546, 560, 562, 563, 674, 696–7
Brief Account of the Present State of the African Trade, 572
Brief Deduction of the … British Woollen Manufacture, 78, 79, 93, 106, 172, 189, 622
Brief Explanation of … The Shortest Way with the Dissenters, 3, 7, 15
Brief Reply to the History of Standing Armies in England, 92
Brief Survey of the Legal Liberties of the Dissenters, 807, 810
British Visions, 558–60
Caledonia, 80, 233, 241, 243, 247, 274, 319, 324, 349, 349, 366, 468, 483, 623
Captain Singleton, 160, 745
Case of the Poor Skippers and Keel-Men of Newcastle, 679, 682
Challenge of Peace, Address'd to the Whole Nation, 26, 31, 32
Character of the Late Dr. Samuel Annesley, 83, 804
Christianity Not as Old as the Creation, 713
Clause Proposed … to Prevent the French Goods being Imported thro' Scotland, 377
Colonel Jack, 343, 713, 828, 830
Commentator, lvi, lxiv–lxv, 344, 489, 554, 662, 794, 829, 851
Compleat English Gentleman, xlix, liv–lvi, lxxv, lxxix, 10, 80, 82, 84, 365, 484, 599, 775, 873–4
Complete English Tradesman, liii–liv, lxxiii, 38, 80, 192, 208, 365, 546, 864
Conduct of Parties in England, lxxi, 20, 143, 454, 465, 468, 672–3, 674, 713
Conjugal Lewdness, 745
Considerations upon the Eighth and Ninth Articles of the Treaty of Commerce, 754, 769
Consolidator, 38, 343, 363, 554
D's self-representation in, 20, 21, 93–4
D's view of, 136
as political allegory, 20, 40, 105, 117, 118, 135, 137–8, 179, 217, 519, 689
read by contemporaries, 141, 197, 367, 655

903

INDEX

Defoe, Daniel, works of, (cont.)
Continuation of Letters written by a Turkish Spy, lv, 49, 79, 82, 220, 599, 802
Counter Queries, 516, 520
Danger of Court Differences, 709, 832
Danger of the Protestant Religion Consider'd, 79, 80, 81, 83, 792
De Foe's Answer, To Dyer's Scandalous News Letter, 429, 430–1
Dialogue between a Dissenter and the Observator, 4, 7
Director, 83, 233
Dissenters Answer to the High-Church Challenge, 31
Dissenters in England Vindicated, 333, 334–5, 339, 348, 363
Dissenter Misrepresented and Represented, 15, 121
Dissenters Vindicated, 333, 335, 348, 360–1, 363, 430
Double Welcome, 52, 117, 143, 179
Due Preparations for the Plague, 709
Dyers News Examined, 110, 430–1, 693
Dyet of Poland,
  praises individuals, 117, 133, 484
  publication of, 48, 51
  satirises individuals, 10, 15, 19, 20, 48, 48, 50, 105, 153, 159, 167, 179
Elegy on the Author of the True-Born-English-Man, 15, 39, 48, 35
Eleven Opinions about Mr. H—y, 78, 522, 579, 596, 689, 786
Encomium on a Parliament, lxv, 172
Enquiry into the Danger and Consequences of a War with the Dutch, 694
Enquiry into the Disposal of the Equivalent, 353
Enquiry into Occasional Conformity, 15
Enquiry into the Occasional Conformity of Dissenters, 79, 82, 93, 94, 839
Essay upon Buying and Selling of Speeches, 83, 794
Essay on the History of Parties and Persecution in Britain, 668, 672, 674
Essay on the History and Reality of Apparitions, 10–11, 79, 187, 873
Essay upon Literature, lv, lxxiv
Essay upon Loans, 505–6, 516
Essay at a Plain Exposition of that Difficult Phrase a Good Peace, 660
Essay upon Projects, liv, lxiv, 11, 16, 79, 117, 122, 190, 358

Essay upon Publick Credit, 494, 499, 501, 505, 516, 578
Essay at Removing National Prejudices against a Union with Scotland ... Part I, 79, 213, 217, 217
Essay at Removing National Prejudices against a Union with Scotland ... Part II, 14, 214, 277
Essay, at Removing National Prejudices against a Union with England. Part III, 217, 225, 226, 231, 235, 236, 243, 246, 247–8
Essay on the South-Sea Trade, 81, 83, 622, 626, 630, 636
Essay upon the Trade to Africa, 571
Essay on the Treaty of Commerce with France, 754, 762, 769
Every-Body's Business, is No-Body's Business, 609
Evident Approach of a War, 770
Experiment, 137–8, 146, 199, 220
Fair Payment No Spunge, 709
Family Instructor, 395, 558, 808
Family Instructor, Volume II, lv, 82, 371
Farther Adventures of Robinson Crusoe, 84, 220, 270, 554
Farther Case Relating to the Poor Keel-Men of Newcastle, 679, 682
Felonious Treaty, 20, 117, 636, 664–5
Fifth Essay, at Removing National Prejudices, 268, 330–1, 332, 337
Fortunate Mistress, 554, 745, 857
Fourth Essay, at Removing National Prejudices, 14, 231, 235, 243, 248, 266, 270, 277, 284, 293, 319, 327, 337, 812
Friendly Epistle by Way of Reproof ... to Thomas Bradbury, 830
Further Search into the Conduct of the Allies, 689, 692–3
General History of Discoveries and Improvements, 630
General History of Trade, 319, 387, 760, 769, 789
Giving Alms no Charity, 121
Greenshields Out of Prison, 269, 386, 555, 565
High-Church Legion, 15, 20, 79, 149, 155, 167, 465
Historical Account of the Bitter Sufferings ... of the Episcopal Church in Scotland, 401, 544
'Historical Collections', xii, xlix
History of the Kentish Petition, 19
History of the Union,

904

INDEX

Anglo-Scottish history in, 79, 82, 217, 440

anti-Union addresses described in, 242, 260

anti-Union writings and sermons described in, 235, 243

Church of Scotland's actions depicted in, 227, 236, 245, 257, 263, 321, 329

Clark, James, dispute with, 255

custom collections described in, 383, 387, 391, 407

D announces he is writing, 337, 339

D's self-representation in, 217–18, 232, 263, 284

Drawback Bill described in, 372–7, 402

English politics described in, 179, 333, 348

Equivalent described in, 296, 353, 387, 399, 401, 407

Jacobite invasion described in, 454

letters, compared to, lxii–lxiii

parliamentary proceedings, recounted in, 246–7, 254, 257, 259, 273–4, 277, 327, 333, 340, 362–3

politicians' treatment in, 246, 255, 260, 327, 366, 389, 408, 448

popular protests against Union in, 226, 231–3, 236, 254–5, 284, 288, 290, 293, 315, 408

Privy Council of Scotland's abolition described in, 415, 652

publishing of, 623, 846

Superiorities denounced in, 415, 610

trade described in, 217, 254, 274, 293, 308–9

'Humanum Est Errare', xii, lxxv

Humble Proposal to the People of England, 630, 769

Hymn to the Mob, 105, 701

Hymn to Peace, 172, 180, 185, 189, 190, 205, 685

Hymn to the Pillory, 15, 20, 21

Hymn to Victory, 52, 95, 105, 107, 108, 143

Imperial Gratitude, 683

Journal of the Plague Year, 28

Jure Divino,

author portrait in, 10, 209

composition of, 107

politicians praised in, 117, 117, 129, 133, 149, 484, 837

politicians satirised in, 20, 48, 122, 153, 167, 196–7

politics and history in, 15, 110

religious allusions in, 599, 693, 701

Scotland, D sells in, 336, 337, 367

subscription publication of, 32, 106, 107, 108, 109, 137, 139, 140, 146, 166, 169, 208, 209, 367

Union mentioned in, 217

Justice and Necessity of a War with Holland, 694, 695

Lay-Man's Sermon upon the Late Storm, 31, 55, 343

Layman's Vindication of the Church of England, 812

Legion's Humble Address to the Lords, 33, 35, 110, 284

Legion's Memorial, lxvi, 7, 19, 21, 117, 135

Letter from Captain Tom to the Mobb, 476, 483

Letter to a Dissenter from his Friend at the Hague, lxv

Letter to the Dissenters, lxx, 762, 773–5, 780–1, 783, 784, 803, 808–9, 810

Letter to Mr. Bisset, xii, 478

Letter to Mr. How, 25, 270

Letter to the Whigs (1710), 596

Letter to the Whigs (1714), 78, 709, 743, 782, 790, 792, 803, 804, 821

Lex Talionis, 48

Manufacturer, 236, 343, 365, 636, 754, 852

Master Mercury, 48–50, 56, 81, 83, 84, 98–9, 104–5, 107

'Meditaćons', 83, 830

Memoirs of a Cavalier, 78–9, 80, 220, 745, 792, 864

Memoirs of the Church of Scotland, 83, 93, 584, 592–4, 657, 745

Memoirs of the Conduct of Her Late Majesty and Her Last Ministry, 817, 821, 828

Memoirs of Count Tariff, 189, 671, 691, 693, 725, 726, 732, 743, 760, 769, 770

Memorial to the Nobility of Scotland, 464–5

Mercator, 599, 783

Commercial Treaty promoted in, 752, 760, 763, 769–70, 810

D's authorship of, 752, 754, 756–7, 759, 823

D's self-representation in, 39, 212, 732

funding of, 765, 809–11

journalistic rivals of, 756, 760, 787, 789, 823

politicisation of trade regretted in, 572, 762, 765, 793

Mercurius Politicus, 831, 832, 834–5, 837, 840–2

INDEX

Defoe, Daniel, works of, (cont.)

Mere Nature Delineated, 138, 854, 856

*Minutes of the Negotiations of Monsr.
Mesnager*, 79, 144, 496, 500, 522, 531,
579, 599, 622, 666, 789, 803

Mock Mourners, 92

Moll Flanders, lxxxii, 11, 516, 830

Monitor, 7, 92, 671, 709, 784, 790, 792,
794, 801, 802, 803, 805, 806–7, 810,
823, 827

More Reformation, 7, 15, 25, 39, 599

More Short-Ways with the Dissenters, 15, 85,
93, 94, 786

New Family Instructor, 526, 745

New Test of the Church of England's Honesty,
15, 85, 92, 94, 395

New Test of the Church of England's Loyalty,
lxvi, 15, 79, 93

New Test of the Sence of the Nation, 122,
415, 494, 496, 537

New Voyage Round the World, 440, 627, 630,
636, 637

*Observations on the Fifth Article of the
Treaty of Union*, 270

Of Royal Education, 79, 80

Old Whig and Modern Whig Revived, 343,
468, 709, 832, 837

*Original Power of the Collective Body of the
People of England*, lxvi, lxxvi, 93, 122,
135, 178, 494

Pacificator, 19, 135, 167

Paralel, 20, 146

Passion and Prejudice, 318, 333, 334–7, 348,
363

Peace without Union, 31, 79–80, 92, 122

Plan of the English Commerce, 38, 93, 135,
630

Political History of the Devil, 79, 395, 519,
554, 713, 735, 745, 792, 873

Poor Man's Plea, 93, 133, 599

Present State of the Parties in Great Britain,
Dissent in, 92, 93, 686, 807, 810
English politics in, 104, 143–4, 205, 435,
494, 500, 544
Scottish affairs in, 217, 281, 348, 415,
455, 538, 544, 557, 584, 587, 592,
593–4, 605, 676
Shortest Way recalled in, 15, 20

Protestant Monastery, 117, 856, 857

Quarrel of the School-Boys at Athens, 709,
832

*Queries upon the Bill against Occasional
Conformity*, 121

Queries to the New Hereditary Right-Men,
537

Question Fairly Stated, 83, 812

Reasons against Fighting, 689, 691, 692–3

*Reasons Concerning the Immediate
Demolishing of Dunkirk*, 786–7, 789,
801

Reasons for Im— the L—d H— T—r, 804

*Reasons against the Succession of the House of
Hanover*, 84, 92, 343, 689, 739, 742,
743, 776, 778

*Reasons why this Nation Ought to put a
Speedy End to this Expensive War*, 627,
648, 655, 659–60, 666, 803

Reformation of Manners, 19, 98, 167, 713,
814

*Remarks on the Bill to Prevent Frauds by
Bankrupts*, 167, 190–1

*Remarks on the Letter to the Author of the
State-Memorial*, 52, 80, 118, 193–4,
465

*Reply to a Pamphlet entituled, The L[or]d
H[aversham]'s Vindication of his Speech*,
39, 48, 79, 185, 192, 205, 208, 217

*Reply to the Scot's Answer, to the British
Vision*, 281

Representation Examined, 593

Review,
circulation of, 118, 137, 139, 144, 237, 367
commences, 30
closure of, 752, 754
D's authorship known, liii, 141, 191
D's self-defences in, xii, 98–9, 105, 108,
110, 118–19, 162, 165–6, 201, 210,
212, 243, 444, 463, 502, 662, 675, 682,
696–7, 700–1, 723, 740, 743
economics, trade, finance in, 134, 136,
190, 192–3, 240, 353, 371–2, 380, 388,
505, 516, 571, 572, 607, 610, 618, 626,
679, 685, 751, 754
Edinburgh edition of, xxx, 475, 482,
498, 623
French bias of, 50–1, 56
international affairs treated in, 52–3,
55–6, 81, 83–4, 430, 770, 771
letters printed in, xii, lvi–lvii, lxxxi, 237,
288, 379, 445–7, 448, 454, 487
ministerial paper, 50–1, 144, 201, 204,
429, 435, 470, 473, 495, 497–8, 516,
596, 662, 682, 745
moderation of, lxviii, 144, 494
pamphlets attacked in, 153–4, 194, 212,
671, 743

INDEX

political reportage of, lxvii, lxxi, 40,
110, 130, 140, 173, 449–50, 461–2,
465, 523, 526, 537, 596, 642, 672,
706, 710
produced in court, 746–7, 837
religious affairs handled in, 154–5, 179,
249, 261, 263, 318–19, 357, 396–7,
398, 475–6, 481, 555, 572, 577–9, 580,
586–7, 668–9, 671–2, 686, 689, 702,
714, 736
rival authors of, lvii, 159, 190, 383, 386,
430, 474, 481, 489, 500, 664, 725,
742, 804
Scandalous Club section, lvi, 120–1, 138
theatre denounced in, 237–9
triweekly publication, 240
Union covered in, lxii, 213–14, 216, 217,
226–7, 236, 246, 281, 339–40, 348,
356, 362–3, 440
War covered in, 49, 52, 99, 104, 122,
205–6, 213–14, 435, 563, 659–60,
683, 689, 693–4, 788–9
Robinson Crusoe, lxxxii, 160, 220, 343–4,
487, 599, 775, 846
Roxana, see Fortunate Mistress
Royal Religion, 80
Scotland in Danger, 465
Scot's Narrative Examin'd, 555
Scots Nation and Union Vindicated, 83, 790,
792
Seasonable Caution to the General Assembly,
255, 584, 585
*Seasonable Expostulation with … Duke of
O——d*, 735, 830
*Seasonable Warning and Caution against the
Insinuations of Papists and Jacobites*,
92, 710
*Second Volume of the Writings of the Author of
The True-Born Englishman*, 93, 367
Secret History of the October Club, 38, 179,
233, 343, 395, 429, 500, 531, 544, 546,
576, 596, 599
*Secret History of the October-Club … Part
II*, 93, 98, 122, 178, 487, 534, 575,
596, 605
Secret History of One Year, 630, 821
*Secret History of the Secret History of the
White-Staff*, 151, 817, 821, 828, 846
Secret History of the White-Staff, lxxii, 79,
138, 478, 522, 804, 807, 814, 816,
818, 820
Secret History of the White-Staff, Part II,
144, 468, 544, 814, 817, 818, 821

Secret History of the White-Staff, Part III, 81,
144, 477, 516, 532, 579, 622, 629, 636,
674, 725, 789, 817
*Secret Memoirs of a Treasonable Conference
at S—— House*, 19, 79, 80, 151, 365,
496, 671
Serious Inquiry into this Grand Question, 31
Serious Reflections … of Robinson Crusoe,
lviii, 187, 220, 365, 554, 599, 600, 713,
837, 839
Sharp Rebuke … to Henry Sacheverell, 481,
830
Short Letter to the Glasgow-Men, 292–3,
294–5
*Short View of the Present State of the
Protestant Religion in Britain*, 80,
358–9, 361, 363
Shortest Way with the Dissenters,
D's justifications of, 14, 14–15, 50, 85,
87, 93–4, 475
pardon of D for, 52
Dissenters' attitudes to, lxxxix, 15, 668,
701
financial consequences for D, lx, 37, 38,
39, 149, 205
irony of, 3, 84
pamphlets compared to, 194, 197, 644,
780
prosecution of D for, lxvi, xci, 3–7, 21,
82, 178, 197, 636, 814
Shortest Way to Peace and Union, 15, 178
Sincerity of the Dissenters Vindicated, 107
*Six Distinguishing Characters of a
Parliament-Man*, lxv, 166, 864
*Some Considerations on a Law for Triennial
Parliaments*, 462
*Some Considerations on … Encreasing and
Encouraging the Seamen*, 123
*Some Reflections … Standing Army is
Inconsistent with a Free Government*,
196
*Some Thoughts of an Honest Tory in the
Country*, 151
*Some Thoughts upon the Subject of Commerce
with France*, 343, 353, 358, 671, 754,
760, 765, 769, 770, 804
Spanish Descent, 40
Spectators Address to the Whigs, 596
Storm, lvi, 129, 151
*Succession to the Crown of England,
Consider'd*, 83
Succession of Spain Consider'd, 622, 662
System of Magick, 395, 599

907

INDEX

Defoe, Daniel, works of, (cont.)
  'To the Athenian Society', 804
  To the Honourable the C—s of England Assembled in P—t, 15, 29–30
  Tour thro' the Whole Island of Great Britain, 16, 153, 158, 167, 172, 186, 188, 189, 197, 236, 254, 269, 312, 366, 377, 379, 455, 517, 607, 657, 679, 701
  Trade of Britain Stated, 389
  True-Born Englishman, lxvi, 80, 636
  True Collection of the Writings of the Author of The True Born Englishman, 10, 15, 337, 367
  True State of the Case between the Government and the Creditors of the Navy, 636
  Trumpet Blown in the North ... Duke of Mar, 534, 830
  Two Great Questions Considered ... Sixth Essay at Removing National Prejudices, 319, 329, 330–1, 332, 333, 360
  Union and No Union, 288, 751
  Validity of the Renunciations of Former Powers, 693–4
  View of the Real Dangers of the Succession, 751
  Vision, xii, 244, 247, 257, 266, 281, 873
  Voice from the South, 371
  Weakest Go to the Wall, 178, 671, 807–8, 810
  What if the Pretender should come?, 671, 739, 776
  Wise as Serpents, 686, 689
  Word Against a New Election, 481, 537
  Ye True-Born Englishmen Proceed, 167
Defoe, Daniel, Jr, 7, 34, 735, 849, 865, 876, 878, 881
Defoe, Hannah, 7, 856, 857, 873, 878
Defoe, Henrietta, 7, 873, 878
Defoe, Maria, 7
Defoe, Martha, 25, 39, 427
Defoe, Mary, xlix, 3, 5, 7, 22, 25, 39, 158, 165, 270, 276, 380, 488, 501, 595, 606, 638, 640, 642, 876–7, 881, 878
Defoe, Sophia, lxxix, lxxxvi, xciii, 7, 854–64, 867–9, *871–3*, 876–81
Delafaye, Charles, l, lvii, lx, lxxii, lxxxii–lxxxvi, lxxxix, xciii, *831–53*
Deloraine, Henry Scott, first Earl of, 304, 305
Denham, Capt., 605
Desbordes, John, 10
Despenser, Hugh, elder, 57
Despenser, Hugh, younger, 57
De Witt, Cornelis, 232

De Witt, Johan, 229, 232–3, 316, 477
Dissenters, li, lxx, lxxxviii–lxxxix, 68, 70–1, 85–92, 145, 156, 174, 178, 194, 197, 212, 331–2, 360–2, 475–6, 483, 517–18, 556, 667–71, 673–4, 676, 686–9, 708, 710, 728, 737, 773–5, 780–4, 807–12, 825
Dissenting Academies, liv, 197–8, 218, 810
Diston, Josiah, 173
Dix, Thomas, 195–6, 198
Dixon, Sir Robert, 386
Dodson, Thomas, 187
Done, Samuel, 188, 195
Dongworth, Richard, 540, 545
Doolittle, Thomas, *A Complete Body of Practical Divinity*, 199
Dormer, George, 827, 834, 838
  Dormer's *News-letter*, 835, 838
Douglas, Archibald Douglas, first Duke of, 532
Douglas, Hon. George, 532
Dowdeswell, Richard, 173
Dowley, Peter, 184, 189, 195, 199
Downie, J. A., 38, 450, 529, 531, 687
Drake, James,
  Memorial of the Church of England, lxxxiv, 145–6, 149–55, 193–4, 220, 464–5
  Mercurius Politicus, 153
Drake, Sir William, 181, 186
Dreer, Ferdinand Julius, 29
Drewry or Drury, Samuel, 217, 218
Duckett, George, 183, 187, 195, 204, 477
Dumbarton, George Douglas, first Earl of, 285, 288
Dunbar, Sir James, 532
Dunbar, Robert Constable, third Viscount, 532
Duncan, John, 527–8
Dunch, Thomas, 130–2, 140
Dundass, Thomas, 527–8
Dundass, William, 527–8
Dundass of Arniston, James, 643–4, 646
  The Faculty of Advocats Loyalty, 644
Dunkirk, *see under* War of the Spanish Succession
Dunlop, William, 520
Dunton, John, lii, lvi, 7, 153, 199, 804, 825
  Dunton's Whipping-Post, 804
  Impeachment, 804
  Neck or Nothing, 800, 804
  Shortest-Way with Whores and Rogues, 10
Dupplin, George Henry Hay, Viscount, *see* Kinnoull, Thomas Hay, seventh Earl of

908

INDEX

Dupplin, Thomas Hay, Viscount, 529, 532, 533, 534, 535, 652

Dyer, John, lvii, lxxxi, xcii, 119, 430, *489–91*, 834

Dyer's News-Letter, 109–10, 119–20, 149, 154, 186, 232, 236, 384, 385, 386, 430–1, 489–91, 497–8, 826–7, 834, 838

Dysart, Lionel Tollemache, third Earl of, 161

East India Company, 149, 439–40

Eborall, Samuel, 477, 481

Edgcumbe, Richard, 187

Edinburgh,
    Faculty of Advocates, 324, 642, 644, 647, 649
    University of, 483, 501, 519, 640, 641, 728

Edinburgh Courant, 459, 462, 482

Edinburgh Gazette, 384, 386, 530, 533, 561

Edward II, King of England, 79

Edward VI, King of England, 79

Edwards, Jonathan, 161

Eglinton, Alexander Montgomerie, ninth Earl of, 468, 540, 652

Elisha, Samuel, l, lxxxii, xci, *94–6*, 106, *107–8*, 195

Elizabeth I, Queen of England, 79, 80, 86, 92–3

Elliott, William, 402, 404

Ellis, Frank H., 516

Elwes, Sir Gervase, 189

Elwill, Sir John, 186

Ellys, John, 189

Emperor, Mr, 191

Equivalent, 245, 247, 248, 250, 251, 264, 266, 273–4, 280, 293, 295–6, 300, 309, 353–4, 387–8, 398–401, 403, 404–8, 436–9, 529, 532, 576

Erle, Lt.-Gen. Thomas, 156, 159, 181

Errol, Charles Hay, thirteenth Earl of, 326–7, 529, 533

Erskine of Carnock, Lt.-Col. John, 269

Erskine of the Sand Haven, Lt.-Col. John, 269

Eveleigh, Josiah, lxxx, 157, 160, 167, 194, 198

Eyles, Francis, 158

Faculty of Advocates, *see* Advocates, Edinburgh Faculty of

Fancourt, Nathaniel, 713

Fane, Col., 824

Farren, Abraham, 188

Fearne, David, 483

Fearns, D., 369

Felton, Sir Thomas, 100, 105

Fenn, Capt., 196

Fenner, Mr, 196, 200

Fenner, John, 160–1, 163, 194

Ferguson, William, 370

Finch, Lord, Daniel, 671

Finch, Heneage, 10

Finch, Robert, 680, 682

Finlay, George, 282, 285, 287, 288, 289, 290–1, 293, 301, 305, 313

Fisher, Peter, 157, 159

Fitzer, John, 195, 198

Fitzer, Thomas, 198

Fitzmaurice, Susan M., lxxiv, 136

Fleming, Robert, 25

Fletcher of Saltoun, Andrew, 244, 246, 267, 270, 288
    Discourse Concerning Militia's and Standing Armies, 246
    State of the Controversy betwixt United and Separate Parliaments, 246

Fletcher, James, 189

Flint, Mrs, 638–9

Flint, David, 639

Flint, George, 837

Flint, John, 639, 659, 663, 715–16, 717

Flying Post, 471, 474, 644, 690, 691, 725–6, 729–32, 740, 742, 746, 754, 794, 801, 805–7, 821–4, 838, 843

Flying Post and Medley, 821–4, 827, 837

Foe, Elisabeth, 7

Foe, James, 7, 309

Fogg, Paul, 846

Foley, Thomas, 794

Forbes, James, 171, 173

Forbes, William Forbes, thirteenth Earl of, 467–9

Forfar, Archibald Douglas, first Earl of, 468, 530, 533

Forster, Eliza, 859

Forster, John (Enfield attorney), 860–1, 872

Forster, John (politician), 398

Forster, John (Victorian critic), lxxxii, 857, 859, 874

Fox, Charles, 159

Fox, Joseph, 101, 104, 105, 109

Fox with his Fire-brand Unkennell'd, 21

Foxe, John, *Acts and Monuments*, 137–8

Franco-Dutch War, 49

Franklin, Benjamin, *Autobiography*, 828, 873

Fransham, Isaac, 119–20

909

INDEX

Fransham, John, xlix, l, lxi, lxii, lxxxv, xci, 105, *109–10, 118–22, 130–2, 137–40, 190–2*, 196, *207–9, 315–19, 430–1*, 735
Criterion, 109
Dialogue between Jack High and Will Low, 109
Exact Account ... Supporting the Poor in ... Norwich, 109
Fraser, Charles, fourth Lord, 530
Freebairn, Robert, 623–5, 653–5
Freke, Thomas, 156, 159, 186
Freman, Ralph, 97–8
Fremantle, Lt.-Col. F. D. E., 445
French Pedlar, 725
French Prophets, 828–30
Fullerton, Thomas, 530, 533
Furbank, P. N. and W. R. Owens, xxx, lviii, lxiv, lxxxvii, 121, 173, 254, 340, 345, 449, 465, 469, 483, 516, 559, 644, 807, 821–2, 823, 831, 837, 838, 847

Gale, Elisha, 195, 198
Gale, John, 198
Galway, Henri de Massue, Earl of, 49
Gaveston, Piers, 57, 79
Gay, Matthew, 194, 197
Gazette a la Main, 471
Gellibrand, John, 151
Gentleman's Journal, 109
George I, King of England, lxxii, lxxxv, lxxxviii, 534, 739, 742, 789–90, 796–7, 815, 818, 821, 824, 825–7, 839, 845
George II, King of England, 789–90
George of Denmark, Prince, 49, 81, 122–3, 128, 348, 392, 469
George of Hesse, Prince, 49
Gery, Thomas, 159
Ghiselyn, John, 39
Gibbons, Mr, 195, 199
Gibbs, Mr, 191
Gill, Abraham, 137–8, 199
Glasgow, David Boyle, first Earl of, 346, 349, 374, 444, 460, 469, 530, 532, 533, 543, 545, 551
Glasgow, University of, 519
Glencairn, William Cunningham, twelfth Earl of, 468
Glencoe Massacre, 81–2
Glenorchy, John Campbell, Lord, 562
Godfrey, Peter, 762
Godolphin, Francis, 160, 531, 535

Godolphin, Sidney, first Earl of,
D, correspondence with, lvii, lxxxv, xci, xcii, 39, *351–3*, 394, 432, *443–5, 458–74*
D employed by, lxxiii, lxxvii, lxxxiv, 22–5, 34, 50–1, 213, 277, 315, 321, 387, 392, 395, 408, 413, 416, 423, 432, 436, 443, 462, 500, 701, 745, 825
D's relationship with, lxviii, 470, 533
D's *Shortest Way* prosecuted by, 3, 16–17
dismissal of, lxix, 492, 497, 498–500, 502, 505, 522, 530, 534, 535, 565, 795
election management in 1705, 157, 179, 187, 188
election management in 1708, lxix, 445, 449, 454, 458–74
Harley, ouster of, lxviii, 433–6
impeachment threatened against, 541–2
receives D's letters to Harley, l, lxii, xci, 264, 306, 310–12, 321, 394–5, 396, 415
Scottish management of, 213, 246, 274, 293, 349, 351–3, 372, 374, 383, 387, 391, 402, 404, 407, 422, 437, 449, 516, 528
Tory alliance of his ministry, 29, 33, 111–16, 117
Treasury, management of, 149, 498, 505, 577, 579
Whig alliance of his ministry, lxvi, lxxi, 133, 149, 156, 344–5, 391–2, 394, 484, 526, 552, 672, 711, 716, 789, 803
Goldsmith, Alexander, *see under* Defoe, Daniel, life of
Goodale, Hanna, 482–3, 487, 522, 638, 641–2, 658
Goodale, John, 482–3, 487, 488
Gordon, Elizabeth, Duchess of, 324, 642
Gordon, George Gordon, first Duke of, 322, 324, 530, 533, 605
Gordon, John, 605
Gordon, William, 462
Goulston, Richard, 200
Grange, James Erskine, Lord, 533
Grantham, John, 745
Granville, John, 182, 187
Gratz, Simon, 852
Gray, Lady Jane, 739
Great Northern War,
Danish siege of Tönning, 54, 77, 84
Narva, Battle and Siege of, 78, 84
renewal of fighting, 660
Swedish invasion of Poland, 52, 54, 55–6, 74, 77–8, 84
Travendal, Treaty of, 55, 84

910

INDEX

Green, Capt. Thomas, 440
Greenshields, James, 555–7, 563–5, 566, 568, 580, 584, 585, 675
Greg, William, 82, 433–5, 644
Grierson, James, 717, 719
Guardian, see under Steele, Sir Richard
Guilot, Claude, *see under* Defoe, Daniel, life of
Guiscard, Antoine, Marquis de, lxi, 596–600, 701, 749, 780
Guise Revolt, 791–2
Gustavus Adolphus, King of Sweden, 59, 80
Gwyn, Francis, 157, 159, 164, 167, 181, 186

Haddington, Thomas Hamilton, sixth Earl of, 280–1, 530
Haddo, William Gordon, Lord, 652
Hales, Sir Christopher, 159
Hales, Capt. Thomas, 824
Halifax, Charles Montagu, Baron, lxxiv, lxxxii, lxxxiii–lxxxiv, xci, *133–6, 141–4, 154–5,* 189, 253–4, 255, 265, 289, 394, 449, 500, 522, 530, 533, 794
Hall, Peter, 188
Hamilton, Mrs, 497, 501, 638, 642
Hamilton, Anne Douglas, Duchess Dowager of, 285, 305, 308, 383
Hamilton, David, 20, 674
Hamilton, Henry, 571
Hamilton, James Douglas, fourth Duke of, election in 1708, 408, 449, 458, 464, 469
election in 1710, 528, 530, 533, 534, 535, 540, 546
Tory ministry, career under, 612, 695, 716
Union, opposition to, 226, 228, 232, 241, 244, 246, 259, 262, 267, 270, 285, 288, 304, 306, 316, 319, 321, 322, 327, 383, 388–9
William III, career under, 448
Hampden, Richard, 788–9
Hanbury, John, 173
Hanmer, Sir Thomas, 775, 789
Harcourt, Simon, first Viscount, 383, 434, 436, 759, 814, 817, 820
Harding, William, 162, 166
Harpur, John, 188
Harley, Edward ('Auditor'), 32, 35, 183, 188, 435
Harley, Edward, Lord (second Earl), 757, 813–14
Harley, Sir Edward, 788

Harley, Robert,
Anne, relationship with, l, 68, 112, 343, 344–5, 492, 494, 498, 502–3, 807, 814, 815, 825
assassination attempt against, 596–600, 617, 700–1
Bolingbroke, partnership with, 54–5, 343, 434, 436, 672, 785, 804, 814
Bolingbroke, rivalry with, 599, 751–2, 754–5, 759, 807, 813, 814, 815, 825
correspondence with D, xlix, l–li, lxi–lxii, lxviii, lxx–lxxiii, lxxv–lxxx, lxxxi, lxxxiii, lxxxv–xcii, *26–8, 29–94, 95–106, 111–18, 141–54, 156–67, 170–2, 180–90, 193–206, 210–37, 240–315, 319–33, 337–50, 353–7, 359–65, 368–429, 432–9, 492–6, 498–501, 502–22, 523–57, 560–86, 596–600, 603–7, 609–10, 612–37, 645–57, 659–62, 664–716, 719–27, 729–75, 778–827*
Chancellor of the Exchequer, 498–9
D, recruitment and employment of, lxvi–lxvii, lxix, 11, 13, 22–4, 29, 33, 50–1, 133, 210, 213–14, 387, 462, 492, 696–7, 701
Dissenters, relationship with, 29, 68, 70–1, 85–94, 198, 669, 807
daughter's death, 779–80
fall in 1708, lxviii, 223, 433–6, 500, 701
fall in 1714, 813–14, 815
illnesses, 342–3, 345, 351, 642, 662, 715–16, 720, 757, 779
impeachment of, 709, 826, 827, 837
peerage, elevation to, lxxviii, 600
political ideas of, lxvi, lxix
Scottish management of, 257, 274, 372, 529, 531–6, 537–8, 540, 544, 551, 557, 565, 571, 572, 580, 604, 605, 612, 617, 643, 645, 649, 652, 685, 694, 714, 736
Secretary of State, lxvii, 30–1, 50–1, 53, 56–84, 111, 113–14, 194, 344–5, 375, 391–2, 394–5, 429, 433, 474, 500, 672
Speaker, 3, 22, 30, 82, 112–13
Treasurer and premier minister, 600, 602, 618, 627, 636, 644, 659, 763, 755, 790, 805, 816–18
William III, career under, lxvi, 68, 82, 112, 116–17
Harris, James, 157
Hart, James, 715, 718

INDEX

Haversham, John Thompson, first Baron, 192, 193, 348, 428, 429, 448, 530, 533, 672
Hay, John, 527–8
Hay of Craignethan, Andrew, 314–15
Hayton, D. W., 242, 824
Healey, G. H., xii, lix, xc, 28, 35, 55, 105, 106, 121, 138, 153, 348, 445, 455, 531, 629, 687, 861, 867, 869
Hearne, Thomas, 153, 154, 237, 431
Heathcote, Sir Gilbert, 525, 526
Hebronites, *see under* Covenanters
Hedges, Sir Charles, xci, 14, 22, 30, 81, 99, 105, 110, 161–2, 166, 183, 187, 344
Heinsius, Antonius, 51, 84, 104
Henley, John, 386–7
Henri III, King of France, 791–2
Henri IV, King of France, 791–2
Henry VIII, King of England, 58, 79–80
Henry, Matthew, 119
Hepburn, John, lxiv, 258, 260, 309, 310–12, 313, 315
Herdman, Mr, 718
Hermitage, René Sauniere de L', 51, 695
Herne, Frederick, 181, 186
Herne, Nathaniel, 181, 186
Hervey, John, 189
Heysham, Robert, 762
Hicks, John, 159
Hincks, Edward, 195, 198
Historical Manuscripts Commission, lxxxv–lxxxvi
Hoare, Sir Richard, 762
Hoblyn, John, 187
Hoblyn, Robert, 159
Hodges, James, 405
  Rights and Interests of the Two British Monarchies, 241, 243, 266, 316
Hog, James, *The Covenants of Redemption and Grace Displayed*, 360, 363
Holmes, Geoffrey, 93, 435, 535
Holt, Sir John, xci, 109–10, 235, 236
Home, Alexander, seventh Earl of, 529, 532, 540, 543
Homer, *Odyssey*, 83
Hone, William, 874
Honour and Prerogative of the Queen's Majesty Vindicated, 789
Hooke, Nathaniel, 396, 399
Hooper, Nicholas, 187
Hopetoun, Charles Hope, first Earl of, 359, 530
Hopkins, Edward, 159
Houblon, James, 408
Houblon, Richard, 187

Howe, John, 25
Howe, W. T. H., 243
Hue and Cry after Daniel Foe, xii, 444
Humorist, 838
Hungarian (Rákóczi's) War of Independence, lxviii, 65, 73–7, 81, 83–4
Hungerford, John, 794
Huntley, Alexander Gordon, Marquess of Huntley, 530, 533
Hurt, Christopher, 41, 48, 103, 145–6, 166
Hurt, William, 724, 725–6, 743, 806, 821–5, 827
Hutchins, Henry C., xc, 441
Hutchinson, William, 527
Hyde, Henry, Lord, 187
Hyland, Paul, 821, 823
Hyndford, James Carmichael, second Earl of, xcii, 543, 545, 546, 574, 576, 604, 608–9, 611, 658–9, 702
Hyndford, John Carmichael, first Earl of, 546

Ibbetson, James, 195, 199
Ireton, Henry, 187
Isaacson, James, 386, 390
Islay, Archibald Campbell, first Earl of, 349, 469, 530, 534, 540–3, 551, 612

Jackson, Mr, 840
Jacobites, li, lxix, lxxxiii, 43, 176, 226, 244, 281, 313, 315, 316–17, 319, 347, 396–8, 403, 406, 410, 431, 450, 453, 465, 522–4, 540–4, 552, 596, 610, 646–7, 650, 675, 681, 711–12, 727, 736, 742, 752, 778, 797, 803, 817, 825, 836, 846
  invasion attempt in 1708, 397, 445, 449, 451, 454–5, 473, 533, 536, 677–8
  uprising in 1715, 379, 462, 623
James I, King of England, 79, 588, 593
James II, King of England, lxv, 16, 83, 86, 93, 94, 97, 297, 363, 445, 446, 448, 532, 688–9
James V, King of Scotland, 593
James, Stephen, 194, 197
Janeway, Richard, 739, 742, 783
Jardin, James, 199
Jardine, Richard, 195, 199
Jellard, Nicholas, 196, 200
Jersey, Edward Villiers, first Earl of, 530, 533
João V, King of Portugal, 770
Job, Elizabeth, xcii–xciii
Johnson, Mr, 196, 200
Johnson, Thomas, 188, 395

912

INDEX

Johnston, Sir Patrick, lxiii, 228–9, 232, 316, 568–9, 571

Johnstone, James, 288, 349

Joseph I, Holy Roman Emperor, 622

Joy, Fred W., 602

Judas Discuver'd, and Catch'd at Last, lii, 740

keelmen (Newcastle upon Tyne), 607, 678–80, 682

Keimer, Samuel, lxi, lxxxi, xciii, *828–30*, 873
Brand Pluck'd from the Burning, 828–30

Keirn, Tim, 571–2

Keith, George, 604–5

Keith, John, 604–5

Kelly, James, 441

Kent, Henry Grey, Duke of, 492, 494, 530

Kent, Walter, 186

Kentish Petition, 7, 16, 19

Ker, Lt.-Gen. William, 304

Ker of Kersland, John, 284

Killicrankie, Battle of, 448

Killingbeck, John, 487

Kilsyth, William Livingston, third Viscount, 540, 543, 546

Kimberley, Jonathan, 174, 178, 220

Kincardine, Alexander Bruce, fourth Earl of, 256

Kinderley, Nathaniel, 195, 199

King, Mr, 840

King, Sir Peter, 478

King, William, Archbishop of Dublin, 435

King, William, *Vindication of the Reverend Henry Sacheverell*, 481

Kinnoull, Thomas Hay, seventh Earl of, 346, 349, 530, 533, 534, 538, 540

Kirkcudbright, James Maclellan, sixth Lord, 530

Knight, Charles, 789, 802

Knox, John, 594

Kynaston, John, 188

Lamb, Henry, 180, 186

Lambe, Aaron, 875

Lane, Thomas, 24

Lawes and Acts of Parliament made by … Kings of Scotland, 592

Leeds, Lady Elizabeth Osborne, Duchess of, 779

Leeds, Thomas Osborne, first Duke of, 530, 534, 779

Lee, William, lxxxiii–lxxxiv, 857

Leicester, Robert Dudley, first Earl of, 57

Leijoncrona, Christoffer, 430, 491

Leith dockyards, 505–7, 513–17, 569, 571

L'Epine, Francesca Margherita de, 535

Leslie, Charles, 20, 153, 154, 220, 481, 500
History of the Church, 219–20
Rehearsal, 19, 153, 194, 197, 260, 430–1

L'Estrange, Roger, 209

Letter Concerning the Consequences of an Incorporating Union, 270

Letter to a Member of Parliament, 354

Leven, David Leslie, third Earl of, 245, 247, 260, 313, 315, 326–7, 349, 378–9, 408, 422, 443–4, 469, 530, 534, 543, 545, 551, 595, 605, 608–9, 611, 638, 640, 644, 655, 659, 667, 695

Lewis, Erasmus, 242, 246, 516, 731, 755, 757, 785

Lewis, Henry, 730–1

Linning, John, 262, 263

Locke, John, liii

Lockhart, George, 314, 327, 530, 534, 557
Memoirs of the Union, lxxxii, 246–7, 254, 255, 259–60, 288, 315, 401

Logan, John, *A Sermon Preached before … the Honourable Estates of Parliament*, 236

London Gazette, 3–4, 10, 49, 119–20, 172, 210, 649, 820, 831, 838

London Post, 140

London Review, lxxxii–lxxxiii, lxxxix, 845

Lothian, Lt.-Gen. William Kerr, second Marquess of, 346, 349, 469, 530, 534, 573

Loudon, Hugh Campbell, third Earl of, 346, 349, 403, 408, 469, 530, 534, 540, 574, 576

Louis XIII, King of France, 78, 79

Louis XIV, King of France, li, 48, 49, 79, 396, 529, 596, 622, 623, 664–5, 739, 743

Love, Daniel, 185, 189

Lowndes, William, 26, 387, 617

Luttrell, Narcissus, 98, 104, 237, 348, 386, 431

Lützen, Battle of, 80

Lyon, Lord, Sir Alexander Areskine of Cambo, 533, 677, 678

Lyttleton, Elizabeth, 599

Mackworth, Sir Humphrey, 118, 121–2, 153, 161, 186

Macky, John, 576

Macmillan of Balmaghie, John, 702–4, 705

Magellan, Ferdinand, 637

Maitland, Lt.-Gen. James, 530, 534, 553, 569, 656, 657

913

INDEX

Malplaquet, Battle of, *see under* War of the
Spanish Succession
Manley, Delarivier, 600
Mansel, Sir Thomas, 434, 436, 498
Mar, John Erskine, twenty-third Earl of, 226,
232, 246, 250, 264, 265, 270, 274, 281,
284, 290, 293, 346, 349, 369, 374, 403,
408, 415, 444, 469, 530, 533, 534, 536,
538, 540–3, 560, 562, 565, 576, 605,
612, 640, 643–4, 695, 793
Marana, Giovanni Paolo, *L'Espion Turc*, 82
Marchmont, Patrick Hume, first Earl of, 293,
530, 576
Marescoe, Peter, 39
Marischal, William Keith, ninth Earl, 326,
327, 530, 534, 540, 543, 546, 694–5
Marlborough, John Churchill, first Duke of,
D's writings on, lxx–lxxi, 141–2, 530,
673–4, 742, 803
diplomat, 116–17, 431
military commander, 52, 56, 81, 83,
119–20, 153, 193, 196, 206, 464,
470–1, 473–4, 534, 535
political alliances of, 111, 117, 146, 345,
372, 392, 394, 429, 433–4, 435, 458,
466, 469, 484, 492, 494, 531, 534,
541–2, 711, 716
removal from command of, 142, 534, 672–4
Whig and Tory views of, 193, 798, 802–3
Marlborough, Sarah Churchill, Duchess of,
141–4, 146, 155, 394, 516, 644
Martin, Henry, 205, 732
Mary I, Queen of England, 86, 92
Mary II, Queen of England, 93, 281
Mary of Modena, 839
Masham, Abigail, 779, 814, 817, 820
Mason, George, xci
Mather, Cotton, xcii
Mathews, Michael, 195, 199
Matthews, John, 140, 235, 237, 483
Maurice, Prince, 60, 80
Maximilian II Emanuel, Elector of Bavaria, 81
Maynwaring, Arthur, lxx, 36, 500, 534
Medley, lxx, 695, 700
Queries, 507, 516
Mazarin, Cardinal, 57, 79, 82
M'Cala, Robert, 386
McClellan, Sir Samuel, 229, 232
Mead, William, 196, 200
Medici, Marie de, 79
Melmoth, William, lxxxi, *237–9*
*Great Importance of a Religious Life
Consider'd*, 239

Melville, Andrew, 594
Melville, George Melville, first Earl of, 378,
379
Melville, Lady Margaret, 379
Memorial of the Church of England, see under
Drake, James
Merchant A-la-Mode, 725
Mercure Gallant, 471
Merivale, Herman, lxxxv
Meriwether, Richard, 180, 185
Messina revolt, 45, 49
Mesnager, Nicolas, 496, 531, 579, 666, 803
Methuen Treaty, 765, 769
Miller, Thomas, 543
Miller, William, 715, 716
Milton, John, 65, 81
Paradise Lost, 711, 713
Mist, Nathaniel, lxxxiv–lxxxv
Weekly Journal: or, Saturday's Post, 745, 831,
835, 838, 839–40, 843–8, 850–2
M'Kneilly or MacNeil, John, 703, 704
Minto, Sir Gilbert Elliot, Lord, 529, 533
Minto, William, lxxxv
Moll, Herman, 627, 630
Monckton, Robert, 377
Monmouth, James Scott, first Duke of, lxiv,
10, 69, 83, 188, 197, 305, 546
Monroe, David, lxxx, 550
Montagu, Edward Wortley, 189
Montagu, George, 189
Montagu, Sir James, 383, 478
Montagu, Capt. Montagu, 874
Montgomery, Andrew, 282, 287–90, 293, 301
Montmorency, Henri, Duke of, 80
Montrose, James Graham, fourth Marquess
of, 272, 274, 346, 469, 530, 534, 643,
644
Moody, Mr, 559
Moore, Arthur, 754, 758, 759, 809, 822, 823
Moore, John Robert, xc, 39, 607, 629, 859, 878
Mordaunt, John, Lord, 171, 172
Morison of Prestongrange, William, 459, 462
Morley, John, 104, 106, 195
Morphew, John, 783, 793, 840–1
Morris, Nicholas, 21
Morrison, Alfred, 243, 602
Morton, Charles, liv–lv, 810
Moule, H. J., 160
Moyle, Joseph, 187
Murray, Lt.-Col. John, 422
Murray, Maurice, 422
Murray of Abercairney, Capt. Robert, 421, 422
Murray of Ochtertyre, Sir Patrick, 652

914

INDEX

Murray of Stanhope, Alexander, 652
Mytton, Richard, 188

Nairne, Sir David, 232, 250, 265, 281, 469
Napier, Sir Nathaniel, 156, 159
Narbrough, John, *An Account of Several Late Voyages & Discoveries*, 627
Narva, Battle and Siege of, *see under* Great Northern War
National Covenant, *see under* Covenanters
Nelson, John, 239
Newcastle, John Holles, first Duke of, 104, 117, 153, 188, 500, 526, 530, 534, 601–2
New-castle Gazette, 558, 560
Newland, Sir George, 762
Newte, John, 159
Newton, Sir Isaac, 720–1
Nine Years' War, 133, 208, 288, 691
    Boyne, Battle of the, 636
    Ryswick, Treaty of, 48, 636
Nokes, William, 196, 199
Norman, Lionel, 386, 530, 535
Norris, Richard, 188
Northesk, David Carnegie, fourth Earl of, 469, 530, 534, 540, 652
Northey, Sir Edward, 743, 759, 776, 778, 824
Norton, Mary, 861
Nottingham, Daniel Finch, second Earl of,
    D's correspondence with, lviii–lix, lxxv, xci, **3–10**
    D's published attacks on, 17, 20, 48, 484, 530, 535, 671, 762
    prosecution of *Shortest Way*, 3–10, 10–12, 15–21, 23, 29, 39, 82, 141, 631, 636
    resignation as Secretary, 20, 30, 85, 93, 111, 187
    supports anti-Dissent legislation, 20, 348, 667–8
Nottingham, Heneage Finch, first Earl of, 10
Novak, Maximillian E., lix, 35, 39, 162, 345, 738, 754, 838, 845, 848
Nowell, Baruch, 194, 197
Nutt, John, 129

Oasland or Osland, Edward, 195, 198
Oaths,
    Abjuration, 250, 297, 299, 311, 325, 328, 331, 333, 338, 342, 444–5, 452–3, 455, 529, 564–5, 580, 675–6, 703–4, 714–15, 716, 718, 736–8, 809–10
    Allegiance, xvii, 297, 298–9, 477, 511, 564–5, 580

Coronation, 160, 250, 257, 297–8
Observations Made in England, on the Trial of Captain Green, 441
Observations Upon the State of the Nation, 671
Observator,
    by Ridpath, 664–6
    by Tutchin, 3, 7, 10, 50, 119, 356
Occasional conformity, lxx, lxxxix, 16, 25, 82, 94, 107, 173
    Acts against, *see under* Acts and Bills of Parliament
Ogilvie, John (Gassion), 422, 429
Oldfield, Joshua, 517–18, 519–20, 525, 530, 539, 553–4, 568, 783, 820
    Israel and Judah made One Kingdom, 519
Oldmixon, John, lii, lxv, 21, 358, 500, 662, 825
    False Steps of the Ministry after the Revolution, 821
    History of England, 197, 198, 742, 754
    Remarks on a Scandalous Libel, 759
Orford, Edward Russell, first Earl of, 522, 530, 535
Original London Post, or Heathcote's Intelligence, 487
Orkney, George Hamilton, first Earl of, 262, 288, 458, 463–5, 469, 471, 474, 530, 535, 540, 656, 657, 673
Orléans, Gaston, Duke of, 80
Ormond, James Butler, second Duke of, lxxi, 435, 689, 799, 803
Osselton, N. E., lxxiv
Oudenarde, Battle of, *see under* War of the Spanish Succession
Oughton, Lt.-Col. Adolphus, 477
Ovalle, Alonso de, *Historical Relation of the Kingdom of Chile*, 626
Overkirk, Henry, Count of Nassau, Lord, 59, 80
Owen, Charles, 195, 198
Owen, Edward, l, 39, *173–9*, 198
Owen, Edward, Jr, 178
Owen, James, 106–7, 198
    Moderation a Virtue, 107
Owens, W. R., *see* Furbank, P. N. and W. R. Owens
Oxford, Robert Harley, first Earl of, *see* Harley, Robert
Oxford, University of, 87, 354, 448
Oxfuird, David Makgill, third Viscount of, 530, 535

Pacy, Capt. John, 196, 199–200
Pacy, Samuel, 199

INDEX

Paget, Henry, 498

Pakington, Sir John, 118, 161

Paper concerning Daniel DeFoe, lii

Paris Gazette, 471–2, 474

Parker, Mr, 282

Parker, Henry, 195, 198

Parker, Hugh, 188

Parker, Sir Thomas, lvii–lviii, 188, 478, 739, 741, 743, 746, 783, 834, 837

Partition Treaties, 17, 20, 133, 636, 664–5

Paterson, Sir Hugh, 652

Paterson, William, xviii, lxxviii, *10–15*, 22, 233, 242, 246, 272–4, 276–7, 293, 306, 365, 377, 626, 629

   Inquiry into the Reasonableness and Consequences of an Union with Scotland, 274

Pedley, John, 189

Pedro II, King of Portugal, 45, 49

Peirce, John, lxiv, xcii, 283, 284, 301, 308, 310, 313, 356

Pembroke, Thomas Herbert, eighth Earl of, 530, 535

Penn, William, lxxxvi, xc–xci, *15–21*, 28–9, 197

Penn, William, Jr, lxxxvi, 17, 28–9

Peter I, King of Russia, 770–1

Peterborough, Charles Mordaunt, third Earl of, 178, 530, 535, 793

Peterson, Spiro, 859

Philip V, King of Spain, 422, 567, 619–20, 622, 659–60, 662, 664–5, 668, 672, 694, 803

Philiphaugh, Sir James Murray, Lord, 259, 291

Phipps, Sir Constantine, 824

Pierrepont, William, 188

Piper, Count, 431

Plaxton, George, 484, 487

Poley, Henry, 150–1

Pollexfen, Nicholas, 186

Polwarth, Lord, *see* Cessnock, Sir Alexander Hume-Campbell, Lord

Pope, Alexander, lxiii

Popham, Alexander, 172, 187

Porter, Aubrey, 189

Porterfield, John, 305

Portland, William Bentinck, first Earl of, 158, 631, 636

Portman, Henry, 181, 186

Portman, Sir William, 186

Post Boy, 151, 471, 474, 559, 742, 743, 786, 824, 830, 839

Poulett, John Poulett, first Earl, 159, 498

Powell, Thomas (D's associate), 21

Powell, Thomas (politician), 186

Pretender, *see* Stuart, James Francis Edward

Price, Jacob M., 395

Price, Robert, 161, 163, 166

Priestley, Nathaniel, 195, 199

Pringle of Haining, John, 617

Psalmanazar, George, 218

Quadruple Alliance, War of the, 847

Queensberry, James Douglas, second Duke of, 226, 230, 233, 246, 252, 255, 260, 261, 263, 293, 304, 312, 315, 337, 340, 346, 354–5, *366–8*, 369, 373, 386, 392, 408, 454, 458, 462, 469, 528, 530, 532–6, 546, 551, 576, 584, 612, 615, 617, 625, 644, 645, 714, 716

Queries, 507, 516

Radcliffe, Sir Ralph, 98

Rákóczi, Ferenc, 75–6, 81, 84

Raleigh, Sir Walter, *History of the World*, 138

Ramillies, Battle of, *see under* War of the Spanish Succession

Rastrick, John, 708–9

Read, Michael, 225–6, 690–1

Read's Weekly Journal, 838, 846, 848, 852

Rebow, Sir Isaac, 189–90, 200

Reformation, 79–80, 93, 246, 263, 363, 587–9, 592–3, 808

Relfe, John, 123, *128–9*

Restoration, 93, 334, 415, 685

Review and Observator Reviewed, lii, 190

Revolution of 1688, lxv, lxxvi, lxix, 82, 93, 98, 236, 249, 281, 330, 447–8, 475–8, 484, 496, 498, 535, 537, 553, 554, 586, 590, 593, 636, 644, 647, 654, 686, 688–9, 704, 809, 811

Reynardson, Jacob, 408

Rich, Sir William, 186

Richardson, Capt., 229, 232

Richelieu, 57, 61–2, 67, 78–82, 113, 362–3

Richetti, John, lx

Ridpath, George, 474, 644, 664, 691, 723, 725–6, 729, 732, 742–3, 746, 780, 821–3

   see also Flying Post

Rigby, Sir Alexander, 386–7, 390–1, 531

Riley, P. W. J., 231, 612

Riseborough, John, 132

Robartes, Russell, 187

Robethon, Jean de, 742

Robertson, Anne, 377

Robinson, John, 84

916

INDEX

Rochester, John Wilmot, second Earl of, 148–9

Rochester, Laurence Hyde, first Earl of, 93, 531, 532, 535, 562

Rogers, Gabriel, 94–5, *106–7*, 108, 200

Rogers, John, 196, 200

Rogers, Pat, 188, 194, 197–200, 849

Roland Laporte, 49

Rolle, James, 186

Rolle, Col. John, 181, 186

Rolle, Robert, 186

Rolle, Samuel, 187

Rooke, Sir George, lvii, lxvii, lxxxvii, 16, 40–50, 55, 66, 81, 98–102, 104–5

Roper, Abel, 150, 151, 474

Roscoe, E. L., lxxxvii

Rosebery, Archibald Primrose, first Earl of, 349, 469, 531, 535, 540

Rosenbloom, Arthur M., 455

Rosewell, Samuel, 315, 318

Ross, Lt.-Gen. Charles, 459, 462

Ross, Walter, lxxx, 550

Ross, William Ross, twelfth Lord, 346, 349

Rothes, John Hamilton-Leslie, ninth Earl of, 346, 349, 469, 531

Roxburghe, John Ker, fifth Earl of, 246, 304, 305, 344, 346, 449, 468–9, 531

Royal African Company, 569, 571–2, 622

Royston Club, 97–8

Rudge, John, 188

Ruggles, John, 200

Ruggles, Thomas, 196, 200

Ruglen, John Douglas-Hamilton, first Earl of, 531

Russell of Braidshaw, John, xcii, *482–3, 487–8, 497–8, 501–2, 522–3*, 560, *594–5, 608–9, 611, 638–42, 658–9, 662–3, 667, 717–19*

Russell, Ursula, 488

Rutland, John Manners, first Duke of, 531, 535

Sacheverell, Henry, lvii, lxix, lxxxiv, lxxxv, 12, 14–15, 87, 93, 98, 150, 186, 475–84, 489, 492, 494, 496, 516, 526, 586, 742, 830
 Perils of False Brethren, 475
 Political Union, 15, 93

Sacheverell, Robert, 188

St. James's Chronicle, 824

St. James's Evening Post, 842

St John, Henry, *see* Bolingbroke, Viscount

Sammen, Nathaniel, 11, 14, 110

Sandilands, John, 383

Sawbridge, George, 150–1

Saywell, Joseph, 558, 560

Schack, Baron, 770–1

Schaepel, Peter J., 754–5, 765

Schellenberg, Battle of, *see under* War of the Spanish Succession

Schomberg, Meinhardt Schomberg, third Duke of, 49

Schonhorn, Manuel, 56

Schütz, Baron Augustus, 790

Scipio Aemilianus, 84

Scotland, Company of, 81, 353, 407

Scots Atalantis, 561, 563

Scots Postman, 483

Scott, George, 217

Scott, Sir Walter, 602

Scrope, John, 604

Seafield, James Ogilvy, first Earl of, 246, 254, 280–1, 288, 346, 404, 415, 422, 439, 464, 469, 543, 545, 551, 695

Secord, Arthur W., lix, 441, 442, 865, 867, 869

Sedgemoor, Battle of, 83

Sempill, Francis Sempill, tenth Lord, 531, 535

Seton of Pitmedden, William, 246

Sexby, Edward, *Killing No Murther*, 844, 846

Seymour, Sir Edward, 93, 111, 157, 160, 161, 164, 167, 181, 186

Shaw, Mr, 491

Shift Shifted, 834, 837

Shrewsbury, Adelhida Talbot, Duchess of, 743

Shrewsbury, Charles Talbot, first Duke of, 492, 495–6, 500, 516, 743, 814, 815, 816–17, 825

Shute, John, *see* Barrington, Viscount

Silk, Capt., 691

Simpson, Samuel, 195, 199

Sinclair, Henry St Clair, tenth Lord, 397

Skelton, Charles, 731

Skippon, Philip, 189

Sloan, William, 194, 197

Smart, Jonathan, 196, 200

Smith, Mr, 477

Smith, John, 175–6, 178–9

Smith, Obadiah, 195, 199

Snell, John, 160

Society for the Promotion of Christian Knowledge, 238–9

Society for the Reformation of Manners, xcii, 527, 567, 638

Solemn League and Covenant, *see under* Covenanters

917

INDEX

Somers, John Somers, first Baron, 81, 111, 115, 117, 377, 394, 449, 469, 522, 531, 535, 536

Somerset, Charles Seymour, sixth Duke of, 157, 159, 181, 433, 644

Somerset, Sir Edward Seymour, first Duke of, 57, 79

Sophia, Electress of Hanover, 193, 605

South Sea Company, lxxvi, 440, 607, 610, 618–23, 626–37, 642, 697, 709

Spademan, John, 25

Speck, W. A., 435

Speech for Mr. D[unda]sse Younger of Arnistown, 644

Spence, Nicol, 567

Squadrone Volante, 226, 231, 344, 349, 447, 449–50, 453–4, 458–9, 464–6, 468–9, 528, 544, 546, 573–5, 650, 656, 678, 694–5, 714–16, 729

Stafford, Hugh, 160–2, 165–7, *168–9*

Stair, John Dalrymple, first Earl of, 255, 326–8, 462

Stair, John Dalrymple, second Earl of, 346, 349, 531, 536, 543, 545, 575–6

Stamper, Robert, 39

Stancliffe, James, *22–6*, 52, 55, 210, 212, 875

Stancliffe, Samuel, 875

Stanhope, Alexander, 84

Stanhope, Lt.-Gen. James (first Earl Stanhope), l, lxxv, lxxxiv–lxxxv, *475–81*, 567, 622, 709, 789, 794, 831–3, 836–7, 841, 852

Stanhope, Philip Henry Stanhope, fifth Earl, lxxxiv–lxxxv

Stanhope, Thomas, 188

Stanisław Leszczyński, King of Poland, 51–2

Stansbury, John, 195, 198

Starhemberg, Guido, 567

Starr, G. A., lx, lxiii

Steele, Sir Richard, 743, 786–804, 807
    Apology for Himself and His Writings, 793
    Crisis, 787, 790, 794, 797–800, 802, 803
    Englishman, 787, 790, 793–7, 801–2
    French Faith Represented in the Present State of Dunkirk, 794, 803
    Guardian, 786, 787, 789, 794, 801
    Importance of Dunkirk Consider'd, 787, 801, 803
    Lover, 789
    Reader, 789, 803
    Spectator, 109, 786
    Tatler, 786, 788

Steen, Sara Jayne, lxxvi

Stenhouse, Henry, 377, 379

Stephen, Jeffrey, 236, 281, 370

Stephens, Robert, 100, 105, 149–53

Stephens, William, *Letter to the Author of the Memorial of the State of England*, 193–4, 196–7

Stepney, George, 474

Steuart, Lt.-Col. James, 536

Steuart, Sir James, 536

Stevens, David, lxxxviii

Stewart of Goodtrees, Sir James, 410, 531, 574, 576, 625, 655, 694

Stewart of Pardovan, Walter, 327, 333

Stewart of Tillicoultry, Robert, 236

Stirling, John, 260, 519

Strafford, Thomas Wentworth, first Earl of, 755

Strange, George, 163

Strangways, Thomas, 156, 159, 181, 186

Strathnaver, William Gordon, Lord, 459, 462

Stuart, James Francis Edward, lxxi, 93, 259, 293, 297, 313, 396–8, 411, 445, 455, 477, 481, 518, 523–4, 526, 530, 534, 541–6, 549, 553–4, 555, 596, 609, 623, 647–8, 653, 671, 675, 677, 678, 706–9, 710–12, 714, 724, 729, 731, 739–40, 743, 751, 776–7, 786, 791, 800, 802, 803, 805, 815, 817, 820, 824, 839, 845

Stuart, Walter, 402, 404

Stuart, William, 536

Stubbs, Philip, 12, 15

Sugg, Charles, 166–7

Sultan Galga, 832, 836, 839, 845

Sunderland, Charles Spencer, third Earl of,
    correspondence with D, l, lxi, lxxx, lxxxv, xcii–xciii, 344, *449–57*
    D's view of, lxviii, 449, 494
    Secretary of State under Anne, 344–5, 348, 349, 373, 375, 391, 394, 429, 450, 458, 466, 468–9, 472, 474, 492, 495, 500, 520, 522, 526, 531, 532, 535, 617, 622
    Secretary and Treasurer under George I, 709, 831–3, 835–8

Sunderland, Robert Spencer, second Earl of, 519, 688–9

Sutherland, James R., lxxxviii–lxxxix, 857, 875

Sutherland, John Gordon, sixteenth Earl of, 267, 270, 346, 459, 462

Sutton, Anne, 865

Sutton, Timothy, 865, 866, 869

Swift, Jonathan, lii, lxxi, 135, 226, 520, 584, 662, 731, 755, 757, 799
    Conduct of the Allies, 672, 674, 690, 732, 783
    Examiner, 580

918

INDEX

Importance of the Guardian Consider'd, 787
Journal to Stella, 685, 709, 716, 720, 725–6, 743
Predictions for the Year 1708, 558
Publick Spirit of the Whigs, 790, 792–3, 802
Short Character of His Ex. T. E. of W., L. L. of I., 536
Some Remarks on the Barrier Treaty, 713
Swift, Samuel, 188
Symmons, Nevill, 195, 199
Symmons, Nevill, Jr, 199
Symmons, Samuel, 199
Szechi, Daniel, 533, 538

T. P., xcii, *642–4*
Tack of Occasional Bill to Land Tax, *see under* Acts and Bills of Parliament
Taverner, Jeremiah, 209
Taylor, Christopher, 315, 318
Taylor, John, 220
Taylor, Robert H., 457
Taylor, William, 220
Temple, R. C., 439
Tenison, Thomas, Archbishop of Canterbury, xcii, 81, 238, 378
Teviot, Sir Thomas Livingstone, Viscount, 531, 536
Thököly, Imre, 84
Thompson, Anthony, 189
Thomson, Mark A., xc
Tillotson, John, Archbishop of Canterbury, 238
Evil of Corrupt Communication, 239
Tilson, George, 461, 463
Tirel, Walter, 12, 15
Titus, Silius, *Killing No Murther*, 844, 846
Toke, John, 100, 105
Toland, John, 643
Memorial of the State of England, 193–4
Tonge, John, 196, 200
Tory party,
addresses to Queen Anne, 492
anti-Unionism of, 374, 395
D's views of, lxix, 176, 179, 541, 841
divisions within, 751–2, 807, 815, 817–18
High Church Party, *see under* Church of England
Jacobitism within, lxxi–lxxii, 836
October Club, 186, 568, 596, 599, 755
Queen Anne's views of, *see under* Anne, Queen of England
Scottish management of, 537, 540, 544, 549, 642

support for Occasional Conformity bills, 111, 117–18, 669
Toulouse, Louis-Alexandre de Bourbon, Comte de, 49
Townshend, Charles Townshend, second Viscount, lxxxviii, 474, 709, 831–2, 832, 834–5, 837–8, 841, 851
Treby, George, 181, 187
Trelawney, Sir Jonathan, 157, 159
Trelawny, Maj. Gen. Charles, 187
Trent, W. P., lxxxvii–lxxxviii
Trevelyan, George Macaulay, lxxxviii, 39
Treves, Battle of, 657
Trevor, Sir Thomas, 357–8
Trotman, Samuel, 187
Tuffley, Samuel, 691, 881
Tugghe, Ignace, 796, 801
Tunnah, Charles, 720–1
Turner, Dawson, 859
Turner, Capt. James, lxxx, 160–2, 166, 572
Tutchin, John, 105, 119, 120
Foreigners, 80
Observator, 3, 7, 10, 356
Western Martyrology, 197
Tweeddale, John Hay, second Marquess of, 344, 346, 349, 531, 536
Tyrell, James, *General History of England*, 15

Upcott, William, 874
Urquhart of Burdysyards, Capt. Robert, 536
Urquhart of Cromarty, Col. James, 536
Utrecht, Treaty of, *see under* War of the Spanish Succession

Vachell, Tanfield, 180, 186
Valdivia, Pedro Gutiérrez de, 633, 637
van der Gucht, Michael, 209
Vendôme, Louis Joseph, duc de, 81, 567
Vernon, James, 116
Vernon, Sir Richard, 789
Victor Amadeus II, Duke of Savoy, 343
Vienna, Siege of, 74, 84
View of the Coasts, Countrys, & Islands within the Limits of the South-Sea Company, 627
Villars, Marshall Claude Louis Hector de, 43, 48
Virgoe, George, 865

Wace, John, 838
Wade, John, 183, 188
Wade, Maj. Nathaniel, 183, 188

919

INDEX

Wade, Thomas, 188
Wake, William, Bishop of Lincoln, 160, 540
Walker, Capt., 824
Walker, Sue, lxxv
Walpole, Horatio, 109
Walpole, Sir Robert, 109, 478, 707, 709, 794, 832, 837, 881
Walsh, William, 435
Walsingham, Sir Francis, 58, 80
War of the Spanish Succession, 10, 205, 288, 664–5, 691, 803
    Almansa, Battle of, 422, 433, 435
    Barcelona and Catalonia, 45, 49, 176, 178, 205, 799, 803–4
    Blenheim, Battle of, 52, 56, 81, 95, 107, 111, 116, 422
    Brabant, Lines of, 153
    Brihuega, Battle of, 567
    Bühl-Stollhofen Line, 422
    Cadiz assault, 40
    Denain, Battle of, 732
    Dunkirk, 66, 529, 786–9, 793–803
    Malplaquet, Battle of, 492
    Oudenarde, Battle of, 473–4
    Quebec expedition, 599
    Ramillies, Battle of, 206, 435
    Schellenberg, Battle of, 52
    Utrecht, Treaty of, 683, 743, 751, 786, 801–2, 803
    Vélez-Málaga, Battle of, 50, 99, 101–2, 105
    Vigo Bay raid, 40
    Villaviciosa, Battle of, 567
Ward, John (D's business partner), 857
Ward, John (politician), 762
Warkman, Thomas, 188
Warner, G. F., lxxxvii
Warner, Thomas, 745, 847
Warre, Sir Francis, 187
Warton, Michael, 226, 533
Watson, James, 623, 653, 655
Watts, John, lxxxi, *873–5*
Welsh-Monster, lxv, 14, 223, 436
Webb, John Richmond, 186
Webb, Thomas, 195, 197
Webster, James, lxxxi, 330–3, *334–7*, 338, 346, 348, 357, 360–3, 446, 531, 536, 715–16
Weir, James, 305
Wells, Edward, 199
Welwood, Dr James, 280–1
Wemyss, David Wemyss, fourth Earl of, 349, 469, 531, 533, 536
Wesley, Charles, 198

Wesley, John, 198
Wesley, Samuel, 198
Wesley, Timothy, 195, 198
West, Stanley, 117
Westfield, Mr, 159, 181
Wharton, Philip, first Duke of, lxxxiv, 484
Wharton, Thomas Wharton, first Marquess of, lxxxi, lxxxiv, 394, 434, 449, 454, 469, *484–7*, 516, 522, 531, 536, 711, 713, 793
Whately, Stephen, 821
Wheely, John, 196, 200
Whig Party,
    Anne's views of, *see under* Anne, Queen of England
    Anne, fortunes under, 87, 111–13, 411, 433, 435, 475–6, 495, 497–8, 502, 506, 520, 536, 552, 577, 622, 648, 667–8, 672–3, 710, 751, 763, 787, 790, 802–3, 805, 813, 815
    D's relationship with, *see under* Defoe, Daniel, life of
    Dissenters, alliance with, li, 667–8, 686, 773, 807–11
    George I, fortunes under, 465, 709, 818, 837
    Junto Lords of, 117, 133, 156, 344, 391, 449, 484, 492, 535, 667–8, 801
    'New' Whigs, 116, 465, 716
    'Old' Whigs, 465, 522, 716
    propaganda of, lxxxviii, 3, 691, 693, 723, 725, 729, 742, 755, 756, 831–2, 843
    Schism within, 831–2
    Scottish alliances of, 449–50, 454, 465, 470, 528, 541, 645, 650, 676, 706, 714–15
    William III, fortunes under, 113, 194
Whitaker, Charles, 196, 200
Whitaker, Joseph, 21
White, John, 543, 546
White, Walter, 170, 172, 182
White, William, 132
White-Hall Evening Post, xciii, 830, 848, 852
Whitehurst, Paul, 25
Whitmore, William, 188
Willcocks, George, 865
Willcocks, Jarvis, 865
William II, King of England, 15
William III, King of England, lxv–lxvi, lxxii, lxxvi, 7, 11, 17, 19, 38, 59, 67, 80–2, 93, 97–8, 113, 114, 117, 123, 133, 135–6, 137, 167, 188, 194, 245, 247, 270, 281, 309, 330, 366, 447–8, 475, 477, 481, 484, 496, 538, 551, 626, 636, 650, 664, 739, 808

920

INDEX

Williams, Daniel, 519, 531, 669
Willis, Richard, Bishop of Gloucester, 850, 852
Wilson, Walter, lxxxi–lxxxii, lxxxiii–lxxxiv, 50, 487, 857, 874, 881
Windervis, Col., 824
Winn, James Anderson, 39
Winnington, Salwey, 188
Winstanley, James, 188–9
Wishart, James, 49
Withers, Jeremy, 176, 179
Withers, Sir William, 762
Wodrow, Robert, 274, 282, 386, 554, 565, 567, 570–1, 605, 643, 701–2, 704, 714, 716, 732
Woodcock, Josiah, 196, 200
Woodhouse, Dr John, 195
Woolley, David, 435

Worcester affair, 217, 439–40
Wraxall, John, 194, 197
Wraxall, Nathaniel, 197
Wright, Sir Nathan, 185
Wright, Stephen, 176, 179
Wright, Thomas, lxxxi, lxxxvi–lxxxvii, 857, 861, 867, 869
Wroth, John, 190
Wroth, Sir Thomas, 187
Wylde, Thomas, 188
Wylie, Robert, 531, 536
Wyndham, Sir William, 807

Yarmouth, William Paston, second Earl of, 531, 536
Yate, Robert, 172
Yester, Charles Hay, Lord, 531, 536, 573, 652
Young, Mr, lxxx, 551